Sound Films, 1927–1939

Sound Films, 1927–1939

A United States Filmography

by

ALAN G. FETROW

McFarland & Company, Inc., Publishers
Jefferson, North Carolina, and London

British Library Cataloguing-in-Publication data are available

Library of Congress Cataloguing-in-Publication Data

Fetrow, Alan G., 1945 –
   Sound films, 1927–1939 : a United States filmography / by Alan G.
Fetrow.
     p. cm.
   Includes bibliographical references and index.
   ISBN 0-89950-546-5 (lib. bdg. : 50# alk. paper) ∞
   1. Motion pictures – United States – Catalogs. 2. Sound motion
pictures – Catalogs. I. Title.
PN1993.5.U6F46 1992
016.79143'75'0973 – dc20   91-52635
                                                                CIP

Manufactured in the United States of America

McFarland & Company, Inc., Publishers
 Box 611, Jefferson, North Carolina 28640

Table of Contents

Introduction

Talking pictures ushered in a new era of film entertainment, adding dialogue and song where before had only been titles, synchronized music and sound effects. It was an era in the history of the United States of America when movie-going was a mainstay in the lives of many people, particularly in the early '30s when many folks came up with the price of a ticket, just to erase the worries of the Depression—if only for just three hours or so.

It was a time when people could laugh their worries away with the hilarious antics of the many comedy stars of the period or ride the range with their favorite cowboy star. The big budget musicals began with the coming of talkies and as it seemed a formidable use of the new medium Hollywood began cranking out the big budget musicals in abundance to the point that the public eventually tired of them.

Information on these films of varying genres is spread throughout numerous volumes, with none having nearly a complete focus on the era as a whole. The major films are usually well documented with little or no notice given to the many B productions of the period, those movies usually referred to as fillers or programmers. These films often accompanied an A feature to complete the bill for a longer program, giving the audience more for their money. Sometimes two of the Bs made up a complete program, particularly for afternoon matinees.

This work is a documentation of feature-length films produced in the United States of America, most from the many studios in Hollywood, California, but with a number of productions of the early '30s produced at Paramount's Astoria Studio in Long Island, N.Y. A few films have coproduction assistance from other countries, but these are minimal and the work contains no films which were produced abroad—though some had shots on location in faraway places. You will not find *Goodbye, Mr. Chips* or *The Citadel* on these pages as they were British productions, filmed at MGM's British studio.

A feature-length film is generally considered to be five reels or more with an actual running time of 45 to 50 minutes or more.

Herein alphabetically listed by title are feature films produced in the United States from the beginning of the talkie era in 1927 (starting with *The Jazz Singer*) through the blockbuster year of 1939. The films run the gamut from the megahit *Gone with the Wind* to the megabomb *Sutter's Gold* interspersed with the many low budget or B productions of the period, including the many series westerns of the era.

Among the many B productions listed are those of the major studios, those of the independent low budget studios along "poverty row" such as Tiffany, Majestic, Mayfair, Invincible, etc., as well as such independent production companies as Allied, Ambassador, Victory and Superior, etc. The latter were made without benefit of a studio and were often released through the state's rights system.

The basic format of the film listings is as follows: title, studio or production company if known, and the year most associated with the film, be it the year production was completed or the year the film was released to the general public, these often being the same. Some films carry the year as (e.g.) "1938–39," indicating the film's production was completed in 1938, with release the following year. This will also account for those few films which show a date of "1939–40." The amount of information given varies from entry to entry, some listing a plot description while others just give the genre of the film. Other information involves the author and source of the material, be it play, novel or short story, as well as previous versions of the film made in the United States, with some references to versions made abroad, these followed by later remakes where applicable. Also listed are awards and nominations for the films and if that film had a sequel. A list of cast members follows from stars to bit players with a number of the films including the name of the character portrayed by the actor. Where applicable, and the information is known, are listings for film debuts, feature film debuts, talkie debuts and starring debuts. In the case of actors or actresses from abroad making their first American film, the remark "American debut" is made. The final film appearance of a particular actor or actress is also noted, as well as other pertinent facts or tidbits of trivial information of general interest regarding that person.

Following the above is information about the persons behind the cameras, such as the director—with notations such as debut, final film or other relevant information. Other behind the camera credits are listed as they were available, such as producers, screenwriters and songwriters.

Throughout this work no personal criticism has been made of the films, this not being a critical work as much as a documentation of the productions of the era. Critical evaluation of a film's worth is in the eye of the viewer. Likes and dislikes in film viewing are as varied as the human experience itself. But for those who feel a need for some type of critical analysis, all Academy Award winners in all categories are noted as are those that received nominations in all categories. Also listed are those films that were honored and nominated by the New York Film Critics and those that were in the running at the Venice Film Festival. Films which received "Photoplay's Gold Medal Award" as well as the top grossing films from the years 1930 to 1939 are also noted.

Film Daily, a trade paper, the *New York Times* newspaper and the National Board of Review each put out a "10 Best" list and appropriate notations are in the entries of films which placed on these lists. The National Board of Review in 1930 and 1931 listed their "10 Best" alphabetically, while in 1932, 1933, 1934 and 1935, a "Best Film" was chosen, with the other nine placements listed alphabetically. From 1936 to 1939, the films were placed according to the number of votes they received. Acting Awards were also given by the National Board of Review from 1937 to 1939.

Beginning with *The Jazz Singer,* many of the early talkies were only part-talkie, indicating the film had titles, synchronized sound, sound effects and dialogue, sometimes with vocalized songs. Part-talkie films are duly noted.

The major portion of the films listed herein were photographed in black and white. Those that were filmed in 2-color technicolor from 1928 to 1936 are noted as are those films which were mainly black and white, but had one or more color sequences. In 1935, 3-color or full-technicolor processing began with RKO's *Becky Sharp.* The technicolor productions between 1935 and 1939 are designated, but because of the expensive processing, their numbers are few.

The ever-expanding computer age of the 1980s has given us a technique whereby old black and white films are being colored via computer graphics and films of the era covered in this book that have undergone this process (as of this writing) are indicated within the text. Coloring the black and white films via computer graphics has created a major controversy; those against it complain that the original artistic intent is destroyed with the artificial color. Those for computer-colored films maintain that members of the younger generation who have grown up with color films will avoid a black and white production in favor of one that is in color. The key word in this debate is "choice." Computer-colored films are fine as long as original black and white prints are kept available for those who do not choose to view the new coloring technique.

Running times of many of the films listed herein are included where access was available through the various source books used. In some cases these running times were consistent from source to source, but in other cases the films show varying running times, sometimes with differences from ten to twenty minutes. No matter how one seems to approach this issue, there are bound to be discrepancies. In some cases it appears that the original running time listed by the production studio is in error. So the best that can be said on this matter is that the listed running time, if proven inaccurate, may vary more or less from one to four minutes.

Beginning in the silent era, some films underwent title changes when exported to England, these apparently coming about for various reasons. One of the more humorous of these title changes occurred with the film titled *Hallelujah, I'm a Bum,* which was known as *Hallelujah, I'm a Tramp* when shown in

England (where the word "bum" is slang for the human posterior). These British titles are indicated at the end of the individual film by: "(G.B. title)." They are also cross-referenced. Other films which at one time or another were known by more than one title, have these titles listed at the end of the entry along with further alphabetical cross-referencing of these titles.

Films of the era which have been made available on home video cassette (as of this writing) are also noted at the end of the text of the individual film. This merely states that the film has been made available, but does not guarantee that you will be able to find it at your local video store. The films of the era that have been made available on home video run the gamut from classic to trite, and it may be noted through the work that many box office hits and classics are still unavailable. For example, of the 19 Charlie Chan mysteries released in the 1930s, only three (as of this writing) are available on home video.

One final note: Cable television is making many stations and networks available to the entire country and is pioneering sort of a re-emergence of many of these long forgotten films to generations who remember them in nostalgia and to others who have little or no awareness as to their existence. To date, the best sources for seeing films of this era are on "American Movie Classics," "The Nostalgia Channel," "The Family Channel" (formerly CBN) and the newly established "Turner Network Television." Local public broadcasting stations are also a good source for seeing many of the oldies but goodies.

I would like to thank William C. Clogston, of Chicago, for his exceptional aid in the reading and correcting of the publisher's proofs.

Alan G. Fetrow
January 1, 1992

Abbreviations
and Terminology

A.A.   Academy Award (Oscar)

A.A.N.   Academy Award (nomination)

As.P.   Associate Producer

B.A.   Best Actor/Actress (Oscar category)

B.S.A.   Best Supporting Actor/Actress (Oscar category)

D   the film's director

d.   died

G.B. title   a film title usually used only in Great Britain

indie   a film that was independently produced (not a studio production) and released either through a major or minor studio or the State's Rights system.

MGM   Metro-Goldwyn-Mayer

meller   a melodrama

o.k.a.   originally known as

P   the producer of the picture

Poverty Row   Gower Street in Hollywood which in the 1930s was the residence of a number of small independent studios and production companies whose sole output were low budget productions.

q.v.   see also

RKO   Radio-Keith-Orpheum

Sc   the writer or writers of the screenplay or script.

series western   The low budget or B westerns of the 1930s and 1940s were most often produced in series of 4-6-8 productions with some 3-5-7-9s interspersed, the same western star as the attraction in each.

st   the story basis of the film, usually a short story, novel or stageplay and in some cases an idea conceived by an individual who usually worked for (but not necessarily) the studio, which became the basis for the final script or screenplay.

unc.   worked on but was not billed in the film's screen credits

W.B.   Warner Bros.

W.B./F.N.   Warner Bros./First National (First National was a major production studio in the silent era which was purchased by the brothers Warner.)

Xxxx   key information not available

The Filmography

1. Abie's Irish Rose (Paramount; 1928–29). *Cast:* Charles "Buddy" Rogers, Nancy Carroll, Jean Hersholt, J. Farrell MacDonald, Nick Cogley, Camillus Pretal, Rosa Rosanova. *D:* Victor Fleming; *P:* B.P. Schulberg; *Sc:* Jules Furthman, Herman J. Mankiewicz, Julian Johnson; *Titles:* Anne Nichols.

A part-talkie of a catholic girl's marriage into a Jewish family. Based on the 1927 play by Anne Nichols, it was remade in 1946.

2. Above the Clouds (Columbia; 1934). *Cast:* Richard Cromwell, Dorothy Revier, Edmund Breese. *D:* Roy William Neill.

Low-budget actioner.

3. Abraham Lincoln (United Artists/Art Cinema; 1930). *Cast:* Walter Huston (Lincoln), Una Merkel (in her talkie debut as Ann Rutledge), Kay Hammond (Mary Todd Lincoln), Hobart Bosworth (Robert E. Lee), E. Alyn Warren (Stephen A. Douglas, Gen. Ulysses S. Grant), Jason Robards (William Herndon), Oscar Apfel (Edwin Stanton), Frank Campeau (General Sheridan), Edgar Dearing (Armstrong), Cameron Prud'Homme (John Hay), Henry B. Walthall (Colonel Marshall), Ian Keith (John Wilkes Booth), H.L. Thorne (Tom Lincoln), Helen Freeman (Nancy Hanks Lincoln), Gordon Thorpe (Tad Lincoln), Helen Ware (Mrs. Edwards), James Bradbury (General Scott), Russell Simpson, Lucille La Verne, Otto Hoffman, Charles Crockett, Jimmie (James) Eagles, Fred Warren, Robert E. Homans, Mary Forbes. *D:* D.W. Griffith; *P:* Joseph M. Schenck; *adaptation:* Stephen Vincent Benet; *sc:* Benet, Gerrit Lloyd, Griffith (unbilled). (1:37) (video)

The life of Abraham Lincoln from his birth to his assassination at Ford's Theater. The film is notable as the first talking picture (of two) of famed silent director D.W. Griffith. The *New York Times* voted it #9 on their list of "10 Best" films while *Film Daily* placed it at #2.

Absinthe *see* **Madame X** (1929)

4. Absolute Quiet (MGM; 1936). *Cast:* Lionel Atwill, Irene Hervey, Ann Loring, Raymond Walburn, Louis Hayward, Stuart Erwin, Wallace Ford, J. Carrol Naish, Robert Livingston, Matt Moore, Harvey Stephens, Bernadene Hayes, Robert Gleckler. *D:* George B. Seitz; *P:* John W. Considine, Jr.; *st:* George F. Worts; *Sc:* Harry Clork. (1:11)

A melodrama of various characters congregating at the home of a wealthy man following a plane crash.

The Abysmal Brute *see* **Conflict** (1936)

5. Accent on Youth (Paramount; 1935). *Cast:* Sylvia Sidney, Herbert Marshall, Philip Reed, Astrid Allwyn, Holmes Herbert, Catherine Doucet, Lon Chaney, Jr., Fifi D'Orsay, Donald Meek, Ernest Cossart, Samuel S. Hinds, Nick (Dick) Foran, Florence Roberts, Laura Treadwell. *D:* Wesley Ruggles; *P:* Douglas McLean; *Sc:* Herbert Fields, Claude Binyon. (1:17)

Comedy of a secretary who falls for her employer. Based on the hit Broadway play by Samson Raphaelson, it was remade in 1950 as *Mr. Music* and again in 1959 as *But Not for Me.*

1

Accidents Wanted (G.B. title) *see* **The Nuisance**

6. Accidents Will Happen (W.B.; 1938). *Cast:* Ronald Reagan, Gloria Blondell, Dick Purcell, Addison Richards, Hugh O'Connell, Sheila Bromley, Janet Shaw, Anderson Lawler, Kenneth Harlan, Earl Dwire, Max Hoffman, Don Barclay, Spec O'Donnell, Elliott Sullivan, John Butler. *D:* William Clemens; *As.P.:* Bryan Foy; *Sc:* George Bricker, Anthony Coldeway. (1:02)
B melodrama of an insurance claims adjuster who turns crooked.

7. The Accusing Finger (Paramount; 1936). *Cast:* Robert Cummings, Marsha Hunt, Kent Taylor, Paul Kelly, John Carroll, Fred Kohler, Harry Carey, Sam Flint, Ralf Harolde, Hilda Vaughn, Bernadene Hayes, DeWitt Jennings, Bud Flanagan (Dennis O'Keefe). *D:* James Hogan; *P:* A.M. Botsford; *Sc:* John Bright, Brian Marlow, Robert Tasker, Madeleine Ruthven.
Melodrama of the use and misuse of circumstantial evidence.

8. Ace of Aces (RKO; 1933). *Cast:* Richard Dix, Elizabeth Allan, Ralph Bellamy, Theodore Newton, Joseph (Sawyer) Sauers, Nella Walker, Anderson Lawler, Frank Conroy, Arthur Jarrett, Claude Gillingwater, Jr., Clarence Stroud, Claude Stroud, Frank Clark, Helmuth Gorin, Howard Wilson, Grady Sutton, William Cagney, Edward Gargan, Betty Furness. *D:* J. Walter Ruben; *As.P.:* Sam Jaffe; *Sc:* John Monk Saunders, H.W. Hanemann. (G.B. title: *Bird of Prey*) (1:16)
World War I drama of an air ace who begins to suffer from emotional problems. Based on the story "Bird of Prey," the film utilizes aerial footage from *Hell's Angels* (q.v.).

9. Aces and Eights (Puritan; 1936). *Cast:* Tim McCoy, Luana Walters, Rex Lease, Wheeler Oakman, John Merton, Charles Stevens, Jimmy Aubrey, Joseph Girard, J. Frank Glendon, Earle Hodgins, Frank Ellis. *D:* Sam Newfield; *Sc:* George A. Durlam. (1:02) (video)
Western.

10. Aces Wild (Commodore; 1936). *Cast:* Harry Carey, Gertrude Messinger, Phil Dunham, Roger Williams, Fred "Snowflake" Toones, Ed Cassidy, Theodore Lorch, Chuck Morrison, William McCall. *D:* Harry Fraser; *Sc:* Monroe Talbot. (0:57) (video)
Western of outlaws out to shut down a newspaper.

11. Acquitted (Columbia; 1929). *Cast:* Lloyd Hughes, Margaret Livingston, Sam Hardy. *D:* Frank Strayer.
Low-budget melodrama.

12. Across the Plains (Monogram; 1939). *Cast:* Jack Randall, Joyce Bryant, Frank Yaconelli, Dennis Moore, Hal Price, Glenn Strange, Robert Cord, Bud Osborne, Dean Spencer, James Sheridan (Sherry Tansey), Wylie Grant. *D:* Spencer Gordon Bennet; *P:* Robert Tansey; *Sc:* Robert Emmett (Tansey). (0:59)
Western of two young brothers separated after an attack on a wagon train.
Note: Prior to release the film was known as "Riders of the Rio Grande."

13. Across the World with Mr. and Mrs. Johnson (Fox; 1930). A documentary feature of famed American explorers Martin and Osa Johnson and their explorations of remote parts of the world.

Adios (G.B. title) *see* **The Lash**

The Adopted Father *see* **The Working Man**

14. Adorable (Fox; 1933). *Cast:* Janet Gaynor, Henry Garat, C. Aubrey

Smith, Herbert Mundin, Blanche Frederici, Hans von Twardowsky, William Henry. *D:* Wilhelm (William) Dieterle; *St:* Paul Frank, Billy Wilder; *Sc:* George Marion, Jr., Jane Storm. (1:25)

The Ruritanian romance of a princess and a naval officer.

Note: Previously filmed in Germany in 1931 as *Ihre Hoheit befiehlt.*

15. Adventure Girl (RKO/Van Beuren; 1934). The narration was written by Ferrin Fraser and delivered by Miss Lowell, being based on her book of the same name. Also featured are Captain Nicholas Wagner, William Sawyer and Otto Siegler. *D:* Herman Raymaker. (1:09)

A low-budget re-enactment of the trek of adventuress Jane Lowell and her 76-year-old father through the dangerous jungles of Guatemala in search of a lost city.

16. Adventure in Manhattan (Columbia; 1936). *Cast:* Joel McCrea, Jean Arthur, Thomas Mitchell, Reginald Owen, Victor Kilian, George Cooper, Herman Bing, John Gallaudet, Emmett Vogan, Robert Warwick. *D:* Edward Ludwig; *St:* Mary Edginton, Joseph Krumgold; *Sc:* Sidney Buchman, Harry Sauber, Jack Kirkland. (G.B. title: *Manhattan Madness*) (1:13)

Comedy-drama of a news reporter and an actress who thwart a bank robbery.

17. Adventure in Sahara (Columbia; 1938). *Cast:* Paul Kelly, Lorna Gray (later Adrian Booth), C. Henry Gordon, Marc Lawrence, Dick Curtis, Stanley Andrews, Robert Fiske, Raphael Bennett, Stanley Brown, Charles Moore, Alan Bridge, Dwight Frye. *D:* D. Ross Lederman; *St:* Samuel Fuller; *Sc:* Maxwell Shane.

A low-budget actioner.

Adventures at Rugby *see* **Tom Brown's School Days** (1939–40)

18. Adventure's End (Universal; 1937). *Cast:* John Wayne, Diana Gibson, Moroni Olsen, Montagu Love, Maurice Black, Paul Wynter, Glenn Strange, Cameron Hall, George Cleveland, P.J. Kelly, Paul White, Oscar V. Sundholm. *D:* Arthur Lubin; *P:* Trem Carr; *St:* Ben Ames Williams; *Sc:* W. Scott Darling, Ben G. Kohn, Sidney Sutherland. (1:03)

A low-budget whaling adventure.

19. The Adventures of Huckleberry Finn (MGM; 1939). *Cast:* Mickey Rooney (Huck Finn), Rex Ingram (Jim), William Frawley (The Duke), Elizabeth Risdon (Widow Douglas), Walter Connolly, Lynne Carver, Victor Kilian, Jo Ann Sayers, Minor Watson, Clara Blandick. *D:* Richard Thorpe; *P:* Joseph L. Mankiewicz; *Sc:* Hugo Butler. (aka: *Huckleberry Finn*) (1:30) (video)

The second sound version of Mark Twain's 1884 classic of a youth and his adventures on the Mississippi River. Previously filmed in 1920 by director William Desmond Taylor and again in 1931 (q.v.) both times as *Huckleberry Finn.* Remade by this studio in 1974 as a musical and again in 1975 as a TV movie. Computer-colored by Turner Entertainment in 1988.

20. The Adventures of Jane Arden (WB; 1939). *Cast:* Rosella Towne, William Gargan, James Stephenson, Benny Rubin, Peggy Shannon, Dennis Moore, Hobart Cavanaugh. *D:* Terry Morse; *As.P.:* Mark Hellinger; *Sc:* Lawrence Kimble, Charles Curran, Vincent Sherman.

The first and only entry in a proposed series of a girl reporter who in this one exposes a gang of jewel smugglers. Based on a popular comic strip of the day by Monte Barrett and Russell E. Ross.

21. The Adventures of Marco Polo (United Artists/Samuel Goldwyn; 1938). *Cast:* Gary Cooper (Marco Polo), Sigrid Gurie (film debut), Basil Rathbone (Ahmed), George Barbier (Kublakhan), Binnie Barnes, Ernest Truex, Alan Hale, Robert Greig, H.B. Warner, Ferdinand Gottschalk, Henry Kolker, Jason Robards, Ward Bond, Harold Huber, Lana Turner (bit as a handmaiden). *D:* Archie Mayo; *P:* Samuel Goldwyn; *St:* N.A. Pogson; *Sc:* Robert E. Sherwood. (1:44)

A lavish production retelling the famed explorer's exploits in the orient.

22. The Adventures of Robin Hood

(WB; 1938). *Cast:* Errol Flynn (Robin Hood), Olivia de Havilland (Maid Marian), Claude Rains (Prince John), Basil Rathbone (Sir Guy of Gisbourne), Eugene Pallette (Friar Tuck), Alan Hale (Little John), Ian Hunter (King Richard), Patric Knowles (Will Scarlett), Melville Cooper (High Sheriff of Nottingham), Herbert Mundin (Much the Miller), Una O'Connor (Bess), Montagu Love (Bishop of Black Canons), Harry Cording (Dicken Malbete), Robert Warwick (Sir Geoffrey), Robert Noble (Sir Ralfe), Kenneth Hunter (Sir Mortimer), Leonard Willey (Essex), Lester Matthews (Sir Ivor), Colin Kenny (Sir Baldwin), Charles McNaughton (Crippen), Lionel Belmore (Humility Prin), Austin Fairman (Sir Nigel), Crauford Kent (Sir Norbett), Herbert Evans (Seneschal), Howard Hill, Ivan Simpson, Janet Shaw, Val Stanton, Ernie Stanton, Olaf Hytten, Alec Harford, Peter Hobbes, Edward Dew, John Sutton, Marten Lamont, Hal Brazeale, Holmes Herbert, Leyland Hodgson. *D:* Michael Curtiz, William Keighley; *As.P.:* (A.A.N. for Best Picture) Henry Blanke; *Sc:* Seton I. Miller, Norman Reilly Raine; *Interior Decorations:* (A.A.) Carl Jules Weyl; *Music:* (A.A.) Erich Wolfgang Korngold; *Editor:* (A.A.) Ralph Dawson. (1:42) (video)

A lavishly produced technicolor swashbuckler of Robin and his men of Sherwood Forest who battle the forces of evil. On the "10 Best" lists of *Film Daily* and the *New York Times,* it placed #7 and #8 respectively. Coming in at $2,000,000, it was the most expensive production of this studio to date, eventually becoming one of the 15 top grossing films of 1937–38. Curiously, James Cagney was the studio's first choice for the title role. Filmed three times before as *Robin Hood,* (Eclair; 1912) with Robert Frazer in his film debut and Barbara Tennant, (Thanhouser; 1913) with William Russell and Gerda Holmes and (United Artists; 1922) with Douglas Fairbanks.

23. The Adventures of Sherlock Holmes

(20th Century–Fox; 1939). *Cast:* Basil Rathbone (Holmes), Nigel Bruce (Watson), Ida Lupino (Ann Brandon), George Zucco (Moriarty), Alan Marshal (Jerrold Hunter), Terry Kilburn (Billy), Henry Stephenson (Sir Ronald Ramsgate), Mary Gordon (Mrs. Hudson), E.E. Clive, Mary Forbes, Holmes Herbert, William Austin, May Beatty, George Regas, Frank Dawson, Anthony Kemble Cooper, George Billings, Peter Willes. *D:* Alfred Werker; *P:* Gene Markey; *Sc:* Edwin Blum, William A. Drake. (G.B. title: *Sherlock Holmes*) (1:25) (video)

This second entry in the Holmes series has the master sleuth and Dr. Watson attempting to thwart a plan by Dr. Moriarty to rob the Tower of London of the Crown jewels. Previously filmed in 1922 as *Sherlock Holmes.* Based on the play of that name by William Gillette.

24. Adventures of the Masked Phantom

(Equity; 1939). *Cast:* Monte "Alamo" Rawlins, Betty Burgess, Art Davis, Boots the dog. *D:* Charles Abbott.

B western.

25. The Adventures of Tom Sawyer

(United Artists/David O. Selznick; 1938). *Cast:* Tommy Kelly (Tom), Jackie Moran (Huck Finn), Ann Gillis (Becky Thatcher), May Robson (Aunt Polly), Victor Jory (Injun Joe), Walter Brennan (Muff Potter), Spring Byington (Widow Douglas), David Holt (Sid Sawyer), Marcia Mae Jones (Mary Sawyer), Victor Kilian (the sheriff), Nana Bryant (Mrs. Thatcher), Mickey Rentschler (Joe Harper), Cora Sue Collins (Amy Lawrence), Charles Richman (Judge Thatcher), Margaret Hamilton (Mrs. Harper), Philip Hurlic (Little Jim), George Billings (Ben Rogers), Byron Armstrong (Billy Fisher), Olin Howland, Donald Meek, Harry C. Myers. *D:* Norman Taurog; *Sc:* John V.A. Weaver; *Art-Set Decoration:* (A.A.N.) Lyle Wheeler, William Cameron Menzies is also credited as art director for the creation of the cave settings. (1:33) (video)

Selznick's technicolor version of Mark Twain's classic novel of a boy and his adventurous life along the Mississippi River. One of the 15 top grossing films of 1937–38 it was voted the "Minister of Popular Culture Award" at the Venice Film Festival. Filmed before in 1919 with Jack Pickford by director William Desmond Taylor and again in 1930 (q.v.). Two more versions were made in 1973, one a TV movie, the other a theatrical musical version—all under the title *Tom Sawyer.*

26. The Adventurous Blonde (WB/FN; 1937). *Cast:* Glenda Farrell (Torchy), Barton MacLane (Steve McBride), Anne Nagel, George E. Stone, Natalie Moorhead, William Hopper, Charles Foy, Virginia Brissac, Carole Landis, Raymond Hatton, Bobby Watson, Tom Kennedy, Charles Wilson, Anderson Lawler, Frank Shannon, Al Herman, Walter Young, George Guhl, Leyland Hodgson, Granville Owen. *D:* Frank McDonald; *P:* Bryan Foy; *Sc:* Robertson White, David Diamond. (aka: *Torchy Blane, the Adventurous Blonde*)

The third entry in the "Torchy Blane—Girl Reporter" series as a fake murder turns out to be the real thing. Based on the characters created by Frederick Nebel.

27. Advice to the Lovelorn (United Artists/20th Century; 1933). *Cast:* Lee Tracy, Sally Blane, Sterling Holloway, Jean Adair, Paul Harvey, Isabel Jewell, Matt Briggs, Charles (Lane) Levison, C. Henry Gordon, Ruth Fallows, May Boley, Judith Wood, Adalyn Doyle. *D:* Alfred Werker; *P:* Darryl Zanuck/20th Century productions; *Sc:* Leonard Praskins. (1:02) (video)

Comedy-drama of a male reporter who is demoted to the lonely-hearts column of his newspaper. Loosely based on Nathanael West's novel "Miss Lonelyhearts." The story was reworked in 1945 as *I'll Tell the World* and remade in 1958 as *Lonelyhearts.*

28. The Affair of Susan (Universal; 1935). *Cast:* ZaSu Pitts, Hugh O'Connell, Inez Courtney, James Burke, Lois January, Walter Catlett, Gertrude Short, Irene Franklin. *D:* Kurt Neumann. (1:02)

A romantic comedy of two shy people in search of soul mates.

29. Affairs of a Gentleman (Universal; 1934). *Cast:* Paul Lukas, Leila Hyams, Onslow Stevens, Lillian Bond, Sara Haden, Dorothy Burgess, Philip Reed, Joyce Compton, Charles C. Wilson, Murray Kinnell, Gregory Gaye, Richard Carle, Dorothy Libaire. *D:* Edwin L. Marin; *Sc:* Cyril Hume, Peter Ruric, Milton Krims. (1:08)

A writer invites his ex-girlfriends to a gathering in this B murder-mystery told in flashbacks.

30. The Affairs of Annabel (RKO; 1938). *Cast:* Lucille Ball, Jack Oakie, Ruth Donnelly, Bradley Page, Fritz Feld, Thurston Hall, Elizabeth Risdon, Granville Bates, James Burke, Lee Van Atta, Anthony Warde, Edward Marr, Leona Roberts. *D:* Ben Stoloff; *P:* Lou Lusty; *St:* "Menial Star" by Charles Hoffman; *Sc:* Bert Granet, Paul Yawitz. (1:08) (video)

Comedy of a daffy Hollywood starlet who with her conniving agent gets involved with gangsters and a case of mistaken identity. Followed by *Annabel Takes a Tour.*

31. The Affairs of Cappy Ricks (Republic; 1937). *Cast:* Walter Brennan (Cappy Ricks), Mary Brian, Phyllis Barry, Lyle Talbot. *D:* Ralph Staub.

Comedy-drama of the lovable old codger, a character created by Peter B. Kyne.

32. The Affairs of Cellini (United Artists/20th Century; 1934). *Cast:* Fredric March (Benvenuto Cellini), Constance Bennett, Frank Morgan (A.A.N. for B.S.A.), Fay Wray, Jessie Ralph, Vince Barnett, Louis Calhern, Jay Eaton, Paul Harvey, John Rutherford, Ward Bond, Lucille Ball (bit). *D:* Gregory LaCava; *P:* Darryl F. Zanuck, William Goetz, Raymond Griffith; *Sc:* Bess Meredyth; *Cinematographer:* (A.A.N.) Charles Rosher; *Art-Set Decoration:* (A.A.N.) Richard Day; *Sound Recording:* (A.A.N.) Thomas T. Moulton. (1:20)

A lavishly produced tongue-in-cheek rendering of the Renaissance painter who has an affair with a woman of royalty. Based on the play "The Firebrand" by Edwin Justus Mayer.

33. Afraid to Talk (Universal; 1932). *Cast:* Edward Arnold (Jim Skelli), Eric Linden, Louis Calhern, Tully Marshall, Sidney Fox, Reginald Barlow, Frank Sheridan, Berton Churchill, Robert Warwick, George Meeker, Mayo Methot, Ian MacLaren, Joyce Compton, Matt McHugh, George Chandler, Arthur Housman, Gustav von Seyffertitz, Edward Martindel, Thomas Jackson. *D:* Edward L. Cahn; *Sc:* Tom Reed. (retitled: *Merry-Go-Round*). (1:09)

An innocent bellboy is railroaded into prison via police corruption. Based on the play "Merry-Go-Round" by Albert Maltz and George Sklar.

34. After Office Hours (MGM; 1935). *Cast:* Constance Bennett, Clark Gable, Stuart Erwin, Billie Burke, Harvey Stephens, Katharine Alexander, Henry Travers, Hale Hamilton, William Demarest, Henry Armetta, Charles Richman, Herbert Bunston. *D:* Robert Z. Leonard; *P:* Bernard B. Hyman, Leonard; *St:* Laurence Stallings, Dale Van Every; *Sc:* Herman J. Mankiewicz. (1:15)

Comedy-melodrama of a society girl who gets a job with a newspaper.

35. After the Dance (Columbia; 1935). *Cast:* Nancy Carroll, George Murphy, Thelma Todd, Victor Kilian, Thurston Hall, Wyrley Birch, Jack Dean. *D:* Leo Bulgakov.

A low-budget musical.

36. After the Thin Man (MGM; 1936). *Cast:* William Powell (Nick Charles), Myrna Loy (Nora Charles), James Stewart (David Graham), Elissa Landi (Selma Landis), Jessie Ralph (Aunt Katherine Forrest), Joseph Calleia (Dancer), Alan Marshal (Robert Landis), Sam Levene (Lt. Abrams), Dorothy McNulty (Penny Singleton — Polly Byrnes), Dorothy Vaughan (Charlotte), Maude Turner Gordon (Helen), Teddy Hart (Floyd Casper), William Law (Lum Kee), William Burress (Lucius), Thomas Pogue (William), George Zucco (Dr. Kammer), Paul Fix (Phil Byrnes), Tom Ricketts (Henry the butler), Joe Caits (Joe), Joe Phillips (Willie), Edith Kingdon (Hattie), John Kelly (Harold), Clarence Kolb (the other Lucius), John T. Murray (Jerry), Zeffie Tilbury (Lucy), Mary Gordon (Rose the cook), Eric Wilton (Peter the butler), Harry Tyler (Fingers), Harlan Briggs (Burton Forrest), Alice H. Smith (Emily), George Taylor (Eddie), Dick Rush, Edgar Dearing, Guy Usher, George Guhl, Jack Norton, Murray Alper, Richard Loo, Vince Barnett, Bobby Watson. *D:* W.S. Van Dyke II; *P:* Hunt Stromberg; *Sc:* (A.A.N.) Frances Goodrich and Albert Hackett; *Songs:* "Smoke Dreams" Nacio Herb Brown, Arthur Freed, "Blow That Horn" Walter

Donaldson, Chet Forrest, Bob Wright. (1:53) (video)

The second entry in the "Thin Man" series has the free-living sleuths Nick and Nora Charles solving another murder case in their own inimitable style. Followed in 1939 by *Another Thin Man* (q.v.). Based on the characters created by Dashiell Hammett, the film was one of the 38 top grossing films of 1936–37.

37. After Tomorrow (Fox; 1932). *Cast:* Charles Farrell, Marian Nixon, William Collier, Sr., Josephine Hull (film debut), Nora Lane, Greta Granstedt, Ferdinand Munier, William Pawley. *D:* Frank Borzage; *St:* Hugh Stanislaus Stange, John Golden; *Sc:* Sonya Levien.

Romantic drama.

38. After Tonight (RKO; 1933). *Cast:* Constance Bennett, Gilbert Roland, Edward Ellis, Sam Godfrey, Lucien Prival, Mischa Auer, Ben Hendricks, Jr., Leonid Snegoff, Evelyn Carter Carrington, Herman Bing, John Wray, Frank Reicher, Virginia Weidler. *D:* George Archainbaud; *As.P.:* H.N. Swanson; *St:* Jane Murfin; *Sc:* Murfin, Albert Shelby LeVino, Worthington Miner; *Song:* Will Jason, Val Burton. (G.B. title: *Sealed Lips*) (1:10)

In World War I Vienna, a romance develops between a Russian spy and an Austrian agent. A box office flop.

Afterwards (G.B. title) *see* **Their Big Moment**

39. Against the Law (Columbia; 1934). *Cast:* Johnny Mack Brown, Sally Blane, Ward Bond, Bradley Page, Arthur Hohl. *D:* Lambert Hillyer.

B western.

40. The Age for Love (United Artists/Howard Hughes; 1931). *Cast:* Billie Dove, Charles Starrett, Lois Wilson, Adrian Morris, Edward Everett Horton, Mary Duncan, Betty Ross Clarke,

Jed Prouty, Joan Standing, Andre Beranger. *D:* Frank Lloyd; *Sc:* Robert E. Sherwood, Lloyd, Ernest Pascal (based on Pascal's novel).

In this marital drama a man changes his mind after marrying with the intent of not having children.

41. The Age of Consent (RKO; 1932). *Cast:* Dorothy Wilson (film debut), Arline Judge, Eric Linden, Richard Cromwell, John Halliday, Aileen Pringle, Reginald Barlow, Grady Sutton, Betty Grable. *D:* Gregory LaCava; *As.P.:* Pandro S. Berman; *St:* Martin Flavin; *Sc:* Sarah Y. Mason, Francis Cockrell. (1:03)

Drama of young people who come to realize they will soon have to face responsibility.

42. Age of Indiscretion (MGM; 1935). *Cast:* Paul Lukas, Helen Vinson, David Jack Holt, Madge Evans, May Robson, Ralph Forbes, Beryl Mercer, Catherine Doucet, Minor Watson, Shirley Ross, Stuart Casey, Adrian Morris. *D:* Edward Ludwig; *P:* Philip Goldstone; *St:* Lenore Coffee; *Sc:* Otis Garrett, Leon Gordon. (1:20)

In this drama an irresponsible wife divorces her husband and seeks custody of their son.

43. Age of Innocence (RKO; 1934). *Cast:* Irene Dunne, John Boles, Lionel Atwill, Laura Hope Crews, Julie Haydon, Helen Westley, Herbert Yost, Theresa Maxwell Conover, Edith Van Cleve, Leonard Carey. *D:* Philip Moeller; *P:* Pandro S. Berman; *Sc:* Victor Heerman, Sarah Y. Mason.

Romantic drama based on a 1920 Pulitzer Prize winning novel by Edith Wharton (the first ever won by a woman) and the play by Margaret Ayer Barnes.

44. Aggie Appleby — Maker of Men (RKO; 1933). *Cast:* Wynne Gibson, Charles Farrell, William Gargan, ZaSu Pitts, Betty Furness, Blanche

Friderici, Jane Darwell. *D:* Mark Sandrich; *P:* Pandro S. Berman; *Sc:* Humphrey Pearson, Edward Kaufman. (retitled: *Aggie Appleby*) (G.B. title: *Cupid in the Rough*) (1:13)

Comedy of a tough city girl who becomes the friend of a meek young man. Based on the play by Joseph Kesselring.

45. Ah, Wilderness (MGM; 1935). *Cast:* Wallace Beery (Sid), Lionel Barrymore (Nat), Eric Linden (Richard), Aline MacMahon (Lily), Cecilia Parker (Muriel), Spring Byington (Essie), Mickey Rooney (Tommy), Charley Grapewin (Mr. McComber), Frank Albertson (Arthur), Bonita Granville (Mildred), Edward Nugent (Wint), Helen Flint (Belle), Helen Freeman (Miss Hawley). *D:* Clarence Brown; *P:* Hunt Stromberg; *Sc:* Frances Goodrich, Albert Hackett. (1:46)

Americana of a small town family and their overly amorous son. Set at the turn-of-the-century it is based on the hit 1933 Broadway play by Eugene O'Neill. Remade in 1948 as the musical *Summer Holiday.*

46. The Air Circus (Fox; 1928). *Cast:* Arthur Lake, Louise Dresser, Sue Carol, Charles Delaney, Charles (Heinie) Conklin. *D:* Howard Hawks, Lewis Seiler; *Sc:* Seton I. Miller, Graham Baker, Andrew Bennison.

Part-talkie of a flyer with acrophobia.

47. Air Devils (Universal; 1938). *Cast:* Dick Purcell, Larry Blake, Mamo Clark, Beryl Wallace, Minerva Urecal. *D:* John Rawlins; *P:* Paul Malvern. (0:58)

B actioner set in the South Seas.

48. Air Eagles (Big Productions; 1931). *Cast:* Lloyd Hughes, Norman Kerry, Berton Churchill. *D:* Phil Whitman.

Minor aerial actioner.

49. Air Hawks (Columbia; 1935). *Cast:* Ralph Bellamy, Tala Birell, Robert Allen, Geneva Mitchell, Wiley Post (who died in 1935 with Will Rogers in a plane crash), Victor Kilian, Edward Van Sloan, Douglass Dumbrille, Peggy Terry, Franklin Parker, Al Hill, William Irving, Robert Middlemass, Wyrley Birch, Billie Seward, Harry Strang. *D:* Albert Rogell; *Sc:* Griffin Jay, Grace Neville.

B aerial actioner.

50. Air Hostess (Columbia; 1933). *Cast:* Evalyn Knapp, James Murray, Thelma Todd, J.M. Kerrigan, Mike Donlin, Arthur Pierson, Jane Darwell, Dutch Hendrian. *D:* Albert Rogell; *Sc:* Keene Thompson, Milton Raison; *St:* Grace Perkins.

B romantic drama.

51. Air Mail (Universal; 1932). *Cast:* Pat O'Brien, Ralph Bellamy, Russell Hopton, Gloria Stuart, Lillian Bond, Slim Summerville, Frank Albertson, Leslie Fenton, Francis Ford, Ward Bond, Jim Thorpe, Tom Carrington, William Daley, David Landau, Hans Furberg. *D:* John Ford; *P:* Carl Laemmle, Jr.; *Sc:* Frank "Spig" Wead, Dale Van Every. (1:25)

Aerial actioner of flyers at a desert airport who carry the U.S. Mail.

Air Patrol (G.B. title) *see* **Happy Landing** (1934)

52. Air Police (Sono Art-World Wide; 1931). *Cast:* Charles Delaney, Kenneth Harlan, Josephine Dunn, Richard Cramer, George Chesebro. *D:* Stuart Paton.

A "Poverty Row" actioner.

Alaska Bound (G.B. title) *see* **North of Nome**

53. Alcatraz Island (WB/F.N.; 1937). *Cast:* John Litel, Ann Sheridan, Mary Maguire, Gordon Oliver, Addison Richards, George E. Stone, Dick Purcell, Ben Welden, Veda Ann Borg, Vladimir Sokoloff, Lane Chandler, Peggy Bates, Charles Trowbridge, Anderson Lawler, Edward Keane, Walter

Young, Edwin Stanley. *D:* William McGann; *P:* Bryan Foy; *Sc:* Crane Wilbur.

B prison drama of a man framed for the murder of another inmate.

54. Alexander Hamilton (WB; 1930–31). *Cast:* George Arliss (recreating his stage role as Hamilton), Doris Kenyon (Betsy Hamilton), Montagu Love (Thomas Jefferson), Alan Mowbray (George Washington), Charles Middleton (John Jay), Lionel Belmore (General Philip Schuyler), John T. Murray (Count Talleyrand), Gwendolin Logan (Martha Washington), Dudley Digges, June Collyer, Ralf Harolde. *D:* John Adolfi; *Sc:* Arliss, Julien Josephson, Maude Howell. (1:13)

Historical drama of the early American financial wizard. Based on the play by George Arliss and Mary Hamlin.

55. Alexander's Ragtime Band (20th Century–Fox; 1938). *Cast:* Tyrone Power (Roger Grant "Alexander"), Alice Faye (Stella Kirby), Don Ameche (Charlie Dwyer), Ethel Merman (Jerry Allen), Jack Haley (Davey Lane), Jean Hersholt (Prof. Heinrich), Helen Westley (Aunt Sophie), Wally Vernon (himself), Ruth Terry (Ruby); Paul Hurst (Bill), Douglas Fowley (Snapper), Chick Chandler (Louie), Eddie Collins (Corp. Collins), Robert Gleckler (Dirty Eddie), Joe King (Charles Dillingham), Grady Sutton (Babe), John Carradine, Joseph Crehan, Dixie Dunbar, Donald Douglas, Charles Coleman, Stanley Andrews, Charles Williams, Jane Jones, Otto Fries, Mel Kalish, The King's Men, Jack Pennick, Cully Richards, Selmer Jackson, Lon Chaney, Jr., Charles Tannen, Arthur Rankin, Paul McVey, James Flavin, Tyler Brooke, Edward Keane, Ralph Dunn, Eleanor Wesselhoeft, Robert Lowery, Horace McMahon, Rondo Hatton. *D:* Henry King; *P:* Darryl F. Zanuck; *As.P.:* Harry Joe Brown; *Original Story:* (A.A.N.) Irving Berlin; *Sc:* Kathryn Scola, Lamar Trotti, Richard Sherman; *Art-Set Decoration:* (A.A.N.) Bernard Herzbrun, Boris Leven; *Music:* (A.A.) Alfred Newman; *Editor:* (A.A.N.) Barbara McLean; *Song:* (A.A.N.) Irving Berlin for "Now It Can Be Told." (1:46)

Sentimental story of a group of musicians from 1911 to the present day, highlighting 26 songs by Irving Berlin including the title song which was his first big hit in 1911. One of the 15 top grossing films of 1937–38, it received an A.A.N. for Best Picture and placed #3 on the list of "10 Best" films of *Film Daily.* It is also Alice Faye's personal favorite of all her films.

56. Algiers (United Artists/Walter Wanger; 1938). *Cast:* Charles Boyer (A.A.N. for B.A. as Pepe Le Moko), Sigrid Gurie (Ines), Hedy Lamarr (in her American debut as Gaby), Joseph Calleia (Acting Award from the National Board of Review), Alan Hale, Johnny Downs, Gene Lockhart (A.A.N. for B.S.A.), Walter Kingsford, Joan Woodbury, Claudia Dell (in her final film as Marie), Stanley Fields, Robert Greig, Leonid Kinskey, Paul Harvey, Charles D. Brown, Nina Koshetz, Bert Roach, Ben Hall, Luana Walters. *D:* John Cromwell; *Sc:* John Howard Lawson, James M. Cain; *Cinematographer:* (A.A.N.) James Wong Howe; *Art-Set Decoration:* (A.A.N.) to Alexander Toluboff. (1:36) (video)

Love and intrigue in the Casbah section of Algiers. The film is a remake of the 1937 French film *Pepe Le Moko.* It was remade by Universal in 1948 as the musical *Casbah.* Based on the novel by Detective Asbelbe.

57. Ali Baba Goes to Town (20th Century–Fox; 1937). *Cast:* Eddie Cantor, Tony Martin, Roland Young, June Lang, John Carradine, Louise Hovick (Gypsy Rose Lee), Douglass Dumbrille, Maurice Cass, Lee J. Cobb, Charles Lane, Paul Hurst, Virginia Field, Jeni Le Gon, the Raymond Scott Quintet, the Pearl Twins, the Peters Sisters. *D:*

David Butler; *P:* Laurence Schwab; *Sc:* Harry Tugend, Jack Yellen; *St:* Gene Towne, Graham Baker, Gene Fowler; *Choreographer:* (A.A.N.) Sammy Lee for his "Swing Is Here to Stay" number. (1:21)

Musical comedy of a man transported back to the days of the Arabian Nights. Songs by Mack Gordon and Harry Revel.

58. Alias French Gertie (RKO; 1930). *Cast:* Bebe Daniels, Ben Lyon, Robert Emmett O'Connor, Betty Pierce, John Ince, Daisy Belmore, Maude Turner Gordon, Nella Walker, Charles Giblyn. *D:* George Archainbaud; *As.P.:* Henry Hobart; *Sc:* Wallace Smith. (G.B. title: *Love Finds a Way*) (1:11)

Comedy of a female crook who intends a jewel robbery in a household where she has taken a job as a "French" maid. Based on the play "The Chatterbox" by Bayard Veiller. Previously filmed in 1925 by FBO (Film Booking Office) as *Smooth as Silk.*

59. Alias Jimmy Valentine (MGM; 1928). *Cast:* William Haines, Lionel Barrymore, Leila Hyams, Tully Marshall, Karl Dane, Howard Hickman. D: Jack Conway; SC: A.P. Younger, Sarah Y. Mason.

A part-talkie crime melodrama with synchronized sound effects and some dialogue at the climax. Previously filmed by Metro in 1920 with Bert Lytell.

60. Alias John Law (Supreme; 1935). *Cast:* Bob Steele, Roberta Gale, Earl Dwire, Jack Rockwell, Buck Connors, Roger Williams, Bob McKenzie, Steve Clark, Horace Murphy. *D:* Robert N. Bradbury (Steele's real life father); *P:* A.W. Hackel; *Sc:* Forbes Parkhill. (0:55)

Bob Steele western of a young man out to get his rightful inheritance.

61. Alias Mary Dow (Universal 1935). *Cast:* Ray Milland, Sally Eilers, Henry O'Neill, Katherine Alexander, Lola Lane, John Carradine, Clarence Muse, Addison Richards, Forrest Halsey, Baby Jane (Quigley). *D:* Kurt Neumann; *St:* Forrest Halsey, William Allen Johnston; *Sc:* Gladys Unger, Rose Franken, Arthur Caesar. (1:05)

B crime melodrama of a millionaire who hires a chorus girl to pose as his long lost daughter.

62. Alias Mary Smith (Mayfair; 1932). *Cast:* John Darrow, Matthew Betz, Myrtle Stedman, Edmund Breese, Raymond Hatton, Alec B. Francis. *D:* E. Mason Hopper.

"Poverty Row" melodrama.

63. Alias the Bad Man (Tiffany; 1931). *Cast:* Ken Maynard, Virginia Brown Faire, Frank Mayo, Charles King, Lafe McKee, Robert Homans, Earl Dwire, Jack Rockwell, Irving Bacon, Ethan Allen, Jim Corey. *D:* Phil Rosen; *P:* Phil Goldstone (Amity Productions); *Sc:* Earle Snell. (1:06)

Ken Maynard western of a cowpoke out to find the man who killed his father.

64. Alias the Deacon (Universal; 1939–40). *Cast:* Bob Burns, Peggy Moran, Dennis O'Keefe, Mischa Auer, Guinn Williams, Edward Brophy, Thurston Hall, Jack Carson, Spencer Charters, Bennie Bartlett, Berton Churchill. *D:* Christy Cabanne; *P:* Ben Pivar; *Sc:* Nat Perrin, Charles Grayson. (1:14)

A cardsharp moves in on a small town, making a small fortune at cards. Based on the play of the same name by John B. Hymer and LeRoy Clemens, it was previously filmed by this studio in 1927 with Jean Hersholt and again in 1934 as *Half a Sinner* (q.v.).

65. Alias the Doctor (WB/F.N.; 1932). *Cast:* Richard Barthelmess, Marian Marsh, Norman Foster, Adrienne Dore, Lucille La Verne, Oscar Apfel, John St. Polis, George Rosener, Boris Karloff, Claire Dodd, Reginald

Barlow, Harold Waldridge, Robert Farfan, Wallis Clark, Arnold Lucy. D: Lloyd Bacon; Sc: Houston Branch, Charles Kenyon.

Drama of a medical student who does a prison stretch by taking the blame for an operation done by his friend which resulted in death. Based on the play by Emric Foeldes.

66. Alibi (United Artists/Art Cinema; 1929). *Cast:* Chester Morris (A.A.N. for B.A. as Chick Williams — "no. 1065"), Eleanor Griffith (Joan Manning), Pat O'Malley (Tommy Glennon), Regis Toomey (film debut as Danny McGann), Mae Busch (Daisy Thomas), Elmer Ballard (Soft Malone), Harry Stubbs (Buck Bachman), Irma Harrison (Toots), Al Hill (Brown), James Bradbury, Jr. (Blake), Kernan Cripps (Trask), Purnell B. Pratt (Pete Manning), DeWitt Jennings (O'Brien), Edward Brady (George Stanislaus David), Virginia Flohri, Edward Jardon. *D:* Roland West; *P:* West; *Sc:* West, C. Gardner Sullivan. (aka: *Nightstick*) (1:30)

Melodrama of a gangster who searches the criminal underworld for an alibi. Based on the play "Nightstick" by John Wray, J.C. Nugent and Elaine Sterne Carrington. Originally filmed as a silent, it was redone as a talkie before release. It received an A.A.N. for Best Picture (1928–29).

67. Alibi for Murder (Columbia; 1936). *Cast:* Marguerite Churchill, William Gargan, Raymond Lawrence, Romaine Callender, Gene Morgan, Drue Leyton, Dwight Frye, Egon Brecher. *D:* D. Ross Lederman.

Mystery.

68/69. Alibi Ike (WB; 1935). *Cast:* Joe E. Brown, Olivia de Havilland, Ruth Donnelly, Roscoe Karns, William Frawley, Eddie Shubert, Paul Harvey, Joseph King, Joseph Crehan, G. Pat Collins, Spencer Charters, Gene Morgan, Adrian Rosley. *D:* Ray Enright; *P:*

Edward Chodorov; *St:* Ring Lardner; *Sc:* William Wister Haines. (1:13)

Comedy of a baseball pitcher who is always in hot water.

70. Alice Adams (RKO; 1935). *Cast:* Katharine Hepburn (A.A.N. for B.A. as Alice Adams), Fred MacMurray (Arthur Russell), Fred Stone (Mr. Adams), Evelyn Venable (Mildred Palmer), Frank Albertson (Walter Adams), Ann Shoemaker (Mrs. Adams), Charley Grapewin (Mr. Lamb), Grady Sutton (Frank Dowling), Hedda Hopper (Mrs. Palmer), Jonathan Hale (Mr. Palmer), Hattie McDaniel (Malena), Janet McLeod (Henrietta Lamb), Virginia Howell (Mrs. Dowling), Zeffie Tilbury (Mrs. Dresser), Ella McKenzie (Ella Dowling). *D:* George Stevens; *P:* Pandro S. Berman; *Sc:* Dorothy Yost, Jane Murfin, Mortimer Offner; *Song:* "I Can't Waltz Alone" by Dorothy Fields and Max Steiner. (1:39) (video)

Americana based on the 1921 Pulitzer Prize-winning novel by Booth Tarkington of a girl who seeks to join society in her small town and fails at each attempt until she learns to be herself. Previously filmed in 1923 by Associated Exhibitors with Florence Vidor, it received an A.A.N. for Best Picture as well as being voted one of the year's "10 Best" films by the National Board of Review.

71. Alice in Wonderland (Xxxxx Xxxx; 1931). *Cast, listed alphabetically:* Gus Alexander, Lillian Ardell, Meyer Berensen, Tom Corliss, N.R. Cregan, Ruth Gilbert, Pat Glasgow, Ralph Hertz, Vie Quinn, Jimmy Rosen, Raymond Schultz, Charles Silvern, Mabel Wright. *D:* Bud Pollard.

An obscure version of Lewis Carroll's (Charles Lutwidge Dodgson) 1865 children's classic "Alice's Adventures in Wonderland."

72. Alice in Wonderland (Paramount; 1933). *Cast:* Charlotte Henry

(Alice), W.C. Fields (Humpty Dumpty), Cary Grant (Mock Turtle), Gary Cooper (White Knight), Edward Everett Horton (Mad Hatter), Edna May Oliver (Red Queen), Jack Oakie (Tweedledum), Roscoe Karns (Tweedledee), Leon Errol (Uncle), Charles Ruggles (March Hare), May Robson (Queen of Hearts), Louise Fazenda (White Queen), Ned Sparks (Caterpillar), Alison Skipworth (Duchess), Richard Arlen (Cheshire Cat), Ford Sterling (White King), Billy Bevan (Two of Spades), Skeets Gallagher (White Rabbit), Sterling Holloway (the Frog), Mae Marsh, Baby LeRoy, William Austin, Colin Kenny, Lillian Harmer, Alice O'Byrne, Jack Duffy, Billy Barty, Harry Ekezian. *D:* Norman Z. McLeod; *P:* Louis D. Lighton; *Sc:* Joseph L. Mankiewicz, William Cameron Menzies. (1:17)

Lavish production with an all-star cast of Lewis Carroll's classic of a young girl's adventures after falling through a rabbit hole. First filmed in 1903 in one reel (about 10 mins.), followed by a 1921 silent feature version and the first talkie version in 1931 (see above). Later versions include a 1950 British production with puppets, the animated 1951 version from Walt Disney, a 1972 British musical production titled *Alice's Adventures in Wonderland,* and a two-part 1986 TV movie in the U.S. with an all-star cast.

73. Alimony Madness (Mayfair; 1933). *Cast:* Helen Chandler, Edward Earle, Alberta Vaughn, Leon (Ames) Waycoff, Blanche Frederici, Arthur Loft, Charlotte Merriam. *D:* B. Reeves Eason; *Sc:* John T. Neville.

A "Poverty Row" drama.

74. The All-American (Universal; 1932). *Cast:* Richard Arlen, Gloria Stuart, John Darrow, James Gleason, Andy Devine, Preston Foster, Robert Ellis, Merna Kennedy, June Clyde, Walter Brennan, Arthur Hoyt, Earle

Foxe, Florence Roberts, Ethel Clayton, Harold Waldridge. *D:* Russell Mack; *St:* Dale Van Every, Richard Schayer; *Sc:* Frank Wead, Ferdinand Reyher. (G.B. title: *Sport of a Nation*) (1:19)

College gridiron drama.

75. The All-American Chump (MGM; 1936). *Cast:* Edward Brophy, Stuart Erwin, Edmund Gwenn, Florence Rice, Robert Armstrong, Betty Furness, E.E. Clive, Harvey Stephens, Dewey Robinson. *D:* Edwin L. Marin; *P:* Lucien Hubbard; *Sc:* Lawrence Kimble. (G.B. title: *The Country Bumpkin*)

Comedy of a small town whiz and his rise to fame and fortune.

76. All-American Sweetheart (Columbia; 1937–38). *Cast:* Jacqueline Wells (Julie Bishop), Scott Colton, Thurston Hall, Allen Brook, Patricia Farr. *D:* Lambert Hillyer.

Romantic comedy.

77. All Men Are Enemies (Fox/Rocket; 1934). *Cast:* Helen Twelvetrees, Hugh Williams, Walter Byron, Henry Stephenson, Herbert Mundin, Una O'Connor, Rafaela Ottiano, Halliwell Hobbes. *D:* George Fitzmaurice.

Melodrama.

78. All of Me (Paramount; 1934). *Cast:* Fredric March, Miriam Hopkins, George Raft, Kitty Kelly, Helen Mack, Nella Walker, William Collier, Jr., Gilbert Emery, Blanche Frederici, Edgar Kennedy, Jason Robards, Guy Usher, John Marston. *D:* James Flood; *P:* Louis D. Lighton; *Sc:* Sidney Buchman, Thomas Mitchell; *Songs:* Ralph Rainger, Leo Robin.

Drama of a professor and his involvement with criminal element. Based on the play "Chrysalis" by Rose Albert Porter.

All One Night (G.B. title) *see* **Love Begins at Twenty**

79. All Over Town (Republic; 1937). *Cast:* Ole Olsen, Chic Johnson, Mary Howard, Gertrude Astor, Fred Kelsey, Stanley Fields, Harry Stockwell, Franklin Pangborn, James Finlayson. *D:* James W. Horne. (1:02) (video)

Low-budget comedy of two nitwits who are attempting to put on a show in a theatre with a reputation for bad luck.

80. All Quiet on the Western Front (Universal; 1930). *Cast:* Lew Ayres (Paul Baumer), Louis Wolheim (Sgt. Katczinsky), John Wray (Himmelstoss), George "Slim" Summerville (Tjaden), Ben Alexander (Kemmerich), Russell Gleason (Muller), William Bakewell (Albert), Raymond Griffith (final film as Gerard Duval), Beryl Mercer (Mrs. Baumer), Scott Kolk (Leer), Arnold Lucy (Kantorek), Owen Davis, Jr. (Peter), Walter Browne Rogers (Behm), Edwin Maxwell (Mr. Baumer), Harold Goodwin (Detering), Marion Clayton (Miss Baumer), Richard Alexander (Westhus), G. (George) Pat Collins (Lt. Bertinck), Yola D'Avril (Suzanne), Bill Irving (Ginger), Edmund Breese (Herr Meyer), Heinie Conklin (Hammacher), Bertha Mann (Sister Libertine), Joan Marsh (poster girl), Poupée Andriot, Renée Damonde, Bodil Rosing, Tom London, Vince Barnett, Fred Zinnemann, Robert Parrish. *D:* (A.A.) Lewis Milestone; *P:* Carl Laemmle, Jr.; *Sc:* (A.A.N.) Maxwell Anderson, Del Andrews, George Abbott and Milestone (unc.). (2:20) (video)

A true classic is this indictment against war, told simply through the eyes of German youths during World War I. The film was highly acclaimed and popular in the U.S. upon its release August 27, 1930, but proved to be very unpopular in Germany. It received the A.A. for Best Picture of the year, *Photoplay*'s Gold Medal Award, was voted Best Film of the year by *Film Daily*, voted one of the "10 Best" films of the year by the National Board of Review and placed #2 on the "10 Best" list of the *New York Times*. Following its initial release, 35 minutes was edited from the film. In the 1980s most of the edited footage was recovered and restored to new prints giving an approximate running time of two hours and ten minutes, being released as such on video cassette. A sequel followed in 1937 titled *The Road Back* (q.v.). Based on the 1929 novel by Erich Maria Remarque, it was remade in 1979 as a TV movie with Ernest Borgnine and Richard Thomas. On a final note, comedienne ZaSu Pitts was originally cast in the role of Mrs. Baumer, but when preview audiences laughed at her performance, the studio immediately reshot all of her footage with Beryl Mercer. Ms. Pitts was seen in European prints.

81. All the King's Horses (Paramount; 1935). *Cast:* Carl Brisson, Mary Ellis, Edward Everett Horton, Katherine de Mille, Eugene Pallette, Phillips Smalley, Edwin Maxwell, Arnold Korff, George MacQuarrie, Rosita, Marina Schubert, Frederick Sullivan, Rolfe Sedan, Eric Mayne, Leo White. *D:* Frank Tuttle; *P:* William LeBaron; *Play:* Laurence Clark, Max Giersberg; *St:* Frederick Herendeen, Edward Horan; *Sc:* Tuttle, Frederick Stephani, Edmund North; *Choreography:* (A.A.N.) to LeRoy Prinz for the "Viennese Waltz" number combined with another dance number from *The Big Broadcast of 1936* (q.v.). (1:27)

A film star and a king trade identities in this musical romance.

All This and Glamour Too (G.B. title) *see* **Vogues of 1938**

82. All Women Have Secrets (Paramount; 1939–40). *Cast:* Virginia Dale, Joseph Allen, Jr., Jeanne Cagney. *D:* Kurt Neumann.

Minor comedy drama of a couples' marital problems. Notable as the film debut of Constance Keane who in the 1940s became better known as peek-a-boo girl Veronica Lake.

83. Allegheny Uprising (RKO; 1939). *Cast:* Claire Trevor, John Wayne (James Smith), George Sanders, Brian Donlevy, Wilfrid Lawson, Robert Barrat, John F. Hamilton, Moroni Olsen, Eddie Quillan, Chill Wills, Ian Wolfe, Wallis Clark, Monte Montague, Olaf Hytten, Eddy Waller, Clay Clement, Forrest Dillon, Charles Middleton. *D:* William A. Seiter; *P:* P.J. Wolfson; *Sc:* Wolfson. (G.B. title: *The First Rebel*) (1:21) (video)

Fact-based story set on the colonial Pennsylvania frontier of 1759 where James Smith and his band of freedom fighters known as "The Black Boys" fight Indians and rum-runners. Based on the book "The First Rebel" by Neil H. Swanson. Computer-colored by Turner Entertainment in 1989.

84. Almost a Gentleman (RKO; 1939). *Cast:* James Ellison, Helen Wood, Ace the Wonder Dog, Robert Kent, June Clayworth, Robert Warwick, Leonard Penn, John Wray, Brandon Tynan, Earle Hodgins, Harlan Briggs. *D:* Leslie Goodwins; *P:* Cliff Reid; *St:* Harold Shumate; *Sc:* Ernest Pagano, David Silverstein. (G.B. title: *Magnificent Outcast*) (1:05)

B drama of a canine saved from the pound that is later accused of murder.

85. Almost Married (Fox; 1932). *Cast:* Ralph Bellamy, Violet Heming, Alexander Kirkland, Herbert Mundin, Mary Gordon. *D:* William Cameron Menzies, Marcel Varnel.

Romance.

86. Aloha (Tiffany; 1931). *Cast:* Ben Lyon, Raquel Torres, Alan Hale, Dickie Moore, Thelma Todd, Robert Ellis, Al St. John, Robert Edeson (final film—d. 1931), T. Roy Barnes, Anne Seymour (film debut). *D:* Albert S. Rogell.

"Poverty Row" romantic comedy.

87. Along Came Love (Paramount; 1936). *Cast:* Charles Starrett, Irene Hervey, Doris Kenyon, H.B. Warner, Irene Franklin. *D:* Bert Lytell (only film as director); *P:* Richard A. Rowland.

B romance of a working girl and a young doctor.

88. Along Came Youth (Paramount; 1931). *Cast:* Charles "Buddy" Rogers, Frances Dee, Stuart Erwin, William Austin, Leo White. *D:* Lloyd Corrigan, Norman Z. McLeod.

B romantic comedy set in London.

89. Always Goodbye (Fox; 1931). *Cast:* Elissa Landi, Paul Cavanagh, Lewis Stone, Frederick Kerr, John Garrick. *D:* Kenneth MacKenna, William Cameron Menzies; *St:* Kate McLaurin.

Romantic drama.

90. Always Goodbye (20th Century–Fox; 1938). *Cast:* Barbara Stanwyck, Herbert Marshall, Ian Hunter, Cesar Romero, Lynn Bari, Binnie Barnes, Mary Forbes, Albert Conti, Gilbert Emery, Ben Welden, George Davis, Marcelle Corday, Herbert Bunston, Eddie Conrad, John Russell. *D:* Sidney Lanfield; *P:* Raymond Griffith; *Sc:* Kathryn Scola, Edith Skouras. (1:15)

Tear-jerker of a woman who decides to give up her illegitimate baby, then changes her mind. Previously filmed in 1933 as *Gallant Lady* (q.v.).

91. Always in Trouble (20th Century–Fox; 1937). *Cast:* Jane Withers, Arthur Treacher, Jean Rogers, Joan Woodbury, Joseph Sawyer, Andrew Tombes, Nana Bryant, Pat Flaherty, Charles Lane, Robert Kellard, Eddie Collins. *D:* Joseph Santley; *St:* Albert Treynor, John Moffitt; *Sc:* Robert Chapin, Karen DeWolf.

Juvenile comedy-drama.

92. Amateur Crook (Victory; 1937). *Cast:* Herman Brix (later Bruce Bennett). *D:* Robert Hill; *P:* Sam Katzman.

Low-budget actioner.

93. Amateur Daddy (Fox; 1932). *Cast:* Warner Baxter, Marian Nixon, Frankie Darro, David Landau, William Pawley, Clarence Wilson, Edwin Stanley, Gail Kornfeld, Lucille Powers, Henry Dunkinson, Joan Breslaw, Joe Hachey. *D:* John G. Blystone.

Sentimental comedy-drama of a man who cares for a group of orphans. Based on a story by Mildred Cram.

Amateur Detective (G.B. title) *see* **Irish Luck**

94. The Amazing Dr. Clitterhouse (WB/F.N.; 1938). *Cast:* Edward G. Robinson (Dr. Clitterhouse), Claire Trevor, Humphrey Bogart, Allen Jenkins, Donald Crisp, Gale Page, Thurston Hall, John Litel, Maxie Rosenbloom, Vladimir Sokoloff, Curt Bois, Robert Homans, William Haade, Ward Bond, Henry O'Neill, Bert Hanlon, Billy Wayne. *D:* Anatole Litvak; *P:* Litvak, Robert Lord; *Sc:* John Huston, John Wexley. (1:27)

Comedy of a doctor who joins a gang in an attempt to understand the workings of the criminal mind. Based on the play by Barré Lyndon.

95. The Amazing Mr. Williams (Columbia; 1939). *Cast:* Melvyn Douglas, Joan Blondell, Ruth Donnelly, Clarence Kolb, Edward Brophy, Donald MacBride, Don Beddoe. *D:* Alexander Hall; *P:* Everett Riskin; *St:* Sy Bartlett; *Sc:* Bartlett, Dwight Taylor, Richard Maibaum. (1:20)

Comedy-mystery of a young couple investigating a murder, has shades of *The Thin Man* (q.v.).

96. Ambassador Bill (Fox; 1931). *Cast:* Will Rogers, Marguerite Churchill, Greta Nissen, Edwin Maxwell, Gustav von Seyffertitz, Arnold Korff, Ferdinand Munier, Tad Alexander, Tom Ricketts, Ernest Wood, Ray Milland. *D:* Sam Taylor; *Sc:* Guy Bolton.

Comedy-drama of a man who makes the world right for others.

97. Ambush (Paramount; 1938–39). *Cast:* Lloyd Nolan, Gladys Swarthout (final film — ret.), Ernest Truex, Polly Moran, William Frawley, William Henry, Ethel Clayton, Raymond Hatton, Clem Bevans. *D:* Kurt Neumann; *St:* Robert Ray; *Sc:* S.J. and Laura Perelman. (1:02)

Low-budget chase melodrama of three people caught up in the escape of bank robbers.

98. Ambush Valley (Reliable; 1936). *Cast:* Bob Custer, Victoria Vinton, Vane Calvert, Eddie Phillips, Roger Williams, Wally Wales (later Hal Taliaferro), Oscar Gahan, Ed Cassidy, Denver Dixon, Wally West, John Elliott. *D:* Raymond Samuels (Bernard B. Ray); *P:* Harry Webb; *Sc:* Bennett Cohen. (0:57)

Bob Custer western of a wealthy rancher who opposes nestors on his land. This was Custer's final starring feature.

99. American Madness (Columbia; 1932). *Cast:* Walter Huston, Pat O'Brien, Kay Johnson, Constance Cummings, Gavin Gordon, Berton Churchill, Robert Ellis, Pat O'Malley, Anderson Lawler, Walter Walker, Edwin Maxwell, Arthur Hoyt, Edward Martindel, Sterling Holloway, Jeanne Sorel. *D:* Frank Capra; *Sc:* Robert Riskin. (1:15)

Depression era story of what happens when a bank failure is apparent.

100. An American Tragedy (Paramount; 1931). *Cast:* Phillips Holmes, Sylvia Sidney, Frances Dee, Irving Pichel, Frederick Burton, Claire Dodd, Richard Cramer, Claire McDowell, Arline Judge, Charles Middleton, Taylor Holmes (the real life father of Phillips), Arnold Korff, Evelyn Pierce, Albert Hart, Emmett Corrigan, Russell Powell, Elizabeth Forrester, Fanny Midgley, Wallace Middleton, Vivian Winston, Imboden Parrish. *D:* Josef von Sternberg; *Sc:* Von Sternberg,

Samuel Hoffenstein, S.K. Lauren (unc.). (1:35)

Drama of a weak-minded young man who hasd difficulty choosing between his poor but pregnant girlfriend and a rich woman who has become attracted to him. Based on Theodore Dreiser's 1925 novel. The author was disgruntled over the final product and took Paramount to court. Curiously, famed Russian director Sergei Eisenstein wrote the original screenplay, but the studio disapproved it. A controversial film of its day, it was remade in 1951 as *A Place in the Sun.* The film was banned in Great Britain.

101. Among the Missing (Columbia; 1934). *Cast:* Richard Cromwell, Henrietta Crosman, Claire DuBrey. *D:* Albert Rogell; *Sc:* Fred Niblo, Jr.; Herbert Asbury; *St:* Florence Wagner.

Low-budget melodrama.

102. And So They Were Married (Columbia; 1935–36). *Cast:* Melvyn Douglas, Mary Astor, Edith Fellows, Jackie Moran, Donald Meek, Dorothy Stickney, Romaine Callender, Douglas Scott, Bud Flanagan (later Dennis O'Keefe). *D:* Elliott Nugent; *P:* B.P. Schulberg; *St:* Sarah Addington; *Sc:* Doris Anderson, Joseph Anthony, Laurie Brazee. (1:14)

Comedy of a widow and a widower who find that their children object to their intended marriage.

103. And Sudden Death (Paramount; 1936). *Cast:* Randolph Scott, Frances Drake, Tom Brown, Fuzzy Knight, Porter Hall, Oscar Apfel, Jimmy Conlin, Charles Arnt, Joseph Sawyer, Maidel Turner, Terry Walker, Billy Lee, John Hyams, Wilma Francis, Don Rowan, Herbert Evans. *D:* Charles Barton; *P:* A.M. Botsford; *St:* Theodore Reeves, Madeleine Ruthven; *Sc:* Joseph Moncure March. (1:10)

B melodrama which tackles the issue of drunk and reckless driving.

104. Andy Hardy Gets Spring Fever (MGM; 1939). *Cast:* Lewis Stone (Judge Hardy), Mickey Rooney (Andy Hardy), Cecilia Parker (Mary Hardy), Fay Holden (Mrs. Emily Hardy), Ann Rutherford (Polly Benedict), Sara Haden (Aunt Milly), Helen Gilbert, Terry Kilburn, John T. Murray, George Breakston, Addison Richards, Charles Peck, Robert Kent, Byron Foulger, Erville Alderson, Sidney Miller, Olaf Hytten. *D:* W.S. Van Dyke; *P:* Lou Ostrow (unc.); *Sc:* Kay Van Riper. (1:25) (video)

The seventh entry in the "Hardy Family" series. In this one Andy writes his own high school play "Adrift in Tahiti" and becomes infatuated with his drama teacher, an older woman. Based on the characters created by Aurania Rouverol.

105. Angel (Paramount; 1937). *Cast:* Marlene Dietrich, Herbert Marshall, Melvyn Douglas, Edward Everett Horton, Laura Hope Crews, Ernest Cossart, Herbert Mundin, Ivan Lebedeff, Dennie Moore, Leonard Carey, Lionel Pape, Michael Visaroff, James Finlayson. *D:* Ernst Lubitsch; *P:* Lubitsch; *Sc:* Samson Raphaelson. (1:38)

A sophisticated comedy of a romantic triangle based on a play by Melchior Lengyel. A box-office bomb which ended Dietrich's current reign at the studio.

106. Angel's Holiday (20th Century–Fox; 1937). *Cast:* Jane Withers, Russell Hopton, Sally Blane, Robert Kent, Joan Davis, Frank Jenks, John Kelly, John Qualen, Harold Huber, Paul Hurst, Al Lydell, Ray Walker, Lon Chaney, Jr. *D:* James Tinling; *P:* John Stone; *Sc:* Lynn Root, Frank Fenton.

Juvenile comedy-drama.

107. Angels Wash Their Faces (WB; 1939). *Cast:* Ann Sheridan, Frankie Thomas, Bobby Jordan, Billy Halop, Leo Gorcey, Gabriel Dell, Huntz Hall, Bernard Punsley, Bonita

Granville, Ronald Reagan, Margaret Hamilton, Marjorie Main, Henry O'Neill, Berton Churchill, Eduardo Cianelli, Bernard Nedell, Cyrus Kendall, John Ridgely, Aldrich Bowker, Minor Watson, Jackie Searle, Egon Brecher, Grady Sutton, DeWolf (William) Hopper, Robert Strange, Dick Rich. *D:* Ray Enright; *As.P.:* Max Siegel; *St:* Jonathan Finn; *Sc:* Michael Fessier, Niven Busch, Robert Buckner. (1:26)

Delinquency melodrama which is a follow-up to the popular *Angels with Dirty Faces* (q.v.).

108. Angels with Dirty Faces (WB/F.N.; 1938). *Cast:* James Cagney (Rocky Sullivan), Pat O'Brien (Jerry Connelly), Humphrey Bogart (James Frazier), Ann Sheridan (Laury Ferguson), George Bancroft (Mac Keefer), Billy Halop (Soapy), Bobby Jordan (Swing), Leo Gorcey (Blim), Gabriel Dell (Patsy), Huntz Hall (Crab), Bernard Punsley (Hunky), Frankie Burke (Rocky as a boy), William Tracy (Jerry as a boy), Marilyn Knowlden (Laury as a girl), Joe Downing (Steve), Adrian Morris (Blackie), Oscar O'Shea (Guard Kennedy), Edward Pawley (Guard Edwards), Mary Gordon (Mrs. Patrick), William Worthington (the Warden), Vera Lewis (Soapy's mother), William Pawley (Bugs), John Hamilton, Earl Dwire, Jack Perrin, James Farley, Chuck Stubbs (Red), Eddie Syracuse, Robert Homans, Harris Berger, Harry Hayden, Dick Rich, Steven Darrell, Joe A. Devlin, William Edmunds, Charles Wilson, Frank Coghlan, Jr., David Durand, Billy Gilbert, Emory Parnell, the St. Brendon Choristers. *D:* (A.A.N.) Michael Curtiz; *As.P.:* Sam Bischoff; *Original Story:* (A.A.N.) Rowland Brown; *Sc:* John Wexley, Warren Duff; *Title Song:* Fred Fisher, Maurice Spitalny. (1:37) (video — b/w and comp. colored)

Drama of two boyhood friends from the slums, one growing up to become a priest (O'Brien), the other a gangster. The gangster (Cagney) begins to see the error of his ways when he finds a gang of tough street kids (the Dead End Kids) who idolize him. For his performance, Cagney received an A.A.N. for B.A., a "Best Actor" award from the New York Film Critics and an Acting Award from the National Board of Review. One of the 16 top-grossing films of 1938–39. Followed in 1939 by *Angels Wash Their Faces* (q.v.). Computer-colored by Turner Entertainment.

109. Animal Crackers (Paramount; 1930). *Cast:* Groucho Marx (Captain Geoffrey T. Spaulding), Harpo Marx (The Professor), Chico Marx (Emanuel Ravelli), Zeppo Marx (Horatio W. Jamison), Lillian Roth (Arabella Rittenhouse), Margaret Dumont (Mrs. Rittenhouse), Hal Thompson (John Parker), Louis Sorin (Roscoe Chandler), Robert Greig (Hives), Margaret Irving (Mrs. Whitehead), Kathryn Reece (Grace Carpenter), Edward Metcalf (Hennessey), Ann Roth, The Music Masters. *D:* Victor Heerman; *P:* Walter Wanger; *Sc:* Morrie Ryskind, Pierre Collings; *Songs:* Bert Kalmar, Harry Ruby. (1:37) (video)

A creaky classic is this second feature film of the Marx Brothers. Based on a stageplay by Morrie Ryskind and George S. Kaufman, the laughs and music are centered around the theft of a valuable painting from a posh Long Island estate. Filmed at Paramount's Astoria Studios in Long Island, New York, the film introduces the song "Hooray for Captain Spaulding" which later was to become Groucho's theme song. One of the 15 top-grossing films of 1930–31.

110. The Animal Kingdom (RKO; 1932). *Cast:* Ann Harding (Daisy Sage), Leslie Howard (recreating his stage role as Tom Collier), Myrna Loy (Cecelia Henry), Neil Hamilton (Owen), William Gargan (recreating his stage role as Regan), Henry Stephenson (Rufus Collier), Ilka Chase (recreating her stage role as Grace), Leni Stengel (Franc), Donald Dillaway (Joe). *D:* Edward H. Griffith; *P:* David O. Selznick; *Adaptation:* Horace Jackson. (G.B. title: *The Woman in His House*) (1:30)

Romantic drama based on a play by Philip Barry. Notable as the first feature film to be shown at RKO's Roxy Theatre upon it's 1932 opening in New York City. One of the 11 top grossing films of 1933. Remade by Warners in 1946 as *One More Tomorrow*.

111. Ann Carver's Profession (Columbia; 1933). *Cast:* Gene Raymond, Claire Dodd, Fay Wray, Diane Bori, Jessie Ralph, Frank Albertson, Robert Barrat, Claude Gillingwater, Frank Conroy, Arthur Pierson, Edward Keane. *D:* Edward Buzzell; *Sc:* Riskin.

A romantic comedy based on the story "Rules for Wives" by Robert Riskin.

112. Ann Vickers (RKO; 1933). *Cast:* Irene Dunne (Ann Vickers), Walter Huston (Barney Dolphin), Edna May Oliver (Malvina Wormser), Bruce Cabot (Captain Resnick), Conrad Nagel (Lindsey Atwell), Mitchell Lewis (Captain Waldo), Sam Hardy (Russell Spaulding), Murray Kinnell, Helen Eby-Rock, Gertrude Michael, J. Carrol Naish, Sarah Padden, Reginald Barlow, Rafaela Ottiano, Jane Darwell. *D:* John Cromwell; *As.P.:* Pandro S. Berman; *Sc:* Jane Murfin. (1:13) (video)

Drama of a woman who becomes a social worker for a prison. Based on the novel by Sinclair Lewis.

113. Anna Christie (MGM; 1929–30). *Cast:* Greta Garbo (Anna Gustafson — "Anna Christie"), Charles Bickford (Matt Burke), George F. Marion (repeating his stage role and 1923 film role as Chris Gustafson), Marie Dressler (Marthy Owens), Lee Phelps (Larry, the bartender), James T. Mack (Johnny the Harp), Salka Steuermann. *D:* (A.A.N.) Clarence Brown; *P:* Irving Thalberg; *Sc:* Frances Marion;

Cinematographer: (A.A.N.) William Daniels. (1:26) (video)

Romantic drama of a woman of questionable morals (in other words a hooker) who finds love with a seaman. Based on the 1921 play by Eugene O'Neill, this was Garbo's first talkie and her anxiously awaited words, first spoken on film were "Gimme a viskey with chincer aile on the saide — and don't be stingy, baby." Curiously enough, Garbo personally hated her performance in this film. The film placed #5 on the "10 Best" list of *Film Daily* and #10 on the same list of the *New York Times*. Previously filmed in 1923 by Thomas H. Ince with Blanche Sweet.

114. Anna Karenina (MGM; 1935). *Cast:* Greta Garbo (voted Best Actress by the New York Film Critics as Anna Karenina), Fredric March (Count Alexei Vronsky), Freddie Bartholomew (Sergei Karenin), Basil Rathbone (Alexei Karenin), Maureen O'Sullivan (Kitty), May Robson (Countess Vronsky), Constance Collier (Countess Lidia), Reginald Owen (Stiva), Phoebe Foster (Dolly), Reginald Denny (Capt. Nicki Yashvin), Gyles Isham (Levin), Buster Phelps (Grisha), Cora Sue Collins (Tania), Guy D'Ennery (Ivanovich the tutor), Harry Allen (Cord), Mary Forbes (Princess Sorokino), Helen Freeman (Barbara), Ethel Griffies (Madame Kartasoff), Harry Beresford (Matve), Joan Marsh (Lily), Mischa Auer (Mahotin), Keith Kenneth (Mr. Kartasoff), Sidney Bracy, Ella Ethridge, Olaf Hytten, Joseph E. Tozer, Sarah Padden, Bud Flanagan (Dennis O'Keefe), Betty Blythe, Robert Warwick, Mahlon Hamilton, Pat Somerset, Harry Cording, Francis McDonald, Larry Steers, Gino Corrado. *D:* Clarence Brown; *P:* David O. Selznick; *Adaptation and Dialogue:* S.N. Behrman; *Sc:* Clemence Dane, Salka Viertel; *Cinematographer:* (A.A.N.) William Daniels. (1:36) (video)

Romantic drama based on the 1877 novel by Leo Tolstoy of a wife and mother's illicit affair with a young cavalry officer. The tragedy was shown at the Venice Film Festival and garnered the "Mussolini Cup" (Best Picture). It was also voted one of the year's "10 Best" films by the National Board of Review as well as placing #10 on the "10 Best" of *Film Daily.* Previously filmed in 1927 with Garbo as *Love.* Remade in Great Britain in 1948 and again in 1985 as a TV movie. A.K. also was one of the 25 top-grossing films of 1935–36.

115. Annabel Takes a Tour (RKO; 1938). *Cast:* Lucille Ball (Annabel), Jack Oakie, Ruth Donnelly, Bradley Page, Ralph Forbes, Alice White, Frances Mercer, Chester Clute, Donald MacBride, Pepito, Jean Rouverol, Cecil Kellaway, James Millican, Clare Verdera. *D:* Lew Landers; *P:* Lou Lusty; *St:* Bert Granet, Joe Bigelow; *Sc:* Granet, Olive Cooper. (1:07) (video)

A flop comedy sequel to the popular *The Affairs of Annabel* (q.v.). Based on the characters created by Charles Hoffman.

116. Annabelle's Affairs (Fox; 1931). *Cast:* Jeanette MacDonald, Victor McLaglen, Sally Blane, Roland Young, Joyce Compton, William Collier, Sr., Louise Beavers, Andre Beranger, Sam Hardy, Walter Walker, Wilbur Mack, Ruth Warren, Ernest Wood, Hank Mann. *D:* Alfred L. Werker.

Romantic comedy based on the play "Good Gracious Annabelle!" by Clare Kummer.

117. Annapolis Farewell (Paramount; 1935). *Cast:* Tom Brown, Richard Cromwell, Sir Guy Standing, John Howard (film debut), Ben Alexander, David Carlyle (later Robert Paige—film debut), Rosalind Keith, Benny Baker, Louise Beavers, Samuel S. Hinds, Minor Watson, Wheeler Oakman. *D:* Alexander Hall; *P:* Louis Lighton; *Sc:* Frank Craven, Dale Van Every. (G.B. title: *Gentlemen of the Navy*)

A naval academy story.

118. Annapolis Salute (RKO; 1937). *Cast:* James Ellison, Marsha Hunt, Van Heflin, Harry Carey, Arthur Lake, Ann Hovey, Dick Hogan, Marilyn Vernon, John Griggs. *D:* Christy Cabanne; *P:* Robert Sisk; *St:* Cabanne; *Sc:* John Twist. (G.B. title: *Salute to Romance*) (1:05)

Two naval cadets are in love with the same girl. This remake of *Midshipman Jack* (q.v.) was filmed on location and was a hit for the studio.

119. Anne of Green Gables (RKO; 1934). *Cast:* Anne Shirley (formerly Dawn O'Day as Anne Shirley), Tom Brown (Gilbert Blythe), O.P. Heggie (Matthew Cuthbert), Helen Westley (Marilla Cuthbert), Sara Haden, Gertrude Messinger, Murray Kinnell, Charley Grapewin, Hilda Vaughn, June Preston. *D:* George Nicholls Jr.; *P:* Kenneth MacGowan; *Sc:* Sam Mintz. (1:19) (video)

Drama of an orphan girl taken in by an elderly couple and her attempts to try and adjust to her new life. Based on the 1908 book (one of a series of six) by Lucy Maude Montgomery. Previously filmed in 1919 by Realart with Mary Miles Minter. Remade for Canadian television in 1985. Followed in 1940 by *Anne of Windy Poplars.* A big hit for the studio.

Annie Doesn't Live Here (G.B. title) *see* **Sweepstake Annie**

120. Annie Oakley (RKO; 1935). *Cast:* Barbara Stanwyck (Annie Oakley), Preston Foster (Toby Walker), Melvyn Douglas, Pert Kelton, Andy Clyde, Chief Thunderbird (Sitting Bull), Moroni Olsen (Buffalo Bill Cody), Delmar Watson, Adeline Craig, Margaret Armstrong. *D:* George Stevens; *As.P.:* Cliff Reid; *St:* Joseph A. Fields, Ewart Adamson; *Sc:* Joel Sayre, John Twist. (1:28) (video) (computer-colored)

A fictionalized account of the famed sharpshooter and her romantic entanglement with another sharpshooter during their tour with Buffalo Bill's Wild West Show in 19th-century America and Europe. A similar story was the basis for the hit Broadway musical "Annie Get Your Gun."

121. Another Dawn (WB; 1937). *Cast:* Kay Francis, Errol Flynn, Ian Hunter, Frieda Inescort, Herbert Mundin, G.P. Huntley, Jr., Clyde Cook, Mary Forbes, Billy Bevan, Reginald Sheffield, David Clyde, Charles Austin, Ben Welden, Eily Malyon. *D:* William Dieterle; *P:* Harry Joe Brown; *Sc:* Laird Doyle. (1:13)

Drama of a romantic triangle at a British army post in the African desert.

122. Another Face (RKO; 1935). *Cast:* Wallace Ford, Brian Donlevy, Phyllis Brooks, Erik Rhodes, Molly Lamont, Alan Hale, Addison (Jack) Randall, Paul Stanton, Charles Wilson, Hattie McDaniel, Si Jenks. *D:* Christy Cabanne; *As.P.:* Cliff Reid; *St:* Thomas Dugan, Ray Mayer; *Sc:* John Twist, Garrett Graham. (G.B. title: *It Happened in Hollywood*) (1:13)

Comedy of an ex-gangster who has his face changed and goes to Hollywood to become a star. A box office hit.

123. Another Language (MGM; 1933). *Cast:* Helen Hayes, Robert Montgomery, John Beal (film debut), Louise Closser Hale, Henry Travers, Margaret Hamilton (film debut), Willard Robertson, Maidel Turner, Minor Watson, Hal K. Dawson, Irene Cattell. *D:* Edward H. Griffith; *P:* Walter Wanger; *Sc:* Herman J. Mankiewicz, Gertrude Purcell, Donald Ogden Stewart. (1:15)

Marital drama of a woman who is not accepted by her in-laws after her marriage. Based on a play by Rose Franken.

124. Another Thin Man (MGM; 1939). *Cast:* William Powell (Nick Charles), Myrna Loy (Nora Charles), Asta, Virginia Grey (Lois MacFay), Otto Kruger (Van Slack), C. Aubrey Smith (Col. Burr MacFay), Ruth Hussey (Dorothy Waters), Nat Pendleton (Lieut. Guild), Patric Knowles (Dudley Horn), Tom Neal (Freddie Coleman), Phyllis Gordon (Mrs. Bellam), Sheldon Leonard (Sam Church), Don Costello ("Diamond Back" Vogel), Harry Bellaver (film debut as "Creeps" Binder), William Anthony Poulsen (Nicky Jr.), Muriel Hutchinson (Smitty), Abner Biberman (Dum-Dum), Marjorie Main (Mrs. Dolley), Martin Garralaga (Pedro), Frank Sully (Pete), Edward Gargan (Quinn), Bert Roach (Cookie), Shemp Howard (Wacky), Nellie V. Nichols (Mrs. Wacky), Joe Devlin (Barney), Murray Alper (Larry), Roy Barcroft (Slim the guard), Alex D'Arcy, Horace MacMahon, Nell Craig, Milton Kibbee, Thomas Jackson, Matty Fain, Joseph Downing, Claire Rochelle, Winstead "Doodles" Weaver, Milton Parsons, Dick Elliott, Nestor Paiva, Edwin Parker, Gladden James, Renee and Stella. *D:* W.S. Van Dyke II; *P:* Hunt Stromberg; *St:* Dashiell Hammett; *Sc:* Frances Goodrich, Albert Hackett. (1:45) (video)

The third entry in the popular series this one concerning a man predicting the deaths of people before they occur. Followed in 1941 by *Shadow of the Thin Man.*

Note: one of the 21 top-grossing films of 1939–40.

125. Anthony Adverse (WB; 1936). *Cast:* Fredric March (Anthony Adverse), Olivia de Havilland (Angela Guisseppi), Anita Louise (Maria), Edmund Gwenn (John Bonnyfeather), Claude Rains (Don Luis), Donald Woods (Vincent Nolte), Louis Hayward (Dennis Moore), Gale Sondergaard (A.A. for B.S.A. in her film debut as Faith), Akim Tamiroff (Carlo Cibo), Luis Alberni (Tony Guisseppi), Fritz Leiber (M. Ouvard), Henry O'Neill (Father Xavier), Steffi Duna (Neleta), Billy Mauch (Anthony—age 10), Ralph Morgan (De Bruille), Marilyn Knowlden (Florence Udney—age 10), Ann Howard (Angela—child), Rollo Lloyd (Napoleon Bonaparte), George E. Stone (Sancho), Joseph Crehan (Capt. Elisha Jorham), Clara Blandick (Mrs. Jorham), Scotty Beckett (Anthony as a little boy), Addison Richards (Capt. Matanze), J. Carrol Naish (Major Doumet), Pedro de Cordoba (Brother Francois), Grace Stafford (Lucia), Eily Malyon (Mother Superior), Leonard Mudie (De Bourrienne), Rafaela Ottiano (Senora Bovina), Paul Sotoff (Ferdinando), Ottola Nesmith (Sister Ursula), Joseph King, Mathilde Comont, Frank Reicher, Joan Woodbury, Frank Lackteen, Martin Garralaga, Zeffie Tilbury, Bess Flowers, Myra Marsh, Boris Nicholai, William Ricciardi. *D:* Mervyn LeRoy; *P:* Jack L. Warner; *Supervisor:* Henry Blanke; *Sc:* Sheridan Gibney; *Cinematographer:* (A.A.) Tony Gaudio; *Art-Set Decoration:* (A.A.N.) Anton Grot; *Musical Score:* (A.A.) Erich Wolfgang Korngold; *Musical Director:* Leo Forbstein; *Editor:* (A.A.) Ralph Dawson. (2:16) (video)

Classic Academy Award-winning film version of Hervey Allen's 1933 bestseller of a young man's adventures in the 19th century. It received an A.A.N. for Best Picture and was one of the 38 top grossing films of 1936–37. *Film Daily* placed it at #8 on their list of "10 Best" films.

126. Anybody's Blonde (Action Pictures; 1931). *Cast:* Dorothy Revier, Reed Howes. *D:* Frank Strayer. (G.B. title: *When Blonde Meets Blonde*)

Minor melodrama.

127. Anybody's War (Paramount; 1930). *Cast:* George Moran, Charles Mack, Neil Hamilton, Joan Peers, Walter McGrail, Betty Farrington, Walter Weems. *D:* Richard Wallace; *Sc:* Lloyd Corrigan.

A World War I comedy.

128. Anybody's Woman (Paramount; 1930). *Cast:* Ruth Chatterton, Paul Lukas, Clive Brook, Sidney Bracey, Cecil Cunningham, Huntley Gordon, Virginia Hammond, Charles Gerrard, Harvey Clark, Tom Patricola, Gertrude Sutton. *D:* Dorothy Arzner; *St:* Gouverneur Morris.

Drama of the marriage of an alcoholic lawyer and a chorus girl.

129. Anything for a Thrill (Ambassador; 1937). *Cast:* Frankie Darro, Kane Richmond, Edward Hearn. *D:* Leslie Goodwins; *P:* Maurice Conn.

B actioner.

130. Anything Goes (Paramount; 1936). *Cast:* Bing Crosby, Ethel Merman, Charles Ruggles, Ida Lupino, Grace Bradley, Arthur Treacher, Margaret Dumont, Chill Wills and the Avalon Boys, Matt Moore, Richard Carle, Robert McWade, Keye Luke, Rolfe Sedan, Bud Flanagan (Dennis O'Keefe—extra). *D:* Lewis Milestone; *P:* Benjamin Glazer; *St:* Guy Bolton, P.G. Wodehouse; *Sc:* Howard Lindsay, Russel Crouse (from their show), Walter DeLeon, Sidney Salkow, John Moffitt, Francis Martin. (TV title: *Tops Is the Limit*) (1:32)

Shipboard musical based on the hit Broadway show which opened in 1934, with songs by Cole Porter including the title song, "You're the Tops" and "I Get a Kick Out of You." Other songs by Hoagy Carmichael (m), Leo Robin (ly), Frederick Hollander (m), Richard A. Whiting (m), Edward Heyman (ly). Remade in 1956 with many of the original songs deleted.

131. The Apache Kid's Escape (Horner Productions; 1930). *Cast:* Jack Perrin, Josephine Hill, Fred Church, Virginia Ashcroft, Henry Rocquemore, Bud Osborne. *D:* Robert J. Horner; *P:* Horner; *Sc:* Horner. (0:50)

Jack Perrin western.

132. Applause (Paramount; 1929). *Cast:* Helen Morgan (film debut as Kitty Darling), Joan Peers (April

Darling), Fuller Mellish, Jr. (Hitch Nelson), Henry Wadsworth (film debut as Tony), Jack Cameron (Joe King), Dorothy Cumming (Mother Superior), Paul Barrett (Slim Lamont), Jack Singer (the producer). *D:* Rouben Mamoulian (in his directorial debut); *P:* Monta Bell; *Sc:* Garrett Fort; *Songs:* "What Wouldn't I Do for That Man" by E.Y. Harburg, Jay Gorney; "Everybody's Doing It," "Doing the New Raccoon" and "Give Your Little Baby Lots of Lovin'" by Dolly Morse and Joe Burke. (1:18) (video)

Musical drama of an alcoholic burlesque queen who protects her daughter from the truth. Based on the novel by Beth Brown, it was filmed at Astoria Studios in Long Island, New York and at various places throughout New York City. A box office flop on original release, the film has gained acclaim in recent years.

133. Are These Our Children? (RKO; 1931). *Cast:* Eric Linden (film debut), Arline Judge, Beryl Mercer, Billy Butts, Rochelle Hudson, William Orlamond, Ben Alexander, Mary Kornman, Bobby Quirk, Roberta Gale, Grady Sutton. *D:* Wesley Ruggles; *As.P.:* Louis Sarecky; *St:* Ruggles; *Adaptation & Sc:* Howard Estabrook. (1:15)

Drama of teens in pursuit of an irresponsible lifestyle, getting involved in murder.

134. Are We Civilized? (Raspin Productions; 1934). *Cast:* Stuart Holmes, Anita Louise, William Farnum, William Humphrey, Oscar Apfel, Frank McGlynn, LeRoy Mason, Harry Burkhart, Allan Cavan, Sidney T. Pink, Conrad Siderman, Bert Lindley, Aaron Edwards, Charles Requa, J. Fowler. *D:* Edwin Carewe (directorial finale); *P:* Carewe; *St:* Harold Sherman; *Sc:* Sherman.

Melodrama.

135. Are You Listening? (MGM; 1932). *Cast:* William Haines, Madge Evans, Anita Page, Karen Morley, Neil Hamilton, Wallace Ford, Jean Hersholt, John Miljan, Joan Marsh, Ethel Griffies. *D:* Harry Beaumont; *St:* J.P. McEvoy; *Sc:* Dwight Taylor.

Low-budget melodrama of newscasting.

136. Are You There? (Fox; 1930). *Cast:* Beatrice Lillie, Lloyd Hamilton, Olga Baclanova. *D:* Hamilton McFadden.

Romantic comedy.

137. The Argyle Case (WB; 1929). *Cast:* Thomas Meighan, Lila Lee, H.B. Warner, Gladys Brockwell, ZaSu Pitts, Douglas Gerrard, Bert Roach, John Darrow, Wilbur Mack, Raymond Gallagher, Lew Harvey, Jimmie Quinn, Alona Marlowe. *D:* Howard Bretherton; *Sc:* Harvey Thew.

A low-budget who-dun-it revolving around the murder of a wealthy man. Filmed before in 1917, it was based on the play by Harriet Ford, Harvey J. O'Higgins and William J. Burns.

138. Arizona (Columbia; 1931). *Cast:* Laura LaPlante, John Wayne, June Clyde, Forrest Stanley, Nina Quartero, Susan Fleming, Loretta Sayers, Hugh Cummings. *D:* George B. Seitz; *Sc:* Robert Riskin. (G.B. title: *Men Are Like That*)

Romantic drama based on a play by Augustus Thomas.

139. Arizona Badman (Willis Kent; 1934). *Cast:* Reb Russell, Rebel (Horse), Edmund Cobb. *D:* S. Roy Luby; *P:* Willis Kent.

Reb Russell western.

140. Arizona Days (Grand National; 1937). *Cast:* Tex Ritter, Eleanor Stewart, Syd Saylor, Ethelind Terry, William Faversham, Forrest Taylor, Snub Pollard, Horace Murphy, Glenn Strange, Earl Dwire, Budd Buster, Salty Holmes, Edward Cassidy, Tommy Bupp, Tex Palmer, William Desmond, White Flash (Ritter's horse). *D:* Jack (John) English; *P:* Edward Finney

(Boots and Saddles Prods.); *St:* Lindsley Parsons; *Sc:* Sherman Lowe. (0:57) (video)

Tex Ritter western with songs of a traveling show.

141. Arizona Gunfighter (Republic-Supreme; 1937). *Cast:* Bob Steele, Jean Carmen, Ted Adams, Ernie Adams, Lew Meehan, Steve Clark, John Merton, Karl Hackett, Frank Ball, Sherry Tansey, Jack Kirk, Hal Price, Budd Buster, Horace Carpenter, Tex Palmer, Allen Greer, Oscar Gahan. *D:* Sam Newfield; *P:* A.W. Hackel; *Sc:* George Plympton. (0:58)

Bob Steele western of a cowboy out to find the killer of his father.

142. The Arizona Kid (Fox; 1930). *Cast:* Warner Baxter, Mona Maris, Carol(e) Lombard, Theodore von Eltz, Arthur Stone, Soledad Jimenez, Walter P. Lewis, Jack Herrick, Wilfred Lucas, Hank Mann, James Gibson, Larry McGrath, De Sacia Mooers. *D:* Alfred Santell; *Sc:* Ralph Block. (1:30)

Romantic western of a bandit lothario.

143. The Arizona Kid (Republic; 1939). *Cast:* Roy Rogers, George "Gabby" Hayes, Sally March, Stuart Hamblen, Dorothy Sebastian, David Kerwin, Earl Dwire, Peter Fargo, Fred Burns, Edward Cassidy, Ted Mapes, Jack Ingram, Frank McCarroll, Robert Middlemass. *D:* Joseph Kane; *P:* Kane; *Sc:* Luci Ward, Gerald Geraghty. (1:01)

Roy Rogers western set during the Civil War period, involving a band of guerillas.

144. Arizona Legion (RKO; 1939). *Cast:* George O'Brien, Laraine (Day) Johnson, Carlyle Moore, Jr., Chill Wills, Tom Chatterton, Edward LeSaint, William Royle, Harry Cording, Glenn Strange, Monte Montague, Bobby Burns, Lafe McKee, John Dilson, Guy Usher, Bob Kortman, Wilfred Lucas, Jim Mason, Art Mix. *D:* David Howard; *P:* Bert Gilroy; *St:* Bernard McConville; *Sc:* Oliver Drake; *Song:* Drake. (0:58)

George O'Brien western of an Arizona Ranger who goes undercover to expose corruption.

145. Arizona Mahoney (Paramount; 1936–37). *Cast:* Robert Cummings, June Martel, Buster Crabbe, Joe Cook, John Miljan, Marjorie Gateson, Fred Kohler, Dave Chasen, Irving Bacon, Richard Carle, Billy Lee, Fuzzy Knight, Si Jenks. *D:* James Hogan; *P:* A.M. Botsford; *Sc:* Robert Yost, Stuart Anthony. (Re-release title: *Arizona Thunderbolt*) (1:01)

Western of an eastern tenderfoot who learns the ways of the west the hard way. Loosely based on Zane Grey's *Stairs of Sand,* (q.v.), the title under which it was filmed in 1929.

146. The Arizona Raiders (Paramount; 1936). *Cast:* Buster Crabbe, Marsha Hunt, Raymond Hatton, Johnny Downs, (Betty) Jane Rhodes, Grant Withers, Richard Carle, Arthur Aylesworth, Don Rowan, Herbert Heywood, Petra Silva. *D:* James Hogan; *P:* Dan Keefe; *Sc:* Robert Yost, John Krafft. (0:54) (video)

Low-budget western of outlaws making life miserable for some settlers. Based on Zane Grey's "Raiders of Spanish Peak."

147. The Arizona Terror (Tiffany/Amity; 1931). *Cast:* Ken Maynard, Lina Basquette, Hooper Atchley, Nena Quartero, Michael Visaroff, Murdock McQuarrie, Charles King, Tom London, Edmund Cobb, Jack Rockwell, Jim Corey, Fred Burns. *D:* Phil Rosen; *P:* Sam Goldstone; *Sc:* John Francis (Jack) Natteford. (1:04)

Ken Maynard western of a cowboy wrongly accused of murder.

Arizona Thunderbolt *see* **Arizona Mahoney**

148. Arizona to Broadway (Fox; 1933). *Cast:* James Dunn, Joan Bennett, Herbert Mundin, Sammy Cohen, Theodore von Eltz, J. Carrol Naish, Merna Kennedy, Walter Catlett, Earle Foxe. *D:* James Tinling; *St & Sc:* William Conselman, Henry Johnson. (1:06)

A woman gets a sideshow con-artist to help her retrieve money from swindlers. Remade in 1943 as *Jitterbugs.*

149. Arizona Trail (Xxxx Xxxx; 1934). *D:* Victor Adamson (Denver Dixon). (No other information available.) Western.

150. The Arizona Wildcat (20th Century-Fox; 1938-39). *Cast:* Jane Withers, Leo Carrillo, Pauline Moore, Henry Wilcoxon, Douglas Fowley, Harry Woods, William Henry, Etienne Girardot. *D:* Herbert I. Leeds; *Sc:* Barry Trivers, Jerry Cady. (1:08)

Juvenile western comedy of a reformed bandit falsely accused of a crime. Previously filmed in 1927 by Fox as a Tom Mix wetsern.

151. The Arizona Wrangler (Xxxx Xxxx; 1935). *Cast:* Roger Williams.

(May be an Ajax Production — no other information available.)

152. The Arizonian (RKO; 1935). *Cast:* Richard Dix (Clay Tallant), Preston Foster (Tex Randolph), Margot Grahame (Kitty Rivers), Louis Calhern, James Bush, J. Farrell MacDonald, Willie Best, Francis Ford, Jack Montgomery, Ray Mayer, Joseph (Sawyer) Sauers, Edward Van Sloan, Robert Kortman, Ted Oliver, Etta McDaniel, Jim Thorpe, Hank Bell. *D:* Charles Vidor; *As.P.:* Cliff Reid; *St:* Dudley Nichols; *Sc:* Nichols. (1:16)

A newly elected lawman cleans up the corrupt town of Silver City. Remade in 1939 as *The Marshal of Mesa City* (q.v.).

153. The Arkansas Traveller (Paramount; 1938). *Cast:* "Bazooka" Bob Burns, Fay Bainter, Jean Parker, Irvin S. Cobb, John Beal, Lyle Talbot, Dickie Moore, Porter Hall. *D:* Alfred Santell; *P:* George M. Arthur; *St:* Jack Cunningham; *Sc:* Viola Brothers Shore, George Sessions Perry. (1:25)

B comedy with "Bazooka" Bob Burns as the traveller who helps a woman save her small-town newspaper.

154. Arm of the Law (Monogram; 1932). *Cast:* Rex Bell, Marceline Day, Lina Basquette, Bryant Washburn, Robert Emmett O'Connor, Robert Frazer, Dorothy Revier, Dorothy Christy, Donald Keith, Larry Banthim, Gilbert Clayton, Wallace McDonald, William V. Mong, Fred "Snowflake" Toones. *D:* Louis King; *P:* Trem Carr; *Sc:* Leon Lee. (1:00)

Low-budget mystery-melodrama involving the murder of a cabaret entertainer. A Trojan production which was based on the story "The Butterfly Mystery" by Arthur Hoerl.

155. Armored Car (Universal; 1937). *Cast:* Robert Wilcox, Judith Barrett, Irving Pichel, Cesar Romero, Harry Davenport, William Lundigan (film debut), Paul Fix, Inez Courtney, John Kelly, Stanley Blystone, Richard Tucker, Wiiliam Pierce, Tony (J. Anthony) Hughes, David Oliver, Rollo Lloyd. *D:* Lewis R. Foster (solo directorial debut); *P:* E.M. Asher; *Sc:* Foster, Robert N. Lee. (1:04)

B melodrama of a detective who goes undercover to capture crooks.

Arms and the Girl (G.B. title) *see* **Red Salute**

156. Army Girl (Republic; 1938). *Cast:* Madge Evans, Preston Foster, Heather Angel, Neil Hamilton, Ralph Byrd, James Gleason, Guinn Williams, H.B. Warner, Ruth Donnelly, Billy Gilbert, Ralph Morgan, Barbara Pepper, Dewey Robinson. *D:* B. Reeves Eason, George Nicholls, Jr.; *P:* Sol C. Siegel; *St:* Charles L. Clifford; *Sc:* Samuel

Ornitz, Barry Trivers; *Cinematographer:* (A.A.N.) Ernest Miller and Harry Wild; *Original Music Score:* (A.A.N.) Victor Young; *Sound Recording:* (A.A.N.) Charles Lootens. (G.B. title: *The Last of the Cavalry*)

A romantic military action drama. Republic productions rarely received Academy Award nominations, but this film got three.

157. Around the Corner (Columbia; 1930). *Cast:* Charlie Murray, George Sidney, Charles Delaney. *D:* Bert Glennon; *St & Sc:* Jo Swerling. Comedy.

158. Around the World in 80 Minutes with Douglas Fairbanks (United Artists; 1931). *D:* Douglas Fairbanks, Victor Fleming; *P:* Fairbanks; *Sc:* Fairbanks, Robert E. Sherwood. (1:20)

A travelogue feature hosted by Douglas Fairbanks, Sr.

159. Arrest Bulldog Drummond (Paramount; 1938–39). *Cast:* John Howard, Heather Angel, H.B. Warner, George Zucco, E.E. Clive, Reginald Denny, John Sutton, John Davidson, Claud Allister, Clyde Cook, Leonard Mudie, George Regas, Jean Fenwick, Neil Fitzgerald, David Clyde, Evan Thomas. *D:* James Hogan; *P:* Stuart Walker; *Sc:* Stuart Palmer. (0:57) (video)

The sixth entry in the series centered around an ex–British army officer who in this one is after a madman with a death ray. Based on a character created in 1919 by "Sapper" (Herman Cyril McNeile). Based on his work, "The Final Count."

160. Arrowsmith (United Artists/ Samuel Goldwyn; 1931). *Cast:* Ronald Colman (Dr. Martin Arrowsmith), Helen Hayes (Leora Tozer), Richard Bennett (Dr. Soldelius), A.E. Anson (Prof. Max Gottlieb), Clarence Brooks (Oliver Marchand), Alec B. Francis (Twyford), Claude King (Dr. Tubbs), Bert Roach (Bert Tozer), Myrna Loy (Joyce Lanyon), Russell Hopton (Terry Wickett), David Landau (the state veterinary), Lumsden Hare (Sir Robert Fairland), DeWitt Jennings (Mr. Tozer), Beulah Bondi (Mrs. Tozer), John M. Qualen (Henry Novak), Adele Watson (Mrs. Novak), Sidney DeGray (Dr. Hesselink), Florence Britton (Miss Twyford), Charlotte Henry, James Marcus, Ward Bond, Pat Somerset, Eric Wilton, Erville Alderson, George Humbert, Raymond Hatton, Theresa Harris. *D:* John Ford; *P:* Samuel Goldwyn; *Sc:* (A.A.N.) Sidney Howard; *Cinematographer:* (A.A.N.) Ray June; *Art-Set Decoration:* (A.A.N.) Richard Day. (1:41) (video)

A research doctor is tempted to give up his calling when he is unable to prevent the death of his beloved wife. Based on the 1925 novel by Sinclair Lewis (who had received the Nobel Prize for literature in 1930). The film received an A.A.N. for Best Picture, placed #4 on the *New York Times* list of "10 Best" films of 1931 as well as receiving the #3 position on the same list of *Film Daily* in 1932. One of the 15 top grossing films of 1932.

161. Arsene Lupin (MGM; 1932). *Cast:* John Barrymore, Lionel Barrymore, Karen Morley, John Miljan, Henry Armetta, Tully Marshall, John Davidson, Mary Jane Irving, James T. Mack, George Davis. *D:* Jack Conway; *Sc:* Carey Wilson, Lenore Coffee, Bayard Veiller. (1:24)

Paris based story of a jewel thief and the detective trying to apprehend him. Based on a character created by Maurice Leblanc, it was previously filmed in 1917 by Vitagraph with Earle Williams. Notable as the first film in which the two Barrymore brothers appeared together. Followed by a sequel (see below).

162. Arsene Lupin Returns (MGM; 1937–38). *Cast:* Melvyn Douglas, Virginia Bruce, Warren William, John Halliday, Nat Pendleton, Monty Woolley, George Zucco, E.E.

Clive, Ian Wolfe, Vladimir Sokoloff, Tully Marshall, Jack Norton, Rollo Lloyd. *D:* George Fitzmaurice; *P:* John W. Considine, Jr.; *Sc:* James Kevin McGuinness, Howard Emmett Rogers, George Harmon Coxe. (1:21)

Comedy-mystery about jewel thieves which is a sequel to the above film.

Arson Gang Busters *see* **Arson Racket Squad**

163. Arson Racket Squad (Republic; 1937–38). *Cast:* Bob Livingston, Dick Wessel, Jackie Moran, Rosalind Keith, Lloyd Whitlock, Clay Clement, Emory Parnell, Warren Hymer, Selmer Jackson, Jack Rico, Walter Sande. *D:* Joe Kane; *Sc:* Norman Burnstine, Alex Gottlieb. (aka: *Arson Gang Busters*)

Crime melodrama.

164. Artists and Models (Paramount; 1937). *Cast:* Jack Benny (Mac Brewster), Ida Lupino (Paula), Richard Arlen (Alan Townsend), Gail Patrick (Cynthia), Martha Raye (specialty), Judy Canova (Toots), Ben Blue (Jupiter Pluvius), Cecil Cunningham (Stella), Donald Meek (Dr. Zimmer), Hedda Hopper (Mrs. Townsend), Andre Kostelanetz and his orchestra (specialty), Louis Armstrong and his orchestra (specialty), Russell Patterson's Personettos (specialty), Judy, Anne & Zeke (the Canovas in a specialty), The Yacht Club Boys (specialty), Connee Boswell (specialty), Madelon Grey (Marjorie), Alan Birmingham (Craig Sheldon), Kathryn Kay (Lois), Del Henderson (Lord), David Newell (Romeo), Little Billy (King), Jane Weir (Miss Gordon), Howard Hickman (Mr. Currie), Sandra Storme (model), Jerry Bergen (bartender), Mary Shepherd and Gloria Wheedon (Water Waltzers), Virginia Brissac (seamstress), Henry and Harry C. Johnson (jugglers), Jack Stary (cycling star), Harvey Poirier (sharpshooter), Pat Moran (tumbler), Edward Earle (Flunkey), Peter Arno, Arthur William Brown, McClelland Barclay, Rube Goldberg, John La Gatta, and Russell Patterson (artists). *D:* Raoul Walsh; *P:* Lewis E. Gensler; *St:* Sig Herzig, Gene Thackrey; *Adaptation:* Eve Greene, Harlan Ware; *Sc:* Walter DeLeon, Francis Martin; *Song:* (A.A.N.) Frederick Hollander and Leo Robin for "Whispers in the Dark"; *Other Songs:* "Mister Esquire" by Ted Koehler, Victor Young; "I Have Eyes" by Ralph Rainger & Robin, "Moonlight and Shadows" by Hollander and Robin, "Pop Goes the Bubble," "Public Enemy No. 1" and "Stop, You're Breaking My Heart" by Koehler and Burton Lane. (1:37)

Comedy of a woman pretending to be a socialite. One of the 38 top grossing films of 1936–37, it was followed by a sequel (see below). Remade in 1955.

165. Artists and Models Abroad (Paramount; 1938). *Cast:* Jack Benny, Joan Bennett, Mary Boland, Charley Grapewin, The Yacht Club Boys, G.P. Huntley, Jr., Georges Renavent, Phyllis Kennedy, Alex Melesh, Andre Cheron. *D:* Mitchell Leisen; *P:* Arthur Hornblow, Jr.; *St:* J.P. McEvoy, Howard Lindsay; *Sc:* Lindsay, Russel Crouse, Ken Englund. (1:30)

Comedy of a group of musicians who are stranded in Paris. A follow-up to the above film.

166. As Good as Married (Universal; 1936–37). *Cast:* John Boles, Doris Nolan, Alan Mowbray, Dorothea Kent, Walter Pidgeon, Esther Ralston, Walter Byron, Harry Davenport, Tala Birell, Katharine Alexander, David Oliver, Mary Philips, Billy Schaeffer, Elsa Christiansen. *D:* Edward Buzzell; *P:* E.M. Asher; *St:* Norman Krasna; *Sc:* F. Hugh Herbert, Lynn Starling. (1:13)

Marital drama of a boss who marries his secretary for the wrong reason.

167. As Husbands Go (Fox; 1933). *Cast:* Warner Baxter, Helen Vinson, Catherine Doucet (film debut),

Beverly Bayne, G.P. Huntley, Jr., Frank O'Connor, Eleanor Lynn, Jay Ward. *D:* Hamilton McFadden.

Marital infidelity as a married woman becomes infatuated with a debonair European. Based on the play by Rachel Crothers.

168. As the Devil Commands (Columbia; 1933). *Cast:* Neil Hamilton, Mae Clarke. *D:* Roy William Neill; *Sc:* Jo Swerling.

Low-budget production.

169. As the Earth Turns (WB; 1934). *Cast:* Donald Woods (Stan Janowski), Jean Muir (Jen Shaw), Russell Hardie, Emily Lowry, Arthur Hohl, Dorothy Appleby, Clara Blandick, David Landau, George A. Billings, William Janney, Marilyn Knowlden, Sarah Padden, Dorothy Peterson, David Durand, Javir Gibbons, Egon Brecher, Joyce Kaye, Dorothy Gray. *D:* Alfred E. Green; *P:* Robert Lord; *Sc:* Ernest Pascal.

A rural drama which depicts the hardships of a farm family in Maine. Based on the novel by Gladys Hasty Carroll.

170. As You Desire Me (MGM; 1932). *Cast:* Greta Garbo (Zara), Melvyn Douglas (Bruno), Erich von Stroheim (Salter), Hedda Hopper (Madame Mantari), Owen Moore (Tony), Rafaela Ottiano (Lena), Albert Conti (captain), Warburton Gamble (Baron), William Ricciardi (Pietro) Roland Varno (Albert). *D:* George Fitzmaurice; *P:* Fitzmaurice; *Sc:* Gene Markey. (1:11)

Drama of an amnesiac who returns to her husband, but remembers nothing of him. Based on the play by Luigi Pirandello. Voted one of the year's "10 Best" by the National Board of Review, it was twice remade by Universal *This Love of Ours* (1945) and *Never Say Goodbye* (1955).

171. Assassin of Youth (B-C-M Productions; 1936–37). *Cast:* Luana

Walters, Arthur Gardner, Dorothy Short, Earl Dwire, Fern Emmett, Henry Rocquemore, Fay McKenzie, Michael Owen, Dorothy Vaughan, Hudson Fausset. *D:* Elmer Clifton; *P:* Leo J. McCarthy; *St:* McCarthy, Clifton; *Sc:* McCarthy, Charles A. Brown. (Re-release title: *Marijuana*) (1:11) (video — 1:07)

Independent exploitation melodrama dealing with the '30s concept of marijuana use and addiction.

172. At the Circus (MGM; 1939). *Cast:* Groucho Marx (I. Cheever Loophole), Harpo Marx (Punchy), Chico Marx (Pirelli), Florence Rice, Kenny Baker, Eve Arden, Margaret Dumont, Nat Pendleton, Fritz Feld, Barnett Parker, Willie Best, James Burke, Byron Foulger, Emory Parnell, Jerry Marenghi. *D:* Edward Buzzell; *P:* Mervyn LeRoy; *Sc:* Irving S. Brecher. (aka: *The Marx Brothers at the Circus* (1:27) (video)

Marx Brothers shenanigans as they save a circus from going bankrupt. This box office hit features Groucho singing his famous "Lydia the Tattooed Lady" with music by Harold Arlen and lyrics by E.Y. Harburg.

173. Atlantic Adventure (Columbia; 1935). *Cast:* Nancy Carroll, Lloyd Nolan, Cornelius Keefe, Harry Langdon, E.E. Clive, Dwight Frye. *D:* Albert S. Rogell.

Low-budget actioner.

Atlantic City Romance (G.B. title) *see* **Convention Girl**

174. Atlantic Flight (Monogram; 1937). *Cast:* Dick Merrill, Paula Stone, Jack Lambie, Weldon Heyburn, Ivan Lebedeff, Milburn Stone. *D:* William Nigh; *P:* William Berke; *St:* W. Scott Darling, Erna Lazarus; *Sc:* Darling, Lazarus. (0:59)

B actioner involving sabotage in an air race. Of minor note is the fact that the star of the film held the world's record for a round-trip Atlantic flight.

175. Attorney for the Defense (Columbia; 1932). *Cast:* Edmund Lowe, Evelyn Brent, Constance Cummings, Nat Pendleton, Clarence Muse, Dorothy Peterson, Donald Dillaway, Bradley Page, Wallis Clark, Dwight Frye, Douglas Haig. *D:* Irving Cummings; *St:* James Kevin McGuinness; *Sc:* Jo Swerling.

Low-budget courtroom drama.

Auction in Souls *see* **The Constant Woman**

176. August Week-End (Chesterfield; 1936). *Cast:* Betty Compson, Claire McDowell. *D:* Charles Lamont. (G.B. title: *Weekend Madness*)

A "Poverty Row" romance.

177. The Avenger (Columbia/Beverly Productions; 1930–31). *Cast:* Buck Jones, Dorothy Revier, Ed Peil, Otto Hoffman, Sidney Bracey, Edward Hearn, Paul Fix, Walter Percival, Frank Ellis, Al Taylor, Charles "Slim" Whitaker. *D:* Roy William Neill; *Sc:* Jack Townley, George Morgan. (1:05)

Buck Jones western set in early California with Jones as Joaquin Murietta, the Robin Hood-bandit. Remade in 1942 as *Vengeance of the West* with Bill Elliott.

178. The Avenger (Monogram; 1933). *Cast:* Ralph Forbes, Adrienne Ames, Arthur Vinton, Claude Gillingwater, Charlotte Merriam, J. Carrol Naish, Berton Churchill, Murray Kinnell, Thomas Jackson, Paul Fix, James Donlan, Leonard Carey, Boothe Howard, Wilson Benge. *D:* Edwin L. Marin; *P:* Trem Carr; *Sc:* Brown Holmes, Tristram Tupper. (1:19)

Low-budget drama of a D.A. wrongfully sentenced to prison, who gets out and sets the record straight with those who sent him up. Based on the novel by John Goodwin.

The Avenging Stranger *see* **God's Country and the Man** (1937)

179. Avenging Waters (Columbia; 1936). *Cast:* Ken Maynard, Beth Marion, John Elliott, Zella Russell, Ward Bond, Wally Wales (later Hal Taliaferro), Tom London, Edmund Cobb, Buffalo Bill, Jr., Glenn Strange, Edward Hearn, Buck Moulton, Cactus Mack. *D:* Spencer Gordon Bennet; *Sc:* Nate Gatzert. (0:56).

Ken Maynard western involving a range feud.

180. The Aviator (WB; 1929). *Cast:* Edward Everett Horton, Patsy Ruth Miller, Johnny Arthur, Lee Moran, Edward Martindel, Bert Roach, Armand Kaliz. *D:* Roy Del Ruth; *Sc:* Robert Lord, Arthur Caesar. (see also *Going Wild*)

Comedy of a successful writer who has his name put on a book about flying so it will sell, only to later find he has to prove his written words. Based on a play by Otto Harbach and the story "The Aviator" by James Montgomery.

181. The Awful Truth (Pathé; 1929). *Cast:* Ina Claire (in her talkie debut), Henry Daniell, Paul Harvey, Theodore von Eltz. *D:* Marshall Neilan.

An early talkie romance.

182. The Awful Truth (Columbia; 1937). *Cast:* Irene Dunne (A.A.N. for B.A. as Lucy Warriner), Cary Grant (Jerry Warriner), Ralph Bellamy (A.A.N. for B.S.A. as Daniel Leeson), Alexander D'Arcy (Armand Duvalle), Cecil Cunningham (Aunt Patsy), Molly Lamont (Barbara Vance), Mary Forbes (Mrs. Vance), Joyce Compton (Toots Bingswanger—"Dixie Belle Lee"), Esther Dale (Mrs. Leeson), Robert Warwick (Mr. Vance), Claud Allister (Lord Fabian), Zita Moulton (Lady Fabian), Robert Allen (Frank Randall), Scott Colton (Mr. Barnsley), Wyn Cahoon (Mrs. Barnsley), Kathryn Curry (Celeste), Bess Flowers (Viola Heath), Edgar Dearing, Alan Bridge, Paul Stanton, Mitchell Harris, Leonard Carey, Miki Morita, Frank Wilson,

Vernon Dent, George C. Pearce, Bobby Watson, Byron Foulger, Edward Peil, Sr., Edward Mortimer, John Tyrrell, Asta. *D:* (A.A.) Leo McCarey; *P:* McCarey; *As.P.:* Everett Riskin; *Sc:* (A.A.N.) Vina Delmar (with the uncredited support of McCarey and Sidney Buchman); *Editor:* (A.A.N.) Al Clark; *Songs:* "My Dreams Have Gone with the Wind" and "I Don't Like Music" by Ben Oakland and Milton Drake. (1:32) (video)

Screwball comedy of a couple with the perfect marriage who decide to divorce to marry richer partners, then proceed to do what they can to screw up each other's plans. Taken from the 1922 play by Arthur Richman, it received an A.A.N. for Best Picture and placed #10 on the list of "10 Best" films of *Film Daily*. It was remade in 1953 as the musical *Let's Do It Again*.

183. Babbitt (WB/F.N.; 1934). *Cast:* Guy Kibbee (George F. Babbitt), Aline MacMahon, Claire Dodd, Maxine Doyle, Glen Boles, Minor Watson, Minna Gombell, Alan Hale, Berton Churchill, Russell Hicks, Nan Grey, Walter Walker, Arthur Aylesworth, Addison Richards, Harry Tyler, Arthur Hoyt, Mary Treen, Hattie McDaniel. *D:* William Keighley; *P:* Sam Bischoff; *Adaptation:* Niven Busch, Tom Reed; *Sc:* Mary McCall, Jr.; *Additional Dialogue:* Ben Markson. (1:15)

Humorous Americana of a small town and the life of the title character. Based on the 1922 novel by Sinclair Lewis, it was previously filmed in 1924 with Willard Louis.

184. Babes in Arms (MGM; 1939). *Cast:* Mickey Rooney (A.A.N. for B.A. as Mickey Moran), Judy Garland (Patsy Barton), Charles Winninger (Joe Moran), Guy Kibbee (Judge Black), June Preisser (film debut as Rosalie Essex), Douglas McPhail (Don Brice), Margaret Hamilton (Martha Steele), Grace Hayes (Florrie Moran), Betty Jaynes (Molly Moran), Rand Brooks (Jeff Steele), Leni Lynn (Dody Martini), John Sheffield (Bobs), Henry Hull (Madox), Barnett Parker (William), Ann Shoemaker (Mrs. Barton), Joseph Crehan (Mr. Essex), George McKay (Brice), Henry Roquemore (Shaw), Lelah Tyler (Mrs. Brice), Lon McAllister. *D:* Busby Berkeley (who also choreographed); *P:* Arthur Freed; *Sc:* Jack McGowan, Kay Van Riper; *Music:* (A.A.N.) Roger Edens, George E. Stoll; *Songs:* title song, "Where or When," "The Lady Is a Tramp" by Richard Rodgers, Lorenz Hart, "You Are My Lucky Star" and "Good Morning" by Nacio Herb Brown, Arthur Freed, "I Cried for You" by Freed, Gus Arnheim and Abe Lyman, and "God's Country" by E.Y. Harburg and Harold Arlen. (1:37) (video)

A musical-comedy of kids putting on a show. Based on the 1937 Rodgers and Hart Broadway musical, retaining only three of the original songs. One of the 21 top-grossing films of 1939–40.

185. Babes in Toyland (MGM/Hal Roach; 1934). *Cast:* Stan Laurel, Oliver Hardy, Charlotte Henry, Harry (Henry) Kleinbach (Henry Brandon), Felix Knight, Jean Darling (of "Our Gang"), Johnny Downs, Florence Roberts, Ferdinand Munier, Marie Wilson (film debut), Billy Bletcher, Virginia Karnes, William Burress. *D:* Gus Meins, Charles R. Rogers; *Sc:* Nick Grinde, Frank Butler. (1:13) (video)

Classic Laurel and Hardy outing based on the operetta by Victor Herbert and Glen MacDonough. Toyland is inhabited by many nursery rhyme and fairy tale characters, this becoming the setting for a basic "good overcomes evil" plot. The film was later edited down by Roach. Remade in 1961 by the Walt Disney Studios and in 1986 as a TV movie.

186. Baboona (Fox; 1935). *P:* Martin and Osa Johnson.

Documentary feature of famed American explorers, Martin and Osa Johnson in Africa.

187. Baby Face (WB; 1933). *Cast:* Barbara Stanwyck, George Brent, Donald Cook, Margaret Lindsay, Arthur Hohl, John Wayne, Henry Kolker, Douglass Dumbrille, James Murray, Alphonse Ethier, Cecil Cunningham, Harry Gribbon, Theresa Harris, Arthur DeKuh, Reneé Whitney. *D:* Alfred E. Green; *Supervisor:* Ray Griffith; *St:* Mark Canfield (Darryl F. Zanuck); *Sc:* Gene Markey, Kathryn Scola. (1:10)

A controversial film of its day is this story of a girl who will do anything to get to the top.

Baby Face (G.B. title) *see* **Baby Face Harrington**

188. Baby Face Harrington (MGM; 1935). *Cast:* Charles Butterworth, Una Merkel, Harvey Stephens, Eugene Pallette, Nat Pendleton, Ruth Selwyn, Donald Meek, Dorothy Libaire, Edward Nugent, Robert Livingston, Stanley Fields, Raymond Brown, Wade Boteler, Bradley Page, Richard Carle, G. Pat Collins, Claude Gillingwater. *D:* Raoul Walsh; *P:* Edgar Selwyn; *Sc:* Nunnally Johnson, Edwin Knopf; *Additional Dialogue:* Charles Lederer. (G.B. title: *Baby Face*) (1:01)

A shy man suddenly finds life turned upside down when he is mistaken for a wanted gangster, with both hoods and cops on his tail. Based on a play by Edgar Selwyn and William LeBaron.

189. Baby, Take a Bow (Fox; 1934). *Cast:* Shirley Temple (in her first starring role), James Dunn, Claire Trevor, Alan Dinehart, Ray Walker, Richard Tucker, Dorothy Libaire, Ralf Harolde, Olive Tell, James Flavin. *D:* Harry Lachman; *St:* James P. Judge; *Sc:* Philip Klein, E.E. Paramore, Jr. (1:16) (video)

A little girl helps her ex-con father prove his innocence in a crime.

190. Bachelor Apartment (RKO; 1931). *Cast:* Lowell Sherman, Irene Dunne, Mae Murray, Claudia Dell, Norman Kerry, Ivan Lebedeff, Noel Francis, Kitty Kelly, Purnell Pratt, Charles Coleman, Arline Judge (film debut — bit), Florence Roberts, Roberta Gale, Arthur Housman, Bess Flowers. *D:* Sherman; *As.P.:* Henry Hobart; *St:* John Howard Lawson; *Sc:* J. Walter Ruben. (1:17)

Romantic comedy of a womanizing bachelor.

191. Bachelor Bait (RKO; 1934). *Cast:* Stuart Erwin, Rochelle Hudson, Pert Kelton, Skeets Gallagher, Grady Sutton, Berton Churchill, Clarence H. Wilson. *D:* George Stevens; *As.P.:* Lou Brock; *St:* Victor and Edward Halperin; *Sc:* Glenn Tryon. (1:15)

Comedy of a marriage license clerk who starts a lonely hearts bureau and finds romance.

192. The Bachelor Father (MGM; 1930–31). *Cast:* Marion Davies, C. Aubrey Smith (repeating his stage role), Ray Milland, Ralph Forbes, Doris Lloyd, Halliwell Hobbes, Guinn Williams, David Torrence, Edgar Norton, Nena Quartero, James Gordon, Elizabeth Murray. *D:* Robert Z. Leonard (who also co-produced); *Sc:* Laurence E. Johnson. (1:30)

Comedy of a lonely old man who wants to get to know his three grown children. Based on the 1929 stage play by Edward Childs Carpenter.

193. The Bachelor Girl (Columbia; 1929). *Cast:* William Collier, Jr., Jacqueline Logan, Thelma Todd. *D:* Richard Thorpe.

A part-talkie romantic comedy.

194. Bachelor Mother (RKO; 1939). *Cast:* Ginger Rogers (Polly Parrish), David Niven, Charles Coburn, Frank Albertson, Ernest Truex, E.E. Clive, Elbert Coplen, Jr. (baby), Ferike Boros, Leonard Penn, Paul Stanton, Frank M. Thomas, Edna Holland, Dennie Moore, June Wilkins, Dorothy Adams, Gerald Oliver-Smith, Nestor

Paiva, Charles Halton and Donald Duck (himself). *D:* Garson Kanin; *As.P.:* B.G. DeSylva; *St:* (A.A.N.) Felix Jackson; *Sc:* Norman Krasna. (1:22) (video) Computer-colored prints have been produced.

Comedy of an unmarried woman who finds an abandoned baby and the situations that ensue when she tries to convince people that it is not her baby. This was the studio's biggest money-maker of 1939. Filmed before in 1935 in Hungary as *Kleine Mutti* (released by Universal in the U.S.). Remade in 1956 as *Bundle of Joy.*

195. Bachelor Mother (Gold-smith; 1932). *Cast:* Evalyn Knapp, James Murray, Astrid Allwyn, Paul Page, Jimmy Aubrey. *D:* Charles Hutchison.

Comedy.

196. Bachelor of Arts (Fox; 1934). *Cast:* Tom Brown, Anita Louise, Arline Judge, Frank Albertson, J. Carrol Naish, Berton Churchill, Stepin Fetchit, Mae Marsh. *D:* Louis King.

Romantic comedy.

197. Bachelor's Affairs (Fox; 1932). *Cast:* Adolphe Menjou, Joan Marsh, Arthur Pierson, Minna Gombell, Irene Purcell, Don Alvarado, Herbert Mundin. *D:* Alfred Werker; *P:* Edmund Grainger; *St:* James Forbes.

Romantic comedy.

198. A Bachelor's Secret (Xxxx Xxxx; 1930). (No information available.)

199. Back Door to Heaven (Paramount; 1939). *Cast:* Wallace Ford, Aline MacMahon, Stuart Erwin, Patricia Ellis, Kent Smith, Van Heflin, Jimmy Lydon (film debut), William Harrigan, Iris Adrian, Billy (William) Redfield (film debut), Robert Wildhack, Raymond Roe, Alfred Webster, Doug McMullen, Kenneth LeRoy, Georgette Harvey, Joe Garry, Hugh Cameron, Bert Frohman, Helen Christian, Bruce Evans, George Lewis, Anita McGee,

Jane Seymour, Robert Vivian. *D:* William K. Howard; *P:* Howard; *Sc:* John Bright, Robert Tasker; *St:* Howard (per on-screen credits). (1:26) (video)

A topical social drama of its day of a poor boy whose life leads him to the wrong side of the law.

200. Back in Circulation (WB/F.N.; 1937). *Cast:* Joan Blondell, Pat O'Brien, Margaret Lindsay, Regis Toomey, Eddie Acuff, George E. Stone, John Litel, Craig Reynolds, Veda Ann Borg, Ben Welden, Frank Faylen, William Hopper, Walter Byron, Granville Bates, Herbert Rawlinson, Gordon Hart. *D:* Ray Enright; *P:* Sam Bischoff; *St:* Adela Rogers St. John; *Adaptation:* Seton I. Miller; *Sc:* Warren Duff, Craig Reynolds. (1:22)

Newspaper melodrama of a girl reporter who solves a crime.

201. The Back Page (Pyramid; 1933). *D:* Anton Lorenze; *St:* Harry E. Chandlee, Douglas W. Churchill; *Cont. & Dial.:* F. McGrew Willis.

202. Back Pay (WB/F.N.; 1930). *Cast:* Grant Withers, Corinne Griffith, Montagu Love, Vivian Oakland, Geneva Mitchell, Bill Bailey, Hallam Cooley, Louise Beavers, Louise Carver. *D:* William A. Seiter; *Sc:* Francis Edwards Faragoh.

Drama of a girl who jilts her hometown boy for a war profiteer. Based on the novel by Fannie Hurst, it was previously filmed in 1924.

203. Back Street (Universal; 1932). *Cast:* Irene Dunne (Ray Schmidt), John Boles (Walter Saxel), George Meeker (Kurt Shendler), ZaSu Pitts (Mrs. Dole), Arletta Duncan (Beth), June Clyde (Freda Schmidt), William Bakewell (Richard), Shirley Grey (Francine), Maude Turner Gordon (Mrs. Saxel, Sr.), Walter Catlett (Bakeless), James Donlan (Prothero), Paul Weigel (Mr. Schmidt), Jane Darwell (Mrs. Schmidt), Paul Fix (Hugo), Robert McWade (Uncle Felix),

Rose Dione, Virginia Pearson, Doris Lloyd, Gloria Stuart. *D:* John M. Stahl; *P:* Carl Laemmle, Jr.; *As.P.:* E.M. Asher; *Sc:* Gladys Lehman, Lynn Starling, Ben Hecht (unc.). (1:33)

Drama of a woman who continues to love a man even after he marries another. Based on the novel by Fannie Hurst, it was remade in 1941 and again in 1961. Voted #9 on *Film Daily's* "10 Best" list.

204. Back to Nature (20th Century-Fox; 1936). *Cast:* Jed Prouty, Spring Byington, Florence Roberts, June Carlson, Kenneth Howell, George Ernest, Billy Mahan, Shirley Deane, Dixie Dunbar, Tony Martin. *D:* James Tinling.

The third entry in the low-budget "Jones Family" comedy series with the family taking to the woods when Pop buys a trailer.

205. Bad Boy (Fox; 1935). *Cast:* James Dunn, Sally Eilers, Beulah Bondi, Allen Vincent, Dorothy Wilson, Victor Kilian, John Carradine. *D:* John G. Blystone; *St:* Vina Delmar; *Sc:* Allen Rivkin.

Drama.

206. Bad Boy (Atlas/Gateway; 1939). *Cast:* Johnny Downs, Matt Moore, Holmes Herbert. *D:* Herbert Meyer. (G.B. title: *Perilous Journey*)

207. Bad Company (RKO-Pathé; 1931). *Cast:* Helen Twelvetrees, Ricardo Cortez, John Garrick, Paul Hurst, Frank Conroy, Frank McHugh, Harry Carey, Kenneth Thomson, Wade Boteler, Robert Keith, Edgar Kennedy, Emma Dunn, Arthur Stone, Al Herman, William V. Mong. *D:* Tay Garnett; *P:* Charles R. Rogers; *As.P.:* Harry Joe Brown; *Sc:* Garnett, Thomas Buckingham. (1:15)

Melodrama of a woman who discovers that her husband is involved with gangsters. Based on the novel "Put on the Spot" by Jack Lait.

208. Bad Girl (Fox; 1931). *Cast:* Sally Eilers, James Dunn (film debut), Minna Gombell, William Pawley, Paul Fix, Frank Darien. *D:* (A.A.) Frank Borzage; *Sc:* (A.A.) Edwin Burke.

A critically acclaimed drama of its day, this film received an A.A.N. for Best Picture, was rated #4 on the "10 Best" list of *Film Daily,* placed #6 on the same list of the *New York Times,* while placing 2nd in the supplementary "10 Best" films of the National Board of Review.

209. Bad Guy (MGM; 1937). *Cast:* Bruce Cabot, Virginia Grey, Edward Norris, Cliff Edwards, Charles Grapewin, Jean Chatburn, Warren Hymer, John Hamilton, Clay Clement. *D:* Edward L. Cahn; *P:* Tom Reed; *St:* J. Robert Bren, Hal Long, Kathleen Shepard; *Sc:* Earl Felton, Harry Ruskin.

B drma of a power lineman's life of corruption.

210. Bad Lands (RKO; 1939). *Cast:* Robert Barrat, Noah Beery, Jr., Guinn Williams, Andy Clyde, Paul Hurst, Robert Coote, Douglas Walton, Addison Richards, Francis Ford, Francis McDonald, Jack (John) Payne. *D:* Lew Landers; *P:* Robert Sisk; *Sc:* Clarence Upson Young. (1:10) (video)

A low-budget western of a nine-man posse whose numbers are decimated one by one by Apache Indians. The film is a remake of 1934's *The Lost Patrol* (q.v.) with a western setting.

211. Bad Little Angel (MGM; 1939-40). *Cast:* Virginia Weidler, Gene Reynolds, Guy Kibbee, Ian Hunter, Elizabeth Patterson, Reginald Owen, Henry Hull, Lois Wilson, Mitchell Lewis, Esther Dale, Cora Sue Collins, Ann (E.) Todd. *D:* William Thiele; *P:* Albert LeVoy; *Sc:* Dorothy Yost. (1:12)

In 1885 an orphaned teen-age girl turns to the Bible for guidance in solving lifes' problems. Based on the book by Margaret Turnbull.

212. The Bad Man (WB/F.N.; 1930). *Cast:* Walter Huston (Pancho Lopez), Dorothy Revier, James Rennie, O.P. Heggie, Sidney Blackmer, Guinn Williams, Arthur Stone, Marion Byron, Edward Lynch, Harry Semels, Erville Alderson, Myrna Loy. *D:* Clarence Badger; *Sc:* Howard Estabrook. (1:30)

Western comedy-drama of an outlaw who can't help but make things right. Based on the play by Porter Emerson Browne and C.H. Towne, this is a remake of the 1923 film by First National with Jack Mulhall. Remade in 1937 as the non-western *West of Shanghai* (q.v.) and again in 1941 as a western.

213. The Bad Man of Brimstone (MGM; 1937–38). *Cast:* Wallace Beery, Virginia Bruce, Noah Beery, Dennis O'Keefe, Lewis Stone, Guy Kibbee, Joseph Calleia, Bruce Cabot, Cliff Edwards, Guinn Williams, Charles Grapewin, Scotty Beckett, Robert Barrat, John Qualen, Raymond Hatton, John Wray, Arthur Hohl, Robert Gleckler. *D:* J. Walter Ruben; *P:* Harry Rapf; *St:* Ruben, Maurice Rapf; *Sc:* Richard Maibaum, Cyril Hume. (1:29)

Western of an outlaw who begins to reform after finding his son.

Bad Man of Harlem *see* **Harlem on the Prairie**

Bad Man of Arizona *see* Arizona Raiders

214. The Bad One (United Artists/Art Cinema; 1930). *Cast:* Dolores Del Rio (in her first all-talkie as Lita), Edmund Lowe (Flannigan), Ullrich Haupt, Yola D'Avril, Don Alvarado, Harry Stubbs, George Fawcett, Blanche Frederici, Charles McNaughton, Boris Karloff, Adrienne D'Ambricourt, John St. Polis, Mitchell Lewis, Ralph Lewis. *D:* George Fitzmaurice; *As.P.:* John W. Considine, Jr.; *St:* John Farrow; *Sc:* Carey Wilson, H.M. Rogers.

Drama of a sailor who jumps ship to be with a female infatuation.

215. The Bad Sister (Universal; 1931). *Cast:* Conrad Nagel (Dr. Dick Lindley), Sidney Fox (film debut as Marianne Madison), Humphrey Bogart (Valentine Corliss), Bette Davis (film debut as Laura Madison), Charles Winninger (Mr. Madison), ZaSu Pitts, Slim Summerville, Emma Dunn, Bert Roach, David Durand. *D:* Hobart Henley; *P:* Carl Laemmle, Jr.; *Sc:* Raymond L. Schrock, Tom Reed. (1:11)

Romantic drama of a girl from a small town who dumps her boyfriend after becoming infatuated with a city slicker. Filmed twice before as *The Flirt;* in 1916 with Marie Walcamp and Grace Benham and again in 1922 with Lydia Knott and George Nicholls, Sr. Based on the story of the same name by Booth Tarkington.

216. Badge of Honor (Mayfair; 1934). *Cast:* Buster Crabbe, Betty Blythe. *D:* Spencer Gordon Bennet.

A "Poverty Row" melodrama.

217. Balalaika (MGM; 1939). *Cast:* Nelson Eddy, Ilona Massey, Charles Ruggles, Frank Morgan, Lionel Atwill, George Tobias, C. Aubrey Smith, Walter Woolf King, Joyce Compton, Dalies Frantz, Abner Biberman, Phillip Terry, Zeffie Tilbury, Frederick Worlock, Alma Kruger, Paul Sutton, William Costello, Mildred Shay, Roland Varno, Paul Irving, Arthur W. Cernitz. *D:* Reinhold Schunzel; *P:* Lawrence Weingarten; *Sc:* Jacques Deval, Leon Gordon; *Songs:* Sigmund Romberg, Gus Kahn; *Sound Recording:* (A.A.N.) Douglas Shearer. (1:42)

Based on the stage play by Eric Maschwitz, this operetta takes place among Russian royalty who have just fled the revolution.

218. The Band Plays On (MGM; 1934). *Cast:* Robert Young, Ted Healy, Betty Furness, Preston Foster, Leo Carrillo, Russell Hardie, Joseph (Sawyer) Sauers, Stuart Erwin, Robert Livingston, Beaudine Anderson, David

Durand, William Tannen, Norman Phillips, Jr., Betty Jane Graham, Sidney Miller. *D:* Russell Mack (final film—ret.); *P:* Edwin L. Marin; *St:* Harry Stuhldreher (of Notre Dame's famed "Four Horsemen"), J. Robert Bren, W. Thornton Smith, Byron Morgan; *Sc:* Bernard Schubert, Harvey Gates, Ralph Spence.

College gridiron comedy.

219. Banjo on My Knee (20th Century-Fox; 1936). *Cast:* Barbara Stanwyck, Joel McCrea, Walter Brennan, Buddy Ebsen, Helen Westley, Tony Martin, Walter Catlett, Katherine de Mille, Minna Gombell, Victor Kilian, Spencer Charters, George Humbert, Louis Mason, The Hall Johnson Choir, Hilda Vaughn, Cecil Weston. *D:* John Cromwell; *P:* Nunnally Johnson; *Sc:* Johnson; *Songs:* Jimmy McHugh, Harold Adamson; *Sound Recording:* (A.A.N.) to E.H. Hansen. (1:36)

This romantic musical based on the novel by Harry Hamilton is set on a riverboat.

220. Bank Alarm (Grand National; 1937). *Cast:* Conrad Nagel, Eleanor Hunt, Vince Barnett, Frank Milan, Wilma Francis, William L. Thorne, Wheeler Oakman, Charles Delaney, Phil Dunham, Sid D'Albrook, Pat Gleason, Wilson Benge, Henry Rocquemore. *D:* Louis J. Gasnier; *P:* George Hirliman; *St:* Cynthia and Laurence Meade; *Sc:* Griffin Jay, David S. Levy. (1:01)

B crime melodrama.

221. Bar 20 Justice (Paramount; 1938). *Cast:* Bill Boyd (Hoppy), Russell Hayden (Lucky Jenkins), George "Gabby" Hayes (Windy Halliday), Gwen Gaze, Paul Sutton, Pat (J.) O'Brien, Joseph DeStephani, William Duncan, Walter Long, H. Bruce Mitchell, John Beach. *D:* Lesley Selander; *P:* Harry M. Sherman; *Sc:* Arnold Belgard, Harrison Jacobs. (1:10)

Number 16 in the "Hopalong Cassidy" series involving dirty dealings with a mine.

222. Bar 20 Rides Again (Paramount; 1935). *Cast:* Bill Boyd (Hoppy), Jimmy Ellison (Johnny Nelson), George "Gabby" Hayes (his first as series regular, Windy Halliday), Jean Rouverol, Harry Worth, Frank McGlynn, Jr., Howard Lang, Chill Wills (in his film debut with the Avalon Boys), Ethel Wales, Paul Fix, J.P. McGowan, Al St. John, Joe Rickson, John Merton, Frank Layton. *D:* Howard Bretherton; *P:* Harry M. Sherman; *Sc:* Doris Schroeder, Gerald Geraghty. (1:02)

Third entry in the "Hopalong Cassidy" series, involving a tyrannical land baron.

223. Bar Z Bad Men (Republic-Supreme; 1937). *Cast:* Johnny Mack Brown, Lois January, Tom London, Ernie Adams, Dick Curtis, Jack Rockwell, Milburn Morante, Horace Murphy, Budd Buster, Frank Ellis, George Morrell, Tex Palmer, Horace B. Carpenter, Art Dillard, Oscar Gahan. *D:* Sam Newfield; *P:* A.W. Hackel; *Sc:* George Plympton. (0:57)

Johnny Mack Brown western of a man falsely accused of cattle-rustling.

224. The Barbarian (MGM; 1933). *Cast:* Ramon Novarro (repeating his role as Jamil), Myrna Loy (Diana), Reginald Denny (Gerald), Louise Closser Hale (Powers), C. Aubrey Smith (Cecil), Edward Arnold (Achmed), Blanche Friderici (Mrs. Hume), Marcelle Corday (Marthe), Hedda Hopper, Leni Stengel. *D:* Sam Wood; *P:* Wood; *As.P.:* Bernard Hyman; *Sc:* Anita Loos, Elmer Harris; *Songs:* "Love Songs of the Night" by Nacio Herb Brown, Arthur Freed. (G.B. title: *A Night in Cairo*) (1:30)

Romantic drama set in the Middle East. Filmed twice previously as *The Arab,* (Lasky/All-Star Feature Films; 1915) with Edgar Selwyn and (Metro-

Goldwyn; 1924) with Ramon Novarro and Alice Terry. Based on the play of that name by Edgar Selwyn.

225. Barbary Coast (United Artists/Samuel Goldwyn; 1935). *Cast:* Miriam Hopkins, Edward G. Robinson, Joel McCrea, Walter Brennan, Frank Craven, Brian Donlevy, Donald Meek, Clyde Cook, J.M. Kerrigan, Harry Carey, Matt McHugh, Otto Hoffman, Rollo Lloyd, David Niven, Roger Gray, Wong Chung, Russ Powell, Frederick Vogeding, Edward Gargan, Herman Bing, Tom London, Art Miles, Jules Cowles, Heinie Conklin, Cyril Thornton, Anders Van Haden, Charles West. *D:* Howard Hawks; *P:* Sam Goldwyn; *Sc:* Ben Hecht, Charles MacArthur; *Cinematographer:* (A.A.N.) Ray June. (1:31) (video)

Lavishly produced action drama set in San Francisco during the gold rush.

226. Barefoot Boy (Monogram; 1938). *Cast:* Jackie Moran, Marcia Mae Jones, Ralph Morgan, Claire Windsor, Matty Fain, Frank Puglia, Charles D. Brown, Helen MacKellar, Marilyn Knowlden, Henry Rocquemore, Roger Gray, Earle Hodgins, Johnny Morris. *D:* Karl Brown; *P:* E.B. Derr; *St & Sc:* John T. Neville. (1:03)

"Poverty row" rural melodrama of a youth who finds a horde of stolen bonds in a deserted house. The first in a series of films by this studio to star Moran and Jones.

227. The Bargain (WB/F.N.; 1931). *Cast:* Lewis Stone, John Darrow, Evalyn Knapp, Doris Kenyon, Una Merkel, Charles Butterworth, Oscar Apfel. *D:* Robert Milton; *Sc:* Robert Presnell. (aka: *You and I*)

Drama of a father's disappointment with his son's choice of career. Based on the play "You and I" by Philip Barry.

228. The Barker (WB/F.N.; 1928). *Cast:* Milton Sills, Betty Compson (A.A.N. for B.A.), Dorothy Mackaill,

George Cooper, Sylvia Ashton, Douglas Fairbanks, Jr., John Irwin. *D:* George Fitzmaurice; *Sc:* Benjamin Glazer; *Titles:* Herman J. Mankiewicz.

This part-talkie of a traveling tent-show based on a play by John Kenyon Nicholson was originally filmed as a silent, but had sound and dialogue added prior to release. Remade as *Hoopla* (q.v.).

229. Barnum Was Right (Universal; 1929–30). *Cast:* Glenn Tryon, Merna Kennedy, Otis Harlan. *D:* Del Lord.

Low-budget comedy of a man who buys an old run-down mansion and attempts to make it livable.

230. The Baroness and the Butler (20th Century–Fox; 1938). *Cast:* William Powell, Annabella (in her American debut), Henry Stephenson, Nigel Bruce, Helen Westley, Joseph Schildkraut, J. Edward Bromberg, Lynn Bari, Maurice Cass, Wilfred Lucas, Claire DuBrey, Alphonse Ethier, Margaret Irving, Ivan Simpson, Frank Baker, George Davis, Eleanor Wesselhoeft. *D:* Walter Lang; *P:* Raymond Griffith; *Sc:* Sam Hellman, Lamar Trotti, Kathryn Scola. (1:19)

Romantic comedy with an European setting. Based on the play "The Lady Has a Heart" by Ladislaus Bus-Fekete.

231. The Barretts of Wimpole Street (MGM; 1934). *Cast:* Norma Shearer (A.A.N. for B.A. as Elizabeth Barrett), Fredric March (Robert Browning), Charles Laughton (Mr. Barrett), Maureen O'Sullivan (Henrietta Barrett), Katharine Alexander (Arabel), Una O'Connor (Wilson), Ian Wolfe (Bevan), Marion Clayton (Bella), Ferdinand Munier (Dr. Chambers), Leo G. Carroll (Dr. Waterloo), Vernon P. Downing (Octavius), Alan Conrad, Neville Clark, Peter Hobbes, Matthew Smith, Robert Carleton (the Barrett brothers), Lowden Adams (butler),

Winter Hall, George Kirby, Leo Carrillo. *D:* Sidney Franklin; *P:* Irving G. Thalberg; *Sc:* Ernest Vajda, Claudine West, Donald Ogden Stewart. (TV title: *Forbidden Alliance*) (1:51)

The romance of Elizabeth Barrett and Robert Browning in 19th-century England. Based on the play by Rudolf Besier, it was voted "Best Film of the Year" by *Film Daily,* as well as receiving an A.A.N. for Best Picture and *Photoplay's* Gold Medal Award.

232. Barricade (20th Century–Fox; 1939). *Cast:* Warner Baxter, Alice Faye, Charles Winninger, Arthur Treacher, Keye Luke, Willie Fung, Doris Lloyd, Moroni Olsen, Philip Ahn, Leonid Snegoff, Harry Hayden, Joan Carroll, Eily Malyon. *D:* Gregory Ratoff; *P:* Edward Kaufman; *St & Sc:* Granville Walker. (1:11)

B romantic adventure set in China.

233. The Barrier (Paramount; 1937). *Cast:* James Ellison, Leo Carrillo, Jean Parker, Otto Kruger, J.M. Kerrigan, Robert Barrat, Andy Clyde, Sally Martin, Sara Haden, Addison Richards, Alan Davis, Fernando Alvarado. *D:* Edward Ludwig, Lesley Selander; *P:* Harry M. Sherman; *Sc:* Bernard Shubert, Harrison Jacobs, Mordaunt Shairp. (1:30)

Melodrama of a sea captain who attempts to prevent the marriage of his daughter. Based on the novel by Rex Beach, it was previously filmed in 1917 (by Beach) in an independent venture. Remade in 1926 by MGM with Lionel Barrymore in his first film for that studio.

234. Bars of Hate (Victory; 1935). *Cast:* Regis Toomey, Sheila Terry. *D:* Al Herman; *P:* Sam Katzman.

B melodrama.

235. The Bat Whispers (United Artists/Art Cinema; 1930). *Cast:* Chester Morris, Una Merkel, Chance Ward, Grayce Hampton (Mrs. Cornelia Van Gorder), Richard Tucker, Maude Eburne, Wilson Benge, DeWitt Jennings, Spencer Charters, Gustav von Seyffertitz, William Bakewell, Ben Bard, Charles Dow Clark. *D:* Roland West (who also directed the 1926 version); *As.P.:* West; *Sc:* West. (1:10)

A classic, this third version of Mary Roberts Rinehart's novel of a group of people in a spooky old house who find themselves at the mercy of a madman called "The Bat." Also based on the stage play by Rinehart and Avery Hopwood. Filmed twice before as *The Bat,* in 1915 and 1926 with the fourth version appearing under the same title in 1959.

236. Batmen of Africa (Republic; 1936). *Cast:* Clyde Beatty, Manuel King, Elaine Shepard, Lucien Prival. *D:* B. Reeves Eason, Joseph Kane; *P:* Barney Sarecky; *Sc:* John Rathmell, Sarecky, Ted Parsons. (aka: *King of the Jungleland*). (1:40)

Latter day feature version of this studio's first serial *Darkest Africa.*

237. The Battle of Broadway (20th Century–Fox; 1938). *Cast:* Victor McLaglen, Brian Donlevy, Louise Hovick (Gypsy Rose Lee), Raymond Walburn, Lynn Bari, Jane Darwell, Hattie McDaniel, Esther Muir, Andrew Tombes, Robert Kellard, Sammy Cohen, Eddie Holden, Paul Irving, Frank Moran. *D:* George Marshall; *P:* Sol M. Wurtzel; *Sc:* Lou Breslow, John Patrick. (1:24)

A comedy of conventioneers in New York City.

238. Battle of Greed (Crescent; 1937). *Cast:* Tom Keene, Gwynne Shipman, James Bush, Jimmy Butler, Budd Buster, Lloyd Ingraham, Bob Callahan, Henry Rocquemore, Rafael Bennett, Robert Fiske, Carl Stockdale, William Worthington. *D:* Howard Higgin; *P:* E.B. Derr; *Sc:* John T. Neville. (0:59)

Historical low-budget western of the discovery of the Comstock Lode in Virginia City.

239. The Battle of Paris (Paramount; 1929). *Cast:* Gertrude Lawrence (film debut), Charles Ruggles, Walter Petrie, Arthur Treacher (film debut), Gladys DuBois, Joseph King. *D:* Robert Florey; *P:* Monta Bell; *Sc:* Gene Markey; *Songs:* Cole Porter, Howard Dietz, Jay Gorney. (1:11)

A romantic comedy with musical interludes. Filmed at Astoria Studios in Long Island, N.Y.

240. The Battle of the Sexes (United Artists/Art Cinema; 1928). *Cast:* Jean Hersholt, Phyllis Haver, Belle Bennett, Sally O'Neil, William Bakewell, Don Alvarado, John Batten. *D:* D.W. Griffith; *Adaptation:* Gerrit Lloyd.

Part-talkie melodrama of marital infidelity instigated by a two-timing gold-digger. The title song is vocalized by Miss Haver while the rest of the film has a synchronized music score and sound effects. Based on the novel "The Single Standard" by Daniel Carson Goodman, this is a remake of Griffith's 1914 success.

The Battling Bellhop *see* **Kid Galahad**

241. The Battling Buckaroo (Willis Kent; 1932). *Cast:* Lane Chandler, Yakima Canutt. *D:* Armand Schaefer; *P:* Kent.

Low-budget western.

The Battling Hoofer *see* **Something to Sing About**

The Baxter Millions (G.B. title) *see* **Three Kids and a Queen**

242. Be Yourself! (United Artists/Art Cinema; 1930). *Cast:* Fanny Brice, Robert Armstrong, Harry Green, Gertrude Astor, G. Pat Collins, Rita Flynn, Marjorie Kane, Budd Fine. *D:* Thornton Freeland; *P:* Joseph M. Schenck; *Sc:* Freeland, Max Marcin; *Songs:* Ralph Rainger, Billy Rose. (1:17)

Romantic melodrama of a nightclub singer and a prizefighter. Based on "The Champ" by Joseph Jackson.

243. The Beast of the City (MGM; 1932). *Cast:* Walter Huston, Jean Harlow, Wallace Ford, Jean Hersholt, Dorothy Peterson, Tully Marshall, John Miljan, Mickey Rooney, Julie Haydon, J. Carrol Naish, Nat Pendleton, Warner Richmond, Emmett Corrigan, Sandy Roth. *D:* Charles Brabin; *Sc:* John Lee Mahin. (1:30)

Melodrama of big city policemen and gangsters with an opening by J. Edgar Hoover. Based on a story by W.R. Burnett.

The Beasts of Berlin *see* **Hitler—Beast of Berlin**

244. Beau Bandit (RKO; 1930). *Cast:* Rod LaRocque, Doris Kenyon, Mitchell Lewis, George Duryea (Tom Keene), Walter Long, Charles Middleton, James Donlan, Nick (Dick) Foran, Charles Brinley, Barney Furey, Bill Patton. *D:* Lambert Hillyer; *As.P.:* Henry Hobart; *Sc:* Wallace Smith. (1:08)

Low-budget western of a wealthy land-grabber.

245. Beau Geste (Paramount; 1939). *Cast:* Gary Cooper (Beau Geste), Ray Milland (John Geste), Brian Donlevy (A.A.N. for B.S.A. as Sgt. Markoff), Robert Preston (Digby Geste), J. Carrol Naish (Rasinoff), Susan Hayward (Isobel Rivers), James Stephenson (Major Henri de Beaujolais), Heather Thatcher (Lady Patricia Brandon), Albert Dekker (Schwartz), Broderick Crawford (Hank Miller), G.P. Huntley (Augustus Brandon), Donald O'Connor (Beau as a child), Billy Cook (John as a child), Marty Spellman (Digby as a child), Ann Gillis (Isobel as a child), David Holt (Augustus as a child), Harvey Stephens (Lieut. Martin), Stanley Andrews (Maris), Harry Woods (Renoir), James Burke (Dufour), Charles

Barton (Buddy), Nestor Paiva, Harold Huber, Arthur Aylesworth, Henry Brandon. *D:* William A. Wellman; *P:* Wellman; *Sc:* Robert Carson; *Art-Set Decoration:* (A.A.N.) Hans Dreier, Robert Odell. (1:54) (video)

Classic film version of Percival Christopher Wren's 1924 novel of three brothers in the French Foreign Legion, lavishly produced and filmed on location in the Arizona desert. A classic silent version was filmed by this studio in 1926 with a remake by Universal in 1966, followed in 1977 by a spoof *The Last Remake of Beau Geste.*

246. Beau Ideal (RKO; 1931). *Cast:* Ralph Forbes, Lester Vail, Don Alvarado, Loretta Young, Irene Rich, Otto Matiesen, Paul McAllister, George Regas, Leni Stengel, Hale Hamilton, Frank McCormack, Bernard Siegel, Myrtle Stedman, Joseph DeStephani, John St. Polis. *D:* Herbert Brenon (who directed the 1926 version of *Beau Geste*); *P:* William LeBaron; *Sc:* Paul Schofield, Elizabeth Meehan. (1:19)

A sequel to *Beau Geste,* based on the novel by Percival Christopher Wren. For what it's worth, RKO considered this their worst production of 1931 and it was a box office bomb to boot.

Beauty! (G.B. title) *see* **Beauty for Sale**

247. The Beauty and the Boss (WB; 1932). *Cast:* Marian Marsh, David Manners, Warren William, Charles Butterworth, Frederick Kerr, Mary Doran, Robert Greig, Lillian Bond, Yola D'Avril, Polly Walters. *D:* Roy Del Ruth; *Sc:* Joseph Jackson. (1:06)

Romantic comedy, based on the play "Church Mouse" by Ladislaus Fodor.

248. Beauty for Sale (MGM; 1933). *Cast:* Madge Evans, Florine McKinney, Una Merkel, Alice Brady, Phillips Holmes, Otto Kruger, May Robson, Hedda Hopper, Charles Grapewin, Louise Carter, Edward Nugent. *D:* Richard Boleslawski; *P:* Lucien Hubbard; *Sc:* Zelda Sears, Eve Greene. (G.B. title: *Beauty!*)

Romantic drama of three female beauty parlor employees. Based on the novel by Faith Baldwin.

249. Beauty for the Asking (RKO; 1939). *Cast:* Lucille Ball, Patric Knowles, Donald Woods, Inez Courtney, Leona Maricle, Frieda Inescort, Frances Mercer, Whitney Bourne, Kay Sutton, Ann Evers. *D:* Glenn Tryon; *P:* B.P. Fineman; *St:* Edmund L. Hartmann; *Sc:* Doris Anderson, Paul Jarrico. (1:08)

B drama of a beautician who markets a new beauty cream. Based on an original idea by Adele Buffington and Grace Norton.

250. Beauty Parlor (Chesterfield; 1932). *Cast:* Barbara Kent, Joyce Compton, Mischa Auer, Dorothy Revier, Wheeler Oakman. *D:* Richard Thorpe.

A "Poverty Row" melodrama.

251. Becky Sharp (RKO/Pioneer Pictures; 1935). *Cast:* Miriam Hopkins (A.A.N. for B.A. as Becky Sharp), Frances Dee, Cedric Hardwicke, Billie Burke, Alison Skipworth, Nigel Bruce, Alan Mowbray, Colin Tapley, Pauline Garon, G.P. Huntley, Jr., Doris Lloyd, William Stack, George Hassell, William Faversham, Charles Richman, Olaf Hytten, Ottola Nesmith, Tempe Pigott, Leonard Mudie, Elspeth Dudgeon, Charles Coleman, James Robinson, Bunny Beatty, May Beatty. *D:* Rouben Mamoulian; *P:* Kenneth MacGowan; *Sc:* Francis Edwards Faragoh. (1:23) (video)

This film is notable as the first full (3-color) technicolor feature film to come out of Hollywood, receiving a special award for it's color at the Venice Film Festival. Based on William Makepeace Thackery's "Vanity Fair" and the play "Becky Sharp" by Langdon Mitchell. This film was originally begun in

1934 by director Lowell Sherman who died during production. When Rouben Mamoulian took over as director, he completely reshot the film. Later re-release prints in cinecolor run (1:07). The entire film was completely restored in 1985. Filmed thrice before as *Vanity Fair:* 1911, 1923 and 1932 (q.v.).

252. Bed of Roses (RKO–Pathé; 1933). *Cast:* Constance Bennett, Joel McCrea, Pert Kelton, Franklin Pangborn, John Halliday, Samuel S. Hinds, Tom Francis, Robert Emmett O'Connor, Eileen Percy, Jane Darwell. *D:* Gregory LaCava; *P:* Pandro S. Berman; *Sc:* Wanda Tuchock, LaCava, Eugene Thackrey. (1:10)

A depression era comedy-drama of two prostitutes on the Mississippi River. Considered risqué in its day.

253. Bedside (WB/F.N.; 1934). *Cast:* Warren William, Jean Muir, Donald Meek, David Landau, Kathryn Sergava, Allen Jenkins, Henry O'Neill, Reneé Whitney, Walter Walker, Marjorie Lytell, Frederick Burton, Philip Faversham, Louise Beavers, Earle Foxe. *D:* Robert Florey; *P:* Sam Bischoff; *St:* Harvey Thew, Manuel Seff; *Sc:* Lillie Hayward, James Wharton; *Additional Dialogue:* Rian James. (1:05)

In this drama a gambler without schooling or credentials sets up a medical practice.

254. A Bedtime Story (Paramount; 1933). *Cast:* Maurice Chevalier, Helen Twelvetrees, Edward Everett Horton, Baby LeRoy (film debut), Adrienne Ames, Gertrude Michael, Earle Foxe, Leah Ray, Betty Lorraine, Ernest Wood, Reginald Mason, Henry Kolker, George MacQuarrie, Paul Panzer, Frank Reicher. *D:* Norman Taurog; *P:* Emanuel Cohen; *Adaptation:* Benjamin Glazer; *Sc:* Waldemar Young, Nunnally Johnson; *Songs:* Ralph Rainger, Leo Robin. (1:29)

Comedy with songs of a Paris playboy who gets stuck with an abandoned baby. Based on the novel "Bellamy the Magnificent" by Roy Horniman.

The Beer Baron (G.B. title) *see* **Song of the Eagle**

255. Before Dawn (RKO; 1933). *Cast:* Stuart Erwin, Dorothy Wilson, Warner Oland, Dudley Digges, Gertrude W. Hoffman, Oscar Apfel, Jane Darwell, Frank Reicher. *D:* Irving Pichel; *As.P.:* Shirley Burden; *Sc:* Garrett Fort. (1:00)

Low-budget thriller about a series of murders in an old mansion where a gangster's loot is believed to be hidden. Based on a story by Edgar Wallace.

256. Before Midnight (Columbia; 1933–34). *Cast:* June Collyer, Ralph Bellamy, Bradley Page, Betty Blythe, Joseph Crehan, Arthur Pierson, Claude Gillingwater, William Jeffrey, Otto Yamaoka. *D:* Lambert Hillyer; *St:* Robert Quigley.

Low-budget melodrama.

257. Before Morning (Greenblatt; 1933). *Cast:* Leo Carrillo, Lora Baxter, Taylor Holmes, Russell Hicks. *D:* Arthur Hoerl; *P:* Arthur Greenblatt. (No other information available.)

258. Beg, Borrow or Steal (MGM; 1937). *Cast:* Frank Morgan, Florence Rice, John Beal, Janet Beecher, Herman Bing, Erik Rhodes, George Givot, E.E. Clive, Reginald Denny, Vladimir Sokoloff, Cora Witherspoon, Tom Rutherford, Harlan Briggs, Frank Reicher. *D:* William Thiele; *P:* Frederick Stephani; *St:* William C. White; *Sc:* Leonard Lee, Harry Ruskin, Marion Parsonnet.

B comedy of an American living in Paris who invites his daughter's wedding guests to his French chateau — which doesn't exist.

259. Beggar's Holiday (Tower; 1934). *Cast:* Hardie Albright, J. Farrell MacDonald. *D:* Sam Newfield.

A low-budget quickie from "Poverty Row."

260. Beggars in Ermine (Monogram; 1934). *Cast:* Lionel Atwill, Henry B. Walthall, Betty Furness, Jameson Thomas, James Bush, Astrid Allwyn, George Hayes, Stephen Gross, Lee Phelps, Clinton Lyle, Sidney DeGrey, Gayle Kaye, Myrtle Stedman, Gordon DeMain. *D:* Phil Rosen; *P:* William T. Lackey; *Sc:* Tristram Tupper. (1:12)

A once wealthy man attempts to regain his fortune in this low-budget drama based on the novel by Esther Lynd Day.

261. Behind Jury Doors (Mayfair; 1933). *Cast:* Helen Chandler, William Collier, Jr., Blanche Frederici. *D:* B. Reeves Eason.

"Poverty Row" melodrama.

262. Behind Office Doors (RKO; 1931). *Cast:* Mary Astor, Robert Ames, Ricardo Cortez, Catherine Dale Owen, Kitty Kelly, Edna Murphy, Charles Sellon, William Morris, George MacFarlane. *D:* Melville Brown; *As.P.:* Henry Hobart; *Sc:* Carey Wilson. (1:22)

A secretary falls for her boss in this romantic drama. Based on the book by Alan Brener Schultz.

Behind Prison Bars *see* **The Outer Gate**

263. Behind Prison Gates (Columbia; 1939). *Cast:* Brian Donlevy, Jacqueline Wells (Julie Bishop), James Craig, Dick Curtis, Paul Fix, George Lloyd, Joseph Crehan, Richard Fiske. *D:* Charles T. Barton; *Sc:* Arthur T. Horman, Leslie T. White.

The title tells all in this B melodrama.

264. Behind Stone Walls (Mayfair; 1932). *Cast:* Eddie Nugent, Priscilla Dean, Ann Christy, George Chesebro. *D:* Frank Strayer.

"Poverty Row" melodrama.

265. Behind That Curtain (Fox; 1929). *Cast:* Warner Baxter, Lois Moran, Gilbert Emery, Boris Karloff (talkie debut), Peter Gawthorne, Claude King, E.L. Park (Charlie Chan), Jamie Hassen, Mercedes de Velasco, Montagu Shaw, Finch Smiles, John Rogers, Philip Strange. *D:* Irving Cummings.

Low-budget action drama.

266. Behind the Evidence (Columbia; 1935). *Cast:* Norman Foster, Sheila Mannors, Donald Cook, Geneva Mitchell, Edward Keane, Samuel S. Hinds, Frank Darien, Pat O'Malley. *D:* Lambert Hillyer.

Low-budget melodrama.

267. Behind the Green Lights (Mascot; 1935). *Cast:* Norman Foster, Judith Allen, Sidney Blackmer, Purnell Pratt, Theodore von Eltz, Ford Sterling, Kenneth Thomson, Lloyd Whitlock, Edward Hearn, Jane Meredith, Edward Gargan, J. Carrol Naish, John Davidson, John Ince, Hooper Atchley, Marc Lobell, Fern Emmett, Ralph Lewis. *D:* Christy Cabanne; *St:* Capt. Cornelius W. Willemse; *Sc:* James Gruen, Colbert Clark. (1:08)

Crime melodrama involving a female attorney.

268. Behind the Headlines (RKO; 1937). *Cast:* Diana Gibson, Lee Tracy, Donald Meek, Philip Huston, Paul Guilfoyle, Frank M. Thomas, Tom Kennedy, Doodles Weaver, Ralph Robertson, Art Thalasso, Edith Craig. *D:* Richard Rosson; *P:* Cliff Reid; *St:* Thomas Ahearn; *Sc:* Edmund L. Hartmann, J. Robert Bren. (0:58)

B crime drama involving a hijacked gold shipment and a kidnapped news reporter.

269. Behind the Make-Up (Paramount; 1929–30). *Cast:* William Powell, Kay Francis, Hal Skelly, Fay Wray, E.H. Calvert. *D:* Robert Milton, Dorothy Arzner (unc.); *P:* Monta Bell; *St:* Mildred Cram.

Romantic drama of a conniving vaudevillian.

270. Behind the Mask (Columbia; 1932). *Cast:* Jack Holt, Constance Cummings, Boris Karloff, Edward Van Sloan, Claude King, Willard Robertson, Bertha Mann. *D:* John Francis Dillon; *St & Sc:* Jo Swerling. (aka: *The Man Who Dared*) (1:10)

Low-budget melodrama of a secret service agent out to smash a drug ring.

271. Behind the Mike (Universal; 1937). *Cast:* William Gargan, Judith Barrett, Don Wilson, Grady Sutton, Sterling Holloway, Minerva Urecal. *D:* Sidney Salkow; *P:* Lou Brock. (1:08)

B comedy of rival radio station managers.

272. Behold My Wife (Paramount; 1934–35). *Cast:* Sylvia Sidney, Gene Raymond, Juliette Compton, Laura Hope Crews, H.B. Warner, Monroe Owsley, Ann Sheridan, Eric Blore, Joseph (Sawyer) Sauers, Charles Middleton, Charles C. Wilson, Jim Thorpe, Fuzzy Knight, Kenneth Thomson, Otto Hoffman, Olin Howland, Dean Jagger, Nella Walker, Ralph Remley, Gwen Gill, Greg Whitespear, Dewey Robinson, Charlotte Granville, Cecil Weston. *D:* Mitchell Leisen; *P:* B.P. Schulberg; *Sc:* Vincent Lawrence, Grover Jones; *Adaptation:* William R. Lippman, Oliver LaFarge. (1:19)

Much to the chagrin of his family, a wealthy young man marries an American Indian girl. Based on the novel "The Translation of a Savage" by Sir Gilbert Parker. Filmed before in 1920 with Milton Sills.

Behold We Live (G.B. title) *see* **If I Were Free**

273. Bellamy Trial (MGM; 1929). *Cast:* Leatrice Joy, Betty Bronson, Margaret Livingston, Edward Nugent, George Barraud, Cosmo Kyrle Bellew, Kenneth Thomson, Charles Middleton, Charles Hill Mailes, Margaret Seddon. *D:* Monta Bell; *Sc:* Bell.

Courtroom drama filmed in flashbacks. Based on the popular best seller of 1927 by Frances Noyes Hart, it was originally filmed as a silent in 1928 and partially reshot in 1929 and released as a part-talkie.

274. Belle of the Nineties (Paramount; 1934). *Cast:* Mae West (Ruby Carter), Roger Pryor (Tiger Kid), John Mack Brown (Brooks Claybourne), Katherine de Mille (Molly Brant), John Miljan (Ace Lamont), Duke Ellington and his orchestra, James Donlan (Kirby), Harry Woods (Slade), Stuart Holmes (Dirk), Tom Herbert (Gilbert), Edward Gargan (Stogie), Libby Taylor (Jasmine), Frederick Burton (Col. Claybourne), Augusta Anderson (Mrs. Claybourne), Benny Baker (Blackie), Morrie Cohan (Butch), Warren Hymer, Wade Boteler, George Walsh, Eddie Borden, Fuzzy Knight, Tyler Brooke, Kay Deslys, Mike Mazurki (film debut — bit). *D:* Leo McCarey; *P:* William Lebaron; *Sc:* Mae West; *Songs:* "My Old Flame," "When a St. Louis Woman Goes Down to New Orleans," "My American Beauty" and "Troubled Waters" by Sam Coslow, Arthur Johnston. (1:13)

Romantic comedy with songs of a saloon singer in love with two men. The original working title "It Ain't No Sin" was objected to by the censors. One of the 15 top-grossing films of 1934.

275. Beloved (Universal; 1934). *Cast:* John Boles, Gloria Stuart, Albert Conti, Dorothy Peterson, Ruth Hall, Anderson Lawler, Morgan Farley, Edmund Breese, Mickey Rooney, Louise Carter, Mae Busch, Lucile Gleason, Bessie Barriscale, Richard Carle, Lucille LaVerne, Edward Woods, Holmes Herbert, Mary Gordon. *D:* Victor Schertzinger; *P:* Carl Laemmle, Jr., B. (Bennie) F. Zeidman; *Sc:* Paul Gangelin, George O'Neil. (1.25)

Drama set in the 19th-century of an Austrian musician who flees his homeland for America.

276. Beloved Bachelor (Paramount; 1931). *Cast:* Paul Lukas, Dorothy Jordan, Vivienne Osborne, Charles Ruggles, Marjorie Gateson (film debut), Alma Chester, Guy Oliver, Leni Stengel, John Breeden, Harold Minjir. *D:* Lloyd Corrigan; *St:* Edward Peple; *Sc:* Sidney Buchman.

Comedy of a philandering bachelor who adopts a child.

277. Beloved Brat (WB/F.N.; 1938). *Cast:* Bonita Granville, Dolores Costello, Donald Crisp, Natalie Moorhead, Lucile Gleason, Emmett Vogan, Donald Briggs, Loia Cheaney, Stymie Beard, Paul Everton, Carmencita Johnson, Ellen Lowe, Doris Brenn, Mary Doyle, Gloria Fischer, Meredith White, Bernice Pilot, Patsy Mitchell, Priscilla Lyon. *D:* Arthur Lubin; *As.P.:* Bryan Foy; *Sc:* Lawrence Kimble. (G.B. title: *A Dangerous Affair*)

Juvenile B drama of a little girl's problems with her parents. Based on the story "Too Much of Everything" by Jean Negulesco.

278. Beloved Enemy (United Artists/Samuel Goldwyn; 1936). *Cast:* Merle Oberon, Brian Aherne, Karen Morley, Ra Hould (later Ronald Sinclair), Jerome Cowan (film debut), Granville Bates, P.J. Kelly, Pat O'Malley, Jack Mulhall, Henry Stephenson, David Niven, Claude King, Theodore von Eltz, David Torrence, Lionel Pape, William Burress, Leo McCabe, Wyndham Standing, Robert Strange, Leyland Hodgson. *D:* H.C. Potter (feature debut); *As.P.:* George Haight; *St:* John Balderston; *Sc:* Balderston; Rose Franken, William Brown Meloney, David Hertz. (1:26) (video)

Drama of the 1921 Irish rebellion with a British woman falling for an Irish revolutionary leader.

279. The Beloved Rogue (Xxxx Xxxx; 1936–37). *Cast:* Walter Long, Sig Rumann.

(No other information available.)

280. Below the Deadline (Chesterfield; 1936). *Cast:* Russell Hopton, Cecilia Parker, Charles Delaney, Warner Richmond, Robert Frazer, John St. Polis. *D:* Charles Lamont.

"Poverty Row" melodrama.

281. Below the Sea (Columbia; 1933). *Cast:* Fay Wray, Ralph Bellamy, Paul Page, Esther Howard, William J. Kelly, Frederick Vogeding, Trevor Bland. *D:* Albert Rogell; *St & Sc:* Jo Swerling.

Low-budget drama with a color sequence.

282. Bengal Tiger (WB; 1936). *Cast:* Barton MacLane, June Travis, Warren Hull, Paul Graetz, Joseph King, Carlyle Moore, Jr., Don Barclay, Gordon Hart, Satan the Tiger. *D:* Louis King; *P:* Bryan Foy; *St & Sc:* Roy Chanslor, Earl Felton. (0:58)

An alcoholic lion-tamer and a trapeze artist are in love with the same girl in this B circus melodrama.

283. The Benson Murder Case (Paramount; 1930). *Cast:* William Powell, William (Bill) Boyd, Paul Lukas, Natalie Moorhead, Eugene Pallette, Richard Tucker, E.H. Calvert, Mischa Auer, May Beatty, Otto Yamaoka, Dick Rush, Charles McMurphy. *D:* Frank Tuttle. (1:09)

The third entry in this studio's Philo Vance mystery series. The story concerns the murder of a Wall Street tycoon. Based on the character created by S.S. Van Dine.

284. Berkeley Square (Fox; 1933). *Cast:* Leslie Howard (A.A.N. for B.A. repeating his stage role as Peter Standish), Heather Angel (Helen Pettigrew), Valerie Taylor (Kate Pettigrew), Irene Browne (Lady Ann Pettigrew), Beryl Mercer (Mrs. Barwick), Alan Mowbray (Major Clinton), David Torrence (Lord Stanley), Colin Keith-Johnston (Tom Pettigrew), Samuel S. Hinds (American Ambassador), Juliette

Compton (Duchess of Devonshire), Betty Lawford (Marjorie Frant), Ferdinand Gottschalk (Mr. Throstle), Olaf Hytten (Sir Joshua Reynolds). *D:* Frank Lloyd; *P:* Jessie L. Lasky; *Adaptation and Sc:* Sonya Levien, John L. Balderston. (1:27)

Romantic fantasy of a contemporary American who finds himself in 18th-century London living the life of one of his ancestors. Based on the story "The Sense of the Past" by Henry James and the play by John Balderston it was voted one of the "10 Best" films of the year by the National Board of Review, placed #6 on the "10 Best" list of the *New York Times,* while placing #10 on the same list of *Film Daily* in 1934. Remade in 1951 by 20th Century–Fox as *I'll Never Forget You* (G.B. title: *The House on the Square*).

285. The Best Man Wins (Columbia; 1935). *Cast:* Edmund Lowe, Florence Rice, Jack Holt, Bela Lugosi, J. Farrell MacDonald, Bradley Page, Forrester Harvey. *D:* Erle C. Kenton; *St:* Ben G. Kohn; *Sc:* Ethel Hill, Bruce Manning.

Romantic comedy.

286. The Best of Enemies (Fox; 1933). *Cast:* Charles "Buddy" Rogers, Marian Nixon, Frank Morgan, Greta Nissen, Arno Frey, Anders Van Haden, William Lawrence. *D:* Rian James; *St & Sc:* Sam Mintz.

Romantic comedy.

The Best of the Blues *see* **St. Louis Blues**

287. Between Fighting Men (World Wide/KBS Productions; 1932–33). *Cast:* Ken Maynard, Ruth Hall, Wallace MacDonald, Josephine Dunn, Albert J. Smith, Walter Law, James Bradbury, Jr., John Pratt, Charles King, Edmund Cobb, Jack Rockwell, Jack Kirk, Bud McClure, Roy Bucko, Jack Ward. *D:* Forrest Sheldon; *Sc:* Sheldon, Betty Burbridge. (0:59) (video)

Ken Maynard western of a range war.

288. Between Men (Supreme; 1935). *Cast:* Johnny Mack Brown, Beth Marion, William Farnum, Lloyd Ingraham, Frank Ball, Forrest Taylor, Earl Dwire, Harry Downing, Horace B. Carpenter, Bud Osborne, Sherry Tansey, Milburn Morante, Artie Ortego. *D:* Robert N. Bradbury; *P:* A.W. Hackel; *Sc:* Charles Francis Royal. (1:00)

Johnny Mack Brown western of a father who avenges the murder of his son, who later turns up alive.

289. Between Two Women (MGM; 1937). *Cast:* Franchot Tone, Maureen O'Sullivan, Virginia Bruce, Leonard Penn, Cliff Edwards, Janet Beecher, Charles Grapewin, Helen Troy, Grace Ford, June Clayworth, Edward Norris, Anthony Nace, Hugh Marlowe. *D:* George B. Seitz; *P:* J.J. Cohn; *Sc:* Frederick Stephani, Marion Parsonnet. (1:28)

Hospital drama. Based on a story by Erich Von Stroheim.

290. Beware of Bachelors (WB/Vitaphone; 1928). *Cast:* Audrey Ferris, William Collier, Jr., Andre Beranger, Tom Ricketts, Dave Morris, Clyde Cook, Margaret Livingston. *D:* Roy Del Ruth; *St:* Mark Canfield (Darryl F. Zanuck); *Sc:* Robert Lord.

A part-talkie comedy of marital infidelity instigated by a greedy relative out to claim a large sum of money.

291. Beware of Ladies (Republic; 1936). *Cast:* Donald Cook, Judith Allen, Russell Hopton, Thomas E. Jackson, Dwight Frye. *D:* Irving Pichel.

Low-budget melodrama.

292. Beware, Spooks! (Columbia; 1939). *Cast:* Joe E. Brown, Mary Carlisle, Clarence Kolb, Marc Lawrence, Don Beddoe, George J. Lewis. *D:* Edward Sedgwick; *P:* Robert Sparks; *St:* Richard Flournoy; *Sc:* Brian Marlow, Albert Duffy. (1:08)

Mystery-comedy set in and around a Coney Island funhouse.

293. Beyond Bengal (Xxxx Xxxx; 1934). Documentary produced, directed and written by Harry Schenk.

294. Beyond the Law (Syndicate; 1930). *Cast:* Lane Chandler, Robert Frazer, Louise Lorraine, Charles King, Jimmy Kane, William Walling, Franklyn Farnum, Harry Holden, George Hackathorne, Ed Lynch, Robert Graves, Al St. John. *D:* J.P. McGowan; *Sc:* George A. Durlam. (1:00)
Lane Chandler western.

295. Beyond the Law (Columbia; 1934). *Cast:* Tim McCoy, Shirley Grey, Lane Chandler, Addison Richards, Dick Rush, Harry Bradley, Morton Laverre (John Merton). *D:* D. Ross Lederman; *Sc:* Harold Schumate. (1:00)
Low-budget action drama of a railroad detective out to prove a man innocent of murder.

296. Beyond the Rio Grande (Big 4; 1930). *Cast:* Jack Perrin, Franklyn Farnum, Charline Burt, Emma Tansey, Buffalo Bill, Jr., Edmund Cobb, Pete Morrison, Henry Roquemore, Henry Taylor. *D:* Harry S. Webb; *P:* John R. Freuler; *Sc:* Carl Krusada. (1:00)
Jack Perrin western.

297. Beyond the Rockies (RKO–Pathé; 1932). *Cast:* Tom Keene, Rochelle Hudson, Marie Wells, Hank Bell, William Welsh, Tom London, Ted Adams, Ernie Adams, Julian Rivero. *D:* Fred Allen; *As.P.:* Harry Joe Brown; *St:* John P. McCarthy; *Sc:* Oliver Drake. (1:00)
Tom Keene western involving a female rancher who may be rustling cattle.

298. Beyond Victory (RKO–Pathé; 1931). *Cast:* Bill Boyd, James Gleason, Lew Cody, ZaSu Pitts, Marion Shilling, Russell Gleason, Lissi Arna, Mary Carr, Fred Scott, Theodore von Eltz, Frank Reicher, E.H. Calvert, Dorothy Burgess, Wade Boteler, Hedwig Reicher, Max Barwyn. *D:* John Robertson, Edward H. Griffith (unc.); *P:* E.B. Derr; *St:* James Gleason, Horace Jackson; *Sc:* Gleason, Jackson. (1:13)
World War I story of four soldiers and why they enlisted.

299. The Big Bluff (Tower; 1933). *Cast:* Reginald Denny, Claudia Dell, Donald Keith, Cyril Chadwick. *D:* Reginald Denny.
"Poverty row" melodrama.

300. Big Boy (WB; 1930). *Cast:* Al Jolson (in blackface), Claudia Dell, Louise Closser Hale, Lloyd Hughes, Eddie Phillips, Lew Harvey, Franklin Batie, John Harron, Tom Wilson, Colin Campbell, Noah Beery. *D:* Alan Crosland; *Sc:* William K. Wells, Rex Taylor, Perry Vekroff. (1:09)
Story of a negro jockey and a big race. Based on a 1925 Broadway musical by Harold Atterridge, Buddy DeSylva, James P. Henley and Joseph Meyer.

301. Big Boy Rides Again (First Division/Beacon; 1935). *Cast:* Guinn "Big Boy" Williams, Connie Bergen, Charles K. French, Lafe McKee, Victor Potel, Bud Osborne, William Gould. *D:* Al Herman; *Sc:* William Nolte. (0:55)
Guinn "Big Boy" Williams comedy western.

302. The Big Brain (RKO/Admiral; 1933). *Cast:* George E. Stone, Fay Wray, Phillips Holmes, Minna Gombell, Lilian Bond, Reginald Owen, Berton Churchill, Reginald Mason, Sam Hardy, Edgar Norton, Charles McNaughton, Lucien Littlefield, Frankie Darro, Douglass Dumbrille. *D:* George Archainbaud; *P:* Sam Bischoff; *St:* Sy Bartlett; *Sc:* Warren Duff. (G.B. title: *Enemies of Society*)
Melodrama of a barber shop bootblack who becomes a professional swindler.

303. The Big Broadcast (Paramount; 1932). *Cast:* Bing Crosby (in his first major screen role), Stuart Erwin, Leila Hyams, Sharon Lynne, George N. Burns and Grace Allen (in their feature film debuts), Kate Smith, Cab Calloway and his band, Mills Brothers, Boswell Sisters, Donald Novis, Arthur Tracy, Vincent Lopez and his orchestra, George Barbier, Ralph Robertson, Major, Sharp and Minor, Spec O'Donnell, Tom Corrigan, Anna Charder, Alex Melesh and radio broadcasters: Don Ball, James Wallington, Norman Brokenshire and William Brenton. *D:* Frank Tuttle; *P:* unc.; *Sc:* George Marion, Jr. (1:27)

Musical-comedy with an all-star radio revue in a story of a failing radio show "The Grip-Tight Girdle Hour" which is saved by "The Big Broadcast." Based on the play "Wild Waves" by William Ford Manley. Hit songs from this film include: "Please" and "Where the Blue of the Night" by Fred Ahlert, Bing Crosby and Roy Turk and "Here Lies Love" by Ralph Rainger and Leo Robin.

304. The Big Broadcast of 1936 (Paramount; 1935). *Cast:* George Burns, Gracie Allen, Jack Oakie, Lyda Roberti, Henry Wadsworth, Wendy Barrie, C. Henry Gordon, Ethel Merman, Charles Ruggles, Mary Boland, Bill "Bojangles" Robinson, Bing Crosby, Amos 'n' Andy (Freeman Gosden & Charles Correll), The Vienna Boys Choir, Virginia Weidler, Sir Guy Standing, Richard Tauber, Ray Noble and his band, Ina Ray Hutton and her Melodears, The Nicholas Brothers (Fay and Harold), Gail Patrick, Samuel S. Hinds, Akim Tamiroff, Jack Mulhall, Charles Hamilton. *D:* Norman Taurog; *P:* Benjamin Glazer; *Sc:* Walter DeLeon, Francis Martin, Ralph Spence, Julius J. Epstein (unc.); *Songs:* Ralph Rainger, Leo Robin; *Choreography:* (A.A.N.) LeRoy Prinz for "It's the Animal in Me" number, combined with a dance number from *All the King's Horses* (q.v.). (1:37)

A lavish production of musical and comedy acts which flopped at the box office.

305. The Big Broadcast of 1937 (Paramount; 1936). *Cast:* Jack Benny, George Burns, Gracie Allen, "Bazooka" Bob Burns, Martha Raye, Shirley Ross, Ray Milland, Frank Forest, Benny Fields, Sam Hearn, Stan Kavanaugh, Benny Goodman and his orchestra, Virginia Weidler, Leopold Stokowski and his symphony orchestra, Billy Lee, David Jack Holt, Louis Da Pron, Eleanore Whitney, Larry Adler, Don Hulbert, Irving Bacon, Ernest Cossart, Cupid Ainsworth, Billie Bellport, Billy Bletcher, Harry Depp, Pat West, Frank Jenks, Avril Cameron, Nora Cecil, Harrison Greene, Gino Corrado, Leonid Kinskey, Henry Arthur, Edward J. LeSaint, Jack Mulhall, Terry Ray (Ellen Drew), Murray Alper, Billy Arnold, Gertrude Short. *D:* Mitchell Leisen; *P:* Lewis E. Gensler; *St:* Erwin Gelsey, Arthur Kober, Barry Trivers; *Sc:* Walter DeLeon, Francis Martin. (1:40)

A variety of musical and comedy acts which was one of the 38 top-grossing films of 1936–37.

306. The Big Broadcast of 1938 (Paramount; 1938). *Cast:* W.C. Fields, Martha Raye, Dorothy Lamour, Lynne Overman, Ben Blue, Leif Erickson, Bob Hope, Shirley Ross, Tito Guizar, Kirsten Flagstad, Shep Fields and his Rippling Rhythm Orchestra, James Craig, Russell Hicks, Grace Bradley, Rufe Davis, Patricia Wilder, Lionel Pape, Dorothy Howe, Leonid Kinskey. *D:* Mitchell Leisen; *P:* Harlan Thompson; *St:* Frederick Hazlitt Brennan; *Sc:* Walter DeLeon, Francis Martin, Ken Englund, Howard Lindsay, Russel Crouse. (1:30)

A musical-comedy with variety acts. Notable as the feature film debut of Bob Hope who with Shirley Ross sings "Thanks for the Memory" which won an A.A. as Best Song for Ralph Rainger and Leo Robin (and later became Hope's theme song).

307. Big Brown Eyes (Paramount; 1936). *Cast:* Cary Grant, Joan Bennett, Walter Pidgeon, Lloyd Nolan, Alan Baxter, Marjorie Gateson, Isabel Jewell, Douglas Fowley, Joseph Sawyer, Helen Brown, Harry Kleinbach (Henry Brandon). *D:* Raoul Walsh; *P:* Walter Wanger; *St:* James Edward Grant; *Sc:* Walsh, Bert Hanlon. (1:16)

Mystery-comedy of a private dick and his girl out to round up a gang of jewel thieves.

308. Big Business (20th Century–Fox; 1937). *Cast:* Jed Prouty, Spring Byington, Florence Roberts, June Carlson, Allan Lane, Marjorie Weaver, Russell Gleason, Shirley Deane, Kenneth Howell, George Ernest, Billy Mahan, Wallis Clark, Frank Conroy. *D:* Frank Strayer; *St:* Eleanor DeLameter, Ron Ferguson; *Sc:* Robert Ellis, Helen Logan.

The fifth entry in the popular low budget "Jones Family" comedy series.

309. Big Business Girl (WB/F.N.; 1931). *Cast:* Loretta Young, Ricardo Cortez, Frank Albertson, Joan Blondell, Frank Darien, Dorothy Christy, Bobby Gordon, George Hayes, Oscar Apfel, Mickey Bennett, Virginia Sale, Nancy Dover. *D:* William A. Seiter; *St:* Patricia Reilly, Harold N. Swanson; *Sc:* Robert Lord. (1:15)

A career woman struggles to make it to the top in this romantic drama.

310. The Big Cage (Universal; 1933). *Cast:* Clyde Beatty (film debut), Anita Page, Mickey Rooney, Andy Devine, Vince Barnett, Raymond Hatton, Wallace Ford, Edward Peil, Jr., Reginald Barlow, Robert McWade, Louise Beavers. *D:* Kurt Neumann; *P:* Carl Laemmle, Jr.; *Sc:* Edward Anthony, Ferdinand Reyher. (1:22)

A circus story of an animal trainer and the young boy who idolizes him. Based on the book by Clyde Beatty and Edward Anthony.

311. Big Calibre (Supreme; 1935). *Cast:* Bob Steele, Peggy Campbell, Forrest Taylor, John Elliott, Georgia O'Dell, Bill Quinn. *D:* Robert N. Bradbury (Steele's real life father); *P:* A.W. Hackel; *Supervisor:* Sam Katzman; *Sc:* Perry Murdock. (0:59)

Bob Steele western of a cowboy in search of his father's killer.

312. The Big Chance (Arthur Greenblatt; 1933). *Cast:* J. Carrol Naish, Mickey Rooney.

(No other information available.)

313. Big City (MGM; 1937). *Cast:* Luise Rainer, Spencer Tracy, Charley Grapewin, Janet Beecher, Eddie Quillan, Victor Varconi, Oscar O'Shea, Helen Troy, William Demarest, John Arledge, Irving Bacon, Guinn Williams, Regis Toomey, Edgar Dearing, Paul Harvey, Andrew J. Tombes, Clem Bevans, Grace Ford, Alice White, Jack Dempsey, James J. Jeffries, Jimmy McLarnin, Maxie Rosenbloom, Jim Thorpe, Frank Wykoff, Jackie Fields, Man Mountain Dean, Gus Sonnenberg, George Godfrey, Joe Rivers, Cotton Warburton, Bull Montana, Snowy Baker, Taski Hagio, Gwen Lee, Ruth Hussey (film debut). *D:* Frank Borzage; *P:* Norman Krasna; *St:* Krasna; *Sc:* Dore Schary, Hugo Butler. (Re-release title: *Skyscraper Wilderness*) (1:20)

A drama of corruption in the taxicab business. The film was a box office flop.

314. Big City Blues (WB; 1932). *Cast:* Eric Linden, Joan Blondell, Inez Courtney, Evalyn Knapp, Guy Kibbee, Humphrey Bogart, Ned Sparks, Josephine Dunn, Walter Catlett, Jobyna Howland, J. Carrol Naish, Grant Mitchell, Clarence Muse, Tom Dugan, Gloria Shea, Thomas Jackson, Betty Gillette. *D:* Mervyn LeRoy; *St:* Ward Morehouse; *Sc:* Morehouse, Lillie Hayward. (1:05)

Low-budget drama of a country boy who becomes disillusioned with

New York City when he becomes involved in a murder.

315. Big Executive (Paramount; 1933). *Cast:* Ricardo Cortez, Elizabeth Young, Richard Bennett, Sharon Lynn, Maude Eburne, Dorothy Peterson, Charles Middleton, Barton MacLane. *D:* Erle C. Kenton.

A Wall Street broker in the midst of an extramarital affair is accused of killing his wife in this B drama.

316. The Big Fight (Sono Art–World Wide; 1930). *Cast:* Ralph Ince, Lola Lane, Guinn Williams, Wheeler Oakman, Stepin Fetchit, Edna Bennett. *D:* Walter Lang.

"Poverty Row" action drama.

317. The Big Gamble (RKO–Pathé; 1931). *Cast:* William (Bill) Boyd, James Gleason, Warner Oland, Dorothy Sebastian, ZaSu Pitts, June MacCloy, William Collier, Jr., Ralph Ince, Geneva Mitchell, Jack Richardson, Fred Walton. *D:* Fred Niblo; *As.P.:* Harry Joe Brown; *St:* Octavus Roy Cohen; *Sc:* Walter DeLeon, F. McGrew Willis. (1:03)

Drama of a man who makes his large creditor the beneficiary in his will. Filmed before in 1926 as *Red Dice* with Rod LaRocque.

318. The Big Game (RKO; 1936). *Cast:* Bruce Cabot, Philip Huston, June Travis, James Gleason, Andy Devine, John Arledge, Guinn Williams, C. Henry Gordon, Barbara Pepper, Frank M. Thomas, Edward Nugent, Margaret Seddon, Billy Gilbert, John Harrington, Murray Kinnell and real-life All-American football players of the day: Frank Alustiza, Jay Berwanger, Robert Hamilton, Irwin Klein, James Moscrip, William Shakespeare, Robert Wilson, Gomer Jones, Chuck Bennis, Ward Bond. *D:* George Nicholls, Jr.; *D (of football scenes):* Edward Killy; *P:* Pandro S. Berman; *Sc:* Irwin Shaw (his first screenplay). (1:14)

Low-budget drama which exposes criminal associations with college football. Based on the novel by Francis Wallace and the play by Irwin Shaw.

319. The Big Guy (Universal; 1939). *Cast:* Jackie Cooper, Victor McLaglen, Peggy Moran, Edward Brophy, Ona Munson, Russell Hicks, Jonathan Hale, George McKay, Edward Pawley, Rondo Hatton, Peggy Moran, Wallis Clark, Alan Davis. *D:* Arthur Lubin; *As.P.:* Burt Kelly; *St:* Wallace Sullivan, Richard K. Polimer; *Sc:* Lester Cole. (1:18)

Drama of a prison warden who must choose between honesty and wealth when a young man he knows to be innocent of a crime is sentenced to die. Remade in 1956 as *Behind the High Wall.*

320. Big Hearted Herbert (WB; 1934). *Cast:* Guy Kibbee, Aline MacMahon, Patricia Ellis, Philip Reed, George Chandler, Helen Lowell, Robert Barrat, Henry O'Neill, Marjorie Gateson, Nella Walker, Hale Hamilton, Trent (Junior) Durkin, Jay Ward, Claudia Coleman. *D:* William Keighley; *P:* James Seymour; *Sc:* Lillie Hayward, Ben Markson. (1:00)

B comedy of a successful plumber who puts his money before his family. Based on the play by Sophie Kerr and Anna Steese Richardson. Remade in 1940 with Grant Mitchell as *Father Is a Prince.*

321. The Big House (MGM/Cosmopolitan; 1930). *Cast:* Chester Morris (John Morgan), Wallace Beery (A.A.N. for B.A. as Butch Schmidt), Lewis Stone (Warden James Adams), Robert Montgomery (Kent Marlowe), Leila Hyams (Anne Marlowe), George F. Marion (Pop Riker), J.C. Nugent (Mr. Marlowe), Karl Dane (Olsen), DeWitt Jennings (Capt. Wallace), Mathew Betz (Gopher), Claire McDowell (Mrs. Marlowe), Robert Emmett O'Connor (Sgt. Donlin), Tom Kennedy (Uncle Jed), Tom Wilson (Sandy—a guard), Eddie Foyer (Dopey), Roscoe Ates (Putnam),

Fletcher Norton (Oliver), Adolph Seidel, Michael Vavitch, Eddie Lambert. *D:* George Hill; *P:* Irving Thalberg; *St:* Frances Marion; *Sc:* (A.A.) Frances Marion; *Additional Dialogue:* Martin Flavin, Joe Farnham; *Sound Recording:* (A.A.) Douglas Shearer. (1:28)

A classic prison drama which set the standards for the genre, receiving an A.A.N. for Best Picture as well as placing #6 on *Film Daily*'s "10 Best" list. Beery's role was originally intended for Lon Chaney who died before production began. A huge hit at the box office, the sets from this film were later reused by Hal Roach in 1931 for *Pardon Us* (q.v.). Also filmed in French, German, Italian and Spanish language versions.

322. Big Money (Pathé; 1930). *Cast:* Eddie Quillan, Margaret Livingston, James Gleason, Robert Armstrong, Miriam Seegar, Robert Edeson, Kit Guard. *D:* Russell Mack.

Melodrama.

323. Big News (Pathé; 1929). *Cast:* Robert Armstrong, Carol(e) Lombard, Frank Reicher, Sam Hardy, Colin Chase, Tom Kennedy, George Hayes, Fred Behrle, Herbert Clark, Robert Dudley, Louis Payne, Gertrude Sutton. *D:* Gregory LaCava; *St:* George S. Brooks; *Sc:* Walter DeLeon; *Dial.:* Frank Reicher.

Comedy.

324. The Big Noise (WB; 1936). *Cast:* Guy Kibbee, Warren Hull, Alma Lloyd, Dick Foran, Marie Wilson, Henry O'Neill, Olin Howland, Virginia Brissac, Andre Beranger, William Davidson, Robert Emmett Keane. *D:* Frank McDonald; *P:* Bryan Foy; *St:* Edmund Hartmann; *Sc:* George Bricker, William Jacobs.

B drama.

325. The Big Party (Fox; 1930). *Cast:* Sue Carol, Frank Albertson, Dixie Lee, Elizabeth Patterson, Walter Catlett, Ilka Chase. *D:* John G. Blystone.

Comedy-drama.

The Big Pay-Off (G.B. title) *see* **Pride of the Legion**

326. The Big Pond (Paramount; 1930). *Cast:* Maurice Chevalier (A.A.N. for B.A. —1929–30), Claudette Colbert, George Barbier, Nat Pendleton, Marion Ballou, Elaine Koch, Andree Corday, Frank Lyon. *D:* Hobart Henley; *P:* Monta Bell; *Sc:* Garrett Fort, Robert Presnell, Preston Sturges. (1:15)

Romantic comedy with songs of an American woman who falls for a Frenchman she brings into the United States. Based on the play by George Middleton and A.E. Thomas.

327. The Big Race (Showmen's Pictures; 1933). *Cast:* Frankie Darro, Boots Mallory, John Darrow, Paul Hurst. *D:* Fred Newmeyer. (G.B. title: *Raising the Wind*)

Low-budget indie actioner.

328. The Big Shakedown (WB/ F.N.; 1934). *Cast:* Bette Davis, Charles Farrell, Ricardo Cortez, Glenda Farrell, Adrian Morris, Allen Jenkins, Henry O'Neill, Samuel S. Hinds, Earle Foxe, George Cooper, Robert Emmett O'Connor, George Pat Collins, Ben Hendricks, Philip Faversham, Dewey Robinson. *D:* John Francis Dillon (final film — d. 1934); *P:* Sam Bischoff; *St:* Niven Busch, Sam G. Engel; *Sc:* Busch, Rian James. (1:04)

Low-budget gangster melodrama set after the repeal of Prohibition.

329. The Big Shot (RKO-Pathé; 1931). *Cast:* Eddie Quillan, Maureen O'Sullivan, Arthur Stone, Mary Nolan, Roscoe Ates, Louis John Bartels, Otis Harlan, William Eugene, Edward Brophy, Sally Eilers, Tom Kennedy, Frank Mayo, Belle Bennett (final film — d. 1932), Frank Darien, Harvey Clark, Charles Thurston, A.S. Byron, Hilliard Carr. *D:* Ralph Murphy; *As.P.:* Harry Joe Brown; *St:* George Dromgold, Hal Conklin; *Sc:* Joseph Fields, Earl Baldwin. (G.B. title: *The Optimist*)

Comedy of a hotel clerk who purchases a worthless tract of swampland, only to learn that it is not worthless.

330. The Big Shot (RKO; 1937). *Cast:* Guy Kibbee, Cora Witherspoon, Dorothy Moore, Gordon Jones, Russell Hicks, Frank M. Thomas, Dudley Clements, George Irving, Maxine Jennings, Barbara Pepper, Tom Kennedy, John Kelly, Eddie Gribbon, Al Hill, Donald Kirke, Edward McWade. *D:* Edward Killy; *St:* Lawrence Pohle, Thomas Ahearn; *Sc:* Arthur T. Horman, Bert Granet. (1:00)

B comedy of a small town veterinarian who gets involved in some racketeering business after inheriting it from an uncle.

331. The Big Show (Republic; 1936). *Cast:* Gene Autry, Smiley Burnette, Kay Hughes, Sally Payne, William Newell, Max Terhune, Sons of the Pioneers with Bob Nolan and Leonard Slye (Roy Rogers), The Jones Boys, The Beverly Hillbillies, The Light Crust Doughboys, The SMU 50, Rex King, Harry Worth, Charles Judels, Mary Russell, Sally Rand, Christine Maple, Jerry Larkin, Jack O'Shea, Charles "Slim" Whitaker, George Chesebro, Edward Hearn, Cliff Lyons, Tracy Layne, Jack Rockwell, Frankie Marvin, Cornelius Keefe, Horace B. Carpenter, Frances Morris, Richard Beach, Art Mix, I. Stanford Jolley. *D:* Mack V. Wright; *P:* Nat Levine; *Sc:* Dorrell & Stuart McGowan. (1:10) (video)

Gene Autry western with many musical acts. Filmed at the Texas Centennial Exposition.

332. The Big Stampede (WB; 1932). *Cast:* John Wayne, Mae Madison, Noah Beery, Luis Alberni, Berton Churchill, Paul Hurst, Sherwood Bailey, Frank Ellis, Hank Bell, Lafe McKee. *D:* Tenny Wright; *St:* Marion Jackson; *Sc:* Kurt Kempler. (0:54)

Early John Wayne western of a deputy who catches some cattle rustlers. Previously filmed by First National in 1927 as *Land Beyond the Law* with Ken Maynard. Remade in 1936 (q.v.) under that title.

333. Big Time (Fox; 1929). *Cast:* Lee Tracy (film debut), Mae Clarke (film debut), Daphne Pollard, Josephine Dunn, Stepin Fetchit, John Ford (himself). *D:* Kenneth Hawks; *St:* Wallace Smith; *Dial. & Sc:* Sidney Lanfield.

Melodrama.

334. Big Time Charlie (Xxxx Xxxx; 1932). (No information available)

335. Big Time or Bust (Tower; 1934). *Cast:* Walter Byron, Charles Delaney. *D:* Sam Newfield.

A "Poverty Row" production.

336. The Big Timer (Columbia; 1932). *Cast:* Ben Lyon, Constance Cummings, Thelma Todd, Charles Delaney, Charles Grapewin, Russell Hopton. *D:* Edward Buzzell.

Low-budget comedy.

337. Big Town Czar (Universal; 1939). *Cast:* Barton MacLane, Tom Brown, Eve Arden, Jack LaRue, Frank Jenks, Horace MacMahon, Ed Sullivan (himself), Esther Dale, Walter Woolf King, Oscar O'Shea, Jerry Marlowe. *D:* Arthur Lubin; *P:* Ken Goldsmith; *Sc:* Edmund L. Hartmann. (1:06)

B crime melodrama centering around the life of a killer up to his death in the electric chair. Based on a story by Ed Sullivan.

338. Big Town Girl (20th Century–Fox; 1937). *Cast:* Donald Woods, Claire Trevor, Alan Baxter, Maurice Cass, George Chandler. *D:* Alfred Werker; *P:* Melton H. Feld; *St:* Frances Whiting Reid, Darrell Ware; *Sc:* Robert Ellis, Helen Logan, John Patrick, Lou Breslow.

Low-budget romance.

339. The Big Trail (Fox; 1930). *Cast:* John Wayne, Marguerite Churchill, El Brendel, Tully Marshall, David Rollins, Tyrone Power, Sr. (his only talkie film and also his final film — d. 1931), Ian Keith, Ward Bond, Helen Parrish, Chief Thundercloud, DeWitt Jennings, Nat Pendleton, Louise Carver, Charles Stevens, George Walsh, Frederick Burton, Russ Powell, William V. Mong, Dodo Newton, Jack Peabody, Marcia Harris, Marjorie Leet, Frank Rainboth, Edmund Emerson, Andy Shuford, Gertrude Van Lent, Lucille Van Lent, Alphonse Ethier, Chief Big Tree. *D:* Raoul Walsh; *Sc:* Jack Peabody, Marie Boyle, Florence Postral, Hal G. Evarts. (1:50) (video)

Epic big-budget western of an arduous wagon train trek. A popular film in its day due to the fact that some scenes were filmed in the wide screen (55 mm.) Fox Grandeur process, but was still a financial loss for the studio. The film originally ran 2 hrs. and 5 mins. with the wide screen footage, but the shortened version minus the wide screen shots which runs 1 hr. 50 mins. is the only version known to exist. The film is particularly notable as the starring debut of John Wayne.

340. Bill Cracks Down (Republic; 1937). *Cast:* Grant Withers, Eddie "Rochester" Anderson. *D:* William Nigh. (G.B. title: *Men of Steel*)

Low-budget comedy.

341. A Bill of Divorcement (RKO; 1932). *Cast:* John Barrymore (Hillary Fairfield), Katharine Hepburn (film debut as Sydney Fairfield), Billie Burke (feature talkie debut as Margaret Fairfield), David Manners (Kit Humphrey), Henry Stephenson (Doctor Alliot), Paul Cavanagh (Gray Meredith), Elizabeth Patterson (Aunt Hester), Gayle Evers (Bassett). *D:* George Cukor; *Ex.P.:* David O. Selznick; *Sc:* Howard Estabrook, Harry Wagstaff Gribble. (O.R.T. 1:16 — now 1:10) (video)

After being released from a mental hospital, a man returns home and gets to know his daughter. Based on the play by Clemence Dane, it was voted one of the "10 Best" films of the year by the National Board of Review. It placed #8 on the "10 Best" lists of both the *New York Times* and *Film Daily*. Previously filmed in Great Britain in 1921. Remade by RKO in 1940.

342. Billion Dollar Scandal (Paramount; 1932–33). *Cast:* Robert Armstrong, Constance Cummings, Frank Morgan, Olga Baclanova, James Gleason, Irving Pichel, Edward Van Sloan, Warren Hymer, Sidney Toler, Berton Churchill, Edmund Breese, Hale Hamilton, Purnell Pratt, Ralf Harolde, Walter Walker. *D:* Harry Joe Brown; *P:* Charles R. Rogers; *St & Sc:* Gene Towne, Graham Baker. (1:21)

B melodrama of ex-cons who are involved in a crooked oil deal.

343. Billy the Kid (MGM; 1930). *Cast:* John Mack Brown (Billy the Kid), Wallace Beery (Pat Garrett), Kay Johnson, Karl Dane, Wyndham Standing, Russell Simpson, Blanche Frederici, Roscoe Ates, Warner P. Richmond, James Marcus, Nelson McDowell, Jack Carlyle, John Beck, Chris (-Pin) Martin, Marguerita Padula, Aggie Herring, Soledad Jimenez, Don Coleman, Lucille Powers, Hank Bell. *D:* King Vidor; *P:* Vidor; *Sc:* Wanda Tuchock, Laurence Stallings; *Additional Dialogue:* Charles MacArthur. (TV title: *The Highwayman Rides*) (1:32)

Marshal Pat Garrett sets out to capture the notorious outlaw. Originally filmed in a wide-screen process. Remade in 1941 with Robert Taylor. Based on the novel "The Saga of Billy the Kid" by Walter Noble Burns.

344. Billy the Kid Returns (Republic; 1938). *Cast:* Roy Rogers, Smiley Burnette, Mary Hart (Lynn Roberts), Fred Kohler, Morgan Wallace, Wade Boteler, Edwin Stanley, Horace Murphy, Joseph Crehan. *D:* Joe Kane; *P:*

Charles E. Ford; *Sc:* Jack Natteford. (0:56) (video)

Roy Rogers western with Roy in a dual role in his second starring feature.

345. Biography of a Bachelor Girl (MGM; 1935). *Cast:* Ann Harding, Robert Montgomery, Edward Everett Horton, Edward Arnold, Una Merkel, Charles Richman, Donald Meek, Mischa Auer, Willard Robertson, Greta Meyer. *D:* Edward H. Griffith; *Sc:* Anita Loos, Horace Jackson. (1:22)

Based on the Broadway play "Biography" by S.N. Behrman, this drama tells of the secret life of a lady portrait painter.

346. Bird of Paradise (RKO; 1932). *Cast:* Dolores Del Rio (Luana), Joel McCrea (Johnny Baker), John Halliday (Mac), Richard "Skeets" Gallagher (Chester), Creighton (Lon) Chaney (Jr.) (Thornton), Bert Roach, Wade Boteler, Arnold Gray, Reginald Simpson, Napoleon Pukui, Sophie Ortego. *D:* King Vidor; *Ex.P.:* David O. Selznick; *Sc:* Wells Root, Wanda Tuchock, Leonard Praskins; *Choreographer:* Busby Berkeley. (1:20) (video)

There's trouble on the island when an European falls for one of its native girls. Based on the play by Richard Walton Tully, it was partially filmed in Hawaii. Remade in 1951 by 20th Century-Fox.

Birds of Prey (G.B. title) *see* **The Ace of Aces**

347. The Bishop Misbehaves (MGM; 1935). *Cast:* Maureen O'Sullivan, Norman Foster, Reginald Owen, Edmund Gwenn (American debut), Lucile Watson, Robert Greig, Dudley Digges, Melville Cooper (American debut), Lillian Bond. *D:* E.A. Dupont; *P:* John Golden; *Sc:* Leon Gordon, George Auerbach (Uncredited). (G.B. title: *The Bishop's Misadventures*) (1:27)

This comedy of an English bishop who gets involved with jewel thieves is based on the play by Frederick Jackson.

348. The Bishop Murder Case (MGM; 1929–30). *Cast:* Basil Rathbone (Philo Vance), Leila Hyams, Alec B. Francis, Roland Young, George F. Marion, Raymond Hackett, Delmer Daves, Clarence Geldart, Carroll Nye, Nellie Bly Baker, Charles Quartermaine, Sidney Bracey, Zelda Sears, Bodil Rosing. *D:* Nick Grinde, David Burton; *Sc:* Lenore Coffee. (1:31)

Philo Vance who-dun-it involving a series of murders which follow various nursery rhymes and a calling card of a black chess bishop. Based on the novel by S.S. Van Dine.

The Bishop's Misadventures (G.B. title) *see* **The Bishop Misbehaves**

349. The Bitter Tea of General Yen (Columbia; 1933). *Cast:* Barbara Stanwyck, Nils Asther, Toshia Mori, Walter Connolly, Gavin Gordon, Lucien Littlefield, Richard Loo, Clara Blandick, Helen Jerome Eddy, Robert Wayne, Emmett Corrigan, Knute Erickson, Arthur Millette, Ella Hall, Moy Ming, Martha Mattox, Jessie Arnold. *D:* Frank Capra; *P:* Walter Wanger; *St:* Grace Zaring Stone; *Sc:* Edward E. Paramore. (1:29)

An American missionary falls for a Chinese warlord after being taken captive by him. Despite the fact that this film was chosen to premiere the opening of Radio City Music Hall in New York, it was a box office flop.

350. Black Aces (Universal; 1936–37). *Cast:* Buck Jones, Kay Linaker, Robert Frazer, Frank Campeau, Forrest Taylor, Charles King, Red Mackaye, W.E. Laurence, Raymond Brown, Robert Kortman, Bernard Phillips, Charles LeMoyne, Arthur Van Slyke, Bob McKenzie. *D:* Jones, Lesley Selander; *P:* Jones; *Sc:* Frances Guihan. (0:59)

Buck Jones western of cattle rustling.

351. The Black Bandit (Universal; 1938). *Cast:* Bob Baker (in a dual role), Marjorie Reynolds, Hal Taliaferro, Jack Rockwell, Forrest Taylor, Glenn Strange, Arthur Van Slyke, Carleton Young, Rex Downing, Dick Dickinson. *D:* George Waggner; *P:* Trem Carr; *Sc:* Joseph West (Waggner). (1:00)

Bob Baker western of twin brothers, one lawless, the other a lawman.

352. Black Beauty (Monogram; 1933). *Cast:* Esther Ralston, Alexander Kirkland, Hale Hamilton, Gavin Gordon, Don Alvarado, George Walsh, Theodore Lorch, John Larkin, Eddie Fetherston, Al Bridge, Bruce Covington. *D:* Phil Rosen; *P:* I.E. Chadwick; *Sc:* Charles Logue. (1:10)

Low-budget equine drama based on the famous novel by Anna Sewell. Previously filmed in 1921. Remade in 1946 and again in Great Britain in 1971.

353. The Black Camel (Fox; 1931). *Cast:* Warner Oland, Sally Eilers, Bela Lugosi, Victor Varconi, Robert Young (film debut), Dwight Frye, Mary Gordon, Dorothy Revier, Frank Yaconnelli, C. Henry Gordon, Robert Homans, Richard Tucker, J.M. Kerrigan, Murray Kinnell, Louis Mackintosh, Otto Yamaoka, Marjorie White, Rita Roselle, William Post, Jr., Violet Dunn. *D:* Hamilton MacFadden; *As.P.:* William Sistrom; *Sc:* Hugh Stange, Barry Connors (based on the character created by Earl Derr Biggers). (1:11)

The second entry in the "Charlie Chan" series involving a fortune-teller and murder. Filmed on location in Hawaii.

354. The Black Cat (Universal; 1934). *Cast:* Boris Karloff (Hjalmar Poelzig), Bela Lugosi (Dr. Vitus Verdegast), David Manners, Jacqueline Wells (later Julie Bishop), Egon Brecher, Harry Cording, Anna Duncan, Lucille Lund, Henry Armetta, Albert Conti, Herman Bing, John Peter Richmond (later John Carradine), Luis Alberni, Andre Cheron. *D:* Edgar G. Ulmer; *P:* Carl Laemmle, Jr.; *St:* Ulmer, Peter Ruric; *Sc:* Ruric. (G.B. title: *House of Doom*) (1:05) (video)

Classic horror film which marks the first teaming of Karloff and Lugosi in a tale of revenge in an old castle inhabited by devil-worshippers. Also notable are the bizarre art-deco sets by Charles D. Hall. A box-office hit which has a cult following.

355. The Black Doll (Universal; 1938). *Cast:* Donald Woods, Nan Grey, Arthur Hoyt, Edgar Kennedy, Holmes Herbert, Addison Richards, C. Henry Gordon, William Lundigan. *D:* Otis Garrett (directorial debut); *P:* Irving Starr; *Sc:* Harold Buckley. (1:06)

B who-dun-it, the second entry in the studio's "Crime Club" series. Based on the novel by William Edward Hayes.

356. Black Fury (WB/F.N.; 1935). *Cast:* Paul Muni, Karen Morley, William Gargan, Barton MacLane, John T. Qualen, J. Carrol Naish, Vince Barnett, Tully Marshall, Henry O'Neill, Joseph Crehan, Mae Marsh, Sara Haden, Willard Robertson, Effie Ellsler, Wade Boteler, Egon Brecher, George Pat Collins, Ward Bond, Akim Tamiroff, Purnell Pratt, Eddie Shubert, Samuel S. Hinds, Mike Mazurki, Pat Moriarty, Mickey Rentschler, Edith Fellows, Bobby Nelson, John Bleifer, Dorothy Gray, Floyd Shackleford, June Ebberling, Dorothy Gray, George Offerman, Jr., Pedro Regas. *D:* Michael Curtiz; *Sc:* Abem Finkel, Carl Erickson. (1:35) (video)

A social drama of coal miners, unions and corruption. Based on the play "Bohunk" by Harry R. Irving and the story "Jan Volkanik" by Judge M.A. Musmanno both of which were based on the real-life murder of Pennsylvania coal miner Mike Shemanski. At the time of release, the film was banned in the state of Pennsylvania and wound up in the deficit column of the studio's ledgers.

357. The Black Ghost (RKO; 1932). *Cast:* Creighton (Lon) Chaney (Jr.), Dorothy Gulliver, Mary Jo Desmond, Francis X. Bushman, Jr., Joe Bonomo, Slim Cole, Richard Neil, William Desmond, LeRoy Mason, Yakima Canutt, Pete Morrison, Claude Peyton, Fritzi Fern, Bill Nestell, Ben Corbett, Fred Burns, Frank Lackteen. *D:* Spencer Gordon Bennet, Tom Storey; *P:* Van Beuren Productions; *Sc:* George Plympton, Robert F. Hill. (1:05)

Feature version of the 12-chapter serial — the only one ever produced by this studio — "The Last Frontier," involving a hooded crusader against a band of outlaws.

358. Black Legion (WB; 1936). *Cast:* Humphrey Bogart (Acting Award from the N.B.R. as Frank Taylor), Erin O'Brien-Moore (Ruth Taylor), Dick Foran (Ed Jackson), Ann Sheridan (Betty Grogan), Joseph Sawyer (Cliff Moore), Helen Flint (Pearl Davis), Paul Harvey (Billings), Charles Halton (Osgood), Samuel S. Hinds (Judge), Addison Richards (prosecuting attorney), Alonzo Price (Alexander Hargrave), Clifford Soubier (Mike Grogan), Dorothy Vaughan (Mrs. Grogan), Dickie Jones (Bud Taylor), Henry Brandon (Sam Dombrowsky), John Litel (Tommy Smith), Eddie Acuff (Metcalf), Harry Hayden (Jones), Egon Brecher (old man Dombrowsky), Pat C. Flick (Nick Strumpas), Paul Stanton (Dr. Barnham), Francis Sayles (Charlie), Don Barclay, Emmett Vogan, Billy Wayne, Frank Sully, Eddy Chandler, Robert E. Homans, Max Wagner, Carlyle Moore, Jr., Dennis Moore, Milton Kibbee, Lee Phelps, Wilfred Lucas, Jack Mower, Fredrich Lindsley (voice only). *D:* Archie Mayo; *As.P.:* Robert Lord; *Original Story:* (A.A.N.) Lord; *Sc:* Abem Finkel, William Wister Haines. (1:23) (video)

A critically acclaimed controversial social drama of a factory worker who becomes involved with a secret organization. The film was voted #3 on the "10 Best" list of the National Board of Review.

359. Black Magic (Micheaux; 1932). A low-budget independent production, directed, produced and written by Oscar Micheaux.

360. Black Market Babies (Xxxx Xxxx; 1933). (No information available)

361. Black Moon (Columbia; 1934). *Cast:* Jack Holt, Fay Wray, Dorothy Burgess, Clarence Muse, Sig Rumann, Lawrence Criner, Arnold Korff, Mme. Sul-Te-Wan, Cora Sue Collins, Eleanor Wesselhoeft. *D:* Roy William Neill; *St:* Clements Ripley; *Sc:* Wells Root.

Low-budget melodrama.

362. The Black Room (Columbia; 1935). *Cast:* Boris Karloff (in a dual role), Marian Marsh, Katherine de Mille, Thurston Hall, Robert Allen, John Buckler, Colin Tapley, Henry Kolker, Edward Van Sloan. *D:* Roy William Neill; *P:* Robert North; *St:* Arthur Strawn; *Sc:* Henry Meyers, Arthur Strawn. (1:07) (video)

A horror thriller of twin brothers, one good the other evil. Based on the writings of Arthur Strawn.

363. Black Sheep (Fox; 1935). *Cast:* Tom Brown, Claire Trevor, Edmund Lowe, Herbert Mundin, Adrienne Ames, David Torrence, Jed Prouty, Akim Tamiroff, Eugene Pallette, Reginald Sheffield, Robert Elliott, Billy Bevan, Ford Sterling (final film — d. 1939). *D:* Allan Dwan; *P:* Sol M. Wurtzel; *St:* Dwan; *Sc:* Allen Rivkin.

Romantic comedy.

364. The Black Watch (Fox; 1929). *Cast:* Victor McLaglen, Myrna Loy, Walter Long, Roy D'Arcy, David

Torrence, Lumsden Hare, Francis Ford, Cyril Chadwick, Frank Reicher, David Rollins, Pat Somerset. *D:* John Ford. (G.B. title: *King of the Khyber Rifles*) The first of John Ford's military trilogy of the British in India. Followed by *Wee Willie Winkie* (q.v.) and *Four Men and a Prayer* (q.v.). Based on the novel "King of the Khyber Rifles" by Talbot Mundy, it was remade under that title in 1954.

365. Blackmail (MGM; 1939). *Cast:* Edward G. Robinson, Ruth Hussey, Gene Lockhart, Bobbs Watson, Guinn Williams, John Wray, Arthur Hohl, Esther Dale, Cyrus Kendall, Mitchell Lewis, Willie Best, Victor Kilian, Charles Middleton. *D:* H.C. Potter; *P:* John W. Considine, Jr.; *As.P.:* Albert E. Levoy; *St:* Dorothy Yost, Endre Bohem; *Sc:* David Hertz, William Ludwig. (1:21)

An innocent man is released from prison and subsequently blackmailed.

366. The Blackmailer (Columbia; 1936). *Cast:* Florence Rice, H.B. Warner, William Gargan, Kenneth Thomson, Paul Hurst, Boyd Irwin. *D:* Gordon Wiles.

B melodrama.

367. Blackwell's Island (WB; 1939). *Cast:* John Garfield, Rosemary Lane, Dick Purcell, Victor Jory, Stanley Fields, Morgan Conway, Granville Bates, Anthony Averill, Peggy Shannon, Charles Foy, Norman Willis, Joe Cunningham. *D:* William McGann; *As.P.:* Bryan Foy; *St:* Crane Wilbur, Lee Katz; *Sc:* Wilbur. (1:11)

B drama of a news reporter out to get an imprisoned hoodlum who is living like a king in his incarceration. Based on an actual incident which occurred in 1934.

Blazing Arrow *see* **Fighting Caravans**

368. Blazing Barriers (Monogram; 1937). *Cast:* Frank (Junior) Coghlan, Jr., Edward Arnold, Jr., Florine McKinney, Irene Franklin, Guy Bates Post, Herbert Corthell, Milburn Stone, Addison (Jack) Randall, Bud Flanagan (Dennis O'Keefe). *D:* Aubrey Scotto; *As.P.:* Ken Goldsmith; *St:* Edwin C. Parsons; *Sc:* Parsons. (1:05)

B drama of two delinquents who reform after being assigned to the Civilian Conservation Corps.

369. Blazing Justice (Spectrum; 1934-36). *Cast:* Bill Cody, Gertrude Messinger, Gordon Griffith, Milburn Morante, Budd Buster, Frank Yaconelli, Charles Tannen. *D:* Albert (Al) Herman; *Sc:* Zara Tazil. (1:00)

Bill Cody oater of a cowboy wrongly accused of theft.

370. Blazing Sixes (WB; 1937). *Cast:* Dick Foran, Mira McKinney, Helen Valkis, John Merton, Glenn Strange, Kenneth Harlan, Milton Kibbee, Gordon Hart, Henry Otho, Wilfred Lucas, Bud Osborne, Tom Forman, Ben Corbett, Malcolm Waite, Tom Burns, Jack Mower, Artie Ortego, Frank Ellis, Cactus Mack, Gene Alsace (Rocky Camron), Smoke the Wonder Horse. *D:* Noel Smith; *As.P.:* Bryan Foy; *St:* Anthony Coldeway; *Sc:* John T. Neville; *Songs:* M.K. Jerome, Jack Scholl. (0:55)

Dick Foran western of an undercover man out to get some gold thieves.

Blazing Trail *see* **Guns for Hire**

371. Blessed Event (WB; 1932). *Cast:* Lee Tracy, Mary Brian, Dick Powell (in his film debut as Bunny Harmon), Ruth Donnelly, Ned Sparks, Frank McHugh, Allen Jenkins, Emma Dunn, Edwin Maxwell, Walter Walker, Isabel Jewell (film debut—recreating her stage role), George Chandler, Tom Dugan, William Halligan, Jesse DeVorska, Milton Maxwell. *D:* Roy Del Ruth; *P:* Ray Griffith; *Sc:* Howard Green. (1:23)

Comedy of a newspaper gossip colmnist whose writing gets him in hot water. Based on the play by Manuel Seff and Forrest Wilson.

372. Blind Adventure (RKO; 1933). *Cast:* Robert Armstrong, Helen Mack, Roland Young, Ralph Bellamy, John Miljan, Laura Hope Crews, Beryl Mercer, Forrester Harvey, Henry Stephenson, John Warburton, Phyllis Barry, Tyrrell Davis, Marjorie Gateson, Ivan Simpson, Charles Irwin, Desmond Roberts, Frederick Sullivan, George K. Arthur. *D:* Ernest B. Schoedsack; *As.P.:* David Lewis; *Sc:* Ruth Rose. (1:05)

Low-budget comedy-mystery of an American newly arrived in London who gets lost in the fog and winds up involved with a gang of crooks.

373. Blind Alibi (RKO; 1938). *Cast:* Richard Dix, Whitney Bourne, Ace the Wonder Dog, Eduardo Ciannelli, Frances Mercer, Paul Guilfoyle, Richard Lane, Jack Arnold, Frank M. Thomas, Solly Ward, Tommy Bupp, Walter Miller, George Irving, Ann Doran. *D:* Lew Landers; *P:* Cliff Reid; *St:* William Joyce Cowan; *Sc:* Lionel Houser, Harry Segall, Ron Ferguson. (1:02)

B crime drama of blackmail and a man who feigns blindness.

374. Blind Alley (Columbia; 1939). *Cast:* Ralph Bellamy, Chester Morris, Ann Dvorak, Joan Perry, Melville Cooper, Rose Stradner, John Eldredge, Marc Lawrence, Milburn Stone, Grady Sutton, Scotty Beckett, Stanley Brown, Marie Blake. *D:* Charles Vidor; *Sc:* Michael Blankfort, Albert Duffy, Philip MacDonald. (1:11)

Psychological drama of a psychiatrist who is being held prisoner by a gangster. Based on the play by James Warwick it was remade in 1948 as *The Dark Past.*

375. Blind Date (Columbia; 1934). *Cast:* Ann Sothern, Paul Kelly, Neil Hamilton, Mickey Rooney, Jane Darwell, Joan Gale, Tyler Brooke, Geneva Mitchell, Ben Hendricks, Theodore Newton, Billie Seward. *D:* Roy William Neill; *St:* Vida Hurst; *Sc:* Ethel Hill. (G.B. title: *Her Sacrifice*) (1:11)

Comedy of a woman and the two men in her life.

Blind Waves (G.B. title) *see* **A Lady Surrenders**

376. Blockade (Film Booking Office; 1928). *Cast:* Wallace MacDonald, Anna Q. Nilsson. *D:* George B. Seitz.

A part-talkie pirate adventure.

377. Blockade (United Artists/ Walter Wanger; 1938). *Cast:* Henry Fonda, Madeleine Carroll, Leo Carrillo, John Halliday, Vladimir Sokoloff, Reginald Denny, Arthur Warwick, Fred Kohler, Katherine de Mille, Lupita Tovar, Carl Stockdale, Arthur Aylesworth, William Davidson, George Houston, Peter Godfrey, Carlos de Valdez, Rosina Galli, Nick Thompson. *D:* William Dieterle; *P:* Walter Wanger; *Original Story:* (A.A.N.) John Howard Lawson; *Sc:* Lawson; *Music:* (A.A.N.) Werner Janssen. (1:25)

A romantic drama of the Spanish Civil War which was in nomination for "Best Film" by the New York Film Critics.

378. Block-Heads (MGM/Hal Roach; 1938). *Cast:* Stan Laurel, Oliver Hardy, Patricia Ellis, Minna Gombell, Billy Gilbert, James Finlayson. *D:* John G. Blystone (final film — d. 1938); *P:* Hal Roach, Stan Laurel; *As.P.:* Hal Roach, Jr.; *St & Sc:* James Parrott, Harry Langdon, Felix Adler, Charles Rogers, Arnold Belgard. (0:55) (video)

Classic Laurel and Hardy comedy with Stan as a soldier who after twenty years finally finds out that World War I is over and his eventual return to society. The last of Roach's films to be released by MGM before signing with United Artists.

379. Blonde Baby (Xxxx Xxxx; 1931). (No information available)

Blonde Bombshell *see* **Bombshell**

380. Blonde Captive (Xxxx Xxxx; 1932). *Narrator:* Lowell Thomas; *P:* Paul Withington.

381. Blond Cheat (RKO; 1938). *Cast:* Joan Fontaine, Derrick de Marney, Cecil Kellaway, Cecil Cunningham, Lillian Bond, Robert Coote, Olaf Hytten, John Sutton, Gerald Hamer, Charles Coleman, Claud Allister, Mary Gordon. *D:* Joseph Santley; *P:* William Sistrom; *St:* Aladar Laszlo; *Sc:* Charles Kaufman, Harry Segall, Viola Brothers Shore, Paul Yawitz; *Song:* Dave Dreyer, Herman Ruby. (1:02)

Romantic comedy of an actress who is paid to break up an Englishman's engagement.

382. Blonde Crazy (WB; 1931). *Cast:* James Cagney, Joan Blondell, Louis Calhern, Ray Milland, Guy Kibbee, Noel Francis, Polly Walters, Charles (Levison) Lane, Maude Eburne, Nat Pendleton, William Burress, Walter Percival, Peter Erkelenz. *D:* Roy Del Ruth; *Sc:* Kubec Glasmon, John Bright.

A low-budget comedy with songs of a small-time conman.

The Blonde Reporter (G.B. title) *see* **Sob Sister**

383. Blonde Trouble (Paramount; 1937). *Cast:* Johnny Downs, Eleanore Whitney, Lynne Overman, El Brendel, Benny Baker, William Demarest, Helen Flint, Terry Walker, John Patterson, Kitty McHugh, Barlowe Borland. *D:* George Archainbaud; *Sc:* Lillie Hayward.

B comedy of a songwriter who is trying to hit the big time on Tin Pan Alley. Based on the 1929 Broadway play by Ring Lardner and George S. Kauf-

man, it was previously filmed in 1931 as *June Moon* (q.v.).

384. Blonde Venus (Paramount; 1932). *Cast:* Marlene Dietrich, Herbert Marshall, Cary Grant, Dickie Moore, Sidney Toler, Cecil Cunningham, Emile Chautard, Rita LaRoy, Robert Emmett O'Connor, Hattie McDaniel, Sterling Holloway, Gene Morgan, Mary Gordon, Francis Sayles, Kent Taylor, Evelyn Preer. *D:* Josef Von Sternberg; *Sc:* S.K. Lauren, Jules Furthman. (1:37) (video)

After her marriage goes on the rocks, a young mother takes to walking the streets to support her child. Notable as the film in which Dietrich sings "Hot Voodoo" in an ape suit. The film was a box office flop.

385. Blondes at Work (WB; 1938). *Cast:* Glenda Farrell (Torchy Blane), Barton MacLane (Steve McBride), Roy Barcroft, Betty Compson, Tom Kennedy, Rosella Towne, John Ridgely, Richard Loo, Carole Landis, Robert Middlemass. *D:* Frank McDonald; *As.P.:* Bryan Foy; *Sc:* Albert de Mond.

The fourth entry in the "Torchy Blane" B series with the girl reporter out to solve the murder of a department store owner. Based on the characters created by Frederick Nebel.

386. Blondie (Columbia; 1938). *Cast:* Penny Singleton (Blondie), Arthur Lake (Dagwood Bumstead), Larry Simms (Baby Dumpling), "Daisy," Jonathan Hale (Mr. Dithers), Gene Lockhart, Ann Doran, Gordon Oliver, Willie Best, Ian Wolfe, Stanley Andrews, Kathleen Lockhart, Dorothy Moore, Irving Bacon (mailman). *D:* Frank R. Strayer; *Sc:* Richard Flournoy. (1:08)

Premiere entry in the series dealing with the wacky goings-on in the Bumstead household. Based on the comic strip by Chic Young. The series itself which ran into the early 1950s was highly successful and profitable for Columbia, but a later attempt at a TV series was not so successful.

387. Blondie Brings Up Baby (Columbia; 1939). *Cast:* Penny Singleton (Blondie), Arthur Lake (Dagwood), Larry Simms (Baby Dumpling), "Daisy," Danny Mummert, Jonathan Hale (Mr. J.C. Dithers), Fay Helm, Peggy Ann Garner, Helen Jerome Eddy, Ian Wolfe, Robert Middlemass, Selmer Jackson, Irving Bacon (mailman). *D:* Frank Strayer. (1:07)

The fourth entry in the popular low-budget comedy series based on the comic strip of Chic Young.

388. Blondie Johnson (WB/F.N.; 1933). *Cast:* Joan Blondell, Chester Morris, Allen Jenkins, Claire Dodd, Earle Foxe, Arthur Vinton, Sterling Holloway, Mae Busch, Olin Howland, Toshia Mori, Sam Godfrey, Donald Kirke. *D:* Ray Enright; *Supervisor:* Lucien Hubbard; *Sc:* Earl Baldwin. (1:07)

Comedy-drama of a woman who works her way up in the rackets and meets her ultimate downfall.

389. Blondie Meets the Boss (Columbia; 1939). *Cast:* Penny Singleton (Blondie), Arthur Lake (Dagwood), Larry Simms (Baby Dumpling), Dorothy Moore, "Daisy," Jonathan Hale (Mr. Dithers), Stanley Brown, Inez Courtney, Don Beddoe, Grady Sutton, Wallis Clark, Richard Fiske, Linda Winters, Joel Dean, Irving Bacon (mailman). *D:* Frank Strayer; *Sc:* Kay Van Riper, Richard Flournoy. (0:58)

The second entry in the "Blondie" comedy series.

390. Blondie of the Follies (MGM; 1932). *Cast:* Marion Davies, Robert Montgomery, Billie Dove, Jimmy Durante, ZaSu Pitts, Sidney Toler, Louise Carter, James Gleason, Douglass Dumbrille, Clyde Cook, Billy Gilbert, Sarah Padden. *D:* Edmund Goulding; *P:* Marion Davies; *Sc:* Frances Marion, Anita Loos.

Musical-drama of two showgirls in love with the same man.

391. Blondie Takes a Vacation (Columbia; 1939). *Cast:* Penny Singleton (Blondie), Arthur Lake (Dagwood), Larry Simms (Baby Dumpling), "Daisy," Danny Mummert, Donald Meek, Elizabeth Dunne, Robert Wilcox, Irving Bacon (mailman). *D:* Frank Strayer. (1:01)

The third entry in the "Blondie" series.

Blood Brothers *see* **Brothers**

392. Blood Money (United Artists/20th Century; 1933). *Cast:* George Bancroft, Frances Dee, Judith Anderson (feature film debut), Chick Chandler, Blossom Seeley, Kathlyn Williams, Theresa Harris, Etienne Girardot, Ann Brody, George Regas, Joseph (Sawyer) Sauers, Lucille Ball (bit). *D:* Rowland Brown (final film as director before becoming a screenwriter); *As.P.:* William Goetz, Raymond Griffith; *St & Sc:* Brown, Hal Long. (1:05)

Drama of a bail-bondsman who falls for a fast-living socialite.

393. Blossoms on Broadway (Paramount; 1937). *Cast:* Edward Arnold, Shirley Ross, John Trent, Rufe Davis, William Frawley, Weber and Fields (a vaudeville act), Frank Craven, Edward Brophy, Charles Halton, Johnny Arthur, The Radio Rogues, Kitty Kelly, Frederick Clarke. *D:* Richard Wallace; *P:* B.P. Schulberg; *Sc:* Theodore Reeves; *Songs:* Frank Loesser, Ralph Rainger. (1:28)

Low-budget film involving a kidnapping.

394. Blue Montana Skies (Republic; 1939). *Cast:* Gene Autry, Smiley Burnette, June Storey, Harry Woods, Tully Marshall, Al Bridge, Glenn Strange, Dorothy Granger, Walt Shrum and his Colorado Hillbillies, Edmund Cobb, Elmo Lincoln (the first screen

Tarzan in 1918), Jack Ingram, John Beach, Allan Cavan, Buffalo Bill, Jr., Champion. *D:* B. Reeves Eason; *P:* Harry Grey; *St:* Norman S. Hall, Paul Franklin; *Sc:* Gerald Geraghty. (0:56)

Gene Autrey western with songs involving fur thieves.

395. Blue Steel (Monogram–Lone Star; 1934). *Cast:* John Wayne, Eleanor Hunt, George Hayes, Ed Peil, Sr., Yakima Canutt, George Cleveland, George Nash, Lafe McKee, Hank Bell, Earl Dwire, Artie Ortego, Horace B. Carpenter, Theodore Lorch, Silver Tip Baker. *D:* Robert N. Bradbury; *St & Sc:* Bradbury; *P:* Paul Malvern. (0:54) (video)

John Wayne western involving a town that was built over a goldmine and a ruthless outlaw known as the "Polka Dot Bandit."

396. Bluebeard's Eighth Wife (Paramount; 1938). *Cast:* Claudette Colbert, Gary Cooper, David Niven, Edward Everett Horton, Elizabeth Patterson, Herman Bing, Leon Ames, Warren Hymer, Franklin Pangborn, Tyler Brooke, Lenore Aubert (American debut), Lawrence Grant, Charles Halton, Armand Cortez, Rolfe Sedan, Terry Ray (Ellen Drew). *D:* Ernst Lubitsch; *P:* Lubitsch; *Adaptation:* Charlton Andrews; *Sc:* Charles Brackett, Billy Wilder. (1:20)

This comedy of an oft-married millionaire is based on the play by Alfred Savoir. Previously filmed by this studio in 1923 with Gloria Swanson and Huntley Gordon.

397. Body and Soul (Fox; 1931). *Cast:* Charles Farrell, Elissa Landi (American debut), Humphrey Bogart, Myrna Loy, Donald Dillaway, Ian MacLaren, Bruce Warren, Dennis d'Auburn, Harold Kinney, Douglas Dray, Pat Somerset, Crauford Kent. *D:* Alfred Santell; *Sc:* Jules Furthman.

World War I drama set among American flyers in Great Britain. Based

on the play "Squadrons" by Elliott White Springs and A.E. Thomas.

398. The Bohemian Girl (MGM/Hal Roach; 1936). *Cast:* Stan Laurel, Oliver Hardy, Mae Busch, Antonio Moreno, Jacqueline Wells (Julie Bishop), Darla Hood (of "Our Gang" game), Zeffie Tilbury, James Finlayson, Thelma Todd (final film), Felix Knight, Mitchell Lewis, William P. Carleton. *D:* James Horne, Charles Rogers; *P:* Hal Roach; *Sc:* Alfred Bunn. (1:15) (video)

Comic operetta of a princess who is kidnapped by gypsies. Based on the operetta by Michael W. Balfe, it was previously filmed in Great Britain in 1922. Notable as the final film appearance of actress-comedienne Thelma Todd who died in 1935 at the age of 30 under mysterious circumstances. A box-office hit.

399. The Boiling Point (Allied; 1932). *Cast:* Hoot Gibson, George Hayes, Helen Foster, Lafe McKee, Wheeler Oakman, Tom London, "Skeeter" Bill Robbins, William Nye, Charles Bailey, Billy Bletcher, Frank Ellis, Lew Meehan, Hattie McDaniel, Bob Burns, Art Mix, Merrill McCormack, Artie Ortego. *D:* George Melford; *P:* M.H. Hoffman, Jr.; *Sc:* Donald W. Lee, Tom Gallaghan, Harry Neumann (who also photographed). (1:10) (video)

Hoot Gibson comic western of a cowboy who makes a bet he can control his temper.

400. The Bold Caballero (Republic; 1936). *Cast:* Bob Livingston, Heather Angel, Sig Rumann, Ian Wolfe, Robert Warwick, Emily Fitzroy, Charles Stevens, Walter Long, Ferdinand Munier, King (Chris-Pin) Martin, John Merton, Jack Kirk, Charles "Slim" Whitaker, George Plues, Chief Thundercloud, Carlos De Valdez. *D:* Wells Root; *Sc:* Root. (1:09) (video)

Western actioner in color (the first for this studio), with Zorro coming to the aid of peasants who are being terrorized by a tyrannical military commandant.

401. Bolero (Paramount; 1934). *Cast:* George Raft, Carole Lombard, Sally Rand (final film — ret.), Frances Drake, William Frawley, Ray Milland, Gertrude Michael, Phillips Smalley, Paul Panzer, Gloria Shea, Clara Lou (Ann) Sheridan. *D:* Wesley Ruggles; *P:* William LeBaron; *Sc:* Carey Wilson, Kubec Glasmon (based on an idea by Ruth Ridenour and Horace Jackson). (1:23) (video)

A dancer hits the big time while neglecting aspects of his personal life. Much of the dancing (choreography by LeRoy Prinz) is done by professionals (Veloz and Yolanda) replacing Raft and Lombard via tricky photographic techniques.

402. Bombay Mail (Universal; 1934). *Cast:* Edmund Lowe (Inspector Dyke), Shirley Grey (Sonia Smeganoff), Walter Armitage (Maharajah of Zungore), Hedda Hopper (Mrs. Anthony Daniels), Onslow Stevens, Ralph Forbes, John Wray, Brandon Hurst, Ferdinand Gottschalk, Tom Moore, Georges Renavent, Jameson Thomas, John Davidson. *D:* Edwin L. Marin; *Sc:* Tom Reed. (1:10)

Low-budget actioner about the investigation of a man's death aboard a train bound from Calcutta to Bombay. Based on the novel by L.G. Blochman.

403. Bombshell (MGM; 1933). *Cast:* Jean Harlow (Lola), Lee Tracy (Space), Frank Morgan (Pops), Franchot Tone (Gifford), Pat O'Brien (Brogan), Una Merkel (Mac), Ted Healy (Junior), Ivan Lebedeff, Isabel Jewell, Louise Beavers, Leonard Carey, Mary Forbes, C. Aubrey Smith, June Brewster, Ethel Griffies, Shirley Ross (film debut — bit). *D:* Victor Fleming; *Ex.P.:* Howard Hughes; *P:* Hunt Stromberg; *Sc:* John Lee Mahin, Jules Furthman. (G.B. title — re-release title — TV title: *Blonde Bombshell*). (1:37)

Classic comedy of a sexy Hollywood starlet who is manipulated and used by virtually everyone she comes in contact with, as well as family members. Events in the film tend to parallel those in Harlow's real life. Based on the play by Caroline Francke and Mack Crane.

404. Bondage (Fox; 1933). *Cast:* Dorothy Jordan, Isabel Jewell, Alexander Kirkland, Edward Woods, Jane Darwell, Nydia Westman, Rafaela Ottiano, Merle Tottenham, Dorothy Libaire. *D:* Alfred Santell.

Romantic drama based on a book by Grace Sothcote Leake.

Bonds of Honour (G.B. title) *see* **No Ransom**

405. Bonnie Scotland (MGM/ Hal Roach; 1935). *Cast:* Stan Laurel, Oliver Hardy, June Lang, William Janney, Anne Grey, Vernon Steele, James Finlayson, David Torrence, Maurice Black, Daphne Pollard, Mary Gordon, Lionel Belmore, Charles Hall, Minerva Urecal. *D:* James Horne; *P:* Hal Roach; *Sc:* Frank Butler, Jeff Moffitt. (1:20) (video)

The misadventures of two Scottish misfits amidst a military regiment in India. Somewhat of a parody on *Lives of a Bengal Lancer* (q.v.), the film was a big box office hit.

406. Booloo (Paramount; 1938). *Cast:* Colin Tapley, Jayne Regan, William Stack, Claude King, Lionel Pape, Ivan Simpson, Mamo Clark, Colin Kenny, Herbert DeSouza, Clive Morgan, Phillips Smalley, Napier Ralkes. *D:* Clyde Elliott; *P:* Elliott; *St:* Elliott; *Sc:* Robert E. Welsh.

Jungle drama set in Malaya of hunters using human bait to trap a white tiger.

407. Boothill Brigade (Republic–Supreme; 1937). *Cast:* Johnny Mack Brown, Claire Rochelle, Dick Curtis, Horace Murphy, Frank LaRue, Frank Ellis, Frank Ball, Ed Cassidy, Bobby Nelson, Steve Clark, Lew Meehan, Jim Corey, Tex Palmer, Sherry Tansey. *D:*

Sam Newfield; *P:* A.W. Hackel; *Sc:* George Plympton. (0:58)

Johnny Mack Brown western of a ranch foreman who comes to the aid of his employer. Brown's final film for Hackel before moving to a Universal contract.

408. Boots and Saddles (Republic; 1937). *Cast:* Gene Autry, Smiley Burnette, Judith Allen, Ra Hould (later Ronald Sinclair), Gordon (Bill) Elliott, Guy Usher, John Ward, Frankie Marvin, Chris-Pin Martin, Stanley Blystone, Bud Osborne, Merrill McCormack, Champion. *D:* Joe Kane; *As.P.:* Sol C. Siegel; *St:* Jack Natteford; *Sc:* Natteford, Oliver Drake. (0:59) (video)

Gene Autry western involving rival horse dealers. Includes the song "Take Me Back to My Boots and Saddles."

409. Boots of Destiny (Grand National; 1937). *Cast:* Ken Maynard, Claudia Dell, Vince Barnett, Ed Cassidy, Walter Patterson, Martin Garralaga, George Morrell, Fred Cordova, Carl Mathews, Wally West, Sid D'Albrook, Tarzan. *D:* Arthur Rosson; *P:* M.H. Hoffman, Jr.; *St:* E. Morton Hough; *Sc:* Rosson. (0:56)

Ken Maynard western of mistaken identity.

410. Border Brigands (Universal; 1935). *Cast:* Buck Jones, Lona Andre, Fred Kohler, Frank Rice, Edward Keane, J.P. McGowan, Hank Bell, Alan Bridge, Lew Meehan. *D:* Nick Grinde; *Sc:* Stuart Anthony. (0:56)

Buck Jones adventure of a Canadian Mountie in search of the man who killed his brother.

411. Border Caballero (Puritan; 1936). *Cast:* Tim McCoy, Lois January, Ralph Byrd, Ted Adams, J. Frank Glendon, Earle Hodgins, John Merton, Bob McKenzie, Oscar Gahan, Bill Patton, Frank McCarroll, Tex Phelps, George Morrell, Jack Evans. *D:* Sam Newfield; *P:* Sig Neufeld (brother to

Sam Newfield), Leslie Simmonds; *Sc:* Joseph O'Donnell. (0:57)

Tim McCoy western of a former government agent who rejoins the service to bring in a gang of outlaws.

412. Border Cafe (RKO; 1937). *Cast:* Harry Carey, John Beal, Armida, George Irving, J. Carrol Naish, Lee Patrick, Marjorie Lord (film debut), Paul Fix, Leona Roberts, Max Wagner, Walter Miller. *D:* Lew Landers; *P:* Robert Sisk; *Sc:* Lionel Houser. (1:07)

A cowboy and a young easterner get the goods on a phony cattlemen's association in this B western with comic overtones and musical numbers. Based on the story "In the Mexican Quarter" by Thomas Gill.

413. Border Devils (Artclass; 1931–32). *Cast:* Harry Carey, Kathleen Collins, Niles Welch, Ray Gallagher, Olive Gordon, Murdock MacQuarrie, George Hayes, Al Smith, Maston Williams, Merrill McCormick, Art Mix. *D:* William Nigh; *Sc:* Harry C. Crist (Harry Fraser). (1:00)

Harry Carey western of a man who breaks jail to prove his innocence.

414. Border Flight (Paramount; 1936). *Cast:* Robert Cummings, Frances Farmer, John Howard, Grant Withers, Roscoe Karns, Samuel S. Hinds, Frank Faylen, Donald Kirke, Ted Oliver, Paul Barrett. *D:* Otho Lovering; *P:* A.M. Botsford; *St:* Ewing Scott; *Sc:* Stuart Anthony, Arthur Beckhard.

B action melodrama of a pilot and his girl who are captured by smugglers.

415. Border G-Man (RKO; 1938). *Cast:* George O'Brien, Laraine (Day) Johnson, Ray Whitley, John Miljan, Rita LaRoy, Edgar Dearing, William Stelling, Edward Keane, Ethan Laidlaw, Hugh Sothern, Bobby Burns. *D:* David Howard; *P:* Bert Gilroy; *St:* Bernard McConville; *Sc:* Oliver Drake. (1:00)

George O'Brien western involving a smuggling ring.

416. Border Guns (Aywon; 1935). *Cast:* Bill Cody, Franklyn Farnum, Janet Morgan (Blanche Mehaffey), George Chesebro, Fred Church, William Desmond, James Aubrey, Wally Wales (Hal Taliaferro). *D:* Robert L. Horner; *P:* Horner; *Sc:* Horner. (0:55)

Bill Cody oater of a cowboy and a known gunman who pair up to corral a gang of outlaws.

417. Border Law (Columbia; 1931). *Cast:* Buck Jones, Lupita Tovar, Frank Rice, Jim Mason, Don Chapman, Louis Hickus, F.R. Smith, John Wallace, Bob Burns, Glenn Strange, Fred Burns, Art Mix. *D:* Louis King; *Sc:* Stuart Anthony. (1:03)

Buck Jones western of a cowboy out to avenge the death of his brother. Remade in 1933 as *The Fighting Ranger* (q.v.) with Jones.

418. The Border Legion (Paramount; 1930). *Cast:* Richard Arlen, Fay Wray, Jack Holt, Eugene Pallette, Syd Saylor, E.H. Calvert, Stanley Fields, Ethan Allen. *D:* Otto Brower, Edwin H. Knopf; *Sc:* Percy Heath, Edward E. Paramore, Jr. (1:20)

Western of a notorious gang and its leader who has a change of heart and dies to save others. Based on the 1916 novel by Zane Grey, it was previously filmed in 1919 by Samuel Goldwyn, with Hobart Bosworth. Filmed by this studio in 1924 with Antonio Moreno and Helen Chadwick. Remade in 1934 as *The Last Roundup* (q.v.).

419. The Border Legion (Republic; 1939–40). *Cast:* Roy Rogers, George "Gabby" Hayes, Carol Hughes, Joseph Sawyer, Maude Eburne, Jay Novello, Hal Taliaferro, Dick Wessel, Paul Porcasi, Robert Emmett Keane, Ted Mapes, Fred Burns. *D:* Joe Kane; *Sc:* Olive Cooper, Louis Stevens. (0:58)

Roy Rogers western of a singing doctor from the east who goes up against an outlaw gang. Loosely based on the Zane Grey novel.

420. Border Menace (Aywon; 1935). *Cast:* Bill Cody, Miriam Rice, George Chesebro, James Aubrey, Benny Corbett, Frank Clark, Jim Donnelly. *D:* Jack Nelson; *P:* Robert Horner; *Sc:* Horner. (0:55)

Bill Cody western of a crooked banker attempting to get his hands on rich oil lands.

421. The Border Patrolman (20th Century–Fox; 1936). *Cast:* George O'Brien, Polly Ann Young, (Le)Roy Mason, Mary Doran, Smiley Burnette, Tom London, Al Hill, Murdock MacQuarrie, John St. Polis, Cyril Ring, William P. Carlton, Martin Garralaga, Chris-Pin Martin. *D:* David Howard; *P:* Sol Lesser (Atherton Productions); *Sc:* Dan Jarrett, Bennett Cohen. (1:00)

George O'Brien western of a man hired by a wealthy family to keep their errant daughter out of trouble.

422. Border Phantom (Republic–Supreme; 1937). *Cast:* Bob Steele, Harley Wood, Don Barclay, Karl Hackett, Horace Murphy, Miki Morita, John Peters, Perry Murdock, Frank Ball, Hans Joby. *D:* S. Roy Luby; *P:* A.W. Hackel; *Sc:* Fred Myton. (0:59) (video)

Offbeat Bob Steele western of a cowboy who goes after a gang of white-slavers.

423. Border Romance (Tiffany; 1930). *Cast:* Armida, Don Terry, Marjorie "Babe" Kane, Victor Potel, Wesley Barry, Nita Martan, (J.) Frank Glendon, Harry Von Meter, William Costello. *D:* Richard Thorpe; *Sc:* John Francis (Jack) Natteford. (1:00)

"Poverty row" western of attempts to retrieve some stolen cattle from south of the border.

424. Border Vengeance (Willis Kent; 1934–35). *Cast:* Reb Russell, Mary Jane Carey, Clarence Geldart, Kenneth MacDonald, June Bupp, Ed Phillips, Norman Feusier, Ben Corbett, Charles "Slim" Whitaker, Marty Joyce,

Fred Burns, Pat Harmon, Glenn Strange, Eddie Parker, Silvertip Baker, Bud Pope, Rex Bell, Monte Montana, Bart Carre, Hank Bell, Ben Gillis, Mabel Strickland, Rebel (horse). *D:* Ray Heinz; *P:* Willis Kent. (0:57)

Reb Russell western of a rodeo performer's attempts to clear his family's name.

425. Border Wolves (Universal; 1938). *Cast:* Bob Baker, Constance Moore, Dickie Jones, Frank Ellis, Glenn Strange, Fuzzy Knight, Frank Campeau, Ed Cassidy, Oscar O'Shea, Jack Montgomery, Willie Fung, Dick Dorrell, Hank Bell, Jack Kirk, Ed Brady, Jack Evans. *D:* Joseph H. Lewis; *P:* Trem Carr; *Sc:* Norton S. Parker. (0:56)

Bob Baker oater set in the days of the California gold rush.

426. Borderland (Paramount; 1937). *Cast:* Bill Boyd (Hoppy), Jimmy Ellison, George Hayes (Windy Halliday), Nora Lane, Trevor Bardette, Stephen Morris (later Morris Ankrum), George Chesebro, Charlene Wyatt, John Beach, Earle Hodgins, Al Bridge, John St. Polis, Charles "Slim" Whitaker, Cliff Parkinson, Karl Hackett, Robert Walker, Frank Ellis, Ed Cassidy, J.P. McGowan, Jack Evans. *D:* Nate Watt; *P:* Harry M. Sherman, Eugene Strong; *Sc:* Harrison Jacobs. (1:22)

"Hopalong Cassidy" western (#9) with Hoppy undercover as a bad man to help capture one. The final film with Jimmy Ellison as "Johnny Nelson" (he gets killed).

427. Bordertown (WB; 1935). *Cast:* Paul Muni, Bette Davis, Eugene Pallette, Margaret Lindsay, Robert Barrat, Henry O'Neill, Hobart Cavanaugh, Chris-Pin Martin, Arthur Treacher, Frank Puglia, Jack Norton, William Davidson, Gavin Gordon, Samuel S. Hinds, Soledad Jimenez, Arthur Stone, Vivian Tobin. *D:* Archie Mayo; *P:* Robert Lord; *Adaptation:* Lord

(from the novel by Carroll Graham); *Sc:* Laird Doyle, Wallace Smith. (1:30)

In Mexico, a lawyer becomes involved with the mentally unstable wife of a local cafe owner.

428. Born Reckless (Fox; 1930). *Cast:* Edmund Lowe, Lee Tracy, Marguerite Churchill, Frank Albertson, Paul Page, Catherine Dale Owen, Roy Stewart, J. Farrell MacDonald, Warren Hymer, Ben Bard, William Harrigan, Ward Bond, Eddie Gribbon, Paul Porcasi, Ferike Boros, Pat Somerset, Mike Donlin, Joe Brown. *D:* John Ford; *Sc:* Dudley Nichols.

Western based on the novel "Louis Beretti" by Donald Henderson Clarke.

429. Born Reckless (20th Century–Fox; 1937). *Cast:* Robert Kent, Rochelle Hudson, Brian Donlevy, Rita (Hayworth) Cansino, Chick Chandler, Harry Carey, Joyce Compton, Lon Chaney, Jr., Francis McDonald, William Pawley, George Wolcott, Pauline Moore, Joseph Crehan. *D:* Mal St. Clair; *Sc:* John Patrick, Robert Ellis, Helen Logan.

B action melodrama, a remake of the above.

430. Born to Battle (Reliable; 1935). *Cast:* Tom Tyler, Jean Carmen, Earl Dwire, Julian Rivero, Nelson McDowell, William Desmond, Richard Alexander, Charles King, Ralph Lewis, Ben Corbett, Jimmy Aubrey, Roger Williams, Robert Walker, George Morrell, Blackie Whiteford. *D:* Harry S. Webb; *Sc:* Rose Gordon, Carl (Krusada) Hartman. (0:58)

Tom Tyler oater of a cowboy working for the cattlemen to get the goods on a gang of rustlers.

431. Born to Be Bad (United Artists/20th Century; 1934). *Cast:* Loretta Young, Cary Grant, Jackie Kelk, Marion Burns, Henry Travers, Russell Hopton, Andrew Tombes, Harry Green. *D:* Lowell Sherman; *P:* William

Goetz, Raymond Griffith; *St:* Ralph Graves; *Sc:* Graves, Harrison Jacobs. (1:01)

A woman seeks to snare the man who adopted her son.

432. Born to Be Wild (Republic; 1938). *Cast:* Ralph Byrd, Ward Bond, Doris Weston, Byron Foulger. *D:* Joseph Kane.

Low-budget actioner.

433. Born to Dance (MGM; 1936). *Cast:* Eleanor Powell (Nora Paige), James Stewart (replacing Allan Jones as Ted Barker), Virginia Bruce (Lucy James), Una Merkel (Jenny Saks), Sid Silvers (Gunny Saks), Frances Langford (replacing Judy Garland as Peppy Turner), Raymond Walburn (Captain Dingby), Buddy Ebsen (Mush Tracy), Alan Dinehart (McKay), Reginald Gardiner (American debut as the policeman), Juanita Quigley (Sally Saks), Georges & Jalna (themselves), Barnett Parker (floorwalker), J. Marshall Smith, L. Dwight Snyder, Jay Johnson, Del Porter, Mary Dees, John Kelly, Helen Troy, William and Joe Mandel (acrobats), Leona and Naomi Keene (acrobats), Anita Brown, Charles (Levison) Lane, Robert Watson, Charles Coleman, James Flavin, Jonathan Hale, Billy Watson, Fuzzy Knight, Sherry Hall, Bud Flanagan (Dennis O'Keefe), David Horsley. *D:* Roy Del Ruth; *P:* Jack Cummings; *St:* Jack McGowan, Sid Silvers, B.G. DeSylva; *Sc:* McGowan, Silvers; *Choreographer:* (A.A.N.) Dave Gould for his "Swingin' the Jinx Away" number; *Other Songs by Cole Porter:* "Easy to Love," "Love Me, Love My Pekinese," "I'm Nuts About You," "Rap-Tap on Wood," "Rollin' Home," "Hey, Babe, Hey." (1:48) (video)

A box office smash musical with songs by Cole Porter including "I've Got You Under My Skin" which became a big hit and received an A.A.N. for Best Song. One of the 38 top-grossing films of 1936–37.

434. Born to Fight (Ambassador; 1936). *Cast:* Frankie Darro, Kane Richmond, Eddie Phillips. *D:* Charles Hutchison; *P:* Maurice Conn.

Low-budget boxing drama.

435. Born to Gamble (Republic; 1935–36). *Cast:* H.B. Warner, Lois Wilson, Ben Alexander, Onslow Stevens, William Janney. *D:* Phil Rosen.

B melodrama.

436. Born to Love (RKO–Pathé; 1931). *Cast:* Constance Bennett, Joel McCrea, Paul Cavanagh, Frederick Kerr, Louise Closser Hale, Anthony Bushell, Edmund Breon, Mary Forbes, Elizabeth Forrester, Claude King, Reginald Sharland, Eily Malyon (debut), Daisy Belmore, Martha Mattox. *D:* Paul L. Stein; *St & Sc:* Ernest Pascal. (1:22)

Shades of "Enoch Arden" in this World War I drama of a flier who is reported killed after having an affair with a nurse who finds herself pregnant with his child.

437. Born to the West (Paramount; 1937). *Cast:* John Wayne, Johnny Mack Brown, Marsha Hunt, Syd Saylor, Monte Blue, Lucien Littlefield, John Patterson, Nick Lukats, James Craig, Jack Kennedy, Lee Prather. *D:* Charles Barton; *Sc:* Stuart Anthony, Robert Yost. (aka: *Hell Town*)

Western of a long-standing feud. Based on the novel by Zane Grey, it was previously filmed in 1926 with Jack Holt and Margaret Morris.

438. Born to Trouble (Columbia; 1932). *Cast:* Charles "Buck" Jones.

Low-budget actioner.

(No other information available)

439. Borneo (20th Century–Fox; 1937). *Narrators:* Lew Lehr, Lowell Thomas; *P:* The Johnsons. (1:16) (video)

The final documentary feature of famed American explorers Martin and

Osa Johnson. Mr. Johnson was killed in a plane crash in 1937 and Mrs. Johnson critically injured. In the 1940s Mrs. Johnson produced two more documentaries on her own.

440. Borrowed Wives (Tiffany; 1930). *Cast:* Rex Lease, Vera Reynolds. *D:* Frank Strayer.

A romantic comedy from "poverty row."

441. Borrowing Trouble (20th Century–Fox; 1937). *Cast:* Jed Prouty, Spring Byington, Florence Roberts, Russell Gleason, June Carlson, Shirley Deane, Kenneth Howell, George Ernest, Billy Mahan, Dick Wessel, Wade Boteler. *D:* Frank Strayer.

The sixth entry in the low-budget "Jones Family" comedy series.

442. The Boss Cowboy (Superior; 1934). *Cast:* Buddy Roosevelt, Frances Morris, Sam Pierce, Fay McKenzie, George Chesebro, Bud Osborne, Lafe McKee, William McCormick, Allen Holbrook, Clyde McClary. *D:* Victor Adamson (Denver Dixon); *P:* Dixon; *Sc:* Betty Burbridge. (0:52)

Buddy Roosevelt western of a ranch foreman's dilemma with his girl.

443. Boss of Lonely Valley (Universal; 1937). *Cast:* Buck Jones, Muriel Evans, Lee Phelps, Harvey Clark, Walter Miller, Ted Adams, Matty Fain, Ezra Pallette, Dickie Howard. *D:* Ray Taylor; *Sc:* Frances Guihan. (1:00)

Buck Jones horse opera involving a land-grabbing scheme.

444. The Boss Rider of Gun Creek (Universal; 1936). *Cast:* Buck Jones, Muriel Evans, Harvey Clark, Lee Phelps, Tom Chatterton, Josef Swickard, Ernest Hilliard, Mahlon Hamilton, Edward Hearn, Alphonse Ethier. *D:* Lesley Selander; *Sc:* Frances Guihan. (1:00)

Buck Jones western with Jones in a dual role. The story of a cattle drive.

445. Bottoms Up (Fox; 1934). *Cast:* Spencer Tracy, Pat Paterson (American debut), John Boles, Harry Green, Herbert Mundin, Sid Silvers, Thelma Todd, Robert Emmett O'Connor, Lucille Ball (bit), Douglas Wood, Del Henderson, Suzanne Kaaren. *D:* David Butler; *P:* B.G. DeSylva; *St:* DeSylva, Sid Silvers; *Sc:* DeSylva, Butler, Silvers; *Songs:* Gus Kahn, Burton Lane, Harold Adamson. (1:29)

Musical of a Hollywood promoter who finds his friends jobs by passing them off as British nobility.

446. The Boudoir Diplomat (Universal; 1930). *Cast:* Ian Keith, Lawrence Grant, Betty Compson, Lionel Belmore, Mary Duncan, André Beranger, Jeanette Loff. *D:* Malcolm St. Clair; *P:* Carl Laemmle, Jr.; *Sc:* Benjamin Glazer, Tom Reed (unc.). (1:08)

B romantic comedy of foreign diplomacy.

447. Bought (WB; 1931). *Cast:* Constance Bennett, Richard Bennett (real life father of Constance), Ben Lyon, Dorothy Peterson, Ray Milland, Doris Lloyd, Maude Eburne, Edward J. Nugent, Paul Porcasi, Mae Madison, Arthur S. Hull. *D:* Archie Mayo; *Sc:* Charles Kenyon, Raymond Griffith. (1:10)

Drama of a girl from the slums who seeks a rich husband. Based on the novel "Jackdaw's Strut" by Harriet Henry.

448. Boulder Dam (WB; 1936). *Cast:* Ross Alexander (starring debut), Patricia Ellis, Lyle Talbot, Eddie Acuff, Henry O'Neill, Egon Brecher, Eleanor Wesselhoeft, George Breakston, Joseph Crehan. *D:* Frank McDonald; *P:* Sam Bischoff; *St:* Dan M. Templin; *Sc:* Sy Bartlett, Ralph Block. (1:10)

Melodrama of a man accused of murder who hides out as a construction worker on the site of Boulder Dam.

449. The Bowery (United Artists/20th Century; 1933). *Cast:* Wallace

Beery, George Raft (Steve Brodie), Pert Kelton, Jackie Cooper, Fay Wray, Herman Bing, Oscar Apfel, Harold Huber, George Walsh, Esther Muir, Fred (Ferdinand) Munier, Andrew Tombes (debut), Tammany Young, John Kelly, Elsie Harmer, Fletcher Norton. *D:* Raoul Walsh; *P:* Darryl F. Zanuck, Raymond Griffith, William Goetz; *Sc:* Howard Estabrook, James Gleason. (1:30)

New York City's Bowery of the gay '90s is the setting for the story of Steve Brodie, best known for jumping from the Brooklyn Bridge on a bet. Based on the novel by Michael L. Simmons and Bessie Roth Solomon, the film is notable as the premiere production of Darryl F. Zanuck's newly formed 20th Century production company. Reworked in 1943 as *Coney Island* and its 1950 remake *Wabash Avenue.*

450. Boy Friend (20th Century–Fox; 1939). *Cast:* Jane Withers, Arleen Whelan, Douglas Fowley, Warren Hymer. *D:* James Tinling.

Low-budget juvenile comedy.

The Boy from Barnardos (G.B. title) *see* **Lord Jeff**

451. Boy Meets Girl (WB; 1938). *Cast:* James Cagney, Pat O'Brien, Marie Wilson, Ralph Bellamy, Frank McHugh, Dick Foran, Bruce Lester, Ronald Reagan, James Stephenson, Penny Singleton, Clem Bevans, Paul Clark, Dennie Moore, William Haade, John Ridgely, Bert Hanlon, Harry Seymour. *D:* Lloyd Bacon; *P:* Hal Wallis; *As.P.:* Sam Bischoff; *Sc:* Bella and Samuel Spewack; *Song:* "With a Pain in My Heart" by M.K. Jerome, Jack Scholl. (1:26)

Screwball comedy of two Hollywood screenwriters which spoofs the movie-making industry. Based on the hit play by Bella and Samuel Spewack, the film was a box office hit.

452. Boy of the Streets (Monogram; 1937–38). *Cast:* Jackie Cooper,

Maureen O'Connor, Kathleen Burke, Robert Emmett O'Connor, Marjorie Main, Guy Usher, Matty Fain, George Cleveland, Gordon (Bill) Elliott, Don Latorre, Paul White. *D:* William Nigh; *St:* Rowland Brown; *Sc:* W. Scott Darling, Gilson Brown. (1:16)

B juvenile melodrama of a boy's devotion to his no-good father.

453. Boy Slaves (RKO; 1939). *Cast:* Anne Shirley, Roger Daniel, James McCallion, Alan Baxter, Johnny Fitzgerald, Walter Ward, Charles Powers, Walter Tetley, Frank Malo, Paul White, Arthur Hohl, Charles Lane, Norman Willis, Roy Gordon, Paul Guilfoyle, George Breakston, Carl Stockdale. *D:* P.J. Wolfson; *P:* Wolfson; *Sc:* Albert Bein, Ben Orkow. (1:10)

Drama of a gang of tough runaway boys who are forced to work on a brutally run turpentine farm. An offbeat production for this studio and a box office flop.

454. Boy Trouble (Paramount; 1939). *Cast:* Donald O'Connor, Mary Boland, Billy Lee, Charles Ruggles, Andrew Tombes, Dick Elliott, Joyce Mathews. *D:* George Archainbaud; *Sc:* Laura S.J. Perelman.

Juvenile comedy-drama of the adoption of two boys by a department store clerk at his wife's insistence.

455. Boys' Reformatory (Monogram; 1939). *Cast:* Frankie Darro, Grant Withers, David Durand, Ben Welden, Warren McCollum, Albert Hill, Jr., Bob McClung, George Offerman, Jr., Frank (Junior) Coghlan, Jr., Lillian Elliott, Tempe Pigott, John St. Polis, Jack McHugh, Kathryn Sheldon, Robert Smith. *D:* Howard Bretherton; *P:* Lindsley Parsons; *St:* Ray Trampe, Norman S. Hall; *Sc:* Trampe, Wellyn Totman. (1:01)

B melodrama of a youth who confesses to a crime to protect another and is subsequently sent to reform school.

456. Boys Town (MGM/Loew's Inc.; 1938). *Cast:* Spencer Tracy (A.A. for B.A. and an Acting Award from the National Board of Review as Father Flanagan), Mickey Rooney (Whitey Marsh), Henry Hull (Dave Morris), Leslie Fenton (Dan Farrow), Gene Reynolds (Tony Ponessa), Edward Norris (Joe Marsh), Addison Richards (judge), Jonathan Hale (John Hargraves), Bobs Watson (Pee Wee), Martin Spellman (Skinny), Mickey Rentschler (Tommy Anderson), Frankie Thomas (Freddie Fuller), Jimmy Butler (Paul Ferguson), Sidney Miller (Mo Kahn), Robert Emmett Keane (Burton), Tommy Noonan (Red), Murray Harris (Hillbilly), Al Hill, Jr. (Apples), Wesley Giraud (Butch), Donald Haines (Alabama), Bennie Chorr (Young Thunder), John Wray (Weasel), John Hamilton (Warden), Minor Watson (Bishop), Ronald Paige (Jimmy), Robert Glecker (Mr. Reynolds), Orville Caldwell (Warden), Victor Kilian (Sheriff), Arthur Aylesworth (Tim), Al Hill (Rod), Roger Converse (Lane the reporter), Walter Young (Judge), William Worthington (governor), George Humbert (Calateri), Kane Richmond (Jackson the reporter), Johnny Walsh (Charley Haines), Barbara Bedford, Gladden James, Phillip Terry, Jay Novello. *D:* (A.A.N.) Norman Taurog; *P:* John W. Considine, Jr.; *Original Story:* (A.A.) Dory Schary, Eleanore Griffin; *Sc:* (A.A.N.) Schary, John Meehan. (1:30) (video)

Sentimental story of Father Edward J. Flanagan and the founding of Boys Town, Nebraska, a home for wayward boys with no barriers to race or creed. The film received an A.A.N. for Best Picture, while placing #4 on the "10 Best" list of *Film Daily.* Followed in 1941 by the sequel *Men of Boys Town.* One of the 16 top grossing films of 1938–39. Computer-colored prints produced in 1989 by Turner Entertainment.

457. Brand of Hate (Supreme; 1934). *Cast:* Bob Steele, Lucille Brown(e), William Farnum, George Hayes, Archie Ricks, James Flavin, Charles K. French, Jack Rockwell, Mickey Rentschler. *D:* Lewis D. Collins; *P:* A.W. Hackel, William Steiner; *Sc:* John F. (Jack) Natteford. (1:03)

Bob Steele oater of cattle rustling.

458. Brand of the Outlaws (Supreme; 1936). *Cast:* Bob Steele, Margaret Marquis, Jack Rockwell, Virginia True Boardman, Charles King, Ed Cassidy, Frank Ball, Robert Kortman, Bud Osborne. *D:* Robert N. Bradbury; *P:* A.W. Hackel; *Sc:* Bradbury. (1:00)

Bob Steele western of a cowboy who unknowingly becomes involved with a gang of cattle rustlers.

459. Branded (Columbia; 1931). *Cast:* Buck Jones, Ethel Kenyon, Wallace MacDonald, Al Smith, Fred Burns, Philo McCullough, John Oscar, Robert Kortman, Clark Burroughs, Sam McDaniel. *D:* D. Ross Lederman; *Sc:* Randall Faye. (1:01)

Buck Jones western of a man who inherits a ranch and finds himself targeted by cattle rustlers.

460. Branded a Coward (Supreme; 1935). *Cast:* Johnny Mack Brown, Billie Seward, Syd Saylor, Lloyd Ingraham, Lee Shumway, Roger Williams, Yakima Canutt, Frank McCarroll, Rex Downing, Robert Kortman, Ed Peil, Sr., Joseph Girard. *D:* Sam Newfield; *P:* A.W. Hackel; *St:* Richard Martinsen; *Adaptation:* Earle Snell. (0:58)

Johnny Mack Brown western of a gunshy cowboy turned lawman.

461. Branded Men (Tiffany/Amity Prods.; 1931). *Cast:* Ken Maynard, June Clyde, Charles King, Donald Keith, Irving Bacon, Jack Rockwell, Hooper Atchley, Edmund Cobb, Slim Whitaker, Billy Bletcher, Bud McClure, Al Taylor. *D:* Phil Rosen; *P:* Phil Goldstone; *St:* Goldstone; *Sc:* Earle Snell. (1:10) (video)

Ken Maynard "poverty row" western.

462. Brat (Fox; 1931–32). *Cast:* June Collyer, Frank Albertson, William Collier, Sr., Virginia Cherrill, Sally O'Neil, Alan Dinehart, Albert Gran, J. Farrell MacDonald, Mary Forbes. *D:* John Ford; *St:* Maude Fulton; *Sc:* S.N. Behrman, Sonya Levien.

A comedy which was previously filmed in 1919 by Metro with Nazimova.

463. Breach of Promise (Sono Art–World Wide; 1932). *Cast:* Clive Brook, Mae Clarke, Chester Morris, Philo McCullough, Elizabeth Patterson, Mary Doran, Charles Middleton. *D:* Paul Stein; *Sc:* Ben Verschleiser.

"Poverty row" romantic drama.

464. Break of Hearts (RKO; 1935). *Cast:* Katharine Hepburn, Charles Boyer (who replaced Francis Lederer), Jean Hersholt, John Beal, Sam Hardy, Inez Courtney, Jean Howard, Lee Kohlmar, Ferdinand Gottschalk, Helene Millard, Susan Fleming, Anne Grey. *D:* Philip Moeller (his second and last film); *P:* Pandro S. Berman; *St:* Lester Cohen; *Sc:* Sarah Y. Mason, Victor Heerman, Anthony Veiller. (1:20) (video)

Romantic drama of a woman composer who falls for an alcoholic conductor.

465. Breakfast for Two (RKO; 1937). *Cast:* Barbara Stanwyck (Valentine Ransom), Herbert Marshall (Joe Blair), Glenda Farrell, Donald Meek, Eric Blore, Etienne Girardot, Frank M. Thomas, Pierre Watkin. *D:* Alfred Santell; *P:* Edward Kaufman; *St:* David Garth; *Sc:* Charles Kaufman, Paul Yawitz, Viola Brothers Shore. (1:07)

Romantic comedy of an heiress and a playboy producer.

466. Breaking the Ice (RKO/ Principal; 1938). *Cast:* Bobby Breen, Dolores Costello, Charles Ruggles, Charlie Murray, Irene Dare (film debut at age 5), Robert Barrat, Dorothy Peterson, Billy Gilbert, John King, Margaret Hamilton, Jonathan Hale, Spencer Charters, Maurice Cass. *D:* Edward Cline; *P:* Sol Lesser; *St:* Fritz Falkenstein, N. Brewster Morse; *Sc:* Mary McCall, Jr., Manuel Seff, Bernard Schubert; *Songs:* Victor Young, Paul Webster, Frank Churchill; *Music:* (A.A.N.) Victor Young. (1:19) (video)

Musical-comedy of a young boy who runs away from his Pennsylvania Dutch farm family to become an ice-skater.

467. Breakwater (Xxxx Xxxx; 1934). (No information available)

468. Breed of the Border (Monogram; 1933). *Cast:* Bob Steele, Marion Byron, George Hayes, Ernie Adams, Wilfred Lucas, Henry Rocquemore, Fred Cavens, Robert Cord, Perry Murdock. *D:* Robert N. Bradbury; *P:* Trem Carr; *St & Sc:* Harry O. Jones (Harry Fraser). (G.B. title: *Speed Brent Wins*) (0:58)

Bob Steele in an offbeat modern western of a racecar driver who gets involved with a gang of cattle rustlers.

469. Breezing Home (Universal; 1937). *Cast:* Binnie Barnes, William Gargan, Wendy Barrie, Alan Baxter, Raymond Walburn, Alma Kruger, Michael Loring, Willie Best, Elisha Cook, Jr. *D:* Milton Carruth; *P:* Edmund Grainger; *St:* Finley Peter, Jr., Philip Dunne; *Adaptation:* Charles Grayson; *Songs:* "I'm Hitting the High Spots" and "You're in My Heart Again" by Jimmy McHugh and Harold Adamson. (1:05)

B race track drama involving skullduggery in the stable and on the track.

470. Bridal Suite (MGM; 1939). *Cast:* Robert Young, Annabella, Walter Connolly, Billie Burke, Reginald Owen, Arthur Treacher, Gene Lockhart, Virginia Field, Felix Bressart. *D:* William Thiele; *P:* Edgar Selwyn; *St:* Gottfried

Reinhardt, Virginia Faulkner; *Sc:* Samuel Hoffenstein. (1:10)

Comedy of a playboy who plans to marry at various times in his life but never follows through.

471. The Bride Comes Home (Paramount; 1935). *Cast:* Claudette Colbert (Jeannette Desmereau), Fred MacMurray (Cyrus Anderson), Robert Young (Jack Bristow), William Collier, Sr. (Alfred Desmereau), Richard Carle (Frank the butler), Edgar Kennedy (Henry), Johnny Arthur (Otto), Kate MacKenna (Emma), James Conlin (Len Noble), Belle Mitchell (Helene the maid), Tom Kennedy (Husky), Donald Meek (judge), William R. (Billy) Arnold, Edward Gargan, Robert McKenzie, Ruth Warren, Frank Mills, Tom Dugan, Eddie Dunn, Charles West, Charles Sylber, C.L. Sherwood, A.S. "Pop" Byron, Jerry Mandy. *D:* Wesley Ruggles; *P:* Ruggles; *St:* Elizabeth Sanxay Holding; *Sc:* Claude Binyon. (1:22)

Comedy of a fickle female who can't decide whether to marry a millionaire or his bodyguard. One of the 25 top grossing films of 1935–36.

472. A Bride for Henry (Monogram; 1937). *Cast:* Anne Nagel, Warren Hull, Henry Mollison, Claudia Dell, Betty Ross Clark, Harrison Greene. *D:* William Nigh; *P:* Dorothy Reid; *Sc:* Dean Spencer. (0:58)

B romantic drama of a jilted girl who marries on the rebound. Based on the story by Josephine Bentham which appeared in Liberty Magazine.

473. The Bride of Frankenstein (Universal; 1935). *Cast:* Boris Karloff (monster), Colin Clive (Dr. Henry Frankenstein), Valerie Hobson (Elizabeth), Elsa Lanchester (in a dual role as Mary Shelley and the monster's mate), Ernest Thesiger (Dr. Pretorius), Dwight Frye (Karl), O.P. Heggie (hermit), E.E. Clive (burgomaster), Una O'Connor (Minnie), Douglas Walton (Percy B.

Shelley), Anne Darling (shepherdess), Gavin Gordon (Lord Byron), Reginald Barlow (Hans), Mary Gordon (Hans' wife), Neil Fitzgerald (Rudy), Ted Billings (Ludwig), Lucien Prival (Albert the butler), Sarah Schwartz (Marta), Norman Ainsley (little archbishop), Joan Woodbury (little queen), Arthur S. Byron (little King Henry VIII), Josephine McKim (mermaid), Kansas DeForrest (little ballerina), John Carradine, Rollo Lloyd, Billy Barty, Walter Brennan, Robert Adair, Brenda Fowler, John Curtis, Mary Stewart, Helen Parrish, Frank Terry, Ed Peil, Sr., Anders Van Haden, John George. *D:* James Whale; *P:* Carl Laemmle, Jr.; *Adaptation:* William Hurlbut, John L. Balderston; *Sc:* Hurlbut; *Sound Recording:* (A.A.N.) Gilbert Kurland. (1:20)

Classic horror film of the mad Dr. Pretorius who coerces Dr. Frankenstein into creating a mate for the monster. The film had the working title of "The Return of Frankenstein." A sequel to the 1931 *Frankenstein* (q.v.). Followed by *The Son of Frankenstein* (q.v.) in 1939. Based on events in Mary Shelley's "Frankenstein" (1816).

Note: Approximately five minutes of original footage missing, giving current running prints of 1:15. (video— 1:15)

474. Bride of the Desert (Rayart; 1929). *Cast:* LeRoy Mason, Alice Calhoun (final film—ret.). *D:* Duke Worne; *P:* Trem Carr.

Low-budget romantic drama.

475. Bride of the Regiment (WB/F.N.; 1930). *Cast:* Vivienne Segal, Allan Prior, Walter Pidgeon, Louise Fazenda, Ford Sterling, Lupino Lane (final American film), Myrna Loy, Harry Cording, Herbert Clark, Claude Fleming. *D:* John Francis Dillon.

Costume operetta adapted from "The Lady in Ermine" and filmed in 2-color technicolor.

476. The Bride Walks Out (RKO; 1936). *Cast:* Barbara Stanwyck, Gene Raymond, Robert Young, Ned Sparks, Helen Broderick, Willie Best, Robert Warwick, Billy Gilbert, Wade Boteler, Hattie McDaniel, Irving Bacon, Anita Colby, Vivian Oakland, Ward Bond, Edgar Dearing. *D:* Leigh Jason; *P:* Edward Small; *St:* Howard Emmett Rogers; *Sc:* P.J. Wolfson, Philip G. Epstein. (1:15) (video)

This comedy of a young married couple trying to get by on the husband's meager salary was a hit at the box office.

477. The Bride Wore Red (MGM; 1937). *Cast:* Joan Crawford, Franchot Tone, Robert Young, Billie Burke, Reginald Owen, George Zucco, Lynne Carver, Mary Phillips, Paul Porcasi, Ann Rutherford, Dickie Moore, Frank Puglia. *D:* Dorothy Arzner; *P:* Joseph L. Mankiewicz; *Sc:* Tess Slesinger, Bradbury Foote. (1:43)

A chorus girl is seeking a wealthy husband at a posh resort in this box office flop. Based on the play "The Girl from Trieste" by Ferenc Molnar.

478. Brides Are Like That (WB/ F.N.; 1936). *Cast:* Ross Alexander, Anita Louise, Dick Purcell, Joseph Cawthorn, Mary Treen, Joseph Crehan, Gene Lockhart, Kathleen Lockhart, Craig Reynolds, Alma Lloyd. *D:* William McGann; *P:* Bryan Foy; *Sc:* Ben Markson.

B comedy of romantic pursuits. Based on the 1925 play "Applesauce" by Barry Connors. Remade in 1940 as *Always a Bride.*

479. The Bridge of San Luis Rey (MGM; 1929). *Cast:* Lily Damita, Ernest Torrence (Uncle Pio), Henry B. Walthall (Father Juniper), Raquel Torres, Duncan Renaldo, Tully Marshall, Don Alvarado, Emily Fitzroy, Eugenie Besserer, Mitchell Lewis, Paul Ellis, Jane Winton, Gordon Thorpe, Michael Vavitch. *D:* Charles Brabin; *P:* Hunt Stromberg; *Sc:* Alice D.G. Miller; *Titles:* Ruth Cummings, Marian Ainslee; *Art-Set Decoration:* (A.A.) Cedric Gibbons.

Part-talkie drama of a priest who investigates the collapse of a bridge in Peru which killed five people. Based on the 1927 Pulitzer Prize–winning novel by Thornton Wilder, it was remade in 1944.

480. The Bridge of Sighs (Invincible; 1935–36). *Cast:* Walter Byron, Onslow Stevens, Mary Doran, Lafe McKee, Paul Fix, Oscar Apfel, Selmer Jackson. *D:* Phil Rosen (who also directed the '25 version).

"Poverty row" romantic drama of a girl and the spoiled son of a wealthy businessman. Previously filmed in 1925 by Warner Brothers.

481. Brief Moment (Columbia; 1933). *Cast:* Gene Raymond, Carole Lombard, Donald Cook, Jameson Thomas, Herbert Evans, Theresa Maxwell Conover, Irene Ware, Reginald Mason, Monroe Owsley, Florence Britton. *D:* David Burton.

Romantic comedy of a night club singer who marries a "man about town" with the intent of reforming him.

482. Bright Eyes (Fox; 1934). *Cast:* Shirley Temple, James Dunn, Lois Wilson, Judith Allen, Jane Withers, Charles Sellon, Jane Darwell, Dorothy Christy, Theodore von Eltz, Walter Johnson, Brandon Hurst. *D:* David Butler; *P:* Sol M. Wurtzel; *St:* Butler, Edwin Burke; *Sc:* William Conselman. (1:24) (video)

Moppet drama of a newly orphaned little girl who becomes the object of a custody fight. Shirley introduces her most popular song, "On the Good Ship Lollipop" by Richard A. Whiting and Sidney Clare. Computer-colored in 1988.

483. Bright Lights (WB/F.N.; 1930–31). *Cast:* Dorothy Mackaill, Frank Fay, Noah Beery, Inez Courtney, Eddie Nugent, Edmund Breese, Daphne Pollard, Frank McHugh, James Murray,

John Peter Richmond (John Carradine), Tom Dugan, Philip Strange. *D:* Michael Curtiz; *Supervisor:* Robert North; *Sc:* Humphrey Pearson, Henry McCarty; *St:* Humphrey Pearson.

Drama, photographed in 2-color technicolor of an actress who marries but cannot find happiness.

484. Bright Lights (WB/F.N.; 1935). *Cast:* Joe E. Brown, Ann Dvorak, Patricia Ellis, William Gargan, Joseph Cawthorn, Henry O'Neill, Joseph Crehan, William Demarest, Arthur Treacher, Tom Kennedy, Gordon Westcott, The Maxellos. *D:* Busby Berkeley; *St:* Lois Leeson; *Sc:* Bert Kalmar, Harry Ruby; *Choreographer:* Berkeley; *Songs:* "She Was an Acrobat's Daughter" by Kalmar & Ruby, "Toddling Along with You" and "You're an Eyeful of Heaven" by Mort Dixon and Alli Wrubel, and "Nobody Cares If I'm Blue" by Grant Clarke and Harry Akst. (G.B. title: *Funny Face*) (1:23)

Musical-comedy of a vaudevillian who lets success go to his head after making it big on the Great White Way.

485. Brilliant Marriage (Invincible; 1936). *Cast:* Joan Marsh, Holmes Herbert, Barbara Bedford, Dick Elliott, Ann Codee, Inez Courtney, George Cleveland, Olive Tell. *D:* Phil Rosen.

"Poverty row" romance.

486. Bring 'em Back Alive (RKO/Van Beuren Prods.; 1932). *D:* Clyde E. Elliott; *P:* Buck. (1:05)

A documentary photographed by Carl Berger and Nick Cavaliere of the RKO/Van Beuren expedition into the Malaysian jungles for wild animals, headed by Frank Buck. The film is narrated by Buck, based on the book written by him with Edward Anthony. One of the 15 top grossing films of 1932.

487. Bringing Up Baby (RKO; 1938). *Cast:* Cary Grant (David Huxley), Katharine Hepburn (Susan Vance), Charles Ruggles (Major Applegate), May Robson (Aunt Elizabeth),

Barry Fitzgerald (Mr. Gogarty), Asta (George—the culprit who stole the bone), Virginia Walker (Alice Swallow), Leona Roberts (Mrs. Gogarty), Walter Catlett (sheriff), Fritz Feld (Doc Lehman), Tala Birell (Mrs. Lehman), Ward Bond (constable), John Kelly, Jonathan Hale, George Irving, Jack Carson. *D:* Howard Hawks; *P:* Hawks; *As.P.:* Cliff Reid; *St:* Hagar Wilde; *Sc:* Wilde, Dudley Nichols. (1:42) (video— b/w and computer-colored)

Classic screwball comedy of a paleontologist in search of a missing dinosaur bone who gets mixed-up with a wacky heiress and "Baby" her pet leopard. The film was a box office flop when first released, but became the inspiration for *What's Up Doc?* in 1971. Computer-colored in 1989.

488. British Agent (WB/F.N.; 1934). *Cast:* Leslie Howard, Kay Francis, William Gargan, Philip Reed, Irving Pichel, Ivan Simpson, Halliwell Hobbes, J. Carrol Naish, Walter Byron, Cesar Romero, Arthur Aylesworth, Alphonse Ethier, Frank Reicher, Tenen Holtz, Doris Lloyd, Mary Forbes, Marina Schubert, George Pearce, Gregory Gaye, Paul Porcasi, Walter Armitage, Addison Richards. *D:* Michael Curtiz; *P:* Henry Blanke; *Sc:* Laird Doyle. (1:21)

Romantic espionage melodrama set in pre–World War I Russia. Based on the autobiographical book by R.H. Bruce Lockhart.

489. Broadminded (WB/F.N.; 1931). *Cast:* Joe E. Brown, Ona Munson, William Collier, Jr., Marjorie White, Margaret Livingston, Holmes Herbert, Thelma Todd, Bela Lugosi, Grayce Hampton. *D:* Mervyn LeRoy; *St & Sc:* Bert Kalmar, Harry Ruby. (1:12)

B comedy of a man who chaperones his younger cousin, leading to complications and misunderstandings galore.

490. Broadway (Universal; 1929). *Cast:* Glenn Tryon, Merna Kennedy, Robert Ellis, Evelyn Brent, Thomas E.

Jackson (film debut—recreating his stage role), Otis Harlan, Paul Porcasi (recreating his stage role), Fritz Feld, Leslie Fenton, Gus Arnheim and His Cocoanut Grove Ambassadors, Marion Lord, Arthur Housman, George Davis, Betty Francisco, Ruby McCoy, Edythe Flynn, Florence Dudley. *D:* Paul Fejos; *P:* Carl Laemmle, Jr.; *Sc:* Edward T. Lowe, Jr., Charles Furthman; *Choreographer:* Maurice Kusell; *Songs:* Title song, "The Chicken or the Egg," "Hot Footin' It," "Hittin' the Ceiling" and "Sing a Little Love Song" by Con Conrad, Sidney Mitchell and Archie Gottler.

Lavishly produced musical drama of a Broadway dancer who becomes involved with bootleggers and murder. Based on the hit 1927 Broadway success by George Abbott and Philip Dunning, some scenes were filmed in "natural" color. Universal spent $1,000,000 on the production which it remade in 1942 with George Raft.

491. Broadway Babies (WB/ F.N.; 1929). *Cast:* Alice White, Charles Delaney, Fred Kohler, Sally Eilers, Tom Dugan, Bodil Rosing, Marion Byron. *D:* Mervyn LeRoy; *St:* Jay Gelzer; *Sc:* Monte Katterjohn, Humphrey Pearson; *Songs:* "Wishing and Waiting for Love" and "Jig Jig Jigaloo" by Grant Clarke, Harry Akst and "Broadway Baby Doll" by Al Bryan and George W. Meyer.

Part-talkie romantic melodrama with songs.

492. Broadway Bad (Fox; 1933). *Cast:* Joan Blondell, Ricardo Cortez, Ginger Rogers, Adrienne Ames, Spencer Charters, Donald Crisp, Victor Jory, Francis McDonald, Allen Vincent, Philip Tead, Ronnie Cosbey, Frederick Burton, Margaret Seddon. *D:* Sidney Lanfield; *St:* William R. Lipman, A.W. Pezet; *Sc:* Arthur Kober, Maude Fulton. (G.B. title: *Her Reputation*) (1:00)

Melodrama of a scheming chorus girl.

493. Broadway Bill (Columbia; 1934–35). *Cast:* Warner Baxter, Myrna Loy, Walter Connolly, Helen Vinson, Douglass Dumbrille, Raymond Walburn, Lynne Overman, Clarence Muse, Margaret Hamilton, Paul Harvey, Claude Gillingwater, Charles (Lane) Levison, Ward Bond, Jason Robards, Alan Hale, Frankie Darro, Clara Blandick, Charles Wilson, George Cooper, Helen Flint, George Meeker, Helene Millard, James Blakely, Harry Todd, Ed Tucker, Bob Tansill, Charles Middleton, Lucille Ball (bit). *D:* Frank Capra (who also directed the '51 remake); *P:* Capra; *St:* Mark Hellinger; *Sc:* Robert Riskin, Sidney Buchman (unc.). (1:44)

Sentimental romantic comedy of a horse trainer and his charge. Remade in 1951 as *Riding High*.

494. Broadway Gondolier (WB; 1935). *Cast:* Dick Powell, Joan Blondell, Adolphe Menjou, Louise Fazenda, Mills Brothers, William Gargan, Grant Mitchell, Ted Fio Rito and his band, Canova Family (with Judy), Hobart Cavanaugh, Joseph (Sawyer) Sauers, Bob Murphy, Rafael Storm, Jack Norton. *D:* Lloyd Bacon; *Sc:* Hans Kräly, E.Y. Harburg, Sig Herzig; *Sc:* Herzig, Warren Duff, Julius Epstein; *Songs:* "The Rose in Her Hair," "Lonely Gondolier," "Outside of You," "You Can Be Kissed," "The Pig and the Cow," "Sweet and Low" and "Lulu's Back in Town" (sung by the Mills Brothers) by Al Dubin and Harry Warren. (1:38)

Musical-comedy of a taxi driver who wants to become a star.

495. The Broadway Hoofer (Columbia; 1930). *Cast:* Jack Egan, Marie Saxon, Eileen Percy, Howard Hickman. *D:* George Archainbaud.

Low-budget romantic musical.

496. Broadway Hostess (WB/ F.N.; 1935). *Cast:* Winifred Shaw, Genevieve Tobin, Phil Regan, Lyle Talbot, Allen Jenkins, Marie Wilson,

Spring Byington, Joseph King, Harry Seymour, Donald Ross, Frank Dawson. *D:* Frank McDonald (directorial debut); *P:* Bryan Foy; *Sc:* George Bricker; *Songs:* "He Was Her Man," "Let It Be Me," "Weary," "Who But You" by Mort Dixon and Allie Wrubel and "Only the Girl" by Herman Ruby and M.K. Jerome; *Choreographer:* (A.A.N.) Bobby Connolly for the number "Playboy from Paree" (Dixon-Wrubel) combined with another from *Go Into Your Dance* (q.v.).

Musical of a chorus girl's rise to stardom.

497. The Broadway Melody (MGM; 1928–29). *Cast:* Bessie Love (A.A.N. for B.A. as Hank Mahoney), Anita Page (Queenie Mahoney), Charles King (1894–1944 as Eddie Kearns), Jed Prouty (Uncle Jed), Kenneth Thomson (Jack Warriner), Mary Doran (Flo), Edward Dillon (stage manager), Eddie Kane (Francis Zanfield), James Gleason (Jimmy Gleason, the music publisher), J. Emmett Beck (Babe Hatrick), Marshall Ruth (Stew), Drew Demarest (Turpe), Nacio Herb Brown (piano player), William Demarest, James Burrows, Ray Cooke. *D:* (A.A.N.) Harry Beaumont; *P:* Harry Rapf, Lawrence Weingarten; *St:* Edmund Goulding; *Sc:* Sarah Y. Mason, Norman Houston, James Gleason; *Songs:* "Give My Regards to Broadway" by George M. Cohan, "Truthful Deacon Brown" by Willard Robison, Title song, "The Wedding of the Painted Doll," "You Were Meant for Me," "Boy Friend," "Love Boat," and "Harmony Babies from Melody Lane" by Nacio Herb Brown and Arthur Freed. (1:50) (video)

Hollywood's first all-talking, all-singing and all-dancing musical and the first all-talkie for this studio. The story of two stage-struck sisters trying to hit the big time who fall for the same man. The film received the A.A. for Best Picture (1928–29) and placed #2 on the "10 Best" list of *Film Daily.* The premiere showing in February 1929 at New York City's

Capital Theatre commanded an unheard of $2.00 admission price, raking in big bucks for MGM. 2-color technicolor was used for "The Wedding of the Painted Doll" production number. Remade by this studio in 1940 as *Two Girls on Broadway.*

498. The Broadway Melody of 1936 (MGM; 1935). *Cast:* Jack Benny (Bert Keeler), Eleanor Powell (Irene—Mlle. Arlette), Robert Taylor (Bob Gordon), Una Merkel (Kitty Corbett), Sid Silvers (Snoop Blue), Buddy Ebsen (film debut as Buddy Burke), Vilma Ebsen (Buddy's sister as Sally), June Knight (Lillian), Robert Wildhack (Hornblow), Nick Long, Jr. (Basil Newcombe), Frances Langford, Harry Stockwell, Don Wilson, Paul Harvey, Irene Coleman, Beatrice Coleman, Georgina Gray, Mary Jane Halsey, Lucille Lund, Ada Ford, Theresa Harris, Max Barwyn, Bernadene Hayes, Treva Lawler, Bud Williams, Lee Phelps, Andre Cheron, Rolfe Sedan, Eddie Tamblyn, Bert Moorehouse, Neely Edwards, Bobby Gordon, Anya Teranda, Luana Walters, Patricia Gregory. *D:* Roy Del Ruth; *P:* John W. Considine, Jr.; Original Story: (A.A.N.) Moss Hart; *Sc:* Jack McGowan, Sid Silvers; *Additional Dialogue:* Harry Conn; *Choreographer:* (A.A.) Dave Gould for the "I've Got a Feeling You're Fooling" number combined with another from *Folies Bergere* (q.v.); Other songs by Nacio Herb Brown and Arthur Freed: "Broadway Rhythm," "You Are My Lucky Star" (choreography by Albertina Rasch), "On a Sunday Afternoon," and "Sing Before Breakfast." (1:43) (video)

Musical-comedy variety with many production numbers. The film received an A.A.N. for Best Picture as well as placing #8 on the "10 Best" list of *Film Daily.* One of the 25 top grossing films of 1935–36.

499. The Broadway Melody of 1938 (MGM; 1937). *Cast:* Robert Taylor, Eleanor Powell, George Murphy,

Buddy Ebsen, Sophie Tucker (singing her famous "Some of These Days"), Judy Garland (feature film debut singing "You Made Me Love You" to a photograph of Clark Gable), Charles Igor Gorin, Binnie Barnes, Raymond Walburn, Charley Grapewin, Willie Howard, Robert Benchley, Robert Wildhack, Billy Gilbert, Barnett Parker, Helen Troy. *D:* Roy Del Ruth; *P:* Jack Cummings; *St:* Sid Silvers, Jack McGowan; *Sc:* McGowan; *Songs:* Nacio Herb Brown, Arthur Freed; *Choreographer:* Dave Gould. (1:50) (video)

A lavish production musical, the third in the series by this studio.

500. The Broadway Melody of 1940 (MGM; 1939–40). *Cast:* Fred Astaire (his first for MGM after leaving RKO), Eleanor Powell, George Murphy, Douglas MacPhail, Frank Morgan, Florence Rice, Ian Hunter, Lynne Carver, Trixie Frischke, Herman Bing, Jack Mulhall, Barbara Jo Allen (later Vera Vague), Joe Yule, Irving Bacon. *D:* Norman Taurog; *P:* Jack Cummings; *St:* Dore Schary, Jack McGowan; *Sc:* Leon Gordon, George Oppenheimer; *Songs by Cole Porter Include:* "I Concentrate on You" and "Begin the Beguine" (from his 1935 Broadway musical "Jubilee"); *Choreography:* Bobby Connolly, Fred Astaire. (1:42) (video)

A lavish production musical.

501. Broadway Musketeers (WB; 1938). *Cast:* Ann Sheridan, Marie Wilson, Margaret Lindsay, John Litel, Dick Purcell, Janet Chapman, Dorothy Adams, Horace McMahon, Maris Wrixon, Richard Bond, Anthony Averill, John Ridgely, Jimmy Conlin, Jan Holm. *D:* John Farrow; *As.P.:* Bryan Foy; *St & Sc:* Don Ryan, Ken Gamet; *Songs:* "Who Said That This Isn't Love?" and "Has It Ever Occurred to You?" by M.K. Jerome, Jack Scholl. (1:02)

Three girls brought up in the same orphanage, meet years later in New York City. A remake of *Three on a Match* (q.v.).

502. Broadway Scandals (Columbia; 1929). *Cast:* Carmel Myers, Sally O'Neil, Jack Egan, John Hyams, Doris Dawson, J. Barney Sherry, Charles Wilson, Gordon (Bill) Elliott (talkie debut). *D:* George Archainbaud; *Sc:* Howard Green; *Song:* "Kickin' the Blues Away" by Sam Coslow.

Musical romance.

503. Broadway Serenade (MGM; 1938–39). *Cast:* Jeanette MacDonald, Lew Ayres, Frank Morgan, Ian Hunter, Rita Johnson, Virginia Grey, William Gargan, Wally Vernon, Al Shean, Esther Dale, Katherine Alexander, Mary Beth Hughes (film debut), Franklin Pangborn, Leon Belasco, Hobart Cavanaugh, Paul Hurst, Arthur Housman, Mary Gordon. *D:* Robert Z. Leonard; *P:* Leonard; *St:* Lew Lipton, John T. Foote, Hans Kräly; *Sc:* Charles Lederer; *Songs:* Sigmund Romberg, Gus Kahn; *Choreographer:* Busby Berkeley. (1:54) (aka: *Serenade*)

A singer and her songwriter husband have marital problems in this flop musical-drama.

Broadway Singer (G.B. title) *see* **Torch Singer**

504. Broadway Thru a Keyhole (United Artists/20th Century; 1933). *Cast:* Constance Cummings, Russ Columbo, Paul Kelly, Blossom Seely, Gregory Ratoff, Texas Guinan (herself, final film — d. 1934), Hobart Cavanaugh, C. Henry Gordon, Eddie Foy, Jr., Helen Jerome Eddy, Ann Sothern (bit), Lucille Ball (film debut — bit), Frances Williams, Billy Gilbert. *D:* Lowell Sherman; *P:* William Goetz, Raymond Griffith; *Sc:* Gene Towne, Graham Baker; *Songs:* Mack Gordon, Harry Revel. (1:30)

This gangster drama set in New York City was based on a story by Walter Winchell.

Broadway to Cheyenne (G.B. title) *see* **From Broadway to Cheyenne**

505. Broadway to Hollywood (MGM; 1933). *Cast:* Alice Brady, Frank Morgan, Jackie Cooper, Russell Hardie, Madge Evans, Mickey Rooney (in his MGM debut), Eddie Quillan, Jimmy Durante, Nelson Eddy (film debut), May Robson, Una Merkel, Edward Brophy, Moe Howard, Tad Alexander, Jean Howard, Ruth Channing. *D:* Willard Mack (final film—d. 1933); *St:* Mack, Edgar Allan Woolf; *Sc:* Mack; *Choreographer:* Albertina Rasch. (1:25)

A generational story of a show business family which utilizes footage from an uncompleted MGM feature of 1930 titled "The March of Time."

506. Broadway Tornado (Xxxx Xxxx; 1932). (No information available)

Broken Dishes *see* **Too Young to Marry**

507. Broken Dreams (Monogram; 1933). *Cast:* Randolph Scott, Martha Sleeper, Joseph Cawthorn, Beryl Mercer, Buster Phelps, Charlotte Merriam, Sidney Bracey, Adele St. Maur, Phyllis Lee, Martin Burton, Finis Barton, Edward LeSaint, Sam Flint; *D:* Robert Vignola; *P:* Ben Verschleiser; *St:* Olga Printzlau; *Sc:* Maude Fulton. (1:08)

Low-budget drama of a doctor who remarries, only to encounter problems with his son.

508. Broken Hearted (Trinity Pictures; 1929). *Cast:* Agnes Ayres, Eddie Brownell. *D:* Frank S. Mattison.

An early independent part-talkie romantic melodrama.

Broken Links (G.B. title) *see* **Leftover Ladies**

Broken Lullaby *see* **The Man I Killed**

509. The Broken Wing (Paramount; 1932). *Cast:* Lupe Velez, Leo Carrillo, Melvyn Douglas, George Barbier, Willard Robertson, Claire Dodd, Arthur Stone, Soledad Jimenez, Julian Rivero, Pietro Sosso. *D:* Lloyd Corrigan; *Sc:* Gordon Jones, William Slavens McNutt. (1:11)

Romantic melodrama of a Mexican girl and an American pilot. Previously filmed: (Preferred; 1923) with Richard Tucker and Miriam Cooper, it was based on a play by Paul Dickey and Charles Goddard.

510. The Bronze Buckaroo (Sack Amusement; 1938). *Cast:* Herb Jeffreys, Spencer Williams, Rellie Hardin, Artie Young, Clarence Brooks, F.E. Miller, The Four Tunes. *D:* Richard C. Kahn; *Sc:* Kahn. (1:00) (video)

Low-budget indie western with an all black cast of two cowboys who help a girl whose father has been killed.

511. Brother Rat (WB/F.N.; 1938). *Cast:* Wayne Morris, Eddie Albert (film debut), Ronald Reagan, Priscilla Lane, Jane Bryan, Jane Wyman, Johnnie "Scat" Davis, Henry O'Neill, Gordon Oliver, William Tracy (film debut—recreating his stage role), Louise Beavers, Larry Williams, Jessie Busley, Isabel Withers. *D:* William Keighley; *As.P.:* Robert Lord; *Sc:* Richard Macaulay, Jerry Wald. (1:30)

Comic hi-jinks at a southern military academy. Based on the popular Broadway play by Fred F. Finklehoffe and John Monks, Jr. Followed in 1940 by the sequel *Brother Rat and a Baby.* Remade in 1952 as the musical *About Face.*

512. Brothers (Columbia; 1929–30). *Cast:* Bert Lytell, Dorothy Sebastian, Francis McDonald, Barbara Bedford, Howard Hickman, William Morris, Richard Tucker, George Chesebro, Claire McDowell, Maurice Black, Frank McCormack, Jessie Arnold, Richard Carle, Rita Carlyle. *D:* Walter Lang; *St:* Herbert Ashton, Jr. (aka: *Blood Brothers*)

Romantic drama.

513. Brothers of the West (Victory; 1937). *Cast:* Tom Tyler, Bob Terry, Roger Williams. *D:* Sam Katzman; *P:* Katzman; *Sc:* Basil Dickey.
Tom Tyler western.

514. The Buccaneer (Paramount; 1938). *Cast:* Fredric March (Jean Lafitte), Franciska Gaal (Gretchen — American debut), Margot Grahame (Annette de Remy), Akim Tamiroff (Dominique You), Walter Brennan (Ezra Peavey), Ian Keith (Crawford), Spring Byington (Dolly Madison), Douglass Dumbrille (Governor Claiborne), Hugh Sothern (Andrew Jackson), Robert Barrat (Captain Brown), Beulah Bondi (Aunt Charlotte), Anthony Quinn (who directed the 1958 remake, as Beluche), Montague Love (Admiral Cockburn), Louise Campbell (Marie de Remy), Eric Stanley (General Ross), Fred Kohler (Gramby), James Craig (creole), Gilbert Emery (Captain Lockyer), Holmes Herbert (Captain McWilliams), John Rogers (Mouse), Hans Steinke (Tarsus), Evan Thomas (Sir Harry Smith), Thaddeus Jones (John Freeman), Reginald Sheffield (ship's surgeon), Eugene Jackson (James Smith), Davison Clark (Colonel Butler), Richard Denning (Lt. Reed), Jack Hubbard (Charles), Evelyn Keyes (film debut as Madeleiene), Lina Basquette (Roxanne), Luana Walters (Suzette), J.P. McGowan (jailer), Barry Norton (Villere), Charles Trowbridge (Daniel Carrol), Alex Hill (Scipio), Charles Brokaw (Vincent Nolte), Alphonse Martell (Major Latour), Paul Fix (dying pirate), Stanley Andrews (collector of Port), Ethel Clayton, Mae Busch, Terry Ray (Ellen Drew), Philo McCullough. *D:* Cecil B. de Mille; *P:* de Mille; *As.P.:* William H. Pine; *Adaptation:* Jeanie MacPherson; *Sc:* Edwin Justus Mayer, Harold Lamb, C. Gardner Sullivan; *Cinematographer:* (A.A.N.) Victor Milner. (2:04)
Epic scale production of Jean Lafitte and the War of 1812. The 1958 remake was the last film produced by

de Mille prior to his death in 1959. Based on "Lafitte, the Pirate" by Lyle Saxon. One of the 15 top grossing films of 1937–38.
Note: Some prints (1:30).

Buffalo Stampede *see* **The Thundering Herd**

515. Bulldog Courage (Puritan; 1935). *Cast:* Tim McCoy, Joan Woodbury, Paul Fix, Eddie Buzzard, Hooper Atchley, Karl Hackett, John Elliott, Ed Cassidy, Edmund Cobb, George Morrell, Jack Rockwell, Bud Osborne. *D:* Sam Newfield; *Sc:* Joseph O'Donnell, Frances Guihan. (1:06) (video)
Tim McCoy western with McCoy in a dual role as father and son, of which the latter avenges the death of the former.

516. Bulldog Drummond (United Artists/Samuel Goldwyn; 1929). *Cast:* Ronald Colman (A.A.N. for B.A. in combination wiht his performance in *Condemned* [q.v.], talkie debut as Bulldog Drummond), Joan Bennett (Phyllis Clavering in her talkie debut), Claude Allister (Algy Longworth — American debut), Lilyan Tashman (Erma), Montagu Love (Peterson), Lawrence Grant (Dr. Lakington), Wilson Benge (Danny), Adolph Milar (Marcovitch), Charles Sellon (Travers), Tetsu Komai (Chong). *D:* F. Richard Jones (final film); *P:* Sam Goldwyn; *Sc:* Sidney Howard, Wallace Smith; *Art-Set Decoration:* (A.A.N.) William Cameron Menzies; *Song:* "(I Says to Myself Says I) There's the One for Me" by Jack Yellen and Harry Akst. (1:30) (video)
Adventurer Captain Hugh Drummond is hired by a girl to rescue her father. Previous version: (Hodkinson; 1923) with Carlyle Blackwell and Evelyn Greeley. Based on the play by Sapper (Herman Cyril McNeile). Voted #6 on the "10 Best" lists of the *New York Times* and *Film Daily*. Followed by the sequel *Bulldog Drummond Strikes Back,* (q.v.).

517. Bulldog Drummond Comes Back (Paramount; 1937). *Cast:* John Howard, John Barrymore, Louise Campbell, Reginald Denny, E.E. Clive, J. Carrol Naish, John Sutton, Helen Freeman, John Rogers, Ivo Henderson. *D:* Louis King; *P:* Edward T. Lowe; *Sc:* Lowe. (1:04) (video)

The second entry in the low-budget series by this studio, this one involving a kidnap plot. Based on "Female of the Species" by Sapper (Herman Cyril McNeile).

518. Bulldog Drummond Escapes (Paramount; 1937). *Cast:* Ray Milland (Capt. Hugh "Bulldog" Drummond), Sir Guy Standing (final film—d. 1937), Heather Angel, Porter Hall, Reginald Denny, E.E. Clive, Fay Holden, Clyde Cook, Walter Kingsford. *D:* James Hogan; *P:* Edward T. Lowe; *Sc:* Lowe. (1:05) (video)

Premiere entry in the B series by this studio and a box office hit. Based on the book "Bulldog Drummond Saves a Lady" by "Sapper" and Gerard Fairlie.

519. Bulldog Drummond in Africa (Paramount; 1938). *Cast:* John Howard (Capt. Hugh "Bulldog" Drummond), H.B. Warner, Heather Angel, J. Carrol Naish, Reginald Denny, Anthony Quinn, Michael Brooke, E.E. Clive, Rollo Dix, Forrester Harvey, Matthew Boulton, William von Brincken. *D:* Louis King; *P:* Edward T. Lowe; *Sc:* Garnett Weston, Harold Hurley. (1:00) (video)

The fifth entry in the series based on "Sapper's" "Challenge." Followed by *Arrest Bulldog Drummond,* (q.v.).

520. Bulldog Drummond Strikes Back (United Artists/20th Century; 1934). *Cast:* Ronald Colman (Bulldog Drummond), Loretta Young, C. Aubrey Smith (Inspector Nielson), Charles Butterworth (Algy Longworth), Warner Oland (Achmed), Mischa Auer, Una Merkel, Halliwell Hobbes, E.E. Clive, Kathleen Burke, George Regas, Douglas Gerrard, Adia Kuznetzoff, Ethel Griffies, Lucille Ball (bit). *D:* Roy Del Ruth; *P:* Darryl F. Zanuck; *Sc:* Nunnally Johnson. (1:23)

A light mystery which is a sequel to *Bulldog Drummond* (q.v.).

521. Bulldog Drummond's Bride (Paramount; 1939). *Cast:* John Howard, Heather Angel, H.B. Warner, E.E. Clive, Reginald Denny, Elizabeth Patterson, Eduardo Ciannelli, John Sutton, Adrienne D'Ambricourt, George Davis, Louis Mercier, Jacques Lory, Gerald Hamer. *D:* James Hogan; *P:* Stuart Walker; *Sc:* Stuart Palmer, Garnett Weston. (0:55) (video)

Eighth and final film in the series which has Drummond's wedding being interrupted. Based on "Bulldog Drummond and the Oriental Mind" by "Sapper."

522. Bulldog Drummond's Peril (Paramount; 1938). *Cast:* John Howard, John Barrymore, Louise Campbell, Reginald Denny, E.E. Clive, Porter Hall, Elizabeth Patterson, Nydia Westman, Clyde Cook, Halliwell Hobbes, Matthew Boulton, Michael Brooke. *D:* James Hogan; *P:* Stuart Walker; *Sc:* Stuart Palmer. (1:06) (video)

Fourth entry in the series, based on "The Third Round" by "Sapper."

523. Bulldog Drummond's Revenge (Paramount; 1937). *Cast:* John Howard, John Barrymore, Louise Campbell, Reginald Denny, E.E. Clive, Nydia Westman, Lucien Littlefield, John Sutton, Frank Puglia, Miki Morita, Robert Gleckler, Bennie Bartlett. *D:* Louis King; *P:* Edward T. Lowe; *Sc:* Lowe. (1:00) (video)

A scientist is murdered and his formula stolen in this third entry in the popular B series. Based on Herman Cyril "Sapper" McNeil's "The Return of Bulldog Drummond."

524. Bulldog Drummond's Secret Police (Paramount; 1939). *Cast:*

John Howard, Heather Angel, H.B. Warner, Reginald Denny, E.E. Clive, Leo G. Carroll, Elizabeth Patterson, Clyde Cook, Forrester Harvey, Wyndham Standing, David Clyde, Neil Fitzgerald, Gerald Rogers, Dick Rush, Dutch Hendrian, Elspeth Dudgeon. *D:* James Hogan; *P:* Stuart Walker; *Sc:* Garnett Weston. (0:56) (video)

The seventh entry in the series with Drummond encountering a madman with a house of torture. Previously filmed in 1930 as *Temple Tower* (q.v.) and based on the book of that name by H.C. "Sapper" McNeile.

525. Bulldog Edition (Republic; 1936). *Cast:* Regis Toomey, Evalyn Knapp, Ray Walker, Betty Compson, Oscar Apfel. *D:* Charles Lamont.

Low-budget newspaper comedy-drama.

526. Bullets or Ballots (WB/ F.N.; 1936). *Cast:* Edward G. Robinson (Johnny Blake), Joan Blondell (Lee Morgan), Humphrey Bogart ("Bugs" Fenner), Barton MacLane (Al Kruger), Frank McHugh (Herman), Dick Purcell (Ed Driscoll), Joseph King (Capt. Dan MacLaren), George E. Stone (Wires), Henry O'Neill (Bryant), Henry Kolker (Hollister), Louise Beavers (Nellie LaFleur), Gilbert Emery (Thorndyke), Herbert Rawlinson (Caldwell), Norman Willis (Vinci), Frank Faylen (Gatley), Joe Connors (Eddie), Virginia Dabney (Mary), William Pawley (Crail), Ed Butler (Garber), Ralph Remley (Kelly), Edna Mae Harris (Rose the maid), Wallace Gregory (Lambert), Chic Bruno (Ben), John Lester Johnson (Timothy), Rosalind Marquis, Addison Richards (voice only), Ray Brown, Max Wagner, Ed Stanley, Milton Kibbee, Frank Marlowe, Carlyle Moore, Jr., Gordon (Bill) Elliot, Anne Nagel, Tom Wilson, Tom Brower, Ralph Dunn, Joseph Crehan, Mary Gordon. *D:* William Keighley; *P:* Louis Edelman; *St:* Seton I. Miller, Martin Mooney; *Sc:* Miller. (1:21)

A cops and gangsters drama which

was one of the 25 top grossing films of 1935–36.

527. Bunker Bean (RKO; 1936). *Cast:* Owen Davis, Jr., Louise Latimer, Robert McWade, Jessie Ralph, Lucille Ball, Berton Churchill, Edward Nugent, Hedda Hopper, Ferdinand Gottschalk, Leonard Carey, Russell Hicks, Sybil Harris, Joan Davis, Pierre Watkin, Charles Arnt, Patricia Wilder, Maxine Jennings. *D:* William Hamilton, Edward Killy; *As.P.:* William Sistrom; *Sc:* Edmund North, James Gow, Dorothy Yost. (1:07)

A male secretary overcomes his inferiority complex while making a big deal involving the rights of a patent that he owns. Based on the novel by Harry Leon Wilson and the play by Lee Wilson Dodd, it was previously filmed as *His Majesty, Bunker Bean* in 1918 by Famous Players–Lasky and again in 1925 by Warner Brothers.

528. Bureau of Missing Persons (WB/F.N.; 1933). *Cast:* Pat O'Brien, Bette Davis, Lewis Stone, Allen Jenkins, Hugh Herbert, Ruth Donnelly, Glenda Farrell, Alan Dinehart, George Chandler, Marjorie Gateson, Tad Alexander, Adrian Morris. *D:* Roy Del Ruth; *Supervisor:* Henry Blanke; *St:* Carol Bird, John H. Ayres; *Sc:* Robert Presnell. (1:15)

Partially based on fact is this story of a cop who takes a job with the bureau, thinking things will be less hectic there, but finds out otherwise.

529. Buried Alive (Producers Distributing Corp.; 1939). *Cast:* Robert Wilcox, Beverly Roberts (final film — ret.), Paul McVey, Ted Osborn, George Pembroke, Alden Chase, Don Rowan, Peter Lynn, Norman Budd, Clem Wilenchick (later Crane Whitley), Bob McKenzie, Wheeler Oakman, Robert Fiske, Joe Caits, Edward Earle, James H. McNamara. *D:* Victor Halperin; *P:* Ben Judell; *St:* William A. Ullman, Jr.; *Sc:* George Bricker. (1:02)

Low-budget prison melodrama of a wrongly incarcerated man.

530. Burn 'em Up Barnes (Majestic/Mascot; 1934). *Cast:* Jack Mulhall, Lola Lane, Frankie Darro, Julian Rivero, Edwin Maxwell, Jason Robards, Francis McDonald, Lloyd Whitlock, Robert Kortman, Tom London, Stanley Blystone, Alan Bridge, Edward Hearn. *D:* Armand Schaefer, Colbert Clark; *St:* Clark, John Rathmell; *Sc:* Schaefer, Al Martin, Barney Sarecky, Sherman Lowe. (G.B. title: *Devil on Wheels*) (1:08)

Feature version of the 12-chapter serial of the same name. This auto-racing drama is a loose remake of the 1921 feature of the same name by Affiliated. Produced by Mascot Studios, but released by Majestic Studios.

531. Burn 'em Up O'Connor (MGM; 1938). *Cast:* Dennis O'Keefe, Cecilia Parker, Nat Pendleton, Harry Carey, Addison Richards, Charley Grapewin, Alan Curtis, Tom Neal, Tom Collins, Frank Orth, Phillip Terry, Truman Bradley, Herman Bing, Tom London. *D:* Edward Sedgwick; *P:* Harry Rapf; *Sc:* Milton Merlin, Byron Morgan. (1:09)

B auto-racing drama involving murder. Based on "Salute to the Gods" by Sir Malcolm Campbell.

532. Burning Gold (Republic; 1936). *Cast:* Bill Boyd, Judith Allen, Frank Mayo, Lloyd Ingraham, Fern Emmett, Bud Flanagan (Dennis O'Keefe). *D:* Sam Newfield; *P:* George A. Hirliman; *St:* Stuart Anthony; *Sc:* Earle Snell. (0:58)

Low-budget actioner of the oil fields.

533. The Burning Question (G&H Productions; 1938). *Cast:* Dave O'Brien, Dorothy Short, Warren McCollum, Lillian Miles, Carleton Young, Thelma White, Kenneth Craig. *D:* Louis Gasnier; *P:* George A. Hirliman; *As.P.:* Samuel Dege; *St:* Lawrence Meade; *Sc:* Arthur Hoerl. (TV and video title: *Reefer Madness*) (1:07) (video)

Melodrama of reefer smokers and what happens to them — at least in this film. This low-budget quickie became a camp phenomenon with the drug culture of the late 1960s and subsequent generations. First re-released as *Tell Your Children,* but is much better known under its second re-release title *Reefer Madness.*

534. Burning Up (Paramount; 1930). *Cast:* Richard Arlen, Mary Brian, Tully Marshall, Clara Blandick, Francis McDonald, Sam Hardy, Charles Sellon. *D:* A. Edward Sutherland.

B auto racing drama.

Burnt Offering (G.B. title) *see* **A Passport to Hell**

535. Business and Pleasure (Fox; 1932). *Cast:* Will Rogers, Jetta Goudal, Joel McCrea, Jed Prouty, Dorothy Peterson, Oscar Apfel, Boris Karloff, Peggy Ross, Vernon Dent, Cyril Ring. *D:* David Butler; *St:* Booth Tarkington.

This folksy comedy was an early attempt to film "The Jones Family" which became popular later in the decade when a second attempt was made. One of the fifteen top grossing films of 1932.

The Busybody (G.B. title) *see* **The Kibitzer**

536. But the Flesh Is Weak (MGM; 1932). *Cast:* Robert Montgomery, C. Aubrey Smith, Heather Thatcher (American debut), Edward Everett Horton, Nora Gregor, Frederick Kerr, Forrester Harvey, Nils Asther, Desmond Roberts. *D:* Jack Conway; *Sc:* Ivor Novello. (1:22)

Comedy of a widower and his son who both plan to marry for money. Based on "The Truth Game" by Ivor Novello. Remade in 1941 as *Free and Easy.*

537. By Appointment Only (Invincible; 1933). *Cast:* Marceline Day,

Sally O'Neil, Lew Cody, Aileen Pringle, Pauline Garon, Claire McDowell. *D:* Frank Strayer.

"Poverty row" romantic comedy.

538. By Candlelight (Universal; 1934). *Cast:* Paul Lukas, Elissa Landi, Nils Asther, Dorothy Revier, Lawrence Grant, Esther Ralston, Warburton Gamble, Lois January. *D:* James Whale; *P:* Carl Laemmle, Jr.; *Sc:* Hans Kräly, F. Hugh Herbert, Karen de Wolf, Ruth Cummings (based on the German play "Candlelight" by Siegfried Geyer. (1:10)

Romantic comedy of assumed and mistaken identity.

539. By Whose Hand? (Columbia; 1932). *Cast:* Ben Lyon, Barbara Weeks, Kenneth Thomson, Nat Pendleton, Dwight Frye. *D:* Ben Stoloff.

Melodrama filmed previously in 1927 by director Walter Lang.

540. By Your Leave (RKO; 1935). *Cast:* Frank Morgan, Genevieve Tobin, Neil Hamilton, Marion Nixon, Gene Lockhart, Margaret Hamilton, Betty Grable, Glenn Anders, Charles Ray, Lona Andre. *D:* Lloyd Corrigan; *P:* Pandro S. Berman; *Sc:* Allan Scott. (1:32)

Comedy of a husband who decides to sew some wild oats while on vacation with his wife. Based on a play by Gladys Hurlbut and Emma B.C. Wells.

541. Bye-Bye Buddy (Trinity Pictures; 1929). *Cast:* Agnes Ayres (final starring role), Buddy Shaw. *D:* Frank S. Mattison.

A part-talkie romantic comedy. A Hercules film.

542. The Cabin in the Cotton (WB/F.N.; 1932). *Cast:* Richard Barthelmess, Dorothy Jordan, Bette Davis, Hardie Albright, David Landau, Berton Churchill, Dorothy Peterson, Russell Simpson, Tully Marshall, Henry B. Walthall, Edmund Breese, John Marston, Erville Alderson, William LeMaire, Clarence Muse, J. Carrol Naish, Virginia Hammond, Harry Cording, Walter Percival, Bud Flanagan (Dennis O'Keefe). *D:* Michael Curtiz; *P:* Hal Wallis; *Sc:* Paul Green. (1:17)

Melodrama of a southern sharecropper and his involvement with a local belle. Based on the novel by Harry Harrison Kroll.

543. The Cactus Kid (Reliable; 1935). *Cast:* Jack Perrin, Jayne Regan, Slim Whitaker, Tom London, Fred Humes, Wally Wales (Hal Taliaferro), Philo McCullough, Joe de la Cruz, Kit Guard, Tina Menard, Lew Meehan, George Chesebro, Gordon DeMain, George Morrell. *D:* Harry S. Webb; *P:* Bernard B. Ray; *Sc:* Carl Krusada. (0:56)

Jack Perrin western of a cowboy out to find the killer of his partner.

544. Cafe Hostess (Columbia; 1939-40). *Cast:* Veda Ann Borg, Ann Dvorak, Preston Foster, Dick Wessel, Peggy Shannon, Douglas Fowley, Linda Winters, Bradley Page, Wynne Gibson, Arthur Loft. *D:* Sidney Salkow; *St:* Howard Higgin; *Sc:* Harold Shumate. (aka: *Street of Missing Women*)

Low-budget melodrama.

545. Cafe Metropole (20th Century-Fox; 1937). *Cast:* Loretta Young, Tyrone Power, Adolph Menjou, Charles Winninger, Gregory Ratoff, Helen Westley, Christian Rub, Leonid Kinskey, Georges Renavent, Hal K. Dawson, Frederick Vogeding. *D:* Edward H. Griffith; *P:* Nunnally Johnson; *St:* Gregory Ratoff; *Sc:* Jacques Deval. (1:24)

Comedy of an indigent American in Paris who poses as a Russian prince.

546. Cafe Society (Paramount; 1939). *Cast:* Madeleine Carroll, Fred MacMurray, Shirley Ross, Claude Gillingwater (final film — d. 1939), Jessie Ralph, Allyn Joslyn, Don Alvarado,

Hilda Plowright, Paul Hurst, Mary Parker, Charles Trowbridge, Cupid Ainsworth, Mira McKinney, Frank Dawson. *D:* Edward H. Griffith; *P:* Jeff Lazarus; *St & Sc:* Virginia Van Upp; *Songs:* Burton Lane. (1:23)

Romantic comedy.

547. Cain and Mabel (WB; 1936). *Cast:* Marion Davies, Clark Gable, David Carlyle (Robert Paige), Allen Jenkins, Roscoe Karns, Walter Catlett, Pert Kelton, Ruth Donnelly, Hobart Cavanaugh, E.E. Clive, William Collier, Sr., Joseph Crehan, Eily Malyon, Sammy White, Allen Pomeroy. *D:* Lloyd Bacon; *P:* Sam Bischoff; *St:* H.C. Witwer; *Sc:* Laird Doyle; *Choreographer:* (A.A.N.) Bobby Connolly for the $1,000 Love Songs" number; "Coney Island," "Here Comes Chiquita," "I'll Sing You a Thousand Love Songs," "The Shadow Waltz," "Those Endearing Young Charms" and "The Rose in Her Hair" by Al Dubin and Harry Warren. (1:30)

Flop musical-comedy of the romance of a boxer and a showgirl.

548. California Frontier (Columbia; 1937-38). *Cast:* Buck Jones, Carmen Bailey, Milburn Stone, Jose Perez, Soledad Jimenez, Glenn Strange, Stanley Blystone, Carlos Villarios, Paul Ellis, Ernie Adams, Forrest Taylor. *D:* Elmer Clifton; *P:* Monroe Shaff; *St & Sc:* Shaff, Arthur Hoerl. (0:55)

Buck Jones western of an army captain sent to California to investigate allegations that Mexicans are being forced from their land.

California in 1978 *see* **Fightin' Thru** (1930)

549. California Mail (WB; 1936-37). *Cast:* Dick Foran, Linda Perry, James Farley, Gene Alsace (Rocky Camron), Glenn Strange, Dick Botiller, Edmund Cobb, Tom Brower, Bob Woodward, Wilfred Lucas, Fred Burns, Milton Kibbee, Edward Keane, Jack Kirk, Lew Meehan, The Sons of the Pioneers, Tex Palmer. *D:* Noel Smith; *P:* Bryan Foy; *Sc:* Roy Chanslor, Harold Buckley; *Songs:* "Ridin' the Mail," "Love Begins at Evening" by M.K. Jerome, Jack Scholl. (0:56)

Dick Foran western with songs of a stage line that receives a mail contract. Filmed before in 1929 with Ken Maynard.

550. California Straight Ahead (Universal; 1936-37). *Cast:* John Wayne, Louise Latimer, Robert McWade, Tully Marshall, Theodore Von Eltz, LeRoy Mason, Grace Goodall. *D:* Arthur Lubin; *P:* Trem Carr; *St:* Herman Boxer; *Sc:* W. Scott Darling. (1:07)

Action-adventure of a cross-country race between a train and a fleet of trucks.

551. The California Trail (Columbia; 1933). *Cast:* Buck Jones, Helen Mack, Emile Chautard, George Humbert, Charles Stevens, Evelyn Sherman, Chris-Pin Martin, Carmen LaRoux, Allan Garcia. *D:* Lambert Hillyer; *Sc:* Jack Natteford. (1:07)

Buck Jones western of two brothers involved in a land swindle.

552. The Californian (20th Century–Fox/Principal; 1937). *Cast:* Ricardo Cortez, Marjorie Weaver, Katherine de Mille, Maurice Black, Morgan Wallace, Nigel de Brulier, Ann Gillis, Helen Holmes, James Farley, Dick Botiller, Tom Forman, Bud Osborne. *D:* Gus Meins; *P:* Sol Lesser; *Sc:* Gilbert Wright. (1:01)

B western of a man returning from Spain to find lawlessness rampant.

553. Call a Messenger (Universal; 1938-39). *Cast:* Billy Halop, Huntz Hall, Billy Benedict, David Gorcey, Robert Armstrong, Mary Carlisle, Anne Nagel, Victor Jory, El Brendel, Buster Crabbe. *D:* Arthur Lubin; *P:* Kenneth Goldsmith; *Sc:* Arthur T. Horman. (1:05)

B entry in the "Little Tough Guys" series.

554. Call Her Savage (Fox; 1932). *Cast:* Clara Bow, Gilbert Roland, Monroe Owsley, Thelma Todd, Estelle Taylor, Fred Kohler, Margaret Livingston, Arthur Hoyt, Mischa Auer, Weldon Heyburn, John Elliott, Dorothy Peterson, John St. Polis, Hale Hamilton, Willard Robertson, Mary Gordon, Kathryn Perry, Anthony Jowitt. *D:* John Francis Dillon; *P:* Sam E. Rork; *Sc:* Edwin Burke. (1:28)

Melodrama of a half-breed Indian girl's problems in life. Based on the novel by Tiffany Thayer.

555. Call It a Day (WB; 1937). *Cast:* Olivia de Havilland, Ian Hunter, Anita Louise, Alice Brady, Roland Young, Frieda Inescort, Bonita Granville, Peggy Wood, Walter Woolf King, Una O'Connor, Marcia Ralston, Beryl Mercer, Elsa Buchanan, Mary Field, Peter Willes. *D:* Archie Mayo; *P:* Henry Blanke (a Cosmopolitan Production); *Sc:* Casey Robinson. (1:29)

Comedy of the problems encountered in one day within an uppercrust British family. Based on the play by Dodie Smith.

556. Call It Luck (Fox; 1934). *Cast:* Herbert Mundin, Pat Paterson, Charles Starrett, Susan Fleming, Theodore Von Eltz, Gordon Westcott, Ernest Wood, Georgia Caine, Reginald Mason, Ethel Griffies. *D:* James Tinling; *St:* Dudley Nichols, George Marshall; *Adaptation:* Joseph Cunningham, Harry McCoy; *Sc:* Nichols, Lamar Trotti.

Comedy of horse-racing.

Call It Murder *see Midnight* (1934)

557. Call of the Circus (Xxxx Xxxx; 1930). *Cast:* Francis X. Bushman, Ethel Clayton. *D:* Frank O'Connor; *Sc:* Maxine Altan.

(No other information available)

558. Call of the Flesh (MGM; 1930). *Cast:* Ramon Novarro, Dorothy Jordan, Ernest Torrence, Renee Adoree (final film—d. 1933), Marie Dressler, Russell Hopton, Nance O'Neil, Mathilde Comont. *D:* Charles Brabin, Novarro; *Sc:* John Colton. (G.B. title: *The Singer of Seville*)

2-color technicolor romantic drama of a cabaret entertainer and the young novice who leaves her convent for him.

559. Call of the Prairie (Paramount; 1936). *Cast:* Bill Boyd (Hoppy), James Ellison (Johnny Nelson), George Hayes (Windy Halliday), Chill Wills and the Avalon Boys, John Merton, Muriel Evans, Chester Conklin, Alan Bridge, Hank Mann, Willie Fung, Howard Lang, Al Hill, Jim Mason. *D:* Howard Bretherton; *P:* Harry M. Sherman; *Sc:* Doris Schroeder, Vernon Smith. (1:05)

Johnny Nelson is being framed in this 4th entry in the "Hopalong Cassidy" series.

560. Call of the Rockies (Columbia; 1938). *Cast:* Charles Starrett, Iris Meredith, Donald Grayson, The Sons of the Pioneers with Bob Nolan, Dick Curtis, Edward LeSaint, Edmund Cobb, Art Mix, John Tyrrell, George Chesebro, Glenn Strange, Jack Rockwell. *D:* Alan James; *Sc:* Ed Earl Repp. (0:54)

Charles Starrett western of a cowboy coming to the aid of a woman about to lose her ranch.

561. Call of the Savage (Xxxx Xxxx; 1935). *D:* Ray Taylor.

(No other information available)

562. Call of the West (Columbia; 1930). *Cast:* Dorothy Revier, Matt Moore, Kathrin Clare Ward, Tom O'Brien, Alan Roscoe, Victor Potel, Nick De Ruiz, Joe de la Cruz, Blanche Rose, Bud Osborne. *D:* Albert Ray; *St:* Florence Ryerson, Colin Clements; *Sc:* Clements. (1:10)

A New York girl marries a rancher but has trouble enduring the life.

563. Call of the Wild (United Artists/20th Century; 1935). *Cast:* Clark Gable, Loretta Young, Jack Oakie, Reginald Owen, Frank Conroy, Katherine de Mille, Sidney Toler, James Burke, Charles Stevens, Lalo Encinas, Thomas Jackson, Russell Powell, George MacQuarrie, Herman Bing, Duke Green, Buck the dog. *D:* William Wellman; *P:* Darryl F. Zanuck; *As.P.:* William Goetz, Raymond Griffith; *Sc:* Gene Fowler, Leonard Praskins. (1:35) (re-release prints run 1:21)

Yukon adventure based on events in the 1903 book by Jack London. This was the final production of 20th Century Pictures before merging with Fox. Previously filmed in 1923. Remade in 1972 in Finland with an European co-production and again in 1976 as a TV movie.

Call of the Wilderness *see* **Trailing the Killer**

564. Call of the Yukon (Republic; 1938). *Cast:* Richard Arlen, Beverly Roberts, Lyle Talbot, Ray Mala, Garry Owen, Ivan Miller, Al St. John, James Lono, Emory Parnell (film debut), J. Anthony Hughes, Nina Campana, Billy Dooley, Buck the Dog. *D:* B. Reeves Eason, John T. Coyle; *Sc:* William Bartlett, Gertrude Orr. (1:10)

Romantic drama of a trapper and a lady writer in the Yukon.

A Call on the President *see* **Joe and Ethel Turp Call on the President**

565. Call the Mesquiteers (Republic; 1938). *Cast:* Bob Livingston (Stony Brooke), Ray Corrigan (Tucson Smith), Max Terhune (Lullaby Joslin), Lynne Roberts (Nee: Mary Hart), Sammy McKim, Eddy Waller, Earle Hodgins, Maston Williams, Eddie Hart, Pat Gleason, Roger Williams, Warren Jackson, Hal Price, Frank Ellis, Curley Dresden, Jack Ingram, Ralph Peters, Ethan Laidlaw, Tom Steele, Al Taylor. *D:* John English; *Sc:* Luci Ward. (0:54)

"Three Mesquiteers" western with the boys being accused of robbery and forced to split up to apprehend the guilty parties.

566. Calling All Cars (Empire; 1934–35). *Cast:* Jack LaRue. *D:* Spencer Gordon Bennet.

Crime melodrama.

(No other information available)

567. Calling All Marines (Republic; 1939). *Cast:* Robert Kent, Helen Mack, Donald Barry, Janet McLeary, Leon Ames, Warren Hymer, Cyrus Kendall, Walter McGrail, Jay Novello, George Chandler, James Flavin, Selmer Jackson. *D:* John H. Auer; *Sc:* Earl Felton.

Action drama.

568. Calling Dr. Kildare (MGM; 1939). *Cast:* Lew Ayres (Dr. Kildare), Lionel Barrymore (Dr. Gillespie), Laraine Day (Mary Lamont), Lana Turner, Nat Pendleton, Samuel S. Hinds, Emma Dunn, Alma Kruger, Marie Blake, Phillip Terry, Walter Kingsford, Nell Craig, Donald Barry, Harlan Briggs, George Offerman, Jr., Dorothy Adams, Reed Hadley, Clinton Rosemond, Lynne Carver, Henry Hunter, Roger Converse, Johnny Walsh. *D:* Harold S. Bucquet; *Sc:* Harry Ruskin, Willis Goldbeck. (1:26)

Second entry in the popular series in which Drs. Kildare and Gillespie get involved in murder.

569. The Calling of Dan Matthews (Columbia; 1935–36). *Cast:* Richard Arlen, Charlotte Wynters, Douglass Dumbrille, Mary Kornman, Donald Cook, Carlyle Blackwell, Jr., Lee Moran (final film — ret.), Tom Dugan, Edward McWade, Lee Burton. *D:* Phil Rosen; *Sc:* Dan Jarrett, Don Swift, Karl Brown. (1:03)

Modern western of a minister who attacks the local lawless element. Based on the novel by Harold Bell Wright.

570. Calling Philo Vance (WB; 1939–40). *Cast:* James Stephenson (Philo Vance), Margot Stevenson, Henry O'Neill, Edward Brophy, Ralph Forbes, Martin Kosleck. *D:* William Clemens; *As.P.:* Bryan Foy; *St:* S.S. Van Dine; *Sc:* Tom Reed. (1:02)

B remake of *The Kennel Murder Case* (q.v.).

571. Calm Yourself (MGM; 1935). *Cast:* Robert Young, Madge Evans, Betty Furness, Hardie Albright, Nat Pendleton, Ralph Morgan, Herman Bing, Raymond Hatton, Ward Bond, Paul Hurst, Claude Gillingwater, Clyde Cook. *D:* George B. Seitz; *P:* Lucien Hubbard; *St:* Edward Hope; *Sc:* Arthur Kober.

B comedy of two girls who create difficulties for an ex-advertising man.

572. Cameo Kirby (Fox; 1930). *Cast:* J. Harold Murray, Norma Terris, Myrna Loy, Charles Morton, Stepin Fetchit, Douglas Gilmore, Robert Edeson, Beulah Hall Jones, Mme. (Carrie) Daumery, John Hyams. *D:* Irving Cummings; *Sc:* Tarkington & Harry Leon Wilson.

A 19th-century costume drama based on the 1908 play by Booth Tarkington. Previous versions: (Lasky Feature Plays; 1915) with Dustin Farnum, (Fox; 1923) directed by John Ford and starring John Gilbert and Gertrude Olmstead, and marking the film debut of Jean Arthur.

573/574. Camille (MGM; 1936). *Cast:* Greta Garbo (A.A.N. for B.A., an Acting Award from the National Board of Review and "Best Actress of the Year" by the New York Film Critics as Marguerite Gautier), Robert Taylor (Armand), Lionel Barrymore (General Duval), Elizabeth Allan (Nichette), Laura Hope Crews (Prudence), Henry Daniell (Baron de Varville), Lenore Ulric (Olympe), Jessie Ralph (Nanine), Rex O'Malley (Gaston), Marion Ballou (Corinne), Joan (Leslie) Brodel (film debut as Marie Jeanette), Russell Hardie (Gustave), E.E. Clive (St. Gadeau), Douglas Walton (Henri), Fritz Leiber (Valentine), June Wilkins (Louise), Elsie Esmond (Madame Duval), Edwin Maxwell (doctor), Eily Malyon (Therese), John Bryan (DeMusset), Mabel Colcord (Madame Barjon), Chappel Dossett (priest), Ferdinand Munier (other priest), Effie Ellsler (Grandma Duval), Sybil Harris (Georges Sand), Maude Hume (Aunt Henriette), Barry Norton (Emille), Olaf Hytten (croupier), Mariska Aldrich, Rex Evans, Eugene King, Adrienne Matzenauer, Georgia Caine, Elspeth Dudgeon, Gwendolyn Logan, John Picorri, Guy Bates Post, Zeffie Tilbury, Gertrude Astor. *D:* George Cukor; *As.P.:* David Lewis; *Sc:* Zoe Akins, Frances Marion, James Hilton. (1:48) (video)

The romance of a consumptive prostitute and a young aristocrat, much to the disapproval of the latter's father. Set in mid–19th-century Paris, it is based on the novel and play "The Lady of the Camellias" by Alexander Dumas. The "10 Best" lists of 1937 from the National Board of Review and the New York Times voted it #4 and #9 respectively. Previous versions: (Champion; 1912) with Gertrude Shipman, (World-Selznick; 1915) with Clara Kimball Young, (Fox; 1917) with Theda Bara and Albert Roscoe, (Metro; 1921) with Nazimova and Valentino and (First National; 1927) with Norma Talmadge and Gilbert Roland. It was remade in 1984 as a TV movie in the U.S.

575/576. Campus Confessions (Paramount; 1938). *Cast:* Betty Grable, Eleanore Whitney, Fritz Feld, William Henry, Matty Kemp, Lane Chandler, Thurston Hall, Hank Luisetti, John Arledge, Roy Gordon, Summer Getchell. *D:* George Archainbaud; *P:* William Thomas; *St & Sc:* Lloyd Corrigan, Erwin Gelsey. (G.B. title: *Fast Play*)

B college comedy with a basketball theme.

577. Can This Be Dixie? (20th Century–Fox; 1936). *Cast:* Jane Withers, Donald Cook, Slim Summerville, Sara Haden, Hattie McDaniel, William Worthington, Claude Gillingwater. *D:* George Marshall; *P:* Sol M. Wurtzel; *Sc:* Marshall (co-writer).

B musical-comedy.

578. The Canary Murder Case (Paramount; 1929). *Cast:* William Powell (Vance), Jean Arthur, James Hall, Eugene Pallette, Charles (Levison) Lane, Gustav von Seyffertitz, Louise Brooks (voice dubbed by Margaret Livingston), Ned Sparks, E.H. Calvert, Lawrence Grant, Louis Jean Bartels. *D:* Frank Tuttle, Malcolm St. Clair; *Sc:* Florence Ryerson, Albert LeVino; *Additional Dialogue:* S.S. Van Dine; *Titles:* Herman J. Mankiewicz. (1:21)

"Philo Vance" mystery revolving around the murder of a beautiful Broadway star. Based on the book by S.S. Van Dine, this was the first of his works to be filmed. Originally photographed in 1928 as a silent, but dialogue was added for release in '29.

579. The Cannonball Express (Sono Art–World Wide; 1932). *Cast:* Rex Lease, Tom Moore, Leon (Ames) Waycoff. *D:* Wallace Fox.

"Poverty Row" melodrama.

580. Canyon Hawks (Big 4; 1930). *Cast:* Yakima Canutt, Buzz Barton, Rene Borden, Wally Wales, Robert Walker, Bob Reeves, Cliff Lyons, Bobby Dunn. *D:* Alvin J. Neitz (Alan James); *P:* John R. Freuler; *Sc:* Neitz. (0:55)

Yakima Canutt western of a cowboy aiding a girl and her brother who are raising sheep.

Cap'n Jericho (G.B. title) *see* **Hell and High Water**

581. Cappy Ricks Returns (Republic; 1935). *Cast:* Robert McWade (Cappy Ricks), Florine McKinney, Lois Wilson, Bradley Page, Ray Walker, Richard Cramer, Oscar Apfel. *D:* Mack V. Wright.

B comedy-drama based on the character created by Peter B. Kyne. This was the first film in a proposed series which was followed by *Affairs of Cappy Ricks* (q.v.). A previous film titled *Cappy Ricks,* based on Kyne's character appeared in 1921.

582. Captain Applejack (WB; 1931). *Cast:* John Halliday, Kay Strozzi, Arthur Edmund Carewe, Mary Brian, Louise Closser Hale, Alec B. Francis, Claud Allister, Julia Swayne Gordon. *D:* Hobart Henley; *Sc:* Maude Fulton.

A man thwarts the attempts by crooks who plan to tear up his home in search of hidden loot. Based on the play "Ambrose Applejohn's Adventure" by Walter Hackett. Filmed before in 1923.

583. Captain Blood (WB/F.N.; 1935). *Cast:* Errol Flynn (starring debut as Dr. Peter Blood, a role originally intended for British actor Robert Donat), Olivia de Havilland (Arabella Bishop), Lionel Atwill (Colonel Bishop), Basil Rathbone (Captain Levasseur), Ross Alexander (Jeremy Pitt), Guy Kibbee (Hagthorpe), Robert Barrat (Wolverstone), Henry Stephenson (Lord Willoughby), George Hassell (Governor Steed), Forrester Harvey (Honesty Nuthall), Hobart Cavanaugh (Dr. Bronson), Donald Meek (Dr. Whacker), Frank McGlynn, Sr. (Rev. Ogle), David Torrence (Andrew Baynes), J. Carrol Naish (Cahusac), Pedro de Cordoba (Don Diego), Leonard Mudie (Lord Jeffries), Jessie Ralph (Mrs. Barlowe), Stuart Casey (Capt. Hobart), Halliwell Hobbes (Lord Sunderland), Colin Kenny (Lord Chester Dyke), Holmes Herbert (Capt. Gardiner), Mary Forbes (Mrs. Steed), Reginald Barlowe (Dixon), Denis D'Auburn (Lord Gilroy), Vernon Steele (King James II), Harry Cording (Kent), E.E.

Clive, Ivan Simpson, Georges Rena-vent, Murray Kinnell, Maude Leslie, Stymie Beard, Gardner James, Sam Appel, Chris-Pin Martin, Yola D'Avril, Tina Menard, Frank Puglia, Gene Alsace (Rocky Camron), Artie Ortego, Kansas Moehring, Tom Steele, Blackie Whiteford, Jim Thorpe, Jim Mason, Buddy Roosevelt, William Yetter, Rex Ingram. *D:* Michael Curtiz; *As.P.:* Harry Joe Brown; *Sc:* Casey Robinson; *Sound Recording:* (A.A.N.) Nathan Levinson. (1:59) (video) (shorter prints exist).

Swashbuckler of an exiled doctor who turns to piracy on the high seas. The film received an A.A.N. for Best Picture as well as being one of the 25 top grossing films of 1935–36. Based on Rafael Sabatini's 1922 novel, it was previously filmed in 1923–24 by Vitagraph with J. Warren Kerrigan. Loosely remade in France in 1960. In 1962, Errol Flynn's son Sean made a sequel in Europe titled *Son of Captain Blood,* shortly before he disappeared in Vietnam. Computer-colored prints were produced by Turner Entertainment.

584. Captain Calamity (Grand National/Regal; 1936). *Cast:* George Houston, Marian Nixon (final film — ret.), Vince Barnett, Juan Torres, Movita, Crane Wilbur, George Lewis, Roy D'Arcy, Margaret Irving, Barry Norton, Louis Natheaux, Lloyd Ingraham. *D:* John Reinhardt; *P:* George A. Hirliman; *St:* Gordon Young; *Sc:* Crane Wilbur. (Formerly known as: *Captain Hurricane*) (1:06)

A low-budget color (Hirlicolor) south seas adventure.

585. Captain Fury (United Artists/Hal Roach; 1939). *Cast:* Brian Aherne, Victor McLaglen, Paul Lukas, June Lang, John Carradine, Douglass Dumbrille, Charles Middleton, George Zucco, Virginia Field, Lawrence Grossmith, Lumsden Hare, Mary Gordon,

Claud Allister, Billy Bevan, Rondo Hatton, Margaret Roach, John Warburton, Will Stanton, Edgar Norton. *D:* Hal Roach; *P:* William de Mille; *St:* W.L. Stevens; *Sc:* de Mille, Grover Jones, Jack Jevne; *Art-Set Decoration:* (A.A.N.) Charles D. Hall. (1:31)

Comedy-adventure of a revolt in an early Australian penal colony.

586. The Captain Hates the Sea (Columbia; 1934). *Cast:* John Gilbert (final film — d. 1936), Victor McLaglen, Walter Connolly, Wynne Gibson, Helen Vinson, Alison Skipworth, Leon Errol, Walter Catlett, Akim Tamiroff, Donald Meek, Arthur Treacher, The Three Stooges, John Wray, Claude Gillingwater, Inez Courtney, Fred Keating. *D:* Lewis Milestone; *St & Sc:* Wallace Smith. (1:33)

Romance, mystery and intrigue aboard an ocean liner — all played for laughs.

587. Captain Hurricane (RKO; 1935). *Cast:* James Barton (film debut), Helen Westley, Helen Mack, Gene Lockhart, Henry Travers, Douglas Walton, Otto Hoffman, Harry Stubbs, J. Farrell MacDonald, Forrester Harvey, Stanley Fields, Lon Chaney, Jr., Nydia Westman. *D:* John S. Robertson; *As.P.:* Frank O'Heron; *Sc:* Josephine Lovett. (1:12)

Comedy-drama of three Cape Cod fishermen who become involved with a girl they save from drowning. Based on the novel "The Taming of Zenas Henry" by Sara Ware Bassett. A box office flop.

Captain Hurricane (1936) *see* **Captain Calamity**

588. The Captain Is a Lady (MGM; 1939–40). *Cast:* Charles Coburn, Billie Burke, Beulah Bondi, Dan Dailey, Virginia Grey, Helen Broderick, Helen Westley. *D:* Robert Sinclair; *Sc:* Harry Clork. (1:03)

Comedy of a man who sends his wife to an old folks home, then dresses as a woman so he can be with her. Based on a play by Rachel Crothers.

589. Captain January (20th Century–Fox; 1936). *Cast:* Shirley Temple, Guy Kibbee, Buddy Ebsen, Slim Summerville, June Lang, Sara Haden, Jane Darwell, Nella Walker, George Irving, Si Jenks, John Carradine, Jerry Tucker. *D:* David Butler; *P:* Darryl F. Zanuck; *Sc:* Sam Hellman, Gladys Lehman, Harry Tugend. (1:15) (video)

A little girl becomes attached to a lighthouse keeper who saves her from a shipwreck. Based on the novel by Laura E. Richards, it was previously filmed in 1924 with Baby Peggy and Hobart Bosworth. Computer-colored in 1988.

590. Captain of the Guard (Universal; 1930). *Cast:* John Boles, Laura La Plante, Lionel Belmore (Colonel of Hussars), Sam DeGrasse (Bazin), James Marcus, Otis Harlan, Stuart Holmes (Louis XVI), Richard Cramer (Danton), Evelyn Hall (Marie Antionette), George Hackathorne (Robespierre), Claude Fleming, Harry Cording, Ervin Renard, Murdock McQuarrie. *D:* Paul Fejos, John S. Robertson; *P:* Carle Laemmle, Jr.; *Sc:* Arthur Ripley, George Manker Watters; *Songs:* "Song of the Guard," "Can It Be?" "For You," "It's a Sword," "Maids on Parade," "You, You Alone" by Heinz Roemheld and William Francis Dugan. (1:23)

Historically inaccurate musical-melodrama of the French Revolution and the composition of the French national anthem "La Marseillaise." Taken from a story by Houston Branch. The film had the working title of "La Marseillaise."

591. Captain Swagger (Pathé; 1928–29). *Cast:* Sue Carol, Ullrich Haupt, Victor Potel, Richard Tucker. *D:* Edward H. Griffith; *St:* "Sapper" as creator.

Part-talkie melodrama originally released in 1928 as a silent with synchronised music score and sound effects and re-released the following year with brief dialogue inserts.

592. Captain Thunder (WB; 1931). *Cast:* Victor Varconi (talkie debut), Fay Wray, Charles Judels, Robert Elliott, Natalie Moorhead, Bert Roach, Frank Campeau, Don Alvarado, John (St. Polis) Sainpolis, Robert Emmett Keane. *D:* Alan Crosland; *St:* Hal Devitt, Pierre Couderc; *Sc:* Gordon Rigby, William K. Wells. (1:06)

Comedy-melodrama of a Mexican outlaw.

593. The Captain's Kid (WB/F.N.; 1936). *Cast:* Guy Kibbee, May Robson, Sybil Jason, Jane Bryan, Fred Lawrence, Mary Treen, George E. Stone, Dick Purcell. *D:* Nick Grinde; *St:* Earl Felton; *Sc:* Tom Reed; *Songs:* "Drifting Along" and "I'm the Captain's Kid" by M.K. Jerome and Jack Scholl. (1:12)

A retired sea captain's telling of tall tales gets him involved in a court case involving murder.

594. The Captain's Wife (Xxxx Xxxx; 1932). (No information available)

595. Captains Courageous (MGM; 1937). *Cast:* Spencer Tracy (A.A. for B.A. as Manuel), Freddie Bartholomew (Harvey), Melvyn Douglas (Mr. Cheyne), Lionel Barrymore (Capt. Disko Troop), Mickey Rooney (Dan Troop), John Carradine (Long Jack), Walter Kingsford (Dr. Finley), Charley Grapewin (Uncle Salters), Leo G. Carroll (Burns), Jack LaRue (Priest), Oscar O'Shea (Cushman), Donald Briggs (Tyler), Sam McDaniel (Doc), Billy Burrud (Charles), Christian Rub (Old Clement), Dave Thursby (Tom), Charles Trowbridge (Dr. Walsh), William Stack (Elliott), Jay

Ward (Pogey), Kenneth Wilson (Alvin), Roger Gray (Nate Rogers), Norman Ainsley (Robbins), Dave Wengren (Lars), Katherine Kenworthy (Mrs. Troop), Richard Powell, Bobby Watson, Billy Gilbert, Gladden James, Tommy Bupp, Wally Albright, Murray Kinnell, Dora Early, Gertrude Sutton. *D:* Victor Fleming; *P:* Louis D. Lighton; *Sc:* (A.A.N.) Marc Connelly, John Lee Mahin, Dale Van Every; *Songs:* Franz Waxman, Gus Kahn; *Ed:* (A.A.N.) Elmo Veron. (1:56) (video)

Classic of a spoiled brat who falls overboard from a cruise ship and is picked up by a Portuguese fishing ship where he learns some things about people and life. Box office gold for the studio the film received an A.A.N. for Best Picture, was in nomination for Best Picture by the New York Film Critics, received *Photoplay's* Gold Medal Award, placed #4 on the "10 Best" list of the *New York Times,* #8 with the National Board of Review among their "10 Best" and #3 on the same list of *Film Daily.* One of the 38 top grossing films of 1936–37. Computer-colored by Turner Entertainment in 1989.

596. Captured (WB; 1933). *Cast:* Leslie Howard, Douglas Fairbanks, Jr., Paul Lukas, Margaret Lindsay, Robert Barrat, Arthur Hohl, John Bleifer, William LeMaire, J. Carrol Naish, Philip Faversham, Frank Reicher, Joyce Coad, Bert Sprotte, Harry Cording, Halliwell Hobbes. *D:* Roy Del Ruth; *P:* Hal Wallis; *Sc:* Edward Chodorov. (1:12)

Following World War I, a P.O.W. returns home to England to find his wife and his best friend had an affair. Based on the story "Fellow Prisoners" by Sir Philip Gibbs.

597. Captured in Chinatown (Superior; 1935). *Cast:* Charles Delaney, Marion Shilling, Bobby Nelson, Philo McCullough. *D:* Elmer Clifton; *Sc:* Clifton (co-writer).

Low-budget melodrama.

598. Car 99 (Paramount; 1935). *Cast:* Fred MacMurray, Ann Sheridan, Sir Guy Standing, Frank Craven, William Frawley, Russell Hopton, Joseph (Sawyer) Sauers, Robert Kent (film debut), Dean Jagger, Charles Wilson, Marina Schubert, Eddie Chandler, Nora Cecil, Howard Wilson, Mack Gray, Alfred Delcambre, Douglas Blackley, John Cox. *D:* Charles Barton; *P:* Bayard Veiller; *St:* Karl Detzer; *Sc:* Detzer, C. Gardner Sullivan.

A rookie state trooper apprehends banks robbers in this B.

599. Caravan (Fox; 1934). *Cast:* Loretta Young, Charles Boyer, Jean Parker, Phillips Holmes, Louise Fazenda, Eugene Pallette, C. Aubrey Smith, Charley Grapewin, Noah Beery, Dudley Digges, Billy Bevan, Richard Carle, Lynn Bari, Lionel Belmore, Armand Kaliz, Harry C. Bradley. *D:* Erik Charell; *St:* Melchior Lengyel; *Sc:* Samson Raphaelson; *Songs:* Werner B. Heymann, Gus Kahn. (1:41)

Offbeat musical-drama of marriage between a gypsy and a countess. A box office flop.

Cardigan's Last Case (G.B. title) *see* **State's Attorney**

600. Cardinal Richelieu (United Artists/20th Century; 1935). *Cast:* George Arliss (Richelieu), Edward Arnold (King Louis XIII), Maureen O'Sullivan, Cesar Romero, Francis Lister, Reginald Sheffield, Douglass Dumbrille (Barados), Russell Hicks, Halliwell Hobbes, Violet (Kemble) Cooper (Queen Marie), Katherine Alexander (Queen Anne), Robert Harrigan, Lumsden Hare, Gilbert Emery, Arthur Treacher, Holmes Herbert, Leonard Mudie, Keith Kenneth, Boyd Irwin, William Worthington, Guy Bellis, Joseph Tozer, David Clyde, Charles Evans, Frank Dunn. *D:* Rowland V. Lee; *P:* Darryl F. Zanuck; *As.P.:* William Goetz, Raymond Griffith; *Sc:* Maude Howell, Cameron Rogers, W.P. Lipscomb. (1:22)

Historically based drama of the cardinal who strongly influences France's King Louis XIII. Based on the play by Sir Edward Bulwer-Lytton.

601. Career (RKO; 1939). *Cast:* Anne Shirley, Edward Ellis, Samuel S. Hinds, Janet Beecher, Leon Errol, Alice Eden (real name: Rowena Cook — won her role in a Hollywood talent contest promoted by Jesse L. Lasky), John Archer (real name: Ralph Bowman — who also won his role in the talent search), Raymond Hatton, Maurice Murphy, Harrison Greene, Charles Drake (debut), Hobart Cavanaugh, John Qualen, Robert Frazer. *D:* Leigh Jason; *P:* Robert Sisk; *Adaptation:* Bert Granet; *Sc:* Dalton Trumbo. (1:19)

Sentimental drama of a benevolent store-keeper, his long-standing feud with the local banker and their offspring who fall in love. Based on the novel by Phil Stong.

602. Career Woman (20th Century–Fox; 1936). *Cast:* Claire Trevor, Michael Whalen, El Brendel, Edward Brophy, Isabel Jewell, Eric Linden, Gene Lockhart, Eily Malyon, Guinn Williams, Sterling Holloway, Charles Middleton, J. Frank McGlynn. *D:* Lewis Seiler.

B romance.

603. Careers (WB/F.N.; 1929). *Cast:* Antonio Moreno, Billie Dove, Noah Beery, Carmel Myers, Holmes Herbert, Thelma Todd, Sojin, Kithnou, Robert Frazer, Gustav von Seyffertitz. *D:* John Francis Dillon; *Sc:* Forrest Halsey; *Song:* Al Bryan, George W. Meyer.

Part-talkie marital drama, based on a play by Alfred Schirokauer and Paul Rosenhayn.

604. Carefree (RKO; 1938). *Cast:* Fred Astaire (who also choreographed with Hermes Pan), Ginger Rogers, Ralph Bellamy, Luella Gear, Jack Carson, Clarence Kolb, Franklin Pangborn, Walter Kingsford, Hattie McDaniel, Kay Sutton, Robert B. Mitchell, St. Brendan's Boys Choir, Tom Tully (film debut). *D:* Mark Sandrich; *P:* Pandro S. Berman; *Original Idea:* Guy Endore, Marian Ainsley; *St & Adaptation:* Dudley Nichols, Hagar Wilde; *Sc:* Allan Scott, Ernest Pagano; *Art-Set Decoration:* (A.A.N.) Van Nest Polglase; *Music:* (A.A.N.) Victor Baravalle; *Songs:* "Change Partners and Dance With Me" (A.A.N. — Best Song), "I Used to Be Color Blind," "Since They Turned 'Loch Lomond' Into Swing" and "The Yam" by Irving Berlin. (1:25) (video)

Musical-comedy with the accent on song and dance. Notable as the first Astaire-Rogers musical to lose money for RKO.

605. The Careless Age (WB/F.N.; 1929). *Cast:* Douglas Fairbanks, Jr., Carmel Myers, Loretta Young, Kenneth Thomson, Holmes Herbert, Wilfred Noy, Ilka Chase, Doris Lloyd. *D:* John Griffith Wray; *Adaptation:* Harrison Macklyn.

Jealousy rears its ugly head in this romantic drama, based on the play "Diversion" by John Van Druten.

606. Careless Lady (Fox; 1932). *Cast:* Joan Bennett, John Boles, J.M. Kerrigan, Josephine Hull, Minna Gombell, Nora Lane, Weldon Heyburn, Fortunio Bonanova (film debut), Maude Turner Gordon, William Pawley, Richard Tucker, Martha Mattox, James Todd, Raul Roulien, Howard Phillips. *D:* Kenneth MacKenna; *St:* Reita Lambert; *Sc:* Guy Bolton.

A small town girl is introduced to sophistication and romance.

607. The Carnation Kid (Paramount; 1929). *Cast:* Frances Lee, Douglas McLean, Lorraine Eddy, Maurice Black, Bert Swor, Jr., Carl Stockdale, Francis McDonald, Charles Hill Mailes. *D:* E. Mason Hopper; *P:* Al Christie (for Christie Film Co.); *Sc:* Alfred A. Cohn.

Part-talkie melodrama of a salesman who saves the life of the local D.A.

608. Carnival (Columbia; 1935).
Cast: Jimmy Durante, Lee Tracy, Sally
Eilers, Florence Rice, Thomas Jackson,
Lucille Ball, Paul Hurst, Dickie
Walters, Fred Kelsey. *D:* Walter Lang;
St & Sc: Robert Riskin. (G.B. title: *Car-
nival Nights*)
Comedy.

609. Carnival Boat (RKO-
Pathé; 1932). *Cast:* Bill Boyd, Ginger
Rogers, Hobart Bosworth, Fred Kohler,
Marie Prevost, Edgar Kennedy, Harry
Sweet, Charles Sellon, Eddie Chandler,
Walter Percival, Robert Perry. *D:*
Albert S. Rogell; *P:* Charles R. Rogers;
As.P.: Harry Joe Brown; *St:* Marion
Jackson, Don Ryan; *Sc:* James
Seymour. (1:01)
A young man rejects his father's
lumber business and joins a carnival
boat where he finds romance.

610. Carnival Lady (Goldsmith;
1933). *Cast:* Boots Mallory, Jason
Robards, Gertrude Astor, Kit Guard.
D: Howard Higgin; *P:* Ken Goldsmith.
Romantic melodrama.

Carnival Nights (G.B. title) *see*
Carnival

611. Carnival Queen (Universal;
1937). *Cast:* Dorothea Kent, Robert
Wilcox, Hobart Cavanaugh. *D:* Nate
Watt; *P:* Robert Presnell. (1:06)
B melodrama of a traveling carnival and its involvement with the
criminal element.

612. Carolina (Fox; 1934). *Cast:*
Janet Gaynor, Lionel Barrymore,
Robert Young, Henrietta Crosman,
Richard Cromwell, Mona Barrie, Shir-
ley Temple, Stepin Fetchit, Ronnie
Cosbey, Jackie Cosbey, Almeda Fowler,
Alden Chase. *D:* Henry King; *P:* Darryl
F. Zanuck; *Sc:* Reginald Berkeley.
(G.B. title: *The House of Connelly*) (1:25)
The romance of a southern planta-
tion owner and a Yankee's daughter.

Based on the play "The House of Connelly" by Paul Green.

613. Caryl of the Mountains
(Reliable; 1936). *Cast:* Rin-Tin-Tin, Jr.,
Francis X. Bushman, Jr., Lois Wild(e),
Josef Swickard, Earl Dwire, Robert
Walker, George Chesebro, Steve Clark,
Jack Hendricks. *D:* Bernard B. Ray; *P:*
Harry S. Fraser; *St:* James Oliver Cur-
wood; *Sc:* Tom Gibson. (1:00)
The low-budget adventures of a
Mountie and his dog. Filmed before in
1914, directed by and starring Tom Sant-
schi. See also *Trails of the Wild* (q.v.).

**614. The Case Against Mrs.
Ames** (Paramount; 1936). *Cast:*
Madeleine Carroll (American debut),
George Brent, Arthur Treacher, Alan
Baxter, Beulah Bondi, Alan Mowbray,
Esther Dale, Ed Brophy, Richard Carle,
Guy Bates Post, June Brewster, Brenda
Fowler, Ward Bond. *D:* William A.
Seiter; *P:* Walter Wanger; *St:* Arthur
Somers Roche; *Sc:* Gene Towne,
Graham Baker. (1:25)
A D.A. falls for a woman he is pro-
secuting in a murder case.

The Case of Mrs. Pembroke
(G.B. title) *see* **Two Against the World**

**615. The Case of Sergeant
Grischa** (RKO; 1930). *Cast:* Chester
Morris (Sgt. Grischa), Jean Hersholt,
Betty Compson, Alec B. Francis, Gus-
tav von Seyffertitz, Paul McAllister,
Leyland Hodgson, Bernard Siegel,
Frank McCormack, Raymond Whi-
taker. *D:* Herbert Brenon; *P:* William
LeBaron; *Sc:* Elizabeth Meehan,
Brenon; *Sound Recording:* (A.A.N.) John
Tribby (1929–30).
Wartime drama of a Russian sol-
dier who escapes a P.O.W. camp, tak-
ing refuge with a German girl. Based on
the novel by Arnold Zweig. A box office
flop.

616. The Case of the Black Cat
(WB/F.N.; 1936). *Cast:* Ricardo Cortez
(Perry Mason), June Travis (Della
Street), Harry Davenport, Jane Bryan,

Carlyle Moore, Jr., Craig Reynolds, Gordon (Bill) Elliott, Clarence Wilson, Nedda Harrigan, Garry Owen, Guy Usher, George Rosener. *D:* William McGann; *P:* Bryan Foy; *Sc:* F. Hugh Herbert. (1:06)

The fifth entry in this studio's low-budget mystery series of "Perry Mason" mysteries, this one concerning the murder of a millionaire. Based on the book by Erle Stanley Gardner. The original director Alan Crosland was killed six days into production in an unrelated auto crash at the age of 41-years.

617. The Case of the Curious Bride (WB/F.N.; 1935). *Cast:* Warren William (Perry Mason), Margaret Lindsay, Donald Woods, Claire Dodd, Allen Jenkins, Philip Reed, Winifred Shaw, Barton MacLane, Warren Hymer, Paul Hurst, Henry Kolker, Thomas Jackson, Charles Richman, Olin Howland, Errol Flynn, Robert Gleckler, James Donlan, Mayo Methot, George Humbert. *D:* Michael Curtiz; *P:* Harry Joe Brown; *Sc:* Tom Reed. (1:20)

Second entry in the "Perry Mason" series with a woman thinking her husband dead, only to find he is still alive. Based on the book by Erle Stanley Gardner.

618. The Case of the Howling Dog (WB; 1934). *Cast:* Warren William (Perry Mason), Mary Astor, Allen Jenkins, Grant Mitchell, Helen Trenholme (film debut), Dorothy Tree, Helen Lowell, Gordon Westcott, Harry Tyler, Russell Hicks, Arthur Aylesworth, Addison Richards, Eddie Shubert, Frank Reicher, Harry Seymour, James Burtis. *D:* Alan Crosland; *P:* Sam Bischoff; *Sc:* Ben Markson. (1:15)

Premiere entry in the "Perry Mason" series, involving the mystery of two men, both claiming to be the husband of the same woman. Based on the book by Erle Stanley Gardner.

619. The Case of the Lucky Legs (WB/F.N.; 1935). *Cast:* Warren William

(Perry Mason), Genevieve Tobin (Della Street), Allen Jenkins, Patricia Ellis, Lyle Talbot, Barton MacLane, Peggy Shannon, Porter Hall, Mary Treen, Henry O'Neill, Craig Reynolds, Olin Howland, Charles Wilson, Anita Kerry, Joseph Crehan, Joseph Downing. *D:* Archie Mayo; *P:* Henry Blanke; *Adaptation:* Jerome Chodorov; *Sc:* Ben Markson, Brown Holmes. (1:17)

The third entry in the "Perry Mason" series, involving the murder of a beauty contest promoter. Based on the book by Erle Stanley Gardner.

The Case of the Missing Blonde (G.B. title) *see* **Lady in the Morgue**

620. The Case of the Missing Man (Columbia; 1935). *Cast:* Roger Pryor, Joan Perry (film debut), Paul Guilfoyle, Arthur Hohl, Tom Dugan, James Burke, Ann Doran, George McKay, Arthur Rankin, Thurston Hall. *D:* D. Ross Lederman; *St & Sc:* Harold Buchman, Lee Loeb.

B mystery melodrama.

621. The Case of the Stuttering Bishop (WB/F.N.; 1937). *Cast:* Donald Woods (Perry Mason), Ann Dvorak, Anne Nagel, Linda Perry, Craig Reynolds, Gordon Oliver, Joseph Crehan, Helen MacKellar, Veda Ann Borg, Edward McWade, Frank Faylen, Selmer Jackson, Tom Kennedy. *D:* William Clemens; *P:* Bryan Foy; *Sc:* Don Ryan, Kenneth Gamet. (1:10)

Sixth and final entry in the "Perry Mason" series with Mason trying to prove the heir to a fortune is the legitimate one. Based on the book by Erle Stanley Gardner.

622. The Case of the Velvet Claws (WB/F.N.; 1936). *Cast:* Warren William (Perry Mason), Claire Dodd (Della Street), Winifred Shaw, Gordon (Bill) Elliott, Paula Stone, Clara Blandick, Addison Richards, Eddie Acuff, Dick Purcell, Stuart Holmes, Kenneth Harlan, Joseph King, Olin Howland,

Robert Middlemass, Ruth Robinson. *D:* William Clemens; *P:* Bryan Foy; *Sc:* Tom Reed. (1:03)

Fourth entry in the "Perry Mason" series with Perry investigating a case of blackmail and murder. Based on the book by Erle Stanley Gardner.

Casino De Paree (G.B. title) *see* **Go Into Your Dance**

623. The Casino Murder Case (MGM; 1935). *Cast:* Paul Lukas (Philo Vance), Rosalind Russell, Eric Blore, Donald Cook, Louise Fazenda, Ted Healy, Isabel Jewell, Leo G. Carroll, Arthur Byron, Alison Skipworth, Leslie Fenton, Claudelle Kaye, Keye Luke, William Demarest, Louise Henry, Charles Sellon, Purnell Pratt. *D:* Edwin L. Marin; *P:* Lucien Hubbard; *Sc:* Hubbard, Florence Ryerson, Edgar Allan Woolf. (1:25)

A "Philo Vance" murder-mystery concerning the murder of a member of an eccentric family. Based on the book by S.S. Van Dine.

624. Cassidy of the Bar 20 (Paramount; 1938). *Cast:* Bill Boyd (Hoppy), Russell Hayden (Lucky Jenkins), Frank Darien, Nora Lane, Robert Fiske, John Elliott, Margaret Marquis, Carleton Young, Gertrude Hoffman, Gordon Hart, Ed Cassidy. *D:* Lesley Selander; *P:* Harry M. Sherman; *Sc:* Norman Houston. (0:56)

The 22nd entry in the "Hopalong Cassidy" series with the boys going to the aid of Hoppy's ex-girlfriend.

Cast Iron (G.B. title) *see* **The Virtuous Sin**

625. Castle on the Hudson (WB; 1939–40). *Cast:* John Garfield, Pat O'Brien, Ann Sheridan, Burgess Meredith, Jerome Cowan, Henry O'Neill, Guinn Williams, John Litel, Willard Robertson, Barbara Pepper, Robert Strange, Billy Wayne, Nedda Harrigan. *D:* Anatole Litvak; *As.P.:* Sam Bischoff;

Sc: Seton I. Miller, Brown Holmes, Courtney Terrett. (1:17)

Prison melodrama of the conflict between a hardened criminal and the prison warden. A remake of *20,000 Years in Sing Sing* (q.v.). Based on the book of that title by Warden Lewis E. Lawes.

626. The Cat and the Canary (Paramount; 1939). *Cast:* Bob Hope (starring debut), Paulette Goddard, Gale Sondergaard, John Beal, Douglass Montgomery, George Zucco, Nydia Westman, Elizabeth Patterson, Willard Robertson, Charles Lane, John Wray, Dwight Frye. *D:* Elliott Nugent; *P:* Arthur Hornblow, Jr.; *Sc:* Walter DeLeon, Lynn Starling. (1:12)

Classic comedy-thriller of an old dark house where a number of people are invited to the reading of a will. Based on the play by John Willard, it was previously filmed in 1927 by this studio with Laura La Plante and Tully Marshall by director Paul Leni and is considered the fore-runner of all "old dark house" mysteries. Remade in 1930 as *The Cat Creeps* (q.v.). A British version under the original title appeared in 1978. The success of this Hope-Goddard venture led in 1940 to a remake of *The Ghost Breaker(s)*.

627. The Cat and the Fiddle (MGM; 1933). *Cast:* Jeanette MacDonald (in her MGM debut), Ramon Novarro, Charles Butterworth, Frank Morgan, Jean Hersholt, Vivienne Segal (final film — ret.), Henry Armetta, Frank Conroy, Joseph Cawthorn, Adrienne D'Ambricourt, Sterling Holloway, Leonid Kinskey. *D:* William K. Howard; *P:* Bernard Hyman; *Sc:* Sam and Bella Spewack; *Choreographer:* Albertina Rasch. (1:30)

Comic operetta of Bohemian life in Brussels, Belgium, by Jerome Kern and Otto Harbach, based on their show. The final scene is in 2-color technicolor.

628. The Cat Creeps (Universal; 1930). *Cast:* Raymond Hackett, Helen

Twelvetrees, Jean Hersholt, Neil Hamilton, Lilyan Tashman, Theodore von Eltz, Lawrence Grant, Montagu Love, Elizabeth Patterson, Lupita Tovar, Blanche Frederici. *D:* Rupert Julian (final film); *Sc:* Gladys Lehman, William Hurlbut. (1:15)

Remake of the silent 1927 classic *The Cat and the Canary.* Based on the 1922 play by John Willard, it was remade in 1939 (q.v.) and again in 1978.

629. The Cat's Paw (Fox/Harold Lloyd Productions; 1934). *Cast:* Harold Lloyd, Una Merkel, George Barbier, Nat Pendleton, Grant Mitchell, Vince Barnett, Alan Dinehart, Grace Bradley, J. Farrell MacDonald, Warren Hymer, Frank Sheridan, Edwin Maxwell, Dewey Robinson, Fred Warren. *D:* Sam Taylor; *P:* Lloyd; *Sc:* Lloyd, Taylor. (1:30)

A missionary's son returns to the United States, only to become the pawn of crooked politicians. The comedy is based on a story by Clarence Budington Kelland.

630. The Cattle Raiders (Columbia; 1938). *Cast:* Charles Starrett, Donald Grayson, Iris Meredith, The Sons of the Pioneers with Bob Nolan, Dick Curtis, Allen Brook, Edward LeSaint, Edmund Cobb, George Chesebro, Art Mix, Ed Coxen, Steve Clark, Allan Sears, Ed Peil, Jim Thorpe, Hank Bell, Blackie Whiteford, Jack Clifford, Frank Ellis, Curley Dresden. *D:* Sam Nelson; *Sc:* Joseph Poland, Ed Earl Repp. (1:01)

Charles Starrett western of a man falsely accused of murder by his friend.

631. The Cattle Thief (Columbia; 1936). *Cast:* Ken Maynard, Geneva Mitchell, Ward Bond, Roger Williams, Jim Marcus, Sheldon Lewis, Edward Cecil, Jack Kirk, Edward Hearn, Al Taylor, Glenn Strange, Bud McClure, Jack King. *D:* Spencer Gordon Bennet; *St:* J.A. Duffy; *Sc:* Nate Gatzert. (0:58)

Ken Maynard western with May-nard posing as an itinerant peddler to get the goods on an outlaw gang.

632. Caught (Paramount; 1931). *Cast:* Richard Arlen, Louise Dresser (Calamity Jane), Frances Dee, Tom Kennedy, Syd Saylor, Edward LeSaint, Martin Burton, Marcia Manners, Guy Oliver, Charles K. French, Jim Mason, Jack Clifford. *D:* Edward Sloman; *St:* Sam and Bella Spewack; *Sc:* Agnes Brand Leahy, Keene Thompson. (1:11)

Western of a cavalry officer who discovers that his mother is Calamity Jane.

Caught by Television (G.B. title) *see* **Trapped by Television**

633. Caught Cheating (Tiffany; 1931). *Cast:* Charlie Murray, George Sidney, Dorothy Christy, Robert Ellis. *D:* Frank Strayer.

"Poverty Row" comedy.

634. Caught in the Fog (WB–Vitaphone; 1928). *Cast:* May McAvoy, Conrad Nagel, Mack Swain, Ruth Cherrington, Charles Gerrard, Hugh Herbert, Emile Chautard. *D:* Howard Bretherton; *St:* Jerome Kingston; *Adaptation:* Charles Condon.

Part-talkie comedy-drama of impersonation sparked by the search for a valuable necklace aboard a houseboat.

635. Caught Plastered (RKO; 1931). *Cast:* Bert Wheeler, Robert Woolsey, Dorothy Lee, Lucy Beaumont, DeWitt Jennings, Jason Robards, Charles B. Middleton, Josephine Whittell, James Farley, Nora Cecil, William Scott, Arthur Housman. *D:* William A. Seiter; *As.P.:* Douglas MacLean; *St:* MacLean; *Sc:* Ralph Spence; *Additional Dialogue:* Eddie Welch. (1:08)

Comedy of two zanies who help a woman save her drugstore from a villain.

636. Caught Short (MGM; 1930). *Cast:* Marie Dressler, Polly Moran,

Charles Morton, Anita Page, Greta Grandstedt, T. Roy Barnes, Roscoe Ates, Douglas Haig, Edward Dillon, Greta Mann, Thomas Conlin, Nanci Price, Herbert Prior. *D:* Charles Reisner; *Sc:* Willard Mack, Robert Hopkins.

Dressler-Moran comedy of two feuding boarding house owners whose children are in love with each other. A Cosmopolitan Production.

637. Cauliflower Alley (Columbia; 1932). *Cast:* Thelma Todd, Leo Carrillo, Nat Pendleton, Dickie Moore, Henry Armetta. *D:* Xxxx Xxxx.

Low-budget comedy.

638. Cavalcade (Fox; 1933). *Cast:* Clive Brook (Robert Marryot), Diana Wynyard (A.A.N. for B.A. as Jane Marryot), Ursula Jeans (Fanny Bridges), Una O'Connor (American debut as Ellen Bridges), Herbert Mundin (Alfred Bridges), Frank Lawton (Joe Marryot), John Warburton (Edward Marryot), Merle Tottenham (Annie), Irene Browne (Margaret Harris), Beryl Mercer (cook), Margaret Lindsay (Edith Harris), Tempe Pigott (Mrs. Snapper), Billy Bevan (George Grainger), Desmond Roberts (Ronnie James), Frank Atkinson (Uncle Dick), Ann Shaw (Mirabelle), Adele Crane (Ada), Will Stanton (Tommy Jolly), Stuart Hall (Lt. Edgar), Mary Forbes (Duchess of Churt), C. Montague Shaw (Major Domo), Lionel Belmore (Uncle George), Dick Henderson, Jr. (young Edward), Douglas Scott (young Joey), Sheila MacGill (young Edith), Bonita Granville (young Fanny), Howard Davies, Betty Grable, David Torrence, Lawrence Grant, Winter Hall, Claude King, Pat Somerset, Douglas Walton, Tom Ricketts, Brandon Hurst, Harry Allen, John Rogers. *D:* (A.A.) Frank Lloyd; *P:* Winfield Sheehan; *Sc:* Reginald Berkeley, Sonya Levien; *Art-Set Decoration:* (A.A.) William S. Darling; *Choreography:* Sammy Lee; *Song:* "Twentieth Century Blues" by Noel Coward. (1:49)

33 years in the lives of members of a British family who endure war, scandal, death and disaster. Based on the play by Noel Coward. This film received the Academy Award for Best Picture of 1933, voted "Best Film of the Year" by *Film Daily,* placed #1 on the "10 Best" list of the *New York Times,* as well as being voted one of the "10 Best" films of the year by the National Board of Review. One of the 11 top grossing films of 1933.

639. Cavalcade of the West (Diversion; 1936). *Cast:* Hoot Gibson, Rex Lease, Earl Dwire. *D:* Harry Fraser; *P:* Walter Futter.

Hoot Gibson western.

640. Cavalier of the West (Artclass; 1931). *Cast:* Harry Carey, Kane Richmond, Carmen LaRoux, Paul Panzer, Ted Adams, Ben Corbett, Maston Williams, Carlotta Monti, George Hayes. *D:* J.P. McCarthy; *Sc:* McCarthy. (1:05)

Harry Carey western of an impending conflict between Indians and whites.

641. Cavalry (Republic-Supreme; 1936). *Cast:* Bob Steele, Frances Grant, Karl Hackett, William Welch, Earle Ross, Hal Price, Ed Cassidy, Perry Murdock, Budd Buster, Earl Dwire, William Desmond, Horace B. Carpenter. *D:* Robert N. Bradbury (Steele's real-life father); *P:* A.W. Hackel; *Sc:* George Plympton. (1:03)

Post Civil War Bob Steele western.

The Cave-In (G.B. title) *see* **Draegerman Courage**

642. Ceiling Zero (WB/F.N.; 1935). *Cast:* James Cagney (Dizzy Davis), Pat O'Brien (Jack Lee), June Travis (Tommy Thomas), Stuart Erwin (Texas Clark), Barton MacLane (Al Stone), Henry Wadsworth (Tay Lawson), Martha Tibbetts (Mary Lee), Isabel Jewell (Lou Clark), Craig Reynolds (Joe Allen), Richard (Dick) Purcell (film debut as Smiley Johnson), Carlyle

Moore, Jr. (Eddie Payson), Addison Richards (Fred Adams), James H. Bush (Buzz Gordon), Robert Light (Les Bogan), Pat West (Baldy Wright), Edward Gargan (Doc Wilson), Garry Owen (Mike Owens), Mathilde Comont (Mama Gini), Carol Hughes (Birdie), Gordon (Bill) Elliott, Frank Tomick, Paul Mantz, Grover Liggon. *D:* Howard Hawks; *P:* Harry Joe Brown; *Sc:* Frank Wead, Morrie Ryskind (unc.). (1:35)

This drama of a reckless and irresponsible air mail carrier placed #7 on the "10 Best" list of the National Board of Review in 1936. A Cosmopolitan production based on the play by Frank Wead. Remade in 1939 as *International Squadron* (q.v.), a film not released until 1941.

643. Central Airport (WB/F.N.; 1933). *Cast:* Richard Barthelmess, Sally Eilers, Tom Brown, Grant Mitchell, James Murray, Willard Robertson, Arthur Vinton, Charles Sellon, Louise Beavers, Glenda Farrell, Harold Huber, J. Carrol Naish, Claire McDowell, John Wayne (bit-part). *D:* William A. Wellman; *Sc:* Rian James, James Seymour. (1:09)

Aerial drama of a love-triangle. Based on the story "Hawk's Mate" by John Moffitt.

644. Central Park (WB/F.N.; 1932). *Cast:* Joan Blondell, Wallace Ford, Guy Kibbee, Henry B. Walthall, Patricia Ellis, Charles Sellon, Wade Boteler, Holmes Herbert, John Wray, Harold Huber, Henry Armetta, George Pat Collins, William Pawley, Harry Holman, Bud Flanagan (Dennis O'Keefe). *D:* John Adolfi; *St:* Ward Morehouse; *Sc:* Morehouse, Earl Baldwin. (1:01)

A young woman unknowingly gets involved with gangsters planning to rob a benefit dinner dance at the Central Park Casino in this B melodrama.

645. Chained (MGM; 1934). *Cast:* Joan Crawford (Diana), Clark Gable (Mike), Otto Kruger (Mr. Fields), Stuart Erwin (Johnny), Una O'Connor (Ann), Marjorie Gateson (Mrs. Field), Adrian Rosley, Louis Natheaux, Ward Bond, Lee Phelps, Ernie Alexander, Nora Cecil, Grace Hayle, Mickey Rooney, Akim Tamiroff, Paul Porcasi, Chris-Pin Martin, George Humbert, Gino Corrado, William Stack, Sam Flint, Wade Boteler, Kendall McComas. *D:* Clarence Brown; *P:* Hunt Stromberg; *St:* Edgar Selwyn; *Sc:* John Lee Mahin. (1:17)

This romantic drama of a woman torn between her husband and a new love was one of the 15 top grossing films of 1934.

The Challenge (G.B. title) *see* **Woman Hungry**

Challenge of the Frontier *see* **Man of the Forest**

The Challenger *see* **Lady and Gent**

646. The Champ (MGM; 1931). *Cast:* Wallace Beery (A.A. for B.A. as Champ, shared with Fredric March in *Dr. Jekyll and Mr. Hyde* (q.v.), Jackie Cooper (Dink), Irene Rich (Linda Carson), Roscoe Ates (Sponge), Edward Brophy (Tim), Hale Hamilton (Tony), Marcia Mae Jones (Mary Lou), Jesse Scott (Jonah), Frank Hagney (Manuel), Lee Phelps (Louie the bartender). *D:* (A.A.N.) King Vidor; *As.P.:* Harry Rapf; *Original Story:* (A.A.) Frances Marion; *Sc:* Marion, Leonard Praskins; *Additional Dialogue:* Wanda Tuchock. (1:27) (video)

The classic sentimental story of a young boy's belief in his father, a has-been prize-fighter. The film received an A.A.N. for Best Picture, as well as placing #2 on the "10 Best" list of *Film Daily*. Remade in 1953 as *The Clown* with Red Skelton and in 1979 as *The Champ.*

647. Champagne Charlie (20th Century-Fox; 1936). *Cast:* Herbert

Mundin, Helen Wood, Paul Cavanagh, Montagu Love, Noel Madison, Thomas Beck, Minna Gombell. *D:* James Tinling; *P:* Edward T. Lowe; *Sc:* Allen Rivkin.

B comedy which was remade in 1944.

648. Champagne for Breakfast (Columbia; 1935). *Cast:* Lila Lee, Hardie Albright, Joan Marsh, Bradley Page, Sidney Toler, Vince Barnett, Mary Carlisle. *D:* Melville Brown.

B romantic comedy.

649. Champagne Waltz (Paramount; 1937). *Cast:* Fred MacMurray, Gladys Swarthout, Jack Oakie, Herman Bing, Vivienne Osborne, Maude Eburne, Ernest Cossart, Martha O'Driscoll, Fritz Leiber, Maurice Cass, Benny Baker, Veloz & Yolanda, Guy Bates Post, Michael Visaroff, Frank Forest. *D:* A. Edward Sutherland; *P:* Harlan Thompson; *St:* Billy Wilder, Hy Kraft; *Sc:* Don Hartman, Frank Butler; *Songs:* Sam Coslow, Burton Lane, Leo Robin. (1:27)

This romantic comedy of a clash between a jazz cafe and a neighboring waltz palace flopped at the box office.

650. Chance at Heaven (RKO; 1933). *Cast:* Joel McCrea, Marion Nixon, Ginger Rogers, Virginia Hammond, Andy Devine, George Meeker, Lucien Littlefield, Ann Shoemaker. *D:* William A. Seiter; *As.P.:* H.N. Swanson; *St:* Vina Delmar; *Sc:* Julien Josephson, Sarah Y. Mason. (1:11)

Small town romantic drama.

651. Chances (WB/F.N.; 1930–31). *Cast:* Douglas Fairbanks, Jr., Anthony Bushell, Rose Hobart, Mary (Forbes) Forbestein, Holmes Herbert, William Austin, Florence Britton, Robert Bennett, Mae Madison, Edmund Breon, Harry Allen, Ethel Griffies, Edward Morgan. *D:* Allan Dwan; *Sc:* Waldemar Young. (G.B. title: *Changes*) (1:12)

Romantic war drama of two brothers on leave in London who fall for the same girl. Based on the novel by A. Hamilton Gibbs.

652. Chandu on Magic Island (Principal; 1934). *Cast:* Bela Lugosi, Maria Alba. *D:* Ray Taylor; *P:* Sol Lesser; *Sc:* Barry Barringer. (see also *The Return of Chandu*)

Feature-version of the last eight chapters of the serial "The Return of Chandu."

653. Chandu the Magician (Fox; 1932). *Cast:* Edmund Lowe (Chandu), Bela Lugosi, Irene Ware, Herbert Mundin, Henry B. Walthall, June (Lang) Vlasek, Weldon Heyburn, Virginia Hammond, Nestor Aber. *D:* Marcel Varnel, William Cameron Menzies; *St:* Harry A. Earnshaw, Vera M. Oldham, R.R. Morgan; *Sc:* Philip Klein, Barry Connors. (1:10) (video)

Chandu is a spiritualist who is out to save the world from a madman with a death ray.

654. Change of Heart (Fox; 1934). *Cast:* Janet Gaynor, Charles Farrell, Ginger Rogers, James Dunn, Beryl Mercer, Gustav von Seyffertitz, Shirley Temple, Fiske O'Hara, Mary Carr, Theodore von Eltz, Irene Franklin, Mischa Auer, Jane Darwell, Kenneth Thomson, Barbara Barondess, Drue Leyton, Nella Walker. *D:* John G. Blystone; *Sc:* Sonya Levien, James Gleason, Samuel Hoffenstein. (1:14)

Romantic drama which is the final film (of twelve) to team the popular duo of Charles Farrell and Janet Gaynor. Based on the novel by Kathleen Norris, it was remade in 1938 (see below).

655. Change of Heart (20th Century–Fox; 1938). *Cast:* Gloria Stuart, Lyle Talbot, Michael Whalen, Delmar Watson, Jane Darwell. *D:* James Tinling.

A low-budget remake of the above.

Changes (G.B. title) *see* **Chances**

656. The Charge of the Light Brigade (WB; 1936). *Cast:* Errol Flynn (Capt. Geoffrey Vickers), Olivia de Havilland (Elsa Campbell), Patric Knowles (Capt. Perry Vickers), Henry Stephenson (Sir Charles Macefield), Nigel Bruce (Sir Benjamin Warrenton), Donald Crisp (Colonel Campbell), David Niven (Capt. James Randall), G.P. Huntley, Jr. (Major Jowett), Spring Byington (Lady Octavia Warrenton), C. Henry Gordon (Surat Khan), Robert Barrat (Count Igor Volonoff), E.E. Clive (Sir Humphrey Harcourt), Lumsden Hare (Colonel Woodward), Walter Holbrook (Cornet Barclay), Charles Sedgwick (Cornet Pearson), J. Carrol Naish (Subahdar Major Singh), Scotty Beckett (Prema Singh), Princess Beigum (Prema's mother), Helen Sanborn (Mrs. Jowett), George Regas (wazir), Crauford Kent (Capt. Brown), George David (Suristani), Reginald Sheffield (Bentham), Georges Renavent (General Canrobert), Charles Croker King (Lord Cardigan), Brandon Hurst (Lord Raglan), Boyd Irwin (General Dunbar), Gordon Hart (Colonel Coventry), Holmes Herbert (General O'Neill), Carlos San Martin, Jimmy Aubrey, Herbert Evans, Harry Semels, Michael Visaroff, Frank Lackteen, Martin Garralaga, Colin Kenny. *D:* Michael Curtiz; *P:* Hal B. Wallis; *Assistant Producer:* Sam Bischoff; *St:* Michel Jacoby (based on Alfred Lord Tennyson's poem); *Sc:* Jacoby, Rowland Leigh; *Music:* (A.A.N.) Max Steiner; *Assistant Director:* (A.A.) Jack Sullivan; *Sound Recording:* (A.A.N.) Nathan Levinson. (1:56) (video)

Romance in the midst of warfare in the Middle East in 1850 is the central theme of this lavish production, the highlight being the final charge at Balaklava, which itself was directed by 2nd unit director, B. Reeves Eason. One of the 38 top grossing films of 1936-37, it was previously filmed in 1912 by Edison. Computer-colored by Turner Entertainment in 1987.

657. Charley's Aunt (Columbia; 1930). *Cast:* Charles Ruggles, June Collyer, Hugh Williams (film debut), Doris Lloyd, Phillips Smalley, Rodney McLennon, Flora Sheffield, Halliwell Hobbes, Flora LeBreton. *D:* Al Christie; *Sc:* F. McGrew Willis.

An Oxford student gets his roommate to pose as his maiden aunt to chaperone a date, setting the stage for a series of comic consequences. Based on the famous 1896 play by Brandon Thomas, it was previously filmed in 1915, in 1925 by Al Christy for Producers Distributing Corporation with Sydney Chaplin, with later versions in 1941 for 20th-Fox with Jack Benny and a British musical version in 1952 entitled *Where's Charley?*

658. Charlie Chan at Monte Carlo (20th Century-Fox; 1937). *Cast:* Warner Oland (film finale—d. 1937), Keye Luke (Lee Chan), Virginia Field, Sidney Blackmer, Harold Huber, Louis Mercier, Robert Kent, Georges Renavent, George Davis, George Lynn, Edward Raquello, John Bleifer. *D:* Eugene Forde; *P:* John Stone; *St:* Robert Ellis, Helen Logan (based on the character created by Earl Derr Biggers); *Sc:* Jerry Cady, Charles Belden. (1:11)

Murder in Monaco.

659. Charlie Chan at the Circus (20th Century-Fox; 1936). *Cast:* Warner Oland (Charlie Chan), Keye Luke (Lee Chan), Olive Brasno, George Brasno, Francis Ford, Maxine Reiner, John McGuire, Shirley Deane, J. Carrol Naish, Drue Leyton, Paul Stanton, Shia Jung, Boothe Howard. *D:* Harry Lachman; *P:* John Stone; *Sc:* Robert Ellis, Helen Logan. (1:12)

Chan can't even take his family on an outing to the circus without getting involved in murder.

660. Charlie Chan at the Olympics (20th Century-Fox; 1937). *Cast:* Warner Oland (Charlie Chan), Keye Luke (Lee Chan), Katherine de Mille,

Pauline Moore, C. Henry Gordon, Jonathan Hale, Allan Lane, John Eldredge, Andrew Tombes, Morgan Wallace, Howard Hickman, Layne Tom, Jr. (Charlie Chan, Jr.), Frederick Vogeding. *D:* H. Bruce Humberstone; *As.P.:* John Stone; *St:* Paul Burger; *Sc:* Robert Ellis, Helen Logan. (1:11)

Chan goes to the 1936 Berlin Olympics to retrieve a stolen airplane robot control.

661. Charlie Chan at the Opera (20th Century–Fox; 1936). *Cast:* Warner Oland (Charlie Chan), Keye Luke (Lee Chan), Boris Karloff (Gravelle), Charlotte Henry, Thomas Beck, Gregory Gaye, Nedda Harrigan, William Demarest, Frank Conroy, Margaret Irving, Guy Usher, Tom McGuire, Maurice Cass. *D:* H. Bruce Humberstone; *As.P.:* John Stone; *St:* Bess Meredyth; *Sc:* W. Scott Darling, Charles Belden. (1:08) (video)

An escape from a mental asylum is followed by two murders at an opera house. The opera in production is "Carnival" by Oscar Levant, William Kernell (libretto) and Charles Maxwell (orchestration).

662. Charlie Chan at the Race Track (20th Century–Fox; 1936). *Cast:* Warner Oland (Charlie Chan), Keye Luke (Lee Chan), Helen Wood, Thomas Beck, Alan Dinehart, Gavin Muir, Frankie Darro, Paul Fix, G.P. Huntley, Jr., John H. Allen, Jonathan Hale, Conn Rogers, Frank (Junior) Coghlan, Jr., Gloria Ray, Harry Jans. *D:* H. Bruce Humberstone; *St:* Lou Breslow, Saul Elkins; *Sc:* Robert Ellis, Helen Logan, Edward T. Lowe. (1:10)

A photo-finish camera is the solution to a race track murder.

663. Charlie Chan at Treasure Island (20th Century–Fox; 1939). *Cast:* Sidney Toler (Chan), Cesar Romero, Pauline Moore, Sen Yung, Douglass Dumbrille, Sally Blane, Billie Seward, Louis Jean Heydt, Charles Halton,

Douglas Fowley, Gerald Mohr, Trevor Bardette, June Gale, Wally Vernon, Donald MacBride. *D:* Norman Foster; *As.P.:* Edward Kaufman; *St & Sc:* John Larkin. (1:14)

Charlie goes up against a blackmailing mystic at the San Francisco Exposition.

664. Charlie Chan Carries On (Fox; 1931). *Cast:* Warner Oland, Marguerite Churchill, John Garrick, George Brent, Warren Hymer, C. Henry Gordon, Lumsden Hare, Jason Robards, Peter Gawthorne, John T. Murray, William Holden, Zeffie Tilbury, John Rogers, Marjorie White, John Swor, Harry Beresford, Betty Francisco, J. Gunnis Davis, Goodee Montgomery. *D:* Hamilton MacFadden. *Sc:* Philip Klein, Barry Connors.

Premiere entry in the B series with Warner Oland making his debut as "Charlie Chan," a character created by Earl Derr Biggers. In 1926 the character of "Charlie Chan" (played by George Kuwa), first appeared in a serial titled *House Without a Key* in a supporting role, followed by another supporting role in *The Chinese Parrot* (Fox; 1928), a silent in which Kamiyama Sojin played the oriental sleuth. *Behind the Curtain* (q.v.) was the first talkie to display Chan's talents.

665. Charlie Chan in City in Darkness (20th Century–Fox; 1939). *Cast:* Sidney Toler (Charlie Chan), Lynn Bari, Richard Clarke, Pedro de Cordoba, Douglass Dumbrille, Lon Chaney, Jr., Leo G. Carroll, Noel Madison, Harold Huber, Adrienne D'Ambricourt, Frederick Vogeding, George Davis, Dorothy Tree, Louis Mercier, C. Henry Gordon, Barbara Leonard. *D:* Herbert I. Leeds; *Sc:* Robert Ellis, Helen Logan. (G.B. title: *City in Darkness*) (1:15)

Paris during a blackout is the setting for this Chan mystery. Based on a play by Gina Kaus and Ladislaus Fodor.

666. Charlie Chan in Egypt (Fox; 1935). *Cast:* Warner Oland (Charlie Chan), Patricia (Pat) Paterson, Thomas Beck, Rita (Hayworth) Cansino, Jameson Thomas, Frank Conroy, Nigel de Brulier, Paul Porcasi, Stepin Fetchit, Frank Reicher, James Eagles, Arthur Stone. *D:* Louis King; *P:* Edward T. Lowe; *Sc:* Robert Ellis, Helen Logan. (1:12)

Murder among the pyramids.

667. Charlie Chan in Honolulu (20th Century–Fox; 1938). *Cast:* Sidney Toler, Phyllis Brooks, Sen Yung, Eddie Collins, John King, Claire Dodd, George Zucco, Robert Barrat, Philip Ahn, Marc Lawrence, Layne Tom, Jr., Richard Lane. *D:* H. Bruce Humberstone; *P:* John Stone; *Sc:* Charles Belden. (1:07)

Murder aboard a tramp steamer in Honolulu Harbor. This entry in the series marks Sidney Toler's debut as the Honolulu detective, following the death of Warner Oland in 1937.

668. Charlie Chan in London (Fox; 1934). *Cast:* Warner Oland (Charlie Chan), Ray Milland, Mona Barrie, Drue Leyton, Alan Mowbray, David Torrence, Madge Bellamy, E.E. Clive, Ann Doran (film debut), Douglas Walton, Murray Kinnell, John Rogers, George Barraud, Perry Ivins, Walter Johnson, Elsa Buchanan. *D:* Eugene Forde; *St & Sc:* Philip MacDonald. (1:19)

This time it's murder in the United Kingdom.

669. Charlie Chan in Paris (Fox; 1935). *Cast:* Warner Oland (Chan), Mary Brian, Thomas Beck, Erik Rhodes, John Miljan, Murray Kinnell, Minor Watson, John Qualen, Keye Luke (Lee Chan), Henry Kolker, Dorothy Appleby, Ruth Peterson, Perry Ivins. *D:* Lewis Seiler; *P:* John Stone; *St:* Philip MacDonald; *Sc:* Edward T. Lowe, Stuart Anthony. (1:10) (video)

The murder of an Apache dancer leads Chan into a mystery concerning forged bonds.

670. Charlie Chan in Reno (20th Century–Fox; 1939). *Cast:* Sidney Toler (Chan), Ricardo Cortez, Phyllis Brooks, Slim Summerville, Kane Richmond, Sen Yung, Pauline Moore, Eddie Collins, Kay Linaker, Louise Henry, Robert Lowery, Charles D. Brown, Morgan Conway, Iris Wong, Hamilton Mac-Fadden. *D:* Norman Foster; *As.P.:* John Stone; *Sc:* Albert Ray, Frances Hyland, Robert E. Kent, Foster (unc.). (1:10)

Chan investigates when a woman seeking a divorce is murdered. Based on the story "Death Makes a Decree" by Philip Wylie.

671. Charlie Chan in Shanghai (Fox; 1935). *Cast:* Warner Oland (Chan), Irene Hervey, Russell Hicks, Keye Luke (Lee Chan), Halliwell Hobbes, Charles Locher (Jon Hall), Frederick Vogeding, Max Wagner, Neil Fitzgerald. *D:* James Tinling; *St:* Gerard Fairlie; *Sc:* Fairlie, Edward T. Lowe. (1:10)

Murder in the Orient.

672. Charlie Chan on Broadway (20th Century–Fox; 1937). *Cast:* Warner Oland (Charlie Chan), Keye Luke (Lee Chan), Donald Woods, J. Edward Bromberg, Joan Marsh, Leon Ames, Joan Woodbury, Douglas Fowley, Louise Henry, Lon Chaney, Jr., Marc Lawrence, Harold Huber, Toshia Mori, Eugene Borden, Charles Williams. *D:* Eugene Forde; *St:* Art Arthur, Robert Ellis, Helen Logan; *Sc:* Jerry Cady, Charles Belden. (1:08)

This time it's murder in a night club on the Great White Way.

673. Charlie Chan's Chance (Fox; 1932). *Cast:* Warner Oland (Chan), H.B. Warner, Marian Nixon, Linda Watkins, Ralph Morgan, James Kirkwood, Alexander Kirkland, Edward Peil, James Wang, James Todd, Herbert Bunston, Charles McNaughton. *D:* John G. Blystone.

The second entry in the popular B series.

674. Charlie Chan's Courage (Fox; 1934). *Cast:* Warner Oland (Chan), Donald Woods, Harvey Clark, Paul Harvey, Drue Leyton, Murray Kinnell. *D:* George Hadden.

The fifth entry in the mystery series.

675. Charlie Chan's Greatest Case (Fox; 1933). *Cast:* Warner Oland (Chan), Heather Angel, Walter Byron, Virginia Cherrill, Clara Blandick, Robert Warwick, Francis Ford, Gloria Roy, Ivan Simpson, John Warburton, Roger Imhof, Claude King, Frank McGlynn, Sr., Cornelius Keefe, William Stack. *D:* Hamilton MacFadden.

The third entry in the mystery series of the wise oriental sleuth from Honolulu.

676. Charlie Chan's Secret (20th Century–Fox; 1936). *Cast:* Warner Oland (Charlie Chan), Rosina Lawrence, Charles Quigley, Henrietta Crosman, Herbert Mundin, Edward Trevor, Astrid Allwyn, Arthur Edmund Carewe (final film—d. 1937), Gloria Roy, William Norton Bailey, Ivan Miller. *D:* Gordon Wiles; *As.P.:* John Stone; *St:* Robert Ellis, Helen Logan; *Sc:* Ellis, Logan, Joseph Hoffman. (1:11) (video)

The Honolulu detective investigates the murder of the prodigal son of a wealthy woman.

677. Charlie Chaplin Carnival (Xxxx Xxxx; 1938). *Cast:* Charles Chaplin, Edna Purviance, Eric Campbell. (1:20) (video)

Four of Chaplin's classic comedies from his period at Mutual, all of which were directed and writen by him. They include: *Behind the Screen* (1916), *The Count* (1916), *The Fireman* (1916) and *The Vagabond* (1916).

678. Charlie Chaplin Cavalcade (Xxxx Xxxx; 1938). *Cast:* Charles Chaplin, Edna Purviance, Eric Campbell. (1:21) (video)

Four more of Chaplin's classic comedies from his period at Mutual, all directed and written by him. They include: *One A.M.* (solo–1916), *The Rink* (1916), *The Pawnshop* (1916) and *The Floorwalker* (his first for Mutual—1916).

679. Charlie Chaplin Festival (Xxxx Xxxx; 1938). *Cast:* Charles Chaplin, Edna Purviance, Eric Campbell. (1:20) (video)

The final four Chaplin comedy classics (of 12) done for Mutual which he directed and wrote. They include: *The Adventurer* (his last for Mutual—1917), *The Cure* (1917), *Easy Street* (1917) and *The Immigrant* (1917).

680. Charlie McCarthy, Detective (Universal; 1939). *Cast:* Edgar Bergen, "Charlie McCarthy," Constance Moore, Robert Cummings, Louis Calhern, Edgar Kennedy, John Sutton, Samuel S. Hinds, Warren Hymer, Harold Huber, Milburn Stone. *D:* Frank Tuttle; *P:* Tuttle; *St:* Robertson White, Darrell Ware; *Sc:* Edward Eliscu, Harold Shumate, Richard Mack. (1:05)

The title tells all in this B comedy-mystery.

681. Charming Sinners (Paramount; 1929). *Cast:* Ruth Chatterton, William Powell, Clive Brook, Mary Nolan, Florence Eldridge, Laura Hope Crews (film debut), Montagu Love, Claude Allister, Juliette Crosby, Lorraine Eddy. *D:* Robert Milton (stage director doing his first film); *Sc:* Doris Anderson. (1:06)

Drawing room comedy based on the popular 1926 stage success "The Constant Wife" by W. Somerset Maugham.

682. Chase Me, Charlie (Xxxx Xxxx; 1932). *Cast:* Charles Chaplin, Edna Purviance, Ben Turpin. (1:01)

Early footage from various Charlie Chaplin comedies (mostly 1914 for Keystone) pieced together to form a story. Narrated by Teddy Bergman.

683. The Chaser (MGM; 1938). *Cast:* Dennis O'Keefe, Ann Morriss, Lewis Stone, Nat Pendleton, Henry O'Neill, John Qualen, Jack Mulhall, Ruth Gillette, Robert Emmett Keane, Pierre Watkin, Irving Bacon. *D:* Edwin L. Marin; *P:* Frank Davis; *St:* Howard Emmett Rogers, Chandler Sprague; *Sc:* Everett Freeman, Harry Ruskin, Sam and Bella Spewack. (1:15)

A lawyer attempts to elude an insurance company in this B remake of *The Nuisance* (q.v.).

684. Chasing Danger (20th Century-Fox; 1939). *Cast:* Preston Foster, Wally Vernon, Lynn Bari, Henry Wilcoxon, Harold Huber, Jody Gilbert, Joan Woodbury, Roy D'Arcy. *D:* Ricardo Cortez; *P:* Sol M. Wurtzel.

Action-adventure which was the second and last entry in the "Camera Daredevils" series as they seek to photograph revolting Arab tribesmen — no pun intended. See also *Sharpshooters*.

685. Chasing Rainbows (MGM; 1929-30). *Cast:* Bessie Love, Charles King (1894-1944), Marie Dressler, Polly Moran, Jack Benny, George K. Arthur, Gwen Lee, Eddie Phillips, Youcca Troubetzkoy, Nita Martan. *D:* Charles Reisner; *Sc:* Bess Meredyth; *Other Songs:* Ager & Yellen. (G.B. title: *The Road Show*) (1:20)

A backstage romantic musical which includes a 2-color technicolor sequence and the smash hit song "Happy Days Are Here Again" by Milton Ager and Jack Yellen. Prior to release the film had the working title "The Road Show."

686. Chasing Through Europe (Fox; 1929). *Cast:* Sue Carol, Nick Stuart, Gustav von Seyffertitz. *D:* David Butler, Alfred Werker.

Low-budget part-talkie romantic comedy.

687. Chasing Trouble (Monogram; 1939-40). *Cast:* Frankie Darro, Marjorie Reynolds, Mantan Moreland, Milburn Stone, Cheryl Walker, Donald Kerr, George Cleveland, Alex Callam, Lillian Elliott, Tristram Coffin, I. Stanford Jolley, William Costello. *D:* Howard Bretherton; *P:* Grant Withers; *Sc:* Mary McCarthy. (1:04)

B mystery-comedy of a floral delivery boy — cum amateur sleuth who discovers his employer is an enemy agent.

688. Chasing Yesterday (RKO; 1935). *Cast:* Anne Shirley, O.P. Heggie (Sylvestre Bonnard), Helen Westley, Elizabeth Patterson, Etienne Girardot, John Qualen, Trent (Junior) Durkin, Doris Lloyd, Hilda Vaughn. *D:* George Nicholls, Jr.; *As.P.:* Cliff Reid; *Sc:* Francis Edwards Faragoh. (1:18)

Sentimental B drama of a French orphan who changes the life of a lonely old man. Based on the book "The Crime of Sylvestre Bonnard" by Anatole France.

689. Chatterbox (RKO; 1935-36). *Cast:* Anne Shirley, Phillips Holmes, Edward Ellis, Erik Rhodes, Margaret Hamilton, Granville Bates, Allen Vincent, Lucille Ball, George Offerman, Jr., Maxine Jennings, Richard Abbott, Wilfred Lucas, Margaret Armstrong. *D:* George Nicholls, Jr.; *As.P.:* Robert Sisk; *Sc:* Sam Mintz. (1:08)

B drama of a girl who following a misunderstanding, leaves home and joins a theater group. Based on a play by David Carb.

690. The Cheat (Paramount; 1931). *Cast:* Tallulah Bankhead, Irving Pichel, Arthur Hohl, Harvey Stephens, Ann Andrews, Jay Fassett, Robert Strange, Tamaki Yoshiwara, Henry Warren, Willard Dasiell, William Ingersoll. *D:* George Abbott; *St:* Hector Turnbull; *Adaptation:* Harry Hervey; *Sc:* Abbott.

Third go-round for a story which when initially made in 1915 by Lasky caused a sensation due to its racial issue of a wayward wife who throws herself at an oriental man. That version was directed, produced and edited by Cecil B. deMille and starred Fanny Ward and Sessue Hayakawa. The second version in 1923 (Paramount) by director George Fitzmaurice starred Pola Negri and Jack Holt. Remade in France in 1937 as *Forgaiture*.

691. Cheaters (Liberty; 1934). *Cast:* Bill Boyd, June Collyer, Dorothy Mackaill, William Collier, Sr., Alan Mowbray, Guinn Williams, Louise Beavers. *D:* Phil Rosen; *P:* Bert Lubin; *St & Sc:* Adele Buffington.

Low-budget melodrama.

692. Cheaters at Play (Fox; 1932). *Cast:* Thomas Meighan, Barbara Weeks, James Kirkwood, Charlotte Greenwood, William Bakewell, Ralph Morgan, Linda Watkins, Olin Howland, William Pawley, Anders Van Haden, Dewey Robinson. *D:* Hamilton MacFadden; *St:* Louis Joseph Vance.

Low-budget romance.

693. Cheating Blondes (Capital; 1933). *Cast:* Thelma Todd, Dorothy Gulliver, William Humphrey, Inez Courtney, Ralf Harolde, Brooks Benedict, Ben Savage, Mae Busch, Earl McCarthy, Milton Wallis, Eddie Fetherston. *D:* Joseph Levering; *St:* Gertie Des Wentworth James.

"Poverty row" romantic comedy.

694. Cheating Cheaters (Universal; 1934). *Cast:* Fay Wray, Cesar Romero, Minna Gombell, Hugh O'Connell, Henry Armetta, Francis L. Sullivan, Harold Huber. *D:* Richard Thorpe; *St:* Max Marcin (play); *Sc:* Gladys Unger, Allen Rivkin. (1:07)

B romance of rival jewel thieves. Previously filmed in 1919 by Allan Dwan and again in 1927 with Betty Compson and Kenneth Harlan.

695. Check and Double Check (RKO; 1930). *Cast:* Freeman F. Gosden (Amos), Charles J. Correll (Andy), Sue

Carol (Jean Blair), Charles Morton (Richard Williams), Irene Rich (Mrs. Blair), Ralf Harolde (Ralph Crawford), Edward Martindel (John Blair), Rita LaRoy (Elinor Crawford), Russell Powell (Kingfish), Duke Ellington and his orchestra, The Rhythm Boys with Bing Crosby. *D:* Melville Brown; *As.P.:* Bertram Milhauser; *St:* Bert Kalmar, Harry Ruby; *Adaptation:* J. Walter Ruben; *Songs:* "Ring Dem Bells" and "Three Little Words" by Kalmar & Ruby; "Old Man Blues" by Irving Mills and Duke Ellington. (1:20) (video)

This film is notable as the only starring feature film appearance of popular radio comedians Amos 'n' Andy (played in blackface). RKO's biggest commercial success of the year and one of the 15 top grossing films of 1930–31.

696. Checkers (20th Century–Fox; 1938). *Cast:* Jane Withers, Stuart Erwin, June Carlson, Marvin Stephens, Una Merkel. *D:* H. Bruce Humberstone.

Juvenile comedy-drama. Previously filmed in 1919.

697. Cheer Up and Smile (Fox; 1930). *Cast:* John Darrow, Arthur Lake, Olga Baclanova, Johnny Arthur, J. Carrol Naish, Franklin Pangborn, John Wayne (bit). *D:* Sidney Lanfield (directorial debut).

Comedy.

698. Cheers of the Crowd (Monogram; 1935). *Cast:* Russell Hopton, Irene Ware, Bradley Page, Harry Holman, Betty Blythe, Wade Boteler, Roberta Page, John Qualen, John H. Dilson. *D:* Vin Moore; *P:* Trem Carr; *St & Sc:* George Waggner. (1:00)

Low-budget drama of a publicity stunt which has an unexpected outcome. This was the final production of this studio prior to their merger with Mascot and Herbert J. Yates to form Republic Productions, Inc. (later Republic Pictures Corp.).

699. The Cherokee Strip (WB/ F.N.; 1937). *Cast:* Dick Foran, Jane Bryan, Tommy Bupp, Tom Brower, Joseph Crehan, Gordon (Bill) Elliott, Frank Faylen, Glenn Strange. *D:* Noel Smith; *P:* Bryan Foy; *St:* Ed Earl Repp; *Sc:* Joseph K. Watson, Luci Ward. (0:55)

Dick Foran western centered around the Oklahoma land rush. "My Little Buckaroo," a hit song of its day by M.K. Jerome and Jack Scholl comes from this B western.

700. Cheyenne Cyclone (Willis Kent; 1932). *Cast:* Lane Chandler, Connie LaMont, Frankie Darro, Edward Hearn, J. Frank Glendon, Henry Rocquemore, Yakima Canutt, Marie Quillan, Jay Hunt, Slim Whitaker, Jack Kirk, Hank Bell. *D:* Armand L. Schaefer; *P:* Willis Kent; *Sc:* Oliver Drake. (0:57)

Lane Chandler western of a cowboy stranded in a small town with a troupe of actors.

701. The Cheyenne Kid (RKO–Pathé; 1933). *Cast:* Tom Keene, Mary Mason, Roscoe Ates, Otto Hoffman, Alan Bridge, Alan Roscoe, Anderson Lawler. *D:* Robert Hill; *St:* "Sir Pregan Passes By" by W.C. Tuttle; *Sc:* Jack Curtis. (1:01) (video)

Tom Keene western of a cowboy wrongly accused of murder. Previously filmed by FBO in 1928 as *Man in the Rough* with Bob Steele. Remade by RKO in 1940 as *The Fargo Kid* with Tim Holt.

702. Cheyenne Rides Again (Victory; 1937). *Cast:* Tom Tyler, Lucille Browne, Jimmie Fox, Lon Chaney, Jr., Roger Williams, Ed Cassidy, Theodore Lorch, Bud Pope, Francis Walker, Carmen LaRoux, Jed Martin, Slim Whitaker, Bob Hill, Oscar Gahan, Merrill McCormack. *D:* Robert Hill; *P:* Sam Katzman; *Sc:* Basil Dickey. (0:56)

Tom Tyler western of a cowboy who joins an outlaw gang, undercover.

703. The Chicken Wagon Family (20th Century–Fox; 1939). *Cast:* Jane Withers, Leo Carrillo, Spring Byington, Marjorie Weaver, Kane Richmond, Hobart Cavanaugh. *D:* Herbert I. Leeds.

Low-budget comedy-drama.

704. The Chief (MGM; 1933). *Cast:* Ed Wynn, Charles "Chic" Sale, Dorothy Mackaill, William "Stage" Boyd, Effie Ellsler, C. Henry Gordon, Nat Pendleton, Purnell Pratt, Bradley Page, George Givot (film debut), Mickey Rooney, Bob Perry, Tom Wilson. *D:* Charles F. Reisner; *P:* Harry Rapf; *Sc:* Arthur Caesar, Robert Hopkins. (G.B. title: *My Old Man's a Fireman*) (1:04)

Comedy which showcased radio comedian Ed Wynn in his character "The Perfect Fool." A box office flop.

705. Child Bride (Xxxx Xxxx; 1938). *D:* Harry Revier (final film). (No other information available)

706. A Child Is Born (WB; 1939–40). *Cast:* Geraldine Fitzgerald, Jeffrey Lynn, Gladys George, Gale Page, Spring Byington, Henry O'Neill, John Litel, Gloria Holden, Eve Arden, Nanette (Fabray) Fabares, Hobart Cavanaugh, Johnny Downs, Fay Helm, Johnnie "Scat" Davis. *D:* Lloyd Bacon; *As.P.:* Sam Bischoff; *Sc:* Robert Rossen. (1:19)

Episodes in the lives of various characters in a hospital maternity ward. A remake of *Life Begins* (q.v.). Based on the play by Mary M. Axelson.

707. Child of Manhattan (Columbia; 1933). *Cast:* Nancy Carroll, John Boles, Charles "Buck" Jones, Jane Darwell, Jessie Ralph, Clara Blandick, Betty Grable, Tyler Brooke, Garry Owen, Luis Alberni, Betty Kendall, Warburton Gamble. *D:* Eddie Buzzell; *Sc:* Gertrude Purcell.

Big city gangster melodrama, based on the play by Preston Sturges.

708. Children of Dreams (WB/ F.N.; 1931). *Cast:* Paul Gregory, Margaret Schilling, Tom Patricola, Charles Winninger, Bruce Winston, Marion Byron. *D:* Alan Crosland; *Sc:* Oscar Hammerstein II, Sigmund Romberg; *Songs:* "The Fruit Pickers Song," "Oh, Couldn't I Love That Girl," "Her Professor," title song, "Sleeping Beauty," "If I Had a Girl Like You," "Seek Love" and "Yes Sir" by Hammerstein II and Romberg.

Romantic operetta of California apple pickers.

709. Children of Loneliness (Xxxx Xxxx; 1935). *St & D:* Richard C. Kahn.

An exploitation film on lesbianism. (No other information available)

710. Children of Pleasure (MGM; 1930). *Cast:* Lawrence Gray, Wynne Gibson, Helen Johnson, May Boley, Benny Rubin, Kenneth Thomson. *D:* Harry Beaumont; *Sc:* Richard Schayer, Crane Wilbur.

Low-budget musical about a group of songwriters. Based on a play by Crane Wilbur.

711. Chills and Fever (Xxxx Xxxx; 1933). (No information available)

712. China Bandit (Xxxx Xxxx; 1937). (No information available)

713. China Clipper (WB/F.N.; 1936). *Cast:* Pat O'Brien, Beverly Roberts, Ross Alexander, Humphrey Bogart, Marie Wilson, Henry B. Walthall (final film—died during production), Joseph Crehan, Addison Richards, Anne Nagel, Wayne Morris (film debut), Joseph King, Kenneth Harlan, Milburn Stone, Marjorie Weaver, Will Wright (film debut), Carlyle Moore, Jr., Dennis Moore, Ruth Robinson, Owen King, Lyle Moraine. *D:* Ray Enright; *As.P.:* Louis F. Edelman; *Production Supervisor:* Sam Bischoff; *Sc:* Frank Wead. (1:20)

A man obsessed with developing trans-Pacific flights begins to neglect other aspects of his life.

714. China Passage (RKO; 1937). *Cast:* Constance Worth, Vinton (Hayworth) Haworth, Leslie Fenton, Gordon Jones, Alec Craig, Dick Elliott, Frank M. Thomas, George Irving, Billy Gilbert, Lotus Liu, Tetsu Komai, Joyce Compton, Philip Ahn, Lotus Long, Huntley Gordon, Anita Colby. *D:* Edward Killy; *As.P.:* Cliff Reid; *St:* Taylor Caven; *Sc:* Edmund L. Hartmann, J. Robert Bren. (1:05)

B mystery adventure set in China as three people search for a stolen diamond.

715. China Seas (MGM; 1935). *Cast:* Clark Gable (Capt. Alan Gaskell), Jean Harlow (Dolly "China Doll" Portland), Wallace Beery (Jamesy MacArdle), Rosalind Russell (Sybil Barclay), Lewis Stone (Tom Davids), C. Aubrey Smith (Sir Guy Wilmerding), Hattie McDaniel (Isabel McCarthy), Dudley Digges (Dawson), Robert Benchley (Charlie McCaleb), Liev de Maigret (Mrs. Vollberg), William Henry (Rockwell), Lillian Bond (Mrs. Timmons), Edward Brophy (Wilbur Timmons), Soo Yong (Yu-Lan), Carol Ann Beery (Carol Ann), Akim Tamiroff (Romanoff), Ivan Lebedeff (Ngah), Donald Meek, Emily Fitzroy, Pat Flaherty, Tom Gubbins, Forrester Harvey, Charles Irwin, Willie Fung, Ferdinand Munier, Chester Gan, John Ince. *D:* Tay Garnett; *P:* Albert Lewin; *Sc:* Jules Furthman, James Kevin McGuinness; *Title Song:* Arthur Freed, Nacio Herb Brown. (1:29) (video)

Drama set aboard a cruise ship bound for Hong Kong. Based on the 1931 novel by Crosbie Garstin, It was one of the 15 top grossing films of 1935.

716. Chinatown After Dark (Tiffany; 1931). *Cast:* Frank Mayo, Rex Lease, Carmel Myers, Barbara Kent, Billy Gilbert, Edmund Breese. *D:* Stuart Paton.

"Poverty row" melodrama.

717. Chinatown Nights (Paramount; 1929). *Cast:* Florence Vidor (final film — ret.), Wallace Beery, Warner Oland, Jack Oakie, Tetsu Komai, Jack McHugh, Freeman Wood, Frank Chew, Peter Morrison, Mrs. (Wong) Wing. *D:* William Wellman; *P:* David O. Selznick; *St:* Samuel Ornitz; *Sc:* Ben Grauman Kohn.

Melodrama of a wealthy society woman who becomes involved with a powerful Tong leader.

718. Chinatown Squad (Universal; 1935). *Cast:* Lyle Talbot, Valerie Hobson, Andy Devine, Leslie Fenton, Jack Mulhall, King Baggot, Bradley Page, Edward Earle, Arthur Hoyt, Toshia Mori, Clay Clement, Hugh O'Connell, E. Alyn Warren, Wallis Clark. *D:* Murray Roth; *St:* L.G. Blochman; *Sc:* Dore Schary, Ben Ryan. (1:15)

B crime melodrama of a detective in search of money stolen from some Chinese communists.

719. Chip of the Flying U (Universal; 1939). *Cast:* Johnny Mack Brown, Bob Baker, Fuzzy Knight, Doris Weston, Ferris Taylor, Forrest Taylor, Anthony Warde, Karl Hackett, Henry Hall, Claire Whitney, Cecil Kellogg. *D:* Ralph Staub; *Sc:* Andrew Bennison, Larry Rhine. (0:55)

Johnny Mack Brown western of a ranch foreman accused of bank robbery. Based on the story by Bertha Muzzy Bowers, it was previously filmed in 1914 with Tom Mix, in 1920 as *The Galloping Dude* with Bud Osborne and again in 1926 with Hoot Gibson.

720. Chisellers of Hollywood (Xxxx Xxxx; 1931). *D:* William O'Connor; *Sc:* Ida May Park.

(No other information available)

721. Chloe (Pinnacle; 1934). *D:* Marshall Neilan.

(No other information available)

722. Christina (Fox; 1929). *Cast:* Janet Gaynor, Charles Morton, Rudolph Schildkraut, Harry Cording, Lucy Dorraine. *D:* William K. Howard; *St:* Tristram Tupper; *Sc:* Marion Orth.

Part-talkie romantic drama.

723. A Christmas Carol (MGM; 1938). *Cast:* Reginald Owen (Ebenezer Scrooge), Gene Lockhart (Bob Cratchit), Kathleen Lockhart (Mrs. Cratchit), Terry Kilburn (Tiny Tim), Leo G. Carroll (Marley's Ghost), Lynne Carver, Barry MacKay (Fred), D'Arcy Corrigan (Ghost of Christmas Future), Ann Rutherford (Ghost of Christmas Past), Lionel Braham (Ghost of Christmas Present), Ronald Sinclair (Young Scrooge), June Lockhart (film debut at age 12), D'Arcy Corrigan. *D:* Edwin L. Marin; *P:* Joseph L. Mankiewicz; *Sc:* Hugo Butler. (1:09) (video)

The famous Christmas classic based on the 1843 book by Charles Dickens. Remade in Great Britain in 1951 and in the U.S.A. as a TV movie. A TV movie variation was filmed in 1979 titled *An American Christmas Carol.* Also filmed in Great Britain in 1935, 1951 and 1970 as *Scrooge* and the American variation of 1988 titled *Scrooged.* Computer-colored by Turner Entertainment in 1987.

724. Christopher Bean (MGM; 1933). *Cast:* Marie Dressler (final film — d. 1934), Lionel Barrymore (Christopher Bean), Beulah Bondi, Helen Mack, George Couleris (film debut), H.B. Warner, Jean Hersholt, Russell Hardie, Helen Shipman, Ellen Lowe. *D:* Sam Wood; *P:* Harry Rapf; *Sc:* Laurence Johnson, Sylvia Thalberg. (G.B. title: *The Late Christopher Bean*) (1:20)

Comedy-drama of a dying artist who appoints his housekeeper as executor to his estate. Based on the play "The Late Christopher Bean" by Sidney Howard.

725. Christopher Strong (RKO; 1933). *Cast:* Katharine Hepburn (Lady Cynthia Darrington — a role originally intended for Ann Harding), Colin Clive (Sir Christopher Strong), Billie Burke, Helen Chandler, Ralph Forbes, Irene Browne, Jack LaRue, Desmond Roberts, Margaret Lindsay. *D:* Dorothy Arzner; *As.P.:* Pandro S. Berman; *Sc:* Zoe Akins. (1:17) (video)

Romantic drama of a lady flyer who falls for a married man. This was Katharine Hepburn's second film and a box office flop. Based on the novel by Gilbert Frankau.

726. A Chump at Oxford (United Artists/Hal Roach; 1939–40). *Cast:* Stan Laurel, Oliver Hardy, James Finlayson, Forrester Harvey, Wilfred Lucas, Forbes Murray, Frank Baker, Gerald Fielding, Gerald Rogers, Victor Kendall, Charles Hall, Anita Gavin, Peter Cushing (in his second film), Rex Lease. *D:* Alfred Goulding; *P:* Hal Roach; *Sc:* Charles Rogers, Harry Langdon, Felix Adler. (1:03) (video)

Laurel and Hardy romp through the hallowed halls of Oxford University after receiving a free education in payment for capturing a bank robber.

727. Cimarron (RKO; 1930–31). *Cast:* Richard Dix (A.A.N. for B.A. as Yancy Cravat), Irene Dunne (A.A.N. for B.A. as Sabra Cravat), Estelle Taylor (Dixie Lee), Edna May Oliver (Mrs. Tracy Wyatt), Nance O'Neil (Felice Venable), William Collier, Jr. ("The Kid"), George E. Stone (Sol Levy), Roscoe Ates (Jess Rickey), Stanley Fields (Lon Yountis), Robert McWade (Louis Hefner), Frank Darien (Mr. Bixby), Eugene Jackson (Isaiah), Dolores Brown (elder Ruby Big Elk), Gloria Vonic (younger Ruby Big Elk), Otto Hoffman (Murch Rankin), William Orlamond (Grat Gotch), Frank Beal (Louis Venable), Nancy Dover (Donna Cravat), Helen Parrish (Donna—child), Donald Dillaway (Cim Cravat), Junior Johnson (Cim—child), Douglas Scott (Cim—younger child), Reginald Streeter (Yancy II), Lois Jane Campbell (Felice II), Ann Lee (Aunt Cassandra), Tyrone Brereton (Dabney Venable), Lillian Lane (Cousin Bella), Henry Rocquemore (Jouett Goforth), Nell Craig (Arminta Greenwood), Robert McKenzie (Pat Leary), Clara Hunt, Bud Flanagan (Dennis O'Keefe), Robert Kortman, Edith Fellows. *D:* (A.A.N.) Wesley Ruggles; *P:* William LeBaron; *As.P.:* Louis Sarecky; *Screenplay Adaptation:* (A.A.) Howard Estabrook; *Cinematographer:* (A.A.N.) Edward Cronjager; *Interior Decoration:* (A.A.) Max Ree. (2:11) (video)

Generational story spanning forty years of a family from the time they settled in Oklahoma to the present day of 1930. Based on the novel by Edna Ferber, the film is notable for its recreation of the Oklahoma land-rush. The film came in at a cost of $1,500,000, the biggest budgeted feature for the studio to date. Despite the fact that the film was one of the 15 top grossing films of 1930–31, the studio still wrote it off as a box office flop, later selling it and the rights to the book to MGM. Notable as the only western in the history of Hollywood (until 1990's *Dances with Wolves*) to win the Academy Award for "Best Picture" as well as being only one of two films by this studio ever to win that honor for one of their films. It received *Photoplay's* Gold Medal Award, was voted "Best Film of the Year" by *Film Daily,* as well as being voted one of the "10 Best" films of the year by the National Board of Review. MGM did a remake in 1961.

728. Cipher Bureau (Grand National/Fine Arts; 1938). *Cast:* Leon Ames, Charlotte Wynters, Joan Woodbury, Donald Dillaway, Tenen Holtz, Gustav von Seyffertitz, Walter Bohn, Si Wills, Peter Lynn, Robert Frazer, Jason Robards, Joe Romantini. *D:* Charles Lamont; *P:* Franklyn Warner; *St:* Arthur Hoerl, Monroe Shaff; *Sc:* Hoerl. (1:10)

Low-budget melodrama concerning a bureau of experts who through their tactics, break coded messages of foreign agents. Followed by a sequel: *Panama Patrol* (q.v.).

729. Circle Canyon (Superior; 1933). *Cast:* Buddy Roosevelt, June Mathews, Clarise Woods, Robert Williamson, Allen Holbrook, Clyde McClary, Harry Leland. *D:* Victor Adamson (Denver Dixon); *Sc:* B.R. Tuttle. (0:48)

Buddy Roosevelt western of two feuding outlaw gangs. Based on a magazine story titled "Gun Glory."

730. Circle of Death (Willis Kent; 1935). *Cast:* Monte Montana, Tove Lindan, Yakima Canutt, Henry Hall, Ben Corbett, J. Frank Glendon, Jack Carson, John Ince, Princess Ah-Tee-Ha, Chief Standing Bear, Dick Botiller, Hank Bell, Budd Buster, Bart Carre. *D:* J. Frank Glendon; *P:* Montana. (1:00) (video)

Monte Montana western involving a white boy raised by Indians. This was one of two attempts by Montana to establish himself as a western cowboy star, but to no avail.

731. Circumstantial Evidence (Chesterfield; 1935). *Cast:* Lloyd Ingraham, Dorothy Revier, Chick Chandler, Robert Frazer, Lee Moran, Barbara Bedford, Robert Elliott, Carl Stockdale. *D:* Charles Lamont.

"Poverty row" melodrama.

732. The Circus Clown (WB/F.N.; 1934). *Cast:* Joe E. Brown (in a dual role as father and son), Patricia Ellis, Dorothy Burgess, Donald Dillaway, Gordon Westcott, Charles Wilson, Harry Woods, Ronnie Cosbey, John Sheehan, Tom Dugan, Spencer Charters, Gordon Evans, William Demarest, Lee Moran. *D:* Ray Enright; *P:* James Seymour; *Sc:* Bert Kalmar, Harry Ruby, Paul Gerard Smith (unc.). (1:08)

Comedy-drama of a circus performer's father who disapproves of his son's line of work. A box office flop.

The Circus Comes to Town (G.B. title) *see* **Under the Big Top**

733. Circus Girl (Republic; 1937). *Cast:* Donald Cook, June Travis, Betty Compson, Bob Livingston, Charlie Murray. *D:* John H. Auer.

Low-budget romantic drama of the big-top.

734. The Circus Kid (FBO; 1928). *Cast:* Joe E. Brown, Frankie Darro (title role), Poodles Hanneford. *D:* George B. Seitz.

Low-budget part-talkie comedy.

735. The Circus Queen Murder (Columbia; 1933). *Cast:* Adolph Menjou (Colt), Donald Cook, Greta Nissen, Harry Holman, George Rosener, Ruthelma Stevens, Dwight Frye. *D:* Roy William Neill; *Adaptation:* Jo Swerling; *Sc:* Anthony Abbot.

Low-budget murder-mystery featuring police detective "Thatcher Colt," a character created by Anthony Abbot (Fulton Oursler) in a series of books. This was the second and last of two books by him, filmed by Columbia.

The Circus Shadow (G.B. title) *see* **The Shadow**

736. The Cisco Kid (Fox; 1931). *Cast:* Warner Baxter (Cisco Kid), Edmund Lowe, Conchita Montenegro, Nora Lane, Chris-Pin Martin, Willard Robertson, Frederic Burt, James Bradbury, Jr., John (Jack) Dillon, Charles Stevens, Douglas Haig, Marilyn Knowlden. *D:* Irving Cummings; *Sc:* Alfred A. Cohn (based on the character created by O'Henry). (1:00)

A sequel to the Academy Award winning *In Old Arizona* (q.v.). The kid steals money to pay off a girl's ranch, and winds up with a price on his head. Followed by another sequel *The Return of the Cisco Kid* (q.v.).

737. The Cisco Kid and the Lady (20th Century–Fox; 1939–40). *Cast:* Cesar Romero, Marjorie Weaver, Chris-Pin Martin, George Montgomery, Virginia Field, Robert Barrat,

Harry Green, John Beach, Ward Bond, J. Anthony Hughes, James Burke, Harry Hayden, James Flavin, Ruth Warren, Gloria Ann White. *D:* Herbert I. Leeds; *P:* Sol M. Wurtzel; *St:* Stanley Rauh; *Sc:* Frances Hyland. (1:13)

Premiere entry in a series of six films, the balance of which were made in the 1940s. Plot revolves around a gold mine, a baby and "the lady" of the title.

738. City Girl (Fox; 1930). *Cast:* Charles Farrell, Mary Duncan, David Torrence, Edith Yorke, Dawn O'Day (Anne Shirley), Roscoe Ates. *D:* F.W. Murnau; *Sc:* Berthold Viertel, Marion Orth. (1:17)

Rural drama of an urban girl who moves to the country only to find that life there is not as simple as she originally thought. Based on the play "The Mud Turtle" by Elliott Lester.

739. City Girl (20th Century-Fox; 1937–38). *Cast:* Douglas Fowley, Ricardo Cortez, Esther Muir, Phyllis Brooks, Adrienne Ames, Robert Wilcox, Paul Stanton, Chick Chandler, Lon Chaney, Jr., Charles Lane, Marjorie Main, Bobby Watson, George Lynn. *D:* Alfred Werker; *P:* Sol M. Wurtzel; *Sc:* Frances Hyland, Robin Harris, Lester Ziffren.

B melodrama of a waitress who will stop at nothing to get what she wants.

City in Darkness (G.B. title) *see* **Charlie Chan in City in Darkness**

740. City Limits (Monogram; 1934). *Cast:* Frank Craven, Sally Blane, Ray Walker, Claude Gillingwater, James Burke, James Conlin, Jane Keckley, Henry Rocquemore, Harry Bradley, George Hayes, George Cleveland, Fern Emmett, George Nash. *D:* William Nigh; *P:* William T. Lackey; *St & Sc:* George Waggner. (1:07)

Low-budget comedy of a wealthy railroad president, suffering from fatigue who falls from one of his trains

and is befriended by two "kings of the road" who teach him a few things about life and living. Based on the novel by Jack Woodford (Josiah Pitts Woolfolk), it was remade by this studio in 1941 as *Father Steps Out.*

741/742. City Park (Chesterfield; 1934). *Cast:* Sally Blane. *D:* Richard Thorpe.

"Poverty row" production.

743. City Streets (Paramount; 1931). *Cast:* Gary Cooper (The Kid), Sylvia Sidney (in her starring debut, replacing Clara Bow who had suffered a nervous breakdown prior to production as Nan), Paul Lukas (Big Fellow Maskal), Wynne Gibson (Aggie), Guy Kibbee (Pop Cooley), William "Stage" Boyd (McCoy), Stanley Fields (Blackie), Betty Sinclair (Pansy), Terry Carroll (sister of Nancy Carroll as Esther March), Robert E. Homans (Inspector), Willard Robertson (detective), Allan Cavan (cop), Bert Hanlon (Baldy), Matty Kemp, Edward LeSaint, Hal Price, Ethan Laidlaw, George Regas, Bob Kortman, Leo Willis, Gordon (Bill) Elliott. *D:* Rouben Mamoulian (his second film); *P:* Mamoulian, E. Lloyd Sheldon; *St:* Dashiell Hammett (his only written directly for the screen); *Adaptation:* Max Marcin; *Sc:* Oliver H.P. Garrett. (1:10)

Melodrama of a man who joins a gang of hoodlums in hopes of springing his girlfriend from jail. The film was voted one of the year's "10 Best" films by the National Board of Review. It also was one of the 15 top grossing films of 1930–31.

744. City Streets (Columbia; 1938). *Cast:* Leo Carrillo, Edith Fellows, Tommy Bond, Mary Gordon, Ann Doran, Arthur Loft, Joseph King, Frank Sheridan, Helen Jerome Eddy, George Humbert, Grace Goodall, Frank Reicher. *D:* Albert S. Rogell; *St:*

I. Bernstein; *Sc:* Lou Breslow, Fred Niblo, Jr. (1:08)

Low-budget sentimental drama of a crippled orphan and her benefactor.

745. Clancy in Wall Street (Fox; 1930). *Cast:* Charlie Murray (Clancy), Edward Nugent, Miriam Seegar, Aggie Herring, Lucien Littlefield, Reed Howes. *D:* Ted Wilde; *P:* Edward Small.

Comedy.

746. Clarence (Paramount; 1937). *Cast:* Roscoe Karns (title role), Johnny Downs, Eleanore Whitney, Eugene Pallette, Spring Byington, Inez Courtney. *D:* George Archainbaud.

B comedy of a man who gets involved in the affairs of a screwball family. Based on a story by Booth Tarkington, it was previously filmed in 1922 by Paramount with Wallace Reid and Agnes Ayres.

747. Clear All Wires (MGM; 1933). *Cast:* Lee Tracy, Benita Hume (American debut), James Gleason, C. Henry Gordon, Una Merkel, Lya Lys, Alan Edwards, John Bleifer, Guy Usher, Ari Kutai, Eugene Sigaloff. *D:* George Hill (final film — d. 1934); *Sc:* Delmer Daves, Sam and Bella Spewack.

A news correspondent who lacks principle is sent on assignment to Moscow in this drama. Based on the hit Broadway play by Sam and Bella Spewack.

748. Clear the Decks (Universal; 1929). *Cast:* Reginald Denny, Olive Hasbrouck, Lucien Littlefield, Elinor Leslie, Robert Anderson, Otis Harlan, Brooks Benedict, Collette Marten. *D:* Joseph E. Henabery; *St:* E.J. Rath; *Sc:* Earle Snell, Gladys Lehman, Albert DeMond, Charles H. Smith.

Part-talkie shipboard comedy of assumed identity followed by mistaken identity.

749. Clearing the Range (Allied; 1931). *Cast:* Hoot Gibson, Sally Eilers (later Mrs. Hoot Gibson), Hooper Atchley, Robert Homans, Edward Peil, George Mendoza, Edward Hearn, Maston Williams, Eva Grippon. *D:* Otto Brower; *P:* M.H. Hoffman; *Sc:* Jack Natteford. (1:05)

Hoot Gibson western (his first for this company) of a cowboy who assumes two disguises to find the killer of his brother. Remade as *The Dude Bandit* (q.v.).

750. Cleopatra (Paramount; 1934). *Cast:* Claudette Colbert (Cleopatra), Warren William (Julius Caesar), Henry Wilcoxon (American debut as Marc Antony), Gertrude Michael (Calpurnia), Joseph Schildkraut (Herod), Irving Pichel (Apollodorus), Ian Keith (Octavian), C. Aubrey Smith (Enobarbus), Ian MacLaren (Cassius), Arthur Hohl (Brutus), Leonard Mudie (Pothinos), Claudia Dell (Octavia), Eleanor Phelps (Charmian), John Rutherford (Drussus), Grace Durkin (Iras), Robert Warwick (Achillas), Edwin Maxwell (Casca), Charles Morris (Cicero), Harry Beresford (soothsayer), Ferdinand Gottschalk (Glabrio), Olga Celeste (slave girl), Florence Roberts (Flora), Kenneth Gibson, William Farnum, Wedgwood Nowell, John Peter Richmond (later John Carradine), Jayne Regan, Celia Ryan, Robert Manning, Lionel Belmore, Dick Alexander, Wilfred Lucas, Jack Mulhall, Hal Price, Edgar Dearing, Ecki the leopard. *D:* Cecil B. de Mille; *P:* de Mille; *Sc:* Waldemar Young, Vincent Lawrence; *Cinematographer:* (A.A.) Victor Milner; *Assistant Director:* (A.A.N.) Cullen Tate; *Editor:* (A.A.N.) Anne Bauchens; *Sound Recording:* (A.A.N.) Franklin Hansen. (1:43) (video)

Epic spectacle of the queen of the Nile which received an A.A.N. for "Best Picture." Previous feature versions: (Vitagraph; 1912) with Helen Gardner and (Fox; 1917) with Theda Bara. Refilmed as a lavish multi-million dollar spectacle in 1963 by 20th Century-Fox.

751. The Climax (Universal; 1930). *Cast:* Kathryn Crawford, John Reinhardt, Jean Hersholt, LeRoy Mason, Henry Armetta. *D:* Renaud Hoffman. (1:05)

B romantic drama of a female opera singer's affairs. Remade in 1944 with Susanna Foster and Boris Karloff. Based on the play by Edward Locke.

752. Clip Joint (Majestic; 1933). *Cast:* Paul Lukas, Leila Hyams, Joyce Compton, Ruth Donnelly, Donald Dillaway, George E. Stone, John St. Polis, Charles McNaughton, Arthur Hoyt, Walter Brennan, Arthur Housman. *D:* Howard Christy; *St & Sc:* Wilson Collison. (alternate and G.B. title: *Sing, Sinner, Sing*)

"Poverty row" melodrama set in a crooked gambling house.

753. Clipped Wings (Xxxx Xxxx; 1938). *Cast:* Lloyd Hughes, Jason Robards, William Janney, Richard Cramer. *D:* Stuart Paton.

B film.

754. Clive of India (United Artists/20th Century; 1935). *Cast:* Ronald Colman (Baron Robert Clive), Loretta Young (Lady Clive), Colin Clive, Francis Lister, Ferdinand Munier, Montagu Love, Robert Greig, Leo G. Carroll, C. Aubrey Smith, Mischa Auer, Cesar Romero, Gilbert Emery, Lumsden Hare, Doris Lloyd, Ian Wolfe, Keith Kenneth, Charles Evans, Edward Cooper, Phyllis Clare, Vernon Downing, Leonard Mudie, Desmond Roberts, Ann Shaw, Peter Shaw, Pat Somerset, Lila Lance, Connie Lee, Vesey O'Davoren, Joseph Tozer. *D:* Richard Boleslawski; *P:* Darryl F. Zanuck, William Goetz, Raymond Griffith; *Sc:* W.P. Lipscomb, R.J. Minney. (1:30)

Romantic adventure of the famed Englishman, except with a happy ending. This box office hit was based on the play by W.P. Lipscomb and R.J. Minney.

The Clock Strikes 8 (G.B. title) *see* **College Scandal**

755. Close Harmony (Paramount; 1929). *Cast:* Nancy Carroll, Charles "Buddy" Rogers, Jack Oakie, Richard "Skeets" Gallagher, Harry Green, Greta Granstedt, Wade Boteler, Ricca Allen, Gus Partos, Matty Roubert, Oscar Smith, Baby Mack. *D:* John Cromwell, A. Edward Sutherland; *St:* Elsie Janis, Gene Markey; *Sc:* Percy Heath, John V.A. Weaver; *Titles:* Joseph L. Mankiewicz; *Songs:* Richard A. Whiting, Leo Robin.

Romantic musical.

756. Coast Guard (Columbia; 1939). *Cast:* Randolph Scott, Frances Dee, Ralph Bellamy, Walter Connolly, Warren Hymer, Robert Middlemass, Stanley Andrews, James Millican, J. Farrell MacDonald, Ann Doran. *D:* Edward Ludwig; *P:* Fred Kohlmar; *Sc:* Richard Maibaum, Albert Duffy, Harry Segall. (1:12)

Adventure drama of two coast guardsmen in love with the same girl.

757. Cocaine Fiends (Willis Kent; 1936–37). *Cast:* Noel Madison, Lois January, Sheila Mannors, Dean Venton, Lois Lindsay. *D:* William A. O'Connor; *P:* Willis Kent. (1:14) (video) (original title: *The Pace That Kills*)

Campy indie melodrama in the same anti-drug vein as *Reefer Madness* (q.v.), about a dope peddler. A PG rating was added for re-release in the 1980s.

758. Cock o' the Walk (Sono Art–World Wide; 1930). *Cast:* Joseph Schildkraut, Myrna Loy, Wilfred Lucas, Edward Peil, Olive Tell, John Beck, Natalie Joyce, Frank Jonasson, Philip Sleeman, Sally Long. *D:* Roy William Neill, Walter Lang; *St:* Arturo S. Mom.

"Poverty row" melodrama of a gigolo who marries a suicide prone girl.

759. Cock of the Air (United Artists/Howard Hughes; 1932). *Cast:* Chester Morris, Billie Dove, Walter Catlett, Matt Moore, Luis Alberni, Katya Sergeiva, Yola D'Avril, Vivian Oakland, John Mack Brown, Helen Chandler, Emile Chautard, Walter Byron, Ethel Sutherland, Peggy Watts. *D:* Tom Buckingham; *P:* Howard Hughes; *St & Sc:* Charles Lederer, Robert E. Sherwood.

Comedy of a French actress whose passion in life is men in uniform.

760. Cockeyed Cavaliers (RKO; 1934). *Cast:* Bert Wheeler, Robert Woolsey, Thelma Todd, Dorothy Lee, Noah Beery, Robert Greig, Henry Sedley, Franklin Pangborn, Snub Pollard, Robert Orwig, Billy Gilbert, Jack Norton (film debut), Alf P. James. *D:* Mark Sandrich; *As.P.:* Lou Brock; *Sc:* Edward Kaufman, Ben Holmes; *Additional Dialogue:* Grant Garrett, Ralph Spence; *Song:* "I Went Hunting and the Big Bad Wolf Was Dead" by Will Jason and Val Burton. (1:12) (video)

Costume musical-comedy with the team of Wheeler and Woolsey on the loose in merry olde England.

761. The Cock-Eyed World (Fox; 1929). *Cast:* Victor McLaglen (Top Sgt. Flagg), Edmund Lowe (Sgt. Harry Quirt), Lily Damita (Mariana Elenita), El Brendel (Olsen), Bobby Burns (Connors), Lelia Karnelly (Olga), Jean Bary (Fanny), Joe Brown (Brownie), Stuart Erwin (Buckley), Ivan Linow (Sanovich), Albert "Curley" Dresden (O'Sullivan), Joe Rochay (Jacobs), Soledad Jimenez (innkeeper), Jeanette Dagna (Katinka), Warren Hymer (Scout), Con Conrad, William K. Wells, "Sugar" Willie Keeler, Lee Houck, Joe Herrick, Charles Sullivan, the Mexican Marimba Band of Agua Caliente, Jose Arias Spanish String Band Serenaders, Kamerko Balalaika Orchestra, Mare Island Navy Band, San Diego Marine Band. *D:* Raoul Walsh; *Sc:* Laurence Stallings, Maxwell

Anderson, Wilson Mizner, Tom Barry, William K. Wells; *Songs:* "So Long," "Elenita" and "So Dear to Me" by Con Conrad, Sidney Mitchell and Archie Gottler. (1:55)

This sequel to *What Price Glory?* (Fox; 1927) has Sgts. Flagg and Quirt heading for the south seas where they go at it over a local beauty. Location shoots include Mare Island Navy Yard at Vallejo, California, the U.S. Marine Base at San Diego and aboard the U.S.S. Henderson. Number 8 on the "10 Best" of *Film Daily.* Based on the play by Laurence Stallings.

762. Cocktail Hour (Columbia; 1933). *Cast:* Randolph Scott, Bebe Daniels, Sidney Blackmer, Barry Norton, Muriel Kirkland, Larry Steers, Marjorie Gateson, Oscar Smith, Jessie Ralph, Phillips Smalley, Paul McVey, Willie Fung, Jay Eaton, George Nardelli. *D:* Victor Schertzinger; *St:* James Kevin McGuinness; *Sc:* Gertrude Purcell, Richard Schayer.

Romantic comedy.

763. Cocoanut Grove (Paramount; 1938). *Cast:* Fred MacMurray, Harriet Hilliard (Nelson), The Yacht Club Boys, Harry Owens Orchestra, Ben Blue, Eve Arden, Billy Lee, Rufe Davis, Monte Blue, Charles Lane, Ethel Clayton, Dorothy Howe, Roy Gordon, Gloria Williams, George Walcott, Terry Ray (Ellen Drew), Red Stanley. *D:* Alfred Santell; *P:* George M. Arthur; *Sc:* Sy Bartlett, Olive Cooper. (1:25)

Romantic musical of a band traveling from Chicago to Los Angeles for an engagement at the Cocoanut Grove. The film includes two popular songs of the day, "You Leave Me Breathless" by Frederick Hollander & Ralph Freed and "Says My Heart" by Burton Lane and Frank Loesser.

764. The Cocoanuts (Paramount; 1929). *Cast:* Groucho Marx, Harpo Marx, Chico Marx, Zeppo Marx, Mary Eaton, Margaret Dumont (film debut),

Oscar Shaw, Kay Francis, Basil Ruysdael, Cyril Ring, Sylvan Lee, Barton MacLane (bit). *D:* Robert Florey, Joseph Santley; *P:* Walter Wanger; *Sc:* George S. Kaufman and Morrie Ryskind; *Songs:* Irving Berlin, including "When My Dreams Come True" written directly for the film. (1:36) (video)

Landmark comedy farce which marked the film debuts of the four Marx Brothers. Based on the stage success by George S. Kaufman, it was filmed at Astoria Studios in L.I., N.Y. and was a box office hit.

765. Code of the Cactus (Victory; 1939). *Cast:* Tim McCoy, Dorothy Short, Ben Corbett (Magpie), Dave O'Brien, Ted Adams, Alden Chase, Forrest Taylor, Bob Terry, Slim Whitaker, Kermit Maynard, Frank Wayne, Carl Mathews, Art Davis, Jimmy Aubrey. *D:* Sam Newfield; *P:* Sam Katzman; *Sc:* Edward Halperin. (0:57)

Tim McCoy in a "Lightnin' Bill Carson" horse opera involving cattle rustlers on wheels.

766. Code of the Desert (Xxxx Xxxx; 1935). *Cast:* Roger Williams.

(No other information available, but possibly an Ajax production)

767. Code of the Fearless (Spectrum; 1938–39). *Cast:* Fred Scott, Claire Rochelle (film debut), John Merton, Walter McGrail, George Sherwood, Harry Harvey, Carl Mathews, William Woods, Don Gallagher, Roger Williams, Frank LaRue, Gene Howard, James "Buddy" Kelly, Art Mix. *D:* Raymond K. Johnson; *P:* C.C. Burr; *Sc:* Fred Myton. (0:56) (video)

Fred Scott oater with songs.

768. Code of the Mounted (Ambassador; 1935). *Cast:* Kermit Maynard, Robert Warwick, Roger Williams, Dick Curtis, Wheeler Oakman, Jim Thorpe. *D:* Sam Newfield; *P:* Maurice Conn.

Kermit Maynard Canadian Mountie actioner.

769. Code of the Range (Columbia; 1936). *Cast:* Charles Starrett, Mary Blake, Ed Coxen, Allan Cavan, Ed Peil, Edmund Cobb, Edward LeSaint, Ralph McCullough, George Chesebro, Art Mix, Albert J. Smith. *D:* C.C. Coleman, Jr.; *Sc:* Ford Beebe. (0:55)

Charles Starrett western of cattlemen vs. sheepmen.

770. Code of the Rangers (Monogram; 1938). *Cast:* Tim McCoy, Rex Lease, Judith Ford, Wheeler Oakman, Frank LaRue, Roger Williams, Kit Guard, Frank McCarroll, Jack Ingram, Loren Riebe, Budd Buster, Ed Peil, Hal Price, Zeke Clements, Herman Hack. *D:* Sam Newfield; *P:* Maurice Conn; *St:* Stanley Roberts; *Sc:* Roberts. (0:56)

Tim McCoy western of a U.S. Ranger and his lawman brother who has turned lawless.

771. Code of the Secret Service (WB/F.N.; 1939). *Cast:* Ronald Reagan (Brass Bancroft), Rosella Towne, Eddie Foy, Jr., Moroni Olsen, Edgar Edwards, Jack Mower. *D:* Noel Smith; *P:* Bryan Foy; *Sc:* Lee Katz, Dean Franklin. (0:58)

Second entry in the "Brass Bancroft" series. In this one agent Bancroft is in pursuit of counterfeiters.

772. Code of the Streets (Universal; 1939). *Cast:* Billy Benedict, James McCallion, Leon Ames, El Brendel, Paul Fix, Mary Gordon, Harry Carey, Frankie Thomas, Marc Lawrence. *D:* Harold Young; *P:* Burt Kelly; *Sc:* Arthur T. Horman.

"Little Tough Guys" juvenile melodrama of an innocent youth convicted of murder and sentenced to death.

773. The Cohens and Kellys in Africa (Universal; 1930–31). *Cast:* George Sidney (Mr. Cohen), Vera Gordon (Mrs. Cohen), Charles Murray (Mr. Kelly), Kate Price (Mrs. Kelly), Lloyd Whitlock, Frank Davis, Louis John Bartels, Nick Cogley. *D:* Vin Moore. (1:08)

Entry in the popular low-budget ethnic series which started in the silent era and ran into the early 1930s. In this one, they trek to the dark continent in search of the reason an ivory shortage is putting the crimps to their piano business.

774. The Cohens and Kellys in Atlantic City (Universal; 1929). *Cast:* George Sidney, Charles Murray, Vera Gordon, Kate Price, Mack Swain, Tom Kennedy, Nora Lane, Cornelius Keefe, Virginia Sale. *D:* William James (W.J.) Craft; *St:* Jack Townley.

In this entry in the series, the Cohens and Kellys own a bathing suit business which is in financial trouble. A part-talkie.

775. The Cohens and Kellys in Hollywood (Universal; 1932). *Cast:* George Sidney (Mr. Cohen), Vera Gordon (Mrs. Cohen), Charles Murray (Mr. Kelly), Kate Price (Mrs. Kelly), June Clyde, Eileen Percy, Frank Albertson, Robert Greig, Emma Dunn, Edwin Maxwell, Esther Howard, John Roche, Lew Ayres (cameo), Norman Foster (cameo), Sidney Fox (cameo), Boris Karloff (cameo), Genevieve Tobin (cameo). *D:* John Francis Dillon; *St & Sc:* Howard Green. (1:15)

The title tells all in this entry in the popular low-budget series of the friendship and rivalry between an Irish and a Jewish couple.

776. The Cohens and Kellys in Scotland (Universal; 1930). *Cast:* George Sidney, Vera Gordon, Charles Murray, Kate Price, Lloyd Whitlock (Prince of Morania), E.J. Ratcliffe, William Colvin, John McDermott. *D:* William James Craft; *Adaptation:* Albert DeMond; *Sc:* DeMond, John McDermott. (1:24)

A feud erupts over the sale of tartan cloth in Scotland in this first all-talkie entry in the series.

777. The Cohens and Kellys in Trouble (Universal; 1933). *Cast:* George

Sidney, Charles Murray, Vera Gordon, Kate Price, Maureen O'Sullivan, Frank Albertson, Andy Devine, Henry Armetta, Jobyna Howland. *D:* Fred Guiol and George Stevens (in his feature directorial debut); *St:* Homer Croy, Vernon Smithl *Sc:* Albert Austin, Fred Guiol, Jack Jungmeyer. (1:07)

The foursome have comic misadventures aboard a tugboat in this, the last entry in the series.

778. Colleen (WB; 1936). *Cast:* Dick Powell, Ruby Keeler, Jack Oakie, Joan Blondell, Hugh Herbert, Louise Fazenda, Paul Draper, Marie Wilson, Luis Alberni, Hobart Cavanaugh, Berton Churchill, Mary Treen, Spencer Charters, J.M. Kerrigan, Addison Richards, Ward Bond, Paula Stone, Andre Beranger. *D:* Alfred E. Green; *P:* Robert Lord; *St:* Lord; *Sc:* Peter Milne, F. Hugh Herbert, Sig Herzig; *Songs:* "I Don't Have to Dream Again," "You've Gotta Know How to Dance," "An Evening with You" and "A Boulevardier from the Bronx" by Al Dubin and Harry Warren. (1:29)

A musical of the "boy meets girl" variety with choreography by Bobby Connolly.

779. College Coach (WB; 1933). *Cast:* Pat O'Brien, Dick Powell, Ann Dvorak, Hugh Herbert, Herman Bing, Lyle Talbot, Nat Pendleton, Guinn Williams, Berton Churchill, Arthur Byron, Donald Meek, Arthur Hohl, Harry Beresford, John Wayne, Philip Reed, Joseph (Sawyer) Sauers, Ward Bond. *D:* William Wellman; *P:* Robert Lord; *St & Sc:* Niven Busch, Manuel Seff; *Songs:* "Lonely Lane" and "Men of Calvert" by Sammy Fain, Irving Kahal, "Just One More Chance" by Sam Coslow, Arthur Johnston, "Meet Me in the Gloaming" by Arthur Freed, Al Hoffman & Al Goodhart, and "What Will I Do Without You" by Johnny Mercer and Hilda Gottlieb. (G.B. title: *Football Coach*) (1:15)

Campus romantic drama with songs of a ruthless football coach who will stop at nothing to make a winning team.

780. College Coquette (Columbia; 1929). *Cast:* William Collier, Jr., Ruth Taylor, Jobyna Ralston, Eddie Clayton, John Holland, Adda Gleason, Frances Lyons, Gretchen Hartman, Ed Peil, Jr., Maurice Murphy, Billy Taft. *D:* George Archainbaud.

Low-budget romantic comedy.

781. College Holiday (Paramount; 1936). *Cast:* Jack Benny (J. Davis Bowster), George Burns (George Hymen), Gracie Allen (Calliope Dove), Mary Boland (Carola Gaye), Martha Raye (Daisy Schloggenheimer), Etienne Girardot (Prof. Hercules Dove), Marsha Hunt (Sylvia Smith), Leif Erickson (Dick Winters), Eleanore Whitney (Eleanor Wayne), Johnny Downs (Johnny Jones), Louis DaPron (Barry Taylor), Olympe Bradna (Felice L'Hommedieu), Jed Prouty (Sheriff John J. Trimble), Richard Carle (Judge Bent), Margaret Seddon (Mrs. Schloggenheimer), Nick Lukats (Wisconsin), Spec O'Donnell (Lafayette), Ben Blue (stagehand), Jack Chapin (Colgate), Lal Chand Mehra (Rahma), Nora Cecil (Miss Elkins), Harry Hayden (Mr. Smith), Fred "Snowflake" Toones, Terry Ray (Ellen Drew in her film debut), Priscilla Lawson, Kay Griffith, Gail Sheridan, Barlowe Borland, Charles Arnt, Edward LeSaint, Eddie Foy, Jr., Buddy Messinger, Dorothy Lamour (bit). *D:* Frank Tuttle; *P:* Harlan Thompson; *Sc:* J.P. McEvoy, Harlan Ware, Jay Gorney, Henry Myers; *Songs:* "A Rhyme for Love," "I Adore You," "So What?" and "Love in Bloom" (originally written for *She Loves Me Not*) (q.v.) by Ralph Rainger and Leo Robin, "The Sweetheart Waltz" and "Who's That Knockin' at My Heart" by Burton Lane and Ralph Freed; *Choreographer:* LeRoy Prinz. (1:27)

Musical-comedy of a woman hotel owner who does sex research on visiting college types. One of the 38 top grossing films of 1936–37.

782. College Humor (Paramount; 1933). *Cast:* Bing Crosby, Jack Oakie, Mary Carlisle, George Burns, Gracie Allen, Richard Arlen, Mary Kornman, Joseph (Sawyer) Sauers, Jimmy Conlin, Eddie Nugent, Frank Jenks (film debut), James Burke (film debut), Grady Sutton. *D:* Wesley Ruggles; *P:* William LeBaron; *St:* Dean Fales; *Sc:* Claude Binyon, Frank Butler. (1:20)

Hit campus comedy with music which features Bing Crosby singing his hit song "Learn to Croon" (Sam Coslow-Arthur Johnston).

783. College Love (Universal; 1929). *Cast:* George Lewis, Dorothy Gulliver, Eddie Phillips, Churchill Ross, Hayden Stevenson, Sumner Getchell, Russ Saunders. *D:* Nat Ross; *P:* Carl Laemmle, Jr.; *Sc:* John B. Clymer, Pierre Couderc, Leonard Fields, Albert DeMond; *St:* Leonard Fields.

Campus gridiron story.

784. College Lovers (WB/F.N.; 1930). *Cast:* Marian Nixon, Russell Hopton, Jack Whiting, Guinn Williams, Frank McHugh, Wade Boteler, Phyllis Crane, Richard Tucker. *D:* John Adolfi; *St:* Earl Baldwin; *Sc:* Douglas Doty.

Low-budget campus comedy.

785. College Rhythm (Paramount; 1934). *Cast:* Jack Oakie, Lyda Roberti, Joe Penner, Lanny Ross, Helen Mack, Mary Brian, Franklin Pangborn, Ben Blue, Clara Lou (Ann) Sheridan, Robert McWade, Harold Minjir, Monte Blue, George Barbier, Joseph (Sawyer) Sauers, Dean Jagger, Bud Flanagan (Dennis O'Keefe). *D:* Norman Taurog; *P:* Louis D. Lighton; *St:* George Marion, Jr.; *Sc:* Walter DeLeon, John McDermott, Francis Martin; *Hit Song:* "Stay as Sweet as You Are."

Comedy with music.

786. College Scandal (Paramount; 1935). *Cast:* Kent Taylor, Arline

Judge, Wendy Barrie, Johnny Downs, Mary Nash, Joyce Compton, William Frawley, Samuel S. Hinds, Billy Benedict. *D:* Elliott Nugent; *P:* Albert Lewis; *Sc:* Charles Brackett (co-writer). (G.B. title: *The Clock Strikes 8*)

B mystery of a killer loose on a college campus. Remade by this studio in 1942 as *Sweater Girl.*

787. College Swing (Paramount; 1938). *Cast:* George Burns, Gracie Allen, Bob Hope, Martha Raye, Edward Everett Horton, Florence George, Ben Blue, Betty Grable, Jackie Coogan, John Payne, Cecil Cunningham, Robert Cummings, Skinnay Ennis and the Slade Brothers, Jerry Bergen, Edward LeSaint, St. Brendan Choristers. *D:* Raoul Walsh; *P:* Lewis E. Gensler; *Sc:* Walter DeLeon, Francis Martin, Morrie Ryskind, Preston Sturges; *St:* Frederick Hazlitt Brennan, Ted Lesser. (G.B. title: *Swing, Teacher, Swing*) (1:26)

Campus musical-comedy of a daffy girl who inherits a college. Based on "The Charm School" by Alice Duer Miller (a work which seems to have been the basis for many films). Includes three popular songs of the day, "I Fall in Love with You Every Day" by Frank Loesser, Manning Sherwin and Arthur Altman, "How'dja Like to Love Me?" and "Moments Like This" by Loesser and Burton Lane.

788/789. Collegiate (Paramount; 1936). *Cast:* Jack Oakie, Joe Penner, Frances Langford, Betty Grable, Ned Sparks, Lynne Overman, Betty Jane Cooper, Henry Kolker, Marjorie (Reynolds) Moore, Martha O'Driscoll (film debut), Donald Gallagher, Mack Gordon, Harry Revel. *D:* Ralph Murphy; *P:* Louis D. Lighton; *Sc:* Walter De Leon, Francis Martin; *Songs:* "You Hit the Spot" and "I Feel Like a Feather in the Breeze" by Mack Gordon and Harry Revel. (G.B. title: *The Charm School*)

B musical-comedy of a man who finds himself heir to a girls school. Based on Alice Duer Miller's "The Charm

School," it was previously filmed in 1921 as *The Charm School* with Wallace Reid, in 1928 as *Someone to Love* with Buddy Rogers, in 1929 as *Sweetie* (q.v.) with Nancy Carroll. Remade in 1938 as *College Swing* (see above).

790. The Colorado Kid (Republic-Supreme; 1937). *Cast:* Bob Steele, Marion Weldon, Karl Hackett, Ted Adams, Ernie Adams, Frank LaRue, Horace Murphy, Kenne Duncan, Budd Buster, Frank Ball, John Merton, Horace B. Carpenter, Wally West. *D:* Sam Newfield; *P:* A.W. Hackel; *Sc:* Charles Francis Royal. (1:00)

Bob Steele western of innocent man escaping from jail to find the party who committed the crime he was sentenced for.

791. Colorado Sunset (Republic; 1939). *Cast:* Gene Autry, Smiley Burnette, June Storey, Barbara Pepper, Larry "Buster" Crabbe, Robert Barrat, Patsy Montana, Purnell Pratt, William Farnum, Kermit Maynard, Jack Ingram, Elmo Lincoln, The CBS-KMBC Texas Rangers, Cactus Mack, Champion. *D:* George Sherman; *P:* William Berke; *St:* Luci Ward, Jack Natteford; *Sc:* Betty Burbridge, Stanley Roberts. (1:01)

Gene Autry western of a group of musicians who buy a cattle ranch only to find the bovines are milkers instead of beefers.

792. The Colorado Trail (Columbia; 1938). *Cast:* Charles Starrett, Iris Meredith, The Sons of the Pioneers with Pat Brady and Bob Nolan, Dick Curtis, Art Mix, Robert Fiske, Edward LeSaint, Alan Bridge, Hank Bell, Ed Peil, Edmund Cobb, Jack Clifford, Richard Botiller. *D:* Sam Nelson; *Sc:* Charles Francis Royal. (0:55)

Charles Starrett western of a range feud which erupts between cattlemen.

793. Come Across (Universal; 1929). *Cast:* Lina Basquette, Reed Howes, Flora Finch. *D:* Ray Taylor.

Low-budget part-talkie crime melodrama.

794. Come and Get It (United Artists/Samuel Goldwyn; 1936). *Cast:* Edward Arnold (Barney Glasgow), Joel McCrea (Richard Glasgow), Frances Farmer (in a dual role as Lotta Morgan & Lotta Bostrom), Walter Brennan (A.A. for B.S.A. as Swan Bostrom), Andrea Leeds (film debut as Evvie Glasgow), Frank Shields (film debut as Tony Schwerke), Edwin Maxwell (Sid Le Maire), Robert Lowery (film debut—bit), Mady Christians (Karie), Mary Nash (Emma Louise Glasgow), Clem Bevans (Gunnar Gallagher), Cecil Cunningham (Josie), Harry Bradley (Gubbins), Charles Halton (Hewitt), Al K. Hall (Goodnow), Rollo Lloyd, Phillip Cooper. *D:* Howard Hawks, William Wyler; *As.P.:* Merritt Hulburd; *Adaptation:* Jules Furthman, Jane Murfin; *Editor:* (A.A.N.) Edward Curtiss. (re-release title: *Roaring Timber*) (1:39) (video)

Adventure drama of a ruthless Wisconsin lumber baron. Based on the novel by Edna Ferber (1935). One of the 38 top grossing films of 1936–37.

795. Come Closer, Folks (Columbia; 1936). *Cast:* James Dunn, Marian Marsh, Gene Lockhart, Wynne Gibson, John Gallaudet, Herman Bing, George McKay, Gene Morgan. *D:* D. Ross Lederman; *St:* Aben Kandel; *Sc:* Harold Buchman, Lee Loeb.

B comedy.

796. Come On, Cowboys! (Republic; 1937). *Cast:* Robert Livingston (Stony Brooke), Ray Corrigan (Tucson Smith), Max Terhune (Lullaby Joslin), Maxine Doyle, Ed Peil, Horace Murphy, Ann Bennett, Ed Cassidy, Roger Williams, Willie Fung, Fern Emmett, Yakima Canutt, Merrill McCormack, Al Taylor, George Plues, George Morrell, Milburn Morante, Carleton Young, Ernie Adams, Jim Corey, Jack Kirk. *D:* Joe Kane; *Sc:* Betty Burbridge. (0:59) (video)

Three Mesquiteers western involving a circus.

797. Come On, Danger (RKO; 1932). *Cast:* Tom Keene, Julie Haydon, Roscoe Ates, Robert Ellis, William Scott, Frank Lackteen, Wade Boteler, Roy Stewart, Harry Tenbrook, Bud Osborne, Nell Craig, Monte Montague. *D:* Robert Hill; *St:* Bennett Cohen; *Sc:* David Lewis, Lester Ilfield. (1:00)

Tom Keene western of a ranger who goes after a gang headed by a girl who he believes killed his brother. The first Keene oater to be released under the RKO-Radio label. Prior to this they were released under the Pathé label. Remade in 1938 with George O'Brien and Tim Holt as *Renegade Ranger* (q.v.) and again in 1942 with Holt as *Come On, Danger*.

798. Come On, Leathernecks! (Republic; 1938). *Cast:* Richard Cromwell, Marsha Hunt, Leon Ames, Edward Brophy, James Bush, Howard Hickman, Robert Warwick, Bruce MacFarlane, Alan Ladd (bit). *D:* James Cruze (final film—ret.); *Sc:* Dorrell McGowan, Stuart McGowan, Sidney Salkow.

B actioner.

799. Come On, Marines (Paramount; 1934). *Cast:* Richard Arlen, Grace Bradley, Ida Lupino, Roscoe Karns, Monte Blue, Lona Andre, Edmund Breese, Clara Lou (Ann) Sheridan, Toby Wing, Colin Tapley, Virginia Hammond, Gwenllian Gill, Fuzzy Knight, Julian Madison, Leo Chalzel, Roger Gray. *D:* Henry Hathaway; *St:* Philip Wylie; *Sc:* Joel Sayre, Byron Morgan.

Comedy of a group of marines who set out to rescue ship-wrecked children, only to find the children are actually a group of gorgeous women. Needless to say, a pre-code release.

800. Come On, Rangers (Republic; 1938). *Cast:* Roy Rogers, Mary Hart (Lynne Roberts), Raymond Hatton, J. Farrell MacDonald, Purnell Pratt, Harry Woods, Bruce McFarlane, Lane Chandler, Lee Powell, Bob Kortman, Chester Gunnels, George (Montgomery) Letz, Robert Wilke, Frank McCarroll, Chick Hannon, Jack Kirk, Al Taylor, Horace B. Carpenter, Al Ferguson, Allan Cavan, Ben Corbett, Burr Caruth. *D:* Joseph Kane; *As.P.:* Charles E. Ford; *Sc:* Gerald Geraghty, Jack Natteford. (Re-release title: *Texas Legionnaires*) (0:57)

Early Roy Rogers western with a story of the Texas Rangers.

801. Come On, Tarzan (World Wide; 1932). *Cast:* Ken Maynard, Merna Kennedy, Kate Campbell, Niles Welch, Roy Stewart, Ben Corbett, Robert Kortman, Jack Rockwell, Nelson McDowell, Jack Mower, Edmund Cobb, Robert Walker, Hank Bell, Slim Whitaker, Blackjack Ward, Jim Corey, Al Taylor, Bud McClure, Tarzan. *D:* Alan James (Alvin J. Neitz); *Sc:* James. (1:01) (video)

Not a Tarzan movie, but a Ken Maynard western of a ranch foreman looking into the allegation that horses are being killed for dog food. Maynard's horse, Tarzan was named after the Edgar Rice Burroughs' jungle hero.

Come Up Smiling (G.B. title) *see* **Sing Me a Love Song**

802. Comet Over Broadway (WB/F.N.; 1938). *Cast:* Kay Francis, Ian Hunter, John Litel, Donald Crisp, Minna Gombell, Melville Cooper, Sybil Jason, Susan Hayward, Ian Keith, Ray Mayer, Clem Bevans, Vera Lewis, Leona Maricle. *D:* Busby Berkeley; *As.P.:* Bryan Foy; *Sc:* Robert Buckner, Mark Hellinger. (1:09)

B drama of a girl who will stop at nothing to attain stardom on the Great White Way. Based on a magazine short story by Faith Baldwin.

803. Comin' 'Round the Mountain (Republic; 1936). *Cast:* Gene Autry, Smiley Burnette, Ann Rutherford, LeRoy Mason, Raymond Brown, Ken Cooper, Tracy Layne, Bob McKenzie, Laurita Puente, John Ince, Frank Lackteen, Frankie Marvin, Jim Corey, Al Taylor, Steve Clark, Frank Ellis, Hank Bell, Richard Botiller. *D:* Mack V. Wright; *P:* Nat Levine; *St:* Oliver Drake; *Sc:* Drake, Dorrell & Stuart McGowan. (0:55)

Gene Autry musical western of a cowboy who saves a girl's ranch.

804. Coming Out Party (Fox; 1934). *Cast:* Frances Dee, Gene Raymond, Alison Skipworth, Nigel Bruce, Harry Green, Jessie Ralph, Gilbert Emery, Lynn Bari, Clifford Jones, Germaine de Neel. *D:* John G. Blystone; *St:* Becky Gardiner, Gladys Unger; *Sc:* Jesse Lasky, Jr., Unger. (1:19)

Girl loves musician. Girl's socialite mother disapproves.

805. Command Performance (Tiffany; 1930–31). *Cast:* Neil Hamilton, Thelma Todd, Mischa Auer, Una Merkel. *D:* Walter Lang.

"Poverty row" romance of mistaken identity.

806. Common Clay (Fox; 1930). *Cast:* Constance Bennett, Lew Ayres, Tully Marshall, Matty Kemp, Purnell Pratt, Beryl Mercer, Hale Hamilton, Ada Williams, Genevieve Blinn, Charles McNaughton. *D:* Victor Fleming; *Sc:* Jules Furthman. (1:08)

Romantic drama of class distinction. Based on the play by Cleves Kinkead. A box office hit, it was remade in 1936 as *Private Number* (q.v.). Previously filmed in 1919 by Pathé with Fannie Ward.

807. Common Ground (Xxxx Xxxx; 1933). (No information available)

808. The Common Law (RKO-Pathé; 1931). *Cast:* Constance Bennett,

Joel McCrea, Hedda Hopper, Lew Cody, Walter Walker, Marion Shilling, Robert Williams (film debut), Paul Ellis, Yola D'Avril. *D:* Paul Stein; *As.P.:* Harry Joe Brown; *Sc:* John Farrow, Horace Jackson. (1:17)

Drama of a girl with a past who works as a model in a Paris art colony. Previous versions: (World–Selznick; 1916) with Conway Tearle and Clara Kimball Young, (First National; 1923) with Conway Tearle and Corinne Griffith. Based on the novel by Robert W. Chambers, this remake was a box office success.

809. Compromised (WB/F.N.; 1931). *Cast:* Ben Lyon, Rose Hobart, Juliette Compton, Claude Gillingwater, Bert Roach, Emma Dunn, Louise Mackintosh, Edgar Norton, Delmar Watson, Virginia Sale, Adele Watson, Florence Britton. *D:* John Adolfi; *Sc:* Waldemar Young, Florence Ryerson. (G.B. title: *We Three*)

B drama of a poor girl who marries a rich young man and through love, saves him from the bottle and himself. Based on the play by Edith Fitzgerald.

Concealment (G.B. title) *see* **The Secret Bride**

810. The Concentratin' Kid (Universal; 1930). *Cast:* Hoot Gibson, Kathryn Crawford, Duke R. Lee, Jim Mason, Robert E. Homans. *D:* Arthur Rosson; *P:* Gibson; *Sc:* Harold Tarshis. (0:57)

Hoot Gibson comedy western of a cowboy in love with a radio singer he never met. Gibson's final film for this studio.

811. Condemned (United Artists/ Samuel Goldwyn; 1929). *Cast:* Ronald Colman (A.A.N. for B.A. combined with *Bulldog Drummond* (q.v.), Ann Harding, Dudley Digges (film debut), Louis Wolheim, William Elmer, William Vaughn. *D:* Wesley Ruggles; *P:* Samuel Goldwyn; *Sc:* Sidney Howard. (G.B. title: *Condemned to Devil's Island*) (1:26)

Drama of a man's escape from the notorious French island prison, Devil's Island. Based on the novel "Condemned to Devil's Island" by Blair Niles.

Condemned to Devil's Island (G.B. title) *see* **Condemned**

812. Condemned to Live (Invincible; 1935). *Cast:* Ralph Morgan, Russell Gleason, Mischa Auer, Pedro De Cordoba. *D:* Frank Strayer.

"Poverty row" horror thriller.

813. Condemned Women (RKO; 1938). *Cast:* Sally Eilers, Louis Hayward, Anne Shirley, Esther Dale, Lee Patrick, Leona Roberts, George Irving, Richard Bond, Netta Packer, Rita LaRoy, Florence Lake, Dorothy Adams (film debut). *D:* Lew Landers; *P:* Robert Sisk; *St:* Lionel Houser; *Sc:* Houser. (1:17)

Hit melodrama set in a women's prison.

814. Confession (WB/F.N.; 1937). *Cast:* Kay Francis, Ian Hunter, Basil Rathbone, Jane Bryan, Donald Crisp, Laura Hope Crews, Mary Maguire, Robert Barrat, Veda Ann Borg, Dorothy Peterson, Sig Rumann, Ben Welden. *D:* Joe May; *P:* Hal B. Wallis; *Supervisor:* Henry Blanke; *Adaptation:* Julius J. Epstein, Margaret LeVino. (1:25)

Drama of a woman who shoots her no-good boyfriend to protect her daughter. Based on an original screenplay by Hans Rameau which was supposedly based on actual events. Previously filmed in 1925 by Paramount as *The Coast of Folly* with Gloria Swanson, and as a 1936 German production titled *Mazurka.*

815. Confessions of a Co-ed (Paramount; 1931). *Cast:* Sylvia Sidney, Phillips Holmes, Norman Foster, Claudia Dell, Martha Sleeper, Bruce Coleman, Florence Britton, Dorothy Libaire, Eulalie Jensen, Marguerite

Warner, Winter Hall. *D:* David Burton, Dudley Murphy. (G.B. title: *Her Dilemma*)

Romantic drama of an unwed mother.

816. Confessions of a Nazi Spy (WB; 1939). *Cast:* Edward G. Robinson (Ed Renard), Francis Lederer (Acting Award by the National Board of Review as Schneider), George Sanders (Schlager), Paul Lukas (Acting Award by the National Board of Review as Dr. Kassel), Henry O'Neill (D.A. Kellogg), James Stephenson (Scotland Yard man), Lya Lys (Erika Wolff), Grace Stafford (Mrs. Schneider), Sig Rumann (Krogman), Fred Tozere (Phillips), Dorothy Tree (Hilda), Celia Sibelius (Mrs. Kassel), Joseph Sawyer (Renz), Lionel Royce (Hintze), Hans von Twardowsky (Wildebrandt), Frederick Vogeding (Capt. Richter), Henry Victor (Helldorf), George Rosener (Klauber), Robert O. Davis (Straubel), John Voight (Westphal), Will Kaufman (Gruetzwald), William (Von Brincken) Vaughn (Capt. Von Eichen), Jack Mower (McDonald), Robert Emmett Keane (Harrison), Eily Malyon (Mrs. MacLaughlin), Frank Mayo (Staunton), Lucien Prival (Kranz), Bodil Rosing (Anna), Charles Sherlock (Young), Martin Kosleck (Joseph Goebbels), John Deering (narrator), Alec Craig, Jean Brooks, Niccolai Yoshkin, Frederick Burton, Ward Bond, Charles Trowbridge, John Ridgely. *D:* Anatole Litvak; *As.P.:* Robert Lord; *Sc:* Milton Krims, John Wexley. (1:42)

Semi-documentary style propaganda film of government men who route out a network of Nazis working in the United States. Based on information gathered by Leon G. Turrou, a former F.B.I. agent, it was voted "Best Film of the Year" by the National Board of Review. Banned in several European countries.

817. Confidential (Republic/Mascot; 1936). *Cast:* Donald Cook, Evalyn Knapp, Warren Hymer, J. Carrol Naish, Herbert Rawlinson, Theodore von Eltz, Morgan Wallace, Kane Richmond, Clay Clement, Reed Howes, Edward Hearn, Alan Bridge, Earl Eby, Lynton Brent, George Chesebro, Monte Carter, Mary Gwynne, Frank Marlowe, James Burtis, Lillian Castle, Donald Kerr, Edwin Argus, Jack Gustin, David Worth, Allen Connor, Tom Brower. *D:* Edward L. Cahn; *St:* John Rathmell, W. Scott Darling; *Sc:* Wellyn Totman; *Additional Dialogue:* Olive Cooper. (1:05) (video)

Melodrama of a G-Man who goes undercover to expose a numbers racket.

Conflict (1930) (G.B. title) *see* **Sweet Mama**

818. Conflict (Universal; 1936). *Cast:* John Wayne, Jean Rogers, Bryant Washburn, Lloyd Ingraham, Tommy Bupp, Ward Bond, Harry Woods, Frank Sheridan, Frank Hagney, Margaret Mann, Eddie Borden. *D:* David Howard; *P:* Trem Carr; *Sc:* Charles Logue, Walter Weems. (aka: *The Abysmal Brute*) (1:00)

B boxing actioner, suggested by a novel by Jack London. A remake of *The Abysmal Brute* (Universal; 1923) with Reginald Denny and Mabel Julienne Scott.

819. Congo Maisie (MGM; 1939–40). *Cast:* Ann Sothern (Maisie), John Carroll, Rita Johnson, Shepperd Strudwick, J.M. Kerrigan, Leonard Mudie, E.E. Clive, Everett Brown, Lionel Pape, Martin Wilkins, Ernest Whitman, Jack Beutel. *D:* H.C. Potter; *P:* J. Walter Ruben; *Sc:* Mary McCall, Jr. (1:10)

Second entry in the "Maisie" series with her adventures in darkest Africa. A hit for the studio, it was a remake of *Red Dust* (q.v.). Remade in 1953 as *Mogambo*. Based on Wilson Collison's "Congo Landing."

820. Congorilla (Fox; 1932). *P:* The Johnsons.

Documentary feature by and featuring famed American explorers Martin and Osa Johnson, as they photograph the African gorilla.

821. A Connecticut Yankee (Fox; 1931). *Cast:* Will Rogers (Hank — "Sir Boss"), Maureen O'Sullivan (Alisande), Myrna Loy (Morgan Le Fay), Frank Albertson (Clarence), William Farnum (King Arthur), Mitchell Harris (Merlin the Magician), Brandon Hurst (Sagramor). *D:* David Butler; *Adaptation & Sc:* William Conselman. (1:36)

A modern man finds himself back in time. This comedy was based on Mark Twain's 1889 "A Connecticut Yankee in King Arthur's Court" and the 1927 stageplay, "A Connecticut Yankee." It was one of the 15 top grossing films of 1930–31 and placed #10 on the "10 Best" list of the *New York Times.* Previously filmed by this studio in 1921 with Harry C. Myers. Remade in 1949 by Paramount as *A Connecticut Yankee in King Arthur's Court.* A variation titled *Unidentified Flying Oddball* was made in 1979 by the Disney Studios.

822. The Conquering Horde (Paramount; 1931). *Cast:* Richard Arlen, Fay Wray, James (Junior) Durkin, Claude Gillingwater, George Mendoza, Ian MacLaren, Kathrin Clare Ward, Charles Stevens, Arthur Stone, Chief Standing Bear, Frank Rice, Edwin J. Brady, Bob Kortman, Harry Cording, John Elliott. *D:* Edward Sloman; *Sc:* Grover Jones, William Slavens McNutt. (1:16)

Western of a government agent who helps a girl get her herd to market after the Civil War. A remake of *North of '36* (Paramount; 1924), it was based on a book by Emerson Hough.

823. The Conquerors (RKO; 1932). *Cast:* Richard Dix, Ann Harding, Edna May Oliver, Guy Kibbee, Julie Haydon, Donald Cook, Walter Walker, Wally Albright, Marilyn Knowlden, Harry Holman, Jason Robards, E.H.

Calvert, Jed Prouty, Richard "Skeets" Gallagher, J. Carrol Naish, Elizabeth Patterson. *D:* William A. Wellman; *Ex.P.:* David O. Selznick; *St:* Howard Estabrook; *Sc:* Robert Lord. (TV and re-release title: *The Pioneer Builders*) (1:28)

Generational story of a banking empire from 1873 to 1929. A failed attempt by RKO to capitalize on the popularity and success of *Cimarron* (q.v.).

824. Conquest (WB; 1929). *Cast:* Monte Blue, Lois Wilson, H.B. Warner, Tully Marshall, Edmund Breese. *D:* Roy Del Ruth; *St:* Mary Imlay Taylor; *Sc:* C. Graham Baker, Eve Unsell.

Melodrama of two pilots in love with the same girl.

825. Conquest (MGM; 1937). *Cast:* Charles Boyer (A.A.N. for B.A. and an Acting Award from the National Board of Review as Napoleon), Greta Garbo (Countess Walewska), Reginald Owen (Talleyrand), Henry Stephenson (Count Walewska), Alan Marshal, Leif Erickson, Dame May Whitty, Maria Ouspenskaya (Acting Award from the National Board of Review), Scotty Beckett, Betty Blythe, George Zucco, Vladimir Sokoloff, C. Henry Gordon, Claude Gillingwater, Henry Kolker, Ivan Lebedeff, George Houston, Robert Warwick, Ian Wolfe, Henry Brandon, Noble Johnson. *D:* Clarence Brown; *P:* Bernard Hyman; *Sc:* Samuel Hoffenstein, Salka Viertel, S.N. Behrman; *Art-Set Decoration:* (A.A.N.) to Cedric Gibbons, William Horning. (G.B. title: *Marie Walewska*) (1:51) (video)

Lavishly produced costume drama of the romance between Napoleon and the Countess Walewska. Based on the Polish play by Waclaw Gasiorowski (English dramatization by Helen Jerome), the film marked Garbo's final dramatic role. A hit at the box office overseas, but not in the United States.

826. Consolation Marriage (RKO; 1931). *Cast:* Irene Dunne, Pat

O'Brien, John Halliday, Myrna Loy, Lester Vail, Matt Moore, Otis Harlan, Baby Pauline Stevens. *D:* Paul L. Sloane; *As.P.:* Myles Connolly; *St:* Bill Cunningham; *Sc:* Humphrey Pearson. (G.B. title: *Married in Haste*) (1:22) (video)

Drama of a couple, jilted by their lovers who fall in love and marry.

827. Conspiracy (RKO; 1930). *Cast:* Bessie Love, Ned Sparks, Hugh Trevor (film finale — d. 1933), Ivan Lebedeff, Rita LaRoy, Gertrude Howard, Otto Matiesen, Bert Moorhouse, Walter Long, Donald MacKenzie, Jane Keckley, Dwight Frye. *D:* Christy Cabanne; *As.P.:* Bertram Millhauser; *Sc:* Beulah Marie Dix. (1:09)

Drama with comic overtones of a stenographer who kills her boss after finding he is a drug dealer responsible for the death of her father. Based on the play by Robert Baker and John Emerson, it was previously filmed as a silent by Famous Players/Lasky. A box office flop.

828. Conspiracy (RKO; 1939). *Cast:* Allan Lane, Linda Hayes (starring debut), Robert Barrat, Lester Matthews, Charles Foy, Lionel Royce, J. Farrell MacDonald, Henry Brandon, William von Brincken, Solly Ward, Al Herman, John Laird, Fred Rapport. *D:* Lew Landers; *P:* Cliff Reid; *St:* John McCarthy, Faith Thomas; *Sc:* Jerome Chodorov; *Song:* Lew Brown, Sammy Fain. (0:59)

B adventure drama of a radio operator who get involved in a foreign revolution.

829. The Constant Woman (Sono Art–World Wide; 1933). *Cast:* Conrad Nagel, Leila Hyams, Claire Windsor, Robert Ellis, Alexander Carr, Stanley Fields. *D:* Victor Schertzinger; *Sc:* Warren Duff; *Adaptation:* F. Hugh Herbert. (aka: *Auction in Souls*)

"Poverty row" romantic drama.

830. Contraband (Xxxx Xxxx; 1933). (No information available)

831. Convict's Code (Monogram–Crescent Pictures; 1938–39). *Cast:* Robert Kent, Anne Nagel, Sidney Blackmer, Norman Willis, Victor Kilian, Maude Eburne, Ben Alexander, Pat Flaherty, Carleton Young, Howard Hickman, Joan Barclay, Harry Strang. *D:* Lambert Hillyer; *P:* E.B. Derr; *Sc:* John Krafft. (1:02)

B melodrama of a man wrongfully sentenced to jail who gets out to find the party responsible for framing him. Filmed before in 1930 by director Harry Revier for Syndicate, a film which was the last for actor Cullen Landis before retiring from the screen.

832. Convicted (Artclass; 1931). *Cast:* Jameson Thomas, Aileen Pringle, Dorothy Christy, Wilfred Lucas. *D:* Christy Cabanne.

Melodrama.

833. Convicted (Columbia; 1938). *Cast:* Charles Quigley, Rita Hayworth, Marc Lawrence, Donald Douglas, Edgar Edwards, Phyllis Clare, George McKay, Doreen MacGregor, William Irving, Grant MacDonald, Bob Rideout, Eddie Laughton, Michael Heppell. *D:* Leon Barsha. *Sc:* Edgar Edwards; *St:* Cornell Woolrich.

Prison melodrama.

834. Convicts at Large (Xxxx Xxxx; 1939). *Cast:* Ralph Forbes, Paula Stone. *D:* Scott E. Beal, David Friedman.

Melodrama.

835. Coquette (United Artists/ Mary Pickford; 1929). *Cast:* Mary Pickford (A.A. for B.A. in her all-talkie debut — as well as her first film without her long curls), John Mack Brown, John (St. Polis) Sainpolis, Matt Moore, William Janney, Henry Kolker, Louise Beavers, George Irving. *D:* Sam Taylor; *P:* Mary Pickford; *Sc:* John Grey, Allen McNeil, Taylor (unc.).

Drama of a southern girl who lies in court to protect her father from a murder charge. Based on the Broadway play by George Abbott and Ann Preston Bridgers, the film is notable as the first all-talkie released by U.A.

836. Cornered (Columbia; 1932). *Cast:* Tim McCoy, Claire McDowell, Noah Beery, Raymond Hatton, Shirley Grey, Niles Welch, Walter Long, Walter Brennan, Charles King, John Elliott, Art Mix, Merrill McCormack, Artie Ortego, Jim Corey, Ed Peil, Sr., Ray Jones, Blackie Whiteford. *D:* B. Reeves Eason; *Sc:* Wallace MacDonald. (1:00)

Tim McCoy western of a ranch foreman blamed for a murder he didn't commit.

837. Coronado (Paramount; 1935). *Cast:* Johnny Downs, Jack Haley, Jacqueline Wells (Julie Bishop), Leon Errol, Eddy Duchin and his orchestra, Alice White, Andy Devine, Berton Churchill, Jameson Thomas, James Burke, Nella Walker. *D:* Norman Z. McLeod; *P:* William LeBaron; *Sc:* Don Hartman, Frank Butler.

Light B musical-comedy set at a beach resort.

838. Corruption (Imperial; 1933). *Cast:* Evalyn Knapp, Preston Foster, Huntley Gordon, Natalie Moorhead, Warner Richmond, Gwen Lee, Mischa Auer, Lane Chandler, Sidney Bracey, Nick Thompson, Jason Robards, Kit Guard. *D:* C. Edward Roberts; *Sc:* Roberts.

Melodrama.

839. Corsair (United Artists/Roland West; 1931). *Cast:* Chester Morris, Alison Lloyd (Thelma Todd), Emmett Corrigan, William Austin, Frank McHugh, Fred Kohler, Frank Rice, Ned Sparks, Mayo Methot, Gay Seabrook, Addie McPhail, Henry Kolker. *D:* Roland West (final film before retiring); *P:* West; *Sc:* Josephine Lovett.

An ex-football hero turns to a life of crime in order to fund a false impression for his spoiled girlfriend and her Wall Street tycoon father. Based on a novel by Walon Green, the film was a fizzle at the box office.

840. The Costello Case (Sono Art–World Wide; 1930). *Cast:* Tom Moore, Lola Lane, Roscoe Karns, Russell Hardie, Wheeler Oakman. *D:* Walter Lang; *P:* James Cruze; *St & Sc:* F. McGrew Willis.

"Poverty row" murder-mystery.

841. Cougar, the King Killer (Sidney A. Snow Productions; 1933). *Cast:* Jay Bruce. *P:* Sidney A. Snow. (1:10)

Documentary of a hunting party combing the California hills for cougars and other game.

Couldn't Possibly Happen (G.B. title) *see* **Radio Ranch**

842/843. Counsel for Crime (Columbia; 1937). *Cast:* Douglass Montgomery, Jacqueline Wells (Julie Bishop), Otto Kruger, Gene Morgan, Thurston Hall, Robert Warwick, Marc Lawrence, Nana Bryant, Stanley Fields. *D:* John Brahm; *St:* Harold Shumate; *Sc:* Harold Buchman, Lee Loeb, Fred Niblo, Jr., Grace Neville.

Low-budget melodrama of a ruthless lawyer.

844. Counsellor at Law (Universal; 1933). *Cast:* John Barrymore, Bebe Daniels, Melvyn Douglas, Doris Kenyon, Onslow Stevens, Isabel Jewell, Thelma Todd, Mayo Methot, John Qualen, Vincent Sherman (film debut), Richard Quine, Victor Adams, Bobby Gordon, Clara Langsner, Barbara Perry, Elmer Brown, John Hammond Dailey, Marvin Kline, Malka Kornstein, Frederick Burton, T.H. Manning, Conway Washburn. *D:* William

Wyler; *P:* Henry Henigson; *Sc:* Elmer Rice. (1:27)

Critically acclaimed drama of a Jewish lawyer in New York City. Based on the hit Broadway play of 1931 by Elmer Rice, the film was also a box office success.

845. The Count of Monte Cristo (United Artists/Reliance; 1934). *Cast:* Robert Donat (his only American film, as Edmond Dantes), Elissa Landi (Mercedes de Rosas), Louis Calhern (Raymond de Villefort, Jr.), Sidney Blackmer (Fernand de Mondego), Raymond Walburn (Danglars), O.P. Heggie (Abbe Faria), Luis Alberni (Jacopo), Irene Hervey (Valentine de Villefort), William Farnum (Capt. Leclere), Georgia Caine (Madame de Rosas), Walter Walker (Morrel), Lawrence Grant (Raymond de Villefort, Sr.), Douglas Walton (Albert de Mondego), Juliette Compton (Clothilde), Clarence H. Wilson (Fouquet), Eleanor Phelps (Haydee), Ferdinand Munier (Louis XVIII), Paul Irving (Napoleon), Mitchell Lewis (Capt. Vampa), Holmes Herbert (judge), Clarence Muse (Ali), Tom Ricketts (Cockeye), Edward Keane (Bertrand), Lionel Belmore (prison governor), Wilfred Lucas (detective), Sydney Jarvis (Ali Pasha), Desmond Roberts (Blaca), John Marsden (Pellerin), Alphonse Martell (Batistino), Russell Powell (Manouse), Wally Albright (Albert as a child), Leon (Ames) Waycoff (Beauchamp), Fred Cavens (fencing master), Paul Fix. *D:* Rowland V. Lee; *P:* Edward Small; *Sc:* Philip Dunne, Dan Totheroh, Lee; *Song:* "The World Is Mine" by E.Y. Harburg, Johnny Green. (1:59) (video)

Classic filming of the classic Alexandre Dumas novel of a man unjustly imprisoned, who escapes to seek revenge on those who imprisoned him. Voted one of the "10 Best" films of the year by the National Board of Review, it also placed #9 on the "10 Best" list of *Film Daily.* First filmed in 1907 in one reel (approx. 10 minutes running time), con-

sidered to be the first film ever shot in California, predating by two years Selig's *In the Sultan's Power* (1909), considered to be the first dramatic film shot in an established California studio. Other silent versions: (Selig; 1912) starring Hobart Bosworth, (Famous Players; 1912-13) with James O'Neill, co-directed by Edwin S. Porter and Joseph Golden, and *Monte Cristo* (Fox; 1922) with John Gilbert. Three French versions followed, 1942, 1953 and 1961 as well as a TV movie in 1975 (U.S.A.). Many variations on the original story too numerous to mention here have also been filmed.

Counted Out (G.B. title) *see* **The Swellhead** (1930)

846. Counterfeit (Columbia; 1936). *Cast:* Chester Morris, Margot Grahame, Lloyd Nolan, Marc Lawrence, Marian Marsh, Gene Morgan, John Gallaudet, George McKay, Pierre Watkin, Claude Gillingwater. *D:* Erle C. Kenton; *P:* B.P. Schulberg; *St:* William Rankin; *Sc:* Rankin, Bruce Manning.

B melodrama of a G-Man posing as a killer to get in with criminal element he hopes to apprehend.

847. Counterfeit Lady (Columbia; 1937). *Cast:* Ralph Bellamy, Joan Perry, Douglass Dumbrille, John Harrington, George McKay, John Tyrrell, Max Hoffman, Jr., Edward LeSaint, Henry Mollison. *D:* D. Ross Lederman; *St:* Harold Shumate; *Sc:* Tom Van Dycke.

B melodrama.

848. The Countess of Monte Cristo (Universal; 1933). *Cast:* Fay Wray, Paul Lukas, Patsy Kelly, Reginald Owen, Carmel Myers, Robert Watson, Richard Tucker, Paul Page, John Sheehan, Robert McWade, Frank Reicher, Matthew Betz, Dewey Robinson. *D:* Karl Freund; *P:* Carl Laemmle, Jr.; *St:* Walter Fleisher; *Sc:* Karen De Wolf, Gene Lewis; *Additional Dialogue:* Gladys Unger. (1:14)

Romantic comedy of a girl pretending to be royalty. Remade in 1948 with Sonja Henie.

849. The Country Beyond (20th Century–Fox; 1936). *Cast:* Rochelle Hudson, Paul Kelly, Robert Kent, Alan Hale, Alan Dinehart, Matt McHugh, Andrew Tombes, Paul McVey, Claudia Coleman, Holmes Herbert, Buck the dog, Prince the dog. *D:* Eugene Forde; *P:* Sol M. Wurtzel; *Sc:* Lamar Trotti, Adele Commandini. (1:09)

Northwoods adventure of two Canadian Mounties, a girl and her dog, all in pursuit of fur thieves. A remake of Fox's 1926 production of the same name.

The Country Bumpkin (G.B. title) *see* **The All-American Chump**

850. The Country Doctor (20th Century–Fox; 1936). *Cast:* The Dionne Quintuplets, Jean Hersholt (Dr. Roy Luke), Dorothy Peterson (Nurse Andrews), June Lang (Mary), Slim Summerville (Ogden), Michael Whalen (Tony), Robert Barrat (Mac Kenzie), John M. Qualen (Asa Wyatt), Jane Darwell (nurse), J. Anthony Hughes (Mike), George Chandler (Greasy), Montagu Love (Sir Basil), Frank Reicher (Dr. Paul Luke), George Meeker (Dr. Wilson), David Torrence (Governor General), William Conlon (Peg-leg Walter), Joseph Sawyer (Joe), Edward McWade (editor), Helen Jerome Eddy (Mrs. Ogden), Carry Ovon (Jerry), Paul McVey (Mack), Harry C. Bradley (minister), Aileen Carlyle (Mrs. Wyatt), Richard Carlyle (bishop), Florence Roberts (grandmother), William (Billy) Benedict, Harry Cording, Kane Richmond, Mary Carr, Cecil Weston, Wilfred Lucas, Dillon Ober, Margaret Fielding, Claude King, John Dilson. *D:* Henry King; *P:* Darryl F. Zanuck; *As.P.:* Nunnally Johnson; *St:* Charles E. Blake; *Sc:* Sonya Levien. (1:50)

One of the 25 top grossing films of 1935–36, made primarily to capitalize on and exploit the Dionne quintuplets. The

popularity of this film begat two sequels, namely: *Reunion* (q.v.) and *Five of a Kind* (q.v.).

851. Country Gentlemen (Republic; 1936). *Cast:* Ole Olsen, Chic Johnson, Joyce Compton, Lila Lee, Ray Corrigan, Wade Boteler. *D:* Ralph Staub. (0:54) (video)

B rural comedy of two con-men whose congame backfires on them.

852. The County Chairman (Fox; 1935). *Cast:* Will Rogers, Evelyn Venable, Mickey Rooney, Louise Dresser, Kent Taylor, Stepin Fetchit, Charles Middleton, Berton Churchill, Gay Seabrook, William V. Mong, Jan Duggan, Frank Melton, Erville Alderson. *D:* John G. Blystone; *P:* Edward Butcher; *Sc:* Gladys Lehman, Sam Hellman.

Comedy-drama of rural life, based on the 1903 play by George Ade. Previous version: (Famous Players; 1915) with Maclyn Arbuckle and Harold Lockwood.

853. The County Fair (Monogram; 1932). *Cast:* Hobart Bosworth, Marion Shilling, Ralph Ince, William Collier, Jr., Kit Guard, George Chesebro, Otto Hoffman, Arthur Millett, Thomas R. Quinn, Edward Kane, Fred "Snowflake" Toones. *D:* Louis King; *P:* Trem Carr; *St:* Roy Fitzroy; *Sc:* Harvey Harris Gates. (1:11)

Some gamblers are out to stop an important horse race in this "poverty row" production.

854. County Fair (Monogram; 1937). *Cast:* John Arledge, Mary Lou Lender, J. Farrell MacDonald, Fuzzy Knight, Jimmy Butler, Harry Worth, Matty Roubert, William Hunter. *D:* Howard Bretherton; *P:* E.B. Derr (for Crescent Pictures); *St & Sc:* John T. Neville. (1:12)

Win the race and pay the mortgage is the theme of this "poverty row" production.

855. Courage (WB; 1930). *Cast:* Belle Bennett, Marian Nixon, Don Marion, Byron Sage, Rex Bell, Richard Tucker, Leon Janney, Carter De Haven, Jr., Charlotte Henry (debut, recreating her stage role), lanche Frederici, Dorothy Ward. *D:* Archie Mayo; *Sc:* Walter Anthony.

Drama of a widow raising her seven children, six of them thankless towards her long-suffering efforts. Based on the play by Tom Barry, it was remade as *My Bill* (q.v.).

856. Courage of the North (Empire/Stage & Screen Attractions; 1935). *Cast:* John Preston (Morton of the Mounted), Dynamite the Wonder Horse, Captain the King of the Dogs, William Desmond, June Love, Jimmy Aubrey, Tom London, Jim Thorpe, Charles King, James Sheridan (later Sherry Tansey). *D:* Robert Emmett (Tansey); *P:* Emmett; *St:* Barry Barringer; *Sc:* Emmett. (0:55)

Low-budget northwoods adventure of Mounties vs. fur thieves.

857. Courage of the West (Universal; 1937). *Cast:* Bob Baker, Lois January, Fuzzy Knight, J. Farrell Mac-Donald, Carl Stockdale, Buddy Cox, Harry Woods, Albert Russell, Charles K. French, Oscar Gahan, Richard Cramer, Jack Montgomery, Thomas Monk. *D:* Joseph H. Lewis; *P:* Trem Carr; *Sc:* Norton S. Parker. (0:56)

Singing cowboy Bob Baker makes his film debut in this first of twelve starring features for this studio. The story of an adopted boy who grows up to join the side of law and order, only to find his real father is the head of a ruthless gang.

Courageous (G.B. title) *see* **A Lost Lady**

858. The Courageous Avenger (Supreme; 1935). *Cast:* Johnny Mack Brown, Helen Erickson, Warner Richmond, Ed Cassidy, Frank Ball, Eddie Parker, Forrest Taylor, Bob Burns, Earl Dwire. *D:* Robert N. Bradbury; *P:* A.W. Hackel; *Sc:* Charles Francis Royal. (0:58)

Johnny Mack Brown western of a sheriff who finds some outlaws are stealing from a local silver mine.

859. The Covered Trailer (Republic; 1939). *Cast:* James Gleason, Lucille Gleason, Russell Gleason, Harry Davenport, Tommy Ryan, Mary Beth Hughes, Maude Eburne, Willie Best, Tom Kennedy, Hobart Cavanaugh. *D:* Gus Meins.

Fourth entry in the low-budget "Higgins Family" comedy series.

860. The Cowboy and the Bandit (Superior; 1935). *Cast:* Rex Lease, Janet Morgan (Blanche Mehaffey), Bobby Nelson, Richard Alexander, Wally Wales (Hal Taliaferro), William Desmond, Bill Patton, Franklyn Farnum, Art Mix, Lafe McKee, Ben Corbett, George Chesebro, Victor Potel, Alphonse Martel, Jack Kirk. *D:* Al Herman; *Sc:* Jack Jevne. (0:57)

Rex Lease western of a cowboy who helps a damsel in distress.

861. The Cowboy and the Kid (Universal; 1935–36). *Cast:* Buck Jones, Billy Burrud, Dorothy Revier, Lafe McKee, Harry Worth, Charles LeMoyne, Dick Rush, Robert McKenzie, Burr Caruth, Eddie Lee, Kernan Cripps. *D:* Ray Taylor; *Sc:* Frances Guihan. (0:58)

Buck Jones western of a cowboy who befriends a fatherless boy. A remake of *Just Pals* (Fox; 1920).

862. The Cowboy and the Lady (United Artists/Samuel Goldwyn; 1938). *Cast:* Gary Cooper, Merle Oberon, Patsy Kelly, Walter Brennan, Fuzzy Knight, Harry Davenport, Emma Dunn, Henry Kolker, Walter Walker, Berton Churchill, Charles Richman, Arthur Hoyt, Mabel Todd, Frederick Vogeding, Ernie Adams, Russell Powell, Jack Baxley, Johnny

Judd, Mabel Colcord. *D:* H.C. Potter; *P:* Sam Goldwyn; *St:* Leo McCarey, Frank R. Adams; *Sc:* S.N. Behrman, Sonya Levien; *Music:* (A.A.N.) Alfred Newman; *Song:* "The Cowboy and the Lady" (A.A.N.) Lionel Newman and Arthur Quenzer; *Sound Recording:* (A.A.) Thomas Moulton. (1:31)

An aristocratic girl falls for a rodeo star in this romantic comedy.

863. The Cowboy Counsellor (Allied; 1932). *Cast:* Hoot Gibson, Sheila Mannors, "Skeeter" Bill Robbins, Bobby Nelson, Fred Gilman, Jack Rutherford, William Humphrey, Gordon DeMain, Merrill McCormack, Alan Bridge, Frank Ellis. *D:* George Melford; *P:* M.H. Hoffman, Jr.; *Sc:* Jack Natteford. (1:02)

Hoot Gibson comic western of a law book salesman accused of a stagecoach robbery.

864. The Cowboy from Brooklyn (WB; 1938). *Cast:* Dick Powell, Pat O'Brien, Priscilla Lane, Dick Foran, Ann Sheridan, Johnnie "Scat" Davis, Ronald Reagan, Emma Dunn, Jeffrey Lynn, Hobart Cavanaugh, John Ridgely, Dennie Moore, Mary Field, James Stephenson, Donald Briggs, Rosella Towne, Mary Gordon, Harry Barris, Candy Candido. *D:* Lloyd Bacon; *P:* Hal Wallis; *As.P.:* Lou Edelman; *Sc:* Earl Baldwin; *Title Song:* Harry Warren, Johnny Mercer; *Other Songs:* Richard Whiting, Mercer. (G.B. title: *Romance and Rhythm*) (1:20)

Musical-comedy based on the play "Howdy Stranger" by Louis Pelletier, Jr., and Robert Sloane. A Cosmopolitan production, it was remade in 1948 as *Two Guys from Texas.*

865. Cowboy Holiday (Beacon; 1934–35). *Cast:* Guinn "Big Boy" Williams, Janet Chandler, Julian Rivero, Richard Alexander, John Elliott, Alma Chester, Frank Ellis, Julia Bejarano. *D:* Robert Hill; *Sc:* Rock Hawley (Robert Hill). (0:57)

Guinn "Big Boy" Williams comedy-western of a cowboy out to apprehend an outlaw disguised as a Mexican bandit.

866. The Cowboy Millionaire (Fox; 1935). *Cast:* George O'Brien, Evelyn Bostock, Edgar Kennedy, Alden Chase (Stephen Chase; Guy Chase), Maude Allen, Dan Jarrett, Lloyd Ingraham, Thomas Curran. *D:* Edward Cline; *P:* Sol Lesser (Atherton Productions); *Sc:* George Waggner, Dan Jarrett. (1:14)

Romantic western of an English girl visiting a dude ranch who falls for a cowpoke.

867. Cowboy Quarterback (WB; 1939). *Cast:* Bert Wheeler, Marie Wilson, Gloria Dickson, William Demarest, Eddie Foy, Jr., DeWolf (William) Hopper, William Gould, Charles Wilson, Frederic Tozere, John Harron, John Ridgely, Eddie Acuff, Clem Bevans. *D:* Noel Smith; *As.P.:* Bryan Foy; *Sc:* Fred Niblo, Jr. (0:56)

Based on a play by Ring Lardner and George M. Cohan, this is a B comedy of a westerner hired as a gridiron player. Previously filmed in 1929 as *Fast Company* (q.v.) and again as *Elmer the Great* (q.v.).

Cowboy Roundup *see* **Ride 'Em Cowboy**

868. The Cowboy Star (Columbia; 1936). *Cast:* Charles Starrett, Iris Meredith, Si Jenks, Marc Lawrence, Ed Peil, Wally Albright, Ralph McCullough, Landers Stevens, Dick Terry, Winifred Hari, Nick Copeland, Lew Meehan. *D:* David Selman; *Sc:* Frances Guihan. (0:56)

Modern Charles Starrett western of a movie cowboy who goes to a small town for a rest and winds up corralin' a bunch of racketeers.

869. Cowboys from Texas (Republic; 1939). *Cast:* Robert Livingston (Stony Brooke), Raymond Hatton (Rusty Joslin), Duncan Renaldo (Rico),

Carole Landis, Betty Compson, Ethan Laidlaw, Yakima Canutt, Walter Willis, Ed Cassidy, Bud Osborne, Charles King, Forbes Murray, Horace Murphy, Harry Strang, Jack Kirk, David Sharpe, Lew Meehan, Jack O'Shea, Charles Miller, Ivan Miller. *D:* George Sherman; *Supervisor:* Harry Grey; *Sc:* Oliver Drake. (0:57)

"Three Mesquiteers" western involving a range war between homesteaders and cattlemen.

870. Coyote Trails (Reliable; 1935). *Cast:* Tom Tyler, Alice Dahl, Ben Corbett, Lafe McKee, Richard Alexander, Slim Whitaker, George Chesebro, Lew Meehan, Jack Evans, Art Dillard, Jimmy Aubrey, Bud McClure, Tex Palmer, Phantom the horse. *D:* Bernard B. Ray; *P:* Harry S. Fraser; *Sc:* Rose Gordon. (1:00)

Tom Tyler western involving a wild stallion accused of stealing ranchers' horses.

871. Crack-Up (20th Century–Fox; 1936). *Cast:* Peter Lorre, Brian Donlevy, Helen Wood, Ralph Morgan, Thomas Beck, Lester Matthews, Lynn Bari, Howard Hickman, Paul Stanton, Gloria Roy. *D:* Malcolm St. Clair; *P:* Samuel G. Engel; *St:* John Goodrich; *Sc:* Charles Kenyon, Sam Mintz. (1:05)

B espionage thriller.

872. Cracked Nuts (RKO; 1931). *Cast:* Bert Wheeler, Robert Woolsey, Edna May Oliver, Dorothy Lee, Stanley Fields, Leni Stengel, Boris Karloff, Roscoe Ates, Frank Thornton, Ben Turpin. *D:* Edward Cline; *As.P.* Douglas MacLean; *Sc:* Al Boasberg; *Dialogue:* Ralph Spence & Al Boasberg. (1:05)

Satirical comedy farce set in the mythical kingdom of El Dorania. A box office hit.

873. Cradle Song (Paramount; 1933). *Cast:* Dorothea Wieck (American debut), Evelyn Venable (film debut),

Louise Dresser, Sir Guy Standing, Kent Taylor, Gail Patrick, Gertrude Michael, Nydia Westman, Mischa Auer, Georgia Caine, Eleanor Wesselhoeft, David Durand, Yvonne Pelletier, Gertrude Norman, Marion Ballou, Rosita Butler, Howard Lang, R.D. McLean, Diane Sinclair. *D:* Mitchell Leisen (solo directorial debut); *Adaptation:* Marc Connelly; *Sc:* Frank Partos, Robert Sparks.

Drama of a nun longing for a child of her own, who finds an abandoned baby girl on the convent steps and raises her to adulthood. Based on the Spanish play by Gregorio Martinez Sierra, the film is no relation to the 1941 Universal film of the same name.

874. Craig's Wife (Columbia; 1936). *Cast:* Rosalind Russell (Harriet Craig), John Boles, Billie Burke, Jane Darwell, Dorothy Wilson (final film—ret.), Alma Kruger, Thomas Mitchell, Elizabeth Risdon, Raymond Walburn, Nydia Westman. *D:* Dorothy Arzner; *Sc:* Mary McCall, Jr., George Kelly, Edward Chodorov. (1:15) (video)

Drama of a woman who thinks more of her material things than she does of her husband. Based on the hit Broadway play by George Kelly. Filmed before by Pathé in 1928 with Warner Baxter and Irene Rich. Remade by Columbia in 1950 as *Harriet Craig.*

875. The Crash (WB/F.N.; 1932). *Cast:* George Brent, Ruth Chatterton, Paul Cavanagh, Barbara Leonard, Henry Kolker, Lois Wilson, Hardie Albright, Helen Vinson, Ivan Simpson, Richard Tucker, Virginia Hammond, Edith Kingdon. *D:* William Dieterle; *Sc:* Larry Barretto, Earl Baldwin (based on Barretto's novel). (0:58)

Drama of the effects on a stockbroker who loses it all in the "Crash of '29." The film was a box office flop as apparently few people wanted to be reminded.

876. Crash Donovan (Universal; 1936). *Cast:* Jack Holt, Nan Grey, John

King, Eddie Acuff, Douglas Fowley, Hugh Buckler, Ward Bond, Paul Porcasi, Joseph Sawyer, Gardner James, Huey White, Al Hill, William Tannen. *D:* William Nigh; *P:* Julian Bernheim; *St:* Harold Shumate; *Sc:* Eugene Solow, Charles Grayson, Karl Detzer. (0:57)

B actioner dealing with the training of a California highway motorcycle patrolman. A box office success.

877. Crashing Broadway (Monogram; 1933). *Cast:* Rex Bell, Doris Hill, Harry Bowen, George Hayes, Charles King, Louis Sargent, G.D. Wood (aka: Gordon DeMain), Ann Howard, John "Blackie" Whiteford, Perry Murdock, Henry Rocquemore, Max Asher, Allan Lee, George Morrell, Archie Ricks, Tex Palmer. *D:* John P. McCarthy; *P:* Paul Malvern; *Sc:* Wellyn Totman. (0:55) (video)

Offbeat Rex Bell western of a cowboy who heads for New York to become an actor.

878. Crashing Hollywood (RKO; 1937). *Cast:* Lee Tracy, Joan Woodbury, Paul Guilfoyle, Lee Patrick, Richard Lane, Bradley Page, Tom Kennedy, George Irving, Frank M. Thomas, Jack Carson, Alec Craig, James Conlin. *D:* Lew Landers; *P:* Cliff Reid; *Sc:* Paul Yawitz, Gladys Atwater. (1:01)

B comedy spoof of bank robbers who get upset when a Hollywood screenwriter fictionalizes their robbery for a movie. Based on the play "Lights Out" by Paul Dickey and Mann Page. Filmed before as *Lights Out* (FBO; 1923).

879. Crashing Society (Xxxx Xxxx; 1935). (No information available)

880. Crashing Thru (Monogram–Criterion Pictures; 1938–39). *Cast:* James Newill (Renfrew), Jean Carmen, Warren Hull, Iron Eyes Cody (film debut), Milburn Stone, Walter Byron, Robert Frazer, Joseph Girard, Dave O'Brien, Roy Barcroft, Guinn

Williams, Whip Wilson (film debut — who later had his own cowboy series for Monogram), Ted Adams, Earl Douglas, Stanley Fields. *D:* Elmer Clifton; *P:* Philip N. Krasne; *Sc:* Sherman L. Lowe. (1:05)

Renfrew the singing Mountie is after some gold thieves. Based on a story by Laurie York Erskine, the film was originally scheduled to be released by Grand National.

881. Crazy That Way (Fox; 1930). *Cast:* Joan Bennett, Kenneth MacKenna, Jason Robards, Sharon Lynn. *D:* Hamilton MacFadden; *Sc:* MacFadden, Marion Orth.

Comedy of a girl and the three men who romance her.

882. Crime Afloat (Treo; 1938). *Cast:* William Bakewell, Duncan Renaldo, Wilfred Lucas. *D:* Elmer Clifton.

Melodrama.

883. Crime and Punishment (Columbia; 1935). *Cast:* Peter Lorre, Edward Arnold, Tala Birell, Marian Marsh, Elizabeth Risdon, Mrs. Patrick Campbell (final film — ret.), Douglass Dumbrille, Thurston Hall, Gene Lockhart, Johnny Arthur, Rafaela Ottiano, Robert Allen, Charles Waldron. *D:* Josef Von Sternberg; *P:* B.P. Schulberg; *Sc:* S.K. Lauren, Joseph Anthony. (1:25)

Drama of a youth who kills a pawnbroker and goes on a guilt trip. Based on the 1866 novel by Feodor Mikhailovich Dostoyevsky. Previous version: (Pathé; 1917). Remade in France in 1958 and retitled *The Most Dangerous Sin.* Also filmed in the U.S.A. in 1959 in an updated modern version titled *Crime and Punishment U.S.A.*

884. The Crime Doctor (RKO; 1934). *Cast:* Otto Kruger, Karen Morley, Donald Crisp, Nils Asther, William Frawley, J. Farrell MacDonald, Pat O'Malley, Judith Wood,

Frank Conroy, Fred Kelsey, George Pat Collins, Samuel S. Hinds. *D:* John S. Robertson; *As.P.:* David Lewis; *St:* Israel Zangwill; *Sc:* Jane Murfin.

Low-budget mystery melodrama of a mastermind who "creates" the perfect crime. A remake of *The Perfect Crime* (FBO; 1928) (q.v.).

885. The Crime Nobody Saw (Paramount; 1937). *Cast:* Lew Ayres, Vivienne Osborne, Eugene Pallette, Colin Tapley, Benny Baker, Hattie McDaniel, Ruth Coleman, Robert Emmett O'Connor, Ferdinand Gottschalk, Howard Hickman, Terry Ray (Ellen Drew). *D:* Charles Barton; *St:* Ellery Queen, Lowell Brentano; *Sc:* Bertram Millhauser.

B murder-mystery involving three playwrights.

886. The Crime of Dr. Crespi (Republic; 1935). *Cast:* Erich Von Stroheim, Dwight Frye, Harriet Russell, Paul Guilfoyle, John Bohn, Geraldine Kay, Patsy Berlin, Dean Raymond, Joe Verdi, Jeanne Kelly. *D:* John H. Auer; *P:* Auer; *St:* Auer; *Sc:* Edwin Olmstead, Lewis Graham. (1:03) (video)

Thriller of a doctor seeking revenge on another. Based on Edgar Allan Poe's "The Premature Burial."

887. The Crime of Dr. Forbes (20th Century–Fox; 1936). *Cast:* J. Edward Bromberg, Robert Kent, Gloria Stuart, Paul McVey, Henry Armetta, Sara Haden, Alan Dinehart, Taylor Holmes, Charles Lane, Paul Stanton, DeWitt Jennings, Charles Croker-King. *D:* George Marshall; *P:* Sol M. Wurtzel; *St & Sc:* Frances Hyland, Saul Elkins. (1:15)

B mystery of a scientist, injured in an experiment who wants to die and seeks help from his assistant.

888. The "Crime" of Dr. Hallet (Universal; 1938). *Cast:* Ralph Bellamy, William Gargan, Josephine Hutchinson, Barbara Read, John King, Nella Walker, Charles Stevens, Honorable Wu, Eleanor Hansen. *D:* S. Sylvan Simon; *P:* Edmund Grainger; *Sc:* Lester Cole, Brown Holmes. (1:08)

A doctor working on a cure for jungle fever assumes the identity of his dead assistant. Remade in 1946 by this studio as *Strange Conquest.*

889. The Crime of Helen Stanley (Columbia; 1934). *Cast:* Gail Patrick, Ralph Bellamy, Kane Richmond, J. Carrol Naish, Shirley Grey, Arthur Hohl, Vincent Sherman, Bradley Page, Ward Bond. *D:* D. Ross Lederman.

Low-budget melodrama.

890. The Crime of the Century (Paramount; 1933). *Cast:* Jean Hersholt, Wynne Gibson, Stuart Erwin, Frances Dee, Samuel S. Hinds, Gordon Westcott, David Landau, William Janney, Robert Elliott, Torben Meyer, Bodil Rosing. *D:* William Beaudine; *Sc:* Brian Marlow, Florence Ryerson.

A who-dun-it of a doctor who confesses to murders before they occur. The film has the slight novelty of the screen going blank for a minute to give the viewer time to guess the killer. Based on the play by Walter Maria Espe.

891. The Crime Patrol (Empire; 1936). *Cast:* Ray Walker. *D:* Eugene Cummings; *Story:* Arthur T. Horman; *Cont. & Dial.:* Betty Burbridge.

Police melodrama.

892. Crime Ring (RKO; 1938). *Cast:* Allan Lane, Frances Mercer, Clara Blandick, Inez Courtney, Bradley Page, Ben Welden, Walter Miller, Frank M. Thomas, Jack Arnold (Vinton Howard), Morgan Conway, George Irving, Leona Roberts, Charles Trowbridge, Tom Kennedy, Paul Fix, Jack Mulhall. *D:* Leslie Goodwins; *P:* Cliff Reid; *St:* Reginald Taviner; *Sc:* J. Robert Bren, Gladys Atwater. (1:09)

B melodrama of a reporter who uncovers a fortune-telling scam.

893. Crime School (WB; 1938). *Cast:* Humphrey Bogart, Gale Page (film debut), Billy Halop, Bobby Jordan, Huntz Hall, Leo Gorcey, Bernard Punsley, Gabriel Dell, George Offerman, Jr., Weldon Heyburn, Cy Kendall, Charles Trowbridge, Spencer Charters, Donald Briggs, Frank Jaquet, Helen MacKellar, Paul Porcasi, Alan Bridge, Milburn Stone, John Ridgely, Jack Mower, Sybil Harris, James B. Carson, Frank Otto. *D:* Lewis Seiler; *As.P.:* Bryan Foy; *St:* Crane Wilbur; *Sc:* Wilbur, Vincent Sherman. (1:26) (video)

B melodrama of a boys reformatory with Humphrey Bogart as the warden and the "Dead End Kids" as inmates. Elements from this film were borrowed from two earlier Warners' productions.

894. Crime Takes a Holiday (Columbia; 1938). *Cast:* Jack Holt, Marcia Ralston, Russell Hopton, Douglass Dumbrille, William Frawley, Paul Fix, Thomas Jackson, Arthur Hohl, John Wray, William Pawley, Joseph Crehan. *D:* Lewis Collins; *Sc:* Henry Altimus, Charles Logue, Jefferson Parker.

B melodrama.

895. Crime Without Passion (Paramount; 1934). *Cast:* Claude Rains (Lee Gentry), Margo (film debut as Carmen Brown), Whitney Bourne (Katy Costello), Stanley Ridges (Eddie White), Esther Dale (film debut as Miss Keeley), Paula Trueman (Buster Malloy), Leslie Adams (O'Brien), Greta Granstedt (Della), Charles Kennedy (Lt. Norton), Fuller Mellish, Jr. (judge), Marjorie Main, Ben Hecht and Charles MacArthur (reporters), Helen Hayes (Mrs. Charles MacArthur in a cameo), Fanny Brice (cameo). *Directed by, Produced by, Adaptation and Screenplay by* Ben Hecht and Charles MacArthur. (1:20)

An offbeat melodrama of a lawyer and his fits of jealousy. Filmed at Paramount's Astoria studios in Long Island, N.Y., it was voted one of the year's "10 Best" films by the National Board of Review. Based on the story "Caballero of the Law" by Ben Hecht and Charles MacArthur.

Crime's End (G.B. title) *see* **My Son Is Guilty**

Crime's Highway (G.B. title) *see* **Desert Justice**

896. The Criminal Code (Columbia; 1930–31). *Cast:* Walter Huston, Phillips Holmes, Constance Cummings (film debut), Boris Karloff, Mary Doran, DeWitt Jennings, Ethel Wales, Clark Marshall, John St. Polis, Otto Hoffman, John Sheehan, Arthur Hoyt, Paul Porcasi, Andy Devine, Russell Hopton, Lee Phelps, James Guilfoyle, Nicholas Soussanin, Hugh Walker, Jack Vance. *D:* Howard Hawks; *P:* Harry Cohn; *Sc:* (A.A.N.) Seton I. Miller, Fred Niblo, Jr. (1:36) (video)

Drama of a D.A. turned prison warden who tries to keep the peace in a prison where he is hated by many. Based on the play by Martin Flavin, it was remade as *Penitentiary* (q.v.) and again in 1950 as *Convicted*.

897. Criminal Lawyer (RKO; 1938). *Cast:* Lee Tracy, Margot Grahame, Eduardo Ciannelli, Erik Rhodes, Wilfred Lucas, Betty Lawford, Frank M. Thomas, William Stack, Lita Chevret, Aileen Pringle, Kenneth Thomson, Theodore von Eltz. *D:* Christy Cabanne; *P:* Cliff Reid; *St:* Louis Stevens; *Sc:* G.V. (Gladys) Atwater, Thomas Lennon. (1:12)

B drama of a D.A. who has to prosecute the gangster who had him appointed to his position. A remake of *State's Attorney* (q.v.).

The Criminal Within (G.B. title) *see* **Murder at Glen Athol**

898. Criminals of the Air (Columbia; 1937). *Cast:* Ralph Byrd, Charles Quigley, Rita Hayworth, John

Hamilton, Marc Lawrence, John Tyrrell, Rosalind Keith, Russell Hicks, Matty Kemp, Lester Dorr, Patricia Farr, John Gallaudet, Walter Soderling. *D:* C.C. Coleman, Jr.; *St:* Jack Cooper; *Sc:* Owen Francis.

B melodrama.

899. Crimson Romance (Mascot; 1934). *Cast:* Ben Lyon, Sari Maritza, Erich Von Stroheim (who was also the technical advisor), Hardie Albright, James Bush, William Bakewell, Herman Bing, Bodil Rosing, Arthur Clayton, Vince Barnett, Oscar Apfel, Purnell Pratt, Jason Robards, William von Brincken, Eric Arnold, Frederick Vogeding, Harry Schultz. *D:* David Howard; *St:* Al Martin, Sherman Lowe; *Sc:* Milton Krims; *Additional Dialogue:* Doris Schroeder. (1:11) (video)

Low-budget World War I drama of two flyers in love with the same girl.

900. The Crimson Trail (Universal; 1934–35). *Cast:* Buck Jones, Polly Ann Young, Ward Bond, Carl Stockdale, Paul Fix, Charles K. French, Charles Brinley, Robert Kortman, Bud Osborne, Robert Walker. *D:* Al Raboch; *P:* Irving Starr; *Sc:* Jack Natteford. (0:58)

Buck Jones western of a cowboy who mediates a feud between two ranchers.

901. The Crooked Circle (World Wide; 1932). *Cast:* Ben Lyon, Irene Purcell, James Gleason, ZaSu Pitts, C. Henry Gordon, Raymond Hatton, Roscoe Karns, Robert Frazer, Berton Churchill, Frank Reicher, Ethel Clayton. *D:* H. Bruce Humberstone; *Sc:* Ralph Spence; *Addit. Dial.:* Tim Whelan.

"Poverty row" mystery-comedy.

902. The Crooked Trail (Supreme; 1936). *Cast:* Johnny Mack Brown, Lucille Browne, John Merton, Charles King, Ted Adams, Dick Curtis, John Van Pelt, Ed Cassidy, Horace Murphy. *D:* S. Roy Luby; *P:* A.W. Hackel; *Sc:* George Plympton. (1:00)

Johnny Mack Brown western of a sheriff who saves a man in the desert, only to find he is wanted by the law.

Crooks in Clover (G.B. title) *see* **Penthouse**

903. Crooner (WB; 1932). *Cast:* David Manners, Ken Murray, Ann Dvorak, Sheila Terry, William Janney, Edward Nugent, J. Carrol Naish, Guy Kibbee, Claire Dodd, Sumner Getchell, Clarence Nordstrom, William Ricciardi, William Halligan, Betty Gillette, Teddy Joyce, Allen Vincent, Bud Flanagan (Dennis O'Keefe). *D:* Lloyd Bacon; *St:* Rian James; *Sc:* Charles Kenyon.

Drama of a radio singer and what happens when sudden fame goes to his head.

904. The Crosby Case (Universal; 1934). *Cast:* Wynne Gibson, Alan Dinehart, Onslow Stevens, Warren Hymer, Leon (Ames) Waycoff, Mischa Auer, Skeets Gallagher, Edward Van Sloan, John Wray, J. Farrell MacDonald, William Collier, Sr., Harold Huber. *D:* Edwin L. Marin; *Sc:* Warren G. Duff, Gordon Kahn. (G.B. title: *The Crosby Murder Case*) (1:18)

Who-dun-it of two people who have to clear themselves after being charged with murdering a doctor.

The Crosby Murder Case (G.B. title) *see* **The Crosby Case**

905. Cross Country Cruise (Universal; 1934). *Cast:* Lew Ayres, Alan Dinehart, Minna Gombell, June Knight, Eugene Pallette, Robert McWade, Alice White, Henry Armetta, Craig Reynolds, Arthur Vinton. *D:* Edward Buzzell; *St:* Stanley Rauh; *Sc:* Elmer Harris. (1:15)

Low-budget fare of romance and murder aboard a cross country bus.

906. Cross Examination (Artclass; 1932). *Cast:* H.B. Warner, Sally

Blane, Edmund Breese, Donald Dillaway, Richard Tucker, Wilfred Lucas, William V. Mong, Natalie Moorhead, Lee Phelps, Margaret Fealy, Sarah Padden, B. Wayne Lamont, Niles Welch, Alexander Pollard, John Webb Dillon, Nita Cavalier, Frank Clark. *D:* Richard Thorpe; *St & Sc:* Arthur Hoerl.

Low-budget courtroom melodrama.

907. Cross-Fire (RKO; 1933). *Cast:* Tom Keene, Edgar Kennedy, Betty Furness, Edward Phillips, Lafe McKee, Nick Cogley, Jules Cowles, Thomas Brower, Stanley Blystone, Murdock MacQuarrie, Kid Wagner, Charles K. French. *D:* Otto Brower; *As.P.:* David Lewis; *Sc:* Harold Shumate, Tom McNamara. (1:00)

Tom Keene western (his last for this studio) of five old-timers who hit the outlaw trail when one of them is unjustly accused of murder.

908. Cross Streets (Chesterfield; 1934). *Cast:* John Mack Brown, Anita Louise, Kenneth Thomson, Edith Fellows, Claire Windsor, Josef Swickard. *D:* Frank Strayer.

B drama from "Poverty row."

909. The Crowd Roars (WB/F.N.; 1932). *Cast:* James Cagney, Joan Blondell, Ann Dvorak, Eric Linden, Guy Kibbee, Frank McHugh, Regis Toomey, Leo Nomis, William Arnold. *D:* Howard Hawks; *St:* Hawks; *Sc:* Kubec Glasmon, John Bright, Niven Busch, Seton I. Miller. (1:25)

Auto-racing drama which was a hit in its day. Remade as *Indianapolis Speedway* (q.v.).

910. The Crowd Roars (MGM; 1938). *Cast:* Robert Taylor, Edward Arnold, Frank Morgan, Maureen O'Sullivan, William Gargan, Lionel Stander, Jane Wyman, Nat Pendleton, Charles D. Brown, Gene Reynolds, Donald Douglas, Isabel Jewell, J. Farrell Mac-Donald, Donald Barry, Frank Craven, Charlotte Merriam. *D:* Richard Thorpe; *P:* Sam Zimbalist; *St:* George Bruce; *Sc:* Bruce, Thomas Lennon, George Oppenheimer. (1:27)

Melodrama of the fight game and racketeers who muscle in. Remade in 1947 as *Killer McCoy*.

911. Crusade Against Rackets (JDK Productions; 1937). *Cast:* Donald Reed, Lona Andre, John Merton, Louise Small, Wheeler Oakman. *D:* Elmer Clifton; *P:* J.D. Kendis; *Sc:* Robert A. Dillon.

Independent low-budget exploitation melodrama.

912. The Crusader (Majestic; 1932). *Cast:* H.B. Warner, Walter Byron, Marceline Day, Evelyn Brent, Lew Cody, Ned Sparks, Arthur Hoyt, Lloyd Ingraham, Syd Saylor, Joseph Girard, John St. Polis, Ara Naswell. *D:* Frank Strayer; *St:* Wilson Collison; *Sc:* Edward T. Lowe.

"Poverty Row" melodrama of criminal element that is trying to blackmail an honest D.A.

913. The Crusades (Paramount; 1935). *Cast:* Loretta Young (Berengaria, Princess of Navarre), Henry Wilcoxon (King Richard the Lionhearted), Ian Keith (Saladin, Sultan of Islam), Katherine de Mille (Princess Alice), C. Aubrey Smith (hermit), Joseph Schildkraut (Conrad, Marquis of Montferrat), Alan Hale (Blondel), C. Henry Gordon (King Philip II), George Barbier (Sancho, King of Navarre), Montagu Love (blacksmith), Lumsden Hare (Robert, Earl of Leicester), William Farnum (Duke Hugo of Burgundy), Hobart Bosworth (Duke Frederick), Pedro de Cordoba (Karakush), Mischa Auer (monk), Albert Conti (Duke Leopold of Austria), Maurice Murphy (Alan), Ramsay Hill (Prince John), Sven-Hugo Borg (Sverre, the Norse king), Paul Sotoff (Prince Michael of Russia), Fred W. Malatesta (King William of Sicily), Hans Von Twardowski (Count Nicholas of Hungary), Anna Demetrio (Duenna), Winter Hall, Emma Dunn, Perry Askam, Edwin Maxwell, Jason Robards, Georgia Caine, J. Carrol Naish, Ann Sheridan, Josef Swickard, Jean Fenwick, Alphonse Ethier, Jack Rutherford, Colin Tapley, Harry Cording, Stanley Andrews, Addison Richards, Maurice Black, William B. Davidson, Guy Usher, Boyd Irwin, Gordon Griffith, Sam Flint, John Carradine, Dewey Robinson. *D:* Cecil B. De Mille; *P:* De Mille; *Sc:* Harold Lamb, Waldemar Young, Dudley Nichols; *Cinematographer:* (A.A.N.) Victor Milner; *Song:* "Song of the Crusades" by Leo Robin, Richard Whiting, Rudolph Kopp. (2:03)

Lavish spectacle of medieval times and the titled events. Based on the book by Harold Lamb. One of the 25 top grossing films of 1935–36.

914. The Cuban Love Song (MGM; 1931). *Cast:* Lawrence Tibbett (his final film), Lupe Velez, Jimmy Durante, Ernest Torrence, Karen Morley, Louise Fazenda, Hale Hamilton, Phillip Cooper, Mathilde Comont. *D:* W.S. Van Dyke; *P:* Albert Lewin; *St:* C. Gardiner Sullivan; *Sc:* Bess Meredyth, John Lynch and others. (1:26)

Drama of a marine who returns to Cuba to claim his illegitimate child after learning the mother has died. An expensive box office fizzle.

915. The Cuckoos (RKO; 1930). *Cast:* Bert Wheeler, Robert Woolsey, June Clyde, Dorothy Lee, Ivan Lebedeff, Hugh Trevor, Mitchell Lewis, Jobyna Howland, Marguerita Padula, Raymond Maurel. *D:* Paul Sloane; *As.P.:* Louis Sarecky; *Sc:* Cyrus Wood, Guy Bolton; *Songs:* Kalmar, Ruby, & others. (1:30)

Musical-comedy farce of two fortune hunters who try to rescue a kidnapped girl. The story was adapted from the play "The Ramblers" by Bert Kalmar and Harry Ruby and was a box office hit. Some scenes were photographed in 2-color technicolor.

Cupid in the Rough (G.B. title) *see* **Aggie Appleby, Maker of Men**

916. Curly Top (Fox; 1935). *Cast:* Shirley Temple, Rochelle Hudson, John Boles, Jane Darwell, Rafaela Ottiano, Esther Dale, Arthur Treacher, Etienne Girardot, Maurice Murphy. *D:* Irving Cummings; *P:* Darryl F. Zanuck; *As.P.:* Winfield Sheehan; *Sc:* Patterson McNutt, Arthur Beckhard; *Songs:* include "Animal Crackers in My Soup" by Ray Henderson, Ted Koehler, Irving Caesar. (1:15) (video)

A little girl makes everything right for everyone in this re-working of *Daddy Long Legs* (q.v.).

917. Curtain at Eight (Majestic; 1934). *Cast:* Dorothy Mackaill, Jack Mulhall, Russell Hopton, C. Aubrey Smith, Natalie Moorhead, Paul Cavanagh. *D:* E. Mason Hopper (final film—ret.); *Sc:* Edward T. Lowe.

"Poverty row" murder-mystery set in a theater.

918. The Curtain Falls (Chesterfield; 1934). *Cast:* Henrietta Crosman, Holmes Herbert, Lloyd Ingraham, Dorothy Revier, Tom Ricketts, Jameson Thomas. *D:* Charles Lamont (feature film debut).

"Poverty row" drama.

919. Custer's Last Stand (Stage and Screen; 1936). *Cast:* Rex Lease, Lona Andre, William Farnum, Ruth Mix, Dorothy Gulliver, Nancy Caswell, Reed Howes, Helen Gibson, George Chesebro, Jack Mulhall, Ted Adams, William Desmond, Robert Walker, Bobby Nelson, Chief Thundercloud, Chief Big Tree, Frank McGlynn, Jr., High Eagle, Josef Swickard, Creighton Hale, Milburn Morante, George Morrell, Cactus Mack, Budd Buster, Franklyn Farnum, Carl Mathews, Artie Ortego, Lafe McKee, Iron Eyes Cody. *D:* Elmer Clifton; *P:* George M. Merrick (Weiss Productions); *Sc:* George Arthur Durlam, Eddy Granemann, Bob Lively. (1:31)

Feature version of the independent 15-chapter serial of the same name, detailing the famous battle as well as an army scout who comes to the aid of a wagon train attacked by Indians.

920. The Cyclone Kid (Big 4; 1931). *Cast:* Buzz Barton, Francis X. Bushman, Jr., Caryl Lincoln, Ted Adams, Lafe McKee, Blackie Whiteford. *D:* J.P. McGowan; *P:* John R. Freuler; *Sc:* George Morgan. (1:00)

Buzz Barton juvenile western of a youth who helps a ranch foreman get the outlaws and then the girl. The first of three films in a series to star Barton. The series was not successful.

921. Cyclone of the Saddle (Superior; 1935). *Cast:* Rex Lease, Bobby Nelson, Janet Chandler, Milburn Morante, Helen Gibson, Yakima Canutt, Chick Davis, Chief Standing Bear, Chief Thundercloud, George Chesebro, Art Mix, William Desmond, Black Fox the horse. *D:* Elmer Clifton; *P:* Louis Weiss (Weiss Productions); *St:* Clifton, George M. Merrick; *Sc:* Clifton, Merrick. (0:53)

Rex Lease western of an undercover government man combating a treacherous white renegade stirring the Indians to attack local whites.

922. The Cyclone Ranger (Spectrum; 1935). *Cast:* Bill Cody, Nena Quartero, Eddie Gribbon, Soledad Jimenez, Earle Hodgins, Zara Tazil, Donald Reed, Colin Chase, Budd Buster. *D:* Robert Hill; *Sc:* Oliver Drake. (1:00)

Bill Cody western of a man pretending to be the son of a blind woman after the son was killed by outlaws.

923. Cynara (United Artists/ Samuel Goldwyn; 1932). *Cast:* Ronald Colman, Kay Francis, Phyllis Barry, Henry Stephenson, Viva Tattersall, Florine McKinney, George Kirby, Paul Porcasi, Clarissa Selwynne, Donald Stewart, Wilson Benge. *D:* King Vidor;

P: Sam Goldwyn; *Sc:* Frances Marion, Lynn Starling. (1:18)

Relationship drama of a London barrister who plays while the wife is away. Based on the novel "Imperfect Lover" by Robert Gore Brown and the play by Brown and H.M. Harwood.

924. The Czar of Broadway (Universal; 1930). *Cast:* John Harron, Betty Compson, John Wray, King Baggot, Claud Allister, Edmund Breese, Wilbur Mack. *D:* William James Craft. (1:19)

Low-budget newspaper melodrama of a reporter investigating a big-time gambler.

Czar of the Slot Machines *see* **King of Gamblers**

925. Daddy Long Legs (Fox; 1931). *Cast:* Janet Gaynor (Judy Abbott), Warner Baxter (Jervis Pendleton), Una Merkel (Sally McBride), John Arledge (Jimmy McBride), Claude Gillingwater, Sr. (Riggs), Kathlyn Williams (Mrs. Pendleton), Louise Closser Hale (Miss Pritchard), Elizabeth Patterson (Mrs. Lippett), Kendall McComas (Freddie Perkins), Sheila Mannors (Gloria Pendleton), Edwin Maxwell (Wykoff), Effie Ellsler (Mrs. Semple), Martha Lee Sparks (Katie), Billy Barty (Billy), Edith Fellows. *D:* Alfred Santell; *Sc:* Sonya Levien, S.N. Behrman. (1:13)

A playboy sponsors a young girl's education. Based on the novel and play by Jean Webster, it was one of the 15 top grossing films of 1930–31. Previously filmed in 1919 by First National with Mary Pickford. Reworked in 1935 as *Curly Top* (q.v.) and remade by 20th Century-Fox in 1955 with Fred Astaire.

926. Damaged Goods (Grand National/Condor; 1937–38). *Cast:* Pedro de Cordoba, Phyllis Barry, Douglas Walton, Arletta Duncan, Ferdinand Munier, Esther Dale, Clarence Wilson, Frank Melton, Wheeler Oakman, Gretchen Thomas. *D:* Phil Goldstone;

P: Goldstone, Irving Starr; *Adaptation:* Upton Sinclair; *Sc:* Joseph Hoffman. (0:56)

Low-budget production dealing with venereal disease. Based on a 1912 play by Eugene Brieux, it was previously filmed in 1914 with Richard Bennett.

927. Damaged Lives (Weldon Pictures; 1933). *Cast:* Diane Sinclair, Lyman Williams, Cecilia Parker, Marceline Day (final film — ret.), Jason Robards, Charlotte Merriam, Harry Myers (final film — d. 1938), Almeda Fowler. *D:* Edgar G. Ulmer; *St & Sc:* Ulmer, Donald Davis. (1:01)

Quickie melodrama sponsored by The American Social Hygiene Association, dealing with V.D. The second half of the film includes a graphic lecture on the disease and its prevention by "Dr." Murray Kinnell. Not shown in New York City until 1937.

928. Damaged Love (Sono Art–World Wide; 1930–31). *Cast:* Betty Garde, Charles Starrett, June Collyer, Eloise Taylor, Charles Trowbridge. *D:* Irvin Willat; *St & Sc:* Thomas W. Broadhurst; *Adaptation:* Frederic & Fanny Hatton; *Orig. play:* Broadhurst.

"Poverty row" romantic drama.

929. Dames (WB; 1934). *Cast:* Joan Blondell, Dick Powell, Ruby Keeler, ZaSu Pitts, Hugh Herbert, Guy Kibbee, Arthur Vinton, Phil Regan, Arthur Aylesworth, Johnny Arthur, Leila Bennett, Berton Churchill, Robert Barrat, Richard Quine, Sammy Fain (bit). *D:* Ray Enright; *P:* Robert Lord; *St:* Lord, Delmer Daves; *Sc:* Daves; *Songs:* "I Only Have Eyes for You," "The Girl at the Ironing Board," "Dames" by Al Dubin and Harry Warren; "Try to See It My Way" by Mort Dixon and Allie Wrubel and "When You Were a Smile on Your Mother's Lips and a Twinkle in Your Daddy's Eye" by Irving Kahal and Sammy Fain. (1:30) (video)

This musical is the final big-budget production by this studio to feature Busby Berkeley's grandiose production numbers, prior to the advent of the "movie code."

930. Dames Ahoy! (Universal; 1930). *Cast:* Glenn Tryon, Eddie Gribbon, Helen Wright, Otis Harlan, Gertrude Astor, Zelma O'Neal. *D:* William James Craft; *Sc:* Matt Taylor, Albert De Mond; *St:* Sherman Lowe. (1:04)

B comedy of three sailors out to find a blonde that swindled one of them.

931. A Damsel in Distress (RKO; 1937). *Cast:* Fred Astaire, Joan Fontaine, George Burns, Gracie Allen, Constance Collier, Reginald Gardiner (with the singing voice of Mario Berini), Montagu Love, Ray Noble, Harry Watson, Jan Duggan, Mary Gordon. *D:* George Stevens; *P:* Pandro S. Berman; *Sc:* P.G. Wodehouse, S.K. Lauren, Ernest Pagano; *Art-Set Decoration:* (A.A.N.) Carroll Clark and Van Nest Polglase; *Choreographer:* (A.A.) Hermes Pan for his "Fun House" number; *Additional Choreography:* Astaire; *Songs:* George and Ira Gershwin include "Foggy Day in London Town" and "Nice Work If You Can Get It." (1:38) (video)

A musical-comedy set in London with a dancer in pursuit of an heiress. A box office flop. Previously filmed in 1920 by Pathé.

932. Dance, Charlie, Dance (WB/F.N.; 1937). *Cast:* Stuart Erwin, Jean Muir, Glenda Farrell, Allen Jenkins, Addison Richards, Charles Foy, Chester Clute, Frank Faylen, Mary Treen, Harvey Clark, Tommy Wonder, Collette Lyons, Olive Olson. *D:* Frank McDonald; *P:* Bryan Foy; *Sc:* Crane Wilbur, William Jacobs; *Songs:* M.K. Jerome and Jack Scholl.

B comedy of a man duped into backing a bad play. Based on the play *The Butter and Egg Man* by George S. Kaufman, it was previously filmed under that title in 1928. Remade as *The Tenderfoot* (q.v.) and *An Angel from Texas* in 1940.

933. Dance, Fools, Dance (MGM; 1930). *Cast:* Joan Crawford, Lester Vail, Cliff Edwards, William Bakewell, William Holden (1872–1932), Clark Gable, Earle Foxe, Purnell B. Pratt, Hale Hamilton, Natalie Moorhead, Joan Marsh, Russell Hopton. *D:* Harry Beaumont; *Sc:* Aurania Rouverol, Richard Schayer; *Song:* Dorothy Fields. (1:22) (video)

Drama of a girl reporter who sets out to get the goods on a notorious hoodlum. Based on a story by Aurania Rouverol of the real-life gangland killing of news reporter Jake Lingle.

934. Dance, Girl, Dance (Invincible; 1933). *Cast:* Evalyn Knapp, Edward Nugent, Alan Dinehart, Theodore von Eltz, Gloria Shea, George Grandee, Ada May, Mae Busch. *D:* Frank Strayer; *St & Sc:* Robert Ellis.

"Poverty row" production.

935. Dance Hall (RKO; 1929). *Cast:* Arthur Lake, Olive Borden, Ralph Emerson, Joseph Cawthorn, Margaret Seddon, Lee Moran, Helen Kaiser, Tom O'Brien, George Irving, Patricia Caron, Natalie Joyce. *D:* Melville Brown; *As.P.:* Henry Hobart; *St:* Vina Delmar; *Sc:* Jane Murfin, J. Walter Ruben. (1:09)

Low-budget romantic comedy.

936. Dance Hall Hostess (Mayfair; 1933). *Cast:* Helen Chandler, Edward Nugent, Clarence Geldert, Jason Robards. *D:* B. Reeves Eason.

"Poverty row" quickie.

937. The Dance of Life (Paramount; 1929). *Cast:* Hal Skelly, Nancy Carroll, Dorothy Revier, Ralph Theodore, May Boley, Richard "Skeets" Gallagher, Oscar Levant, Charles D. Brown, George Irving, Al St. John, James Farley, Jimmie Quinn. *D:* John Cromwell, A. Edward Sutherland; *P:* David O. Selznick; *Sc:* George M. Watters, Benjamin Glazer; *Songs:* Sam Coslow, Richard A. Whiting and Leo Robin include the popular "True Blue Lou."

Musical-drama with a 2-color technicolor sequence of a stage comedian who hits the skids after leaving his loving wife. Based on the stage hit "Burlesque" by George Manker Watters and Arthur Hopkins it was remade by this studio as *Swing High, Swing Low* (q.v.) and again in 1948 as *When My Baby Smiles at Me.*

938/939. Dance Team (Fox; 1932). *Cast:* James Dunn, Sally Eilers, Ralph Morgan, Nora Lane, Russell Hopton, Edward Crandall, Harry Beresford, Charles Williams. *D:* Sidney Lanfield; *St:* Sarah Addington; *Sc:* Edwin Burke.

Light low-budget romantic musical.

940. The Dancers (Fox; 1930). *Cast:* Walter Byron, Lois Moran, Phillips Holmes, Mae Clarke, Mrs. Patrick Campbell (film debut). *D:* Chandler Sprague.

Romantic drama based on a 1923 play.

941. Dancers in the Dark (Paramount; 1932). *Cast:* Miriam Hopkins, Jack Oakie, George Raft, William Collier, Jr., Lyda Roberti (film debut), Eugene Pallette, Claire Dodd, Walter Hiers, Alberta Vaughn, Paul Fix, Paul Hurst, Maurice Black, DeWitt Jennings, Mary Gordon, Frances Moffett. *D:* David Burton; *St:* James Ashmore Creelman; *Sc:* Herman J. Mankiewicz, Brian Marlow, Howard Emmett Rogers. (1:00)

Drama of a taxi-dancer with a past.

942. Dancing Co-ed (MGM; 1939). *Cast:* Lana Turner, Richard Carlson, Artie Shaw (film debut), Leon Errol, Ann Rutherford, Lee Bowman, Monty Woolley, Roscoe Karns, June Preisser, Walter Kingsford, Mary Beth Hughes, Chester Clute, Mary Field, Minerva Urecal, Thurston Hall. *D:* S. Sylvan Simon; *P:* Edgar Selwyn; *St:*

Albert Treynor; *Sc:* Albert Mannheimer. (G.B. title: *Every Other Inch a Lady*) (1:30)

Tailored for Lana Turner was this musical romance of a girl who makes it in college and show business.

943. Dancing Dynamite (Capitol; 1931). *Cast:* Richard Talmadge, Robert Ellis, Dot Farley, Richard Cramer, Walter Brennan. *D:* Noel Mason (Smith).

"Poverty row" production.

944. Dancing Feet (Republic; 1936). *Cast:* Ben Lyon, Joan Marsh, Edward Nugent, Isabel Jewell, James Burke, Lillian Harmer, Vince Barnett, Herbert Rawlinson, Purnell Pratt, Nick Condos, Herbert Corthell. *D:* Joseph Santley; *St:* Robert Eden; *Sc:* Jerome Chodorov, Olive Cooper, Wellyn Totman.

B musical-comedy.

Dancing Fool (G.B. title) *see* **Harold Teen**

945. Dancing Lady (MGM; 1933). *Cast:* Joan Crawford, Clark Gable, Franchot Tone, Fred Astaire (film debut), May Robson, Ted Healy and his Stooges, Grant Mitchell, Winnie Lightner, Robert Benchley, Nelson Eddy, Sterling Holloway, Eunice Quedens (Eve Arden), Gloria Foy, Arthur Jarrett, Lynn Bari (film debut — bit as a showgirl). *D:* Robert Z. Leonard; *As.P.:* John W. Considine, Jr.; *Sc:* Allen Rivkin, Zelda Sears, P.J. Wolfson; *Songs:* "Everything I Have Is Yours" by Burton Lane and Harold Adamson, "That's the Rhythm of the Day" by Richard Rodgers and Lorenz Hart; *Other Songs:* Jimmy McHugh and Dorothy Fields. (1:34) (video)

Backstage romantic comedy with music, based on the novel by James Warner Bellah.

946. Dancing Man (Pyramid; 1934). *Cast:* Robert Ellis, Judith Allen, Reginald Denny, Natalie Moorhead, Donald Stuart, Edwin Maxwell, Edmund Breese, Douglas Cosgrove, Charlotte Merriam, Huntley Gordon, Maude Truax. *D:* Albert Ray; *St:* Beulah Poynter; *Sc:* Ray.

Low-budget drama.

The Dancing Partner (G.B. title) *see* **Just a Gigolo**

947. The Dancing Pirate (RKO/Principal; 1936). *Cast:* Frank Morgan, Charles Collins; Steffi Duna, Cyrus Kendall, Victor Varconi, Luis Alberni, Jack LaRue, Alma Real, William V. Mong, Mitchell Lewis, Julian Rivero, John Eberts, The Royal Cansinos, Max Wagner, Ellen Lowe, Vera Lewis, Harold Waldridge, Nora Cecil. *D:* Lloyd Corrigan; *P:* John Speaks; *St:* Emma Lindsay-Squier; *Adaptation:* Jack Wagner, Boris Ingster; *Sc:* Ray Harris, Francis Edwards Faragoh; *Songs:* Richard Rodgers, Lorenz Hart; *Choreography:* (A.A.N.) Richard Lewis for his "Finale" number.

Shades of "Pirates of Penzance" in this technicolor musical-comedy of pirates who invade a small town. This was the third 3-color technicolor production from Hollywood and it flopped at the box office.

948. Dancing Sweeties (WB; 1930). *Cast:* Sue Carol, Grant Withers, Vince Barnett, Billy Bletcher, Edna Murphy, Tully Marshall, Eddie Phillips, Kate Price, Ada Mae Vaughn. *D:* Ray Enright; *St:* Harry Fried; *Sc:* Gordon Rigby, Joseph Jackson.

Drama of the ups and downs experienced by a dance team.

949. Danger Ahead (Victory; 1934–35). *Cast:* Lawrence Gray, Eddie Phillips, Fuzzy Knight, Fred Kelsey, J. Farrell MacDonald, George Chesebro, Bryant Washburn. *D:* Al Herman; *P:* Sam Katzman.

B actioner.

950. Danger Flight (Monogram; 1939). *Cast:* John Trent (Tommy), Marjorie Reynolds (Betty Lou), Milburn Stone (Skeeter), Jason Robards (Paul), Tommy Baker, Dennis Moore, Julius Tannen, Edwin Parker, Joe Bernard, Harry Harvey, Jr., Walter Wills. *D:* Howard Bretherton; *P:* Paul Malvern; *Sc:* Byron Morgan, Edwin C. Parsons. (G.B. title: *Scouts of the Air*) (1:05)

The fourth and final entry in the "Tailspin Tommy" series as crooks try to steal a payroll from a plane in flight. Based on the popular comic strip characters created by Hal Forrest.

Danger Island *see* **Mr. Moto in Danger Island**

951. Danger Lights (RKO; 1930). *Cast:* Louis Wolheim, Jean Arthur, Robert Armstrong, Hugh Herbert, Robert Edeson, Frank Sheridan, Alan Roscoe, James Farley, William P. Burt. *D:* George B. Seitz; *As.P.:* Myles Connolly; *Sc:* James Ashmore Creelman. (1:13) (video)

Drama of a romantic triangle with a railroading background originally photographed in the "wide stereoscopic" process, a pioneering venture engineered by George K. Spoor and P.J. Berrggren.

952. Danger—Love at Work (20th Century–Fox; 1937). *Cast:* Ann Sothern, Jack Haley, Mary Boland, Edward Everett Horton, Walter Catlett, John Carradine, Etienne Girardot, Maurice Cass, Bennie Bartlett, Alan Dinehart, E.E. Clive, Stanley Fields, Margaret McWade, Claud Allister, Elisha Cook, Jr., Margaret Seddon, Charles Lane, Franklin Pangborn, Paul Hurst. *D:* Otto Preminger; *P:* Harold Wilson; *Sc:* Ben Markson, James Edward Grant. (1:21)

Screwball comedy of a rich but nutty family.

953. The Danger Man (Cosmos; 1930). *Cast:* Charles Hutchinson, Edith Thornton. *D:* Bud Pollard; *Sc:* Pollard.

A feature version of 1926 serial "Lightning Hutch."

954. Danger on the Air (Universal; 1938). *Cast:* Donald Woods (Benjamin Butts), Nan Grey (Reenie McCorkle), Jed Prouty, Berton Churchill, William Lundigan, Skeets Gallagher, Edward Van Sloan, George Meeker, Lee J. Cobb, Johnny Arthur. *D:* Otis Garrett; *P:* Irving Starr; *Sc:* Betty Laidlaw, Robert Lively. (1:07)

B comic murder-mystery involving the on-air murder of a radio sponsor. An entry in the "Crime Club" series by this studio, it was based on the novel "Death Catches Up with Mr. Kluck" by Xantippe.

955. Danger on Wheels (Universal; 1939–40). *Cast:* Richard Arlen, Jack Arnold (Vinton Haworth), Herbert Corthell. *D:* Christy Cabanne; *P:* Ben Pivar. (1:01)

B actioner of a man who tests racing cars.

956. Danger Patrol (RKO; 1937). *Cast:* John Beal, Sally Eilers, Harry Carey, Frank M. Thomas, Paul Guilfoyle, Herman Brix (Bruce Bennett), Crawford Weaver, Lee Patrick, Edward Gargan, Solly Ward, Ann Hovey, Richard Lane, Walter Miller, George Shelley, Vinton Haworth (Hayworth). *D:* Lew Landers; *St:* Helen Vreeland, Hilda Vincent; *Sc:* Sy Bartlett. (1:00)

Much to the chagrin of his family, a law student gets a side job carrying nitro-glycerine in this B melodrama.

Danger Rides the Range (G.B. title) *see* **Three Texas Steers**

957. Danger Trails (Beacon/First Division; 1935). *Cast:* Guinn "Big Boy" Williams, Marjorie Gordon, Wally Wales (Hal Taliaferro), Edmund Cobb, John Elliott, George Chesebro, Steve Clark, Ace Cain. *D:* Robert Hill; *St:* Williams; *Sc:* Rock Hawley (Robert Hill). (1:02)

Guinn "Big Boy" Williams western

of a man who returns from the east to get those responsible for killing his family.

958. Danger Valley (Monogram; 1937). *Cast:* Jack Randall, Lois Wilde, Charles King, Hal Price, Frank LaRue, Chick Hannon, Earl Dwire, Jimmy Aubrey, Glenn Strange, Bud Osborne, Tex Palmer, Merrill McCormack, Oscar Gahan, Denver Dixon (Victor Adamson). *D:* Robert N. Bradbury; *P:* Bradbury; *Supervisor:* Scott R. Dunlap; *Sc:* Robert Emmett (Tansey). (0:58)

Jack Randall western involving claim-jumpers.

959. Dangerous (WB; 1935). *Cast:* Bette Davis (A.A. for B.A. as Joyce Heath), Franchot Tone (Don Bellows), Margaret Lindsay (Gail Armitage), Alison Skipworth (Mrs. Williams), John Eldredge (Gordon Heath), Richard (Dick) Foran (Teddy), William B. Davidson (Reed Walsh), Pierre Watkin (George Sheffield), Walter Walker (Roger Farnsworth), George Irving (Charles Melton), Douglas Wood (Elmont), Richard Carle (Pitt Hanley), Milton Kibbee (Williams the chauffeur), Miki Morita (Cato), Pauline Garon (Betty the maid), Libby Taylor (Beulah), Mary Treen (Nurse), Edward Keane (doctor), George Andre Beranger, Frank O'Connor, Larry McGrath, Eddie Shubert, Florence Fair, Gordon (Bill) Elliott, Craig Reynolds, Billy Wayne, Eddie Foster. *D:* Alfred E. Green; *P:* Harry Joe Brown; *St & Sc:* Laird Doyle. (1:18) (video)

Sentimental drama of a woman on the down-and-out and her eventual salvation. Remade in 1941 as *Singapore Woman*.

960. A Dangerous Adventure (Columbia; 1937). *Cast:* Don Terry, Billy Benedict, Joseph Sawyer. *D:* Ross Lederman; *St:* Owen Francis; *Sc:* John B. Rathmell.

B romantic drama localed in a steel mill.

961. A Dangerous Affair (Columbia; 1931). *Cast:* Jack Holt, Esther Muir (film debut), Ralph Graves, Edward Brophy, Sally Blane, Blanche Frederici, Charles Middleton, Tyler Brooke, Sidney Bracey, DeWitt Jennings, William V. Mong, Frederic Stanley, Susan Fleming. *D:* Edward Sedgwick; *St & Sc:* Howard Green.

Melodrama.

962. Dangerous Corner (RKO; 1934). *Cast:* Melvyn Douglas, Conrad Nagel, Virginia Bruce, Erin O'Brien-Moore, Ian Keith, Betty Furness, Henry Wadsworth, Doris Lloyd. *D:* Phil Rosen; *As.P.:* B.P. Fineman; *Sc:* Anne Morrison Chapin, Madeleine Ruthven. (1:07)

Story of a suicide and the events leading up to it. Based on the play by J.B. Priestley.

963. Dangerous Crossroads (Columbia; 1933). *Cast:* Preston Foster, Frank Albertson, Jackie Searle. *D:* Lambert Hillyer.

Low-budget melodrama.

964. Dangerous Curves (Paramount; 1929). *Cast:* Richard Arlen, Clara Bow, Kay Francis, David Newell, Anders Randolf, Stuart Erwin, May Boley, T. Roy Barnes, Joyce Compton, Charles D. Brown, Jack Luden. *D:* Lothar Mendes; *St:* Lester Cohen; *Sc:* Donald Davis, Florence Ryerson. (1:15)

Circus melodrama of a high-wire artist who takes to the bottle.

Dangerous Days (G.B. title) *see* **Wild Boys of the Road**

Dangerous Female *see* **The Maltese Falcon**

Dangerous Ground (G.B. title) *see* **Escapade**

965/966. Dangerous Holiday (Republic; 1937). *Cast:* Carleton Young,

Mary Hart (later Lynn Roberts—film debut), Guinn Williams, William Bakewell, Franklin Pangborn, Wade Boteler, Jack Mulhall, Grady Sutton. *D:* Nicholas Barrows.

B melodrama.

967. Dangerous Intrigue (Columbia; 1936). *Cast:* Ralph Bellamy, Gloria Shea, Fred Kohler, Ann Doran, George Billings. *D:* David Selman.

B melodrama.

968. Dangerous Nan McGrew (Paramount; 1930). *Cast:* Helen Kane, Victor Moore, Stuart Erwin, James Hall, Louise Closser Hale, Frank Morgan, Roberta Robinson. *D:* Malcolm St. Clair; *Sc:* Paul Gerard Smith, Pierre Collings. (1:02)

Romantic comedy of a singing female sharpshooter.

969. Dangerous Number (MGM; 1937). *Cast:* Ann Sothern, Robert Young, Cora Witherspoon, Reginald Owen, Dean Jagger, Marla Shelton, Franklin Pangborn, Clem Bevans, Barnett Parker, Charles Trowbridge. *D:* Richard Thorpe; *P:* Lou Ostrow; *Sc:* Carey Wilson.

A married actress and her ex-stripper mother get involved in various escapades, much to the disapproval of her stick-in-the-mud husband.

970. Dangerous Paradise (Paramount; 1930). *Cast:* Richard Arlen, Nancy Carroll, Warner Oland, Gustav von Seyffertitz, Francis McDonald, Willie Fung, Clarence Wilson, Evelyn Selbie, Dorothea Wolbert, Lillian Worth, George Kotsonaros, Wong Wing. *D:* William A. Wellman; *Sc:* Grover Jones, William Slavens McNutt.

Melodrama of a south sea island hotel which is invaded by three rowdies. Suggested by the novel "Victory" by Joseph Conrad. Filmed before in 1919 as *Victory* and remade under that title in 1940.

971. Dangerous to Know (Paramount; 1938). *Cast:* Akim Tamiroff, Anna May Wong, Gail Patrick, Lloyd Nolan, Harvey Stephens, Pierre Watkin, Roscoe Karns, Hedda Hopper, Hugh Sothern, Anthony Quinn, Porter Hall, Dewey Robinson, Terry Ray (Ellen Drew), Barlowe Borland, Edward Pawley. *D:* Robert Florey; *P:* Edward T. Lowe; *Sc:* William R. Lipman, Horace McCoy. (1:10)

Drama of a hoodlum who tries to ditch his oriental mistress in order to marry a wealthy socialite. Based on the Edgar Wallace play "On the Spot."

972. Dangerous Waters (Universal; 1936). *Cast:* Jack Holt, Robert Armstrong, Grace Bradley, Charles Murray, Billy Gilbert, Willard Robertson, Diana Gibson, Guy Usher, Richard Alexander. *D:* Lambert Hillyer; *P:* Fred S. Mayer; *St:* Theodore Reeves; *Sc:* Richard Schayer, Hazel Jamieson, Malcolm Stuart Boylan. (1:10)

B shipboard drama.

973. A Dangerous Woman (Paramount; 1929). *Cast:* (Olga) Baclanova (talkie and starring debut), Clive Brook, Neil Hamilton, Leslie Fenton, Clyde Cook, Snitz Edwards. *D:* Rowland V. Lee; *P:* Louis D. Lighton; *Sc:* John Farrow, Edward E. Paramore.

Drama of a seductive married woman who leads other men to their doom. With a British colonial setting, it was based on the best selling novel "The Woman Who Needed Killing" by Margery H. Lawrence.

974. Dangerously Yours (Fox; 1933). *Cast:* Warner Baxter, Miriam Jordan, Florence Eldridge, Mischa Auer, Robert Greig, Herbert Mundin, Arthur Hoyt, Tyrell Davis, Edmund Burns, Nella Walker, Florence Roberts. *D:* Frank Tuttle; *St:* Paul Hervey Fox; *Sc:* Horace Jackson.

Romantic melodrama.

975. Dangerously Yours (20th Century-Fox; 1937). *Cast:* Cesar

Romero, Phyllis Brooks, Leon Ames, Earle Foxe, Douglas Wood, Leonid Snegoff, Jane Darwell, Natalie Garson, John Harrington. *D:* Malcolm St. Clair; *St & Sc:* Lou Breslow, John Patrick.

B remake of the above.

976. Daniel Boone (RKO; 1936). *Cast:* George O'Brien (Daniel Boone — in his first film for this studio after leaving Fox), Heather Angel, Ralph Forbes, John Carradine (Simon Girty), Dickie Jones, Clarence Muse, George Regas, Huntley Gordon, Harry Cording, Aggie Herring, Crauford Kent, Keith Kenneth. *D:* David Howard; *P:* George A. Hirliman; *St:* Edgecumb Pinchon; *Sc:* Daniel Jarrett. (1:20 (video)

In 1775, the famed frontiersman encounters treachery from white renegade Simon Girty while leading a wagon train of thirty settlers in the Kant-u-kee land.

977. Dante's Inferno (Fox; 1935). *Cast:* Spencer Tracy (Jim Carter), Claire Trevor (Betty McWade), Henry B. Walthall (Pop McWade), Alan Dinehart (Jonesy), Scott(y) Beckett (Alexander Carter), Willard Robertson (Inspector Harris), Robert Gleckler (Dean), Rita (Hayworth) Cansino (film debut in a dance sequence with Gary Leon), Morgan Wallace (Capt. Morgan), Jack Norton (drunk). *D:* Harry Lachman; *P:* Sol M. Wurtzel; *Sc:* Philip Klein, Robert M. Yost. (1:28)

The owner of a Coney Island concession exhibit called "Dante's Inferno" is driven by greed until his world starts crumbling around him. Notable is the eerie sequence with its concept of hell. The film climaxes with a fire at sea created by technicians Fred M. Sersen, Ralph Hammeras, Louis J. Witte and Willy Pogany. A remake of the 1924 film by this studio.

978. Daredevil Drivers (WB/ F.N.; 1938). *Cast:* Dick Purcell, Beverly Roberts, Gloria Blondell, Gordon Oliver, Charles Foy, Al Herman, Ferris Taylor, DeWolf (William) Hopper, Earl

Dwire, Donald Briggs, Eric Stanley. *D:* B. Reeves Eason; *As.P.:* Bryan Foy; *St:* Charles Condon; *Sc:* Sherman Lowe.

B actioner of dirt track auto-racing.

979. Daring Danger (Columbia; 1932). *Cast:* Tim McCoy, Alberta Vaughn, Wallace MacDonald, Robert Ellis, Richard Alexander, Bobby Nelson, Murdock MacQuarrie, Max Davidson. *D:* D. Ross Lederman; *St:* William Colt MacDonald; *Sc:* Michael Trevelyan. (1:00)

Tim McCoy western of a cowboy vs. cattle rustlers.

980. Daring Daughters (Capitol; 1933). *Cast:* Marian Marsh, Joan Marsh, Kenneth Thomson, Bert Roach, Richard Tucker, Allen Vincent, Arthur Hoyt, Florence Roberts, Bryant Washburn, Jr., Charlotte Merriam, Lita Chevret. *D:* Christy Cabanne; *St:* Sam Mintz; *Sc:* Barry Barringer, F. Hugh Herbert.

"Poverty row" melodrama.

981. The Daring Young Man (Fox; 1935). *Cast:* James Dunn, Mae Clarke, Madge Bellamy, Neil Hamilton, Sidney Toler, Raymond Hatton, Arthur Treacher, Phil Tead, Warren Hymer, Stanley Fields, Dorothy Christy, Robert Gleckler, William Pawley, Frank Melton, Bud Flanagan (Dennis O'Keefe). *D:* William A. Seiter; *P:* Robert T. Kane; *St:* Claude Binyon, Sidney Skolsky; *Sc:* William Hurlbut.

Drama.

982. The Dark Angel (United Artists/Samuel Goldwyn; 1935). *Cast:* Fredric March, Merle Oberon (A.A.N. for B.A.), Herbert Marshall, Janet Beecher, John Halliday, Henrietta Crosman, Frieda Inescort (film debut), George Breakston, Claud Allister, David Torrence, Lawrence Grant, Olaf Hytten, Douglas Walton, John Miltern, Randolph Connolly, Sarah Edwards, Jimmy Butler, Ann Fielder, Fay Chaldecott, Denis Chaldecott, Jimmy Baxter, Cora Sue Collins, Helena

Byrne-Grant. *D:* Sidney Franklin; *P:* Sam Goldwyn; *Sc:* Lillian Hellman, Mordaunt Shairp; *Interior Set Decoration:* (A.A.) Richard Day; *Sound Recording:* (A.A.N.) Thomas T. Moulton. (1:50)

World War I story of two men in love with the same woman, one of the men losing his sight. Based on the play by Guy Bolton it was previously filmed in 1925 by Goldwyn/First National with Ronald Colman and Vilma Banky.

983. Dark Hazard (WB/F.N.; 1934). *Cast:* Edward G. Robinson, Glenda Farrell, Robert Barrat, Genevieve Tobin, Hobart Cavanaugh, Henry B. Walthall, Sidney Toler, Gordon Westcott, George Meeker, William V. Mong, Barbara Rogers, Willard Robertson. *D:* Alfred E. Green; *P:* Robert Lord; *Sc:* Ralph Block, Brown Holmes (based on the novel by W.R. Burnett). (1:12)

Low-budget drama of a gambler who tries to keep it all together. Remade as *Wine, Women and Horses* (q.v.).

984. The Dark Horse (WB/F.N.; 1932). *Cast:* Guy Kibbee, Warren William, Bette Davis, Frank McHugh, Vivienne Osborne, Robert Warwick, Sam Hardy, Harry Holman, Berton Churchill, Charles Sellon. *D:* Alfred E. Green; *P:* Samuel Bischoff; *St:* Melville Crossman (Darryl F. Zanuck), Joseph Jackson, Courtney Terrett; *Sc:* Jackson, Wilson Mizner. (1:15)

B spoof on political campaigning and elections.

985. The Dark Hour (Chesterfield; 1936). *Cast:* Irene Ware, Lloyd Whitlock, Berton Churchill, Hedda Hopper, Hobart Bosworth, E.E. Clive, William V. Mong, John St. Polis. *D:* Charles Lamont.

"Poverty row" drama.

986. Dark Rapture (Universal; 1938). Documentary feature by Armand Denis of the Denis–Roosevelt expedition to the Belgian Congo. The film is notable for its photography, depicting animals, natives, etc.

987. Dark Skies (Biltmore; 1929). *Cast:* Evelyn Brent, Shirley Mason, Wallace MacDonald. *D:* Harry S. Webb, Harry O. Hoyt.

Low-budget melodrama.

988. Dark Streets (WB; 1929). *Cast:* Jack Mulhall (in a dual role), Lila Lee, William Walling, Maurice Black, Earl Pingree. *D:* Frank Lloyd; *St:* Richard Connell; *Sc:* Bradley King.

Low-budget melodrama of twin brothers on opposite sides of the law who fall for the same girl.

989. Dark Victory (WB; 1939). *Cast:* Bette Davis (A.A.N. for B.A. as Judith Traherne, a role which also garnered her an Acting Award from the National Board of Review in conjunction with her performance in *The Old Maid* (q.v.), George Brent (Dr. Frederick Steele), Humphrey Bogart (Michael O'Leary), Geraldine Fitzgerald (Acting Award from the National Board of Review as Ann King), Ronald Reagan (Alec Hamin), Cora Witherspoon (Carrie Spottswood), Dorothy Peterson (Miss Wainwright), Henry Travers (Dr. Parsons), Virginia Brissac (Martha), Herbert Rawlinson (Dr. Carter), Charles Richman (Colonel Mantle), Leonard Mudie (Dr. Driscoll), Lottie Williams (Lucy), Fay Helm (Miss Dodd), Diane Bernard (Agatha), Jack Mower (veterinarian), William Worthington, Alexander Leftwich, Stuart Holmes, Ila Rhodes, Frank Darien, John Harron, John Ridgely, Sidney Bracey, Rosella Towne, Edgar Edwards. *D:* Edmund Goulding; *P:* Hal B. Wallis; *As.P.:* David Lewis; *Sc:* Casey Robinson; *Music:* (A.A.N.) Max Steiner; *Song:* "Oh Give Me Time for Tenderness" by Elsie Janis and Edmund Goulding. (1:46) (video)

Based on the 1934 play by George Brewer, Jr., and Bertram Bloch, this classic soaper of a woman with a terminal illness was a big hit for the studio. It received an A.A.N. for Best Picture, placed #4 on the "10 Best" list of the *New York Times,* as well as #5 on the same list by *Film Daily.* Remade in Great Britain in 1963 with Susan Hayward as *Stolen Hours* and again in the U.S. in 1976 as a TV movie with Elizabeth Montgomery. Computer-colored by Turner Entertainment in the 1980s.

990. Darkened Rooms (Paramount; 1929). *Cast:* Neil Hamilton, Evelyn Brent, David Newell, E.H. Calvert, Doris Hill, Wallace MacDonald, Gale Henry, Blanche Craig. *D:* Louis Gasnier; *Sc:* Melville Baker, Patrick Kearney.

Fake spiritualism is the theme of this low-budget drama based on a novel by Philip Gibbs.

991. Darktown Revue (Micheaux; 1931). Low-budget independent feature produced, directed and written by Oscar Micheaux.

Daughter of Luxury (G.B. title) *see* **Five and Ten**

992. Daughter of Shanghai (Paramount; 1937). *Cast:* Anna May Wong, Charles Bickford, Buster Crabbe, Philip Ahn, Cecil Cunningham, Anthony Quinn, Fred Kohler, J. Carrol Naish, Evelyn Brent, Paul Fix, Pierre Watkin, Frank Sully, Guy Bates Post, Ching Wah Lee, Mrs. Wong Wing, Archie Twitchell, Maurice Liu, John Patterson, Ernest Whitman, Mae Busch. *D:* Robert Florey; *P:* Harold Hurley; *St:* Garnett Weston; *Sc:* Gladys Unger, Weston. (G.B. title: *Daughter of the Orient*) (1:03)

B melodrama of a girl who goes after the smugglers who killed her father.

993. Daughter of the Congo (Micheaux; 1930). Low-budget independent feature produced, directed and written by Oscar Micheaux.

994. Daughter of the Dragon (Paramount; 1931). *Cast:* Warner Oland, Anna May Wong, Sessue Hayakawa, Bramwell Fletcher, Frances Dade, Holmes Herbert, Tetsu Komai, Lawrence Grant, E. Alyn Warren, Nella Walker, Harold Minjir, Nicholas Soussanin, Oie Chan, Olaf Hytten, H. Reynolds. *D:* Lloyd Corrigan; *Sc:* Sidney Buchman; *Adaptation:* Corrigan, Monte Katterjohn; *Dial.:* Signey Buchman. (1:12)

Melodrama of the evil Dr. Fu Manchu's equally evil daughter. Based on the characters created in 1911 by Sax Rohmer, this was the third and final entry in a short series by this studio.

Daughter of the Orient (G.B. title) *see* **Daughter of Shanghai**

995. Daughter of the Tong (Times Pictures; 1939). *Cast:* Grant Withers, Evelyn Brent, Dave O'Brien, Richard Loo, Robert Frazer. *D:* Raymond K. Johnson.

B melodrama.

996. Daughters Courageous (WB; 1939). *Cast:* John Garfield, Claude Rains, Jeffrey Lynn, Fay Bainter, Donald Crisp, May Robson, Frank McHugh, Dick Foran, Priscilla Lane, Rosemary Lane, Lola Lane, Gale Page, Berton Churchill, William (DeWolf) Hopper, James Millican, Hobart Cavanaugh. *D:* Michael Curtiz; *As.P.:* Henry Blanke; *Sc:* Julius J. and Philip G. Epstein. (1:47)

Family drama of a prodigal father who returns to his wife and daughters after many years absence. A film which sought to capitalize on the popularity of the highly successful *Four Daughters* (q.v.). Based on the play "Fly Away Home" by Irving White and Dorothy Bennett.

997. David Copperfield (MGM; 1934–35). *Cast:* Freddie Bartholomew (American debut as David the boy), Frank Lawton (David the man), W.C. Fields (Mr. Micawber), Basil Rathbone (Mr. Murdstone), Edna May Oliver

(Aunt Betsey), Roland Young (Uriah Heep), Maureen O'Sullivan (Dora), Violet Kemble-Cooper (Miss Murdstone), Lennox Pawle (Mr. Dick), Madge Evans (Agnes), Jessie Ralph (Peggotty), Elizabeth Allan (David's mother), Lionel Barrymore (Dan Peggotty), Hugh Williams (Steerforth), Lewis Stone (Mr. Wickfield), Herbert Mundin (Barkis), Elsa Lanchester (American debut as Clickett), Jean Cadell (Mrs. Micawber), Una O'Connor (Mrs. Gummidge), John Buckler (Ham), Hugh Walpole (vicar), Arthur Treacher (Donkey Man), Ivan Simpson (Limmiter), Fay Chaldecott (Little Em'ly the child), Florine McKinney (Little Em'ly the woman), Marilyn Knowlden (child Agnes), Harry Beresford (Dr. Chillip), Mabel Colcord (Mary Ann), Renée Gadd (Janet). *D:* George Cukor; *P:* David O. Selznick; *Sc:* Hugh Walpole, Howard Estabrook; *Assistant Director:* (A.A.N.) Joseph Newman; *Editor:* (A.A.N.) Robert J. Kern. (2:13) (video)

Classic version of the Charles Dickens novel. The film received an A.A.N. for Best Picture, was voted "Best Film of 1935" by *Film Daily,* voted one of the "10 Best" films of 1935 by the National Board of Review, placed #3 on the "10 Best" of 1935 by the *New York Times* as well as being in nomination at the Venice Film Festival. Previously filmed in 1911 by Thanhouser and again in 1923 by Associated Exhibitors. Remade in 1970 as a TV movie in the U.S. Computer-colored by Turner Entertainment in 1988. One of the 15 top grossing films of 1935.

998. David Harum (Fox; 1934). *Cast:* Will Rogers, Evelyn Venable, Kent Taylor, Louise Dresser, Stepin Fetchit, Noah Beery, Charles Middleton, Jane Darwell, Sleep 'n' Eat (Willie Best), Sarah Padden, Roger Imhof, Frank Melton, William Stuart. *D:* James Cruze; *Sc:* Walter Woods. (1:23)

Small town folksy comedy-drama of a wise old matchmaker. Based on the 1898 book by Edward Noyes Westcott

who wrote the book in 1896 shortly before he died. Previously filmed in 1915 by Famous Players with William H. Crane.

The Dawn of Life (G.B. title) *see* **Life Begins**

999. The Dawn Patrol (WB/ F.N.; 1930). *Cast:* Richard Barthelmess, Douglas Fairbanks, Jr., Neil Hamilton, William Janney, James Finlayson, Clyde Cook, Edmund Breon, Frank McHugh, Gardner James, Henry Allen, Jack Ackroyd, Dave O'Brien (feature debut in an unbilled bit). *D:* Howard Hawks (his first talkie); *P:* Hal B. Wallis; *Supervisor:* Robert North; *St:* (A.A.) John Monk Saunders; *Sc:* Hawks, Saunders, Seton I. Miller, Dan Totheroh. (TV title: *Flight Commander*) (1:35)

The adventures of various fliers in a fighter squadron during World War I. Remade in 1938 (see below).

1000. The Dawn Patrol (WB; 1938). *Cast:* Errol Flynn, Basil Rathbone, David Niven, Donald Crisp, Melville Cooper, Barry Fitzgerald, Carl Esmond (American debut), James Burke, Peter Willes, Herbert Evans, Stuart Hall, Michael Brooke, Morton Lowry. *D:* Edmund Goulding; *As.P.:* Robert Lord; *Sc:* Seton I. Miller, Dan Totheroh. (1:43) (video)

World War I story of flyers and their missions. A remake of the preceding film which also utilizes much of that version's aerial footage. Based on the story "Flight Commander" by John Monk Saunders.

1001. The Dawn Rider (Monogram–Lone Star; 1935). *Cast:* John Wayne, Marion Burns, Yakima Canutt, Reed Howes, Denny Meadows (Dennis Moore), Bert Dillard, Jack Jones, Nelson McDowell, Archie Ricks, Tex Phelps, James Sheridan (Sherry Tansey). *D:* Robert N. Bradbury; *P:* Paul Malvern; *St:* Lloyd Nosler; *Sc:* Bradbury; *Supervisor:* Trem Carr. (0:57) (video)

John Wayne western of a cowboy who goes after the gang that killed his father.

1002. The Dawn Trail (Columbia/Beverly Productions; 1930). *Cast:* Buck Jones, Miriam Seegar, Charles Morton, Charles King, Hank Mann, Erville Alderson, Edward LeSaint, Vester Pegg, Bob Burns, Slim Whitaker, Buck Connors. *D:* Christy Cabanne; *Sc:* John T. Neville. (1:06)

Buck Jones oater of a range feud.

1003. A Day at the Races (MGM; 1937). *Cast:* Groucho Marx (Dr. Hugo Z. Hackenbush), Harpo Marx (Stuffy), Chico Marx (Tony), Allan Jones (Gil Stewart), Margaret Dumont (Emily Upjohn), Maureen O'Sullivan (Judy Standish), Douglass Dumbrille (Morgan), Leonard Ceeley (Whitmore), Esther Muir (Flo Marlowe), Sig Rumann (Dr. Leopold X. Steinberg), Robert Middlemass (sheriff), Charles Trowbridge (Dr. Wilmerding), Vivian Fay, Frank Dawson, Max Lucke, Frankie Darro, Pat Flaherty, Si Jenks, Hooper Atchley, John Hyams, Wilbur Mack, Mary MacLaren, Edward LeSaint, Jack Norton, Carole Landis (film debut – bit), Ivie Anderson and the Crinoline Choir, Byron Foulger, Dorothy Dandridge (film debut in an unbilled bit), Richard Farnsworth (film debut in an unbilled performance as a stuntman). *D:* Sam Wood; *P:* Lawrence Weingarten; *As.P.:* Max Siegel; *St:* Robert Pirosh, George Seaton; *Sc:* Pirosh, Seaton, George Oppenheimer; *Songs:* "A Message from the Man in the Moon," "On Blue Venetian Waters," "Tomorrow Is Another Day" and "All God's Chillun Got Rhythm" by Bronislau Kaper, Walter Jurmann and Gus Kahn; *Choreographer:* (A.A.N.) Dave Gould for "All God's Chillun. . . ." (1:49) (video)

A zany trio helps a girl save her racehorse. A classic Marx Brothers comedy with a ballet sequence which was originally photographed in blue tint.

1004. Day of Reckoning (MGM; 1933). *Cast:* Richard Dix (in his only film for this studio), Madge Evans, Clarence Wilson, Conway Tearle, Una Merkel, Stuart Erwin, Raymond Hatton, Paul Hurst, Samuel S. Hinds, Spanky McFarland, John Larkin, Wilfred Lucas. *D:* Charles Brabin; *P:* Lucien Hubbard; *St:* Morris Lavine; *Sc:* Zelda Sears, Eve Greene.

B drama.

1005. The Day the Bookies Wept (RKO; 1938). *Cast:* Joe Penner, Betty Grable, Richard Lane, Tom Kennedy, Thurston Hall, Bernadene Hayes, Carol Hughes, Jack Arnold (Vinton Haworth). *D:* Leslie Goodwins; *P:* Robert Sisk; *St:* Daniel Fuchs; *Sc:* Bert Granet, George Jeske. (1:04)

Low-budget comedy farce about a tippling racehorse named Hiccup whose pedigree stems from "out of Bourbon by Distillery." A hit for the studio.

1006. Day-Time Wife (20th Century–Fox; 1939). *Cast:* Tyrone Power, Linda Darnell, Warren William, Joan Davis, Binnie Barnes, Wendy Barrie, Leonid Kinskey, Mary Gordon, Renie Riano, Joan Valerie, Mildred Gover. *D:* Gregory Ratoff; *P:* Darryl F. Zanuck; *St:* Rex Taylor; *Sc:* Art Arthur, Robert Harari. (1:11)

Comedy of a housewife who takes an office job.

1007. Daybreak (MGM; 1931). *Cast:* Ramon Novarro, Helen Chandler, C. Aubrey Smith, Jean Hersholt, William Bakewell, Karen Morley, Kent Douglass (Douglass Montgomery), Glenn Tryon, Clyde Cook, Sumner Getchell, Clara Blandick, Edwin Maxwell, Jackie Searle, Sidney Blackmer. *D:* Jacques Feyder; *Adaptation:* Ruth Cummings; *Sc:* Zelda Sears, Cyril Hume. (1:12)

Romantic drama of an Austrian army officer and a piano teacher. A box office flop which was based on the book by Arthur Schnitzler.

1008. Days of Jesse James (Republic; 1938–39). *Cast:* Roy Rogers, George "Gabby" Hayes, Pauline Moore, Donald Barry (Jesse James), Harry Woods, Arthur Loft, Wade Boteler, Ethel Wales, Scotty Beckett, Harry Worth, Glenn Strange, Olin Howland, Monte Blue, Jack Rockwell, Fred Burns, Bud Osborne, Jack Ingram, Carl Sepulveda, Lynton Brent, Pasquel Perry, Eddie Acuff, Horace B. Carpenter. *D:* Joe Kane; *As.P.:* Kane; *St:* Jack Natteford; *Sc:* Earl Snell. (1:03) (video)

Historically flavored Roy Rogers western.

1009. Dead End (United Artists/ Samuel Goldwyn; 1937). *Cast:* Sylvia Sidney (Drina), Joel McCrea (Dave), Humphrey Bogart (Baby Face Martin), Wendy Barrie (Kay), Claire Trevor (A.A.N. for B.S.A. as Francie), Marjorie Main (Mrs. Martin), Allen Jenkins (Hunk), Billy Halop (Tommy), Huntz Hall (Dippy), Bobby Jordan (Angel), Leo Gorcey (Spit), Gabriel Dell (T.B.), Bernard Punsley (Milty), Charles Peck (Philip Griswold), Minor Watson (Mr. Griswold), James Burke (Mulligan), Elizabeth Risdon (Mrs. Connell), Esther Dale (Mrs. Fenner), George Humbert (Pascagli), Marcelle Corday (governess), Charles Halton (Whitey), Jerry Cooper (Milty's brother), Kath Ann Lujan (Milty's sister), Ward Bond (doorman), Robert E. Homans, Bill Dagwell, Tom Ricketts, Gertrude Valerie, Charlotte Treadway, Maude Lambert, Frank Shields, Lucille Brown, Bud Geary, Mickey Martin, Wesley Girard, Esther Howard, Gilbert Clayton, Earl Askam, Mona Monet, Donald Barry. *D:* William Wyler; *P:* Sam Goldwyn; *As.P.:* Merritt Hulburd; *Sc:* Lillian Hellman; *Cinematographer:* (A.A.N.) Gregg Toland; *Art Director:* (A.A.N.) Richard Day. (1:33) (video)

Classic drama of tenement life in New York City which received an A.A.N. for Best Picture. It also placed #8 on the "10 Best" list of *Film Daily,* marking the film debuts of the "Dead End Kids" who appeared in the original stage production by Sidney Kingsley.

The Dead End Kids on Dress Parade *see* **On Dress Parade**

1010. The Dead March (Xxxx Xxxx; 1937). *Cast:* Solo Doudauz, Al Rigali, Al Ritchie. *D:* Bud Pollard; *P:* Bud Pollard; *Sc:* Samuel Taylor Moore. Semi-doc, anti-war film.

1011. Dead Yesterday (Xxxx Xxxx; 1937).
(No information available)

1012. Deadline (Columbia; 1931). *Cast:* Buck Jones, Loretta Sayers, Robert Ellis, Raymond Nye, Ed Brady, Knute Erickson, George Ernest, Harry Todd, Jack Curtis, James Farley, Robert Kortman. *D:* Lambert Hillyer; *Sc:* Hillyer. (1:00)

Buck Jones western of a cowboy paroled from jail, only to find trouble waiting for him.

1013. The Deadly Ray from Mars (Universal; 1938). *Cast:* Buster Crabbe (Flash Gordon), Jean Rogers (Dale Arden), Charles Middleton (Ming), Frank Shannon (Dr. Zarkoff), Donald Kerr, Beatrice Roberts, Kane Richmond, Wheeler Oakman. *D:* Ford Beebe, Robert Hill. (1:39)

The first feature version of this studio's 15-chapter serial "Flash Gordon's Trip to Mars."

1014. Deadwood Pass (Monarch; 1933). *Cast:* Tom Tyler, Wally Wales (Hal Taliferro), Alice Dahl, Lafe McKee, Edmund Cobb, Slim Whitaker, Merrill McCormack, Carlotta Monti, Buffalo Bill, Jr., Duke Lee, Blackie Whiteford. *D:* J.P. McGowan; *P:* John R. Freuler; *St:* John Wesley Patterson; *Sc:* Oliver Drake. (1:01)

Tom Tyler horse opera of a government agent who poses as an outlaw called "The Hawk" in order to retrieve some stolen loot.

1015. Dealers in Death (Xxxx Xxxx; 1934). *P:* Monroe Shaff; *St:* Burnett Hershey; *Narrator:* Basil Ruysdael.

Documentary.

1016. Death Flies East (Columbia; 1935). *Cast:* Conrad Nagel, Florence Rice, George Hayes, Irene Franklin, Raymond Walburn, Robert Allen, Oscar Apfel. *D:* Phil Rosen.

B melodrama.

1017. Death from a Distance (Invincible; 1935). *Cast:* Russell Hopton, Lola Lane, Robert Frazer, John St. Polis, Wheeler Oakman. *D:* Frank Strayer.

"Poverty row" mystery set in a planetarium.

1018. Death in the Air (Puritan; 1937). *Cast:* John Carroll, Lona Andre, Reed Howes, Leon Ames, Wheeler Oakman, Gaston Glass. *D:* Elmer Clifton.

B mystery.

1019. The Death Kiss (World Wide/Tiffany; 1933). *Cast:* Bela Lugosi, David Manners, Adrienne Ames, John Wray, Vince Barnett, Edward Van Sloan, Mona Maris, Edmund Burns, Lee Moran, Harold Minjir, Al Hill, Alan Roscoe, Harold Waldridge. *D:* Edwin L. Marin (directorial debut); *Sc:* Gordon Kahn, Barry Barringer; *St:* Madelon St. Denis. (1:15) (video)

"Poverty row" murder-mystery set in a movie studio. Produced by Tiffany, but released by World Wide.

1020. Death of a Champion (Paramount; 1939). *Cast:* Lynne Overman, Virginia Dale, Donald O'Connor, Joseph Allen, Jr., Susan Paley, Robert Paige, Harry Davenport, Frank M. Thomas, May Boley, Pierre Watkin, David Clyde, Bob McKenzie, Walter Soderling, Hal Brazeale. *D:* Robert Florey; *Sc:* Cortland Fitzsimmons, Stuart Palmer.

Based on the novel by Frank Gruber, this comedy-mystery is centered around the mysterious death of a champion great Dane at a dog show.

1021. Death on the Diamond (MGM; 1934). *Cast:* Madge Evans, Robert Young, Paul Kelly, Nat Pendleton, Mickey Rooney, Robert Livingston, Willard Robertson, Joseph (Sawyer) Sauers, Ted Healy, C. Henry Gordon, Marc Lawrence, Edward Brophy, James Ellison, DeWitt Jennings, David Landau, Jack Norton. *D:* Edward Sedgwick; *P:* Lucien Hubbard; *St:* Cortland Fitzsimmons; *Sc:* Harvey Thew, Joe Sherman, Ralph Spence.

Low-budget murder-mystery involving a baseball team.

The Death Ray (G.B. title) *see* **Murder at Dawn** (1932)

1022. Death Rides the Range (Colony; 1939–40). *Cast:* Ken Maynard, Fay McKenzie, Ralph Peters, Julian Rivero, Charles King, John Elliott, William Costello, Sven-Hugo Borg, Julian Madison. *D:* Sam Newfield; *P:* Max & Arthur Alexander; *Sc:* Bill Lively. (0:58)

Independent Ken Maynard western concerning the control of a deposit of helium gas.

1023. Death Takes a Holiday (Paramount; 1934). *Cast:* Fredric March (Death—"Prince Sirki"), Evelyn Venable (Grazia), Sir Guy Standing (Duke Lambert), Gail Patrick (Rhoda), Katherine Alexander (Alda), Helen Westley (Stephanie), Kathleen Howard (film debut as Princess Maria), Henry Travers (Baron Cesarea), Kent Taylor (Prince Corrado), Edward Van Sloan (Dr. Valle), G.P. Huntley, Jr. (Eric), Otto Hoffman (Fedele), Hector Sarno (Pietro), Frank Yaconelli, Anna De Linsky. *D:* Mitchell Leisen; *P:* E. Lloyd Sheldon; *Sc:* Maxwell Anderson, Gladys Lehman, Walter Ferris. (1:18)

Classic romantic fantasy which has Death taking human form for three days to find out why men fear him. Based on the play by Alberto Casella and another by Maxwell Anderson. A hit at the box office, it was remade in 1971 as a TV movie.

1024. Death Watch (Xxxx Xxxx; 1934). (No information available)

Deceit (G.B. title) *see* **Unholy Love**

1025. The Deceiver (Columbia; 1931). *Cast:* Lloyd Hughes, Dorothy Sebastian, George Byron, Ian Keith, Natalie Moorhead, Greta Granstedt, DeWitt Jennings, Allan Garcia, Frank Halliday, Richard Tucker, Harvey Clark, Nick Copeland, Sidney Bracey, Murray Kinnell. *D:* Louis King; *St:* Abem Finkel, Bella Muni; *Sc:* Jo Swerling.
Low-budget romantic melodrama.

1026. Deception (Columbia; 1932). *Cast:* Leo Carrillo, Thelma Todd, Nat Pendleton, Barbara Weeks, Frank Sheridan, Dickie Moore, Hans Steinke. *D:* Lewis Seiler; *St & Sc:* Nat Pendleton.
Low-budget comedy.

1027. Defenders of the Law (Xxxx Xxxx; 1931). *Cast:* Philo McCullough, Edmund Breese, Joseph Girard, Kit Guard.
Low-budget production.
(No other information available)

1028. The Defense Rests (Columbia; 1934). *Cast:* Jack Holt, Jean Arthur, Nat Pendleton, Raymond Hatton, Donald Meek, J. Carrol Naish, John Wray, Ward Bond, Harold Huber, Raymond Walburn, Samuel S. Hinds, Selmer Jackson, Robert Gleckler, Sarah Padden, Arthur Hohl, Shirley Grey. *D:* Lambert Hillyer; *St & Sc:* Jo Swerling.
B courtroom melodrama.

1029. Delicious (Fox; 1931). *Cast:* Janet Gaynor (Heather Gordon), Charles Farrell (Jerry Beaumont), El

Brendel (Jansen), Lawrence O'Sullivan (O'Flynn), Virginia Cherrill (Diana Van Bergh), Raoul Roulien (Sascha), Olive Tell (Mrs. Van Bergh), Manya Roberti (Olga), Mischa Auer (Mischa), Marvine Maazel (Tosha), Jeanette Gegna (Momotschka), Crauford Kent. *D:* David Butler; *St:* Guy Bolton; *Sc:* Bolton, Sonya Levien; *Songs:* "You Started It," "New York Rhapsody," "Somebody from Somewhere" and "Delicious" by George and Ira Gershwin. (1:46)
A romantic musical which was one of the 15 top grossing films of 1932.

1030. The Delightful Rogue (RKO; 1929). *Cast:* Rod La Rocque, Rita LaRoy, Charles Byer, Bert Moorhouse, Ed Brady, Harry Semels, Samuel Blum, Gladden James, Hugh Crumplin. *D:* A. Leslie Pearce; *Pictorial Director:* Lynn Shores; *As.P.:* Henry Hobart; *Sc:* Wallace Smith; *Song:* "Gay Love" by Oscar Levant, Sidney Clare. (1:11)
Low-budget romantic drama.

1031. Delinquent Parents (Progressive Pictures Corp.; 1938). *Cast:* Doris Weston, Maurice Murphy. *D:* Nick Grinde; *Sc:* Nick Barrows, Robert St. Clair.
B melodrama.

1032. Deluge (RKO/Admiral; 1933). *Cast:* Sidney Blackmer, Peggy Shannon, Lois Wilson, Fred Kohler, Edward Van Sloan, Matt Moore, Ralf Harolde, Samuel S. Hinds. *D:* Felix E. Feist (feature directorial debut); *As.P.:* Sam Bischoff; *Sc:* John Goodrich, Warren B. Duff. (1:10) (video)
Disaster melodrama with special effects by Ned Mann which shows the destruction of New York City by earthquake and tidal waves and the survival of a handful of people afterward. Based on the novel by S. Fowler Wright.

1033. A Demon for Trouble (Supreme; 1934). *Cast:* Bob Steele (his first for this independent company), Gloria Shea, Lafe McKee, Jimmy Aubrey,

Nick Stuart, Walter McGrail, Don Alvarado, Carmen LaRoux, Perry Murdock, Blackie Whiteford. *D:* Robert Hill; *P:* A.W. Hackel; *Sc:* Jack Natteford. (0:58)

Bob Steele western involving the investigation into the reason some landowners were murdered.

1034. Deported (Xxxx Xxxx; 1932). (No information available)

1035. Derelict (Paramount; 1930). *Cast:* George Bancroft, Jessie Royce Landis (film debut), Bill Boyd, Marie Dressler, Dorothy Jordan, William Stack, Donald Stuart, Wade Boteler. *D:* Rowland V. Lee; *Sc:* Grover Jones, William Slavens McNutt.

B drama of shipboard rivalry for the love of a girl.

1036. Desert Gold (Paramount; 1936). *Cast:* Buster Crabbe, Tom Keene, Robert Cummings, Marsha Hunt, Raymond Hatton, Robert Frazer, Glenn (Leif) Erickson, Frank Mayo, Monte Blue. *D:* James Hogan; *P:* Harold Hurley; *Sc:* Stuart Anthony, Robert Yost. (0:58)

B western based on a book by Zane Grey of an Easterner who goes west to help a friend capture a wanted killer. Filmed before in 1926 by this studio with Neil Hamilton.

1037. Desert Guns (Beaumont; 1936). *Cast:* Conway Tearle, Margaret Morris, Charles K. French, Budd Buster, William Gould, Marie Werner, Kate Brinkler, Duke Lee, Art Felix, Slim Whitaker, Bull Montana. *D:* Charles Hutchison, *St:* Jacques Jaccard. (1:00)

B western of a lawman who helps a girl save her inheritance.

1038. Desert Justice (Atlantic; 1936). *Cast:* Jack Perrin, Maryan Downing, Warren Hymer, David Sharpe, Dennis (Moore) Meadows, Roger Williams, Budd Buster, William Gould, Fred "Snowflake" Toones, Earl Dwire, Starlight the horse, Braveheart the dog.

D: Lester Williams (William Berke); *P:* Berke; *Sc:* Gordon Phillips, Lewis Kingdon. (G.B. title: *Crime's Highway*) (1:00)

Jack Perrin western of a border patrolman on the trail of smugglers.

1039. Desert Mesa (Security; 1936). *D:* Denver Dixon; *P:* Dixon.

Obscure independent B western which attempted to launch stuntman Wally West into a career as a cowboy star, this flop being the only such effort.

1040. Desert Patrol (Republic-Supreme; 1938). *Cast:* Bob Steele, Marion Weldon, Rex Lease, Ted Adams, Forrest Taylor, Budd Buster, Steve Clark, Jack Ingram, Tex Palmer. *D:* Sam Newfield; *P:* A.W. Hackel; *Sc:* Fred Myton. (1:00)

Bob Steele western of a Texas Ranger who pursues a gang that killed a fellow ranger.

1041. The Desert Phantom (Supreme; 1936). *Cast:* Johnny Mack Brown, Sheila Mannors, Ted Adams, Karl Hackett, Hal Price, Nelson McDowell, Charles King, Forrest Taylor. *D:* S. Roy Luby; *P:* A.W. Hackel; *Sc:* Earle Snell. (1:06)

Johnny Mack Brown oater of a man hired to protect a girl's ranch from marauding outlaws. A remake of *The Night Rider* (q.v.).

1042. The Desert Song (WB; 1929). *Cast:* John Boles, Carlotta King, Louise Fazenda, John Miljan, Edward Martindel, Johnny Arthur, Otto Hoffman, Jack Pratt, Myrna Loy, Del Elliott, Robert E. Guzman, Marie Wells. *D:* Roy Del Ruth; *St:* Otto Harbach, Laurence Schwab, Frank Mandel; *Sc:* Harvey Gates; *Lyrics:* Oscar Hammerstein II; *Songs:* "The Riff Song," "The French Military Marching Song," "Then You Will Know," "Love's Yearning," "The Desert Song," "Song of the Brass Key," "Sabre Song" and "Romance." (1:46)

Notable as the first all-talkie operetta to reach the silver screen. Based on the successful 1926 stage production by Sigmund Romberg, some sequences are in 2-color technicolor. Remade in 1943–44 and 1953.

1043. The Desert Trail (Monogram–Lone Star; 1935). *Cast:* John Wayne, Mary Kornman, Paul Fix, Eddy Chandler, Carmen LaRoux, Lafe McKee, Al Ferguson, Henry Hall, Frank Ball, Artie Ortego, Lew Meehan, Wally West, Frank Brownlee, Frank Ellis, Dick Dickinson. *D:* Cullen Lewis (Lewis Collins); *P:* Paul Malvern; *St & Sc:* Lindsley Parsons. (0:54) (video)

John Wayne western of two pals out to clear their names of robbery charges.

1044. Desert Vengeance (Columbia/Beverly Productions; 1930–31). *Cast:* Buck Jones, Barbara Bedford, Douglas Gilmore, Al Smith, Ed Brady, Buck Connors, Gilbert "Pee Wee" Holmes, Slim Whitaker, Robert Ellis, Bob Fleming, Joe Girard, Barney Bearsley. *D:* Louis King; *Sc:* Stuart Anthony. (0:55)

Buck Jones western of a man who saves a girl after she is left in the desert to die.

1045. Design for Living (Paramount; 1933). *Cast:* Fredric March, Gary Cooper, Miriam Hopkins, Edward Everett Horton, Franklin Pangborn, Isabel Jewell, Wyndham Standing, Jane Darwell, Adrienne D'Ambricourt, Emile Chautard, Nora Cecil, Mary Gordon, Harry Phillips, George Savidan, Mrs. Treboal. *D:* Ernst Lubitsch; *P:* Lubitsch; *Sc:* Ben Hecht. (1:35)

Hit sophisticated comedy of a woman who chooses to marry for wealth rather than love. Based on the play by Noel Coward.

1046. Desirable (WB; 1934). *Cast:* Verree Teasdale, Jean Muir, George Brent, Arthur Aylesworth, Joan Wheeler, Barbara Leonard, Jane Darwell, Russell Hopton, John Halliday, Charles Starrett, Virginia Hammond, Doris Atkinson, Jim Miller, Pauline True. *D:* Archie Mayo; *P:* Edward Chodorov; *Sc & St:* Mary McCall, Jr. (1:08)

Comedy-drama of a woman who keeps her daughter in school longer than necessary to conceal her (the mother's) age.

1047. Desire (Paramount; 1936). *Cast:* Marlene Dietrich, Gary Cooper, John Halliday, William Frawley, Ernest Cossart, Akim Tamiroff, Alan Mowbray, Zeffie Tilbury, Stanley Andrews, Marc Lawrence, Enrique Acosta, Alice Feliz. *D:* Frank Borzage; *P:* Ernst Lubitsch; *Sc:* Edwin Justus Mayer, Waldemar Young, Samuel Hoffenstein. (1:36) (video)

A sophisticated romantic story about the reformation of a jewel thief. Originally scheduled to be shot in technicolor with Ernst Lubitsch directing, but due to illness Lubitsch was forced to bow out. Based on the German film *Die schönen Tage von Aranjuex* and a play by Hans Szekely and Robert A. Stemmle.

1048. Desire of Death (Xxxx Xxxx; 1930). (No information available)

1049. A Desperate Adventure (Republic; 1938). *Cast:* Ramon Novarro, Marian Marsh, Lois Collier (film debut), Eric Blore, Andrew Tombes, Margaret Tallichet. *D:* John H. Auer. (G.B. title: *It Happened in Paris*)

A painter finds romance in Paris while searching for a stolen painting.

1050. Desperate Trails (Universal; 1939). *Cast:* Johnny Mack Brown, Fuzzy Knight, Frances Robinson, Bob Baker, Russell Simpson, Clarence Wilson, Billy Cody, Jr., Ralph Dunn, Charles Stevens, Ed Cassidy, Horace Murphy, Fern Emmett, Frank Ellis, Frank McCarroll, Cliff Lyons, Eddie Parker. *D:* Albert Ray; *Sc:* Andrew Bennison. (0:58)

Johnny Mack Brown western (his first of six for this studio) of a cowboy who uncovers skullduggery on a girl's ranch.

1051. Destination Saturn (Universal; 1939). *Cast:* Buster Crabbe, Constance Moore, Jackie Moran, Jack Mulhall, Anthony Warde, C. Montague Shaw. *D:* Ford Beebe, Saul Goodkind. (aka: *Planet Outlaws*) (1:31) (video)

Feature version of the 12-chapter serial "Buck Rogers" in which Rogers is revived in the distant future and does battle with Killer Kane.

1052. Destination Unknown (Universal; 1933). *Cast:* Pat O'Brien, Betty Compson, Ralph Bellamy, Tom Brown, Russell Hopton, Alan Hale, Stanley Fields, Charles Middleton, Noel Madison, Willard Robertson, Rollo Lloyd, Forrester Harvey, George Regas, Richard Alexander. *D:* Tay Garnett; *St & Sc:* Tom Buckingham. (1:05)

Low-budget melodrama of rum-running.

1053. Destry Rides Again (Universal; 1932). *Cast:* Tom Mix, Tony (his horse), Claudia Dell, Andy Devine, ZaSu Pitts, George Ernest, Stanley Fields, Earle Foxe, Ed Peil, Sr., Francis Ford, Frederick Howard, John Ince, Edward LeSaint, Charles K. French. *D:* Ben Stoloff; *Sc:* Richard Schayer, Robert Keith, Isadore Bernstein. (TV title: *Justice Rides Again*) (1:04) (video)

Tom Mix western of a man who is framed and sent to prison only to get out and seek vengeance on those who framed him. The title of the film is taken from the book by Max Brand. This was Mix's first talking picture; also his first of nine features for this studio.

1054. Destry Rides Again (Universal; 1939). *Cast:* Marlene Dietrich (Frenchy), James Stewart (Tom Destry), Mischa Auer (Boris Callahan),

Charles Winninger ("Wash" Dimsdale), Brian Donlevy (Kent), Allen Jenkins (Gyp Watson), Warren Hymer (Bugs Watson), Irene Hervey (Janice Tyndall), Una Merkel (Lily Belle Callahan), Billy Gilbert (Loupgerou), Samuel S. Hinds (Hiram Slade), Jack Carson (Jack Tyndall), Tom Fadden (Lem Claggett), Virginia Brissac (Sophie Claggett), Lillian Yarbo (Clara), Edmund MacDonald (Rockwell), Ann (E.) Todd (Sis Claggett), Dickie Jones (Eli Whitney Claggett), Joe King (Sheriff Keogh), Minerva Urecal (Mrs. DeWitt), Lloyd Ingraham (Turner), Carmen D'Antonio (dancer), Loren Brown and Harold DeGarro (jugglers), Harry Cording, Richard Alexander, Bob McKenzie, Billy Bletcher, Bill Cody, Jr., Bill Steele Gettinger, Harry Tenbrook, Bud McClure, Alex Woloshin, Chief John Big Tree. *D:* George Marshall; *P:* Joe Pasternak; *As.P.:* Islin Auster; *St:* Felix Jackson; *Sc:* Jackson, Gertrude Purcell, Henry Myers. (1:34) (video)

Classic western which is another of the films of Hollywood's block-buster year of 1939. Loosely based on the novel by Max Brand. The story concerns a lawman without guns summoned to the town of Bottleneck to clean up the lawless element overrunning the town. A winner for the studio, it was one of the 21 top grossing films of 1939-40.

Note: Loosely remade in 1950 as *Frenchie,* with a remake following in 1954 titled *Destry* (both Universal).

Detective, Clive Bart (G.B. title) *see* **Scotland Yard**

1055. Determination (Xxxx Xxxx; 1931). (No information available)

1056. The Devil and the Deep (Paramount; 1932). *Cast:* Tallulah Bankhead, Charles Laughton, Gary Cooper, Cary Grant, Paul Porcasi, Henry Kolker, Dorothy Christy, Kent Taylor, Juliette Compton, Arthur Hoyt. *D:* Marion Gering; *P:* Emanuel

Cohen; *St:* Harry Hervey; *Sc:* Benn Levy. (1:18)

Melodrama of a submarine commander's jealousy over his wife's lover.

1057. The Devil Diamond (Ambassador; 1937). *Cast:* Frankie Darro, Kane Richmond. *D:* Xxxx Xxxx; *P:* Maurice Conn.

B melodrama of jewel thieves.

1058. Devil Dogs of the Air (WB; 1934–35). *Cast:* James Cagney, Pat O'Brien, Margaret Lindsay, Frank McHugh, Helen Lowell, John Arledge, Robert Barrat, Russell Hicks, Ward Bond, William Davidson, Gordon (Bill) Elliott, Samuel S. Hinds, Bud Flanagan (Dennis O'Keefe). *D:* Lloyd Bacon; *P:* Louis Edelman; *Sc:* Malcolm Stuart Boylan, Earl Baldwin. (1:26)

Comedy-drama of the Marine Flying Corps, notable for its stunt flying sequences. Based on the novel by John Monk Saunders, the film is dedicated to the U.S.M.C.

1059. The Devil-Doll (MGM; 1936). *Cast:* Lionel Barrymore, Maureen O'Sullivan, Frank Lawton, Rafaela Ottiano, Robert Greig, Lucy Beaumont, Henry B. Walthall, Grace Ford, Pedro de Cordoba, Arthur Hohl, Juanita Quigley, Claire DuBrey, Rollo Lloyd, E. Alyn Warren, Billy Gilbert. *D:* Tod Browning; *P:* E.J. Mannix; *St:* Browning; *Sc:* Garrett Fort, Guy Endore, Erich Von Stroheim. (1:19) (video)

A horror classic notable for its special effects of a Devil's Island escapee seeking revenge on those who wrongly imprisoned him. Based on the book "Burn, Witch, Burn" by Abraham Merritt.

1060. The Devil-Horse (Mascot; 1932). *Cast:* Harry Carey, Noah Beery, Frankie Darro, Greta Granstedt, Barrie O'Daniels, Ed Peil, Jack Mower, Alan Bridge, Jack Byron, J. Paul Jones, Carli Russell, Lou Kelley, Dick Dickinson, Lane Chandler, Fred Burns, Yakima Canutt, Ken Cooper, Wes Warner, Al Taylor, Apache the horse. *D:* Otto Brower; *P:* Nat Levine; *Sc:* George Morgan, Barney A. Sarecky, George Plympton, Wyndham Gittens.

Feature version of the 12-chapter serial of the same name involving wild horses and revenge. Previously filmed in 1926 as a feature by Pathé.

1061. The Devil Is a Sissy (MGM; 1936). *Cast:* Freddie Bartholomew (Claude), Mickey Rooney (Gig Stevens), Jackie Cooper (Buck Murphy), Ian Hunter (Mr. Pierce), Peggy Conklin (Rose), Katharine Alexander (Mrs. Pierce), Gene Lockhart (Mr. Murphy), Kathleen Lockhart (Mrs. Murphy), Dorothy Peterson (Mrs. Stevens), Jonathan Hale (judge), Etienne Girardot (principal), Mary Doran (Mrs. Robbins), Sherwood Bailey (Bugs), Buster Flavin (Six Toes), John Kelly (Roy), Rollo Lloyd (pawnbroker), John Wray (priest), Andrew Tombes (Mr. Muldoon), Harold Huber (Willie), Jason Robards (Kraus), Grant Mitchell (Krump), Stanley Fields (Joe), Ian Wolfe (the other pawnbroker), Charles Coleman, Stanley Andrews, George Guhl, Myra Marsh, Harry Tyler, Christian Rub, Frank Puglia, Etta McDaniel. *D:* W.S. Van Dyke; *P:* Frank Davis; *Sc:* John Lee Mahin, Richard Schayer; *St:* Rowland Brown; *Song:* Nacio Herb Brown, Arthur Freed. (G.B. title: *The Devil Takes the Count*) (1:32)

A boy from England moves to a tenement area of New York City and seeks to join a local youth gang. It placed #6 on the "10 Best" list of the National Board of Review.

1062. The Devil Is a Woman (Paramount; 1935). *Cast:* Marlene Dietrich, Lionel Atwill, Cesar Romero, Edward Everett Horton, Alison Skipworth, Don Alvarado, Morgan Wallace, Tempe Pigott, Donald Reed, Hank Mann. *D:* Josef Von Sternberg; *Sc:* John Dos Passos, S.K. Winston; *Songs:* Ralph Rainger, Leo Robin. (1:23)

Lavishly produced romantic drama set against the Spanish Civil War of 1890 of a cold-hearted woman who leads various men on. The last of Dietrich's films to be directed by Von Sternberg. Based on the novel "La Femme et le Pantin" by Pierre Loüys, it was a box office flop in 1935. A remake of 1920's *The Woman and the Puppet* with Geraldine Farrar for Sam Goldwyn. Filmed twice in France, in 1958 as *A Woman Like Satan* (aka: *The Female*) with Brigitte Bardot and in 1977 as *That Obscure Object of Desire*.

1063. The Devil Is Driving (Paramount; 1932). *Cast:* Edmund Lowe, James Gleason, Wynne Gibson, Francis McDonald, Lois Wilson, Guinn Williams, Tom Kennedy, Dickie Moore, John Kelly, Charles Williams, George Rosener, Geneva Mitchell. *D:* Ben Stoloff; *St:* Frank Mitchell Dazey; *Sc:* Louis Weitzenkorn; *Adaptation:* P.J. Wolfson, Allen Rivkin.

B melodrama of an auto mechanic who uncovers skullduggery at his place of employment.

1064. The Devil Is Driving (Columbia; 1937). *Cast:* Richard Dix, Ann Rutherford, Elisha Cook, Jr., Ian Wolfe, Frank C. Wilson, Charles C. Wilson, Joan Perry, Nana Bryant, James Millican. *D:* Harry Lachman; *St:* Harold Buchman, Lee Loeb; *Sc:* Richard Blake, Jo Milward.

Low-budget melodrama on reckless driving.

1065. Devil-May-Care (MGM; 1929). *Cast:* Ramon Novarro (talkie debut), Dorothy Jordan, Marion Harris, John Miljan, William Humphrey, Clifford Bruce, George Davis. *D:* Sidney Franklin; *St:* Eugene Scribe, Ernest Legouve; *Adaptation:* Richard Schayer; *Sc:* Hans Kräly, Zelda Sears.

Part-talkie costume operetta set in 18th-century France. A hit for the studio, it was based on an 1851 French play titled "Batailles des Dames."

1066. The Devil on Deck (Sono Art–World Wide; 1932). *Cast:* Reed Howes, Molly O'Day, June Marlowe, Wheeler Oakman. *D:* Wallace Fox.

"Poverty row" melodrama.

1067. Devil on Horseback (Grand National; 1936). *Cast:* Lili Damita, Del Campo, Fred Keating, Tiffany Thayer, Jean Chatburn, Renee Torres, Juan Torena, Ann Miller (film debut—bit). *D:* Crane Wilbur; *P:* George A. Hirliman; *St & Sc:* Wilbur. (1:11)

Low-budget color musical of a kidnapped troupe of entertainers in South America.

Devil on Wheels (G.B. title) *see* **Indianapolis Speedway**

1068. The Devil Plays (Chesterfield; 1931). *Cast:* Robert Ellis, Edmund Burns, Carmelita Geraghty, Lillian Rich, Jameson Thomas. *D:* Richard Thorpe (who also edited).

"Poverty row" production.

The Devil Takes the Count (G.B. title) *see* **The Devil Is a Sissy**

1069. Devil Tiger (Fox; 1934). *Cast:* Kane Richmond, Marion Burns, Harry Woods, Ah Lee, "The Devil Tiger." *D:* Clyde E. Elliott; *St & Sc:* James O. Spearing, Russell Shields, Lew Lehr.

Melodrama.

1070. The Devil to Pay (United Artists/Samuel Goldwyn; 1930). *Cast:* Ronald Colman, Frederick Kerr, Loretta Young, David Torrence, Florence Britton, Myrna Loy, Paul Cavanagh, Crauford Kent, Mary Forbes. *D:* George Fitzmaurice; *P:* Sam Goldwyn; *Adaptation:* Benjamin Glazer; *St & Sc:* Frederick Lonsdale. (1:13)

Drawing room comedy of the son of a millionaire who has trouble with responsibility. The film placed #5 on the list of "10 Best" films of the *New York Times*.

1071/1072. A Devil with Women (Fox; 1930). *Cast:* Victor McLaglen,

Mona Maris, Humphrey Bogart (feature film debut), Michael Vavitch, John St. Polis, Joe de la Cruz, Mona Rico, Luana Alcaniz. *D:* Irving Cummings; *P:* George Middleton; *Sc:* Dudley Nichols, Henry M. Johnson. (1:16)

A romantic tale of two soldiers of fortune. Based on the story "Dust and Son" by Clements Ripley.

The Devil's Brother *see* **Fra Diavolo**

1073. Devil's Canyon (Xxxx Xxxx; 1935). (No information available)

The Devil's Daughter *see* **Pocomania**

1074. The Devil's Holiday (Paramount; 1929–30). *Cast:* Nancy Carroll (A.A.N. for B.A. 1929–30), Phillips Holmes, Paul Lukas, Ned Sparks, ZaSu Pitts, James Kirkwood, Hobart Bosworth, Jed Prouty, Wade Boteler, Morgan Farley, Guy Oliver, Morton Downey. *D:* Edmund Goulding; *Sc:* Goulding.

A romantic comedy of a gold-digging manicurist who is reformed by true love. The film was originally scheduled to star Jeanne Eagels who died before production began.

1075. The Devil's in Love (Fox; 1933). *Cast:* Loretta Young, Victor Jory, Vivienne Osborne, C. Henry Gordon, David Manners, J. Carrol Naish, Bela Lugosi, Herbert Mundin, Emile Chautard, Akim Tamiroff. *D:* William Dieterle; *St:* Harry Hervey; *Sc:* Howard Estabrook. (1:11)

Foreign legion melodrama of a doctor falsely accused of murder.

1076. Devil's Island (WB; 1939–40). *Cast:* Boris Karloff, James Stephenson, Nedda Harrigan, Adia Kuznetzoff, Robert Warwick, Pedro de Cordoba,

Will Stanton, Edward Keane, Paul Fix. *D:* William Clemens; *As.P.:* Bryan Foy; *St:* Anthony Coldeway, Raymond L. Schrock; *Sc:* Kenneth Gamet, Don Ryan. (1:03)

Low-budget drama of an innocent doctor sent to the famed island prison. The film was briefly released in 1939 but shelved for political reasons, receiving full release in 1940.

1077. The Devil's Lottery (Fox; 1932). *Cast:* Victor McLaglen, Elissa Landi, Paul Cavanagh, Ralph Morgan, Beryl Mercer, Herbert Mundin, Barbara Weeks, Alexander Kirkland, Ruth Warren, Ethel Griffies, Halliwell Hobbes. *D:* Sam Taylor; *St:* Nalbro Bartley; *Sc:* Guy Bolton.

After they win the Calcutta sweepstakes, a couple learn that money can't buy happiness.

1078. Devil's Mate (Monogram; 1933). *Cast:* Preston Foster, Peggy Shannon, Ray Walker, Hobart Cavanaugh, Barbara Barondess, Paul Porcasi, Harold Waldridge, Jason Robards, Bryant Washburn, Harry Holman, George Hayes, James Durkin, Gordon DeMain, Paul Fix, Sam Flint, Henry Otho, Henry Hall. *D:* Phil Rosen; *P:* Ben Verschleiser; *St:* Leonard Fields, David Silverstein; *Sc:* Fields, Silverstein. (G.B. title: *He Knew Too Much*) (1:08)

An investigation ensues when a convicted killer is murdered just before he is to be electrocuted. Remade in 1941 as *I Killed That Man.*

1079. The Devil's Party (Universal; 1938). *Cast:* Victor McLaglen, William Gargan, Paul Kelly, Beatrice Roberts, Samuel S. Hinds, Frank Jenks, John Gallaudet, Mickey Rentschler, Scotty Beckett, Tommy Bupp, Dickie Jones, Juanita Quigley, Arthur Hoyt, Joseph Downing, Ed Gargan, Gordon (Bill) Elliott, David Oliver. *D:* Ray McCarey; *P:* Edmund Grainger; *Sc:* Roy Chanslor. (1:05) (video)

Melodrama of a reunion of friends who grew up together in Hell's Kitchen in New York City. Based on a novel by Borden Chase.

1080. The Devil's Pit (Universal; 1930). *Produced, directed and written by* Lewis Collins.

A documentary feature of life among the Maori tribes of New Zealand.

1081. Devil's Playground (Columbia; 1937). *Cast:* Richard Dix, Dolores Del Rio, Chester Morris, Pierre Watkin, Ward Bond, Ann Doran, John Gallaudet, Stanley Andrews, George McKay, Don Rowan, Francis McDonald. *D:* Erle C. Kenton; *P:* George Vanderbilt; *St:* Norman Springer; *Sc:* Dalton Trumbo, Jerome Chodorov, Liam O'Flaherty. (1:14)

Action-adventure involving a romantic triangle. A remake of Frank Capra's *Submarine* (1928).

1082. The Devil's Saddle Legion (WB; 1937). *Cast:* Dick Foran, Anne Nagel, Gordon Hart, Ernie Stanton, Max Hoffman, Jr., Granville Owen, Willard Parker, Glenn Strange, Carlyle Moore, Jr., John "Skins" Miller, Frank Orth, Jack Mower, Milton Kibbee, George Chesebro, Walter Young, Charles LeMoyne, Raphael (Ray) Bennett, Gordon (Bill) Elliott, Smoke the Wonder Horse. *D:* Bobby Connolly (choreographer in his directorial debut); *P:* Gordon Hollingshead; *St & Sc:* Ed Earl Repp; *Songs:* "Ridin' to My Home in Texas," "Dog's Country" and "When Moonlight Is Riding the Range" by M.K. Jerome and Jack Scholl. (0:52)

Dick Foran western of a group of escaped convicts who band together to bring justice to the range.

1083. Devil's Squadron (Columbia; 1936). *Cast:* Richard Dix (his first film for this studio), Karen Morley, Lloyd Nolan, Shirley Ross, Thurston Hall, Gene Morgan, Gordon Jones,

William Stelling, Gertrude Green, Boyd Irwin, Henry Mollison. *D:* Erle C. Kenton; *P:* Robert North; *Sc:* Lionel Houser, Bruce Manning, Howard Green.

B action drama.

1084. Devotion (RKO–Pathé; 1931). *Cast:* Ann Harding, Leslie Howard, Robert Williams, O.P. Heggie, Louise Closser Hale, Dudley Digges, Olive Tell, Douglas Scott, Alison Skipworth, Doris Lloyd, Ruth Weston, Joan Carr, Tempe Pigott, Forrester Harvey, Claude King, Pat Somerset, Joyce Coad, Donald Stuart, Margaret Daily, Cyril Delevanti. *D:* Robert Milton; *P:* Charles R. Rogers; *Sc:* Graham John, Horace Jackson. (1:20)

Tear-jerker of a London barrister who decides to play while the wife is away. Based on the novel "A Little Flat in the Temple" by Pamela Wynne.

1085. Diamond Jim (Universal; 1935). *Cast:* Edward Arnold (Brady), Jean Arthur (in a dual role), Binnie Barnes (Lillian Russell), Cesar Romero, Eric Blore, George Sidney, Hugh O'Connell, Henry Kolker, William Demarest, Otis Harlan, Purnell Pratt, Robert McWade, Tully Marshall, Arthur Housman, Fred Kelsey, Bill Hoolahahn, Charles Sellon, Lew Kelly. *D:* A. Edward Sutherland; *P:* Edmund Grainger; *Adaptation:* Harry Clork, Doris Malloy; *Sc:* Preston Sturges. (1:28)

Lavishly produced and partially fictionalized story of 19th-century millionaire Diamond Jim Brady, his love of good food and actress Lillian Russell. Based on the biography by Parker Morell.

1086. The Diamond Trail (Monogram; 1932). *Cast:* Rex Bell, Frances Rich, Bud Osborne, Lloyd Whitlock, Norman Feusier, Jerry Storm, John Webb Dillon, Billy West, Larry Lamont. *D:* Harry Fraser; *P:*

Trem Carr; *St:* Sherman Lowe; *Sc:* Lowe, Fraser. (1:01)

Rex Bell western of an eastern reporter who heads west to scoop some diamond smugglers.

1087. Dick Tracy (Republic; 1937). *Cast:* Ralph Byrd, Kay Hughes, Smiley Burnette, Roy Barcroft, Byron Foulger. *D:* Alan James (Alvin J. Neitz). *P:* Nat Levine. (1:30)

Feature version of the 15-chapter serial of the same name with the fearless detective going after the Spider Gang, a group of terrorists who have taken his brother.

1088. Dick Tracy Returns (Republic; 1938). *Cast:* Ralph Byrd, Lynn Roberts, Charles Middleton, David Sharpe, Clayton Moore. *D:* John English, William Witney; *P:* Nat Levine.

Feature version of the 15-chapter serial of the same name with Tracy battling a West Coast crime family.

1089. Dick Tracy's G-Men (Republic; 1939). *Cast:* Ralph Byrd, Irving Pichel, Phyllis Isley (Jennifer Jones), George Cleveland. *D:* John English, William Witney; *P:* Nat Levine. (1:30)

Feature version of the serial of the same name with Tracy attempting to stop an international spy from sabotaging the U.S. defense system.

1090. Dimples (20th Century–Fox; 1936). *Cast:* Shirley Temple, Frank Morgan, Helen Westley, Berton Churchill, Robert Kent, Astrid Allwyn, Delma Byron, Herman Bing, John Carradine, Stepin Fetchit, Douglas Fowley, Jack Clifford, Arthur Aylesworth, Paul Stanton, Julius Tannen, The Hall Johnson Choir, Betty Jean Hainey, Billy McClain. *D:* William A. Seiter; *As.P.:* Nunnally Johnson; *Sc:* Arthur Sheekman, Nat Perrin; *Song:* Jimmy McHugh, Ted Koehler. (1:19) (video)

Musical comedy-drama of a little girl and her grandfather who reside in New York's Bowery of the mid 19th-century.

1091. Dinky (WB; 1935). *Cast:* Jackie Cooper, Mary Astor, Roger Pryor, Henry Armetta, Betty Jean Hainey, Henry O'Neill, Jimmy Butler, Edith Fellows, Richard Quine, George Ernest, Sidney Miller, Frank Gernardi, Clay Clement, Addison Richards, Florence Fair, James Burke, Joseph Crehan. *D:* Howard Bretherton, D. Ross Lederman; *P:* Sam Bischoff; *St:* John Fante, Frank Fenton, Samuel Gilson Brown; *Sc:* Harry Sauber. (1:05)

Sentimental B drama of a mother accused of fraud who protects her son, a cadet in a military school.

1092. Dinner at Eight (MGM; 1933). *Cast:* Marie Dressler (Carlotta Vance), John Barrymore (Larry Renault), Wallace Beery (Dan Packard), Jean Harlow (Kitty Packard), Lionel Barrymore (Oliver Jordan), Lee Tracy (Max Kane), Edmund Lowe (Wayne Talbot), Billie Burke (Millicent Jordan), Madge Evans (Paula Jordan), Jean Hersholt (Joe Stengel), Karen Morley (Mrs. Wayne Talbot), Phillips Holmes (Ernest DeGraf), May Robson (cook), Louise Closser Hale (Hattie Loomis), Grant Mitchell (Ed Loomis), Phoebe Foster (Miss Alden), Hilda Vaughn (Tina), John Davidson (Mr. Hatfield), Harry Beresford (Fosdick), Herman Bing (waiter), Edwin Maxwell (Mr. Fitch), Edward Woods (Eddie), George Baxter (Gustav), Anna Duncan (Dora), Constance Collier (American debut — bit), Taylor Holmes. *D:* George Cukor; *P:* David O. Selznick; *Sc:* Frances Marion, Herman J. Mankiewicz, Donald Ogden Stewart. (1:53) (video)

Classic sophisticated comedy of New York society and the preparations for an elaborate dinner party. Based on the play by George S. Kaufman and Edna Ferber, it placed #5 on the "10 Best" list of the *New York Times* of 1933 while placing #8 on the same list of *Film Daily* in 1934. Remade as a TV movie in 1989.

1093. Diplomaniacs (RKO; 1933). *Cast:* Bert Wheeler (Willy Nilly), Robert Woolsey (Hercules Grub), Marjorie White, Louis Calhern, Hugh Herbert, Edgar Kennedy, Phyllis Barry, Richard Carle, Billy Bletcher, Edward Cooper, Neely Edwards. *D:* William A. Seiter; *As.P.:* Sam Jaffe; *St:* Joseph L. Mankiewicz; *Sc:* Mankiewicz, Henry Myers; *Songs:* Harry Akst, Edward Eliscu. (1:03) (video)

Musical farce of two barbers from an American Indian reservation who journey to the Geneva Peace Convention.

1094. The Diplomats (Fox; 1929). *Cast:* Bobby Clark, Cissy Fitzgerald. *D:* Norman Taurog.

Low-budget comedy.

1095. Dirigible (Columbia; 1931). *Cast:* Jack Holt, Ralph Graves, Fay Wray, Hobart Bosworth, Roscoe Karns, Selmer Jackson, Alan Roscoe, Harold Goodwin, Emmett Corrigan, Clarence Muse, Richard Loo (film debut). *D:* Frank Capra; *St:* Frank Wead; *Sc:* Jo Swerling, Dorothy Howell. (1:33)

Airship experimentation in Antarctica ends in disaster in this action-drama.

1096. Disbarred (Paramount; 1939). *Cast:* Gail Patrick, Otto Kruger, Robert Preston, Sidney Toler, Charles D. Brown, Paul Fix, Clay Clement, Harry Worth, Edward Marr, Helen Mackellar, Virginia Dabney, John Hart. *D:* Robert Florey; *P:* Stuart Walker; *Sc:* Lillie Hayward, Robert Presnell. (0:58)

B melodrama of a lady lawyer and a gangster she is going to defend.

1097. Discarded Lovers (Tower; 1932). *Cast:* Russell Hopton, Natalie Moorhead, Sharon Lynn, J. Farrell MacDonald, Roy D'Arcy, Robert Frazer, Fred Kelsey, Jason Robards. *D:* Fred Newmeyer.

"Poverty row" melodrama.

1098. Disgraced (Paramount; 1933). *Cast:* Helen Twelvetrees, Bruce Cabot, Ken Murray, Adrienne Ames, Charles Middleton, William Harrigan. *D:* Erle C. Kenton; *St:* Alice Duer Miller.

B drama of a jilted girl who threatens to kill her lover.

1099. Dishonored (Paramount; 1931). *Cast:* Marlene Dietrich, Victor McLaglen, Lew Cody, Warner Oland, Gustav von Seyffertitz, Barry Norton, Wilfred Lucas, Davison Clark, Tom London. *D:* Josef von Sternberg; *St:* "X-27" by von Sternberg; *Sc:* Daniel N. Rubin, von Sternberg. (1:31)

A girl, posing as a peasant is actually a German spy. With its World War I setting, the film was a box office hit as well as being voted one of the "10 Best" films of the year by the National Board of Review.

1100. Disorderly Conduct (Fox; 1932). *Cast:* Spencer Tracy, Sally Eilers, Ralph Morgan, Ralph Bellamy, El Brendel, Sally Blane, Charley Grapewin, Geneva Mitchell, Nora Lane, Frank Conroy, Claire Maynard, James Todd, Cornelius Keefe. *D:* John W. Considine, Jr.; *St & Sc:* William Anthony McGuire.

A cop gets involved in unlawful activities in this low-budget melodrama.

1101. Disputed Passage (Paramount; 1939). *Cast:* Dorothy Lamour, Akim Tamiroff, John Howard, Judith Barrett, Victor Varconi, William Collier, Sr., Keye Luke, Elizabeth Risdon, Philip Ahn, Gordon Jones, Dorothy Adams, William Pawley, Renie Riano, Dave Alison, Alma Eidnea, Lee Ya-ching, Jack Chapin, Billy Cook, Mary Akaiek. *D:* Frank Borzage; *P:* Harlan Thompson; *Sc:* Anthony Veiller, Sheridan Gibney. (1:30)

Hit drama of scientists with conflicting ideas and ideals, based on the bestseller by Lloyd C. Douglas.

1102. Disraeli (WB; 1929). *Cast:* George Arliss (A.A. for B.A. 1929–30 as Benjamin Disraeli), Joan Bennett (Lady Clarissa Pevensey of Glastonbury), Florence Arliss (Lady Mary Beaconsfield), Anthony Bushell (film debut as Lord Charles Deeford), David Torrence (Sir Michael, Lord Probert), Ivan Simpson (Hugh Meyers), Doris Lloyd (Mrs. Agatha Travers), Gwendolyn Logan (Duchess of Glastonbury), Henry Carvill (Duke of Glastonbury), Charles E. Evans (Potter), Norman Cannon (Foljambe), Cosmo Kyrle Bellew (Mr. Terle), Jack Deery (Bascot), Michael Visaroff (Count Bosrinov), Shayle Gardner (Dr. Williams), Powell York (Flookes), Margaret Mann (Queen Victoria), George Atkinson. *D:* Alfred E. Green; *Adaptation:* (A.A.N.) Julien Josephson. (1:29)

Events in the life of the famed British Prime Minister as he attempts to outwit the Russians in the purchase of the Suez Canal. Based on the 1911 play by Louis N. Parker, it was first filmed as an independent production in 1917 by Paul Cromelin. Remade in 1921 with Mr. and Mrs. Arliss for United Artists release. This highly acclaimed film received an A.A.N. for Best Picture (1929–30), *Photoplay's* Gold Medal Award, was voted "Best Film of the Year" by *Film Daily* and placed #2 on the "10 Best" list of the *New York Times.*

Divine Love (G.B. title) *see* **No Greater Love**

1103. Divorce Among Friends (WB; 1930). *Cast:* James Hall, Irene Hervey, Natalie Moorhead, Lew Cody, Edward Martindel, Irene Delroy, Margaret Seddon. *D:* Roy Del Ruth; *St:* Jack Townley; *Sc:* Arthur Caesar, Harvey Thew.

Low-budget triangular romantic drama.

1104. Divorce in the Family (MGM; 1932). *Cast:* Conrad Nagel, Jackie Cooper, Lois Wilson, Lewis Stone, Louise Beavers, Jean Parker (film debut), Maurice Murphy. *D:* Charles F. Reisner; *Sc:* Delmer Daves.

Low-budget production aptly described by the title.

1105. Divorce Made Easy (Paramount; 1929). *Cast:* Douglas MacLean (in his final film as an actor), Marie Prevost, Johnny Arthur, Frances Lee. *D:* Walter Graham; *P:* Al Christie.

Low-budget drama of a man who attempts to get rid of his wife in order to gain an inheritance.

1106. The Divorcee (MGM; 1930). *Cast:* Norma Shearer (A.A. for B.A. 1929–30 as Jerry), Chester Morris (Ted), Conrad Nagel (Paul), Robert Montgomery (Don), Florence Eldridge (Helen), Helene Millard (Mary), Robert Elliott (Bill), Mary Doran (Janice), Tyler Brooke (Hank), George Irving (Dr. Bernard), Zelda Sears (Hannah), Helen Johnson (Dorothy), Theodore Von Eltz. *D:* (A.A.N.) Robert Z. Leonard; *P:* Leonard; *Sc:* (A.A.N.) Nick Grinde, Zelda Sears, John Meehan. (1:23)

A married man has affairs with other women, but gets upset when he finds his wife is seeing other men. Based on the novel "Ex-Wife" by Ursula Parrott, this critically praised tear-jerker of the old double-standard was a smash hit at the box office, receiving an A.A.N. for Best Picture and placing #8 on the "10 Best" list by *Film Daily.*

1107. Dixiana (RKO; 1930). *Cast:* Bebe Daniels, Everett Marshall, Bert Wheeler, Robert Woolsey, Jobyna Howland, Bill Robinson (film debut), Joseph Cawthorn, Dorothy Lee, Ralf Harolde, Eugene Jackson, Eddie Chandler, Bruce Covington, Raymond Maurel. *D:* Luther Reed; *P:* William LeBaron; *St:* Anne Caldwell; *Sc:* Reed; *Title Song:* Benny Davis; *Other Songs:* Anne Caldwell, Harry Tierney. (1:39)

Musical-comedy with color sequences of a man from an aristocratic southern family who falls for a circus performer. The film, set in 19th-century New Orleans, was a box office flop.

1108. Dizzy Dames (Liberty; 1935). *Cast:* Marjorie Rambeau, Inez Courtney, Lawrence Gray, Berton Churchill, Mary Forbes. *D:* William Nigh; *P:* M.H. Hoffman, Jr.; *Sc:* George Waggner.

Low-budget comedy.

1109. Docks of San Francisco (Mayfair; 1932). *Cast:* Mary Nolan, Jason Robards, Max Davidson. *D:* George B. Seitz.

"Poverty row" melodrama.

1110. Dr. Bull (Fox; 1933). *Cast:* Will Rogers (Dr. Bull), Marian Nixon, Ralph Morgan, Rochelle Hudson, Berton Churchill, Louise Dresser, Elizabeth Patterson, Robert Parrish, Andy Devine, Vera Allen, Nora Cecil, Effie Ellsler, Ethel Griffies, Veda Buckland, Helen Freeman, Howard Lally, Patsy O'Byrne. *D:* John Ford; *St:* James Gould Cozzens; *Sc:* Paul Green, Jane Storm. (1:15)

A common sense doctor heals bodies and minds of the residents of a small town. A hit for the studio.

1111. Dr. Jekyll and Mr. Hyde (Paramount; 1931–32). *Cast:* Fredric March (A.A. for B.A., shared with Wallace Beery for *The Champ* [q.v.] as the dual role of Dr. Jekyll/Mr. Hyde), Miriam Hopkins (Ivy Pearson), Rose Hobart (Muriel Carew), Holmes Herbert (Dr. Lanyan), Halliwell Hobbes (Brig. Gen. Sir Danvers Carew), Edgar Norton (Poole the butler), Arnold Lucy (Utterson), Colonel MacDonnell (Hobson the butler), Tempe Pigott (Mrs. Hawkins), Eric Wilton (Briggs the butler), Douglas Walton, John Rogers, Murdock MacQuarrie, Major Sam Harris, Tom London. *D:* Rouben Mamoulian; *P:* Mamoulian; *Sc:* (A.A.N.) Percy Heath, Samuel Hoffenstein; *Cinematographer:* (A.A.N.) Karl Struss. (video — restored to 1:37)

Classic version of Robert Louis Stevenson's 1885 horror story "The Strange Case of Dr. Jekyll and Mr. Hyde," first adapted to the stage in 1887. At the Venice Film Festival it was voted "the most original and dramatic film." It placed #5 on the "10 Best" list of the *New York Times* and #6 on the same list of *Film Daily.* Censored for re-release in the late 1930s, the film was fully restored in 1989 by Turner Entertainment for home video release. Silent versions: (Selig; 1908), (Denmark; 1909), (Thanhouser; 1912) with James Cruze, (Universal; 1913) with King Baggot and Jane Gail, (Great Britain; 1913), 1919 with Sheldon Lewis, (Paramount; 1920) with John Barrymore, Martha Mansfield and Nita Naldi, and (Germany; 1920). Along with many variations, latter day versions include (MGM; 1941), *The Two Faces of Dr. Jekyll* (Great Britain; 1961), *Edge of Sanity* (1989) and a 1990 TV movie. One of the 15 top grossing films of 1932.

1112. Dr. Monica (WB; 1934). *Cast:* Kay Francis (title role), Warren William, Jean Muir, Verree Teasdale, Emma Dunn, Philip Reed, Herbert Bunston, Ann Shoemaker, Hale Hamilton, Virginia Pine, Louise Beavers, Virginia Hammond. *D:* William Keighley; *P:* Henry Blanke; *English Language Adaptation:* Laura Walker Mayer; *Sc:* Charles Kenyon. (0:51)

The wandering husband of a lady doctor fathers a child by another. Based on the Polish play by Marja Morozowicz Sczepokowska, it was a hit for the studio with primary appeal to the female audience.

1113. Doctor Rhythm (Paramount; 1938). *Cast:* Bing Crosby, Beatrice Lillie, Mary Carlisle, Andy Devine, Laura Hope Crews, Rufe Davis, Henry Wadsworth, Sterling Holloway, Emory Parnell, Louis Armstrong, Fred Keating, Franklin Pangborn, William Austin, Gino Corrado, John Hamilton, Frank Elliott, Alphonse Martel, Dolores Casey, Desmond

Gallagher, Charles Moore, Harold Minjir, Harry Stubbs, Allen Mathews. *D:* Frank Tuttle; *P:* Emanuel Cohen; *Sc:* Jo Swerling, Richard Connell; *Songs:* James V. Monaco, Johnny Burke. (1:20)

Hit musical of a veterinarian who moonlights as a bodyguard with an eye on show business. Based on the story "The Badge of Policeman O'Roon" by O'Henry.

1114. Dr. Socrates (WB; 1935). *Cast:* Paul Muni, Ann Dvorak, Barton MacLane, Robert Barrat, John Eldredge, Hobart Cavanaugh, Helen Lowell, Mayo Methot, Samuel S. Hinds, Henry O'Neill, Grace Stafford, June Travis, Raymond Brown, Olin Howland, Joseph Downing, Marc Lawrence, Carl Stockdale, John Kelly, William Burress, Hal K. Dawson, Ivan Miller, Sam Wren, Adrian Morris, Edward McWade, Ralph Remley, Jack Norton. *D:* William Dieterle; *P:* Robert Lord; *Adaptation:* Mary C. McCall, Jr.; *Sc:* Lord. (1:10)

A small town doctor patches up a wounded gangster and finds events in his life taking a different turn. Based on the novel by W.R. Burnett, it was twice remade, in 1939 as *King of the Underworld* (q.v.) and in 1942 as the low-budget *Bullet Scars*.

1115. Doctor X (WB/F.N.; 1932). *Cast:* Lionel Atwill, Fay Wray, Lee Tracy, Preston Foster, John Wray, Harry Beresford, Arthur Edmund Carewe, Leila Bennett, Robert Warwick, George Rosener, Willard Robertson, Thomas Jackson, Harry Holman, Mae Busch, Tom Dugan. *D:* Michael Curtiz; *P:* Hal Wallis; *Sc:* Earl Baldwin, Robert Tasker. (1:20) (video)

Classic 2-color technicolor horror thriller centering around a series of stranglings during the full moon. Based on the play by Howard Warren Comstock and Allen C. Miller, it was a hit for the studio.

1116. A Doctor's Diary (Paramount; 1937). *Cast:* George Bancroft, Helen Burgess, Molly Lamont, Sidney Blackmer, Sue Carol, Milburn Stone, Charles Waldron, Ra Hould (Ronald Sinclair), John Trent, Ruth Coleman. *D:* Charles Vidor; *P:* B.P. Schulberg.

Low-budget melodrama involving a hospital trial.

1117. The Doctor's Secret (Paramount; 1929). *Cast:* Ruth Chatterton, John Loder (American debut), H.B. Warner, Robert Edeson, Ethel Wales, Wilfred Noy, Nancy Price, Frank Finch-Smiles. *D:* William C. de Mille; *Sc:* de Mille.

Low-budget drama of an extramarital affair. Based on a play by Sir James Barrie, it was filmed in 1920 as *Half an Hour* with Dorothy Dalton and Charles Richman.

1118. Doctor's Wives (Fox; 1931). *Cast:* Warner Baxter, Joan Bennett, Victor Varconi, George Chandler, John St. Polis, Minna Gombell, Helene Millard, Paul Porcasi, Cecilia Loftus, Violet Dunn, Nancy Gardner, William Maddox, Ruth Warren, Louise Mackintosh. *D:* Frank Borzage; *St:* Henry & Sylvia Lieferant.

Marital drama.

1119. Dodge City (WB; 1939). *Cast:* Errol Flynn (Wade Hatton), Olivia de Havilland (Abbie Irving), Ann Sheridan (Ruby Gilman), Bruce Cabot (Jeff Surrett), Frank McHugh (Joe Clemens), Alan Hale (Rusty Hart), John Litel (Matt Cole), Victor Jory (Yancy), William Lundigan (Lee Irving), Henry Travers (Dr. Irving), Henry O'Neill (Colonel Dodge), Cora Witherspoon (Mrs. McCoy), Guinn "Big Boy" Williams (Tex Baird), Gloria Holden (Mrs. Cole), Ward Bond (Bud Taylor), Douglas Fowley (Munger), Georgia Caine (replacing Elizabeth Risdon as Mrs. Irving), Bobs Watson (Harry Cole), Nat Carr (Crocker), Russell Simpson (Orth), Clem Bevans

(Charlie the Barber), Joseph Crehan (Hammond), Thurston Hall (Twitchell), Chester Clute (Coggins), Charles Halton (lawyer), Monte Blue (Barlow the Indian agent), George Guhl (Marshal Jason), Fred Graham (Al), James Burke, Robert Homans, Spencer Charters, Bud Osborne, Wilfred Lucas, Richard Cramer, Milton Kibbee, Vera Lewis, Earle Hodgins, Tom Chatterton, Pat O'Malley, Pat Flaherty. *D:* Michael Curtiz; *P:* Robert Lord; *Sc:* Robert Buckner. (1:45) (video)

Lavish technicolor western of Dodte City, Kansas in its wild and lawless days. One of the 16 top grossing films of 1938–39.

1120. Dodge City Trail (Columbia; 1938). *Cast:* Charles Starrett, The Sons of the Pioneers, Donald Grayson. *D:* C.C. Coleman, Jr.; *Sc:* Harold Shumate. (1:04)

Charles Starrett western.

1121. Dodsworth (United Artists/Samuel Goldwyn; 1936). *Cast:* Walter Huston (A.A.N. for B.A. and "Best Actor of the Year" by the New York Film Critics as Sam Dodsworth), Ruth Chatterton (Fran Dodsworth), Paul Lukas (Arnold Iselin), Mary Astor (Edith Cortwright), David Niven (Lockert), Maria Ouspenskaya (A.A.N. for B.S.A. in her film debut as Baroness von Obersdorf), Gregory Gaye (Kurt von Obersdorf), Odette Myrtil (Madame de Penable), Kathryn Marlowe (Emily), John Payne (film debut as Harry), Spring Byington (Matey Pearson), Harlan Briggs (Tubby Pearson), Beatrice Maude. *D:* (A.A.N.) William Wyler; *P:* Samuel Goldwyn; *As.P.:* Merritt Hulburd; *Sc:* (A.A.N.) Sidney Howard; *Art Director:* (A.A.) Richard Day for Interior Decoration; *Sound Recording:* (A.A.N.) Oscar Lagerstrom. (1:41) (video)

A Hollywood classic of an American industrialist who retires and moves to Europe with his wife to live, only to find that living abroad is a whole new experience. Based on the novel by Sinclair

Lewis which also spawned a play. It received an A.A.N. for Best Picture, was in nomination for "Best Film of the Year" by the New York Film Critics, placed #2 on the "10 Best" list of the *New York Times* and on the same list of *Film Daily* it placed #5. One of the 38 top grossing films of 1936–37.

1122. A Dog of Flanders (RKO; 1935). *Cast:* Frankie Thomas (Nello), Helen Parrish (Maria), O.P. Heggie, DeWitt Jennings, Ann Shoemaker, Christian Rub, Lightning the dog, Richard Quine, Frank Reicher, Nella Walker, Addison Richards, Josef Swickard, Sarah Padden, Harry Beresford, Henry Kolker. *D:* Edward Sloman; *As.P.:* William Sistrom; *Adaptation:* Dorothy Yost; *Sc:* Ainsworth Morgan. (1:12)

Sentimental story of a poor Flemish boy who yearns to become a great painter and the mistreated dog he befriends. Based on the classic 1872 book by Ouida it was previously filmed by Metro-Goldwyn in 1924 as *A Boy of Flanders* with Jackie Coogan. Remade in 1959 by Fox.

1123. Don't Bet on Blondes (WB; 1935). *Cast:* Warren William, Guy Kibbee, Claire Dodd, Walter Byron, William Gargan, Hobart Cavanaugh, Vince Barnett, Spencer Charters, Maude Eburne, Herman Bing, Marc Lawrence, Mary Treen, Jack Norton, Eddie Shubert, Clay Clement, Errol Flynn (bit). *D:* Robert Florey; *P:* Sam Bischoff; *St:* Isabel Dawn, Boyce de Gaw; *Sc:* Dawn, de Gaw.

B comedy of a man who assures a Kentucky colonel that his daughter will not marry.

1124. Don't Bet on Love (Universal; 1933). *Cast:* Lew Ayres, Ginger Rogers, Charley Grapewin, Shirley Grey, Merna Kennedy, Robert Emmett O'Connor, Thomas Dugan, Lucile Gleason, Henry Armetta. *D:* Murray Roth; *P:* Carl Laemmle, Jr.; *St:* Roth;

Sc: Roth, Howard Emmett Rogers, Ben Ryan. (1:02)

B comedy of romance between a manicurist and a lover of race horses.

1125. Don't Bet on Women (Fox; 1931). *Cast:* Jeanette MacDonald, Edmund Lowe, Una Merkel, Roland Young, Louise Beavers, Helene Millard, J.M. Kerrigan. *D:* William K. Howard; *St:* William Anthony McGuire; *Sc:* Lynn Starling, Leon Gordon. (G.B. title: *More Than a Kiss*)

Low-budget romantic comedy.

1126/1127. Don't Gamble with Love (Columbia; 1936). *Cast:* Ann Sothern, Bruce Cabot, Ian Keith, George McKay, Clifford Jones, Franklin Pangborn, Richard Livernoin. *D:* Dudley Murphy; *St & Sc:* Harold Buchman, Lee Loeb.

Low-budget romantic comedy.

1128. Don't Get Personal (Universal; 1936). *Cast:* Sally Eilers, James Dunn, Pinky Tomlin, George Cleveland, Spencer Charters, Jean Rogers, Lillian Harmer. *D:* William Nigh; *P:* David Diamond; *St:* Thiele; *Co-St:* William Thiele, Edmund L. Hartmann; *Sc:* George Waggner. (1:10)

B comedy of a girl who embarks on a road trip with some ousted college students.

Don't Pull Your Punches (G.B. title) *see* **The Kid Comes Back**

1129. Don't Tell the Wife (RKO; 1937). *Cast:* Guy Kibbee, Una Merkel, Lynne Overman, Lucille Ball, Guinn Williams, Thurston Hall, Frank M. Thomas, William Demarest, Harry Tyler, George Irving, Bradley Page, Harry Jans, Si Jenks, Hattie McDaniel. *D:* Christy Cabanne; *P:* Robert Sisk; *Sc:* Nat Perrin (based on the play "Once Over Lightly" by George Holland). (1:03)

B comedy of a man who has trouble overcoming his bad habit of conning people.

1130. Don't Turn 'Em Loose (RKO; 1936). *Cast:* Lewis Stone, Bruce Cabot, James Gleason, Betty Grable, Louise Latimer, Grace Bradley, Nella Walker, Frank M. Thomas, Harry Jans, John Arledge, Frank Jenks, Maxine Jennings, Gordon Jones, Addison (Jack) Randall, John Ince. *D:* Ben Stoloff; *As.P.:* Robert Sisk; *St:* "Homecoming" by Thomas Walsh; *Sc:* Harry Segall, Ferdinand Reyher. (1:05)

B melodrama of family conflict between a father and his hoodlum son with a social statement on lenient parole regulations.

1131. The Donovan Affair (Columbia; 1929). *Cast:* Jack Holt, Agnes Ayres, Dorothy Revier, William Collier, Jr., Hank Mann, Alphonse Ethier, Edward Hearn, John Wallace, John Roche, Ethel Wales, Fred Kelsey. *D:* Frank Capra; *St:* Owen Davis; *Sc:* Howard Green, Dorothy Howell.

Action melodrama.

Donovan's Kid (G.B. title) *see* **Young Donovan's Kid**

1132. Doomed at Sundown (Republic-Supreme; 1937). *Cast:* Bob Steele, Lorraine Hayes (Laraine Day), Warner Richmond, David Sharpe, Earl Dwire, Horace B. Carpenter, Sherry Tansey, Harold Daniels, Budd Buster, Jack Kirk, Horace Murphy, Charles King, Lew Meehan, Jack Ingram. *D:* Sam Newfield; *P:* A.W. Hackel; *Sc:* George Plympton. (1:00)

Bob Steele western of a cowboy who takes on a gang of hooded riders.

1133. The Doomed Battalion (Universal; 1932). *Cast:* Luis Trenker, Tala Birell, Victor Varconi, Albert Conti, Gustav von Seyffertitz, Henry Armetta, Ferdinand Gottschalk, Gibson Gowland. *D:* Cyril Gardner; *St:* Luis Trenker; *Adaptation & Screenplay:*

Trenker, Carl Hartl, Patrick Kearney. (1:35)

World War I drama of the war's effects on an Austrian man and his wife. Partially filmed in Austria's Tyrolean Alps. Remade in 1940 as *Ski Patrol.*

1134. Doorway to Hell (WB; 1930). *Cast:* Lew Ayres, Charles Judels, Dorothy Mathews, Leon Janney, Robert Elliott, James Cagney (his second film), Dwight Frye, Noel Madison, Cameron Prud'Homme, Kenneth Thomson, Jerry Mandy. *D:* Archie Mayo; *St:* (A.A.N.) Rowland Brown for his original story "A Handful of Clouds"; *Sc:* George Rosener. (1:18)

A Chicago gangster story.

1135. Double Cross Roads (Fox; 1930). *Cast:* Lila Lee, Robert Ames, Edythe Chapman, J. Carrol Naish, Ned Sparks, Thomas Jackson, Charlotte Walker, George MacFarlane, William V. Mong, Thomas Jefferson, Montagu Love. *D:* Alfred Werker; *Assoc. P:* George Middleton; *St:* William R. Lipman; *Sc:* Howard Estabrook.

Low-budget production.

1136. Double Danger (RKO; 1938). *Cast:* Preston Foster, Whitney Bourne, Donald Meek, Samuel S. Hinds, Paul Guilfoyle, Cecil Kellaway, June Johnson, Arthur Lake, Edythe Elliott, Alec Craig, Harry Hayden, Vivian Oakland. *D:* Lew Landers; *St:* Arthur T. Horman; *Sc:* Horman, J. Robert Bren. (1:02)

B mystery of efforts to uncover a jewel thief.

Double Daring (G.B. title) *see* **Fixer Dugan**

1137. The Double Door (Paramount; 1934). *Cast:* Evelyn Venable, Mary Morris (recreating her stage role), Anne Revere (film debut—recreating her stage role), Sir Guy Standing, Kent Taylor, Colin Tapley, Halliwell Hobbes, Virginia Howell, Helen Shipman, Leonard Carey, Ralph Remley,

Frank Dawson, Burr Caruth. *D:* Charles Vidor; *Sc:* Gladys Lehman, Jack Cunningham.

An "old dark house" mystery based on a popular 1933 Broadway play by Elizabeth McFadden.

1138. Double Harness (RKO; 1933). *Cast:* William Powell, Ann Harding, Lillian Bond, Kay Hammond, Henry Stephenson, Lucile Browne, George Meeker, Leigh Allen, Reginald Owen, Hugh Huntley, Wallis Clark, George Weeks. *D:* John Cromwell; *As.P.:* Kenneth MacGowan; *Sc:* Jane Murfin.

Drawing room comedy based on the play by Edward Poor Montgomery.

1139. Double or Nothing (Paramount; 1937). *Cast:* Bing Crosby, Martha Raye, Andy Devine, Mary Carlisle, William Frawley, Fay Holden, Frances Faye, William Henry, Gilbert Emery, Samuel S. Hinds, Benny Baker, John Gallaudet. *D:* Jay Theodore Reed; *P:* Benjamin Glazer; *St:* M. Coates Webster; *Sc:* Charles Lederer, Erwin Gelsey, Duke Atteberry, John Moffitt; *Songs:* Burton Lane, Arthur Johnston, Johnny Burke (includes "The Moon Got in My Eyes"). (1:35)

Musical-comedy of four people who each have to double their money in thirty days after each is given $5,000.

1140. Double Wedding (MGM; 1937). *Cast:* William Powell, Myrna Loy, John Beal, Florence Rice, Edgar Kennedy, Sidney Toler, Barnett Parker, Katherine Alexander, Donald Meek, Mary Gordon, Jessie Ralph, Priscilla Lawson, Horace McMahon. *D:* Richard Thorpe; *P:* Joseph L. Mankiewicz; *Sc:* Jo Swerling. (1:27)

Romantic comedy based on the play "Great Love" by Ferenc Molnar.

1141. Doubting Thomas (Fox; 1935). *Cast:* Will Rogers, Alison Skipworth, Gail Patrick, Billie Burke, T. Roy Barnes, Sterling Holloway, Andrew Tombes, Billy Benedict, Frank Albertson, John Qualen, George Cooper, Johnny Arthur, Helen Freeman, Helen Flint, Fred Wallace, Ruth Warren, Frances Grant, Bud Flanagan (Dennis O'Keefe). *D:* David Butler; *P:* B.G. DeSylva; *Sc:* William Conselman, Bartlett Cormack.

Homespun comedy of a simple man trying to deal with the theatrical aspirations of his wife. A hit for the studio, it was based on the play "The Torch Bearers" by George Kelly.

1142. Doughboys (MGM; 1930). *Cast:* Buster Keaton, Sally Eilers, Cliff Edwards, Edward Brophy, Victor Potel, Frank Mayo, Pitzy Katz, Arnold Korff, William Steele, Harriette Lake (Ann Sothern — bit). *D:* Edward Sedgwick; *P:* Buster Keaton; *Sc:* Richard Schayer. (G.B. title: *Forward March*) (1:19)

Army comedy with Buster Keaton front and center. A box office hit.

1143. Doughnuts and Society (Republic/Mascot; 1935–36). *Cast:* Louise Fazenda, Maude Eburne, Ann Rutherford, Edward Nugent, Hedda Hopper, Franklin Pangborn, Rafael Corio, Smiley Burnette, Harold Minjir, Olaf Hytten, Robert Light, Claudell Kaye. *D:* Lewis Collins; *Supervisor:* William Berke; *St & Sc:* Karen deWolf, Robert St. Clair, Wallace MacDonald; *Additional Dialogue:* Gertrude Orr, Matt Brooks. (1:03)

B comedy of two mothers who are co-owners in a coffee shoppe. A Mascot production released by Republic.

The Dove (G.B. title) *see* **Girl of the Rio**

The Dover Road (G.B. title) *see* **Where Sinners Meet**

1144. Down in "Arkansaw" (Republic; 1938). *Cast:* Frank Weaver (Cicero), Leon Weaver (Abner), June Weaver (Elviry), Ralph Byrd, June Storey, Paula Stone, Pinky Tomlin,

Guinn Williams, Berton Churchill, Selmer Jackson. *D:* Nick Grinde.

Rural B comedy featuring the down-home humor and hillbilly music of The Weaver Brothers and Elviry. The film was a big hit prompting the studio to start a continuing series into the 1940s featuring the Weavers.

1145. Down on the Farm (20th Century-Fox; 1938). *Cast:* Jed Prouty, Spring Byington, Florence Roberts, Kenneth Howell, George Ernest, Billy Mahan, June Carlson, William Haade. *D:* Malcolm St. Clair.

Entry in the popular "Jones Family" comedy series, aptly described by the title.

1146. Down the Stretch (WB/F.N.; 1936). *Cast:* Mickey Rooney, Patricia Ellis, Dennis Moore, William (Willie) Best, Gordon (Bill) Elliott, Charles C. Wilson, Gordon Hart, Virginia Brissac, Joseph Crehan, Mary Treen, Robert Emmett Keane, Charles Foy, Crauford Kent, Frank Faylen, Andre Beranger, Stanley Morner (Dennis Morgan). *D:* William Clemens; *P:* Bryan Foy; *St & Sc:* William Jacobs. (1:05)

B racetrack drama of a young jockey trying to live with his disgraced father's reputation. A remake of the 1927 feature.

1147. Down the Wyoming Trail (Monogram; 1939). *Cast:* Tex Ritter, Mary Brodel, Horace Murphy, Bobby Lawson, Charles King, Bob Terry, Jack Ingram, Earl Douglas, Frank LaRue, Ernie Adams, Charles Sargent, Ed Coxen, Jean Southern, The Northwesterners (Merle & Ray Scobee, A.J. Brier, Wilson Rasch, Charles Davis), White Flash the horse. *D:* Al Herman; *P:* Edward Finney (Boots and Saddles Prods.); *St & Sc:* Peter Dixon, Roger Merton. (0:56)

Tex Ritter western with songs of a cowboy framed by cattle rustlers. Prior to release the film was known as "The Wild Herd."

1148. Down to Earth (Fox; 1932). *Cast:* Will Rogers, Irene Rich, Dorothy Jordan, Mary Carlisle, Matty Kemp, Brandon Hurst, Clarence Wilson, Harvey Clark, Louise Mackintosh, Theodore Lodi. *D:* David Butler. (1:13)

Hit comedy of a man who declares himself broke to curb the extravagant expenditures of his family. Based on a book by Homer Croy, the film is a sequel to *They Had to See Paris* (Fox; 1928).

1149. Down to Their Last Yacht (RKO; 1934). *Cast:* Ned Sparks, Mary Boland, Polly Moran, Sterling Holloway, Sidney Blackmer, Tom Kennedy, Charles Coleman, Sidney Fox, Marjorie Gateson, Irene Franklin, Hazel Forbes, Marie Wilson, Gigi Parrish, Ramsey Hill, Alice Moore, Lorimer Johnson. *D:* Paul Sloane; *As.P.:* Lou Brock; *St:* Brock, Herbert Fields; *Sc:* Marion Dix, Lynn Starling (G.B. title: *Hawaiian Nights*) (1:04)

Offbeat musical-comedy of carefree down-and-out socialites who whoop it up on a tropical island after being stranded. This film ran way over budget and turned into a financial disaster for the studio. At the time of its release it was considered the worst ever by this studio—see it, you'll probably agree.

1150. Down Under the Sea (Republic; 1936). *Cast:* Ben Lyon, Ann Rutherford, Russell Hardie, Paul Porcasi, Victor Potel, Mike Tellegen, Fritz Leiber, Vince Barnett, Maurice Murphy, Frank Yaconelli, John Picorri, Francisco Maran. *D:* Lewis Collins; *St:* Eustace L. Adams, William A. Ullman, Jr., Wellyn Totman; *Sc:* Totman, Robert Lee Johnson.

B action drama.

1151. Downstairs (MGM; 1932). *Cast:* John Gilbert, Paul Lukas, Virginia Bruce, Hedda Hopper, Reginald Owen, Olga Baclanova, Lucien Littlefield, Otto Hoffman, Bodil Rosing, Marion Lessing. *D:* Monta Bell; *St:* John Gilbert; *Sc:* Lenore Coffee, Melville Baker. (1:17)

Drama of a blackmailing chauffeur.

1152. Dracula (Universal; 1931). *Cast:* Bela Lugosi (Count Dracula), Helen Chandler (Mina Seward), David Manners (Jonathan Harker), Edward Van Sloan (film debut as Prof. Van Helsing), Dwight Frye (Renfield), Frances Dade (Lucy Weston), Herbert Bunston (Dr. Seward), Charles Gerrard (Martin), Moon Carroll (Briggs), Michael Visaroff (innkeeper), Joan Standing (maid), Josephine Velez (nurse), Daisy Belmore. *D:* Tod Browning; *P:* Carl Laemmle, Jr.; *As.P.:* E.M. Asher; *Sc:* Garrett Fort. (1:24) (video)

Classic horror film based on Bram Stoker's 1897 book which was also adapted to the stage in 1925 by Hamilton Deane and John Balderston. Early plans for the film had Lon Chaney in the title role, but his death in 1930 lead to the casting of Bela Lugosi who had also appeared in the 1927 stageplay. This was Universal's biggest money-maker for 1931. First filmed in Germany in 1922 as *Nosferatu* starring Max Schreck and directed by F.W. Murnau. The name "Dracula" was not used as rights had not been secured from the author. The German version was remade in that country in 1979 as *Nosferatu the Vampyr* starring Klaus Kinski. *Dracula* was remade in Great Britain in 1958 (known in the U.S.A. as *Horror of Dracula*) in the U.S.A., in 1973 as a TV movie with Jack Palance and followed the original story more closely than any other version. Filmed again in 1979 with Frank Langella recreating his stage role in the play's revival. Many variations utilizing the central character have been filmed over the years in the U.S.A. and abroad, these being too numerous to mention here. Followed in 1936 by the sequel *Dracula's Daughter* (see below).

1153. Dracula's Daughter (Universal; 1936). *Cast:* Gloria Holden (Countess Zaleska), Otto Kruger (Jeffrey Garth), Marguerite Churchill (Janet), Edward Van Sloan (Prof. Van Helsing), Gilbert Emery (Sir Basil Humphrey), Irving Pichel (Sandor),

Halliwell Hobbes (Hawkins), Billy Bevan (Albert), Nan Grey (Lili), Hedda Hopper (Lady Esme Hammond), Claude Allister (Sir Aubrey), Edgar Norton (Hobbs), E.E. Clive (Sgt. Wilkes), Eily Malyon, Christian Rub, Gordon Hart, William von Brincken, Fred Walton, Joseph Tozer, Douglas Wood. *D:* Lambert Hillyer; *As.P.:* E.M. Asher; *St:* Suggested by Oliver Jeffries; *Sc:* Garrett Fort. (1:10)

Semi-classic sequel to the 1931 film with a female descendant of the count terrorizing the populace.

1154. Draegerman Courage (WB/F.N.; 1937). *Cast:* Barton MacLane, Jean Muir, Henry O'Neill, Robert Barrat, Addison Richards, Helen MacKellar, Gordon Oliver, Joseph Crehan. *D:* Louis King; *P:* Bryan Foy; *Sc:* Anthony Coldeway. (G.B. title: *The Cave-In*) (1:00)

B action thriller of the rescue of miners after a cave-in in Nova Scotia. Based on fact.

1155. Drag (WB/F.N.; 1929). *Cast:* Richard Barthelmess, Alice Day, Lucien Littlefield, Kathrin Clare Ward, Charlie Parker, Margaret Fielding, Tom Dugan, Lila Lee. *D:* (A.A.N.) Frank Lloyd; *Sc:* Bradley King; *Songs:* Al Bryan, George W. Meyer.

A husband's in-laws move in with him and his wife, making life a "drag." Based on a story by William Dudley Pelley.

1156. The Dragnet (Burroughs-Tarzan; 1936). *Cast:* Rod La Rocque, Marian Nixon, Betty Compson, Joseph Girard. *D:* Xxxx Xxxx.

B crime melodrama, previously filmed in 1928.

1157. Dragnet Patrol (Mayfair; 1931). *Cast:* Glenn Tryon, Vera Reynolds, Walter Long, George Hayes. *D:* Frank Strayer. (G.B. title: *Love Redeemed*)

"Poverty row" crime melodrama.

1158. The Dragon Murder Case (WB/F.N.; 1934). *Cast:* Warren William, Margaret Lindsay, Lyle Talbot, Eugene Pallette, Helen Lowell, Robert McWade, Robert Barrat, Dorothy Tree, George E. Stone, Etienne Girardot, George Meeker, Robert Warwick, William Davidson, Arthur Aylesworth, Charles C. Wilson. *D:* H. Bruce Humberstone; *P:* Henry Blanke; *Adaptation:* Rian James; *Sc:* F. Hugh Herbert, Robert N. Lee. (1:08)

The second entry in this studio's Philo Vance series with Warren William replacing William Powell, following *The Kennel Murder Case* (q.v.). The story involves a mysterious death by drowning. Based on the character created by S.S. Van Dine (Willard Huntingdon Wright).

1159. The Drake Case (Universal; 1929). *Cast:* Gladys Brockwell (final film—d. 1929), Forrest Stanley, Robert Frazer, James Crane, Tom Dugan, Francis Ford, Barbara Leonard, W.L. Thorne, Edward Hearn, Amber Norman. *D:* Edward Laemmle; *Sc:* Charles Logue.

A man believed dead, is proved to be otherwise by his wife in this low-budget mystery-melodrama.

1160. Dramatic School (MGM; 1938). *Cast:* Luise Rainer, Paulette Goddard, Alan Marshal, Lana Turner, Anthony Allan (John Hubbard), Henry Stephenson, Genevieve Tobin, Gale Sondergaard, Melville Cooper, Erik Rhodes, Ann Rutherford, Margaret Dumont, Virginia Grey, Dorothy Granger, Minerva Urecal, Hans Conried (film debut), Rand Brooks (film debut), Dick Haymes, Frank Puglia, Jean Chatburn, Marie Blake, Cecilia Callejo. *D:* Robert B. Sinclair; *P:* Mervyn LeRoy; *Sc:* Ernst Vajda, Mary McCall, Jr. (1:20)

A theatrical drama of aspiring thespians. Based on the Hungarian stage play "School of Drama" by Hans Szekely and Zoltan Egyed.

Dream Mother (G.B. title) *see* **The Midnight Lady**

1161. Dressed to Thrill (Fox; 1935). *Cast:* Clive Brook, Tutta Rolf, Robert Barrat, Nydia Westman. *D:* Harry Lachman; *Sc:* Samson Raphaelson.

Low-budget production.

1162. Drift Fence (Paramount; 1936). *Cast:* Buster Crabbe, Tom Keene, Katherine de Mille, Glenn (Leif) Erickson, Walter Long, Benny Baker, Richard Carle, Effie Ellsler, Jack Pennick, Jan Duggan, Richard Alexander. *D:* Otho Lovering; *P:* Harold Hurley; *Sc:* Robert Yost, Stuart Anthony. (Re-release title: *Texas Desperadoes*). (0:56) (video)

B western based on a book by Zane Grey of an assumed identity.

1163. The Drifter (Willis Kent; 1932). *Cast:* William Farnum, Noah Beery, Phyllis Barrington, Charles Sellon, Bruce Warren, Russell Hopton, Ann Brody, Ynez Seabury. *D:* William O'Connor; *P:* Willis Kent; *Sc:* Oliver Drake. (1:00)

Low-budget western involving a lumber feud.

1164. Drifting Souls (Tower; 1932). *Cast:* Lois Wilson, Theodore von Eltz, Guinn Williams, Mischa Auer, Raymond Hatton, Edmund Breese. *D:* Louis King.

"Poverty row" drama.

1165. Drifting Westward (Monogram; 1939). *Cast:* Jack Randall, Frank Yaconelli, Edna Duran, Stanley Blystone, Carmen Bailey, Julian Rivero, Dave O'Brien, Octavio Giraud, Dean Spencer, James Sheridan (Sherry Tansey), Rusty the Wonder Horse. *D:* Robert Hill; *P:* Scott R. Dunlap; *Sc:* Robert Emmett (Tansey). (0:57)

Jack Randall western of a cowboy who comes to the aid of a family being harrassed by outlaws.

1166. Drum Taps (World Wide; 1932). *Cast:* Ken Maynard, Dorothy Dix, Hooper Atchley, Alan Bridge, Charles Stevens, Junior Coghlan, Harry Semels, Jim Mason, Slim Whitaker, Neal Hart, Art Mix, Kermit Maynard (brother to Ken), Leo Willis, Boy Scout Troop 107. *D:* J.P. McGowan; *Sc:* Alan James. (1:01) (video)

Ken Maynard western of a cowboy who helps a troop of boy scouts put the crimps to some land-grabbers.

1167. Drums Along the Mohawk (20th Century–Fox; 1939). *Cast:* Claudette Colbert (Magdelana "Lana" Martin), Henry Fonda (Gilbert Martin), Edna May Oliver (A.A.N. for B.S.A. as Mrs. Sarah McKlennar), Eddie Collins (Christian Reall), John Carradine (Caldwell), Dorris Bowdon (Mary Reall), Jessie Ralph (Mrs. Weaver), Robert Lowery (John Weaver), Ward Bond (Adam Helmer), Arthur Shields (Rev. Rosenkrantz), Chief John Big Tree (Blue Back), Arthur Aylesworth (George Weaver), Roger Imhof (Gen. Nicholas Herkimer), Francis Ford (Joe Boleo), Russell Simpson (Dr. Petry), Beulah Hall Jones (Daisy), Si Jenks (Jacob Small), J. Russell (Jack) Pennick (Amos Hartman), Elizabeth Jones (Mrs. Reall), Charles Tannen (Dr. Robert Johnson), Paul McVey (Capt. Mark DeMooth), Kay Linaker (Mrs. DeMooth), Edwin Maxwell (Rev. Daniel Gross), Robert Greig (Mr. Borst), Clara Blandick (Mrs. Borst), Tom Tyler (Morgan), Lionel Pape, Noble Johnson, Clarence H. Wilson, Mae Marsh. *D:* John Ford; *As.P.:* Raymond Griffith; *Sc:* Lamar Trotti, Sonya Levien. (1:43) (video)

Lavishly produced technicolor classic colonial frontier adventure of Revolutionary upstate New York as colonists battle marauding Indians and primitive living conditions in the Mohawk Valley. Based on the novel by Walter D. Edmonds.

1168. Drums of Destiny (Crescent; 1937). *Cast:* Tom Keene, Edna Lawrence, Budd Buster, Rafael Bennett, Robert Fiske, David Sharpe, John Merton, Carlos de Valdez, Chief Flying Cloud. *D:* Ray Taylor; *P:* E.B. Derr; *Sc:* Roger Whatley, John T. Neville. (1:04)

Historically flavored drama set in 1815 of attempts to put down an uprising of Creek Indians in Spanish Florida.

1169. Drums of Jeopardy (Tiffany; 1931). *Cast:* Lloyd Hughes, Warner Oland, June Collyer, Mischa Auer, Wallace MacDonald, Ann Brody. *D:* George B. Seitz.

"Poverty row" mystery-adventure.

Du Barry (G.B. title) *see* **DuBarry, Woman of Passion**

1170. DuBarry, Woman of Passion (United Artists/Art Cinema; 1930). *Cast:* Norma Talmadge (DuBarry, in her final film — ret.), William Farnum (Louis XV), Conrad Nagel (Duc de Brissac), Hobart Bosworth, Ulrich Haupt, Alison Skipworth, E. Alyn Warren, Edgar Norton, Henry Kolker, Edwin Maxwell. *D:* Sam Taylor; *P:* Joseph M. Schenck; *Adaptation:* Taylor. (G.B. title: *DuBarry*) (1:30)

Costume drama of the famed Madame DuBarry, a milliner who became the mistress of King Louis XV of France. Based on the play by David Belasco. Previous films on the same subject were in 1915 with Mrs. Leslie Carter, *DuBarry* (aka: *Madame DuBarry*) (Fox; 1918) with Theda Bara, (Germany; 1919) with Pola Negri, as *Madame DuBarry* (aka: *Passion*). Also filmed in 1934 as *Madame DuBarry* (q.v.), followed in 1943 by the spoof *DuBarry Was a Lady* (MGM).

1171. Duck Soup (Paramount; 1933). *Cast:* Groucho Marx (Rufus T. Firefly), Harpo Marx (Pinky), Chico Marx (Chicolini), Zeppo Marx (in his final film with his brothers as Robert Roland), Margaret Dumont, Louis Calhern, Raquel Torres, Edgar Kennedy, Leonid Kinskey, Charles Middleton, Edmund Breese, Edwin Maxwell, Bud Flanagan (Dennis O'Keefe — bit). *D:* Leo McCarey; *P:* Herman J. Mankiewicz; *Sc:* Bert Kalmar, Harry Ruby, Arthur Sheekman, Nat Perrin; *Songs:* Kalmar and Ruby. (1:12) (video)

Classic satiric Marx Brothers romp with Groucho as the prime minister of the mythical kingdom of Freedonia who declares war on neighboring Sylvania on a whim. The one liners are in abundance and there is a singularly classic sequence involving a mirror. This was the last of five pictures for this studio before moving over to MGM. The film was a box office bomb when released.

1172. The Dude Bandit (Allied; 1932-33). *Cast:* Hoot Gibson, Gloria Shea, Hooper Atchley, "Skeeter" Bill Robbins, Neal Hart, Lafe McKee, Gordon DeMain, Fred Burns, Art Mix, Fred Gilman, George Morrell, Merrill McCormack. *D:* George Melford; *P:* M.H. Hoffman, Jr.; *Sc:* Jack Natteford. (1:02)

Hoot Gibson western of a cowboy who goes to lengths to find out who killed his friend. A remake of *Clearing the Range* (q.v.).

1173. Dude Ranch (Paramount; 1931). *Cast:* Jack Oakie, June Collyer (Mrs. Stuart Erwin), Stuart Erwin, Mitzi Green, Eugene Pallette, Charles Sellon, Guy Oliver, George Webb, James Crane, Cecil Weston. *D:* Frank Tuttle; *St:* Milton Krims; *Sc:* Percy Heath, Grover Jones, Lloyd Corrigan, Joseph L. Mankiewicz. (1:12)

Low-budget comedy of an actor who goes to a dude ranch to impress a girl, only to find the place invaded by bad guys.

1174. The Dude Ranger (Fox; 1934). *Cast:* George O'Brien, Irene Hervey, Syd Saylor, LeRoy Mason, Henry Hall, Jim Mason, Lloyd Ingraham, Earl Dwire, Si Jenks, Lafe

McKee, Hank Bell, Alma Chester, Jack Kirk. *D:* Edward F. Cline; *P:* Sol Lesser (Atherton Prods.); *Sc:* Barry Barringer. (1:08) (video)

George O'Brien western of a man who inherits an Arizona ranch from his uncle as well as the trouble that goes along with it. Based on Zane Grey's book of the same name it was remade as *Roll Along Cowboy* (q.v.).

1175. The Dude Wrangler (Sono Art–World Wide; 1930). *Cast:* George Duryea (Tom Keene), Lina Basquette, Francis X. Bushman, Clyde Cook, Sojin, Julia Swayne Gordon, Margaret Seddon, Ethel Wales, Wilfred North, Alice Davenport, Virginia Sale, Louis Payne, Fred Parker, Aileen Carlyle, Jack Richardson. *D:* Richard Thorpe; *Co-producer:* Dorothy Reid; *Sc:* Robert N. Lee. (1:00)

Light western romance from "poverty row" of a man who borrows money to buy a dude ranch, and another who plans to sabotage the deal.

1176. Dugan of the Badlands (Monogram; 1931). *Cast:* Bill Cody, Andy Shuford, Blanche Mehaffey, Ethan Laidlaw, Julian Rivero, Earl Dwire, John Elliott. *D:* Robert N. Bradbury; *P:* Trem Carr; *St & Sc:* Bradbury. (1:06)

Bill Cody western of a cowboy and an orphan who helped corral an outlaw deputy.

1177. The Duke Comes Back (Republic; 1937). *Cast:* Allan Lane, Genevieve Tobin, Heather Angel, Selmer Jackson, George Cooper, Byron Foulger, John Russell (film debut — bit). *D:* Irving Pichel. (G.B. title: *The Call of the Ring*)

Low-budget fight drama.

1178. The Duke of West Point (United Artists/Edward Small; 1938). *Cast:* Louis Hayward, Joan Fontaine, Tom Brown, Richard Carlson, Alan Curtis, Donald Barry, Gaylord (Steve) Pendleton, Jed Prouty, Marjorie Gateson, Charles D. Brown, Emma Dunn, Jonathan Hale, William Bakewell, Mary MacLaren, Kenneth Harlan, George McKay, James Flavin, Nick Lukats. *D:* Alfred E. Green; *P:* Edward Small; *Sc:* George Bruce. (1:49)

A new cadet at the military academy has difficulty adjusting to the rigid routine.

1179. The Duke Steps Out (MGM; 1929). *Cast:* William Haines, Joan Crawford, Delmer Daves, Karl Dane, Edward Nugent, Jack Roper, Irving Bacon. *D:* James Cruze; *Sc:* Raymond Schrock, Dale Van Every; *Song:* "Just You."

Low-budget part-talkie college romance of a student who leaves college to become a boxer and then returns for his girl and the big fight.

1180. Dumbbells in Ermine (WB; 1930). *Cast:* Barbara Kent, Beryl Mercer, Robert Armstrong, James Gleason, Julia Swayne Gordon, Claude Gillingwater, Arthur Hoyt, Mary Foy, Charlotte Merriam. *D:* John Adolfi; *Adaptation & Sc:* Harvey Thew; *Dial.:* James Gleason.

B comedy of a girl who falls for a boxer. Based on the play "Weak Sisters" by Lynn Starling.

1181. The Dummy (Paramount; 1929). *Cast:* Fredric March (film debut), Ruth Chatterton, Mickey Bennett, ZaSu Pitts, Eugene Pallette, John Cromwell, Fred Kohler, Jack Oakie, Richard Tucker, Vondell Darr. *D:* Robert Milton; *P:* Hector Turnbull; *St:* Harriet Ford, Harvey J. O'Higgins; *Sc:* Herman J. Mankiewicz.

Low-budget drama of an office boy who pretends to be deaf and dumb in order to thwart kidnappers. Filmed before in 1917 (Paramount) with Jack Pickford.

1182. Durango Valley Raiders (Republic-Supreme; 1938). *Cast:* Bob Steele, Louise Stanley, Karl Hackett,

Forrest Taylor, Ted Adams, Steve Clark, Horace Murphy, Jack Ingram, Ernie Adams, Budd Buster, Frank Ball. *D:* Sam Newfield; *P:* A.W. Hackel; *Sc:* George Plympton. (1:00) (video)

Bob Steele western of a cowboy helping some people in their fight against some outlaws.

1183. Dust Be My Destiny (WB; 1939). *Cast:* John Garfield, Priscilla Lane, Alan Hale, Frank McHugh, Billy Halop, Bobby Jordan, Charley Grapewin, Henry Armetta, Stanley Ridges, John Litel, Victor Kilian, Marc Lawrence, Ward Bond, Moroni Olsen, Frank Jaquet. *D:* Lewis Seiler; *As.P.:* Lou Edelman; *Sc:* Robert Rossen. (1:28)

Melodrama of an angry young man in search of himself. Based on the novel by Jerome Odlum.

1184. Dynamite (MGM; 1929). *Cast:* Kay Johnson (film debut), Conrad Nagel, Charles Bickford, Julia Faye, Leslie Fenton, Joel McCrea, Russ Columbo, William Holden (1872–1832), Tyler Brooke, Ernest Hilliard, Henry Stockbridge, Neely Edwards, Robert Edeson, Mary Gordon, Nancy Dover, Barton Hepburn, Muriel McCormack, June Nash, Jerry Zier. *D:* Cecil B. De Mille; *P:* De Mille; *Sc:* Jeanie MacPherson, John Howard Lawson, Gladys Unger; *Art-Set Decoration:* (A.A.N.) Mitchell Leisen. (2:09)

A girl is forced to marry a man she doesn't love via a clause in her father's will. This drama climaxes with a mine cave-in and is notable as the first talkie film of Cecil B. de Mille.

1185. Dynamite Delaney (Imperial; 1938). *Cast:* Weldon Heyburn, Eve Farrell, Donald Dillaway. *D:* Joseph Rothman.

"B" cup drama.

1186. Dynamite Denny (Mayfair; 1932). *Cast:* Jay Wilsey, Blanche Mehaffey. *D:* Frank Strayer.

"B" railroad drama.

1187. Dynamite Ranch (World Wide; 1932). *Cast:* Ken Maynard, Ruth Hiatt, Alan Roscoe, Jack Perrin, Arthur Hoyt, Al Smith, John Beck, George Pierce, Lafe McKee, Martha Mattox, Edmund Cobb, Charles LeMoyne, Cliff Lyons, Kermit Maynard (Ken's brother). *D:* Forrest Sheldon; *Sc:* Sheldon, Barry Barringer. (1:00) (video)

Ken Maynard western (his first for this "poverty row" studio). A cowboy is blamed for a train robbery and thrown in jail, only to escape and prove his innocence.

1188. Each Dawn I Die (WB; 1939). *Cast:* James Cagney, George Raft, Jane Bryan, George Bancroft, Maxie Rosenbloom, Stanley Ridges, Alan Baxter, Victor Jory, Thurston Hall, Emma Dunn, Louis Jean Heydt, John Wray, John Ridgely, Paul Hurst, Abner Biberman, William B. Davidson, Willard Robertson, Clay Clement, Charles Trowbridge, Edward Pawley. *D:* William Keighley; *As.P.:* David Lewis; *Sc:* Norman Reilly Raine, Warren Duff, Charles Perry. (1:32) (video)

Drama of a reporter who becomes hardened after being framed for manslaughter and sent to prison. Based on the novel by Jerome Odlum.

1189. Eager Lips (Xxxx Xxxx; 1930). (No information available)

1190. The Eagle and the Hawk (Paramount; 1933). *Cast:* Fredric March, Cary Grant, Carole Lombard, Sir Guy Standing, Jack Oakie, Forrester Harvey, Douglas Scott, Kenneth Howell, Crauford Kent, Virginia Hammond, Robert Manning, Russell Scott, Leyland Hodgson, Bud Flanagan (Dennis O'Keefe). *D:* Stuart Walker; *St:* John Monk Saunders; *Sc:* Bogart Rogers, Seton I. Miller. (1:12)

Melodrama of an American flyer in France during World War I.

1191. The Eagle's Brood (Paramount; 1935). *Cast:* Bill Boyd (Hopalong Cassidy), James Ellison (Johnny Nelson), Joan Woodbury, Dorothy Revier, George Hayes, William Farnum, Lois January, Paul Fix, John Merton, Addison Richards. *D:* Howard Bretherton; *P:* Harry M. Sherman; *Sc:* Doris Schroeder, Harrison Jacobs. (0:59)

Second entry in the "Hopalong Cassidy" series, based on the book "Hopalong Cassidy and the Eagle's Brood" by Clarence E. Mulford.

1192. Early to Bed (Paramount; 1936). *Cast:* Mary Boland, Charles Ruggles, George Barbier, Gail Patrick, Robert McWade, Lucien Littlefield, Sidney Blackmer, Colin Tapley, Billy Gilbert, Arthur Hoyt, Helen Flint. *D:* Norman Z. McLeod; *P:* Harlan Thompson; *St:* Lucien Littlefield, Chandler Sprague, Arthur Kober; *Sc:* S.J. Perelman. (1:15)

B comedy of a sleepwalker who gets involved with gangsters.

1193. Earthworm Tractors (WB/ F.N.; 1936). *Cast:* Joe E. Brown, June Travis, Guy Kibbee, Dick Foran, Carol Hughes, Gene Lockhart, Olin Howland, Joseph Crehan, Rosalind Marquis, Charles C. Wilson, William B. Davidson, Irving Bacon, Stuart Holmes, Sarah Edwards. *D:* Ray Enright; *P:* Sam Bischoff; *Sc:* Richard Macauley, Joe Traub, Hugh Cummings. (G.B. title: *A Natural Born Salesman*) (1:09) (video)

Comedy of a man who becomes a crack tractor salesman after creating much chaos. Based on the stories of William Hazlett Upson which appeared in *The Saturday Evening Post.*

1194. The Easiest Way (MGM; 1931). *Cast:* Constance Bennett, Robert Montgomery, Adolphe Menjou, Anita Page, Marjorie Rambeau, J. Farrell MacDonald, Clark Gable, Clara Blandick. *D:* Jack Conway; *Sc:* Edith Ellis. (1:26)

Rags-to-riches story of a girl with loose morals. Based on the play by Eugene Walter which was previously filmed in 1917 with Clara Kimball

Young and Rockliffe Fellows by Clara Kimball Young Prods.

East End Chant *see* **Limehouse Blues**

1195. East Is West (Universal; 1930). *Cast:* Lupe Velez, Edward G. Robinson, Lew Ayres, E. Alyn Warren, Tetsu Komai, Jean Hersholt, Mary Forbes, Edgar Norton, Henry Kolker, Charles Middleton. *D:* Monta Bell; *Sc:* Winifred Eaton Reeve, Tom Reed. (1:15)

Chinatown based melodrama of a father selling his daughter into slavery. A remake of the 1922 First National production with Constance Talmadge and Warner Oland. Based on an old play by Samuel Shipman and John B. Hymer.

1196. East Lynne (Fox; 1931). *Cast:* Ann Harding, Clive Brook, O.P. Heggie, Conrad Nagel, Cecilia Loftus, Beryl Mercer, Flora Sheffield, David Torrence, Leslie Fenton, Snub Pollard, Ronnie Cosbey, Wally Albright, J. Gunnis Davis, Eric Mayne. *D:* Frank Lloyd; *Sc:* Tom Barry, Bradley King. (1:42)

Hit soaper of its day based on the novel by Mrs. Henry Wood, of a woman divorced by her husband after she is caught in an affair. It received an A.A.N. for Best Picture (1930–31). Two silent American versions preceded it: 1916 with Theda Bara and 1925 with Alma Rubens, both for Fox.

1197. East of Borneo (Univeral; 1931). *Cast:* Rose Hobart, Charles Bickford, Georges Renavent, Lupita Tovar, Noble Johnson. *D:* George Melford; *St:* Dale Van Every; *Sc:* Edwin Knopf. (1:17) (video)

Jungle adventure of a woman in search of her doctor-husband. A volcano erupts for the grand finale.

1198. East of Fifth Avenue (Columbia; 1933). *Cast:* Mary Carlisle, Walter Byron, Walter Connolly, Louise Carter, Wallace Ford, Maude Eburne, Dorothy Tree. *D:* Albert Rogell; *Sc:* Jo Swerling. (G.B. title: *Two in a Million*).

Low-budget comedy.

1199. East of Java (Universal; 1935). *Cast:* Charles Bickford, Elizabeth Young, Frank Albertson, Leslie Fenton, Clarence Muse, Sig Rumann, Jay Gilbuena, Edgar Norton, Richard Loo, *D:* George Melford; *Sc:* James Ashmore Creelman, Paul Perez. (G.B. title: *Java Seas*). (1:12)

Survival drama of people and animals taking refuge on an island following a shipwreck. Based on the story "Tiger Island" by Gouverneur Morris.

1200. East Side of Heaven (Universal; 1938–39). *Cast:* Bing Crosby, Joan Blondell, Baby Sandy (Sandra Lee Henville—film debut), Mischa Auer, C. Aubrey Smith, Irene Hervey, Edward Earle, Jerome Cowan, Robert Kent, The Music Maids, Jane Jones, Arthur Hoyt, Emory Parnell, J. Farrell MacDonald, Russell Hicks, Douglas Wood, Mary Carr, Jackie Gerlich, Jack Powell. *D:* David Butler; *St:* Butler, Herbert Polesie; *Sc:* William Conselman; *Songs:* James V. Monaco, Johnny Burke. (1:30)

Comedy of a singing cab driver who finds himself with an abandoned baby boy (actually played by a girl).

1201. Eastside (Xxxx Xxxx; 1931). (No information available)

Easy Go *see* **Free and Easy**

1202. Easy Living (Paramount; 1937). *Cast:* Jean Arthur, Ray Milland, Edward Arnold, Luis Alberni, Mary Nash, Franklin Pangborn, William Demarest, Andrew Tombes, Esther Dale, Robert Greig, Robert E. Homans, William B. Davidson, Nora Cecil, Harlan Briggs, Bud Flanagan (Dennis O'Keefe), Barlowe Borland. *D:* Mitchell Leisen; *P:* Arthur Hornblow, Jr.; *St:* Vera Caspary; *Sc:* Preston Sturges. (1:28)

Critically acclaimed screwball comedy of what happens when a man throws his wife's fur coat out the window.

1203. Easy Millions (Monarch; 1933). *Cast:* Dorothy Burgess, Skeets Gallagher, Merna Kennedy, Noah Beery, Johnny Arthur. *D:* Fred Newmeyer; *P:* John R. Freuler.

Low-budget indie melodrama.

1204. Easy Money (Invincible; 1936). *Cast:* Onslow Stevens, Kay Linaker, Barbara Barondess, Noel Madison, Robert Frazer, Selmer Jackson, Robert E. Homans. *D:* Phil Rosen.

"Poverty row" melodrama.

1205. Easy Street (Micheaux; 1930). Low-budget independent production produced, directed and written by Oscar Micheaux.

1206. Easy to Love (WB; 1933). *Cast:* Adolphe Menjou, Genevieve Tobin, Mary Astor, Edward Everett Horton, Patricia Ellis, Hugh Herbert, Guy Kibbee, Hobart Cavanaugh, Robert Greig, Harold Waldridge, Paul Kaye. *D:* William Keighley (solo directorial debut); *Adaptation:* David Boehm; *Sc:* Carl Erickson, Manuel Seff; *Title Song:* Irving Kahal, Sammy Fain. (1:10)

Marital comedy of extra-marital affairs. Based on the play by Thompson Buchanan.

1207. Easy to Take (Paramount; 1936). *Cast:* John Howard, Marsha Hunt, Carl "Alfalfa" Switzer, Eugene Pallette, Jan Duggan. *D:* Glenn Tryon; *P:* Jack Cunningham.

B comedy of a radio star who becomes "heir" to a spoiled brat.

1208. Eat 'em Alive (Xxxx Xxxx; 1933). *P:* Harold Austin.

Documentary.

1209. Ebb Tide (Paramount; 1937). *Cast:* Ray Milland, Frances Farmer, Oscar Homolka (American debut), Lloyd Nolan, Barry Fitzgerald, David Torrence, Lina Basquette, Charles Judels, Charles Stevens, George Piltz, Arthur Allen, Joe Molina,

Manuella Kalili. *D:* James Hogan; *P:* Lucien Hubbard; *Sc:* Bertram Millhauser. (1:32)

Technicolor drama of seafarers stranded on an island with a madman. Based on the book by Robert Louis Stevenson and Lloyd Osbourne, it was first produced on the screen in 1915 by Selig, with a 1922 Paramount remake following. Remade in 1947 as *Adventure Island* (Paramount).

1210. Educating Father (20th Century–Fox; 1936). *Cast:* Jed Prouty, Spring Byington, Florence Roberts, Kenneth Howell, June Carlson, George Ernest, Shirley Deane, Billy Mahan, Dixie Dunbar, Tony Martin, Charles C. Wilson, Erville Alderson, J. Anthony Hughes, Clarence Wilson, Francis Ford, David Newell, Charles Tannen. *D:* James Tinling; *Sc:* John Patrick, Edward T. Lowe, Katharine Kavanaugh.

Following *Every Saturday Night* (q.v.), this became the second entry in what was to become the popular low-budget "Jones Family" comedy series, in fact the family was first named "Jones" in this one.

1211. Eight Bells (Columbia; 1935). *Cast:* Ann Sothern, Ralph Bellamy, Charley Grapewin, Franklin Pangborn, Keye Luke, John Buckler. *D:* Roy William Neill.

B shipboard comedy mystery.

1212. Eight Girls in a Boat (Paramount; 1934). *Cast:* Douglass Montgomery, Kay Johnson, Dorothy Wilson, Walter Connolly, Jean Rogers (film debut), Baby Peggy (Peggy Montgomery), Billy Gilbert, Kay Hammond, Ferike Boros, Barbara Barondess, Virginia Hall, James Bush, Margaret Marquis, Marjorie Cavalier. *D:* Richard Wallace; *P:* Charles R. Rogers; *St:* Helmut Brandis; *Sc:* Casey Robinson.

B drama set in a girls finishing school.

1213. Eight to Five (Xxxx Xxxx; 1935). (No information available)

1214. El Diablo Rides (Metropolitan; 1939). *Cast:* Bob Steele, Claire Rochelle, Carleton Young, Ted Adams, Kit Guard, Robert Walker. *D:* Ira Webb; *P:* Harry S. Webb; *Sc:* Carl Krusada. (0:55)

Bob Steele horse opera with a range feud story.

Elephants Never Forget (G.B. title) *see* **Zenobia**

Eleven Men and a Girl *see* **Maybe It's Love** (1930)

1215. The Eleventh Commandment (Allied; 1933). *Cast:* Marian Marsh, Lee Moran, Alan Hale, Theodore von Eltz, Marie Prevost, Arthur Hoyt. *D:* Christy Cabanne, George Melford; *P:* M.H. Hoffman, Jr.

"Poverty row" production.

1216. Elinor Norton (Fox; 1935). *Cast:* Claire Trevor, Norman Foster, Hugh Williams, Gilbert Roland, Henrietta Crosman, Cora Sue Collins. *D:* Hamilton MacFadden.

B mystery based on a book by Mary Roberts Rinehart.

Elizabeth the Queen *see* **The Private Lives of Elizabeth and Essex**

1217. Ellis Island (Invincible; 1936). *Cast:* Donald Cook, Joyce Compton. *D:* Phil Rosen.

"Poverty row" mystery-melodrama.

1218. Elmer and Elsie (Paramount; 1934). *Cast:* George Bancroft, Frances Fuller, Roscoe Karns, Charles Sellon, Vera Stedman, Marie Wells, Nella Walker, William Robyns, George Barbier, Ruth Clifford, Alfred P. James, Duke York, Helena Phillips Evans, Thomas Dempsey, Floyce Brown, Eddie Baker. *D:* Gilbert Pratt.

This is not a film about two bovines, but a B comedy about a trucker (pre–women's movement) who believes that women should be obedient to men. Based on the play by George S. Kaufman and Marc Connelly, it was previously filmed in 1923 as *To the Ladies* with Edward Everett Horton and Louise Dresser.

1219. Elmer the Great (WB; 1933). *Cast:* Joe E. Brown, Patricia Ellis, Frank McHugh, Claire Dodd, Preston S. Foster, Russell Hopton, Sterling Holloway, Emma Dunn, Charles Wilson, Charles Delaney, Berton Churchill, J. Carrol Naish, Gene Morgan, Douglass Dumbrille, Jessie Ralph, Ruth Clifford. *D:* Mervyn LeRoy; *Sc:* Tom Geraghty. (1:14)

Hit comedy about a country boy who makes it big as a baseball player. Based on the play by Ring Lardner and George M. Cohan it was previously filmed as *Fast Company* (1929) (q.v.). Remade as *The Cowboy Quarterback* (q.v.).

1220. Elsa Maxwell's Hotel for Women (20th Century–Fox; 1939). *Cast:* Linda Darnell (film debut), Ann Sothern, Elsa Maxwell (acting debut), Lynn Bari, Sidney Blackmer, Alan Dinehart, John Halliday, Jean Rogers, James Ellison, Chick Chandler, Ivan Lebedeff, Joyce Compton, Katharine (Kay) Aldridge, June Gale, Charles C. Wilson, Mary Healy, Amanda Duff, Herbert Ashley. *D:* Gregory Ratoff; *P:* Raymond Griffith; *Sc:* Kathryn Scola, Darrell Ware. (Retitled and better known as: *Hotel for Women*) (1:23)

Hit comedy about a woman who runs a hotel for women in search of husbands. Followed in 1940 by a sequel, *Free, Blonde and 21*.

1221. Embarrassing Moments (Universal; 1930). *Cast:* Merna Kennedy, Reginald Denny, Otis Harlan, Virginia Sale, William Austin, Greta Granstedt. *D:* William James Craft. (0:58)

B comedy of a female artist who creates a fictitious husband to avoid marriage, only to have the imaginary man turn up as a real person.

1222. Embarrassing Moments (Universal; 1934). *Cast:* Chester Morris, Marion Nixon, Walter Woolf King, Herman Bing, Henry Armetta, Jane Darwell, George E. Stone, Alan Mowbray. *D:* Edward Laemmle. (1:07)

No relation to the above named film is this B comedy of a practical joker who comes to believe that one of his jokes backfired and caused a suicide.

Embassy Girl (G.B. title) *see* **Hat Check Girl**

1223. Emergency Call (RKO; 1933). *Cast:* William Boyd, Wynne Gibson, William Gargan, George E. Stone, Betty Furness, Reginald Mason, Merna Kennedy, Edwin Maxwell, Oscar Apfel, Ruth Fellows, Jane Darwell, Alberta Vaughn, Paul Fix. *D:* Edward Cahn; *As.P.:* Sam Jaffe; *St:* John B. Clymer, James Ewens; *Sc:* Joseph L. Mankiewicz, Houston Branch. (1:10)

B melodrama of a doctor who uncovers corruption in a big city hospital. Based on a play by Joseph L. Mankiewicz and Houston Branch.

1224. Emma (MGM; 1932). *Cast:* Marie Dressler (A.A.N. for B.A. [1931–32] as Emma), Richard Cromwell (Ronnie Smith), Jean Hersholt (Mr. Smith), Myrna Loy (Isabelle), John Miljan (District Attorney), Leila Bennett (Matilda), Purnell B. Pratt (Haskins), Kathryn Crawford (Sue), George Meeker (Bill), Wilfred Noy (Drake), Andre Cheron (Count Pierre), Dale Fuller (maid), Barbara Kent, Edith Fellows, Dawn O'Day (Anne Shirley). *D:* Clarence Brown; *St:* Frances Marion; *Sc:* Leonard Praskins, Zelda Sears. (1:13)

Hit sentimental story of a lady who works many years as a housekeeper and nanny, eventually marrying her employer. Number 7 on the "10 Best" list of *Film Daily*.

1225. The Emperor Jones (United Artists; 1933). *Cast:* Paul Robeson (film debut as Brutus Jones, recreating his stage role), Dudley Digges, Frank C. Wilson, Fredi Washington, Ruby Elzy, Rex Ingram, "Blue Boy" O'Connor, Brandon Evans, Jackie "Moms" Mabley, George Haymid Stamper. *D:* Dudley Murphy; *P:* John Krimsky, Gifford Cochran; *Sc:* Dubose Heyward. (1:12) (video)

A train porter escapes from a chain gang and becomes ruler of his own jungle empire. Based on the 1921 play by Eugene O'Neill. The production was filmed in New York state.

1226. The Emperor's Candlesticks (MGM; 1937). *Cast:* William Powell, Luise Rainer, Robert Young, Maureen O'Sullivan, Frank Morgan, Henry Stephenson, Bernadene Hayes, Donald Kirke, Douglass Dumbrille, Charles Waldron, Ien Wulfe (Ian Wolfe), Barnett Parker, Frank Reicher, Bert Roach, Paul Porcasi, E.E. Clive, Emma Dunn, Frank Conroy. *D:* George Fitzmaurice; *P:* John W. Considine, Jr.; *Sc:* Monckton Hoffe, Harold Goldman, Herman J. Mankiewicz (unc.). (1:29)

Lavishly produced romance of pre–Russian revolutionary spies who are on opposing sides. Based on the novel by Baroness Orczy, the film was a box office flop.

1227. Employee's Entrance (WB/F.N.; 1933). *Cast:* Warren William, Loretta Young, Alice White, Wallace Ford, Allen Jenkins, Marjorie Gateson, Ruth Donnelly, Albert Gran, Hale Hamilton, Frank Reicher, Charles Sellon, Zita Moulton, Harry C. Bradley, Helen Mann. *D:* Roy Del Ruth; *P:* Lucien Hubbard; *Sc:* Robert Presnell. (1:15)

Comedy-melodrama with pre-code spicy humor of a ruthless department store manager. Considered offbeat in it's day. Based on the play by David Boehm.

1228. Empty Holsters (WB/F.N.; 1937). *Cast:* Dick Foran, Pat Walthall, Emmett Vogan, Wilfred Lucas, Earl Dwire, Charles LeMoyne, Glenn Strange, Edmund Cobb, George Chesebro, J.P. McGowan, Milton Kibbee, Art Mix, Artie Ortego, Jack Mower, Ben Corbett, Merrill McCormack. *D:* B. Reeves Eason; *P:* Bryan Foy; *St:* Ed Earl Repp; *Sc:* John Thomas Neville; *Songs:* "Old Corral" and "I Gotta Get Back to My Gal" by M.K. Jerome, Jack Scholl. (1:02)

Dick Foran western of a cowboy wrongly sent to prison.

1229. Empty Saddles (Universal; 1936). *Cast:* Buck Jones, Louise Brooks, Harvey Clark, Gertrude Astor, Charles Middleton, Lloyd Ingraham, Frank Campeau, Earl Askam, Niles Welch, Claire Rochelle, Robert Adair, Ben Corbett. *D:* Lesley Selander; *Sc:* Frances Guihan. (1:02)

Buck Jones western of a range feud.

1230. Enchanted April (RKO; 1935). *Cast:* Ann Harding, Frank Morgan, Katherine Alexander, Reginald Owen, Jane Baxter, Jessie Ralph, Ralph Forbes, Charles Judels, Rafaela Ottiano, Ethel Griffies. *D:* Harry Beaumont; *P:* Kenneth MacGowan; *Sc:* Samuel Hoffenstein, Ray Harris. (1:06)

Romantic comedy of four women spending their vacation at an Italian villa. Based on the novel by "Elizabeth" and the play by Kane Campbell, it was a box office dud.

1231. End of the Trail (Columbia; 1932). *Cast:* Tim McCoy, Wheeler Oakman, Luana Walters, Wally Albright, Wade Boteler, Lafe McKee, Chief White Eagle. *D:* D. Ross Lederman; *Sc:* Stuart Anthony. (1:00)

Tim McCoy western with much stock footage of a U.S. Cavalry captain who exposes the white man's greed and lies as being the main reason the Indians go on the warpath. Filmed at the Arapaho Wind River Reservation in Wyoming.

1232. The End of the Trail (Columbia; 1936). *Cast:* Jack Holt, Louise

Henry, Guinn Williams, Douglass Dumbrille, George McKay, Gene Morgan, C. Henry Gordon, Erle C. Kenton (Teddy Roosevelt), "Black Jack" Ward, Edward J. LeSaint, Blackie Whiteford, Art Mix. *D:* Erle C. Kenton; *Sc:* Harold Shumate. (1:10)

Offbeat western of a Spanish-American War veteran who is unable to adjust and hits the outlaw trail. Based on a Zane Grey novel, the film was theatrically re-released by the studio in 1987.

Enemies of Society (G.B. title) *see* **The Big Brain**

1233. Enemies of the Law (Xxxx Xxxx; 1931). *Cast:* Lou Tellegen (final film — suicide 1934), Mary Nolan, Johnny Walker (final film), Gordon Westcott, John Dunsmuir, Alan Brooks, Dewey Robinson, Dee Dee Green, Danny Hardin, Harold Healy, Bert West. *D:* Lawrence C. Windom; *St:* Charles Reed Jones.

Low-budget crime melodrama.

Enemies of the Public (G.B. title) *see* **The Public Enemy**

1234. Enemy of Men (Xxxx Xxxx; 1930). (No information available)

1235. Enlighten Thy Daughter (Exploitation Pictures; 1934). *Cast:* Robert (Bob) Livingston (film debut), Lillian Walker (final film — ret.). *D:* John Varley.

Low-budget melodrama.

1236. Enter Madame (Paramount; 1935). *Cast:* Elissa Landi (singing voice dubbed by Nina Koshetz), Cary Grant, Lynne Overman, Sharon Lynn, Paul Porcasi, Frank Albertson, Cecilia Parker, Clara Lou (Ann) Sheridan, Gino Corrado, Diana Lewis, Adrian Rosley, Bud Galea, Wilfred Hari, Michelette Burani. *D:* Elliott Nugent; *P:* Benjamin Glazer; *Sc:* Charles Brackett, Gladys Lehman. (1:23)

Comedy of a millionaire who marries an opera singer, only to find he has to contend with her operatic career. A remake of the 1922 Metro production with Clara Kimball Young, Elliott Dexter and Louise Dresser. The film which was a box office dud was based on the hit Broadway play of 1920 by Gilda Varesi Archibald and Dorothea Donn-Byrne.

1237. Escapade (Invincible; 1932). *Cast:* Sally Blane, Phillips Smalley, Walter Long, Anthony Bushell, Thomas Jackson, Jameson Thomas, Carmelita Geraghty, David Mir. *D:* Richard Thorpe; *St & Sc:* Edward T. Lowe. (G.B. title: *Dangerous Ground*)

"Poverty row" melodrama.

1238. Escapade (MGM; 1935). *Cast:* William Powell, Luise Rainer (American debut), Virginia Bruce, Mady Christians, Reginald Owen, Frank Morgan, Laura Hope Crews, Henry Travers, Paul Cavanagh, Billy Gilbert, Mathilde Comont. *D:* Robert Z. Leonard; *P:* Bernard Hyman; *St:* Walter Reisch; *Sc:* Herman J. Mankiewicz. (1:27)

Romantic drama of a Viennese artist. Based on a 1934 German film titled *Maskerade*.

1239. The Escape (20th Century-Fox; 1939). *Cast:* Edward Norris, Amanda Duff, Kane Richmond, Jack Carson, Henry Armetta, June Gale, Richard Lane, Matt McHugh, Leona Roberts, Jimmy Butler, Scotty Beckett, Rex Downing, Helen Ericson, Frank Reicher, Roger McGee. *D:* Ricardo Cortez; *P:* Sol M. Wurtzel; *Sc:* Robert Ellis, Helen Logan.

B crime drama told in flashbacks.

1240. Escape by Night (Republic; 1937). *Cast:* William Hall, Anne Nagel, Dean Jagger, Ward Bond, Steffi Duna, Arthur Aylesworth. *D:* Hamilton MacFadden.

B melodrama.

1241. Escape from Devil's Island (Columbia; 1935). *Cast:* Victor Jory,

Norman Foster, Florence Rice, Daniel Haynes, Herbert Heywood, Frank Lackteen, Noble Johnson. *D:* Albert Rogell; *St:* Fred de Gresac; *Sc:* Fred Niblo, Jr., Earle Snell. (aka: *Song of the Damned*)
B melodrama of incarceration.

Escape from Yesterday (G.B. title) *see* **Ride a Crooked Mile**

Escape to Happiness (G.B. title) *see* **Intermezzo, a Love Story**

1242. Escape to Paradise (RKO/ Principal; 1939). *Cast:* Bobby Breen, Kent Taylor, Marla Shelton, Joyce Compton, Pedro de Cordoba, Robert O. Davis, Rosina Galli, Frank Yaconelli, Anna Demetrio. *D:* Erle C. Kenton; *As.P.:* Barney Briskin; *St:* Ian McLellan Hunter, Herbert C. Lewis; *Sc:* Weldon Melick; *Songs:* Nilo Menendez, Eddie Cherkose.
Romance with music localed in South America.

1243. Eskimo (MGM; 1933). *Cast:* Mala and an all native Eskimo cast, Joseph (Sauers) Sawyer and other unbilled caucasian actors. *D:* W.S. Van Dyke; *P:* Hunt Stromberg; *Translated to the Screen:* John Lee Mahin; *Editor:* (A.A.) Conrad Nervig. (G.B. title: *Mala the Magnificent*) (1:51)
Critically acclaimed semi-documentary on Eskimo life and the dilemma created when white men interfere. Based on "Der Eskimo" and "Die Flucht ins weisse Land" two books by Peter Freuchen on the moral code of the Eskimo. Filmed on location in Northern Alaska between April/1932 and November/1933. Voted one of the "10 Best" films of the year by the National Board of Review. All native dialogue is subtitled.

1244. Espionage (MGM; 1937). *Cast:* Edmund Lowe, Madge Evans, Paul Lukas, Ketti Gallian, Skeets Gallagher, Leonid Kinskey, Barnett Parker, Frank Reicher, Ann Rutherford, Billy

Gilbert, Mitchell Lewis, Gaston Glass. *D:* Kurt Neumann; *P:* Harry Rapf; *Sc:* Manuel Seff, Leonard Lee, Ainsworth Morgan. (1:07)
B comedy of a pair of reporters posing as newlyweds on the Orient Express. Based on the play by Walter Hackett.

1245. Espionage Agent (WB; 1939). *Cast:* Joel McCrea, Brenda Marshall (film debut), Jeffrey Lynn, George Bancroft, Stanley Ridges, James Stephenson, Nana Bryant, Martin Kosleck, Addison Richards, Hans von Twardowsky, Edwin Stanley, Howard Hickman, DeWolf (William) Hopper, Robert O. Davis, Lucien Richards. *D:* Lloyd Bacon; *As.P.:* Louis F. Edelman; *St:* Robert Henry Buckner; *Sc:* Warren Duff, Michael Fessier, Frank Donaghue. (1:23)
Spy melodrama.

1246. Eternally Yours (United Artists; 1939). *Cast:* Loretta Young, David Niven, Broderick Crawford, Hugh Herbert, C. Aubrey Smith, Billie Burke, Raymond Walburn, ZaSu Pitts, Eve Arden, Virginia Field, Lionel Pape, May Beatty, Ralph Graves, Franklin Parker, Dennie Moore, Mary Field, Edwin Stanley, Leyland Hodgson, Fred Keating, Douglas Wood, Billy Wayne, Ralph Norwood, Paul Le Paul, Frank Jaquet, Lieut. Pat Davis, George Cathrey, Tay Garnett (bit), Herman the Rabbit. *D:* Tay Garnett; *P:* Garnett; *Sc:* Gene Towne, Graham Baker; *Music:* (A.A.N.) Werner Janssen. (1:35) (video)
Romantic comedy of a woman who marries a magician.

1247. Evelyn Prentice (MGM; 1934). *Cast:* Myrna Loy, William Powell, Una Merkel, Harvey Stephens, Isabel Jewell, Rosalind Russell (film debut), Henry Wadsworth, Edward Brophy, Frank Conroy, Jessie Ralph, Billy Gilbert, Stanley Andrews, Samuel S. Hinds, Cora Sue Collins. *D:* William K. Howard; *P:* John W. Considine, Jr.; *Sc:* Lenore Coffee. (1:20)

A lawyer's wife has an affair with a man who later blackmails her. Based on the novel by W.E. Woodward, it was remade as *Stronger Than Desire* (q.v.).

1248. Evenings for Sale (Paramount; 1932). *Cast:* Herbert Marshall, Sari Maritza, Mary Boland, Charles Ruggles, Lucien Littlefield, Clay Clement, George Barbier, Bert Roach, Arnold Korff. *D:* Stuart Walker; *Sc:* S.K. Lauren, Agnes Brand Leahy. (1:08)

Romance set in Vienna of a titled gigolo and a wealthy American woman. Based on the novel by I.A.R. Wylie.

Eventful Journey (G.B. title) *see* **Hitch Hike Lady**

1249. Ever in My Heart (WB; 1933). *Cast:* Barbara Stanwyck, Otto Kruger, Ralph Bellamy, Ruth Donnelly, Frank Albertson, Laura Hope Crews, Donald Meek, Clara Blandick, Harry Beresford, Wallis Clark, Henry O'Neill, Florence Roberts, Ronnie Cosbey, Frank Reicher. *D:* Archie Mayo; *P:* Robert Presnell; *St:* Beulah Marie Dix, Bertram Millhauser; *Sc:* Millhauser. (1:08)

Marital tear-jerker of a young couple who marry only to find their lives disrupted by World War I.

1250. Ever Since Eve (Fox; 1934). *Cast:* George O'Brien, Mary Brian, Herbert Mundin, George Meeker, Betty Blythe, Roger Imhof. *D:* George Marshall; *St:* Paul Armstrong; *Sc:* Henry Johnson, Stuart Anthony.

A romantic comedy which was previously filmed in 1921.

1251. Ever Since Eve (WB/F.N.; 1937). *Cast:* Marion Davies (final film—ret.), Robert Montgomery, Frank McHugh, Patsy Kelly, Louise Fazenda, Barton MacLane, Mary Treen, Allen Jenkins, Marcia Ralston, Arthur Hoyt, Harry Hayden, Frank Faylen, George Meeker, John T. Murray, Pierre Watkin, Frederick Clarke, Minerva Urecal.

D: Lloyd Bacon; *P:* Earl Baldwin; *St:* Gene Baker, Margaret Lee; *Sc:* Lawrence Riley, Earl Baldwin, Lillie Hayward; *Title Song:* M.K. Jerome, Jack Scholl. (1:20)

Comedy of a man who falls for a beautiful girl, not realizing she is his plain-Jane secretary. A Cosmopolitan production that flopped so badly at the box office that Marion Davies gave up acting.

1252. Every Day's a Holiday (Paramount/Major Productions; 1937). *Cast:* Mae West (Peaches O'Day), Edmund Lowe, Charles Butterworth, Charles Winninger, Walter Catlett, Lloyd Nolan, Louis Armstrong, Herman Bing, Roger Imhof, Chester Conklin, Lucien Prival, George Rector. *D:* A. Edward Sutherland; *P:* Emanuel Cohen; *St:* Jo Swerling; *Sc:* Mae West; *Art-Set Decoration:* (A.A.N.) Wiard Ihnen; *Song:* Hoagy Carmichael. (1:19)

Mae West as a con-woman who sells the Brooklyn Bridge, in this her last film for this studio. Set in the gay '90s.

1253. Every Night at Eight (Paramount; 1935). *Cast:* George Raft, Alice Faye, Frances Langford (film debut), Patsy Kelly, Walter Catlett, Herman Bing, Radio Rogues (Jimmy Hollywood, Eddie Bartel, Henry Taylor), Harry Barris, Charles Forsythe, Boothe Howard, John Dilson, Mary Jo Mathews, Florence Gill, Bud Flanagan (Dennis O'Keefe). *D:* Raoul Walsh; *P:* Walter Wanger; *Sc:* Gene Towne, Graham Baker. (1:20)

Musical-comedy of three singing sisters who hit it big on radio. Based on the story "Three on a Mike" by Stanley Garvey. Two songs to later become hits are from this film: "I Feel a Song Coming On" by Dorothy Fields, Jimmy McHugh and George Oppenheimer and "I'm in the Mood for Love" by Fields and McHugh. A box office hit for the studio.

Every Other Inch a Lady (G.B. title) *see* **Dancing Co-ed**

1254. Every Saturday Night (20th Century-Fox; 1936). *Cast:* Jed Prouty, Spring Byington, Florence Roberts, Kenneth Howell, George Ernest, June Carlson (film debut), June Lang, Billy Mahan, Kay Hughes, Paxton Sisters, Paul Stanton, Thomas Beck, Tom London, Phyllis Fraser, Fred Wallace, Oscar Apfel. *D:* James Tinling; *P:* Max H. Golden; *Sc:* Edward Eliscu.

First film in what later became known as the "Jones Family" comedy series — the family being named "Evers" in this one. The series was designed to run a competition with MGM's "Hardy Family — Andy Hardy" series. Based on a play by Katharine Kavanaugh.

Every Woman's Man (G.B. title)
see **The Prizefighter and the Lady**

1255. Everybody Sing (MGM; 1937). *Cast:* Judy Garland, Allan Jones, Fanny Brice, Reginald Owen, Billie Burke, Lynne Carver, Reginald Gardiner, Monty Woolley, Henry Armetta, Helen Troy, Andrew Tombes, Mary Forbes, Adia Kuznetzoff, Michelette Burani. *D:* Edwin L. Marin; *P:* Harry Rapf; *St:* Edgar Allan Woolf; *Sc:* Woolf, Florence Ryerson; *Songs:* Bert Kalmar, Harry Ruby, Gus Kahn. (1:20)

Musical-comedy centered around a screwball theatrical family.

1256. Everybody's Baby (20th Century-Fox; 1939). *Cast:* Jed Prouty, Spring Byington, Florence Roberts, Kenneth Howell, George Ernest, Billy Mahan, Hattie McDaniel, Claire DuBrey. *D:* Malcolm St. Clair.

Number 12 in the "Jones Family" comedy series.

1257. Everybody's Doing It (RKO; 1938). *Cast:* Preston Foster, Sally Eilers, Cecil Kellaway, William Brisbane, Guinn Williams, Richard Lane, Arthur Lake, Frank M. Thomas, Lorraine Krueger, Jack Carson, Willie Best. *D:* Christy Cabanne; *P:* William

Sistrom; *St:* George Beck; *Sc:* J. Robert Bren, Harry Segall, Edmund Joseph; *Song:* Hal Borne, Mort Greene. (1:06)

B comedy of a promotional contest which is invaded by racketeers.

1258. Everybody's Hobby (WB/F.N.; 1939). *Cast:* Irene Rich, Henry O'Neill, Jane Sharon, Aldrich Bowker, Jackie Moran, John Ridgely, Peggy Stewart, Nat Carr. *D:* William McGann; *As.P.:* Bryan Foy; *Sc:* Kenneth Gamet, William Brockway.

B production of a family of which each member has a hobby which comes in handy at various times. A proposed series which went no farther than this entry.

1259. Everybody's Old Man (20th Century-Fox; 1936). *Cast:* Irvin S. Cobb (in the title role), Norman Foster, Rochelle Hudson, Sara Haden, Johnny Downs, Warren Hymer, Donald Meek, Lynn Bari, Charles Coleman. *D:* James Flood; *P:* Bogart Rogers; *St:* Edgar Franklin; *Sc:* A.E. Thomas, Patterson McNutt.

B comedy.

1260. Everyman's Law (Supreme; 1936). *Cast:* Johnny Mack Brown, Beth Marion, Frank Campeau, Roger Gray, Lloyd Ingraham, John Beck, Horace Murphy, Slim Whitaker, Ed Cassidy, Jim Corey. *D:* Albert Ray; *P:* A.W. Hackel; *Sc:* Earle Snell. (1:01)

Johnny Mack Brown oater of a rancher who is making things rough for the local homesteaders.

1261. Everything Happens at Night (20th Century-Fox; 1939). *Cast:* Sonja Henie, Ray Milland, Robert Cummings, Maurice Moscovich, Leonid Kinskey, Alan Dinehart, Fritz Feld, Victor Varconi, Jody Gilbert, Holmes Herbert, Lester Matthews, Frank Reicher, Christian Rub, Michael Visaroff, Roger Imhof, Paul Porcasi, George Davis, William Edmunds, Eleanor Wesselhoeft, Ferdinand Munier, Rolfe

Sedan, John Bleifer. *D:* Irving Cummings; *P:* Harry Joe Brown; *Sc:* Art Arthur, Robert Harari. (1:17) (video)

Romantic comedy of two reporters in pursuit of the daughter of a Nobel Prize winner who is attempting to evade the Gestapo.

1262. Everything's on Ice (RKO/Principal; 1939). *Cast:* Irene Dare, Roscoe Karns, Edgar Kennedy, Lynn Roberts, Eric Linden, Bobby Watson, George Meeker, Mary Currier, Maxine Stewart, Wade Boteler, Paul Winchell. *D:* Erle C. Kenton; *P:* Sol Lesser; *Sc:* Adrian Landis, Sherman Lowe; *Title Song:* Milton Drake, Fred Stryker.

A drama to showcase 6-year-old ice skating star Irene Dare who made her debut the previous year in Lesser's *Breaking the Ice* (q.v.).

1263. Everything's Rosie (RKO; 1931). *Cast:* Robert Woolsey (his only film without Bert Wheeler), Anita Louise, John Darrow, Florence Roberts, Clifford Dempsey, Lita Chevret, Alfred P. James, Frank Beal. *D:* Clyde Bruckman; *As.P.:* Louis Sarecky; *St:* Al Boasberg; *Sc:* Tim Whelan, Boasberg, Ralph Spence. (1:07)

Comedy of a carnival medicine man who adopts an orphan.

1264. Evidence (WB; 1929). *Cast:* Pauline Frederick, Conway Tearle, Lowell Sherman, William Courtenay, Alec B. Francis, Freddie Burke Frederick, Myrna Loy. *D:* John Adolfi; *Sc:* J. Grubb Alexander; *Song:* Al Dubin, M.K. Jerome.

Drama of a man who suspects his wife of marital infidelity. Based on the play by J. Du Rocher MacPherson, it was previously filmed in 1922.

Evidence in Camera (G.B. title) *see* **Headline Shooter**

1265. Ex-Bad Boy (Universal; 1931). *Cast:* Jean Arthur, Robert Armstrong, Jason Robards, George Brent, Grayce Hampton, Mary Doran, Lola Lane, Eddie Kane, Edward Hearn. *D:* Vin Moore; *Sc:* Dale Van Every. (G.B. title: *His Temporary Affair*) (1:07)

Low-budget comedy of a man who creates an exciting past for himself to impress his fiancee. Loosely based on the short story "Jail Break" by W.R. Burnett and the play "The Whole Town's Talking" by Anita Loos and John Emerson.

1266. Ex-Champ (Universal; 1939). *Cast:* Victor McLaglen, Tom Brown, Nan Grey, Constance Moore, Donald Briggs, William Frawley, Thurston Hall, Marc Lawrence, Samuel S. Hinds, Charles Halton, Noble "Kid" Chissell. *D:* Phil Rosen; *P:* Burt Kelly; *St:* Gordon Kahn; *Sc:* Edmund L. Hartmann, Alex Gottlieb. (G.B. title: *Golden Gloves*) (1:12)

B melodrama of a boxer who seeks to help his son pay financial debts he owes to gamblers.

1267. Ex-Flame (Tiffany; 1930). *Cast:* Marian Nixon, Neil Hamilton, Judith Barrie, Roland Drew, Norman Kerry, Billie Haggerty, Jose Bohr, Snub Pollard, Joan Standing, Cornelius Keefe, Lorimer Johnson, Joseph North, May Beatty, Charles Crockett. *D:* Victor Halperin; *St:* Halperin; *Adapt. Dial.:* George Draney; *Dial. D:* Farjeon.

"Poverty row" romance.

1268. Ex-Lady (WB; 1933). *Cast:* Bette Davis (in her starring debut), Gene Raymond, Frank McHugh, Monroe Owsley, Claire Dodd, Ferdinand Gottschalk, Kay Strozzi, Alphonse Ethier, Bodil Rosing. *D:* Robert Florey; *P:* Lucien Hubbard; *St:* Edith Fitzgerald, Robert Riskin; *Sc:* David Boehm. (1:10) (video)

Romantic drama of a lady artist who has liberal views on sex and marriage—at least until the love bug bites her. The openness of the film made it controversial in its day, but nevertheless flopped at the box office. A remake of *Illicit* (q.v.).

Ex-Mistress (G.B. title) *see* **My Past**

1269. The Ex-Mrs. Bradford (RKO; 1936). *Cast:* William Powell, Jean Arthur, James Gleason, Eric Blore, Robert Armstrong, Lila Lee, Grant Mitchell, Ralph Morgan, Erin O'Brien-Moore, Lucile Gleason, Frank M. Thomas, Frank Reicher, John Sheehan, Paul Fix, Charles Richman, Frankie Darro. *D:* Stephen Roberts (final film—d. 1936); *As.P.:* Edward Kaufman; *St:* James Edward Grant; *Sc:* Anthony Veiller. (1:21) (video)

Hit comedy of a doctor and his ex-wife who get involved in sleuthing a murder.

1270. Exclusive (Paramount; 1937). *Cast:* Fred MacMurray, Charles Ruggles, Frances Farmer, Lloyd Nolan, Fay Holden, Ralph Morgan, Horace McMahon (film debut), Willard Robertson, Harlan Briggs, Chester Clute, William Henry. *D:* Alexander Hall; *P:* Benjamin Glazer; *St:* John C. Moffitt; *Sc:* Rian James, Sidney Salkow. (1:25)

Drama of a newspaper editor's daughter who goes to work for a sleazy tabloid run by a local hoodlum.

1271. Exclusive Story (MGM; 1936). *Cast:* Franchot Tone, Madge Evans, Joseph Calleia, Stuart Erwin, J. Carrol Naish, Robert Barrat, J. Farrell MacDonald, Louise Henry, Wade Boteler, Margaret Irving, Raymond Hatton, Charles Trowbridge, William Henry. *D:* George B. Seitz; *P:* Lucien Hubbard; *St:* Martin Mooney; *Sc:* Michael Fessier. (1:15)

B newspaper melodrama.

1272. The Exile (Micheaux; 1931). Low-budget indie production which was produced, directed and written by Oscar Micheaux.

1273. Exile Express (Grand National; 1939). *Cast:* Alan Marshal, Anna Sten, Jed Prouty, Walter Catlett, Jerome Cowan, Stanley Fields, Leonid Kinskey, Irving Pichel, Harry Davenport, Addison Richards, Feodor Chaliapin, Jr., Spencer Charters, Byron Foulger, Etienne Girardot, Don Brodie, Henry Rocquemore, Maude Eburne, Vince Barnett, Charles Richman, George Chandler. *D:* Otis Garrett; *P:* Eugene Frenke; *St:* Edwin Justus Mayer; *Sc:* Mayer, Ethel LaBlanche. (1:11)

B mystery-drama of a lady seeking American citizenship who becomes implicated in murder and faces deportation. A United Players production.

1274. Exiled to Shanghai (Republic; 1937). *Cast:* June Travis, William Bakewell, Wallace Ford, Arthur Lake, Dean Jagger, Johnny Arthur, Minerva Urecal. *D:* Nick Grinde.

B romantic drama of two news reporters after the same girl.

1275. Expensive Husbands (WB; 1937–38). *Cast:* Patric Knowles, Beverly Roberts, Allyn Joslyn, Gordon Oliver, Vladimir Sokoloff, Eula Guy, Robert C. Fischer, Fritz Feld, John Butler, Ann Codee, George Humbert, Otto Fries. *D:* Bobby Connolly; *P:* Bryan Foy; *St:* Kyrill de Shishmareff; *Sc:* Jean Negulesco, Lillie Hayward, Jay Brennan; *Song:* M.K. Jerome, Jack Scholl. (0:58)

B comedy of a film actress who marries into royalty to impress others.

1276. Expensive Women (WB/F.N.; 1931). *Cast:* Warren William, Dolores Costello, Anthony Bushell, Joe Donahue, H.B. Warner, Allan Lanc, Morgan Wallace, Polly Walters, William House, Mae Madison, Adele Watson. *D:* Hobart Henley; *St:* Wilson Collison; *Sc:* Harvey Thew, Raymond Griffith.

Drama of a woman's fickleness in love.

1277. The Expert (WB; 1932). *Cast:* Charles "Chic" Sale, Earle Foxe, Lois Wilson, Dickie Moore, Ralf

Harolde, May Boley, Noel Francis, Louise Beavers, Walter Catlett, Elizabeth Patterson, Adrienne Dore, William Robyns, Charles Evans, Elsa Peterson, Zita Moulton, Dorothea Wolbert. *D:* Archie Mayo; *Sc:* Julien Josephson, Maude Howell.

Comedy-drama of an elderly man who comes to Chicago to live with his son. Based on the novel by Edna Ferber it was remade as *No Place to Go* (q.v.).

1278. Explorers of the World (Raspin Productions; 1931). *Cast:* James L. Clark, Laurence M. Gould, Gene Lamb, Harold McCracken, Harold Noice, Lieutenant-Commander J.R. Stenhouse. *D:* Harold Noice.
Documentary.

1279. Exposed (Eagle Productions; 1932). *Cast:* William Collier, Jr., Barbara Kent. *D:* Albert Herman.
"B" gangster drama.

1280. Exposed (Universal; 1938). *Cast:* Glenda Farrell, Otto Kruger, Charles D. Brown, Bernard Nedell, Herbert Mundin, Eddie "Rochester" Anderson, Maurice Cass, David Oliver, James Blaine, Lorraine Krueger, John Kelly, Richard Lane, John Butler. *D:* Harold Schuster; *P:* Max H. Golden; *Sc:* Charles Kaufman, Franklin Coen. (1:03)
B melodrama of a female fotog who gets the goods on some hoods.

1281. Exposure (Capital; 1932). *Cast:* Walter Byron, Lila Lee, Lee Moran, Tully Marshall, Raymond Hatton, Mary Doran, Nat Pendleton, Roy Stewart, Pat O'Malley, Sidney Bracey. *D:* Xxxx Xxxx.
"Poverty row" melodrama.

1282. Extortion (Columbia; 1938). *Cast:* Scott Colton, Ann Doran, Mary Russell, Albert Dekker, J. Farrell MacDonald, Thurston Hall, Arthur Loft, Frank Wilson, Edward Keane, Gene Morgan, Roland Got. *D:* Lambert Hillyer.
B crime melodrama.

1283. Extravagance (Tiffany; 1930). *Cast:* June Collyer, Lloyd Hughes, Owen Moore, Gwen Lee, Arthur Hoyt, Joan Standing, Nella Walker, Jameson Thomas (American debut), Robert Agnew, Dorothy Christy, Addie McPhail. *D:* Phil Rosen.
A "poverty row" comedy, previously filmed in 1921 by director Rosen.

1284. Eyes of the World (United Artists/Inspiration Prods.; 1930). *Cast:* Una Merkel (Sybil), Fern Andra (American debut as Gertrude), Brandon Hurst, John Holland, Hugh Huntley, Nance O'Neil, Frederic Burt, Eulalie Jensen, Florence Roberts, William Jeffrey. *D:* Henry King; *P:* Sol Lesser; *St:* Harold Bell Wright; *Sc:* Clarke Silvernail, N. Brewster Morse.
Melodrama of a mountain girl involved with seduction and jealousy.

1285. F-Man (Paramount; 1936). *Cast:* Jack Haley, Grace Bradley, William Frawley, Onslow Stevens, Billy Gilbert, Robert Middlemass, Adrienne Marden. *D:* Edward Cline; *P:* Val Paul; *St:* Richard Connell; *Sc:* Paul Gerard Smith, Henry Johnson, Eddie Welch.
B comedy of a soda-jerk who yearns to be a G-man.

1286. Face in the Fog (Victory; 1936). *Cast:* June Collyer, Lloyd Hughes. *D:* Robert F. Hill; *Sc:* Al Martin; *Sc:* Peter B. Kyne.
"B" newspaper drama.

1287. Face in the Sky (Fox; 1933). *Cast:* Spencer Tracy, Marion Nixon, Lila Lee, Stuart Erwin, Frank McGlynn, Jr., Sarah Padden, Sam Hardy, Guy Usher, Billy Platt. *D:* Harry Lachman (American debut); *St:* Myles Connolly.
Romantic musical.

1288/1289. The Face on the Bar-room Floor (Xxxx Xxxx; 1936). *Cast:* Dulcie Cooper, Bramwell Fletcher. *D:* Bert Bracken.

"B" prohibition drama.

1290. Fair Warning (Fox; 1930–31). *Cast:* George O'Brien, Louise Huntington, George Brent, Mitchell Harris, Nat Pendleton, Willard Robertson, Ernie Adams. *D:* Alfred Werker; *Sc:* Ernest Pascal. (1:14)

George O'Brien western based on a novel by Max Brand. A remake of Tom Mix's *The Untamed* (Fox; 1920).

1291. Fair Warning (20th Century-Fox; 1937). *Cast:* J. Edward Bromberg, Betty Furness, John Howard Payne (John Payne), Victor Kilian, Gavin Muir, Paul McVey, Andrew Tombes, Billy Burrud, Ivan Lebedeff, John Eldredge. *D:* Norman Foster; *St:* Philip Wylie; *Sc:* Foster. (1:10)

Murder in Death Valley.

1292. Faith (Xxxx Xxxx; 1932). (No information available)

1293. Faithless (MGM; 1932). *Cast:* Tallulah Bankhead, Robert Montgomery, Hugh Herbert, Maurice Murphy, Louise Closser Hale, Henry Kolker, Lawrence Grant, Sterling Holloway. *D:* Harry Beaumont; *Sc:* Carey Wilson. (1:16)

Riches-to-rags story. Based on the novel "Tinfoil" by Mildred Cram.

1294. The Fall Guy (RKO; 1930). *Cast:* Jack Mulhall, Pat O'Malley, Mae Clarke, Wynne Gibson, Ned Sparks, Thomas Jackson, Tom Kennedy, Alan Roscoe, Ann Brody, Elmer Ballard. *D:* Leslie Pearce; *As.P.:* William Sistrom; *Sc:* Tim Whelan. (G.B. title: *Trust Your Wife*) (1:10)

Comedy-drama of a drug store clerk who after losing his job finds himself involved with crooks dealing in illegal drugs. Based on the hit Broadway play by George Abbott and James Gleason.

1295. The Fall of Eve (Columbia; 1929). *Cast:* Patsy Ruth Miller, Ford Sterling, Gertrude Astor, Jed Prouty, Betty Farrington, Arthur Rankin. *D:* Frank Strayer; *St:* Anita Loos, John Emerson; *Adaptation:* Gladys Lehman; *Sc:* Frederick & Fanny Hatton.

Comedy.

1296. Falling Star (Xxxx Xxxx; 1931). (No information available)

1297. False Faces (Sono Art–World Wide; 1932). *Cast:* Lowell Sherman, Lila Lee, Peggy Shannon, Joyce Compton, David Landau, Berton Churchill, Geneva Mitchell, Nance O'Neil, Purnell Pratt, Oscar Apfel, Edward Martindel, Miriam Seegar, Harold Waldridge. *D:* Lowell Sherman; *St & Sc:* Kubec Glasmon, Llewelyn Hughes. (G.B. title: *What Price Beauty?*)

"Poverty row" hospital drama.

False Faces (1935) (G.B. title) *see* **Let 'em Have It**

The False Idol (G.B. title) *see* **The False Madonna**

1298. The False Madonna (Paramount; 1931). *Cast:* Kay Francis, William "Stage" Boyd, Conway Tearle. *D:* Stuart Walker. (G.B. title: *The False Idol*)

In order to get an inheritance, a woman masquerades as another she knows to be deceased.

1299. False Pretenses (Chesterfield; 1935). *Cast:* Russell Hopton, Irene Ware, Betty Compson, Sidney Blackmer, Dot Farley. *D:* Charles Lamont.

"Poverty row" production.

False Witness (G.B. title) *see* **Transient Lady**

Fame Street *see* **Police Court**

1300. A Family Affair (MGM; 1937). *Cast:* Lionel Barrymore, Spring Byington, Mickey Rooney, Eric

Linden, Cecilia Parker, Sara Haden, Charley Grapewin, Julie Haydon, Selmer Jackson, Allen Vincent, Harlan Briggs, Margaret Marquis. *D:* George B. Seitz; *P:* Lucien Hubbard; *Sc:* Kay Van Riper. (1:09)

Low-budget family comedy based on the 1928 Broadway play "Skidding" by Aurania Rouverol. The premiere entry in what was later to emerge as the "Hardy Family" or "Andy Hardy" series. In the series, Lionel Barrymore and Spring Byington were replaced by Lewis Stone and Fay Holden.

1301. The Family Next Door (Universal; 1939). *Cast:* Hugh Herbert, Eddie Quillan, Ruth Donnelly, Joy Hodges, Frances Robinson, James Bush, Juanita Quigley, Bennie Bartlett, Thomas Beck, Cecil Cunningham, Lillian Yarbo, Spooks the dog. *D:* Joseph Santley; *P:* Max H. Golden; *Sc:* Mortimer Offner. (1:00)

B comedy of a screwball family with their own share of problems.

1302. The Famous Ferguson Case (WB/F.N.; 1932). *Cast:* Joan Blondell, Tom Brown, Adrienne Dore, Vivienne Osborne, Walter Miller, Leslie Fenton, J. Carrol Naish, Russell Hopton, Leon (Ames) Waycoff, Grant Mitchell, Kenneth Thomson, Purnell Pratt, George Meeker, Willard Robertson, Miriam Seegar. *D:* Lloyd Bacon; *Sc:* Courtney Terrett, Harvey Thew.

B drama which deals with the dangers of "yellow journalism." Based on the story "Circulation" by Granville Moore.

1303. Fancy Baggage (WB; 1929). *Cast:* Audrey Ferris, Wallace MacDonald, Myrna Loy, Edmund Breese. *D:* John Adolfi; *St:* Jerome Kingston; *Sc:* C. Graham Baker.

Part-talkie low-budget drama of a girl who poses as a rival businessman's secretary in order to get some important papers for her father.

1304. Fang and Claw (RKO/Van Beuren; 1935). *Narration:* Frank Buck. (1:10)

The third documentary to be produced and directed by famed adventurer Frank Buck, this one dealing with the capture of wild animals in Malaya.

1305. Fanny Foley Herself (RKO; 1931). *Cast:* Edna May Oliver (Fanny Foley), Rochelle Hudson, Helen Chandler, John Darrow, Hobart Bosworth, Florence Roberts, Robert Emmett O'Connor, Harry Stubbs. *D:* Melville Brown; *P:* John E. Burch; *Sc:* Carey Wilson, Bernard Schubert. (G.B. title: *Top of the Bill*)

Sentimental technicolor drama of a lady vaudevillian and her concern for the happiness and welfare of her two daughters. Filmed in 2-color technicolor, this was the studio's first attempt to make Edna May Oliver a star attraction. Based on the story by Juliet Wilbur Tompkins.

1306. A Farewell to Arms (Paramount; 1932). *Cast:* Helen Hayes (Catherine Barkley), Gary Cooper (Frederic Henry), Adolphe Menjou (Major Rinaldi), Mary Philips (Helen Ferguson), Jack LaRue (priest), Blanche Frederici (head nurse), Henry Armetta (Bonello), Gilbert Emery (British major), Mary Forbes (Miss Van Campen), George Humbert (Piani), Tom Ricketts (Count Greffi), Robert Cauterio (Gordoni), Fred Malatesta (Manera). *D:* Frank Borzage; *Adaptation:* Benjamin Glazer, Oliver H.P. Garrett; *Cinematographer:* (A.A.) Charles B. Lang, Jr.; *Art-Set Decoration:* (A.A.N.) Hans Dreier, Roland Anderson; *Sound Recording:* (A.A.) Harold C. Lewis. (1:18) (video)

Classic World War I story of the ill-fated love of an American soldier and a British nurse. Based on the novel by Ernest Hemingway, it received an A.A.N. for Best Picture (1932–33), was voted one of the "10 Best" films of the year by the National Board of Review in 1932 as well as placing #6 on the same list

of *Film Daily* in 1933. Remade by
Warners in 1951 as *A Force of Arms* (aka:
A Girl for Joe) and by 20th Century–Fox
in 1957 under the original title.

1307. Fargo Express (World
Wide; 1932–33). *Cast:* Ken Maynard,
Helen Mack, Paul Fix, William Des-
mond, Roy Stewart, Jack Rockwell. *D:*
Alan James (Alvin J. Neitz); *Sc:* James,
Earle Snell. (1:01) (video)
    Ken Maynard western of a cow-
poke who poses as another to prove that
man innocent of robbery.

1308. The Farmer in the Dell
(RKO; 1936). *Cast:* Fred Stone, Jean
Parker, Esther Dale, Moroni Olsen,
Frank Albertson, Maxine Jennings,
Ray Mayer, Lucille Ball, Rafael Corio,
Frank Jenks, Spencer Charters, John
Beck, Tony Martin. *D:* Ben Holmes;
As.P.: Robert Sisk; *Sc:* Sam Mintz, John
Grey. (1:07)
    B comedy of an Iowa family who
sell their farm and move to Hollywood
with hopes of getting their daughters
into movies—with unexpected results.
One might take note of the famous
"Hollywood" sign at the beginning of the
film as opposed to the way it appears to-
day. Based on the novel by Phil Stong.

1309. The Farmer Takes a Wife
(Fox; 1935). *Cast:* Janet Gaynor, Henry
Fonda (in his film debut, recreating his
stage role), Charles Bickford, Slim Sum-
merville, Andy Devine, Roger Imhof,
Jane Withers, Margaret Hamilton, Sig
Rumann, John Qualen, Ruth Hall,
Kitty Kelly. *D:* Victor Fleming; *P:*
Winfield Sheehan; *Sc:* Edwin Burke.
(1:31) (video)
    Drama of farm life along the Erie
Canal in the 1820s. Based on the play by
Frank B. Elser and Marc Connelly
which was adapted from the novel
"Rome Haul" by Walter D. Edmonds.
Remade in 1953 as a musical.

Fashion Follies of 1934 (G.B. title)
see **Fashions of 1934**

Fashions *see* **Fashions of 1934**

1310. Fashions in Love (Para-
mount; 1929). *Cast:* Adolphe Menjou,
Fay Compton (American debut), John
Miljan, Miriam Seegar, Joan Standing,
Robert Wayne, Russell Powell, Billie
Bennett, Jacques Vanaire. *D:* Victor
Schertzinger.
    Low-budget romantic comedy of a
concert pianist-cum-lothario.

1311. Fashions of 1934 (WB;
1934). *Cast:* William Powell, Bette
Davis, Frank McHugh, Hugh Herbert,
Verree Teasdale, Reginald Owen,
Henry O'Neill, Phillip Reed, Gordon
Westcott, Dorothy Burgess, Etienne
Girardot, William Burress, Nella
Walker, Spencer Charters, George
Humbert, Frank Darien, Harry Beres-
ford, Martin Kosleck (American debut).
D: William Dieterle; *P:* Henry Blanke;
St: Harry Collins, Warren Duff; *Sc:* F.
Hugh Herbert, Carl Erickson, Gene
Markey (unc.); *Songs:* "Spin a Little
Web of Dreams" and "Broken Melody"
by Irving Kahal and Sammy Fain.
(Retitled: *Fashions*) (G.B. title: *Fashion
Follies of 1934*) (1:18) (video)
    A musical-comedy set in the world
of French fashion design with
choreography by Busby Berkeley.

1312. Fast and Furious (MGM;
1939). *Cast:* Franchot Tone, Ann
Sothern, Ruth Hussey, Lee Bowman,
Allyn Joslyn, John Miljan, Bernard
Nedell, Frank Orth, Mary Beth
Hughes, Cliff Clark, Margaret Roach,
Gladys Blake. *D:* Busby Berkeley; *P:*
Frederick Stephani; *Sc:* Marco Page
(Harry Kurnitz).
    Husband and wife detectives Joel
and Garda Page sleuth murder at a
beauty contest in this B mystery-
comedy, the final entry in a series of
three films.

1313. Fast and Loose (Paramount; 1930). *Cast:* Miriam Hopkins
(film debut), Frank Morgan, Charles
Starrett, Ilka Chase, Henry Wads-

worth, David Hutcheson, Winifred Harris, Carole Lombard (bit), Herbert Yost, Herschel Mayall. *D:* Fred Newmeyer; *Adaptation and Dialogue:* Preston Sturges; *Sc:* Doris Anderson, Jack Kirkland. (1:15)

Comedy of upper crust parents who disapprove of their offspring's potential marriage partners. A remake of *The Best People* (Paramount; 1925) with Esther Ralson and Warner Baxter which was based on the hit 1924 play of that name by Avery Hopwood and David Gray. Filmed at Astoria Studios in Long Island, N.Y.

1314. Fast and Loose (MGM; 1939). *Cast:* Robert Montgomery, Rosalind Russell, Ralph Morgan, Reginald Owen, Etienne Girardot, Alan Dinehart, Joan Marsh, Tom Collins, Ian Wolfe, Sidney Blackmer, Jo Ann Sayers, Donald Douglas, Mary Forbes, Winifred Harris, Anthony Allan (John Hubbard). *D:* Edwin L. Marin; *P:* Frederick Stephani; *Sc:* Harry Kurnitz. (1:20)

Husband and wife detectives Joel and Garda Page investigate the theft of a rare Shakespearian manuscript in this B mystery-comedy, the second of three films in a series.

1315. Fast Bullets (Reliable; 1936). *Cast:* Tom Tyler, Rex Lease, Margaret Nearing, Alan Bridge, William Gould, Robert Walker, Slim Whitaker, Jimmy Aubrey, George Chesebro, Charles King. *D:* Henri Samuels (Harry S. Webb); *P:* B.B. Ray; *Sc:* Carl Krusada, Rose Gordon. (0:59)

Tom Tyler western of a ranger in pursuit of a gang of smugglers.

1316. Fast Companions (Universal; 1932). *Cast:* Tom Brown, Maureen O'Sullivan, Mickey Rooney, Andy Devine, James Gleason, Berton Churchill, Russell Hopton. *D:* Kurt Neumann. (aka: *The Information Kid*) (1:10)

A crooked jockey is reformed by love and friendship in this B film.

1317. Fast Company (Paramount; 1929). *Cast:* Jack Oakie, Evelyn Brent, Richard "Skeets" Gallagher, Chester Conklin, Gwen Lee, Sam Hardy, Arthur Housman. *D:* A. Edward Sutherland, Edwin H. Knopf (directorial debut—unc.); *St:* Ring Lardner, George M. Cohan; *Sc:* Florence Ryerson, Patrick Kearney, Walton Butterfield; *Dial.:* Joseph L. Mankiewicz.

Low-budget baseball comedy.

1318. Fast Company (MGM; 1938). *Cast:* Melvyn Douglas, Florence Rice, Claire Dodd, Louis Calhern, George Zucco, Horace McMahon, Nat Pendleton, Douglasss Dumbrille, Shepperd Strudwick (film debut), Thurston Hall, Dwight Frye, Don Douglas, Minor Watson, Mary Howard. *D:* Edward Buzzell; *P:* Frederick Stephani; *Sc:* Harold Tarshis, Marco Page (Harry Kurnitz—based on his novel). (TV title: *The Rare Book Murder*) (1:15)

Premiere entry in the short mystery-comedy series featuring Joel and Garda Page, husband and wife detectives. In this one they solve a murder in the rare book business.

1319. Fast Life (WB/F.N.; 1929). *Cast:* Douglas Fairbanks, Jr., Loretta Young, Chester Morris, William Holden (1872–1932), Frank Sheridan, Ray Hallor, Purnell Pratt, John St. Polis. *D:* John Francis Dillon; *Sc:* John F. Goodrich; *Song:* Ray Perkins.

Melodrama of a man on trial for a murder he didn't commit. Based on the play by Samuel Shipman and John B. Hymer.

1320. Fast Life (MGM; 1932). *Cast:* William Haines, Madge Evans, Conrad Nagel, Cliff Edwards, Arthur Byron, Kenneth Thomson, Karen Morley, Ben Hendricks, Jr., Albert Gran, Warburton Gamble. *D:* Harry Pollard (final film—d. 1934); *St:* E.J. Rath; *Sc:* Byron Morgan, Ralph Spence.

A man invents a motorboat engine in this low-budget comedy.

Fast Play (G.B. title) *see* **Campus Confessions**

1321. Fast Workers (MGM; 1933). *Cast:* John Gilbert, Robert Armstrong, Mae Clarke, Muriel Kirkland, Vince Barnett, Virginia Cherrill, Muriel Evans, Sterling Holloway, Guy Usher, Warner Richmond, Robert Burns. *D:* Tod Browning; *Sc:* Karl Brown, Ralph Wheelwright, Laurence Stallings. (1:08) (working title: "Rivets")

The friendship of two high-rise riveters begins to deteriorate over the affections of a girl. A box office dud which was the final starring role of Gilbert. Based on the play "Rivets" by John W. McDermott.

1322. Fatal Lady (Paramount; 1936). *Cast:* Mary Ellis, Walter Pidgeon, Norman Foster (final film as an actor), John Halliday, Ruth Donnelly, Alan Mowbray, Edgar Kennedy, Ward Bond, Samuel S. Hinds, Jean Rouverol, Irene Franklin, Guy Bates Post. *D:* Edward Ludwig; *P:* Walter Wanger; *St:* Harry Segall; *Sc:* Samuel Ornitz. (1:17)

Melodrama of an opera singer who becomes involved in murder.

1323. Father and Son (Columbia; 1929). *Cast:* Jack Holt, Dorothy Revier, Wheeler Oakman, Noah Beery, Jr., Helene Chadwick, Mickey McBan. *D:* Erle C. Kenton; *P:* Harry Cohn; *St:* Elmer Harris.

Part-talkie low-budget melodrama.

1324. Father Brown, Detective (Paramount; 1934–35). *Cast:* Walter Connolly (Father Brown), Paul Lukas, Gertrude Michael, Una O'Connor, E.E. Clive, Halliwell Hobbes, King Baggot. *D:* Edward Sedgwick; *P:* Bayard Veiller; *Sc:* C. Gardner Sullivan, Henry Myers.

B mystery based on G.K. Chesterton's character-creation of a detective-priest who catches a jewel thief.

1325. Father's Son (WB/F.N.; 1930–31). *Cast:* Lewis Stone, John Halliday, Irene Rich, Leon Janney, Mickey Bennett, Robert Dandridge, George Reed, Gertrude Howard, Grover Liggon, Bertha Mann. *D:* William Beaudine; *Sc:* Hope Loring.

Family drama of a boy who feels misunderstood by his father. Based on a story by Booth Tarkington it was remade in 1941.

1326. A Feather in Her Hat (Columbia; 1935). *Cast:* Pauline Lord, Basil Rathbone, Louis Hayward, Billie Burke, Wendy Barrie, J.M. Kerrigan, Victor Varconi, Nydia Westman, Thurston Hall, E.E. Clive, Nana Bryant, David Niven. *D:* Alfred Santell; *St:* I.A.R. Wylie; *Sc:* Lawrence Hazard. (1:12)

Mother-love drama.

1327. Federal Agent (Republic; 1936). *Cast:* William Boyd, Irene Ware, Don Alvarado, George Cooper. *D:* Sam Newfield; *P:* George A. Hirliman.

B crime melodrama.

1328. Federal Bullets (Monogram; 1937). *Cast:* Milburn Stone, Zeffie Tilbury, Terry Walker, Selmer Jackson, William Harrigan, Matty Fain, Lyle Moraine, Warner Richmond, Eddie Phillips, Betty Compson, Helen MacKellar, John Merton. *D:* Karl Brown; *P:* Lon Young; *St:* Major George Fielding Eliot; *Sc:* Brown. (1:01)

B crime melodrama of a government agent who infiltrates a gang of crooks run by an elderly woman.

1329. Federal Man Hunt (Republic; 1938–39). *Cast:* Bob Livingston, June Travis, Ben Welden, Horace McMahon, Charles Halton, John Gallaudet, Matt McHugh, Jerry Tucker, Gene Morgan, Sybil Harris, Frank Conklin, Margaret Mann. *D:* Nick Grinde; *Sc:* Maxwell Shane. (G.B. title: *Flight from Justice*)

F.B.I. melodrama on a low budget.

1330. Feet First (Paramount/ Harold Lloyd Prods.; 1930). *Cast:*

Harold Lloyd, Robert McWade, Barbara Kent, Lillian Leighton, Alec B. Francis, Sleep 'n' Eat (Willie Best — film debut), Noah Young, Arthur Housman. *D:* Clyde Bruckman; *Sc:* Lex Neal, Felix Adler, Paul Gerard Smith. (1:28)

Flop comedy of a Honolulu shoe salesman who gets involved with crooks.

1331. Female (WB/F.N.; 1933). *Cast:* Ruth Chatterton, George Brent, Lois Wilson, Johnny Mack Brown, Ruth Donnelly, Ferdinand Gottschalk, Philip Reed (film debut), Gavin Gordon, Kenneth Thomson, Huey White, Douglass Dumbrille, Spencer Charters, Charles C. Wilson, Jean Muir, Rafaela Ottiano, Sterling Holloway, Samuel S. Hinds, Edward Cooper, Walter Walker. *D:* Michael Curtiz, William Dieterle (unc.); *P:* Henry Blanke; *St:* Donald Henderson Clarke; *Sc:* Gene Markey, Kathryn Scola. (1:00)

A corporate female exec uses men in business and pleasure until she meets one who won't be used.

1332. Female Fugitive (Monogram/Crescent Pictures; 1938). *Cast:* Evelyn Venable, Craig Reynolds, Reed Hadley (film debut), John Kelly, Martha Tibbetts, Charlotte Treadway, Reginald Sheffield, Raphael (Ray) Bennett, John Merton, Emmett Vogan, Lee Phelps. *D:* William Nigh; *P:* E.B. Derr; *St:* Bennett R. Cohen; *Sc:* John T. Neville, Cohen. (0:58)

After learning of her husband's criminal activities, a woman leaves and takes up with an artist in this B melodrama.

1333. The Ferocious Pal (Principal; 1934). *Cast:* Ruth Sullivan, Gene Toler, Robert Manning, Kazan the dog, Tom London, Grace Wood, Edward Cecil. *D:* Spencer Gordon Bennet; *P:* Sol Lesser; *Sc:* Joe Roach. (0:55)

A boy and his dog help thwart crooks in this B quickie.

1334. The Feud Maker (Republic-Supreme; 1938). *Cast:* Bob Steele,

Marion Weldon, Karl Hackett, Frank Ball, Budd Buster, Lew Meehan, Roger Williams, Forrest Taylor. *D:* Sam Newfield; *P:* A.W. Hackel; *Sc:* George Plympton. (1:00)

Bob Steele western of a feud between ranchers and homesteaders.

1335. Feud of the Range (Metropolitan; 1939). *Cast:* Bob Steele, Gertrude Messinger, Richard Cramer, Frank LaRue, Jean Cranford, Robert Burns, Budd Buster, Jack Ingram, Charles King. *D:* Harry S. Webb; *P:* B. (Bernard) B. Ray; *Sc:* Carl Krusada. (0:55)

Bob Steele western (his first for this indie company) of a range war.

1336. Feud of the Trail (Victory; 1937). *Cast:* Tom Tyler, Harley Wood, Milburn Morante, Roger Williams, Lafe McKee, Richard Alexander, Slim Whitaker, Jim Corey. *D:* Robert Hill; *P:* Sam Katzman; *Sc:* Basil Dickey (0:56)

Tom Tyler western of a cowboy out to recover some stolen gold.

1337. Feud of the West (Diversion; 1936). *Cast:* Hoot Gibson, Joan Barclay, Buzz Barton, Reed Howes, Robert Kortman, Ed Cassidy, Nelson McDowell, Roger Williams, Allen Greer, Richard Cramer. *D:* Harry Fraser; *P:* Walter Futter; *Sc:* Phil Dunham. (1:02)

Hoot Gibson western of a cowboy who takes flight when wrongly accused of murder.

1338. Fever (Xxxx Xxxx; 1932–33). (No information available)

1339. The Fiddlin' Buckaroo (Universal; 1933). *Cast:* Ken Maynard, Gloria Shea, Frank Rice, Fred Kohler, Jack Rockwell, Jack Mower, Bob McKenzie, Joseph Girard, Slim Whitaker, Pascale Perry, Frank Ellis, Roy Bucko, Buck Bucko, Hank Bell. *D & P:* Ken Maynard; *Sc:* Nate Gatzert. (1:03)

Ken Maynard western with musical numbers of a cowboy accused of a hold-up he didn't commit.

1340. 15 Maiden Lane (20th Century–Fox; 1936). *Cast:* Claire Trevor, Cesar Romero, Douglas Fowley, Lloyd Nolan, Lester Matthews, Holmes Herbert, Howard Hickman, Murray Kinnell. *D:* Allan Dwan; *Sc:* Lou Breslow, John Patrick, David Silverstein. (1:05)

B crime melodrama about jewel thieves.

1341. Fifteen Wives (Invincible; 1934). *Cast:* Conway Tearle, Noel Francis, Robert Frazer, Ralf Harolde, Margaret Dumont, Raymond Hatton, Oscar Apfel. *D:* Frank Strayer. (G.B. title: *The Man with the Electric Voice*)

"Poverty row" romantic comedy.

1342. 5th Avenue Girl (RKO; 1939). *Cast:* Ginger Rogers, Walter Connolly, Verree Teasdale, Tim Holt, James Ellison, Kathryn Adams, Franklin Pangborn, Louis Calhern, Ferike Boros, Alexander D'Arcy, Theodore von Eltz, Jack Carson, Robert Emmett Keane, Cornelius Keefe, Manda Lane. *D:* Gregory LaCava; *P:* LaCava; *Sc:* Allan Scott. (1:23) (video)

Hit comedy of a millionaire who hires a girl to pose as a golddigger and has her move into his home.

The Fifth Round (G.B. title) *see* **Tough Kid**

1343. Fifty Fathoms Deep (Columbia; 1931). *Cast:* Jack Holt, Richard Cromwell, Mary Doran, Wallace MacDonald, Loretta Sayers. *D:* Roy William Neill; *St:* Dorothy Howell.

Low-budget melodrama.

1344. Fifty Million Frenchmen (WB; 1931). *Cast:* Ole Olsen, Chick Johnson, William Gaxton (recreating his stage role), Claudia Dell, Helen Broderick (recreating her stage role), John Halliday, Charles Judels, Carmelita Geraghty, Vera Gordon, Evalyn Knapp, Bela Lugosi, Marian Marsh, Nat Carr, Norman Phillips, Jr., Lester Crawford. *D:* Lloyd Bacon; *Sc:* Joseph Jackson, Eddie Welch.

2-color technicolor comedy based on the 1929 stage musical by Herbert Fields, dialogue by Al Boasberg and Eddie Welch, adapted by Joseph Jackson, with music by Cole Porter.

1345. Fifty Roads to Town (20th Century–Fox; 1937). *Cast:* Don Ameche, Ann Sothern, Slim Summerville, Jane Darwell, John Qualen, Douglas Fowley, Stepin Fetchit, Oscar Apfel, Russell Hicks, Allan Lane, Paul Hurst, Arthur Aylesworth, Bradley Page. *D:* Norman Taurog; *P:* Raymond Griffith; *Sc:* George Marion, Jr., William Conselman. (1:20)

Hit comedy of people who are snowbound at an inn and nobody is who they appear to be.

1346. 52nd Street (United Artists/Walter Wanger; 1937). *Cast:* Kenny Baker, Ella Logan, Leo Carrillo, Ian Hunter, ZaSu Pitts, Dorothy Peterson, Pat Paterson, Jerry Colonna (film debut—bit), Georgie Tapps (bit), Pat Harrington, Sr. (bit), Sid Silvers, Jack White, Al Shean, Billy Burrud, Marla Shelton, Collette Lyons, Roman Bohnen, Wade Boteler, Al Norman, Cook and Brown, Rocco and Saulter. *D:* Harold Young; *P:* Wanger; *Sc:* Grover Jones. (1:23)

Romantic comedy with music of "nightclub row" in New York City from 1912 to the present day (1937).

1347. The Fight for Peace (Monogram/Warwick Pictures; 1938). *Narrator:* David Ross.

Independent documentary on the horrors of the war in Europe in the 1930s with the focus on Hitler, Mussolini and Stalin. The film was re-released in 1939 by Monogram. (1:05)

1348. Fight for Your Lady (RKO; 1937). *Cast:* John Boles, Jack

Oakie, Ida Lupino, Margot Grahame, Erik Rhodes, Billy Gilbert, Paul Guilfoyle, Georges Renavent, Charles Judels, Maude Eburne, Charles Coleman, Leona Roberts, Forrester Harvey. *D:* Ben Stoloff; *P:* Albert Lewis; *St:* Jean Negulesco, Isabel Leighton; *Sc:* Ernest Pagano, Harry Segall, Harold Kusell; *Song:* "Blame It on the Danube" by Harry Akst and Frank Loesser. (1:10)

B comedy of romantic misunderstandings.

1349. A Fight to the Finish (Columbia; 1937). *Cast:* Don Terry, Rosalind Keith, Ward Bond, Tom Chatterton, Frank Sheridan, Lucille Lund, George McKay, Wade Boteler, Harold Goodwin, Ivan Miller. *D:* C.C. Coleman, Jr.; *St & Sc:* Harold Shumate.

B melodrama of feuding taxi-cab companies.

1350. Fightin' Thru (Tiffany; 1930). *Cast:* Ken Maynard, Jeannette Loff, Wallace MacDonald, Carmelita Geraghty, William L. Thorne, Charles Mix, Chuck Baldra, Jack Kirk, Bud McClure, Jim Corey. *D:* William Nigh; *P:* Phil Goldstone; *Sc:* John Francis (Jack) Natteford. (aka: *California in 1878*) (1:01)

Ken Maynard "poverty row" western (his first for this studio) of a gold miner accused of killing his partner.

1351. The Fighting Caballero (Superior; 1935). *Cast:* Rex Lease, Dorothy Gulliver, Earl Douglas, George Chesebro, Wally Wales (Hal Taliaferro), Robert Walker, Milburn Moranti, George Morrell, Franklyn Farnum. *D:* Elmer Clifton; *P:* Louis Weiss; *Sc:* Clifton, George M. Merrick. (0:59)

A Rex Lease western.

1352. Fighting Caravans (Paramount; 1931). *Cast:* Gary Cooper, Lily Damita, Ernest Torrence, Tully Marshall, Fred Kohler, Eugene Pallette, Syd Saylor, Roy Stewart, Charles Winninger, Frank Campeau, Eve Southern, James Farley, May Boley, Jane Darwell, E. Alyn Warren, Donald MacKenzie, Frank Hagney. *D:* Otto Brower, David Burton; *Sc:* Edward E. Paramore, Jr., Agnes Brand Leahy, Keene Thompson. (1:31) (video — 1:20)

Large scale western based on a book by Zane Grey of a wanted man leading a wagon train west. The film offers comedy, romance and the inevitable climactic Indian attack. Remade as *Wagon Wheels* (q.v.).

1353. The Fighting Champ (Monogram; 1932). *Cast:* Bob Steele, Arletta Duncan, Charles King, Kit Guard, George Chesebro, Frank Ball, Lafe McKee, George Hayes, Henry Rocquemore. *D:* John P. McCarthy; *P:* Trem Carr; *St & Sc:* Wellyn Totman. (0:59)

Offbeat Bob Steele western with a prize-fighting background.

1354. The Fighting Code (Columbia; 1933–34). *Cast:* Buck Jones, Diane Sinclair, Niles Welch, Ward Bond, Richard Alexander, Louis Natheaux, Alfred P. James, Erville Alderson, Gertrude Howard, Robert Kortman, Charles Brinley, Buck Moulton. *D:* Lambert Hillyer; *Sc:* Hillyer. (1:05)

Buck Jones oater of a cowboy seeking the killer of a girl's father.

1355. The Fighting Coward (Victory Pictures; 1935). *Cast:* Roger Williams, Joan Woodbury. *D:* Dan Milner; *Sc:* Al Martin.

B western.

1356. The Fighting Cowboy (Superior; 1933). *Cast:* Buffalo Bill, Jr., Genee Boutell, Allen Holbrook, William Ryno, Marin Sais, Tom Palky, Bart Carre, Jack Evans, Boris Bullock, Ken Broeker, Betty Butler, Clyde McClary. *D:* Denver Dixon (Victor Adamson); *P:* Dixon; *Sc:* L.V. Jefferson. (0:58)

Buffalo Bill, Jr., western involving thefts from a tungsten mine.

1357. The Fighting Deputy
(Spectrum; 1937). *Cast:* Fred Scott, Al
St. John, Phoebe Logan, Marjorie
Beebe, Charles King, Lafe McKee,
Frank LaRue, Eddie Holden, Sherry
Tansey, Jack C. Smith, Chick Hannon,
Jack Evans. *D:* Sam Newfield; *Sc:*
William Lively. (1:00)
   Fred Scott western with songs of a
cowboy taking a job as lawman to find
the man who ambushed him.

1358. The Fighting Fool (Co-
lumbia; 1932). *Cast:* Tim McCoy,
Marceline Day, Mary Carr, Robert
Ellis, Ethel Wales, Dorothy Granger,
Robert Kortman, Arthur Rankin,
Harry Todd, William V. Mong. *D:*
Lambert Hillyer; *Sc:* Frank Clark.
(0:58)
   Tim McCoy western.

1359. Fighting for Justice (Co-
lumbia; 1932). *Cast:* Tim McCoy, Joyce
Compton, Hooper Atchley, William
Norton Bailey, Lafe McKee, Walter
Brennan, Harry Todd, Harry Cording,
Robert Frazer, Murdock MacQuarrie,
Charles King, William V. Mong. *D:*
Otto Brower; *Sc:* Robert Quigley. (1:00)
   Tim McCoy horse opera involving
the sale of a cattle ranch in which the
seller is killed and the buyer blamed.

1360. Fighting Fury (J.D. Trop;
1934). *Cast:* John King, Bonita Baker,
Tom London, Lafe McKee, Philo Mc-
Cullough, Bart Carre, Del Morgan,
Jack Donovan, Kazan the dog, Cactus
the horse. *D:* Robert Hill; *P:* John King;
Sc: Myron Dattlebaum. (1:01)
   B actioner of a dog and a white stal-
lion who help a cowboy capture a gang
of outlaws.

1361. The Fighting Gentleman
(Monarch; 1932). *Cast:* William Collier,
Jr., Pat O'Malley, Lee Moran, Crau-
ford Kent, Josephine Dunn. *D:* Fred
Newmeyer; *P:* John R. Freuler.
   "Poverty row" boxing drama.

1362. The Fighting Gringo
(RKO; 1939). *Cast:* George O'Brien,
Lupita Tovar, Bill Cody, Sr., Lucio Vil-
legas, LeRoy Mason, William Royle,
Glenn Strange, Slim Whitaker, Mary
Field, Martin Garralaga, Dick Botiller,
Cactus Mack, Chris-Pin Martin. *D:*
David Howard; *P:* Bert Gilroy; *St:*
Oliver Drake; *Sc:* Drake. (0:59)
   George O'Brien western with a
"save the ranch" formula plot.

1363. The Fighting Hero (Reli-
able; 1934). *Cast:* Tom Tyler, Renee
Borden, Edward Hearn, Dick Botiller,
Ralph Lewis, Murdock MacQuarrie,
George Chesebro, Tom London, Nel-
son McDowell, Rosa Rosanova, J.P.
McGowan, Lew Meehan, Chuck Bal-
dra, Jimmy Aubrey. *D:* Harry S. Webb;
P: Bernard B. Ray; *Sc:* Carl Krusada,
Rose Gordon. (0:55)
   Tom Tyler oater.

1364. The Fighting Lady (Fanchon Royer Pictures; 1935). *D:* Carlos
Borcosque; *Sc:* John Francis Natteford.

1365. The Fighting Legion (Uni-
versal; 1930). *Cast:* Ken Maynard,
Frank Rice, Dorothy Dwan, Ernie
Adams, Stanley Blystone, Jack Fowler,
Harry Todd, Robert Walker, Les Bates,
Slim Whitaker, Bill Nestel. *D:* Harry
Joe Brown; *P:* Maynard; *Sc:* Bennett
Cohen. (1:15)
   Part-talkie Ken Maynard western
with musical sequences of a cowboy
wrongfully accused of murder. It might
be noted here that Ken Maynard was *the
first singing cowboy,* introducing songs
into his westerns years before Gene
Autry began the singing cowboy craze of
the mid–1930s. Remade as *The Lone
Avenger* (q.v.).

1366. Fighting Mad (Mono-
gram/Criterion; 1939). *Cast:* James
Newill (Renfrew), Sally Blane, Dave
O'Brien, Benny Rubin, Milburn Stone,
Walter Long, Warner Richmond, Ted
Adams, Chief Thundercloud, Ole Ol-
sen, Horace Murphy. *D:* Sam Newfield;

P: Philip N. Krasne; *Sc:* George Rosener, John Rathmell. (1:00)

"Renfrew" adventure as the singing Mountie and his partner go after some American gangsters in the wilderness. Based on the Laurie York Erskine story "Renfrew Rides North."

1367. The Fighting Marines (Republic/Mascot; 1935–36). *Cast:* Grant Withers, Adrian Morris, Ann Rutherford, Robert Warwick, George Lewis, Pat O'Malley, Victor Potel, Jason Robards, Warner Richmond, Robert Frazer, J. Frank Glendon, Donald Reed, Max Wagner, Richard Alexander, Tom London, Jim Corey. *D:* Joseph Kane, B. Reeves Eason; *P:* Barney Sarecky; *St:* Wallace MacDonald, Maurice Geraghty, Ray Trampe; *Sc:* Sarecky, Sherman Lowe. (1:09) (video)

Feature version of the 12-chapter serial of the same name of military attempts to establish a landing field on a remote Pacific island. The serial was a Mascot production, featurized following the merger of Mascot and Monogram into Republic Pictures.

1368. The Fighting Marshal (Columbia; 1931). *Cast:* Tim McCoy, Dorothy Gulliver, Matthew Betz, Mary Carr, Pat O'Malley, Edward J. LeSaint, Lafe McKee, Ethan Laidlaw, Harry Todd, Dick Dickinson, Blackie Whiteford. *D:* D. Ross Lederman; *Sc:* Frank Clark. (1:00)

Tim McCoy western of a man escaping from prison to prove his innocence.

1369. The Fighting Parson (Allied; 1933). *Cast:* Hoot Gibson, Marceline Day, "Skeeter" Bill Robbins, Robert Frazer, Stanley Blystone, Charles King, Jules Cowan, Ethel Wales, Frank Nelson, Phil Dunham, Frank Ellis, Merrill McCormack, Blackie Whiteford, J. Farrell MacDonald. *D:* Harry Fraser; *P:* M.H. Hoffman, Jr.; *Sc:* Fraser. (1:10)

Hoot Gibson western of a cowboy who is mistaken for a man of the cloth leading to various comic complications. Gibson's final film for producer Hoffman.

1370. The Fighting Pilot (Ajax; 1935). *Cast:* Richard Talmadge, Gertrude Messinger, Robert Frazer. *D:* Noel Smith.

Low-budget actioner.

1371. The Fighting Pioneers (Resolute; 1935). *Cast:* Rex Bell, Ruth Mix, Buzz Barton, Lew Meehan, Stanley Blystone, Earl Dwire, John Elliott, Chief Thundercloud, Roger Williams, Chuck Morrison, Guate Mozin, Chief Standing Bear, Bob Burns, Blackjack Ward, Francis Walker. *D:* Harry Fraser; *Sc:* Fraser, Chuck Roberts. (0:54)

Rex Bell western of gun runners stirring up trouble between whites and Indians.

1372. The Fighting President (Universal; 1933). *Written & Narrated by:* Edwin C. Hill.

Documentary feature on events in the life of President Franklin Delano Roosevelt as compiled by Allyn Butterfield.

1373. The Fighting Ranger (Columbia; 1933–34). *Cast:* Buck Jones, Dorothy Revier, Frank Rice, Ward Bond, Bradley Page, Paddy O'Flynn, Art Smith, Frank LaRue, Jack Wallace, Bud Osborne, Lew Meehan, Denver Dixon, Jim Corey, Steve Clemente, Frank Ellis, Mozelle Britton. *D:* George B. Seitz; *Sc:* Harry O. Hoyt. (1:00)

Buck Jones western of a ranger who quits the service so he can apprehend a gang of outlaws in Mexico. A remake of *Border Law* (q.v.).

1374. The Fighting Renegade (Victory; 1939). *Cast:* Tim McCoy (Lightnin' Bill Carson), Joyce Bryant, Ben Corbett (Magpie), Budd Buster, Dave O'Brien, Forrest Taylor, Ted

Adams, Reed Howes, Carl Mathews, John Elliott. *D:* Sam Newfield; *P:* Sam Katzman; *Sc:* William Lively. (1:00)

Tim McCoy western as a masquerading cowboy out to clear his name.

1375. The Fighting Rookie (Mayfair; 1934). *Cast:* Jack LaRue, Matthew Betz. *D:* Spencer Gordon Bennet.

"Poverty row" crime-actioner.

1376. Fighting Shadows (Columbia; 1935). *Cast:* Tim McCoy, Robert Allen, Geneva Mitchell, Ward Bond, Si Jenks, Otto Hoffman, Edward J. LeSaint, Ethan Laidlaw, Bud Osborne. *D:* David Selman; *Sc:* Ford Beebe. (1:00)

Tim McCoy Canadian Mountie actioner of a constable in pursuit of some fur thieves.

1377. The Fighting Sheriff (Columbia/Beverly Prods.; 1931). *Cast:* Buck Jones, Loretta Sayers, Robert Ellis, Harlan Knight, Paul Fix, Lillian Worth, Clarence Muse, Nena Quartero, Lillian Leighton. *D:* Louis King; *Sc:* Stuart Anthony. (1:07)

Buck Jones oater of a sheriff maligned by the leader of an outlaw gang.

1378. The Fighting 69th (WB; 1939–40). *Cast:* James Cagney (Jerry Plunkett), Pat O'Brien (Father Duffy), George Brent (Wild Bill Donovan), Jeffrey Lynn (Joyce Kilmer), Alan Hale (Sgt. Big Mike Wynn), Frank McHugh ("Crepe Hanger" Burke), Dennis Morgan (Licut. Amcs), Dick Foran (Lieut. Long John Wynn), William Lundigan (Timmy Wynn), Guinn Williams (Paddy Dolan), John Litel (Capt. Mangan), Henry O'Neill (colonel), Frank Wilcox (Lieut. Norman), Tom Dugan (Pvt. McManus), Harvey Stephens (Major Anderson), Charles Trowbridge (Chaplain Holmes), Sammy Cohen (Mike Murphy), De-Wolf (William) Hopper (Pvt. Turner), George Reeves (Jack O'Keefe), John

Ridgely (Moran), Herbert Anderson (Casey), J. Anthony Hughes (Healey), Frank Mayo (Capt. Bootz), John Harron (Carroll), George Kilgen (Ryan), Richard Clayton (Tierney), Eddie Dew (Regan), Frank Coghlan, Jr. (Jimmy), George O'Hanlon (Eddie), Wilfred Lucas, Emmett Vogan, Frank Sully, Joseph Crehan, James Flavin, Jack Perrin, Trevor Bardette, John Arledge, Frank Melton, Edmund Glover, Johnny Day, Frank Faylen, Edgar Edwards, Saul Gorss, Ralph Dunn. *D:* William Keighley; *As.P.:* Louis F. Edelman; *Sc:* Norman Reilly Raine, Fred Niblo, Jr., Dean Franklin. (1:29)

World War I drama which was one of the 21 top grossing films of 1939–40. Computer-colored by Turner Entertainment in 1987.

1379. The Fighting Texan (Ambassador; 1936). *Cast:* Kermit Maynard, Elaine Shepard, Frank LaRue, Budd Buster, Ed Cassidy, Bruce Mitchell, Murdock, MacQuarrie, Art Miles, Merrill McCormack, Blackie Whiteford, John Merton. *D:* Charles Abbott; *P:* Maurice Conn; *Sc:* Joseph O'Donnell. (0:59)

Kermit Maynard western of feuding ranchers.

1380. The Fighting Texans (Monogram; 1933). *Cast:* Rex Bell, Luana Walters, Betty Mack, George Hayes, Wally Wales (Hal Taliaferro), Yakima Canutt, Lafe McKee, Anne Howard, Alan Bridge, Frank LaRue, George Nash, Gordon DeMain (Gordon Wood). *D:* Armand Schaefer; *P:* Paul Malvern; *St:* Wellyn Totman; *Sc:* Totman, Charles Roberts. (G.B. title: *Randy Strikes Oil*). (0:58)

Rex Bell western of dirty deeds in the oil fields.

1381. Fighting Thoroughbreds (Republic; 1939). *Cast:* Mary Carlisle, Ralph Byrd, George "Gabby" Hayes, Victor Kilian, Robert Allen. *D:* Sidney Salkow.

Race track story.

1382. Fighting Through (Willis Kent/Cristo; 1934). *Cast:* Reb Russell, Lucille Lund, Yakima Canutt, Edward Hearn, Charles King, Wally Wales (Hal Taliaferro), Lew Meehan, Chester Gan, Slim Whitaker, Steve Clemente, Bill Patton, Frank McCarroll, Ben Corbett, Hank Bell, Nelson McDowell, Rebel the horse. *D:* Harry Fraser; *P:* Willis Kent; *Sc:* Fraser. (0:55)

Reb Russell western of two cowboys who become friends after one saves the life of the other in a crooked poker game.

1383. Fighting to Live (Principal; 1934). *Cast:* Gaylord (Steve) Pendleton, Marion Shilling, Reb Russell, Eddie Phillips, Lloyd Ingraham, Henry Hall, John Strohback, Bruce Mitchell, Captain the dog, Lady the dog. *D:* Edward F. Cline; *P:* Sol Lesser; *Sc:* Robert Ives. (1:00)

Juvenile canine adventure of two dogs accused of killing chickens and left in the desert to die.

1384. The Fighting Trooper (Ambassador; 1934). *Cast:* Kermit Maynard, Barbara Worth, Walter Miller, Robert Frazer, LeRoy Mason, George Regas, Charles Delaney, Joseph Girard, George Chesebro, Charles King, Artie Ortego, Milburn Morante, Lafe McKee, George Morrell. *D:* Ray Taylor; *P:* Maurice Conn; *Sc:* Forrest Sheldon. (0:57) (video)

Kermit Maynard Canadian Mountie actioner. The first in a series of 16 films for producer Maurice Conn.

The Fighting Westerner *see* **Rocky Mountain Mystery**

1385. Fighting Youth (Universal; 1935). *Cast:* Charles Farrell, Ann Sheridan, June Martel, Andy Devine, J. Farrell MacDonald, Edward Nugent, Herman Bing, Phyllis Fraser, Jean Rogers, Clara Kimball Young, Charles C. Wilson, Herbert Bunston, David Worth, Jeff Cravath, Glen Boles, Walter Johnson, Alden Chase (Stephen Chase). *D:* Hamilton MacFadden; *Sc:* MacFadden, Florabel Muir, Henry Johnson. (1:25)

Offbeat college story of a subversive co-ed who bangs heads with a flag-waving football player.

1386. File 113 (Allied; 1932). *Cast:* William Collier, Jr., June Clyde, Mary Nolan, Lew Cody, George E. Stone, Roy D'Arcy, Clara Kimball Young, Harry Cording, Crauford Kent. *D:* Chester M. Franklin; *P:* M.H. Hoffman, Jr.

Low-budget detective yarn, based on the works of Frenchman Emile Gaboriau.

1387. The Final Edition (Columbia; 1932). *Cast:* Pat O'Brien, Mae Clarke, Wallis Clark, Bradley Page, Phil Tead, Morgan Wallace, Mary Doran, Bertha Mann. *D:* Howard Higgin; *St & Sc:* Roy Chanslor; *Adapt. & Dial.:* Dorothy Howell.

Low-budget newspaper melodrama.

1388. The Final Hour (Columbia; 1936). *Cast:* Marguerite Churchill, Ralph Bellamy, Lina Basquette, Marc Lawrence, Jean Howard, John Gallaudet, George McKay, John Dilson. *D:* D. Ross Lederman; *St & Sc:* Harold Shumate.

B melodrama.

1389. Find the Witness (Columbia; 1937). *Cast:* Rosalind Keith, William Humphrey, John Tyrrell, Harry Tyler. *D:* David Selman.

B melodrama.

1390. The Finger Points (WB/F.N.; 1931). *Cast:* Richard Barthelmess, Fay Wray, Regis Toomey, Robert Elliott, Clark Gable, Robert Gleckler, Oscar Apfel. *D:* John Francis Dillon; *St:* W.R. Burnett; *Sc:* John Monk Saunders, Robert Lord. (1:28)

Melodrama of a crusading journalist and his ties to local crime figures.

1391. Finishing School (RKO; 1934). *Cast:* Frances Dee, Ginger Rogers, Bruce Cabot, Billie Burke, John Halliday, Beulah Bondi, Sara Haden, Helen Freeman, Marjorie Lytell, Adalyn Doyle, Dawn O'Day (Anne Shirley), Jane Darwell. *D:* George Nicholls, Jr., Wanda Tuchock; *As.P.:* Kenneth Macgowan; *St:* David Hempstead; *Sc:* Tuchock, Laird Doyle. (1:13)

The romance of an intern and a girl from an exclusive private school.

1392. Finn and Hattie (Paramount; 1930–31). *Cast:* Leon Errol, ZaSu Pitts, Mitzi Green, Jackie Searle, Regis Toomey, Lilyan Tashman, Mack Swain, Harry Beresford. *D:* Norman Taurog, Norman Z. McLeod; *Sc:* Sam Mintz, Joseph L. Mankiewicz. (1:17)

Hit comedy of an American who takes his family abroad. Based on the novel "Mr. & Mrs. Haddock Abroad" by Donald Ogden Stewart.

Fire Alarm *see* **Flames**

1393. The Fire Trap (Empire; 1935). *Cast:* Norman Foster, Evalyn Knapp, Ben Alexander, Sidney Blackmer, Oscar Apfel, Arthur Housman. *D:* Burt Lynwood.

B melodrama.

1394. The Firebird (WB; 1934). *Cast:* Ricardo Cortez, Anita Louise, Lionel Atwill, Verree Teasdale, C. Aubrey Smith, Nan Grey, Dorothy Tree, Helen Trenholme, Hobart Cavanaugh, Robert Barrat, Florence Fair, Jane Darwell, Hal K. Dawson. *D:* William Dieterle; *Sc:* Charles Kenyon.

B who-dun-it involving the murder of a mime artist. Based on the play by Lajos Zilahy, it is set in Vienna, Austria.

1395. Firebrand Johnson (Big 4; 1930). *Cast:* Lane Chandler, Aline Goodwin, Yakima Canutt, Sheldon Lewis, Marguerite Ainslee, Tom Lon-

don, Lew Meehan, Frank Yaconelli, Alfred Hewston. *D:* Alvin J. Neitz (Alan James); *P:* John R. Freuler; *Sc:* Carl Krusada. (1:00)

Lane Chandler (in his starring debut) western of a cowboy on the trail of some counterfeiters.

1396. The Firefly (MGM; 1937). *Cast:* Jeanette MacDonald (Nina Maria Azaria), Allan Jones (Don Diego Manrique de Lara/Captain Francois DeCoucourt), Warren William (Colonel De Rougemont), Billy Gilbert (innkeeper), Henry Daniell (General Savary), George Zucco (St. Clair), Douglass Dumbrille (Marquis DeMelito), Leonard Penn (film debut as Etienne), Ian Wolfe (Minister Izquierdo), Tom Rutherford (King Ferdinand), Belle Mitchell (Lola), Corbet Morris (Duval), Matthew Boulton (Duke of Wellington), Robert Spindola (Juan), Manuel Alvarez Maciste (Pedro), Frank Puglia (Pablo), John Picorri, James B. Carson, Alan Curtis, Jason Robards, Bud Flanagan (Dennis O'Keefe), Ralph Byrd, Sam Appel, Maurice Cass, Maurice Black, Rolfe Sedan, Inez Palange, Harry Worth, John Merton, Hooper Atchley, Stanley Price, Brandon Hurst, Pedro de Cordoba, Theodore von Eltz, Edward Keane, Lane Chandler, Sidney Bracey, Eddie Phillips, Russell Powell, Agostino Borgato, Robert Z. Leonard (bit), Albertina Rasch (bit). *D:* Robert Z. Leonard; *P:* Hunt Stromberg; *Adaptation:* Ogden Nash (of the book by Otto Harbach, music by Rudolf Friml stage production of 1912); *Sc:* Albert Hackett, Frances Goodrich; *Songs:* "Love Is Like a Firefly," "Sympathy," "Giannina Mia," "When a Maid Comes Knocking at Your Heart," "A Woman's Kiss," "When the Wine Is Full of Fire" and "He Who Loves and Runs Away" all from the original score; and "Donkey Serenade" adapted from a piano piece from the original for the film by Bob Wright, Chet Forrest and Rudolf Friml. (2:18)

Dramatic operetta set during the Napoleonic wars of 1808–1812. Lavishly produced in sepia tint, it became one of the 15 top grossing films of 1937–38.

1397. Fireman, Save My Child (WB/F.N.; 1932). *Cast:* Joe E. Brown, Evalyn Knapp, Lillian Bond, Guy Kibbee, Richard Carle, George MacFarlane, Frank Shallenbach, Virginia Sale, Curtis Benton, George Meeker, George Ernest, Ben Hendricks, Jr., Walter Walker, Louis Robinson. *D:* Lloyd Bacon; *Sc:* Ray Enright, Robert Lord, Arthur Caesar. (1:07)

B comedy of a fireman whose first love is baseball. A remake of the 1927 production.

1398. Fires of Youth (Universal; 1931). *Cast:* Genevieve Tobin, Dorothy Peterson. *D:* Monta Bell; *St:* Bell.

Low-budget drama previously filmed by this studio in 1918.

1399. First Aid (Sono Art World Wide; 1931). *Cast:* Grant Withers, Donald Keith, Paul Panzer, Wheeler Oakman, George Chesebro. *D:* Stuart Paton. (G.B. title: *In Strange Company*)

Low-budget melodrama.

1400. The First Baby (20th Century–Fox; 1936). *Cast:* Gene Lockhart, Shirley Deane, Johnny Downs, Dixie Dunbar, Hattie McDaniel, Jane Darwell, Taylor Holmes, Willard Robertson. *D:* Lewis Seiler.

B domestic comedy.

1401. The First Hundred Years (MGM; 1938). *Cast:* Robert Montgomery, Virginia Bruce, Warren William Binnie Barnes, Lee Bowman, Harry Davenport, E.E. Clive, Alan Dinehart, Nydia Westman, Jonathan Hale, Torben Meyer, Bodil Rosing. *D:* Richard Thorpe; *P:* Norman Krasna; *St:* Krasna; *Sc:* Melville Baker.

Marital comedy which was previously filmed in 1924 as a Harry Langdon short.

1402. First Lady (WB; 1937). *Cast:* Kay Francis, Preston Foster, Anita Louise, Walter Connolly, Verree Teasdale, Victor Jory, Marjorie Rambeau, Louise Fazenda, Marjorie Gateson, Henry O'Neill, Harry Davenport, Sara Haden, Grant Mitchell, Lucile Gleason, Olaf Hytten, Eric Stanley. *D:* Stanley Logan; *P:* Harry Joe Brown; *Sc:* Rowland Leigh. (1:22)

Washington D.C. political comedy based on a 1935 play by George S. Kaufman and Katherine Dayton.

1403. First Love (Universal; 1939). *Cast:* Deanna Durbin, Robert Stack (film debut giving Durbin her much publicized first screen kiss), Helen Parrish, Eugene Pallette, Leatrice Joy, Marcia Mae Jones, Frank Jenks, Lewis Howard, Mary Treen, June Storey, Jack Mulhall, Charles Coleman, Samuel S. Hinds, Kathleen Howard, Jessie Royce Landis, Thurston Hall, Dorothy Vaughan, Lucille Ward. *D:* Henry Koster; *P:* Joe Pasternak; *Sc:* Bruce Manning, Lionel Houser; *Art-Set Decoration:* (A.A.N.) Jack Otterson & Martin Obzina; *M.D.:* (A.A.N.) Charles Previn; *Songs:* "Spring Is in My Heart" by Hans Salter & Ralph Freed, adapted from a work by Johann Strauss, "Amapola" by Albert Gamse & Joseph LaCalle, "Home Sweet Home" by John Howard Payne & Sir Henry Bishop, and "One Fine Day" from Puccini's "Madame Butterfly." (1:18)

Cinderella-type story of a young girl and her first love. A hit for the studio.

1404. First Offenders (Republic; 1939). *Cast:* John Hamilton, Beverly Roberts, Walter Abel. *D:* Frank McDonald.

B melodrama.

The First Rebel (G.B. title) *see* **Allegheny Uprising**

1405. The First World War (Fox; 1934). *Narration & Dialogue delivered by:* Lew Lehr, Pedro de Cordoba, Bonney Powell, Laurence Stallings, Russell Shields, Louis de Rochemont. *P:* Truman Talley.

Documentary of the great conflict of 1914-1918. Voted one of the "10 Best" films of the year by the National Board of Review.

1406. The First Year (Fox; 1932). *Cast:* Janet Gaynor, Charles Farrell, Robert McWade, Minna Gombell, George Meeker, Maude Eburne, Leila Bennett, Dudley Digges, Elda Vokel. *D:* William K. Howard.

Another film pairing the popular box office team of Janet Gaynor and Charles Farrell. A romance, based on the play by Frank Craven it was previously filmed in 1926.

1407. Fish (20th Century-Fox; 1936). *Cast:* Warren Hull, Anita Kerry, Walter Johnson, Henry O'Neill, Johnny Arthur, Florence Fair, Alma Lloyd, Mary Treen, Spec O'Donnell. *D:* William McGann; *Sc:* Earl Felton, George Bricker.

B romantic comedy.

1408. Fisherman's Wharf (RKO/Principal; 1939). *Cast:* Bobby Breen, Henry Armetta, Leo Carrillo, Lee Patrick, Slicker the seal, Tommy Bupp, Rosina Galli, George Humbert, Leon Belasco, Pua Lani, Leonard Kibrick, Jackie Salling, Ronnie Paige, Milo Marchetti, Jr. *D:* Bernard Vorhaus; *P:* Sol Lesser; *Sc:* Bernard Schubert, Ian McLellan Hunter, Herbert Clyde Lewis; *Songs:* Victor Young, Charles Newman, Farlan Myers, Frank Churchill, William Howe, Paul Webster.

Musical-drama of three fishermen and their domestic problems, highlighted by singing juvenile Bobby Breen.

1409. Fit for a King (RKO/Loew; 1937). *Cast:* Helen Mack, Joe E. Brown, Harry Davenport, Paul Kelly, Halliwell Hobbes, John Qualen, Donald Briggs, Frank Reicher, Russell Hicks, Charles Trowbridge. *D:* Edward Sedgwick; *P:* David L. Loew; *Sc:* Richard Flournoy.

Hit slapstick comedy of a news reporter attempting to prevent a royal assassination.

1410. Five and Ten (MGM; 1931). *Cast:* Marion Davies, Leslie Howard, Richard Bennett, Irene Rich, Kent Douglass (Douglass Montgomery), Halliwell Hobbes, Mary Duncan, Ruth Selwyn, Henry Armetta, Lee Beranger, Charles Giblyn, Arthur Housman. *D:* Robert Z. Leonard; *P:* Marion Davies; *Sc:* A.P. Younger, Edith Fitzgerald. (G.B. title: *Daughter of Luxury*) (1:28)

Drama based on the novel by Fannie Hurst of an heiress who elopes with a married man.

1411. Five Bad Men (Sunset Pictures; 1935). *Cast:* Noah Beery, Jr. *D:* Cliff Smith; *P:* Anthony J. Xydias.

B western.

1412. Five Came Back (RKO; 1939). *Cast:* Chester Morris, Lucille Ball, Wendy Barrie, John Carradine, Allen Jenkins, Joseph Calleia, C. Aubrey Smith, Patric Knowles, Elizabeth Risdon, Kent Taylor, Casey Johnson, Dick Hogan, Frank Faylen. *D:* John Farrow (who also directed the remake); *P:* Robert Sisk; *St:* Richard Carroll; *Sc:* Jerry Cady, Dalton Trumbo, Nathanael West. (1:15) (video)

Critically acclaimed B drama of the interactions between passengers on a plane called the "Silver Queen" downed in the Amazon jungle and surrounded by headhunters. Remade as *Back from Eternity* (RKO; 1956).

1413. Five Little Peppers and How They Grew (Columbia; 1939). *Cast:* Edith Fellows, Dorothy Peterson, Dorothy Ann Seese, Clarence Kolb, Ronald Sinclair, Tommy Bond, Charles Peck, Jimmy Leake. *D:* Charles Barton; *Sc:* Nathalie Bucknall, Jefferson Parker.

Premiere entry in a sentimental juvenile oriented series based on the stories by Margaret Sidney. Followed in

1940 by the other three entries in the series, all directed by Barton. They include: *Five Little Peppers at Home, Out West with the Peppers* and *Five Little Peppers in Trouble.*

1414. Five of a Kind (20th Century-Fox; 1938). *Cast:* The Dionne quints (Annette, Cecile, Emilie, Marie and Yvonne), Jean Hersholt, Claire Trevor, Slim Summerville, Andrew Tombes, Cesar Romero, John Qualen, Jane Darwell, David Torrence, Marion Byron, Pauline Moore, Hamilton Mac-Fadden, John Russell. *D:* Herbert I. Leeds; *P:* Sol M. Wurtzel; *Sc:* John Patrick, Lou Breslow.

A sequel to *Reunion* (q.v.) which continued the movie popularity and exploitation of the famous Dionne quintuplets.

1415. Five Star Final (WB; 1931). *Cast:* Edward G. Robinson (Joseph Randall), H.B. Warner (Michael Townsend), Frances Starr (Nancy Voorhees Townsend), Marian Marsh (Jenny Townsend), Anthony Bushell (Phillip Weeks), George E. Stone (Ziggie Feinstein), Ona Munson (Kitty Carmody), Robert Elliott (Brannegan), Aline MacMahon (Miss Taylor), Gladys Lloyd (Miss Edwards), Boris Karloff (T. Vernon Isopod), Evelyn Hall (Mrs. Weeks), David Torrence (Mr. Weeks), Polly Walters (telephone operator), Harold Waldridge (Arthur Goldberg), Oscar Apfel (Bernard Hinchecliffe), Purnell Pratt (Robert French), James Donlan, Frank Darien. *D:* Mervyn LeRoy; *P:* Hal B. Wallis; *Sc:* Robert Lord, Byron Morgan. (1:29)

Story of a newspaper that will stop at nothing to get a sensational story. Based on a play by Louis Weitzenkorn the film received an A.A.N. for Best Picture (1931–32) and placed #7 on the "10 Best" list of *Film Daily.* Previously filmed in 1922 by First National. Remade as *Two Against the World* (q.v.) (aka: *One Fatal Hour*).

1416. Fixer Dugan (RKO; 1939). *Cast:* Lee Tracy, Virginia Weidler, Peggy Shannon, Bradley Page, William Edmunds, Edward Gargan, Jack Arnold (Vinton Haworth), Rita LaRoy, Irene Franklin, John Dilson, Edythe Elliott. *D:* Lew Landers; *P:* Cliff Reid; *Sc:* Bert Granet, Paul Yawitz. (1:08)

B drama of a fast-talking promoter who makes an orphan girl a main circus attraction. Based on the play "What's a Fixer For?" by H.C. Potter. A box office bomb.

1417. The Flame Within (MGM; 1935). *Cast:* Ann Harding, Maureen O'Sullivan, Louis Hayward (American debut), Henry Stephenson, Herbert Marshall, Margaret Seddon, George Hassell, Claudelle Kaye, Eily Malyon. *D:* Edmund Goulding; *P:* Goulding; *St & Sc:* Goulding. (1:13)

Romantic drama of a lady psychiatrist and her "flame within."

1418. Flames (Monogram; 1932). *Cast:* John Mack Brown, Noel Francis, George Cooper, Marjorie Beebe, Richard Tucker, Russell Simpson, Kit Guard. *D:* Karl Brown; *P:* Trem Carr; *St:* Brown, I.E. Chadwick; *Sc:* Brown, Chadwick. (aka: *Fire Alarm*) (1:03)

Low-budget drama about firefighters. Prior to release the film had the working title: "Fatal Alarm."

1419. Flaming Frontiers (Universal; 1938). *Cast:* John Mack Brown, Eleanor Hansen, Charles Middleton, Ralph Bowman (John Archer — film debut), Chief Thundercloud, Horace Murphy, Roy Barcroft, Charles King, James Blaine, Charles Stevens, Eddy Waller, Ed Cassidy. *D:* Ray Taylor, Alan James (Alvin J. Neitz); *P:* Henry MacRae; *Sc:* Wyndham Gittens, Paul Perez, Basil Dickey, George Plympton, Ella O'Neill. (0:56)

The feature version of this studio's 15-chapter serial of the same name of an Indian scout who helps a girl and her brother get what is rightfully theirs.

Based on the story "The Tie That Binds" by Peter B. Kyne.

1420. Flaming Gold (RKO; 1933). *Cast:* Bill Boyd, Mae Clarke, Pat O'Brien, Robert McWade, Helen Ware, Rollo Lloyd. *D:* Ralph Ince; *As.P.:* Sam Jaffe; *St:* Houston Branch; *Sc:* Malcolm Stuart Boylan, John Goodrich. (0:54)

Two oil drillers in the tropics are in love with the same girl in this B drama. A box office dud.

1421. Flaming Guns (Universal; 1932). *Cast:* Tom Mix, Ruth Hall, Tony, Jr., Duke Lee, William Farnum, Fred Burns, George Hackathorne, Clarence H. Wilson. *D:* Arthur Rosson; *Sc:* Jack Cunningham. (0:57)

Tom Mix western with a modern setting and a sophisticated comedy style. A remake of *The Buckaroo Kid* (Universal; 1926) with Hoot Gibson.

1422. Flaming Lead (Colony; 1939). *Cast:* Ken Maynard, Eleanor Stewart, Dave O'Brien, Ralph Peters, Walter Long, Tom London, Carleton Young, Reed Howes, Kenne Duncan, John Merton, Carl Mathews, Bob Terry. *D:* Sam Newfield; *P:* Max & Arthur Alexander; *Sc:* Joseph O'Donnell. (0:57)

Ken Maynard horse opera of a cowboy coming to the aid of a rancher having his horses rustled.

1423. The Flaming Signal (Xxxx Xxxx; 1933). *Cast:* Marceline Day, Noah Beery, Mischa Auer, Carmelita Geraghty. *D:* C.E. Roberts, George Jeske.

Low-budget melodrama.

Flash Gordon *see* **Spaceship to the Unknown** and **Perils from the Planet Mongo**

1424. Flesh (MGM; 1932). *Cast:* Wallace Beery, Karen Morley, Ricardo Cortez, John Miljan, Jean Hersholt, Herman Bing, Edward Brophy, Vince Barnett, Greta Meyer. *D:* John Ford; *St:* Edmund Goulding; *Sc:* Moss Hart; *Adapt.:* Leonard Praskins, Edgar Allan Woolf; *Dial.:* Moss Hart. (1:35)

Flop romantic melodrama of a naive German wrestler who falls for a girl of the New York streets who is having an affair with another.

1425. Flight (Columbia; 1929). *Cast:* Jack Holt, Ralph Graves, Lila Lee, Alan Roscoe, Harold Goodwin, Jimmy de la Cruze. *D:* Frank Capra; *St:* Ralph Graves; *Sc:* Howard J. Green, Capra. (1:56)

The story of buddies in the Marine Flying Corps sent to rescue U.S. Marines in Nicaragua.

1426. Flight at Midnight (Republic; 1939). *Cast:* Phil Regan, Barbara Pepper, Robert Armstrong, Noah Beery, Jr., Raymond Bailey, Harlan Briggs, Harry Hayden, Helen Lynd, Colonel Roscoe Turner. *D:* Sidney Salkow; *St:* Hugh King, Daniel Moore; *Sc:* Eliot Gibbons.

B mystery-melodrama.

Flight Commander *see* **The Dawn Patrol** (1930)

1427. Flight from Glory (RKO; 1937). *Cast:* Chester Morris, Onslow Stevens, Van Heflin, Whitney Bourne, Richard Lane, Paul Guilfoyle, Solly Ward, Douglas Walton, Rita LaRoy, Walter Miller, Pasha Khan. *D:* Lew Landers; *P:* Robert Sisk; *St:* Robert D. Andrews; *Sc:* John Twist, David Silverstein. (1:07) (video)

Hit B action drama of pilots in debt to their boss who fly his unsafe planes over the Andes Mountains in South America.

Flight from Justice (G.B. title) *see* **Federal Manhunt**

1428. Flight Into Nowhere (Columbia; 1938). *Cast:* Jack Holt, Dick Purcell, Jacqueline Wells (Julie Bishop), Ward Bond, Fritz Leiber, Howard Hickman, Robert Fiske, James Burke,

Karen Sorrell, Hector V. Sarno. *D:* Lewis Collins; *St:* Clarence Jay Schneider, William Bloom; *Sc:* Jefferson Parker, Gordon Rigby.

B melodrama.

1429. Flight to Fame (Columbia; 1938). *Cast:* Charles Farrell, Jacqueline Wells (Julie Bishop), Jason Robards, Reed Howes, Selmer Jackson. *D:* C.C. Coleman, Jr.

1430. Flirtation Walk (WB/ F.N.; 1934). *Cast:* Dick Powell (Dick "Canary" Dorcy), Ruby Keeler (Kathleen Fitts), Pat O'Brien (Sgt. "Scrapper" Thornhill), Ross Alexander (Oskie), Guinn Williams (Sleepy), Glen Boles (Eight Ball), Henry O'Neill (Gen. John Brent Fitts), John Arledge (Spike), John Eldredge (Lieut. Robert Biddle), Frederick Burton (Gen. Paul Landacre), John Darrow (Chase), Colonel Tim Lonergan (superintendent), Tyrone Power, Paul Fix, Gertrude Keeler, Lieut. Joe Cummins, Cliff Saum, Sol Bright, William J. Worthington, Emmett Vogan, Maude Turner Gordon, Frances Lee, Frank Dawson, Avis Johnson, Mary Russell, Carlyle Blackwell, Jr., Dick Winslow, Sol Hoopii's Native Orchestra, U.S.C. Polo Team, U.S. Army Polo Team. *D:* Frank Borzage; *P:* Borzage, Robert Lord; *St:* Delmer Daves, Lou Edelman; *Sc:* Daves; *Songs:* "Flirtation Walk," "Mr. and Mrs. Is the Name," "No Horse, No Wife, No Mustache," "I See Two Lovers," "Smoking in the Dark," and "When Do We Eat" by Mort Dixon and Allie Wrubel; *Sound Recording:* (A.A.N.) Nathan Levinson. (1:37)

Set at West Point, this hit romantic story received an A.A.N. for Best Picture.

1431. The Flirting Widow (WB/ F.N.; 1930). *Cast:* Dorothy Mackaill, Basil Rathbone, William Austin, Leila Hyams, Wilfred Noy, Claude Gillingwater, Emily Fitzroy, Anthony Bushell, Flora Bramley. *D:* William A. Seiter; *Sc:* John F. Goodrich.

Low-budget romantic comedy of a woman who writes to an imaginary beau who to her chagrin turns out to be a real person, creating comic confusion when he shows up. Based on the novel "Green Stockings" by A.E.W. Mason. A remake of *Slightly Used* (First National; 1927) with May McAvoy.

1432. Flirting with Danger (Monogram; 1934). *Cast:* Robert Armstrong, William Cagney, Edgar Kennedy, Marion Burns, Maria Alba, William von Brincken, Gino Corrado, Ernest Hilliard, Guy Usher. *D:* Vin Moore; *P:* George Bertholon; *St:* Bertholon; *Sc:* Albert E. DeMond; *Additional Dialogue:* Norman S. Hall. (1:10)

Comic actioner of three dynamite experts who are sent to South America. Prior to release, the film had two working titles: "Dames and Dynamite" and "Reckless Romeos."

1433. Flirting with Fate (MGM/ Loew; 1938). *Cast:* Joe E. Brown, Leo Carrillo, Beverly Roberts, Wynne Gibson, Steffi Duna, Stanley Fields, Charles Judels, Leonid Kinskey, Irene Franklin, George Humbert, Jay Novello. *D:* Frank McDonald; *P:* David L. Loew; *St:* Dan Jarrett, A. Dorian Otvos; *Sc:* Harry Clork, Ethel LaBlanche, Joseph March, Charles Melson. (1:09)

Comedy of a troupe of vaudevillians who are stranded in a South American country.

1434. The Flood (Columbia; 1931). *Cast:* Monte Blue, Eleanor Boardman, Arthur Hoyt, Frank Sheridan, David Newell, Violet Barlowe, Ethan Allen, Buddy Ray, William V. Mong, Eddie Tamblyn, Ethel Wales. *D:* James Tinling; *St & Sc:* John T. Neville.

Low-budget romance.

1435. The Florodora Girl (MGM; 1930). *Cast:* Marion Davies, Lawrence Gray, Walter Catlett, Louis John Bartels, Ilka Chase, Vivian Oakland, Claud Allister, Jed Prouty, Sam

Hardy, Anita Louise, George Chandler, Maude Turner Gordon, Nance O'Neil, Jane Keithly, Robert Bolder, Mary Jane Irving. *D:* Harry Beaumont; *P:* Marion Davies; *Sc:* Gene Markey; *Additional Dialogue:* Ralph Spence, Al Boasberg, Robert Hopkins; *Songs:* Herbert Stothart, Clifford Grey, Andy Rice. (G.B. title: *The Gay Nineties*) (1:19)

Gay '90s romantic comedy-drama with songs based on the play of the same name by Gene Markey. Some scenes originally filmed in 2-color technicolor with some locale shooting at Marion Davies' beachfront home in Santa Monica, California.

Note: Shown on Turner Network Television on 7/23/90 with original technicolor sequences in b/w.

1436. The Florentine Dagger (WB; 1935). *Cast:* Margaret Lindsay, Donald Woods, Robert Barrat, C. Aubrey Smith, Henry O'Neill, Henry Kolker, Florence Fair, Herman Bing, Rafaela Ottiano, Frank Reicher, Eily Malyon. *D:* Robert Florey; *P:* Harry Joe Brown; *Sc:* Brown Holmes, Tom Reed. (1:09)

B who-dun-it of a murdered art dealer. Based on the novel by Ben Hecht.

1437. The Florida Special (Paramount; 1936). *Cast:* Jack Oakie, Sally Eilers, Kent Taylor, Frances Drake, J. Farrell MacDonald, Sam (Schlepperman) Hearn, Claude Gillingwater, Sidney Blackmer, Dwight Frye, Dewey Robinson, Sam Flint, Harry C. Bradley, Matthew Betz, Jean Bary, Clyde Dilson. *D:* Ralph Murphy; *P:* Albert Lewis; *St:* Clarence Buddington Kelland; *Sc:* S.J. Perelman, Marguerite Roberts, David Boehm, Laura Perelman. (1:10)

B romantic mystery with music set aboard a Florida bound train.

1438. Fly Away Baby (WB; 1937). *Cast:* Glenda Farrell (Torchy), Barton MacLane (Steve McBride), Gordon Oliver, Hugh O'Connell, Marcia Ralston, Harry Davenport, Tom Kennedy, Raymond Hatton, Emmett Vogan, Gordon Hart, Anderson Lawler, Joseph King, George Guhl. *D:* Frank McDonald; *P:* Bryan Foy; *St:* Dorothy Kilgallen; *Sc:* Don Ryan, Kenneth Gamet.

"Torchy Blane," girl reporter travels to track down a murderer in this entry in the B series. Based on the characters created by Frederick Nebel.

Flying Aces (G.B. title) *see* **The Flying Deuces**

The Flying Circus (G.B. title) *see* **Flying Devils**

1439. The Flying Deuces (RKO; 1939). *Cast:* Stan Laurel, Oliver Hardy, Jean Parker, James Finlayson, Reginald Gardiner, Charles Middleton, Jean Del Val, Clem Wilenchick (later more prolifically billed as "Crane Whitley"). *D:* A. Edward Sutherland; *P:* Boris Morros; *St & Sc:* Ralph Spence, Harry Langdon, Charles Rogers, Alfred Schiller. (G.B. title: *Flying Aces*) (1:07) (video)

Hit Laurel and Hardy comedy with the duo again in the French Foreign Legion for Ollie to forget a sour romance.

1440. Flying Devils (RKO; 1933). *Cast:* Bruce Cabot, Eric Linden, Arline Judge, Ralph Bellamy, Cliff Edwards, June Brewster, Frank LaRue, Mary Carr. *D:* Russell Birdwell; *As.P.:* David Lewis; *St:* Louis Stevens; *Sc:* Stevens, Byron Morgan. (G.B. title: *The Flying Circus*) (1:00)

Hit actioner with a triangular romantic angle, of veteran pilots who join a flying circus.

1441. Flying Down to Rio (RKO; 1933). *Cast:* Dolores Del Rio (Belinha de Rezende), Gene Raymond (Roger Bond), Raul Roulien (Julio Rubeiro), Ginger Rogers (Honey Hale), Fred Astaire (Fred Ayres), Blanche Frederici (Dona Elena), Eric Blore (assistant manager), Franklin Pangborn (Hammerstein), Walter

Walker (Senor de Rezende), Etta Moten, Roy D'Arcy, Maurice Black, Armand Kaliz, Reginald Barlow, Paul Porcasi, Alice Gentle, Ray Cooke, Luis Alberni, Gino Corrado, Wallace MacDonald, Clarence Muse, Mary Kornman, Harry Semels, Jack Rice, Eddie Borden, Betty Furness, Lucille Browne, Julian Rivero, Pedro Regas, Movita Castaneda, Martha La Venture, Brazilian Turunas Band, Sidney Bracey, American Clippers Band. *D:* Thornton Freeland; *As.P.:* Lou Brock; *St:* Brock; *Sc:* Cyril Hume, H.W. Hanemann, Erwin Gelsey; *Songs:* "Music Makes Me," "Orchids in the Moonlight," "Flying Down to Rio" and "The Carioca" (A.A.N. for Best Song—1934) by Edward Eliscu, Vincent Youmans and Gus Kahn. (1:29) (video)

Musical which is notable as the first screen teaming of Fred Astaire and Ginger Rogers. This is the film with the production number of girls dancing on the wings of an airborne plane. Based on the play by Anne Caldwell, the film was a big hit for the studio.

1442. Flying Fists (Treo; 1938). *Cast:* Herman Brix (Bruce Bennett), Guinn Williams, Dickie Jones, Fuzzy Knight, J. Farrell MacDonald. *D:* Robert F. Hill.

B actioner.

1443. The Flying Fool (Pathé; 1929). *Cast:* William Boyd, Marie Prevost, Russell Gleason. *D:* Tay Garnett; *Dial.:* James Gleason; *Song:* "If I Had My Way" by George Waggner.

Low-budget comic actioner.

Flying Fury (G.B. title) *see* **The Strawberry Roan**

1444. Flying High (MGM; 1931). *Cast:* Bert Lahr (American film debut recreating his stage role), Charlotte Greenwood, Pat O'Brien, Charles Winninger, Guy Kibbee, Hedda Hopper, Kathryn Crawford, Herbert Braggiotti. *D:* Charles Reisner; *Sc:* Robert Hopkins, A.P. Younger,

Reisner; *Songs:* Buddy DeSylva, Lew Brown, Ray Henderson & Jimmy McHugh. (1:20) (G.B. title: *Happy Landing*)

Musical-comedy of a screwball inventor and his flying machine. Based on a Broadway play by George White, the film with choreography by Busby Berkeley was a box office flop.

1445. Flying Hostess (Universal; 1936). *Cast:* William Gargan, Judith Barrett, Ella Logan (film debut), Astrid Allwyn, Andy Devine, Addison (Jack) Randall, William Hall, Marla Shelton, Richard Tucker, Diana Gibson, Michael Loring, Mary Alice Rice, Russell Wade, Dorothea Kent, Maxine Reiner, Pat Flaherty. *D:* Murray Roth; *P:* Charles R. Rogers; *St:* "Sky Fever" by George Sayre; *Sc:* Brown Holmes, Harvey Gates, Harry Clork; *Song:* Irving Actman, Frank Loesser. (1:06)

This production dealing with the training of air-hostesses climaxes with one of the ladies bringing in a plane on her own.

1446. The Flying Irishman (RKO; 1939). *Cast:* Douglas "Wrong Way" Corrigan (playing himself), Paul Kelly, Robert Armstrong, Gene Reynolds, Donald MacBride, Eddie Quillan, J.M. Kerrigan, Dorothy Peterson, Scotty Beckett, Joyce Compton, Dorothy Appleby, Minor Watson, Cora Witherspoon, Spencer Charters, Peggy Ryan, Charles Lane, Grady Sutton. *D:* Leigh Jason; *P:* Pandro S. Berman; *Sc:* Trumbo, Ernest Pagano. (1:12)

Based-on-fact story of an American flyer who in 1939 set out from New York to Los Angeles, eventually arriving in Ireland, thus gaining the title "Wrong Way" Corrigan. Based on the book by Dalton Trumbo, the film was a flop.

1447. The Flying Marine (Columbia; 1929). *Cast:* Ben Lyon, Jason Robards, Shirley Mason. *D:* Albert Rogell.

Part-talkie actioner.

1448. Fog (Columbia; 1933–34). *Cast:* Donald Cook, Reginald Denny, Mary Brian, Samuel S. Hinds, Maude Eburne, Ethel Griffies. *D:* Albert Rogell.

Low-budget mystery-melodrama.

1449. Fog Over Frisco (WB/ F.N.; 1934). *Cast:* Bette Davis, Donald Woods, Margaret Lindsay, Lyle Talbot, Hugh Herbert, Arthur Byron, Robert Barrat, Douglass Dumbrille, Henry O'Neill, Irving Pichel, Alan Hale, William Demarest, William B. Davidson, Gordon Westcott, George Chandler, Harold Minjir, Douglas Cosgrove, Bud Flanagan (Dennis O'Keefe). *D:* William Dieterle; *P:* Henry Blanke; *Sc:* Eugene Solow, Robert N. Lee. (1:07)

Hit mystery-melodrama which centers around the murder of an heiress. The film is noted for its break-neck pace. Based on the novel by George Dyer it was remade as *Spy Ship* (W.B.; 1942).

1450. Folies-Bergère (United Artists/20th Century; 1935). *Cast:* Maurice Chevalier (in a dual role and his final American film for over 20 years), Ann Sothern, Merle Oberon (American debut), Eric Blore, Ferdinand Munier, Walter Byron, Lumsden Hare, Robert Greig, Halliwell Hobbes, Philip Dare, Barbara Leonard, Georges Renavent, Olin Howland, Albert Pollet. *D:* Roy Del Ruth; *P:* Darryl F. Zanuck; *Sc:* Bess Meredyth, Hal Long; *Choreographer:* (A.A.) Dave Gould for his "Straw Hat" number—combined with his work on *The Broadway Melody of 1936* (q.v.). (G.B. title: *The Man form the Folies-Bergère*) (1:24)

Lavishly produced musical based on the play "The Red Cat" by Rudolph Lothar and Hans Adler. Twice remade: *That Night in Rio* (20th Century–Fox; 1941) and *On the Riviera* (20th Century–Fox; 1951).

1451. Follow the Fleet (RKO; 1936). *Cast:* Fred Astaire (Baker),

Ginger Rogers (Sherry Martin), Randolph Scott (Bilge Smith), Harriet Hilliard (Connie Martin), Astrid Allwyn (Iris Manning), Russell Hicks (Jim Nolan), Ray Mayer (Dopey), Harry Beresford (Capt. Hickey), Addison (Jack) Randall (Lieut. Williams), Brooks Benedict (Sullivan), Lucille Ball (Kitty Collins), Herbert Rawlinson (Webber), Betty Grable, Joy Hodges, Jeanne Gray, Tony Martin (film debut), Maxine Jennings, Edward Burns, Jane Hamilton, Frank Mills, Frank Jenks. *D:* Mark Sandrich; *P:* Pandro S. Berman; *Sc:* Dwight Taylor, Allan Scott; *Songs:* "Let's Face the Music and Dance," "We Saw the Sea," "Let Yourself Go," "I'm Puttin' All My Eggs in One Basket," "I'd Rather Lead a Band," "Get Thee Behind Me, Satan," and "Here Am I, But Where Are You?" by Irving Berlin. (1:50) (video)

Musical which has its origins in the 1922 Broadway play "Shore Leave" by Hubert Osborne. Other films based on that work are *Shore Leave* (First National/ Inspiration; 1925), *Hit the Deck* (RKO; 1930) (q.v.) and *Hit the Deck* (MGM; 1951), with songs by Vincent Youmans. One of the 25 top grossing films of 1935–36.

1452. Follow the Leader (Paramount; 1930). *Cast:* Ed Wynn (recreating his stage role), Ginger Rogers, Stanley Smith, Lou Holtz, Robert Watson, Ethel Merman (film debut), Preston Foster, James C. Morton, Donald Kirke, Holly Hall, Lida Kane, William Halligan. *D:* Norman Taurog; *Songs:* Arthur Schwartz, E.Y. Harburg. (aka: *Manhattan Mary*)

Musical-comedy of a dimwit waiter who by a fluke becomes a mob leader. Based on a stageplay, it was filmed at Astoria Studios in Long Island, N.Y.

1453. Follow Thru (Paramount; 1930). *Cast:* Nancy Carroll, Charles "Buddy" Rogers, Thelma Todd, Jack Haley (film debut—recreating his stage role), Zelma O'Neal (film debut—recreating her stage role), Eugene Pallette, Claude King, Albert Gran, Kathryn Givney, Frances Dee. *D:* Lloyd Corrigan, Laurence Schwab; *P:* Frank Mandel, Schwab; *Sc:* Corrigan, Schwab; *Songs:* "Button Up Your Overcoat," "I Want to Be Bad," "Lucky Star," "You Wouldn't Fool Me, Would You?" and "A Peach of a Pair" by George Marion, Jr., and Richard A. Whiting.

Technicolor musical-comedy centered around the game of golf and based on the hit play by Laurence Schwab and Frank Mandel. Filmed in 2-color Technicolor.

1454. Follow Your Heart (Republic; 1936). *Cast:* Marion Talley (in her only film), Vivienne Osborne, Nigel Bruce, Ben Blue, Henrietta Crosman, Clarence Muse, Walter Catlett, Michael Bartlett, John Eldredge, Si Jenks, Margaret Irving, Mickey Rentschler, Josephine Whittell, Eunice Healy, Hall Johnson Choir. *D:* Aubrey Scotto; *P:* Nat Levine; *St:* Dana Burnet; *Sc:* Nathanael West, Samuel Ornitz, Lester Cole; *Songs:* Schertzinger, Walter Bullock, Sidney Mitchell.

Romantic musical of an opera singer.

1455. A Fool's Advice (Xxxx Xxxx; 1933). (No information available)

1456. Fools for Scandal (WB; 1938). *Cast:* Carole Lombard, Fernand Gravet, Ralph Bellamy, Allen Jenkins, Isabel Jeans, Marie Wilson, Ottola Nesmith, Marcia Ralston, Heather Thatcher, Jane Wyman, Tempe Pigott, Jeni LeGon, Michelette Burani, Jacques Lory, Les Hite and his Orchestra. *D:* Mervyn LeRoy; *P:* LeRoy; *Sc:* Herbert Fields, Joseph Fields, Irving S. Brecher (unc.); *Songs:* Richard Rodgers, Lorenz Hart. (1:21)

Musical-comedy of the romance between a Hollywood star and a French nobleman. Based on the play "Return Engagement" by Nancy Hamilton, Rosemary Casey and James Shute.

Fools of Desire *see* **It's All in Your Mind**

Football Coach (G.B. title) *see* **College Coach**

1457. Footlight Parade (WB; 1933). *Cast:* James Cagney (Chester Kent), Joan Blondell (Nan Prescott), Ruby Keeler (Bea Thorn), Dick Powell (Scotty Blair), Frank McHugh (Francis), Guy Kibbee (Silas Gould), Ruth Donnelly (Harriet Bowers Gould), Hugh Herbert (Charlie Bowers), Claire Dodd (Vivian Rich), Gordon Westcott (Harry Thompson), Arthur Hohl (Al Frazer), Reneé Whitney (Cynthia Kent), Barbara Rogers (Gracie), Philip Faversham (Joe Farrington), Juliet Ware (Miss Smythe), Herman Bing (Fralick), Paul Porcasi (George Appolinaris), Hobart Cavanaugh (title-thinker-upper), William Granger, Charles C. Wilson, Billy Taft, Marjean Rogers, Pat Wing, Donna Mae Roberts, Dave O'Brien, George Chandler, William V. Mong, Lee Moran, Billy Barty, Harry Seymour, Sam McDaniel, Fred Kelsey, Jimmy Conlin, Roger Gray, John Garfield (film debut—bit), Duke York, Donna LaBarr, Henry O'Neill, Dorothy Lamour (film debut—bit). *D:* Lloyd Bacon; *P:* Robert Lord, Hal Wallis, Darryl F. Zanuck; *St & Sc:* Manuel Seff, James Seymour; *Other Songs:* "Ah, the Moon Is Here" and "Sittin' on a Backyard Fence" by Sammy Fain and Irving Kahal. (1:44) (video)

Musical-comedy of a theatrical producer putting on the "big show" with the usual headaches. Three production numbers choreographed by Busby Berkeley highlight the production, namely: "By a Waterfall" by Sammy Fain and Irving Kahal, "Honeymoon Hotel" and "Shanghai Lil" by Harry Warren and Al Dubin. The film was a huge success at the box office.

1458. Footlights and Fools (WB/ F.N.; 1929). *Cast:* Colleen Moore, Raymond Hackett, Fredric March, Virginia

Lee Corbin, Mickey Bennett, Edward Martindel. *D:* William A. Seiter; *St:* Katherine Brush; *Sc:* Brush, Tom Geraghty, Carey Wilson; *Songs:* "If I Can't Have You," "You Can't Believe My Eyes" and "Ophelia Will Fool You" by Al Bryan and George W. Meyer.

Musical-romance of a girl who leads a double life between show business and romance.

1459. The Footloose Heiress (WB; 1937). *Cast:* Ann Sheridan, Craig Reynolds, Anne Nagel, Hugh O'Connell, Teddy Hart, DeWolf (William) Hopper, Frank Orth, Loia Cheaney, William Eberhardt, Hal Neiman. *D:* William Clemens; *P:* Bryan Foy; *Sc:* Robertson White.

B comedy of a girl who makes a bet she will be married by midnight of her eighteenth birthday.

1460. For Love or Money (Universal; 1939). *Cast:* Robert Kent, June Lang, Ed Brophy, Etienne Girardot, Richard Lane, Edward Gargan, Horace McMahon, Lois Wilson. *D:* Albert Rogell; *P:* Max H. Golden; *St:* Julian Blaustein, Daniel Taradash, Bernard Fein; *Sc:* Arthur T. Horman, Charles Grayson. (1:07)

B comedy of two guys who lose track of $50,000 belonging to some crooks who want their money back or else. Remade as *The Noose Hangs High* (Eagle-Lion; 1948).

1461. For the Defense (Paramount; 1930). *Cast:* William Powell, Kay Francis, Scott Kolk, James Finlayson, George Hayes, William B. Davidson, Thomas Jackson, John Elliott, Edward LeSaint, Charles West, Bertram Marburgh, Harry Walker, Charles Sullivan, Ernie Adams. *D:* John Cromwell; *P:* David O. Selznick; *St:* Charles Furthman; *Sc:* Oliver H.P. Garrett.

Hit drama of a boozing D.A. who is convicted of bribing a jury. The title character was based on real life New York attorney William Fallon who was much in the news in his day.

1462. For the Love o' Lil (Columbia; 1930). *Cast:* Sally Starr, Jack Mulhall, Elliott Nugent, Margaret Livingston, Julia Swayne Gordon, Claire DuBrey, Billy Bevan. *D:* James Tinling. Romantic comedy.

1463. For the Service (Universal; 1935). *Cast:* Buck Jones, Beth Marion, Clifford Jones, Allan Sears, Charles "Slim" Whitaker, Frank McGlynn, Fred Kohler, Edward Keane, Ben Corbett, Chief Thunderbird. *D:* Jones, Lesley Selander; *P:* Jones; *Sc:* Isadore Bernstein. (1:05)

Buck Jones western of an army scout who saves the day at an army post.

For You Alone (G.B. title) *see* **When You're in Love**

1464. Forbidden (Columbia; 1932). *Cast:* Barbara Stanwyck, Adolphe Menjou, Ralph Bellamy, Dorothy Peterson, Henry Armetta, Halliwell Hobbes, Charlotte Henry, Tom Ricketts, Thomas Jefferson (final film—d. 1932). *D:* Frank Capra; *Sc:* Capra, Jo Swerling. (1:23)

Romantic drama of a woman who falls for a married man while on a pleasure cruise.

Forbidden Adventure (1931) *see* **Newly Rich**

1465. Forbidden Adventure (Xxxx Xxxx; 1937). Low-budget independent exploitation melodrama dealing with relations between humans and simians. The film had a limited release after a title change from *Love Life of a Gorilla*, a title which the censors would not pass.

Forbidden Alliance *see* **The Barrets of Wimpole Street**

1466. Forbidden Company (Invincible; 1932). *Cast:* John Darrow, Sally

Blane, Josephine Dunn, John St. Polis, Myrtle Stedman. *D:* Richard Thorpe. "Poverty row" melodrama.

1467. Forbidden Heaven (Republic; 1935). *Cast:* Charles Farrell, Charlotte Henry, Phyllis Barry, Beryl Mercer. *D:* Reginald Barker (his final film).

Low-budget tear-jerker.

Forbidden Love *see* **Freaks**

1468. Forbidden Trail (Columbia; 1932). *Cast:* Buck Jones, Barbara Weeks, Mary Carr, Al Smith, George Cooper, Frank Rice, Frank LaRue, Tom Forman, Ed Brady, Wallis Clark, Dick Rush. *D:* Lambert Hillyer; *Sc:* Milton Krims. (1:11) (video)

Buck Jones "range-war" western with comic overtones.

1469. Forbidden Valley (Universal; 1937–38). *Cast:* Noah Beery, Jr., Robert Barrat, Samuel S. Hinds, Frances Robinson, Glenn Strange, Charles Stevens, Fred Kohler, Henry Hunter, Stanley Andrews, Spencer Channing, Margaret McWade, John Ridgely. *D:* Wyndham Gittens; *Sc:* Gittens. (1:07)

B western of an accused man and his son who flee the law to prove the former's innocence of horse stealing. Remade as *Sierra* (Universal-International; 1950).

1470. Forced Landing (Republic; 1935). *Cast:* Edward Nugent, Esther Ralston, Kane Richmond, Onslow Stevens, Toby Wing, Barbara Pepper, Sidney Blackmer, Barbara Bedford, Willard Robertson, George Cleveland, Bradley Page. *D:* Melville Brown; *P:* M.H. Hoffman, Jr.

B aerial murder-mystery.

1471. The Forest Ring (Xxxx Xxxx; 1930). *Cast:* Emily Graham, Isabel Keightley, Marvin Kline, Betty Lancaster, Walter Roach, Lois Shore, Cordelia Spivey. *D:* David Gaither, Kyra Markham; *St:* William de Mille.

1472. Forged Passport (Republic; 1939). *Cast:* Paul Kelly, June Lang, Cliff Nazarro, Lyle Talbot, Maurice Murphy, Billy Gilbert, Dewey Robinson. *D:* John H. Auer; *P:* Auer; *St:* James Webb, Lee Loeb; *Sc:* Loeb, Franklin Coen.

A murder and some smuggled aliens draw the attention of the border patrol in this B.

1473. Forgotten (Invincible; 1933). *Cast:* Lee Kohlmar, June Clyde, William Collier, Jr., Natalie Kingston, Tom Ricketts, Leon (Ames) Waycoff, Selmer Jackson. *D:* Richard Thorpe.

Sentimental drama from "poverty row" of a lonely and forgotten old codger.

1474. Forgotten Commandments (Paramount; 1932). *Cast:* Gene Raymond, Sari Maritza, Marguerite Churchill, Irving Pichel, Edward Van Sloan, John Peter Richmond (John Carradine), Harry Beresford, Helen Carlyle, John Deering, Kent Taylor, Joseph (Sauers) Sawyer, Allen Fox, Florence Shreve, Frankie Adams, William Shawhan, Boris Bullock, Harry Cording. *D:* Louis Gasnier, William Schorr; *St:* Agnes Brand Leahy, James Bernard Fagan.

Low-budget melodrama utilizing footage from Cecil B. de Mille's *The Ten Commandments* (1923) of loose-living youth at a Russian university.

1475. Forgotten Faces (Paramount; 1936). *Cast:* Herbert Marshall (Heliotrope Harry), Gertrude Michael, Robert Cummings, Mary Gordon, (Betty) Jane Rhodes, Arthur Hohl, Robert Gleckler, Pierre Watkin, Ann Evers, James Burke, Alonzo Price, Brian Marlow, Alan Edwards, Dora Clement. *D:* E.A. Dupont; *P:* A.M. Botsford; *Sc:* Marguerite Roberts, Robert Yost, Brian Marlow.

B drama of an ex-con who works as a domestic for the family who adopted his daughter fifteen years earlier. Based on the 1918 story "A Whiff of Heliotrope" by Richard Wasburn Child. First filmed in 1920 as *Heliotrope*, with Frederick Burton. Remade as *Forgotten Faces* in 1928 with Clive Brook and William Powell by director Victor Schertzinger—both for Paramount. Remade in 1942 as *A Gentleman After Dark* with Brian Donlevy for U.A. release.

1476. Forgotten Men (Jewel Prod.; 1933). *Presented by* Public Welfare Pictures Corp.; *Supervised by:* Samuel Cummings.
Documentary.

1477. The Forgotten Million (Xxxx Xxxx; 1932). (No information available)

1478. The Forgotten Woman (Universal; 1939). *Cast:* Sigrid Gurie, William Lundigan, Eve Arden, Elizabeth Risdon, Virginia Brissac, Donald Briggs, Norman Willis, Ray Walker, Joseph Downing, George Walcott, Donnie Dunagan. *D:* Harold Young; *P:* Edmund Grainger; *Sc:* Harold Buchman, Lionel Houser. (1:07)
B melodrama of a woman framed by gangsters who must prove her innocence.

1479. Forgotten Women (Monogram; 1931). *Cast:* Marion Shilling, Rex Bell, Beryl Mercer, Virginia Lee Corbin, Carmelita Geraghty, Edna Murphy, Edward Earle, Jack Carlyle, Edward Kane, G.D. Wood (aka: Gordon DeMain). *D:* Richard Thorpe; *St:* Wellyn Totman; *Sc:* Adele Buffington. (1:07)
"Poverty row" drama set in Hollywood, of several aspiring actresses.

1480. Forlorn River (Paramount; 1937). *Cast:* Buster Crabbe, Ruth Warren, Harvey Stephens, Syd Saylor, June Martel, John Patterson, Robert Homans, Ray Bennett, William Duncan, Chester Conklin, Lew Kelly, Lee Powell. *D:* Charles Barton; *Sc:* Stuart Anthony, Robert Yost. (TV title: *River of Destiny*) (0:56) (video)

B western of ranchers who are harrassed by cattle rustlers. Based on the novel by Zane Grey, it was previously filmed by this studio in 1926 with Jack Holt and Arlette Marchal.

1481. Forsaking All Others (MGM; 1934). *Cast:* Joan Crawford (Mary), Clark Gable (Jeff), Robert Montgomery (Dill), Charles Butterworth (Shep), Billie Burke (Paula), Frances Drake (Connie), Rosalind Russell (Eleanor), Arthur Treacher (Johnson), Tom Ricketts (Wiffens), Greta Meyer (Bella), Eily Malyon. *D:* W.S. Van Dyke; *P:* Bernard H. Hyman; *Sc:* Joseph L. Mankiewicz; *Title Song:* Gus Kahn, Walter Donaldson. (1:24)
Based on the 1933 stageplay by Edward Barry Roberts and Frank Morgan Cavett, this all-star comedy drama was one of the 15 top grossing films of 1935.

1482. .45 Calibre Echo (Xxxx Xxxx; 1932). *Cast:* Jack Perrin, Alec B. Francis, Jimmy Aubrey, George Chesebro. *D:* Xxxx Xxxx.
Jack Perrin western.

1483. 45 Fathers (20th Century-Fox; 1937). *Cast:* Jane Withers, Louise Henry, Leon Ames, Romaine Callender, George Givot, Andrew Tombes, Nella Walker, Thomas Beck, Richard Carle, Hattie McDaniel, Ruth Warren, Sammy Cohen, The Hartmans. *D:* James Tinling; *P:* John Stone; *St:* Mary Bickel, John Kobler; *Sc:* Albert Ray, Frances Hyland.
B juvenile comedy-drama.

1484. Forty Naughty Girls (RKO; 1937). *Cast:* James Gleason (Oscar Piper), Zasu Pitts (Hildegarde Withers), Marjorie Lord, George Shelley, Joan Woodbury, Frank M. Thomas, Tom Kennedy, Alan Edwards, Alden Chase (Stephen Chase), Edward Marr, Ada Leonard, Donald Kerr, Barbara Pepper. *D:* Edward Cline; *P:* William Sistrom; *St:* Stuart Palmer; *Sc:* John Grey. (1:03)
B mystery-comedy of some back-

stage murders investigated by an old maid schoolteacher and her cranky old police inspector friend. Sixth and final entry in the Hildegarde Withers–Oscar Piper mysteries for this studio. The misleading title is actually the name of the stage show.

1485. Forty-Niners (Monarch; 1932). *Cast:* Tom Tyler, Betty Mack, Alan Bridge, Gordon Wood (aka: Gordon DeMain), Fern Emmett, Mildred Rogers, Fred Ritter, Frank Ball, Florence Wells. *D:* John P. McCarthy; *P:* John R. Freuler; *Sc:* F. McGrew Willis. (0:49)

Tom Tyler western of a cowboy who comes to the aid of a wagon train.

1486. Forty-Second Street (WB; 1933). *Cast:* Warner Baxter (Julian Marsh), Ruby Keeler (Peggy Sawyer—in her film debut), George Brent (Pat Denning), Bebe Daniels (Dorothy Brock—a role originally intended for Kay Francis), Dick Powell (Billy Lawler), Guy Kibbee (Abner Dillon), George E. Stone (Andy Lee), Allen Jenkins (MacElroy), Harry Akst (Jerry), Una Merkel (Lorraine Fleming), Ginger Rogers (Anytime Annie), Robert McWade (Al Jones), Ned Sparks (Thomas Barry), Edward J. Nugent (Terry Neil), Clarence Nordstrom (groom in "Shuffle Off to Buffalo"), Henry B. Walthall (actor), Al Dubin & Harry Warren (songwriters), Tom Kennedy (Slim Murphy), Wallis Clark (Dr. Chadwick), Louise Beavers (Pansy), Patricia Ellis (secretary), Toby Wing, Pat Wing, Jack LaRue, Dave O'Brien, Charles (Lane) Levison (film debut), George Irving, Milton Kibbee, Rolfe Sedan, Lyle Talbot, Ruth Donnelly, and as the chorus girls: Gertrude Keeler, Helen Keeler, Geraine Grear (later Joan Barclay), Ann Hovey, Reneé Whitney, Dorothy Coonan, Barbara Rogers, June Glory, Jayne Shadduck, Adele Lacey, Loretta Andrews, Margaret La Marr, Mary Jane Halsey, Ruth Eddings, Edna Callaghan, Patsy Farnum, Maxine Cantway, Lynn Browning, Donna Mae Roberts, Lorena Layson, Alice Jans. *D:* Lloyd Bacon; *Sc:* James Seymour, Rian James, Lucien Hubbard (unc.); *Sound Recording:* (A.A.N.) Nathan Levinson; *Songs:* "42nd Street," "Shuffle Off to Buffalo," "You're Getting to Be a Habit with Me," "Young and Healthy," and "It Must Be June" by Al Dubin and Harry Warren. (1:29) (video—b/w and comp.-colored)

Classic musical with choreography by Busby Berkeley about the problems of putting on a big show. Based on the novel by Bradford Ropes, this became a block-buster for the studio, grossing $2.25 million at the box office and becoming one of the 11 top grossing films of 1933. Released on March 11th, it garnered an A.A.N. for Best Picture (1932–33) and placed #2 on the "10 Best" list of *Film Daily*. Computer-colored by Turner Entertainment in 1986.

Forward March (G.B. title) *see* **The Doughboys**

1487. The Forward Pass (WB/ F.N.; 1929). *Cast:* Douglas Fairbanks, Jr., Loretta Young, Bert Rome, Lane Chandler, Guinn Williams, Allen (Allan) Lane, Marion Byron, Floyd Shackleford, Phyllis Crane. *D:* Edward Cline; *Sc:* H.E. Rogers; *St:* Harvey Gates.

Romantic college football comedy.

1488. Found Alive (Olympic; 1934). *Cast:* Robert Frazer, Barbara Bedford, Edwin Cross, Harry Griffith, Maurice Murphy. *D:* Charles Hutchison; *St:* Captain Jacob Conn.

Low-budget drama.

1489. The Fountain (RKO; 1934). *Cast:* Ann Harding, Brian Aherne, Paul Lukas, Jean Hersholt, Ralph Forbes, Violet Kemble-Cooper, Sara Haden, J.M. Kerrigan, Ian Wolfe (film debut), Christian Rub, Frank

Reicher, Ferike Boros, William Stack, Douglas Wood, Barbara Barondess, Charles McNaughton, Betty Alden, Rich Abbott, Desmond Roberts, Rudolph Amendt. *D:* John Cromwell; *P:* Pandro S. Berman; *Sc:* Jane Murfin, Samuel Hoffenstein. (1:23)

World War I romantic drama of a woman torn between her husband and her lover. A box office flop, it was based on the bestseller by Charles Morgan.

1490. Four Daughters (WB; 1938). *Cast:* Claude Rains (Adam Lemp), Priscilla Lane (Ann Lemp), Gale Page (Emma Lemp) Rosemary Lane (Kay Lemp), Lola Lane (Thea Lemp), John Garfield (A.A.N. for B.S.A. and an Acting Award from the National Board of Review as Mickey Borden), Jeffrey Lynn (Felix Deitz), Dick Foran (Ernest Talbot), Frank McHugh (Ben Crowley), May Robson (Aunt Etta), Vera Lewis (Mrs. Ridgefield), Tom Dugan (Jake), Eddie Acuff (Sam), Donald Kerr (Earl), Wilfred Lucas (doctor), Jerry Mandy, Joe Cunningham. *D:* (A.A.N.) Michael Curtiz; *As.P.:* Henry Blanke; *Sc:* (A.A.N.) Lenore Coffee, Julius J. Epstein; *Sound Recording:* (A.A.N.) Nathan Levinson. (1:30)

Classic drama of small town family life and the romances of four daughters of one family. Based on the story "Sister Act" by Fannie Hurst which appeared in *Cosmopolitan,* the film received an A.A.N. for Best Picture, while placing #10 on the "10 Best" list of the *New York Times.* A box office hit that made an overnight star of John Garfield and brought forth two sequels: *Four Wives* (q.v.) and *Four Mothers* (1940). Remade in 1954 as *Young at Heart.*

1491. Four Days Wonder (Universal; 1937). *Cast:* Jeanne Dante (in her only film), Kenneth Howell, Walter Catlett, Martha Sleeper, Harry Davenport, Alan Mowbray. *D:* Sidney Salkow; *P:* Robert Presnell. (1:00)

B drama of a teen who runs away following the death of her aunt, fearing

she will somehow be blamed. Based on the story by A.A. Milne.

1492. Four Devils (Fox; 1928). *Cast:* J. Farrell MacDonald, Janet Gaynor, Claire McDowell, Charles Morton, Barry Norton, Nancy Drexel, George Davis, Anita (Louise) Fremault, Mary Duncan, Michael Visaroff, Jack Parker, Wesley Lake, Dawn O'Day (Anne Shirley). *D:* F.W. Murnau; *St:* Herman J. Bang; *Cinematographer:* (A.A.N.) Ernest Palmer.

Part-talkie circus story of a high-wire act. No copies are known to remain of this film, but it placed #10 on the "10 Best" list of the *New York Times.*

1493. Four Frightened People (Paramount; 1934). *Cast:* Claudette Colbert, Herbert Marshall, William Gargan, Mary Boland, Leo Carrillo, Nella Walker, Tetsu Komai, Ethel Griffies, Teru Shimada, Chris-Pin Martin, Delmar Costello, Joe de la Cruz, Minoru Nishida, E.R. Jinadas. *D:* Cecil B. De Mille; *P:* De Mille; *Sc:* Bartlett Cormack, Lenore Coffee. (1:18)

To escape a plague, four people leave a ship via lifeboat and upon landing, find that they are forced to trek through a dense jungle to safety. Based on the novel by E. Arnot Robertson, the critics tended to favor this film while the movie-going public did not, making it a box office flop, a rarity for a De Mille film. Filmed on location in Hawaii.

1494. Four Girls in White (MGM; 1938–39). *Cast:* Florence Rice, Alan Marshal, Ann Rutherford, Una Merkel, Buddy Ebsen, Mary Howard, Kent Taylor, Jessie Ralph, Sara Haden, Phillip Terry, Tom Neal. *D:* S. Sylvan Simon; *P:* Nat Levine; *St:* Nathalie Bucknall, Endre Bohem; *Sc:* Dorothy Yost. (1:28)

A hospital drama of four student nurses which climaxes with a spectacular train wreck.

1495. Four Hours to Kill (Paramount; 1935). *Cast:* Richard Barthelmess, Ray Milland, Gertrude Michael, Joe Morrison, Helen Mack, Dorothy Tree, Roscoe Karns, Henry Travers, John Howard, Charles Wilson, Noel Madison, Olive Tell, Craig Reynolds, Paul Harvey, Bodil Rosing, Lee Kohlmar, Lois Kent. *D:* Mitchell Leisen; *P:* Arthur Hornblow, Jr.; *Sc:* Norman Krasna (based on his play "Small Miracle"). (1:14)

Offbeat melodrama of a killer who escapes into a vaudeville theater on the way to his execution.

1496. Four Men and a Prayer (20th Century–Fox; 1938). *Cast:* Loretta Young, Richard Greene, George Sanders, David Niven, William Henry, C. Aubrey Smith, J. Edward Bromberg, John Carradine, Alan Hale, Reginald Denny, Barry Fitzgerald, Berton Churchill, John Sutton, William Stack, Claude King, Frank Dawson. *D:* John Ford; *P:* Kenneth MacGowan; *Sc:* Richard Sherman, Sonya Levien, Walter Ferris. (1:25)

Drama of the effects on the four sons of a murdered man as they try to find the reason for the act. Based on the novel by David Garth, this was the third installment in John Ford's "British in India" trilogy.

1497. Four Sons (Fox; 1928). *Cast:* James Hall, Margaret Mann, Earle Foxe, Charles Morton, Francis X. Bushman, Jr., George Meeker, June Collyer, Robert Parrish, Ruth Mix, Frank Reicher, Hughie Mack, August Tollaire, Ferdinand Schumann-Heink, Archduke Leopold of Austria. *D:* John Ford; *St:* I.A.R. Wylie; *Song:* "Little Mother" by Erno Rapee. (1:40)

In this part-talkie drama which premiered 2/13/28 at the Gaiety Theater in New York, the four sons of a Bavarian widow choose different sides in World War I. A hit film of its day it received *Photoplay*'s Gold Medal Award and placed #4 on the "10 Best" list of *Film Daily*. Remade in 1940.

1498. Four Wives (WB; 1939). *Cast:* Priscilla Lane, Rosemary Lane, Lola Lane, Gale Page, Claude Rains, Jeffrey Lynn, Eddie Albert, May Robson, Frank McHugh, Dick Foran, John Garfield (in a retrospective from *Four Daughters*), John Qualen, Vera Lewis. *D:* Michael Curtiz; *As.P.:* Henry Blanke; *Sc:* Julius J. Epstein, Philip G. Epstein, Maurice Hanline; *Mickey Borden's Theme:* Max Rabinowitz. (1:50)

This sequel to *Four Daughters* (q.v.) has three of the daughters of the Lemp family trying to find a husband for their widowed sister. Suggested by the story "Sister Act" by Fannie Hurst. *Four Mothers,* another sequel followed in 1940.

1499. Four's a Crowd (WB; 1938). *Cast:* Errol Flynn, Olivia de Havilland, Rosalind Russell, Patric Knowles, Walter Connolly, Hugh Herbert, Melville Cooper, Franklin Pangborn, Herman Bing, Margaret Hamilton, Joseph Crehan, Joe Cunningham, Dennie Moore, Gloria Blondell, Carole Landis, George Meeker, Scotty Beckett, Marilyn Knowlden, Renie Riano, Alma Kruger. *D:* Michael Curtiz; *As.P.:* David Lewis; *St:* Wallace Sullivan; *Sc:* Casey Robinson, Sig Herzig. (1:31)

A comedy of mixed-up relationships.

1500. The Fourth Alarm (Ray Johnston; 1930). *Cast:* Nick Stuart. *D:* Philip H. Whitman; *St:* Scott Littleton. "B" fireman drama.

1501. The Fourth Horseman (Universal; 1932). *Cast:* Tom Mix, Margaret Lindsay, Fred Kohler, Rosita Marstini, Raymond Hatton, Buddy Roosevelt, Richard Cramer. *D:* Hamilton MacFadden; *Sc:* Jack Cunningham. (1:03)

In this Tom Mix western, a cowpoke tries to prevent the outlaws from getting a woman's land. The fifth of nine features that Mix did for this studio.

1502. The Fox Movietone Follies of 1929 (Fox; 1929). *Cast:* Lola

Lane, John Breeden, Dixie Lee, Sue Carol, David Rollins, Sharon Lynn, Jackie Cooper (film debut), Stepin Fetchit, Warren Hymer, Robert Burns, Archie Gottler, Melva Cornell, Arthur Stone, Arthur Kay, David Percy, Mario Dominici, DeWitt Jennings, Frank Richardson, Paula Langlen. *D:* David Butler, Marcel Silver; *Sc:* Butler, Wells. (aka: *The William Fox Movietone Follies of 1929*) (G.B. title: *Movietone Follies of 1929*) (1:22)

Musical acts with an all-star cast from the lot of Fox Film with a 2-color technicolor sequence.

1503. Fra Diavolo (MGM/Hal Roach; 1933). *Cast:* Stan Laurel (Stanlio), Oliver Hardy (Ollio), Dennis King (Fra Diavolo), Thelma Todd (Lady Pamela), James Finlayson (Lord Rocburg), Lucille Browne (Zerlina), Arthur Pierson (Lorenzo), Henry Armetta (Matteo), Matt McHugh (Francesco), Lane Chandler (Lieutenant), James E. Morton (woodchopper), Nena Quartero (Rita), Wilfred Lucas (Alessandro), Carl Harbaugh. *D:* Hal Roach, Charles R. Rogers; *P:* Roach; *Sc:* Jeanie MacPherson. (1:30) (Retitled and better known as: *The Devil's Brother*)

Two incompetents become assistants to a notorious bandit. Based on the 1830 opera by Frank Auber, this was Laurel and Hardy's first attempt at "comic opera."

1504. The Frame-Up (Columbia; 1937). *Cast:* Paul Kelly, Jacqueline Wells (Julie Bishop), Ted Oliver, John Tyrrell, Edward Earle, Wade Boteler, George McKay, Raphael (Ray) Bennett, Horace Murphy, Leona Maricle. *D:* D. Ross Lederman; *St:* Richard E. Wormser; *Sc:* Harold Shumate.

B crime melodrama.

1505. **Framed** (RKO; 1930). *Cast:* Evelyn Brent, Regis Toomey, Ralf Harolde, William Holden, Maurice Black, Robert Emmett O'Connor, Eddie Kane, Charles Middleton. *D:* George Archainbaud; *As.P.:* Henry Hobart; *Sc:* Paul Schofield, Wallace Smith. (1:08)

B melodrama of a woman seeking revenge on the police inspector who killed her father.

1506. Frankenstein (Universal; 1931). *Cast:* Colin Clive (Dr. Henry Frankenstein), Mae Clarke (Elizabeth), John Boles (Victor Moritz), Boris Karloff (monster), Edward Van Sloan (Dr. Waldman), Frederick Kerr (Baron Frankenstein), Dwight Frye (Fritz), Lionel Belmore (Burgomaster Vogel), Marilyn Harris (Maria), Michael Mark (Ludwig, Maria's father), Arletta Duncan, Pauline Moore, Francis Ford. *D:* James Whale; *P:* Carl Laemmle, Jr.; *As.P.:* E.M. Asher; *Adaptation:* John L. Balderston; *Sc:* Garrett Fort, Francis Edwards Faragoh. (Sequel: *The Bride of Frankenstein* — q.v.) (1.11) (video)

Classic horror film of a doctor who creates human life, accidentally endowing his creation with a criminal brain. Based on the 1816 book by Mary Wollstonecraft Shelley and the play by Peggy Webling, the film was in nomination at the Venice Film Festival in 1932. It also received a #7 placement on the "10 Best" list of the *New York Times* of 1931, as well as being one of the 15 top grossing films of 1932. First filmed in 1910 by Edison with Charles Ogle playing the monster. Remade in 1957 in Great Britain by Hammer Films as *The Curse of Frankenstein* and again in 1973 as the 2-part TV movie *Frankenstein: The True Story.* Many other variations utilizing the titled character have been made over the years, both in the U.S. and abroad. Prior to release two scenes were censored by the Breen office, with these censored scenes being restored in 1987 to home video prints. The film had a brief release on 11/21/31 but did not receive general release until 1932.

1507. Frankie and Johnnie (RKO; 1934–36). *Cast:* Helen Morgan (her final film), Chester Morris, Lilyan Tashman, Florence Reed, Walter Kingsford. *D:* John H. Auer; *Sc:* Moss Hart. (1:06) (video)

Low-budget musical-drama based on the old folk song. Completed in 1934 with release held up until 1936.

Fraternally Yours (G.B. title) *see* **Sons of the Desert**

1508. Fraternity House (Xxxx Xxxx; 1931). (No information available)

1509. Freaks (MGM; 1932). *Cast:* Wallace Ford (Phroso), Leila Hyams (Venus), Olga Baclanova (Cleopatra), Roscoe Ates (Roscoe), Henry Victor (Hercules), Harry Earles (Hans), Daisy Earles (Frieda), Rose Dione (Madame Tetrallini), Edward Brophy and Matt McHugh (Rollo Brothers), Daisy & Violet Hilton (Siamese twins), Olga Roderick (bearded lady), Prince Randian (Hindu living torso), Johnny Eck (half-torso boy), Schlitzie, Elvira and Jennie Lee Snow (pinheads), Pete Robinson (living skeleton), Koo Coo (bird girl), Joseph-Josephine (half man—half woman), Martha Morris (armless wonder), Frances O'Connor (turtle girl), Angelo Rossito (midget), Michael Visaroff (caretaker Jean), Louise Beavers (maid), Zip and Pip, Elizabeth Green, Albert Conti, Ernie S. Adams. *D:* Tod Browning; *P:* Browning/A Dwain Esper Presentation; *Sc:* Willis Goldbeck, Leon Gordon, Edgar Allan Woolf, Al Boasberg. (aka: *Nature's Mistakes, Forbidden Love* and *The Monster Show*) (1:04) (video)

A one-of-a-kind film of love and close comradship among the freaks of a traveling sideshow which depicts them as human beings with human emotions. Suggested by a short story titled "Spurs" by Tod Robbins which appeared in *Munsey's Magazine* in 1923, this film so repulsed and outraged critics, theater owners and the movie-going public that the studio was forced to withdraw it from circulation. In recent years the film has

been critically acclaimed and attracted a cult following, agreement being that the film was ahead of its time.

1510. Freckles (RKO; 1935). *Cast:* Tom Brown, Virginia Weidler, Carol Stone, James Bush, Lumsden Hare, Dorothy Peterson, Addison Richards, Richard Alexander, George Lloyd, Louis Natheaux, Wade Boteler. *D:* Edward Killy, William Hamilton; *P:* Pandro S. Berman; *Sc:* Dorothy Yost, Mary Mayes.

Americana of a youth who seeks acceptance in a rowdy Indiana lumber camp. First filmed by Paramount in 1917, remade by FBO in 1928, with another remake by Fox in 1960. Based on the 1904 novel by Gene Stratton-Porter.

1511. Free and Easy (MGM; 1930). *Cast:* Buster Keaton (talkie debut), Anita Page, Robert Montgomery, Trixie Friganza, William Collier, Sr., John Miljan, Don Alvarado, Edgar Dearing, Gwen Lee, William Haines (cameo), Jackie Coogan (cameo), Lionel Barrymore (cameo), Cecil B. De Mille (cameo), Fred Niblo (cameo), Edward Brophy, Karl Dane, Dorothy Sebastian, Raquel Torres. *D:* Edward Sedgwick; *Sc:* Al Boasberg, Richard Schayer. (aka: *Easy Go*)

This Hollywood based musical-comedy offers many cameo appearances. A hit for the studio.

1512. Free Love (Universal; 1930–31). *Cast:* Conrad Nagel, Genevieve Tobin, Monroe Owsley, ZaSu Pitts, Slim Summerville, Ilka Chase, Bertha Mann, George Irving, Sidney Bracey, Reginald Pasch. *D:* Hobart Henley; *Sc:* Winifred Dunn, Edwin Knopf. (1:10)

Based on the play "Half Gods" by Sidney Howard, this romantic drama deals with a woman who decides to leave her husband.

1513. A Free Soul (MGM; 1931). *Cast:* Norma Shearer (A.A.N. for B.A.

1930–31 as Jan Ashe), Lionel Barrymore (A.A. for B.A. as Steve Ashe — as well as a lifetime contract with MGM), Leslie Howard (Dwight Winthrop), Clark Gable (Ace Wilfong), James Gleason (Eddie), Lucy Beaumont (Grandmother Ashe), Claire Whitney (Aunt Helen), Frank Sheridan (prosecuting attorney), E. Alyn Warren (Bottomley), George Irving (defense attorney Johnson), Edward Brophy (Slouch), William Stacy (Dick), James Donlan (reporter), Sam McDaniel (valet), Lee Phelps (court clerk), Roscoe Ates, Larry Steers, Henry Hall, Francis Ford. *D:* (A.A.N.) Clarence Brown; *Sc:* John Meehan. (1:31)

A lawyer defends a gambler successfully on a murder charge only to have his daughter succumb to the gambler's charms. Her fiance kills the gambler and the lawyer must also defend him. Based on the novel by Adela Rogers St. John and its dramatization by Willard Mack. Remade by this studio in 1953 as *The Girl Who Had Everything.* The film placed #9 on the "10 Best" list of *Film Daily.*

Free to Live (G.B. title) *see* **Holiday** (1938)

1514. Free, White and 21 (Xxxx Xxxx; 1932). (No information available)

1515. The Freedom (Xxxx Xxxx; 1937). (No information available)

1516. Freighters of Destiny (RKO–Pathé; 1931). *Cast:* Tom Keene, Barbara Kent, Mitchell Harris, Charles "Slim" Whitaker, Frederick Burton, Frank Rice, Billy Franey, William Welsh, Fred Burns. *D:* Fred Allen; *Sc:* Adele Buffington. (1:00)

Tom Keene western dealing with a wagon train harassed by outlaws.

1517. Freshman Love (WB; 1936). *Cast:* Patricia Ellis, Frank McHugh, Warren Hull, Walter Johnson, Joseph Cawthorn, George E.

Stone, Mary Treen, Henry O'Neill, Joe Sawyer, Johnny Arthur, Alma Lloyd, Anita Kerry, Spec O'Donnell, Florence Fair. *D:* William McGann; *P:* Bryan Foy; *Sc:* Earl Felton, George Bricker; *Songs:* M.K. Jerome, Jack Scholl; "Freshman Love," "Collegiana," "That's What I Mean" and "Romance After Dark." (G.B. title: *Rhythm on the River*)

B college comedy of a coach's effort to make a winning football team. Based on the play "The College Widow" by George Ade. A remake of the 1927 film of that title (First National).

1518. Freshman Year (Universal; 1938). *Cast:* William Lundigan, Constance Moore, Dixie Dunbar (final film — retired at 19 to marry), Three Murtha Sisters, Ernest Truex, Three Diamond Brothers, Lucky Seven Choir, Stanley Hughes, Frank Melton, Alan Ladd, Arthur O'Connell (American debut — his second film, making his initial debut in Great Britain). *D:* Frank McDonald; *P:* F. George Bilson; *St:* Thomas Ahearn, F. Maury Grossman; *Sc:* Charles Grayson; *Songs:* "Chasin' You Around" by Frank Loesser and Irving Actman, "Ain't That Marvellous" and "Swing That Cheer" by Joe McCarthy, Harry Barris. (1:05)

Light low-budget college musical.

1519. Friends and Lovers (RKO; 1931). *Cast:* Adolphe Menjou, Lily Damita, Laurence Olivier, Erich Von Stroheim, Hugh Herbert, Frederick Kerr, Blanche Frederici, Vadim Uraneff, Jean Del Val, Dorothea Wolbert, Yvonne D'Arcy, Lal Chand Mehra. *D:* Victor Schertzinger; *P:* William LeBaron; *Sc:* Wallace Smith, Jane Murfin (unc.). (1:07)

Comedy-drama of two friends in the British Indian service who find their friendship is stronger than their love for a widow. Based on the novel "The Sphinx Has Spoken" by Maurice DeKobra, the film flopped at the box office.

1520. Friends of Mr. Sweeney (WB; 1934). *Cast:* Charles Ruggles, Eugene Pallette, Berton Churchill, Robert Barrat, Ann Dvorak, Harry Tyler, William Davidson, Dorothy Tree, Dorothy Burgess, Harry Beresford, Fred MacMurray (film debut — bit). *D:* Edward Ludwig; *P:* Sam Bischoff; *Sc:* Warren Duff, Sidney Sutherland, F. Hugh Herbert, Erwin Gelsey. (1:08)

Hit low-budget comedy based on the book by Elmer Davis of a timid quiet man who undergoes a personality change after meeting an old college chum.

1521. Frisco Jenny (WB/F.N.; 1932–33). *Cast:* Ruth Chatterton, Donald Cook, Louis Calhern, J. Carrol Naish, James Murray, Hallam Cooley, Helen Jerome Eddy, Robert Emmett O'Connor, Pat O'Malley, Harold Huber, Frank McGlynn, Sr., Robert Warwick, Franklin Parker, Sam Godfrey, Berton Churchill. *D:* William A. Wellman; *P:* Ray Griffith; *St:* Lillie Hayward, Gerald Beaumont, John Francis Larkin; *Sc:* Wilson Mizner, Robert Lord. (1:13)

Melodrama of a woman with a past, which is set on the Barbary Coast in San Francisco.

1522. Frisco Kid (WB; 1935). *Cast:* James Cagney, Margaret Lindsay, Ricardo Cortez, Lily Damita, Donald Woods, Barton MacLane, George E. Stone, Joseph King, Addison Richards, Robert McWade, Joseph Crehan, Robert Strange, Joseph Sawyer, Fred Kohler, Edward McWade, Claudia Coleman, John Wray, Charles Middleton, Bill Dale, Alice Lake, Vera Steadman, Helene Chadwick. *D:* Lloyd Bacon; *P:* Sam Bischoff; *Sc:* Warren Duff, Seton I. Miller. (1:17)

Slam-bang actioner set on San Francisco's 19th-century Barbary Coast.

1523. Frisco Waterfront (Republic; 1935). *Cast:* Russell Hopton, Rod La Rocque, Ben Lyon, Helen Twelvetrees, Lee Shumway. *D:* Arthur Lubin.

B melodrama.

1524. From Broadway to Cheyenne (Monogram; 1932). *Cast:* Rex Bell, Marceline Day, Matthew Betz, Huntley Gordon, Roy D'Arcy, Robert Ellis, Gwen Lee, Alan Bridge, Rae Daggett, John Elliott, George Hayes, Earl Dwire. *D:* Harry Fraser; *P:* Trem Carr; *St:* Wellyn Totman; *Sc:* Totman. (G.B. title: *Broadway to Cheyenne*) (1:00)

Rex Bell western of a detective out to stop some New York gangsters from setting up operations out west.

1525. From Headquarters (WB; 1929). *Cast:* Monte Blue, Guinn Williams, Gladys Brockwell, Lionel Belmore, Henry B. Walthall, Ethylyne Clair, Pat Hartigan. *D:* Howard Bretherton; *St:* Samuel Hartridge; *Sc:* Harvey Gates.

Part-talkie action-drama of a group of marines sent to Central America to search for sightseers lost in the jungle.

1526. From Headquarters (WB; 1933). *Cast:* George Brent, Margaret Lindsay, Eugene Pallette, Hugh Herbert, Hobart Cavanaugh, Robert Barrat, Henry O'Neill, Edward Ellis, Dorothy Burgess, Ken Murray, Kenneth Thomson, Theodore Newton. *D:* William Dieterle; *P:* Samuel Bischoff; *St:* Robert N. Lee; *Sc:* Lee, Peter Milne. (1:03)

B police drama which is no relation to the preceding film.

1527. From Hell to Heaven (Paramount; 1933). *Cast:* Carole Lombard, David Manners, Jack Oakie, Adrienne Ames, Sidney Blackmer, Berton Churchill, Rita LaRoy, Bradley Page, Shirley Grey, Verna Hillie, Walter Walker, Cecil Cunningham, Donald Kerr, Nydia Westman, Clarence Muse, Thomas Jackson, Del Henderson, Allen Wood, James Eagles, Bud Flanagan (Dennis O'Keefe). *D:* Erle C. Kenton; *St:* Lawrence Hazard; *Sc:* Sidney Buchman, Percy Heath.

Comedy-drama of a race track bookie and his daughter.

1528. From Nine to Nine (Xxxx Xxxx; 1935). (No information available)

1529. The Front Page (United Artists/Howard Hughes; 1931). *Cast:* Adolphe Menjou (Walter Burns), Pat O'Brien (Hildy Johnson), Mary Brian (Peggy Grant), Edward Everett Horton (Bensinger), Walter Catlett (Murphy), George E. Stone (Earl Williams), Mae Clarke (Molly Malloy), Frank McHugh (McCue), Spencer Charters (Woodenshoe), Matt Moore (Kruger), Slim Summerville, (Pincus), Clarence H. Wilson (Sheriff Hartman), Fred Howard (Schwartz), Phil Tead (Wilson), Eugene Strong (Endicott), Maurice Black (Diamond Louie), Effie Ellsler (Mrs. Grant), Dorothea Wolbert (Jenny), James Gordon (mayor), Richard Alexander (Jacobi), James Donlan (reporter), Lewis Milestone (bit), Herman J. Mankiewicz (bit). *D:* (A.A.N.) Lewis Milestone; *P:* Howard Hughes; *Sc:* Bartlett Cormack, Charles Lederer. (1:43) (video)

Critically acclaimed comedy based on the 1928 play by Ben Hecht and Charles MacArthur which is set in the pressroom of a criminal court. A Caddo production which received an A.A.N. for Best Picture, was voted one of the "10 Best" films of the year by the National Board of Review, as well as placing #6 on the same list of *Film Daily*. Remade three times: *His Girl Friday* (Columbia; 1939-40) (q.v.), *The Front Page* (Universal-International; 1974) and in 1988 as *Switching Channels.*

1530. Front Page Woman (WB; 1935). *Cast:* Bette Davis, George Brent, Roscoe Karns, Winifred Shaw, J. Carrol Naish, Walter Walker, J. Farrell MacDonald, Addison Richards, Selmer Jackson, Joseph King, Georges Renavent, Gordon Westcott, Dorothy Dare, June Martel, Miki Morita, Grace Hayle, Jack Norton. *D:* Michael Curtiz; *P:* Samuel Bischoff; *St:* Richard Macaulay; *Sc:* Laird Doyle, Lillie Hayward, Roy Chanslor. (1:22)

Hit comedy-drama of rival newspaper reporters.

1531. Frontier Days (Spectrum; 1934). *Cast:* Bill Cody (Pinto Kid), Ada Ince, Wheeler Oakman, Franklyn Farnum, Bill Cody, Jr., Lafe McKee, Victor Potel, Bill Desmond, Bob McKenzie. *D:* Robert Hill; *P:* Al Altmont; *Sc:* Jimmy Hawkeye. (1:01)

Bill Cody western of a cowboy wrongly accused of killing a rancher.

Frontier Horizon *see* **The New Frontier** (1938-39) (video title)

1532. Frontier Justice (Diversion; 1935-36). *Cast:* Hoot Gibson, Jane Barnes, Richard Cramer, Franklyn Farnum, Lloyd Ingraham, Joseph Girard, Fred "Snowflake" Toones, Roger Williams, Lafe McKee, John Elliott, George Yeoman. *D:* Robert McGowan; *P:* Walter Futter; *Sc:* W. Scott Darling. (0:58)

Hoot Gibson western of a man who returns to his father's ranch to find skullduggery afoot.

1533. Frontier Marshal (Fox; 1933-34). *Cast:* George O'Brien, George E. Stone, Irene Bentley, Alan Edwards, Ruth Gillette, Berton Churchill, Frank Conroy, Ward Bond, Edward LeSaint, Russell Simpson, Jerry Foster, Richard Alexander. *D:* Lewis Seiler; *Sc:* William Conselman, Stuart Anthony. (1:06)

George O'Brien western of Wyatt Earp and his cleaning up of Tombstone, Arizona. Based on the book "Wyatt Earp, Frontier Marshal" by Stuart N. Lake. Remade in 1939 (see below), in 1946 as *My Darling Clementine* and in 1953 as *Powder River.*

1534. Frontier Marshal (20th Century-Fox; 1939). *Cast:* Randolph Scott, Nancy Kelly, Cesar Romero, Binnie Barnes, John Carradine, Joseph Sawyer, Lon Chaney, Jr., Ward Bond, Edward Norris, Eddie Foy, Jr., Pat O'Malley, Tom Tyler, Harry Hayden, Charles Stevens, Del Henderson, Margaret Brayton, Gloria Roy, Ventura Ybarra, Si Jenks. *D:* Allan Dwan; *P:* Sol M. Wurtzel; *Sc:* Sam Hellman. (1:11)

A remake of the preceding film.

1535. Frontier Pony Express (Republic; 1939). *Cast:* Roy Rogers, Mary Hart (Lynn Roberts), Raymond Hatton, Edward Keane, Noble Johnson, Monte Blue, Donald Dillaway, William Royle, Ethel Wales, Bud Osborne, George (Montgomery) Letz, Fred Burns, Charles King, Jack Kirk, Ernie Adams, Hank Bell, Jack O'Shea. *D:* Joseph Kane; *P:* Kane; *Sc:* Norman Hall. (0:58) (video)

Roy Rogers western set in 1861.

1536. Frontier Scout (Grand National/Fine Arts; 1938). *Cast:* George Houston (starring western debut as Wild Bill Hickok), Al St. John, Beth Marion, Dave O'Brien, Jack Ingram, Charles "Slim" Whitaker, Kenne Duncan, Carl Mathews, Alden Chase (Stephen Chase), Dorothy Fay, Mantan Moreland, Bob Woodward, Jack C. Smith, Walter Byron, Budd Buster, Kit Guard, Minerva Urecal, Frank LaRue, Roger Williams, Joseph Girard. *D:* Sam Newfield; *P:* Franklyn Warner, Maurice Conn; *Sc:* Frances Guihan. (1:01)

B western.

1537. Frontier Town (Grand National/Boots and Saddles; 1938). *Cast:* Tex Ritter, Snub Pollard, Horace Murphy, Ann Evers, Charles King, Forrest Taylor, Jack C. Smith, Ed Cassidy, Karl Hackett, Lynton Brent, Hank Worden, Don Marion, John Elliott, Babe Lawrence, Jimmy LeFieur's Saddle Pals, White Flash the horse. *D:* Ray Taylor; *P:* Edward Finney; *Sc:* Edmund Kelso. (1:00)

Tex Ritter western with songs, a "rodeo days" plot—and much stock footage.

1538. Frontiers of '49 (Columbia; 1938). *Cast:* Bill Elliott, Hal Taliaferro (Wally Wales), Luana de Alcaniz, Charles King, "Slim" Whitaker, Al Ferguson, Jack Walters, Octavio Girard, Carlos Villarias, Jose de la Cruz, Kit Guard, Bud Osborne, Jack Ingram, Ed Cassidy, Lee Shumway, Tex Palmer. *D:* Joseph Levering; *Sc:* Nate Gatzert. (0:54)

Bill Elliott western—his second starring feature—in a story of old California.

1539. The Frontiersman (Paramount; 1938). *Cast:* Bill Boyd (Hoppy), Evelyn Venable, Russell Hayden (Lucky), George "Gabby" Hayes (Windy), William Duncan (Buck Peters), Clara Kimball Young, Roy Barcroft, Dickie Jones, Charles Hughes, Emily Fitzroy, John Beach, George Morrell, Jim Corey. *D:* Lesley Selander; *P:* Harry M. Sherman; *Sc:* Norman Houston, Harrison Jacobs. (1:14) (video—0:58)

The 20th entry in the "Hopalong Cassidy" series, as the Bar 20 boys come to the aid of a school marm.

Frou Frou (G.B. title) *see* **The Toy Wife**

1540. Frozen Justice (Fox; 1929). *Cast:* Lenore Ulric, Robert Frazer, Louis Wolheim, El Brendel, Warren Hymer, Gertrude Astor, Alice Lake, Ullrich Haupt, Tom Patricola, Laska Winter. *D:* Allan Dwan; *Sc:* Sonya Levien.

Outdoor melodrama.

1541. Frozen River (WB; 1929). *Cast:* Rin-Tin-Tin, Davey Lee, Nena Quartero, Josef Swickard, Raymond McKee, Duane Thompson, Frank Campeau. *D:* F. Harmon Weight; *St:* John F. Fowler; *Sc:* Anthony Coldeway.

Rin-Tin-Tin part-talkie, part-barking adventure with Rinty getting the crooks and saving the gold. Rinty's 18th picture for this studio.

1542. The Fugitive (Monogram; 1933). *Cast:* Rex Bell, Cecilia Parker, George Hayes, Robert Kortman, Tom London, Gordon DeMain, Phil Dunham, Theodore Lorch, Dick Dickinson, Earl Dwire, George Nash. *D:* Harry

Fraser; *P:* Paul Malvern; *St & Sc:* Harry O. Jones (Fraser). (0:56)

Rex Bell western.

1543. Fugitive at Large (Columbia; 1939). *Cast:* Jack Holt, Patricia Ellis (final film — ret.), Guinn Williams, Stanley Fields, Leon Ames, Ben Welden, Weldon Heyburn, Don Douglas, Arthur Hohl, Cyrus Kendall, Ernie Adams, Lou Natheaux, Cy Schindell. *D:* Lewis Collins; *St:* Eric Taylor; *Sc:* Taylor, Harvey Gates.

B melodrama.

1544. Fugitive in the Sky (WB; 1936). *Cast:* Warren Hull, Jean Muir, John Litel, Howard Phillips, Carlyle Moore, Jr., Winifred Shaw, Gordon Oliver, Lillian Harmer, Nedda Harrigan, Gordon Hart, Thomas Jackson, John Kelly, Don Barclay, Mary Treen, Joe Cunningham, Charles Foy, Gordon (Bill) Elliott, Spencer Charters. *D:* Nick Grinde; *P:* Bryan Foy; *St & Sc:* George Bricker. (0:57)

B melodrama of a killer's attempt to hi-jack a passenger plane.

1545. Fugitive Lady (Columbia; 1934). *Cast:* Florence Rice (film debut), Donald Cook, Neil Hamilton, Rita La-Roy, William Demarest, Wade Boteler, Clara Blandick, Lucille Ball (bit). *D:* Albert Rogell.

B melodrama.

1546. Fugitive Lovers (MGM; 1933-34). *Cast:* Robert Montgomery, Madge Evans, Nat Pendleton, Ted Healy, C. Henry Gordon, The Three Stooges, Ruth Selwyn, Akim Tamiroff. *D:* Richard Boleslawski; *P:* Lucien Hubbard; *St:* Ferdinand Reyher, Frank Wead; *Sc:* Albert Hackett, Frances Goodrich, George B. Seitz. (1:24) (video)

Among the passengers on a cross-country bus are an escaped prisoner and a runaway dancer.

1547. Fugitive Road (Invincible; 1934). *Cast:* Erich Von Stroheim, Leslie Fenton, Wera (Vera) Engels, Ferdinand Schumann-Heink, Leonid Kinsky. *D:* Frank Strayer; *Sc:* Von Stroheim (co-writer); *Adapt.:* Charles S. Belden, Robert Ellis.

"Poverty row" triangular romantic drama set in World War I.

1548. The Fugitive Sheriff (Columbia; 1936). *Cast:* Ken Maynard, Beth Marion, Edmund Cobb, Walter Miller, Frank Ball, John Elliott, Hal Price. *D:* Spencer Gordon Bennet. (G.B. title: *Law and Order*)

Ken Maynard western, his last for this studio.

1549. Fugitives for a Night (RKO; 1938). *Cast:* Frank Albertson, Eleanor Lynn, Allan Lane, Bradley Page, Russell Hicks, Adrienne Ames, Jonathan Hale, Paul Guilfoyle, Cornelius Keefe, Ward Bond, Jack Arnold (Vinton Haworth). *D:* Leslie Goodwins; *P:* Lou Lusty; *St:* Richard E. Wormser; *Sc:* Dalton Trumbo. (1:03)

B melodrama of an actor and his girl who take it on the lam after a film executive is murdered.

1550. Full Confession (RKO; 1939). *Cast:* Victor McLaglen, Barry Fitzgerald, Sally Eilers, Joseph Calleia, Elizabeth Risdon, Adele Pearce, Malcolm McTaggart, John Bleifer, William Haade, George Humbert. *D:* John Farrow; *P:* Robert Sisk; *St:* Leo Birinski; *Sc:* Farrow, Jerry Cady. (1:13)

B melodrama of a man who confesses his crime of murder to a priest and then waits as an innocent man is convicted of the crime and sentenced to die.

1551. Full of Notions (Xxxx Xxxx; 1931). (No information available)

Funny Face (G.B. title) *see* **Bright Lights** (1935)

1552. A Funny Thing Called Love (Xxxx Xxxx; 1934). (No information available)

1553. The Furies (WB/F.N.; 1930). *Cast:* Lois Wilson, H.B. Warner,

Montagu Love, Jane Winton, Carl Stockdale, Natalie Moorhead, Theodore von Eltz, Tyler Brooke, Dorothy Peterson. *D:* Alan Crosland; *Sc:* Forrest Halsey.

Low-budget melodrama of a young man who believes his mother and her lover are responsible for the death of his father. Based on the play by Zoe Akins.

1554. Fury (MGM; 1936). *Cast:* Spencer Tracy (Joe Wilson), Sylvia Sidney (her only film for this studio as Katherine Grant), Walter Abel (District Attorney), Bruce Cabot (Kirby Dawson), Edward Ellis (Sheriff Hummel), Walter Brennan (Bugs Meyers), George Walcott (Tom Wilson), Frank Albertson (Charlie Wilson), Arthur Stone (Durkin), Morgan Wallace (Fred Garrett), George Chandler (Milton Jackson), Edwin Maxwell (Vickery), Howard C. Hickman (governor), Jonathan Hale (defense attorney), Leila Bennett (Edna Hooper), Roger Gray (stranger), Esther Dale (Mrs. Whipple), Helen Flint (Franchette), Frederick Burton (Judge Hopkins), Carlos Martin (Donelli), Ben Hall (Goofy), Victor Potel (Jorgeson), Clarence Kolb (Pippin), Gertrude Sutton (Mrs. Tuttle), Minerva Urecal (Bessie), Harry Harvey (Anderson), Si Jenks (Uncle Billy), Esther Muir, Edward LeSaint, George Offerman, Jr., Mira McKinney, Frank Sully, Guy Usher, Bert Roach, Raymond Hatton, Ward Bond, Daniel Haynes, William Newell, Eddie Quillan, Syd Saylor. *D:* Fritz Lang (American directorial debut); *P:* Joseph L. Mankiewicz; *Original Story:* (A.A.N.) Norman Krasna; *Sc:* Lang, Bartlett Cormack. (1:34) (video)

A critically acclaimed hit film of it's day as an innocent man becomes the victim of mob rule. It was voted "Best Film of the Year" by the *New York Times,* was in nomination for "Best Film" by the New York Film Critics and placed #4 on the list of "10 Best" films of the National Board of Review.

1555. Fury and the Woman (Rialto; 1937). *Cast:* William Gargan, Molly Lamont, Arthur Kerr, Bob Rideout, David Clyde, Harry Hastings, Libby Taylor, Reginald Hincks, J.P. McGowan, Ernie Impett, James McGrath. *D:* Lewis D. Collins; *Sc:* Philip Conway.

B action melodrama.

1556. Fury Below (Treo Productions; 1938). *Cast:* Russell Gleason, Maxine Doyle, LeRoy Mason, Sheila Terry. *D:* Harry Fraser; *Sc:* Phil Dunham.

B melodrama.

1557. Fury of the Jungle (Columbia; 1934). *Cast:* Donald Cook, Peggy Shannon, Dudley Digges, Harold Huber, Clarence Muse. *D:* Roy William Neill.

Low-budget action melodrama.

G-Man's Wife (G.B. title) *see* **The Public Enemy's Wife**

1558. G-Men (WB/F.N.; 1935). *Cast:* James Cagney (James "Brick" Davis), Ann Dvorak (Jean Morgan), Margaret Lindsay (Kay McCord), Robert Armstrong (Jeff McCord), Barton MacLane (Brad Collins), Lloyd Nolan (Hugh Farrell), William Harrigan (McKay), Russell Hopton (Gerard), Noel Madison (Durfee), Edward Pawley (Danny Leggett), Regis Toomey (Eddie Buchanan), Addison Richards (Bruce J. Gregory), Harold Huber (Venke), Edwin Maxwell (Joseph Kratz), Raymond Hatton, Monte Blue, Mary Treen, Adrian Morris, James Flavin, Emmett Vogan, Ed Keane, Stanley Blystone, Pat Flaherty, James T. Mack, Charles Sherlock, Jonathan Hale, Gordon (Bill) Elliott, Wheeler Oakman, Perry Ivins, Eddie Dunn, Gertrude Short, Frank Marlowe, Marie Astaire, Florence Dudley, Frances Morris, Al Hill, Huey White, Glen Cavender, John Impilito, Bruce Mitchell, Monte Vandergrift, Frank Shannon, Frank Bull, Martha Merrill, Gene Morgan, Joseph DeStefani, Ward Bond, George Daly, Tom Wilson, Henry Hall, Lee Phelps, Marc Lawrence, Brooks Benedict. *D:* William Keighley; *P:* Louis Edelman; *Sc:* Seton I. Miller; *Song:* "You Bother Me an Awful Lot" by Sammy Fain and Irving Kahal. (1:25)

A young lawyer joins the FBI to find the killers of his best friend. Based on Gregory Rogers' (Darryl F. Zanuck) "Public Enemy No. 1," the film is noted for it's fast pace. Re-released in 1949 on the 25th anniversary of the FBI with an added prologue by David Brian and Douglas Kennedy. Computer-colored by Turner Entertainment in 1988.

1559. Gabriel Over the White House (MGM; 1933). *Cast:* Walter Huston, Karen Morley, Franchot Tone, C. Henry Gordon, Samuel S. Hinds, Jean Parker, Dickie Moore, Arthur Byron, Akim Tamiroff, Claire DuBrey, David Landau. *D:* Gregory LaCava; *P:* Walter Wanger; *Sc:* Carey Wilson, Bertram Bloch. (1:27)

A critically praised offbeat fantasy of a crooked politician who becomes president of the United States and begins to reform under mysterious circumstances. Based on the novel "Rinehard" by T.F. Tweed.

1560. Gallant Defender (Columbia; 1935). *Cast:* Charles Starrett, Joan Perry, Harry Woods, George Chesebro, Edward LeSaint, Sons of the Pioneers with Dick Weston (Roy Rogers), Glenn Strange. *D:* David Selman; *St:* Peter B. Kyne; *Sc:* Ford Beebe. (1:00)

Charles Starrett western of cattlemen vs. homesteaders. This was Starrett's first feature for this studio of which 131 more followed, including the "Durango Kid" series which would culminate in 1952 with his last feature *The Kid from Broken Gun.*

1561. The Gallant Fool (Monogram; 1933). *Cast:* Bob Steele, Arletta Duncan, George Hayes, John Elliott, Theodore Lorch, Perry Murdock, George Nash, Pascale Perry. *D:* Robert N. Bradbury; *P:* Trem Carr; *St:* John P. McCarthy; *Sc:* Bradbury, Harry O. Jones (Harry Fraser). (1:00)

Bob Steele in an offbeat western of an accused man who joins a traveling circus.

1562. Gallant Lady (United Artists/20th Century; 1933–34). *Cast:* Ann Harding, Clive Brook, Otto Kruger, Tullio Carminati, Dickie Moore, Janet Beecher (film debut), Betty Lawford, Ivy Merton, Theresa Maxwell Conover, Gilbert Emery, Charles Coleman, Adrienne D'Ambricourt. *D:* Gregory La Cava; *P:* William Goetz, Raymond Griffith; *St:* "Gilbert Emery," Douglas Doty; *Sc:* Sam Mintz. (1:24)

Soaper of a woman who gives her baby up for adoption and years later marries the boy's stepfather after the adoptive mother dies. Remade as *Always Goodbye* (20th Century–Fox; 1938) (q.v.).

1563. Galloping Dynamite (Ambassador; 1937). *Cast:* Kermit Maynard, Ariane Allen, John Merton, Stanley Blystone, John Ward, David Sharpe, Earl Dwire, Francis Walker, Tracy Layne, Bob Burns, Allen Greer, Budd Buster. *D:* Harry Fraser; *P:* Maurice Conn; *Sc:* Sherman Lowe, Charles Condon. (0:58)

Kermit Maynard western of a Texas Ranger out to get the men who killed his brother. The film features Maynard's fancy horsemanship.

1564. Galloping Romeo (Monogram; 1933). *Cast:* Bob Steele, George Hayes, Doris Hill, Frank Ball, Ernie Adams, Lafe McKee, Ed Brady, George Nash, Earl Dwire. *D:* Robert N. Bradbury; *P:* Trem Carr, Paul Malvern; *St:* Bradbury; *Sc:* Harry O. Jones (Harry Fraser). (1:00)

Bob Steele western of a pair of saddle pals who have trouble keeping out of trouble.

1565. Galloping Thru (Monogram; 1931). *Cast:* Tom Tyler, Betty

Mack, Al Bridge, Stanley Blystone, G.D. Wood (Gordon DeMain), John Elliott, Si Jenks, Artie Ortego. *D:* Lloyd Nosler; *P:* Trem Carr; *St & Sc:* Wellyn Totman. (0:58)

Tom Tyler western of a cowboy who returns to the town where he grew up—then his father is murdered.

1566. The Gamblers (WB; 1929). *Cast:* H.B. Warner, Lois Wilson, Jason Robards, Pauline Garon, George Fawcett, Johnny Arthur, Frank Campeau, Charles Sellon. *D:* Michael Curtiz; *Sc:* J. Grubb Alexander.

Stock market drama which was based on a play by Charles Klein.

1567. Gambling (Fox; 1934). *Cast:* George M. Cohan, Wynne Gibson, Dorothy Burgess, Walter Gilbert, Cora Witherspoon, Robert Strange, Joseph Allen, David Morris, Fred Miller, John T. Doyle, Percy Ames, Hunter Gardner, E.J. DeVarney, Harold Healy, Theodore Newton. *D:* Rowland V. Lee; *P:* Harold B. Franklin; *Sc:* Garrett Graham.

Drama which spotlights song 'n' dance man George M. Cohan, based on his own play.

1568. Gambling Lady (WB; 1934). *Cast:* Barbara Stanwyck, Joel McCrea, Pat O'Brien, Claire Dodd, C. Aubrey Smith, Robert Barrat, Philip Reed, Arthur Treacher, Robert Elliott, Willard Robertson, Huey White, Philip Faversham, Arthur Vinton, Ferdinand Gottschalk. *D:* Archie Mayo; *P:* Henry Blanke; *St:* Doris Malloy; *Sc:* Ralph Block, Malloy. (1:06)

B melodrama of a man's family who disapproves after he marries the daughter of a gambler who took his own life.

1569. The Gambling Sex (Monarch; 1932). *Cast:* Grant Withers, Ruth Hall, John St. Polis. *D:* Fred Newmeyer; *P:* John R. Freuler.

"Poverty row" melodrama.

1570. Gambling Ship (Paramount; 1932). *Cast:* Cary Grant, Glenda Farrell, Benita Hume, Roscoe Karns, Jack LaRue, Edward Gargan, Marc Lawrence, Reed Howes, Edwin Maxwell, Charles Williams. *D:* Louis Gasnier, Max Marcin; *St:* Peter Ruric; *Adaptation:* Claude Binyon.

B melodrama of a gambling ship rivalry and a gambler caught in the middle.

1571. Gambling Ship (Universal; 1938–39). *Cast:* Robert Wilcox, Helen Mack, Selmer Jackson, Edward Brophy, Sam McDaniel, Joseph Sawyer, Arthur Vinton, Al Hill, Tim Davis, Dorothy Vaughan, John Harmon, Rudolph Chavers. *D:* Aubrey H. Scotto; *P:* Irving Starr; *St:* George Carleton Brown, Emanuel Manheim; *Sc:* Alex Gottlieb.

B entry in the "Crime Club" series of the owner of a gambling ship who is thought to be a respected member of the community.

1572. The Gambling Terror (Republic-Supreme; 1936). *Cast:* Johnny Mack Brown, Iris Meredith, Charles King, Ted Adams, Earl Dwire, Dick Curtis, Horace Murphy, Bobby Nelson, Frank Ellis, Frank Ball, Budd Buster, Lloyd Ingraham. *D:* Sam Newfield; *P:* A.W. Hackel; *Sc:* George Plympton, Fred Myton. (1:00)

Johnny Mack Brown western of a man out to break up a cattle protection racket.

1573. Gambling with Souls (JDK Productions; 1936). *Cast:* Robert Frazer, Gaston Glass, Myrtle Stedman, Wheeler Oakman. *D:* Elmer Clifton; *P:* J.D. Kendis.

B indie melodrama.

1574. The Game That Kills (Columbia; 1937). *Cast:* Charles Quigley, Rita Hayworth, J. Farrell MacDonald, Paul Fix, Dick Wessel, Arthur Loft, Harry Strang, Bud Weiser. *D:* D. Ross Lederman.

B melodrama dealing with the dangers of ice hockey.

1575. Gang Bullets (Monogram; 1938). *Cast:* Anne Nagel, Robert Kent, Charles Trowbridge, Morgan Wallace, J. Farrell MacDonald, John T. Murray, Arthur Loft, John Merton, Donald Kerr, Carleton Young, Isabelle LaMal, Bennie Bartlett. *D:* Lambert Hillyer; *P:* E.B. Derr; *As.P.:* Frank Melford; *Sc:* John T. Neville. (1:03)

A D.A. is accused of criminal connections in this B melodrama.

1576. The Gang Buster (Paramount; 1930–31). *Cast:* Jack Oakie, Jean Arthur, Wynne Gibson, William "Stage" Boyd, Francis McDonald, Tom Kennedy, Joseph Girard, Harry Stubbs, Ernie Adams, William Morris, Pat Harmon, Constantine Romanoff, Eddie Dunn. *D:* A. Edward Sutherland; *Sc:* Joseph L. Mankiewicz.

An insurance salesman gets involved with a gangland rivalry in this B comedy.

1577. Gang Smashers (Xxxx Xxxx; 1938). (No information available)

1578. Gang War (Film Booking Office; 1928). *Cast:* Jack Pickford (final film — ret.), Olive Borden, Eddie Gribbon, Walter Long. *D:* Bert Glennon; *St:* James Ashmore Creelman; *Sc:* Fred Myton, Edgar Allan Woolf.

Part-talkie crime melodrama.

1579. Gangs of New York (Republic; 1938). *Cast:* Charles Bickford, Ann Dvorak, Alan Baxter, Wynne Gibson, Fred Kohler, Maxie Rosenbloom, Maurice Cass, Willard Robertson, Horace McMahon, John Wray, Harold Huber, Robert Gleckler, Charles Trowbridge, Jonathan Hale, Howard Phillips, Elliott Sullivan. *D:* James Cruze; *St:* Herbert Asbury, Samuel Fuller; *Sc:* Fuller, Charles Francis Royal, Wellyn Totman.

A cop poses as a wanted hoodlum in this hit low-budget gangster melodrama.

1580. Gangster's Boy (Monogram; 1938). *Cast:* Jackie Cooper, Lucy Gilman, Robert Warwick, Louise Lorimer, Tommy Wonder, Selmer Jackson, Bobby Stone, Betty Blythe, Bradley Metcalfe, Huntley Gordon, William Gould, Jack Kennedy, Herbert Evans. *D:* William Nigh; *P:* William T. Lackey; *St:* Robert D. Andrews, Karl Brown; *Sc:* Andrews. (1:20)

A young high school student comes under fire when his father, a former racketeer returns to town.

1581. The Garden Murder Case (MGM; 1936). *Cast:* Edmund Lowe (Philo Vance), Virginia Bruce, Benita Hume, Douglas Walton, Nat Pendleton, H.B. Warner, Gene Lockhart, Frieda Inescort, Henry B. Walthall, Kent Smith (film debut), Jessie Ralph, Grant Mitchell, Charles Trowbridge, Rosalind Ivan (film debut). *D:* Edwin L. Marin; *P:* Lucien Hubbard, Ned Marin; *Sc:* Bertram Millhauser. (1:02)

Philo Vance investigates a series of murders involving hypnotic suggestion in this B mystery. Based on the book by S.S. Van Dine (Willard Wright).

1582. The Garden of Allah (United Artists/Selznick International; 1936). *Cast:* Marlene Dietrich (in a role originally intended for Merle Oberon), Charles Boyer, Tilly Losch, Basil Rathbone, Joseph Schildkraut, Henry (Brandon) Kleinbach, John Carradine, Lucile Watson, C. Aubrey Smith, Charles Waldron, Marcia Mae Jones, Nigel de Brulier, John Bryan, Robert Frazer, Pedro de Cordoba, Helen Jerome Eddy, Alan Marshal (film debut), Ferdinand Gottschalk, Ann Gillis (film debut), Leonid Kinskey, Frank Puglia. *D:* Richard Boleslawski (his final complete film); *P:* David O. Selznick; *Sc:* W.P. Lipscomb, Lynn Riggs; *Music:* (A.A.N.) Max Steiner; *Assistant Director:* (A.A.N.) Eric G. Stacey. (1:25) (video)

A technicolor desert romance which received an A.A. (special plaque) for W. Howard Greene and Harold

Rosson for their color cinematography. Filmed twice before, in 1917 (Selig) with Tom Santschi and Helen Ware and 1927 (MGM) with Ivan Petrovich and Alice Terry. Based on the novel by Robert Hichens.

1583. Garden of the Moon (WB/F.N.; 1938). *Cast:* Pat O'Brien, Margaret Lindsay (in a role originally intended for Bette Davis), John Payne (in a role originally intended for Dick Powell), Melville Cooper, Isabel Jeans, Johnnie "Scat" Davis, Penny Singleton, Jerry Colonna, John Ridgely, Edward McWade, Dick Purcell, Larry Williams, Jimmie Fidler, Mabel Todd. *D:* Busby Berkeley; *As.P.:* Lou Edelman; *Sc:* Jerry Wald, Richard Macaulay; *Songs:* title song, "The Girl Friend of the Whirling Dervish," "Love Is Where You Find It," "Confidentially" and "The Lady on the Two-Cent Stamp" by Al Dubin, Harry Warren and Johnny Mercer. (1:34)

Romantic musical set around the feud between a bandleader and a nightclub owner.

The Gates of Alcatraz (G.B. title) *see* **Those High Grey Walls**

1584. Gateway (20th Century–Fox; 1938). *Cast:* Don Ameche, Arleen Whelan, Gregory Ratoff, Raymond Walburn, Binnie Barnes, Gilbert Roland, John Carradine, Harry Carey, E.E. Clive, Lyle Talbot, Fritz Leiber, Maurice Moscovich, Edward Gargan, Warren Hymer, Mary Gordon, Marjorie Gateson, Gerald Oliver Smith, Russell Hicks, Charles Coleman, Eddie Conrad. *D:* Alfred L. Werker; *P:* Samuel G. Engel; *St:* Walter Reisch; *Sc:* Lamar Trotti. (1:15)

Romantic drama of the difficulties encountered by an Irish girl on Ellis Island.

1585. The Gay Bride (MGM; 1934). *Cast:* Carole Lombard (her only film for MGM), Chester Morris, ZaSu Pitts, Nat Pendleton, Leo Carrillo, Sam Hardy, Gene Lockhart, Walter Walker. *D:* Jack Conway; *P:* John W. Considine, Jr.; *Sc:* Bella and Sam Spewack. (1:20)

Comedy-melodrama of a girl who marries a gangster, becomes a widow, marries another gangster, etc. A box office dud based on the story "Repeal" by Charles Francis Coe.

1586. The Gay Buckaroo (Allied; 1931–32). *Cast:* Hoot Gibson, Merna Kennedy, Roy D'Arcy, Ed Peil, Sr., Charles King, Lafe McKee, Sidney DeGrey, Hoot Gibson Cowboys. *D:* Phil Rosen; *P:* M.H. Hoffman, Jr.; *Sc:* Philip Graham White. (1:01)

Hoot Gibson western of a romantic rivalry.

1587. The Gay Caballero (Fox; 1932). *Cast:* George O'Brien, Victor McLaglen, Conchita Montenegro, Linda Watkins, C. Henry Gordon, Weldon Heyburn, Willard Robertson, Wesley Giraud, Juan Torena, Martin Garralaga. *D:* Alfred Werker; *Sc:* Barry Connors, Philip Klein. (1:00)

George O'Brien western of a football hero who returns to the ranch where he grew up to find cattle rustlers at work. Based on the story "The Gay Bandit of the Border" by Tom Gill.

1588. The Gay Deception (Fox; 1935). *Cast:* Francis Lederer, Frances Dee, Benita Hume, Alan Mowbray, Akim Tamiroff, Lennox Pawle, Richard Carle, Lionel Stander, Luis Alberni, Iris Adrian, Robert Greig, Lenita Lane, Barbara Fritchie, Adele St. Maur. *D:* William Wyler; *P:* Jesse L. Lasky; *St & Sc:* (A.A.N.) Stephen Morehouse Avery, Don Hartman. (1:19)

Light romance of a prince, posing as a doorman, who marries a secretary.

1589. The Gay Desperado (United Artists; 1936). *Cast:* Nino Martini, Ida Lupino, Leo Carrillo, Harold Huber, Mischa Auer, James Blakely,

Stanley Fields, Adrian Rosley, Paul Hurst, Chris-Pin Martin, Allan Garcia, Frank Puglia, Harry Semels, Michael Visaroff, Lew Brixton, Alfonso Pedroza, George DuCount, Travadores Chinacos. *D:* Rouben Mamoulian ("Best Director" from the New York Film Critics); *P:* Mary Pickford, Jesse L. Lasky; *St:* Leo Birinski; *Sc:* Wallace Smith. (1:28)

Hit musical spoof of a gang of desperadoes who are holding an heiress prisoner. Songs include "The World Is Mine Tonight."

1590. The Gay Diplomat (RKO; 1931). *Cast:* Genevieve Tobin, Betty Compson, Ivan Lebedeff, Ilka Chase, Purnell Pratt, Colin Campbell, Arthur Edmund Carewe, Edward Martindel, John St. Polis, Judith Vosselli, George Irving, Rita LaRoy, Onslow Stevens. *D:* Richard Boleslawski; *P:* Pandro S. Berman (his first for RKO); *St:* Benn W. Levy; *Sc:* Doris Anderson, Alfred Jackson. (1:07)

B espionage drama of a Russian officer sent to Hungary to discover the identity of a spy.

The Gay Divorce (G.B. title) *see* **The Gay Divorcee**

1591. The Gay Divorcee (RKO; 1934). *Cast:* Fred Astaire (recreating his stage role as Guy Holden), Ginger Rogers (Mimi Glossup), Alice Brady (Aunt Hortense), Edward Everett Horton (Egbert Fitzgerald), Erik Rhodes (film debut as Rodolfo Tonetti), Eric Blore (waiter), Betty Grable (dancer), Charles Coleman (valet), William Austin (Cyril Glossup), Lillian Miles, George Davis, Alphonse Martell, Paul Porcasi, Charles Hall, E.E. Clive. *D:* Mark Sandrich; *P:* Pandro S. Berman; *Sc:* George Marion, Jr., Dorothy Yost, Edward Kaufman; *Choreographers:* Hermes Pan, Dave Gould, Astaire; *Art-Set Decoration:* (A.A.N.) Van Nest Polglase, Carroll Clark; *Musical Score:* (A.A.N.) Kenneth Webb, Samuel Hoffenstein and musical director Max

Steiner; *Sound Recording:* (A.A.N.) Hugh McDowell, Jr., Carl Dreher; *Songs:* "Night and Day" by Cole Porter, "Looking for a Needle in a Haystack' and "The Continental" (the first song to receive an A.A. for "Best Song" in that newly established category) by Con Conrad and Herb Magidson, "Don't Let It Bother You" and "Let's K-nock K-nees" by Mack Gordon and Harry Revel. (G.B. title: *The Gay Divorce*) (1:47) (video)

Hit musical of its day involving a divorce case and mistaken identity. Based on the novel by J. Hartley Manners and the succeesful 1932 stage musical by Dwight Taylor, Kenneth Webb and Samuel Hoffenstein, the film received an A.A.N. for Best Picture.

The Gay Imposters (G.B. title) *see* **Gold Diggers in Paris**

The Gay Lady (G.B. title) *see* **Lady Tubbs**

The Gay Nineties (G.B. title) *see* **The Floradora Girl**

1592. General Crack (WB; 1929–30). *Cast:* John Barrymore (feature talkie debut), Marian Nixon, Armida, Hobart Bosworth, Lowell Sherman, Julanne Johnston, Jacqueline Logan, Douglas Gerrard, Theodore Lodi, Otto Matieson, Andre De Segurola, Curt Rehfeld. *D:* Alan Crosland; *St:* George Preddy; *Adaptation:* Thomas Broadhurst; *Sc:* J. Grubb Alexander, Walter Anthony.

Lavishly produced swashbuckler.

1593. The General Died at Dawn (Paramount; 1936). *Cast:* Gary Cooper, Madeleine Carroll, Akim Tamiroff (A.A.N. for B.S.A.), Dudley Digges, Porter Hall, William Frawley, Leonid Kinskey, J.M. Kerrigan, Philip Ahn (film debut), Lee Tung Foo, John O'Hara (bit), Lewis Milestone (bit), Clifford Odets (bit). *D:* Lewis Milestone; *P:* William LeBaron; *Sc:* Clifford Odets; *Cinematographer:* (A.A.N.) Victor Milner; *Musical Score:* (A.A.N.) Werner Janssen and musical director Boris Morros. (1:38) (video)

Hit action-drama set in the orient of a mercenary who falls for a female spy while attempting to subdue an evil warlord. Based on the novel by Charles G. Booth.

1594. General Spanky (MGM/ Hal Roach; 1936). *Cast:* "Spanky" Mc-Farland, Phillips Holmes, Billie "Buckwheat" Thomas, Ralph Morgan, Irving Pichel, Rosina Lawrence, Carl "Alfalfa" Switzer, Hobart Bosworth, Louise Beavers, Robert Middlemass, James Burtis, Willie Best. *D:* Fred Newmeyer, Gordon Douglas (directorial debut); *P:* Hal Roach; *St & Sc:* Richard Flournoy, Hal Yates, John Guedel; *Sound Recording:* (A.A.N.) William Randall, Elmer A. Raguse. (1:15)

Comedy of an orphan boy and his involvement in a Civil War battle.

Generals of Tomorrow (G.B. title) *see* **Touchdown Army**

1595. Gentle Julia (20th Century–Fox; 1936). *Cast:* Jane Withers, Marsha Hunt, Jackie Searle, Francis Ford, Hattie McDaniel, George Meeker, Maurice Murphy, Myra Marsh, Jackie Hughes. *D:* John G. Blystone; *P:* Sol M. Wurtzel; *Sc:* Lamar Trotti.

Juvenile comedy-drama based on a story by Booth Tarkington.

Gentleman for a Day (G.B. title) *see* **Union Depot**

1596. The Gentleman from Arizona (Monogram; 1939). *Cast:* John King, J. Farrell MacDonald, Joan Barclay, Craig Reynolds, Ruth Reece, Johnny Morris, Nora Lane, Doc Pardee. *D:* Earl Haley; *P:* Charles E. Goetz; *Sc:* Haley, Jack O'Donnell. (1:11)

Light western filmed in cinecolor of a singing caballero and his efforts to train a wild stallion and a "hot tamale."

Gentleman from California *see* **The Californian**

1597. The Gentleman from Louisiana (Republic; 1936). *Cast:* Charles "Chic" Sale, Eddie Quillan, Charlotte Henry, John Miljan, Holmes Herbert, Marjorie Gateson, Gertrude W. Hoffman, Snub Pollard, Charles C. Wilson. *D:* Irving Pichel.

Horse racing drama.

1598. Gentleman Jim McKee (Xxxx Xxxx; 1936). (No information available)

1599. A Gentleman's Fate (MGM; 1931). *Cast:* John Gilbert, Louis Wolheim (final film – d. 1931), Leila Hyams, Anita Page, John Miljan, Marie Prevost, Frank Reicher, Paul Porcasi, Ralph Ince, Ferike Boros, George Cooper. *D:* Mervyn LeRoy; *Sc:* Leonard Praskins.

Crime melodrama of rival bootleggers who happen to be brothers. Based on the book by Ursula Parrott, the film was a flop.

1600/1601. Gentlemen Are Born (WB/F.N.; 1934). *Cast:* Franchot Tone, Ross Alexander, Nick (Dick) Foran, Jean Muir, Robert Light, Margaret Lindsay, Ann Dvorak, Charles Starrett, Russell Hicks, Arthur Aylesworth, Henry O'Neill, Jane Darwell, Addison Richards, Bradley Page. *D:* Alfred E. Green; *P:* Edward Chodorov; *St:* Robert Lee Johnson; *Sc:* Eugene Solow, Johnson; *Songs:* "Alma Mater," "When You Call the Roll" by Irving Kahal, Sammy Fain. (1:14)

Drama with songs of college graduates attempting to secure jobs.

Gentlemen of the Navy (G.B. title) *see* **Annapolis Farewell**

1602. Gentlemen of the Press (Paramount; 1929). *Cast:* Walter Huston (film debut), Katherine (Kay) Francis (film debut), Charles Ruggles, Betty Lawford, Norman Foster (film debut), Lawrence Leslie, Victor Kilian (film debut — bit), Duncan Penwarden. *D:* Millard Webb; *P:* Monta Bell; *Sc:* Bartlett Cormack.

A newspaper comedy-drama of a reporter whose secretary is also his mistress. Based on the play by theater critic Ward Morehouse, production was accomplished at Astoria Studios in Long Island, N.Y.

1603. George White's Scandals (Fox; 1934). *Cast:* Rudy Vallee, Jimmy Durante, Alice Faye (debut), Adrienne Ames, Gregory Ratoff, Cliff Edwards, Dixie Dunbar (film debut), Gertrude Michael, George White, Warren Hymer, George Irving, Thomas Jackson, William Norton Bailey, Edna Mae Jones, Armand Kaliz, Roger Gray, Edward LeSaint. *D:* George White, Thornton Freeland, Harry Lachman; *P:* Winfield Sheehan; *Sc:* Jack Yellen. (1:19)

Big budget romantic musical highlighted by Alice Faye in her film debut singing "Oh, You Nasty Man." Based on the Broadway show.

1604. George White's 1935 Scandals (Fox; 1935). *Cast:* Alice Faye, James Dunn, Ned Sparks, Lyda Roberti, Cliff Edwards, Arline Judge, Eleanor Powell (in her dancing film debut), George White, Benny Rubin, Jed Prouty, Fuzzy Knight, Jack Mulhall, Lynn Bari, Emma Dunn, Charles Richman, Sam McDaniel. *D:* George White; *P:* Winfield Sheehan; *Sc:* Jack Yellen, Patterson McNutt. (1:23)

A producer brings a group of small-towners to the big city to put on a musical show. A follow-up to the popularity of the preceding film.

1605. Geraldine (Pathé; 1929). *Cast:* Eddie Quillan, Marian Nixon, Gaston Glass, Albert Gran. *D:* Melville Brown.

Low-budget part-talkie romantic comedy, based on a story by Booth Tarkington.

1606. Geronimo (Paramount; 1939). *Cast:* Preston Foster, Ellen Drew, Andy Devine, Gene Lockhart, Ralph Morgan, Marjorie Gateson, Chief Thundercloud (Geronimo), Monte Blue, Addison Richards, Richard Denning, Francis Ford, Akim Tamiroff, William Haade, Kitty Kelly, Henry Brandon, Gaylord (Steve) Pendleton, Eddy Waller, Syd Saylor, Hank Bell, William Henry, Pat West, Pierre Watkin, Ivan Miller, Archie Twitchell, Cecil Kellogg, Philip Warren, Harry Templeton, William Edmunds, Jack Chapin. *D:* Paul Sloane; *Sc:* Sloane. (1:29)

Western remake of *Lives of a Bengal Lancer* (q.v.) with cavalry vs. Indians and much stock footage to save the budget.

Get-Rich-Quick Wallingford (G.B. title) *see* **The New Adventures of Get-Rich-Quick Wallingford**

1607. Get That Girl (Capital; 1932). *Cast:* Richard Talmadge, Lloyd Ingraham, Carl Stockdale. *D:* George Crone.

"Poverty row" production.

1608. Get That Man (Empire; 1935). *Cast:* Wallace Ford, Leon Ames. *D:* Spencer Gordon Bennet.

B melodrama.

1609. Get That Venus (Regent; 1933). *Cast:* Jean Arthur, Harry Davenport. *D:* Grover Lee.

Low-budget comedy.

1610. Ghost City (Monogram; 1931–32). *Cast:* Bill Cody, Andy Shuford, Helen Foster, Walter Miller, Kate Campbell, Charles King, Walter Shumway, Al Taylor, Jack Carlisle, Thomas Curran. *D:* Harry Fraser; *P:* Trem Carr; *St:* Fraser; *Sc:* Wellyn Totman. (1:00)

Bill Cody western of a cowboy coming to the aid of a woman and her mining operation.

The Ghost of John Holling (G.B. title) *see* **Mystery Liner**

1611. Ghost Patrol (Puritan; 1936). *Cast:* Tim McCoy, Claudia Dell, Walter Miller, Wheeler Oakman, Lloyd Ingraham, Dick Curtis, Slim Whitaker. *D:* Sam Newfield; *St:* Joseph O'Donnell. (0:57) (video)

Tim McCoy western with science fiction elements of a scientist who invents a machine which emits a ray that forces mail planes from the sky.

1612. The Ghost Rider (Superior/Argosy; 1935). *Cast:* Rex Lease, Bobby Nelson, Ann Carol, Franklyn Farnum, Lloyd Ingraham, William Desmond, Art Mix, Bill Patton, Denver Dixon, Blackie Whiteford, Roger Williams, Lafe McKee, Eddie Parker. *D:* Jack Jevne; *Sc:* John West (Jevne). (0:56)

Rex Lease western of a phantom rider on the side of law and order.

1613. The Ghost Talks (Fox; 1929). *Cast:* Helen Twelvetrees (film debut), Stepin Fetchit, Carmel Myers, Mickey Bennett, Earle Foxe, Charles Eaton, Joe Brown, Clifford Dempsey, Arnold Lucy, Dorothy McGowan, Baby Mack, Henry Sedley, Bess Flowers. *D:* Lewis Seiler; *St & Sc:* Edward Hammond, Max Marcin.

Low-budget mystery-comedy.

1614. Ghost Town (Commodore; 1936). *Cast:* Harry Carey, Jane Novak, Ruth Findlay, David Sharpe, Ed Cassidy, Earl Dwire, Roger Williams, Lee Shumway, Phil Dunham, Chuck Morrison, Sonny the horse. *D:* Harry Fraser; *P:* William Berke; *Sc:* Monroe Talbot. (1:00)

Harry Carey oater of a cowboy who comes to the aid of a miner plagued by claim jumpers.

1615. Ghost Town Gold (Republic; 1936). *Cast:* Bob Livingston (Stony Brooke), Ray Corrigan (Tucson Smith), Max Terhune (with Elmer—as Lullaby Joslin), Kay Hughes, Yakima Canutt, LeRoy Mason, Frank Hagney, Burr Carruth, Bob Kortman, Milburn Morante, Horace Murphy, Earle Hodgins, Ed Peil, Sr., Harry Harvey, Hank Worden, Bud Osborne, Bob Burns, I. Stanford Jolley, Wally West. *D:* Joseph Kane; *Sc:* John Rathmell, Oliver Drake. (0:54) (video)

"Three Mesquiteers" western (the second in the series) involving a gang of outlaws who hide their loot in a ghost town.

1616. Ghost Town Riders (Universal; 1938). *Cast:* Bob Baker, Fay Shannon, George Cleveland, Hank Worden, Forrest Taylor, Glenn Strange, Jack Kirk, Martin Turner, Reed Howes, Murdock McQuarrie, Merrill McCormack, George Morrell, Oscar Gahan, Frank Ellis, Tex Phelps. *D:* George Waggner; *P:* Trem Carr; *Sc:* Joseph West (Waggner). (0:54)

Bob Baker western of two cowboys who encounter outlaws planning a fake gold boom in a ghost town.

1617. The Giant Swing (Xxxx Xxxx; 1931). (No information available)

1618. Ghost Valley (RKO-Pathé; 1932). *Cast:* Tom Keene, Merna Kennedy, Mitchell Harris, Billy Franey, Harry Bowen, Kate Campbell, Ted Adams, George Hayes. *D:* Fred Allen; *As.P.:* Harry Joe Brown; *St & Sc:* Adele Buffington. (0:54)

Tom Keene western of a girl who inherits a ghost town, not knowing it contains a gold mine.

1619. The Ghost Walks (Chesterfield; 1934-35). *Cast:* John Miljan, June Collyer (her final film before retiring to become Mrs. Stuart Erwin), Richard Carle, Sally Blane, Henry Kolker, Spencer Charters, Johnny Arthur, Eve

Southern, Douglas Gerrard, Wilson Benge, Donald Kirke. *D:* Frank Strayer; *Sc:* Charles S. Belden. (1:10)

"Poverty row" comedy-thriller set in an old dark house.

1620. The Gift of Gab (Universal; 1934). *Cast:* Edmund Lowe, Gloria Stuart, Ruth Etting, Phil Baker, Alexander Woollcott, Ethel Waters, Victor Moore, Boris Karloff, Bela Lugosi, Paul Lukas, Chester Morris, Binnie Barnes, Douglass Montgomery, Winifred Shaw, Gene Austin, Ted Healy and His Stooges (Moe, Larry and Curly), Helen Vinson, Alice White, Henry Armetta, Andy Devine, Douglas Fowley, Gus Arnheim and his orchestra, Sterling Holloway, Edwin Maxwell, John Miller, Warner Richmond, Tammany Young, Maurice Black, James Flavin, Richard Elliott, Marion Byron, Tom Hanlon, Sid Walker, Hugh O'Connell, Billy Barty, Florence Enright, Leighton Noble. *D:* Karl Freund; *St:* Jerry Wald, Philip G. Epstein; *Sc:* Rian James, Lou Breslow; *Songs:* title song, "Talking to Myself" by Herb Magidson, Con Conrad, "Somebody Looks Good" George Whiting, Albert von Tilzer, "Walkin' on Air" by von Tilzer, Jack Meskill. (1:11)

Musical-comedy-drama of a conceited radio announcer.

1621. Gigolette (RKO/Select; 1935). *Cast:* Adrienne Ames, Donald Cook, Ralph Bellamy, Robert Armstrong, Harold Waldridge, Robert T. Haines, Grayce Hampton, Gilbert Roland. *D:* Charles Lamont; *As.P.:* Burt Kelly; *St & Sc:* Gordon Kahn. (G.B. title: *Night Club*)

Low-budget romantic drama involving misunderstandings.

1622. Gigolettes of Paris (Equitable; 1933). *Cast:* Gilbert Roland, Jetta Goudal (final film—ret.). *D:* Alphonse Martell. (G.B. title: *Tarnished Youth*)

Low-budget romantic melodrama.

1623. The Gilded Lily (Paramount; 1935). *Cast:* Claudette Colbert, Fred MacMurray, Ray Milland, C. Aubrey Smith, Edward Craven, Luis Alberni, Donald Meek, Warren Hymer, Charles Wilson, Leonid Kinskey, Jack Norton, Michelette Burani, Ferdinand Munier, Claude King, Charles Irwin. *D:* Wesley Ruggles; *P:* Albert Lewis; *St:* Jack Kirkland, Melville Baker; *Sc:* Claude Binyon. (1:20)

Romance of a woman who has to choose between two men. Voted one of the year's "10 Best" films by the National Board of Review, it was previously filmed in 1921 by this studio with Mae Murray and Lowell Sherman.

1624. Ginger (Fox; 1935). *Cast:* Jane Withers, Jackie Searle, Katherine Alexander, O.P. Heggie, Walter Woolf King. *D:* Lewis Seiler; *P:* Sol M. Wurtzel; *St & Sc:* Arthur Kober.

Hit B juvenile comedy-drama.

1625. The Girl and the Gambler (RKO; 1939). *Cast:* Leo Carrillo, Steffi Duna, Tim Holt, Donald MacBride, Chris-Pin Martin, Edward Raquello, Paul Fix, Julian Rivero, Frank Puglia, Esther Muir, Paul Sutton, Charles Stevens, Frank Lackteen. *D:* Lew Landers; *P:* Cliff Reid; *Sc:* Joseph Fields, Clarence Upson Young; *Songs:* Aaron Gonzales. (1:03)

Post turn-of-the-century low-budget western of a Mexican bandit who kidnaps a saloon dancer to win a bet. Previously filmed as *The Dove* (United Artists; 1928) and *Girl of the Rio* (RKO; 1932) (q.v.). Based on Willard Mack's play "The Dove."

1626. Girl Crazy (RKO; 1932). *Cast:* Bert Wheeler, Robert Woolsey, Dorothy Lee, Eddie Quillan, Stanley Fields, Arline Judge, Mitzi Green, Lita Chevret, Creighton (Lon) Chaney (Jr.), Chris-Pin Martin, Kitty Kelly, Dick Curtis, Brooks Benedict. *D:* William A. Seiter; *P:* William LeBaron; *Sc:* Herman J. Mankiewicz, Eddie Welch, Walter De Leon, Tim Whelan; *Songs:* George and Ira Gershwin.

A flop big budget comedy farce of guys trying to forget girls. Based on the play by Guy Bolton and Jack McGowan, the rights were sold to MGM who remade it in 1943 as a Mickey Rooney–Judy Garland vehicle, with songs added. *When the Boys Meet the Girls* was a 1965 remake.

1627. The Girl Downstairs (MGM; 1938–39). *Cast:* Franchot Tone, Franciska Gaal (her last of three American films), Walter Connolly, Rita Johnson, Reginald Owen, Reginald Gardiner, Franklin Pangborn, Robert Coote, Barnett Parker, Billy Gilbert, James B. Carson. *D:* Norman Taurog; *P:* Harry Rapf; *Sc:* Harold Goldman, Felix Jackson, Karl Noti. (1:17)

Romantic comedy of a rich bachelor in Europe.

1628. The Girl Friend (Columbia; 1935). *Cast:* Roger Pryor, Ann Sothern, Jack Haley, Victor Kilian, Thurston Hall, Inez Courtney, Margaret Seddon, Ray Walker. *D:* Edward Buzzell; *St:* Gene Towne, Graham Baker; *Sc:* Benny Rubin, Gertrude Purcell.

Comedy with music.

1629. The Girl from Calgary (Monogram; 1932). *Cast:* Fifi D'Orsay, Paul Kelly, Robert Warwick, Edwin Maxwell, Astrid Allwyn, Eddie Fetherston. *D:* Phil Whitman, Leon D'Usseau; *P:* I.E. Chadwick; *St:* D'Usseau, Sig Schlager; *Sc:* Lee Chadwick. (1:04)

"Poverty row" musical of a press agent who turns a girl into a Broadway star. This film utilizes footage from *The Great Gabbo* (q.v.) with several sequences in a process called magnacolor.

1630. The Girl from Chicago (Micheaux; 1933). *Produced, Directed and Written by:* Oscar Micheaux.

Low-budget independent production.

1631. The Girl from Havana (Fox; 1929). *Cast:* Lola Lane, Paul Page,

Warren Hymer, Natalie Moorhead, Kenneth Thomson, Adele Windsor, Dorothy Brown, Marcia Chapman, Raymond Lopez, Juan Sedillo. *D:* Benjamin Stoloff; *St & Sc:* Edwin Burke, John Stone.

Low-budget comedy.

1632. The Girl from Mandalay (Republic; 1936). *Cast:* Esther Ralston, Donald Cook, Conrad Nagel. *D:* Howard Bretherton.

Low-budget drama.

The Girl from Mexico (G.B. title) *see* **Mexicali Rose** (1929–30)

1633. The Girl from Mexico (RKO; 1939). *Cast:* Lupe Velez (Carmelita Fuentes), Donald Woods (Dennis), Linda Hayes (Elizabeth), Leon Errol (Uncle Matt), Elizabeth Risdon (Aunt Della), Donald MacBride, Edward Raquello, Ward Bond. *D:* Leslie Goodwins; *P:* Robert Sisk; *St:* Lionel Houser; *Sc:* Houser, Joseph A. Fields. (1:11)

Hit screwball B comedy of a brunette bombshell with a penchant for trouble who catches the eye of an ad man looking for a singer. This was followed by seven more films which became the "Mexican Spitfire" series which ran into the early 1940s.

1634. The Girl from Missouri (MGM; 1934). *Cast:* Jean Harlow, Franchot Tone, Lionel Barrymore, Lewis Stone, Patsy Kelly, Alan Mowbray, Clara Blandick, Henry Kolker, Hale Hamilton, Nat Pendleton, Douglas Fowley. *D:* Jack Conway; *P:* Bernard Hyman; *Sc:* John Emerson, Anita Loos. (G.B. title: *100% Pure*) (1:15)

Comedy of a virtuous girl who is determined to stay that way until the right Mr. Big-Bucks comes along.

1635. The Girl from Scotland Yard (Paramount/Major Productions; 1937). *Cast:* Karen Morley, Robert Baldwin, Katherine Alexander, Eduardo Ciannelli, Bud Flanagan (Dennis O'Keefe), Milli Monti, Lloyd Crane (Jon Hall), Odette Myrtil, Lynn Anders, Alphonse Martel, Philip Sleeman, Don Brodie. *D:* Robert Vignola (final film—ret.); *P:* Emanuel Cohen; *St:* Conigsby Dawson; *Sc:*Doris Anderson, Dore Schary. (1:02)

Minor fantasy style melodrama of a Scotland Yard girl who is trying to stop a madman with a death ray.

The Girl from State Street (G.B. title) *see* **State Street Sadie**

1636. The Girl from 10th Avenue (WB/F.N.; 1935). *Cast:* Bette Davis, Ian Hunter (American debut), Colin Clive, Alison Skipworth, Katherine Alexander, John Eldredge, Philip Reed, Heinie Conklin, Phil Regan, Helen Jerome Eddy, Gordon (Bill) Elliott, André Cheron, Edward McWade, Adrian Rosley. *D:* Alfred E. Green; *P:* Henry Blanke; *Sc:* Charles Kenyon. (G.B. title: *Men on Her Mind*) (1:09)

After being jilted by his intended a lawyer gets drunk and marries another only to find his original love wants him back. Though it sounds as though it ought to be a comedy, the film is actually a serious drama. Based on the play by Hubert Henry Davies.

1637. Girl from Rio (Monogram; 1939). *Cast:* Movita, Warren Hull, Alan Baldwin, Kay Linaker, Clay Clement, Adele Pearce, Soledad Jimenez, Richard Tucker, Dennis Moore, Byron Foulger. *D:* Lambert Hillyer; *P:* E.B. Derr; *Sc:* Milton Raison, John T. Neville. (1:02)

B melodrama of a girl who must come to New York from South America to clear her brother's name when he is accused of arson and murder.

1638. The Girl from Woolworth's (WB/F.N.; 1929). *Cast:* Alice White, Charles Delaney, Wheeler Oakman, Ben Hall, Rita Flynn. *D:* William Beaudine; *Sc:* Adele Comman-

dini, Richard Weil, Edward Luddy; *Song:* "Crying for Love" by Al Bryan, George W. Meyer.

Low-budget musical about a singing salesgirl.

1639. The Girl Habit (Paramount; 1931). *Cast:* Charles Ruggles, Sue Conroy, Tamara Geva, Margaret Dumont, Donald Meek, Betty Garde, Allen Jenkins (film debut), Jerome Daley, Douglas Gilmore, Paulette Goddard (bit). *D:* Edward Cline; *St:* A.E. Thomas, Clayton Hamilton; *Sc:* Owen Davis, Gertrude Purcell.

B comedy of a man-about-town who has his marriage interrupted by an old flame. A remake of *Thirty Days* (Paramount; 1922) with Wallace Reid and Wanda Hawley.

The Girl I Made (G.B. title) *see* **Made on Broadway**

1640. Girl in Danger (Columbia; 1934). *Cast:* Shirley Grey, Ralph Bellamy, J. Carrol Naish, Vincent Sherman, Ward Bond. *D:* D. Ross Lederman.

B melodrama.

1641. The Girl in 419 (Paramount; 1933). *Cast:* Gloria Stuart, David Manners, James Dunn, Vince Barnett, Kitty Kelly, William Harrigan, Johnny Hines, Effie Ellsler, Hal Price, Clarence Wilson, Gertrude Short. *D:* Alexander Hall, George Somnes; *P:* B.P. Schulberg; *St:* Jules Furthman; *Sc:* P.J. Wolfson, Allen Rivkin, Manuel Seff.

B hospital mystery of an assaulted female patient who won't divulge what happened to her.

The Girl in Pawn (G.B. title) *see* **Little Miss Marker**

1642. The Girl in the Glass Cage (WB/F.N.; 1929). *Cast:* Loretta Young, Carroll Nye, Ralph Lewis, Mathew Betz, George E. Stone, Lucien Littlefield. *D:* Ralph Dawson; *St:* George Kibbe Turner; *Sc:* James Gruen.

Part-talkie drama of a moviebox cashier with problems.

1643. The Girl in the Show (MGM; 1930). *Cast:* Bessie Love, Raymond Hackett, Edward Nugent, Mary Doran, Jed Prouty, Ford Sterling, Nanci Price, Lucy Beaumont, Richard Carlyle, Alice Moe, Frank Nelson, Jack McDonald, Ethel Wales, John F. Morrissey. *D:* Edgar Selwyn (directorial debut); *Adaptation and Additional Dialogue:* Selwyn. (1:21)

Drama of a touring company which travels the country putting on productions of "Uncle Tom's Cabin." Based on the play "Eva the Fifth" by John Kenyon Nicholson and John Golden.

1644. The Girl Is Mine (Xxxx Xxxx; 1934). (No information available)

1645. Girl Loves Boy (Grand National; 1937). *Cast:* Cecilia Parker, Eric Linden, Dorothy Peterson, Roger Imhof, Pedro de Cordoba, Bernadene Hayes, Otto Hoffman, Patsy O'Connor, Rollo Lloyd, Buster Phelps, John T. Murray, Spencer Charters, Sherwood Bailey, Edwin Mordant, Jameson Thomas. *D:* Duncan Mansfield; *P:* B.F. Zeidman; *St:* Karl Brown, Hinton Smith; *Sc:* Mansfield, Carroll Graham. (1:17)

B Americana of life and love in a rural community.

1646. Girl Missing (WB; 1933). *Cast:* Ben Lyon, Glenda Farrell, Mary Brian, Lyle Talbot, Peggy Shannon, Edward Ellis, Guy Kibbee, Harold Huber, Ferdinand Gottschalk, Helen Ware, Louise Beavers, Fred Kelsey, George Pat Collins, Bud Flanagan (Dennis O'Keefe). *D:* Robert Florey; *P:* Henry Blanke; *Sc:* Carl Erickson, Don Mullaly, Ben Markson.

B mystery-melodrama of shady goings-on at a Palm Beach hotel. Based on a story by S.S. Van Dine (Willard Wright). A dud at the box office.

1647. Girl o' My Dreams (Monogram; 1934). *Cast:* Eddie Nugent, Mary Carlisle, Creighton (Lon) Chaney (Jr.), Arthur Lake, Sterling Holloway, Gigi Parrish, Jeanie Roberts, Tom Dugan, Lee Shumway, Beverly Crane, Betty Mae Crane, George Cleveland, Ted Dahl and his orchestra. *D:* Ray McCarey; *P:* William T. Lackey; *Sc:* George Waggner. (1:05)

"Poverty row" collegiate comedy-drama involving a conceited athlete.

Girl of My Dreams (G.B. title) *see* **The Sweetheart of Sigma Chi** (1933)

1648. Girl of the Golden West (WB/F.N.; 1930). *Cast:* Ann Harding (Minnie), James Rennie (Johnson), Harry Bannister (Jack Rance), Ben Hendricks, Jr., J. Farrell MacDonald, George Cooper, Arthur Stone, Johnnie Walker, Joseph Girard, Richard Carlyle, Arthur Housman. *D:* John Francis Dillon; *P:* Robert North; *Sc:* Waldemar Young. (1:21)

Western romance based on the Broadway play by David Belasco. Previously filmed by Lasky in 1914–15, with House Peters and Mabel Van Buren, and by First National in 1923 with Sylvia Breamer and J. Warren Kerrigan by director Edwin Carewe. Remade in 1938 (see below).

1649. Girl of the Golden West (MGM; 1938). *Cast:* Jeanette MacDonald (Mary Robbins), Nelson Eddy (Ramerez "Lt. Johnson"), Walter Pidgeon (Sheriff Jack Rance), Leo Carrillo (Mosquito), Buddy Ebsen (Alabama), Leonard Penn (Pedro), H.B. Warner (Father Sienna), Noah Beery (general), Priscilla Lawson (Nina Martinez), Monty Woolley (governor), Bob Murphy (Sonora Slim), Olin Howland (Trinidad Joe), Cliff Edwards (Minstrel Joe), Billy Bevan (Nick), Brandon Tynan (professor), Charley Grapewin (Uncle Davy), Bill Cody, Jr. (Gringo), Jeanne Ellis (girl Mary), Ynez Seabury (Wowkle), Victor Potel (stage driver), Nick Thompson (Billy Jack Rabbit),

Tom Mahoney (Handsome Charlie), Phillip Armenta (Long Face), Gene Coogan (Manuel), Sergei Arabeloff (Jose), Alberto Morin (Juan), Joe Dominguez (Felipe), Frank McGlynn (Pete), Cy Kendall (Hank), Hank Bell (deputy), Walter Bonn (Lieut. Johnson), Richard Tucker (colonel), Chief Big Tree, Russell Simpson, Armand "Curley" Wright, Pedro Regas, E. Alyn Warren, Francis Ford, Virginia Howell. *D:* Robert Z. Leonard; *P:* William Anthony McGuire; *Sc:* Isabel Dawn, Boyce DeGaw; *Songs:* "Mariachi," "There's a Brand New Song in Town," "The Golden West," "The West Ain't Wild Anymore," "Señorita," "Soldiers of Fortune," "Who Are We to Say?" and "From Sun-Up to Sundown" by Sigmund Romberg and Gus Kahn. (2:00) (video)

Photographed in sepia tones by Oliver Marsh, this remake of the preceding film has added songs by Sigmund Romberg and Gus Kahn along with "Ave Maria" by Charles Gounod. One of the 15 top grossing films of 1937–38.

1650. A Girl of the Limberlost (Monogram; 1934). *Cast:* Louise Dresser (Mrs. Comstock), Marian Marsh (Elnora Comstock), Ralph Morgan, Henry B. Walthall, Edward Nugent, Helen Jerome Eddy, Gigi Parrish, Betty Blythe, Robert Ellis (Mr. Comstock — final film d. 1935), Barbara Bedford, Tommy Bupp. *D:* Christy Cabanne; *P:* William T. Lackey; *Sc:* Adele Commandini. (1:16)

Low-budget rural drama of an unwanted and unloved girl who finds happiness with a neighboring family. Based on the 1909 novel by Gene Stratton-Porter.

1651. Girl of the Ozarks (Paramount; 1936). *Cast:* Virginia Weidler, Leif Erickson, Elizabeth Russell, Henrietta Crosman, Arthur Aylesworth. *D:* William Shea; *P:* A.M. Botsford.

B rural drama of a little girl from a poor family who is helped by the town's newspaper.

1652. Girl of the Port (RKO; 1929–30). *Cast:* Reginald Sharland, Sally O'Neil, Mitchell Lewis, Arthur Clayton, Crauford Kent, Duke Kahanamoko, Gerald Barry, Renée Macready, John Webb Dillon. *D:* Bert Glennon; *As.P.:* Bertram Millhauser; *St:* John Russell; *Sc:* Beulah Marie Dix; *Dialogue:* Frank Reicher. (1:09)

Romantic melodrama of an English lord who falls for an Irish showgirl. Filmed on location on the South Sea isle of Fiji.

1653. Girl of the Rio (RKO; 1932). *Cast:* Dolores Del Rio, Norman Foster, Leo Carrillo, Ralph Ince, Stanley Fields, Lucile Gleason, Edna Murphy, Frank Campeau. *D:* Herbert Brenon; *As.P.:* Louis Sarecky; *Sc:* Elizabeth Meehan; *Song:* "Guerida" by Victor Schertzinger. (G.B. title: *The Dove*) (1:09)

South-of-the-border romance of a cafe entertainer and an American. Based on the play "The Dove" by Willard Mack which was a Broadway success by producer David Belasco. Mack's play was based on a magazine short story by Gerald Beaumont. This film was a box office flop, but was previously filmed in 1928 as a success with Gloria Swanson. Remade as *The Girl and the Gambler* (q.v.).

1654. The Girl on the Barge (Universal; 1929). *Cast:* Sally O'Neil, Jean Hersholt, Malcolm McGregor, Henry West, J. Francis Robertson, Rupert Hughes, Nancy Kelly, Morris McIntosh, George Offerman, Jr. *D:* Edward Sloman; *Sc:* Charles Kenyon, Nan Cochrane, Tom Reed, Charles H. Smith.

Part-talkie romantic drama.

1655. The Girl on the Front Page (Universal; 1936). *Cast:* Gloria Stuart, Edmund Lowe, Reginald

Owen, Spring Byington, Gilbert Emery, Robert Gleckler, David Oliver, Clifford Jones, Maxine Reiner. *D:* Harry Beaumont; *P:* Charles R. Rogers; *Sc:* Austin Parker, Albert R. Perkins, Alice Duer Miller. (1:15)

B newspaper story.

1656. Girl Overboard (Universal; 1929). *Cast:* Fred Mackaye, Mary Philbin, Edmund Breese, Otis Harlan, Francis McDonald. *D:* Wesley Ruggles.

Part-talkie melodrama of a prison parolee who saves a girl from drowning.

1657. Girl Overboard (Universal; 1937). *Cast:* Gloria Stuart, Walter Pidgeon, Sidney Blackmer, Hobart Cavanaugh, Billy Burrud, Robert Emmett O'Connor, David Oliver, Charlotte Wynters, Edward McNamara, Jack Smart, Gerald Oliver Smith. *D:* Sidney Salkow; *P:* Robert Presnell; *St:* Sarah Elizabeth Rodger; *Sc:* Tristram Tupper. (0:58)

B shipboard drama of a girl accused of murder. No relation to the preceding film of the same name.

1658. The Girl Said No (MGM; 1930). *Cast:* William Haines, Leila Hyams, Marie Dressler, Polly Moran, Francis X. Bushman, Jr., William Janney, Frank (Junior) Coghlan, William V. Mong, Phyllis Crane, Clara Blandick, Edward Brophy, Wilbur Mack. *D:* Sam Wood; *St:* A.P. Younger; *Sc:* Charles MacArthur, Sarah Y. Mason.

Low-budget comedy of a college football hero who continues his carefree lifestyle after he graduates.

1659. The Girl Said No (Grand National; 1937). *Cast:* Paula Stone, Robert Armstrong, Irene Hervey, Vivian Hart, William Danforth, Holmes Herbert, Gwili Andre, Josef Swickard, Max Davidson, Horace Murphy, Bert Roach, Harry Tyler, Mildred Rogers, Arthur Kay, Vera Ross, Carita Crawford, Allan Rogers, Frank Moulan, Richard Tucker. *D:* Andrew L. Stone;

P: Stone; *St:* Stone; *Sc:* Robert Lively, Betty Laidlaw; *Songs:* Gilbert and Sullivan; *Sound Recording:* (A.A.N.) A.E. Kaye. (1:16)

Musical romance.

1660. The Girl Who Came Back (Chesterfield; 1935). *Cast:* Shirley Grey, Noel Madison, Sidney Blackmer, Matthew Betz. *D:* Charles Lamont.

"Poverty row" melodrama.

1661. A Girl with Ideas (Universal; 1937). *Cast:* Walter Pidgeon, Wendy Barrie, Kent Taylor, George Barbier, Dorothea Kent, Ted Osborne, Henry Hunter, Samuel S. Hinds, Edward Gargan, Horace MacMahon, George Humbert, Norman Willis. *D:* S. Sylvan Simon (directorial debut); *St:* William Rankin; *Sc:* Bruce Manning, Robert T. Shannon. (G.B. title: *Mightier Than the Sword*) (1:10)

Romantic comedy of a girl who inherits a newspaper.

1662. Girl Without a Room (Paramount; 1933). *Cast:* Charles Farrell, Marguerite Churchill, Charles Ruggles, Mischa Auer, Leonid Kinskey, Gregory Ratoff, Grace Bradley, Walter Woolf King, Adrian Rosley, Leonid Snegoff, Sam Ash, Alex Melesh, August Tollaire, Perry Ivins, William Colvin. *D:* Ralph Murphy; *P:* Charles R. Rogers; *St & Sc:* Jack Lait.

B comedy of American youths studying in Paris.

1663. Girls About Town (Paramount; 1931). *Cast:* Kay Francis, Joel McCrea, Lilyan Tashman, Eugene Pallette, Alan Dinehart, Claire Dodd, Louise Beavers, Adrienne Ames, Judith Wood, Lucile Gleason, George Barbier, Robert McWade, Anderson Lawler, Hazel Howell, Lucile Brown, Patricia Caron. *D:* George Cukor; *St:* Zoë Akins; *Sc:* Brian Marlow, Raymond Griffith. (1:22)

Made prior to the establishment of the censorship code, this comedy of two

party girls was considered adult entertainment in it's day.

1664. Girls Can Play (Columbia;
1937). *Cast:* Charles Quigley, Rita
Hayworth, Jacqueline Wells (Julie
Bishop), Guinn Williams, Joseph
Crehan. *D:* Lambert Hillyer.

B murder-mystery involving the
members of an all-girl softball team.

1665. Girls Demand Excitement
(Fox; 1931). *Cast:* Marguerite Churchill,
Edward Nugent, William Janney,
Virginia Cherrill, Helen Jerome Eddy,
Martha Sleeper, Marion Byron, Winter
Hall, Addie McPhail, Jerry Mandy,
Ralph Welles, Terrance Ray, Ray
Cooke, John Wayne (bit). *D:* Seymour
Felix (better known as a choreographer
in his directorial debut); *Sc:* Harlan
Thompson.

Romantic college comedy.

1666. Girls Dormitory (20th
Century–Fox; 1936). *Cast:* Herbert
Marshall, Simone Simon (American
debut), Ruth Chatterton, Constance
Collier, J. Edward Bromberg, Dixie
Dunbar, Tyrone Power, Frank Reicher,
John Qualen, Shirley Deane, Christian
Rub, Lillian West, George Hassell,
Lynne Berkeley, Rita Gould, Symona
Boniface, June Storey. *D:* Irving Cum-
mings; *Sc:* Gene Markey. (1:06)

Romantic story of a college girl who
falls for the school's head master. Based
on a story by Ladislaus Fodor.

1667. Girls on Probation (WB/
F.N.; 1938). *Cast:* Jane Bryan, Ronald
Reagan, Anthony Averill, Sheila
Bromley, Henry O'Neill, Elizabeth
Risdon, Sig Rumann, Dorothy Peter-
son, Susan Hayward, Larry Williams,
Arthur Hoyt, Janet Shaw, Joseph
Crehan, Esther Dale, Peggy Shannon,
Emory Parnell, James Nolan. *D:* Wil-
liam McGann; *As.P.:* Bryan Foy; *Sc:*
Crane Wilbur. (1:03)

B melodrama aptly described by
the title.

1668. Girls School (Columbia;
1938). *Cast:* Anne Shirley, Ralph Bel-
lamy, Nan Grey, Doris Kenyon, Noah
Beery, Jr., Gloria Holden, Heather
Thatcher, Marjorie Main, Peggy
Moran (film debut), Martha O'Driscoll,
Kenneth Howell, Pierre Watkin,
Margaret Tallichet, Dorothy Moore,
Virginia Howell, Joanne Tree. *D:* John
Brahm; *P:* Samuel Marx; *St:* Tess Sle-
singer; *Sc:* Slesinger, Richard Sherman;
Music: (A.A.N.) Morris Stoloff, Greg-
ory Stone.

B drama.

1669. Git Along Little Dogies
(Republic; 1937). *Cast:* Gene Autry,
Smiley Burnette, Judith Allen, Weldon
Heyburn, William Farnum, Willie
Fung, Carleton Young, Maple City
Four, Will and Gladys Ahern, Cabin
Kids, Champion. *D:* Joe Kane; *P:* Ar-
mand Schaefer; *Sc:* Dorrell and Stuart
McGowan; *Songs Include:* "Wait for the
Wagon," "Red River Valley," "Long,
Long Ago," "Goodnight Ladies," "After
You've Gone," and "Happy Days Are
Here Again." (G.B. title: *Serenade of the
West*) (1:00) (video)

Gene Autry western of a cowboy
who protects the oil rights of a girl and
her father.

1670. Give and Take (Universal;
1928). *Cast:* George Sidney, George
Lewis, Jean Hersholt, Sam Hardy,
Sharon Lynn, Charles Hill Mailes. *D:*
William Beaudine; *St:* Aaron Hoffman;
Sc: Albert De Mond, Harvey Thew.

Part-talkie comedy-drama of an industrialist who has to deal with the
unrest at his factory that was stirred up
by his son. Mostly synchronized music
and sound effects with a few passages of
spoken dialogue.

1671. Give Me a Sailor (Para-
mount; 1938). *Cast:* Martha Raye,
Bob Hope, Betty Grable, Jack Whit-
ing, Clarence Kolb, J.C. Nugent,
Nana Bryant, Eddie Dunn, John
H. Allen, Edward Earle, Eddie

Kane, Archie Twitchell, Dorothy White, Ralph Sandford, Barbara Salisbury, Carol Parker, Bonnie Jean Churchill, Don Brodie, Eddie Borden, Ned Glass, George Magrill, Bosy Roth, Jerry Storm, Gloria Williams, Emerson Treacy, Philip Warren, Scotty Groves, Harriette Haddon, Franklin Parker. *D:* Elliott Nugent; *P:* Jeff Lazarus; *Sc:* Doris Anderson, Frank Butler. (1:20) (video)

Musical-comedy of a homely girl who wins a "beautiful legs" contest. Based on the play by Anne Nichols.

1672. Give Me Your Heart (WB; 1936). *Cast:* Kay Francis, George Brent, Patric Knowles (American debut), Roland Young, Henry Stephenson, Frieda Inescort, Helen Flint, Halliwell Hobbes, Zeffie Tilbury. *D:* Archie Mayo; *P:* Robert Lord; *Sc:* Casey Robinson. (G.B. title: *Sweet Aloes*) (1:28)

Tear-jerker of a woman who has a baby by a married man and then marries another. Based on the play "Sweet Aloes" by Joyce Carey (Jay Mallory).

1673. Give Us This Night (Paramount; 1936). *Cast:* Jan Kiepura, Gladys Swarthout, Philip Merivale, William Collier, Sr., Alan Mowbray, Sidney Toler, Benny Baker, Michelette Burani, Billy Gilbert, Mattie Edwards, John Miltern. *D:* Alexander Hall; *P:* William LeBaron; *St:* Jacques Bachrach; *Sc:* Edwin Justus Mayer, Lynn Starling; *Songs:* Erich Wolfgang Korngold, Oscar Hammerstein II.

Flop musical starring Jan Kiepura, the famous Polish operatic tenor in his only American film as a fisherman who becomes a singing sensation.

1674. The Glad Rag Doll (WB; 1929). *Cast:* Dolores Costello, Claude Gillingwater, Ralph Graves, Audrey Ferris, Lee Moran, Andre Beranger, Dale Fuller, Louise Beavers, Douglas Gerrard, Tom Ricketts, Albert Gran, Arthur Rankin, Maude Turner Gordon. *D:* Michael Curtiz; *St:* Harvey

Gates; *Sc:* C. Graham Baker; *Title Song:* Jack Yellen, Dan Dougherty, Milton Ager.

Drama of a wealthy man who becomes infatuated with a showgirl.

1675. The Gladiator (Columbia/ Loew; 1938). *Cast:* Joe E. Brown, Man Mountain Dean, June Travis, Dickie Moore, Lucien Littlefield, Robert Kent, Lee Phelps, Ethel Wales, Eddie Kane, Don Douglas. *D:* Edward Sedgwick; *P:* David L. Loew; *Sc:* Arthur Sheekman, Charles Melson. (1:10)

College comedy of a youth who takes an elixir, changing from a wimp to a college hero. Based on Philip Wylie's 1930 book, this film was supposedly the basis for the original idea of "Superman."

1676. Glamour (Universal; 1934). *Cast:* Constance Cummings, Paul Lukas, Philip Reed, Joseph Cawthorn, Doris Lloyd, Olaf Hytten, Lyman Williams, Luis Alberni, Louise Beavers, Alice Lake (final film—ret.), Yola D'Avril. *D:* William Wyler; *P:* Carl Laemmle, Jr.; *St:* Edna Ferber; *Sc:* Doris Anderson, Gladys Unger. (1:13)

The story of a Broadway love triangle.

1677. Glamour Boy (Xxxx Xxxx; 1939). (No information available)

1678. The Glass Key (Paramount; 1935). *Cast:* Edward Arnold, George Raft, Claire Dodd, Rosalind Keith, Guinn Williams, Ray Milland, Emma Dunn, Ann Sheridan, Charles Richman, Robert Gleckler, Charles C. Wilson, Pat Moriarty, Herbert Evans, Frank Marlowe, Harry Tyler, Tammany Young. *D:* Frank Tuttle; *P:* E. Lloyd Sheldon; *Sc:* Kathryn Scola, Harry Ruskin, Kubec Glasmon. (1:20)

Hit melodrama of a politician who becomes involved in a strange murder. Based on the best-seller by Dashiell Hammett, it was remade in 1942.

1679. Glorifying the American Girl (Paramount; 1929). *Cast:* Mary Eaton, Edward Crandall, Eddie Cantor, Helen Morgan, Rudy Vallee, Norman Brokenshire, Sarah Edwards, Dan Healy, Kaye Renard, Olive Shea, Mayor and Mrs. Jimmy Walker (of New York City as themselves), Otto Kahn (a famous banker as himself), Texas Guinan (herself), Adolph Zukor (himself), Florenz Ziegfeld (himself), Billie Burke (Mrs. Florenz Ziegfeld in an unbilled cameo), Ring Lardner (himself), Noah Beery (himself), Johnny Weissmuller (film debut as himself), Irving Berlin (himself). *D:* Millard Webb, John Harkrider; *P:* Florenz Ziegfeld; *St:* J.P. McEvoy; *Sc:* Webb, McEvoy; *Songs Include:* "I'm Just a Vagabond Lover" by Rudy Vallee and Leon Zimmerman (sung by Vallee), "What Wouldn't I Do for That Man" by E.Y. Harburg and Jay Gorney (originally written for *Applause* (q.v.), again sung here by Helen Morgan), and "Blue Skies." (video — restored to 1:36)

A musical revue of showbiz greats amidst a standard plot line for this genre. The film with 2-color technicolor sequences could be considered somewhat of a time-capsule due to all the name people that appear. Filmed at Astoria Studios in Long Island, N.Y.

1680. Glorious Betsy (WB; 1928). *Cast:* Dolores Costello (Elizabeth "Betsy" Patterson), Conrad Nagel (Jerome Bonaparte), John Miljan, Marc MacDermott, Betty Blythe, Paul Panzer, Michael Vavitch, Pasquale Amato (Napoleon Bonaparte), Andre de Segurola. *D:* Alan Crosland; *Adaptation:* (A.A.N.) Anthony Coldeway.

A Vitaphone part-talkie with a based on fact story of Napoleon Bonaparte's younger brother who falls for Elizabeth Patterson, a young girl of Baltimore, Maryland. In reality, Napoleon broke up the romance, but not in the film as to create a happy ending and thus a successful film. Based on a play by Rida Johnson Young it was remade in 1936 as *Hearts Divided* (q.v.).

1681. The Glory Parade (Xxxx Xxxx; 1936). (No information available)

1682. The Glory Trail (Crescent; 1936–37). *Cast:* Tom Keene, Joan Barclay, E.H. Calvert, Frank Melton, William Royle, Walter Long, Allen Greer, William Crowell, Harve Foster, Ann Hovey, John Lester Johnson, Etta McDaniel, James Bush. *D:* Lynn Shores; *P:* E.B. Derr; *Sc:* John T. Neville. (1:04)

Historical western drama of events leading up to the Bozeman massacre.

1683. Go Chase Yourself (RKO; 1938). *Cast:* Joe Penner, Lucille Ball, June Travis, Richard Lane, Jack Carson, Fritz Feld, Tom Kennedy, Granville Bates, Bradley Page, George Irving, Arthur Stone, Frank M. Thomas. *D:* Edward F. Cline; *P:* Robert Sisk; *St:* Walter O'Keefe; *Sc:* Paul Yawitz, Bert Granet. (1:10)

Slapstick B comedy of a bank teller (Joe Penner) who unknowingly participates in a bank robbery.

1684. Go-Get-'em Haines (Republic; 1936). *Cast:* William Boyd, Sheila Terry, Jimmy Aubrey, Lee Shumway, Lloyd Ingraham, Clarence Geldart. *D:* Sam Newfield; *P:* George A. Hirliman.

B actioner.

1685. The Go-Getter (WB; 1936–37). *Cast:* Charles Winninger, George Brent, Anita Louise, John Eldredge, Henry O'Neill, Willard Robertson, Eddie Acuff, Joseph Crehan, Ward Bond, John Shelton, Minerva Urecal, Harry Beresford, Herbert Rawlinson. *D:* Busby Berkeley; *As.P.:* Sam Bischoff; *Sc:* Delmer Daves; *Song:* "It Shall Be Done" by M.K. Jerome-Jack Scholl. (1:30)

Comedy-drama built around the character of "Cappy Ricks," a disabled American veteran who seeks to make it on his own. Based on the story by Peter B. Kyne, it was previously filmed in 1923 by First National.

1686. Go Into Your Dance (WB/ F.N.; 1935). *Cast:* Al Jolson (Al Howard), Ruby Keeler, Glenda Farrell, Barton MacLane, Patsy Kelly, Akim Tamiroff, Sharon Lynne, Benny Rubin, Phil Regan, Gordon Westcott, William B. Davidson, Joyce Compton, Joseph Crehan, John Carroll, Arthur Treacher, Joseph Cawthorn, Marc Lawrence, Ward Bond, Al Dubin (bit), Harry Warren (bit); Gordon (Bill) Elliott (bit). *D:* Archie Mayo; *P:* Sam Bischoff; *St:* Bradford Ropes; *Sc:* Earl Baldwin; *Choreographer:* (A.A.N.) Bobby Connolly for the "She's a Latin from Manhattan" number, combined with another from *Broadway Hostess* (q.v.); *Songs:* "About a Quarter to Nine," "I'll Sing About You," "A Good Old-Fashioned Cocktail with a Good Old-Fashioned Girl," title song, "Casino de Paree," "Mammy" and "...Latin from Manhattan" by Al Dubin and Harry Warren. (G.B. title: *Casino de Paree*) (1:29)

Hit backstage musical drama of an irresponsible entertainer.

1687. Go West, Young Man (Paramount; 1936). *Cast:* Mae West, Randolph Scott, Warren William, Lyle Talbot, Alice Brady, Isabel Jewell, Elizabeth Patterson, Jack LaRue, Margaret Perry, Etienne Girardot, Xavier Cugat and his orchestra, Alice Ardell, Nicodemus Stewart. *D:* Henry Hathaway; *P:* Emanuel R. Cohen; *Sc:* Mae West. (1:20)

Romantic comedy based on the hit Broadway play of 1934 by Lawrence Riley titled "Personal Appearance." A movie star falls for a local farm boy after her car breaks down in the backwoods of Pennsylvania.

1688. God's Country and the Man (Syndicate; 1931). *Cast:* Tom Tyler, Lillian Bond, Alan Bridge, Andy Shuford, Jack Perrin, Ted Adams, Gordon DeMain, Slim Whitaker, Fern Emmett, George Hayes. *D:* John P. McCarthy; *Sc:* Wellyn Totman. (0:59)

Tom Tyler western.

1689. God's Country and the Man (Monogram; 1937). *Cast:* Tom Keene, Betty Compson, Charlotte Henry, Charles King, Billy Bletcher, Eddie Parker, Bob McKenzie, Merrill McCormack, James Sheridan (Sherry Tansey). *D:* Robert N. Bradbury; *P:* Bradbury; *Sc:* Robert Emmett (Tansey). (aka: *The Avenging Stranger*) (0:56)

Tom Keene western of a cowpoke who saves a girl and her gold mine.

1690. God's Country and the Woman (WB; 1936-37). *Cast:* George Brent, Beverly Roberts, Barton MacLane, Robert Barrat, Alan Hale, El Brendel, Addison Richards, Roscoe Ates, Billy Bevan, Joseph Crehan, Joseph King, Bert Roach, Victor Potel, Mary Treen, Herbert Rawlinson, Harry Hayden, Pat Moriarty, Max Wagner, Susan Fleming, Minerva Urecal, Eily Malyon. *D:* William Keighley; *As.P.:* Louis Edelman; *St:* Peter Milne, Charles Belden; *Sc:* Norman Reilly Raine. (1:20)

Technicolor outdoor melodrama of competing lumber companies. Based on the novel by James Oliver Curwood.

1691. God's Gift to Women (WB; 1931). *Cast:* Frank Fay, Laura La Plante, Joan Blondell, Charles Winninger, Alan Mowbray (film debut), Arthur Edmund Carewe, Charles Judels, Yola D'Avril, Louise Brooks, Margaret Livingston, Nena Quartero, Tyrell Davis, Billy (William) House. *D:* Michael Curtiz; *Sc:* Joseph Jackson, Raymond Griffith. (G.B. title: *Too Many Women*)

Light romantic comedy of a Frenchman in pursuit of an American heiress. Based on the play "The Devil Was Sick" by Jane Hinton.

1692. God's Stepchildren (Micheaux; 1937). *Produced, directed and written by:* Oscar Micheaux.

Low-budget independent production.

1693. The Godless Girl (Pathé; 1929). *Cast:* Lina Basquette, George Duryea (Tom Keene), Marie Prevost, Noah Beery, Eddie Quillan, George Irving. *D:* Cecil B. De Mille; *St & Sc:* Jeanie MacPherson.

Part-talkie melodrama.

1694. Goin' to Town (Paramount; 1935). *Cast:* Mae West, Paul Cavanagh, Gilbert Emery, Ivan Lebedeff, Tito Coral, Marjorie Gateson, Fred Kohler, Monroe Owsley, Grant Withers, Francis Ford, Leonid Kinskey, Luis Alberni, Adrienne D'Ambricourt, Dewey Robinson, Mona Rico, Lucio Villegas. *D:* Alexander Hall; *P:* William LeBaron; *St:* Marion Morgan, George B. Dowell; *Sc:* Mae West; *Songs:* "He's a Bad, Bad Man But He's Good Enough for Me" by Sammy Fain, Irving Kahal and an aria from "Samson and Delilah" by Saint-Saëns. (1:14)

Hit romantic musical-comedy of a wealthy western girl who sets her sights on becoming a member of high society. One of the 12 top grossing films of 1935.

1695. Going Highbrow (WB; 1935). *Cast:* Guy Kibbee, ZaSu Pitts, Ross Alexander, June Martel, Edward Everett Horton, Judy Canova, Nella Walker, Gordon Westcott, Arthur Treacher, Jack Norton. *D:* Robert Florey; *P:* Sam Bischoff; *Sc:* Edward Kaufman, Sy Bartlett; *Songs:* Louis Alter, Jack Scholl.

B comedy of a couple who want to break into society. Based on a play by Ralph Spence.

1696. Going Hollywood (MGM; 1933). *Cast:* Marion Davies, Bing Crosby, Patsy Kelly (feature film debut), Stuart Erwin, Fifi D'Orsay, Ned Sparks, Robert Watson, Clara Blandick, Sterling Holloway, Harvey Clark. *D:* Raoul Walsh; *P:* Walter Wanger; *St:* Frances Marion; *Sc:* Donald Ogden Stewart; *Songs:* Brown and Freed. (1:20)

Hit romantic comedy with songs of a woman in pursuit of a popular crooner. Bing Crosby as the crooner sings "Temptation" by Nacio Herb Brown and Arthur Freed which became a big hit for him along with "After Sundown."

1697. Going Places (WB; 1938). *Cast:* Dick Powell, Anita Louise, Allen Jenkins, Ronald Reagan, Walter Catlett, Harold Huber, Louis Armstrong, Maxine Sullivan, Eddie "Rochester" Anderson, Thurston Hall, John Ridgely, Joyce Compton, Ward Bond, Joe Cunningham, Robert Warwick, George Reed, Larry Williams. *D:* Ray Enright; *As.P.:* Benjamin Glazer; *Sc:* Sig Herzig, Jerry Wald, Maurice Leo. (1:24)

Musical romance of a sporting goods salesman who poses as a famous jockey. Based on the 1920 play "The Hottentot" by Victor Mapes and William Collier, Sr. Two previous filmings under that title were in 1922 by First National and 1929 by Warners (q.v.). The song "Jeepers Creepers" by Harry Warren and Johnny Mercer was introduced in this film, receiving an A.A.N. for "Best Song," being rendered by Louis Armstrong and Maxine Sullivan. The song became a big hit, but the film didn't. A Cosmopolitan Production.

1698. Going Wild (WB/F.N.; 1930–31). *Cast:* Joe E. Brown, Lawrence Gray, Ona Munson (film debut), Walter Pidgeon, Laura Lee, Frank McHugh, May Boley, Anders Randolph, Johnny Arthur, Fred Kelsey, Harvey Clark, Arthur Hoyt, Sam Cantor. *D:* William A. Seiter; *Adaptation:* Humphrey Pearson; *Sc:* Henry McCarty, Pearson. (1:07) See also: *The Aviator* (1929) (q.v.)

Comedy of an unemployed news reporter who poses as a famous flyer and novelist. Based on "The Aviator" by James Montgomery, it was previously filmed by First National in 1923 as *Going Up*.

1699. Gold (Majestic; 1932). *Cast:* Jack Hoxie, Alice Day, Hooper Atchley, Tom London, Robert Kortman, Lafe

McKee, Matthew Betz, Jack Clifford, Jack Byron, Jack Kirk, Dynamite the horse. *D:* Otto Brower; *P:* Max and Arthur Alexander; *Sc:* W. Scott Darling. (0:58)

Jack Hoxie "poverty row" western of a cowboy accused of killing his partner, who sets the record straight.

1700. Gold Diggers in Paris (WB; 1938). *Cast:* Rudy Vallee, Rosemary Lane, Hugh Herbert, Allen Jenkins, Gloria Dickson, Melville Cooper, Mabel Todd, Fritz Feld, Curt Bois, The Schnickelfritz Band, Victor Kilian, Georges Renavent, Armand Kaliz, Maurice Cass, Eddie "Rochester" Anderson, Edward Brophy, Rosella Towne, Janet Shaw, Carole Landis, Peggy Moran, Diana Lewis, Lois Lindsay, Poppy Wilde. *D:* Ray Enright; *As.P.:* Sam Bischoff; *Sc:* Earl Baldwin, Warren Duff; *Songs:* "The Latin Quarter," "I Wanna Go Back to Bali," "Put That Down in Writing" and "A Stranger in Paree" by Al Dubin, Harry Warren and "Day Dreaming All Night Long," "Waltz of the Flowers" and "My Adventure" by Johnny Mercer and Harry Warren. (G.B. title: *The Gay Imposters*) (1:35)

Musical-comedy which was the last of the "Gold Digger" series. The original (?) idea by Jerry Horwin and James Seymour of a dance troupe in Paris was developed into a story by Jerry Wald, Maurice Leo and Richard Macaulay. Busby Berkeley choreographed the production numbers.

1701. Gold Diggers of Broadway (WB; 1929). *Cast:* Nancy Welford (Jerry), Conway Tearle (Stephen Lee), Winnie Lightner (Mabel), Lilyan Tashman (Eleanor), William Bakewell (Wally), Ann Pennington (Ann Collins), Nick Lucas (Nick), Helen Foster (Violet), Albert Gran (Blake), Gertrude Short (Topsy), Neely Edwards (stage manager), Julia Swayne Gordon (Cissy Gray), Lee Moran (choreographer), Armand Kaliz (Barney Barnett), Louise

Beavers. *D:* Roy Del Ruth; *Sc:* Robert Lord; *Songs include:* "Painting the Clouds with Sunshine," "Tip-Toe Through the Tulips," and "And They Still Fall in Love," by Al Dubin and Joe Burke. (1:38)

2-color technicolor musical of three showgirls on the prowl for rich husbands. Based on Avery Hopwood's play *The Gold Diggers,* it was previously filmed under that title by this studio in 1923. Remade as *Gold Diggers of 1933* (q.v.) and *Painting the Clouds with Sunshine* (WB; 1951). It placed #5 on the "10 Best" list of *Film Daily.*

1702. Gold Diggers of 1933 (WB; 1933). *Cast:* Warren William (J. Lawrence Bradford), Joan Blondell (Carol), Aline MacMahon (Trixie Lorraine), Ruby Keeler (Polly Parker), Dick Powell (Robert Treat Bradford "Brad Roberts"), Guy Kibbee (Thaniel H. Peabody), Ned Sparks (Barney Hopkins), Ginger Rogers (Fay Fortune), Clarence Nordstrom (Gordon), Robert Agnew (choreographer), Tammany Young (Gigolo Eddie), Sterling Holloway, Ferdinand Gottschalk, Lynn Browning, Charles C. Wilson, Theresa Harris, Fred "Snowflake" Toones, Billy Barty, Joan Barclay, Wallace MacDonald, Wilbur Mack, Grace Hayle, Charles (Levison) Lane, Hobart Cavanaugh, Gordon (Bill) Elliott, Bud Flanagan (Dennis O'Keefe), Busby Berkeley (bit), Fred Kelsey, Frank Mills, Etta Moten. *D:* Mervyn LeRoy; *P:* Hal Wallis, Robert Lord, Darryl F. Zanuck; *Sc:* Erwin Gelsey, James Seymour, David Boehm, Ben Markson. *Songs:* "The Gold Diggers Song (We're in the Money)," "I've Got to Sing a Torch Song," "Pettin' in the Park," "The Shadow Waltz" and "Remember My Forgotten Man" by Al Dubin and Harry Warren; *Sound Recording:* (A.A.N.) Nathan Levinson. (1:36) (video)

Hit musical loosely based on the 1919 play "The Gold Diggers" by Avery Hopwood. A remake of *Gold Diggers of Broadway* (q.v.). With choreography by

Busby Berkeley, the film became one of the 11 top grossing films of 1933.

1703. Gold Diggers of 1935 (WB/F.N.; 1935). *Cast:* Dick Powell (Dick Curtis), Adolphe Menjou (Nikolai Nicoleff), Gloria Stuart (Amy Prentiss), Alice Brady (Matilda Prentiss), Hugh Herbert (T. Mosley Thorpe), Glenda Farrell (Betty Hawes), Frank McHugh (Humbolt Prentiss), Joseph Cawthorn (August Schultz), Grant Mitchell (Louis Lampson), Dorothy Dare (Arline Davis), Winifred Shaw (Wini Shaw), Thomas Jackson (Haggerty), Virginia Grey, Emily LaRue (film debut), Ramon and Rosita, Matty Kemp, Phil Tead, Nora Cecil, Eddie Kane, Arthur Aylesworth, Gordon (Bill) Elliott, John Qualen, Don Brodie, George Riley, Eddie Fetherston, Billy Newell, Harry Seymour, Ray Cooke, Franklyn Farnum, E.E. Clive, Charles Coleman, Leo White, Bud Flanagan (Dennis O'Keefe). *D:* Busby Berkeley; *P:* Robert Lord; *St:* Lord, Peter Milne; *Sc:* Milne, Manuel Seff; *Songs:* "The Words Are in My Heart," "I'm Going Shopping with You" and "Lullaby of Broadway" (which received the A.A. for "Best Song") by Al Dubin and Harry Warren; *Choreographer:* (A.A.N.) Berkeley for the "Lullaby of Broadway" and "The Words Are in My Heart" numbers. "Lullaby of Broadway" which became a big hit song is sung here by Wini Shaw. (1:35) (video)

Hit musical with more showgirls in search of rich husbands.

1704. Gold Diggers of 1937 (WB/F.N.; 1936). *Cast:* Dick Powell, Joan Blondell, Glenda Farrell, Victor Moore, Lee Dixon, Osgood Perkins, Charles D. Brown, Jane Wyman (film debut), Rosalind Marquis, Irene Ware, Olin Howland, William Davidson, Iris Adrian, Jack Norton, Frank Faylen, Charles Halton, Susan Fleming, Paul Irving. *D:* Lloyd Bacon; *P:* Earl Baldwin; *Sc:* Warren Duff; *Songs:* "With Plenty of Money" by Al Dubin, Harry

Warren, "Speaking of the Weather" and "Let's Put Our Heads Together" by Harold Arlen and E.Y. Harburg; *Choreographer:* (A.A.N.) Busby Berkeley for his "All's Fair in Love and War" number. (1:40)

A musical with the story line of an insurance salesman who is conned into selling a million dollar policy to a theatrical producer who he later finds could be living on borrowed time. Based on the 1935 Broadway play "Sweet Mystery of Life" by Richard Maibaum, Michael Wallach and George Haight.

1705. Gold Dust Gertie (WB; 1931). *Cast:* Winnie Lightner, Ole Olsen, Chic Johnson, Dorothy Christy, Claude Gillingwater, Vivian Oakland, Arthur Hoyt, George Byron, Charley Grapewin, Charles Judels, Virginia Sale. *D:* Lloyd Bacon; *Sc:* William K. Wells, Ray Enright; *Dialogue:* Arthur Caesar. (G.B. title: *Why Change Your Husband?*) (1:04)

B comedy of two men, both previously married to the same woman who dodge her constant attempts to collect alimony. Based on the play "The Wife of the Party" by Len D. Hollister.

1706. Gold Is Where You Find It (WB/F.N.; 1938). *Cast:* George Brent, Olivia de Havilland, Claude Rains, Margaret Lindsay, John Litel, Barton MacLane, Tim Holt, Marcia Ralston, George Hayes, Clarence Kolb, Moroni Olsen, Sidney Toler, Henry O'Neill, Harry Davenport, Charles Halton, Willie Best, Granville Bates. *D:* Michael Curtiz; *As.P.:* Sam Bischoff; *Sc:* Warren Duff, Robert Buckner. (1:30)

A story of the California gold rush produced in technicolor on a large budget, and a bomb at the box office. A Cosmopolitan production it was based on a serialized story which appeared in Cosmopolitan magazine by Clements Ripley.

1707. Gold Mine in the Sky (Republic; 1938). *Cast:* Gene Autry, Smiley

Burnette, Carol Hughes, Craig Reynolds, Cupid Ainsworth, LeRoy Mason, J.L. Frank's Golden West Cowboys, Frankie Marvin, Robert Homans, Ben Corbett, George (Montgomery) Letz, Charles King, Anita Bolster, Earl Dwire, Maude Prickett, Al Taylor, Stafford Sisters, Art Dillard, Eddie Cherkose, Milburn Morante, Fred "Snowflake" Toones. *D:* Joe Kane; *P:* Charles E. Ford; *St:* Betty Burbridge; *Sc:* Burbridge, Jack Natteford; *Title Song:* Nick and Charles Kenney. (1:00)

Gene Autry western of a cowboy out to save a stubborn girl's ranch.

1708. The Gold Racket (Grand National; 1937). *Cast:* Conrad Nagel, Eleanor Hunt, Fuzzy Knight, Charles Delaney, Frank Milan, Karl Hackett, Warner Richmond, Albert J. Smith, Edward LeSaint, William L. Thorne, Paul Weigel, Fred Malatesta. *D:* Louis Gasnier; *P:* George A. Hirliman; *St:* Howard Higgin; *Sc:* Griffin Jay, David Levy. (1:06)

B melodrama of gold smugglers.

1709. Goldberg (Xxxx Xxxx; 1931). (No information available)

1710. The Golden Arrow (WB/F.N.; 1936). *Cast:* Bette Davis, George Brent, Eugene Pallette, Dick Foran, Carol Hughes, Catherine Doucet, Ivan Lebedeff, Earle Foxe, Hobart Cavanaugh, Frank Faylen, Craig Reynolds, E.E. Clive, Henry O'Neill, Selmer Jackson, Sarah Edwards, G.P. Huntley, Jr., Rafael Storm, Bess Flowers. *D:* Alfred E. Green; *P:* Sam Bischoff; *Sc:* Charles Kenyon. (1:08)

B comedy of a scheming heiress who tricks a newspaper reporter into marriage. Based on a play by Michael Arlen, this film is only notable as the one which started Bette Davis' war with the Brothers Warner for better scripts.

1711. Golden Boy (Columbia; 1939). *Cast:* Barbara Stanwyck (Lorna Moon), William Holden (in his starring debut as Joe Bonaparte), Adolphe Men-

jou (Tom Moody), Lee J. Cobb (Mr. Bonaparte), Joseph Calleia (Eddie Fuseli), Sam Levene (Siggie), Edward Brophy (Roxy Lewis), Don Beddoe, Howard da Silva, Minerva Urecal, Charles Halton, William Strauss, Beatrice Blinn, Charles Lane. *D:* Rouben Mamoulian; *P:* William Perlberg; *Sc:* Lewis Meltzer, Daniel Taradash, Sarah Y. Mason, Victor Heerman; *Original Music Score:* (A.A.N.) Victor Young. (1:41) (video)

A basic story of a violinist who decides to become a prizefighter, but still retains his love for playing music. Based on the play by Clifford Odets.

The Golden Calf *see* **Her Golden Calf**

1712. Golden Dawn (WB/F.N.; 1930). *Cast:* Vivienne Segal, Walter Woolf King, Noah Beery (in blackface), Alice Gentle, Lupino Lane, Dick Henderson, Sojin, Otto Matiesen, Lee Moran, Marion Byron, Nena Quartero. *D:* Ray Enright; *Sc:* Walter Anthony; *Songs:* "Whip Song," "Dawn," "My Bwana" and "We Two" by Otto Harbach, Oscar Hammerstein II and Emmerich Kalman, "My Heart's Love Call," "Africa Smiles No More," "Mooda's Song" and "In a Jungle Bungalow" by Grant Clarke and Harry Akst.

Operetta filmed in 2-color technicolor of a native uprising in East Africa during World War I. Based on the 1927 Broadway play by Hammerstein II, Harbach, Kalman and Herbert Stothart.

Golden Gloves (G.B. title) *see* **Ex-Champ**

1713. Golden Harvest (Paramount; 1933). *Cast:* Chester Morris, Richard Arlen, Julie Haydon, Genevieve Tobin, Lawrence Gray, Henry Kolker, Berton Churchill, Richard Carle, Roscoe Ates, Elizabeth Patterson. *D:* Ralph Murphy; *St:* Nina Wilcox Putnam; *Adaptation:* Casey Robinson.

Offbeat depression era drama of the

plight of wheat farmers and one family's involvement.

1714. The Golden West (Fox; 1932). *Cast:* George O'Brien (in a dual role), Janet Chandler, Marion Burns, Arthur Pierson, Onslow Stevens, Hattie McDaniel (film debut), Edmund Breese, Julia Swayne Gordon, Everett Corrigan, Sam West, Bert Hanlon, Charles Stevens, Stanley Blystone, George Regas, Dorothy Ward, Sam Adams, Ed Dillon, Chief Big Tree, John War Eagle. *D:* David Howard; *Sc:* Gordon Rigby. (1:10)

An elaborately produced western which spans two generations. A white boy raised by Indians after his father is killed grows up to hate the white man. Based on the novel by Zane Grey.

1715. Goldfish Bowl (Xxxx Xxxx; 1931). (No information available)

1716. Goldie (Fox; 1931). *Cast:* Jean Harlow, Spencer Tracy, Lina Basquette, Warren Hymer, Maria Alba, Eleanor Hunt. *D:* Ben Stoloff.

A romantic comedy which was filmed before in 1928 by Howard Hawks as *A Girl in Every Port.*

1717. Goldie Gets Along (RKO/King Motion Pictures; 1933). *Cast:* Lili Damita (Goldie LaFarge), Sam Hardy, Charles Morton, Nat Pendleton, Lita Chevret, Lee Moran, Arthur Hoyt, Henry Fink, Bradley Page, Hugh Herbert, Walter Brennan (unbilled bit). *D:* Malcolm St. Clair; *P:* J.G. Bachmann; *Sc:* William A. Drake. (1:08)

Low-budget comedy of a girl traveling cross-country, determined to get to Hollywood. Based on a book by Hawthorne Hurst.

1718. The Goldwyn Follies (United Artists/Samuel Goldwyn; 1938). *Cast:* Kenny Baker (Danny Beecher), Zorina (Olga Samara), Adolphe Menjou (Oliver Merlin), The Ritz Brothers (themselves), Edgar Bergen and Charlie McCarthy (themselves), Andrea Leeds (Hazel Dawes), Helen Jepson (film debut as Leona Jerome), Bobby Clark (A. Basil Crane, Jr.), Phil Baker (Michael Day), Ella Logan (Glory Wood), Jerome Cowan (director Lawrence), Nydia Westman (Ada), Charles Kullmann (Alfredo in "La Traviata"), Walter Sande, Alan Ladd, Frank Shields, Joseph Crehan, Roland Drew, Frank Mills, American Ballet of the Metropolitan Opera (under the direction of George Balanchine). *D:* George Marshall; *As.P.:* George Haight; *St & Sc:* Ben Hecht; *Art-Set Decoration:* (A.A.N.) Richard Day; *Music:* (A.A.N.) Alfred Newman; *Songs:* "Love Walked In," "Love Is Here to Stay," "I Was Doing All Right" and "I Love to Rhyme" by George and Ira Gershwin, "Spring Again" and "I'm Not Complaining" by Kurt Weill and Ira Gershwin, "Here Pussy Pussy" by Sid Kuller, Ray Golden; also arias from "La Traviata." (2:00) (video)

Lavish technicolor musical-comedy which is notable on two counts, as the first all-color production of Sam Goldwyn and the last songs written by George Gershwin who died in 1938. One of the 15 top grossing films of 1937–38.

1719. Gone with the Wind (MGM/Selznick International; 1939). *Cast:* **At Tara:** Fred Crane (Brent Tarleton), George Reeves (film debut as Stuart Tarleton), Vivien Leigh (A.A. for B.A. and the "Best Actress Award" from the New York Film Critics in her American film debut as Scarlett O'Hara), Hattie McDaniel (A.A. for B.S.A. as Mammy), Everett Brown (Big Sam), Zack Williams (Elijah), Thomas Mitchell (Gerald O'Hara), Oscar Polk (Pork), Barbara O'Neil (Ellen O'Hara), Victor Jory (Jonas Wilkerson), Evelyn Keyes (Suellen O'Hara), Ann Rutherford (Careen O'Hara), Butterfly McQueen (film debut as Prissy). **At Twelve Oaks:** Howard Hickman (John Wilkes), Alicia Rhett (India Wilkes), Leslie Howard (Ashley Wilkes), Olivia de Havilland (A.A.N. for B.S.A. as Melanie Hamilton), Rand Brooks (Charles

Hamilton), Carroll Nye (Frank Kennedy), Marcella Martin (Cathleen Calvert), Clark Gable (A.A.N. for B.A. as Rhett Butler), James Bush (gentleman). **At the Atlanta Bazaar:** Laura Hope Crews (Aunt Pittypat Hamilton), Harry Davenport (Doctor Meade), Leona Roberts (Caroline Meade), Jane Darwell (Dolly Merriwether), Albert Morin (Rene Picard), Mary Anderson (film debut as Maybelle Merriwether), Terry Shero (Fanny Elsing), William McClain (Old Levi). **Outside the Examiner Office:** Eddie "Rochester" Anderson (Uncle Peter), Jackie Moran (Phil Meade). **At the Hospital:** Cliff Edwards (reminiscent soldier), Ona Munson (Belle Watling), Ed Chandler (sergeant), George Hackathorne (wounded soldier in pain), Roscoe Ates (convalescent soldier), John Arledge (dying soldier), Eric Linden (amputee), Guy Wilkerson (wounded card player). **During the Evacuation:** Tom Tyler (commanding officer), Frank Faylen (soldier aiding Doctor Meade). **During the Siege:** William Bakewell (mounted officer), Lee Phelps (bartender). **Georgia After Sherman:** Paul Hurst (Yankee deserter), Ernest Whitman (carpetbagger's friend), William Stelling (returning veteran), Louis Jean Heydt (hungry soldier), Isabel Jewell (Emmy Slattery). **During Reconstruction:** Robert Elliott (Yankee Major), George Meeker and Wallis Clark (poker playing captains), Irving Bacon (corporal), Adrian Morris (carpetbagger orator), J.M. Kerrigan (Johnny Gallagher), Olin Howland (Yankee businessman), Yakima Canutt (renegade), Blue Washington (renegade's companion), Ward Bond (Tom, a Yankee captain), Cammie King (Bonnie Blue Butler), Mickey Kuhn (Beau Wilkes), Lillian Kemble Cooper (Bonnie's nurse), Si Jenks (Yankee on the street), Harry Strang (Tom's aide). *D:* (A.A.) Victor Fleming (with the directorial support of Sam Wood, George Cukor and David O. Selznick — unc.); *P:* (A.A. for Best Picture) David O. Selznick; *Sc:* (A.A.)

Sidney Howard (and the uncredited support of others including Ben Hecht); *Color Cinematography:* (A.A.) Ernest Haller and Ray Rennahan; *Art Director:* (A.A.) Lyle Wheeler; *Production Design:* (A.A. — special plaque) William Cameron Menzies "for use of color in production to enhance dramatic moods"; *Original Music Score:* (A.A.N.) Max Steiner; *Editors:* (A.A.) Hal C. Kern and James E. Newcom; *Sound Recording:* (A.A.N.) Thomas T. Moulton; *Special Effects:* (A.A.N. — the burning of Atlanta) John R. Cosgrove, Fred Albin, Arthur Jones (directed by B. Reeves Eason and photographed by Lee Garmes); with a scientific and technical Oscar to Don Musgrave and Selznick International for "pioneering in the use of coordinated equipment." (3:29) (video)

Since its much publicized and anticipated release in Atlanta, Georgia, on December 15, 1939, this one-of-a-kind sprawling technicolor American Civil War epic romance has successfully captured the attention of generation after generation and remains one of the glossiest and most popular productions ever to come out of Hollywood. The life, loves, trials and tribulations of its fickle, self-centered heroine, Scarlett O'Hara are themselves legendary. The lavish production which opens at the O'Hara plantation of Tara and ends with the era of reconstruction after the war finished up in the vicinity of $4,000,000, an unheard of film budget in the 1930s. Much could be written about this film, but one famous Hollywood quote stands out, that made to Louis B. Mayer head of MGM by Irving Thalberg, head of production at the studio in 1936 after Mayer made the decision to do the picture: "Forget it Louis, no Civil War picture ever made a nickel." As of January, 1979, according to Variety, "GWTW" ranked #9 in the top box office receipts in the U.S. and Canada at $76,700,000. In 1967 a wide-screen 70mm print was produced from the original in stereophonic sound for theatrical release. In 1989 Turner Entertainment completely restored "GWTW" to its original sharp technicolor images of the initial release. Being the 50th anniversary of its release, it also had a limited re-release with the newly restored prints also being released to home video. In the 1970s a stage musical based on the film toured with some success. Based on the runaway best-seller by Margaret Mitchell, "GWTW" received thirteen Academy Award nominations, winning eight of the thirteen including "Best Picture" and a special plaque to William Cameron Menzies (see credits). "GWTW" also received *Photoplay*'s Gold Medal Award, placed #10 on the "10 Best" list of the *New York Times* in 1939, placed #9 on the "10 Best" list of the National Board of Review in 1940, was in nomination for "Best Picture" by the New York Film Critics in 1939, was one of the 21 top grossing films of 1939–40, and voted "Best Film of the Year" by *Film Daily* in 1941.

1720. The Good Bad Girl (Columbia; 1931). *Cast:* James Hall, Mae Clarke, Robert Ellis, Marie Prevost, Wheeler Oakman, Paul Fix, Paul Porcasi, Nance O'Neil, Edmund Breese, George Berliner. *D:* Roy William Neill; *St:* Winifred Van Duzer; *Sc:* Jo Swerling.
Low-budget romantic melodrama.

1721. Good-Bye Again (WB/ F.N.; 1933). *Cast:* Warren William, Joan Blondell, Genevieve Tobin, Hugh Herbert, Helen Chandler, Ruth Donnelly, Wallace Ford, Hobart Cavanaugh, Ray Cooke, Jay Ward. *D:* Michael Curtiz; *P:* Henry Blanke; *Sc:* Ben Markson. (1:05)
Light romantic comedy of an author, his ex-girl friend and his secretary. Based on the play by George Haight and Allan Scott. Remade in 1941 as *Honeymoon for Three*.

1722. Good-Bye Broadway (Universal; 1938). *Cast:* Alice Brady (Mrs. Molloy), Charles Winninger (Pat Molloy), Frank Jenks, Tom Brown,

Dorothea Kent, Jed Prouty, Willie Best, Donald Meek, Virginia Howell, Rollo Lloyd, Charles Sullivan, Del Henderson, Tommy Riggs and his Betty Lou, Steve Strelich, Henry Rocquemore, Jack Daley. *D:* Ray McCarey; *P:* Edmund Grainger; *Sc:* Roy Chanslor, A. Dorian Otvos. (1:05)
Comedy-drama of a vaudevillian couple who buy a seedy rundown hotel in a small town. A remake of *The Shannons of Broadway* (q.v.). Based on the play of that name by James Gleason.

1723. Good-Bye Love (RKO/ Jefferson; 1933). *Cast:* Charles Ruggles, Verree Teasdale, Sidney Blackmer, Mayo Methot, Phyllis Barry, Ray Walker, John Kelly, Grace Hayle, Luis Alberni. *D:* H. Bruce Humberstone; *P:* Joseph I. Schnitzer, Samuel Zierler; *St:* Hampton Del Ruth; *Sc:* Del Ruth, George Rosener, John Howard Lawson.
A romantic comedy which was the final production of Jefferson Pictures Corporation before it folded.

1724. Good Dame (Paramount; 1934). *Cast:* Fredric March, Sylvia Sidney, Jack LaRue, Noel Francis, Russell Hopton, Helene Chadwick, Walter Brennan, Kathleen Burke, Bradley Page, William Farnum, Guy Usher. *D:* Marion Gering; *P:* B.P. Schulberg; *St:* William R. Lipman; *Sc:* Lipman, Vincent Lawrence, Frank Partos, Sam Hellman. (G.B. title: *Good Girl*) (1:17)
Romantic drama of two misfits which was a box office flop.

1725. The Good Earth (MGM; 1937). *Cast:* Paul Muni (Wang Lung), Luise Rainer (A.A. for B.A. and an Acting Award from the National Board of Review as O-lan), Walter Connolly (Uncle), Tilly Losch (Lotus with voice dubbed by Lotus Liu), Charley Grapewin (Old Father), Jessie Ralph (Cuckoo), Soo Yong (Old Mistress Aunt), Keye Luke (Elder Son), Harold

Huber (Cousin), Roland Lui (Younger Son), Ching Wah Lee (Ching), William Law (gateman), Mary Wong (Little Bride), Charles Middleton (banker), Suzanna Kim (Little Fool), Caroline Chew, Chester Gan, Olaf Hytten, Miki Morita, Philip Ahn, Sammee Tong, Richard Loo. *D:* (A.A.N.) Sidney Franklin, (Victor Fleming—unc.); *P:* Irving Thalberg, Bernard Hyman; *As.P.:* Albert Lewin; *Sc:* Talbot Jennings, Tess Slesinger, Claudine West; *Cinematographer:* (A.A.) Karl Freund for his sepia tone photography; *Editor:* (A.A.N.) Basil Wrangell. (2:18) (video)

Critically acclaimed classic drama of life and love in the China of the 1930s amidst revolution, famine and a plague of locusts. The lavish $2,800,000 production entails authentic sets shipped from China with additional footage shot in that country. The film had much appeal in the states and abroad, bringing in a gross of $3,500,000 at the box office. Based on the 1931 Pulitzer Prize winning novel by Pearl Buck and the stage adaptation by Owen and Donald Davis, "TGE" received an A.A.N. for "Best Picture" while also being nominated for "Best Picture" by the New York Film Critics. It also placed #2 on the "10 Best" lists of both *Film Daily* and the *New York Times,* while placing #6 on the same list of the National Board of Review. This was the final production of Irving Grant Thalberg who died in 1936 at the age of 37 years. One of the 38 top grossing films of 1936-37.

1726. The Good Fairy (Universal; 1935). *Cast:* Margaret Sullavan (Luisa Ginglebusher), Herbert Marshall, Frank Morgan, Reginald Owen, Alan Hale, Beulah Bondi, Cesar Romero, Eric Blore, Alan Bridge, George Davis, Hugh O'Connell. *D:* William Wyler; *P:* Henry Henigson; *Sc:* Preston Sturges. (1:21)

Critically praised romantic comedy of affairs and relationships which was based on the play by Ferenc Molnar. Remade by this studio as *I'll Be Yours* (1947).

Good Girl (G.B. title) *see* **Good Dame**

1727. Good Girls Go to Paris (Columbia; 1939). *Cast:* Joan Blondell, Melvyn Douglas, Walter Connolly, Alan Curtis, Joan Perry, Isabel Jeans, Alexander D'Arcy, Clarence Kolb, Don Beddoe, Howard Hickman, Henry Hunter, Stanley Brown. *D:* Alexander Hall; *P:* William Perlberg; *St:* Lenore Coffee, William Joyce Cowen; *Sc:* Gladys Lehman, Ken Englund. (1:18)

Screwball type comedy of a gold digger who is torn between a rich man and the one she loves.

1728. Good Intentions (Fox; 1930). *Cast:* Edmund Lowe, Marguerite Churchill, Regis Toomey, J. Carrol Naish, Earle Foxe, Robert McWade, Hale Hamilton, Pat Somerset, Eddie Gribbon. *D:* William K. Howard; *St:* Howard; *Sc:* Howard (co-writer).

Romantic comedy.

1729. Good News (MGM; 1930). *Cast:* Bessie Love, Stanley Smith, Gus Shy (film debut—recreating his stage role), Mary Lawlor (film debut—recreating her stage role), Lola Lane, Dorothy McNulty (Penny Singleton—film debut), Cliff Edwards, Thomas Jackson, Frank McGlynn, Delmer Daves. *D:* Nick Grinde, Edgar MacGregor; *Sc:*Frances Marion, Joe Farnham; *Songs Include:* "The Varsity Drag," "The Best Things in Life Are Free," and "Lucky in Love" by DeSylva-Brown-Henderson and George Waggner.

Musical with a college football theme. Based on the 1927 Broadway musical. Remade by this studio in 1947.

1730. The Good Old Soak (MGM; 1937). *Cast:* Wallace Beery, Betty Furness, Eric Linden, Una Merkel, Ted Healy, Janet Beecher, Robert McWade, Margaret Hamilton, Judith Barrett, George Sidney (final film—ret.), James Bush. *D:* J. Walter Ruben; *P:* Harry Rapf; *Sc:* A.E. Thomas.

B comedy-drama of a small town family. Based on the play "The Old Soak" by Don Marquis.

1731. Good Sport (Fox; 1931). *Cast:* John Boles, Greta Nissen, Linda Watkins, Joyce Compton, Sally Blane, Louise Beavers, Betty Francisco, Ethel Kenyon, Claire Maynard. *D:* Kenneth MacKenna; *St:* William Hurlbut.
Romantic comedy.

1732. Goona Goona (First Division; 1932). *D:* Andre Roosevelt, *St:* Armand Denis.
Documentary.

1733. The Goose and the Gander (WB; 1935). *Cast:* Kay Francis, George Brent, Genevieve Tobin, John Eldredge, Claire Dodd, Ralph Forbes, William Austin, Wade Boteler, Gordon (Bill) Elliott, Charles Coleman, Eddie Shubert, Olive Jones, Helen Lowell, John Sheehan. *D:* Alfred E. Green; *P:* James Seymour; *St & Sc:* Charles Kenyon. (1:05)
B romantic comedy of a woman who tries to save the marriage of her ex-husband.

Goose Step *see* **Hitler—Beast of Berlin**

1734. The Gorgeous Hussy (MGM; 1936). *Cast:* Joan Crawford (Peggy O'Neal Eaton), Robert Taylor (Bow Timberlake), Lionel Barrymore (Andrew Jackson), Franchot Tone (John Eaton), Melvyn Douglas (John Randolph), James Stewart (Rowdy "Roderick" Dow), Alison Skipworth (Mrs. Beall), Beulah Bondi (A.A.N. for B.S.A. as Rachel Jackson), Louis Calhern (Sunderland), Edith Atwater (Lady Vaughn), Melville Cooper (Cuthbert), Sidney Toler (Daniel Webster), Gene Lockhart (Major O'Neal), Phoebe Foster (Emily Donaldson), Clara Blandick (Louisa Abbott), Frank Conroy (John C. Calhoun), Nydia Westman (Maybelle), Louise Beavers (Aunt Sukey), Charles Trowbridge (Martin Van Buren), Willard Robertson (Secretary Ingham), Greta Meyer (Mrs. Oxenrider), Fred "Snowflake" Toones (Horatius), William Orlamond (Herr Oxenrider), Rubye de Remer (Mrs. Bellamy), Betty Blythe (Mrs. Wainwright), George Reed (Braxton), Oscar Apfel (Tompkins), Zeffie Tilbury (Mrs. Daniel Beall), William Stack (W.R. Earle), Lee Phelps (bartender), Bert Roach, Franklin Parker, Harry Holman, Morgan Wallace, Harry C. Bradley, Ward Bond, Sam McDaniel, Samuel S. Hinds. *D:* Clarence Brown; *P:* Joseph L. Mankiewicz; *Sc:* Ainsworth Morgan, Stephen Morehouse Avery; *Cinematographer:* (A.A.N.) George Folsey. (1:42)
Historical costume drama of Andrew Jackson and his lady and the scandal that surrounded her. Based on the novel by Samuel Hopkins Adams, the film was one of the 38 top grossing films of 1936–37.

1735. The Gorilla (WB/F.N.; 1930). *Cast:* Joe Frisco, Harry Gribbon, Edwin Maxwell, Lila Lee, Walter Pidgeon (who also appeared in the '27 version), Roscoe Karns, Purnell Pratt, Landers Stevens, Will Philbrick. *D:* Bryan Foy; *P:* Edward Small; *Sc:* Ralph Spence, Herman Ruby, W. Harrison Orkow.
Mystery-comedy set in an old dark house. Previously filmed by First National in 1927. Remade in 1939 (see below). Based on the popular play by Ralph Spence.

1736. The Gorilla (20th Century–Fox; 1939). *Cast:* The Ritz Brothers (Al, Harry and Jimmy), Anita Louise, Patsy Kelly, Lionel Atwill, Bela Lugosi, Joseph Calleia, Edward Norris, Wally Vernon, Art Miles. *D:* Allan Dwan; *As.P.:* Harry Joe Brown; *Sc:* Rian James, Sid Silvers. (1:06) (video)
Low-budget mystery-comedy, a remake of the preceding film based on the play by Ralph Spence.

1737. Gorilla Ship (Mayfair; 1932). *Cast:* Ralph Ince, Vera Reynolds (final film — ret.), Wheeler Oakman, George Chesebro. *D:* Frank Strayer. Low-budget mystery-melodrama.

1738. The Gracie Allen Murder Case (Paramount; 1939). *Cast:* Gracie Allen, Warren William (Philo Vance), Ellen Drew, Kent Taylor, Jerome Cowan, Judith Barrett, Donald MacBride, William Demarest, H.B. Warner, Horace McMahon, William Haade, James Flavin, Willie Fung, Harry Tyler, Al Shaw, Walter Soderling, Lee Moore, Jack Baxley, Don Brodie, Rube Demarest, Tiny Newlan, Sammy Lee. *D:* Alfred E. Green; *P:* George M. Arthur. (1:14)

Philo Vance murder-mystery which was especially written for the talents of the dingbat comedienne by S.S. Van Dine.

1739. Graft (Universal; 1931). *Cast:* Sue Carol, Regis Toomey, Boris Karloff, Dorothy Revier, William Davidson. *D:* Christy Cabanne. (1:12)

Low-budget newspaper melodrama involving politics and murder.

1740. Grand Canary (Fox; 1934). *Cast:* Warner Baxter, Madge Evans, Marjorie Rambeau, H.B. Warner, Zita Johann, Barry Norton, Gilbert Emery, Roger Imhof, John Rogers, Desmond Roberts, Gerald Rogers, Carrie Daumery. *D:* Irving Cummings; *P:* Jesse L. Lasky; *Sc:* Ernest Pascal.

Drama based on a novel by A.J. Cronin.

1741. Grand Exit (Columbia; 1935). *Cast:* Edmund Lowe, Ann Sothern, Onslow Stevens, Iris Adrian, Edward Van Sloan, Selmer Jackson, Guy Usher, Wyrley Birch. *D:* Erle C. Kenton; *St:* Gene Towne, Graham Baker; *Sc:* Lionel Houser, Bruce Manning.

B mystery-melodrama.

1742. Grand Hotel (MGM; 1932). *Cast:* Greta Garbo (Grusinskaya), Joan Crawford (Flaemmchen), Wallace Beery (Preysing), John Barrymore (Baron Felix von Geigern), Lionel Barrymore (Otto Kringelein), Lewis Stone (Dr. Otternschlag), Jean Hersholt (Senf), Ferdinand Gottschalk (Pimenov), Rafaela Ottiano (Suzette), Frank Conroy (Rohna), Robert McWade (Meierheim), Tully Marshall (Gerstenkorn), Purnell Pratt (Zinnowitz), Murray Kinnell (Schweimann), Edwin Maxwell (Dr. Waitz), Morgan Wallace (chauffeur), Mary Carlisle (honeymooner), John Davidson (hotel manager), Sam McDaniel (bartender), Rolfe Sedan & Herbert Evans (hotel clerks), Lee Phelps, John Miljan, Lawrence Grant. *D:* Edmund Goulding; *Adaptation:* William A. Drake. (1:55) (video)

Classic drama of various people whose lives cross while staying at a posh hotel. Based on the novel by Vicki Baum which was originally a magazine serial in Germany, this is the film where Garbo says "I vant to be alone." It was also adapted for the stage by Max Reinhardt. One of the 15 top grossing films of 1932, it received the A.A. for "Best Picture," while also receiving the same honors from *Film Daily*. It was in nomination for "Best Film" at the Venice Film Festival, while placing #4 on the "10 Best" list of the *New York Times* of 1932. Remade as *Weekend at the Waldorf* (MGM; 1945).

1743. Grand Jury (RKO; 1936). *Cast:* Fred Stone, Louise Latimer, Owen Davis, Jr., Moroni Olsen, Guinn Williams, Frank M. Thomas, Harry Beresford, Harry Jans, Russell Hicks, Charles Wilson, Billy Gilbert, Ed Gargan, Margaret Armstrong, Robert Emmett Keane, G. Pat Collins, Billy Arnold. *D:* Albert S. Rogell; *P:* Lee Marcus; *St:* James Edward Grant, Thomas Lennon; *Sc:* Joseph A. Fields, Philip G. Epstein. (1:01)

B melodrama of a citizen's crusade against local crime.

1744. Grand Jury Secrets (Paramount; 1939). *Cast:* John Howard, Gail Patrick, Richard Denning, Porter Hall, Morgan Conway, Elisha Cook, Jr., William Frawley, Jane Darwell, Harvey Stephens, John Hartley, Jack Norton. *D:* James Hogan; *P:* Samuel Engel; *St:* Maxwell Shane, Irving Reis; *Sc:* Reis, Robert Yost.

B courtroom melodrama.

1745. Grand Old Girl (RKO; 1935). *Cast:* May Robson, Fred MacMurray, Alan Hale, Mary Carlisle, Etienne Girardot, William Burress, Hale Hamilton, Edward Van Sloan, Fred Kohler, Jr., Onest Conley, Ben Alexander, George Offerman, Jr., Gavin Gordon, Ward Bond. *D:* John S. Robertson; *As.P.:* Cliff Reid; *St:* Wanda Tuchock; *Adaptation:* Arthur T. Horman; *Sc:* Milton Krims, John Twist. (1:12)

Sentimental story of a female teacher-principal in a small town who loses her job after many years of service. The film is dedicated to the school teachers of America.

1746. The Grand Parade (Pathe; 1930). *Cast:* Helen Twelvetrees, Fred Scott, Richard Carle, Russell Powell, Bud Jamison, Marie Astaire. *D:* Fred C. Newmeyer; *P:* Edmund Goulding; *Sc:* Goulding; *Director of Musical Numbers:* Richard Boleslawski.

Musical.

1747. Grand Slam (WB; 1933). *Cast:* Loretta Young, Paul Lukas, Frank McHugh, Glenda Farrell, Helen Vinson, Roscoe Karns, Walter Byron, Mary Doran, Lee Moran, DeWitt Jennings, Tom Dugan, Paul Porcasi, Lucien Prival, Reginald Barlow, Maurice Black, Ruthelma Stevens. *D:* William Dieterle; *P:* Hal Wallis; *Sc:* David Boehm, Erwin Gelsey. (1:07)

Low-budget comedy with its main focus, a bridge tournament. Based on the novel by B. Russell Herts.

1748. Granny Get Your Gun (WB; 1939-40). *Cast:* May Robson, Harry Davenport, Margot Stevenson, Hardie Albright, Arthur Aylesworth, Clem Bevans, William Davidson. *D:* George Amy; *As.P.:* Bryan Foy; *Sc:* Kenneth Gamet. (0:56)

Programmer comedy of an elderly lady who becomes a deputy sheriff to solve a murder she took the blame for. Based on the book "The Case of the Dangerous Dowager" by Erle Stanley Gardner.

1749. The Great Commandment (20th Century-Fox; 1939-41). *Cast:* John Beal, Albert Dekker, Lloyd Corrigan, Ian Wolfe, Maurice Moscovich. *D:* Irving Pichel; *Sc:* Dana Burnet.

Costumer completed in 1939 with release held up until 1941.

The Great Decision (G.B. title) *see* **Men of America**

1750. The Great Divide (WB/ F.N.; 1929). *Cast:* Dorothy Mackaill, Ian Keith, Lucien Littlefield, Myrna Loy, George Fawcett, Ben Hendricks, Jr., Claude Gillingwater, Creighton Hale, Roy Stewart. *D:* Reginald Barker; *St:* William Vaughn Moody; *Sc:* Fred Myton.

Melodrama of a crude miner who heads for the city to find himself a girl to take home and share his life. A remake of MGM's 1925 production of the same name with Wallace Beery and Alice Terry. Remade as *Woman Hungry* (q.v.).

1751. Great Expectations (Universal; 1934). *Cast:* Phillips Holmes (Pip), Jane Wyatt (Estella), Henry Hull (Magwitch), Florence Reed (Miss Haversham), Alan Hale (Joe Gargery), Rafaela Ottiano (Mrs. Joe), Francis L. Sullivan (Jaggers), Walter Armitage (Herbert Pocket), George Breakston (young Pip), Taylor Holmes, Robert Middlemass, Eily Malyon, Walter Brennan (unbilled bit). *D:* Stuart Walker; *Sc:* Gladys Unger. (1:40) (video)

An orphan boy is made wealthy by a mysterious benefactor in this adaptation of Charles Dickens novel. First filmed in 1917. A critically praised version came out of Great Britain in 1946 with another remake as a British-American co-produced TV movie in 1974.

1752. The Great Flirtation (Paramount; 1934). *Cast:* Elissa Landi, Adolphe Menjou, David Manners, Lynne Overman, Raymond Walburn, Akim Tamiroff, Paul Porcasi, Judith Vosselli, Adrian Rosley, George Baxter, Vernon Steele. *D:* Ralph Murphy; *St:* Gregory Ratoff.

Sentimental story of an actress's rise to fame as her husband's fame is fading.

1753. The Great Gabbo (Sono Art-World Wide; 1929–30). *Cast:* Erich Von Stroheim, Don Douglas, Marjorie Kane, Betty Compson. *D:* James Cruze; *P:* Cruze; *St:* Ben Hecht; *Sc:* F. Hugh Herbert. (1:29) (video)

Released on New Year's Day of 1930, this early musical-drama is centered around an egomaniacal ventriloguist. Some sequences originally filmed in color.

1754. The Great Gambini (Paramount; 1937). *Cast:* Akim Tamiroff, Marian Marsh, Genevieve Tobin, William Demarest, Reginald Denny, Roland Drew, Edward Brophy, John Trent, Lya Lys, Ralph Peters, Alan Birmingham. *D:* Charles Vidor; *P:* B.P. Schulberg; *Sc:* Frank Partos, Frederick Jackson, Howard Irving Young. (1:10)

B melodrama of a mystic who predicts the deaths of others.

1755. The Great Garrick (WB; 1937). *Cast:* Brian Aherne (David Garrick), Olivia de Havilland, Edward Everett Horton, Melville Cooper, Lionel Atwill, Luis Alberni, Lana Turner, Marie Wilson, Etienne Girardot, Albert Dekker (film debut), Fritz Leiber, Dorothy Tree, Craig Reynolds, Chester Clute, Ben Welden, E.E. Clive, Harry Davenport, Henry O'Neill, Jack Norton, Trevor Bardette, Linda Perry, Paul Everton, Milton Owen. *D:* James Whale; *P:* Whale; *Supervisor:* Mervyn LeRoy; *Sc:* Ernest Vajda. (1:31)

A fictitious comedy farce set in 1750 with members of the Comedie Francaise of Paris perpetrating a joke on real life British actor David Garrick. Based on Ernest Vajda's story "Ladies and Gentlemen."

1756. Great God Gold (Monogram; 1935). *Cast:* Sidney Blackmer, Martha Sleeper, Regis Toomey, Gloria Shea, Edwin Maxwell, Ralf Harolde, Maria Alba, John T. Murray. *D:* Arthur Lubin; *St:* Albert J. Meserow, Elynore Dalkhart; *Sc:* Norman Houston; *Additional Dialogue:* Jefferson Parker. (1:11)

B crime melodrama.

1757. Great Guy (Grand National; 1936–37). *Cast:* James Cagney, Mae Clarke, James Burke, Edward Brophy, Henry Kolker, Bernadene Hayes, Edward J. McNamara, Dwight Frye, Mary Gordon, Robert Gleckler, Joseph Sawyer, Edward Gargan, Matty Fain, Wallis Clark, Douglas Wood, Jeffrey Sayre, Eddy Chandler, Henry Rocquemore, Murdock MacQuarrie, Kate Price, Frank O'Connor, Arthur Hoyt, Jack Pennick, Lynton Brent, John Dilson, Bud Geary, Bud Flanagan (Dennis O'Keefe), Robert Lowery, Bobby Barber, Ethelreda Leopold, Gertrude Green, Bruce Mitchell, James Ford, Frank Mills, Ben Hendricks, Jr., Kernan Cripps, Bill O'Brien, Lester Dorr, Harry Tenbrook, Lee Shumway, Gertrude Astor, Vera Steadman, Mildred Harris, Bert Kalmar, Jr., Walter D. Clarke, Jr. *D:* John G. Blystone; *P:* Douglas MacLean; *St:* James Edward Grant (the "Johnny Cave" stories); *Sc:* Henry McCarty, Henry Johnson, Grant, Harry Ruskin; *Additional Dialogue:* Harry McCoy. (G.B. title: *Pluck of the Irish*) (1:13) (video)

A melodrama of corruption in the meat business. This was the first film for Cagney for another studio since being signed as a contract player by Warners. It achieved moderate success at the box office.

1758. The Great Hospital Mystery (20th Century–Fox; 1937). *Cast:* Jane Darwell, Joan Davis, Sig Rumann, Sally Blane, Thomas Beck, William Demarest, Wade Boteler, Howard Phillips, George Walcott. *D:* James Tinling; *Sc:* Bess Meredyth, William Conselman, Jerry Cady. (0:59)

B murder-mystery set in a big city hospital. Based on the book by Mignon Eberhart.

1759. The Great Hotel Murder (Fox; 1934–35). *Cast:* Edmund Lowe, Victor McLaglen, Rosemary Ames, Mary Carlisle, Madge Bellamy, Herman Bing, John Qualen, Henry O'Neill, Robert Gleckler, C. Henry Gordon, Charles Wilson, William Janney, Clarence Wilson. *D:* Eugene Forde; *P:* John Stone; *St:* Vincent Starrett; *Sc:* Arthur Kober. (1:10)

"Flagg and Quirt" type detectives compete to solve a murder in this low-budget comedy-mystery.

1760. The Great Impersonation (Universal; 1935). *Cast:* Edmund Lowe (in a dual role), Valerie Hobson, Wera Engels, Henry Mollison, Spring Byington, Lumsden Hare, Charles Waldron, Dwight Frye, Frank Reicher, Leonard Mudie, Brandon Hurst, Claude King. *D:* Alan Crosland (final film—d. 1936 in an auto accident); *Sc:* Frank Wead, Eve Greene. (1:21)

Melodrama of a German spy posing as the owner of an English castle. Based on the novel by E. Phillips Oppenheim, it was previously filmed in 1921 by Paramount with James Kirkwood. Remade in 1942 with Ralph Bellamy.

1761. The Great Jasper (RKO; 1933). *Cast:* Richard Dix (Jasper Horn),

Florence Eldridge (Mrs. Horn), Edna May Oliver (Madame Telma), Wera Engels, Walter Walker, David Durand, Bruce Cabot, Betty Furness, James Bush, Herman Bing. *D:* J. Walter Ruben; *P:* David O. Selznick; *As.P.:* Kenneth MacGowan; *Sc:* H.W. Hanemann, Robert Tasker. (1:25)

Drama of an irresponsible married womanizer who becomes involved with the wife of his employer. Set in Atlantic City, it is based on the book by Fulton Oursler.

1762. The Great Lover (MGM; 1931). *Cast:* Adolphe Menjou, Irene Dunne, Neil Hamilton, Cliff Edwards, Olga Baclanova, Ernest Torrence, Hale Hamilton, Lillian Bond, Roscoe Ates, Herman Bing, Elsa Janssen; *D:* Harry Beaumont; *St:* Leo Ditrichstein, Frederick & Fanny Hatton; *Sc:* Gene Markey, Edgar Allan Woolf. (1:17)

An aging operatic baritone loses his protege to a much younger man.

1763. The Great Man Votes (RKO; 1939). *Cast:* John Barrymore (Gregory Vance), Peter Holden, Virginia Weidler, Donald MacBride, Katherine Alexander, William Demarest, Elizabeth Risdon, Bennie Bartlett, J.M. Kerrigan, Brandon Tynan, Roy Gordon, Luis Alberni, Granville Bates. *D:* Garson Kanin; *P:* Cliff Reid; *St:* Gordon Malherbe Hillman; *Sc:* John Twist. (1:12)

Critically acclaimed political comedy of a tippling ex-college prof who becomes popular with the candidates during an election.

1764. The Great Meadow (MGM; 1931). *Cast:* John Mack Brown, Eleanor Boardman, Lucille La Verne, Anita Louise, Gavin Gordon, Guinn Williams, Russell Simpson, John Miljan, Julie Haydon, Helen Jerome Eddy, Sarah Padden. *D:* Charles Brabin; *Sc:* Brabin, Edith Ellis. (1:18)

Colonial frontier drama of hardships suffered by the pioneers trekking from Virginia to a new homeland in what is now known as Kentucky in the 1770s. Based on the novel by Elizabeth Madox Roberts.

1765. The Great O'Malley (WB; 1936–37). *Cast:* Pat O'Brien, Sybil Jason, Humphrey Bogart, Ann Sheridan, Frieda Inescort, Donald Crisp, Henry O'Neill, Hobart Cavanaugh, Mary Gordon, Frank Reicher, Mabel Colcord, Frank Sheridan. *D:* William Dieterle; *As.P.:* Harry Joe Brown; *Sc:* Milton Krims, Tom Reed. (1:11)

Melodrama of a cop who cares for the wife and crippled daughter of a crook he sent to prison. Based on the story "The Making of O'Malley" by Gerald Beaumont. A remake of *The Making of O'Malley* (First National; 1923).

1766. The Great Power (MGM/ Franklyn Warner; 1929). *Cast:* Minna Gombell, Herschel Mayall. *D:* Joe Rock; *P:* Franklyn Warner (independent).

A minor early talkie which was filmed in New York, marking the film debut of Minna Gombell in the lead recreating her stage role from the same production.

The Great Radio Mystery (G.B. title) *see* **Take the Stand**

The Great Schnozzle (G.B. title) *see* **Palooka**

1767. The Great Victor Herbert (Paramount; 1939). *Cast:* Walter Connolly (in his final film before his death, as Victor Herbert), Allan Jones, Mary Martin (in her starring film debut), Lee Bowman, Susanna Foster (starring debut), Jerome Cowan, Judith Barrett, Richard Tucker (final film — d. 1942), John Garrick, Hal K. Dawson, Pierre Watkin, James Finlayson, Emmett Vogan. *D:* Andrew L. Stone; *P:* Stone; *St:* Stone, Robert Lively; *Sc:* Lively, Russel Crouse; *Musical Score:* (A.A.N.) Phil Boutelje, Arthur Lange; *Sound Recording:* (A.A.N.) Loren Ryder. (1:24)

Filmed biography of the famed composer, featuring over twenty-five of Herbert's compositions in various forms.

1768. The Great Waltz (MGM; 1938). *Cast:* Luise Rainer (Poldi Vogelhuber), Fernand Gravet (Johann Strauss II), Miliza Korjus (Hungarian actress making her only American film and receiving an A.A.N. for B.S.A. as Carla Donner), Hugh Herbert (Hofbauer), Lionel Atwill (Count Hohenfriend), Curt Bois (Keinzl), Leonid Kinskey (Dudelman), Al Shean (Cellist), Minna Gombell (Mrs. Hofbauer), George Houston (Schiller), Bert Roach (Vogelhuber), Greta Meyer (Mrs. Vogelhuber), Herman Bing (Dommayer), Alma Kruger (Mrs. Strauss), Henry Hull (Franz Josef), Sig Rumann (Wertheimer), Christian Rub, Billy Gilbert. *D:* Julian Duvivier; *P:* Bernard Hyman; *St:* Gottfried Reinhardt; *Sc:* Walter Reisch, Samuel Hoffenstein; *Cinematographer:* (A.A.) Joseph Ruttenberg; *Editor:* (A.A.N.) Tom Held. (1:43)

A lavishly produced fictionalized biography of Austrian composer, Johann Strauss II. Much of Strauss' music is used throughout the film with Oscar Hammerstein II writing the lyrics for "I'm in Love with Vienna" and "One Day When We Were Young." Remade in 1972.

1769. The Great Ziegfeld (MGM; 1936). *Cast:* William Powell (Flo Ziegfeld), Luise Rainer (A.A. for B.A. as well as the "Best Actress" Award from the New York Film Critics as Anna Held), Myrna Loy (Billie Burke), Frank Morgan (Billings), Reginald Owen (Sampston), Nat Pendleton (Sandow), Virginia Bruce (Audrey Lane), Fanny Brice (herself), Ray Bolger (himself), Ernest Cossart (Sidney), Robert Greig (Joe), Raymond Walburn (Sage), Jean Chatburn (Mary Lou), Ann Pennington (herself), Harriett Hoctor (herself), Charles Trowbridge (Julian Mitchell), Gilda Gray (herself), A.A. Trimble

(Will Rogers), Jean Holland (Patricia
Ziegfeld), Buddy Doyle (Eddie Cantor),
Charles Judels (Pierre), Leon Errol
(himself), Marcelle Corday (Marie),
Esther Muir (prima donna), Paul Irving
(Erlanger), William Demarest (Gene
Buck), Miss Morocco (Little Egypt),
Suzanne Kaaren (Miss Blair), Herman
Bing, Richard Tucker, Clay Clement,
Selmer Jackson (customers), Alice Keat-
ing (Alice), Rosina Lawrence (Marilyn
Miller), Edwin Maxwell (Charles Fro-
man), Ruth Gillette (Lillian Russell),
John Hyams (Dave Stamper), Boothe
Howard (Willie Zimmerman), Mickey
Daniels, Susan Fleming, Stanley Mor-
ner (Dennis Morgan), Virginia Grey,
Joseph Cawthorn. *D:* (A.A.N.) Robert
Z. Leonard; *P:* Hunt Stromberg;
Original Story: (A.A.N.) William An-
thony McGuire; *Sc:* McGuire; *Art-Set
Decorations:* (A.A.N.) Cedric Gibbons,
Eddie Imazu, Edwin B. Willis; *Choreog-
rapher:* (A.A.) Seymour Felix for the "A
Pretty Girl Is Like a Melody" number
(originally from Ziegfeld's 1919 Follies);
Editor: (A.A.N.) William S. Gray; *Songs:*
"I Wish You'd Come and Play With
Me," "It's Delightful to Be Married," "A
Circus Must Be Different in a Ziegfeld
Show," "It's Been So Long," "You Gotta
Pull Strings," "You," "Queen of the
Jungle," "She's a Follies Girl," and "You
Never Looked So Beautiful" by Walter
Donaldson–Harold Adamson, and "A
Pretty Girl Is Like a Melody" by Irving
Berlin. (3:04) (video)

Ultra-lavish film biography of
Broadway showman Florenz Ziegfeld,
his two marriages and his establishment
of the famous "Ziegfeld Follies." This
proved to be the most expensive production of this studio since their 1926 production of *Ben-Hur.* It was their second
biggest money-maker of 1936 as well as
one of the 25 top grossing films of 1935–
36. It won the A.A. for "Best Picture"
and was also in nomination for "Best
Film" at the Venice Film Festival. It
placed #3 on the "10 Best" list of *Film
Daily,* while placing #10 on the same list
of the *New York Times.*

**1770. The Greeks Had a Word
for Them** (United Artists/Samuel
Goldwyn; 1932). *Cast:* Joan Blondell
(Schatze), Madge Evans (Polaire), Ina
Claire (Jean), David Manners, Lowell
Sherman, Phillips Smalley, Sidney
Bracey, Frances Dean (Betty Grable).
D: Lowell Sherman; *P:* Goldwyn; *Sc:*
Sidney Howard. (Retitled: *Three Broad-
way Girls*) (1:17) (video)

Comedy based on the play by Zoe
Akins of three New York gold diggers in
search of rich husbands. Remade in 1938
as *Three Blind Mice* (q.v.), in 1941 as *Moon
Over Miami,* in 1946 as *Three Little Girls in
Blue* and in 1953 as *How to Marry a
Millionaire.*

1771. Green Eyes (Chesterfield;
1934). *Cast:* Lloyd Whitlock, Charles
Starrett, Shirley Grey, Dorothy Revier,
Claude Gillingwater. *D:* Richard
Thorpe; *Sc:* Andrew Moses.

"Poverty row" mystery-drama.

1772. The Green Goddess (WB/
Vitaphone; 1930). *Cast:* George Arliss
(A.A.N. for B.A. repeating his role in
the 1923 version as the Rajah of Rukh),
Alice Joyce (who also appeared in the '23
version as Mrs. Crespin), H.B. Warner
(Major Crespin), Ralph Forbes (Dr.
Basil Traherne), Ivan Simpson (Lord
Chamberlain Watkins), Reginald
Sheffield (Lieut. Cardew), Nigel de
Brulier (temple priest), David Tearle
(high priest), Betty Boyd (Ayah). *D:*
Alfred E. Green; *Sc:* Julien Josephson.
(1:20)

In a remote kingdom in the Hima-
layas a self righteous and vengeful
potentate holds three British passengers
captive after their plane crash lands. A
melodrama based on the stage play by
William Archer, it was previously filmed
by First National in 1923. Remade in
1942 as *Adventure in Iraq.*

1773. Green Light (WB/F.N.;
1937). *Cast:* Errol Flynn, Anita Louise,
Margaret Lindsay, Sir Cedric Hardwicke, Walter Abel, Henry O'Neill,

Spring Byington, Erin O'Brien-Moore, Henry Kolker, Russell Simpson, Pierre Watkin, Myrtle Stedman. *D:* Frank Borzage; *P:* Henry Blanke; *Sc:* Milton Krims. (1:25)

This melodrama of a surgeon who gives up his medical practice when one of his patients dies was one of the 38 top grossing films of 1936–37. A Cosmopolitan production which was based on the novel by Lloyd C. Douglas.

1774. The Green Pastures (WB; 1936). *Cast:* Rex Ingram (De Lawd/Adam/Hezdrel), Oscar Polk (Gabriel), Eddie "Rochester" Anderson (Noah), Frank C. Wilson (Moses/Sexton), Ernest Whitman (Pharaoh), George Reed (Deshee/Isaac), George Randol (high priest), William Cumby (Abraham/King of Babylon/head magician), Edna M. Harris (Zeba), Slim Thompson (Master of Ceremonies/man on ground), Ida Forsythe (Mrs. Noah), Al Stokes (Cain), Myrtle Anderson (Eve), Reginald Fenderson (Joshua), David Bethea (Aaron), Abraham Gleaves (archangel), Jimmy Fuller (Cain the sixth), John Alexander (dancer #1), Clinton Rosemond (prophet), Rosena Weston (Zipporah), William Broadus (Mr. Randall), Amanda Drayton (Mrs. Randall), Fred "Snowflake" Toones (Zubo), Charles Andrews (Flatfoot/Gambler), Dudley Dickerson (Ham), Ray Martin (Shem), James Burress (Japheth), Minnie Gray (Mrs. Ham), Bessie Guy (Mrs. Shem), Dorothy Bishop (Mrs. Japheth), Ben Carter (gambler), Ivory Williams (Jacob), Jesse Graves (general), Lillian Davis (Viney Prohack), Bessie Lyle (Mrs. Prohack), Duke Upshaw (Abel/dancer #2), Charlotte Sneed (Carlotta Prohack), Willie Best (Henry the angel), Johnny Lee (angel), Philip "Lucky" Hurlic (Carlisle), Hall Johnson Choir (chorus of angels). *D:* William Keighley, Marc Connelly; *P:* Hal B. Wallis; *As.P.:* Henry Blanke; *Sc:* Marc Connelly (from his play which was inspired by Roark Bradford's sketches "Ol' Man Adam An'

His Chillun") Sheridan Gibney; *Songs:* (arranged by Hall Johnson) include "Joshua Fit de Battle of Jericho and the Walls Came Tumbling Down," "De Old Ark's a Moverin," "Let My People Go," "Run, Sinner, Run," "Death Gwinter Lay His Hands on Me" and "When the Saints Come Marchin' In." (1:33) (video)

Classic offbeat film with an all-black cast, depicting various biblical characters and "life in heaven." Based on the 1930 Pulitzer Prize winning play by Marc Connelly, this film received no Oscar nominations but on the "10 Best" lists of the *New York Times,* the National Board of Review and *Film Daily* respectively it placed #6, #9 and #10. Considered a prestigious film of its day, it was popular at the box office, being one of the 25 top grossing films of 1935–36. Being the first all-black film to receive general theatrical release, it is looked upon today by many as demeaning to blacks, though initially it was conceived in the simplicity of faith.

1775. The Greene Murder Case (Paramount; 1929). *Cast:* William Powell (Philo Vance), Florence Eldridge, Ullrich Haupt, Jean Arthur, Eugene Pallette, E.H. Calvert, Morgan Farley, Brandon Hurst, Gertrude Norman, Marcia Harris, Helena Phillips, Augusta Burmeister. *D:* Frank Tuttle; *Sc:* Louise Long, Bartlett Cormack. (1:09)

Philo Vance mystery, the second in this studio's series. Based on the book by S.S. Van Dine.

1776. The Greyhound Limited (WB; 1929). *Cast:* Monte Blue, Grant Withers, Edna Murphy, Lucy Beaumont, Lew Harvey, Ernie Shields. *D:* Howard Bretherton; *St:* Albert Howson; *Sc:* Anthony Coldeway.

Part-talkie melodrama of a man accused of murder.

1777. Gridiron Flash (RKO; 1934). *Cast:* Eddie Quillan, Betty

Furness, Grant Mitchell, Lucien Little-field, Edgar Kennedy, Grady Sutton, Joseph (Sawyer) Sauers, Allen Wood, Margaret Dumont. *D:* Glenn Tryon; *As.P.:* Louis Sarecky; *St:* Nicholas Barrows, Earle Snell; *Sc:* Tryon. (G.B. title: *Luck of the Game*)

Low-budget comedy-drama of a prison inmate who is hired for a college football team.

1778. Grief Street (Chesterfield; 1931). *Cast:* Barbara Kent, Lillian Rich, Lafe McKee, Larry Steers, Crauford Kent. *D:* Richard Thorpe (also editor). "Poverty row" melodrama.

1779. Grumpy (Paramount; 1930). *Cast:* Cyril Maude (film debut — recreating his stage role), Phillips Holmes, Frances Dade, Halliwell Hobbes, Paul Cavanagh, Paul Lukas, Olaf Hytten, Colin Kenny, Doris Luray, Robert Bolder. *D:* George Cukor (his directorial debut), Cyril Gardner; *Sc:* Doris Anderson.

Comedy of an old barrister who solves the mystery of a stolen diamond. Based on the popular stage play by Horace Hodges and Thomas Percyval which was previously filmed in 1923 by this studio with Theodore Roberts and May McAvoy. Filmed at Astoria Studios in Long Island, N.Y.

1780. Guard That Girl! (Columbia; 1935). *Cast:* Florence Rice, Robert Allen, Barbara Kent, Elizabeth Risdon, Thurston Hall, Arthur Hohl, Ward Bond. *D:* Lambert Hillyer; *St & Sc:* Hillyer.

B production.

1781. The Guardsman (MGM; 1931). *Cast:* Alfred Lunt (A.A.N. for B.A. 1931–32 as the actor), Lynn Fontanne (A.A.N. for B.A. 1931–32 as the actress), Roland Young (critic), ZaSu Pitts (Liesl, the maid), Maude Eburne (Mama), Herman Bing (creditor), Ann Dvorak (fan). *D:* Sidney Franklin; *P:* Albert Lewin; *Adaptation:* Ernest Vajda,

Claudine West. (aka: *Son of Russia*) (1:23)

Marital comedy of a jealous actor who assumes another identity to romance his wife. Lunt and Fontanne in their only starring film together, repeating their 1924 Broadway roles in an adaptation of Ferenc Molnar's play. A box office flop that was voted "Best Film of the Year" by the *New York Times,* one of the "10 Best" films of the year by the National Board of Review and a #4 place on the list of "10 Best" films by *Film Daily* in 1932.

Note: Remade in 1941 as *The Chocolate Soldier.*

1782. Guilty? (Columbia; 1930). *Cast:* Robert T. Haines, Virginia Valli, Eddie Clayton, John St. Polis, Richard Carlyle, Clarence Muse, Lydia Knott, John Holland. *D:* George B. Seitz.

Low-budget melodrama from "poverty row."

Guilty as Charged (G.B. title) *see* **Guilty as Hell**

1783. Guilty as Hell (Paramount; 1932). *Cast:* Richard Arlen, Edmund Lowe, Victor McLaglen, Henry Stephenson, Adrienne Ames, Noel Francis, Ralph Ince, Elizabeth Patterson, Claire Dodd, Willard Robertson, Richard Tucker, William Davidson, Gordon Westcott (film debut), Lillian Harmer, Fred Kelsey, Arnold Lucy, Oscar Smith, Harold Berquist, Charles Sylber, Clifford Dempsey, Elsa Peterson, Earl Pingree. *D:* Erle C. Kenton; *Sc:* Frank Partos, Arthur Kober.

Mystery-melodrama of a doctor who kills his adulterous wife and blames her lover. Based on the novel "Riddle Me This" by Daniel Rubin, it was remade as *Night Club Scandal* (q.v.).

1784. The Guilty Generation (Columbia; 1931). *Cast:* Robert Young, Constance Cummings, Leo Carrillo, Leslie Fenton, Boris Karloff, Emma Dunn, Murray Kinnell, Ruth Warren,

Elliott Roth. *D:* Rowland V. Lee; *St:* J. Kirby Hawkes, Jo Milward.

Melodrama of the offspring of rival gang bosses who fall in love.

1785. Guilty Hands (MGM; 1931). *Cast:* Lionel Barrymore, Kay Francis, Madge Evans, William Bakewell, C. Aubrey Smith, Polly Moran, Alan Mowbray, Forrester Harvey, Charles Crockett, Henry Barrows. *D:* W.S. Van Dyke II; *P:* Hunt Stromberg; *St & Sc:* Bayard Veiller. (1:07)

A D.A. kills the man he believes is going to marry his daughter and attempts to cover his crime in this low-budget drama.

1786. Guilty or Not Guilty (Monogram; 1932). *Cast:* Betty Compson, Claudia Dell, Tom Douglas, George Irving, Wheeler Oakman, Luis Alberni, Walter Percival, William Davidson, Erin La Bissoniere. *D:* Al (Albert) Ray; *Sc:* Frances Hyland. (1:10)

Low-budget mystery-melodrama which is based on a syndicated news story by Arthur Hoerl.

1787. Guilty Parents (Syndicate Exchange; 1934). *Cast:* Jean Lacy, Donald Keith, Robert Frazer, Gertrude Astor, John St. Polis. *D:* Jack Townley.

Exploitation melodrama of a naive girl not informed by her parents of the "facts of life" who runs off with her no-good boyfriend and ultimately down the road to self-destruction.

1788. Guilty Trails (Universal; 1938). *Cast:* Bob Baker, Marjorie Reynolds, Fuzzy Knight, Jack Rockwell, Glenn Strange, Hal Taliaferro, Georgia O'Dell, Carleton Young, Murdock MacQuarrie, Tom London, Jack Kirk, Tex Palmer. *D:* George Waggner; *P:* Trem Carr; *Sc:* Joseph West (Waggner) (0:57)

Bob Baker western of a cowboy who saves a girl's ranch from the bad guys.

1789. Gulliver's Travels (Paramount; 1939). *D:* Dave Fleischer; *P:* Max Fleischer; *Adaptation:* Edmond Seward; *Sc:* Ted Pierce, Dan Gordon, Cal Howard, Isidor Sparber; *Singing Voices:* Lanny Ross, Jessica Dragonette. (1:14) (video)

Animated technicolor production of Jonathan Swift's satire on the political structure of the England of his time told through the animation of Max Fleischer. One of 21 top grossing films of 1939–40, this was the second color animated feature film to come out of Hollywood, preceded by Disney's *Snow White and the Seven Dwarfs* (q.v.). Remade in 1976–77 as a live action-animated co-production of Great Britain and Belgium. 1960 also saw the British production of *The Three Worlds of Gulliver*.

1790. Gun Grit (Atlantic; 1936). *Cast:* Jack Perrin, Ethel Beck, David Sharpe, Jimmy Aubrey, Ed Cassidy, Earl Dwire, Horace Murphy, Roger Williams, Ralph Peters, Frank Hagney, Oscar Gahan, Budd Buster, Starlight the horse, Braveheart the dog. *D:* Lester Williams (William Berke); *P:* Harry Fraser; *Sc:* Gordon Phillips. (1:00)

Jack Perrin western of a government agent sent west to put the crimps to a cattle protection racket established by big city racketeers.

1791. Gun Justice (Universal; 1933). *Cast:* Ken Maynard, Cecilia Parker, Walter Miller, Hooper Atchley, Sheldon Lewis, Lafe McKee, Jack Rockwell, Jack Richardson, Francis Ford, Fred Mackaye, William Dyer, Ed Coxen, William Gould, Ben Corbett, Bob McKenzie, Horace B. Carpenter, Frank Ellis, Hank Bell, Bud McClure, Roy Bucko, Buck Bucko, Pascale Perry, Cliff Lyons, Blackjack Ward. *D:* Alan James (Alvin J. Neitz); *Sc:* Robert Quigley. (0:59) (video)

Ken Maynard horse opera of a cowboy who inherits a ranch and encounters trouble with his neighbors.

1792. Gun Law (Majestic; 1933). *Cast:* Jack Hoxie, Betty Boyd, J. Frank Glendon, Mary Carr, Harry Todd, Edmund Cobb, Ben Corbett, Paul Fix, Richard Botiller, Bob Burns, Horace B. Carpenter, Jack Kirk. *D:* Lewis D. Collins; *P:* Max & Arthur Alexander; *Sc:* Collins, Oliver Drake. (0:59)

"Poverty row" Jack Hoxie oater centered around an outlaw called the Sonora Kid.

1793. Gun Law (RKO; 1938). *Cast:* George O'Brien, Paul Everton, Rita Oehmen (film debut), Ray Whitley, Robert Gleckler, Ward Bond, Francis McDonald, Edward Pawley, Paul Fix, Frank O'Connor, Hank Bell, Ethan Laidlaw, Lloyd Ingraham, Bob Burns, Jim Mason, Neal Burns, Ken Card. *D:* David Howard; *P:* Bert Gilroy; *Sc:* Oliver Drake; *Songs:* Ray Whitley, Drake. (1:00)

George O'Brien western of a U.S. marshal who works his way into a treacherous gang of outlaws. A remake of *When the Law Rides* (FBO; 1928) with Tom Tyler and *The Reckless Ranger* (q.v.).

1794. Gun Lords of Stirrup Basin (Republic-Supreme; 1937). *Cast:* Bob Steele, Louise Stanley, Karl Hackett, Ernie Adams, Frank LaRue, Frank Ball, Steve Clark, Lew Meehan, Frank Ellis, Jim Corey, Budd Buster, Lloyd Ingraham, Jack Kirk, Horace Murphy, Milburn Morante, Bobby Nelson, Tex Palmer, Horace B. Carpenter. *D:* Sam Newfield; *P:* A.W. Hackel; *Sc:* George Plympton, Fred Myton. (1:00)

Bob Steele western of a family feud.

1795. Gun Packer (Monogram; 1938). *Cast:* Jack Randall, Louise Stanley, Charles King, Barlowe Borland, Glenn Strange, Raymond Turner, Lloyd Ingraham, Lowell Drew, Ernie Adams, Forrest Taylor, Curley Dresden, Sherry Tansey, Rusty the horse. *D:* Wallace Fox; *P:* Robert Tansey; *St & Sc:* Robert Emmett (Tansey). (0:51)

Jack Randall western.

1796. Gun Play (Beacon/Equity; 1935). *Cast:* Guinn "Big Boy" Williams, Marion Shilling, Frank Yaconelli, Wally Wales (Hal Taliaferro), Charles K. French, Tom London, Roger Williams, Gordon Griffith, Barney Beasley, Si Jenks, Dick Botiller, Julian Rivero. *D:* Al Herman; *Sc:* William L. Nolte. (Retitled: *Lucky Boots*) (0:59)

Guinn "Big Boy" Williams western of two cowboys on a treasure hunt for hidden loot from a dead Mexican bandit.

1797. The Gun Ranger (Republic-Supreme; 1937). *Cast:* Bob Steele, Eleanor Stewart, Hal Taliaferro, John Merton, Ernie Adams, Earl Dwire, Budd Buster, Frank Ball, Horace Murphy, Lew Meehan, Horace B. Carpenter, Jack Kirk, George Morrell, Tex Palmer. *D:* Robert N. Bradbury; *P:* A.W. Hackel; *Sc:* George Plympton. (1:00)

Bob Steele oater of a ranger in search of the party who killed a girl's father.

1798. Gun Smoke (Paramount; 1931). *Cast:* Richard Arlen, Mary Brian, William ("Stage") Boyd, Eugene Pallette, Charles Winninger, Louise Fazenda, J. Carrol Naish, Jack Richardson, James (Junior) Durkin, Dawn O'Day (Anne Shirley), Guy Oliver, Brooks Benedict, Willie Fung, William V. Mong, William Arnold, Stanley Mack. *D:* Edward Sloman; *St & Sc:* Grover Jones, William Slavens McNutt. (1:06)

B western of a wild horse wrangler who wrangles up a gang of big city gangsters in a small town.

1799. Gun Smoke (Willis Kent; 1935). *D:* Bartlett Carre.

Buck Coburn (Gene Alsace/Rocky Camron) indie western, one of two films in a failed attempt to establish a series.

Monte Montana, a trick roper who also made a bid for cowboy stardom and failed also appears in the film as well as producing it.

1800. Gunfire (Resolute; 1934–35). *Cast:* Rex Bell, Ruth Mix, Buzz Barton, Milburn Morante, Theodore Lorch, Philo McCullough, Ted Adams, Lew Meehan, Willie Fung, Mary Jane Irving, Jack Baston, Fern Emmett, Howard Hickey, Chuck Morrison, Mary Jo Ellis, William Demarest, Slim Whitaker. *D:* Harry Fraser; *Sc:* Harry C. Crist (Fraser). (0:56)

Rex Bell western — one in a series of four — of a cowboy who with the help of a girl from the east prove a rancher innocent of murder.

1801. Gunga Din (RKO; 1939). *Cast:* Cary Grant (Cutter), Victor McLaglen (MacChesney), Douglas Fairbanks, Jr. (Ballantine), Sam Jaffe (Gunga Din), Eduardo Ciannelli (Gura), Joan Fontaine (Emmy), Montagu Love (Colonel Weed), Robert Coote (Higginbotham), Abner Biberman (Chota), Lunsden Hare (Major Mitchell), Cecil Kellaway (Mr. Stebbins), Reginald Sheffield (journalist), Olin Francis (Fulad), Lal Chand Mehra (Jadoo), Roland Varno (Lieut. Markham), Ann Evers, Audrey Manners, Fay McKenzie, Charles Bennett, Les Sketchley, Frank Levya, George Ducount, Jamiel Hasson, George Regas, Bryant Fryer, Clive Morgan, Rodd Redwing. *D:* George Stevens; *P:* Stevens; *Adaptation:* Ben Hecht, Charles MacArthur; *Sc:* Joel Sayre, Fred Guiol. (1:57) (video)

Action-adventure of the British Army battling warring Punjabs in 19th-century India. Based on the poem by Rudyard Kipling, this was the most expensive production of this studio, coming in at $1,900,000. It turned out to be one of the 16 top grossing films of 1938–39. A Hollywood classic, it was filmed at Lone Pine, California. Remade in 1961 as *Sergeants 3*, for U.A. release, Computer-colored by Turner Entertainment in 1989.

1802. Gunners and Guns (Beaumont; 1935). *Cast:* Black King the horse (in the first of his two starring features), Edwin (Edmund) Cobb, Edna Aslin, Edward Allen Bilby, Eddie Davis, Ned Norton, Lois Glaze, Felix Valee, Jack Cheatham, Ruth Runnell, Frank Walker. *D:* Jerry Callahan, Robert Hoyt; *P:* Mitchell Leichter; *Sc:* Ruth Runnell. (0:57) (video)

B western with the focus on the murder of a dude ranch owner, who it turns out had a dark past.

Note: Originally released in 1934 as *Racketeer Round-Up* with additional footage added for this 1935 release.

Guns A-Blazin' *see* **Law and Order** (1932)

1803. Guns and Guitars (Republic; 1936). *Cast:* Gene Autry, Smiley Burnette, Dorothy Dix, Earle Hodgins, J.P. McGowan, Tom London, Charles King, Frankie Marvin, Eugene Jackson, Jack Rockwell, Ken Cooper, Tracy Layne, Wes Warner, Jack Kirk, Audry Davis, Jim Corey, Al Taylor, Frank Stravenger, Robert E. (Bob) Burns, Jack Don, Harrison Greene, Pascale Perry, Champion. *D:* Joseph Kane; *P:* Nat Levine; *Supervisor:* Robert Beche; *St & Sc:* Dorrell & Stuart McGowan; *Songs:* Autry, Burnette, Oliver Drake. (0:56)

Gene Autry western with songs and a story of infected cattle.

1804. Guns for Hire (Willis Kent; 1932). *Cast:* Lane Chandler, Sally Darling, Neal Hart, Yakima Canutt, John Ince, Slim Whitaker, Jack Rockwell, Ben Corbett, Steve Clemente, Bill Patton, Hank Bell, John P. McGuire, Frances Morris, Nelson McDowell, John Bacon, Roy Bucko, Buck Bucko, Edward Porter, Gene Alsace (Rocky Camron), Bud McClure, Bud Pope, Jack O'Shea, Ray Jones. *D:* Oliver Drake; *P:* Willis Kent; *Sc:* Drake. (0:59) (TV title: *Blazing Trail*)

Lane Chandler western.

1805. Guns in the Dark (Republic-Supreme; 1937). *Cast:* Johnny Mack Brown, Claire Rochelle, Syd Saylor, Ted Adams, Frank Ellis, Budd Buster, Merrill McCormack, Richard Cramer, Jack C. Smith, Roger Williams, Jim Corey, Dick Curtis, Steve Clark, Julian Madison, Slim Whitaker, Lew Meehan, Oscar Gahan, Tex Palmer, Chick Hannon, Sherry Tansey. *D:* Sam Newfield; *P:* A.W. Hackel; *Sc:* Charles Francis Royal. (0:56)

Johnny Mack Brown western of a cowboy who turns gunshy, believing he killed his friend in a barroom brawl.

1806. Guns of the Pecos (WB/F.N.; 1937). *Cast:* Dick Foran, Anne Nagel, Gaby Fay (Fay Holden), Gordon Hart, Joseph Crehan, Eddie Acuff, Gordon (Bill) Elliott, Robert Middlemass, Monte Montague, Glenn Strange, Robert E. (Bob) Burns, Milton Kibbee, Bud Osborne, Douglas Wood, Gene Alsace (Rocky Camron), Bob Woodward, Frank McCarroll, Jack Kirk, Ray Jones. *D:* Noel Smith; *P:* Bryan Foy; *St:* Anthony Coldeway; *Sc:* Harold Buckley; *Songs:* "When a Cowboy Takes a Wife" and "The Prairie Is My Home" by M.K. Jerome, Jack Scholl. (0:57)

Dick Foran horse opera with songs, of a group of geriatric Texas Rangers on the trail of rustlers who killed an army officer.

1807. Gunsmoke on the Guadalupe (Willis Kent; 1935). *Cast:* Roger Williams.

(No other information available) (Possibly an Ajax production)

1808. Gunsmoke Ranch (Republic; 1937). *Cast:* Bob Livingston (Stony Brooke), Ray Corrigan (Tucson Smith), Max Terhune (Lullaby), Julia Thayer (Jean Carmen), Kenneth Harlan, Sammy McKim, Yakima Canutt, Oscar & Elmer (dummies), Burr Caruth, Horace B. Carpenter, Robert Walker, Fred "Snowflake" Toones, Jack Kirk, Jack Ingram, Jack Padjan, John Mer-

ton, Bob McKenzie, Ed Peil, Sr., Fred Burns. *D:* Joe Kane; *Sc:* Jack Natteford, Oliver Drake. (0:56)

Hit "Three Mesquiteers" western of flood victims who are further being victimized by a crooked politician.

1809. Gunsmoke Trail (Monogram; 1938). *Cast:* Jack Randall, Louise Stanley, Al St. John, John Merton, Henry Rocquemore, Ted Adams, Al Bridge, Hal Price, Harry Strang, Kit Guard, Jack Ingram, Charles "Slim" Whitaker, Art Dillard, Carleton Young, Sherry Tansey, George Morrell, Oscar Gahan, Blackjack Ward, Glenn Strange. *D:* Sam Newfield; *P:* Maurice Conn; *St:* Robert Emmett (Tansey); *Sc:* Fred Myton. (0:57)

Jack Randall western of a cowboy who comes to the aid of a girl in distress.

1810. Hair Trigger Casey (Atlantic; 1936). *Cast:* Jack Perrin, Betty Mack, Wally Wales (Hal Taliaferro), Fred "Snowflake" Toones, Ed Cassidy, Robert Walker, Phil Dunham, Denny Meadows (Dennis Moore). *D:* Harry S. Fraser; *P:* William Berke; *Sc:* Monroe Talbot. (0:59)

Jack Perrin western of border smugglers.

1811. Half a Sinner (Universal; 1934). *Cast:* Berton Churchill (recreating his stage role as "The Deacon"), Joel McCrea, Sally Blane, Mickey Rooney, Guinn Williams, Walter Brennan, Russell Hopton, Bert Roach, Theresa Maxwell Conover, Gay Seabrook, Reginald Barlow, Alexander Carlisle. *D:* Kurt Neumann. (1:11)

A cardsharp-conman makes his money whenever and wherever he can in the mid-west, posing as a character known as "The Deacon." A remake of *Alias the Deacon* (Universal; 1927). Remade under that title in 1939 for 1940 release. Based on the play of that name by John B. Hymer and LeRoy Clemens.

1812. Half a Sinner (Universal/Grand National; 1939–40). *Cast:* John

King, Heather Angel, Constance Collier, Walter Catlett. *D:* Al Christie; *P:* Christie; *St:* Dalton Trumbo; *Sc:* Frederick Jackson. (1:00)

B melodrama of a girl who steals a car only to find a corpse in the back seat. A production of Grand National released by Universal after that studio folded.

1813. Half Angel (20th Century–Fox; 1936). *Cast:* Frances Dee, Brian Donlevy, Charles Butterworth, Helen Westley, Henry Stephenson, Sara Haden, Etienne Girardot, Gavin Muir (film debut), Paul Stanton, Julius Tannen, Nigel de Brulier. *D:* Sidney Lanfield; *As.P.:* Kenneth MacGowan; *St:* F. Tennyson Jesse; *Sc:* Bess Meredyth, Gene Fowler, Allen Rivkin. (1:05)

B mystery of a newsman who helps a girl accused of murder.

1814. Half Marriage (RKO; 1929). *Cast:* Olive Borden, Morgan Farley, Ken Murray (film debut), Ann Greenway, Anderson Lawler, Sally Blane, Hedda Hopper, Richard Tucker. *D:* William J. Cowan; *As.P.:* Henry Hobart; *St:* George Kibbe Turner; *Sc:* Jane Murfin; *Songs:* Oscar Levant, Sidney Clare. (1:12)

Low-budget melodrama of a couple who are secretly married.

1815. The Half-Naked Truth (RKO; 1932). *Cast:* Lupe Velez, Lee Tracy, Eugene Pallette, Frank Morgan, Shirley (Ross) Chambers, Franklin Pangborn, Robert McKenzie, Mary Mason. *D:* Gregory La Cava; *As.P.:* Pandro S. Berman; *St:* Ben Markson, H.N. Swanson; *Sc:* Corey Ford, La Cava, Bartlett Cormack (unc.). (1:17) (video)

Hit comedy farce of a publicity agent and the female star he is trying to create. Based on the story "Phantom Fame" by David Freeman.

1816. Half-Shot at Sunrise (RKO; 1930). *Cast:* Bert Wheeler, Robert Woolsey, Dorothy Lee, George McFarlane, Edna May Oliver, Leni Stengel, Hugh Trevor, Roberta Robinson, John Rutherford, Tiller Sunshine Girls, Ivan Lebedeff, Cameron Prud'Homme, E.H. Calvert, Alan Roscoe, Eddie de Lange. *D:* Paul Sloane; *As.P.:* Henry Hobart; *St:* James Ashmore Creelman; *Sc:* Anne Caldwell, Ralph Spence. (1:15) (video)

Comedy of two A.W.O.L. doughboys who invade Paris and proceed to turn it upside down in search of "a good time." The second starring film for Wheeler and Woolsey.

1817. Halfway to Heaven (Paramount; 1929). *Cast:* Charles "Buddy" Rogers, Jean Arthur, Paul Lukas, Guy Oliver, Dick French, Oscar Apfel, Irving Bacon, Helen Ware, Lucille Williams, Al Hill, Ford West, Edna West. *D:* George Abbott; *St:* H.L. Gates.

Low-budget triangular romantic drama with a circus setting.

1818. Hallelujah! (MGM; 1929). *Cast:* Daniel L. Haynes (Zeke), Nina Mae McKinney (film debut replacing Honey Brown as Chick), William Fountaine (Hot Shot), Harry Gray (former slave making his film debut at age 86 as the minister), Fannie Belle de Knight (Mammy), Everett McGarrity (Spunk), Victoria Spivey (Missy Rose), Milton Dickerson, Walter Tait, Robert Couch (Johnson kids), Evelyn Pope Burwell, Eddie Connors, William Allen "Slickem" Garrison, Dixie Jubilee Singers. *D:* (A.A.N.) King Vidor; *P:* Vidor; *St:* Vidor; *Sc:* Wanda Tuchock; *Dialogue:* Ransom Rideout; *Adaptation:* Richard Schayer; *Songs:* "Waiting at the End of the Road" and "Swanee Shuffle" by Irving Berlin, with many other traditional folk songs and spirituals. (1:46)

Critically praised drama of a man who decides to become a minister after killing a man, then finds he is always susceptible to the sins of the flesh. Partially filmed in Memphis, Tennessee, this is notable as the first all-black feature film. The *New York Times* placed it at #3 on their "10 Best" list of the year, while *Film Daily* placed it at #10 on theirs.

1819. Hallelujah I'm a Bum (United Artists/Art Cinema; 1933). *Cast:* Al Jolson, Harry Langdon, Madge Evans, Frank Morgan, Chester Conklin, Edgar Connor, Tammany Young, Tyler Brooke, Bert Roach, Louise Carver, Dorothea Wolbert, Richard Rodgers (bit), Lorenz Hart (bit). *D:* Lewis Milestone; *P:* Joseph M. Schenck, Milestone; *St:* Ben Hecht; *Sc:* S.N. Behrman; *Rhymes & Music:* Rodgers and Hart. (G.B. titles: *Hallelujah I'm a Tramp* & *Lazy Bones*) (TV title: *The Heart of New York*) (1:22) (video)

Offbeat musical of depression-era tramps in New York's Central Park. A box office dud.

Hallelujah I'm a Tramp (G.B. title) *see* **Hallelujah I'm a Bum**

1820. Handcuffed (Rayart; 1929). *Cast:* Wheeler Oakman, Virginia Brown Faire, Dean Jagger. *D:* Duke Worne; *P:* Trem Carr.

Low-budget crime melodrama.

A Handful of Clouds (G.B. title) *see* **Doorway to Hell**

1821. Handle with Care (Fox; 1932). *Cast:* James Dunn, Boots Mallory (film debut), El Brendel, Jane Withers (film debut), George Ernest, Pat Hartigan, Buster Phelps, Frank O'Connor. *D:* David Butler; *St:* Butler; *Sc:* Frank Craven, Sam Mintz.

Low-budget comedy.

1822. Hands Across the Table (Paramount; 1935). *Cast:* Carole Lombard, Fred MacMurray, Ralph Bellamy, Astrid Allwyn, Ruth Donnelly, Marie Prevost, William Demarest, Ed Gargan, Herman Bing, Ferdinand Munier, Marcelle Corday, Harold Minjir, Joseph Tozer. *D:* Mitchell Leisen; *P:*

E. Lloyd Sheldon; *St:* Vina Delmar; *Sc:* Norman Krasna, Vincent Lawrence, Herbert Fields. (1:21)

Hit romantic comedy of a manicurist in search of a rich husband.

The Hands of Orlac (G.B. title) *see* **Mad Love**

1823. Handy Andy (Fox; 1934). *Cast:* Will Rogers, Peggy Wood, Conchita Montenegro (final American film), Mary Carlisle, Roger Imhof, Robert Taylor (film debut), Paul Harvey, Gregory Gaye, Grace Goodall, Frank Melton, Jessie Pringle. *D:* David Butler; *P:* Sol M. Wurtzel; *Sc:* William Conselman, Henry Johnson. (1:22)

Hit comedy of a small town druggist and his social-climbing wife. Based on the play "Merry Andrew" by Lewis Beach.

1824. Happiness Ahead (WB/F.N.; 1934). *Cast:* Dick Powell, Josephine Hutchinson (film debut), Frank McHugh, John Halliday, Allen Jenkins, Ruth Donnelly, Jane Darwell, Dorothy Dare, Mary Forbes, Marjorie Gateson, J.M. Kerrigan, Russell Hicks (film debut), Mary Russell, Mary Treen (film debut). *D:* Mervyn LeRoy; *P:* Sam Bischoff; *Sc:* Harry Sauber, Brian Marlow; *Songs:* "There Must Be Happiness Ahead," "Pop Goes Your Heart," and "All On Account of a Strawberry Sundae" by Mort Dixon and Allie Wrubel, "Beauty Must Be Loved" by Irving Kahal and Sammy Fain, and "Massaging Window Panes" by Bert Kalmar and Harry Ruby. (1:26)

A romance with songs of an heiress pretending to be poor. Filmed before in 1928.

1825. Happiness C.O.D. (Chesterfield; 1935). *Cast:* Lona Andre, Irene Ware, William Bakewell, Frank (Junior) Coghlan, Polly Ann Young, Maude Eburne, Donald Meek, Malcolm McGregor, Richard Carlyle. *D:* Charles Lamont.

"Poverty row" romantic comedy.

1826. Happy Days (Fox; 1930). *Cast:* Janet Gaynor, Charles Farrell, Warner Baxter, Victor McLaglen, Stuart Erwin, Will Rogers, George Jessel, El Brendel, William Collier, Sr., Edmund Lowe, Sharon Lynn, Paul Page, Walter Catlett, Dixie Lee, Ann Pennington, Whispering Jack Smith, David Rollins, Richard Keene, George McFarlane, James J. Corbett, J. Harold Murray, George Olsen, Tom Patricola, J. Farrell MacDonald, Frank Richardson, Marjorie White, Betty Grable (film debut in a chorus line bit). *D:* Ben Stoloff; *Sc:* Sidney Lanfield, Edwin Burke.

An all-star revue which was filmed in Fox's wide-screen "Grandeur" process.

The Happy Family (G.B. title) *see* **The Merry Frinks**

1827. Happy-Go-Lucky (Republic; 1936). *Cast:* Phil Regan, Evelyn Venable, Carleton Young. *D:* Xxxx Xxxx.

A low-budget musical-comedy.

Happy Landing (G.B. title) *see* **Flying High**

1828. Happy Landing (Monogram; 1934). *Cast:* Ray Walker, Jacqueline Wells (Julie Bishop), William Farnum, Noah Beery, Hyram Hoover, Morgan Conway, Warner Richmond, Donald Reed, Billy Erwin, Ruth Romaine, Eddie Fetherston, Gertrude Simpson. *D:* Robert N. Bradbury; *P:* Paul Malvern; *St:* Stuart Anthony; *Sc:* Anthony. (1:03)

B actioner of a border patrolman who is suspected of being in league with a gang of payroll thieves.

1829/1830. Happy Landing (20th Century–Fox; 1938). *Cast:* Sonja Henie (Trudy Erickson), Don Ameche (Jimmy Hall), Ethel Merman (Flo Kelly), Cesar Romero (Sargent), Jean Hersholt (Herr Erickson), Billy Gilbert (counter man), Wally Vernon (Al Mahoney), Raymond Scott Quintet, El Brendel (Yonnie), Joseph Crehan (agent), Alex Novinsky (count), William B. Davidson (manager), Marcel de Labrosse (Rajah), William Wagner (justice of the peace), Condos Brothers, Peters Sisters, Leah Ray, Ben Welden, Syd Saylor, Matt McHugh, Harvey Parry, Louis Adlon, Jr., Marcelle Corday, Eddy Conrad, Fred Kelsey, June Storey, Robert Lowery, Lon Chaney, Jr. *D:* Roy Del Ruth; *As.P.:* David Hempstead; *St & Sc:* Milton Sperling, Boris Ingster; *Songs:* "Hot and Happy," "Yonny and His Oompah," "You Are the Words to the Music in My Heart" by Samuel Pokrass and Jack Yellen, "A Gypsy Told Me" and "You Appeal to Me" by Harold Spina and Walter Bullock. (1:42)

A romantic musical with ice-skating which was one of the 15 top grossing films of 1937–38.

1831. Hard-Boiled Rose (WB; 1929). *Cast:* Myrna Loy, Ralph Emerson, William Collier, Jr., Gladys Brockwell, Edward Martindel, John Miljan. *D:* F. Harmon Weight; *St:* Melville Crossman (Darryl Zanuck); *Sc:* Robert Lord.

Part-talkie low-budget drama of a girl who talks her boyfriend into taking the blame for criminal escapades committed by her father.

1832. The Hard Hombre (Allied; 1931). *Cast:* Hoot Gibson, Lina Basquette, "Skeeter" Bill Robbins, Jessie Arnold, Mathilde Comont, G. Raymond Nye, Glenn Strange, Christian Frank. *D:* Otto Brower; *P:* M.H. Hoffman, Jr.; *Sc:* Jack Natteford. (1:05)

Hoot Gibson western with a dose of mother-love of a cowpoke who is mistaken for a wanted outlaw. Remade as *Trailin' Trouble* (q.v.).

1833. Hard Luck Dames (Xxxx Xxxx; 1936). *Cast:* Arthur Treacher. (No other information available)

1834. Hard Rock Harrigan (Fox; 1935). *Cast:* George O'Brien, Irene Hervey, Fred Kohler, Dean Benton, Frank Rice, Victor Potel, Olin Francis, William Gould, George Humbert, Lee Shumway, Edward Keane, Glenn Strange, David Clyde. *D:* David Howard; *P:* Sol Lesser (Atherton Prods.); *Sc:* Raymond L. Schrock, Dan Jarrett. (1:10)

A comedy-adventure of two tunnel drillers in love with the same girl. Based on the story by Zane Grey.

1835. Hard to Get (WB/F.N.; 1929). *Cast:* Dorothy Mackaill, Charles Delaney, Edmund Burns, James Finlayson, Louise Fazenda, Jack Oakie, Clarissa Selwynne, Irving Bacon. *D:* William Beaudine; *Sc:* Richard Weil, James Gruen; *Song:* "The Things We Want Most Are Hard to Get" by Al Bryan, George W. Meyer.

Comedy-romance of a girl who marries a poor auto mechanic rather than a millionaire. Based on a story by Edna Ferber.

1836. Hard to Get (WB; 1938). *Cast:* Dick Powell, Olivia de Havilland, Charles Winninger, Allen Jenkins, Bonita Granville, Melville Cooper, Isabel Jeans, Grady Sutton, Thurston Hall, John Ridgely, Granville Bates, Penny Singleton, Jack Mower, Arthur Housman. *D:* Ray Enright; *As.P.:* Sam Bischoff; *St:* Wally Klein, Joseph Schrank, Stephen Morehouse Avery; *Sc:* Jerry Wald, Maurice Leo, Richard Macaulay; *Song:* "You Must Have Been a Beautiful Baby" by Harry Warren and Johnny Mercer. (1:20)

A rich girl meets and falls for a poor boy in this romantic comedy.

1837. Hard to Handle (WB; 1933). *Cast:* James Cagney, Ruth Donnelly, Mary Brian, Allen Jenkins, Claire

Dodd, Emma Dunn, Paul Fix, Berton Churchill, Sterling Holloway, John Sheehan, Matt McHugh, Louise Mackintosh. *D:* Mervyn LeRoy; *P:* Robert Lord; *Supervisor:* Ray Griffith; *St:* Houston Branch; *Sc:* Wilson Mizner, Lord. (1:15)

Comedy of a go-getter who organizes a dance marathon. Prior to release te film had two working titles: "A Bad Boy" and "The Inside."

1838. Hard to Hold (Xxxx Xxxx; 1937). (No information available)

1839. The Hardys Ride High (MGM; 1939). *Cast:* Lewis Stone (Judge Hardy), Mickey Rooney (Andy Hardy), Cecilia Parker (Marian Hardy), Fay Holden (Mrs. Hardy), Ann Rutherford (Polly Benedict), Sara Haden (Aunt Milly), Virginia Grey, Marsha Hunt, William T. Orr, John King, Halliwell Hobbes, Minor Watson, Truman Bradley, Donald Briggs, John T. Murray. *D:* George Seitz; *P:* Lou Ostrow (unc.); *Sc:* Kay Van Riper, Agnes Christine Johnston, William Ludwig. (1:21)

The sixth entry in the "Andy Hardy" series with the family coming into a windfall of one million dollars. One of the 16 top grossing films of 1938–39.

1840. Harlem After Midnight (Micheaux; 1934). *Cast:* Rex Lease.

Low-budget independent production, produced, directed and written by Oscar Micheaux.

1841. Harlem on the Prairie (Associated Features; 1938). *Cast:* Herb Jeffreys, Flourney E. Miller, Mantan Moreland, Connie Harris, Maceo Sheffield, William Spencer, Jr., George Randall, Nathan Curry, Four Tones, Edward Brandon, James Davis, Four Blackbirds. *D:* Sam Newfield; *P:* Jed Buell; *Sc:* Fred Myton, Flourney E. Miller. (aka: *Bad Man of Harlem*) (0:54)

Novelty B western of a black cowboy who confronts a crooked L.A. cop. An independent feature which catered to the black audience.

1842. Harlem Rides the Range (Hollywood Pictures; 1939). *Cast:* Herb Jeffreys, Lucius Brooks, Spencer Williams, Flourney E. Miller, Artie Young, Clarence Brooks, Tom Southern, Four Tones, John Thomas. *D:* Richard C. Kahn; *Sc:* Spencer Williams, Flourney E. Miller. (0:58) (video)

B western with an all-black cast involving stolen rights to a radium mine.

1843. Harmony at Home (Fox; 1930). *Cast:* William Collier, Sr., Rex Bell, Marguerite Churchill, Elizabeth Patterson, Charles Eaton, Charlotte Henry, Dot Farley. *D:* Hamilton MacFadden; *Adaptation:* Seton I. Miller, William Collier, Sr., Clare Kummer, Charles J. McGuirk.

Folksey comedy based on the play "The Family Upstairs" by Harry Delf. Remade as *Stop, Look and Love* (q.v.).

1844. Harmony Lane (Mascot; 1935). *Cast:* Douglass Montgomery (Foster), Evelyn Venable (Susan Pentland), Adrienne Ames (Jane McDowell), William Frawley (Ed "E.P." Christy), Clarence Muse, Joseph Cawthorn, Gilbert Emery, Florence Roberts, James Bush, David Torrence, Victor DeCamp, Edith Craig, Cora Sue Collins, Lloyd Hughes, Smiley Burnette, Ferdinand Munier, Mildred Gover, James B. Carson, Mary MacLaren, Rodney Hildebrand, Al Herman, Earle Hodgins. *D:* Joseph Santley; *P:* Colbert Clark; *St:* Milton Krims; *Sc:* Santley, Elizabeth Meehan. (1:29) (video)

Low-budget sentimental biography on the tragic life of 19th-century songwriter Stephen Collins Foster, filled with many of his old standards. See also *Swanee River* (q.v.), another filmed biography of Foster.

Harmony Parade (G.B. title) *see* **Pigskin Parade**

1845. Harold Teen (WB; 1934). *Cast:* Hal LeRoy, Rochelle Hudson, Patricia Ellis, Guy Kibbee, Hobart Cavanaugh, Chick Chandler, Eddie Tamblyn, Douglass Dumbrille, Mayo Methot, Hugh Herbert, Clara Blandick, Charles Wilson. *D:* Murray Roth; *P:* Robert Lord; *Sc:* Paul Gerard Smith, Al Cohn; *Songs:* "How Do You Know It's Sunday," "Simple and Sweet," "Two Little Flies on a Lump of Sugar" and "Collegiate Wedding" by Irving Kahal and Sammy Fain. (G.B. title: *The Dancing Fool*) (1:06)

Low-budget teen comedy set in a small town. Based on the popular comic strip by Carl Ed. A remake of the 1928 production with Arthur Lake and Mary Brian.

1846. The Harvester (Republic; 1936). *Cast:* Edward Nugent, Ann Rutherford, Frank Craven, Alice Brady, Joyce Compton, Russell Hardie, Emma Dunn, Cora Sue Collins, Harry Bowen, Phyllis Fraser, Grace Hayle, Roy Atwell, Lucille Ward. *D:* Joseph Santley; *Sc:* Robert Lee Johnson, Elizabeth Meehan, Homer Croy, Gertrude Orr.

Rustic romance based on the 1911 novel by Gene Stratton-Porter. Previously filmed in 1927.

1847. Hat Check Girl (Fox; 1932). *Cast:* Sally Eilers, Ben Lyon, Ginger Rogers, Noel Madison, Eddie Anderson, Joyce Compton, Purnell Pratt, Arthur Pierson, Monroe Owsley, Burr Caruth, Eulalie Jensen, Harold Goodwin, Dewey Robinson, Arthur Housman. *D:* Sidney Lanfield; *St:* Rian James; *Sc:* Barry Conners, Philip Klein, Arthur Kober. (G.B. title: *Embassy Girl*)

Romantic comedy.

1848. Hat, Coat and Glove (RKO; 1934). *Cast:* Ricardo Cortez (replacing John Barrymore, originally scheduled for the role), John Beal, Barbara Robbins, Margaret Hamilton, Sara Haden, Samuel S. Hinds, Murray Kinnell, Dorothy Burgess, Frederick Sullivan, Paul Harvey, Gayle Evers, Wilbur Higby, David Durand, Louise Beavers. *D:* Worthington Miner; *As.P.:*

Kenneth MacGowan; *Sc:* Francis Edwards Faragoh. (1:04)

B courtroom drama of a lawyer who defends his wife's boyfriend when he is accused of murder. Based on the play by Wilhelm Speyer, it was remade as *A Night of Adventure* (RKO; 1944).

1849. The Hatchet Man (WB/F.N.; 1932). *Cast:* Edward G. Robinson, Loretta Young, Dudley Digges, Leslie Fenton, Edmund Breese, Tully Marshall, J. Carrol Naish, Noel N. Madison, Blanche Frederici, Ralph Ince, Charles Middleton, Willie Fung, E. Alyn Warren, Otto Yamaoka, Edward Peil, Sr., Toshia Mori, Anna Chang, Evelyn Selbie. *D:* William Wellman; *Sc:* J. Grubb Alexander (based on the play by Achmed Abdullah and David Belasco). (G.B. title: *The Honourable Mr. Wong*) (1:14)

Melodrama of the Tong Society in Chinatown with all caucasians playing the major oriental roles.

1850. Hats Off (Grand National; 1936). *Cast:* Mae Clarke, John Payne (starring debut in which he sings "Twinkle, Twinkle Little Star"), Helen Lynd, Skeets Gallagher, Luis Alberni, Franklin Pangborn, Robert Middlemass, George Irving, Clarence Wilson, Val & Ernie Stanton, Radio Rogues (Jimmy Hollywood, Eddie Bartell, Henry Taylor), Bud Flanagan (Dennis O'Keefe). *D:* Boris Petroff; *P:* Petroff; *St & Sc:* Sam Fuller, Edmund Joseph; *Additional Dialogue:* Lawrence Thiele; *Songs:* Ben Oakland, Herb Magidson. (1:06)

A hit at the box office was this light musical-comedy of rival press agents.

1851. Haunted (Xxxx Xxxx; 1933). (No information available)

1852. Haunted Gold (WB/Vitagraph; 1932). *Cast:* John Wayne, Sheila Terry, Harry Woods, Erville Alderson, Otto Hoffman, Martha Mattox, Blue Washington, Slim Whitaker, Bud Osborne, Jim Corey, Ben Corbett, Duke the horse. *D:* Mack V. Wright; *As.P.:* Sid Rogell; *Sc:* Adele Buffington. (0:58) (video)

John Wayne western (his first for this studio) concerning the search for a lost gold mine. A remake of *The Phantom City* (First National; 1928) with Ken Maynard.

1853. Havana Widows (WB/F.N.; 1933). *Cast:* Joan Blondell, Glenda Farrell, Lyle Talbot, Guy Kibbee, Frank McHugh, Ralph Ince, Allen Jenkins, Ruth Donnelly, Hobart Cavanaugh, Maude Eburne, George Cooper. *D:* Ray Enright; *P:* Robert Lord; *Sc:* Earl Baldwin.

Low-budget romantic drama of two gold diggers in Cuba.

1854. Have a Heart (MGM; 1934). *Cast:* Jean Parker, James Dunn, Una Merkel, Stuart Erwin, Willard Robertson, Samuel S. Hinds, Paul Page, Kate Price, Muriel Evans, Pepi Sinoff. *D:* David Butler; *P:* John W. Considine, Jr.; *Sc:* Florence Ryerson, Edgar Allan Woolf; *St:* B.G. DeSylva, Butler. (1:22)

A sentimental comedy of a woman who is left standing at the altar.

1855. Having Wonderful Time (RKO; 1938). *Cast:* Ginger Rogers, Douglas Fairbanks, Jr., Peggy Conklin, Lucille Ball, Lee Bowman, Eve Arden, Richard "Red" Skelton (film debut), Donald Meek, Ann Miller, Jack Carson, Grady Sutton, Dorothea Kent, Clarence H. Wilson, Allan Lane, Shimman Ruskin, Dorothy Tree, Leona Roberts, Harlan Briggs, Inez Courtney, Juanita Quigley, Kirk Windsor. *D:* Alfred Santell, George Stevens (unc.); *P:* Pandro S. Berman; *Sc:* Arthur Kober; *Songs:* Sam Stept, Charles Tobias. (1:11) (video)

Romantic comedy situated at a resort in New York's Catskill Mountains. Based on the hit stage play by Arthur Kober, the film was not a hit.

1856. Hawaii Calls (RKO/Principal; 1937–38). *Cast:* Bobby Breen, Irvin S. Cobb, Ned Sparks, Warren Hull, Mamo Clark, Gloria Holden, Herbert Rawlinson, Juanita Quigley, Raymond Page and his orchestra, William Harrigan, Cyrus Kendall, William Abbey, Philip Ahn, Ward Bond, Donald Kirke, Pua Lani, Jerry Mandy, Aggie Auld, Uilani Silva, Dora Clement, Laurence Duran, Ruben Duran, Ruben Maldonado, Birdie DeBolt. *D:* Edward F. Cline; *P:* Saul Lesser; *Sc:* Wanda Tuchock; *Songs:* Johnny Noble, Harry Owens.

Musical-drama of two boys who stowaway on a ship bound for Hawaii and then hide out there. Based on the novel "Stowaways in Paradise" by Don Blanding.

1857. Hawaiian Buckaroo (20th Century–Fox/Principal; 1938). *Cast:* Smith Ballew, Evalyn Knapp, Harry Woods, Pat J. O'Brien, Carl Stockdale, Benny Burt, George Regas, Fred "Snowflake" Toones. *D:* Ray Taylor; *P:* Sol Lesser; *Sc:* Dan Jarrett. (1:00)

Offbeat western with a modern setting on a Hawaiian cattle ranch (located in California).

Hawaiian Nights (G.B. title) *see* **Down to Their Last Yacht**

1858. Hawaiian Nights (Universal; 1939). *Cast:* Johnny Downs, Constance Moore, Mary Carlisle, Eddie Quillan, Thurston Hall, Etienne Girardot, Samuel S. Hinds, Princess Luana. *D:* Albert S. Rogell; *P:* Max H. Golden; *St:* John Grey; *Sc:* Lee Loeb, Charles Grayson; *Songs:* "Hawaii Sang Me to Sleep," "Hey, Good Lookin!," "I Found My Love," and "Then I Wrote the Minuet in G" (using a melody from Beethoven by Frank Loesser and Matty Malneck.

A low-budget romance with music.

The Hawk (1932) (G.B. title) *see* **Ride Him Cowboy**

The Hawk *see* **Trail of the Hawk** (1935)

1859. He Couldn't Say No (WB; 1938). *Cast:* Frank McHugh, Jane Wyman, Cora Witherspoon, Diana Lewis, Berton Churchill, Ferris Taylor, William Haade, Tom Kennedy, Raymond Hatton, John Ridgely, Chester Clute, Cliff Clark, Rita Gould, *D:* Lewis Seiler; *As.P.:* Bryan Foy; *St:* Norman Matson; *Sc:* Robertson White, Joseph Schrank, Ben Grauman Kohn. (0:57)

B comedy of a shy man who's life is dominated by things he doesn't like or by being forced to do things he doesn't want to do. Based on the play by Joseph Schrank.

1860. He Couldn't Take It (Monogram; 1933). *Cast:* Ray Walker, Virginia Cherrill, George E. Stone, Stanley Fields, Dorothy Granger, Jane Darwell, Paul Porcasi, Donald Douglas, Astrid Allwyn, Franklin Parker, Jack Kennedy. *D:* William Nigh; *P:* William T. Lackey; *St:* Dore Schary; *Sc:* Schary; *Additional Dialogue:* George Waggner. (1:03)

B comedy of a hot-tempered youth who gets a job as a process server. Remade as *Here Comes Kelly* (Monogram; 1943) and as *Live Wires* (Monogram; 1946). Prior to release, the film had two working titles: "Born Tough" and "The Process Server."

1861. He Knew Women (RKO; 1930). *Cast:* Lowell Sherman, Alice Joyce, Frances Dade, David Manners. *D:* F. Hugh Herbert; *As.P.:* Myles Connolly; *Sc:* Herbert, William Jutte. (1:07)

A writer romances a wealthy widow, soaking her for all he can. Based on the play "The Second Man" by S.N. Behrman.

1862. He Learned About Women (Paramount; 1933). *Cast:* Stuart Erwin, Alison Skipworth, Susan Fleming, Sidney Toler, Claude King, Grant Mitchell, Gordon Westcott, Tom

Ricketts. *D:* Lloyd Corrigan; *St:* Corrigan.

B comedy of a naive young man who inherits $50,000,000 and soon finds nearly everyone is out to separate him from it.

He Lived to Kill *see* **Night of Terror**

1863. He Trusted His Wife (Xxxx Xxxx; 1935). (No information available)

1864. He Was Her Man (WB; 1934). *Cast:* James Cagney, Joan Blondell, Victor Jory, Frank Craven, Sarah Padden, Harold Huber, Russell Hopton, Ralf Harolde, John Qualen, Bradley Page, Samuel S. Hinds, George Chandler, James Eagles. Edward Earle, Gino Corrado. *D:* Lloyd Bacon; *P:* Robert Lord; *St:* Lord; *Sc:* Niven Busch, Tom Buckingham. (1:10)

Romantic comedy-drama of a hooker and an ex-con.

He Wore a Star (G.B. title) *see* **Star Packer**

1865. Headin' East (Columbia/Coronet; 1937). *Cast:* Buck Jones, Ruth Coleman, Donald Douglas, Elaine Arden, Shemp Howard, Earle Hodgins, John Elliott, Stanley Blystone, Frank Faylen, Dick Rich, Al Herman, Harry Lash. *D:* Ewing Scott; *P:* L.G. Leonard (Leonard Goldstein), Monroe Shaff; *St:* Shaff, Joseph Hoffman; *Sc:* Ethel LaBlanche, Paul Franklin. (1:07)

Buck Jones "eastern" western of a cowboy tangling with gangsters in the big city.

1866. Headin' for God's Country (Republic; 1937). *Cast:* William Lundigan, Virginia Dale, Harry Davenport, Harry Shannon, Addison Richards, J. Frank Hamilton, Eddie Acuff, Wade Crosby, Skelton Knaggs, John Bleifer, Eddy Waller, Charlie Lung, Ernie Adams, Eddie Lee, James B. Leong,

Anna Q. Nilsson. *D:* William Morgan; *Sc:* Elizabeth Meehan, Houston Branch. (1:18)

B adventure drama of a prospector who as a point of spite, tells the residents of an Alaskan village that the U.S. is at war.

1867. Headin' for the Rio Grande (Grand National; 1936). *Cast:* Tex Ritter, Eleanor Stewart, Warner Richmond, Syd Saylor, Snub Pollard, Charles King, Earl Dwire, Forrest Taylor, William Desmond, Charles K. French, Bud Osborne, Budd Buster, Tex Palmer, Jack C. Smith, Bill Woods, Sherry Tansey, Jim Mason, Ed Cassidy. *D:* Robert N. Bradbury; *P:* Edward Finney (for Boots and Saddles productions); *Sc:* Robert Emmett (Tansey); *St:* Lindsley Parsons. (1:00) (video)

Tex Ritter western — his second — with songs.

1868. Headin' for Trouble (Big 4; 1931). *D:* J.P. McGowan; *P:* John R. Freuler.

Bob Custer western.

1869. Headin' North (Tiffany; 1930). *Cast:* Bob Steele, Barbara Luddy, Perry Murdock, Walter Shumway, Eddie Dunn, Fred Burns, Gordon De-Main, Jim Welsh. *D:* John P. McCarthy; *P:* Trem Carr; *Sc:* McCarthy. (1:00)

Offbeat Bob Steele western with the hero hiding out on the vaudeville circuit to escape a murder charge.

1870. The Headleys at Home (Standard; 1938). *Cast:* Evelyn Venable, Grant Mitchell, Vince Barnett, Edward Earle, Louise Beavers, Benny Rubin. *D:* Chris Beute. (G.B. title: *Among Those Present*)

Domestic comedy.

1871. Headline Crasher (Ambassador; 1937). *Cast:* Frankie Darro, Kane Richmond, Jack Ingram, Edward Earle, Charles King. *D:* Leslie Goodwins; *P:* Maurice Conn.

B newspaper melodrama.

1872. Headline Shooter (RKO; 1933). *Cast:* William Gargan, Frances Dee, Ralph Bellamy, Jack LaRue, Gregory Ratoff, Wallace Ford, Betty Furness, Hobart Cavanaugh, Robert Benchley, June Brewster, Franklin Pangborn, Dorothy Burgess, Purnell Pratt, Henry B. Walthall. *D:* Otto Brower; *As.P.:* David Lewis; *St:* Wallace West; *Sc:* Agnes Christine Johnston, Allen Rivkin, Arthur Kober. (G.B. title: *Evidence in Camera*) (0:59)

B quickie depicting the adventures of a newsreel cameraman and a reporter, utilizing much stock-footage.

1873. The Headline Woman (Mascot; 1935). *Cast:* Heather Angel, Roger Pryor, Jack LaRue, Ford Sterling, Conway Tearle, Franklin Pangborn, Jack Mulhall, Russell Hopton, Syd Saylor, Theodore von Eltz, George Lewis, Ward Bond, Harry Bowen, Wade Boteler, Wheeler Oakman, Warner Richmond, Lynton Brent, Edward Hearn, George Hayes, Jack Raymond, Lillian Miles, Robert Gleckler, Alan Bridge, Joan Standing, Lloyd Ingraham, Tony Martelli, Charles Regan, Guy Kingsford. *D:* William Nigh; *St & Sc:* Jack Natteford, Claire Church. (G.B. title: *The Woman in the Case*) (1:11)

B comedy-melodrama with a newspaper story.

1874. Heads Up! (Paramount; 1930). *Cast:* Charles "Buddy" Rogers, Helen Kane (final film—ret.), Victor Moore (recreating his stage role), John Hamilton, Margaret Breen, Harry Shannon (film debut), Charles Anthony Hughes, Billy Taylor, Helen Carrington, Gene Gowing. *D:* Victor Schertzinger (who also composed some song lyrics).

Romantic musical of a coast guard officer who sets out to nab some bootleggers. Based on the moderately successful 1929 stage play by Paul Gerard Smith and John McGowan with songs by Richard Rodgers and Lorenz Hart.

1875. The Healer (Monogram; 1935). *Cast:* Ralph Bellamy, Karen Morley, Mickey Rooney, Judith Allen, Robert McWade, Bruce Warren, J. Farrell MacDonald, Vessie Farrell. *D:* Reginald Barker; *Sc:* James Knox Millen, John Goodrich (based on the novel by Robert Herrick). (Re-release title: *Little Pal*) (1:17)

Low-budget drama of a doctor who becomes infatuated with a society girl and begins to neglect his responsibilities.

1876. The Heart of Arizona (Paramount; 1938). *Cast:* Bill Boyd (Hoppy), George "Gabby" Hayes (Windy), Russell Hayden (Lucky), Natalie Moorhead, John Elliott, Billy King, Dorothy Short, Stephen (Alden) Chase, John Beach, Lane Chandler, Leo McMahon, Lee Phelps, Bob McKenzie *D:* Lesley Selander; *P:* Harry M. Sherman; *Sc:* Norman Houston, Harrison Jacobs. (1:08)

The 15th entry in the "Hopalong Cassidy" series involving a woman's ranch in the hands of a crooked foreman.

1877. The Heart of New York (WB; 1932). *Cast:* Joe Smith, Charles Dale (better known as "Smith & Dale"), George Sidney, Anna Appel, Aline MacMahon, Donald Cook, Oscar Apfel, Marion Byron, Ann Brody, Ruth Hall, George McFarlane, Harold Waldridge. *D:* Mervyn LeRoy; *Sc:* LeRoy, Arthur Caesar, Houston Branch. (1:14)

Comedy of a Jewish plumber who invents the washing machine and hits the big time. Based on the play "Mendel, Inc." by David Freedman.

The Heart of New York (1933) *see* **Hallelujah I'm a Bum**

1878. Heart of the North (WB/ F.N.; 1938). *Cast:* Dick Foran, Gloria Dickson, Gale Page, Russell Simpson, Allen Jenkins, Patric Knowles, Janet Chapman, James Stephenson, Anthony Averill, Joseph Sawyer, Joseph King,

Garry Owen, Pedro de Cordoba, Robert Homans, Arthur Gardner. *D:* Lewis Seiler; *As.P.:* Bryan Foy; *St:* William Byron Mowery; *Sc:* Lee Katz, Vincent Sherman. (1:25)

Technicolor romantic outdoor action adventure of the Northwest Mounted Police.

1879. The Heart of the Rockies (Republic; 1937). *Cast:* Bob Livingston (Stony Brooke), Ray Corrigan (Tucson Smith), Max Terhune (Lullaby Joslin), Mary Hart (Lynne Roberts), J.P. McGowan, Sammy McKim, Yakima Canutt, Hal Taliaferro, Guy Wilkerson, Maston Williams, Ranny Weeks, Nelson McDowell, Herman's Mountaineers. *D:* Joseph Kane; *Sc:* Jack Natteford, Oliver Drake. (0:56)

The "Three Mesquiteers" go after poachers in a game preserve. This was the 9th in a series of 51 films.

1880. Heart of the West (Paramount; 1936). *Cast:* Bill Boyd (Hoppy), James Ellison (Johnny Nelson), George Hayes (Windy), Lynn Gilbert, Sidney Blackmer, Charles Martin, John Rutherford, Warner Richmond, Walter Miller, Ted Adams, Fred Kohler. *D:* Howard Bretherton; *P:* Harry M. Sherman; *Sc:* Doris Schroeder. (1:00)

The 6th entry in the "Hopalong Cassidy" series with Hoppy and Johnny getting involved in a grazing land feud.

1881. The Heart Punch (Mayfair; 1932). *Cast:* Lloyd Hughes, Wheeler Oakman. *D:* B. Reeves Eason.

A "poverty row" action-melodrama.

1882. Heartbreak (Fox; 1931). *Cast:* Charles Farrell, Madge Evans, Hardie Albright, Paul Cavanagh, John Arledge, Claude King, John St. Polis. *D:* Alfred L. Werker; *St:* Llewellyn Hughes.

Low-budget romantic drama.

1883. Hearts Divided (WB/F.N.; 1938). *Cast:* Marion Davies (Betsy), Dick Powell (Jerome Bonaparte), Edward Everett Horton, Claude Rains (Napoleon), Charles Ruggles, Arthur Treacher, Henry Stephenson, Walter Kingsford, Beulah Bondi, Hobart Cavanaugh, Hattie McDaniel, Sam McDaniel (Hattie's brother), Halliwell Hobbes, George Irving, Clara Blandick. *D:* Frank Borzage; *P:* Harry Joe Brown; *Sc:* Laird Doyle, Casey Robinson; *Songs:* Al Dubin, Harry Warren; *Spirituals Sung by:* Hall Johnson Choir.

Musical remake of *Glorious Betsy* (q.v.) involving the marriage of Napoleon's brother to an American girl. A Cosmopolitan production based on the play by Rida Johnson Young.

1884. Hearts in Bondage (Republic; 1936). *Cast:* Mae Clarke, James Dunn, David Manners, Lane Chandler, Ben Alexander, Charlotte Henry, Smiley Burnette, George Hayes, Lloyd Ingraham, Fritz Leiber, George Irving, Warner Richmond, Oscar Apfel. *D:* Lew Ayres (in his only solo directorial job).

Civil War drama concerning the events leading to the battle between the Monitor and Merrimac.

1885. Hearts in Dixie (Fox; 1929). *Cast:* Clarence Muse (film debut), Eugene Jackson, Stepin Fetchit, Gertrude Howard, Rex Ingram (1895–1969), Richard Carlyle, Robert Brooks, A.C.H. Billbrew, Clifford Ingram, Dorothy Morrison, Mildred Washington, Vivian Smith, Bernice Pilot, Zack Williams. *D:* Paul Sloane; *Sc:* Walter Weems.

Deep south melodrama.

1886. Hearts in Exile (WB; 1929). *Cast:* Dolores Costello, Grant Withers, James Kirkwood, Olive Tell, George Fawcett, William Irving, Lee Moran, Rose Dione, Tom Dugan, David Torrence. *D:* Michael Curtiz; *Sc:* Harvey Gates; *Song:* "Like a Breath of Springtime."

Drama of Siberian exiles filmed with two different endings, one happy, the other not. Based on the play by John Oxenham.

Hearts in Reunion (G.B. title) *see* **Reunion**

1887. Hearts of Humanity (Majestic; 1932). *Cast:* Claudia Dell, Jean Hersholt, Jackie Searle, J. Farrell MacDonald, Charles Delaney. *D:* Christy Cabanne.

"Poverty row" drama.

1888. Heat Lightning (WB; 1934). *Cast:* Aline MacMahon (starring debut as Olga), Ann Dvorak, Preston Foster, Lyle Talbot, Glenda Farrell, Frank McHugh, Ruth Donnelly, Theodore Newton, Jane Darwell, Edgar Kennedy, Willard Robertson, Muriel Evans, James Durkin (1879–1934), Harry C. Bradley. *D:* Mervyn LeRoy; *P:* Sam Bischoff; *Sc:* Brown Holmes, Warren Duff. (1:03)

Low-budget drama set in the arrid southwest as a woman, owner of a gas station, becomes involved with two murderers on the lam. Based on the play by George Abbott and Leon Abrams, it was remade in 1941 as *Highway West.*

1889. Heaven on Earth (Universal; 1931). *Cast:* Lew Ayres, Anita Louise, Harry Beresford, Elizabeth Patterson, Slim Summerville, Alf P. James, John Peter Richmond (John Carradine), Harlan Knight, Louise Beavers, Mme. Sul-Te-Wan, Jules Cowles, Lew Kelly, Robert E. (Bob) Burns, Jack Duffy. *D:* Russell Mack; *Sc:* Ray Doyle. (1:10)

Mississippi River drama of a man who finds that his "father" is actually the killer of his real father. Based on the novel "Mississippi" by Ben Lucien Burman.

1890. Heaven with a Barbed Wire Fence (20th Century–Fox; 1939). *Cast:* Glenn Ford (film debut), Jean Rogers, Nicholas (Richard) Conte (film debut), Raymond Walburn, Marjorie Rambeau, Eddie Collins, Ward Bond, Paul Hurst. *D:* Ricardo Cortez; *St:* Dalton Trumbo; *Sc:* Trumbo, Leonard Hoffman, Ben Grauman Kohn. (1:01)

B drama of a New Yorker who hitch hikes to Arizona where he has bought land.

1891. Heidi (20th Century–Fox; 1937). *Cast:* Shirley Temple (Heidi), Jean Hersholt (grandfather), Arthur Treacher, Helen Westley, Pauline Moore, Mary Nash, Thomas Beck, Sidney Blackmer, Mady Christians, Sig Rumann, Marcia Mae Jones, Christian Rub, Delmar Watson, George Humbert, Egon Brecher. *D:* Allan Dwan; *P:* Raymond Griffith; *Sc:* Walter Ferris, Julien Josephson. (1:28) (video)

Popular adaptation of Johanna Spyri's children's classic of a Swiss orphan girl and her grandfather. Computer-colored in 1987.

1892. Heir to Trouble (Columbia; 1935). *Cast:* Ken Maynard, Joan Perry, Harry Woods, Wally Wales, Martin Faust, Harry Brown, Dorothea Wolbert, Fern Emmett, Pat O'Malley, Art Mix, Frank Yaconelli, Hal Price, Frank LaRue, Lafe McKee, Jack Rockwell, Slim Whitaker. *D:* Spencer Gordon Bennet; *Sc:* Nate Gatzert. (0:59)

Ken Maynard western of a cowboy who adopts the young son of his late friend.

1893. Held for Ransom (Grand National; 1938). *Cast:* Blanche Mehaffey, Grant Withers, Bruce Warren, Jack Mulhall, Kenneth Harlan, Harry Harvey, Sr., Edward Foster, Walter McGrail, George Moore, Robert McKenzie, Richard Lancaster, John McCallum, Joseph Girard. *D:* Clarence Bricker; *St & Sc:* Barry Barringer. (0:59)

A female FBI agent pursues kidnappers in this B melodrama.

1894. Hell and High Water
(Paramount; 1933). *Cast:* Richard
Arlen, Judith Allen, Sir Guy Standing,
Charley Grapewin, William Frawley,
Barton MacLane, Selmer Jackson, Ger-
trude W. Hoffman, Matsui, Robert
Knettles. *D:* Grover Jones, William
Slavens McNutt; *St:* Max Miller; *Sc:*
Jones, McNutt, Agnes Brand Leahy.
(G.B. title: *Cap'n Jericho*)
Low-budget drama of a garbage
scow operator who saves a girl from
drowning.

1895. Hell Below (MGM; 1933).
Cast: Robert Montgomery, Walter
Huston, Madge Evans, Jimmy Durante, Eugene Pallette, Robert Young,
Edwin Styles, John Lee Mahin, Sterling
Holloway, David Newell, Charles Irwin. *D:* Jack Conway; *Sc:* John Lee
Mahin, John Meehan; *Additional Dialogue:* Laird Doyle, Raymond Schrock.
(1:45)
World War I submarine drama set
in the Mediterranean sea. Based on the
novel "Pigboats" by Commander Edward Ellsberg.

1896. Hell Below Zero (Xxxx
Xxxx; 1931). *Narrated by:* Carveth Wells.
Documentary.

1897. Hell Bent for Frisco (Sono
Art-World Wide; 1931). *Cast:* Charles
Delaney, Vera Reynolds, Carroll Nye,
William Desmond. *D:* Stuart Paton.
"Poverty row" melodrama.

1898. Hell Bent for Love (Co-
lumbia; 1934). *Cast:* Tim McCoy,
Lillian Bond, Vincent Sherman, Brad-
ley Page, Lafe McKee. *D:* D. Ross
Lederman.
B actioner.

1899. Hell Bound (Tiffany; 1931).
Cast: Lloyd Hughes, Lola Lane, Leo
Carrillo, Russ Columbo, Gertrude
Astor, Helene Chadwick, Ralph Ince,
Martin Faust, William Lawrence, Bill
O'Brien, Jack Grey, Richard Tucker,
Harry Strang. *D:* Walter Lang; *St & Sc:*

Adele Commandini, Edward Dean Sul-
livan; *Adaptation:* Julien Josephson; *Sc:*
Josephson.
"Poverty row" drama.

1900. The Hell Cat (Columbia;
1934). *Cast:* Ann Sothern, Robert Arm-
strong, J. Carrol Naish, Minna Gom-
bell, Purnell Pratt, Benny Baker, Guy
Usher, Charles Wilson. *D:* Albert S.
Rogell; *St:* Adele Buffington; *Sc:* Fred
Niblo, Jr.
B newspaper drama.

1901. Hell Divers (MGM; 1931).
Cast: Wallace Beery (Windy), Clark
Gable (Steve), Conrad Nagel (Duke),
Dorothy Jordan (Ann), Marjorie Ram-
beau (Mame Kelsey), Marie Prevost
(Lulu), Cliff Edwards (Baldy), John
Miljan (Griffin), Landers Stevens (ad-
miral), Reed Howes (Lieut. Fisher),
Alan Roscoe (captain), Frank Conroy
(chaplain), Robert Young (young
officer), Jack Pennick, Tom London,
John Kelly, Virginia Bruce (bit). *D:*
George Hill; *Adaptation:* Harvey Gates,
Malcolm Stuart Boylan. (1:53)
Drama of the rivalry between two
naval air force officers which is notable
for its action sequences and was one of
the 15 top grossing films of 1932. Based
on a story by Lieutenant Commander
Frank "Spig" Wead, the location shooting was done aboard the aircraft carrier
"Saratoga" while on naval maneuvers in
Panama.

1902. Hell-Fire Austin (Tiffany/
Amity; 1932). *Cast:* Ken Maynard, Nat
Pendleton, Ivy Merton, Jack Perrin,
Charles LeMoyne, Lafe McKee, Alan
Roscoe, William Robyns, Fargo
Bussey, Jack Rockwell, Jack Ward, Bud
McClure, Lew Meehan, Slim
Whitaker, Ben Corbett, Jim Corey,
Jack Pennick. *D:* Forrest Sheldon; *P:*
Phil Goldstone; *Sc:* Betty Burbridge.
(1:10) (video)
Ken Maynard western of difficul-
ties encountered by two World War I
vets after returning home to Texas.

Maynard's 11th and final film for this "poverty row" studio.

1903. Hell Harbor (United Artists/Inspiration Prods.; 1930). *Cast:* Lupe Velez, John Holland, Gibson Gowland, Jean Hersholt, Al St. John, Rondo Hatton (film debut), Harry Allen, Paul E. Burns, George Book-Asta. *D:* Henry King; *P:* King; *St:* Rida Johnson Young; *Sc:* Fred de Gresac, N. Brewster Morse, Clark Silvernail.

Romantic actioner set on an island inhabited by the descendants of Sir Henry Morgan's band of notorious pirates.

1904. Hell in the Heavens (Fox; 1934). *Cast:* Warner Baxter, Conchita Montenegro, Ralph Morgan, Herbert Mundin, J. Carrol Naish, Johnny Arthur, Andy Devine, Vince Barnett, William Stack, William Stelling, Arno Frey, Vincent Carato, Rudolph Amendt. *D:* John G. Blystone; *P:* Al Rockett; *St:* Herman Rossmann; *Sc:* Byron Morgan, Ted Parsons.

A drama of World War I fighter pilots.

1905. Hell-Ship Morgan (Columbia; 1936). *Cast:* George Bancroft, Ann Sothern, Victor Jory, Ralph Byrd (film debut). *D:* D. Ross Lederman.

Low-budget actioner.

Hell Town *see* **Born to the West**

1906. Hell's Angels (United Artists/Caddo Co.; 1930). *Cast:* Ben Lyon (Monte Rutledge), James Hall (Roy Rutledge), Jean Harlow (replacing Greta Nissen as Helen), John Darrow (Karl Arnstedt), Lucien Prival (Baron von Kranz), Frank Clark (Lieut. von Bruen), Roy Wilson (Baldy Maloney), Douglas Gilmore (Capt. Redfield), Jane Winton (Baroness von Kranz), Evelyn Hall (Lady Randolph), Wyndham Standing (squadron commander of the Royal Flying Corps), William B. Davidson (staff major), Carl Von Hartmann (zeppelin commander), Ferdinand Schumann-Heink (zeppelin first officer), Stephen Carr (Elliott), Pat Somerset (Marryat), William von Brincken (Baron Von Richtofen), Hans Joby (Von Schlieben), Lena Malena (Gretchen), Harry Semels (anarchist), Marilyn Morgan (later Marian Marsh as the girl selling kisses), Thomas Carr, J. Granville-Davis, Stuart Murphy, Ira Reed, Maurice "Loop the Loop" Murphy, Leo Nomis, Frank Tomick, Al Wilson, Roscoe Turner, Al Johnson (flier killed during production), Phil Jones (flier killed during production). *D:* Howard Hughes, James Whale (unc.), Howard Hawks (unc.), Lewis Milestone (unc.); *P:* Howard Hughes; *St:* Marshall Neilan, Joseph Moncure March; *Sc:* Howard Estabrook, Harry Behn, Whale (unc.); *Cinematographers:* (A.A.N.) Antonio (Tony) Gaudio, Harry Perry, E. Burton Steene (who succumbed to a stroke during production), Harry Zech, Dewey Wrigley, Elmer Dyer. (Original running time: 2:15) (Restored prints run 2:05, apparently missing some widescreen footage from the original).

Howard Hughes production of World War I aviation which premiered at Grauman's Chinese Theater on May 27, 1930, in Hollywood, a much publicized event of its day. The spectacular aerial dogfight sequences have never been surpassed according to many critics. When production began in 1927, the film was originally intended as a silent, but as filming ran into the talkie era, last minute additions of sound track and dialogue were added prior to release. The party sequences are filmed in 2-color technicolor. One of the 15 top grossing films of 1930–31, it also placed #9 on the "10 Best" list of *Film Daily.*

Hell's Cargo *see* **Below the Sea**

Hell's Devils *see* **Hitler — Beast of Berlin**

1907. Hell's Headquarters (Capital; 1932). *Cast:* Jack Mulhall, Frank Mayo. *D:* Andrew L. Stone.

1908. Hell's Heroes (Universal; 1929). *Cast:* Charles Bickford (Sangster),

Raymond Hatton (Gibbons), Fred Kohler (Kearney), Fritzi Ridgeway (mother), John Huston, Tom London. *D:* William Wyler (in his talkie directorial debut); *Sc:* Tom Reed. (1:05)

Hit western of three outlaws who care for a baby after the mother dies. Based on the story by Peter B. (Bernard) Kyne it was filmed in 1916, 1936 (q.v.) and 1948 as *Three Godfathers.* Also filmed in 1920 as *Marked Men* and again in 1975 as a TV movie *The Godchild.* The same story idea was also used in the 1909 production of *Broncho Billy and the Baby.* Filmed on location in the Mojave Desert and the Panamint Valley, this was Universal's first all-talkie to be filmed outdoors.

1909. Hell's Highway (RKO; 1932). *Cast:* Richard Dix, Tom Brown, Rochelle Hudson, C. Henry Gordon, Oscar Apfel, Stanley Fields, Warner Richmond, Charles Middleton, Louise Carter, Sandy Roth, Clarence Muse, Fuzzy Knight (film debut), Eddie Hart, Harry Smith, Bert Starkey, Jed Kiley, Louise Beavers, Bob Perry. *D:* Rowland Brown; *P:* David O. Selznick; *Sc:* Brown, Sam Ornitz, Robert Tasker. (1:02)

Brutal conditions spark a revolt against authority on a southern chain gang. A controversial film of its day.

1910. Hell's House (Capital Film Exchange; 1932). *Cast:* James (Junior) Durkin, Pat O'Brien, Bette Davis, Frank (Junior) Coghlan, Charley Grapewin, Emma Dunn, Morgan Wallace, Hooper Atchley, James Marcus, Wallis Clark, Mary Alden. *D:* Howard Higgin; *St:* Higgin; *Sc:* Paul Gangelin, B. Harrison Orkow. (1:12) (video)

"Poverty row" melodrama of an innocent youth sentenced to a cruel reformatory after his mother is killed.

1911. Hell's Island (Columbia; 1930). *Cast:* Jack Holt, Dorothy Sebastian, Ralph Graves, Lionel Belmore,

Richard Cramer, Carl Stockdale. *D:* Edward Sloman; *Sc:* Jo Swerling.

Seafaring action-melodrama.

1912. Hell's Kitchen (WB; 1939). *Cast:* Billy Halop, Bobby Jordan, Leo Gorcey, Huntz Hall, Gabriel Dell, Bernard Punsley, Margaret Lindsay, Ronald Reagan, Stanley Fields, Frankie Burke, Grant Mitchell, Fred Tozere, Arthur Loft, Vera Lewis, Robert Homans, Charles Foy, Raymond Bailey, Clem Bevans, George Irving, Ila Rhodes. *D:* Lewis Seiler, E.A. Dupont; *As.P.:* Bryan Foy, Mark Hellinger; *St:* Crane Wilbur; *Sc:* Wilbur, Fred Niblo, Jr. (1:21)

B delinquency melodrama. A remake of *The Mayor of Hell* (q.v.) and *Crime School* (q.v.).

1913. Hell's Valley (Big 4; 1931). *D:* Alvin J. Neitz.

(No other information available)

1914. Helldorado (Fox; 1934-35). *Cast:* Richard Arlen (replacing Spencer Tracy), Madge Evans, Ralph Bellamy, Stepin Fetchit, James Gleason, Henry B. Walthall, Helen Jerome Eddy, Berton Churchill, Gertrude Short, Patricia Farr, Philip Hurlic. *D:* James Cruze; *P:* Jesse L. Lasky; *St:* Frank Mitchell Dazey; *Sc:* Frances Hyland; *Adapt.:* Rex Taylor. (1:15) (video)

Comedy-drama of a drifter who discovers a gold mine in an old western ghost town.

1915. Hello, Everybody! (Paramount; 1933). *Cast:* Kate Smith, Sally Blane, Randolph Scott, Charley Grapewin, Julia Swayne Gordon (final film — d. 1933), George Barbier, Frank Darien, Fern Emmett, Paul Kruger, Edwards Davis, Ted Collins, Jerry Tucker, Marguerite Campbell, Bud Flanagan (Dennis O'Keefe). *D:* William A. Seiter; *St:* Fannie Hurst.

A girl becomes a popular radio singing star and saves the family farm.

1916. Hello Sister (Sono Art-World Wide; 1930). *Cast:* Lloyd Hughes, Wilfred Lucas. *D:* Walter Lang.
"Poverty row" feature.

1917. Hello, Sister (Fox; 1933). *Cast:* James Dunn, Boots Mallory, ZaSu Pitts, Minna Gombell, Marion Nixon, Terrance Ray, Will Stanton. *D:* Erich Von Stroheim, Alfred Werker; *P:* Winfield Sheehan; *Sc:* Von Stroheim, Leonard Spigelgass (based on the novel by Dawn Powell). (1:02)
Boy meets girl story which was originally filmed as *Walking Down Broadway,* but later re-edited and renamed with many sections completely reshot. Despite all that, the film was still a box office dud.

1918. Hello Trouble (Columbia; 1932). *Cast:* Buck Jones, Lina Basquette, Wallace MacDonald, Spec O'Donnell, Ruth Warren, Otto Hoffman, Ward Bond, Frank Rice, Russell Simpson, Alan Roscoe, Al Smith, King Baggot, Bert Roach, Walter Brennan, Morgan Galloway. *D:* Lambert Hillyer; *P:* Hillyer; *Sc:* Hillyer. (1:07)
Buck Jones western of a Texas Ranger who quits the service after killing a suspected cattle rustler who turns out to be his friend.

1919. Henry Goes Arizona (MGM; 1939–40). *Cast:* Frank Morgan, Virginia Weidler, Gordon Jones, Douglas Fowley, Guy Kibbee, Slim Summerville, Owen Davis, Jr., Porter Hall, Mitchell Lewis. *D:* Edwin L. Marin; *P:* Harry Rapf; *St:* W.C. Tuttle; *Sc:* Florence Ryerson, Milton Merlin. (G.B. title: *Spats to Spurs*) (1:06)
B comedy of a vaudevillian who inherits his late brother's debt-ridden ranch and finds trouble with landgrabbers when he goes to claim it.

1920. Her Bodyguard (Paramount; 1933). *Cast:* Edward Arnold, Wynne Gibson, Edmund Lowe, Johnny Hines, Fuzzy Knight, Marjorie White, Louise Beavers, Zolla Conan. *D:* William Beaudine; *St:* Corey Ford; *Sc:* Ralph Spence, Walter De Leon; *Adapt.:* Frank Partos, Francis Martin.
B comedy of a Broadway star who falls for her bodyguard.

Her Dilemma (G.B. title) *see* **Confessions of a Co-ed**

1921. Her First Mate (Universal; 1933). *Cast:* ZaSu Pitts, Slim Summerville, Una Merkel, Warren Hymer, Berton Churchill, George F. Marion, Henry Armetta. *D:* William Wyler; *St:* Frank Craven, John Golden, Dan Jarrett; *Sc:* Earle Snell, Clarence Marks. (1:05)
Hit marital comedy of a peanut vendor who yearns to sail the seas rather than hawk peanuts on the local ferry. Based on the play "Salt Water" by Frank Craven.

1922. Her Forgotten Past (Mayfair; 1933). *Cast:* Barbara Kent, Monte Blue, Dewey Robinson. *D:* Wesley Ford.
"Poverty row" drama.

1923. Her Golden Calf (Fox; 1930). *Cast:* Sue Carol, Jack Mulhall, Marjorie White, El Brendel, Paul Page, Walter Catlett, Ilka Chase, Richard Keene. *D:* Millard Webb; *St:* Aaron Davis.
Romantic comedy.

1924. Her Husband Lies (Paramount; 1936–37). *Cast:* Ricardo Cortez, Gail Patrick, Louis Calhern, Tom Brown, Akim Tamiroff, Bradley Page, Dorothy Peterson, Ralf Harolde, Ray Walker, Adrian Morris, June Martel. *D:* Edward Ludwig; *P:* B.P. Schulberg; *St:* Oliver H.P. Garrett; *Sc:* Eve Greene, Wallace Smith.
B gangster melodrama, a remake of *Street of Chance* (q.v.).

1925. Her Husband's Secretary (WB/F.N.; 1937). *Cast:* Warren Hull,

Beverly Roberts, Jean Muir, Stuart Holmes, Pauline Garon (final film—ret.), Clara Blandick, Joseph Crehan, Addison Richards, Harry Davenport, Minerva Urecal, Gordon Hart. *D:* Frank McDonald; *P:* Bryan Foy; *St:* Crane Wilbur; *Sc:* Lillie Hayward.

B triangular romantic comedy.

1926. Her Jungle Love (Paramount; 1938). *Cast:* Dorothy Lamour, Ray Milland, Lynne Overman, J. Carrol Naish, Dorothy Howe (Virginia Vale), Jonathan Hale, Archie Twitchell, Edward Earle, Richard Denning, Tony Urchell, Sonny Choree, Philip Warren, Jiggs the chimp. *D:* George Archainbaud; *P:* George M. Arthur; *St:* Curt Siodmak, Gerald Geraghty; *Sc:* Joseph Moncure March, Lillie Hayward, Eddie Welch. (1:21)

Hit technicolor romantic-comedy adventure of two downed flyers who encounter a sarong clad beauty on a tropical island. The studio made a huge profit off of this venture.

1927. Her Mad Night (Mayfair; 1932). *Cast:* Mary Carlisle, Conway Tearle, Irene Rich, Kenneth Thomson, William Davidson. *D:* E. Mason Hopper; *Sc:* John T. Neville.

"Poverty row" drama of a thrill-seeking girl who gets tangled up with the wrong guy.

1928. Her Majesty, Love (WB/F.N.; 1931). *Cast:* Marilyn Miller (final film), Ben Lyon, W.C. Fields, Leon Errol, Chester Conklin, Ford Sterling, Virginia Sale, Harry Stubbs, Ruth Hall, Maude Eburne, Clarence Wilson, William Irving, Mae Madison, Harry Holman. *D:* William Dieterle; *St:* Rudolph Bernauer, Rudolph Oesterreicher; *Adaptation:* Robert Lord, Arthur Caesar; *Dialogue:* Henry Blanke, Joseph Jackson; *Songs:* "Because of You," "You're Baby Minded Now," "Don't Ever Be Blue" and "Though You're Not the First Wine." (1:16)

Romantic musical-comedy with German locales.

1929. Her Man (Pathé; 1930). *Cast:* Helen Twelvetrees, Ricardo Cortez, James Gleason, Phillips Holmes, Marjorie Rambeau, Franklin Pangborn, Rafaela Ottiano, Slim Summerville, Ruth Hiatt, Thelma Todd, Matthew Betz. *D:* Tay Garnett; *St:* Garnett, Howard Higgin; *Sc:* Tom Buckingham.

Romantic drama.

1930. Her Master's Voice (Paramount; 1936). *Cast:* Edward Everett Horton, Peggy Conklin, Laura Hope Crews, Grant Mitchell, Elizabeth Patterson, Dick Elliott. *D:* Joseph Santley; *P:* Walter Wanger.

B comedy of a man with marital and in-law problems who is able to take control after becoming a popular radio crooner.

1931. Her Private Affair (Pathé; 1929). *Cast:* Ann Harding, John Loder, Harry Bannister, Kay Hammond (film debut), Elmer Ballard, William Orlamond, Lawford Davidson, Frank Reicher. *D:* Paul Stein; *St:* Leo Orvantov; *Sc:* Francis Edwards Faragoh.

Part-talkie romantic drama.

1932. Her Private Life (WB/F.N.; 1929). *Cast:* Billie Dove, Roland Young, Montagu Love, Walter Pidgeon, Holmes Herbert, Thelma Todd, ZaSu Pitts, Mary Forbes. *D:* Alexander Korda; *Sc:* Forrest Halsey.

Drama of marriage, indiscretions and divorce, based on the play "Declassee" by Zoe Akins. A remake of the 1925 production by First National.

Her Reputation (G.B. title) *see* **Broadway Bad**

1933. Her Resale Value (Mayfair; 1933). *Cast:* June Clyde. *D:* B. Reeves Eason.

"Poverty row" drama.

Her Sacrifice (G.B. title) *see* **Blind Date**

1934. Her Secret (Xxxx Xxxx; 1933). *Cast:* Sari Maritza, William Collier, Jr., Alan Mowbray. *D:* Xxxx Xxxx.

Melodrama.

1935. Her Splendid Folly (Progressive Pictures; 1933). *Cast:* Lillian Bond, Lloyd Whitlock, Theodore von Eltz, Alexander Carr, Louise Beavers. *D:* William O'Connor.

"Poverty row" romantic comedy.

Her Unlisted Man *see* **Red Salute**

1936. Her Wedding Night (Paramount; 1930). *Cast:* Clara Bow, Ralph Forbes, Charles Ruggles, Richard "Skeets" Gallagher, Natalie Kingston, Lillian Elliott, Geneva Mitchell, Wilson Benge, Rosita Moreno. *D:* Frank Tuttle (who also directed the '25 version); *P:* E. Lloyd Sheldon; *St:* Avery Hopwood.

Romantic comedy of misunderstandings and mix-ups on the French Riviera. A remake of *Miss Bluebeard* (Paramount; 1925) with Bebe Daniels and Raymond Griffith.

1937. Here Comes Carter! (WB/ F.N.; 1936). *Cast:* Ross Alexander, Anne Nagel, Glenda Farrell, Hobart Cavanaugh, Craig Reynolds, George E. Stone, Wayne Morris, John Sheehan. *D:* William Clemens; *P:* Bryan Foy; *St:* Michel Jacoby; *Sc:* Roy Chanslor; *Songs:* "Through the Courtesy of Love" and "You on My Mind" by M.K. Jerome, Jack Scholl.

B comedy-drama of a Hollywood press agent who does an expose on "tinsel town."

1938. Here Comes Cookie (Paramount; 1935). *Cast:* George Burns, Gracie Allen, Betty Furness, Andrew Tombes, Lee Kohlmar, George Barbier, Frank Darien, Milla Davenport, Rafael Storm, Jack Powell. *D:* Norman Z. McLeod; *P:* William LeBaron; *St:* Don Hartman, Sam Mintz; *Sc:* Hartman. (G.B. title: *The Plot Thickens*) (1:06)

B comedy of a tycoon who takes steps to protect his daughter from fortune hunters.

1939. Here Comes the Band (MGM; 1935). *Cast:* Harry Stockwell, Virginia Bruce, Ted Lewis and his band, Ted Healy, Billy Gilbert, Nat Pendleton, Donald Cook, Spanky McFarland, Bert Roach, Ferdinand Gottschalk, Charles (Lane) Levison, Tyler Brooke. *D:* Paul Sloane; *P:* Lucien Hubbard; *Sc:* Ralph Spence, Victor Mansfield, Paul Sloane; *Songs:* Burton Lane, Walter Donaldson, Harold Adamson.

B musical of a songwriter who can't sell his latest song—then plagiarists make it a hit.

1940. Here Comes the Groom (Paramount; 1934). *Cast:* Jack Haley, Mary Boland, Neil Hamilton, Patricia Ellis, Isabel Jewell, E.H. Calvert, Arthur Treacher, Sidney Toler, Lawrence Gray, Ward Bond. *D:* Edward Sedgwick; *St:* Richard Flournoy; *Sc:* Casey Robinson, Leonard Praskins.

B romantic comedy of a feigned marriage.

1941. Here Comes the Navy (WB; 1934). *Cast:* James Cagney (Chesty), Pat O'Brien (Biff), Gloria Stuart (Dorothy), Dorothy Tree (Gladys), Frank McHugh (Droopy), Robert Barrat (Commander Denny), Willard Robertson (Lieut. commander), Maude Eburne (Droopy's Ma), Guinn Williams (floor manager), Martha Merrill, Lorena Layson, Ida Darling, Henry Otho, Pauline True, Sam McDaniel, Frank LaRue, Joseph Crehan, James Burtis, Edward Chandler, Leo White, Niles Welch, Fred "Snowflake" Toones, Eddie Shubert, George Irving, Howard Hickman, Edward Earle, Gordon (Bill) Elliott, Emmett Vogan. *D:* Lloyd Bacon; *P:* Louis Edelman; *Sc:* Ben Markson, Earl Baldwin; *Song:* "Hey, Sailor" by Irving Kahal, Sammy Fain. (1:26)

Hit naval story which received an A.A.N. for Best Picture. Prior to release the film had the working title of "Hey, Sailor!"

1942. Here Comes Trouble (20th Century–Fox; 1936). *Cast:* Arline Judge, Paul Kelly, Mona Barrie, Edward Brophy, Gregory Ratoff, Mischa Auer, Andrew Tombes, Halliwell Hobbes, George Chandler, Wade Boteler. *D:* Lewis Seiler.

B comedy.

1943. Here I Am a Stranger (20th Century–Fox; 1939). *Cast:* Richard Dix, Richard Greene, Gladys George, Brenda Joyce, Roland Young, George Zucco, Russell Gleason, Edward Norris, Kay Aldrich, Minor Watson, Charles Wilson, Richard Bond. *D:* Roy Del Ruth; *P:* Harry Joe Brown; *St:* Gordon Malherbe Hillman; *Sc:* Milton Sperling, Sam Hellman. (1:22)

Drama of a man who meets his long-lost father, an ex-alcoholic.

1944. Here Is My Heart (Paramount; 1934). *Cast:* Bing Crosby, Kitty Carlisle, Roland Young, Alison Skipworth, Reginald Owen, Cecilia Parker, William Frawley, Akim Tamiroff, Cromwell McKechnie, Charles Arnt, Marian Mansfield, Albert Petit, Charles Wilson, Arthur Housman. *D:* Frank Tuttle; *P:* Louis D. Lighton; *Sc:* Edwin Justus Mayer, Harlan Thompson, Dorothy Parker (unc.); *Songs:* "June in January" and "With Every Breath I Take" by Ralph Rainger and Leo Robin. (1:17)

Hit romantic musical of a radio singer in love with a princess. A remake of *The Grand Duchess and the Waiter* (Paramount; 1926) with Adolphe Menjou and Florence Vidor, which was a huge hit for the studio. Based on the play of that name by Alfred Savoir.

1945. Here's Flash Casey (Grand National; 1937–38). *Cast:* Eric Linden, Boots Mallory, Cully Richards, Holmes Herbert, Joseph Crehan, Howard Lang, Victor Adams, Harry Harvey, Sr., Suzanne Kaaren, Matty Kemp, Dorothy Vaughan, Maynard Holmes. *D:* Lynn Shores; *P:* Max & Arthur Alexander; *St:* George Harmon Coxe; *Sc:* John Krafft. (0:58)

Mystery-drama of a young man who sets out to make it big in photography.

1946. Here's to Romance (Fox; 1935). *Cast:* Nino Martini, Anita Louise, Reginald Denny, Genevieve Tobin, Keye Luke, Miles Mander (American debut), Elsa Buchanan, Armand Kaliz, Adrian Rosley, Pat Somerset, Egon Brecher, Mathilde Comont, Ernestine Schumann-Heink, Vincent Escudero. *D:* Alfred E. Green; *P:* Jesse Lasky, Jr.; *St:* Sonya Levien, Ernest Pascal; *Sc:* Pascal, Arthur Richman.

Romantic musical.

1947. Heritage of the Desert (Paramount; 1932). *Cast:* Randolph Scott, Sally Blane, David Landau, Guinn Williams, Vince Barnett, J. Farrell MacDonald, Gordon Westcott, Susan Fleming, Fred Burns, Charles Stevens. *D:* Henry Hathaway (directorial debut); *Sc:* Harold Shumate, Frank Partos. (Re-release title: *When the West Was Young*) (1:02)

B western based on the 1910 book by Zane Grey, previously filmed by this studio in 1924. The story of a cowboy who thwarts claim-jumpers was remade in 1939 (see below).

1948. Heritage of the Desert (Paramount; 1939). *Cast:* Donald Woods, Evelyn Venable, Russell Hayden, Robert Barrat, Sidney Toler, C. Henry Gordon, Paul Guilfoyle, Paul Fix, Willard Robertson, Reginald Barlow, John Miller. *D:* Lesley Selander; *P:* Harry M. Sherman; *Sc:* Norman Houston. (1:14)

A remake of the preceding film based on the book by Zane Grey of an easterner who goes west and runs afoul of claim-jumpers.

1949. Hero for a Day (Universal; 1939). *Cast:* Charley Grapewin, Dick Foran, Anita Louise, Berton Churchill, Samuel S. Hinds, Frances Robinson. *D:* Harold Young; *P:* Kenneth Goldsmith. (1:05)

B effort of a football hero returning to his alma mater for one more game.

The Hero of Pine Ridge (G.B. title) *see* **Yodelin' Kid from Pine Ridge**

1950. Heroes for Sale (WB/F.N.; 1933). *Cast:* Richard Barthelmess, Aline MacMahon, Loretta Young, Gordon Westcott, Robert Barrat, Berton Churchill, Grant Mitchell, Charley Grapewin, Robert McWade, George Pat Collins, James Murray, Edwin Maxwell, Margaret Seddon, Arthur Vinton, Robert Elliott, John Marston, Willard Robertson, Douglass Dumbrille, Ward Bond. *D:* William Wellman; *P:* Hal Wallis; *St:* Wilson Mizner; *Sc:* Robert Lord, Mizner. (1:13)

Drama of a World War I veteran who encounters difficulties in adjusting after the war. A box office flop.

1951. Heroes in Blue (Monogram; 1939). *Cast:* Dick Purcell, Charles Quigley, Bernadene Hayes, Edward Keane, Julie Warren, Lillian Elliott, Frank Sheridan. *D:* William Watson; *P:* T.R. Williams; *St:* "Detective First Class" by C.B. Williams and Charles Curran; *Sc:* C.B. Williams. (1:01)

B melodrama of two brothers, both cops who have different ideas about their profession.

1952. Heroes of the Alamo (Columbia/Sunset Pictures; 1937–38). *Cast:* Earle Hodgins (Stephen Austin), Lane Chandler (Davy Crockett), Rex Lease (Col. William B. Travis), Edward Peil, Sr. (Sam Houston), Julian Rivero (Gen. Santa Anna), Roger Williams, Jack C. Smith, Bruce Warren, Ruth Findlay,

Lee Valianos, William Costello, Steve Clark, Sherry Tansey, Denver Dixon (Victor Adamson), George Morrell, Tex Cooper, Oscar Gahan, Ben Corbett. *D:* Harry S. Fraser; *P:* Anthony J. Xydias; *Sc:* Roby Wentz. (aka: *Remember the Alamo*) (1:14)

Independent production of the famed battle for Texan independence against Santa Anna's troops.

1953. Heroes of the Hills (Republic; 1938). *Cast:* Bob Livingston (Stony Brooke), Ray Corrigan (Tucson Smith), Max Terhune (Lullaby Joslin), Priscilla Lawson, LeRoy Mason, James Eagles, Roy Barcroft, Carleton Young, Forrest Taylor, Maston Williams, John Beach, Roger Williams, Kit Guard, Jack Kirk, Curley Dresden. *D:* George Sherman; *Sc:* Betty Burbridge, Stanley Roberts. (0:56)

The "Three Mesquiteers" encounter trouble when they decide to turn their ranch into a prison work farm.

1954. Heroes of the Range (Columbia; 1936). *Cast:* Ken Maynard, June Gale, Harry Woods, Harry Ernest, Robert Kortman, Tom London, Bud McClure, Bud Osborne, Frank Hagney, Jack Rockwell, Lafe McKee, Wally Wales (Hal Taliaferro), Buffalo Bill, Jr., Bud Jamison, Bob Reeves. *D:* Spencer Gordon Bennet; *St & Sc:* Nate Gatzert. (0:58)

Ken Maynard oater of a government man who saves a girl's brother and gets the bad guys. The highlight of the film has got to be Maynard singing and fiddling "Give Us Back Our Old .45s."

1955. Heroic Lover (General Pictures; 1929–30). *Cast:* Barbara Bedford, Stuart Holmes. *D:* Noel Mason (Smith).

Low-budget independent production.

1956. Hi, Gaucho! (RKO; 1935). *Cast:* John Carroll (starring debut), Steffi Duna, Rod La Rocque, Montagu Love, Ann Codee, Tom Ricketts, Paul Porcasi, Enrique De Rosas, Billy

Gilbert. *D:* Tommy Atkins; *As.P.:* John E. Burch; *St:* Atkins; *Sc:* Adele Buffington; *Songs:* Albert Hay Malotte. (1:00)

B musical drama of a South American gaucho who romances the girl despite their feuding families.

1957. Hi, Nellie! (WB; 1934). *Cast:* Paul Muni, Glenda Farrell, Ned Sparks, Robert Barrat, Hobart Cavanaugh, Berton Churchill, Donald Meek, Douglass Dumbrille, Edward Ellis, John Qualen, Frank Reicher, George Chandler, Harold Huber, Pat Wing, Sidney Miller, George Meeker. *D:* Mervyn LeRoy; *P:* Robert Presnell; *St:* Roy Chanslor; *Sc:* Abem Finkel, Sidney Sutherland.

Comedy-melodrama of a newsman of questionable ethics who is demoted to the "advice to the lovelorn" column. A box office flop which was remade as *Love Is on the Air* (q.v.), *You Can't Escape Forever* (W.B.; 1942) and *The House Across the Street* (WB; 1949).

1958. Hi-Yo Silver! (Republic; 1938–40). *Cast:* Lee Powell, Chief Thundercloud, Lane Chandler, Hal Taliaferro, Herman Brix (Bruce Bennett), George (Montgomery) Letz, George Cleveland, Frank McGlynn, Stanley Andrews, Lynn Roberts, William Farnum, John Merton, Sammy McKim. *D:* William Witney, John English; *P:* Nat Levine; *Sc:* Barry Shipman, George Worthing Yates, Franklyn Adreon, Ronald Davidson, Lois Eby. (1:09)

Feature version of the 1938 15-chapter serial "The Lone Ranger," released as a feature in 1940.

1959. Hidden Gold (Universal; 1932). *Cast:* Tom Mix, "Tony," Judith Barrie, Raymond Hatton, Eddie Gribbon, Donald Kirke, Wallis Clark, Roy Moore. *D:* Arthur Rosson; *Sc:* Jack Natteford, James Mulhauser. (1:01)

Tom Mix western of a cowboy who infiltrates a gang of bank robbers.

Note: During the filming of a chase scene, Tony, Mix's horse stepped in a gopher hole, threw Mix from his back and landed on top of him, injuring Mix seriously. Tony himself suffered a permanent hip injury and was retired from films following this one, being replaced by Tony, Jr., in the rest of the features in this series.

1960. Hidden Power (Columbia; 1939). *Cast:* Jack Holt, Gertrude Michael, Dickie Moore, Regis Toomey, Holmes Herbert, Oscar Homolka, Marilyn Knowlden, Harry Hayden, Helen Brown. *D:* Lewis D. Collins; *Sc:* Gordon Rigby.

Low-budget melodrama.

1961. Hidden Valley (Monogram; 1932). *Cast:* Bob Steele, Gertrude Messinger, Francis McDonald, Ray Hallor, John Elliott, Arthur Millett, V.L. Barnes, Joe (Jose) de la Cruz, Dick Dickinson, George Hayes, Captain Verner L. Smith, Tom London. *D:* Robert N. Bradbury; *P:* Trem Carr; *St & Sc:* Wellyn Totman. (1:00)

Bob Steele western with the offbeat premise of a lawman searching the desert for a wanted man, via an airship. Steele's first for this studio.

1962. Hide-Out (Universal; 1930). *Cast:* James Murray, Dorothy Dwan, Edward Hearn, Robert Elliott, Lee Moran, Carl Stockdale, Kathryn Crawford. *D:* Reginald Barker; *Sc:* Arthur Ripley, Lambert Hillyer. (0:59)

B of a wanted bootlegger who finds romance while hiding out at a college under an assumed identity.

1963. Hide-Out (MGM; 1934). *Cast:* Robert Montgomery, Maureen O'Sullivan, Edward Arnold, Elizabeth Patterson, Whitford Kane, Mickey Rooney, C. Henry Gordon, Muriel Evans, Edward Brophy, Henry Armetta, Herman Bing, Louise Henry, Harold Huber, Douglass Dumbrille. *D:* W.S. Van Dyke; *P:* Hunt Stromberg;

Original Story: (A.A.N.) Mauri Grashin; *Sc:* Frances Goodrich, Albert Hackett. (1:23) (video)

A wounded gangster learns about life and love while recovering from gunshot wounds amidst a simple farm family. A hit film of its day, it was remade as *I'll Wait for You* (MGM; 1941).

1964. Hideaway (RKO; 1937). *Cast:* Fred Stone, Emma Dunn, Marjorie Lord, J. Carrol Naish, William Corson, Ray Mayer, Bradley Page, Paul Guilfoyle, Tommy Bond, Dudley Clements, Alec Craig, Charles Withers, Otto Hoffman, Bob McKenzie, Lee Patrick. *D:* Richard Rosson; *P:* Cliff Reid; *Sc:* J. Robert Bren, Edmund L. Hartmann (based on the play by Melvin Levy). (0:58)

Comedy of a family of squatters who move into an abandoned house, only to have the owner, a big city gangster show up with some of his boys.

1965. Hideaway Girl (Paramount; 1937). *Cast:* Martha Raye, Shirley Ross, Robert Cummings, Edward Brophy, Chill Wills and the Avalon Boys, Robert Middlemass, Monroe Owsley, Ray Walker, Elizabeth Russell, Louis DaPron, Wilma Francis. *D:* George Archainbaud; *P:* A.M. Botsford; *St:* David Garth; *Sc:* Joseph Moncure March.

B comedy of a girl who takes refuge on a playboy's yacht after a jewel robbery.

1966. The Higgins Family (Republic; 1938). *Cast:* James Gleason, Lucile Gleason, Russell Gleason, Harry Davenport, Tommy Ryan, Lynn Roberts, William Bakewell. *D:* Gus Meins.

Premiere entry in a hit series of nine B comedy features of the misadventures of the "Higgins Family." In this entry the man of the house has his career hampered by family problems.

Note: The Higgins Family features were Republic's answer to MGM's "Hardy Family" series and Fox's "Jones Family" series.

1967. High Flyers (RKO; 1937). *Cast:* Bert Wheeler (Jerry Lane), Robert Woolsey (final film as Pierre—d. 1938), Lupe Velez (Sonora), Marjorie Lord (Arlene Arlington), Margaret Dumont (Mrs. Arlington), Paul Harvey (Mr. Horace Arlington), Jack Carson (David), Squeezie the dog, Charles Judels, Lucien Prival, Herbert Evans, Herbert Clifton, George Irving. *D:* Edward Cline; *P:* Lee Marcus; *Sc:* Benny Rubin, Bert Granet, Byron Morgan; *Songs:* Herman Ruby, Dave Dreyer. (1:10)

Comedy of two Bozo flying instructors who unknowingly smuggle gems and crashland a plane at a large country estate. The final film of the comedy team of Wheeler and Woolsey, due to the death of the latter the following year. Based on the play by Victor Mapes.

1968. High Gear (Ken Goldsmith Prods.; 1933). *Cast:* Joan Marsh, James Murray, Jackie Searle, Lee Moran, Ann Brody, Theodore von Eltz, Eddie Lambert, Mike Donlin. *D:* Leigh Jason; *P:* Ken Goldsmith; *St & Sc:* Jason, Charles Saxton, Rex Taylor.

Low-budget independent production.

1969. High Hat (Imperial; 1938). *Cast:* Franklin Pangborn, Dorothy Dare, Lona Andre, Gavin Gordon. *D:* Clifford Sanforth; *Sc:* Sherman L. Lowe.

(No other information available)

1970. High Pressure (WB; 1932). *Cast:* William Powell, Evelyn Brent, George Sidney, Frank McHugh, Guy Kibbee, Evalyn Knapp, Ben Alexander, Lillian Bond, John Wray, Robert Watson, Harry Beresford, Charles Judels, Alison Skipworth, Luis Alberni, Lucien Littlefield, Oscar Apfel, Maurice Black, Harold Waldridge. *D:* Mervyn LeRoy; *St:* S.J. Peters; *Sc:* Joseph Jackson. (1:14)

Comedy of a man trying to sell people on artificial rubber. Based on the play "Hot Money" by Aben Kandel.

The High Road (G.B. title) *see* **The Lady of Scandal**

1971. High School Girl (Fox; 1935). *Cast:* Cecilia Parker, Mahlon Hamilton, Crane Wilbur, Mildred Gover, Helen MacKellar, Carlyle Moore, Jr., Noel Warwick, Treva Scott. *D:* Crane Wilbur; *P:* Bryan Foy; *Sc:* Wallace Thurman, Wilbur.
Hit exploitation film of a young girl who finds out about sex the hard way.

1972. High Society Blues (Fox; 1930). *Cast:* Janet Gaynor, Charles Farrell, William Collier, Sr., Hedda Hopper, Louise Fazenda, Lucien Littlefield, Joyce Compton, Brandon Hurst. *D:* David Butler; *Sc:* Howard J. Green; *Song:* Joe McCarthy, James Hanley. (1:42)
A romance with music which capitalized on the popularity of its stars.

1973. High Speed (Columbia; 1932). *Cast:* Charles "Buck" Jones, Loretta Sayers, Wallace MacDonald, Mickey Rooney, Ward Bond. *D:* D. Ross Lederman.
B drama of race car drivers.

1974. High Stakes (RKO; 1931). *Cast:* Lowell Sherman, Mae Murray (final film—ret.), Karen Morley, Edward Martindel, Leyland Hodgson, Ethel Levey, Alan Roscoe, Maude Turner Gordon, Charles Coleman, Phillips Smalley. *D:* Lowell Sherman; *As.P.:* Henry Hobart; *Sc:* J. Walter Ruben. (1:09)
Drama of a good-natured drunk who tries to save his brother from the clutches of a golddigger. Based on the play by Willard Mack.

1975. High Tension (20th Century–Fox; 1936). *Cast:* Brian Donlevy, Norman Foster, Glenda Farrell, Helen Wood, Robert McWade, Joe Sawyer, Theodore von Eltz, Murray Alper, Romaine Callender. *D:* Allan Dwan; *Sc:* Lou Breslow, Edward Eliscu, John Patrick. (1:03)

B comedy of cable layers in Hawaii.

1976. High Voltage (Pathé; 1929). *Cast:* Owen Moore, Bill Boyd, Carole Lombard, William Bevan, Diane Ellis, Phillips Smalley, James Gleason. *D:* Howard Higgin. (0:57) (video)
Action melodrama.

1977. High, Wide and Handsome (Paramount; 1937). *Cast:* Irene Dunne, Randolph Scott, Dorothy Lamour, Raymond Walburn, Alan Hale, Elizabeth Patterson, Charles Bickford, William Frawley, Akim Tamiroff, Ben Blue, Irving Pichel, Lucien Littlefield, Russell Hopton, Claire McDowell, Billy Bletcher, James Burke, Helen Lowell, Frank Sully, Edward Gargan, Roger Imhof, Stanley Andrews, Raymond Brown, Tommy Bupp, Monte Blue, George O'Neil, Jack Clifford. *D:* Rouben Mamoulian; *P:* Arthur Hornblow, Jr.; *Sc:* Oscar Hammerstein II, Mamoulian (unc.); *Songs:* title song, "The Folks Who Live on the Hill" and "Can I Forget You" by Jerome Kern & Oscar Hammerstein II. (1:50)
In 1859, oil was discovered in rural Pennsylvania, setting the stage for this musical about the romance of a farmer turned oilman and a circus girl.

1978. Highway Patrol (Columbia; 1938). *Cast:* Robert Paige, Jacqueline Wells (Julie Bishop), Ann Doran, Arthur Loft, George McKay, Alan Bridge, Robert Middlemass, Eddie Foster, Eddie Laughton. *D:* C.C. Coleman, Jr.; *St:* Lambert Hillyer; *Sc:* Robert E. Kent, Stuart Anthony.
B crime melodrama.

The Highwayman Rides *see* **Billy the Kid**

1979. Hills of Old Wyoming (Paramount; 1937). *Cast:* Bill Boyd (Hopalong Cassidy), Russell Hayden (Lucky Jenkins), George Hayes (Windy Halliday), William Duncan, Stephen

Morris (Morris Ankrum in his film debut), Earle Hodgins, Chief John Big Tree, Clara Kimball Young, Steve Clemente, George Chesebro, John Beach. *D:* Nate Watt; *P:* Harry M. Sherman; *Sc:* Maurice Geraghty. (1:19)

"Hopalong Cassidy" and the Bar 20 boys encounter trouble on the Indian reservation in this, the 10th entry in the series.

1980. Hips, Hips, Hooray! (RKO; 1934). *Cast:* Bert Wheeler, Robert Woolsey, Dorothy Lee, Thelma Todd, Ruth Etting, George Meeker, Phyllis Barry, James Burtis, Matt Briggs, Spencer Charters. *D:* Mark Sandrich; *As.P.:* H.N. Swanson; *Sc:* Bert Kalmar, Harry Ruby, Edward Kaufman, Aben Kandel; *Songs by:* Kalmar and Ruby include: "Keep On Doing What You're Doing." (1:08) (video)

Musical-comedy spoof of the beauty business, flavored lipstick salesmen and motor races.

1981. Hired Wife (Pinnacle; 1934). *Cast:* Weldon Heyburn, Molly O'Day, James Kirkwood. *D:* George Melford.

Low-budget romantic comedy.

His Affair (G.B. title) *see* **This Is My Affair**

His Best Man (G.B. title) *see* **Times Square Playboy**

1982. His Brother's Wife (MGM; 1936). *Cast:* Robert Taylor, Barbara Stanwyck, John Eldredge, Joseph Calleia, Jean Hersholt, Samuel S. Hinds, Leonard Mudie, Jed Prouty, Pedro de Cordoba, Phyllis Clare, Rafael Corio (Rafael Storm), William Stack, Edgar Edwards. *D:* W.S. Van Dyke II; *P:* Lawrence Weingarten; *St:* George Auerbach; *Sc:* Leon Gordon, John Meehan. (1:31)

Romantic melodrama of a scientist whose girl friend marries his brother.

1983. His Captive Woman (WB/F.N.; 1929). *Cast:* Milton Sills, Dorothy Mackaill, Gladden James, Jed Prouty, Sidney Bracey, George Fawcett, William Holden, Frank Reicher, Marion Byron, Gertrude Howard, August Tollaire. *D:* George Fitzmaurice; *St:* Donn Byrne; *Sc:* Carey Wilson.

Part-talkie courtroom drama told in flashbacks of a woman charged with murder.

1984. His Double Life (Paramount/Atlantic; 1933). *Cast:* Roland Young, Lillian Gish (in her last film appearance until 1943), Montagu Love, Lucy Beaumont, Charles Richman, Lumsden Hare, Gerald Oliver Smith, Philip Tonge, Audrey Ridgewell. *D:* Arthur Hopkins. (1:07) (video)

A famous artist seeks anonymity by assuming the identity of his deceased butler, setting the stage for various mix-ups and misunderstandings. A hit comedy of its day, it had three previous filmings in the silent era. Remade as *Holy Matrimony* (20th Century–Fox; 1943). Based on the novel "Buried Alive" and the play "The Great Adventure" by Arnold Bennett.

1985. His Exciting Night (Universal; 1938). *Cast:* Charles Ruggles, Ona Munson, Marion Martin, Maxie Rosenbloom, Stepin Fetchit. *D:* Gus Meins; *P:* Kenneth Goldsmith. (0:55)

B comedy of newlyweds and the misunderstandings and complications that the bridegroom gets involved in on his wedding night.

1986. His Family Tree (RKO; 1935). *Cast:* James Barton, Margaret Callahan, Addison (Jack) Randall, Maureen Delaney, William Harrigan, Marjorie Gateson, Clifford Jones, Ray Mayer, Herman Bing, Pat Moriarty, Ferdinand Munier. *D:* Charles Vidor; *As.P.:* Cliff Reid; *Sc:* Joel Sayre, John Twist. (1:09)

An Irish immigrant changes his

name from Murphy to Murphree and gets involved in midwestern politics in this B comedy-drama. Based on the play "Old Man Murphy" by Patrick Kearney and Harry Wagstaff Gribble.

1987. His Fighting Blood (Ambassador; 1935). *Cast:* Kermit Maynard, Polly Ann Young, Paul Fix, Ben Hendricks, Jr., Ted Adams, Joseph Girard, Frank LaRue, Frank O'Connor, Charles King, Jack Cheatham, Ed Cecil, Theodore Lorch, Singing Constables (Glenn Strange, Chuck Baldra, Jack Kirk). *D:* John English (a former film editor in his directorial debut); *P:* Maurice Conn; *Sc:* Joseph O'Donnell. (1:00)

A Kermit Maynard actioner of the Canadian Northwest Mounted Police.

1988. His Girl Friday (Columbia; 1939–40). *Cast:* Rosalind Russell, Cary Grant, Ralph Bellamy, Gene Lockhart, Porter Hall, Ernest Truex, Cliff Edwards, Clarence Kolb, Roscoe Karns, Frank Jenks, Regis Toomey, Abner Biberman, Frank Orth, John Qualen, Helen Mack, Billy Gilbert, Alma Kruger, Edwin Maxwell, Pat West, George E. Stone. *D:* Howard Hawks; *P:* Hawks; *Sc:* Charles Lederer. (1:32) (video)

A classic and critically acclaimed newspaper farce. A remake of *The Front Page* (q.v.) and based on the play of that name by Charles MacArthur and Ben Hecht. Remade under that title in 1974 and again in 1988 as *Switching Channels* with a TV studio replacing the newspaper office.

1989. His Glorious Night (MGM; 1929–30). *Cast:* John Gilbert (his first all-talkie), Catherine Dale Owen, Nora Gregor, Hedda Hopper, Gustav von Seyffertitz, Nance O'Neil, Peter Gawthorne. *D:* Lionel Barrymore; *Sc:* Willard Mack.

Romantic drama based on Ferenc Molnar's play "Olympia." A box office flop that was remade as *A Breath of Scandal* (Paramount; 1960).

1990. His Greatest Gamble (RKO; 1934). *Cast:* Richard Dix, Dorothy Wilson, Bruce Cabot, Erin O'Brien-Moore, Shirley Grey, Leonard Carey, Edith Fellows, Eily Malyon. *D:* John S. Robertson; *As.P.:* Myles Connolly; *St:* Salisbury Field; *Sc:* Sidney Buchman, Harry Hervey. (1:10)

B drama of a man who escapes from prison after learning of the negative effects his ex-wife's over protective influence has had on their daughter.

1991. His Last Hour (Xxxx Xxxx; 1934). (No information available)

1992. His Lucky Day (Universal; 1929). *Cast:* Reginald Denny, Lorayne Du Val, Otis Harlan, Eddie Phillips. *D:* Edward Cline.

Part-talkie comedy of mistaken identity.

His Majesty Bunker Bean *see* **Bunker Bean**

1993. His Night Out (Universal; 1935). *Cast:* Edward Everett Horton, George Cleveland, Irene Hervey, Oscar Apfel, Willard Robertson, Clara Kimball Young, Ward Bond, Jack Norton, Lola Lane, Jack Mulhall, Dewey Robinson, Theodore von Eltz. *D:* William Nigh; *St:* Charles Christensen; *Sc:* Harry Clork, Doris Malloy. (1:07)

Low-budget comedy of a man who finds he is terminally ill and decides to live it up, but gets more than he bargained for.

1994. His Private Secretary (Showman's Pictures; 1933). *Cast:* Evalyn Knapp, John Wayne, Reginald Barlow, Al St. John, Natalie Kingston (final film—ret.), Alec B. Francis, Arthur Hoyt. *D:* Philip H. Whitman.

Low-budget independent romantic comedy.

His Temporary Affair (G.B. title) *see* **Ex-Bad Boy**

1995. His Woman (Paramount; 1931). *Cast:* Gary Cooper, Claudette Colbert, Averell Harris, Richard Spiro, Douglass Dumbrille, Joseph Calleia (film debut), Harry Davenport, Edward Keane, Charlotte Wynters, John T. Doyle, Joan Blair, Herschel Mayall, Sidney Easton, Lon Haschal. *D:* Edward Sloman; *Sc:* Adelaide Heilbron, Melville Baker. (1:20)

Comedy-drama set aboard a freighter of a captain who rescues a baby. Based on the book, "The Sentimentalist" by Dale Collins. Filmed at Astoria Studios in Long Island, N.Y. this is a remake of *Sal of Singapore* (q.v.).

1996. History Is Made at Night (United Artists/Walter Wanger; 1937). *Cast:* Jean Arthur, Charles Boyer, Leo Carrillo, Colin Clive, Adele St. Maur, Oscar Apfel, Ivan Lebedeff, Barry Norton, George Meeker, Lucien Prival, Georges Renavent, Jack Mulhall, George Davis. *D:* Frank Borzage; *P:* Walter Wanger; *Sc:* Gene Towne, Graham Baker. (1:37) (video)

Comedy-drama of a divorced woman and her new lover who are being pursued by her jealous ex-husband. The film has a sea disaster finale.

Hit Me Again (G.B. title) *see* **Smarty**

1997. Hit of the Show (Film Booking Office; 1928). *Cast:* Joe E. Brown. *D:* Ralph Ince.

Part-talkie comedy originally released in July, 1928, as a silent, withdrawn and re-released in September of that year with two songs and some dialogue added.

1998. The Hit Parade (Republic; 1937). *Cast:* Phil Regan, Pert Kelton, Frances Langford, J. Farrell Mac-Donald, Eddy Duchin and his orchestra, Duke Ellington and his orchestra, Max Terhune, Oscar & Elmer (dummies), Inez Courtney, Edward Brophy, William Demarest, Louise Henry, George

Givot, Carl Hoff and his orchestra, Pierre Watkin, Monroe Owsley, Al Pearce, Ed Thorgersen, Sammy White, Gentle Maniacs, Voice of Experience, Toc Toc Girls, Pick and Pat. *D:* Gus Meins; *P:* Nat Levine; *St:* Bradford Ropes; *Sc:* Ropes, Sam Ornitz.

Hit musical-comedy with many specialty acts.

1999. Hit the Deck (RKO; 1929–30). *Cast:* Jack Oakie (Bilge Smith), June Clyde, Polly Walker, Ethel Clayton, George Ovey, Marguerita Padula, Wallace MacDonald, Harry Sweet, Franker Woods, Roger Gray, Del Henderson, Grady Sutton, Charles Sullivan, Nate Slott, Andy Clark. *D:* Luther Reed; *P:* William LeBaron; *Sc:* Reed; *Songs:* Leo Robin, Clifford Grey, Vincent Youmans, Sidney Clare, Harry Tierney. (Originally filmed with a 2-color technicolor sequence).

Comedy of a sailor on leave in search of romance. A remake of *Shore Leave* (First National; 1925), but more appropriately a film adaptation of the 1927 Broadway musical by Herbert Fields and Vincent Youmans. Based on the play "Shore Leave" (1922) by Hubert Osborne, it was remade as *Follow the Fleet* (q.v.). The property was then sold to MGM who remade it in 1954 as *Hit the Deck*.

2000. Hit the Saddle (Republic; 1937). *Cast:* Bob Livingston (Stony Brooke), Ray Corrigan (Tucson Smith), Max Terhune (Lullaby Joslin), Rita (Hayworth) Cansino, Sammy McKim, Yakima Canutt, J.P. McGowan, Ed Cassidy, Harry Tenbrook, Robert Smith, Ed Boland, Jack Kirk, George Plues. *D:* Mack V. Wright; *Sc:* Oliver Drake. (1:01) (video)

The fifth entry in the "Three Mesquiteers" series with a story of a wild horse roundup.

2001. Hitch Hike Lady (Republic; 1936). *Cast:* James Ellison, Alison Skipworth, Mae Clarke, Smiley Burnette, Russell Gleason, Warren Hymer, George Hayes, Arthur Treacher, J. Farrell MacDonald, Charles Wilson. *D:* Aubrey Scotto. (G.B. title: *Eventful Journey*)

B romantic comedy.

2002. Hitch Hike to Heaven (Invincible; 1936). *Cast:* Anita Page (final film — ret.), Henrietta Crosman, Crauford Kent. *D:* Frank Strayer.

"Poverty row" romantic comedy.

2003. Hitler — Beast of Berlin (Producers Pictures; 1939). *Cast:* Roland Drew, Steffi Duna, Greta Granstedt, Vernon Dent, Allan (Alan) Ladd, Bodil Rosing, Hans Joby, Lucien Prival, John Ellis, George Rosener, Hans Von Twardowski, Willie Kaufman, Frederick Giermann, Clem Wilenchick (later known as "Crane Whitley"), Henry von Zynda, John Voight, Hans Schumm, John Peters, Hans Von Morhart, Walter Stahl, Paul Panzer, Dick Wessel. *D:* Sherman Scott (Sam Newfield); *P:* Ben Judell. (1:24)

In Nazi Germany a man and his wife, members of the underground are caught and imprisoned in a concentration camp. Prior to release the film was known as "Goose Step," the name of the book on which it is based by Shepard Traube. Shortly after release the film underwent a title change to *Beasts of Berlin,* the title under which it is best known.

2004. Hittin' the Trail (Grand National; 1937). *Cast:* Tex Ritter, Jerry Bergh, Tommy Bupp, Earl Dwire, Jack C. Smith, Heber Snow (Hank Worden), Ed Cassidy, Snub Pollard, Archie Ricks, Charles King, Ray Whitley and His Range Ramblers (Ken Card, the Phelps Brothers), Tex Ritter's Texas Tornadoes, Smokey the dog, White Flash the horse. *D:* Robert N. Bradbury; *P:* Edward Finney (Boots and Saddles prods.); *Sc:* Robert Emmett (Tansey). (0:58)

Tex Ritter western with songs of a cowboy who unknowingly becomes involved with rustlers.

2005. Hitting a New High (RKO; 1937). *Cast:* Lily Pons, Jack Oakie, Edward Everett Horton, Lucille Ball, Eric Blore, Eduardo Ciannelli, John Howard, Luis Alberni, Jack Arnold (nee: Vinton Haworth), Leonard Carey. *D:* Raoul Walsh; *P:* Jesse L. Lasky, Jr.; *St:* Maxwell Shane, Robert Harari; *Sc:* Gertrude Purcell, John Twist; *Songs:* Jimmy McHugh, Harold Adamson; *Sound Recording:* (A.A.N.) John Aalberg. (1:25)

A musical which was a disaster at the box office and wiped out Lily Pon's career at RKO.

2006. Hold 'em Jail (RKO; 1932). *Cast:* Bert Wheeler, Robert Woolsey, Edna May Oliver, Robert Armstrong, Roscoe Ates, Edgar Kennedy, Betty Grable, Warren Hymer, Paul Hurst, G. Pat Collins, Stanley Blystone, Jed Prouty, Spencer Charters. *D:* Norman Taurog; *As.P.:* Harry Joe Brown; *St:* Tim Whelan, Lew Lipton; *Sc:* Walter DeLeon, S.J. Perelman, Eddie Welch; *Radio Dialogue:* John P. Medbury. (1:06) (video)

A Wheeler and Woolsey comedy spoof of football and prison films which flopped at the box office.

2007. Hold 'em Navy (Paramount; 1937). *Cast:* Lew Ayres, Mary Carlisle, John Howard, Benny Baker, Elizabeth Patterson, Richard Denning (film debut), Pat Flaherty, Harold Adams, Oscar Smith, Lee Bennett, Billy Daniels, Lambert Rogers, Gwen Kenyon, Priscilla Moran, Alston Cockrell, Dick French, John Hubbard, George Lollier, Archie Twitchell, Alan Ladd (bit). *D:* Kurt Neumann; *St:* Albert Shelby LeVino; *Sc:* Lloyd Corrigan, Erwin Gelsey. (G.B. title: *That Navy Spirit*) (1:04)

B gridiron romance set at Annapolis.

2008. Hold 'em Yale (Paramount; 1935). *Cast:* Buster Crabbe,

Patricia Ellis, Cesar Romero, Grant Withers, William Frawley, Rod La-Rocque, George E. Stone, Andy Devine, Ethel Griffies, Ruth Clifford, Garry Owen, Leonard Carey, Hale Hamilton, George Barbier, Oscar Smith, Guy Usher, Warren Hymer, Kendall Evans, Theodore Lorch, Arthur Housman. *D:* Sidney Lanfield; *P:* Charles R. Rogers; *St:* Damon Runyon; *Sc:* Eddie Welch; Paul Gerard Smith. (G.B. title: *Uniform Lovers*) (1:05)

B comedy involving con-men and a footloose heiress.

2009. Hold Everything (WB; 1930). *Cast:* Joe E. Brown, Sally O'Neil, Georges Carpentier (former French heavyweight champion), Winnie Lightner, Bert Roach, Dorothy Revier, Edmund Breese, Jimmie Quinn, Jack Curtis, Tony Stabeneau, Lew Harvey. *D:* Roy Del Ruth; *Sc:* Robert Lord; *Songs:* "Take It on the Chin," "When Little Red Roses Get the Blues for You," "Sing a Little Theme Song," "Physically Fit," "Girls We Remember," "All Alone Together," "Isn't This a Cockeyed World" and "You're the Cream in My Coffee" by Al Dubin and Joe Burke.

2-color technicolor musical-comedy of a man pretending to be a championship boxer. Based on the musical play by B.G. DeSylva and John McGowan.

2010. Hold Me Tight (Fox; 1933). *Cast:* James Dunn, Sally Eilers, June Clyde, Kenneth Thomson, Dorothy Peterson, Clay Clement. *D:* David Butler; *St:* Gertrude Rigdon; *Sc:* Gladys Lehman.

Low-budget comedy.

2011. Hold That Co-ed (20th Century–Fox; 1938). *Cast:* John Barrymore, George Murphy, Joan Davis, Marjorie Weaver, Jack Haley, George Barbier, Ruth Terry, Donald Meek, Johnny Downs, Guinn Williams, Fred Kohler, Jr., Paul Hurst, Russell Hicks, Clem Bevans, Glenn Morris, Stanley Andrews, Brewster Twins, Billy Bene-dict, Dora Clement, Frank Sully. *D:* George Marshall; *P:* David Hempstead; *Sc:* Karl Tunberg, Don Ettinger, Jack Yellen; *Songs:* Jule Styne. (G.B. title: *Hold That Girl*) (1:20)

A musical-comedy with some politics thrown in for diversion.

2012. Hold That Girl (Fox; 1934). *Cast:* Claire Trevor, James Dunn, John Davidson, Gertrude Michael, Charles Wilson, Alan Edwards, Effie Ellsler, Jay Ward, Lucille Ball. *D:* Hamilton MacFadden; *St & Sc:* Dudley Nichols, Lamar Trotti.

Low-budget newspaper comedy.

Hold That Girl (1938) (G.B. title) *see* **Hold That Co-ed**

2013. Hold That Kiss (MGM; 1938). *Cast:* Dennis O'Keefe (in his starring debut), Maureen O'Sullivan, Mickey Rooney, George Barbier, Fay Holden, Jessie Ralph, Edward Brophy, Ruth Hussey, Frank Albertson, Phillip Terry, Barnett Parker. *D:* Edwin L. Marin; *P:* John W. Considine, Jr.; *St & Sc:* Stanley Rauh.

B romantic comedy.

2014. Hold the Press (Columbia; 1933). *Cast:* Tim McCoy, Wheeler Oakman, Samuel S. Hinds, Oscar Apfel, Joseph Crehan. *D:* Phil Rosen.

Low-budget newspaper melodrama.

2015. Hold Your Man (Universal; 1929). *Cast:* Laura La Plante, Scott Kolk, Mildred Van Dorn, Eugene Borden. *D:* Emmett J. Flynn; *St:* Maxine Alton; *Sc:* Harold Shumate.

Marital comedy of a wife who goes to Europe to become an artist, prompting her husband to have an affair.

2016. Hold Your Man (MGM; 1933). *Cast:* Clark Gable, Jean Harlow, Stuart Erwin, Dorothy Burgess, Muriel Kirkland, Elizabeth Patterson, Blanche (Frederici) Friderici, Garry Owen, Barbara Barondess, Inez Courtney, Helen

Freeman, Paul Hurst, Louise Beavers, Theresa Harris, George Reed. *D:* Sam Wood; *P:* Wood, Bernard Hyman; *St:* Anita Loos; *Sc:* Loos, Howard Emmett Rogers; *Song:* Nacio Herb Brown, Arthur Freed. (1:28)

Hit comedy-drama of a woman who is waiting for her man to finish a jail sentence.

2017. The Hole in the Wall (Paramount; 1928–29). *Cast:* Edward G. Robinson (talkie debut), Claudette Colbert (talkie debut), David Newell, Nelly Savage, Donald Meek (film debut), Louise Closser Hale, Alan Brooks, Helen Crane, Barry Macollum, Marcia Kagno, Katherine Emmett, George MacQuarrie. *D:* Robert Florey; *P:* Monta Bell; *Sc:* Pierre Collings. (1:13)

Crude early talkie melodrama of a phony clairvoyant involved in the kidnapping of a young child. Based on the play by Fred Jackson.

2018. Holiday (RKO-Pathé; 1930). *Cast:* Ann Harding (A.A.N. for B.A. 1930–31 as Linda Seton), Mary Astor (Julia Seton), Edward Everett Horton (Nick Potter), Robert Ames (John Case), Hedda Hopper (Susan Potter), Monroe Owsley (Ned Seton), William Holden (Edward Seton), Hallam Cooley (Seton Cram), Mabel Forrest (Mary Jessup), Elizabeth Forrester (Laura), Creighton Hale (Pete Hedges), Mary Elizabeth Forbes (Mrs. Pritchard Ames). *D:* Edward H. Griffith; *P:* E.B. Derr; *Sc:* (A.A.N.) Horace Jackson. (1:29)

Romantic comedy of two sisters who fall for the same man. Based on the play by Philip Barry, it was voted one of the year's "10 Best" films by the National Board of Review, while placing #3 and #8 respectively on the "10 Best" lists of *Film Daily* and the *New York Times.* Remade in 1938 (see below).

2019. Holiday (Columbia; 1938). *Cast:* Katharine Hepburn (Linda Seton), Cary Grant (Johnny Case), Lew

Ayres (Acting Award from the National Board of Review for his portrayal of Ned Seton), Doris Nolan (Julia Seton), Edward Everett Horton (repeating his role of Nick Potter from the '30 production), Binnie Barnes (Laura Cram), Henry Daniell (Seton Cram), Jean Dixon (final film — ret. as Susan Potter), Henry Kolker (Edward Seton), Charles Trowbridge (banker), George Pauncefort (Henry), Charles Richman (Thayer), Mitchell Harris (Jennings), Neil Fitzgerald (Edgar), Marion Ballou (grandmother), Mabel Colcord (cook), Bess Flowers (countess), Esther Peck (Mrs. Jennings), Lillian West (Mrs. Thayer), Luke Cosgrave (grandfather), Howard Hickman, Hilda Plowright, Harry Allen, Edward Cooper, Margaret McWade, Frank Shannon, Aileen Carlyle, Matt McHugh, Maurice Brierre. *D:* George Cukor; *P:* Everett Riskin; *Sc:* Donald Ogden Stewart; *Art-Set Decoration:* (A.A.N.) Stephen Goosson, Lionel Banks. (G.B. titles: *Free to Live* and *Unconventional Linda*). (1:33) (video)

A remake of the preceding film of a man who gets involved with a New York City society family and their two daughters. One of the 15 top grossing films of 1937–38.

2020. Hollywood Boulevard (Paramount; 1936). *Cast:* John Halliday, Marsha Hunt, Robert Cummings, C. Henry Gordon, Frieda Inescort, Esther Dale, Esther Ralston, Albert Conti, Thomas Jackson, Frank Mayo, Gary Cooper (cameo), Francis X. Bushman, Mae Marsh, Bryant Washburn, Maurice Costello, Charles Ray, Jane Novak, Jack Mulhall, Bert Roach, Betty Compson, Creighton Hale, Harry Myers, Rita LaRoy, Ruth Clifford, Edmund Burns (final film — ret.), Charles Morton, William Desmond, Gregory Gaye, Pat O'Malley, Herbert Rawlinson, Mabel Forrest, Kitty McHugh, Terry Ray (Ellen Drew), Jack Mower. *D:* Robert Florey; *P:* A.M. Botsford; *Sc:* Marguerite Roberts. (1:15)

Melodrama on what happens to various people after a has-been actor writes his memoirs. Many greats from the silent era of films have bits and cameos in this film which is based on the novel by Faith Thomas.

2021. Hollywood Cavalcade (20th Century–Fox; 1939). *Cast:* Don Ameche (Michael Linnett Connors), Alice Faye (Molly Adair), J. Edward Bromberg (Dave Spingold), Alan Curtis (Nicky Hayden), Stuart Erwin (Pete Tinney), Jed Prouty (chief of police), Buster Keaton (himself), Rin-Tin-Tin, Jr. (Rin-Tin-Tin), Donald Meek (Lyle P. Stout), George Givot (Claude the actor), Heinie Conklin, James Finlayson, Hank Mann, Eddie Collins (four of the original Keystone Kops, recreating their roles), Chick Chandler (Chick, the assistant director), Robert Lowery (Henry Potter), Russell Hicks (Roberts), Ben Welden (agent), Willie Fung (Willie), Paul Stanton (lawyer), Mary Forbes (Mrs. Gaynes), Joseph Crehan (Bill, the attorney), Irving Bacon (clerk), Ben Turpin (bartender), Chester Conklin (sheriff), Marjorie Beebe (telephone operator), Frederick Burton (Thomas), Lee Duncan (owner and trainer of Rin-Tin-Tin as himself), Mack Sennett (himself), Al Jolson (himself), Harold Goodwin (prop boy), Fred "Snowflake" Toones (porter), Victor Potel, Edward Earle, John Ince, Franklyn Farnum, J. Anthony Hughes, Lynn Bari. *D:* Irving Cummings; *As.P.:* Harry Joe Brown; *St:* Brown Holmes, Hilary Lynn; *Sc:* Ernest Pascal. (1:36)

Big Budget technicolor production of the life and career of a Hollywood producer of old time silent comedies. The film is offbeat in that the first half of the film restages and recreates many of the old silent comedies, including the Keystone Kops. The balance of the film relates to the producer's personal life. One of the 21 top grossing films of 1939–40).

2022. Hollywood Cowboy (RKO; 1937). *Cast:* George O'Brien,

Cecilia Parker, Maude Eburne, Charles Middleton, Lee Shumway, Walter De Palma, Al Hill, William Royle, Al Herman, Frank Hagney, Dan Wolheim, Slim Balch, Lester Dorr, Harold Daniels, Joe Caits, Frank Milan. *D:* Ewing Scott; *As.P.:* Leonard Goldstein (for George A. Hirliman productions); *Sc:* Scott, Dan Jarrett. (aka: *Wings Over Wyoming*) (1:03) (video)

George O'Brien comedy-western of a film company who gets involved in range warfare while on location filming a western movie.

2023. Hollywood Hoodlum (Xxxx Xxxx; 1934). *Cast:* June Clyde, Frank Albertson. *D:* Breezy Eason; *Sc:* John Thomas Neville.

2024. Hollywood Hotel (WB; 1937). *Cast:* Dick Powell, Rosemary Lane, Lola Lane, Hugh Herbert, Ted Healy, Glenda Farrell, Johnnie "Scat" Davis, Alan Mowbray, Mabel Todd, Allyn Joslyn, Grant Mitchell, Edgar Kennedy, Louella Parsons (herself), Frances Langford, Raymond Paige and his orchestra, Fritz Feld, Gene Krupa, Lionel Hampton, Teddy Wilson, Harry James (film debut), Curt Bois, Susan Hayward (film debut). *D:* Busby Berkeley; *P:* Sam Bischoff; *St:* Maurice Leo, Jerry Wald; *Sc:* Leo, Wald, Richard Macaulay; *Songs:* Johnny Mercer, Dick (Richard) Whiting includes: "Hooray for Hollywood." (1:49) (video)

Big budget musical-comedy with an all-star cast and many guest stars.

Hollywood Mystery *see* **Hollywood Hoodlum**

2025. Hollywood Party (MGM; 1934). *Cast:* Jimmy Durante, Stan Laurel, Oliver Hardy, Lupe Velez, Charles Butterworth, Polly Moran, Eddie Quillan, Ted Healy and the Stooges (Larry, Moe & Curly), June Clyde, George Givot, Jack Pearl, "Mickey Mouse" (in a 5-minute Walt Disney cartoon), Tom Kennedy, Arthur Treacher, Leonid Kinskey, Ben Bard, Frances

Williams, Richard Carle. *D:* Richard Boleslawski (unc.), Allan Dwan (unc.), Roy Rowland (unc.); *P:* Harry Rapf; *St:* Arthur Kober; *Sc:* Howard Deitz, Kober; *Songs:* Nacio Herb Brown, Arthur Freed, Gus Kahn. (1:08)

An all-star cast in a comedy where the title tells all. No director received credit for his work on this film.

The Hollywood Revue *see* **The Hollywood Revue of 1929**

2026. The Hollywood Revue of 1929 (MGM; 1929). *Cast:* Jack Benny (film debut as an M.C.), Conrad Nagel (M.C.), Charles King (1894–1944), Cliff Edwards (film debut), Joan Crawford, Anita Page, Karl Dane, George K. Arthur, William Haines, Gwen Lee, Bessie Love, Marie Dressler, Polly Moran, Oliver Hardy & Stan Laurel (in their feature film debuts), Marion Davies, Buster Keaton, Nils Asther, Gus Edwards, Norma Shearer, John Gilbert, Lionel Barrymore, MGM Chorus, Rounders, Brox Sisters, Albertina Rasch ballet, Natasha Natova & Company, Biltmore Quartet, Ernest Belcher's Dancing Tots, Ann Dvorak (film debut — bit as a chorus girl). *D:* Charles F. Reisner; *P:* Harry Rapf; *Dialogue:* Al Boasberg, Robert E. Hopkins; *Art-Set Decoration:* (A.A.N.) Cedric Gibbons & Richard Day (1928–29); *Songs:* "Singing' in the Rain," "You Were Meant for Me" and "Tommy At kins on Parade" by Nacio Herb Brown & Arthur Freed; "Low-Down Rhythm" by Jesse Greer & Raymond Klages; "For I'm the Queen" (sung by Dressler in her talkie debut) by Martin Broones and Andy Rice; "Gotta Feelin' for You" by Louis Alter & Joe Trent; "Bones and Tambourines," "Strike Up the Band" and "Tableaux of Jewels" by Fred Fisher; "Lon Chaney Will Get You If You Don't Watch Out" (sung by Gus Edwards), "Strolling Through the Park One Day," "Your Mother and Mine," "Orange Blossom Time," "Minstrel Days," "Nobody But You" and "I Never Knew I Could Do a Thing Like That" by Gus Edwards and Joe Goodwin. (2:10)

An all-star musical-comedy revue with "Romeo and Juliet," "Orange Blossom Time" and the grand finale of "Singin' in the Rain" in 2-color technicolor. A.A.N. for Best Picture (1928–29).

2027. Hollywood Roundup (Columbia/Coronet; 1937). *Cast:* Buck Jones, Helen Twelvetrees, Grant Withers, Shemp Howard, Dickie Jones, Eddie Kane, Monte F. Collins, Warren Jackson, Lester Dorr, Lee Shumway, Edward Keane, George (Andre) Beranger. *D:* Ewing Scott; *P:* L.G. Leonard (Leonard Goldstein), Monroe Shaff; *St:* Shaff; *Sc:* Joseph Hoffman, Shaff. (1:03)

Buck Jones vehicle involving a Hollywood stuntman and cowboy stand-in.

2028/2029. Hollywood Speaks (Columbia; 1932). *Cast:* Pat O'Brien, Genevieve Tobin, Rita LaRoy, Claire Dodd, Thomas Jackson, Anderson Lawler, Ralf Harolde, Lorena Layson, Leni Stengel, Lucien Prival. *D:* Edward Buzzell; *St:* Norman Krasna; *Sc:* Krasna, Jo Swerling.

Low-budget drama.

The Hollywood Stadium Mystery *see* **The Stadium Murders**

2030. A Holy Terror (Fox; 1931). *Cast:* George O'Brien, Sally Eilers, James Kirkwood, Humphrey Bogart, Rita LaRoy, Stanley Fields, Robert Warwick, Richard Tucker, Earl Pingree. *D:* Irving Cummings; *P:* Edmund Grainger; *Sc:* Ralph Block. (0:53)

A remake of the Tom Mix western *Trailin'* (Fox; 1921), disguised as a small town drama of an eastern playboy who heads west to find the party responsible for his father's death. Based on Max Brand's novel "Trailin'."

2031. The Holy Terror (20th Century–Fox; 1937). *Cast:* Jane Withers, Tony Martin, Joan Davis, El Brendel, Gavin Muir, Leah Ray, Andrew Tombes, John Eldredge, Victor Adams, Fred Kohler, Jr., Joe E. Lewis. *D:* James Tinling; *St & Sc:* Lou Breslow, John Patrick; *Songs:* Harry Akst, Sidney Clare.

B juvenile comedy.

2032. Home on the Prairie (Republic; 1939). *Cast:* Gene Autry, Smiley Burnette, June Storey, George Cleveland, Jack Mulhall, Walter Miller, Gordon Hart, Hal Price, Earle Hodgins, Ethan Laidlaw, John Beach, Jack Ingram, Bob Woodward, Sherven Brothers, Rodeoliers, Champion. *D:* Jack Townley; *P:* Harry Grey; *Sc:* Paul Franklin, Charles Arthur Powell. (aka: *Ridin' the Range*) (0:58)

Gene Autry western with songs of a gang of crooks trying to ship diseased cattle.

2033. Home on the Range (Paramount; 1934–35). *Cast:* Randolph Scott, Jackie Coogan, Evelyn Brent, Dean Jagger, Addison Richards, Fuzzy Knight, Richard Carle, Clara Lou (Ann) Sheridan, Francis Sayles. *D:* Arthur Jacobson; *P:* Harold Hurley; *Sc:* Ethel Doherty, Grant Garrett. (0:54)

Western of homesteaders and land-grabbers. A remake of *Code of the West* (Paramount; 1925) with Owen Moore and Constance Bennett. Remade under that title in 1947 by RKO. Based on the book of that name by Zane Grey.

2034. The Home Towners (WB; 1928). *Cast:* Richard Bennett, Doris Kenyon, Robert McWade, Stanley Taylor, Robert Edeson, Vera Lewis, Gladys Brockwell, John Miljan, Patricia Caron, James T. Mack. *D:* Bryan Foy; *Adaptation:* Addison Burkhart, Murray Roth. (1:24)

An old coot falls for a girl half his age and a friend tries to prove that she is only after his money. Based on the play by George M. Cohan, this was the third all-talkie by this studio. Twice remade, in 1936 as *Times Square Playboy* (q.v.) and in 1940 as *Ladies Must Live*.

2035. Homicide Bureau (Columbia; 1939). *Cast:* Bruce Cabot, Robert Paige, Marc Lawrence, Rita Hayworth, Richard Fiske, Moroni Olsen, Stanley Andrews, Lee Prather, Norman Willis, Eddie Fetherston, Gene Morgan. *D:* C.C. Coleman, Jr.; *Sc:* Earle Snell. (0:58)

B police melodrama.

2036. Homicide Squad (Universal; 1931). *Cast:* Leo Carrillo, Russell Gleason, Mary Brian, George Brent, Noah Beery, J. Carrol Naish, Walter Percival. *D:* Edward L. Cahn (directorial debut), George Melford; *St:* Henry La Cossitt. (G.B. title: *The Lost Men*) (1:10)

B melodrama of a gangster who finds his long-lost son.

2037. Honey (Paramount; 1930). *Cast:* Nancy Carroll, Stanley Smith, Lillian Roth, Skeets Gallagher, Harry Green, ZaSu Pitts, Jobyna Howland, Mitzi Green, Charles Sellon. *D:* Wesley Ruggles; *P:* David O. Selznick; *Sc:* Herman J. Mankiewicz; *Songs:* Sam Coslow, W. Franke Harling include "Sing You Sinners."

Comedy with music of a down-and-out southern family who lease their mansion to a wealthy New Yorker. A remake of *Come Out of the Kitchen* (Famous Players-Lasky; 1917) based on the 1916 hit Broadway play by A.E. Thomas, adapted from a book by Alice Duer Miller, the '17 version starring Marguerite Clark.

2038. Honeymoon in Bali (Paramount; 1939). *Cast:* Fred MacMurray, Madeleine Carroll, Allan Jones, Osa Massen (film debut), Helen Broderick, Akim Tamiroff, Astrid Allwyn, John Qualen, Bennie Bartlett, Carolyn Lee, Edward Van Sloan, William Davidson, Georgia Caine. *D:* Edward H. Griffith;

P: Jeff Lazarus; *St:* Katherine Brush, Grace Sartwell Mason; *Sc:* Virginia Van Upp. (aka: *My Love for Yours*) (G.B. title: *Husbands and Lovers*) (1:30) (video)

A hit romantic comedy of its day.

2039. Honeymoon Lane (Paramount/Sono Art Productions; 1931). *Cast:* Eddie Dowling (repeating his stage role as Tim Dugan), Ray Dooley, June Collyer, Noah Beery, Raymond Hatton, Mary Carr, Lloyd Whitlock, Armand Kaliz, Corliss Palmer, Ethel Wales, George Kotsonaros, Gene Lewis. *D:* William James Craft; *Sc:* Eddie Dowling, James Hanley.

Low-budget comedy set in a honeymoon hotel. Based on a 1926 Broadway play of the same name by Eddie Dowling and James Hanley.

2040. Honeymoon Limited (Monogram; 1935). *Cast:* Neil Hamilton, Irene Hervey, Lloyd Hughes, Russell Hicks, Lorin Raker, Joy Filmer, June Filmer, George Hayes, Henry Kolker, Gertrude Astor, Virginia Brissac, Lee Moran. *D:* Arthur Lubin; *P:* Mrs. Wallace (Dorothy) Reid; *St:* Vida Hurst; *Sc:* Reid, Betty Burbridge.

Low-budget comedy of an author who takes a bet from his publisher that he can write a novel while walking from New York to San Francisco.

Note: The film previewed at (1:23), then cut to its present running time (1:10).

2041. The Honeymoon's Over (20th Century–Fox; 1939). *Cast:* Stuart Erwin, Marjorie Weaver, Hobart Cavanaugh, E.E. Clive, June Gale, Russell Hicks, Jack Carson. *D:* Eugene Forde; *Sc:* Leonard Hoffman, Hamilton MacFadden, Clay Adams.

B romantic comedy.

2042. Hong Kong Nights (FD; 1935). *Cast:* Tom Keene, Wera Engels. *D:* E. Mason Hopper.

B adventure.

2043. Honky Tonk (WB; 1929). *Cast:* Sophie Tucker, Audrey Ferris, Lila Lee, George Duryea (Tom Keene), Mahlon Hamilton, John T. Murray. *D:* Lloyd Bacon; *St:* Leslie S. Barrows; *Sc:* C. Graham Baker, Jack Yellen; *Songs:* "Some of These Days" (which became Tucker's theme song), "I'm the Last of the Red Hot Mamas," "I'm Doin' What I'm Doin' for Love," "He's a Good Man to Have Around," and "I'm Feathering a Nest (for a Little Bluebird)" by Jack Yellen and Milton Ager.

Hit sentimental tear-jerker of a woman who sacrifices all for a thankless daughter.

2044. Honolulu (MGM; 1938–39). *Cast:* Robert Young (in a dual role), Eleanor Powell, George Burns, Gracie Allen, Rita Johnson, Ruth Hussey, Clarence Kolb, Sig Rumann, Willie Fung, Eddie "Rochester" Anderson, Jo Ann Sayers, Ann Morriss, Cliff Clark, Edgar Dearing. *D:* Edward Buzzell; *P:* Jack Cummings; *St:* Frank Partos; *Sc:* Herbert Fields, Partos. (1:23)

Comedy with music involving mistaken identities.

2045. Honor Among Lovers (Paramount; 1931). *Cast:* Claudette Colbert, Fredric March, Pat O'Brien, Ginger Rogers, Ralph Morgan (talkie debut), Charles Ruggles, Avonne Taylor, John Kearney, Leonard Carey, Monroe Owsley, Charles Halton (feature film debut), Jules Epailly, Janet McLeary. *D:* Dorothy Arzner; *St:* Austin Parker; *Sc:* Parker, Gertrude Purcell.

Comedy-drama of a husband who doesn't appreciate his wife's boss' attention to her. Filmed at Astoria Studios in Long Island, N.Y.

2046. Honor of the Family (WB; 1931). *Cast:* Warren William, Bebe Daniels, Frederick Kerr, Alan Mowbray, Dita Parlo, Harry Cording, Allan Lane, Cameron Prud'Homme, Blanche Frederici, Alphonse Ethier, Murray Kinnell, Carl Miller. *D:* Loyd Bacon; *Sc:* James Ashmore Creelman, Roland Pertwee.

An old man is infatuated with a

loose woman. Adapted from a story by Honoré de Balzac.

2047. Honor of the Mounted (Monogram; 1932). *Cast:* Tom Tyler, Cecilia Ryland, Francis McDonald, Charles King, Tom London, Stanley Blystone, William Dwire, Arthur Millett, Gordon Wood (Gordon DeMain), Theodore Lorch. *D:* Harry Fraser; *P:* Trem Carr; *St & Sc:* Fraser. (1:02)

Tom Tyler western of a Canadian Mountie who enters the United States to clear himself of murder charges.

2048. Honor of the Press (Mayfair; 1932). *Cast:* Dorothy Gulliver, Eddie Nugent, Wheeler Oakman, Franklyn Farnum, Charles K. French. *D:* B. Reeves Eason.

"Poverty row" newspaper story.

2049. Honor of the Range (Universal; 1934). *Cast:* Ken Maynard, Cecilia Parker, Fred Kohler, James Marcus, Frank Hagney, Eddie Barnes, Franklyn Farnum, Jack Rockwell, Albert J. Smith, Slim Whitaker, Ben Corbett, Fred Mackaye, Wally Wales (Hal Taliaferro), Jack Kirk, Hank Bell, Art Mix, Lafe McKee, Pascale Perry, Bill Patton, Bud McClure. *D:* Alan James (Alan J. Neitz); *Sc:* Nate Gatzert. (1:02)

Ken Maynard western with Maynard in a dual role as a lawman and his twin brother who happens to be crooked.

2050. Honor of the West (Universal; 1939). *Cast:* Bob Baker, Fuzzy Knight, Marjorie Bell (Marge Champion), Dick Dickinson, Carleton Young, Glenn Strange, Jack Kirk, Frank O'Connor, Reed Howes, Forrest Taylor, Murdock MacQuarrie. *D:* George Waggner; *P:* Trem Carr; *Sc:* Joseph West (Waggner). (1:00)

Bob Baker western with songs and cattle rustlers.

The Honourable Mr. Wong (G.B. title) *see* **The Hatchet Man**

2051. Hook Line and Sinker (RKO; 1930). *Cast:* Bert Wheeler, Robert Woolsey, Dorothy Lee, Ralf Harolde, Jobyna Howland, Natalie Moorhead, Hugh Herbert, George F. Marion, Sr., Stanley Fields, Ben Hendricks, Jr., William Davidson. *D:* Edward Cline; *As.P.:* Myles Connolly; *Sc:* Tim Whelan, Ralph Spence. (1:15)

An early spoof of gangster films with Wheeler and Woolsey taking over a run-down old hotel, only to find the place is soon overrun by visiting gangsters.

2052. Hoop-la (Fox; 1933). *Cast:* Clara Bow (final film — ret.), Richard Cromwell, Preston Foster, Herbert Mundin, James Gleason, Minna Gombell, Roger Imhof, Florence Roberts. *D:* Frank Lloyd; *Sc:* Bradley King, J.M. March. (1:25)

Melodrama of a carnival dancer who marries the son of the carnival's owner. A remake of *The Barker* (q.v.) and based on the play of that name by John Kenyon Nicholson.

2053. Hooray for Love (RKO; 1935). *Cast:* Ann Sothern, Gene Raymond, Pert Kelton, Bill Robinson, Maria Gambarelli, Fats Waller (film debut), Thurston Hall, Etienne Girardot, Georgia Caine, Sam Hardy, Lionel Stander, Eddie Kane, Perry Ivins, Harry Kernell, Jeni Le Gon. *D:* Walter Lang; *As.P.:* Felix Young; *St:* Marc Lachmann; *Sc:* Lawrence Hazard, Ray Harris; *Songs:* Dorothy Fields, Jimmy McHugh. (1:12)

Musical-comedy of a producer and his problems.

2054. Hoosier Schoolboy (Monogram; 1937). *Cast:* Mickey Rooney, Anne Nagel, Frank Shields, Edward Pawley, William Gould, Bradley Metcalfe, Dorothy Vaughan. *D:* William Nigh; *P:* Ken Goldsmith; *Sc:* Robert Lee Johnson. (1941 re-release title: *Forgotten Hero*) (1:02)

Small town drama of a school

teacher who takes a young boy under his wing, knowing the boy's father is a war veteran and the town drunk. Based on the novel by Edward Eggleston.

2055. The Hoosier Schoolmaster (Monogram; 1935). *Cast:* Norman Foster, Charlotte Henry, Sarah Padden, William V. Mong, Dorothy Libaire, Otis Harlan, Russell Simpson, Fred Kohler, Jr., Tommy Bupp, Wallace Reid, Jr., George Hayes, Joe Bernard. *D:* Lewis D. Collins; *P:* Trem Carr; *Sc:* Charles Logue. (G.B. title: *The Schoolmaster*) (1:15)

A post American Civil War drama of an ex-soldier turned schoolmaster in Indiana who uncovers the dealings of some crooked politicians. Based on the 1871 novel by Edward Eggleston, it was previously filmed in 1924 by Producers Distributing Corporation with Tom Brown.

2056. Hop-a-Long Cassidy (Paramount; 1935). *Cast:* William Boyd (Hop-a-Long Cassidy), Jimmy Ellison (Johnny Nelson), George Hayes (Uncle Ben), Paula Stone (film debut as Mary Meeker), Charles Middleton (Buck Peters), Robert Warwick (Jim Meeker), Kenneth Thomson (Jack Anthony), Frank McGlynn, Jr. (Red Connors), Willie Fung, Franklyn Farnum, Frank Campeau, Ted Adams. *D:* Howard Bretherton; *P:* Harry M. Sherman; *As.P.:* George Green; *Sc:* Doris Schroeder; *Additional Dialogue:* Harrison Jacobs; *Song:* "I'm Following a Star" by Samuel H. Stept and Dave Franklin. (Re-release, TV and video title: *Hopalong Cassidy Enters*). (1:03)

A gold mine for the studio was this premiere entry in what eventually became a series of 52 western features and started the "Hopalong Cassidy" craze of the late 1930s. Cassidy, with a limp in this one (giving him his nickname), joins the boys of the Bar 20 Ranch in time for some trouble with a neighboring ranch. Based on the 1910 book by Clarence E. Mulford.

Hopalong Cassidy Enters *see* **Hop-a-Long Cassidy**

2057. Hopalong Cassidy Returns (Paramount; 1936). *Cast:* Bill Boyd (Cassidy), Gail (Ann) Sheridan, George Hayes (Windy), Evelyn Brent, William Janney, Stephen Morris (Morris Ankrum), Al St. John, Ray Whitley, Ernie Adams, Irving Bacon. *D:* Nate Watt; *P:* Harry M. Sherman; *Sc:* Harrison Jacobs. (1:11)

This "Hopalong Cassidy" western is the 7th entry in the series and has Hoppy dealing with a greedy and vicious woman, the head of an outlaw gang. Based on Clarence E. Mulford's book of the same name.

2058. Hopalong Rides Again (Paramount; 1937). *Cast:* Bill Boyd (Hoppy), Russell Hayden (Lucky), George Hayes (Windy), Nora Lane, Harry Worth, William Duncan, Lois Wilde, Billy King, John Rutherford, Ernie Adams, Frank Ellis, John Beach, Artie Ortego, Ben Corbett. *D:* Lesley Selander (his first "Bar 20" feature); *P:* Harry M. Sherman; *Sc:* Norman Houston. (1:07)

Thirteenth entry in the "Hopalong Cassidy" series as the Bar 20 boys deal with a paleontologist searching for dinosaur bones, who in reality is a cattle rustler.

2059. Horse Feathers (Paramount; 1932). *Cast:* Groucho Marx (Professor Quincey Adams Wagstaff), Harpo Marx (Pinky), Chico Marx (Baravelli), Zeppo Marx (Frank Wagstaff), Thelma Todd, Robert Greig, David Landau, Nat Pendleton, Florine McKinney, Reginald Barlow, James Pierce, Ben Taggart, Vince Barnett. *D:* Norman Z. McLeod; *P:* Herman J. Mankiewicz; *Sc:* Bert Kalmar, Harry Ruby, S.J. Perelman, Will B. Johnston; *Songs:* Kalmar & Ruby. (1:12) (video)

Classic Marx Brothers romp with the new college president (Groucho) stopping at nothing to create a winning football team.

2060. Horsehoofs (Xxxx Xxxx; 1931). A Harry Carey western. (No other information available)

2061. The Horseman (Xxxx Xxxx; 1933). (No information available)

2062. Horseplay (Universal; 1933). *Cast:* Slim Summerville, Leila Hyams, Andy Devine, Cornelius Keefe, Ethel Griffies. *D:* Edward Sedgwick. (1:10)

Comedy of a simple-minded down-home rancher who becomes a millionaire and heads to London with his gal for a high time.

2063. Hot Curves (Tiffany; 1930). *Cast:* Benny Rubin, Mary Carr, Rex Lease, Alice Day, Pert Kelton, Paul Hurst, John Ince. *D:* Norman Taurog. "Poverty row" college comedy.

2064. Hot for Paris (Fox; 1929). *Cast:* Victor McLaglen, El Brendel, Fifi D'Orsay, Polly Moran, Yola D'Avril, Charles Judels, George Fawcett, Anita Murray, August Tollaire, Edward Dillon, Rosita Marstini, Lennox Pawle, Dave Valles. *D:* Raoul Walsh; *St:* Walsh.

Comedy.

2065. The Hot Heiress (WB/ F.N.; 1931). *Cast:* Ona Munson, Ben Lyon, Walter Pidgeon, Thelma Todd, Tom Dugan, Inez Courtney, Holmes Herbert, Nella Walker. *D:* Clarence Badger; *Sc:* Herbert Fields; *Songs:* Richard Rodgers, Lorenz Hart. (1:18)

Musical-comedy of a society woman who passes a riveter off as an architect. A box office fizzle.

2066. Hot Money (WB; 1936). *Cast:* Ross Alexander, Beverly Roberts, Joseph Cawthorn, Paul Graetz, Andrew Tombes, Cyrus Kendall, Frank Orth, Andre Beranger, Joe Cunningham, Anne Nagel, Eddie Conrad, Harry Burns, Addison Richards, Charles Foy, Robert Emmett Keane, Edwin Stanley.

D: William McGann; *P:* Bryan Foy; *Sc:* William Jacobs; *Song:* "What Can I Do? I Love Him"by Ruth and Louis Herscher. (1:09)

B comedy of a man who invents a gasoline substitute, incurring the wrath of the big oil companies. Based on the play by Aben Kandel.

2067. Hot Off the Press (Victury; 1935). *D:* Al Herman; *Sc:* Victor Potel, Gordon S. Griffith; *St:* Peter B. Kyne. (No other information available)

2068. Hot Pepper (Fox; 1933). *Cast:* Victor McLaglen (Flagg), Edmund Lowe (Quirt), Lupe Velez, El Brendel, Lillian Bond, Boothe Howard, Gloria Roy.*D:* John G. Blystone; *St:* Dudley Nichols; *Sc:* Barry Connors, Philip Klein. (1:16)

Flagg and Quirt are still at it, this time as night club owners quarrelling over Lupe Velez. The last of the series offshoots of *What Price, Glory?* (a silent feature which introduced the battling buddies).

2069. Hot Saturday (Paramount; 1932). *Cast:* Nancy Carroll, Cary Grant, Randolph Scott, Edward Woods, Lillian Bond, Jane Darwell, William Collier, Sr., Rita LaRoy, Oscar Apfel, Marjorie Main, Grady Sutton, Jessie Arnold, Rose Coghlan. *D:* William A. Seiter; *Sc:* Seton I. Miller, Josephine Lovett, Joseph Moncure March. (1:13)

Drama of the effects that small-town gossip has on a girl. Based on the novel by Harvey Ferguson.

2070. Hot Tip (RKO; 1935). *Cast:* James Gleason, ZaSu Pitts, Margaret Callahan, Russell Gleason, Ray Mayer, Willie Best, J.M. Kerrigan, Arthur Stone, Rollo Lloyd, Del Henderson, Donald Kerr, Kitty McHugh. *D:* James Gleason, Ray McCarey; *As.P.:* William Sistrom; *St:* William Slavens McNutt; *Sc:* Hugh Cummings, Olive Cooper, Louis Stevens. (1:09)

B drama of a man who risks the family fortune at the race track.

2071. Hot Water (20th Century-Fox; 1937). *Cast:* Jed Prouty, Spring Byington, Florence Roberts, June Carlson, Joan Marsh, Kenneth Howell, George Ernest, Billy Mahan, Russell Gleason, Marjorie Weaver, Shirley Deane, Willard Robertson, Robert Gleckler, Arthur Hohl, Joseph King, Selmer Jackson. *D:* Frank Strayer; *St:* Eleanor DeLamater, Ron Ferguson; *Sc:* Karen de Wolf, Robert Chapin.

Seventh entry in the "Jones Family" comedy series.

2072. Hotel Continental (Tiffany; 1932). *Cast:* Peggy Shannon, Alan Mowbray, J. Farrell MacDonald, Mary Carlisle, Theodore von Eltz, Henry B. Walthall, Ethel Clayton, Rockliffe Fellowes, Bert Roach, William Scott. *D:* Christy Cabanne; *St:* Paul Perez, F. Hugh Herbert; *Sc:* Herbert.

A "poverty row" comedy.

Hotel for Women *see* **Elsa Maxwell's Hotel for Women**

2073. Hotel Haywire (Paramount; 1937). *Cast:* Leo Carrillo, Lynne Overman, Mary Carlisle, Benny Baker, Spring Byington, George Barbier, Porter Hall, Lucien Littlefield, John Patterson, Franklin Pangborn, Terry Ray (Ellen Drew). *D:* George Archainbaud; *P:* Harold Hurley; *Sc:* Preston Sturges. (1:06)

This B comedy farce of misunderstandings involving an astrologer named Zodiac Z. Zippe was originally scheduled for George Burns and Gracie Allen. Preston Sturges original script was revised by the studio prior to production.

2074. Hotel Imperial (Paramount; 1939). *Cast:* Ray Milland, Isa Miranda (American debut), Reginald Owen, Gene Lockhart, J. Carrol Naish, Curt Bois, Henry Victor, Albert Dekker. *D:* Robert Florey; *Sc:* Gilbert Gabriel, Robert Thoeren. (1:07)

Espionage melodrama of a girl seeking the person responsible for her sister's death. Based on the play by Lajos Biro, the film is a remake of the 1927 production with Pola Negri. Reworked in 1943 as *Five Graves to Cairo.* A box office deficit due to many production problems encountered over the three years the film was in the works.

2075. Hotel Variety (Capital/Screencraft; 1935). *Cast:* Hal Skelly, Olive Borden, Sally Rand. *D:* Raymond Cannon; *P:* Arthur Hoerl; *Sc:* Hoerl.

"Poverty row" hotel drama.

2076. The Hottentot (WB; 1929). *Cast:* Edward Everett Horton, Patsy Ruth Miller, Douglas Gerrard, Edward Earle, Stanley Taylor, Gladys Brockwell, Otto Hoffman, Edmund Breese. *D:* Roy Del Ruth; *Sc:* Harvey Thew. (1:17)

Comedy of a horse lover mistaken for a champion jockey. A remake of the 1922 production by First National with Douglas MacLean, it is based on the 1920 stage play by Victor Mapes and William Collier, Sr. Remade as *Going Places* (q.v.).

2077. The Hound of the Baskervilles (20th Century-Fox; 1939). *Cast:* Basil Rathbone (Sherlock Holmes), Nigel Bruce (Dr. Watson), Richard Greene, Wendy Barrie, Lionel Atwill, Morton Lowry, John Carradine, Barlowe Borland, Beryl Mercer, Ralph Forbes, E.E. Clive, Eily Malyon, Mary Gordon, Nigel de Brulier. *D:* Sidney Lanfield; *P:* Gene Markey; *Sc:* Ernest Pascal. (1:20) (video)

Based on the 1902 novel by Sir Arthur Conan Doyle, this was the first film in the Fox series featuring Sherlock Holmes. The plot involves a "phantom" hound roaming the moors of Dartmoor near Baskerville Hall. First filmed in Great Britain in 1922. Remade there in 1959 by Hammer Films, in 1972 in the U.S.A. as a TV movie, in Great Britain in 1977 as a satire and as a TV movie in 1983.

The Hounds of Zaroff (G.B. title) *see* **The Most Dangerous Game**

The Hours Between (G.B. title) *see* **Twenty-Four Hours**

2078. A House Divided (Universal; 1931). *Cast:* Walter Huston, Kent Douglass (Douglass Montgomery), Helen Chandler, Vivian Oakland, Frank Hagney, Mary Fay, Marjorie Main (film debut), Lloyd Ingraham, Charles Middleton. *D:* William Wyler; *P:* Paul Kohner; *Sc:* John B. Clymer, Dale Van Every; *Additional Dialogue:* John Huston. (1:08)

A critically acclaimed dramatic triangle involving a widowed fisherman, his new wife and his son. A hit for the studio, it was based on the story "Heart and Hands" by Olive Edens.

2079. The House of a Thousand Candles (Republic; 1936). *Cast:* Phillips Holmes, Mae Clarke, Irving Pichel, Rosita Moreno, Mischa Auer, Lawrence Grant, Rafael Storm, Frederick Vogeding, Fred Walton, Hedwig Reicher, Keith Daniels, Michael Fitzmaurice, Charles DeRavenne, Paul Ellis. *D:* Arthur Lubin; *P:* Nat Levine; *Sc:* H.W. Hanemann, Endre Bohem. (0:54)

B mystery of a man who must live in a mansion in order to gain his inheritance. Previously filmed in 1916, it was based on the novel by Meredith Nicholson.

The House of Connelly (G.B. title) *see* **Carolina**

2080. House of Danger (Hollywood Film Exchange; 1934). *Cast:* Onslow Stevens, Janet Chandler. *D:* Charles Hutchison; *Sc:* John Francis (Jack) Natteford.

Melodrama.

House of Doom (G.B. title) *see* **The Black Cat**

The House of Fate (G.B. title) *see* **Muss 'Em Up**

2081. House of Fear (Universal; 1938–39). *Cast:* William Gargan, Irene Hervey, Alan Dinehart, Walter Woolf King, Dorothy Arnold, El Brendel, Harvey Stephens, Robert Coote, Tom Dugan, Jan Duggan, Emory Parnell. *D:* Joe May; *P:* Edmund Grainger; *St:* Thomas F. Fallon; *Sc:* Peter Milne. (1:06)

B comedy-mystery of a murderer who strikes at a New York City theater. A remake of *The Last Warning* (Universal; 1928) (q.v.).

2082. The House of Horror (WB/F.N.; 1929). *Cast:* Louise Fazenda, Chester Conklin, Thelma Todd, James Ford, William V. Mong, Dale Fuller, Emile Chautard. *D:* Benjamin Christensen; *Sc:* Richard Bee, William Irish.

Part-talkie slapstick comedy of the misadventures of two loonies who get involved with crooks in an old antique shop.

House of Menace *see* **Kind Lady**

2083. The House of Mystery (Monogram; 1934). *Cast:* Ed Lowry, Verna Hillie, John Sheehan, Brandon Hurst, Liya Joy (Joyzelle Joyner), Fritzi Ridgeway, Clay Clement, George Hayes, Dale Fuller, Harry C. Bradley, Irving Bacon, Mary Foy, Samuel Godfrey, George Cleveland, Bruce Mitchell, Dick Botiller, James C. Norton. *D:* William Nigh; *P:* Adam Hull Shirk; *Supervisor;* Paul Malvern; *Sc:* Albert E. DeMond. (1:02)

B comedy-mystery involving a group of people who must spend a week in an old dark house in order to collect an inheritance. Prior to release the film was known as "The Ape," the title of the stage play by Adam Hull Shirk on which it was based. The story was reworked and filmed by this studio in 1940 as *The Ape*.

2084. The House of Mystery (Columbia; 1938). *Cast:* Jack Holt, Beverly Roberts, Craig Reynolds, Sheila Bromley, Marjorie Gateson, Tom Kennedy, Gilbert Emery. *D:* Lewis D. Collins.

B who-dun-it.

2085. The House of Rothschild
(United Artists/20th Century; 1934).
Cast: George Arliss (in a dual role as
Mayer Rothschild and Nathan Roths-
child), Loretta Young (Julie Roths-
child), Boris Karloff (Count Ledrantz),
Robert Young (Capt. Fitzroy), C.
Aubrey Smith (Duke of Wellington),
Arthur Byron (Baring), Helen Westley
(Gudula Rothschild), Reginald Owen
(Herries), Florence Arliss (Hannah
Rothschild), Alan Mowbray (Metter-
nich), Noel Madison (Carl Rothschild),
Lumsden Hare (Prince Regent),
Georges Renavent (Talleyrand),
Holmes Herbert (Rowerth), Paul Har-
vey (Solomon Rothschild), Ivan Simp-
son (Amschel Rothschild), Murray Kin-
nell (James Rothschild), Charles Evans
(Nesselrode), Oscar Apfel, Leo Mc-
Cabe, Gilbert Emery, Desmond Rob-
erts, Earl McDonald, Ethel Griffies, Lee
Kohlmar, William Strauss, Reginald
Sheffield, Matthew Betz, Brandon
Hurst, Harold Minjir, Horace Claude
Cooper, Crauford Kent, Milton Kahn,
Gerald Pierce, George Offerman, Jr.,
Cullen Johnson, Bobbie La Manche,
Leonard Mudie, Wilfred Lucas, Walter
Long. *D:* Alfred Werker; *P:* Darryl F.
Zanuck; *As.P.:* Raymond Griffith,
William Goetz; *Sc:* Nunnally Johnson.
(1:26)
    Lavish historical documentation of
the famous banking family. It received
an A.A.N. for Best Picture while on
both the "10 Best" lists of the *New York
Times* and *Film Daily* it placed #2. The
final sequence is in 2-color technicolor.
Based on an unproduced play by George
Hembert Westley.

2086. The House of Secrets
(Chesterfield; 1929). *Cast:* Marcia Man-
ning, Joseph Striker. *D:* Edmund
Lawrence.
    "Poverty row" mystery-melodrama.
Remade in 1936 (see below).

2087. House of Secrets (Chesterfield; 1936–37). *Cast:* Muriel Evans,
Sidney Blackmer, Noel Madison,

Holmes Herbert, Leslie Fenton, Syd
Saylor, Jameson Thomas, Morgan Wallace, Ian MacLaren, George Rosener.
D: Roland D. Reed.
    "Poverty row" murder-mystery. A
remake of the preceding film.

2088. The House on 56th Street
(WB; 1933). *Cast:* Kay Francis, Ricardo
Cortez, Gene Raymond, Margaret
Lindsay, Frank McHugh, Sheila Terry,
William ("Stage") Boyd, Philip Reed,
Henry O'Neill, John Halliday, Hardie
Albright, Samuel S. Hinds, Walter
Walker, Nella Walker, Philip Faver-
sham, Bud Flanagan (Dennis O'Keefe).
D: Robert Florey; *P:* James Seymour;
Sc: Austin Parker, Sheridan Gibney.
    Melodrama of a woman who sacri-
fices all for her daughter, including
spending 20-years in prison. Based on
the novel by Joseph Santley.

**2089. The Housekeeper's Daugh-
ter** (United Artists/Hal Roach; 1939).
Cast: Joan Bennett, John Hubbard,
Adolphe Menjou, William Gargan,
George E. Stone, Peggy Wood, Donald
Meek, Victor Mature (film debut),
Marc Lawrence, Lillian Bond, Luis Al-
berni, Tom Dugan, Josephine Hutchin-
son, Gene Morgan, Leila McIntyre,
Rosina Galli. *D:* Hal Roach; *P:* Roach;
Sc: Rian James, Gordon Douglas. (1:21)
    Comedy-mystery of a gangster's
girl friend who stops by to visit her
mother, a housekeeper in a wealthy
household. Based on the novel by
Donald Henderson Clarke.

2090. Housewife (WB; 1934).
Cast: George Brent, Bette Davis, Ann
Dvorak, John Halliday, Ruth Donnelly,
Hobart Cavanaugh, Robert Barrat, Jo-
seph Cawthorn, Phil Regan, Willard
Robertson, Ronnie Cosbey, Leila Ben-
nett, Harry Tyler, Charles Coleman,
Claire Dodd. *D:* Alfred E. Green; *St:*
Robert Lord, Lillie Hayward; *Sc:*
Manuel Seff, Hayward. (1:09)
    Drama of a man who leaves his wife
for his old girl friend. Upon viewing this

film Bette Davis exclaimed "Dear God! What a horror!"

2091. Huckleberry Finn (Paramount; 1931). *Cast:* Jackie Coogan (Tom Sawyer), James (Junior) Durkin (Huck Finn), Clarence Muse (Jim), Jane Darwell (Widow Douglas), Jackie Searle (Sid Sawyer), Mitzi Green (Becky Thatcher), Eugene Pallette, Clara Blandick (Aunt Polly), Edith Fellows, Charlotte Henry, Oscar Apfel, Guy Oliver, Warner Richmond, Frank McGlynn, Sr., Cecil Weston, Lillian Harmer, Aileen Manning, Doris Short. *D:* Norman Taurog; *P:* Louis D. Lighton; *Sc:* Grover Jones, William Slavens McNutt. (1:20)

The first talkie version of Mark Twain's book of life along the Mississippi in the mid–19th-century. Previously filmed in 1920 with Lewis Sargent by director William Desmond Taylor. Remade in 1939 as *The Adventures of Huckleberry Finn* (q.v.), again by the same studio in 1960 (MGM), in 1974 as a musical for United Artists release and again in 1975 as a TV movie.

Huckleberry Finn (1939) *see* **The Adventures of Huckleberry Finn**

2092. Huddle (MGM; 1932). *Cast:* Ramon Novarro, Madge Evans, Una Merkel, Conrad Nagel, Arthur Byron, Cliff Edwards, Kane Richmond, Ralph Graves, Martha Sleeper, John Arledge, Ferike Boros, Frank Albertson, Henry Armetta, Joseph (Sawyer) Sauers, Rockliffe Fellowes. *D:* Sam Wood; *St:* Francis Wallace, Jerry Wald; *Sc:* Robert Lee Johnson, C. Gardner Sullivan, Arthur Hyman, Walton Smith. (G.B. title: *The Impossible Years*). (1:44)

Drama of an unpopular youth attending a university on a scholarship who finds love and a rival, eventually becoming a football hero.

2093. Human Cargo (20th Century–Fox; 1936). *Cast:* Claire Trevor, Brian Donlevy, Ralph Morgan, Rita (Hayworth) Cansino, Herman Bing, Wade Boteler, Helen Troy, Harry Woods. *D:* Allan Dwan; *St:* Kathleen Shepard; *Sc:* Doris Malloy, Jefferson Parker.

B melodrama of the smuggling of illegal aliens into the country.

2094. The Human Side (Universal; 1934). *Cast:* Adolphe Menjou, Doris Kenyon, Reginald Owen, Dickie Moore, Lois January, Charlotte Henry, Charles Wilson, Ward Bond, George Ernest, Dick Winslow, Betty Lawford. *D:* Edward Buzzell; *St:* Christine Ames.

B drama of a financially down-and-out man who tries to get his ex-wife to marry for money (for the sake of the kids).

2095. Human Targets (Big 4; 1932). *Cast:* Rin-Tin-Tin, Jr., Buzz Barton, Francis X. Bushman, Jr., Nanci Price, Tom London, Edmund Cobb, Ted Adams, Leon Kent, John Ince, Edgar Lewis, Pauline Parker, Helen Gibson, Franklyn Farnum. *D:* J.P. McGowan; *P:* John R. Freuler; *Sc:* George Morgan. (0:55)

B indie of a boy, a dog and a cowboy against some claim jumpers.

2096. Humanity (Fox; 1933). *Cast:* Ralph Morgan, Boots Mallory, Noel Madison, Nella Walker, Christian Rub, Alexander Kirkland, Irene Ware, Wade Boteler, Betty Jane Graham, Ferike Boros, Crauford Kent. *D:* John Francis Dillon; *St:* Harry Fried.

Low-budget drama.

2097. The Hunchback of Notre Dame (RKO; 1939). *Cast:* Charles Laughton (Quasimodo), Maureen O'Hara (American debut as Esmeralda), Cedric Hardwicke (Frollo), Thomas Mitchell (Clopin, King of Beggars), Edmond O'Brien (film debut as Gringoire), Harry Davenport (King Louis XI), Alan Marshal (Captain Phoebus), Walter Hampden (archbishop), Helen Whitney (Fleur), Katherine Alexander (Madame de Lys—Fleur's mother), George Zucco (procurator), Minna Gombell (Queen of Beggars), Fritz Leiber (old nobleman), Etienne Girardot (doctor), Arthur Hohl (Olivier), George Tobias (beggar), Rod La Rocque (Phillipo), Spencer Charters (court clerk), Rondo Hatton. *D:* William Dieterle; *P:* Pandro S. Berman; *Adaptation:* Bruno Frank; *Sc:* Sonya Levien; *Music:* (A.A.N.) Alfred Newman; *Sound Recording:* (A.A.N.) John Aalberg, John E. Tribby. (1:57) (video)

Lavishly produced version of the classic Victor Hugo story of a deformed bellringer and his love for a beautiful gypsy girl he rescues from a mob. First filmed as *The Darling of Paris* (Fox; 1917) with Theda Bara. Remade in 1923 (Universal) in the classic version with Lon Chaney and Patsy Ruth Miller. Remade in 1957 in a French-Italian coproduction with Anthony Quinn and again in 1982 as a TV movie. The story was also the basis for the 1979 Broadway musical "Quasimodo." One of the 21 top grossing films of 1939–40. Computer-colored by Turner Entertainment in 1989.

2098. Hunted Men (Paramount; 1938). *Cast:* Lloyd Nolan, Lynne Overman, Mary Carlisle, J. Carrol Naish, Anthony Quinn, Dorothy Peterson, Regis Toomey, Buster Crabbe, Johnny Downs, Hooper Atchley, Fern Emmett, Delmar Watson, Lu Miller, George Davis. *D:* Louis King; *P:* Stuart Walker; *St:* Albert Duffy, Marian Grant; *Sc:* Horace McCoy, William R. Lipman. (1:05)

A wanted killer takes over a private household, holding the family at bay.

2099. Hurricane (Columbia; 1929–30). *Cast:* John Mack Brown, Leila Hyams, Hobart Bosworth. *D:* Ralph Ince (talkie directorial debut).

Low-budget production.

2100. The Hurricane (United Artists/Samuel Goldwyn; 1937). *Cast:* Dorothy Lamour (Marama), Jon Hall (in a role originally intended for Joel McCrea as Terangi), Mary Astor (Madame De Laage), Thomas Mitchell (A.A.N. for B.S.A. as Dr. Kersaint), Raymond Massey (Governor De Laage), C. Aubrey Smith (Father Paul), John Carradine (jailer), Jerome Cowan (Captain Nagle), Al Kikume (Chief Mehevi), Kuulei De Clercq (Tita), Layne Tom, Jr. (Mako), Flora Hayes (Mama Rua), Mamo Clark (Hitia), Movita Castenada (Arai), Reri (Reri), Francis Kaai (Tavi), Pauline Steele (Mata), Mary Shaw (Marunga), Spencer Charters (judge), Roger Drake (Captain of the Guards), Inez Courtney, Paul Stader. *D:* John Ford; Stuart Heisler (storm sequences only); *As.P.:* Merritt Hulburd; *Adaptation:* Oliver H.P. Garrett; *Sc:* Dudley Nichols, Ben Hecht (unc.); *Music:* (A.A.N.) Alfred Newman; *Sound Recording:* (A.A.) Thomas T. Moulton; *Song:* "Moon of Manakoora" by Frank Loesser, Alfred Newman. (1:50) (video — 1:42)

Classic romantic adventure of peaceful south sea islanders and a disastrous hurricane which disrupts their lives forever. Based on the book by Charles Nordhoff and James Norman Hall, this box office bonanza was released the day before Christmas in '37 and became one of the 15 top grossing films of 1937–38. The much acclaimed special effects for the hurricane were engineered by James Basevi with four months of production time at a cost of $400,000, to produce what became only twenty minutes of film footage. No oscars were given for special effects until 1939. *Film Daily* placed it at #10 on their "10 Best" list of 1938. Remade in 1979 as *Hurricane*.

2101. Hurricane Express (Mascot; 1932). *Cast:* Tully Marshall, Conway Tearle, John Wayne, J. Farrell MacDonald, Shirley Grey, Edmund Breese, Lloyd Whitlock, Alan Bridge, Matthew Betz, Joseph Girard, James Burtis, Ernie S. Adams, Charles King, Al Ferguson, Glenn Strange. *D:* John P. McGowan, Armand Schaefer; *St:* Colbert Clark, Barney A. Sarecky, Wyndham Gittens; *Sc:* George Morgan, John P. McGowan. (1:20) (video)

Railroad action-adventure feature which was edited down from the serial of the same name. The basic story of a man out to avenge the death of his father.

2102. Hurricane Horseman (Willis Kent; 1931). *Cast:* Lane Chandler, Marie Quillan, Walter Miller, Yakima Canutt, Lafe McKee, Richard Alexander. *D:* Armand L. Schaefer; *P:* Willis Kent; *Sc:* Oliver Drake. (0:50)

Lane Chandler western of a gunsmith who saves a girl from outlaws.

2103. The Hurricane Rider (Xxxx Xxxx; 1931). A Harry Carey western.

(No other information available)

2104. Husband's Holiday (Paramount; 1931). *Cast:* Clive Brook, Charles Ruggles, Vivienne Osborne, Juliette Compton, Charles Winninger, Dickie Jones, Marilyn Knowlden, Dorothy Tree, Elizabeth Patterson, Berton Churchill, Adrienne Ames, Leni Stengel, Harry Bannister. *D:* Robert Milton; *St & Sc:* Ernest Pascal, Viola Brothers Shore.

Low-budget story of a man who decides to leave his wife for another woman.

Husbands and Lovers (G.B. title) *see* **Honeymoon in Bali**

2105. Hush Money (Fox; 1931). *Cast:* Joan Bennett, Hardie Albright, George Raft, Myrna Loy, Owen Moore, C. Henry Gordon, Claude King, Henry Armetta, Douglas Cosgrove, Huey White. *D:* Sidney Lanfield; *St:* Courtney Terrett; *Sc:* Dudley Nichols, Philip Klein, Terrett.

Low-budget melodrama.

2106. Hypnotised (Sono Art-World Wide; 1932). *Cast:* Charlie Murray, Ernest Torrence, Wallace Ford, Marjorie Beebe, George Moran & Charles Emmett Mack (better known as the comedy team of Moran & Mack), Luis Alberni, Hattie McDaniel, Mitchell Harris, Maria Alba, Harry Schultz, Matt McHugh. *D:* Mack Sennett; *St:* Arthur Ripley; *Sc:* Sennett, Ripley.

"Poverty row" comedy of the slapstick variety which is notable as the final feature film of comedy director Mack Sennett.

I Accuse (G.B. title) *see* **The Life of Emile Zola**

2107. I Am a Criminal (Monogram/Crescent Pictures; 1938). *Cast:* John Carroll, Kay Linaker, Martin Spellman, Craig Reynolds, Lester Matthews, Mary Kornman, May Beatty, Robert Fiske, Byron Foulger, Edward Earle, Jack Kennedy, Allan Cavan. *D:* William Nigh; *P:* E.B. Derr; *St:* Harrison Jacobs; *Sc:* John Krafft. (1:13)

B drama of a racketeer who adopts an orphan when he learns he is to be tried for murder. Remade by this studio in 1943 as *Smart Guy.*

I Am a Fugitive (G.B. title) *see* **I Am a Fugitive from a Chain Gang**

2108. I Am a Fugitive from a Chain Gang (WB; 1932). *Cast:* Paul Muni (A.A.N. for B.A. as James Allen), Glenda Farrell (Marie Woods), Helen Vinson (Helen), Preston Foster (Pete), Edward Ellis (Bomber Wells), Allen Jenkins (Barney Sykes), Louise Carter (Mrs. Allen), Hale Hamilton (Reverend Robert Clinton Allen), Noel Francis (Linda), Robert McWade (replacing Morgan Wallace as Ramsey), John Wray (Nordine), Harry Woods (guard), David Landau (warden), Edward J. McNamara (warden), Willard Robertson (replacing John Marston as the police commissioner), Berton Churchill (Judge), Sheila Terry (Allen's secretary), James Bell (film debut as Red), Sally Blane (Alice), Edward Le Saint (replacing Oscar Apfel as the chamber of commerce chairman), Douglass Dumbrille (replacing C. Henry Gordon as the D.A.), Robert Warwick (Fuller), Charles Middleton (train conductor), Reginald Barlow (Parker), Jack LaRue (Ackerman), Charles Sellon (hot dog stand owner), Erville Alderson (replacing Russell Simpson as the chief of police), George Pat Collins (Wilson), William Pawley (Doggy), Lew Kelly (Mike), Everett Brown (replacing Sam Baker as Sebastian T. Yale), William LeMaire (Texas), George Cooper (vaudevillian), Wallis Clark (replacing Edward Arnold as a lawyer), Walter Long (replacing Dewey Robinson as the blacksmith), Frederick Burton (Georgia prison official), Irving Bacon (Bill the barber), Lee Shumway, J. Frank Glendon, Bud Flanagan (Dennis O'Keefe). *D:* Mervyn LeRoy; *P:* Hal Wallis; *Sc:* Sheridan Gibney, Brown Holmes, Howard J. Green; *Sound Recording:* (A.A.N.) Nathan Levinson. (TV and G.B. title: *I Am a Fugitive*) (1:33) (video)

This indictment on the penal system of the southern states of the 1930s shocked audiences of its day, bringing about some eventual reform in the system. A Hollywood classic which received an A.A.N. for Best Picture, it was also voted "Best Picture of the Year" by the National Board of Review. Based on the autobiographical book "I Am a Fugitive from a Georgia Chain Gang" by Robert E. Burns, it also placed #8 on the "10 Best" list of *Film Daily* in 1933.

2109. I Am a Thief (WB; 1934). *Cast:* Mary Astor, Ricardo Cortez, Dudley Digges, Robert Barrat, Irving Pichel, Arthur Aylesworth, Ferdinand Gottschalk, Hobart Cavanaugh, Frank Reicher, Oscar Apfel, Florence Fair. *D:* Robert Florey; *P:* Henry Blanke; *St & Sc:* Ralph Block, Doris Malloy. (1:04)

B melodrama of intrigue on the Orient Express.

2110. I Am Suzanne (Fox; 1934). *Cast:* Gene Raymond, Lillian Harvey,

Geneva Mitchell, Leslie Banks, Halliwell Hobbes, Georgia Caine, Murray Kinnell, Edward Keane, Lionel Belmore. *D:* Rowland V. Lee; *St & Sc:* Lee, Edwin Justus Mayer.

Low-budget musical.

2111. I Am the Law (Columbia; 1938). *Cast:* Edward G. Robinson, Otto Kruger, John Beal, Barbara O'Neil, Wendy Barrie, Arthur Loft, Louis Jean Heydt, Marc Lawrence, Fay Helm, Donald Woods, Byron Foulger, Emory Parnell, James Millican, Horace McMahon, Charles Halton, Robert Middlemass, Douglas Wood, Ivan Miller. *D:* Alexander Hall; *P:* Everett Riskin; *St:* Fred Allhoff; *Sc:* Jo Swerling. (1:23) (video)

Melodrama of a D.A. who is hired to clean up the rackets.

2112. I Believed in You (Fox; 1934). *Cast:* John Boles, Leslie Fenton, Gertrude Michael, Victor Jory, Rosemary Ames, George Meeker, Gilbert Emery, Morgan Wallace, Joyzelle Joyner, Louise Beavers. *D:* Irving Cummings; *St:* William Anthony McGuire; *Sc:* William Conselman.

Romantic drama.

2113. I Can't Escape (Beacon; 1934). *Cast:* Onslow Stevens, Lila Lee, Russell Gleason. *D:* Otto Brower.

B drama.

2114. I Conquer the Sea! (Academy Pictures; 1936). *Cast:* Stanley Morner (Dennis Morgan), Steffi Duna, Douglas Walton, George Cleveland. *D:* Victor Halperin; *P:* Edward Halperin; *Sc:* The Halperins; *Story Adapt.:* Richard Carroll; *Dial.:* Rollo Lloyd, Howard Higgin.

Low-budget independent romantic drama of Portuguese fishermen which ends tragically.

2115. I Cover Chinatown (20th Century–Fox; 1936). *Cast:* Norman Foster, Vince Barnett, Arthur Lake, Theodore von Eltz, George Hackathorne. *D:* Norman Foster (directorial debut); *P:* Fenn Kimball.

B melodrama of a driver of a sight-seeing bus who gets involved in murder.

2116. I Cover the War (Universal; 1937). *Cast:* John Wayne, Gwen Gaze, Major Sam Harris, James Bush, Don Barclay, Arthur Aylesworth, Jack Mack, Franklin Parker, Earle Hodgins, Pat Somerset, Charles Brokaw, Frank Lackteen, Abdulla, Olaf Hytten, Keith Kenneth. *D:* Arthur Lubin; *P:* Trem Carr; *St:* Bernard McConville; *Sc:* George Waggner. (1:08)

B actioner of a newsreel correspondent in Arabia in search of a story. Filmed in California.

2117. I Cover the Waterfront (United Artists/Reliance; 1933). *Cast:* Claudette Colbert, Ben Lyon, Ernest Torrence (in a critically acclaimed performance in his final film as Captain Eli Kirk—d. 1933), Hobart Cavanaugh, Maurice Black, Purnell Pratt, Wilfred Lucas, Harry Beresford, Vince Barnett, George Humbert, Claudia Coleman, Rosita Marstini. *D:* James Cruze; *P:* Edward Small; *Sc:* Wells Root, Jack Jevne. (1:10) (video)

Low-budget melodrama of a reporter who romances a girl with the intent of nailing her father, suspected of smuggling Chinese aliens into the country. Based on the book by Max Miller, this was considered a tough melodrama in its day. Remade in 1961 as *The Secret of Deep Harbor.*

2118. I Demand Payment (Imperial; 1938). *Cast:* Jack LaRue, Betty Burgess, Matty Kemp, Guinn Williams. *D:* Clifford Sanforth; *P:* Sanforth; *Sc:* Sherman L. Lowe.

"Poverty row" crime drama.

2119. I Dream Too Much (RKO; 1935). *Cast:* Lily Pons (film debut), Henry Fonda, Eric Blore, Osgood Perkins, Lucien Littlefield, Lucille Ball, Mischa Auer, Paul Porcasi, Scotty Beckett, Esther Dale, Billy Gilbert. *D:* John Cromwell; *P:* Pandro S. Berman; *St:* Elsie Finn, David G. Wittels; *Sc:* Edmund North, James Gow; *Songs:* Jerome Kern, Dorothy Fields; "Bell Song" from the opera "Lakme" by (Clement) Leo Delibes; "Caro Nome" from "Rigoletto" by Guiseppe Verdi (conducted by Andre Kostelanetz); *Sound Recording:* (A.A.N.) Carl Dreher, Hugh McDowell, P.J. Faulkner, J.G. Stewart. (1:35) (video)

A box office flop set in the south of France of a married couple with career problems.

2120. I Found Stella Parish (WB/F.N.; 1935). *Cast:* Kay Francis, Paul Lukas, Ian Hunter, Sybil Jason, Jessie Ralph, Barton MacLane, Eddie Acuff, Joseph Sawyer (nee: Sauers), Walter Kingsford, Robert Strange. *D:* Mervyn LeRoy; *P:* Harry Joe Brown; *St:* John Monk Saunders; *Sc:* Casey Robinson. (1:24)

An actress with a past tries to protect her daughter in this hit tear-jerker of its day.

2121. I Give My Love (Universal; 1934). *Cast:* Wynne Gibson, Paul Lukas, Eric Linden, John Darrow, Anita Louise, Dorothy Appleby, Kenneth Howell, Louise Beavers, Tad Alexander. *D:* Karl Freund. (1:05)

B tear-jerker of a woman who after serving a prison term, meets her son who believes his mother to be dead.

2122. I Hate Women (Ken Goldsmith; 1934). *Cast:* Wallace Ford. *D:* Aubrey H. Scotto; *Sc:* Mary E. McCarthy.

(No other information available)

2123. I Have Lived (Chesterfield; 1933). *Cast:* Gertrude Astor, Anita Page, Matthew Betz, Eddie Boland, Allen Vincent, Maude Truax, Del Henderson. *D:* Richard Thorpe; *St:* Lou Heifetz.

"Poverty row" melodrama.

2124. I Like It That Way (Universal; 1934). *Cast:* Gloria Stuart, Roger

Pryor, Marian Marsh, Shirley Grey, Lucile Gleason, Noel Madison, Merna Kennedy, Mae Busch, Mickey Rooney, Gloria Shea. *D:* Harry Lachman; *St:* Harry Sauber; *Sc:* Chandler Sprague, Joseph Santley; *Songs:* "Blue Sky Avenue" by Herb Magidson, Con Conrad, title song, "Let's Put Two and Two Together" and "Goin' to Town" by Sidney Mitchell and Archie Gottler. (1:07)

B musical.

2125. I Like Your Nerve (WB/ F.N.; 1931). *Cast:* Douglas Fairbanks, Jr., Loretta Young, Henry Kolker, Edmund Breon, Boris Karloff, Claud Allister, Ivan Simpson, Cameron Prud'Homme, Paul Porcasi, Andre Cheron, Henry Bunston. *D:* William McGann; *St:* Roland Pertwee; *Sc:* Houston Branch.

Comedy of a girl who is put up in lieu of a gambling debt.

2126. I Live for Love (WB; 1935). *Cast:* Dolores Del Rio, Everett Marshall, Allen Jenkins, Guy Kibbee, Berton Churchill, Eddie Conrad, Don Alvarado, Hobart Cavanaugh, Mary Treen, Montague Shaw, Miki Morita, Robert Greig. *D:* Busby Berkeley; *P:* Bryan Foy; *St:* Robert Andrews, Jerry Wald; *Sc:* Wald, Julius J. Epstein, Andrews; *Song:* "Mine Alone," "Silver Wings," title song, "I Wanna Play House" and "A Man Must Shave" by Mort Dixon and Allie Wrubel. (G.B. title: *I Live for You*) (1:04)

Hit programmer musical of a temperamental actress taken by the charms of a street singer.

I Live for You (G.B. title) *see* **I Live for Love**

2127. I Live My Life (MGM; 1935). *Cast:* Joan Crawford, Brian Aherne, Frank Morgan, Aline MacMahon, Eric Blore, Jessie Ralph, Fred Keating, Arthur Treacher, Hedda Hopper, Etienne Girardot, Ed Brophy, Lionel Stander, Vince Barnett, Frank Conroy. *D:* W.S. Van Dyke II; *P:* Bernard Hyman; *Sc:* Joseph L. Mankiewicz, Gottfried Reinhardt. (1:25)

The romance of a society girl and an archaeologist. Based on the story "Claustrophobia" by A. Carter Goodloe.

2128. I Love a Soldier (Xxxx Xxxx; 1936). (No information available)

2129. I Love That Man (Paramount; 1933). *Cast:* Nancy Carroll, Edmund Lowe, Robert Armstrong, Lew Cody, Pat O'Malley, Inez Courtney, Warren Hymer, Dorothy Burgess, Grant Mitchell. *D:* Harry Joe Brown; *P:* Charles R. Rogers; *St & Sc:* Gene Towne, Casey Robinson, Graham Baker.

B drama of a couple of con-artists who decide to go straight.

2130. I Loved a Woman (WB/ F.N.; 1933). *Cast:* Edward G. Robinson, Kay Francis, Genevieve Tobin, J. Farrell MacDonald, Henry Kolker, Robert Barrat, Henry O'Neill (feature film debut), E.J. Ratcliffe, Paul Porcasi, William V. Mong, Walter Walker, George Blackwood, Lorena Layson, Sam Godfrey. *D:* Alfred E. Green; *P:* Henry Blanke; *Sc:* Charles Kenyon, Sidney Sutherland. (1:30)

Comedy-melodrama of a meat packer who is thwarted at every turn by his ambitious wife. Based on the novel by David Karsner.

2131. I Loved You Wednesday (Fox; 1933). *Cast:* Warner Baxter, Elissa Landi, Miriam Jordan, Victor Jory, Anne Nagel, Laura Hope Crews. *D:* Henry King, William Cameron Menzies.

Romantic drama of a ballerina. Based on a stage play by William DuBois and Molly Ricardel.

2132. I Married a Doctor (WB/ F.N.; 1936). *Cast:* Josephine Hutchinson, Pat O'Brien, Ross Alexander, Guy Kibbee, Louise Fazenda, Olin Howland, Robert Barrat, Margaret Irving, Gaby Fay (Fay Holden in her film debut), Harry Hayden, George Hayes, Willard Robertson, Alma Lloyd, Ray Mayer, Dora Clement, Grace Stafford, Thomas Pogue, Edythe Elliott, Frank Rhodes, Hedwig Reicher, Sam Wren, Janet Young. *D:* Archie Mayo; *P:* Harry Joe Brown; *Sc:* Casey Robinson, Harriet Ford, Harvey O'Higgins. (1:27)

A city girl marries a small town doctor and becomes the victim of malicious gossip and scandal. A remake of *Main Street* (First National; 1923) and based on the novel of that name by Sinclair Lewis, with a happy ending replacing the original in this film version.

2133. I Met Him in Paris (Paramount; 1937). *Cast:* Claudette Colbert, Melvyn Douglas, Robert Young, Lee Bowman, Mona Barrie, Fritz Feld, Hans Joby, George Davis, Rudolph Amendt, Alexander Cross, Egon Brecher. *D:* Wesley Ruggles; *P:* Ruggles; *St:* Helen Meinardi; *Sc:* Claude Binyon. (1:26)

Romantic comedy with an European setting. The film was voted #7 on the "10 Best" list of the *New York Times* as well as being one of the 38 top grossing films of 1936–37.

2134. I Met My Love Again (United Artists/Walter Wanger; 1937–38). *Cast:* Henry Fonda, Joan Bennett, Alan Marshal, Dorothy Stickney, Dame May Whitty, Alan Baxter, Louise Platt (film debut), Tim Holt, Florence Lake, Genee Hall, Alice Cavenna. *D:* Joshua Logan (directorial debut) & Arthur Ripley (also in his directorial debut); *P:* Walter Wanger; *Sc:* David Hertz. (1:17)

Flop tear-jerker of a woman who returns to the man she first loved after her husband dies. Based on the magazine serial "Summer Lightning" by Allene Corliss.

2135. I Promise to Pay (Columbia; 1937). *Cast:* Chester Morris, Helen Mack, Thomas Mitchell, Leo Carrillo, Marc Lawrence, Thurston Hall, Harry Woods, Wallis Clark, John Gallaudet, Henry Brandon, Edward Keane. *D:* D. Ross Lederman; *Sc:* Lionel Houser, Mary McCall, Jr.

B melodrama.

2136. I Sell Anything (WB/F.N.; 1934). *Cast:* Pat O'Brien, Ann Dvorak, Claire Dodd, Roscoe Karns, Hobart Cavanaugh, Russell Hopton, Robert Barrat, Harry Tyler, Gus Shy, Leonard Carey, Ferdinand Gottschalk, Clay Clement. *D:* Robert Florey; *P:* Sam Bischoff; *St:* Albert J. Cohen, Robert T. Shannon; *Sc:* Brown Holmes, Sidney Sutherland. (1:08)

Story of a high-minded auctioneer who tries to make it on New York's Park Avenue by selling antiques — which are actually reproductions.

2137. I Stand Accused (Republic; 1938). *Cast:* Robert Cummings, Robert Paige, Helen Mack, Lyle Talbot, Gordon Jones, Robert Middlemass, John Hamilton, Leona Roberts, Harry Stubbs, Howard Hickman, Thomas Beck, Robert Strange. *D:* John H. Auer; *P:* Auer (co); *Sc:* Gordon Kahn.

B melodrama.

2138. I Stole a Million (Universal; 1939). *Cast:* George Raft, Claire Trevor, Dick Foran, Henry Armetta, Victor Jory, Joseph Sawyer, George Chandler, Irving Bacon, Ralph Dunn, Hobart Cavanaugh, Jason Robards, Emory Parnell, Tom Fadden, Robert Elliott. *D:* Frank Tuttle; *P:* Burt Kelly; *St:* Lester Cole; *Sc:* Nathanael West. (1:29)

Melodrama of a cab driver who takes to a life of crime to support his family.

2139. I Take This Woman (Paramount; 1931). *Cast:* Gary Cooper, Carole Lombard, Helen Ware, Lester Vail, Charles Trowbridge, Clara Blandick, David Landau, Guy Oliver. *D:* Marion Gering, Slavko Vorkapich (usually noted for his montage work);

Sc: Vincent Lawrence (based on the novel "Lost Ecstasy" by Mary Roberts Rinehart). (1:14)

Comedy-drama of a free-spirit society girl who falls for a ranchhand.

Note: No relation to the 1940 film by MGM of the same title.

2140. I Was a Convict (Republic; 1939). *Cast:* Barton MacLane, Beverly Roberts, Clarence Kolb, Leon Ames, Janet Beecher, Horace MacMahon, Ben Welden, Russell Hicks, Willard Robertson, John Harmon, Clara Blandick, Chester Clute, Crauford Kent. *D:* Aubrey Scotto; *Sc:* Ben Markson, Robert D. Andrews. (aka: *I Was in Prison*)

B drama of a man who attempts to go straight after being released from prison.

I Was in Prison *see* **I Was a Convict**

2141. I'd Give My Life (Paramount; 1936). *Cast:* Sir Guy Standing, Frances Drake, Tom Brown, Robert Elliott, Paul Hurst, Janet Beecher, Charles Richman, Robert Gleckler, Charles Wilson, Helen Lowell. *D:* Edwin L. Marin; *P:* Richard A. Rowland; *St:* H.H. Van Loan, Willard Mack; *Sc:* George O'Neil.

A remake of *The Noose* (First National; 1928) is this B drama of a state governor and his involvement with his stepson, a known gangster.

2142. I'll Fix It (Columbia; 1934). *Cast:* Jack Holt, Mona Barrie, Winnie Lightner (final film — ret.), Edward Van Sloan, Edward Brophy, Selmer Jackson, Nedda Harrigan, Clarence Wilson, Jimmy Butler, Helena Phillips Evans, Wallis Clark, Charles Moore. *D:* Roy William Neill; *St:* Leonard Spigelgass; *Sc:* Ethel Hill, Dorothy Howell.

Comedy.

2143. I'll Give a Million (20th Century–Fox; 1938). *Cast:* Warner Baxter, Lynn Bari, Peter Lorre, Marjorie Weaver, Jean Hersholt, John Carradine, J. Edward Bromberg, Fritz Feld, Sig Rumann, Luis Alberni, Charles Halton, Rafaela Ottiano, Frank Reicher, Georges Renavent, Harry Hayden, Christian Rub, Stanley Andrews, Frank Dawson. *D:* Walter Lang; *P:* Darryl F. Zanuck; *St:* Cesare Zavattini; *Sc:* Giaci Mondaini, Boris Ingster, Milton Sperling. (1:10)

Satirical story of local bums who are given the royal treatment after a millionaire announces he is posing as one and giving big bucks for acts of kindness.

2144. I'll Love You Always (Columbia; 1935). *Cast:* Nancy Carroll, George Murphy, Raymond Walburn, Robert Allen, Arthur Hohl, Jean Dixon. *D:* Leo Bulgakov; *St:* Lawrence Hazard, Vera Caspary; *Sc:* Sidney Buchman, Caspary.

B musical.

2145. I'll Take Romance (Columbia; 1937). *Cast:* Grace Moore (American film debut), Melvyn Douglas, Helen Westley, Stuart Erwin, Margaret Hamilton, Walter Kingsford, Esther Muir, Barry Norton, Franklin Pangborn, Marek Windheim, Walter Stahl, Gennaro Curci, Frank Forest, Lucio Villegas. *D:* Edward H. Griffith; *P:* Everett Riskin; *St:* Stephen Morehouse Avery; *Sc:* George Oppenheimer, Jane Murfin. (1:25)

Musical-comedy of an opera singer who is kidnapped by her manager.

2146. I'll Tell the World (Universal; 1934). *Cast:* Lee Tracy (who also starred in the '45 remake), Roger Pryor, Gloria Stuart, Onslow Stevens, Leon (Ames) Waycoff, Herman Bing, Alec B. Francis, Arthur Stone, Willard Robertson, Hugh Enfield (Craig Reynolds), Dorothy Granger. *D:* Edward Sedgwick; *St:* Frank Wead, Lincoln Quarberg; *Sc:* Dale Van Every, Ralph Spence. (1:25)

A journalist discovers a lost airship

in a mythical country that is experiencing political upheaval. Remade in 1945.

2147. I'm from Missouri (Paramount; 1939). *Cast:* Bob Burns, Gladys George, Patricia Morison, Gene Lockhart, William Henry, George P. Huntley, Jr., Judith Barrett, Melville Cooper, E.E. Clive, Raymond Hatton, Ethel Griffies, Charles Halton, Eddy Waller, Dennie Moore, Tom Dugan, Doris Lloyd, Lawrence Grossmith. *D:* Theodore Reed; *P:* Paul Jones; *St:* Julian Street, Homer Croy; *Sc:* Duke Atteberry, John C. Moffitt. (1:20)

B comedy of a rural American delivering a load of army mules in London.

2148. I'm from the City (RKO; 1938). *Cast:* Joe Penner, Richard Lane, Kay Sutton, Paul Guilfoyle, Lorraine Krueger, Kathryn Sheldon, Ethan Laidlaw, Lafayette (Lafe) McKee, Edmund Cobb, Clyde Kinney, Willie Best. *D:* Ben Holmes; *P:* William Sistrom; *St:* Holmes; *Sc:* Nicholas T. Barrows, Robert St. Clair, John Grey; *Songs:* Hal Raynor. (1:06)

B comedy of a simpleton who is turned into a circus bareback rider through hypnotism.

2149. I'm No Angel (Paramount; 1933). *Cast:* Mae West (Tira), Cary Grant (Jack Clayton), Edward Arnold (Bill Barton), Gertrude Michael (Alicia Hatton), Kent Taylor (Kirk Lawrence), Ralf Harolde (Slick Wiley), Russell Hopton (Flea Madigan), Gregory Ratoff (Benny Pinkowitz), Dorothy Peterson (Thelma), Getrude Howard (Beulah Thorndyke), William Davidson (Ernest Brown, the chump), Nigel de Brulier (Rajah), Irving Pichel (Bob the attorney), George Bruggeman (Omnes), Nat Pendleton (Harry), Morrie Cohan (chauffeur), Walter Walker (judge), Monte Collins & Ray Cooke (sailors), Hattie McDaniel (maid), Libby Taylor (Libby the maid), Bud Flanagan (Dennis O'Keefe as the re-

porter). *D:* Wesley Ruggles; *P:* William LeBaron; *St:* Mae West, Lowell Brentano; *Adaptation:* Harlan Thompson; *Dialogue:* West; *Songs:* "They Call Me Sister Honky Tonk," "No One Loves Me Like That Dallas Man," "I Found a New Way to Go to Town," "I Want You, I Need You" and the title song by Ben Ellison, Gladys DuBois and Harvey Brooks. (1:27)

Comedy of a gold digging lion tamer out to nab a wealthy playboy. This is a good example of Mae West at her naughtiest and the spicy double entendres outraged many audiences of the period, subsequently making the film a huge success at the box office, being one of the 11 top grossing films of 1933.

2150. I've Been Around (Universal; 1934). *Cast:* Rochelle Hudson, Chester Morris, G.P. Huntley, Jr., Gene Lockhart, Henry Armetta, Mary (Phyllis) Brooks (film debut), Isabel Jewell, Ralph Morgan. *D:* Philip Cahn. (1:03)

B romantic drama of a fickle woman who leaves her first love in search of something better, but eventually returns to him.

2151. I've Got Your Number (WB; 1934). *Cast:* Joan Blondell, Pat O'Brien, Allen Jenkins, Glenda Farrell, Eugene Pallette, Gordon Westcott, Henry O'Neill, Renee Whitney, Hobart Cavanaugh, Robert Ellis, Louise Beavers, Selmer Jackson, Wallis Clark, Douglas Cosgrove, Henry Kolker. *D:* Ray Enright; *P:* Sam Bischoff; *St:* William Rankin; *Sc:* Warren Duff, Sidney Sutherland. (1:08)

B production of a girl who is proven innocent of burglary by some telephone workers.

2152. The Ice Follies of 1939 (MGM; 1939). *Cast:* Joan Crawford, James Stewart, Lew Ayres, Lewis Stone, Lionel Stander, Bess Ehrhardt, Charles D. Brown, Roy Shipstad, Eddie

Shipstad, Oscar Johnson and the International Ice Follies. *D:* Reinhold Schunzel; *P:* Harry Rapf; *St:* Leonard Praskins; *Sc:* Praskins, Florence Ryerson, Edgar Allan Woolf. (1:22)

A big budgeted ice show which turned out to be one of the studio's biggest bombs of the year. A remake of *Excess Baggage* (MGM; 1928). The final ice show sequence is in technicolor.

2153. The Idaho Kid (Colony; 1936). *Cast:* Rex Bell, Marion Shilling, David Sharpe, Earle Dwire, Lafe McKee, Lane Chandler, Charles King, Phil Dunham, Dorothy Woods, Herman Hack, Ed Cassidy, George Morrell, Jimmy Aubrey, Sherry Tansey, Dick Botiller. *D:* Robert Hill; *P:* Paul Malvern; *Sc:* George Plympton. (0:54)

Rex Bell western of feuding ranchers.

Identity Parade (G.B. title) *see* **The Line-Up**

2154. Idiot's Delight (MGM; 1939). *Cast:* Clark Gable, Norma Shearer, Edward Arnold, Charles Coburn, Burgess Meredith, Joseph Schildkraut, Laura Hope Crews, Skeets Gallagher, Virginia Grey, Pat Paterson, Fritz Feld, Joan Marsh, Joe Yule, Virginia Dale, Peter Willes, Bernadene Hayes, Clem Bevans, Hobart Cavanaugh, Paula Stone, William Edmunds, Lorraine Krueger. *D:* Clarence Brown; *P:* Hunt Stromberg; *Sc:* Robert E. Sherwood. (1:45) (video)

At the outbreak of World War II, various characters are staying at a hotel on the Swiss border. Based on the play by Robert E. Sherwood which originally starred Alfred Lunt and Lynn Fontanne. Notable is Gable singing and dancing to "Puttin' on the Ritz."

2155. The Idle Rich (MGM; 1929). *Cast:* Conrad Nagel, Leila Hyams, Bessie Love, James Neill, Edythe Chapman, Kenneth Gibson, Paul Kruger, Robert Ober. *D:* William de Mille.

Comedy of the strange behavior encountered from his in-laws when a millionaire marries a typist. Based on the hit Broadway play "White Collars" by Edith Ellis.

2156. The Idol of the Crowds (Universal; 1937). *Cast:* John Wayne, Sheila Bromley, Billy Burrud, Russell Hopton, Clem Bevans, Charles Brokaw, Hal Neiman. *D:* Arthur Lubin; *P:* Paul Malvern; *St:* George Waggner; *Sc:* Waggner, Harold Buckley. (1:02)

B actioner with an ice hockey background.

2157. If I Had a Million (Paramount; 1932). *Cast:* Richard Bennett (millionaire), Mary Boland, Gary Cooper, Frances Dee, W.C. Fields, Wynne Gibson, Roscoe Karns, Charles Laughton, Lucien Littlefield, Jack Oakie, George Raft, Gene Raymond, May Robson, Charles Ruggles, Alison Skipworth, Gail Patrick (film debut), Berton Churchill, Blanche Frederici, Joyce Compton, Samuel S. Hinds (film debut). *D:* James Cruze, H. Bruce Humberstone, Ernst Lubitsch, Norman Z. McLeod, Stephen Roberts, William A. Seiter, Norman Taurog; *St:* Robert D. Andrews; *Sc:* Claude Binyon, Whitney Bolton, Malcolm Stuart Boylan, John Bright, Sidney Buchman, Lester Cole, Isabel Dawn, Boyce DeGaw, Walter de Leon, Oliver H.P. Garrett, Harvey Gates, Grover Jones, Ernst Lubitsch, Lawton MacKaill, Joseph L. Mankiewicz, William Slavens McNutt, Seton I. Miller, Tiffany Thayer. (1:28)

Classic depression-era comedy-drama of a millionaire expecting to die who chooses various unknown persons to whom he gives each a million dollars, rather than leave his fortune to his loathsome relatives. What each of the people does with their million dollars makes up the film.

2158. If I Were Free (RKO; 1933). *Cast:* Irene Dunne, Clive Brook,

Nils Asther, Henry Stephenson, Vivian Tobin, Laura Hope Crews, Tempe Pigott, Lorraine MacLean, Mario Dominici. *D:* Elliott Nugent; *As.P.:* Kenneth MacGowan; *Sc:* Dwight Taylor. (G.B. title: *Behold We Live*) (1:06)

Drama of an extramarital affair. Based on the play "Behold We Live" by John Van Druten.

2159/2160. If I Were King (Paramount; 1938). *Cast:* Ronald Colman (Villon), Frances Dee, Basil Rathbone (A.A.N. for B.S.A. as King Louis XI), Ellen Drew, Ralph Forbes, C.V. France, Henry Wilcoxon, Heather Thatcher (queen), Sidney Toler, John Miljan, William Farnum, Walter Kingsford, Montagu Love, Francis McDonald, Darryl Hickman (film debut), Lester Matthews, Fritz Leiber, William Haade, Stanley Ridges, Henry Brandon, Bruce Lester, Colin Tapley, Barry Macollum, Adrian Morris. *D:* Frank Lloyd; *P:* Lloyd; *Sc:* Preston Sturges; *Art-Set Decoration:* (A.A.N.) Hans Dreier, John Goodman; *Music:* (A.A.N.) Richard Hageman; *Sound Recording:* (A.A.N.) Loren Ryder. (1:41)

An historically inaccurate costume drama of the rogue poet Francois Villon and his confrontation with France's King Louis XI. Based on the play by Justin Huntly McCarthy it was previously filmed in 1920 with William Farnum, in 1928 as *The Beloved Rogue* and again in 1930 as Rudolph Friml's operetta *The Vagabond King* (q.v.). Remade under that title in 1956 by this studio.

2161. If You Could Only Cook (Columbia; 1935). *Cast:* Herbert Marshall, Jean Arthur, Leo Carrillo, Lionel Stander, Frieda Inescort, Alan Edwards, Gene Morgan, Ralf Harolde. *D:* William A. Seiter; *As.P.:* Everett Riskin; *St:* F. Hugh Herbert; *Sc:* Gertrude Purcell, Howard J. Green. (1:12)

Comedy of a wealthy man and a poor girl who pretend to be married so they can get jobs as domestics for a known gangster.

2162. Igloo (Universal; 1932). *Cast:* Chee-Ak, Kyatuk, Toyuk, Lanak, Nah-Shuk, Mala (film debut). *D:* Ewing Scott; *Sc:* Scott. (1:10)

Semi-documentary drama with an all native Eskimo cast which was a box office flop.

The Illegal Divorce (G.B. title) *see* **Second-Hand Wife**

2163. Illegal Traffic (Paramount; 1938). *Cast:* J. Carrol Naish, Mary Carlisle, Robert Preston, Judith Barrett, Buster Crabbe, Monte Blue, Pierre Watkin, George McKay, Philip Warren. *D:* Louis King; *P:* William Thomas; *St:* Robert Yost; *Sc:* Yost, Lewis Foster, Stuart Anthony. (1:07)

B melodrama based on part of J. Edgar Hoover's "Persons in Hiding" concerning the smuggling of criminals out of the United States to escape prosecution.

2164. Illicit (WB; 1931). *Cast:* Miss Barbara Stanwyck, James Rennie, Ricardo Cortez, Joan Blondell, Charles Butterworth, Claude Gillingwater, Natalie Moorhead. *D:* Archie Mayo; *Sc:* Harvey Thew. (1:21)

Hit tear-jerker of a marriage which is taking a turn toward indifference. Based on the play by Robert Riskin and Edith Fitzgerald it was remade in 1933 as *Ex-Lady* (q.v.).

2165. Illusion (Paramount; 1929). *Cast:* Charles "Buddy" Rogers, Nancy Carroll, Kay Francis, June Collyer, Regis Toomey, William Austin, Lillian Roth, Eugenie Besserer, Knute Erickson, Maude Turner Gordon, Eddie Kane, Emilie Melville, Frances Raymond, John E. Nash, Catherine Wallace. *D:* Lothar Mendes; *P:* B.P. Schulberg; *St:* Arthur Train; *Sc:* E. Lloyd Sheldon; *Songs:* Larry Spier.

Romantic drama from the days of vaudeville.

Imaginary Sweetheart (G.B. title) *see* **Professional Sweetheart**

2166. Imitation of Life (Universal; 1934). *Cast:* Claudette Colbert (Beatrice Pullman), Warren William (Stephen Archer), Louise Beavers (Delilah Johnson), Ned Sparks (Elmer), Rochelle Hudson (Jessie Pullman at 18), Fredi Washington (Peola Johnson at 19), Marilyn Knowlden (Jessie at 8), Dorothy Black (Peola at 9), Baby Jane (later Juanita Quigley as Jessie at 3), Sebie Hendricks (Peola at 4), Alan Hale (Martin the furniture man), Clarence Hummel Wilson (landlord), Henry Armetta (painter), Henry Kolker (Dr. Preston), Wyndham Standing (butler), Alice Ardell (French maid), Paul Porcasi (restaurant manager), Walter Walker (Hugh), Noel Francis (Mrs. Eden), Franklin Pangborn (Mr. Carven), Alma Tell (Mrs. Carven), William Austin (Englishman), Edgar Norton (butler), Hazel Washington (maid), Lenita Lane (Mrs. Dale), Reverend Gregg (minister), Curry Lee (chauffeur), Claire McDowell (teacher), Madame Sul-Te-Wan (cook), Stuart Johnston (understaker), William B. Davidson, G.P. Huntley, Jr., Tyler Brooke, Barry Norton, Joyce Compton, Fred "Snowflake" Toones, Hattie McDaniel, Bud Flanagan (Dennis O'Keefe). *D:* John M. Stahl; *P:* Carl Laemmle, Jr.; *Sc:* William Hurlbut, Preston Sturges (unc.); *Assistant Director:* (A.A.N.) Scott Beal; *Sound Recording:* (A.A.N.) Gilbert Kurland. (1:46)

Classic sentimental tear-jerker of a working mother who turns a pancake recipe into a big business. The film with its racial aspects was a huge box office hit and eventually remade in 1959 with Lana Turner. Based on the novel by Fannie Hurst, the film received an A.A.N. for Best Picture.

2167. The Impatient Maiden (Universal; 1931). *Cast:* Mae Clarke (in a role originally intended for Clara Bow), Lew Ayres, Una Merkel, John Halliday, Andy Devine, Berton Churchill, Arthur Hoyt, Ethel Griffies, Cecil Cunningham, Monte Montague, Blanche Payson, Lorin Raker. *D:* James Whale; *Sc:* Richard Schayer, Winifred Dunn. (1:12)

Comedy-drama of a surgeon who teaches a young secretary a few things about life, after saving hers. Based on the novel "The Impatient Virgin" by Donald Henderson Clarke.

The Imperfect Lady (G.B. title) *see* **The Perfect Gentleman**

2168. The Important Witness (Tower; 1933). *Cast:* Robert Ellis, Dorothy Burgess, Noel Madison, Franklin Pangborn, Charles Delaney, Noel Francis. *D:* Sam Newfield.

"Poverty row" melodrama.

The Impossible Lover (G.B. title) *see* **Huddle**

2169. In Caliente (WB/F.N.; 1935). *Cast:* Dolores Del Rio, Pat O'Brien, Edward Everett Horton, Leo Carrillo, Glenda Farrell, Judy Canova (in her film debut with her family), Phil Regan, Winifred Shaw, Herman Bing, Luis Alberni, the elegant de Marcos, Katherine de Mille, Dorothy Dare, George Humbert. *D:* Lloyd Bacon; *St:* Ralph Block, Warren Duff; *Sc:* Jerry Wald, Julius J. Epstein; *Songs:* title song, "The Lady in Red" and "To Call You My Own" by Mort Dixon and Allie Wrubel, and "Muchacha" by Al Dubin and Harry Warren. (1:25)

Romantic musical of a hot tempered Mexican dancer and a magazine critic. Choreography by Busby Berkeley includes a production number of "The Lady in Red."

2170. In Defense of the Law (Xxxx Xxxx; 1931). (No information available)

2171. In Early Arizona (Columbia; 1938). *Cast:* Bill Elliott, Dorothy Gulliver, Harry Woods, Art Davis, Jack Ingram, Franklyn Farnum, Charles King, Ed Cassidy, Slim Whitaker, Frank Ellis, Al Ferguson, Bud Osborne, Lester Dorr, Tom London, Kit Guard, Jack O'Shea, Frank Ball, Tex Palmer, Sherry Tansey, Dick Dorrell, Oscar Gahan, Buzz Barton, Jess Cavan. *D:* Joseph Levering; *Sc:* Nate Gatzert. (0:53)

Bill Elliott western (his starring debut) of a lawman's attempts to clean up a corrupt town.

2172. In Gay Madrid (MGM; 1930). *Cast:* Ramon Novarro (in his 2nd talkie), Lottice Howell, Dorothy Jordan, William V. Mong, Beryl Mercer, Eugenie Besserer, George Chandler, Claude King, Herbert Clark, Nanci Price, David Scott, Bruce Coleman, Nicholas Caruso. *D:* Robert Z. Leonard; *P:* Leonard; *Sc:* Edwin Justus Mayer, Bess Meredyth, Salisbury Field.

Musical-comedy of a Spanish law student with girl problems.

2173. In His Steps (Grand National; 1936). *Cast:* Eric Linden, Cecilia Parker, Olive Tell, Clara Blandick, Henry Kolker, Charles Richman, Harry Beresford, Roger Imhof, Robert Warwick, Warner Richmond, Donald Kirke, Stanley Andrews. *D:* Karl Brown; *P:* B. (Bennie) F. Zeidman; *Sc:* Brown; *Additional Dialogue:* Hinton Smith. (aka: *Sins of the Children*) (1:19)

This was the first production release of this newly organized studio, noted for its low-budget productions. It was an inspirational type drama of love and life and was a box office success. Based on the best seller novel by the Reverend Charles M. Sheldon.

2174. In Line of Duty (Monogram; 1931). *Cast:* Sue Carol, Noah Beery, Francis McDonald, James Murray, Richard Cramer, Frank Seider, Henry Hall. *D:* Bert Glennon; *St:* George Arthur Durlam; *Sc:* Durlam. (1:04)

A Canadian Mountie falls for the daughter of the man he has sworn to bring to justice in this low-budget outdoor drama.

2175. In Love with Life (Chesterfield; 1934). *Cast:* Lila Lee, Lloyd Ingraham, Onslow Stevens, William Arnold, Dickie Moore, Clarence Geldart, Betty Kendig, Milla Davenport, Claude Gillingwater, Tom Ricketts, James T. Mack, Rosita Marstini. *D:* Frank Strayer; *St & Sc:* Robert Ellis. (G.B. title: *Re-Union*)

"Poverty row" drama.

2176. In Name Only (RKO; 1939). *Cast:* Carole Lombard, Cary Grant, Kay Francis, Charles Coburn, Helen Vinson, Katherine Alexander, Jonathan Hale, Nella Walker, Alan Baxter, Maurice Moscovich, Peggy Ann Garner, Grady Sutton, Spencer Charters, Byron Foulger. *D:* John Cromwell; *P:* George Haight; *Sc:* Richard Sherman. (1:34) (video)

Hit romantic drama of a man who seeks a divorce so he can marry another. Based on the novel "Memory of Love" by Bessie Breuer.

2177. In Old Arizona (Fox; 1928). *Cast:* Warner Baxter (A.A. for B.A. in his talkie debut as the Cisco Kid), Edmund Lowe (Sgt. Mickey Dunn), Dorothy Burgess (in her film debut as Tonia Maria), J. Farrell MacDonald (Tad), Ivan Linow (immigrant), Soledad Jimenez (cook), Henry Armetta (barber), Fred Warren (piano player), James Marcus (blacksmith), Roy Stewart (in his talkie debut as the commandant), Alphonse Ethier (sheriff), Frank Campeau, Tom Santschi, Frank Nelson, Duke Martin, Pat Hartigan, James Bradbury, Jr., John (Jack) Dillon, Joe Brown, Lola Salvi, Edward Peil, Sr., Helen Lynch. *D:* (A.A.N.) Raoul Walsh who was originally to play "The Kid" until an accident prior to production cost him an eye and Irving Cummings; *Sc:* (A.A.N.) Tom Barry (1928–29); *Cinematography:* (A.A.N.) Arthur Edeson. (1:35)

Based on O'Henry's character "The Cisco Kid," a Robin Hood-bandit from the story "The Caballero's Way." Premiering on Christmas day of 1928, this was Fox's first all-talkie and also the first all-talkie to use the "sound on film" process as opposed to Warner's and others "sound on disc." Also the first film to utilize outdoor location shooting. The film received an A.A.N. for Best Picture and placed #7 on the "10 Best" list of *Film Daily* in 1929.

Note: *The Cisco Kid* (Fox; 1931) (q.v.) was the sequel to this film. Some sources erroneously list *The Arizona Kid* (Fox; 1930) (q.v.) as the sequel.

2178. In Old Caliente (Republic; 1939). *Cast:* Roy Rogers, Mary Hart (Lynn Roberts), George "Gabby" Hayes, Jack LaRue, Katherine de Mille, Frank Puglia, Harry Woods, Merrill McCormack, Paul Marion, Ethel Wales. *D:* Joe Kane; *Sc:* Norman Houston, Gerald Geraghty (0:57) (video)

Roy Rogers western of a cowboy who discovers the party behind some cattle rustling.

2179. In Old California (Audible Pictures; 1929). *Cast:* Henry B. Walthall, Helen Ferguson, George Duryca (Tom Kccnc). *D:* Burton King.

Low-budget western.

2180. In Old Cheyenne (Sono Art-World Wide; 1931). *Cast:* Rex Lease, Dorothy Gulliver, Jay Hunt, Harry Woods, Harry Todd, Slim Whitaker. *D:* Stuart Paton; *Sc:* Betty Burbridge. (1:00) (video)

Rex Lease horse opera dealing with the taming of a wild stallion.

2181. In Old Chicago (20th Century-Fox; 1937). *Cast:* Tyrone Power (Dion O'Leary), Alice Faye (Belle Faw-cett), Don Ameche (Jack O'Leary), Alice Brady (A.A. for B.S.A. as Mrs. Molly O'Leary), Andy Devine (Pickle Bixby), Brian Donlevy (Gil Warren), Tom Brown (Bob O'Leary), Phyllis Brooks (Ann Colby), June Storey (Gretchen O'Leary), Berton Churchill (Senator Colby), Madame Sul-Te-Wan (Hattie), Sidney Blackmer (Gen. Phil Sheridan), Paul Hurst (Mitch), J. Anthony Hughes (Patrick O'Leary), Tyler Brooke (specialty singer), Rondo Hatton (bodyguard), Thelma Manning (Carrie Donahue), Ruth Gillette (Miss Lou), Gene Reynolds (Dion the child), Bobs Watson (film debut as Bob the child), Billy Watson (Jack the child), Spencer Charters (Beavers), Eddie Collins (film debut as the drunk), Scotty Mattraw (Beef King), Joe Twerp, Charles Lane, Clarence Hummel Wilson, Harry Stubbs, Frank Dae, Francis Ford, Joe King, Robert Murphy, Wade Boteler, Russell Hicks, Gustav von Seyffertitz, Harry Hayden, Vera Lewis, Minerva Urecal, Ed Brady. *D:* Henry King; *P:* Darryl F. Zanuck; *As.P.:* Kenneth MacGowan; *Original Story:* (A.A.N.) Niven Busch's "We the O'Learys"; *Sc:* Lamar Trotti, Sonya Levien; *Assistant Director:* (A.A.) Robert Webb; *Music:* (A.A.N.) Musical director Louis Silvers; *Sound Recording:* (A.A.N.) E.H. Hansen. (1:55) (video – 1:35)

Classic comedy-drama with songs and an ultra-lavish production set in 19th-century Chicago amidst the fictionalized lives of the O'Leary family from the time they settled there until the great fire of 1871 razed the city. The film was originally released at a running time of (1:55), but current TV and video prints are missing twenty minutes of the original footage which consisted of extra musical numbers. One of the 15 top grossing films of 1937–38 it received an A.A.N. for Best Picture, as well as being in nomination for "Best Picture of the Year" by the New York Film Critics. On the "10 Best" list of *Film Daily* in 1938 it placed #6. Fox embarked on this venture when it saw the profits raked in by MGM's *San Francisco* (q.v.). The "Chicago Fire" special effects were directed by H. Bruce Humberstone, photographed by Daniel B. Clark and staged by Fred Sersen, Ralph Hammeras and Louis J. Witte.

2182. In Old Kentucky (Fox; 1935). *Cast:* Will Rogers (Steve Tapley — final film), Dorothy Wilson (Nancy Martingale), Russell Hardie (Lee Andrews), Bill "Bojangles" Robinson (Wash Jackson), Louise Henry (Arlene Shattuck), Alan Dinehart (Slick Doherty), Charles Sellon (Ezra Martingale), Charles Richman (Pole Shattuck), Etienne Girardot (rainmaker), Esther Dale (Dolly Breckenridge), John Ince (sheriff), Everett Sullivan (jailer), Fritz Johannet, Bobby Rose, Eddie Tamblyn (jockies), Edward Le Saint, Allan Cavan, Stanley Andrews (stewards), G. Raymond "Bill" Nye, William J. Worthington, Dora Clement, Ned Norton. *D:* George Marshall; *P:* Edward Butcher; *St:* Charles T. Dazey; *Sc:* Gladys Lehman, Sam Hellman. (1:26)

Folksey rural drama of a family feud. This film was one of the 25 top grossing films of 1935–36 and is notable as the final film of popular humorist-film star Will Rogers prior to his being killed in a plane crash in 1935. Previously filmed in 1920 by director Marshall Neilan for Associated Producers and again by Fox in 1927.

2183. In Old Mexico (Paramount; 1938). *Cast:* Bill Boyd (Hoppy), Russell Hayden (Lucky), George "Gabby" Hayes (Windy), Jane (Jan) Clayton, Glenn Strange, Trevor Bardette, Paul Sutton, Allan Garcia, Betty Amann, Anna Demetrio, Tony Roux, Fred Burns. *D:* Edward D. Venturini; *P:* Harry M. Sherman; *Sc:* Harrison Jacobs. (1:02)

The 18th "Hopalong Cassidy" feature with the Bar 20 boys in New Mexico after a gang of cattle rustlers

led by an individual known as "The Fox."

2184. In Old Montana (Spectrum; 1939). *Cast:* Fred Scott, Jean Carmen (Julia Thayer), John Merton, Harry Harvey, Walter McGrail, Wheeler Oakman, Gene Howard, Frank LaRue, Allan Cavan, Jane Keckley, James Kelly, Richard Cramer, Carl Mathews. *D:* Raymond K. Johnson; *P:* C.C. Burr; *Sc:* Johnson, Jackson Parks, Homer King Gordon, Barney Hutchinson. (1:00)

Fred Scott western with songs involving a story of feuding sheepmen and cattlemen and Montana statehood.

2185. In Old Monterey (Republic; 1939). *Cast:* Gene Autry, Smiley Burnette, George "Gabby" Hayes, June Storey, Hoosier Hot Shots, Sarie & Sally, Ranch Boys, Stuart Hamblen, Billy Lee, Jonathan Hale, Robert Warwick, William Hall, Eddie Conrad, Curley Dresden, Ken Carson, Victor Cox, Robert Wilke, Hal Price, Tom Steele, Jack O'Shea, Rex Lease, Edward Earle, Jim Mason, Fred Burns, Dan White, Frank Ellis, Jim Corey, Champion. *D:* Joseph Kane; *P:* Armand Schaefer; *St:* George Sherman, Gerald Geraghty; *Sc:* Geraghty, Dorrell & Stuart McGowan. (1:14)

Gene Autry western with songs and a story of local ranchers in conflict with the local military.

2186. In Old Santa Fe (Mascot; 1934). *Cast:* Ken Maynard (Kentucky), Evalyn Knapp, H.B. Warner, George Hayes, Tarzan (Maynard's horse), Kenneth Thomson, George Chesebro, George Burton, Jack Rockwell, Wheeler Oakman, Gene Autry (film debut), Lester "Smiley" Burnette (feature film debut), Cliff Lyons, Edward Hearn, Stanley Blystone, Frank Ellis. *D:* David Howard; *P:* Nat Levine; *Supervisor:* Victor Zobel; *St:* Wallace MacDonald, John Rathmell; *Sc:* James Gruen, Colbert Clark. (1:07)

Ken Maynard western of a cowboy who outwits some city dudes. This was Maynard's only feature for this studio.

2187. In Paris A.W.O.L. (Xxxx Xxxx; 1936). (No information available)

2188. In Person (RKO; 1935). *Cast:* Ginger Rogers, George Brent, Alan Mowbray, Grant Mitchell, Samuel S. Hinds, Joan Breslau, Louis Mason, Spencer Charters, Edgar Kennedy. *D:* William A. Seiter; *P:* Pandro S. Berman; *Sc:* Allan Scott (based on the novel by Samuel Hopkins Adams); *Songs:* Oscar Levant, Dorothy Fields. (1:27) (video)

A much sought after film star flees the spotlight for some R. & R. and finds romance.

2189. In Spite of Danger (Columbia; 1935). *Cast:* Wallace Ford, Marian Marsh, Charley Grapewin, Charles Middleton, Dick Wessel. *D:* Lambert Hillyer.

B melodrama.

In Strange Company (G.B. title) *see* **First Aid**

2190. In the Headlines (WB; 1929). *Cast:* Grant Withers, Marion Nixon, Clyde Cook, Edmund Breese, Pauline Garon, Frank Campeau, Vivian Oakland, Hallam Cooley, Spec O'Donnell. *D:* John Adolfi; *St:* James A. Starr; *Sc:* Joseph Jackson.

B crime melodrama of newsreporters investigating a double murder.

2191. In the Money (Chesterfield; 1933–34). *Cast:* Lois Wilson, Skeets Gallagher, Warren Hymer, Louise Beavers, Frank (Junior) Coghlan, Arthur Hoyt. *D:* Frank Strayer.

"Poverty row" comedy.

2192. In the Next Room (WB/ F.N. — Vitaphone; 1930). *Cast:* Alice Day, Jack Mulhall, John St. Polis, Jane Winton, Edward Earle, Claud Allister,

DeWitt Jennings, Robert Emmett O'Connor, Aggie Herring, Lucien Prival, Webster Campbell, Crauford Kent. *D:* Edward Cline; *Sc:* Harvey Gates, James A. Starr.

Low-budget murder-mystery set in an old dark house. Based on the play by Harriet Ford and Eleanor Robson Belmont.

2193. India Speaks (RKO/Futter Corp.; 1933). *P:* Walter Futter; *Dialogue:* Norman Houston.

Narrated by and starring Richard Halliburton, this travelogue-documentary of India (with some staged scenes) is an independent production of the Futter Corporation.

Indian Love Call *see* **Rose-Marie**

2194. Indianapolis Speedway (WB; 1939). *Cast:* Pat O'Brien, Ann Sheridan, John Payne, Gale Page, Frank McHugh, John Ridgely, Regis Toomey, Grace Stafford, Granville Bates, Edward McWade, William Davidson, John Harron (final film — d. 1939, age 36), Charles Halton, Robert Middlemass. *D:* Lloyd Bacon; *As.P.:* Max Siegel; *St:* Howard Hawks, William Hawks; *Sc:* Sig Herzig, Wally Klein. (G.B. title: *Devil on Wheels*) (1:22)

An auto-racing drama which is a remake of *The Crowd Roars* (1932 — q.v.).

2195. Indiscreet (United Artists/ Art Cinema; 1931). *Cast:* Gloria Swanson, Ben Lyon, Monroe Owsley, Barbara Kent, Arthur Lake, Maude Eburne, Henry Kolker, Nella Walker. *D:* Leo McCarey; *P:* Joseph M. Schenck; *Sc:* B.G. "Buddy" DeSylva, Lew Brown, Ray Henderson; *Songs:* DeSylva, Brown & Henderson. (1:32) (video — 1:21)

Triangular romantic comedy-drama involving two sisters. A box office hit of its day, shorter prints are seen on TV.

2196. Infernal Machine (Fox; 1933). *Cast:* Chester Morris, Genevieve

Tobin, J. Carrol Naish, Edward Van Sloan, Victor Jory, Mischa Auer, James Bell, Leonard Carey, Elizabeth Patterson, Arthur Hohl, Josephine Whittell, Robert Littlefield. *D:* Marcel Varnel; *St:* Carl Sloboda.

Low-budget production.

The Information Kid *see* **Fast Companions**

2197. The Informer (RKO; 1935). *Cast:* Victor McLaglen (A.A. for B.A. as Gypo Nolan), Heather Angel (Mary McPhillip), Preston Foster (Dan Gallagher), Margot Grahame (American debut as Katie Madden), Wallace Ford (Frankie McPhillip), Una O'Connor (Mrs. McPhillip), J.M. Kerrigan (Terry), Joseph (Sawyer) Sauers (Mulholland), Neil Fitzgerald (Tommy O'Connor), Donald Meek (Peter Mulligan), D'Arcy Corrigan (blind man), Leo McCabe (Donahue), Gaylord (Steve) Pendleton (Dennis Daly), Francis Ford (Flynn), May Boley ("Aunt" Betty), Denis O'Dea (street singer), Grizelda Harvey, Jack Mulhall, Bob Parrish, Anne O'Neal, Frank Moran, Cornelius Keefe, Eddy Chandler, Pat Moriarty, Frank Marlowe, Harry Tenbrook, Robert E. Homans, Frank Hagney, Bob Perry, Pat Somerset. *D:* John Ford (A.A. as Best Director and voted "Best Director of the Year" by the New York Film Critics); *As.P.:* Cliff Reid; *Sc:* (A.A.) Dudley Nichols for screenplay adaptation; *Music:* (A.A.) Max Steiner; *Editor:* (A.A.N.) George Hively. (1:31) (video)

Classic drama set in 1922 Ireland of a man who informs on a friend for a price and the guilt and persecution that he suffers afterward. At a production cost of $243,000, this turned into a bonanza for the studio. It received an A.A.N. for Best Picture, placed #3 on the "10 Best" list of *Film Daily,* while being voted "Best Film of the Year" by the New York Film Critics, the New York Times and the National Board of Review. It was also in nomination for "Best

Film" at the Venice Film Festival. Based on the 1925 book by Liam O'Flaherty, it was previously filmed in Great Britain in 1929 with Lars Hanson. Remade in 1968 by Paramount with an all-black cast as *Uptight!*

Note: An interesting side-note to this film is the fact that studio heads at RKO were dissatisfied with Ford's final product and were going to shelve it, rather than release it.

2198. Ingagi (Road Show Productions; 1930). An African "documentary" photographed by George Summerton and Harold Williams.

Injustice (G.B. title) *see* **Road Gang**

2199. Innocents of Paris (Paramount; 1929). *Cast:* Maurice Chevalier (feature American debut), Sylvia Beecher, Russell Simpson, George Fawcett, David Durand, John Miljan, Margaret Livingston, Jack Luden, Mrs. George Fawcett, Johnny Morris. *D:* Richard Wallace; *St:* Charles E. Andrews; *Sc:* Ernest Vajda, Ethel Doherty; *Songs Include:* "Louise" by Richard A. Whiting & Leo Robin. (1:09)

Musical of a junk dealer who saves a child from drowning in the Seine River and proceeds to romance his aunt. Paramount's first musical.

2200. Inside Information (Stage & Screen; 1939). *Cast:* Rex Lease, Marion Shilling. *D:* Robert F. Hill.

"Poverty row" crime drama.

2201. Inside Information (Universal; 1939). *Cast:* Dick Foran, June Lang, Harry Carey, Rex Lease, Jean Porter, Philo McCullough, Paul McVey, Jimmy Aubrey, Grant Richards. *D:* Charles Lamont; *P:* Irving Starr. (1:02)

A "Crime Club" series entry of a rookie cop who insists on doing things his way.

2202. Inside Story (20th Century–Fox; 1938–39). *Cast:* Michael

Whalen, Jean Rogers, Chick Chandler, Louise Carter, Douglas Fowley, Jane Darwell, Charles Lane. *D:* Ricardo Cortez; *P:* Sol M. Wurtzel.

The third and final entry in the "Roving Reporters" series which has the reporters coming to the aid of a girl who is in hiding after witnessing a gangland killing.

2203. Inside the Lines (RKO; 1930). *Cast:* Betty Compson, Ralph Forbes, Montagu Love, Ivan Simpson, Reginald Sharland, Betty Carter, Mischa Auer, Evan Thomas, William von Brincken. *D:* Roy Pomeroy; *As.P.:* Pomeroy; *Sc:* Ewart Adamson, John Farrow. (1:16) (video)

The enemy attempts to destroy the British fleet in this World War I espionage drama. Set in 1914 Germany, it is based on the novel by Earl Derr Biggers.

2204. Inspiration (MGM; 1931). *Cast:* Greta Garbo, Robert Montgomery, Lewis Stone, Marjorie Rambeau, Judith Vosselli, Beryl Mercer, John Miljan, Edwin Maxwell, Oscar Apfel, Joan Marsh, Zelda Sears, Karen Morley, Gwen Lee, Paul McAllister, Arthur Hoyt, Richard Tucker. *D:* Clarence Brown; *P:* Brown; *Sc:* Gene Markey. (1:14)

A woman with a past is working as an artist's model in this romantic drama.

2205. Interference (Paramount; 1928–29). *Cast:* Clive Brook, Evelyn Brent (talkie debut), William Powell, Doris Kenyon, Brandon Hurst, Clyde Cook, Raymond Lawrence, Wilfred Noy, Louis Payne, Donald Stuart. *D:* Roy Pomeroy; *Sc:* Hope Loring, Ernest Pascal (based on the play by Roland Pertwee and Harold Dearden. (1:15)

This studio's first all-talkie is a mystery where blackmail and murder surround the return of a man thought killed in the war.

Intermezzo *see* **Intermezzo, A Love Story**

2206. Intermezzo, A Love Story (United Artists/Selznick International; 1939). *Cast:* Leslie Howard (final American film), Ingrid Bergman (American film debut recreating her role in the '36 Swedish production), Edna Best, Cecil Kellaway, John Halliday, Douglas Scott, Eleanor Wesselhoeft, Enid Bennett, Ann (E.) Todd, Maria Flynn. *D:* Gregory Ratoff; *P:* David O. Selznick; *As.P.:* Leslie Howard; *Sc:* George O'Neil (based on the original Swedish scenario by Gosta Stevens and Gustave Molander); *Music:* (A.A.N.) Lou Forbes. (G.B. title: *Escape to Happiness*) (Retitled: *Intermezzo*) (1:10) (video)

The story of a romantic affair between a pianist and a married violinist. A hit film at the box office with its hit love theme by Robert Henning and Heinz Provost. Previously filmed in Sweden in 1936.

2207. International Crime (Grand National; 1938). *Cast:* Rod La Rocque ("The Shadow"), Astrid Allwyn, Thomas Jackson, Oscar O'Shea, William von Brincken, William Pawley, Walter (Bohn) Bonn, William Moore, Lew Hearn, Tenen Holtz, John St. Polis, Lloyd Whitlock, Jack Baxley. *D:* Charles Lamont; *P:* Max & Arthur Alexander; *Sc:* Jack Natteford; *Additional Dialogue:* John Krafft. (1:00)

Low-budget melodrama with "The Shadow" confronting some international spies. Based on stories of "The Shadow" by Maxwell Grant (Walter B. Gibson).

2208. International House (Paramount; 1933). *Cast:* W.C. Fields, George Burns, Gracie Allen, Peggy Hopkins Joyce, Stuart Erwin, Bela Lugosi, Sari Maritza, Edmund Breese, Rudy Vallee, Franklin Pangborn, Sterling Holloway, Baby Rose Marie, Cab Calloway and his orchestra, Lumsden Hare, Colonel Stoopnagle & Budd. *D:* A. Edward Sutherland; *P:* Albert E.

Lewis; *St:* Lou Heifetz, Harrison Greene; *Sc:* Heifetz, Francis Martin, Walter DeLeon, Neil Brant; *Songs:* Ralph Rainger, Leo Robin. (1:13) (video)

Classic all-star madcap comedy of various people who congregate at a hotel in Shanghai with an offbeat plot involving a perfected television experiment. A gigantic hit for the studio.

2209. International Settlement (20th Century–Fox; 1938). *Cast:* George Sanders, Dolores Del Rio, June Lang, Dick Baldwin, Leon Ames, Ruth Terry, John Carradine, Harold Huber, Keye Luke, Pedro de Cordoba. *D:* Eugene Forde; *P:* Sol M. Wurtzel; *St:* Frank Fenton, Lynn Root; *Sc:* Lou Breslow, John Patrick. (1:15)

Melodramatic actioner of smuggling in the orient.

International Spy *see* **The Spy Ring**

2210. Internes Can't Take Money (Paramount; 1937). *Cast:* Joel McCrea (Dr. Kildare), Barbara Stanwyck, Lloyd Nolan, Stanley Ridges, Lee Bowman (film debut), Irving Bacon, Pierre Watkin, Charles Lane, Fay Holden, Terry Ray (Ellen Drew), Gaylord (Steve) Pendleton, Barry Macollum. *D:* Alfred Santell; *P:* Benjamin Glazer; *Sc:* Rian James, Theodore Reeves. (G.B. title: *You Can't Take Money*) (1:15)

This is the B film which introduced "Dr. Kildare" (without Dr. Gillespie) to film audiences and is not part of the hit series created by MGM the following year beginning with *Young Dr. Kildare* (q.v.). A box office hit that was based on the story by Max Brand.

2211. The Intruder (Allied; 1932–33). *Cast:* Monte Blue, Lila Lee, Gwen Lee. *D:* Albert Ray; *P:* M.H. Hoffman, Jr.; *Sc:* Frances Hyland.

"Poverty row" murder drama.

2212. Invisible Enemy (Republic; 1938). *Cast:* Alan Marshal, Tala

Birell, C. Henry Gordon, Herbert Mundin, Ivan Simpson, Ian McLaren, Egon Brecher, Elsa Buchanan, Mady Correll, Leonard Willie, Dwight Frye, Gerald Oliver Smith. *D:* John H. Auer; *St:* Robert T. Shannon, Albert J. Cohen; *Sc:* Cohen, Alex Gottlieb, Norman Burnstine.

B melodrama.

2213. The Invisible Killer (Producers Distributing Corporation; 1939). *Cast:* Grace Bradley, Roland Drew, William Newell, Alex Callam, Jeanne Kelly (Jean Brooks), Sidney Grayler, Boyd Irwin, David Oliver, Harry Worth, Ernie Adams. *D:* Sherman Scott (Sam Newfield); *P:* Ben Judell; *Sc:* Joseph O'Donnell. (1:03)

B mystery-melodrama of two reporters investigating a series of murders. Based on the novel "Murder for Millions" by Carter Wayne, the film had the working title of "Wanted for Murder."

2214. The Invisible Man (Universal; 1933). *Cast:* Claude Rains (film debut as Dr. Griffin), Gloria Stuart, Una O'Connor, William Harrigan, E.E. Clive (film debut), Henry Travers, Dudley Digges, Dwight Frye, Holmes Herbert, Forrester Harvey, John Peter Richmond (John Carradine), Walter Brennan, John Merivale, Donald Stuart, Merle Tottenham, Harry Stubbs. *D:* James Whale; *P:* Carl Laemmle, Jr.; *Sc:* R.C. Sherriff, Philip Wylie (unc.). (1:11) (video)

Classic fantasy of a man who discovers the secret to invisibility and goes mad with his delusions about taking over the world. Based on the book by H.G. Wells, it placed #9 on the "10 Best" list of the *New York Times*. Followed in 1940 by the sequel *The Invisible Man Returns*. Remade in 1975 as a TV movie which was also a pilot for a TV series.

Note: Watch for the footprints in the snow and figure out what is wrong with them.

2215. The Invisible Menace (WB; 1937–38). *Cast:* Boris Karloff

Regis Toomey, Henry Kolker, Cy Kendall, Charles Trowbridge, Eddie Acuff, Frank Faylen, Harland Tucker, William Haade, John Ridgely, Jack Mower, Anderson Lawler, John Harron, Willard Parker. *D:* John Farrow; *As.P.:* Bryan Foy; *Sc:* Crane Wilbur. (aka: *Without Warning*) (0:55)

Programmer murder-mystery set on an island military base. Based on the play by Ralph Spencer Zink, it was remade by this studio in 1943 as *Murder on the Waterfront*.

Invisible Power (G.B. title) *see* **Washington Merry-Go-Round**

2216. The Invisible Ray (Universal; 1936). *Cast:* Boris Karloff, Bela Lugosi, Frances Drake, Frank Lawton, Walter Kingsford, Beulah Bondi, Violet Kemble-Cooper, Nydia Westman, Frank Reicher, Daniel Haynes. *D:* Lambert Hillyer; *P:* Edmund Grainger; *St:* Howard Higgin, Douglas Hodges; *Sc:* John Colton. (1:21) (video)

Following an experiment a mild-mannered scientist slowly becomes a madman.

2217. Invisible Stripes (WB; 1939). *Cast:* George Raft, Humphrey Bogart, William Holden, Jane Bryan, Flora Robson, Paul Kelly, Henry O'Neill, Lee Patrick, Moroni Olsen, Tully Marshall, Marc Lawrence, Joseph Downing, William Haade, DeWolf (William) Hopper. *D:* Lloyd Bacon; *As.P.:* Louis Edelman; *Sc:* Warren Duff. (1:22)

A flop for the studio was this melodrama of an ex-con who finds difficulty going straight after his release from prison. Based on a book by Warden Lewis E. Lawes.

2218. Invitation to Happiness (Paramount; 1939). *Cast:* Irene Dunne, Fred MacMurray, Charles Ruggles, Billy Cook, William Collier, Sr., Marion Martin, Eddie Hogan, Oscar O'Shea, Burr Caruth. *D:* Wesley Ruggles; *P:* Ruggles; *St:* Mark Jerome; *Sc:* Claude Binyon. (1:35)

Drama of the marriage between a society girl and an ambitious boxer. A hit at the box office.

Irish and Proud of It (G.B. title) *see* **King Kelly of the U.S.A.**

2219. The Irish Gringo (Keith Productions; 1936). *Cast:* Pat Carlyle, William Farnum, Bryant Washburn. *D:* William Thompson.

Low-budget independent western with a "Cisco Kid" type of hero.

2220. The Irish in Us (WB/F.N.; 1935). *Cast:* James Cagney, Pat O'Brien, Olivia de Havilland, Frank McHugh, Mary Gordon, Allen Jenkins, J. Farrell MacDonald, Thomas Jackson. *D:* Lloyd Bacon; *P:* Samuel Bischoff; *Sc:* Earl Baldwin. (1:23)

A sentimental comedy of three brothers and their friendly rivalry. Based on a story by Frank Orsatti.

2221. Irish Luck (Monogram; 1939). *Cast:* Frankie Darro, Dick Purcell, Lillian Elliott, Sheila Darcy, Mantan Moreland, James Flavin, Dennis Moore, Howard Mitchell. *D:* Howard Bretherton; *P:* Grant Withers; *St:* Charles M. Brown; *Sc:* Mary McCarthy. (G.B. title: *Amateur Detective*) (0:58)

A bellhop who yearns to be a detective goes after a gang that is selling hot bonds. This was the first entry in a popular low budget mystery-comedy series starring Frankie Darro and Mantan Moreland.

2222. Iron Man (Universal; 1931). *Cast:* Lew Ayres, Jean Harlow, Robert Armstrong, John Miljan, Eddie Dillon, Ned Sparks, Mary Doran, Mike Donlin, Morrie Cohan, Mildred Van Dorn, Sam Blum, Sammy Gervon. *D:* Tod Browning; *P:* Carl Laemmle, Jr.; *Sc:* Francis Edwards Faragoh. (1:13)

A naive boxer is a dupe for his

money-mad girl friend. A melodrama based on the novel "The Iron Man" by W.R. Burnett. Remade as *Some Blondes Are Dangerous* (q.v.) and again in 1951 under the original title.

2223. The Iron Mask (United Artists; 1928–29). *Cast:* Douglas Fairbanks, Belle Bennett, Marguerite de la Motte, Dorothy Revier, Vera Lewis, William Bakewell, Ullrich Haupt, Nigel de Brulier, Robert Parrish, Henry Otto, Stanley Sandford, Rolfe Sedan, Charles Stevens, Gordon Thorpe. *D:* Allan Dwan; *P:* Douglas Fairbanks; *Sc:* Elton Thomas (D. Fairbanks); *Art-Set Decoration:* (A.A.N.) William Cameron Menzies. (1:27) (video)

The classic story of twin brothers at the time of King Louis XIV in France. Early prints of this film had talkie sequences which were later removed. Based on the novel by Alexander Dumas, it was remade as *The Man in the Iron Mask* (q.v.), the title of Dumas' original work.

2224. The Iron Master (Allied; 1932–33). *Cast:* Reginald Denny, Lila Lee, Astrid Allwyn, J. Farrell MacDonald, William Janney, Ronnie Cosbey, Freddie Burke Frederick, Virginia Sale, Richard Tucker, Esther Howard, Otto Hoffman, Tom London, Nola Luxford. *D:* Chester Franklin; *P:* M.H. Hoffman, Jr.; *St:* Georges Ohnet; *Sc:* Adele Buffington.

Low-budget melodrama.

2225. Is Everybody Happy? (WB; 1929). *Cast:* Ted Lewis, Alice Day, Ann Pennington, Lawrence Grant, Julia Swayne Gordon, Otto Hoffman, Purnell Pratt. *D:* Archie Mayo; *St & Sc:* Joseph Jackson, James A. Starr; *Songs:* "Wouldn't It Be Wonderful?" "I'm the Medicine Man for the Blues," "Samoa," and "New Orleans" by Harry Akst and Grant Clarke; "In the Land of Jazz" and "Start the Band" by Ted Lewis; "St. Louis Blues" by W.C. Handy; and "Tiger Rag" by Jelly Roll Morton, Nick La Rocca. (1:20)

Musical drama of a down and out horn player who emerges victorious. Remade by Columbia in 1943.

2226. Is My Face Red? (RKO; 1932). *Cast:* Helen Twelvetrees, Ricardo Cortez, Jill Esmond, Robert Armstrong, Arline Judge, ZaSu Pitts, Clarence Muse, Sidney Toler, Fletcher Norton. *D:* William A. Seiter; *As.P.:* Harry Joe Brown; *Sc:* Ben Markson, Casey Robinson. (1:06)

B drama of a newspaper columnist who deals in scandal. Based on the play by Ben Markson and Allen Rivkin.

2227. Is There Justice? (Tiffany; 1931). *Cast:* Rex Lease, Helen Foster, Robert Ellis, Joseph Girard. *D:* Stuart Paton.

"Poverty row" melodrama.

2228. Island Captives (Principal; 1937). *Cast:* Eddie Nugent, Joan Barclay. *D:* Glenn Kershner; *P:* Sol Lesser; *Sc:* Al Martin.

"Poverty row" crime drama.

2229. Island in the Sky (20th Century-Fox; 1938). *Cast:* Paul Kelly, Michael Whalen, Gloria Stuart, Leon Ames, Paul Hurst, Paula Stone, Willard Robertson, George Humbert, June Storey, Aggie Herring, Robert Kellard. *D:* Herbert I. Leeds; *St:* Jerry Cady; *Sc:* Albert Ray, Frances Hyland.

B action drama.

2230. Island of Lost Men (Paramount; 1939). *Cast:* Anna May Wong, J. Carrol Naish, Broderick Crawford, Anthony Quinn, Eric Blore, Ernest Truex, William Haade, Richard Loo. *D:* Kurt Neumann; *P:* Eugene Zukor; *St:* Norman Reilly Raine; *Sc:* Horace McCoy, William R. Lipman. (1:04)

A girl searches for her father along the waterfront in this B melodrama.

2231. Island of Lost Souls (Paramount; 1933). *Cast:* Charles Laughton (Dr. Moreau), Bela Lugosi, Richard

Arlen, Kathleen Burke, Stanley Fields, Leila Hyams, George Irving, Paul Hurst, Tetsu Komai, Arthur Hohl, Joe Bonomo, John George, Robert Kortman, Hans Steinke, Rosemary Grimes, Harry Ekezian, Alan Ladd (bit), Randolph Scott (bit), Larry "Buster" Crabbe (film debut—bit). *D:* Erle C. Kenton; *Sc:* Waldemar Young, Philip Wylie. (1:14)

Classic horror shocker of its day as a mad doctor transforms animals into half-human creatures. Based on H.G. Wells' 1896 story "The Island of Dr. Moreau," the film was a box office flop. Remade in 1977 as *The Island of Dr. Moreau.*

2232. Isle of Destiny (RKO/Fine Arts Pictures; 1939–40). *Cast:* William Gargan, June Lang, Wallace Ford, Gilbert Roland, Katherine de Mille, Grant Richards, Etienne Girardot, Tom Dugan, Harry Woods, Ted Osborne. *D:* Elmer Clifton; *P:* Franklyn Warner; *St:* Allan Vaughan Elston; *Sc:* Arthur Hoerl, M. Coates Webster, Robert Lively.

Filmed in Cosmocolor, this low-budget South Sea Island actioner of two marines who help a downed lady flyer was originally to be released through Grand National.

2233. Isle of Escape (WB; 1930). *Cast:* Monte Blue, Betty Compson, Noah Beery, Nena Quartero, Duke Kahanamoku, Myrna Loy, Rose Dione. *D:* H.P. (Howard) Bretherton; *St:* Mack McLaren; *Sc:* Lucien Hubbard, J. Grubb Alexander; *Song:* "My Kalua Rose" by Ed Ward, Al Bryan.

South Seas romantic action drama which was based on a play by G.C. Dixon.

2234. Isle of Fury (WB; 1936). *Cast:* Humphrey Bogart, Margaret Lindsay, Donald Woods, Paul Graetz, E.E. Clive, Gordon Hart, Housley Stevenson, Frank Lackteen, Sidney Bracey. *D:* Frank McDonald; *P:* Bryan Foy; *Sc:* Robert Andrews, William Jacobs. (1:00)

B drama of a wanted man who seeks refuge on a South Sea island. A remake of *The Narrow Corner* (q.v.). Based on the novel of that name by Somerset Maugham.

Note: An interesting side-note on this film is that Bogart considered it a blotch on his list of screen credits and denied ever making the film!

2235. Isle of Lost Ships (WB/F.N.; 1929). *Cast:* Noah Beery, Virginia Valli, Jason Robards, Clarissa Selwynne, Robert Emmett O'Connor. *D:* Irvin Willat; *St:* Crittenden Marriott; *Sc:* Fred Myton.

Offbeat and bizarre drama of a passenger steamer that gets trapped in the Sargasso Sea. A remake of the 1923 production of the same name by First National, directed by Maurice Tourneur.

2236. Isle of Paradise (Xxxx Xxxx; 1932). *Narrator:* David Ross; *Sc:* Richard Mack.

Documentary.

2237. It Can Be Done (Universal; 1929). *Cast:* Glenn Tryon, Sue Carol, Richard Carle. *D:* Fred Newmeyer.

Part-talkie comedy of mistaken identity.

2238. It Can't Last Forever (Columbia; 1937). *Cast:* Ralph Bellamy, Betty Furness, Robert Armstrong, Raymond Walburn, Edward Pawley, Thurston Hall, Wade Boteler. *D:* Hamilton MacFadden; *St & Sc:* Harold Buchman, Lee Loeb.

Low-budget comedy.

2239. It Could Happen to You (Republic; 1937). *Cast:* Owen Davis, Jr., Astrid Allwyn, Jack Carson, Frank Yaconelli. *D:* Phil Rosen.

B comedy.

2240. It Could Happen to You (20th Century–Fox; 1939). *Cast:* Stuart Erwin, Gloria Stuart, Douglas Fowley, June Gale, Robert Greig, Paul Hurst, Raymond Walburn, Richard Lane, Clarence Kolb. *D:* Alfred Werker; *Sc:* Allen Rivkin, Lou Breslow.

B comedy of an ad man who keeps having his ideas stolen. Based on the writings of Charles Hoffman.

2241. It Couldn't Have Happened (Invincible; 1936). *Cast:* Evelyn Brent, Reginald Denny, Inez Courtney, Robert Frazer, Hugh Marlowe (film debut), Crauford Kent. *D:* Phil Rosen.

"Poverty row" production.

2242. It Had to Happen (20th Century–Fox; 1936). *Cast:* George Raft, Rosalind Russell, Leo Carrillo, Alan Dinehart, Arline Judge, Andrew Tombes, Paul Hurst, Stanley Fields, Pierre Watkin, Thomas Jackson, Paul Stanton. *D:* Roy Del Ruth; *Sc:* Kathryn Scola, Howard Ellis Smith. (1:19)

An Italian immigrant gets involved in New York City's political game.

It Happened in Hollywood (1935) (G.B. title) *see* **Another Face**

2243. It Happened in Hollywood (Columbia; 1937). *Cast:* Richard Dix, Fay Wray, Franklin Pangborn, Victor Kilian, Billy Burrud, Arthur Loft, Edgar Dearing, Zeffie Tilbury, Granville Bates, Harold Goodwin, Charles Brinley, Charles Arnt. *D:* Harry Lachman; *St:* Myles Connolly; *Sc:* Samuel Fuller, Harvey Ferguson, Ethel Hill. (G.B. title: *Once a Hero*)

A star of silent westerns has a difficult time adapting when talkies arrive. This film sports the gimmick of utilizing star look-a-likes.

2244. It Happened in New York (Universal; 1935). *Cast:* Lyle Talbot, Gertrude Michael, Heather Angel, Herman Bing, King Baggot, Dick Elliott, Wallis Clark, Huntley Gordon, Rafael

Storm, Phil Tead, Bess Stafford, Robert Gleckler, Hugh O'Connell. *D:* Alan Crosland; *St:* Ward Morehouse, Jean Dalrymple; *Sc:* Seton I. Miller, Rian James. (1:05)

B romance of a runaway film star and a New York cabbie.

It Happened in Paris (G.B. title) *see* **A Desperate Adventure**

2245. It Happened One Night (Columbia; 1934). *Cast:* Clark Gable (A.A. for B.A. as Peter Warne), Claudette Colbert (A.A. for B.A. as Ellie Andrews), Walter Connolly (Alexander Andrews), Roscoe Karns (Oscar Shapely), Alan Hale (Danker), Jameson Thomas (King Westley), Arthur Hoyt (Zeke), Blanche Frederici (Zeke's wife — final film, d. 1933), Wallis Clark (Lovington), Harry C. Bradley (Henderson), Charles C. Wilson (Joe Gordon), Ward Bond (bus driver), Eddy Chandler (other bus driver), Charles D. Brown (reporter), Harry Holman (auto camp manager), Maidel Turner (his wife), Irving Bacon (station attendant), Harry Todd (flag man), Frank Yaconelli (Tony), Henry Wadsworth (drunken boy), Claire McDowell (mother), Milton Kibbee (drunk), Mickey Daniel (vender), Bess Flowers (secretary), Oliver Eckhardt (Dykes), Father Dodds (minister), Edmund Burns (best man), Ethel Sykes (maid of honor), Eddie Kane (radio announcer), Hal Price (reporter), James Burke, Joseph Crehan, Frank Holliday and Ky Robinson (4 detectives), Ernie Adams, Billy Engle, Allen Fox, Kit Guard, Marvin Loback, Rita Ross, Bert Starkey and Dave Wengren (bus passengers), George Breakston (boy), Tom Ricketts (old man). *D:* (A.A.) Frank Capra; *P:* Harry Cohn; *St:* "Night Bus" by Samuel Hopkins Adams; *Sc:* (A.A.) Robert Riskin. (1:45) (video)

Classic romance of a reporter and a runaway heiress who meet on a bus trip. This comedy premiered at Radio City Music Hall in New York City and became a phenomenon in its day, being the first film in the history of Hollywood to garner all of the top Oscars starting with an A.A. for "Best Picture." It was also voted "Best Film of the Year" by both the National Board of Review and the *New York Times,* while being in nomination for "Best Film" at the Venice Film Festival. *Film Daily* voted it #3 on their "10 Best" list. One of the 15 top grossing films of 1934 it was remade in 1945 as *Eve Knew Her Apples* and in 1956 as *You Can't Run Away from It* (both by Columbia).

2246. It Happened Out West (20th Century–Fox/Principal; 1937). *Cast:* Paul Kelly, Judith Allen, Johnny Arthur, Frank LaRue, LeRoy Mason, Nina Campana, Steve Clemente, Reginald Barlow. *D:* Howard Bretherton; *P:* Sol Lesser; *St:* Harold Bell Wright; *Sc:* Earle Snell, John Roberts. (0:59)

Crooks try to bilk a girl out of her dairy ranch when they learn of a large silver deposit on it.

2247. It Pays to Advertise (Paramount; 1931). *Cast:* Carole Lombard, Norman Foster, Richard "Skeets" Gallagher, Louise Brooks, Eugene Pallette, Tom Kennedy, Frank (Junior) Coghlan, Lucien Littlefield, Morgan Wallace, Helen Johnson, Marcis Manners. *D:* Frank Tuttle; *Sc:* Arthur Kober; *Adapt.:* Ethel Doherty.

Low-budget comedy of a publicity campaign to sell soap. A remake of the 1919 production of the same name with Bryant Washburn and Lois Wilson. Based on a play by Walter Hackett and Roi Cooper Megrue.

2248. It's a Gift (Paramount; 1934). *Cast:* W.C. Fields (Harold Bissonette), Kathleen Howard (Amelia Bissonette), Tommy Bupp (Norman Bissonette), Jean Rouverol (Mildred Bissonette), Baby LeRoy (Elwood Dunk), Julian Madison (John Durston), Tammany Young (Everett Ricks, the store clerk), Charles Sellon (Mr.

Muckle, the blind man), Morgan Wallace (James Fitchmueller), Josephine Whittell (Mrs. Dunk), Diana Lewis (film debut as Miss Dunk), T. Roy Barnes (insurance salesman), Spencer Charters (gate guard), Guy Usher (Harry Payne Bosterley), Del Henderson (Mr. Abernathy), James Burke, Jerry Mandy, William Tooker, Patsy O'Byrne. *D:* Norman Z. McLeod; *P:* William LeBaron; *St:* Charles Bogle (Fields), J.P. McEvoy; *Sc:* Jack Cunningham. (1:13) (video)

Classic Fields' field day as W.C., a merchant perplexed by everyday living purchases an orange ranch in California after receiving an inheritance and moves there with his disgruntled family. A remake of *It's the Old Army Game* (Paramount; 1926) which was based on the play "The Comic Supplement" by Fields and J.P. McEvoy.

2249. It's a Great Life (MGM; 1929). *Cast:* Vivian Duncan, Rosetta Duncan (real life sisters), Lawrence Gray, Jed Prouty, Benny Rubin. *D:* Sam Wood; *Sc:* Al Boasberg, Willard Mack; *Songs:* Sammy Fain.

A romance with musical numbers of two showbiz sisters in love with the same man.

2250. It's a Great Life (Paramount; 1935–36). *Cast:* Joe Morrison, Paul Kelly, Rosalind Keith, Baby LeRoy (in his final film before retiring, as he was getting too old to be called "Baby" LeRoy), Irving Bacon. *D:* Edward Cline; *P:* Harold Hurley; *St:* Arthur Lake, Sherman Rogers; *Sc:* Paul Gerard Smith, Harlan Thompson.

B drama of a rural youth who becomes a hero during a forest fire.

2251. It's a Small World (Fox; 1935). *Cast:* Spencer Tracy, Wendy Barrie, Raymond Walburn, Astrid Allwyn, Virginia Sale, Frank McGlynn, Sr. *D:* Irving Cummings.

Low-budget small-town comedy which was filmed in Arizona.

2252. It's a Wise Child (MGM; 1931). *Cast:* Marion Davies, Lester Vail, Ben Alexander, James Gleason, Polly Moran, Sidney Blackmer, Johnny Arthur, Marie Prevost, Emily Fitzroy, Clara Blandick, Robert McWade, Hilda Vaughn. *D:* Robert Z. Leonard (who also co-produced); *St & Sc:* Laurence E. Johnson.

Hit romantic comedy based on a play by Laurence Johnson.

2253. It's a Wonderful World (MGM; 1939). *Cast:* Claudette Colbert, James Stewart, Guy Kibbee, Nat Pendleton, Edgar Kennedy, Frances Drake, Ernest Truex, Richard Carle, Cecil Cunningham, Sidney Blackmer, Andy Clyde, Cliff Clark, Hans Conried, Grady Sutton, Frank Faylen, Jack Norton, Leonard Kibrick, Cecilia Callejo. *D:* W.S. Van Dyke II; *P:* Frank Davis; *St:* Herman J. Mankiewicz, Ben Hecht; *Sc:* Hecht. (1:26)

Another of the classic screwball comedies produced in Hollywood in the late '30s. A runaway girl joins forces with a suspected murderer on the lam from the cops. Financially, the film came out in the red.

2254. It's All in Your Mind (Reliable; 1937). A low-budget exploitation film of a man's "mid-life crisis" starring Byron Foulger and produced by Bernard B. Ray. (Retitled: *Fools of Desire*)

2255. It's All Yours (Columbia; 1937–38). *Cast:* Madeleine Carroll, Francis Lederer, Mischa Auer, Grace Bradley, Victor Kilian, J.C. Nugent, Arthur Hoyt, Richard Carle, Franklin Pangborn, George McKay, Charles Waldron. *D:* Elliott Nugent; *Sc:* Mary C. McCall, Jr. (1:20)

Comedy of a millionaire who dies and leaves his entire estate to his secretary.

2256. It's Great to Be Alive (Fox; 1933). *Cast:* Gloria Stuart, Joan Marsh, Edna May Oliver, Dorothy Burgess, Herbert Mundin, Edward Van Sloan, Robert Greig, Raul Roulien. *D:* Alfred Werker; *St:* John D. Swain.

Low-budget comedy.

2257. It's in the Air (MGM; 1935). *Cast:* Jack Benny, Una Merkel, Ted Healy, Nat Pendleton, Mary Carlisle, Grant Mitchell, Harvey Stephens, Johnny Arthur, Purnell Pratt, Bud Flanagan (Dennis O'Keefe). *D:* Charles Reisner; *P:* E.J. Mannix, Harry Rapf; *St:* Lew Lipton; *Sc:* Byron Morgan, Lipton, Herman J. Mankiewicz (unc.). (1:20)

Flop comedy of a con-artist who seeks help from his ex-wife to avoid paying taxes.

2258. It's Love I'm After (WB; 1937). *Cast:* Bette Davis, Leslie Howard, Olivia de Havilland, Patric Knowles, Eric Blore, George Barbier, Spring Byington, Bonita Granville, E.E. Clive, Veda Ann Borg, Georgia Caine, Thomas Pogue, Sarah Edwards, Ed Mortimer, Valerie Bergere, Thomas Mills. *D:* Archie L. Mayo; *P:* Harry Joe Brown; *St:* Maurice Hanline; *Sc:* Casey Robinson.

A critically acclaimed hit comedy of a stage couple whose marriage is anything but wedded bliss. The original working title was "Gentlemen After Midnight."

2259. It's Spring Again (Xxxx Xxxx; 1938). (No information available)

2260. It's Tough to Be Famous (WB/F.N.; 1932). *Cast:* Douglas Fairbanks, Jr., Mary Brian, Walter Catlett, Lillian Bond, Terrence Ray, David Landau, Claire McDowell, Ivan Linow, J. Carrol Naish, Oscar Apfel, Louise Beavers, Berton Churchill, Emma Dunn, Harold Minjir. *D:* Alfred E. Green; *St:* Mary McCall, Jr.; *Sc:* Robert Lord. (1:19)

Comedy of a man who seeks to keep a low profile, but suddenly finds himself a celebrity.

2261. The Ivory-Handled Gun (Universal; 1935). *Cast:* Buck Jones, Frank Rice, Charlotte Wynters, Silver the horse, Walter Miller, Carl Stockdale, Lafe McKee, Lee Shumway, Ben Corbett, Eddie Phillips, Joseph Girard, Robert Kortman, Charles King. *D:* Ray Taylor (who also directed the remake); *Sc:* John Thomas Neville. (0:58)

Offbeat Buck Jones western of a long-standing family feud over the titled gun. Remade as *Law of the Range* (Universal; 1941) with Johnny Mack Brown.

Jailbirds (G.B. title) *see* **Pardon Us**

2262. Jailbreak (WB; 1936). *Cast:* Craig Reynolds, Dick Purcell, June Travis, Barton MacLane, Addison Richards, Joseph King, Eddie Acuff, George E. Stone, Joseph Crehan, Mary Treen, Charles Middleton, Robert Emmett Keane, Henry Hall. *D:* Nick Grinde; *P:* Bryan Foy; *St:* Jonathan Finn; *Sc:* Robert D. Andrews, Joseph Hoffman. (G.B. title: *Murder in the Big House*)

B melodrama of a reporter who investigates murder in a prison. Remade as *Murder in the Big House* (WB; 1942).

2263. Jalna (RKO; 1935). *Cast:* Kay Johnson, Ian Hunter, Peggy Wood, C. Aubrey Smith, Nigel Bruce, David Manners, Forrester Harvey, Jessie Ralph, Molly Lamont, Theodore Newton, Halliwell Hobbes, George Offerman, Jr., Clifford Severn, Willie Best. *D:* John Cromwell; *P:* Kenneth MacGowan; *Adaptation:* Garrett Fort, Larry Bachmann; *Sc:* Anthony Veiller. (1:18)

Domestic drama of two brides brought into a closely knit family, creating dissension among some members. Based on the novel by Mazo de la Roche.

2264. Jamboree (Xxxx Xxxx; 1933). (No information available)

2265. Jane Eyre (Monogram; 1934). *Cast:* Virginia Bruce (Jane), Colin Clive (Rochester), Beryl Mercer, Jameson Thomas, Aileen Pringle, David Torrence, Lionel Belmore, Joan Standing, Edith Fellows, Desmond Roberts, John Rogers, Clarissa Selwynne, Hylda Tyson, Gretta Gould, Claire DuBrey, Ethel Griffies, Edith Kingdon, William Wagner, Olaf Hytten, William Burress, Gail Kaye, Jean Darling, Richard Quine, Anne Howard. *D:* Christy Cabanne; *P:* Ben Verschleiser; *Sc:* Adele Commandini. (1:10) (video)

Low-budget production based on the gothic novel by Charlotte Brontë of a young girl, hired as a governess into a household which harbors a sinister secret. Previously filmed as a featurette (Universal; 1913) with Ethel Grandin and Irving Cummings, (Biograph; 1915) with Louise Vale and Alan Hale and (Hodkinson; 1921) with Mabel Ballin and Norman Trevor. Remade: (20th Century–Fox; 1944) and in 1970 as a British TV movie.

Java Seas (G.B. title) *see* **East of Java**

2266. Jaws of Justice (Principal; 1933). *Cast:* Richard Terry (Jack Perrin), Kazan the dog, Ruth Sullivan, Robert Walker, Lafe McKee, Gene Tolar. *D:* Spencer Gordon Bennet; *P:* Sol Lesser; *Sc:* Joseph Anthony Roach. (0:58)

Northwoods adventure of a Mountie and his dog on the trail of a wanted man.

2267. Jazz Heaven (RKO; 1929). *Cast:* John Mack Brown, Sally O'Neil, Joseph Cawthorn, Albert Conti, Clyde Cook, Blanche Frederici, Henry Armetta, Ole M. Ness, J. Barney Sherry, Adele Watson. *D:* Melville Brown; *As.P.:* Myles Connolly; *St:* Pauline Forney, Dudley Murphy; *Sc:* J. Walter Ruben, Cyrus Wood; *Song:* "Someone" by Oscar Levant, Sidney Clare. (1:11)

A young southerner tries to become a song writer in New York City.

2268. The Jazz Singer (WB; 1927). *Cast:* Al Jolson (Jakie Rabinowitz-Jack Robin), May McAvoy (Mary Dale), Warner Oland (Cantor Rabinowitz), Eugenie Besserer (Sara Rabinowitz), Otto Lederer (Moisha Yudelson), William Demarest (Buster Billings), Roscoe Karns (agent), Richard Tucker (Harry Lee), Nat Carr (Levi), Cantor Josef Rosenblatt (himself), William Walling (doctor), Bobby Gordon (Jakie a boy), Anders Randolf (Dillings), Myrna Loy (chorus girl). *D:* Alan Crosland; *Adaptation:* (A.A.N.) Alfred A. Cohn; *Engineering Effects:* (A.A.N.) Nugent Slaughter; *Songs:* "My Gal Sal" by Paul Dresser, "Waiting for the Robert E. Lee" by L. Wolfe Gilbert, Lewis F. Muir, "Kol Nidre" (a traditional Yiddish song), "Dirty Hands, Dirty Face" by Edgar Leslie, Grant Clarke, Al Jolson, Jimmy Monaco, "Toot Toot Tootsie Good-Bye" by Gus Kahn, Ernie Erdman, Dan Russo, "Yahrzeit" (a traditional Yiddish song), "Blue Skies" by Irving Berlin, "Mother I Still Have You," by Al Jolson, Louis Silvers, "My Mammy" by Sam Lewis, Joe Young and Walter Donaldson. (1:28) (video)

Landmark part-talkie film, credited with being the first American feature film with spoken dialogue and vocalized songs. It profited $3,000,000 for the studio and set the stage for the beginning of the era of talking pictures. The story of a Jewish cantor's son, who against his father's wishes, goes into show business, rather than becoming a cantor. The film premiered October 6, 1927, at the Warner Theater in New York City, eventually winning a special Academy Award for revolutionizing the movie industry. Based on the story "The Day of Atonement" and the 1925 play adaptation by Samson Raphaelson. Remade 1952–53 and 1980.

2269. Jealousy (Paramount; 1929). *Cast:* Jeanne Eagels (final film—

d. 1929), Fredric March, Henry Daniell (film debut), Halliwell Hobbes (film debut), Anthony Bushell, Granville Bates, Blanche Le Clair, Hilda Moore. *D:* Jean de Limur; *Sc:* Garrett Fort, John D. Williams, Eugene Walter.

Drama of a man who kills his wife's former guardian and lover. Based on the play by Louis Verneuil.

2270. Jealousy (Columbia; 1934). *Cast:* Nancy Carroll, Donald Cook, George Murphy, Raymond Walburn, Robert Allen, Inez Courtney, Clara Blandick, Lucille Ball (bit). *D:* Roy William Neill.

B romance.

2271. Jeepers Creepers (Republic; 1939). *Cast:* The Weavers (featuring Leon, Frank, June and Loretta singing and playing their own brand of down-home music), Maris Wrixon, Roy Rogers, Billy Lee, Lucien Littlefield, Thurston Hall, Johnny Arthur, Ralph "Tiny" Sandford, Milton Kibbee, Dan White. *D:* Frank McDonald; *Sc:* Dorrell & Stuart McGowan. (G.B. title: *Money Isn't Everything*) (1:07)

B rural comedy of some rustics who are cheated out of their land.

2272. Jennie Gerhardt (Paramount; 1933). *Cast:* Sylvia Sidney, Donald Cook, Mary Astor, Edward Arnold, H.B. Warner, Theodore von Eltz, Louise Carter, Cora Sue Collins, Jane Darwell, Frank Reicher, Dave O'Brien, Walter Walker, Greta Meyer, Dorothy Libaire, David Durand, Gilda Storm, Betsy Ann Hisle. *D:* Marion Gering; *P:* B.P. Schulberg; *Sc:* Josephine Lovett, Joseph Moncure March, S.K. Lauren, Frank Partos. (1:27)

Turn-of-the-century hanky soaker of the suffering endured by a fallen woman. Based on the novel by Theodore Dreiser.

Jenny Lind (G.B. title) *see* **A Lady's Morals**

2273. Jesse James (20th Century–Fox; 1939). *Cast:* Tyrone Power (Jesse James), Henry Fonda (Frank James), Nancy Kelly (Zee), Randolph Scott (Will Wright), Henry Hull (major), Jane Darwell (Mrs. Samuels), Slim Summerville (jailer), J. Edward Bromberg (Runyon, the Pinkerton man), Brian Donlevy (Barshee), John Carradine (Bob Ford, killer), Donald Meek (McCoy), John Russell (Jesse James, Jr.), Charles Tannen (Charlie Ford), Claire DuBrey (Mrs. Ford), Willard Robertson (Clark), Paul Sutton (Lynch), Ernest Whitman (Pinky), Paul Burns (Bill), Spencer Charters (preacher), Arthur Aylesworth (Tom), Charles Halton (Heywood), George Chandler (Roy), Erville Alderson (old marshal), Harry Tyler (farmer), George Breakston (farm boy), Virginia Brissac (boy's mother), Edward J. LeSaint (Judge Rankin), John Elliott (Judge Matthews), Lon Chaney, Jr., Harry Holman, Wylie Grant, Ethan Laidlaw, Donald Douglas, James Flavin, George O'Hara, Charles Middleton, Eddy Waller, Jo Frances James. *D:* Henry King; *As.P.:* Nunnally Johnson; *P:* Darryl F. Zanuck; *Hist. Research:* Rosalind Schaeffer, Jo Frances James; *Sc:* Nunnally Johnson. (1:45) (video)

Lavish technicolor western based on the exploits of the infamous James brothers. Followed by a sequel *The Return of Frank James* (20th Century–Fox; 1940). Remade in 1957 as *The True Story of Jesse James.*

Note: One of the 16 top grossing films of 1938–39.

2274. The Jewel Robbery (WB; 1932). *Cast:* William Powell, Kay Francis, Hardie Albright, Andre Luguet, Henry Kolker, Spencer Charters, Alan Mowbray, Lee Kohlmar, Helen Vinson (film debut), Lawrence Grant, C. Henry Gordon, Herman Bing, Ruth Donnelly, Clarence Wilson, Harold Waldridge, Ivan Linow, Harold Minjir, Jacques Vanaire. *D:* William Dieterle; *Sc:* Erwin Gelsey. (1:08)

Hit romance of a jewel thief and a wealthy woman who meet during a robbery. Based on the play by Ladislaus Fodor.

2275. Jezebel (WB/F.N.; 1938). *Cast:* Bette Davis (A.A. for B.A. as Julie Marston), Henry Fonda (Preston Dillard), George Brent (Buck Cantrell), Fay Bainter (A.A. for B.S.A. as Aunt Belle), Richard Cromwell (Ted Dillard), Spring Byington (Mrs. Kendrick), Margaret Lindsay (Amy Bradford Dillard), Donald Crisp (Dr. Livingstone), Henry O'Neill (Gen. Bogardus), John Litel (Jean La Cour), Gordon Oliver (Dick Allen), Janet Shaw (Molly Allen), Margaret Early (Stephanie Kendrick), Irving Pichel (Huger), Georges Renavent (De Lautrec), Lew Payton (Uncle Cato), Eddie Anderson (Gros Bat), Theresa Harris (Zetté), Stymie Beard (Ti Bat), Georgia Caine (Mrs. Petion), Fred Lawrence (Bob), Ann Codee (Madame Poulard the dressmaker), Jacques Vanaire (Durette), Suzanne Dulier (Midinette), John Harron (Jenkins), Philip "Lucky" Hurlic (Erronens), Dolores Hurlic (Errata), Daisy Bufford, Jesse A. Graves, Frederick Burton, Edward McWade, Frank Darien, Davison Clark, Trevor Bardette, George Guhl, Jack Norton, Louis Mercier, Alan Bridge, Charles Wagenheim, Jac George. *D:* William Wyler; *As.P.:* Henry Blanke; *Sc:* Clements Ripley, Abem Finkel, John Huston, Robert Buckner (unc.); *Cinematographer:* (A.A.N.) Ernest Haller; *Music:* (A.A.N.) Max Steiner; *Songs:* "Jezebel" by Harry Warren, Johnny Mercer, "Raise a Ruckus" by Harry Warren and Al Dubin. (1:44) (video)

Lavishly produced drama of a fiery southern belle who weaves a web of deceit and jealousy among the men in her life. This film was offered to Davis to appease her disappointment with losing the role of "Scarlett O'Hara." A hit at the box office, it received an A.A.N. for "Best Picture" as well as being in nomination for "Best Film" at the Venice

Film Festival. The National Board of Review placed it at #8 on their "10 Best" list. Based on an unpopular play by Owen Davis, Sr., it was computer-colored by Turner Entertainment in 1989.

2276. Jim Burke's Boy (Xxxx Xxxx; 1936). (No information available)

2277. Jim Hanvey, Detective (Republic; 1937). *Cast:* Tom Brown, Lucie Kaye, Guy Kibbee, Helen Jerome Eddy, Wade Boteler, Edward Gargan, Edward Brophy, Oscar Apfel, Kenneth Thomson. *D:* Phil Rosen.

B mystery-comedy.

2278. Jimmy and Sally (Fox; 1933). *Cast:* James Dunn, Claire Trevor (in a role originally intended for Sally Eilers), Harvey Stephens, Lya Lys, Matt McHugh, Jed Prouty, Alma Lloyd, Gloria Roy. *D:* James Tinling; *St:* Marguerite Roberts, Paul Schofield. (1:08)

Low-budget romance.

2279. Jimmy the Gent (WB; 1934). *Cast:* James Cagney, Bette Davis, Allen Jenkins, Alan Dinehart, Alice White, Arthur Hohl, Philip Reed, Hobart Cavanaugh, Mayo Methot, Renee Whitney, Ralf Harolde, Merna Kennedy, Philip Faversham, Nora Lane, Jane Darwell, Joseph (Sawyer) Sauers, Bud Flanagan (Dennis O'Keefe). *D:* Michael Curtiz; *P:* Robert Lord; *St:* "The Heir Chaser" by Laird Doyle & Ray Nazarro; *Sc:* Bertram Millhauser. (1:07)

Comedy of shady operator who creates heirs to large unclaimed estates.

2280. Joe and Ethel Turp Call on the President (MGM; 1939). *Cast:* Ann Sothern (Ethel Turp), William Gargan (Joe Turp), Lewis Stone (president), Walter Brennan, Marsha Hunt, Tom Neal, Muriel Hutchinson, Louis Jean Heydt, Mary Gordon, Jack Mulhall, Jack Norton, Lon McCallister, Ann Teeman, Aldrich Bowker, Don Costello, James Bush. *D:* Robert B. Sinclair; *P:* Edgar Selwyn; *Sc:* Melville Baker. (aka: *A Call on the President*)

Offbeat B screwball comedy of a Brooklyn couple who go right to Washington for results after their postman loses his job. Based on a story by Damon Runyon, this was the only entry in what was to be a proposed series by the studio.

Joe Palooka *see* **Palooka**

2281. John Meade's Woman (Paramount; 1937). *Cast:* Edward Arnold, Francine Larrimore, Gail Patrick, George Bancroft, Aileen Pringle, Sidney Blackmer, Charles Middleton, Willard Robertson, Robert Strange, Stanley Andrews, John Trent, Harry Hayden. *D:* Richard Wallace; *P:* B.P. Schulberg; *St:* Robert Tasker, John Bright; *Sc:* Vincent Lawrence, Herman J. Mankiewicz.

A timber tycoon marries, but loves another.

2282. Join the Marines (Republic; 1937). *Cast:* Ray Corrigan (Lieut. Hodge), Paul Kelly, Carleton Young, June Travis, Reginald Denny, Warren Hymer, Sterling Holloway, Roy Barcroft, Arthur Hoyt. *D:* Ralph Staub.

Title implies all in this low-budget production.

2283. The Jones Family in Hollywood (20th Century–Fox; 1939). *Cast:* Jed Prouty, Spring Byington, Florence Roberts, Kenneth Howell, George Ernest, Billy Mahan, William Tracy, Mary Gordon. *D:* Mal St. Clair; *St:* Buster Keaton (co).

Again, the title tells all in this entry in the hit comedy series.

2284. Josette (20th Century–Fox; 1938). *Cast:* Simone Simon, Don Ameche, Robert Young, Joan Davis, Bert Lahr, Paul Hurst, William Collier, Sr., Tala Birell, Lynn Bari, William Demarest, Lon Chaney, Jr., Ruth Gillette, Armand Kaliz, Lillian Porter. *D:* Allan Dwan; *P:* Gene Markey; *St:* Laslo

Vadnay; *Sc:* James Edward Grant; *Song:* Harry Revel, Mack Gordon. (1:13) Musical-comedy.

2285. Journal of a Crime (WB/ F.N.; 1934). *Cast:* Ruth Chatterton, Adolphe Menjou, Claire Dodd, Douglass Dumbrille, George Barbier, Walter Pidgeon, Philip Reed, Noel Madison, Frank Reicher, Henry O'Neill, Clay Clement, Edward McWade, Frank Darien, Jane Darwell, Elsa Janssen. *D:* William Keighley; *P:* Henry Blanke; *Sc:* F. Hugh Herbert, Charles Kenyon. (1:05)

B melodrama of a woman who shoots her husband's mistress, letting someone else take the blame. Based on a play by Jacques Deval.

2286. Journey's End (Tiffany; 1930). *Cast:* Colin Clive (film debut recreating his London stage performance as Capt. Stanhope), Ian MacLaren (Lieut. Osborne), David Manners (film debut as Second Lieut. Raleigh), Anthony Bushell (Second Lieut. Hibbert), Billy Bevan (Second Lieut. Trotter), Charles Gerrard (Priv. Mason), Robert Adair (Capt. Hardy), Thomas Whiteley (company sergeant major), Jack Pitcairn (colonel), Werner Klinger (German soldier). *D:* James Whale; *P:* George Pearson; *Sc:* Joseph Moncure March, Gareth Gundrey. (2:10)

Critically acclaimed drama of the World War I trenches is a British-American co-production by Gainsborough-Welsh-Pearson-Tiffany. Produced by Britishers in the United States for better sound reproduction. Based on the British play by R.C. Sherriff, the film is similar in many respects to *All Quiet on the Western Front* (q.v.), except this one is told through the eyes of the Allies. The *New York Times* placed it at #3 on their "10 Best" list, while *Film Daily* placed it at #4 on theirs. Filmed before in Great Britain in 1921 and remade there in 1976 as *Aces High* with an aerial war-drama theme.

2287. Joy of Living (RKO; 1938). *Cast:* Irene Dunne, Douglas Fairbanks, Jr., Alice Brady, Guy Kibbee, Jean Dixon, Eric Blore, Lucille Ball, Warren Hymer, Billy Gilbert, John Qualen, Franklin Pangborn, Frank Milan, Dorothy Steiner, Estelle Steiner, Phyllis Kennedy, James Burke, Spencer Charters, Grady Sutton. *D:* Tay Garnett; *P:* Felix Young; *St:* Dorothy Fields, Herbert Fields; *Sc:* Gene Towne, Allan Scott, Graham Baker; *Songs:* Jerome Kern, Dorothy Fields. (1:31) (video)

Flop screwball comedy with music of a family who is trying to prevent the marriage of their "bread 'n' butter."

The Joy Parade (G.B. title) *see* **Life Begins in College**

2288. Juarez (WB; 1939). *Cast:* Paul Muni (Benito Pablo Juarez), Bette Davis (Empress Carlotta von Habsburg), Brian Aherne (A.A.N. for B.S.A. as Emperor Maximilian von Habsburg), Claude Rains (Louis Napoleon III), John Garfield (Gen. Porfirio Diaz), Gale Sondergaard (Empress Eugenie), Donald Crisp (Marechal Bazaine), Gilbert Roland (Col. Miguel Lopez), Louis Calhern (Le Marc), Joseph Calleia (Alejandro Uradi), Pedro de Cordoba (Riva Palacio), Montagu Love (Jose de Montares), Harry Davenport (Dr. Samuel Basch), Henry O'Neill (Miguel Miramon), Walter Fenner (Achille Fould), Alex Leftwich (Drouyn de Lhuys), Georgia Caine (Countess Battenberg), Robert Warwick (Major DuPont), Gennaro Curci (Senor de Leon), Bill Wilkerson (Tomás Mejia), John Miljan (Mariano Escobedo), Hugh Sothern (John Bigelow), Fred Malatesta (Senor Salas), Carlos de Valdez (tailor), Irving Pichel (Carbajal), Frank Lackteen (coachman), Walter O. Stahl (Senator del Valle), Frank Reicher (Duc de Morny), Holmes Herbert (Marshall Randon), Walter Kingsford (Prince Metternich), Egon Brecher (Baron von Magnus),

Monte Blue (Lerdo de Tajada), Manuel Diaz (Pepe), Mickey Kuhn (Augustin Iturbide), Lillian Nicholson (Josefa Iturbide), Noble Johnson (Regules), Martin Garralaga (Negroni), Vladimir Sokoloff (Camilo), Grant Mitchell (Mr. Harris), Charles Halton (Mr. Roberts). *D:* William Dieterle; *P:* Hal B. Wallis; *As.P.:* Henry Blanke; *Sc:* John Huston, Wolfgang Reinhardt, Aeneas MacKenzie. (2:12) (video)

Lavishly produced historical biography of the famed Mexican leader which sports a cast of 1,186 players. Two works form the basis for the screenplay, namely "Juarez and Maximillian," a play by Franz Werfel and "The Phantom Crown," a novel by Bertita Harding. Voted #5 and #8 respectively on the "10 Best" lists of the *New York Times* and *Film Daily.*

Note: One of the 16 top grossing films of 1938–39.

2289. Judge Hardy and Son (MGM; 1939). *Cast:* Lewis Stone (Judge Hardy), Mickey Rooney (Andy Hardy), Cecilia Parker (Marian Hardy), Fay Holden (Mrs. Hardy), Sara Haden (Aunt Milly), Ann Rutherford (Polly Benedict), June Preisser, Maria Ouspenskaya, Henry Hull, Martha O'Driscoll, Joe Yule (Mickey Rooney's real life father), Leona Maricle, Margaret Early. *D:* George B. Seitz; *P:* Lou Ostrow (unc.); *St & Sc:* Carey Wilson. (1:30)

Eighth entry in the "Hardy Family–Andy Hardy" series with the family becoming increasingly concerned over Mrs. Hardy's serious illness.

2290. Judge Hardy's Children (MGM; 1938). *Cast:* Lewis Stone (Judge Hardy), Mickey Rooney (Andy Hardy), Cecilia Parker (Marian Hardy), Fay Holden (Mrs. Hardy), Betty Ross Clark (replacing Sara Haden as Aunt Milly in this entry), Ann Rutherford (Polly Benedict), Robert Whitney, Ruth Hussey, Janet Beecher, Jacqueline Laurent, Jonathan Hale, Leonard

Penn. *D:* George B. Seitz; *P:* Lou Ostrow (unc.); *Sc:* Kay Van Riper. (1:18)

In this the 3rd entry in the "Hardy" series, the family visits Washington, D.C.

2291. Judge Priest (Fox; 1934). *Cast:* Will Rogers (Judge William Priest), Tom Brown (Jerome Priest), Anita Louise (Ellie May Gillespie), Henry B. Walthall (Rev. Ashby Brand), David Landau (Bob Gillis—final film, d. 1935), Stepin Fetchit (Jeff Poindexter), Hattie McDaniel (Aunt Dilsey), Charley Grapewin (Sgt. Jimmy Bagby), Berton Churchill (Senator Horace Maydew), Rochelle Hudson (Virginia Maydew), Roger Imhof (Billy Gaynor), Frank Melton (Flem Talley), Brenda Fowler (Mrs. Caroline Priest), Francis Ford (12th juror), Robert Parrish. *D:* John Ford; *P:* Sol M. Wurtzel; *Sc:* Dudley Nichols, Lamar Trotti. (1:20) (video)

Post Civil War Americana of a small southern town and a judge whose ethics are questioned by some. Based on stories by Irvin S. Cobb, it was one of the 15 top grossing films of 1934. Remade by Ford in 1953 as *The Sun Shines Bright.*

2292. Judgment Book (Beaumont; 1935). *Cast:* Conway Tearle, Bernadene Hayes, Howard Lang, Richard Cramer, William Gould, Jack Pendleton, Jimmy Aubrey, Roy Rice, Blackie Whiteford, Ray Gallagher, Dick Rush. *D:* Charles Hutchison; *Sc:* E.J. Thornton. (1:01)

Conway Tearle western of a man from the east who goes to a small western town to take over the local newspaper, only to find the town run by ruthless cattlemen.

2293. June Moon (Paramount; 1931). *Cast:* Frances Dee, Jack Oakie, Wynne Gibson, Harry Akst, June MacCloy, Sam Hardy, Frank Darien, Harold Waldridge, Jean Bary, Ernest Wood,

Ethel Sutherland. *D:* A. Edward Sutherland; *Sc:* Joseph L. Mankiewicz, Vincent Lawrence, Keene Thompson; *Songs:* Harry Akst.

Comedy of an electrician who wants to be a song writer. Based on a 1929 Broadway hit by Ring Lardner and George S. Kaufman. Remade as *Blonde Trouble* (q.v.).

2294. Jungle Bride (Monogram; 1933). *Cast:* Anita Page, Charles Starrett, Kenneth Thomson, Eddie Borden, Clarence Geldart, Gertrude Simpson, Jay Emmett, Albert Cross. *D:* Harry O. Hoyt (final film), Albert Kelley; *P:* I.E. Chadwick; *St:* Leah Baird (1:03)

Low-budget melodrama of four people who are shipwrecked off the coast of Africa.

2295. The Jungle Killer (Century Productions; 1932). *Narrator:* Carveth Wells.

Documentary.

2296. Jungle Madness (Xxxx Xxxx; 1931). (No information available)

2297. The Jungle Princess (Paramount; 1936). *Cast:* Dorothy Lamour (starring debut), Ray Milland, Akim Tamiroff, Lynne Overman, Molly Lamont, Hugh Buckler, Mala, Robert Law, Sally Martin. *D:* William Thiele; *P:* E. Lloyd Sheldon; *St:* Max Marcin; *Sc:* Cyril Hume, Gerald Geraghty, Gouverneur Morris, Frank Partos (unc.), Charles Brackett (unc.); *Song:* "Moonlight and Shadow" by Leo Robin, Frederick Hollander. (1:24)

This was Dorothy Lamour's first outing in a sarong as a wild jungle girl who finds romance. The film was a surprise hit at the box office.

2298. The Jury's Secret (Universal; 1938). *Cast:* Kent Taylor, Fay Wray, Nan Grey, Larry Blake, Halliwell Hobbes, Leonard Mudie, Samuel S. Hinds, Bert Roach, Virginia Sale, Jane Darwell, Granville Bates, Fritz Leiber, Ted Oliver, Ferris Taylor, Billy Wayne, Lillian Elliott, John Miller, Harry C. Bradley, Robert Spencer, Drew Demarest, Dick Rush, Edward Broadley. *D:* Edward (Ted) Sloman (final film — ret.); *P:* Edmund Grainger; *St:* Newman Levy; *Sc:* Levy, Lester Cole. (1:02)

B courtroom melodrama of a man sitting on the jury which is trying a man for a murder he committed.

2299. Just a Gigolo (MGM; 1931). *Cast:* William Haines, Lillian Bond, C. Aubrey Smith, Irene Purcell (film debut), Ray Milland, Albert Conti, Charlotte Granville, Maria Alba, Gerald Fielding, Lenore Bushman. *D:* Jack Conway; *Sc:* Richard Schayer, Hans Kräly, Claudine West. (G.B. title: *The Dancing Partner*)

Low-budget comedy of a man who poses as a gigolo to avoid marriage. Based on an old play by Alexander Engel, Alfred Grunwald.

2300. Just Around the Corner (20th Century–Fox; 1938). *Cast:* Shirley Temple, Charles Farrell, Joan Davis, Bert Lahr, Amanda Duff, Bill Robinson, Franklin Pangborn, Cora Witherspoon, Claude Gillingwater, Orville Caldwell, Tony (J. Anthony) Hughes, Marilyn Knowlden, Bennie Bartlett, Hal K. Dawson, Eddie Conrad, Charles Williams. *D:* Irving Cummings; *P:* Darryl F. Zanuck; *As.P.:* David Hempstead; *St:* Paul Gerard Smith; *Sc:* J.P. McEvoy, Ethel Hill, Darrell Ware. (1:10) (video)

A little girl makes everything right for everybody.

2301. Just Imagine (Fox; 1930). *Cast:* El Brendel, Maureen O'Sullivan, John Garrick, Marjorie White, Frank Albertson, Hobart Bosworth, Mischa Auer, Kenneth Thomson, Fifi D'Orsay, Robert Keith, Dorothy Tree (film debut), Ivan Linow, Joyzelle Joyner, Wilfred Lucas, Sidney DeGray, George Irving, J.M. Kerrigan. *D:* David Butler; *Sc:* Butler; *Art-Set Decoration:*

(A.A.N.) Stephen Goosson, Ralph Hammeras; *Songs:* B.G. DeSylva, Lew Brown, Ray Henderson. (1:42)

An early science-fiction musical of a man who dies in 1930 and is revived fifty years later. The futuristic sets boggled the minds of 1930 audiences and is a definite curio as such.

2302. Just Like Heaven (Tiffany; 1930). *Cast:* Anita Louise, Yola D'Avril, Gaston Glass. *D:* Roy William Neill.

"Poverty row" romance.

2303. Just My Luck (Victory; 1936). *Cast:* Edward Nugent, Charles King, Richard Cramer, Snub Pollard, Tom London, John Roche, Matthew Betz, Charles Ray. *D:* Xxxx Xxxx; *P:* Sam Katzman.

B indie production.

Justice for Sale (G.B. title) *see* **Night Court**

2304. Justice of the Range (Columbia; 1935). *Cast:* Tim McCoy, Billie Seward, Ward Bond, Guy Usher, Edward LeSaint, Allan Sears, Jack Rockwell, Jack Rutherford, George Hayes, Bill Patton, Stanley Blystone, Earl Dwire, J. Frank Glendon, Tom London, Dick Rush, Frank Ellis, Bud Osborne, Dick Botiller. *D:* David Selman; *Sc:* Ford Beebe. (0:58)

Tim McCoy western of a cowboy accused of murder while investigating some cattle rustling.

Justice Rides Again *see* **Destry Rides Again** (1932)

2305. Justice Takes a Holiday (Mayfair/Golden Arrow; 1933). *Cast:* H.B. Warner, Robert Frazer. *D:* Spencer Gordon Bennet.

"Poverty row" production.

2306. Juvenile Court (Columbia; 1938). *Cast:* Paul Kelly, Frankie Darro, Rita Hayworth, Hally Chester, Dick Ellis, Charles Hart, Don Latorre, Allan Ramsey, Howard Hickman. *D:* D. Ross

Lederman; *Sc:* Robert E. Kent, Michael Simmons, Henry Taylor.

B delinquency melodrama.

2307. Kansas City Princess (WB; 1934). *Cast:* Joan Blondell, Glenda Farrell, Robert Armstrong, Osgood Perkins, T. Roy Barnes, Hugh Herbert, Hobart Cavanaugh, Gordon Westcott, Ivan Lebedeff, Arthur Hoyt, Arthur Housman, Reneé Whitney, Vince Barnett. *D:* William Keighley; *P:* Lou Edelman; *St & Sc:* Sy Bartlett, Manuel Seff. (1:02)

B comedy of two gold diggers — out for what they can get.

2308. The Kansas Terrors (Republic; 1939). *Cast:* Bob Livingston (in his return to the series as Stoney Brooke), Raymond Hatton (Rusty Joslin), Duncan Renaldo (Rico), Jacqueline Wells (Julie Bishop), Howard Hickman, George Douglas, Frank Lackteen, Myra Marsh, Yakima Canutt, Ruth Robinson, Artie Ortego. *D:* George Sherman; *P:* Harry Grey; *Sc:* Betty Burbridge, Jack Natteford. (0:57)

"Three Mesquiteers" vehicle (#25) with the boys delivering government horses to a Caribbean island.

2309. Kathleen Mavourneen (Tiffany; 1930). *Cast:* Sally O'Neil (Kathleen, a role which she reprised for the '37 version), Charles Delaney, Robert Elliott, Francis Ford. *D:* Albert Ray.

Romantic drama, previously filmed in 1919 by Fox with Theda Bara and remade in Great Britain in 1937.

2310. Keep 'Em Rolling (RKO; 1934). *Cast:* Walter Huston, Frances Dee, Minna Gombell, Frank Conroy, Robert Shayne (film debut). *D:* George Archainbaud; *As.P.:* William Sistrom. (1:05)

Drama with sentimental touches of a hard-drinking career soldier who loves women and horses, especially Rodney, his favorite horse. The film is set in and filmed on location at Fort Myers, Virginia, spanning the years 1915 to 1933. Based on the story "Rodney" by Leonard Nason.

2311. Keep Smiling (20th Century-Fox; 1938). *Cast:* Jane Withers, Gloria Stuart, Robert Allen, Henry Wilcoxon, Douglas Fowley, Helen Westley, Hal K. Dawson, Pedro de Cordoba, Claudia Coleman, Mary McCarty, Carmencita Johnson, Paula Rae Wright, Etta McDaniel, The Three Nelsons (Ozzie, Harriet and David). *D:* Herbert I. Leeds; *P:* John Stone; *St:* Frank Fenton; *Sc:* Albert Ray, Frances Hyland.

A juvenile comedy-drama which is set in Hollywood.

2312. The Keeper of the Bees (Monogram; 1935). *Cast:* Neil Hamilton, Betty Furness, Emma Dunn, Edith Fellows (Little Scout), Hobart Bosworth (Bee Master), Helen Jerome Eddy, Marion Shilling, James Burtis, Barbara Bedford, Lafe McKee, George Cleveland, William Worthington, Gigi Parrish. *D:* Christy Cabanne; *P:* William T. Lackey; *Sc:* Adele Buffington, George Waggner. (1:15)

Drama of a war veteran who finds a new purpose for living while residing at a peaceful seaside village. Based on the 1925 novel by Gene Stratton-Porter, it was previously filmed in 1925 and remade by Columbia in 1947.

2313. Keeping Company (Xxxx Xxxx; 1931). (No information available)

2314. Kelly of the Secret Service (Victory; 1936). *Cast:* Jack Mulhall, Lloyd Hughes, Fuzzy Knight, Forrest Taylor. *D:* Robert Hill; *P:* Sam Katzman.

Low-budget indie actioner.

2315. Kelly the Second (MGM/Hal Roach; 1936). *Cast:* Patsy Kelly, Guinn Williams, Pert Kelton, Charley Chase, Harold Huber, Maxie Rosenbloom, Billy Gilbert, Edward Brophy, Carl "Alfalfa" Switzer, DeWitt Jennings, Syd Saylor. *D:* Hal Roach, Gus Meins; *P:* Roach; *St:* Jeff Moffitt, William Terhune; *Sc:* Jack Jevne, Gordon Douglas and others. (1:10)

Successful slapstick comedy of a woman training a dimwit boxer whose abilities are limited by a minor quirk.

2316. The Kennel Murder Case (WB; 1933). *Cast:* William Powell (Vance), Mary Astor, Eugene Pallette, Ralph Morgan, Robert McWade, Robert Barrat, Frank Conroy, Etienne Girardot, James Lee, Paul Cavanagh, Arthur Hohl, Helen Vinson, Jack LaRue, Charles Wilson, Henry O'Neill, Ned Sparks, Hobart Cavanaugh, Don Brodie. *D:* Michael Curtiz; *P:* Robert Presnell; *Adaptation:* Presnell; *Sc:* Robert Lee, Peter Milne. (1:13) (video)

Hit Philo Vance mystery set around the world of dog shows. Based on the novel "The Return of Philo Vance" by S.S. Van Dine, the film was remade in 1940 as *Calling Philo Vance.*

2317. Kentucky (20th Century-Fox; 1938). *Cast:* Loretta Young (Sally Goodwin), Richard Greene (Jack Dillon), Walter Brennan (A.A. for B.S.A. as Peter Goodwin), Douglass Dumbrille (John Dillon—1861), Karen Morley (Mrs. Goodwin—1861), Moroni Olsen (John Dillon—1938), Russell Hicks (Thad Goodwin—1861), Willard Robertson (Bob Slocum), Charles Waldron (Thad Goodwin—1938), George Reed (Ben), Bobs Watson (Peter Goodwin—1861), Delmar Watson (Thad Goodwin, Jr.—1861), Leona Roberts (Grace Goodwin), Charles Lane (auctioneer), Charles Middleton (southerner), Harry Hayden (racing secretary), Robert Middlemass (track official), Madame Sul-Te-Wan (Lily), Cliff Clark (Melish), Meredith Howard (Susie May), Frederick Burton (presiding officer), Charles Trowbridge (doctor), Eddie "Rochester" Anderson (groom), Stanley Andrews (presiding judge). *D:* David Butler; *As.P.:* Gene Markey; *Sc:* Lamar Trotti, John Taintor Foote. (1:35) (video)

A lavishly produced technicolor drama of rival horse-breeding families from the Civil War to the present day. Based on the novel "The Look of Eagles" by John Taintor Foote.

2318. Kentucky Blue Streak (Puritan; 1935). *Cast:* Edward Nugent, Patricia Scott. *D:* Raymond K. Johnson.

Nineteenth-century costume drama set around the world of horses.

2319. Kentucky Kernels (RKO; 1934). *Cast:* Bert Wheeler, Robert Woolsey, Mary Carlisle, Spanky McFarland, Noah Beery, Lucille La Verne, Sleep 'n' Eat (Willie Best), Margaret Dumont, Louis Mason, Paul Page, Frank McGlynn, Jr., Richard Alexander, William Pawley. *D:* George Stevens; *As.P.:* H.N. Swanson; *St:* Bert Kalmar, Harry Ruby; *Sc:* Kalmar, Ruby, Fred Guiol; *Songs:* "Supper Song," "One Little Kiss" by Kalmar & Ruby. (G.B. title: *Triple Trouble*) (1:15)

The comedy team of Wheeler and Woolsey as two magicians, adopt a small boy and take him down south to collect his rightful inheritance, running headlong into an old family feud. The film which concludes with an old-fashioned slapstick chase scene was one of the 15 top grossing films of 1934.

2320. Kentucky Moonshine (20th Century–Fox; 1938). *Cast:* Tony Martin, Marjorie Weaver, Ritz Brothers, Slim Summerville, John Carradine, Eddie Collins, Claud Allister, Berton Churchill, Mary Treen, Clarence Wilson, Wally Vernon, Frank McGlynn, Jr., Paul Stanton, Si Jenks, Francis Ford, Brian Sisters. *D:* David Butler; *P:* Kenneth McGowan; *St:* Jack Lait, Jr., M.M. Musselman; *Sc:* Musselman, Art Arthur. (G.B. title: *Three Men and a Girl*) (1:25)

A comedy of feuding hillbillies in the backwoods of Kentucky.

2321. Kept Husbands (RKO; 1931). *Cast:* Dorothy Mackaill, Joel McCrea, Ned Sparks, Mary Carr, Clara Kimball Young, Robert McWade, Bryant Washburn, Florence Roberts, Freeman Wood, Lita Chevret. *D:* Lloyd Bacon; *As.P.:* Louis Sarecky; *St:* Sarecky; *Sc:* Forrest Halsey, Alfred Jackson. (1:16)

Domestic comedy-drama of a millionaire's daughter who marries a poor young football hero.

2322. The Key (WB; 1934). *Cast:* William Powell, Edna Best, Colin Clive, Hobart Cavanaugh, Halliwell Hobbes, Henry O'Neill, Phil Regan, Arthur Treacher, Maxine Doyle, Arthur Aylesworth, Gertrude Short, Dawn O'Day (Anne Shirley), Donald Crisp, J.M. Kerrigan. *D:* Michael Curtiz; *P:* Robert Presnell; *Sc:* Laird Doyle; *Song:* Mort Dixon, Allie Wrubel. (1:11)

Romantic drama set in Ireland in the 1920s. Based on the play by R. Gore Brown and J.L. Hardy.

2323. The Keyhole (WB; 1933). *Cast:* Kay Francis, George Brent, Glenda Farrell, Allen Jenkins, Monroe Owsley, Ferdinand Gottschalk, Henry Kolker, Helen Ware. *D:* Michael Curtiz; *P:* Hal Wallis; *Sc:* Robert Presnell. (1:09)

Low-budget drama of a detective hired to follow a married woman. Based on a story by Alice Duer Miller.

2324. The Kibitzer (Paramount; 1929). *Cast:* Harry Green, Mary Brian, Neil Hamilton, Eugene Pallette, E.H. Calvert, Henry Fink, Albert Gran, Eddie Kane, Lee Kohlmar, David Newell, Guy Oliver. *D:* Edward Sloman. (G.B. title: *The Busybody*)

Low-budget comedy of a meddlesome old gambler who interferes in his daughter's romance. Based on the play by Jo Swerling and Edward G. Robinson.

2325. Kick In (Paramount; 1931). *Cast:* Clara Bow, Regis Toomey, Wynne Gibson, James Murray, Donald Crisp, Leslie Fenton, Wade Boteler, Juliette Compton, J. Carrol Naish, Paul Hurst. *D:* Richard Wallace; *Sc:* Bartlett Cormack.

Drama of a young married couple who are drawn into criminal activity. Based on a 1914 Broadway play by Willard Mack which starred John Barrymore. Previous versions: (Pathé; 1917) with William Courtenay and Mollie King and (Paramount; 1922) with Bert Lytell, May McAvoy and Betty Compson.

2326. The Kid Comes Back (WB; 1937–38). *Cast:* Barton MacLane, Wayne Morris, June Travis, Dickie Jones, Maxie Rosenbloom, Joseph Crehan, Herbert Rawlinson, Frank Otto, James Robbins, Ken Niles. *D:* B. Reeves Eason; *P:* Bryan Foy; *Sc:* George Bricker. (G.B. title: *Don't Pull Your Punches*) (1:01)

B boxing melodrama which had the working title of "Don't Pull Your Punches." Based on the story of that name by E.J. Flanagan (Dennis O'Keefe).

2327. Kid Courageous (Supreme; 1935). *Cast:* Bob Steele, Reneé Borden, Arthur Loft, Jack Powell, Lafe McKee, Kit Guard, Vane Calvert, Barry Sevry, Perry Murdock, John Elliott. *D:* Robert N. Bradbury; *P:* A.W. Hackel; *Sc:* Bradbury. (0:53)

Bob Steele western of an eastern athlete who goes west and eventually saves the girl from an unwanted marriage.

2328. The Kid from Arizona (Cosmos; 1931). *Cast:* Jack Perrin, Josephine Hill, Robert Walker, George Chesebro, Henry Rocquemore, Ben Corbett. *D:* Robert J. Horner; *Sc:* Robert Walker. (0:55)

Jack Perrin western of a lawman sent to stop Indian raids in the badlands.

2329. The Kid from Kokomo (WB/F.N.; 1939). *Cast:* Pat O'Brien, Wayne Morris, Joan Blondell, May Robson, Jane Wyman, Maxie Rosenbloom, Stanley Fields, Sidney Toler, Clem Bevans, John Ridgely, Ward Bond, Ed Brophy, Paul Hurst, Morgan Conway, Winifred Harris. *D:* Lewis Seiler; *As.P.:* Sam Bischoff; *St:* Dalton Trumbo; *Sc:* Jerry Wald, Richard Macaulay. (G.B. title: *Orphan of the Ring*)

B comedy of a dim-wit boxer with some strange ideas.

2330. The Kid from Spain (United Artists/Samuel Goldwyn; 1932). *Cast:* Eddie Cantor, Lyda Roberti, Theresa Maxwell Conover, Robert Young, Ruth Hall, John Miljan, Noah Beery, J. Carrol Naish, Stanley Fields, Luis Alberni, Robert Emmett O'Connor, Paul Porcasi, Julian Rivero, Ben Hendricks, Jr., Sidney Franklin, Walter Walker. *D:* Leo McCarey; *P:* Samuel Goldwyn; *Sc:* William Anthony McGuire, Bert Kalmar, Harry Ruby; *Choreography:* Busby Berkeley; *Songs:* Kalmar & Ruby. (1:58)

Lavishly produced musical of a young man who is kicked out of college, only to be mistaken for a famous bullfighter. Another hit for Sam Goldwyn, being one of the 11 top grossing films of 1933. In the chorus line of Goldwyn Girls can be seen Lucille Ball, Paulette Goddard, Frances Dean (Betty Grable), & Virginia Bruce.

Note: Shorter versions are known in TV prints.

2331. The Kid from Texas (MGM; 1939). *Cast:* Dennis O'Keefe (nee: Bud Flanagan), Florence Rice, Buddy Ebsen, Jessie Ralph, Anthony Allan (John Hubbard), Tully Marshall, Jack Carson, Virginia Dale. *D:* S. Sylvan Simon; *P:* Edgar Selwyn; *Sc:* Albert Mannheimer, Florence Ryerson, Edgar Allan Woolf. (1:11)

Offbeat B comedy of a cowboy who becomes a polo player.

2332. Kid Galahad (WB/F.N.; 1937). *Cast:* Edward G. Robinson, Bette Davis (Best Actress Award for her performance in combination with *Marked Woman* [q.v.] at the Venice Film Festival), Humphrey Bogart, Wayne Morris (Kid Galahad), Jane Bryan, Harry Carey, Veda Ann Borg, Joseph Crehan, Frank Faylen, Joyce Compton, William Haade (film debut), Ben Welden (American debut), Horace McMahon, Don Defore, Soledad Jimenez, Harland Tucker, Bob Evans, George Blake, Joe Cunningham, Bob Nestell, Frank Hankinson. *D:* Michael Curtiz; *P:* Samuel Bischoff; *Sc:* Seton I. Miller; *Song:* "The Moon Is in Tears Tonight" by M.K. Jerome, Jack Scholl. (TV title: *The Battling Bellhop*) (1:41)

Classic ringside drma of a boxing promoter who creates a star pugilist. Reworked in 1941 as *The Wagons Roll at Night* with a circus setting. Remade in 1962 by Paramount. Based on the book by Francis Wallace.

2333. Kid Gloves (WB; 1929). *Cast:* Conrad Nagel, John Davidson, Lois Wilson, Tommy Dugan, Maude Turner Gordon, Richard Cramer (film debut), Edward Earle. *D:* Ray Enright; *Sc:* Robert Lord.

Part-talkie crime melodrama based on a play by Fred Kennedy Myton.

2334. Kid Millions (United Artists/Samuel Goldwyn; 1935). *Cast:* Eddie Cantor, Ann Sothern, Ethel Merman, George Murphy (film debut), Berton Churchill, Warren Hymer, Paul Harvey, Jesse Block, Eve Sully, Otto Hoffman, Stanley Fields, Edgar Kennedy, Jack Kennedy, John Kelly, Doris Davenport, Nicholas Brothers, Edith Fellows, Fred Kohler, Ward Bond, Clarence Muse, Stymie Beard, Tommy Bond, Guy Usher, Leonard Kibrick, Tor Johnson (film debut in an unbilled bit—see below). *D:* Roy Del Ruth; *P:* Samuel Goldwyn; *Sc:* Arthur Sheekman, Nat Perrin, Nunnally Johnson; *Songs:* Irving Berlin, Bert Kalmar,

Harry Ruby, Walter Donaldson, Gus Kahn, Burton Lane, Harold Adamson; *Piano Number:* Jacques Fray, Mario Braggiotti. (1:30) (video)

Hit musical-comedy of a slum kid who inherits 77 million dollars with the catch that he has to find its hiding place in Egypt. The film has a lavish technicolor finale entitled "Free Ice Cream Factory" and in the chorus line of Goldwyn Girls can be seen Lucille Ball and Paulette Goddard. The film also includes the popular song "Mandy" by Irving Berlin, as well as another hit song "When My Ship Comes In."

Note: Tor Johnson who made his film debut in this feature was later to become better known for his performance as the beefy bald detective in Edward D. Wood, Jr.'s cheapie-creepie *Plan 9 from Outer Space* (1959).

2335. Kid Nightingale (WB; 1939). *Cast:* John Payne, Jane Wyman, Walter Catlett, Harry Burns, Ed Brophy, Charles D. Brown, John Ridgely, William Haade, Lee Phelps, Max Hoffman, Jr., Helen Troy, Frankie Van, Winifred Harris. *D:* George Amy; *As.P.:* Bryan Foy; *St:* Lee Katz; *Sc:* Charles Belden, Raymond Schrock. (0:57)

B comedy of an opera singer who wants to be a prize-fighter.

2336. The Kid Ranger (Supreme; 1936). *Cast:* Bob Steele, Joan Barclay, William Farnum, Earl Dwire, Charles King, Lafe McKee, Frank Ball, Buck Moulton. *D:* Robert N. Bradbury; *P:* A.W. Hackel; *Sc:* Bradbury. (0:57)

Bob Steele western of a ranger who kills the wrong man.

The Kid's Last Fight (G.B. title) *see* **The Life of Jimmy Dolan**

Kidnapped (1933–34) (G.B. title) *see* **Miss Fane's Baby Is Stolen**

2337. Kidnapped—The Adventures of David Balfour (20th Century-

Fox; 1938). *Cast:* Warner Baxter (Alan Breck), Freddie Bartholomew (David Balfour), Arleen Whelan (film debut as Jean MacDonald), C. Aubrey Smith (Duke of Argyle), Reginald Owen (Capt. Hoseason), John Carradine (Gordon), Nigel Bruce (Neil MacDonald), Miles Mander (Ebenezer Balfour), Ralph Forbes (James), H.B. Warner, Arthur Hohl, E.E. Clive, Halliwell Hobbes, Montagu Love, Donald Haines, Moroni Olsen, Mary Gordon, Forrester Harvey, Clyde Cook, Russell Hicks, Billy Watson, Eily Malyon, Kenneth Hunter, Charles Irwin, John Burton, David Clyde, Holmes Herbert, Brandon Hurst, Vernon Steele, C. Montague Shaw, R.T. Noble. *D:* Alfred L. Werker; *As.P.:* Kenneth MacGowan; *Sc:* Sonya Levien, Eleanor Harris, Ernest Pascal, Edwin Blum. (1:30) (video)

A reworked version of Robert Louis Stevenson's classic novel of a boy sold into slavery. Set in 18th-century Scotland, it was previously filmed in 1918 by Edison as *Kidnapped.* Remade in 1948 and again in Great Britain in 1960 and 1971.

2338. Kiki (United Artists/Art Cinema; 1931). *Cast:* Mary Pickford (title role), Reginald Denny, Joseph Cawthorn, Margaret Livingston, Phil Tead, Fred Walton, Edwin Maxwell, Benay Venuta, Frances Dean (Betty Grable). *D:* Sam Taylor; *P:* Mary Pickford; *Sc:* Taylor. (1:36)

Comedy of a chorus girl who pursues a married musical impresario. This was the next to last film for Mary Pickford before retiring and was also her first film to lose money for United Artists. Her popularity had declined rapidly after cutting off her famous curls in 1929 for her role in *Coquette* (q.v.). Based on a play by David Belasco, it was filmed previously by First National in 1926 with Norma Talmadge.

2339. Killer ar Large (Columbia; 1936). *Cast:* Betty Compson, Mary Brian, George McKay, Thurston Hall, Henry Brandon, Harry Hayden, Lon Chaney, Jr., Boyd Irwin. *D:* David Selman; *Sc:* Harold Shumate.

B melodrama.

2340. Killers of the Sea (Grand National; 1937). *Cast:* Captain Wallace Caswell, Jr., "Spot" Hayes, Bruce Stillwell, Steve Beadon, Hubert Dykes, "Evolution" Henderson, Bryant Lee, Julius Randy. *D:* Ray Friedgen; *P:* Friedgen; *St:* Frederick M. Wagner; *Sc:* Adrian Johnson; *Additional Dialogue:* John P. Medbury. (0:49)

A marine documentary-adventure set in the Gulf of Mexico and narrated by Lowell Thomas.

2341. Kind Lady (MGM; 1935). *Cast:* Aline MacMahon, Basil Rathbone, Mary Carlisle, Frank Albertson, Dudley Digges, Doris Lloyd, Frank Reicher, Donald Meek, Eily Malyon, Robert Graves. *D:* George B. Seitz; *P:* Lucien Hubbard; *St:* "The Silver Casket" by Hugh Walpole; *Sc:* Bernard Schubert. (TV title: *House of Menace*) (1:16)

B suspense melodrama of criminals who take over the house of a reclusive old lady with the intent of doing away with her. Based on the play by Edward Chodorov, it was remade in 1951 with Ethel Barrymore.

2342. The King and the Chorus Girl (WB; 1937). *Cast:* Joan Blondell, Fernand Gravet, Edward Everett Horton, Jane Wyman, Alan Mowbray, Mary Nash, Luis Alberni, Kenny Baker, Ben Welden, Torben Meyer, Armand Kaliz, Leonard Mudie, Georges Renavent, Adrian Rosley, Ferdinand Schumann-Heink, Lionel Pape, Montague Shaw, Velma Wayne. *D:* Mervyn LeRoy; *P:* LeRoy; *Sc:* Norman Krasna and Groucho Marx; *Song:* Werner Heymann, Ted Koehler. (G.B. title: *Romance Is Sacred*) (1:34)

Romantic comedy based on the story "Grand Passion" by Norman Krasna and Groucho Marx.

2343. King for a Night (Universal; 1933). *Cast:* Chester Morris, Helen Twelvetrees, Alice White, John Miljan, Grant Mitchell, George E. Stone, George Meeker, Frank Albertson, Warren Hymer, Maxie Rosenbloom, John Sheehan, Wade Boteler. *D:* Kurt Neumann; *St:* William Anthony McGuire; *Sc:* McGuire, Jack O'Donnell, Scott Pembroke. (1:10)

Melodrama of a boxer who takes the rap for the murder of a fight promoter who was killed by the fighter's sister.

2344. King Kelly of the U.S.A. (Monogram; 1934). *Cast:* Guy Robertson (his only film, as King Kelly), Irene Ware, Edgar Kennedy, Franklin Pangborn, Joyce Compton, Ferdinand Gottschalk, William von Brincken, Lorin Raker, Otis Harlan, Bodil Rosing. *D:* Leonard Fields; *P:* George Bertholon; *St:* Bertholon, Howard Higgin; *Sc:* Fields, David Silverstein. (G.B. title: *Irish and Proud of It*) (1:06)

B musical-comedy of a theatrical troupe which travels to the mythical kingdom of Belgardia where romance blossoms between the king's daughter and the troupe's owner.

2345. King Kong (RKO; 1933). *Cast:* Robert Armstrong (Carl Denham), Fay Wray (Ann Darrow), Bruce Cabot (Jack Driscoll), Frank Reicher (Captain Englehorn), Victor Wong (Charlie), Noble Johnson (native chief), Sam Hardy (Weston), Steve Clemente (witch king), James Flavin (second mate Briggs), Paul Porcasi (apple vendor), Lynton Brent & Frank Mills (reporters), Vera Lewis, Ethan Laidlaw, Dick Curtis, Charlie Sullivan, LeRoy Mason, Ernest B. Schoedsack, Merian C. Cooper (bits as Fliers). *D:* Merian C. Cooper, Ernest B. Schoedsack; *P:* Cooper & Shoedsack; *St:* Cooper & Edgar Wallace; *Sc:* James Ashmore Creelman, Ruth Rose; *Chief Technician:* Willis H. O'Brien. (1:43) (video—b/w and computer-colored—both with re-stored footage originally censored in 1933).

A genuine American classic is the now legendary story of the giant gorilla found on a prehistoric isle, brought back to New York City as a money-making venture, only to escape leaving a path of death and destruction. RKO was in dire financial straits when it decided to take a chance on this production, in turn seeing a monstrous (no pun intended) return at the box office. Prior to release the film had the working titles of "Kong," "The Beast" and "The Eighth Wonder." Upon its release on April 7, 1933, in New York City "Kong" played simultaneously at Radio City Music Hall and the Roxy, being the first film to date to receive such an honor. Re-releases in 1938 and 1953 also brought substanial financial returns. In November of 1933 a hurried sequel titled *Son of Kong* (q.v.) followed close on the success trail of *King Kong.* Remade in 1976 in a contemporary style. The original "Kong" was computer-colored by Turner Entertainment in 1989.

Notes: 1. Many of the sets utilized for the prehistoric island were earlier creations of special effects technician Willis H. O'Brien for an unfulfilled project (at least in his lifetime) titled "Genesis" that he was unable to get financial backing for. O'Brien died in 1962 and seven years later his unfulfilled project was brought to the screen by Warners as *The Valley of Gwangi* (1969). 2. Prior to "Kong" many of the same sets were used for *The Most Dangerous Game* (q.v.).

2346. The King Murder (Chesterfield; 1932). *Cast:* Conway Tearle, Natalie Moorhead, Don Alvarado, Marceline Day, Dorothy Revier, Robert Frazer, Rose Dione. *D:* Richard Thorpe.

Low-budget who-dun-it from "poverty row."

2347. King of Alcatraz (Paramount; 1938). *Cast:* J. Carrol Naish,

Gail Patrick, Lloyd Nolan, Harry Carey, Robert Preston (film debut), Anthony Quinn, Porter Hall, Richard Denning, Richard Stanley (Dennis Morgan), Emory Parnell, Gustav von Seyffertitz, Tom Tyler, Monte Blue, Dorothy Howe (Virginia Vale), Paul Fix, Jack Norton, Nora Cecil, Philip Warren, Virginia Dabney, John Hart. *D:* Robert Florey; *P:* William C. Thomas; *St & Sc:* Irving Reis. (G.B. title: *King of the Alcatraz*) (0:55)

B melodrama of convicts who take over a ship.

2348. King of Burlesque (Fox; 1935). *Cast:* Warner Baxter, Jack Oakie, Alice Faye, Mona Barrie, Dixie Dunbar, Fats Waller, Kenny Baker, Keye Luke, Jane Wyman, Gregory Ratoff, Andrew Tombes, Herbert Mundin, Shirley Deane, Nick Long, Jr., Montague Shaw, Claudia Coleman, Harry Welch, Paxton Sisters, Herbert Ashley, Gareth Johnson, Ellen Lowe, Jerry Mandy. *D:* Sidney Lanfield; *P:* Darryl F. Zanuck; *As.P.:* Kenneth MacGowan; *Sc:* James Seymour, Gene Markey, Harry Tugend; *Choreography:* (A.A.N.) Sammy Lee for two dance numbers, "Lovely Lady" & "Too Good to Be True"; *Songs Include:* "I'm Shootin' High" by Jimmy McHugh. (1:23) (video)

Musical which was remade in 1943 by this studio as *Hello, Frisco, Hello* with a Barbary Coast setting.

2349. King of Chinatown (Paramount; 1939). *Cast:* Anna May Wong, Sidney Toler, Akim Tamiroff, J. Carrol Naish, Anthony Quinn, Roscoe Karns, Philip Ahn, Richard Denning, Bernadene Hayes, Ray Mayer, Charles Trowbridge, George Anderson. *D:* Nick Grinde; *P:* Harold Hurley; *St:* Herbert J. Biberman; *Sc:* Lillie Hayward, Irving Reis. (1:00)

B melodrama of gangsters who are trying to muscle in on Chinatown.

2350. King of Gamblers (Paramount; 1937). *Cast:* Lloyd Nolan, Claire Trevor, Akim Tamiroff, Buster Crabbe,

Porter Hall, Evelyn Brent, Harvey Stephens, Fay Holden, Cecil Cunningham, Colin Tapley, Helen Burgess, Paul Fix, Purnell Pratt, Barlowe Borland. *D:* Robert Florey; *St:* Tiffany Thayer; *Sc:* Doris Anderson. (aka: *Czar of the Slot Machines*) (1:19)

B crime melodrama set in the days before Las Vegas became the big gambling capitol of the U.S.

2351. King of Hockey (WB; 1936). *Cast:* Dick Purcell, Wayne Morris (film debut—see note below), Anne Nagel, Ann Gillis, Marie Wilson, George E. Stone, Joseph Crehan, Gordon Hart, Harry Davenport, Andre Beranger, Frank Faylen. *D:* Noel Smith; *P:* Bryan Foy; *Sc:* George Bricker. (G.B. title: *King of the Ice Rink*) (0:57)

Title tells all in this B action drama.

Note: Hirschhorn in "The Warner Brothers Story" states this film as Morris' film debut, but Halliwell and Katz state it was *China Clipper* (q.v.) (also released in 1936). *C.C.* was released first, but *K.O.H.* may have been produced first with release held up till the end of '36.

2352. The King of Jazz (Universal; 1930). *Cast:* Paul Whiteman & his orchestra, Rhythm Boys (with Bing Crosby in his film debut), John Boles, Jeanette Loff, Glenn Tryon, Walter Brennan, Laura La Plante, Slim Summerville, Otis Harlan, Marcia Mae Jones, Merna Kennedy, John Arledge (film debut), Charles Irwin, Frank Leslie, William Kent, Stanley Smith, G Sisters, Brox Sisters, Russell Markert Dancers, George Chiles, Jacques Cartier. *D:* John Murray Anderson (directorial debut); *P:* Carl Laemmle, Jr.; *Sc:* Harry Ruskin, Charles MacArthur, Edward T. Lowe; *Art-Set Decoration:* (A.A. 1929–30) Herman Rosse; *Songs:* "Mississippi Mud" by Harry Barris & James Cavanaugh (performed by the Rhythm Boys); "Music Hath Charm" (sung by Crosby), "Happy Feet," "A Bench in the Park" by Jack Yellen & Milton Ager; "So the Bluebirds and the

Blackbirds Got Together" by Barris & Billy Moll; "It Happened in Monterey" by Mabel Wayne & Billy Rose; "Ragamuffin Romeo" by Wayne & Harry DeCosta; "When Day Is Done" by Buddy DeSylva & Robert Katscher; "The Aba Daba Honeymoon" by Walter Donovan & Arthur Shields and "Song of the Dawn" (sung by Boles) by Milton Ager & Jack Yellen. (1:45) (video)

Early musical filmed in 2-color technicolor at a cost of $2,000,000. It features many musical production numbers including George Gershwin's "Rhapsody in Blue" which was especially written for and is performed by Paul Whiteman and his orchestra. The film also includes a number of comedy skits and an animated sequence by Walter Lantz.

King of the Alcatraz (G.B. title) *see* **King of Alcatraz**

2353. King of the Arena (Universal; 1933). *Cast:* Ken Maynard, Lucille Brown, Michael Visaroff, Bob Kortman, Jack Rockwell, James Marcus, John St. Polis, Coleman Brothers Circus. *D:* Alan James (Alvin J. Neitz); *Sc:* James. (1:02)

Ken Maynard western with a wild west show setting in a story of a Texas Ranger out to trap some smugglers.

King of the Ice Rink (G.B. title) *see* **King of Hockey**

2354. King of the Jungle (Paramount; 1933). *Cast:* Buster Crabbe (in his starring debut), Frances Dee, Irving Pichel, Sidney Toler, Douglass Dumbrille, Nydia Westman, Robert Barrat, Warner Richmond, Sam Baker, Patricia Farley, Ronnie Cosbey, Robert Adair, Florence Britton. *D:* H. Bruce Humberstone, Max Marcin; *St:* Charles Thurley Stoneham; *Adaptation:* Marcin; *Sc:* Philip Wylie, Fred Niblo, Jr. (1:13)

A man who grew up wild in the jungle is brought to the United States and exploited in a circus. This film, which climaxes with a big top fire

became a phenomenal money-maker for the studio.

King of the Jungleland *see* **Batmen of Africa**

King of the Khyber Rifles (G.B. title) *see* **The Black Watch**

2355. King of the Newsboys (Republic; 1938). *Cast:* Lew Ayres, Helen Mack, Billy Benedict, Alison Skipworth, Sheila Bromley, Alice White, Gloria Rich, Marjorie Main, Horace MacMahon, Byron Foulger, Victor Varconi, Mary Kornman, Oscar O'Shea, Jack Pennick, Victor Ray Cooke. *D:* Bernard Vorhaus; *St:* Horace McCoy, Sam Ornitz; *Sc:* Peggy Thompson, Lewis Weitzenkorn.

B delinquency melodrama.

2356/2357. King of the Pecos (Republic; 1936). *Cast:* John Wayne, Muriel Evans, Cy Kendall, Jack Clifford, J. Frank Glendon, Herbert Heywood, Arthur Aylesworth, John Beck, Mary MacLaren, Yakima Canutt, Bradley Metcalfe, Jr., Edward Hearn, Earl Dwire, Tex Palmer, Jack Kirk. *D:* Joe Kane; *Sc:* Bernard McConville, Dorrell & Stuart McGowan. (0:54)

John Wayne western of a law student who goes after the party who killed his parents ten years before.

2358. King of the Royal Mounted (20th Century–Fox; 1936). *Cast:* Robert Kent, Rosalind Keith, Jack Luden, Alan Dinehart, Frank McGlynn, Grady Sutton, Arthur Loft. *D:* Howard Bretherton; *P:* Sol Lesser (Principal); *Sc:* Earle Snell. (1:01)

B actioner of a Mountie out to stop the theft of a scientist's invention. Based on the comic strip by Zane Grey, it was remade as a serial by Republic in 1940.

2359. King of the Sierras (Grand National; 1938). *Cast:* Rex the horse,

Sheik the horse, Hobart Bosworth, Harry Harvey, Jr., Frank Campeau, Harry Harvey, Sr., Jack Lindell. *D:* Samuel Diege; *P:* George A. Hirliman; *St:* Frank Gay; *Sc:* W. Scott Darling. (0:53)

A horse story.

2360. King of the Turf (United Artists; 1939). *Cast:* Adolphe Menjou, Roger Daniel, Walter Abel, Dolores Costello, Alan Dinehart, William Demarest, Harold Huber, George McKay, Lee M. Moore, Fred "Snowflake" Toones, Milburn Stone, William Bakewell, George Chandler, Cliff Nazarro, Oscar O'Shea, Charles McAvoy. *D:* Alfred E. Green; *P:* Edward Small; *Sc:* George Bruce. (1:28)

This sentimental drama of a young jockey who attempts to rehabilitate a race track derelict was a loser at the box office.

2361. King of the Underworld (WB; 1939). *Cast:* Humphrey Bogart, Kay Francis, James Stephenson, John Eldredge, Jessie Busley, John Ridgely, Arthur Aylesworth, Clem Bevans, Murray Alper, Harland Tucker, Ralph Remley. *D:* Lewis Seiler; *As.P.:* Bryan Foy; *Sc:* Vincent Sherman, George Bricker. (1:09)

Melodrama of a lady doctor who becomes involved with gangsters. A remake of *Dr. Socrates* (q.v.) and based on the novel of that name by W.R. Burnett. Remade as *Bullet Scars* (WB; 1942).

2362. King of the Wild Horses (Columbia; 1933). *Cast:* Rex the horse, William Janney, Dorothy Appleby, Wallace MacDonald, Harry Semels, Art Mix, Ford West, King the horse, Lady the horse. *D:* Earl Haley; *Sc:* Fred Myton. (1:02)

B western of a wild horse and the cowboy who tames him.

2363. King Solomon of Broadway (Universal; 1935). *Cast:* Edmund Lowe, Dorothy Page, Louise Henry, Edward Pawley, Dwight Frye, Charley Grapewin, Bradley Page, Pinky Tomlin, Arthur Vinton, Clyde Dilson. *D:* Alan Crosland; *St & Sc:* Albert J. Cohen, Robert T. Shannon. (1:12)

B melodrama of a night club owner who gets involved with the mob when he tries to save his establishment.

2364. The King Steps Out (Columbia; 1936). *Cast:* Grace Moore, Franchot Tone, Walter Connolly, Raymond Walburn, Herman Bing, Victor Jory, Elizabeth Risdon, Nana Bryant, Frieda Inescort, E.E. Clive, Thurston Hall, Johnny Arthur, DeWolf (William) Hopper, George Hassell, Gustav Holm. *D:* Josef Von Sternberg; *P:* William Perlberg; *Sc:* Sidney Buchman; *Songs:* Fritz Kreisler, Dorothy Fields. (1:25)

Romantic costumer with music set among the aristocracy of Europe. Based on the operetta "Sissy" by Hubert and Ernst Marischka, it was one of the 25 top grossing films of 1935-36.

2365. The King's Vacation (WB; 1933). *Cast:* George Arliss (Philip), Dick Powell, Marjorie Gateson, Florence Arliss (Wilhelmina), Dudley Digges, Patricia Ellis, O.P. Heggie, Douglas Gerrard, Desmond Roberts, Charles Evans, Harold Minjir, Maude Leslie, James Bell, Helena Phillips, Vernon Steele. *D:* John Adolfi; *P:* Lucien Hubbard; *St:* Ernest Pascal; *Sc:* Pascal, Maude T. Howell. (1:02)

A king abdicates his throne and seeks a life-style with a slower pace.

2366. Kismet (WB/F.N.; 1930). *Cast:* Otis Skinner (who also appeared in the 1911 stage production as Haji), Loretta Young (Haji's daughter), David Manners (Caliph), Mary Duncan (Zeleekha), Sidney Blackmer (Wazir), Edmund Breese (Jawan), Ford Sterling, Montagu Love, Theodore von Eltz, Blanche Frederici, John St. Polis, John Sheehan, Richard Carlyle. *D:* John Francis Dillon; *Sc:* Howard Estabrook. (1:30)

An Arabian Nights-type tale of romance and skullduggery. A lavish production, filmed in the 65mm. Vitascope wide-screen process, it is based on the 1911 play by Edward Knoblock. A remake of the 1920 Robertson-Cole production which also starred Skinner. Remade in Germany in 1931, followed by another American remake in 1944. The play was then adapted to the Broadway stage as a musical and was again filmed as such in 1955.

2367. Kiss and Make Up (Paramount; 1934). *Cast:* Cary Grant, Genevieve Tobin, Helen Mack, Edward Everett Horton, Lucien Littlefield, Mona Maris, Henry Armetta, Jacqueline Wells (Julie Bishop), Andre Beranger, Doris Lloyd, Katherine Williams, Clara Lou (Ann) Sheridan, Rafael Storm, Lucille Lund, Toby Wing, Milton Wallace. *D:* Harlan Thompson; *P:* B.P. Schulberg; *Sc:* Thompson, George Marion, Jr., Jane Hinton; *Songs:* Ralph Rainger, Leo Robin. (1:20)

Romantic comedy of a male Parisian beautician. Based on the play by Stephen Bekeffi.

2368. The Kiss Before the Mirror (Universal; 1933). *Cast:* Nancy Carroll, Frank Morgan, Gloria Stuart, Paul Lukas, Charley Grapewin, Jean Dixon, Donald Cook, Walter Pidgeon, Robert Adair, Christian Rub, Reginald Mason, Wallis Clark, Allen Connor. *D:* James Whale; *Sc:* William Anthony McGuire. (1:06)

A lawyer who is defending a man for killing his cheating wife, begins to see the same scenario occurring in his own life. Set in Vienna, the film is based on the play by Ladislaus Fodor and utilizes leftover sets from *Frankenstein* (q.v.). Remade as *Wives Under Suspicion* (q.v.).

2369. Kiss Me Again (WB/F.N.; 1931). *Cast:* Walter Pidgeon, Bernice Claire, Frank McHugh, Edward Everett Horton, Albert Gran, June Collyer, Judith Vosselli, Claude Gillingwater, G

Sisters. *D:* William A. Seiter; *Sc:* Julian Josephson, Paul Perez. (G.B. title: *Toast of the Legion*) (1:14)

Romantic musical filmed in 2-color technicolor of a cabaret singer and a French lieutenant. Based on the operetta "Mademoiselle Modiste" by Victor Herbert and Henry Blossom, the film was a box office flop.

2370. Kiss of Araby (Xxxx Xxxx; 1933). (No information available)

2371. Klondike (Monogram; 1932). *Cast:* Lyle Talbot, Thelma Todd, Captain Frank Hawks, Henry B. Walthall, Priscilla Dean, Tully Marshall, Jason Robards, Ethel Wales, Pat O'Malley, Myrtle Stedman, George Hayes, Lafe McKee. *D:* Phil Rosen; *P:* William T. Lackey; *St & Sc:* Tristram Tupper. (1:08)

Low-budget action drama of a doctor who loses his license after a patient dies on the operating table, ultimately finding himself aboard a plane downed in Alaska. Remade as *Klondike Fury* (Monogram; 1942).

2372. Klondike Annie (Paramount; 1936). *Cast:* Mae West, Victor McLaglen, Philip Reed, Harold Huber, Helen Jerome Eddy, Harry Beresford, Esther Howard, Lucile Webster Gleason, Soo Yong, Conway Tearle, Lawrence Grant, George Walsh (final film—ret.), James Burke, Philip Ahn, Ted Oliver, Tetsu Komai, John Rogers. *D:* Raoul Walsh; *P:* William LeBaron; *St:* Marion Morgan, Frank Dazey, George B. Dowell; *Sc:* Mae West. (1:20)

Romantic comedy with songs of a wanted woman who flees to the Klondike and poses as a missionary worker.

2373. Klondike Gold (Xxxx Xxxx; 1932). (No information available)

2374. Knight of the Plains (Spectrum; 1938). *Cast:* Fred Scott, Al St. John, Marion Weldon, Richard Cramer, John Merton, Frank LaRue, Lafe

McKee, Emma Tansey, Steve Clark, Carl Mathews, Sherry Tansey, Jimmy Aubrey, George Morrell, Cactus Mack, Budd Buster, Tex Palmer, Olin Francis, Bob Burns. *D:* Sam Newfield; *P:* Stan Laurel Productions, Jed Buell; *Sc:* Fred Myton. (0:57)

Fred Scott western with songs of a cowboy who helps some settlers besieged by cattle rustlers.

Konga (G.B. title) *see* **Konga, the Wild Stallion**

2375. Konga, the Wild Stallion (Columbia; 1939–40). *Cast:* Fred Stone, Rochelle Hudson, Richard Fiske, Eddy Waller, Robert Warwick, Carl Stockdale, Don Beddoe, George Cleveland, Burr Caruth. *D:* Sam Nelson; *Sc:* Harold Shumate. (G.B. title: *Konga*) (1:05)

Equine drama of a rancher who kills the man who shot his horse.

2376. Kongo (MGM; 1932). *Cast:* Walter Huston (repeating his stage role as Deadlegs Flint), Lupe Velez, Conrad Nagel, Virginia Bruce, C. Henry Gordon, Mitchell Lewis, Forrester Harvey, Charles Middleton, Curtis Nero. *D:* William J. Cowen (directorial debut); *Sc:* Leon Gordon. (1:26)

Jungle melodrama of a madman who seeks revenge on the daughter of the man who crippled him. A remake of *West of Zanzibar* (MGM; 1928) with Lon Chaney, it was based on the play of that name by Chester DeVonde and Kilbourn Gordon. The earlier version was popular at the box office, but this remake was not.

2377. Laddie (RKO; 1935). *Cast:* John Beal, Gloria Stuart, Donald Crisp, Virginia Weidler, Willard Robertson, Dorothy Peterson, William Bakewell, Charlotte Henry, Gloria Shea, Jimmy Butler, Greta Meyer, Grady Sutton, Mary Forbes. *D:* George Stevens; *P:* Pandro S. Berman; *Sc:* Ray Harris, Dorothy Yost.

Sentimental rural drama of life and love in Indiana. Previously filmed in 1926 by Film Booking Office, it was remade by RKO in 1940. Based on the 1913 novel by Gene Stratton-Porter.

2378. Ladies Beware (Republic; 1936). *D:* Irving Pichel.

(No other information available)

2379. Ladies Courageous (Xxxx Xxxx; 1932). (No information available)

2380. Ladies Crave Excitement (Mascot; 1935). *Cast:* Norman Foster, Evalyn Knapp, Eric Linden, Esther Ralston, Purnell Pratt, Irene Franklin, Emma Dunn, Gilbert Emery, Russell Hicks, Christian Rub, Francis McDonald, Matt McHugh, Syd Saylor, George Hayes, Jason Robards, Stanley Blystone, Milburn Stone, Robert Frazer, Ed Peil, Sr. *D:* Nick Grinde; *P:* Armand Schaefer; *St:* John Rathmell; *Sc:* Wellyn Totman, W. Scott Darling. (1:13)

Low-budget drama of rival newsreel companies.

2381. Ladies in Distress (Republic; 1938). *Cast:* Polly Moran, Alison Skipworth, Bob Livingston, Berton Churchill, Horace MacMahon, Max Terhune. *D:* Gus Meins.

Comedy-drama of the lady mayor of a small town who wants to clean out the criminal element.

2382. Ladies in Love (Chesterfield; 1930). *Cast:* Alice Day, Dorothy Gould, Johnnie Walker, Elinor Flynn, Freeman Wood. *D:* Edgar Lewis; *Sc:* Charles Beahan.

"Poverty row" comedy-drama.

2383. Ladies in Love (20th Century–Fox; 1936). *Cast:* Janet Gaynor, Loretta Young, Constance Bennett, Simone Simon, Don Ameche, Paul Lukas, Tyrone Power, Alan Mowbray, Wilfrid Lawson, J. Edward Bromberg, Virginia Field, Eleanor Wesselhoeft, James Burtis, Frank Dawson, John Bleifer, Egon Brecher, Lynn Bari, Vesey

O'Davoren. *D:* Edward H. Griffith; *P:* B.G. DeSylva; *Sc:* Melville Baker. (1:37)

This romance of women on the hunt for men, based on the play by Ladislaus Bus-Fekete, is set in Budapest, Hungary.

2384. Ladies Love Brutes (Paramount; 1930). *Cast:* George Bancroft, Mary Astor, Fredric March, Margaret Quimby, Stanley Fields, Claud Allister, Crauford Kent, E.H. Calvert, Paul Fix, Ferike Boros, Lawford Davidson, Freddie Burke Frederick, Ben Hendricks, Jr., David Durand. *D:* Rowland V. Lee; *Sc:* Herman J. Mankiewicz, Waldemar Young. (1:23)

Comedy-drama of a gangster who falls for a lady socialite. Based on the play "Pardon My Glove" by Zoe Akins.

2385. Ladies Love Danger (Fox; 1935). *Cast:* Donald Cook, Adrienne Ames, Mona Barrie, Gilbert Roland, Hardie Albright, Herbert Mundin, Billy Benedict. *D:* H. Bruce Humberstone; *Sc:* Co-written by Samson Raphaelson.

Low-budget melodrama.

2386. Ladies' Man (Paramount; 1931). *Cast:* William Powell, Kay Francis, Carole Lombard, Gilbert Emery, Olive Tell, John Holland, Maude Turner Gordon, Martin Burton, Frank Atkinson. *D:* Lothar Mendes; *St:* Rupert Hughes; *Sc:* Herman J. Mankiewicz. (1:10)

Hit sophisticated comedy-drama of a society gigolo and his many female conquests.

2387. Ladies Must Love (Universal; 1933). *Cast:* June Knight, Sally O'Neil, Dorothy Burgess, Mary Carlisle, Neil Hamilton, George E. Stone, Edmund Breese, Arthur Hoyt, Richard Carle, Oscar Apfel, Berton Churchill, Virginia Cherrill, Maude Eburne. *D:* E.A. Dupont; *Sc:* John Francis Larkin. (1:10)

Hit depression-era comedy of four girls who decide to split their paychecks four ways in order to make ends meet— with the expected problems after the agreement is set in motion. Based on the play by William Hurlbut.

2388. Ladies Must Play (Columbia; 1930). *Cast:* Neil Hamilton. *D:* Raymond Cannon; *Dialogue:* Jo Swerling.

Ladies' Night (G.B. title) *see* **Ladies Night in a Turkish Bath**

2389. Ladies' Night in a Turkish Bath (First National; 1928). *Cast:* Dorothy Mackaill, James Finlayson, Guinn Williams, Jack Mulhall, Sylvia Ashton, Reed Howes. *D:* Edward Cline; *St:* Charlton Andrews, Avery Hopwood; *Sc:* Henry McCarty, Gene Towne. (G.B. title: *Ladies' Night*)

Part-talkie comedy.

2390. Ladies of Leisure (Columbia; 1930). *Cast:* Barbara Stanwyck, Lowell Sherman, Ralph Graves, Marie Prevost, Nance O'Neil, George Fawcett, Johnnie Walker. *D:* Frank Capra; *St:* Milton Herbert Gropper; *Sc:* Jo Swerling. (1:38)

Drama of a gold digger who falls for a playboy. Previously filmed in 1926. Remade as *Women of Glamour* (q.v.).

2391. Ladies of the Big House (Paramount; 1931–32). *Cast:* Sylvia Sidney, Gene Raymond, Wynne Gibson, Rockliffe Fellowes, Earle Foxe, Purnell Pratt, Louise Beavers, Jane Darwell, Noel Francis, Esther Howard, Hilda Vaughn, Theodore von Eltz, Roscoe Karns, J. Carrol Naish, Fritzi Ridgeway, Miriam Goldina, Mary Foy, Frank Sheridan, Edna Bennett, Ruth Lyons. *D:* Marion Gering; *St:* Ernest Booth; *Sc:* Louis Weitzenkorn. (1:17)

The title tells all in this hit melodrama of a young couple who are framed for murder. Remade in 1940 as *Women Without Names.*

2392. Ladies of the Jury (RKO; 1932). *Cast:* Edna May Oliver, Jill

Esmond, Roscoe Ates, Ken Murray, Kitty Kelly, Cora Witherspoon, Robert McWade, Charles Dow Clark, Helene Millard, Kate Price, Lita Chevret, Florence Lake, Guinn Williams, Leyland Hodgson, Andre Beranger, George Humbert, Alan Roscoe, Suzanne Fleming, Morgan Galloway, Tom Francis. *D:* Lowell Sherman; *As.P.:* Douglas MacLean; *Sc:* Marion Dix, Salisbury Field, Eddie Welch. (1:03)

Low-budget comedy-drama of a stubborn and feisty society matron who disrupts courtroom proceedings to get to the truth of the case on trial. Based on the play by John Frederick Ballard, it was remade as *We're on the Jury* (q.v.).

2393. Ladies Should Listen (Paramount; 1934). *Cast:* Cary Grant, Frances Drake, Edward Everett Horton, Rosita Moreno, George Barbier, Nydia Westman, Charles Ray, Clara Lou (Ann) Sheridan, Rafael Corio (Rafael Storm), Charles North, Henrietta Burnside, Charles Arnt (film debut). *D:* Frank Tuttle; *P:* Douglas MacLean; *Sc:* Claude Binyon, Frank Butler, Guy Bolton. (1:03)

B romantic comedy of a telephone operator and a businessman.

2394. Ladies They Talk About (WB; 1933). *Cast:* Barbara Stanwyck, Lyle Talbot, Preston Foster, Dorothy Burgess, Lillian Roth (in her final film appearance till 1977 due to a bout with alcoholism), Maude Eburne, Ruth Donnelly, Harold Huber, Grace Cunard, Helen Ware, Robert McWade, Allen Jenkins, Robert Warwick, Cecil Cunningham, Harry Gribbon, Madame Sul-Te-Wan, Helen Mann, Harold Healy. *D:* Howard Bretherton, William Keighley; *P:* Raymond Griffith; *Sc:* Sidney Sutherland, Brown Holmes. (1:09)

Melodrama based on the play "Women in Prison" by Dorothy Mackaye and Carlton Miles.

2395. Lady and Gent (Paramount; 1932). *Cast:* George Bancroft,

Wynne Gibson, Charles Starrett, James Gleason, John Wayne, Joyce Compton, Charley Grapewin, Morgan Wallace, Billy Butts, William Halligan, James Crane. *D:* Stephen Roberts; *St:* (A.A.N.) Grover Jones, William Slavens McNutt. (aka: *The Challenger*)

B drama of a washed up boxer and his girl, a night club hostess. Remade as *Unmarried* (q.v.).

2396. The Lady and the Mob (Columbia; 1939). *Cast:* Fay Bainter, Ida Lupino, Lee Bowman, Henry Armetta, Warren Hymer, Harold Huber, Joseph Sawyer. *D:* Ben Stoloff; *P:* Fred Kohlmar; *Sc:* Richard Maibaum, Gertrude Purcell. (1:05)

B comedy of a rich lady and her "gang."

2397. Lady, Be Careful (Paramount; 1936). *Cast:* Lew Ayres, Mary Carlisle, Buster Crabbe, Grant Withers, Benny Baker, Wesley Barry, Josephine McKim, Jack Chapin, Wilma Francis, Terry Ray (Ellen Drew). *D:* Theodore Reed; *Sc:* Dorothy Parker, Alan Campbell, Harry Ruskin.

B comedy of a sailor who makes a bet with his buddies that he can romance a girl, despite his shyness. Based on the plays "The Fleet's In" by Monte Bria and J. Walter Ruben and "Sailor Beware" by John Kenyon Nicholson and Charles Robinson. Remade in 1941 as *The Fleet's In* and again in 1952 as *Sailor Beware.*

Lady Be Gay (G.B. title) *see* **Laugh It Off**

2398. Lady Behave (Republic; 1937). *Cast:* Sally Eilers, Joseph Schildkraut, Neil Hamilton, Warren Hymer, Marcia Mae Jones, Grant Mitchell, Charles Richman, Patricia Farr, Robert Greig, George Ernest, Mary Gordon. *D:* Lloyd Corrigan; *St:* Joseph Krumgold; *Sc:* Krumgold, Olive Cooper.

B romantic comedy.

Lady Beware (G.B. title) *see* **The Thirteenth Guest**

2399. Lady by Choice (Columbia; 1934). *Cast:* Carole Lombard, May Robson, Walter Connolly, Roger Pryor, Arthur Hohl, Raymond Walburn, James Burke, Henry Kolker, Lillian Harmer, Fred "Snowflake" Toones, John Boyle, Bud Flanagan (Dennis O'Keefe), Abe Dinovitch, Mariska Aldrich. *D:* David Burton; *Sc:* Jo Swerling; *St:* Dwight Taylor. (1:18)

Comedy of a dancer who adopts a female derelict with the intent of receiving publicity. This film followed in the footsteps of *Lady for a Day* (q.v.) to capitalize on that film's popularity.

2400. The Lady Consents (RKO; 1936). *Cast:* Ann Harding, Herbert Marshall, Margaret Lindsay, Walter Abel, Edward Ellis, Hobart Cavanaugh, Ilka Chase. *D:* Stephen Roberts; *As.P.:* Edward Kaufman; *Sc:* P.J. Wolfson, Anthony Veiller. (1:17)

Drama of a man who after having an affair, realizes he still loves his wife. Based on the play "The Indestructible Mrs. Talbot" by P.J. Wolfson, the film was a box office loser.

The Lady Dances *see* **The Merry Widow**

2401. The Lady Escapes (20th Century–Fox; 1937). *Cast:* Gloria Stuart, George Sanders, Michael Whalen, Lon Chaney, Jr., Franklin Pangborn. *D:* Eugene Forde.

B melodrama.

2402. The Lady Fights Back (Universal; 1937). *Cast:* Kent Taylor, Irene Hervey, William Lundigan, Willie Best, Frank Jenks, Paul Hurst, Samuel S. Hinds, Joe Sawyer, Chick Chandler. *D:* Milton Carruth; *P:* Edmund Grainger. (1:01)

B drama of an ecological fight surrounding the site of a proposed dam.

2403. Lady for a Day (Columbia; 1933). *Cast:* Warren William (Dave the Dude), May Robson (Apple Annie), Guy Kibbee (Judge Blake), Glenda Farrell (Missouri Martin), Ned Sparks (Happy), Jean Parker (Louise), Walter Connolly (Count Romero), Nat Pendleton (Shakespeare), Robert Emmett O'Connor (inspector), Wallis Clark (commissioner), Hobart Bosworth (governor), Dad Mills (blind man), Barry Norton (Carlos), Samuel S. Hinds, Halliwell Hobbes. *D:* (A.A.N.) Frank Capra; *Sc:* (A.A.N.) Robert Riskin. (1:35)

This comedy-drama of a gangster who transforms a ragged old apple vendor into the perfect lady was a tremendous hit for the studio and became the first film from that studio to win an A.A.N. for "Best Picture." Based on Damon Runyon's story "Madame La Gimp," it was remade in 1961 as *A Pocketful of Miracles*. It placed #4 on the "10 Best" list of *Film Daily.*

Lady for Frisco *see* **Rebellion**

2404. The Lady from Nowhere (Chesterfield; 1930–31). *Cast:* Alice Day, John Holland, Phillips Smalley, Barbara Bedford, Mischa Auer. *D:* Richard Thorpe; *Sc:* Adrian Johnson, Barney Gerard.

"Poverty row" crime drama.

2405. The Lady from Nowhere (Columbia; 1936). *Cast:* Mary Astor, Charles Quigley, Gene Morgan, John Tyrrell, Victor Kilian, Thurston Hall, Norman Willis, Rita LaRoy, Claudia Coleman. *D:* Gordon Wiles; *St:* Ben G. Kohn; *Sc:* Joseph Krumgold, Fred Niblo, Jr., Arthur Strawn.

B romantic drama.

2406. The Lady in Scarlet (Chesterfield; 1935). *Cast:* Claudia Dell, Reginald Denny, Dorothy Revier, John St. Polis, Jameson Thomas. *D:* Charles Lamont.

"Poverty row" melodrama.

2407. Lady in the Morgue (Universal; 1938). *Cast:* Preston Foster (Bill Crane), Frank Jenks (Doc Williams), Patricia Ellis, Thomas Jackson, Barbara

Pepper, Roland Drew, Morgan Wallace, Gordon Hart, Rollo Lloyd, Byron Foulger, Don Brodie, Brian Burke, James Robbins, Al Hill, Donald Kerr, Gordon (Bill) Elliott, Minerva Urecal. *D:* Otis Garrett; *P:* Irving Starr; *Sc:* Eric Taylor, Robertson White. (1:07) (G.B. title: *The Case of the Missing Blonde*)

Hit B "Crime Club" series mystery of murder, suicide and a missing corpse. Based on the novel by Jonathan Latimer.

2408. Lady Killer (WB; 1933). *Cast:* James Cagney, Mae Clarke, Leslie Fenton, Margaret Lindsay, Henry O'Neill, Raymond Hatton, Willard Robertson, Russell Hopton, George Chandler, Douglass Dumbrille, Marjorie Gateson, Herman Bing, Bud Flanagan (Dennis O'Keefe), Douglas Cosgrove, George Blackwood. *D:* Roy Del Ruth; *P:* Henry Blanke; *Sc:* Ben Markson, Lillie Hayward. (1:17)

Classic comedy of a wanted criminal who takes off for Hollywood and hits it big as a film star. Based on the novel "The Finger Man" by Rosalind Keating Shaffer.

2409. The Lady Lies (Paramount; 1929). *Cast:* Claudette Colbert, Walter Huston, Charles Ruggles, Tom Brown, Virginia True Boardman, Jean Dixon (film debut), Verna Deane, Duncan Penwarden, Betty Garde, Patricia Deering. *D:* Hobart Henley; *St:* John Meehan; *Sc:* Meehan, Garrett Fort. (1:15)

Romance of a widower and a salesgirl amidst his disapproving relatives.

2410. Lady Luck (Chesterfield; 1936). *Cast:* William Bakewell, Iris Adrian, Duncan Renaldo, Jameson Thomas. *D:* Charles Lamont.

"Poverty row" romance.

2411. The Lady Objects (Columbia; 1938). *Cast:* Lanny Ross, Gloria Stuart, Robert Paige, Joan Marsh, Ann Doran. *D:* Erle C. Kenton; *Song:* (A.A.N.) Ben Oakland & Oscar Hammerstein II.

B romantic comedy.

2412. A Lady of Chance (MGM; 1928–29). *Cast:* Norma Shearer, John Mack Brown, Lowell Sherman, Gwen Lee. *D:* Robert Z. Leonard; *Sc:* A.P. Younger.

Part-talkie melodrama of a woman operating a "badger game." Released in 1928 as a silent, with a '29 re-release with some dialogue.

2413. The Lady of Scandal (MGM; 1930). *Cast:* Ruth Chatterton, Ralph Forbes, Basil Rathbone, Frederick Kerr, Nance O'Neil, Cyril Chadwick, Edgar Norton, Effie Ellsler, Moon Carroll, Herbert Bunston, Mackenzie Ward, Robert Bolder. *D:* Sidney Franklin; *Sc:* Hans Kräly, Edwin Justus Mayer, Claudine West. (G.B. title: *The High Road*)

Drama of an actress who chooses her stage career over romance. Based on "The High Road" by Frederick Lonsdale.

2414. Lady of Secrets (Columbia; 1936). *Cast:* Ruth Chatterton, Otto Kruger, Lionel Atwill, Marian Marsh, Lloyd Nolan, Robert Allen, Nana Bryant. *D:* Marion Gering; *P:* B.P. Schulberg; *Sc:* Zoe Akins, Joseph Anthony. (1:13)

Drama of a woman who becomes reclusive after love sours.

Lady of the Boulevards (G.B. title) *see* **Nana**

Lady of the Night *see* **Lady of the Pavements**

2415. Lady of the Pavements (United Artists/Art Cinema; 1929). *Cast:* Jetta Goudal, William Boyd, Albert Conti, George Fawcett, Lupe Velez, William Bakewell, Franklin Pangborn, Henry Armetta. *D:* D.W. Griffith; *P:* Joseph M. Schenck; *St:* Karl Vollmoeller; *Sc:* Sam Taylor, Gerrit Lloyd; *Song:* "Where Is the 'Song of Songs' for Me" by Irving Berlin; (aka: *Lady of the Night*)

Part-talkie romance of misunderstandings at the time of Napoleon III. Originally made with music and some dialogue sequences, only the silent version remains. Griffith's last silent film.

Lady of the Rose (G.B. title) *see* **Bride of the Regiment**

2416. Lady of the Tropics (MGM; 1939). *Cast:* Robert Taylor, Hedy Lamarr, Joseph Schildkraut, Gloria Franklin, Ernest Cossart, Mary Taylor, Charles Trowbridge, Frederick Worlock, Paul Porcasi, Marguerita Padula, Cecil Cunningham, Natalie Moorhead, Zeffie Tilbury. *D:* Jack Conway; *P:* Sam Zimbalist; *St & Sc:* Ben Hecht; *Song:* "Each Time You Say Good-bye (I Die a Little)" by Phil Ohman, Foster Carling. (1:32)

An interracial romantic drama which flopped for the studio.

2417. The Lady Refuses (RKO; 1931). *Cast:* Betty Compson, John Darrow, Gilbert Emery, Margaret Livingston, Ivan Lebedeff, Edgar Norton, Daphne Pollard. *D:* George Archainbaud; *As.P.:* Bertram Millhauser; *St:* Guy Bolton, Robert Milton; *Sc:* Wallace Smith. (1:12)

Drama of a father who tries to protect his son from a gold digger. Set in London.

2418. A Lady Surrenders (Universal; 1930). *Cast:* Conrad Nagel, Rose Hobart, Genevieve Tobin (talkie film debut), Basil Rathbone, Edgar Norton, Carmel Myers, Franklin Pangborn, Vivian Oakland, Grace Cunard. *D:* John M. Stahl; *P:* Carl Laemmle, Jr.; *Sc:* Gladys Lehman. (G.B. title: *Blind Wives*) (1:42)

A triangular romantic melodrama which is based on the novel "Sincerity" by John Erskine.

2419. A Lady to Love (MGM; 1929–30). *Cast:* Edward G. Robinson, Vilma Banky (in her final American film), Robert Ames, Richard Carle,

Henry Armetta, Lloyd Ingraham. *D:* Victor Seastrom; *Sc:* Sidney Howard. (1:32)

Drama based on Sidney Howard's play "They Knew What They Wanted" of a vineyard owner who lures a potential wife by sending her a photograph of his handsome foreman. A remake of *The Secret Love* (Paramount; 1928) with Pola Negri. Remade as *They Knew What They Wanted* (RKO; 1940) with Charles Laughton.

2420. Lady Tubbs (Universal; 1935). *Cast:* Alice Brady, Anita Louise, Douglass Montgomery, Alan Mowbray, Minor Watson, Russell Hicks, Hedda Hopper, June Clayworth, Walter Brennan, Lumsden Hare, Mildred Harris, Mary (Phyllis) Brooks, Virginia Hammond, Sam McDaniel, Harry Tyler, Rafael Storm. *D:* Alan Crosland; *Sc:* Barry Trivers. (G.B. title: *The Gay Lady*) (1:09)

Hit comedy of a logging camp cook who becomes heiress to a fortune and moves into society. Based on the novel by Homer Croy.

2421. The Lady Who Dared (WB/F.N.; 1931). *Cast:* Billie Dove, Conway Tearle, Sidney Blackmer, Judith Vosselli, Cosmo Kyrle Bellew, Ivan Simpson, Lloyd Ingraham, Mathilde Comont. *D:* William Beaudine; *St:* Kenneth J. Saunders; *Sc:* Kathryn Scola, Forrest Halsey. (0:59)

Low-budget melodrama of blackmail.

2422. Lady with a Past (RKO-Pathé; 1932). *Cast:* Constance Bennett, Ben Lyon, David Manners, Don Alvarado, Albert Conti, Merna Kennedy, Astrid Allwyn (film debut), Donald Dillaway, Blanche Frederici, John Roche, Cornelius Keefe, Nella Walker, Arnold Lucy, Freeman Wood, Gordon ("Bill") Elliott. *D:* Edward H. Griffith; *As.P.:* Harry Joe Brown; *Sc:* Horace Jackson. (G.B. title: *Reputation*) (1:10)

Comedy-drama of a shy woman who suddenly finds herself with a reputation. Based on the novel by Harriet Henry.

2423. The Lady's from Kentucky (Paramount; 1939). *Cast:* George Raft, Ellen Drew, ZaSu Pitts, Hugh Herbert, Louise Beavers, Stanley Andrews, Gilbert Emery, Eugene Jackson, Forrester Harvey, George Anderson, Harry Tyler, Edward Pawley, Lew Payton, Jimmy Bristow. *D:* Alexander Hall; *P:* Jeff Lazarus; *Sc:* Malcolm Stuart Boylan; *St:* Rowland Brown. (1:07)

B romantic race track drama.

2424. A Lady's Morals (MGM; 1930). *Cast:* Grace Moore (film debut as Jenny Lind), Reginald Denny, Wallace Beery (P.T. Barnum), Jobyna Howland, Giovanni Martino, Frank Reicher, Paul Porcasi, Gilbert Emery, Bodil Rosing, Joan Standing, Gus Shy, Judith Vosselli, Mavis Villiers, George F. Marion, Sr. *D:* Sidney Franklin; *Sc:* Hans Kraly, Claudine West; *Dial.:* John Meehan, Arthur Richman. (G.B. title: *Jenny Lind*) (1:15)

A romantic musical based around the life of 19th-century singer Jenny Lind, a film designed to introduce audiences to Metropolitan Opera singer Grace Moore. A box office dud.

2425. A Lady's Profession (Paramount; 1933). *Cast:* Alison Skipworth, Roland Young, Sari Maritza, Kent Taylor, Roscoe Karns, Warren Hymer, Ethel Griffies, George Barbier, Edgar Norton, Dewey Robinson, Claudia Braddock. *D:* Norman Z. McLeod; *P:* Albert E. Lewis; *St:* Nina Wilcox Putnam.

Low-budget comedy of two English aristocrats who are running an illegal speakeasy.

2426. Lancer Spy (20th Century–Fox; 1937). *Cast:* George Sanders, Dolores Del Rio, Peter Lorre, Joseph Schildkraut, Virginia Field, Sig Rumann, Fritz Feld, Maurice Moscovich, Luther Adler (film debut), Lester Matthews, Frank Reicher, Lynn Bari, Holmes Herbert, Claude King, Leonard Mudie, Kenneth Hunter, Joan Carol, Carlos de Valdez. *D:* Gregory Ratoff; *P:* Darryl F. Zanuck; *Sc:* Philip Dunne. (1:20)

War drama with a romantic subplot of a man posing as a German officer in order to attain information. Based on the novel by Marthe McKenna.

2427. Land Beyond the Law (WB; 1937). *Cast:* Dick Foran, Linda Perry, Cy Kendall, Glenn Strange, Jim Corey, Harry Woods, Gordon (Bill) Elliott. *D:* B. Reeves Eason; *P:* Bryan Foy; *St:* Marion Jackson; *Sc:* Luci Ward, Joseph K. Watson; *Songs:* "Whisper While You're Waiting" and "Song of the Circle Bar" by M.K. Jerome, Jack Scholl. (0:58)

Dick Foran western with songs of a ranch hand who unknowingly becomes involved with rustlers. Filmed previously by First National in 1927 with Ken Maynard and in 1932 as *The Big Stampede* (q.v.).

2428. Land of Fighting Men (Monogram; 1938). *Cast:* Jack Randall, Herman Brix (Bruce Bennett), Louise Stanley, Dickie Jones, Robert Burns, Wheeler Oakman, John Merton, Lane Chandler, Rex Lease, Ernie Adams, Colorado Hillbillies. *D:* Alan James (aka: "Alvin J. Neitz"); *P:* Maurice Conn; *St:* Stanley Roberts; *Sc:* Joseph O'Donnell. (0:53)

Jack Randall western of a cowboy wrongfully accused of killing a rancher.

2429. The Land of Missing Men (Tiffany; 1930). *Cast:* Bob Steele, Al St. John, Edward Dunn, Caryl Lincoln, Al Jennings, Fern Emmett, Emilio Fernandez. *D:* J.P. McCarthy; *P:* Trem Carr; *Sc:* McCarthy, Bob Quigley. (1:00)

Bob Steele western of two cowboys accused of a stage holdup.

2430. Land of Wanted Men (Monogram; 1931). *Cast:* Bill Cody, Andy Shuford, Gibson Gowland, Sheila

Mannors, Jack Richardson, Frank Lackteen, James Marcus. *D:* Harry Fraser; *P:* Trem Carr; *St & Sc:* Fraser. (1:02)

Bill Cody horse opera of a range feud.

2431. The Laramie Kid (Reliable; 1935). *Cast:* Tom Tyler, Alberta Vaughn, Al Ferguson, Murdock MacQuarrie, George Chesebro, Snub Pollard, Steve Clark, Artie Ortego, Jimmy Aubrey, Wally Wales, Budd Buster, Nelson McDowell. *D:* Harry S. Webb; *P:* Bernard B. Ray; *Sc:* Carl Krusada, Rose Gordon. (0:57)

Tom Tyler western of a cowboy who gives himself up so his ladylove's dad can pay off the ranch.

Larceny Lane (G.B. title) *see* **Blonde Crazy**

2432. Larceny on the Air (Republic; 1937). *Cast:* Robert Livingston, Grace Bradley, Smiley Burnette, Willard Robertson, Byron Foulger. *D:* Irving Pichel.

B crime melodrama.

2433. Lariats and Six-Shooters (Cosmos; 1931). *Cast:* Jack Perrin, Lafe McKee, George Chesebro, Jimmy Aubrey, Olin Francis. *D:* Alvin J. Neitz (aka: Alan James).

Jack Perrin western.

2434. Lasca of the Rio Grande (Universal; 1931). *Cast:* Leo Carrillo, John Mack Brown (in his first film after leaving MGM), Dorothy Burgess, Slim Summerville, Frank Campeau. *D:* Edward Laemmle; *Sc:* Randall Faye. (1:00)

Western tale of romance between a Texas Ranger and a dancer.

2435. The Lash (WB/F.N.; 1930). *Cast:* Richard Barthelmess, Mary Astor, Marion Nixon, Fred Kohler, Barbara Bedford, Robert Edeson, Arthur Stone, James Rennie, Francis McDonald, Erville Alderson, Mathilde Comont. *D:* Frank Lloyd; *P:* Lloyd; *St:* Lanier Bartlett, Virginia Stivers Bartlett; *Sc:* Bradley King. (G.B. title: *Adios*) (1:15)

Romantic adventure of a Spanish nobleman who hits the outlaw trail. Previously filmed in 1916 by Famous Players-Lasky with Marie Doro and Elliott Dexter.

2436. The Last Assignment (Victory; 1936). *D:* Dan Milner; *P:* Sam Katzman; *Sc:* Al Martin.

Alternate title for "Fighting Coward" (1936, Victory).

2437. The Last Dance (Audible Pictures; 1930). *Cast:* Vera Reynolds, Jason Robards, George Chandler. *D:* Scott Pembroke; *Sc:* Jack Townley.

(No other information available)

2438. The Last Days of Pompeii (RKO; 1935). *Cast:* Preston Foster, Basil Rathbone, Alan Hale, David Holt, Louis Calhern, Dorothy Wilson, John Wood, Wyrley Birch, Gloria Shea, Edward Van Sloan, Frank Conroy, Zeffie Tilbury, John Davidson, Henry Kolker, William V. Mong, Murray Kinnell. *D:* Ernest B. Schoedsack; *P:* Merian C. Cooper; *St:* James Ashmore Creelman, Melville Baker; *Adaptation:* Boris Ingster; *Sc:* Ruth Rose; *Chief Technician:* Willis H. O'Brien. (1:36) (video)

A man aspires to wealth in the arena from his gladiatorial expertise. The film utilizes the title of Sir Edward Bulwer-Lytton's novel and was a box office flop on its initial release, recouping financial losses in 1949 when released with another RKO loser of 1935, *She* (q.v.). The film climaxes with the destruction of Pompeii by the eruption of Mt. Vesuvius. Other variations on the story were filmed in Italy in 1912 with a cast of 10,000, followed by another from Italy in 1925, a French version in 1951, another from Italy in 1960 and a three-part mini-series for TV in 1984. Computer-colored in 1990 by Turner Entertainment.

2439. The Last Express (Universal; 1938). *Cast:* Kent Taylor, Don

Brodie, Dorothea Kent, Greta Granstedt, Paul Hurst, Samuel Lee, Charles Trowbridge, Addison Richards, Robert Emmett Keane, Edward Raquello, Al Shaw. *D:* Otis Garrett; *P:* Irving Starr; *Sc:* Edmund L. Hartmann. (1:00)

"Crime Club" series entry of an investigation into the murder of a special prosecutor. Based on the novel by Baynard Kendrick.

2440. The Last Flight (WB/F.N.; 1931). *Cast:* Richard Barthelmess, David Manners, John Mack Brown, Helen Chandler, Elliott Nugent, Walter Byron. *D:* William Dieterle; *Sc:* John Monk Saunders, Byron Morgan. (1:20)

An offbeat film of its day of four American flyers who remain in Paris after World War I to get their lives back together. Based on the novel "Single Lady" by John Monk Saunders. Copies of this film were unknown until 1968.

2441. The Last Gangster (MGM; 1937). *Cast:* Edward G. Robinson (Joe Krozac), Rose Stradner (American debut as Talya Krozac), James Stewart (Paul North), Lionel Stander (Curly), Douglas Scott, John Carradine, Sidney Blackmer, Grant Mitchell, Edward S. Brophy, Alan Baxter, Larry Simms (film debut — later Baby Dumpling of the "Blondie" series), Horace McMahon, Frank Conroy. *D:* Edward Ludwig; *P:* J.J. Cohn; *St:* William Wellman, Robert Carson; *Sc:* John Lee Mahin. (1:21)

Drama of a gangster who gets out of prison to find things are not the same in the outside world, as when he went in.

2442. The Last Gentleman (United Artists/20th Century; 1934). *Cast:* George Arliss, Edna May Oliver, Ralph Morgan, Janet Beecher, Charlotte Henry, Edward Ellis, Donald Meek, Joseph Cawthorn, Frank Albertson, Rafaela Ottiano, Harry C. Bradley. *D:* Sidney Lanfield; *P:* William Goetz, Raymond Griffith; *St:* Katharine Clugston; *Sc:* Leonard Praskins. (1:20)

Comedy of a millionaire who is dying and suddenly finds himself swamped with potential heirs to his estate.

2443. The Last Man (Columbia; 1932). *Cast:* Charles Bickford, Constance Cummings, Robert Ellis, Alec B. Francis, Alan Roscoe, Edward Le Saint, Hal Price, Jack Richardson, Bill Williams, Jack Carlyle, Robert St. Angelo, Al Smith, Bill Sundholm, John Eberts, Kit Guard, James Wang, George Magrill. *D:* Howard Higgin; *St:* Keene Thompson; *Sc:* Francis Edwards Faragoh.

Melodrama.

2444. The Last Mile (Sono Art-World Wide; 1932). *Cast:* Preston S. Foster, Howard Phillips, George E. Stone, Noel Madison, Alan Roscoe, Paul Fix, Alec B. Francis, Edward Van Sloan, Louise Carter, Walter Walker, Jack Kennedy, Al Hill, William Scott, Albert J. Smith, Kenneth MacDonald, Frank Sheridan, Ralph Theodore, Daniel Haynes. *D:* Sam Bischoff (his only film as director); *P:* E.W. Hammons; *St:* John Wexley; *Sc:* Seton I. Miller. (1:24) (video)

Hit "poverty row" prison melodrama of a convicted murderer on death row awaiting execution. The film, noted for its graphic violence was remade in 1959 with Mickey Rooney.

2445. The Last of Mrs. Cheyney (MGM; 1929). *Cast:* Norma Shearer (Mrs. Cheyney), Basil Rathbone (Lord Arthur Dilling), George Barraud (Charles), Hedda Hopper (Lady Maria), Cyril Chadwick (Willie Wynton), Maude Turner Gordon (Mrs. Webley), Herbert Bunston (Lord Elton), Moon Carroll (Joan), Madeline Seymour (Mrs. Wynton), Finch Smiles (William), George K. Arthur (George). *D:* Sidney Franklin; *Adaptation:* Hans Kräly, Claudine West; *Supervisor:* Irving Thalberg. (1:34)

Hit romantic drama of a female jewel thief who is exploited by a rascal. Notable as the first film from this studio with the sound track on film, it placed #9 on the "10 Best" list of *Film Daily*. Based on the play by Frederick Lonsdale. (See below for remakes.)

2446. The Last of Mrs. Cheyney (MGM; 1937). *Cast:* Joan Crawford (Mrs. Cheyney), Robert Montgomery (Lord Dilling), William Powell, Frank Morgan, Jessie Ralph, Nigel Bruce, Benita Hume, Melville Cooper, Sara Haden, Aileen Pringle, Ralph Forbes, Leonard Carey, Wallis Clark, Barnett Parker, Colleen Clare. *D:* Richard Boleslawski (his final credited film as he died during production, with directorial completion by George Fitzmaurice who received no credit); *P:* Lawrence Weingarten; *Sc:* Leon Gordon, Samson Raphaelson, Monckton Hoffe. (1:38)

A remake of the preceding film which became one of the 38 top grossing films of 1936–37. Remade as *The Law and the Lady* (MGM; 1951) and *Frau Cheyney's Ende* (Germany; 1962).

2447. The Last of the Clintons (Ajax; 1935). *Cast:* Harry Carey, Betty Mack, Del Gordon, Victor Potel, Earl Dwire, Ruth Findlay, Tom London, Slim Whitaker, Ernie Adams, Lafe McKee. *D:* Harry Fraser; *P:* William Berke; *Sc:* Weston Edwards. (1:04)

Harry Carey western of a lawman who goes undercover to capture an outlaw gang.

2448. The Last of the Duanes (Fox; 1930). *Cast:* George O'Brien, Lucille Browne, Myrna Loy, Walter McGrail, James Bradbury, Jr., Nat Pendleton, Blanche Frederici, Frank Campeau, Jim Mason, Lloyd Ingraham, Willard Robertson. *D:* Alfred L. Werker; *Sc:* Ernest Pascal. (0:55)

George O'Brien western of the complications that arise when an outlaw's wife falls for a cowboy. Based on the Zane Grey novel, it was filmed twice in the silent era, in 1919 with William Farnum and in 1924 with Tom Mix. Remade by 20th Century–Fox in 1941 with George Montgomery.

2449. Last of the Lone Wolf (Columbia; 1930). *Cast:* Bert Lytell, Patsy Ruth Miller, Henry Daniell. *D:* Richard Boleslawski (solo feature American directorial debut).

Low-budget production featuring the gentleman thief created by Louis Joseph Vance.

2450. The Last of the Mohicans (United Artists/Reliance; 1936). *Cast:* Randolph Scott (Hawkeye), Binnie Barnes (Alice), Heather Angel (Cora), Bruce Cabot (Magua), Henry Wilcoxon (Major Duncan Heyward), Robert Barrat (Chingachgook), Philip Reed (Uncas), Ian McLaren (William Pitt), Olaf Hytten (King George II), Hugh Buckler, Willard Robertson, Ian Wolfe, Frank McGlynn, Sr., Chief John Big Tree. *D:* George B. Seitz, Wallace Fox (unc.); *P:* Edward Small; *Sc:* Philip Dunne, John Balderston, Paul Perez, Daniel Moore; *Assistant Director:* (A.A.N.) Clem Beauchamp. (1:31) (video)

James Fenimore Cooper's novel of the French and Indian War and life in the 18th-century wilderness of New York state. Other filmings include: *Leatherstocking* (Biograph; 1909; *D:* D.W. Griffith), (Thanhouser; 1911), (Pat Powers; 1911), (Associated Producers; 1920), a silent classic by directors Maurice Tourneur and Clarence Brown with George Hackathorne and Noah Beery, (Mascot; 1932) a 12-chapter serial with Harry Carey, *Last of the Redmen* (1947) a loose remake, a "candy coated" 1977 TV movie and a British-Canadian co-produced mini-series, lavishly produced for PBS in the 1980s.

2451. Last of the Pagans (MGM; 1935). *Cast:* Ray Mala (Taro), Lotus (Long) (Lilleo), Teio A. Tematua. *D:* Richard Thorpe; *P:* Philip Goldstone; *Sc:* John Villiers Farrow. (1:11)

Filmed on location in Tahiti, this romantic tale of the South Seas with a predominantly native cast is notable for its underwater photography and a storm sequence.

2452. Last of the Warrens (Supreme; 1936). *Cast:* Bob Steele, Margaret Marquis, Lafe McKee, Charles K. French, Charles King, Horace Murphy, Blackie Whiteford, Jim Corey, Steve Clark. *D:* Robert N. Bradbury; *P:* A.W. Hackel; *Sc:* Bradbury. (0:56)

Bob Steele western of a World War I flyer who returns home to find his land stolen by a crooked businessman.

2453. The Last Outlaw (RKO; 1936). *Cast:* Harry Carey, Tom Tyler, Hoot Gibson, Henry B. Walthall, Margaret Callahan, Fred Scott, Ray Mayer, Harry Jans, Frank M. Thomas, Russell Hopton, Jack Luden, Frank Jenks, Maxine Jennings, Joseph Sawyer. *D:* Christy Cabanne; *As.P.:* Robert Sisk; *St:* John Ford, E. Murray Campbell; *Sc:* Jack Townley, John Twist; *Song:* "My Heart's on the Trail" by Nathaniel Shilkret, Frank Luther. (1:12)

Considered a classic among western buffs, this hit modern-day western tells of the experiences of an aging outlaw, released from prison after 25-years and his attempt to adjust to a rapidly changing world. A comedy-western which was unique for its time.

2454. The Last Outpost (Paramount; 1935). *Cast:* Cary Grant, Claude Rains, Gertrude Michael, Kathleen Burke, Colin Tapley, Akim Tamiroff, Billy Bevan, Jameson Thomas, Georges Renavent, Claude King, Harry Semels, Margaret Swope, William Brown, Meyer Ouhayoun, Nick Shaid. *D:* Charles Barton, Louis Gasnier; *P:* E. Lloyd Sheldon; *Sc:* Philip MacDonald, Frank Partos, Charles Brackett.

Action-drama of the British army in North Africa. Based on a story by F. Britten Austin.

2455. The Last Parade (Columbia; 1931). *Cast:* Jack Holt, Constance Cummings, Gaylord (Steve) Pendleton, Edward LeSaint, Robert Ellis, Tom Moore, Clarence Muse, Gino Corrado, Robert Graham, Edmund Breese, Earle D. Bunn, Jesse DeVorska. *D:* Erle C. Kenton; *St:* Casey Robinson; *Sc:* Dorothy Howell.

Low-budget drama.

2456. The Last Performance (Universal; 1929–30). *Cast:* Conrad Veidt (Erik the magician), Mary Philbin, Leslie Fenton (Buffo), Fred Mackaye, Anders Randolph, Sam De-Grasse, Gustav Partos, William H. Turner, George Irving. *D:* Paul Fejos; *St:* James Ashmore Creelman; *Sc:* Creelman, Walter Anthony, Tom Reed.

Part-talkie romantic melodrama of a magician, his two assistants and a drifter, which ends in murder and suicide.

2457. The Last Ride (Universal; 1931–32). *Cast:* Frank Mayo, Tom Santschi (final film—d. 1931), Dorothy Revier, Charles Morton, Virginia Browne Faire. *D:* Duke Worne. (1:04)

B melodrama of a reporter and his criminal entanglement.

2458. The Last Roundup (Paramount; 1934). *Cast:* Randolph Scott, Barbara Fritchie, Fred Kohler, Monte Blue, Richard Carle, Barton MacLane, Charles Middleton, Fuzzy Knight, Dick Rush, Jim Corey, Buck Connors. *D:* Henry Hathaway.

Western of a cattle rustler who sacrifices himself for the sake of two young lovers. Based on Zane Grey's book "The Border Legion," it had three previous filmings under that title, in 1919 an independent production with Hobart Bosworth, in 1924 and 1930 (q.v.). Loosely remade in 1939–40 (q.v.), also under the original book title.

2459. The Last Stand (Universal; 1938). *Cast:* Bob Baker, Constance Moore, Fuzzy Knight, Earle Hodgins, Glenn Strange, Forrest Taylor, Jack Kirk, Jimmy Phillips, Frank Ellis, Sam

Flint, Jack Montgomery. *D:* Joseph H. Lewis; *P:* Trem Carr; *Sc:* Norton S. Parker, Harry O. Hoyt. (0:57)

Bob Baker western with songs of a cowboy seeking the murderer of his father.

2460. The Last Trail (Fox; 1933). *Cast:* George O'Brien, Claire Trevor (in her second film), J. Carrol Naish, El Brendel, Matt McHugh, Lucille La Verne, Edward J. LeSaint, Ruth Warren, George Reed. *D:* James Tinling; *Sc:* Stuart Anthony. (0:59)

George O'Brien western of a man out to get the crooks who took over his family's ranch. Based on a book by Zane Grey.

2461. The Last Train from Madrid (Paramount; 1937). *Cast:* Dorothy Lamour, Lew Ayres, Gilbert Roland, Karen Morley, Lionel Atwill, Helen Mack, Robert Cummings, Anthony Quinn, Olympe Bradna, Lee Bowman, Evelyn Brent, George Lloyd, Charles Middleton, Alan Ladd, Henry Brandon. *D:* James Hogan; *Assoc. D:* Hugh Bennett; *P:* George M. Arthur; *Sc:* Louis Stevens, Robert Wyler. (1:17)

Hit drama of its day of various people trying to escape from the Spanish Civil War. Based on a story by Elsie and Paul Hervey Fox.

2462. The Last Warning (Universal; 1928–29). *Cast:* John Boles, Laura La Plante, Roy D'Arcy, Margaret Livingston, Montagu Love, D'Arcy Corrigan, Mack Swain, Bert Roach, Burr McIntosh, Carrie Daumery, Slim Summerville, Torben Meyer, Charles K. French, Fred Kelsey, Harry Northrup, Tom O'Brien, Buster Phelps. *D:* Paul Leni (final film — d. 1929); *P:* Carl Laemmle, Jr.; *Sc:* Alfred A. Cohn, Tom Reed.

Part-talkie murder-mystery set in an old theater where a murder occurred years before. Based on the play "The Last Warning" by Thomas F. Fallon and the story "House of Fear" by Wadsworth Camp. Sets are from the 1925 production of *The Phantom of the Opera*.

Note: Remade in 1939 as *House of Fear* (q.v.).

2463. The Last Warning (Universal; 1938). *Cast:* Preston Foster (Bill Crane), Joyce Compton, Frank Jenks, Frances Robinson, Kay Linaker, Robert Paige, Raymond Parker, E.E. Clive, Roland Drew, Orville Caldwell, Henry Brandon, Albert Dekker, Clem Wilenchick (later Crane Whitley). *D:* Albert S. Rogell; *P:* Irving Starr; *Sc:* Edmund L. Hartmann. (1:02)

"Crime Club" mystery-comedy of a kidnapper who calls himself "The Eye." Based on Jonathan Latimer's novel "The Dead Don't Care."

The Late Christopher Bean (G.B. title) *see* **Christopher Bean**

2464. Laugh and Get Rich (RKO; 1931). *Cast:* Hugh Herbert, Edna May Oliver, Dorothy Lee, Russell Gleason, Rochelle Hudson, John Harron, Charles Sellon, George Davis, Robert Emmett Keane, Maude Fealy, Louise MacKintosh, Lita Chevret. *D:* Gregory LaCava; *As.P.:* Douglas MacLean; *St:* MacLean; *Sc:* LaCava, Ralph Spence. (1:12)

Domestic comedy of a middle-class couple who have to deal with sudden wealth after the discovery of oil.

2465. Laugh It Off (Universal; 1939). *Cast:* Constance Moore, Johnny Downs, Cecil Cunningham, Janet Beecher, Marjorie Rambeau, Hedda Hopper, Edgar Kennedy, William Demarest, Horace McMahon, Paula Stone, Chester Clute. *D:* Albert S. Rogell; *P:* Rogell; *St:* Lee Loeb, Mortimer Braus; *Sc:* Harry Clork, Loeb; *Songs:* Sam Lerner, Ben Oakland. (1:03) (G.B. title: *Lady Be Gay*)

A light B musical of four actresses and their fading careers.

2466. Laughing at Death (20th Century–Fox; 1936). *Cast:* Allan Lane,

Lois Wilson, Delma Byron, Margaret Hamilton, Jason Robards, Frank Reicher, Jane Darwell, Billy Benedict, Sara Haden, John Carradine. *D:* Frank Strayer. (G.B. title: *Laughing at Trouble*) B comedy.

2467. Laughing at Life (Mascot; 1933). *Cast:* Victor McLaglen, Conchita Montenegro, William "Stage" Boyd, Regis Toomey, Ruth Hall, Noah Beery, Tully Marshall, J. Farrell MacDonald, Lois Wilson, Guinn Williams, Henry B. Walthall, Dewey Robinson, Ivan Lebedeff, Mathilde Comont, Henry Armetta, Edmund Breese, Frankie Darro, Buster Phelps, Pat O'Malley, William Desmond, Lloyd Whitlock, Philo McCullough, George Humbert. *D:* Ford Beebe; *St:* Beebe; *Adaptation:* Prescott Chaplin, Thomas Dugan. (1:11)
Low-budget drama of a gun-runner who meets the son he deserted years before.

Laughing at Trouble (G.B. title) *see* **Laughing at Death**

2468. Laughing Boy (MGM; 1934). *Cast:* Ramon Novarro, Lupe Velez, Chief Thunderbird, William Davidson. *D:* W.S. Van Dyke (who considered this one of the worst films he ever directed); *P:* Hunt Stromberg; *Sc:* John Colton, John Lee Mahin. (1:20)
Romantic melodrama of a Navajo Indian youth who marries an outcast. The film, based on the Pulitzer Prize winning novel by Oliver La Farge was a box office flop.

2469. Laughing Irish Eyes (Republic; 1936). *Cast:* Phil Regan, Evalyn Knapp, Ray Walker, Betty Compson, Walter C. Kelly, Raymond Hatton, Wallace Sullivan, Russell Hicks, J.M. Kerrigan, Herman Bing, Clarence Muse, Warren Hymer, Mary Gordon. *D:* Joseph Santley; *St:* Sidney Sutherland, Wallace Sullivan; *Sc:* Olive Cooper, Ben Ryan, Stanley Rauh.
B romantic musical-comedy.

2470. The Laughing Lady (Paramount; 1929). *Cast:* Ruth Chatterton, Clive Brook, Dan Healy, Nat Pendleton, Raymond Walburn (feature debut), Nedda Harrigan, Betty Bartley, Herbert Druce, Dorothy Hall, Helen Hawley, Alice Hegeman, Joseph King, Marguerite St. John. *D:* Victor Schertzinger; *Adaptation:* Bartlett Cormack, Arthur Richman.
Drama of a woman who after her divorce, has an affair with her ex-husband's attorney. A remake of *A Society Scandal* (Paramount; 1924) with Gloria Swanson. Based on a play by Alfred Sutro.

2471. Laughing Sinners (MGM; 1931). *Cast:* Joan Crawford, Clark Gable, Neil Hamilton, Marjorie Rambeau, Guy Kibbee, Cliff Edwards, Roscoe Karns, George F. Marion, Henry Armetta, George Cooper, Clara Blandick, Gertrude Short, Bert Woodruff. *D:* Harry Beaumont; *St:* (John) Kenyon Nicholson; *Sc:* Bess Meredyth, Martin Flavin. (1:11)
Hit drama of a girl with a past who joins the Salvation Army in hopes of finding redemption. The film originally premiered with John Mack Brown in Gable's role, but the film was withdrawn and partially reshot using Gable instead of Brown.

2472. Laughter (Paramount; 1930). *Cast:* Nancy Carroll, Fredric March, Frank Morgan, Glenn Anders, Diane Ellis, Leonard Carey, Eric Blore, Ollie Burgoyne, Arthur Vinton. *D:* Harry D'Abbadie D'Arrast (talkie directorial debut); *P:* Herman J. Mankiewicz; *St:* (A.A.N.) Donald Ogden Stewart, d'Arrast, Douglas Doty; *Sc:* Stewart. (1:21)
Sophisticated romantic comedy of a showgirl who marries for money, only to find that her life is lacking and unfulfilled. Voted one of the year's "10 Best" by the National Board of Review.

2473. Laughter in Hell (Universal; 1933). *Cast:* Pat O'Brien, Merna

Kennedy, Douglass Dumbrille, Gloria Stuart, Tom Brown, Noel Madison, Berton Churchill, Dick Winslow, Clarence Muse, Mickey Bennett, Lew Kelly, Tommy Conlon. *D:* Edward L. Cahn; *St:* Jim Tully. (1:10)

Low-budget melodrama of a killer who escapes from a chain gang and takes refuge in a house where the residents are enduring a contagion.

Laughter in the Air (G.B. title) *see* **Myrt and Marge**

Laurel and Hardy in Toyland *see* **Babes in Toyland**

2474. Law and Lawless (Majestic; 1933). *Cast:* Jack Hoxie, Hilda Moore, Wally Wales (Hal Taliaferro), Yakima Canutt, Julian Rivero, Jack Mower, Edith Fellows, Helen Gibson, J. Frank Glendon, Bob Burns, Fred Burns, Al Taylor. *D:* Armand Schaefer; *P:* Max & Arthur Alexander, Larry Darmour; *Sc:* Oliver Drake. (0:58)

Jack Hoxie "poverty row" western of a cowboy who goes after some rustlers. One of a series of six westerns Hoxie did for this studio.

2475. Law and Lead (Colony; 1935–36). *Cast:* Rex Bell, Wally Wales (Hal Taliaferro), Harley Wood, Earl Dwire, Soledad Jimenez, Donald Reed, Roger Williams, Lane Chandler, Lloyd Ingraham, Karl Hackett, Ed Cassidy, Lew Meehan. *D:* Robert Hill; *Sc:* Basil Dickey.

Rex Bell western of a wanted outlaw known as "The Juarez Kid."

2476. Law and Order (Universal; 1932). *Cast:* Walter Huston (Frame Johnson), Harry Carey (Ed Brant), Russell Hopton (Luther Johnson), Raymond Hatton (Deadwood), Ralph Ince, Harry Woods, Richard Alexander, Russell Simpson, Andy Devine, Walter Brennan, Steve Clemente, Alphonse Ethier, Dewey Robinson, Nelson McDowell, D'Arcy Corrigan, George

Dixon, Arthur Wanzer, Neal Hart, Art Mix, Richard Cramer, Hank Bell. *D:* Edward L. Cahn (solo directorial debut); *Adaptation & Dialogue:* John Huston; *Sc:* Tom Reed. (Re-release title: *Guns A-Blazin'*) (1:12)

Western which is a fictionalized account of the cleaning up of Tombstone, Arizona. Based on the novel "Saint Johnson" by W.R. Burnett, it was remade by this studio in 1937 as the serial "Wild West Days" with Johnny Mack Brown, and as the features *Law and Order* in 1940 (also with Brown) and 1953 with Ronald Reagan.

Law and Order (1933) (G.B. title) *see* **The Fugitive Sheriff**

2477. Law Beyond the Range (Columbia; 1935). *Cast:* Tim McCoy, Billie Seward, Robert Allen, Guy Usher, Harry Todd, Walter Brennan, Si Jenks, Tom London, J.B. Kenton, Jack Rockwell, Ben Hendricks, Jr. *D:* Ford Beebe; *St:* Lambert Hillyer; *Sc:* Beebe. (1:00)

Tim McCoy western of a Texas Ranger released from the service after being wrongly accused of murder and escaping custody.

2478. The Law Comes to Texas (Columbia; 1939). *Cast:* Bill Elliott, Veda Ann Borg, Charles King, Bud Osborne, Slim Whitaker, Frank Ellis, Leon Beaumont, Edmund Cobb, Lee Shumway, Paul Everton, Jack Ingram, Frank LaRue, David Sharpe, Forrest Taylor, Lane Chandler, Budd Buster, Dan White, Ben Corbett. *D:* Joseph Levering; *P:* Larry Darmour (unc.); *Sc:* Nate Gatzert. (0:55)

Bill Elliott in a fictionalized western account of the forming of the Texas Rangers.

2479. The Law Commands (Crescent; 1937). *Cast:* Tom Keene, Lorraine Hayes (Laraine Day), Budd Buster, Matthew Betz, John Merton, Robert Fiske, David Sharpe, Carl

Stockdale, Marie Stoddard, Fred Burns, Horace B. Carpenter. *D:* William Nigh; *P:* E.B. Derr; *Sc:* Bennett Cohen. (0:58)

Historically based story of settlers given land in Iowa by the Homestead Act and their plight with land grabbers.

2480. Law for Tombstone (Universal; 1936–37). *Cast:* Buck Jones, Muriel Evans, Harvey Clark, Carl Stockdale, Earle Hodgins, Alexander Cross, Chuck Morrison, Mary Carney, Charles LeMoyne, Francis Walker, Ben Corbett, Bob Kortman, Slim Whitaker, Tom Forman, Bill Patton, Frank McCarroll. *D:* Charles "Buck" Jones, B. Reeves Eason; *P:* Jones; *Sc:* Frances Guihan. (0:59)

Buck Jones oater of a special agent hired to look into the thefts of gold shipments.

2481. The Law in Her Hands (WB/F.N.; 1936). *Cast:* Margaret Lindsay, Warren Hull, Glenda Farrell, Lyle Talbot, Eddie Acuff, Addison Richards, Dick Purcell, Al Shean, Joseph Crehan, Houseley Stevenson, Eddie Shubert, Milton Kibbee, Billy Wayne, Mabel Colcord. *D:* William Clemens; *P:* Bryan Foy; *Sc:* George Bricker, Luci Ward.

B drama of an underworld lady lawyer and her problems with career and marriage.

2482. Law of the 45s (Normandy/First Division; 1935). *Cast:* Guinn Williams (Tucson Smith), Al St. John (Stony Brooke), Molly O'Day, Lafe McKee, Ted Adams, Fred Burns, Martin Garralaga, Curley Baldwin, Sherry Tansey, Glenn Strange, Bill Patton, Jack Kirk, Francis Walker, Jack Evans, Tex Palmer, Merrill McCormack, George Morrell, William McCall, Broderick O'Farrell. *D:* John P. McCarthy; *Sc:* Robert Tansey. (G.B. title: *The Mysterious Mr. Sheffield*) (0:56)

B western based on William Colt MacDonald's 1933 book of the same name which proceeds to introduce the characters of "Tucson Smith" and "Stony

Brooke" (later two of the "Three Mesquiteers").

2483. Law of the North (Monogram; 1932). *Cast:* Bill Cody, Andy Shuford, Nadine Dore, Al St. John, William L. Thorne, Heinie Conklin, Gil Pratt, Jack Carlyle, Lew Short. *D:* Harry Fraser; *P:* Trem Carr; *Sc:* Fraser. (0:55)

Bill Cody western of a cowboy wrongfully accused of murder and sent to jail.

2484. Law of the Pampas (Paramount; 1939). *Cast:* Bill Boyd (Hoppy), Russell Hayden (Lucky), Sidney Toler, Steffi Duna, Sidney Blackmer, Rad Robertson, William Duncan, Glenn Strange, Eddie Dean, Pedro de Cordoba, Anna Demetrio, Tony Roux, Martin Garralaga, King's Men, Jojo LaSavio. *D:* Nate Watt; *P:* Harry M. Sherman; *Sc:* Harrison Jacobs. (1:12)

"Hopalong Cassidy" western, set in Argentina. The 24th entry in the series.

2485. Law of the Plains (Columbia; 1938). *Cast:* Charles Starrett, Iris Meredith, Robert Warwick, Dick Curtis, Sons of the Pioneers with Bob Nolan, Edmund Cobb, Art Mix, Edward LeSaint, Jack Rockwell, George Chesebro, Jack Long, John Tyrrell, Blackie Whiteford. *D:* Sam Nelson; *Sc:* Maurice Geraghty. (0:56)

Charles Starrett western of a ranch foreman who puts the crimps to some outlaws.

2486. Law of the Ranger (Columbia; 1937). *Cast:* Bob Allen, Hal Taliaferro, Elaine Shepard, Lafe McKee, John Merton, Tom London, Lane Chandler, Slim Whitaker, Ernie Adams, Bud Osborne, Jimmy Aubrey. *D:* Spencer Gordon Bennet; *Sc:* Nate Gatzert. (0:57)

Bob Allen "Texas Rangers" western of two rangers sent to investigate illegal control of water rights.

2487. Law of the Rio Grande (Syndicate; 1931). *Cast:* Bob Custer, Edmund Cobb, Betty Mack, Nelson McDowell, Harry Todd. *D:* Forrest Sheldon, Bennett Cohen; *Sc:* Betty Burbridge, Cohen. (0:57)

Bob Custer oater of an ex-outlaw who meets with opposition when he tries to go straight.

2488. Law of the Sea (Monogram; 1931–32). *Cast:* William Farnum, Rex Bell, Sally Blane, Ralph Ince, Priscilla Dean, Eve Southern, Wally Albright, Syd Saylor, Jack Clifford, Frank LaRue, Charles T. Taylor, Heinie Conklin. *D:* Otto Brower; *P:* I.E. Chadwick. (1:01)

Low-budget drama of a cruel and sadistic ship's captain and the living hell he creates for those around him.

2489. Law of the Texan (Columbia; 1938). *Cast:* Buck Jones, Dorothy Fay, Donald Douglas, Kenneth Harlan, Joe Whitehead, Matty Kemp, Dave O'Brien, Jack Ingraham, Forrest Taylor, Robert Kortman, Jose Tortosa, Melissa Sierra, Tommy Mack. *D:* Elmer Clifton; *P:* Monroe Shaff (Coronet prods.); *Sc:* Shaff, Arthur Hoerl. (0:54)

Buck Jones western (his last for this studio) of a Texas Ranger who finds that supposed cattle rustling is a coverup for the theft of ore shipments.

2490. Law of the Tong (Syndicate; 1931). *Cast:* Jason Robards, Dot Farley, Mary Carr, Frank Lackteen. *D:* Lewis Collins.

Low-budget crime melodrama set in Chinatown.

2491. Law of the Underworld (RKO; 1938–39). *Cast:* Chester Morris, Anne Shirley, Eduardo Ciannelli, Walter Abel, Richard Bond, Lee Patrick, Paul Guilfoyle, Frank M. Thomas, Eddie Acuff, Jack Arnold (aka: Vinton Haworth), Jack Carson, Paul Stanton, George Shelley, Cecil Kellaway. *D:* Lew Landers; *P:* Robert Sisk; *Sc:* Edmund L. Hartmann, Bert Granet.

A remake of *The Pay-Off* (q.v.) is this crime melodrama of an innocent young couple who get mixed up with a gang of criminals. Based on the story "The Lost Game," play "Crime" by Samuel Shipman and John B. Hymer.

2492. Law of the West (Sono Art-World Wide; 1932). *Cast:* Bob Steele, Nancy Drexel, Hank Bell, Ed Brady, Charles West, Earl Dwire, Dick Dickinson, Rose Plummer, Frank Ellis. *D:* Robert N. Bradbury; *P:* Trem Carr; *Sc:* Bradbury. (0:50)

Bob Steele western from "poverty row" of a man kidnapped by outlaws as a baby and a pending dilemma.

2493. The Law Rides (Supreme; 1936). *Cast:* Bob Steele, Harley Wood, Charles King, Buck Connors, Margaret Mann, Jack Rockwell, Barney Furey, Ted Mapes. *D:* Robert N. Bradbury; *P:* A.W. Hackel; *Sc:* Al Martin. (0:57)

Bob Steele western of miners being murdered following a gold strike.

2494. The Law West of Tombstone (RKO; 1938). *Cast:* Harry Carey (Judge Bill Parker), Tim Holt (The Tonto Kid), Evelyn Brent, Clarence Kolb, Jean Rouverol, Allan Lane, Esther Muir, Bradley Page, Paul Guilfoyle, Robert Moya, Ward Bond, George Irving, Monte Montague, Robert Kortman, Kermit Maynard, Charles Middleton. *D:* Glenn Tryon; *P:* Cliff Reid; *St:* Clarence Upson Young; *Sc:* Young, John Twist. (1:13)

Fictionalized western based around the real life character of Judge Roy Bean.

2495. Lawful Larceny (RKO; 1930). *Cast:* Bebe Daniels, Lowell Sherman, Purnell Pratt, Olive Tell, Kenneth Thomson, Maude Turner Gordon, Helene Millard, Bert Roach, Louis Payne, Dickie Moore. *D:* Lowell Sherman (in his directorial debut); *As.P.:* Henry Hobart; *Sc:* Jane Murfin.

Low-budget melodrama of a woman who cons a con-artist. Based on the play by Samuel Shipman. Filmed before in 1925.

2496. Lawless Borders (Spectrum; 1935). *Cast:* Bill Cody, Molly O'Day, Martin Garralaga, Ted Adams, John Elliott, Merrill McCormack, Roger Williams, Budd Buster. *D:* John P. McCarthy; *Sc:* Zara Tazil. (0:58)

Bill Cody oater of a cowboy out to get the guys who killed his pal.

2497. The Lawless Frontier (Monogram-Lone Star; 1934). *Cast:* John Wayne, Sheila Terry, George Hayes, Jack Rockwell, Buffalo Bill, Jr., Yakima Canutt, Earl Dwire, Lloyd Whitlock, G.D. Wood (Gordon De-Main), Eddie Parker, Artie Ortego, Herman Hack. *D:* Robert N. Bradbury; *P:* Paul Malvern; *Supervisor:* Trem Carr; *St & Sc:* Bradbury. (0:54) (video)

John Wayne western of a cowpoke accused of a series of crimes, who must apprehend the real culprits to get the law off his back.

2498. Lawless Land (Republic-Supreme; 1936–37). *Cast:* Johnny Mack Brown, Louise Stanley, Ted Adams, Julian Rivero, Horace Murphy, Frank Ball, Ed Cassidy, Roger Williams, Frances Kellogg. *D:* Albert Ray; *P:* A.W. Hackel; *Sc:* Andrew Bennison. (0:55)

Johnny Mack Brown shoot-em-up of a Texas Ranger sent to a small western town to investigate some murders.

2499. The Lawless Nineties (Republic; 1936). *Cast:* John Wayne, George Hayes, Ann Rutherford, Harry Woods, George Chesebro, Lane Chandler, Jack Rockwell, Charles King, Alan Bridge, Sam Flint, Tom London, Fred "Snowflake" Toones, Etta McDaniel, Tom Brower, Cliff Lyons, Al Taylor, Earl Seaman, Tracy Layne, Philo

McCullough. *D:* Joseph Kane; *Sc:* Joseph Poland. (0:56) (video)

John Wayne oater of a town terrorized by outlaws opposing statehood.

The Lawless North (G.B. title) *see* **North of Nome**

2500. The Lawless Range (Republic-Lone Star; 1935). *Cast:* John Wayne, Sheila Mannors, Earl Dwire, Glenn Strange, Frank McGlynn, Jr., Yakima Canutt, Jack Curtis, Wally Howe, Jack Kirk, Fred Burns, Slim Whitaker, Julia Griffin. *D:* Robert N. Bradbury; *P:* Paul Malvern; *Supervisor:* Trem Carr; *Sc:* Lindsley Parsons. (0:59) (video)

John Wayne western of a greedy banker out to secure some gold deposits — by hook or crook.

2501. Lawless Riders (Columbia; 1935). *Cast:* Ken Maynard, Geneva Mitchell, Frank Yaconelli, Harry Woods, Wally Wales (Hal Taliaferro), Slim Whitaker, Frank Ellis, Jack Rockwell, Bob McKenzie, Hank Bell, Bud Jamison, Horace B. Carpenter, Bud McClure, Pascale Perry, Oscar Gahan. *D:* Spencer Gordon Bennet; *St & Sc:* Nate Gatzert. (1:00)

Ken Maynard western involving a series of stagecoach robberies.

2502. Lawless Valley (RKO; 1938). *Cast:* George O'Brien, Kay Sutton, Earle Hodgins, Fred Kohler, Sr., Fred Kohler, Jr., Walter Miller, Lew Kelly, George MacQuarrie, Chill Wills, Dot Farley, Robert Stanton (Kirby Grant), George Chesebro, Carl Stockdale, Ben Corbett, Robert McKenzie. *D:* David Howard; *P:* Bert Gilroy; *Sc:* Oliver Drake. (0:59)

George O'Brien western of a wrongfully convicted man who gets out of prison to find out who framed him. Based on a novel by W.C. Tuttle.

2503. The Lawless Woman (Chesterfield; 1931). *Cast:* Vera

Reynolds, James Burtis, Gwen Lee, Thomas Jackson, Carroll Nye, Wheeler Oakman, Kitty Adams. *D:* Richard Thorpe; *Sc:* Thorpe (co).

"Poverty row" melodrama.

2504. A Lawman Is Born (Republic-Supreme; 1937). *Cast:* Johnny Mack Brown, Iris Meredith, Al St. John, Mary MacLaren, Warner Richmond, Charles King, Dick Curtis, Earle Hodgins, Frank LaRue, Steve Clark, Jack C. Smith, Sherry Tansey, Wally West, Budd Buster, Lew Meehan, Tex Palmer. *D:* Sam Newfield; *P:* A.W. Hackel; *Sc:* George Plympton. (0:58) (video)

Johnny Mack Brown western of a cowboy who thwarts some land grabbers.

2505. Lawyer Man (WB; 1932). *Cast:* William Powell, Joan Blondell, Helen Vinson, Claire Dodd, Alan Dinehart, Allen Jenkins, David Landau, Sheila Terry, Rockliffe Fellowes, Roscoe Karns, Vaughn Taylor (film debut), Sterling Holloway, Harold Huber, Edward McWade, Kenneth Thomson, Curly Wright. *D:* William Dieterle; *Sc:* Rian James, James Seymour. (1:08)

Low-budget melodrama of a lawyer who falls victim to corruption. Based on the novel by Max Trell.

2506. The Lawyer's Secret (Paramount; 1931). *Cast:* Clive Brook, Charles "Buddy" Rogers, Fay Wray, Richard Arlen, Jean Arthur, Claire Dodd, Syd Saylor, Francis McDonald, Harold Goodwin. *D:* Louis Gasnier, Max Marcin; *St:* James Hilary Finn.

Melodrama of a lawyer who knows the truth about a murder, but is unable to reveal it.

Lazy Bones (G.B. title) *see* **Hallelujah, I'm a Bum**

2507. Lazy River (MGM; 1934). *Cast:* Jean Parker, Robert Young, Nat Pendleton, Maude Eburne, C. Henry

Gordon, Ted Healy, Raymond Hatton, Irene Franklin, Erville Alderson, Ruth Channing, George Lewis. *D:* George B. Seitz; *P:* Lucien Hubbard; *St:* Lea David Freeman; *Sc:* Hubbard.

B drama set in the deep south of a prodigal son.

2508. The League of Frightened Men (Columbia; 1937). *Cast:* Walter Connolly (Nero Wolfe), Lionel Stander (Archie Goodwin), Eduardo Ciannelli, Irene Hervey, Victor Kilian, Walter Kingsford, Jameson Thomas, Ian Wolfe, Rafaela Ottiano, Leonard Mudie, James Flavin, Charles Irwin, Allen Brook, Herbert Ashley, Nana Bryant, Kenneth Hunter, Clara Blandick, Edward J. McNamara. *D:* Alfred E. Green; *Sc:* Guy Endore, Eugene Solow. (1:05)

A Nero Wolfe murder-mystery, based on the character created in a series of books by Rex Stout. The story concerns a group of men who attended college together that are being killed off one at a time.

2509. Leathernecking (RKO; 1929–30). *Cast:* Irene Dunne (film debut), Ken Murray, Eddie Foy, Jr., Louise Fazenda, Ned Sparks, Lilyan Tashman, Benny Rubin, Rita LaRoy, Fred Santley, William von Brincken, Claude King. *D:* Edward Cline; *As.P.:* Louis Sarecky; *Sc:* Alfred Jackson, Jane Murfin; *Songs:* Oscar Levant, Sidney Clare, Benny Davis, Harry Akst. (G.B. title: *Present Arms*) (1:20)

In Hawaii, a marine private pretends to be an officer in order to impress a lady socialite. This comedy with music was based on the hit Broadway musical "Present Arms" by Richard Rodgers, Lorenz Hart and Herbert Fields. The film sports a color sequence and has original show tunes dropped and new ones written for the score.

2510. The Leathernecks Have Landed (Republic; 1936). *Cast:* Lew Ayres, James Ellison, Isabel Jewell, Joseph Sawyer, Ray Corrigan, Maynard Holmes, J. Carrol Naish, Ward Bond, James Burke, Paul Porcasi, Clay Clement. *D:* Howard Bretherton; *St:* Wellyn Totman, James Gruen; *Sc:* Seton I. Miller. (G.B. title: *The Marines Have Landed*)

In China, some U.S. Marines become involved in smuggling and murder.

2511. The Leavenworth Case (Republic; 1936). *Cast:* Donald Cook, Norman Foster, Erin O'Brien-Moore, Warren Hymer, Jean Rouverol, Ian Wolfe, Maude Eburne, Carl Stockdale. *D:* Lewis Collins.

B detective yarn based on the 1870 story by Anna Katherine Green.

2512. Left Handed Law (Universal; 1936-37). *Cast:* Buck Jones, Noel Francis, Lee Phelps, Robert Frazer, Frank LaRue, Matty Fain, George Regas, Lee Shumway, Nena Quartero, Charles LeMoyne, Budd Buster, Frank Lackteen, Jim Toney, Bill Wolfe, Jack Evans, Jim Corey. *D:* Lesley Selander; *Sc:* Frances Guihan. (1:02)

Buck Jones western of an army colonel who cleans up a New Mexico town.

2513. Leftover Ladies (Tiffany; 1931). *Cast:* Walter Byron, Claudia Dell, Marjorie Rambeau, Roscoe Karns, Rita LaRoy, Alan Mowbray, Franklyn Farnum, Buster Phelps, J. Farrell MacDonald, Selmer Jackson. *D:* Erle C. Kenton; *St:* Ursula Parrott. (G.B. title: *Broken Links*)

"Poverty row" romantic drama.

2514. Legion of Lost Flyers (Universal; 1939). *Cast:* Richard Arlen, Anne Nagel, Andy Devine, William Lundigan, Guinn Williams, Ona Munson, Jack Carson, Leon Ames, Theodore von Eltz, Dave Willock, Leon Belasco, Eddy Waller, Pat Flaherty, Jerry Marlowe, Edith Mills. *D:* Christy Cabanne; *P:* Ben Pivar; *St:* Pivar; *Sc:* Maurice Tombragel. (1:05)

B actioner of a pilot accused of negligence in a plane crash.

2515. The Legion of Missing Men (Monogram; 1937). *Cast:* Ralph Forbes, Ben Alexander, George Regas, Hala Linda, Jimmy Aubrey, Paul Hurst, Frank Leigh, Roy D'Arcy. *D:* Hamilton MacFadden; *P:* I.E. Chadwick; *St:* Norman S. Hall; *Sc:* Sherman Lowe, Harry O. Hoyt. (1:02)

B action drama of two buddies who join the French Foreign Legion.

2516. Legion of Terror (Columbia; 1936). *Cast:* Bruce Cabot, Marguerite Churchill, John Hamilton, Ward Bond, Harry Davenport, Charles Wilson, Edward J. LeSaint, Nick Copeland, Arthur Loft, John Tyrrell, Crawford Weaver. *D:* C.C. Coleman, Jr.; *Sc:* Bert Granet.

B melodrama of a terrorist organization similar to the Black Legion, a topical issue of the mid to late 1930s with a similar story told by Warners' *Black Legion* (q.v.).

2517. Legion of the Lawless (RKO; 1939-40). *Cast:* George O'Brien, Virginia Vale, Monte Montague, Herbert Heywood, Norman Ellis, Hugh Sothern, William (Billy) Benedict, Edwin (Eddy) Waller, Delmar Watson, Bud Osborne, Slim Whitaker, Mary Field. *D:* David Howard; *P:* Bert Gilroy; *St:* Berne Giler; *Sc:* Doris Schroeder. (1:00)

Offbeat George O'Brien western which makes a statement against vigilante justice.

2518. Lem Hawkin's Confession (Micheaux; 1935). Low-budget production produced, directed and written by Oscar Micheaux.

2519. The Lemon Drop Kid (Paramount; 1934). *Cast:* Lee Tracy, Helen Mack, William Frawley, Baby LeRoy, Minna Gombell, Robert McWade, Henry B. Walthall, Kitty Kelly, Eddie Peabody, Del Henderson, Sam McDaniel, Edward J. LeSaint, Clarence Wilson, Lee Shumway,

Charles C. Wilson. *D:* Marshall Neilan; *Sc:* Howard J. Green, J.P. McEvoy, Seena Owen (uncredited). (1:11)

Sentimental B comedy-melodrama of a race track con-man who endeavors to get away from it all. Based on the story by Damon Runyon, it was remade by this studio in 1951 with Bob Hope.

2520. Lena Rivers (Tiffany; 1932). *Cast:* Charlotte Henry, Beryl Mercer, James Kirkwood, Morgan Galloway, Betty Blythe, John St. Polis, Joyce Compton, Clarence Muse, John Larkin, Russell Simpson, Kentucky Jubilee Singers. *D:* Phil Rosen; *P:* Sam Bischoff; *St:* Mary J. Holmes; *Sc:* Stuart Anthony, Warren Duff. (0:57) (Re-released in 1938 by Monogram as *The Sin of Lena Rivers*)

Drama of a girl born out-of-wedlock who goes to live with a wealthy uncle, but is made unhappy by other family members.

2521. Les Miserables (United Artists/20th Century; 1935). *Cast:* Fredric March (Jean Valjean), Charles Laughton (Javert), John Beal (Marius), Cedric Hardwicke (American debut as Bishop Bienvenu), Rochelle Hudson (Cosette), Frances Drake (Eponine Thernardier), Florence Eldridge (Fantine), Jessie Ralph (Madame Magloire), Marilyn Knowlden (Cosette the child), Mary Forbes (Mlle. Baptieme), Ferdinand Gottschalk (M. Thernardier), Jane Kerr (Madame Thernardier), Eily Malyon (mother superior), Vernon Downing (Brissac), Lyons Wickland (LeMarque), John Carradine (Enjolras), Charles Jockey Hoefli (Brevet), Leonid Kinskey (Genflou), John M. Bleifer (Chenildieu), Harry Semels (Cochepaille), Florence Roberts (Toussaint), Lorin Raker (Valsin), Perry Ivins (Inspector Devereury), Pat Somerset (Francois), Herbert Bunston (judge at Favorelles), Keith Kenneth (senior prefect), G. Raymond (Bill) Nye (Jacques), Robert Greig (prison governor), Virginia Howell (old beggar-

woman), Harry Cording (Beam Warder), Paul Irving (innkeeper), Lowell Drew (Duval), Thomas R. Mills (L'Estrange), Davison Clark (Marcin), Montague Shaw (factory foreman), Margaret Bloodgood (factory forewoman), Sidney Bracey, Cecil Weston, Ian MacLaren, Gilbert Clayton, Leonard Mudie, Olaf Hytten. *D:* Richard Boleslawski; *P:* Darryl F. Zanuck; *As.P.:* William Goetz, Raymond Griffith; *Sc:* W.P. Lipscomb; *Cinematographer:* (A.A.N.) Gregg Toland; *Editor:* (A.A.N.) Barbara McLean; *Assistant Director:* (A.A.N.) Eric Stacey. (1:48) (video)

Classic adaptation of Victor Hugo's novel of the events which follow the theft of a loaf of bread. This was the second highest (of 11) top grossing films of 1935, receiving an A.A.N. for "Best Picture" as well as being voted one of the "10 Best" films of the year by the National Board of Review. On the "10 Best" lists of the *New York Times* and *Film Daily* it placed #5. Other filmings of the story were in 1909 (U.S.A.), 1913 (France), 1917 (U.S.A.), 1923 (France), 1929 (U.S.A.) as *The Bishop's Candlesticks,* 1934 (France), 1946 (Italy), 1952 (U.S.A.), 1956 (France), 1978 as a British TV movie, 1982 (France) and finally it became a stage musical in Great Britain in 1987, eventually becoming a hit on Broadway.

2522. Let 'Em Have It (United Artists/Reliance; 1935). *Cast:* Richard Arlen, Virginia Bruce, Alice Brady, Bruce Cabot, Harvey Stephens, Eric Linden, Dorothy Appleby, Joyce Compton, J. Farrell MacDonald, Gordon Jones, Bodil Rosing, Paul Stanton, Paul Fix, Wesley Barry, Harry Woods, Matthew Betz, Hale Hamilton, Robert Emmett O'Connor, Bud Flanagan (Dennis O'Keefe). *D:* Sam Wood; *P:* Edward Small; *St & Sc:* Joseph Moncure March, Elmer Harris. (G.B. title: *False Faces*) (1:30) (video)

Action-packed melodrama of the F.B.I. vs. gangsters.

2523. Let Freedom Ring (MGM; 1939). *Cast:* Nelson Eddy, Virginia Bruce, Victor McLaglen, Lionel Barrymore, H.B. Warner, Raymond Walburn, Edward Arnold, Guy Kibbee, Charles Butterworth, Billy Bevan, George Hayes, Emory Parnell, Louis Jean Heydt, Trevor Bardette, Dick Rich, Sarah Padden, Eddie Dunn, C.E. Anderson. *D:* Jack Conway; *P:* Harry Rapf; *Sc:* Ben Hecht; *Songs:* Sigmund Romberg, Gus Kahn. (1:40)

Western-type actioner of a man fighting corruption in his home town. A minor hit at the box office.

2524. Let Them Live (Universal; 1937). *Cast:* John Howard, Nan Grey, Edward Ellis, Judith Barrett, Robert Wilcox, Robert Warwick, Bennie Bartlett, Ralph Remley. *D:* Harold Young; *P:* Edmund Grainger; *St:* Richard E. Wormser; *Sc:* Bruce Manning, Lionel Houser. (1:12)

Good vs. evil in this small town B drama.

2525. Let Us Be Gay (MGM; 1930). *Cast:* Norma Shearer, Marie Dressler, Rod La Rocque, Raymond Hackett, Sally Eilers, Hedda Hopper, Tyrrell Davis, Gilbert Emery, Dickie Moore, Johnny Walker, Wilfred Noy, Mary Carr, Sybil Grove, Bill O'Brien. *D:* Robert Z. Leonard; *P:* Leonard; *Sc:* Frances Marion. (1:19)

Romantic comedy of a divorced couple who meet years later. Based on the 1929 play by Rachel Crothers.

2526. Let Us Live (Columbia; 1939). *Cast:* Maureen O'Sullivan, Henry Fonda, Ralph Bellamy, Alan Baxter, Stanley Ridges, John Qualen, Byron Foulger, Martin Spellman, Philip Trent, Forrester Harvey, Peter Lynn, George Douglas. *D:* John Brahm; *St:* Joseph F. Dineen; *Sc:* Anthony Veiller, Allen Rivkin. (1:08)

B melodrama of a cabbie wrongfully convicted of murder and the girl who is out to save him.

2527. Let's Be Ritzy (Universal; 1934). *Cast:* Lew Ayres, Patricia Ellis, Frank McHugh, Robert McWade, Isabel Jewell, Berton Churchill, Hedda Hopper. *D:* Edward Ludwig. (G.B. title: *Millionaire for a Day*) (1:08)

B comedy of a young couple who try to live better than they are financially able.

2528. Let's Fall in Love (Columbia; 1933). *Cast:* Ann Sothern, Miriam Jordan, Edmund Lowe, Gregory Ratoff, Kane Richmond, Betty Furness, John Qualen, Greta Meyer, Arthur Jarrett, Connie Gilchrist, Tala Birell, Selmer Jackson. *D:* David Burton; *St:* Herbert Fields; *Sc:* Fields.

Low-budget musical-comedy.

2529. Let's Get Married (Columbia; 1937). *Cast:* Ida Lupino, Ralph Bellamy, Reginald Denny, Walter Connolly, Raymond Walburn, Robert Allen. *D:* Alfred E. Green.

B romantic comedy.

2530. Let's Go Native (Paramount; 1930). *Cast:* Jeanette MacDonald, Jack Oakie, Kay Francis, James Hall, Skeets Gallagher, Eugene Pallette, Grady Sutton, William Austin, Charles Sellon, David Newell. *D:* Leo McCarey; *Sc:* Percy Heath, George Marion, Jr.

Musical-comedy of castaways on an island paradise.

2531. Let's Go Places (Fox; 1930). *Cast:* Lola Lane, Sharon Lynn, Frank Richardson, Ilka Chase, Dixie Lee, Joseph Wagstaff, Larry Steers, Charles Judels, Betty Grable (bit). *D:* Frank Strayer; *St:* Andrew Bennison; *Sc:* William K. Wells.

B musical.

2532. Let's Live Tonight (Columbia; 1935). *Cast:* Lillian Harvey, Tullio Carminati, Hugh Williams, Tala Birell, Arthur Treacher, Janet Beecher, Claudia Coleman, Luis Alberni, Gilbert

Emery. *D:* Victor Schertzinger; *St:* Bradley King; *Sc:* Gene Markey; *Songs:* Schertzinger, Jack Scholl.

Low-budget romantic musical.

2533. Let's Make a Million (Paramount; 1937). *Cast:* Edward Everett Horton, Charlotte Wynters, Porter Hall. *D:* Ray McCarey; *P:* Harold Hurley.

B comedy of small-town life and a shopkeeper who is swindled by con-men.

2534. Let's Sing Again (RKO/ Principal; 1936). *Cast:* Bobby Breen, Henry Armetta, George Houston, Vivienne Osborne, Grant Withers, Inez Courtney, Richard Carle, Lucien Littlefield, Ann Doran, Gene Reynolds, Clay Clement. *D:* Kurt Neumann; *P:* Sol Lesser; *Sc:* Don Swift, Dan Jarrett; *Songs:* Gus Kahn, Jimmy McHugh, Hugo Riesenfeld, Selma Hautzik, Samuel Pokrass, Charles O. Locke, Richard E. Tyler.

Sentimental musical of an 8-year-old boy who runs away from an orphanage. This was the first in a series of Principal productions featuring the "singing boy wonder" Bobby Breen.

2535. Let's Talk It Over (Universal; 1934). *Cast:* Chester Morris, Mae Clarke, Frank Craven, Otis Harlan, Andy Devine, Frank Reicher, Henry Armetta, Irene Ware, Douglas Fowley, Jane Darwell, Anderson Lawler, Willard Robertson, John Warburton, Goodee Montgomery, Herbert Corthell, Russ Brown. *D:* Kurt Neumann; *St:* Dore Schary, Lewis Foster; *Sc:* John Meehan, Jr. (1:10)

A wealthy woman feigns drowning to attract the attention of a certain man, but she is saved by another who falls for her.

2536. Let's Try Again (RKO; 1934). *Cast:* Clive Brook, Diana Wynyard, Irene Hervey, Helen Vinson, Theodore Newton, Arthur Hoyt, Henry Kolker. *D:* Worthington Miner; *As.P.:* Myles Connolly; *Sc:* Miner. (G.B. title: *The Marriage Symphony*) (1:07)

B marital drama of a couple who separate after 10-years of marriage. Based on the play "Sour Grapes" by Vincent Lawrence.

2537. The Letter (Paramount; 1929). *Cast:* Jeanne Eagels (A.A.N. for B.A. 1928–29), Herbert Marshall, Reginald Owen (film debut), O.P. Heggie (American debut), Irene Browne (American debut), Lady Tsen Mei (American debut), Tamaki Yoshiwara. *D:* Jean De Limur; *P:* Monta Bell; *Sc:* Garrett Fort; *Dialogue:* Bell, De Limur. (1:01)

Romantic drama set on a tropical plantation of a married woman who shoots her lover and the events which follow. Based on the play by Somerset Maugham, it was filmed at Astoria Studios in Long Island, N.Y. Remade in 1940 with Bette Davis, in 1947 by this studio as *The Unfaithful*, in a loosely adapted version from Great Britain in 1976 titled *East of Elephant Rock* and a 1982 TV movie.

2538. A Letter of Introduction (Universal; 1938). *Cast:* Adolphe Menjou, Andrea Leeds, Edgar Bergen & Charlie McCarthy, George Murphy, Eve Arden, Rita Johnson, Ernest Cossart, Ann Sheridan, Frank Jenks, Constance Moore, Frank Reicher, Frances Robinson. *D:* John M. Stahl; *P:* Stahl; *St:* Bernice Boone; *Sc:* Sheridan Gibney, Leonard Spigelgass. (1:38) (video)

A girl seeks to make it on her own without the credited influence of her famous father.

2539. Letty Lynton (MGM; 1932). *Cast:* Joan Crawford, Robert Montgomery, Nils Asther, May Robson, Lewis Stone, Louise Closser Hale, Emma Dunn, Walter Walker, William Pawley. *D:* Clarence Brown; *P:* Hunt Stromberg; *Sc:* John Meehan, Wanda Tuchock. (1:24)

Hit drama of love and murder which helped establish Joan Crawford as a star. Miss Crawford's fashions in this film helped create a trend at the time. Based on the novel by Mrs. Belloc-Lowndes which in turn was based on the true story of Madeleine Smith, a newsworthy murder case of its day. (Refilmed in England, 1950.)

2540. Libeled Lady (MGM; 1936). *Cast:* Jean Harlow (Gladys), William Powell (Bill Chandler), Myrna Loy (Connie Allenbury), Spencer Tracy (Haggerty), Walter Connolly (Mr. Allenbury), Charley Grapewin (Mr. Bane), Cora Witherspoon (Mrs. Burns-Norvell), E.E. Clive (fishing instructor), Bunny Lauri Beatty (Babs), Otto Yamaoka (Ching), Charles Trowbridge (Graham), Greta Meyer (Connie's maid), George Chandler (bellhop), Spencer Charters (magistrate), Billy Benedict (Johnny), Hal K. Dawson (Harvey Allen), William Newell (divorce detective), Duke York (taxi driver), Harry Allen (Jacques), Edwin Stanley, Pat West, Wally Maher, Tom Mahoney, Pat Somerset, Richard Tucker, Libby Taylor, Jack Mulhall, Jed Prouty, Charles Irwin, Eddie Shubert, Hattie McDaniel, Thomas Pogue, George Davis, Charles King, Howard C. Hickman, Inez Palange, Charles Croker-King, Harry C. Bradley, Bodil Ann Rosing, Robin Adair, Barnett Parker, Buster Phelps, Bobs Watson, Tommy Bond. *D:* Jack Conway; *P:* Lawrence Weingarten; *St:* Wallace Sullivan; *Sc:* Maurine Watkins, Howard Emmett Rogers, George Oppenheimer. (1:38)

This comedy of a newspaper editor who does what he has to do to get a good story was a huge hit for the studio, being one of the 38 top grossing films of 1936–37. It received an A.A.N. for "Best Picture" and was remade as *Easy to Wed* (MGM; 1946).

2541. Liberty Road (Xxxx Xxxx; 1932). (No information available)

2542. Life Begins (WB/F.N.; 1932). *Cast:* Loretta Young, Eric Linden, Aline MacMahon, Preston Foster, Glenda Farrell, Vivienne Osborne, Frank McHugh, Clara Blandick, Elizabeth Patterson, Gilbert Roland, Dorothy Tree, Dorothy Peterson, Gloria Shea, Mary Philips, Herbert Mundin, Ruthelma Stevens, Reginald Mason, Helena Phillips, Terrance Ray, Walter Walker. *D:* James Flood, Elliott Nugent; *P:* Raymond Griffith; *Sc:* Earl Baldwin. (G.B. title: *The Dawn of Life*) (1:12)

The stories of various people involved in childbirth in a maternity hospital. Based on the play by Mary McDougal Axelson, the film flopped. Remade as *A Child Is Born* (WB; 1940).

Life Begins at College *see* **Life Begins in College**

2543. Life Begins at Forty (Fox; 1935). *Cast:* Will Rogers, Rochelle Hudson, Richard Cromwell, Jane Darwell, Slim Summerville, George Barbier, Thomas Beck, Sterling Holloway, Roger Imhof, Ruth Gillette, Charles Sellon, John Bradford. *D:* George Marshall; *P:* Sol M. Wurtzel; *St:* Walter B. Pitkin; *Sc:* Lamar Trotti. (1:25)

Another Will Rogers hit for the studio is this Americana of a man trying to clear another who has been convicted of bank robbery.

2544. Life Begins in College (20th Century–Fox; 1937). *Cast:* Ritz Brothers, Joan Davis, Tony Martin, Gloria Stuart, Nat Pendleton, Fred Stone, Marjorie Weaver, Joan Marsh, Jed Prouty, Dixie Dunbar, Elisha Cook, Jr., Fred Kohler, Jr., J.C. Nugent, Maurice Cass, Dick Baldwin, Ed Thorgersen. *D:* William A. Seiter; *P:* Harold Wilson; *St:* Darrell Ware; *Sc:* Karl Tunberg, Don Ettlinger. (G.B. title: *The Joy Parade*) (1:34)

A college football comedy.

2545. Life Begins with Love (Columbia; 1937). *Cast:* Jean Parker, Douglass Montgomery, Edith Fellows.

D: Raymond B. McCarey; *St:* Dorothy Bennett; *Sc:* Thomas Mitchell, Brown Holmes.

(No other information available)

2546. Life Goes On (Million Dollar Productions; 1938). *Cast:* Louise Beavers.

(No other information available)

2547. Life in the Raw (Fox; 1933). *Cast:* George O'Brien, Claire Trevor (film debut), Francis Ford, Greta Nissen, Warner Richmond, Gaylor (Steve) Pendleton, Alan Edwards, Nigel de Brulier. *D:* Louis King; *Sc:* Stuart Anthony. (1:02)

George O'Brien comedy-western of a cowboy who takes on the job of reforming his girl's brother.

2548. Life Is Worth Living (Xxxx Xxxx; 1934). (No information available)

2549. The Life of Emile Zola (WB; 1937). *Cast:* Paul Muni (A.A.N. for B.A. and "Best Actor of the Year" by the New York Film Critics as Emile Zola), Joseph Schildkraut (A.A. for B.S.A. as Alfred Dreyfus), Gale Sondergaard (Lucie Dreyfus), Donald Crisp (Maitre Labori), Gloria Holden (Alexandrine Zola), Erin O'Brien-Moore (Nana), Henry O'Neill (Colonel Picquart), Morris Carnovsky (film debut as Anatole France), Louise Calhern (Major Dort), John Litel (Charpentier), Vladimir Sokoloff (Paul Cezanne), Ralph Morgan (Commandant of Paris), Robert Barrat (Major Walsin-Esterhazy), Grant Mitchell (Georges Clemenceau), Harry Davenport (chief of staff), Robert Warwick (Major Henry), Charles Richman (M. Delagorgue), Gilbert Emery (minister of war), Walter Kingsford (Colonel Sandherr), Paul Everton (assistant chief of staff), Montagu Love (M. Cavaignac), Frank Sheridan (M. Van Cassell), Lumsden Hare (Mr. Richards), Marcia Mae Jones (Helen Richards), Florence Roberts (Madame Zola), Dickie Moore (Pierre Dreyfus), Rolla Gourvitch (Jeanne Dreyfus), Moroni Olsen (Capt. Guignet), Egon Brecher (Brucker), Frank Reicher (M. Perrenx), Walter O. Stahl (Senator Scheurer-Kestner), Frank Darien (Albert), Countess Iphigenie Castiglioni (Madame Charpentier), Arthur Aylesworth (chief censor), Frank Mayo (Mathieu Dreyfus), Alexander Leftwich (Major D'Aboville), Paul Irving (La Rue), Pierre Watkin (prefect of police), Holmes Herbert (Commander of Paris), Robert Cummings, Sr. (General Gillian), Harry Worth (Lieutenant), William von Brincken (Swartzkoppen). *D:* (A.A.N.) William Dieterle; *P:* Jack L. Warner, Hal B. Wallis; *Supervisor:* Henry Blanke; *St:* (A.A.N.) Heinz Herald, Geza Herczeg; *Sc:* (A.A.) Herald, Herczeg & Norman Reilly Raine (based on Matthew Josephson's "Zola and His Times"); *Art Director:* (A.A.N.) Anton Grot; *Assistant Director:* (A.A.N.) Russ Saunders; *Music:* (A.A.N.) Max Steiner; *Music Director:* Leo F. Forbstein; *Sound Recording:* (A.A.N.) Nathan Levinson. (G.B. title: *I Accuse*) (1:56) (video)

Critically acclaimed classic drama of the famed French novelist's attempts to save Alfred Dreyfus from imprisonment on Devil's Island. It received the A.A. for "Best Picture" as well as being voted "Best Film of the Year" by the *New York Times,* the New York Film Critics and *Film Daily.* With the National Board of Review, it placed #2 on their "10 Best" list.

2550. The Life of Jimmy Dolan (WB; 1933). *Cast:* Douglas Fairbanks, Jr., Loretta Young, Aline MacMahon, Guy Kibbee, Lyle Talbot, Fifi D'Orsay, Harold Huber, Shirley Grey, George Meeker, John Wayne, Arthur Hohl, Mickey Rooney, Allen "Farina" Hoskins, David Durand, Dawn O'Day (Anne Shirley). *D:* Archie Mayo; *P:* Hal Wallis; *Sc:* David Boehm, Erwin Gelsey. (G.B. title: *The Kid's Last Fight*) (1:29)

A sentimental drama of mistaken identity and a man wanted for murder.

Based on the play by Bertram Mill-hauser and Beulah Marie Dix. Remade as *They Made Me a Criminal* (q.v.).

2551. The Life of the Party (WB/Vitaphone; 1930). *Cast:* Winnie Lightner (Flo), Irene Delroy (Dot), Jack Whiting (A.J. Smith), Charles Butterworth (film debut as Colonel Joy), Charles Judels (LeMaire), John Davidson (Mr. Smith), Arthur Hoyt (secretary). *D:* Roy Del Ruth; *St:* Melville Crossman (Darryl F. Zanuck); *Sc:* Arthur Caesar. (1:17)

Two-color technicolor comedy of two song pluggers from Brooklyn who head for Havana, Cuba with the intent of finding rich husbands.

Note: Shown on Turner Network Television 8/25/1990 in b/w.

2552. The Life of the Party (RKO; 1937). *Cast:* Joe Penner, Gene Raymond, Harriet Hilliard (Nelson), Ann Miller, Parkyakarkus, Helen Broderick, Victor Moore, Billy Gilbert, Franklin Pangborn, Margaret Dumont, Betty Jane Rhodes, Richard Lane, Ann Shoemaker, Winifred Harris, Charles Judels. *D:* William A. Seiter; *P:* Edward Kaufman; *St:* Joseph Santley; *Sc:* Bert Kalmar, Harry Ruby, Viola Brothers Shore; *Songs:* Allie Wrubel, Herb Magidson, George Jessel, Ben Oakland. (1:17)

Musical-comedy of a girl who decides on show business to avoid an arranged marriage that would give her a possible inheritance of $3,000,000.

2553. The Life of Vergie Winters (RKO; 1934). *Cast:* Ann Harding (Vergie Winters), John Boles, Helen Vinson, Frank Albertson, Creighton (Lon) Chaney, (Jr.), Bonita Granville, Sara Haden, Donald Crisp, Walter Brennan, Ben Alexander, Betty Furness, Molly O'Day, Cecil Cunningham, Maidel Turner, Wesley Barry, Edward Van Sloan, Josephine Whittell, Edwin Stanley. *D:* Alfred Santell; *P:* Pandro S. Berman; *Sc:* Jane Murfin. (1:22)

Small town drama of a married pol-itician and his continued love for his mistress and their daughter. A hit tear-jerker for the ladies in its day. Based on the novel by Louis Bromfield.

2554. Life Returns (Universal; 1934–35). *Cast:* Onslow Stevens, Lois Wilson, Valerie Hobson, Stanley Fields, Frank Reicher, Richard Carle, George Breakston, Lois January, Richard Quine, Dean Benton, Maidel Turner, George MacQuarrie, Otis Harlan, Dr. Robert E. Cornish. *D:* Eugene Frenke, James Hogan; *P:* Lou Ostrow; *St:* Frenke, Hogan; *Sc:* Arthur T. Horman, John F. Goodrich. (1:03)

Offbeat B film of a doctor experimenting with bringing asphyxiation victims back to life who finds he is being backed by criminal element. The film utilizes actual footage of Dr. Robert E. Cornish bringing a dead dog back to life. Re-released in 1938 by Grand National.

2555. Light Fingers (Columbia; 1929). *Cast:* Dorothy Revier, Ian Keith. *D:* Joseph Henabery.

Part-talkie melodrama.

2556. The Light of the Western Stars (Paramount; 1930). *Cast:* Richard Arlen, Mary Brian, Regis Toomey, Fred Kohler, George Chandler, Harry Green, William Le Maire, Syd Saylor, Guy Oliver, Gus Saville. *D:* Otto Brower, Edwin H. Knopf; *Sc:* Grover Jones, William Slavens McNutt. (1:20)

Western based on the book by Zane Grey. Previously filmed in 1918 with Dustin Farnum and (Paramount; 1925) with Jack Holt and Billie Dove. Remade by this studio in 1940.

2557. The Light That Failed (Paramount; 1939). *Cast:* Ronald Colman, Ida Lupino, Walter Huston, Dudley Digges, Muriel Angelus (American debut), Fay Helm, Francis McDonald, Ernest Cossart, Colin Tapley, Halliwell Hobbes, Clyde Cook, Pedro de Cordoba, Ronald Sinclair, Ferike Boros, Charles Irwin, Sarita Wooton, Wilfred Roberts, George Regas. *D:* William Wellman; *Sc:* Robert Carson. (1:37)

Romantic drama of an artist who is determined to finish a girl's portrait before his approaching blindness becomes permanent. Based on the story by Rudyard Kipling, it was previously filmed by Pathé in 1916 with Robert Edeson and Jose Collins and in 1923 by Paramount with Percy Marmont and Jacqueline Logan.

2558. Lightnin' (Fox; 1930). *Cast:* Will Rogers (Bill Jones), Joel McCrea, Louise Dresser, Rex Bell, Sharon Lynn, Joyce Compton, J.M. Kerrigan, Jason Robards, Thomas Jefferson, Frank Campeau, Charlotte Walker, Phil Tead, Ruth Warren, Walter Percival, Bess Flowers, Goodee Montgomery, Luke Cosgrave, Helen Cohan. *D:* Henry King; *Sc:* S.N. Behrman, Sonya Levien.

Another comedy starring Fox's biggest box office attraction of the era, Will Rogers. Rogers' home-spun commonsense outlook on American life endeared him to his multitude of fans, making every one of his films a money-maker. This one was voted #4 on the "10 Best" list of the *New York Times*. Based on the long-running Broadway hit by Frank Bacon and Winchell Smith, it was previously filmed by John Ford in 1925 for this studio with Edythe Chapman, Jay Hunt and Otis Harlan.

2559. Lightnin' Bill Carson (Puritan; 1936). *Cast:* Tim McCoy, Lois January, Rex Lease, Harry Worth, John Merton, Karl Hackett, Lafe McKee, Edmund Cobb, Jack Rockwell, Joseph Girard, Jimmy Aubrey, Frank Ellis, Slim Whitaker, Franklyn Farnum, Oscar Gahan, Artie Ortego. *D:* Sam Newfield; *Sc:* Joseph O'Donnell. (1:11)

Tim McCoy western of a government man who uses various disguises to get the bad guys. Followed by a sequel (see below).

2560. Lightnin' Carson Rides Again (Victory; 1938). *Cast:* Tim McCoy, Joan Barclay, Ben Corbett (Magpie), Walter Patterson, George Champion, Slim Lucas, George Hunter, Paul Hurst, Yakima Canutt. *D:* Sam Newfield; *P:* Sam Katzman; *Sc:* Joseph O'Donnell. (0:59)

Tim McCoy sequel to the preceding film. A government man helps his nephew when he is accused of robbery and murder.

2561. Lightnin' Crandall (Republic-Supreme; 1937). *Cast:* Bob Steele, Lois January, Dave O'Brien, Horace Murphy, Charles King, Ernie Adams, Earl Dwire, Richard Cramer, Frank LaRue, Lew Meehan, Lloyd Ingraham, Ed Carey, Art Felix. *D:* Sam Newfield; *P:* A.W. Hackel; *St:* E.B. Mann; *Sc:* Charles Francis Royal. (1:00)

Bob Steele western of a range war.

2562. Lightnin' Smith Returns (Xxxx Xxxx; 1931). *Cast:* Buddy Roosevelt, Jack Richardson, Tom London. *D:* Jack Irwin.

Buddy Roosevelt western.

2563. Lightning Bill (Superior; 1934). *Cast:* Buffalo Bill, Jr., Alma Rayford, Allen Holbrook, George Hazel, Nelson McDowell, Budd Osborne, William McCall, Lafe McKee, Eva McKenzie, Blackjack Ward. *D:* Victor Adamson (Denver Dixon); *P:* Dixon; *Sc:* L.V. Jefferson. (0:46)

Buffalo Bill, Jr., oater of a cowboy on the trail of horse rustlers.

2564. Lightning Flyer (Columbia; 1931). *Cast:* James Hall, Dorothy Sebastian. *D:* William Nigh.

2565. Lightning Range (Superior; 1934–35). *Cast:* Buddy Roosevelt, Patsy Bellamy, Genee Boutell, Betty Butler, Anne Howard, Si Jenks, Denver Dixon, Jack Evans, Boris Bullock, Clyde McClary, Bart Carre, Lafe McKee, Olin Francis, Ken Broeker, Jack Bronston, Merrill McCormack. *D:* Victor Adamson (Denver Dixon); *P:* Dixon; *Sc:* L.V. Jefferson. (0:50)

Buddy Roosevelt western of a cowboy helping a girl who has had money stolen.

2566. Lightning Strikes Twice (RKO; 1934). *Cast:* Ben Lyon, Thelma Todd, Pert Kelton, Laura Hope Crews, Skeets Gallagher, Walter Catlett, Chick Chandler, Jonathan Hale, Margaret Armstrong, John Davidson, Fred Kelsey, Edgar Dearing, Roger Gray, Walter Long. *D:* Ben Holmes; *As.P.:* Lee Marcus; *St:* Holmes, Marion Dix; *Sc:* Joseph A. Fields, John Grey. (1:05)

B mystery-comedy of the chain of events which follow the scream of a cat and a gunshot.

2567. Lightning Triggers (Marcy Exchange; 1935). *Cast:* Reb Russell, Fred Kohler, Jack Rockwell, Yvonne Pelletier, Edmund Cobb, Lillian Castle, Lew Meehan, William McCall, Rebel the horse. *D:* S. Roy Luby; *P:* Willis Kent. (0:50)

Reb Russell western of a cowboy's attempts to bring an outlaw gang to justice by joining them.

Lights and Shadows (G.B. title) *see* **The Woman Racket**

2568. Lights of New York (WB; 1928). *Cast:* Helene Costello (Kitty Lewis), Cullen Landis (Eddie Morgan), Wheeler Oakman (Hawk Miller), Eugene Pallette (Gene), Gladys Brockwell (Molly Thompson), Tom Dugan (Sam), Mary Carr (Mrs. Morgan), Robert Elliott (Detective Crosby), Tom McGuire (Police Chief Collins), Guy D'Ennery (Tommy), Walter Percival (Jake Jackson), Jere Delaney (Dan Dickson), Roscoe Karns, Jimmy Conlin (film debut). *D:* Bryan Foy; *St:* Charles L. Gaskill; *Sc:* F. Hugh Herbert, Murray Roth. (0:57)

Crime melodrama of a small town boy victimized in the big city. Notable as the first all-talkie to come out of Hollywood, it premiered on July 8, 1928, at the Mark Strand Theatre in New York City. The quality of the sound on disk is considered poor, but this $75,000 production raked in $2,000,000 for the studio.

2569. Lilies of Broadway (Xxxx Xxxx; 1934). (No information available)

2570. Lilies of the Field (WB/ F.N.; 1930). *Cast:* Corinne Griffith (repeating her role in the earlier version as Mildred Harker), Ralph Forbes, May Boley, John Loder, Freeman Wood, Patsy Page, Virginia Bruce, Andre Beranger, Tyler Brooke, Rita LaRoy, Eve Southern. *D:* Alexander Korda; *Sc:* John F. Goodrich.

Musical drama of a woman who hits the downside of life after her divorce. Filmed before by First National 1923–24. Based on the play by William Hurlbut, it was a box office dud.

2571. Liliom (Fox; 1930). *Cast:* Charles Farrell, Rose Hobart (film debut recreating her stage role — which in this film was originally intended for Janet Gaynor), Lee Tracy, Walter Abel, Estelle Taylor, Guinn Williams, H.B. Warner, Dawn O'Day (Anne Shirley), Nat Pendleton, Bert Roach. *D:* Frank Borzage; *Sc:* S.N. Behrman, Sonya Levien. (1:34)

A story of the here and the hereafter which was based on the play by Ferenc Molnar. Remade in Germany in 1933 by director Fritz Lang, it was also the basis for the hit Broadway musical "Carousel" which was filmed in 1956.

2572. Lilly Turner (WB/F.N.; 1933). *Cast:* Ruth Chatterton (title role), George Brent, Frank McHugh, Ruth Donnelly, Guy Kibbee, Gordon Westcott, Marjorie Gateson, Arthur Vinton, Robert Barrat, Hobart Cavanaugh, Mae Busch, Grant Mitchell, Margaret Seddon, Lucille Ward, Kathrin Clare Ward. *D:* William Wellman, George Abbott (unc.); *P:* Hal Wallis; *Sc:* Gene Markey, Kathryn Scola.

Romantic drama of a "hoochie-koochie" dancer who is deserted by her husband, a magician. Based on the play by Philip Dunning and George Abbott.

2573. Limehouse Blues (Paramount; 1934). *Cast:* George Raft, Jean

Parker, Anna May Wong, Kent Taylor, Billy Bevan, Eric Blore, Montagu Love, Eily Malyon, Clara Lou (Ann) Sheridan, Desmond Roberts, John Rogers, Forrester Harvey, Tempe Pigott, Keith Kenneth, Colin Kenny, Robert Adair, Robert Lorraine. *D;* Alexander Hall; *P:* Arthur Hornblow, Jr.; *St:* Arthur Phillips; *Sc:* Phillips, Cyril Hume, Grover Jones. (aka: *East End Chant*) (1:05)

B melodrama of a man who falls for a lady with a past and then must deal with the jealousy of his oriental mistress.

2574. The Line-Up (Columbia; 1934). *Cast:* Marion Nixon, William Gargan, John Miljan, Harold Huber, Paul Hurst, Joseph Crehan, Noel Francis. *D:* Howard Higgin; *Sc:* George Waggner. (G.B. title: *Identity Parade*) B melodrama.

2575. The Lion and the Lamb (Columbia; 1931). *Cast:* Walter Byron, Carmel Myers, Montagu Love, Raymond Hatton, Charles Gerrard, Sidney Bracey. *D:* George B. Seitz.

"Poverty row"—yes, Columbia was originally a "poverty row" studio, located on Gower Street amidst the many low-budget production studios of the early 1930s—romance.

2576. The Lion and the Mouse (WB; 1928). *Cast:* Lionel Barrymore, May McAvoy, William Collier, Jr., Alec B. Francis, Emmett Corrigan, Jack Ackroyd. *D:* Lloyd Bacon; *Sc:* Robert Lord.

A Vitaphone part-talkie (sound on disk) drama of an all-powerful financier. Based on a play by Charles Klein it was previously filmed in 1919 with Alice Joyce. This remake contains 31 minutes of dialogue.

2577. The Lion Man (Normandy; 1936). *Cast:* Charles Locher (Jon Hall), Kathleen Burke, Richard Carlyle. *D:* Xxxx Xxxx.

B action-adventure based on "The Lad and the Lion" by Edgar Rice Burroughs.

2578. The Lion's Den (Puritan; 1936). *Cast:* Tim McCoy, Joan Woodbury, Don Barclay, J. Frank Glendon, John Merton, Arthur Millett, Karl Hackett, Dick Curtis, Jack Evans, Art Felix, Jack Rockwell, Bud McClure, Frank Ellis. *D:* Sam Newfield; *Sc:* John T. Neville. (0:59)

Tim McCoy prairie saga of a sharpshooter mistaken for a hired gun.

2579. Listen, Darling (MGM; 1938). *Cast:* Mary Astor, Judy Garland (who sings "Zing! Went the Strings of My Heart"), Freddie Bartholomew, Scotty Beckett, Walter Pidgeon, Alan Hale, Charley Grapewin, Barnett Parker, Gene Lockhart, Byron Foulger. *D:* Edwin L. Marin; *P:* Jack Cummings; *St:* Katherine Brush; *Sc:* Elaine Ryan, Anne Morrison Chapin. (1:10)

Comedy of three fatherless teen-age siblings who try to find their mother a new husband.

2580. The Little Accident (Universal; 1930). *Cast:* Douglas Fairbanks, Jr., Anita Page, Sally Blane, Joan Marsh, Roscoe Karns, Slim Summerville, ZaSu Pitts, Myrtle Stedman, Henry Armetta, Nora Cecil, Gertrude Short, Bertha Mann, Albert Gran. *D:* William James Craft; *Adaptation:* Gene Towne; *Sc:* Gladys Lehman. (1:22)

Comedy farce of a man who on the night of his re-marriage, finds that his ex-wife is pregnant with his child. Based on the novel "An Unmarried Father" by Floyd Dell which was adapted to the play "The Little Accident" by Dell and Thomas Mitchell. Remade in 1939 (see below) and in 1944 as *Casanova Brown*.

2581. Little Accident (Universal; 1939). *Cast:* Hugh Herbert, Baby Sandy (Sandra Lee Henville), Florence Rice, Richard Carlson, Ernest Truex, Joy Hodges, Edgar Kennedy, Fritz Feld, Etienne Girardot, Peggy Moran, Anne

Gwynne, Emory Parnell, Frances Robinson, Minerva Urecal. *D:* Charles Lamont; *P:* Lamont; *Sc:* Paul Yawitz, Eve Greene. (1:05)

Remake of the preceding film as a male advice columnist finds a baby and decides to keep it.

2582. The Little Adventuress (Columbia; 1938). *Cast:* Edith Fellows, Jacqueline Wells (Julie Bishop). *D:* D. Ross Lederman.

B juvenile entertainment.

2583. Little America (Paramount; 1935). *Photographed by:* John L. Herrmann & Carl O. Peterson.

Feature documentary of Rear Admiral Richard E. Byrd's second expedition to Antarctica in 1933 for further exploration and study of the continent.

2584. Little Big Shot (WB; 1935). *Cast:* Robert Armstrong, Glenda Farrell, Sybil Jason (American debut as the daughter), Edward Everett Horton, Jack LaRue, Arthur Vinton, J. Carrol Naish, Marc Lawrence, Addison Richards, Joseph (Sawyer) Sauers, Ward Bond, Tammany Young, Murray Alper, Mary Foy, Guy Usher, Emma Dunn. *D:* Michael Curtiz; *P:* Sam Bischoff; *St:* Harrison Jacobs; *Sc:* Jerry Wald, Julius J. Epstein, Robert Andrews; *Songs:* "I'm a Little Big Shot Now," "Rolling in Money" and "My Kid's a Crooner" by Mort Dixon & Allie Wrubel. (1:14)

Sentimental B melodrama involving the custody of the daughter of a deceased gangster.

2585. Little Caesar (WB/F.N.; 1930). *Cast:* Edward G. Robinson (Caesar Enrico Bandello), Douglas Fairbanks, Jr. (Joe Massara), Glenda Farrell (Olga Strassoff), William Collier, Jr. (Tony Passa), Ralph Ince (Diamond Pete Montana), Sidney Blackmer ("Big Boy"), George E. Stone (Otero), Thomas Jackson (Lieut. Tom Flaherty), Stanley Fields (Sam Vettori), Armand Kaliz (DeVoss), Landers Stevens (Gabby), Maurice Black (Little Arnie Lorch), Noel Madison (Peppi), Nick Bela (Ritz Colonna), Lucille La Verne (Ma Magdalena), Ben Hendricks, Jr. (Kid Bean), George Daly, Larry Steers, Al Hill, Ernie S. Adams. *D:* Mervyn LeRoy; *P:* Hal Wallis; *Supervisor:* Darryl F. Zanuck; *Adaptation:* Francis Edwards Faragoh, Robert N. Lee. (1:20) (video)

Classic melodrama of the rise and fall of a big city gangster. Based on the novel by W.R. Burnett, this was Warner's first "social conscience" film, and one of the 15 top grossing films of 1930–31.

2586. The Little Colonel (Fox; 1935). *Cast:* Shirley Temple, Lionel Barrymore, Evelyn Venable, Bill Robinson, John Lodge, Sidney Blackmer, Hattie McDaniel, Dave O'Brien, William Burress, Frank Darien, Avonne Jackson, Alden (Stephen) Chase, Nyanza Potts, Geneva Williams. *D:* David Butler; *P:* B.G. DeSylva; *Adaptation:* William Conselman (of the best seller by Annie Fellows Johnston). (1:20) (video)

Comedy-drama with musical interludes of a southern family's problems after the Civil War. The final party sequence was originally filmed in technicolor. The famous "Dance on the Steps" by Shirley Temple and Bill Robinson is from this film. Computer-colored prints were produced in the 1980s.

2587. The Little Giant (WB/F.N.; 1933). *Cast:* Edward G. Robinson (Bugs Ahearn), Mary Astor, Helen Vinson, Russell Hopton, Kenneth Thomson, Shirley Grey, Berton Churchill, Donald Dillaway, Louise Mackintosh, Helen Mann. *D:* Roy Del Ruth; *P:* Ray Griffith; *Sc:* Robert Lord, Wilson Mizner. (1:15)

Hit comedy of a Chicago bootlegger who moves to California with the intent of bettering his reputation by joining the society crowd, but instead finds himself involved with a family of phonies.

2588. Little Johnny Jones (WB/ F.N.; 1929). *Cast:* Eddie Buzzell (Johnny Jones), Alice Day, Edna Murphy, Robert Edeson, Wheeler Oakman, Donald Reed. *D:* Mervyn LeRoy; *Sc:* Adelaide Heilbron; *Songs:* "Yankee Doodle Boy" and "Give My Regards to Broadway" by George M. Cohan, and "Painting the Clouds with Sunshine" by Al Dubin & Joe Burke; and by other composers, "Go Find Somebody to Love," "My Paradise" and "She Was Kicked on the Head by a Butterfly."

An American jockey wins the English Derby on a horse called "Yankee Doodle." Based on the hit Broadway musical of 1904 by George M. Cohan. Filmed before by Warners in 1923 with Johnny Hines and Wyndham Standing.

2589. Little Lord Fauntleroy (United Artists/Selznick International; 1936). *Cast:* Freddie Bartholomew (Ceddie), Dolores Costello (Dearest), C. Aubrey Smith (Grandfather), Mickey Rooney (Dick Tipton), Henry Stephenson (Havisham), Jessie Ralph, Guy Kibbee, E.E. Clive, Helen Flint, Eric Alden, Jackie Searle, May Beatty, Walter Kingsford, Constance Collier, Una O'Connor, Gustav von Seyffertitz, Lawrence Grant, Gilbert Emery, Eily Malyon, Joan Standing, Virginia Field. *D:* John Cromwell; *P:* David O. Selznick; *Sc:* Hugh Walpole, Richard Schayer (unc.), Selznick (unc.). (1:38) (video)

Classic tale based on the 1886 novel by Frances Hodgson Burnett, of a fatherless boy who finds he is heir to a British title. First filmed in 1914. Remade with and by Mary Pickford (in a dual role) in 1921 for U.A. release. Remade in 1980 as a TV movie.

2590. Little Man, What Now? (Universal; 1934). *Cast:* Margaret Sullavan (Lammchen Pinneberg), Douglass Montgomery (Hans Pinneberg), Alan Hale, Muriel Kirkland, Catherine Doucet, Mae Marsh, Alan Mowbray, Hedda Hopper, Fred Kohler, Paul Fix, Monroe Owsley, DeWitt Jennings, Etienne Girardot, Christian Rub, G.P. Huntley, Jr., Frank Reicher, Tom Ricketts, Bodil Rosing, Donald Haines, Max Asher, George Meeker, Sarah Padden, Carlos de Valdez. *D:* Frank Borzage; *P:* Carl Laemmle, Jr.; *Sc:* William Anthony McGuire. (1:31)

Drama of the Weimar Republic in pre–Nazi Germany and a young couple who find themselves in the grip of poverty. Based on the novel by Hans Fallada, the film was considered important in its day.

2591. Little Men (Mascot; 1934). *Cast:* James (Junior) Durkin, Frankie Darro, David Durand, Dickie Moore, Tad Alexander, Richard Quine, Tommy Bupp, Ronnie Cosbey, Bobby Cox, George Ernest, Buster Phelps, Dickie Jones, Donald Buck, Eddie Dale Heiden, Erin O'Brien-Moore, Ralph Morgan, Cora Sue Collins, Hattie McDaniel, Jacqueline Taylor, G.P. Huntley, Jr., Phyllis Fraser. *D:* Phil Rosen; *P:* Ken Goldsmith; *Sc:* Gertrude Orr. (1:12)

Low-budget juvenile tale loosely based on Louisa May Alcott's sentimental 1871 tale of a home for orphaned boys.

2592. Little Men (RKO/The Play's the Thing; 1939–40). *Cast:* Kay Francis (Jo), Jack Oakie (Willie), George Bancroft (Major Burdle), Jimmy Lydon (Daniel), Ann Gillis (Nan), Charles E. (Carl) Esmond (Professor), Richard Nichols (Teddy), Jimmy Zaner, Donald Rackerby, Lillian Randolph, Schuyler Standish, Francesca Santoro, "Elsie" the Borden cow (Buttercup). *D:* Norman Z. McLeod; *P:* Gene Towne, Graham Baker; *Sc:* Mark Kelly, Arthur Caesar. (1:24) (video)

Loosely adapted rural 19th-century Americana based on the 1871 book by Louisa May Alcott. See preceding film for another version.

2593. The Little Minister (RKO; 1934). *Cast:* Katharine Hepburn

(Babbie), John Beal (Gavin), Alan Hale (Rob Dow), Donald Crisp (Dr. Mc-Queen), Lumsden Hare (Tammas), Beryl Mercer (Margaret), Dorothy Stickney (Jean), Frank Conroy (Lord Rintoul), Billy Watson (Micah), Mary Gordon (Nanny), Eily Malyon (Eva-lina), Reginald Denny, Andy Clyde, Leonard Carey, Herbert Bunston. *D:* Richard Wallace; *P:* Pandro S. Berman; *Sc:* Jane Murfin, Sarah Y. Mason, Vic-tor Heerman; *Sc:* (for additional scenes) Mortimer Offner, Jack Wagner. (1:50) (video)

The romance of a 19th-century Scottish minister and a local gypsy girl. Based on a well known 1897 play and best seller novel by James M. Barrie, it was filmed five times in the silent era, four of which include (Vitagraph; 1913) with Clara Kimball Young and James Young, one in 1915, (Vitagraph; 1921) with Alice Calhoun and James Morrison and (Paramount; 1921) with Betty Comp-son and George Hackathorne. In recent years it has twice been adapted for TV.

2594. Little Miss Broadway (20th Century–Fox; 1938). *Cast:* Shirley Temple, Jimmy Durante, George Mur-phy, Edna May Oliver, Phyllis Brooks, George Barbier, Edward Ellis, Jane Darwell, El Brendel, Donald Meek, Claude Gillingwater, Russell Hicks, Syd Saylor, Ben Welden, Robert Gleck-ler, Montague Shaw, Vince Barnett, Claire DuBrey. *D:* Irving Cummings; *As P :* David Hempstead; *Sc:* Harry Tugend, Jack Yellen. (1:10) (video)

Comedy with songs of a little girl who is taken into a theatrical boarding house. Computer-colored.

2595. Little Miss Marker (Para-mount; 1934). *Cast:* Adolphe Menjou (Sorrowful Jones), Shirley Temple (Marthy Jane—"Marky"), Dorothy Dell (Bangles Carson), Charles Bickford (Steve Halloway), Lynne Overman (Regret), Frank McGlynn, Sr. (Doc Chesley), John Sheehan (Sun Rise), Garry Owen (Grinder), Sleep 'n' Eat (later Willie Best as Dizzy Memphis),

Pudgy White (Eddie), Tammany Young (Buggs), Sam Hardy (Bennie the Gouge), Edward Earle (Marky's father), Warren Hymer (Canvas Back), John Kelly (Sore Toe), Frank Conroy (Dr. Ingalls), James Burke (Detective Rear-don), Stanley Price, Don Brodie, Ernie Adams, Mildred Gover, Lucille Ward. *D:* Alexander Hall; *P:* B.P. Schulberg; *Sc:* William R. Lipman, Sam Hellman, Gladys Lehman; *Songs:* "I'm a Black Sheep Who Is Blue," "Low Down Lullaby" and "Laugh You Son-of-a-Gun" by Ralph Rainger and Leo Robin. (1:20) (video)

Hit film of its day as a little girl is left in lieu of a debt with a bookie. Based on a Damon Runyon story it was re-made by this studio in 1949 as *Sorrowful Jones* with Bob Hope, in 1963 by Univer-sal as *Forty Pounds of Trouble* again in 1979–80 as a TV movie.

2596. Little Miss Nobody (20th Century–Fox; 1936). *Cast:* Jane Withers, Ralph Morgan, Sara Haden, Jameson Thomas, Jackie Morrow, Clarence Wilson, Jane Darwell, Harry Carey, Donald Haines, Betty Jean Hainey, Claudia Coleman. *D:* John G. Blystone; *P:* Sol M. Wurtzel; *St:* Frederick Hazlitt Brennan; *Sc:* Edward Eliscu, Lou Breslow, Paul Burger.

Juvenile comedy-drama with a sen-timental touch.

2597. Little Miss Roughneck (Columbia; 1938). *Cast:* Edith Fellows, Leo Carrillo, Jacqueline Wells (Julie Bishop), Scott Colton, Wade Boteler, Thurston Hall. *D:* Aubrey Scotto.

B juvenile comedy-drama.

2598. Little Miss Thoroughbred (WB; 1938). *Cast:* Janet Chapman (film debut), John Litel, Ann Sheridan, Frank McHugh, Eric Stanley, Robert Homans, Peggy Ann Garner (film debut), John Ridgely, James Nolan. *D:* John Farrow; *As.P.:* Bryan Foy; *Sc:* George Bricker, Albert DeMond.

Sentimental B juvenile drama of a little girl who goes in search of her father.

2599. Little Old New York (20th Century–Fox; 1939–40). *Cast:* Alice Faye, Richard Greene, Fred MacMurray, Henry Stephenson, Brenda Joyce, Andy Devine, Fritz Feld, Ward Bond, Theodore von Eltz, Clarence Wilson, Robert Middlemass, Jody Gilbert, Dutch Hendrian, Herbert Heywood, Harry Tyler, Paul Sutton. *D:* Henry King; *P:* Darryl F. Zanuck; *As.P.:* Raymond Griffith; *Play:* Rida Johnson Young; *Sc:* Harry Tugend. (1:40)

Part-fact, part-fiction romantic drama of Robert Fulton and the invention of the first commercially successful steamboat, the "Clermont" in 1807. Previously filmed in 1923 by Samuel Goldwyn with Marion Davies.

2600. Little Orphan Annie (RKO; 1932). *Cast:* Mitzi Green (Annie), Edgar Kennedy (Daddy Warbucks), Buster Phelps, May Robson, Matt Moore, Kate Lawson, Sidney Bracey. *D:* John Robertson; *P:* David O. Selznick; *Sc:* Wanda Tuchock, Tom McNamara. (1:00) (video)

Hit comedy-drama based on Harold Gray's comic strip of a little girl who had to do good in the world. Previously filmed in 1919 by Pioneer. (See below for another version.)

2601. Little Orphan Annie (Paramount; 1938). *Cast:* Ann Gillis (Annie), Robert Kent, J. Farrell MacDonald, Ben Welden, June Travis, J.M. Kerrigan, Sarah Padden, Harry Tyler, Dorothy Vaughan, James Burke, Ian MacLaren. *D:* Ben Holmes; *P:* John Speaks; *Sc:* Budd Schulberg, Samuel Ornitz, Endre Bohem.

Independent B production which was based on the comic strip character created by Harold Gray, this one with a boxing theme.

Little Pal *see* **The Healer**

2602. The Little Princess (20th Century–Fox; 1939). *Cast:* Shirley Temple, Richard Greene, Anita Louise, Ian Hunter, Cesar Romero, Arthur Treacher, Mary Nash, Sybil Jason, Miles Mander, Marcia Mae Jones, Beryl Mercer, E.E. Clive, Clyde Cook, Holmes Herbert, Ira Stevens, Eily Malyon, Guy Bellis, Keith Kenneth, Will Stanton, Evan Thomas, Kenneth Hunter, Deidre Gale, Lionel Braham. *D:* Walter Lang; *As.P.:* Gene Markey; *Sc:* Ethel Hill, Walter Ferris; *Words & Music for the "Fantasy" Ballet by:* Walter Bullock & Samuel Pokrass. (1:33) (video)

Lavishly produced in technicolor, this drama tells of a little girl left at a boarding school when her father goes to fight in the Boer War. Based on the novel by Frances Hodgson Burnett, and set in Queen Victoria's 1899 England it was a hit for the studio. Previously filmed in 1917 by Paramount/Artclass with Mary Pickford.

2603. The Little Red Schoolhouse (Chesterfield; 1936). *Cast:* Dickie Moore, Lloyd Hughes, Ann Doran, Richard Carle. *D:* Charles Lamont.

"Poverty row" rural drama. Previously filmed in 1923.

2604. Little Tough Guy (Universal; 1938). *Cast:* Billy Halop (Johnny Boylan), Huntz Hall (Pig), Gabriel Dell (String), Bernard Punsley (Ape), David Gorcey (Sniper), Hally Chester (Dopey), Helen Parrish, Marjorie Main, Jackie Searle, Robert Wilcox, Edward Pawley, Peggy Stewart, Jason Robards. *D:* Harold Young; *P:* Kenneth Goldsmith; *St:* Brenda Weisberg; *Sc:* Weisberg, Gilson Brown. (1:03) (video)

An offshoot of the "Dead End Kids" as a slum youth is sent to a reformatory. Followed by *Little Tough Guys in Society* (see below).

2605. Little Tough Guys in Society (Universal; 1938). *Cast:* Mary Boland, Mischa Auer, Harris Berger, Edward Everett Horton, Helen Parrish, Charles Duncan, Jackie Searle, Frankie Thomas, William (Billy) Benedict, Hally Chester, David Gorcey, Peggy Stewart, Harold Huber, David Oliver.

D: Erle C. Kenton; *P:* Max H. Golden; *Sc:* Edward Eliscu, Mortimer Offner. (1:03)

A followup to the preceding film is this B comedy of a woman who invites street kids to her mansion in order to straighten out her overbearing son.

2606. The Little Wildcat (WB; 1929). *Cast:* George Fawcett, Audrey Ferris, James Murray, Doris Dawson. *D:* Ray Enright; *St:* Gene Wright; *Sc:* Edward T. Lowe, Jr.

Part-talkie drama of an old Civil War vet who sits around and reminisces with his old captain and friend while his granddaughters have amorous adventures.

2607. Little Women (RKO; 1933). *Cast:* Katharine Hepburn (voted "Best Actress of the Year" at the Venice Film Festival for her portrayal of Jo), Joan Bennett (Amy), Paul Lukas (Fritz Bhaer), Frances Dee (Meg), Jean Parker (Beth), Edna May Oliver (Aunt March), Douglass Montgomery (Laurie), Henry Stephenson (Mr. Lawrence), Spring Byington (feature debut as Marmie), John Davis Lodge (Brooks), Samuel S. Hinds (Mr. March), Mabel Colcord (Hannah), Nydia Westman (Mamie), Marion Ballou. *D:* (A.A.N.) George Cukor; *As.P.:* Kenneth MacGowan; *Sc:* (A.A.) Sarah Y. Mason, Victor Heerman, Gene Towne (unc.). (1:55) (video)

Classic adaptation of Louisa May Alcott's 1869 novel of four sisters growing up prior to the American Civil War. This titanic hit was one of the 11 top grossing films of 1933, receiving *Photoplay's* Gold Medal Award. It received an A.A.N. for "Best Picture," was voted one of the "10 Best" films of the Year by the National Board of Review, as well as placing #8 on the "10 Best" list of the *New York Times* of 1933. It made the "10 Best" list of *Film Daily* in 1934 at #5. First Filmed by World in 1918. Remade by MGM in 1949 and again in 1978 as a 2-part TV movie, which in

turn was followed by a short-lived TV series.

2608/2609. The Littlest Rebel (20th Century–Fox; 1935). *Cast:* Shirley Temple (Virgie Cary), John Boles (Capt. Herbert Cary), Jack Holt (Col. Morrison), Karen Morley (Mrs. Cary), Bill Robinson (Uncle Billy), Guinn Williams (Sgt. Dudley), Willie Best (James Henry), Frank McGlynn, Sr. (Abraham Lincoln), Bessie Lyle (Mammy), Hannah Washington (Sally Ann), James Flavin (guard). *D:* David Butler; *As.P.:* B.G. DeSylva; *Sc:* Edwin Burke, Harry Tugend. (1:10) (video)

Civil War story of a little southern girl who visits President Lincoln in an attempt to get her father released from a Union prison camp. Based on the play by Edward Peple, the film was one of the 25 top grossing films of 1935–36. Filmed before (World; 1914) with Mimi Yvonne and E.K. Lincoln. Computer-colored.

2610. Live, Love and Learn (MGM; 1937). *Cast:* Robert Montgomery, Rosalind Russell, Robert Benchley, Helen Vinson, Mickey Rooney, Monty Woolley (film debut), E.E. Clive, Billy Gilbert, Maude Eburne, Al Shean, June Clayworth, Zeffie Tilbury, Charles Judels, Ann Rutherford, Minerva Urecal, Harlan Briggs, Marion Parsonnet. *D:* George Fitzmaurice; *P:* Harry Rapf; *St:* Helen Grace Carlisle; *Sc:* Charles Brackett, Cyril Hume, Richard Maibaum. (1:18)

Hit romantic tale of a bohemian artist and his marriage which begins to change his attitude on life.

2611. Lives of a Bengal Lancer (Paramount; 1935). *Cast:* Gary Cooper (Capt. McGregor), Franchot Tone (Lieut. Fortesque), Richard Cromwell (Lieut. Stone), Sir Guy Standing (Col. Stone), C. Aubrey Smith (Major Hamilton), Monte Blue (Hamzulla Khan), Kathleen Burke (Tania Volkanskaya),

Colin Tapley (Lieut. Barrett), Douglass R. Dumbrille (Mohammed Khan), Akim Tamiroff (Emir), Jameson Thomas (Hendrickson), Noble Johnson (Ram Singh), Lumsden Hare (Major General Woodley), J. Carrol Naish (grand vizier), Rollo Lloyd (ghazi), Mischa Auer (Afridi), Bhogwan Singh (Shah), Abdul Hassan (Ali Hamdi), Clive Morgan (Lieut. Norton), Leonid Kinskey (snake charmer), Hussain Nasri (Muezzin), James Warwick (Lieut. Gilhooley), George Regas (Kushal Khan), Charles Stevens, Myra Kinch, Eddie Das, Major Sam Harris, Ram Singh, Jamiel Hasson, James Bell, General Ikonnikoff, F.A. Armenta, Claude King, Reginald Sheffield, Lya Lys, Rodd Redwing. *D:* (A.A.N.) Henry Hathaway; *P:* Louis D. Lighton; *Sc:* (A.A.N.) Achmed Abdullah, John L. Balderston, Grover Jones, William Slavens McNutt, Waldemar Young; *Art-Set Decoration:* (A.A.N.) Hans Dreier, Roland Anderson; *Editor:* (A.A.N.) Ellsworth Hoagland; *Sound Recording:* (A.A.N.) Franklin Hansen, Harold Lewis; *Assistant Directors:* (A.A.N.) Clem Beauchamp & Paul Wing. (1:49) (video)

Classic adventure drama set amidst a British regiment in India. Based on the novel by Francis Yeats-Brown, it became one of the 12 top grossing films of 1935. It received an A.A.N. for "Best Picture" and was voted one of the year's "10 Best" by the National Board of Review. On the "10 Best" list of *Film Daily* it placed #2, while on the same list of the *New York Times* it placed #4.

2612. Living on Love (RKO; 1937). *Cast:* James Dunn, Whitney Bourne, Joan Woodbury, Solly Ward, Tom Kennedy, Franklin Pangborn, Kenneth Terrell, James Fawcett, Chester Clute. *D:* Lew Landers; *Sc:* Franklin Coen.

A light romantic comedy of two people who share the same apartment,

but not at the same time. A remake of *Rafter Romance* (q.v.), it is based on the novel by John Wells.

2613. Living on Velvet (WB/ F.N.; 1935). *Cast:* George Brent, Kay Francis, Warren William, Helen Lowell, Henry O'Neill, Russell Hicks, Samuel S. Hinds, Edgar Kennedy, Maude Turner Gordon, Paul Fix, Martha Merrill. *D:* Frank Borzage; *P:* Edward Chodorov; *St:* Jerry Wald; *Sc:* Wald, Julius J. Epstein; *Title Song:* Al Dubin, Harry Warren. (1:17)

Drama of a carefree flyer who finds his life is changed after learning he is responsible for a plane crash.

2614. The Llano Kid (Paramount; 1939–40). *Cast:* Tito Guizar, Jan Clayton, Gale Sondergaard, Glenn Strange, Alan Mowbray, Minor Watson, Harry Worth. *D:* Edward Venturini; *P:* Harry M. Sherman; *Sc:* Wanda Tuchock. (1:10)

B western of a cowboy whose past catches up with him when he poses as a woman's long-lost son. Based on the story "A Double-Eyed Deceiver" by O'Henry (William Sydney Porter), the film is a remake of *The Texan* (1930) (q.v.).

2615. Lloyd's of London (20th Century–Fox; 1936). *Cast:* Freddie Bartholomew (Young Jonathan), Madeleine Carroll (Clementine), Sir Guy Standing (Angerstein), Tyrone Power (Jonathan the man), C. Aubrey Smith (Old "Q"), Virginia Field (Polly), George Sanders (American debut as Lord Stacy), J.M. Kerrigan (Watson), Una O'Connor (Widow Blake), Douglas Scott (Young Nelson), Forrester Harvey (Potts), Gavin Muir (Gavin Gore), E.E. Clive (magistrate), Miles Mander (Jukes), Montagu Love (Hawkins), Arthur Hohl (first captain), Robert Greig (Lord Drayton), Lumsden Hare (Capt. Suckling), Murray Kinnell (Reverend Nelson), Billy Bevan, Georges Renavent (French lieutenant), Ivan Simpson (old man), Will Stanton (Smutt), John Burton (Lord Nelson), May Beatty (Lady Masham), Hugh Huntley (Prince of Wales), Charles Croker-King (Willoughby), Lester Matthews (Capt. Hardy), Barlowe Borland (Joshua Lamb), Vernon Steele (Sir Thomas Lawrence), Winter Hall (Dr. Beatty), Ann Howard (Catherine), Fay Chaldecott (Susannah), Yvonne Severn (Ann), Thomas Pogue (Benjamin Franklin), Yorke Sherwood (Dr. Johnson), William Wagner (Boswell), Charles Coleman, Charles McNaughton, Leonard Mudie, Holmes Herbert, Constance Purdy, Elsa Buchanan. *D:* Henry King; *As.P.:* Kenneth MacGowan; *Sc:* Ernest Pascal, Walter Ferris (based on the novel by Curtis Kenyon); *Art-Set Decoration:* (A.A.N.) William S. Darling; *Editor:* (A.A.N.) Barbara McLean. (1:55) (video)

Fictional drama of the famous London based insurance company. One of the 38 top grossing films of 1936–37, this is the film that gave Tyrone Power his Hollywood star.

2616. The Local Bad Man (Allied; 1932). *Cast:* Hoot Gibson, Sally Blane, Ed Peil, Sr., Hooper Atchley, Edward Hearn, "Skeeter" Bill Robbins, Milton Brown, Jack Clifford. *D:* Otto Brower; *P:* M.H. Hoffman, Jr.; *Sc:* Philip White. (1:00)

Hoot Gibson western of two bankers who plot their own robbery. Based on the story "All for Love" by Peter B. Kyne.

2617. Local Boy Makes Good (WB; 1931). *Cast:* Joe E. Brown, Dorothy Lee, Ruth Hall, Robert Bennett, Edward Woods, Wade Boteler, Edward J. Nugent, John Harrington, William Burress. *D:* Mervyn LeRoy; *Sc:* Robert Lord. (1:07)

Comedy of a timid young man who does what the title implies after pretending to be a popular high school athlete.

Based on the play "The Poor Nut" by J.C. and Elliott Nugent.

2618. London by Night (MGM; 1937). *Cast:* George Murphy, Rita Johnson (film debut), Virginia Field, Leo G. Carroll, George Zucco, Montagu Love, Eddie Quillan, Leonard Mudie, J.M. Kerrigan, Neil Fitzgerald, Harry Stubbs, Ivan Simpson, Forrester Harvey, Corky the dog. *D:* William Thiele; *P:* Sam Zimbalist; *Sc:* George Oppenheimer. *Song:* "Hi Bill" by Dr. William Axt, Bob Wright, Chet Forrest.

B crime melodrama of an American investigating the case of an English killer who mysteriously disposes of his victims. Based on a play by Will Scott.

2619. The Lone Avenger (World Wide; 1933). *Cast:* Ken Maynard, Muriel Gordon, Jack Rockwell, Charles King, Alan Bridge, Jim Mason, Niles Welch, William N. Bailey, Ed Brady, Lew Meehan, Bud McClure, Horace B. Carpenter, Jack Ward. *D:* Alan James (aka: Alvin J. Neitz); *Sc:* James. (1:01)

Ken Maynard western (his last for this "poverty row" studio) of an outlaw gang attempting to take over a town by causing a bank panic.

2620. The Lone Bandit (Empire/ Kinematrade; 1934). *Cast:* Lane Chandler, Doris Brook, Wally Wales (Hal Taliaferro), Slim Whitaker, Ray Gallagher, Ben Corbett, Jack Prince, Philo McCullough, Forrest Taylor. *D:* J.P. McGowan; *Sc:* Ralph Consumana. (1:00)

Lane Chandler western involving a masked bandit.

2621. Lone Cowboy (Paramount; 1934). *Cast:* Jackie Cooper, Lila Lee, John Wray, Addison Richards, Charles Middleton, Barton MacLane, Gavin Gordon, Herbert Corthell, J.M. Kerrigan, Del Henderson, Lillian Harmon. *D:* Paul Sloane; *Sc:* Paul Sloane; *Adapt.:* Agnes Brand Leahy, Bobby Vernon. (1:15)

B western of a juvenile delinquent from Chicago who is sent out west to live on a ranch. Based on the novel of the same name by Will James. Remade in 1971 by Universal as *Shoot-Out.*

The Lone Ranger *see* **Hi-Yo Silver**

2622. The Lone Rider (Columbia/Beverly Prods.; 1930). *Cast:* Buck Jones, Vera Reynolds, Harry Woods, George Pearce. *D:* Louis King; *P:* Sol Lesser; *Sc:* Forrest Sheldon. (1:00)

Buck Jones western (his first all-talkie) of a former outlaw who winds up the head of the town's vigilante committee. This was also Jones' first western for this studio, never released to TV, it was re-released theatrically in 1987. Remade as *Texas Gunfighter* (q.v.) and *Man Trailer* (q.v.).

2623. Lone Star Pioneers (Columbia; 1939). *Cast:* Bill Elliott, Dorothy Gulliver, Lee Shumway, Slim Whitaker, Charles King, Jack Ingram, Harry Harvey, Buzz Barton, Frank LaRue, Budd Buster, David Sharpe, Frank Ellis, Kit Guard, Tex Palmer, Merrill McCormack, Jack Rockwell. *D:* Joseph Levering; *Sc:* Nate Gatzert. (0:56)

Bill Elliott western of Texas after the Civil War. Elliott's third starring feature.

2624. The Lone Star Ranger (Fox; 1930). *Cast:* George O'Brien, Sue Carol, Walter McGrail, Warren Hymer, Russell Simpson, Roy Stewart, Lee Shumway, Colin Chase, Richard Alexander, Joel Franz, Joe Rickson, Elizabeth Patterson, Billy Butts. *D:* A.F. Erickson & H. Van Buren; *Sc:* Seton I. Miller, John Hunter Booth. (1:10)

George O'Brien western of a man wrongly accused of unlawful activities.

Previously filmed by this studio in 1919 with William Farnum and again in 1923 with Tom Mix, it was based on the 1914 novel by Zane Grey. Remade by 20th Century-Fox in 1942.

2625. The Lone Trail (Syndicate/Metropolitan; 1931-32). *Cast:* King the dog, Rex Lease, Virginia Browne Faire, Joe Bonomo, Jack Mower, Josephine Hill, Al Ferguson, Robert Walker, Edmund Cobb, Harry Todd. *D:* Harry S. Webb, Forrest Sheldon; *Sc:* Carl Krusada.

Feature-version of the 10-chapter serial "The Sign of the Wolf," involving the theft of chains which turn sand into jewels.

2626. The Lone Wolf in Paris (Columbia; 1938). *Cast:* Francis Lederer, Frances Drake, Walter Kingsford, Leona Maricle, Olaf Hytten, Albert van Dekker, Maurice Cass, Ruth Robinson, Eddie Fetherston, Pio Peretti, Bess Flowers. *D:* Albert S. Rogell; *Sc:* Arthur T. Horman. (1:06)

Second entry in the series of Michael Lanyard, jewel thief (alias: "The Lone Wolf"). Based on the character created by Louis Joseph Vance.

2627. The Lone Wolf Returns (Columbia; 1936). *Cast:* Melvyn Douglas (Michael Lanyard—"The Lone Wolf"), Gail Patrick, Tala Birell, Arthur Hohl, Thurston Hall, Douglass Dumbrille, Raymond Walburn, Robert Emmett O'Connor, Robert Middlemass, Nana Bryant, Henry Mollison. *D:* Roy William Neill; *Sc:* Lionel Houser, Joseph Krumgold, Bruce Manning. (1:09)

Premiere entry in a hit series which ran up until 1949 of jewel thief Michael Lanyard who eventually winds up on the right side of the law. Various films on this character, created by Louis Joseph Vance were made during the silent era.

2628. The Lone Wolf Spy Hunt (Columbia; 1939). *Cast:* Warren William, Ida Lupino, Rita Hayworth, Virginia Weidler, Ralph Morgan, Don Beddoe, Marc Lawrence, Ben Welden, James Millican, Leonard Carey, Tom Dugan, Brandon Tynan, Helen Lynd, Jack Norton. *D:* Peter Godfrey (directorial debut); *St:* Louis Joseph Vance; *Sc:* Jonathan Latimer. (G.B. title: *The Lone Wolf's Daughter*) (1:07)

Third entry in the hit series with another lead change, this time to Warren William who continued for seven more films in the series into the 1940s beginning with *The Lone Wolf Strikes* (1940). A remake of *The Lone Wolf's Daughter* (Hodkinson; 1919) with Louise Glaum, Bertram Grassky, and Thomas Holding.

The Lone Wolf's Daughter (G.B. title) *see* **The Lone Wolf Spy Hunt**

2629. The Lonely Trail (Republic; 1936). *Cast:* John Wayne, Ann Rutherford, Cy Kendall, Bob Kortman, Fred "Snowflake" Toones, Etta McDaniel, Sam Flint, Denny Meadows (Dennis Moore), Jim Toney, Yakima Canutt, Lloyd Ingraham, Bob Burns, James Marcus, Rodney Hildebrand, Eugene Jackson, Jack Kirk, Jack Ingram, Bud Pope, Tracy Layne. *D:* Joe Kane; *Sc:* Bernard McConville, Jack Natteford. (0:56)

John Wayne western of the attempts to oust carpetbaggers from Texas after the Civil War.

2630. Lonely Wives (RKO-Pathé; 1931). *Cast:* Edward Everett Horton (in a dual role), Esther Ralston, Laura La Plante, Patsy Ruth Miller, Spencer Charters, Maude Eburne, Maurice Black, Georgette Rhodes. *D:* Russell Mack; *P:* E.B. Derr; *St & Sc:* Walter DeLeon. (1:30)

Drawing room comedy of marital problems which cause a lawyer to hire a double to impersonate him. Based on the European play by A.H. Woods.

2631. Lonesome (Universal; 1928). *Cast:* Glenn Tryon, Barbara Kent, Eddie Phillips, Gustav Partos. *D:* Paul Fejos; *P:* Carl Laemmle, Jr.; *St:* Mann Page; *Sc:* Edward T. Lowe, Jr., Tom Reed.

Part-talkie romance of two lonely people who meet on the beach at Coney Island. Synchronized music, sound effects, titles and a few lines of dialogue (the first for this studio).

2632. The Lonesome Trail (Syndicate; 1930). *Cast:* Charles Delaney, Virginia Browne Faire, George Berliner, William von Brincken, George Hackathorne, George Regas, Yakima Canutt, Art Mix, Jimmy Aubrey, Lafe McKee, Ben Corbett, Monte Montague, Bob Reeves, Bill McCall. *D:* Bruce Mitchell; *Sc:* George Arthur Durlam. (1:00)

Early talkie western of cattle and rustling.

2633. The Long, Long Trail (Universal; 1929). *Cast:* Hoot Gibson, Sally Eilers, Kathryn McGuire, Archie Ricks, James (Jim) Mason, Walter Brennan. *D:* Arthur Rosson.

Part-talkie Hoot Gibson western with a rodeo setting.

2634. Long Lost Father (RKO; 1933–34). *Cast:* John Barrymore, Helen Chandler, Donald Cook, Alan Mowbray, Claude King, E.E. Clive, Reginald Sharland, Ferdinand Gottschalk, Natalie Moorhead, Virginia Weidler, Phyllis Barry, Tempe Pigott, Doris Lloyd, Herbert Bunston, Charles Irwin, John Rogers. *D:* Ernest B. Schoedsack; *As.P.:* Kenneth MacGowan; *Sc:* Dwight Taylor. (1:03)

Drama of a girl abandoned by her father many years before who is helped by him when she needs him most. Based on the novel by G.B. Stern.

2635. The Long Shot (Grand National/Fine Arts; 1938–39). *Cast:* Gordon Jones, Marsha Hunt, C. Henry Gordon, George Meeker, Harry Davenport, George E. Stone, Dorothy Fay, Frank Darien, Tom Kennedy, Earle Hodgins, Emerson Treacy, Lee Phelps, Gay Seabrook, Ben Burt, Denmore Chief, James Robinson, Joe Hernandez, James Keefe. *D:* Charles Lamont; *P:* Franklyn Warner; *St:* Harry Beresford, George Callaghan; *Sc:* Ewart Adamson. (1:09)

A couple of young horse trainers run afoul of crooks trying to fix a horse race. The "Long Shot" emerges in the big race finale.

2636. The Longest Night (MGM; 1936). *Cast:* Robert Young, Florence Rice, Julie Haydon, Leslie Fenton, Ted Healy, Catherine Doucet, Sidney Toler, Janet Beecher, Samuel S. Hinds, Paul Stanton. *D:* Errol Taggart; *P:* Lucien Hubbard, Samuel Marx; *St & Sc:* Robert Andrews. (0:50)

B murder mystery set in a department store. Based on the novel by Cortland Fitzsimmons, this film is notable as the shortest feature film ever produced by this studio.

Looking for Trouble (1931) (G.B. title) *see* **The Tip-Off**

2637. Looking for Trouble (United Artists/20th Century; 1933–34). *Cast:* Spencer Tracy, Jack Oakie, Constance Cummings, Morgan Conway (film debut), Arline Judge, Judith Wood, Joseph (Sawyer) Sauers, Franklyn Ardell, Paul Harvey. *D:* William Wellman; *P:* Darryl F. Zanuck; *St:* J. Robert Bren; *Sc:* Leonard Praskins, Elmer Harris. (1:17)

Two telephone linemen become involved in various adventures as they fight over the same girl. A hit film of its day with an earthquake climax.

2638. Looking Forward (MGM; 1933). *Cast:* Lionel Barrymore, Colin Clive, Elizabeth Allan (American debut), Phillips Holmes, Lewis Stone, Benita Hume, Alec B. Francis, Doris Lloyd, Douglas Walton, George K. Arthur, Halliwell Hobbes, Billy Bevan, Viva Tattersall, Lawrence Grant, Charles Irwin, Ethel Griffies, Eily Malyon, E.E. Clive. *D:* Clarence Brown; *As.P.:* Harry Rapf; *Sc:* Bess Meredyth, H.M. Harwood. (G.B. title: *Service*) (Retitled: *The New Deal*) (1:22)

A flop at the box office, this drama is centered around the activities in an English department store. A Cosmopolitan production based on the play "Service" by C.L. Anthony (Dodie Smith).

2639. Loose Ankles (WB/F.N.; 1930). *Cast:* Douglas Fairbanks, Jr., Loretta Young, Edward Nugent, Louise Fazenda, Ethel Wales, Inez Courtney, Daphne Pollard, Otis Harlan. *D:* Ted Wilde; *P:* Robert Lord; *Sc:* Gene Towne.

Romantic comedy of a girl who will only get her inheritance if two maiden aunts approve of her marriage. Based on a play by Sam Janney, it was previously filmed in 1926 by First National.

2640. Lord Byron of Broadway (MGM; 1929–30). *Cast:* Charles Kaley, Ethelind Terry, Cliff Edwards, Gwen Lee, Gino Corrado, Benny Rubin, Marion Shilling, Rita Flynn, John Byron, Drew Demarest, Hazel Craven. *D:* Harry Beaumont, William Nigh; *St:* Nell Martin; *Sc:* Crane Wilbur, Willard Mack; *Songs:* Nacio Herb Brown & Arthur Freed (includes the hit "Should I?").

Early musical which stars the Broadway singing duo of Charles Kaley and Ethelind Terry in their only film together.

2641. Lord Jeff (MGM; 1938). *Cast:* Freddie Bartholomew, Mickey Rooney, Charles Coburn, Herbert Mundin, Terry Kilburn (film debut), Gale Sondergaard, Peter Lawford

(American debut), Walter Tetley, Peter Ellis, George Zucco, Matthew Boulton, John Burton, Emma Dunn, Monty Woolley, Gilbert Emery, Charles Irwin, Walter Kingsford. *D:* Sam Wood; *P:* Wood, Frank Davis; *St:* Bradford Ropes, Val Burton, Endre Bohem; *Sc:* James Kevin McGuinness. (G.B. title: *The Boy from Barnardos*) (1:18)

A good kid gets into trouble and finds himself in a naval military school in this family type drama.

2642. Loser's End (Awyon; 1934). *P:* Bernad B. Ray.

A Jack Perrin western.

The Losing Game (G.B. title) *see* **The Pay-Off**

2643. The Lost City (Krellberg; 1935). *Cast:* William "Stage" Boyd, Kane Richmond, George Hayes, Milburn Morante, Josef Swickard, Ralph Lewis, Gino Corrado, Eddie Fetherston, Jerry Frank, Billy Bletcher, William (Le-Strange) Millman. *D:* Harry Revier; *P:* Sherman S. Krellberg; *St:* George M. Merrick, Zelma Carroll, Robert Dillon; *Sc:* Perley Poore Sheehan, Eddie Grane-mann, Leon D'Usseau.

Action-adventure which is the feature version of the 12-chapter serial of the same name.

2644. Lost Horizon (Columbia; 1937). *Cast:* Ronald Colman (Robert Conway), Jane Wyatt (Sondra Bizet), John Howard (George Conway), Edward Everett Horton (Alexander P. "Lovey" Lovett), Thomas Mitchell (Henry Barnard), H.B. Warner (A.A.N. for B.S.A. as Chang), Isabel Jewell (Gloria Stone), Margo (Maria), Sam Jaffe (High Lama), Hugh Buckler (Lord Gainsford), David Torrence (prime minister), John Miltern (Carstairs), John Burton (Wynant), John T. Murray (Meeker), Max Rabinowitz (Seiveking), Willie Fung (bandit leader), John Tettener (Montaigne), Val Durand (Talu), Milton Owen (Fenner), Victor Wong (bandit leader), George Chan (Chinese priest), Lawrence Grant, Wyrley Birch, Boyd Irwin, Sr., Leonard Mudie, David Clyde, Neil Fitzgerald, Ruth Robinson, Margaret McWade, Noble Johnson, Dennis d'Auburn, Carl Stockdale, Beatrice Curtis, Mary Lou Dix, Beatrice Blinn, Arthur Rankin, Darby Clark, Eric Wilton, Chief Big Tree, Richard Loo. *D:* Frank Capra; *P:* Capra; *Sc:* Robert Riskin, Sidney Buchman (unc.); *Art-Set Decoration:* (A.A.) Stephen Goosson; *Music:* (A.A.N.) Dimitri Tiomkin; *Editors:* (A.A.) Gene Havlick, Gene Milford; *Sound Recording:* (A.A.N.) John Livadary; *Assistant Director:* (A.A.N.) C.C. Coleman, Jr. (Original Running Time: 1:58) (Video Restoration: 2:13)

Classic fantasy-drama of a group of plane crash survivors who find themselves in the mystical land of Shangri-la where peace and tranquility reign and human aging slows down. Based on the best seller by James Hilton and as originally produced by Frank Capra, it had a running time of (2:12), but due to Harry Cohn's (head of Columbia studios) despising of films which ran more than two hours, it's initial theatrical release showed a film which ran (1:58). A 1943 re-release (to recoup losses from the initial release) chopped the film down to (1:49), leaving only a shell of its former intent by Capra. A musical remake in 1973 fell into disfavor with critics and audiences alike and apparently sparked the American Film Society to restore the original which it began in 1973, working into 1987 and restoring the deleted footage of 1943 as well as the studio edited footage prior to initial release, much of which had to be accomplished with freeze-frame restoration with still photos, as much of the early footage is either lost forever or has yet to be found. The film received an A.A.N. for "Best Picture," placed #4 and #10 respectively on the "10 Best" lists of *Film Daily* and the *New York Times*. The restored version is available on home video and runs (2:13) complete with a fully restored sound track.

Note: One of the 38 top grossing films of 1936–37.

2645. Lost in the Stratosphere (Monogram; 1934). *Cast:* William Cagney (yes, he's the brother of James), Edward Nugent, June Collyer, Lona Andre, Edmund Breese, Frank McGlynn, Sr., Pauline Garon, Matt McHugh, Hattie McDaniel. *D:* Melville Brown; *P:* William T. Lackey; *St:* Tristram Tupper; *Sc:* Albert DeMond. (1:04)

B comedy-drama of air force buddies, both in love with the same girl who are assigned to tryout a new flying vehicle. Prior to release, the film had the working title of "Murder in the Stratosphere."

2646. Lost Island of Kioga (Republic; 1938). *Cast:* Bruce Bennett (nee: Herman Brix), Mala, Monte Blue, Jill Martin, Noble Johnson. *D:* William Witney, John English; *P:* Nat Levine; *Sc:* Barry Shipman, Rex Taylor, Norman Hall. (1:40)

Feature version of the serial "Hawk of the Wilderness" which tells a tale of shipwreck survivors further aided by a white he-man.

2647. The Lost Jungle (Majestic/Mascot; 1934). *Cast:* Clyde Beatty, Cecilia Parker, Syd Saylor, Edward LeSaint, Warner Richmond, Wheeler Oakman, Lew Meehan, Max Wagner, Wally Wales (Hal Taliaferro), Ernie Adams, Jack Carlyle, Wes Warner, Charles "Slim" Whitaker, Jim Corey, Mickey Rooney, Lloyd Whitlock, Lloyd Ingraham, Crauford Kent, Maston Williams, George Hayes. *D:* Armand Schaefer, David Howard; *St:* Sherman Lowe, Al Martin; *Sc:* Barney Sarecky, David Howard, Armand Schaefer, Wyndham Gittens. (1:08) (video — serial only)

This action-adventure is the feature version of the 12-chapter serial of the same name, produced by Mascot Pictures but released by Majestic studios.

2648. A Lost Lady (WB/F.N.; 1934). *Cast:* Barbara Stanwyck, Ricardo Cortez, Frank Morgan, Lyle Talbot, Philip Reed, Hobart Cavanaugh, Rafaela Ottiano, Donald Cook, Samuel S. Hinds, Jameson Thomas, Willie Fung, Walter Walker, Robert McWade. *D:* Alfred E. Green; *P:* James Seymour; *Sc:* Gene Markey, Kathryn Scola. (G.B. title: *Courageous*)

Flop marital drama of a woman who marries an older man, falls for a younger one, and realizes her mistake. Based on the Pulitzer Prize winning novel by Willa Cather, the film is a remake of a 1925 First National production with Irene Rich.

The Lost Lady (G.B. title) *see* **Safe in Hell**

The Lost Men (G.B. title) *see* **Homicide Squad**

2649. The Lost Patrol (RKO; 1934). *Cast:* Victor McLaglen (sergeant), Boris Karloff (Sanders), Wallace Ford (Morelli), Reginald Denny (Brown), J.M. Kerrigan (Quincannon), Billy Bevan (Hale), Alan Hale (Cook), Sammy Stein (Abelson), Douglas Walton (Pearson), Brandon Hurst (Corporal Bell), Paul Hanson (Mackay), Neville Clark (Lieut. Hawkins), Howard Wilson (aviator). *D:* John Ford (his first film for this studio); *As.P.:* Cliff Reid; *Adaptation:* Garrett Fort; *Sc:* Dudley Nichols; *Music:* (A.A.N.) Max Steiner. (original running time: 1:14) (video prints: 1:05)

Classic drama of a British patrol lost in the desert whose numbers are gradually being dwindled by the enemy. Based on the story "Patrol" by Philip MacDonald, it was previously filmed in Great Britain in 1929. Current prints seen today are missing approximately nine minutes of the original film's footage. One of the 15 top grossing films of 1934, the film was voted one of the year's "10 Best" by the National Board of Review. The *New York Times* placed it at #8 on their "10 Best" list. Remade as the western *Bad Lands* (q.v.). *Bataan* (MGM; 1943) is a loose remake.

2650. Lost Ranch (Victory; 1937). *Cast:* Tom Tyler, Jeanne Martel, Lafe McKee, Marjorie Beebe, Forrest Taylor, Harry Harvey, Howard Bryant, Slim Whitaker, Roger Williams, Theodore Lorch. *D:* Sam Katzman; *P:* Katzman; *Sc:* Basil Dickey. (0:56)
Tom Tyler oater of a cowboy coming to the aid of two girls from the east who are attacked by outlaws.

2651. The Lost Squadron (RKO; 1932). *Cast:* Richard Dix, Mary Astor, Robert Armstrong, Dorothy Jordan, Joel McCrea, Erich Von Stroheim (Von Furst, the director), Hugh Herbert, Ralph Ince, Marjorie Peterson, Ralph Lewis, William Davidson, Art Gobel, Leo Nomis, Frank Clark. *D:* George Archainbaud; *P:* David O. Selznick; *St:* Dick Grace; *Sc:* Wallace Smith; *Additional Dialogue:* Herman J. Mankiewicz, Robert S. Presnell. (1:19) (video)
Unemployed World War I pilots take jobs as stunt flyers for a maniacal and obsessive film director.
Note: Old TV prints may have a shorter running time.

2652. The Lost Zeppelin (Tiffany; 1929–30). *Cast:* Ricardo Cortez, Virginia Valli, Conway Tearle, Kathryn McGuire, Duke Martin, Winter Hall. *D:* Edward Sloman; *St:* Frances Hyland, Jack Natteford.
"Poverty row" action melodrama.

2653. The Lottery Bride (United Artists/Art Cinema; 1930). *Cast:* Jeanette MacDonald, John Garrick, Joe E. Brown, ZaZu Pitts, Robert Chisholm, Joseph Macaulay, Harry Gribbon, Carroll Nye. *D:* Paul Stein; *P:* Joseph M. Schenck; *Sc:* Horace Jackson, Howard Emmett Rogers; *Production Supervisor:* John W. Considine, Jr.; *Songs:* Rudolf Friml. (1:20) (video)
Romantic musical with a Yukon setting of a girl forced to marry a man she doesn't love. Based on the story "Bride 66" by Herbert Stothart.

2654. Lottery Lover (Fox; 1934–35). *Cast:* Lew Ayres, Reginald Denny, Pat Paterson, Sterling Holloway, Edward Nugent, Alan Dinehart, Rafaela Ottiano. *D:* William Thiele (American directorial debut); *St:* Franz Schulz, Billy Wilder; *Sc:* Sig Herzig, Maurice Hanline. (1:20)
Romantic comedy of a sailor who wins a date with a star of the Folies Bergere. Set in Paris.

2655. Lotus Lady (Audible Pictures; 1930). *Cast:* Fern Andra (in her second and last American film before retiring from the screen). *D:* Phil Rosen.
Low-budget romance.

2656. The Loudspeaker (Monogram; 1934). *Cast:* Ray Walker, Jacqueline Wells (Julie Bishop), Noel Francis, Charley Grapewin, Lorin Raker, Wilbur Mack, Spencer Charters, Sherwood Bailey, Billy Irving, Ruth Romaine, Lawrence Wheat, Mary Carr. *D:* Joseph Santley; *P:* William T. Lackey; *St:* Ralph Spence; *Sc:* Albert E. DeMond. (1:07) (G.B. title: *The Radio Star*)
B comedy-drama of a small town nobody who journeys to New York City and becomes a popular radio star, only to have success go to his head.

Louisiana Gal *see* **Old Louisiana**

2657. Love Affair (Columbia; 1932). *Cast:* Humphrey Bogart, Dorothy Mackaill, Jack Kennedy, Astrid Allwyn, Halliwell Hobbes, Barbara Leonard. *D:* Thornton Freeland; *St:* Ursula Parrott; *Sc:* Jo Swerling. (1:08)

B comedy-drama of the romance of a flying instructor and an heiress.

2658. Love Affair (RKO; 1939). *Cast:* Irene Dunne (A.A.N. for B.A. as Terry McKay), Charles Boyer (Michel Marnet), Maria Ouspenskaya (A.A.N. for B.S.A. as the grandmother), Lee Bowman (Ken Bradley), Astrid Allwyn (Lois Clarke), Maurice Moscovich (Maurice Cobert), Frank McGlynn, Sr. (Picklepuss, the orphanage superintendent), Bess Flowers, Harold Miller, Scotty Beckett, Joan (Leslie) Brodel, Del Henderson, Carol Hughes, Ferike Boros, Leyland Hodgson, Tom Dugan, Oscar O'Shea, Lloyd Ingraham, Phyllis Kennedy, Gerald Mohr. *D:* Leo McCarey; *P:* McCarey; *Original Story:* (A.A.N.) McCarey & Mildred Cram; *Sc:* Delmer Daves, Donald Ogden Stewart; *Art-Set Decoration:* (A.A.N.) Van Nest Polglase, Al Herman; *Song:* "Wishing" (A.A.N.) B.G. DeSylva, "Sing My Heart" by Harold Arlen, Ted Koehler. (1:29) (video)

Critically acclaimed hit sentimental comedy-drama of a shipboard romance which continues sometime afterwards despite a major drawback. It received an A.A.N. for "Best Picture" and was remade as *An Affair to Remember* (20th-Fox; 1957).

2659. Love Among the Millionaires (Paramount; 1930). *Cast:* Clara Bow, Stanley Smith, Stuart Erwin, Mitzi Green, Richard "Skeets" Gallagher, Barbara Bennett (final film—ret.), Claude King, Charles Sellon. *D:* Frank Tuttle; *Sc:* Herman J. Mankiewicz; *Adapt.:* Grover Jones, William Conselman; *Dial.:* Herman J. Mankiewicz.

Romance on the railroad.

2660. Love and Hisses (20th Century-Fox; 1937). *Cast:* Walter Winchell, Ben Bernie and his orchestra (final film), Joan Davis, Bert Lahr, Simone Simon, Ruth Terry, Lon Chaney, Jr.,

Chick Chandler, Douglas Fowley, Hal K. Dawson, Georges Renavent, Harry Stubbs, Charles Williams, Dick Baldwin, Robert Battier, Brewster Twins, Raymond Scott Quintet, Peters Sisters, Rush Hughes, Gary Breckner, Chilton and Thomas. *D:* Sidney Lanfield; *P:* Kenneth MacGowan; *St:* Art Arthur; *Sc:* Arthur, Curtis Kenyon. (1:24)

A sequel to the hit *Wake Up and Live* (q.v.) which was released earlier in the year. The story concerns a comical feud between a news commentator and a band leader.

2661. Love at First Sight (Chesterfield; 1930). *Cast·* Norman Foster, Suzanne Keener, Doris Rankin. *D:* Edgar Lewis; *Sc:* Lester Lee, Charles Levison.

(No information available)

2662. Love Before Breakfast (Universal; 1936). *Cast:* Carole Lombard, Preston Foster, Cesar Romero, Janet Beecher, Bert Roach, Betty Lawford, Douglas Blackley (Robert Kent), E.E. Clive, Richard Carle, John King (feature debut), Joyce Compton, Donald Briggs, Andre Beranger, Bud Flanagan (Dennis O'Keefe). *D:* Walter Lang; *P:* Edmund Grainger; *Sc:* Herbert Fields. (1:05)

B comedy of a wealthy Park Avenue girl who is pursued by two men. Based on the novel "Spinster Dinner" by Faith Baldwin.

2663. Love Begins at 20 (WB/F.N.; 1936). *Cast:* Hugh Herbert, Patricia Ellis, Dorothy Vaughan, Warren Hull, Hobart Cavanaugh, Clarence Wilson, Robert Gleckler, Anne Nagel, Arthur Aylesworth, Mary Treen, Milton Kibbee, Max Wagner, Tom Brower, Tom Wilson, Henry Otho, Saul Gorss. *D:* Frank McDonald; *P:* Bryan Foy; *Sc:* Dalton Trumbo, Tom Reed. (G.B. title: *All One Night*)

B marital tale of a henpecked man who stands up to his domineering wife and gains the right to run his own

Dishes" by Martin Flavin, this is a remake of *Too Young to Marry* (q.v.). Remade again in 1940 by this studio as *Calling All Husbands.*

2664. Love Birds (Universal; 1934). *Cast:* ZaSu Pitts, Slim Summerville, Mickey Rooney, Frederick Burton, Emmett Vogan, Maude Eburne, Gertrude Short, Arthur Stone, Craig Reynolds. *D:* William A. Seiter. (1:02)

B comedy of a conman who sells the same parcel of land to two different people, who in turn scheme revenge.

2665. Love Bound (Peerless; 1932–33). *Cast:* Natalie Moorhead, Jack Mulhall, Edmund Breese, Montagu Love. *D:* Robert Hill.

"Poverty row" shipboard drama.

2666. The Love Captive (Universal; 1934). *Cast:* Nils Asther, Gloria Stuart, Paul Kelly, Alan Dinehart, Russ Brown. *D:* Max Marcin; *Sc:* Karen de Wolf; *St:* Max Marcin. (1:05)

B melodrama of a hypnotist with ulterior motives.

2667. Love Comes Along (RKO; 1930). *Cast:* Bebe Daniels, Lloyd Hughes, Montagu Love, Ned Sparks, Lionel Belmore, Alma Tell, Evelyn Selbie. *D:* Rupert Julian; *As.P.:* Henry Hobart; *Sc:* Wallace Smith; *Songs:* Oscar Levant, Sidney Clare. (1:18)

Melodrama with comic overtones of an Irish actress who falls for an American sailor who wants to take her to America. Based on the play "Conchita" by Edward Knoblock.

2668. The Love Doctor (Paramount; 1929). *Cast:* Richard Dix, June Collyer, Miriam Seegar, Morgan Farley, Lawford Davidson, Winifred Harris. *D:* Melville Brown; *Sc:* Guy Bolton.

Low-budget romance of a matchmaking physician.

Love Finds a Way (G.B. title) *see* **Alias French Gertie**

2669. Love Finds Andy Hardy (MGM; 1938). *Cast:* Lewis Stone (Judge James Hardy), Mickey Rooney (Andy Hardy), Judy Garland (Betsy Booth), Cecilia Parker (Marian "Mary" Hardy), Fay Holden (Mrs. Hardy), Lana Turner (Cynthia Potter), Ann Rutherford (Polly Benedict), Betty Ross Clark (replacing Sara Haden as Aunt Milly), Marie Blake (Augusta), Don Castle (Dennis Hunt), Gene Reynolds (Jimmy MacMahon), Mary Howard (Mrs. Tompkins), George Breakston (Breezy), Raymond Hatton (Peter Dugan), Frank Darien, Rand Brooks, Erville Alderson. *D:* George B. Seitz; *P:* Carey Wilson (unc.); *Sc:* William Ludwig (based on the characters created by Aurania Rouverol & stories by Vivien R. Bretherton); *Songs:* "In Between" by Roger Edens, "What Do You Know About Love?" "Meet the Beat of My Heart," and "It Never Rains But It Pours" by Mack Gordon & Harry Revel. (1:30) (video)

The 4th entry in the "Hardy Family" series with Andy getting into trouble with his regular girl Polly when a new girl moves in next door and sets her sights on him. A big hit at the box office, it placed #9 on the "10 Best" list of *Film Daily.*

2670. Love, Honor and Behave (WB; 1938). *Cast:* Wayne Morris, Priscilla Lane, Thomas Mitchell, John Litel, Barbara O'Neil, Mona Barrie, Dick Foran, Dickie Moore, Margaret Irving, Crauford Kent, Donald Briggs, Minor Watson, Gregory Gaye, Audrey Leonard. *D:* Stanley Logan; *As.P.:* Lou Edelman; *Sc:* Clements Ripley, Robert Buckner, Michel Jacoby, Lawrence Kimble; *Song:* "Bei Mir Bist du Schoen" by Sammy Cahn, Saul Chaplin, Sholom Secunda.

B comedy of a married couple whose union has few peaceful moments. Based on a story by Stephen Vincent Benet.

2671. Love, Honor and Oh Baby! (Universal; 1933). *Cast:* ZaSu

Pitts, Slim Summerville, Verree Teasdale, Evalyn Knapp, George Barbier, Lucile Webster Gleason, Purnell Pratt, Donald Meek, Neely Edwards, Adrienne Dore, Dorothy Granger. *D:* Edward Buzzell; *St:* Bertrand Robinson, Howard Lindsay; *Adaptation:* Norman Krasna.

B comedy of a scheming lawyer and his girlfriend. Remade in 1940 with Donald Woods.

2672. Love in a Bungalow (Universal; 1937). *Cast:* Nan Grey, Kent Taylor, Richard Carle, Hobart Cavanaugh, Minerva Urecal, Louise Beavers, Marjorie Main. *D:* Raymond B. McCarey; *P:* E.M. Asher. (1:07)

B romance of an unmarried couple who win a contest open only to married couples. Remade as *Hi, Beautiful* (Universal; 1944) with Noah Beery, Jr., and Martha O'Driscoll.

2673. Love in Bloom (Paramount; 1935). *Cast:* George Burns, Gracie Allen, Joe Morrison, Dixie Lee, J.C. Nugent, Lee Kohlmar, Jack Mulhall, Wade Boteler, Mary Foy, Richard Carle, Marian Mansfield. *D:* Elliott Nugent; *P:* Benjamin Glazer; *St:* J.P. McEvoy, Frank R. Adams; *Sc:* Frank R. Adams; *Adapt.:* J.P. McEvoy, Keene Thompson. (1:15)

B musical-comedy of the romance of a carnival girl and a songwriter from New York City.

2674. Love in High Gear (Mayfair; 1932). *Cast:* Alberta Vaughn, Fred Kelsey, Harrison Ford (final film — ret.), Arthur Hoyt. *D:* Frank Strayer.

"Poverty row" romance.

2675. Love in the Desert (Film Booking Office; 1929). *Cast:* Noah Beery, Olive Borden, Hugh Trevor. *D:* George Melford.

Part-talkie romance melodrama.

2676. Love in the Rough (MGM; 1930). *Cast:* Robert Montgomery, Dorothy Jordan, J.C. Nugent, Dorothy McNulty (Penny Singleton), Benny Rubin, Roscoe Ates, Allan Lane, Clarence Wilson, Tyrrell Davis, Edwards Davis, Harry Burns, Catherine Moylan. *D:* Charles Reisner; *Sc:* Sarah Y. Mason, Joe Farnham, Robert Hopkins; *Songs:* Jimmy McHugh, Dorothy Fields.

Low-budget comedy-romance with music. A remake of *Spring Fever* (MGM; 1927) with William Haines.

2677. Love Is a Headache (MGM; 1937–38). *Cast:* Franchot Tone, Gladys George, Mickey Rooney, Virginia Weidler, Jessie Ralph, Fay Holden, Ted Healy, Frank Jenks, Barnett Parker, Ralph Morgan, Henry Kolker, Julius Tannen. *D:* Richard Thorpe; *P:* Frederick Stephani; *Sc:* Marion Parsonnet, Harry Ruskin, William R. Lipman.

B comedy of an actress who adopts two orphans.

2678. Love Is a Racket (WB/ F.N.; 1932). *Cast:* Douglas Fairbanks, Jr., Frances Dee, Ann Dvorak, Lee Tracy, Lyle Talbot (film debut), Warren Hymer, William Burress, Cecil Cunningham, Eddie Kane, Marjorie Peterson, Terrance Ray, André Luguet, John Marston. *D:* William Wellman; *St:* Rian James; *Sc:* Courtney Terrett. (G.B. title: *Such Things Happen*) (1:12)

B comedy-drama of a newsman and the girl he is protecting from a murder charge.

2679. Love Is Dangerous (Chesterfield; 1933). *Cast:* Rochelle Hudson, Dorothy Revier. *D:* Richard Thorpe.

"Poverty row" feature.

2680. Love Is Like That (Chesterfield; 1933). *Cast:* Rochelle Hudson, Dorothy Revier, Bradley Page. *D:* Richard Thorpe.

(No other information available)

2681. Love Is News (20th Century-Fox; 1937). *Cast:* Tyrone Power, Loretta Young, Don Ameche, Slim Summerville, Dudley Digges, Walter Catlett, Jane Darwell, Stepin Fetchit, George Sanders, Pauline Moore, Elisha Cook, Jr., Frank Conroy, Lynn Bari. *D:* Tay Garnett; *P:* Earl Carroll, Harold Wilson; *St:* William R. Lipman, Frederick Stephani; *Sc:* Harry Tugend, Jack Yellen. (1:18)

After a reporter embarrasses an heiress with his news stories about her, she marries him — and turns the tables on him. One of the 38 top grossing films of 1936–37. Remade as *Sweet Rosie O'Grady* (20th-Fox; 1943) and *That Wonderful Urge* (20th-Fox; 1948).

2682. Love Is On the Air (WB/F.N.; 1937). *Cast:* Ronald Reagan (film debut), June Travis, Eddie Acuff, Ben Welden, Robert Barrat, Addison Richards, Raymond Hatton, DeWolf (William) Hopper, Mary Hart (Lynn Roberts), Willard Parker, Tommy Bupp, Herbert Rawlinson, Harry Hayden, Spec O'Donnell, Jack Mower. *D:* Nick Grinde; *P:* Bryan Foy; *St:* Roy Chanslor; *Sc:* Morton Grant, George Bricker (unc.). (G.B. title: *The Radio Murder Mystery*) (1:01)

B production of a radio reporter who takes it upon himself to go after some corrupt government officials. A remake of *Hi, Nellie* (q.v.), it was also remade as *You Can't Escape Forever* (WB; 1942) and *The House Across the Street* (WB; 1949).

2683. The Love Kiss (Celebrity Pictures; 1930). *Cast:* Donald Meek, Olive Shea, Forrest Stanley. *D:* Robert R. Snody; *Sc:* Harry G. Smith. (No other information available)

2684. Love Letters of a Star (Universal; 1936). *Cast:* Henry Hunter, Mary Alice Rice, C. Henry Gordon, Ralph Forbes, Warren Hymer, Samuel S. Hinds, Hobart Cavanaugh, Halliwell Hobbes, Walter Coy. *D:* Milton Carruth, Lewis R. Foster (directorial

debut); *P:* E.M. Asher; *St:* Foster (co-writer). (1:06)

B mystery of a man seeking the truth behind his wife's death.

Love Life of a Gorilla *see* **Forbidden Adventure** (1937)

2685. Love, Live and Laugh (Fox; 1929). *Cast:* George Jessel, Lila Lee, Kenneth MacKenna, David Rollins, Dick Winslow Johnson, Henry Kolker, Jerry Mandy, John Reinhart, Marcia Manon. *D:* William K. Howard; *St & Sc:* John B. Hymer, LeRoy Clemens.

Low-budget musical-comedy.

2686. Love Me Forever (Columbia; 1935). *Cast:* Grace Moore, Leo Carrillo, Robert Allen, Spring Byington, Douglass Dumbrille, Thurston Hall, Michael Bartlett, Luis Alberni. *D:* Victor Schertzinger; *St:* Schertzinger; *Sc:* Sidney Buchman, Jo Swerling; *Songs:* Schertzinger, Gus Kahn (including the theme song). (G.B. title: *On Wings of Song*) (1:32)

Musical of a down-on-her-luck singer's sudden rise to stardom. As art imitates life, this film was also instrumental in making Grace Moore a star in real life. The film placed #10 on the "10 Best" list of the *New York Times.*

2687. Love Me Tonight (Paramount; 1932). *Cast:* Maurice Chevalier (Maurice Courtelin), Jeanette MacDonald (Princess Jeanette), Charles Ruggles (Vicomte Gilbert de Vareze), Myrna Loy (Countess Valentine), Charles Butterworth (Count de Savignac), C. Aubrey Smith (Duke), Robert Greig (Major Domo Flamond), Elizabeth Patterson (first aunt), Ethel Griffies (second aunt), Blanche Frederici (third aunt), Mary Doran (Madame Dupont), Joseph Cawthorn (doctor), Herbert Mundin (groom), Ethel Wales (Madame Dutoit, the dressmaker), Bert

Roach (Emile), Cecil Cunningham (laundress), Tyler Brooke (composer), Marion "Peanuts" Byron (bakery girl), Edgar Norton (valet), Rita Owin (chambermaid), Clarence Wilson (shirtmaker), Major Sam Harris (bridge player), Gordon Westcott (film debut as the collector), George Davis (Pierre Dupont), Rolfe Sedan (taxi driver), Tony Merlo (hatmaker), William H. Turner (bootmaker), George Hayes (grocer), George Humbert (chef), Tom Ricketts. *D:* Rouben Mamoulian; *P:* Mamoulian; *Sc:* Samuel Hoffenstein, Waldemar Young, George Marion, Jr.; *Songs:* "The Song of Paree," "How Are You?" "Isn't It Romantic?" "Lover," "Mimi," "Poor Apache," "Love Me Tonight," "A Woman Needs Something Like That" and "The Son-of-a-Gun Is Nothing But a Tailor" by Richard Rodgers, Lorenz Hart. (1:44)

Classic musical, considered by many critics and film buffs as one of the best musicals ever made. The story concerns a princess who falls for a simple tailor. Based on the play "Tailor in the Chateau" by Leopold Marchand and Paul Armont.

2688. Love on a Bet (RKO; 1936). *Cast:* Gene Raymond, Wendy Barrie, Helen Broderick, William Collier, Sr., Spencer Charters, Walter Johnson, Addison (Jack) Randall, Eddie Gribbon, Morgan Wallace, Marc Lawrence. *D:* Leigh Jason; *As.P.:* Lee Marcus; *St:* Kenneth Earl; *Sc:* P.J. Wolfson, Philip G. Epstein. (1:17)

Notable for its witty dialogue, this romantic comedy tells of a young man who takes a cross-country trip on a bet.

2689. Love on a Budget (20th Century–Fox; 1938). *Cast:* Jed Prouty, Spring Byington, Florence Roberts, Joyce Compton, June Carlson, Kenneth Howell, George Ernest, Billy Mahan, Shirley Deane, Russell Gleason, Dixie Dunbar. *D:* Herbert I. Leeds (directorial debut).

Eighth entry in the "Jones Family" low-budget comedy series.

2690. Love on the Run (MGM; 1936). *Cast:* Joan Crawford, Clark Gable, Franchot Tone, Reginald Owen, Mona Barrie, Ivan Lebedeff, Charles Judels, William Demarest, Donald Meek, Billy Gilbert, Leonid Kinskey. *D:* W.S. Van Dyke II; *P:* Joseph L. Mankiewicz; *St:* Alan Green, Julian Brodie; *Sc:* John Lee Mahin, Manuel Seff, Gladys Hurlbut; *Song:* "Gone" by Franz Waxman & Gus Kahn. (1:20)

Due to its star power, a hit romantic comedy of rival newsmen and a runaway heiress.

2691. Love on Toast (Paramount; 1937–38). *Cast:* John Payne, Stella (Adler) Ardler, Benny Baker, Isabel Jewell, Franklin Pangborn, William Davidson. *D:* E.A. Dupont; *P:* Emanuel Cohen.

B romantic comedy of a soda jerk who wins a "Mr. Manhattan" contest.

2692. The Love Parade (Paramount; 1929). *Cast:* Maurice Chevalier (A.A.N. for B.A. as Count Alfred Renard), Jeanette MacDonald (film debut as Queen Louise), Lillian Roth (Lulu), Lionel Belmore (prime minister), Lupino Lane (Jacques), Edgar Norton (Master of Ceremonies), Albert Roccardi (foreign minister), Carl Stockdale (admiral), Eugene Pallette (minister of war), E.H. Calvert (Sylvanian ambassador), Russell Powell (Afghan ambassador), Margaret Fealy & Virginia Bruce (ladies in waiting), Yola D'Avril (Paulette), Andre Cheron (Paulette's husband), Winter Hall (priest), Ben Turpin, Albert de Winton, Helene Friend, Anton Vaverka, William von Hardenburg. *D:* (A.A.N.) Ernst Lubitsch (talkie directorial debut); *P:* Lubitsch; *Adaptation:* Ernest Vajda; *Sc:* Guy Bolton; *Cinematographer:* (A.A.N.) Victor Milner; *Art Director:* (A.A.N.) Hans Dreier; *Sound Recording:*

(A.A.N.) Franklin Hansen; *Songs:* "My Love Parade," "Dream Lover," "Let's Be Common," "Anything to Please the Queen," "March of the Grenadiers," "Paris Stay the Same," "Nobody's Using It Now," "Oo La La" and "The Queen Is Always Right" by Victor Schertzinger & Clifford Grey. (1:50)

An operetta of romance among European royalty. Lavishly produced it became a big box office hit, receiving an A.A.N. for "Best Picture." Voted "Best Film of the Year" by the *New York Times,* it is based on the play "The Prince Consort" by Leon Xanrof and Jules Chancel.

2693. Love Past Thirty (Monarch; 1934). *Cast:* Aileen Pringle, Theodore von Eltz. *D:* Vin Moore; *Sc:* Earle Snell

(No information available)

2694. The Love Racket (WB/ F.N.; 1929). *Cast:* Dorothy Mackaill, Sidney Blackmer, Edmund Burns, Alice Day, Edith Yorke, Myrtle Stedman, Martha Mattox. *D:* William A. Seiter; *Sc:* John F. Goodrich (based on a play by Bernard K. Burns). (G.B. title: *Such Things Happen*)

Low-budget drama of a woman who years after she is left by her husband, finds herself on a jury at a murder trial where the murder victim was her ex-husband.

Love Redeemed (G.B. title) *see* **Dragnet Patrol**

Love Starved *see* **Young Bride**

2695. Love Takes Flight (Grand National; 1937). *Cast:* Bruce Cabot, Beatrice Roberts, John Sheehan, Astrid Allwyn, Elliott Fisher, Gordon (Bill) Elliott, Edwin Maxwell, Harry Tyler, William Moore, Grady Sutton, Arthur Hoyt, William L. Thorne, Brooks Benedict, Henry Rocquemore. *D:* Conrad Nagel (his only film as director); *P:* George A. Hirliman; *St:* Anne Morrison

Chapin; *Sc:* Lionel O. Houser, Mervin Houser. (1:11)

B drama of a romantic triangle. A Condor production.

2696. Love That Man (Xxxx Xxxx; 1933). (No information available)

2697. Love Time (Fox; 1934). *Cast:* Nils Asther, Pat Paterson, Herbert Mundin, Herman Bing, Earle Foxe. *D:* James Tinling.

Low-budget romance.

2698. The Love Trader (Tiffany; 1930). *Cast:* Leatrice Joy, Henry B. Walthall, Roland Drew, Noah Beery, Chester Conklin, Barbara Bedford, Clarence Burton. *D:* Joseph Henabery (who also co-produced).

"Poverty row" romance.

2699. The Love Trap (Universal; 1929). *Cast:* Laura La Plante, Neil Hamilton, Norman Trevor, Robert Ellis, Clarissa Selwynne, Rita LaRoy. *D:* William Wyler; *St:* Edward J. Montagne; *Sc:* John B. Clymer, Clarence J. Marks; *Dial:* Clarence Thompson; *Titles:* Albert De Mond.

Low-budget part-talkie romantic comedy of a girl whose marriage meets with opposition from Hubby's side of the family.

2700. Love Under Fire (20th Century–Fox; 1937). *Cast:* Don Ameche, Loretta Young, Frances Drake, Walter Catlett, John Carradine, Sig Rumann, Holmes Herbert, Harold Huber, E.E. Clive, Katherine de Mille, Borrah Minnevitch and His Rascals, Clyde Cook, Don Alvarado, Georges Renavent, Egon Brecher, George Humbert, Claude King, Juan Torena, David Clyde, George Regas, Francis McDonald. *D:* George Marshall; *P:* Nunnally Johnson; *Sc:* Gene Fowler, Allen Rivkin, Ernest Pascal. (1:15)

During the Spanish Civil War a detective pursues a lady jewel thief. A romantic adventure which is based on the play by Walter Hackett.

Love's Conquest (G.B. title) *see* **The Racketeer**

Lovely to Look At (G.B. title) *see* **Thin Ice**

2701. Lover Come Back (Columbia; 1931). *Cast:* Constance Cummings, Jack Mulhall, Jameson Thomas, Susan Fleming, Betty Bronson, Jack Mack, Kathryn Givney, Loretta Sayers, Frederic Santley. *D:* Erle C. Kenton; *St:* Helen Topping Miller.
"Poverty row" romance.

2702. Lovers Courageous (MGM; 1932). *Cast:* Robert Montgomery, Madge Evans, Frederick Kerr, Roland Young, Reginald Owen, Beryl Mercer, Jackie Searle, Halliwell Hobbes, Alan Mowbray, Ethel Griffies, Norman Phillips, Jr., Eily Malyon, Evelyn Hall. *D:* Robert Z. Leonard; *P:* Leonard; *Sc:* Frederick Lonsdale.
Drama of a playwright who falls for the daughter of a stuffy English admiral in South Africa.

2703. Lovin' the Ladies (RKO; 1930). *Cast:* Richard Dix, Lois Wilson, Allen Kearns, Rita LaRoy, Anthony Bushell, Reneé Macready, Virginia Sale, Henry Armetta, Ernest Hilliard, Selmer Jackson. *D:* Melville Brown; *As.P.:* Louis Sarecky; *Sc:* J. Walter Ruben. (1:08)
Low-budget comedy of two men who make a bet which turns into a major mix-up for a potential romance. Based on the play "I Love You" by William LeBaron.

2704. The Luck of Roaring Camp (Monogram; 1937). *Cast:* Owen Davis, Jr., Joan Woodbury, Charles Brokaw, Forrest Taylor, Bob Kortman, Charles King, Byron Foulger, Bob

McKenzie, John Wallace. *D:* Irvin Willat (final film); *P:* Scott R. Dunlap; *Sc:* Harvey Gates. (0:58)
B western drama of a baby that brings luck to a California gold camp. Based on the story by Bret Harte.

Luck of the Game (G.B. title) *see* **Gridiron Flash**

2705. The Luckiest Girl in the World (Universal; 1936). *Cast:* Jane Wyatt, Louis Hayward, Eugene Pallette, Philip Reed, Nat Pendleton, Catherine Doucet, Viola Callahan, Franklin Pangborn. *D:* Edward Buzzell; *P:* Charles R. Rogers; *Sc:* Herbert Fields, Henry Myers (based on a story by Anne Jordan which appeared in *Ladies Home Journal*). (1:15)
B romance of a girl who tries to prove to her father that she can live in New York City on $150 a month.

Lucky Boots *see* **Gun Play**

2706. Lucky Boy (Tiffany; 1929). *Cast:* George Jessel, Richard Tucker, Mary Doran, Gwen Lee, Rosa Rosanova, William Strauss, Margaret Quimby, Gayne Whitman, Glenda Farrell (film debut—bit). *D:* Norman Taurog; *St:* Viola Brothers Shore; *Songs:* "My Mother's Eyes," "Lucky Boy."
Part-talkie "poverty row" musical romance.

2707. Lucky Devils (RKO; 1933). *Cast:* Bill Boyd, Dorothy Wilson, William Gargan, Robert Rose, Rosco(e) Ates, William Bakewell, Julie Haydon, Bruce Cabot, Rochelle Hudson, Creighton (Lon) Chaney (Jr.), Phyllis Fraser, Betty Furness, Ward Bond, Sylvia Picker, Gladden James. *D:* Ralph Ince; *As.P.:* Merian C. Cooper; *St:* Casey Robinson, Robert Rose; *Sc:* Agnes Christine Johnston, Ben Markson. (1:00)
B drama of a Hollywood stuntman

which is partially based on the life of Bob Rose.

2708. Lucky Dog (Universal; 1933). *Cast:* Charles "Chic" Sale, Buster the Dog, Harry Holman, Tom O'Brien, Clarence Geldert, Mary Gordon. *D:* Zion Myers. (1:00)

A sentimental B story of an elderly man and his devoted canine.

2709. Lucky Ghost (Xxxx Xxxx; 1936). (No information available)

2710. Lucky Larkin (Universal; 1930). *Cast:* Ken Maynard, Nora Lane, James Farley, Harry Todd, Paul Hurst, Charles Clary, Jack Rockwell, Edgar "Blue" Washington. *D:* Harry Joe Brown; *P:* Maynard; *Sc:* Marion Jackson. (1:06)

Part-talkie Ken Maynard western with musical interludes of a cowboy out to win the big race to get the prize money to pay off his girl's Dad's ranch.

2711. Lucky Larrigan (Monogram; 1932). *Cast:* Rex Bell, Helen Foster, George Chesebro, John Elliott, Stanley Blystone, Julian Rivero, G.D. Wood (Gordon DeMain), Wilfred Lucas, Buzz Barton. *D:* John P. McCarthy; *P:* Trem Carr; *St & Sc:* Wellyn Totman. (0:58)

Rex Bell western of a polo player from the east who winds up out west fighting outlaws.

2712. Lucky Night (MGM; 1939). *Cast:* Myrna Loy, Robert Taylor, Joseph Allen, Henry O'Neill, Douglas Fowley, Marjorie Main, Charles Lane, Irving Bacon, Bernard Nedell, Frank Faylen, Bernadene Hayes, Oscar O'Shea, Gladys Blake. *D:* Norman Taurog; *P:* Louis D. Lighton; *St:* Oliver Claxton; *Sc:* Vincent Lawrence, Grover Jones. (1:30)

Comedy of a young married couple who are out to get rich quick overnight. Notable as the only film to star Loy and Taylor.

2713. Lucky Terror (Grand National; 1936). *Cast:* Hoot Gibson, Lona Andre, Charles Hill, George Chesebro, Wally Wales (Hal Taliaferro), Robert McKenzie, Jack Rockwell, Frank Yaconelli, Charles King, Art Mix, Horace B. Carpenter, Hank Bell, Horace Murphy, Nelson McDowell. *D:* Alan James (aka: Alvin J. Neitz); *Sc:* James. (1:01)

Hoot Gibson western of a cowboy who accidentally comes upon a hidden cache of gold.

2714. The Lucky Texan (Monogram-Lone Star; 1933–34). *Cast:* John Wayne, George Hayes, Barbara Sheldon, Lloyd Whitlock, Yakima Canutt, Gordon DeMain, Edward Parker, Earl Dwire, Jack Rockwell, Artie Ortego, Tex Palmer, Tex Phelps, George Morrell. *D:* Robert N. Bradbury; *P:* Paul Malvern; *Supervisor:* Trem Carr; *St & Sc:* Bradbury. (0:56) (video)

John Wayne western of a cowboy who attempts to prove his partner innocent of robbery and murder.

The Lullaby (G.B. title) *see* **The Sin of Madelon Claudet**

2715. Lummox (United Artists/ Art Cinema; 1930). *Cast:* Winifred Westover, Ben Lyon, Dorothy Janis, Myrtle Stedman, Lydia Yeamans Titus, Robert Ullman, William Collier, Jr., William Bakewell, Edna Murphy, Anita Bellew, Cosmo Kyrle Bellew, Ida Darling, Myrta Bonillas. *D:* Herbert Brenon; *P:* Joseph M. Schenck; *Sc:* Elizabeth Meehan.

Tear-jerker based on the novel by Fannie Hurst of a mother who gives up her illegitimate child for adoption and then watches him grow to manhood without ever revealing herself.

2716. Lure of the Wasteland (Al Lane Pictures; 1939). *Cast:* Grant Withers, LeRoy Mason, Marion Arnold, Snub Pollard, Karl Hackett, Henry Rocquemore, Tom London, Sherry Tansey. *D:* Harry Fraser; *P:* Al Lane; *Sc:* Monroe Talbot. (0:55)

B color western of a government man out to find the loot stolen in a robbery years before. Filmed in a process called Telco color.

2717. Luxury Liner (Paramount; 1933). *Cast:* George Brent, Zita Johann, Vivienne Osborne, Frank Morgan, Alice White, Verree Teasdale, C. Aubrey Smith, Henry Wadsworth, Billy Bevan, Theodore von Eltz, Wallis Clark. *D:* Lothar Mendes; *Sc:* Gene Markey, Kathryn Scola. (1:12)

The stories of various passengers on an ocean liner sailing from New York. Based on the best seller by Gina Kaus.

2718. Mad About Music (Universal; 1938). *Cast:* Deanna Durbin, Herbert Marshall, Gail Patrick, Arthur Treacher, Helen Parrish, Jackie Moran, Marcia Mae Jones, William Frawley, Martha O'Driscoll, Franklin Pangborn, Elizabeth Risdon, Christian Rub, Cappy Barra's Harmonica Band, Vienna Boys Choir, Sid Grauman, Joanne Tree, Charles Peck. *D:* Norman Taurog; *P:* Joe Pasternak; *Original Story:* (A.A.N.) Marcella Burke, Frederick Kohner; *Sc:* Bruce Manning, Felix Jackson; *Cinematographer:* (A.A.N.) Joseph Valentine; *Art-Set Decoration:* (A.A.N.) Jack Otterson; *Music:* (A.A.N.) Charles Previn & Frank Skinner. (1:38)

Critically acclaimed musical about a girl in a private Swiss school who "creates" a father to impress her schoolmates. A hit for the studio, it was remade as *Toy Tiger* (Universal-International; 1956).

2719. The Mad Game (Fox; 1933). *Cast:* Spencer Tracy, Claire Trevor, Ralph Morgan, J. Carrol Naish, Paul Fix, John Miljan, Kathleen Burke, Willard Robertson, Matt McHugh, John Davidson, Mary Mason, Douglas Fowley (film debut), Jerry Devine, Howard Lally. *D:* Irving Cummings; *St:* Edward Dean Sullivan.

Melodrama of a bootlegger and a news reporter.

2720. The Mad Genius (WB/F.N.; 1931). *Cast:* John Barrymore, Donald Cook, Marian Marsh, Carmel Myers, Charles Butterworth, Mae Madison, Frankie Darro, Luis Alberni, Boris Karloff, André Luguet. *D:* Michael Curtiz; *Sc:* J. Grubb Alexander, Harvey Thew. (1:21)

A follow-up to the hit *Svengali* (q.v.), this offbeat story tells of a dance entrepreneur who lives vicariously through the career of another. Based on the play "The Idol" by Martin Brown, the film flopped at the box office.

2721. Mad Holiday (MGM; 1936). *Cast:* Edmund Lowe, Elissa Landi, ZaSu Pitts, Gustav von Seyffertitz, Ted Healy, Edmund Gwenn, Edgar Kennedy, Walter Kingsford, Harlan Briggs, Raymond Hatton, Soo Yong, Rafaela Ottiano, Herbert Rawlinson. *D:* George B. Seitz; *P:* Harry Rapf; *Sc:* Florence Ryerson, Edgar Allan Woolf.

B mystery-comedy based on Joseph Santley's "Murder in a Chinese Theatre."

2722. Mad Love (MGM; 1935). *Cast:* Peter Lorre, Colin Clive, Frances Drake, Ted Healy, Sara Haden, Edward Brophy, Henry Kolker, Keye Luke, May Beatty, Ian Wolfe, Charles Trowbridge, Billy Gilbert, Harold Huber. *D:* Karl Freund (final film as director); *P:* John W. Considine, Jr.; *Adaptation:* Guy Endore; *Sc:* P.J. Wolfson, John Balderston. (G.B. title: *The Hands of Orlac*) (1:10)

Classic horror tale of a pianist who has his hands severed in an accident and to resume his career, has the hands of a murderer grafted on. Based on the French novel "The Hands of Orlac" by Maurice Renard (translated and adapted by Florence Crewes-Jones). Various other versions of this story have been filmed abroad over the years.

The Mad Masquerade (G.B. title) *see* **Washington Masquerade**

2723. The Mad Miss Manton
(RKO; 1938). *Cast:* Barbara Stanwyck
(Melsa Manton), Henry Fonda (Peter
Ames), Sam Levene, Frances Mercer,
Stanley Ridges, Whitney Bourne, Hat-
tie McDaniel, Vicki Lester, Miles
Mander, Penny Singleton, Grady Sut-
ton, Ann Evers, Linda Terry, Catherine
O'Quinn, Eleanor Hansen, James
Burke, Paul Guilfoyle, Leona Maricle,
Kay Sutton, John Qualen, Olin How-
land, Emory Parnell, Charles Halton.
D: Leigh Jason; *As.P.:* P.J. Wolfson; *St:*
Wilson Collison; *Sc:* Philip G. Epstein.
(1:20) (video)
    Screwball comedy of a socialite who
gets her Park Avenue debutante girl
friends involved in a murder mystery.

2724. The Mad Parade (Para-
mount; 1931). *Cast:* Irene Rich, Evelyn
Brent, Lilyan Tashman, Marceline
Day, Louise Fazenda, June Clyde,
Fritzi Ridgeway, Helen Keating, Eliza-
beth Keating. *D:* William Beaudine; *P:*
A Liberty prod.; *St:* Doris Malloy, Ger-
trude Orr; *Sc:* Henry McCarthy, Frank
R. Conklin.
    World War I drama of women in
the service of their country.

2725. Mad Youth (JDK Productions; 1939). *D:* Melville Shyer; *P:* J.D.
Kendis.
    Low-budget teen exploitation
melodrama.

2726. Madam Satan (MGM;
1930). *Cast:* Kay Johnson (Angela
Brooks—"Madam Satan"), Reginald
Denny (Bob Brooks), Lillian Roth
(Trixie), Roland Young (Jimmy Wade),
Elsa Peterson (Martha), Jack King
(Herman), Edward Prinz (Biff), Boyd
Irwin (zeppelin captain), Wallace Mac-
Donald (zeppelin's first mate), Tyler
Brooke (Romeo), Ynez Seabury (Babo),
Theodore Kosloff (Electricity), Julanne
Johnston (Miss Conning Tower), Mar-
tha Sleeper (fish girl), Doris McMahon
(Water), Vera Marsh (Call of the Wild),
Albert Conti (Empire Officer), Earl

Askam (pirate), Countess DeLiguoro
(Spain), Katherine Irving (spider girl),
Lotus Thompson (Eve), Aileen Ransom
(Victory), Abe Lyman & His Band,
Vera Gordon, Allan Lane, Mary Carlisle, Wilfred Lucas. *D:* Cecil B. De
Mille; *P:* De Mille; *Sc:* Jeanie MacPherson, Gladys Unger, Elsie Janis; *Music &
Lyrics:* Clifford Grey, Herbert Stothart,
Elsie Janis, Jack King. (1:45)
    Lavishly produced marital comedy
of a woman who disguises herself as a
vamp in order to win back her wayward
husband. The film climaxes with a wild
party aboard an ill-fated zeppelin.
Popular at the box office in its day, but
due to excessive expenditures in production, it was a financial flop.

2727. Madame Butterfly (Para-
mount; 1932). *Cast:* Cary Grant (Lieut.
Pinkerton), Sylvia Sidney (Madame
Butterfly), Charles Ruggles, Sandor
Kallay, Irving Pichel (Yamadori),
Helen Jerome Eddy, Berton Churchill,
Edmund Breese, Louise Carter, Sheila
Terry, Dorothy Libaire, Judith Vosselli. *D:* Marion Gering; *Sc:* Josephine
Lovett, Joseph Moncure March. (1:28)
    Non-musical romantic drama of
the tragic love of a westerner and a
Japanese geisha girl. Based on the 1900
play by David Belasco, it was previously
filmed in 1915 by Famous Players-Lasky
with Mary Pickford and Marshall
Neilan. Belasco's play was based on an
1898 story by John Luther Long. The
well known operatic adaptation was conceived and written by Giacomo Puccini
in 1904.

2728. Madame DuBarry (WB;
1934). *Cast:* Dolores Del Rio (DuBarry),
Reginald Owen (King Louis XV), Vic-
tor Jory (d'Aiguillon), Anita Louise
(Marie Antoinette), Osgood Perkins
(Cardinal Richelieu), Verree Teasdale,
C. Aubrey Smith, Arthur Treacher,
Dorothy Tree, Hobart Cavanaugh,
Halliwell Hobbes, Henry O'Neill, Nella
Walker, Phillips Smalley, Ferdinand
Gottschalk, Leo White, Virginia Sale,
Helen Lowell, Joan Wheeler, Jessie

Scott, Camille Rovelle, Bud Flanagan (Dennis O'Keefe). *D:* William Dieterle; *P:* Henry Blanke; *Sc:* Edward Chodorov. (1:17)

The life (partially fictionalized) of the famous courtesan of Versailles, France. Other American versions of the story were *DuBarry* (1915) with Mrs. Leslie Carter, *DuBarry* (Fox; 1917) with Theda Bara, *DuBarry, Woman of Passion* (q.v.) and the comic *DuBarry Was a Lady* (MGM; 1943)

Madame Julie (G.B. title) *see* **The Woman Between**

2729. Madame Racketeer (Paramount; 1932). *Cast:* Alison Skipworth, Richard Bennett, George Raft, Evalyn Knapp, Gertrude Messinger, J. Farrell MacDonald, Robert McWade, Arthur Hoyt, Oscar Apfel, Eleanor Wesselhoeft, John Breeden. *D:* Alexander Hall, Henry (Harry) Wagstaff Gribble; *St & Sc:* Malcolm Stuart Boylan, Harvey Gates. (G.B. title: *The Sporting Widow*) (1:11)

A notorious con-woman known as "The Countess" begins to reform after meeting her two grown daughters. The film was voted one of the years "10 Best" by the National Board of Review.

2730. Madame Spy (Universal; 1934). *Cast:* Fay Wray (B-24), Nils Asther, Edward Arnold, John Miljan, David Torrence, Douglas Walton, Oscar Apfel, Noah Beery, Richard Bennett, Vince Barnett, Robert Ellis, Rollo Lloyd, Alden Chase, Mabel Marden. *D:* Karl Freund; *P:* Edmund Grainger; *St:* Max Kimmich, Joseph Than (based on the 1932 German film *Under False Flags*); *Sc:* William Hurlbut. (1:10)

Low-budget espionage melodrama of a German officer seeking the identity of a wanted spy — who it turns out, is his own wife.

2731. Madame X (MGM; 1929). *Cast:* Ruth Chatterton (A.A.N. for B.A. 1928-29 as Jacqueline), Raymond

Hackett (Raymond), Mitchell Lewis (Colonel Hanby), Sidney Toler (film debut as Merivel), Lewis Stone (Floriot), Carroll Nye (Darrell), Richard Carle (Perissard), Eugenie Besserer (Rose), Holmes Herbert (Noel), John P. Eddington (doctor), Ullrich Haupt (Laroque), Claude King (Valmorin), Chappell Dossett (judge), Mary Gordon (baby's nurse), Edith Fellows (film debut—bit). *D:* (A.A.N.) Lionel Barrymore (for his directorial debut); *Sc:* Willard Mack. (TV title: *Absinthe*) (1:35)

Tear-jerker of a woman who hits the skids and eventually finds herself being defended against a murder charge by her son who doesn't know her true identity. Based on the old play by Alexandre Bisson, it was previously filmed in 1909 with Jane Harding, in 1915 by Pathé with Dorothy Donnelly, 1920 by Samuel Goldwyn with Pauline Frederick. (See below for additional versions). *Film Daily* placed it at #3 on their "10 Best" list of the year.

2732. Madame X (MGM; 1937). *Cast:* Gladys George, John Beal, Warren William, Reginald Owen, William Henry, Henry Daniell, Philip Reed, Ruth Hussey, Lynne Carver, Cora Witherspoon, Emma Dunn, Stanley Andrews, Adia Kuznetzoff, Luis Alberni, George Zucco, Jonathan Hale. *D:* Sam Wood; *P:* James Kevin McGuinness; *Sc:* John Meehan. (1:11)

A remake of the preceding film. Remade in Great Britain in 1955 as *The Trial of Madame X,* in 1966 by Universal with Lana Turner and in 1981 as a TV movie with Tuesday Weld.

2733. Made for Each Other (United Artists/Selznick International; 1939). *Cast:* Carole Lombard (Jane Mason), James Stewart (John Mason), Lucile Watson (Mrs. Mason), Charles Coburn, Alma Kruger, Esther Dale, Ruth Weston, Harry Davenport, Donald Briggs, Fern Emmett. *D:* John Cromwell; *P:* David O. Selznick; *Sc:* Jo

Swerling. (1:33) (video—b/w & computer-colored)

Hit comedy-drama of a young married couple and their multitude of problems in creating a life for themselves. Based on a story suggested by Rose Franken it was voted "Best Film of the Year" by the *New York Times.*

2734. Made on Broadway (MGM; 1933). *Cast:* Robert Montgomery, Madge Evans, Sally Eilers, Eugene Pallette, Jean Parker, C. Henry Gordon, John Miljan, Raymond Hatton, Ivan Lebedeff, Mae Clark, Vince Barnett, David Newell. *D:* Harry Beaumont; *P:* Lucien Hubbard; *St:* Courtney Terrett; *Sc:* Terrett. (G.B. title: *The Girl I Made*)

Triangular romantic comedy of a star who is created through publicity.

Madelon *see* **Melody of Love**

2735. Madison Square Garden (Paramount; 1932). *Cast:* Jack Oakie, Marian Nixon, Thomas Meighan, William "Hopalong Cassidy" Boyd, Lew Cody, ZaSu Pitts, William Collier, Sr., Warren Hymer, Mushy Callahan, Lou Magnolia, Robert Elliott. *D:* Harry Joe Brown; *P:* Charles R. Rogers; *St:* Thomson Burtis; *Sc:* P.J. Wolfson, Allen Rivkin.

B boxing melodrama involving fixed fights.

2736. Madonna of Avenue "A" (WB; 1929). *Cast:* Dolores Costello, Louise Dresser, Grant Withers, William Russell, Douglas Gerrard, Otto Hoffman, Lee Moran. *D:* Michael Curtiz; *Sc:* Ray Doyle; *Dial.:* Francis Powers; *St:* Mark Canfield (Darryl F. Zanuck); *Adaptation:* Ray Doyle; *Dialogue:* King; *Song:* "My Madonna" by Fred Fisher, Louis Silvers.

Part-talkie melodrama of a young girl who finds her mother is a dance hall hostess.

2737. Madonna of the Streets (Columbia; 1930). *Cast:* Evelyn Brent,

Richard Tucker, Josephine Dunn, Edwards Davis, Ivan Linow. *D:* John S. Robertson; *St:* W.B. Maxwell; *Sc:* Jo Swerling.

Low-budget drama, a remake of a 1924 First National silent with Milton Sills and Nazimova.

2738. The Magnificent Brute (Universal; 1936). *Cast:* Victor McLaglen, Binnie Barnes, William Hall, Jean Dixon, Billy Burrud, Edward Norris, Ann Preston, Selmer Jackson, Henry Armetta, Thomas Jackson, Charles Wilson, Etta McDaniel, Adrian Rosley, Zeni Vatori. *D:* John G. Blystone; *P:* Edmund Grainger; *St:* Bertram Millhauser; *Sc:* Owen Francis, Lewis R. Foster, Francis Millhauser; *Art-Set Decoration:* (A.A.N.) Albert D'Agostino, Jack Otterson. (1:17)

Melodrama of two steel workers who are after the same woman.

2739. The Magnificent Fraud (Paramount; 1939). *Cast:* Akim Tamiroff, Patricia Morison, Mary Boland, Lloyd Nolan, Steffi Duna, Ernest Cossart, Nestor Paiva, Frank Reicher, Robert Warwick, Edward McWade, Virginia Dabney, Barbara Pepper, Donald Gallaher, Robert Middlemass, Julius Tannen. *D:* Robert Florey; *P:* Harlan Thompson; *Sc:* Gilbert Gabriel, Walter Ferris. (1:18)

B melodrama of a man who impersonates an assassinated South American dictator.

2740. The Magnificent Lie (Paramount; 1931). *Cast:* Ruth Chatterton, Charles Boyer, Ralph Bellamy, Stuart Erwin, Tyler Brooke, Tyrell Davis, Jean Del Val. *D:* Berthold Viertel; *Sc:* Samson Raphaelson.

Drama of romantic deception which turns into love.

2741. Magnificent Obsession (Universal; 1935). *Cast:* Irene Dunne, Robert Taylor, Ralph Morgan, Sara Haden, Betty Furness, Charles Butterworth, Arthur Hoyt, Gilbert Emery,

Arthur Treacher, Beryl Mercer, Edward Earle, Inez Courtney, Joyce Compton, Theodore von Eltz, Lucien Littlefield, Frank Reicher, Henry Armetta, Cora Sue Collins, Gino Corrado, Alan Davis, Leonard Mudie, Purnell Pratt, Walter Walker, Sam Hardy, Marion Clayton, Mickey Daniels, Lowell Durham, Crauford Kent. *D:* John M. Stahl; *P:* Stahl; *Sc:* George O'Neil, Sarah Y. Mason, Victor Heerman. (1:50)

Drama of a reckless playboy who feels responsible for a woman's blindness following an auto accident. Based on the novel by Lloyd C. Douglas it was one of the 25 top grossing films of 1935–36. Remade in 1954 by this studio.

The Magnificent Outcast (G.B. title) *see* **Almost a Gentleman**

2742. Maid of Salem (Paramount; 1937). *Cast:* Claudette Colbert, Fred MacMurray, Harvey Stephens, Louise Dresser, Gale Sondergaard, Beulah Bondi, Bonita Granville, Edward Ellis, Virginia Weidler, Donald Meek, Madame Sul-Te-Wan, Halliwell Hobbes, Bennie Bartlett, E.E. Clive, William Farnum, Tom Ricketts, Zeffie Tilbury, Pedro de Cordoba, Stanley Fields, Sterling Holloway, Henry Kolker, Ivan Simpson, Barbara Nelson. *D:* Frank Lloyd; *P:* Lloyd, Howard Estabrook; *Sc:* Bradley King, Walter Ferris, Durward Grinstead. (1:26)

Salem, Massachusetts in 1692 is the setting for this flop melodrama of witchcraft hysteria, based on historical fact with the usual Hollywood fiction thrown in.

2743. Maid to Order (Weil; 1931). *Cast:* Julian Eltinge, Jane Reid. *D:* Elmer Clifton; *Sc:* Grace Elliott.

(No other information available)

2744. Maid's Night Out (RKO; 1937–38). *Cast:* Joan Fontaine, Allan Lane, Billy Gilbert, Hedda Hopper, Cecil Kellaway, George Irving, William

Brisbane, Hilda Vaughn, Frank M. Thomas, Solly Ward, Eddie Gribbon, Lee Patrick. *D:* Ben Holmes; *P:* Robert Sisk; *St:* Willoughby Speyers; *Sc:* Bert Granet. (1:05) (video)

Low-budget screwball comedy of mistaken identities.

2745. The Main Event (Columbia; 1938). *Cast:* Ann Doran, Robert Paige, Jacqueline Wells (Julie Bishop), Oscar O'Shea, Nick Copeland, Arthur Loft, Thurston Hall, Lester Dorr, Pat Flaherty, John Gallaudet, Gene Morgan, John Tyrell. *D:* Daniel Dare; *St:* Harold Shumate; *Sc:* Lee Loeb.

Low-budget production, a remake of a 1927 silent.

2746. Main Street Lawyer (Republic; 1939). *Cast:* Edward Ellis, Anita Louise, Beverly Roberts, Ferris Taylor, Margaret Hamilton, Harold Huber, Robert Baldwin, Richard Lane, Wallis Clark, Clem Bevans, Willard Robertson. *D:* Dudley Murphy; *St:* Harry Hamilton; *Sc:* Joseph Krumgold. (G.B. title: *Small Town Lawyer*)

B crime melodrama involving blackmail. Remade by this studio in 1956 as *When Gangland Strikes.*

2747. Maisie (MGM; 1939). *Cast:* Ann Sothern (Maisie Ravier), Robert Young, Ian Hunter, Ruth Hussey, Anthony Allan (John Hubbard), Cliff Edwards, Art Mix, George Tobias (film debut), Richard Carle, Minor Watson, Harlan Briggs, Paul Everton, Joseph Crehan, Frank Puglia, Willie Fung, Robert Middlemass, Clem Bevans. *D:* Edwin L. Marin; *P:* J. Walter Ruben; *Sc:* Mary C. McCall, Jr. (1:14)

Premiere entry in a series of ten films made between 1939 and 1947 with the main character, a tough blonde with the proverbial heart-of-gold. Followed by *Congo Maisie* (q.v.). A big hit at the box office, it was based on the novel "Dark Dame" by Wilson Collison.

2748. Make a Million (Monogram; 1935). *Cast:* Charles Starrett,

Pauline Brooks, George E. Stone, James Burke, Norman Houston, Monte Carter, Jimmy Aubrey, George Cleveland, Guy Usher, John Elliott. *D:* Lewis Collins; *St:* Emmett Anthony; *Sc:* Charles Logue. (1:06) (video)

B comedy of an ex-college professor who devises a plan which starts the big bucks rolling in, only to find others are out to get a piece of his pie.

2749. Make a Wish (RKO/Principal; 1937). *Cast:* Bobby Breen, Basil Rathbone, Marion Claire, Leon Errol, Henry Armetta, Ralph Forbes, Donald Meek, Fred Scott, Billy Lee, Herbert Rawlinson, Johnny Arthur, Leonid Kinskey. *D:* Kurt Neumann; *P:* Sol Lesser; *As.P.:* Edward Cross; *St:* Gertrude Berg; *Sc:* Berg, Bernard Schubert, Earle Snell; *Music:* (A.A.N.) Hugo Riesenfeld; *Songs:* Oscar Straus, Louis Alter, Paul Francis Webster. (1:20) (video)

Hit musical of a child prodigy which was designed for the singing boy wonder, Bobby Breen.

2750. Make Me a Star (Paramount; 1932). *Cast:* Stuart Erwin, Joan Blondell, ZaSu Pitts, Ben Turpin, Florence Roberts, Kent Taylor, Charles Sellon, Helen Jerome Eddy, Sam Hardy, Ruth Donnelly, Arthur Hoyt, Snub Pollard, Oscar Apfel, Frank Mills, Polly Walters, George Templeton, Kathrin Clare Ward; Tallulah Bankhead, Maurice Chevalier, Gary Cooper, Clive Brook, Claudette Colbert, Fredric March, Jack Oakie, Charles Ruggles, Sylvia Sidney (cameos). *D:* William Beaudine; *P:* E. Lloyd Sheldon; *Sc:* Sam Mintz, Walter De Leon, Arthur Kober. (1:20)

The story of a simple man who goes to Hollywood and becomes a film star. Based on the 1922 novel by Harry Leon Wilson, it was adapted for the stage by Marc Connelly and George S. Kaufman in 1923. A remake of *Merton of the Movies* (Paramount; 1924), with Glenn Hunter, which is also the title of the original book. Remade as *Merton of the Movies* (MGM; 1947).

2751. Make Way for a Lady (RKO; 1936). *Cast:* Herbert Marshall, Anne Shirley, Gertrude Michael, Margot Grahame, Taylor Holmes, Clara Blandick, Frank (Junior) Coghlan, Maxine Jennings, Mary Jo Ellis, Murray Kinnell, Helen Parrish, Willie Best, John Butler, Maidel Turner, Del Henderson, Alan Edwards, Grace Goodall. *D:* David Burton; *As.P.:* Zion Myers; *Sc:* Gertrude Purcell. (1:05)

A young girl plays matchmaker for her widowed father in this B comedy. Based on the novel "Daddy and I" by Elizabeth Jordan.

2752. Make Way for Tomorrow (Paramount; 1937). *Cast:* Victor Moore (Barkley Cooper), Beulah Bondi (Lucy Cooper), Fay Bainter (Anita Cooper), Thomas Mitchell (George Cooper), Porter Hall (Harvey Chase), Barbara Read (Rhoda Cooper), Louise Beavers (Mamie), Maurice Moscovich (Max Rubens), Gene Lockhart (Mr. Henning), Elizabeth Risdon (Cora Payne), Louis Jean Heydt (film debut as the doctor), Ferike Boros (Mrs. Rubens), Ralph M. Remley (Bill Payne), Gene Morgan (Carlton Gorman), Del Henderson (auto salesman), Minna Gombell (Nellie Chase), Ray Mayer (Robert Cooper), Ruth Warren (secretary), Paul Stanton (hotel manager), George Offerman, Jr. (Richard Payne), Tommy Bupp (Jack Payne), Granville Bates (Mr. Hunter), Byron Foulger (Mr. Dale), Avril Cameron (Mrs. McKenzie), Nick Lukats, Terry Ray (Ellen Drew), Kitty McHugh, Ralph Brooks, Ethel Clayton, Ralph Lewis, Phillips Smalley, Don Brodie, Howard Mitchell, William Newell, Rosemary Theby, Richard R. Neill, Helen Dickson, Leo McCarey (several bits). *D:* Leo McCarey; *P:* McCarey; *Sc:* Vina Delmar; *Title Song:* Leo Robin, Sam Coslow, Jean Schwartz. (1:34)

Critically acclaimed drama of an elderly couple who after encountering financial difficulty, are separated, each living with a different one of their grown children. Based on the novel "The Years Are So Long" by Josephine Lawrence which was adapted for the stage by Helen and Nolan Leary. The *New York Times* placed it at #6 on their "10 Best" list while the National Board of Review gave it a #5 placement on their same list.

2753. Maker of Men (Columbia; 1931). *Cast:* Richard Cromwell, Jack Holt, John Wayne, Joan Marsh, Walter Catlett, Richard Tucker, Natalie Moorhead, Ethel Wales, Corbet Morris, Robert Alden. *D:* Edward Sedgwick; *St:* Sedgwick, Howard Green; *Sc:* Green.

B drama of a football player who sells out his team to gamblers.

2754. Making the Grade (Fox; 1929). *Cast:* Lois Moran, Edmund Lowe. *D:* Alfred E. Green.

A low-budget part-talkie.

2755. Making the Headlines (Columbia; 1938). *Cast:* Jack Holt, Beverly Roberts, Craig Reynolds, Sheila Bromley, Marjorie Gateson, Gilbert Emery, Maurice Cass, Tom Kennedy, Corbet Morris, Dorothy Appleby. *D:* Lewis Collins; *St:* Howard Green; *Sc:* Green, Jefferson Parker.

B melodrama.

Mala the Magnificent (G.B. title) *see* **Eskimo**

2756. Malay Nights (Weeks/ Mayfair; 1932–33). *Cast:* John Mack Brown, Dorothy Burgess, Ralph Ince, Raymond Hatton, Carmelita Geraghty. *D:* E. Mason Hopper. (G.B. title: *Shadows of Singapore*)

Low-budget melodrama.

Malibu *see* **Sequoia**

2757. The Maltese Falcon (WB; 1931). *Cast:* Bebe Daniels (Brigid), Ricardo Cortez (Sam Spade), Dudley Digges (Gutman), Una Merkel, Robert Elliott, Otto Matieson, Walter Long, Thelma Todd, Dwight Frye, J. Farrell MacDonald, Oscar Apfel. *D:* Roy Del Ruth; *Sc:* Maude Fulton, Lucien Hubbard (unc.), Brown Holmes. (TV title: *Dangerous Female*) (1:20) (video)

Early version of Dashiell Hammett's detective novel of the search for the statue of a bird. Remade in 1936 by this studio as *Satan Met a Lady* (q.v.), and again in the 1941 classic version under the original title with Humphrey Bogart and Mary Astor. A 1975 feature titled *The Black Bird* was a satire.

2758. Mama Loves Papa (Paramount; 1933). *Cast:* Mary Boland, Charles Ruggles, Lilyan Tashman, Walter Catlett, George Barbier, Andre Beranger, Warner Richmond, Gail Patrick, Tom Ricketts, Morgan Wallace, Ruth Warren. *D:* Norman Z. McLeod; *P:* Douglas MacLean; *St:* Keene Thompson, Douglas MacLean; *Sc:* Johnson, Arthur Kober.

Domestic comedy of an elderly married couple. Voted one of the year's "10 Best" films by the National Board of Review. Paramount sold the rights to RKO who remade it as a B feature in 1945 with Leon Errol.

2759. Mama Runs Wild (Republic; 1937). *Cast:* Mary Boland, Ernest Truex, William Henry, Mary Hart (Lynn Roberts), Max Terhune, Joseph Crehan, Dewey Robinson. *D:* Ralph Staub.

B domestic comedy.

2760. Mama Steps Out (MGM; 1937). *Cast:* Alice Brady, Guy Kibbee, Betty Furness, Stanley Morner (Dennis Morgan), Ivan Lebedeff, Heather Thatcher, Gregory Gaye, Gene Lockhart, Edward Norris. *D:* George B. Seitz; *P:* John Emerson; *Sc:* Anita Loos.

B comedy of a screwball family who heads for the French Riviera after receiving a windfall. Based on the play "Ada Beats the Drum" by John Kirkpatrick.

2761. Mamba (Tiffany; 1930). *Cast:* Ralph Forbes, Eleanor Boardman, Jean Hersholt, Arthur Stone, William von Brincken, Will Stanton, Josef Swickard, Andres DeSegurola, Claude Fleming. *D:* Albert S. Rogell; *St:* John Reinhardt, Ferdinand Schumann-Heink; *Sc:* Tom Miranda, Winifred Dunn.

"Poverty row" melodrama.

2762. Mammy (WB; 1930). *Cast:* Al Jolson, Lois Moran, Louise Dresser, Lowell Sherman, Hobart Bosworth, Tully Marshall, Lee Moran, Stanley Fields, Noah Beery, Ray Cooke. *D:* Michael Curtiz; *P:* Walter Morosco; *Sc:* Gordon Rigby, Joseph Jackson; *Music & Songs:* Irving Berlin. (1:24)

Musical drama of the old minstrel circuit and a man who flees after another is shot onstage. Based on a play by James Gleason and Irving Berlin titled "Mr. Bones," the film which originally included a 2-color technicolor sequence was a major hit for the studio.

2763. Man About Town (Fox; 1932). *Cast:* Warner Baxter, Karen Morley, Conway Tearle, Lillian Bond, Alan Mowbray, Noel Madison, Halliwell Hobbes, Leni Stengel. *D:* John Francis Dillon.

Low-budget romance.

2764. Man About Town (Paramount; 1939). *Cast:* Jack Benny, Dorothy Lamour (replacing Betty Grable who had been stricken with appendicitis), Edward Arnold, Binnie Barnes, Phil Harris, Eddie "Rochester" Anderson, Monty Woolley, Betty Grable, Isabel Jeans, E.E. Clive, Matty Malneck Band, Herbert Evans, Noel Madison, Leonard Mudie, Cyril Thornton, Clifford Severn, Kay Linaker. *D:* Mark Sandrich; *P:* Arthur Hornblow, Jr.; *St:* Morrie Ryskind, Allan Scott, Zion Myers; *St:* Ryskind; *Songs:* (Including "Strange Enchantment") by Frank Loesser. (1:25)

Hit musical comedy of its day of Americans in London.

2765. Man Against Woman (Columbia; 1932). *Cast:* Walter Connolly, Jack Holt, Lillian Miles, Emmett Corrigan, Arthur Vinton, Harry Seymour, Clarence Muse. *D:* Irving Cummings; *St:* Keene Thompson; *Sc:* Jo Swerling.

Low-budget drama.

2766. The Man and the Moment (WB/F.N.; 1929). *Cast:* Billie Dove, Rod La Rocque, Gwen Lee, Doris Dawson, Robert Schable, Charles Sellon, George Bunny. *D:* George Fitzmaurice; *St:* Elinor Glyn; *Sc:* Agnes Christine Johnston.

Part-talkie story of the lifestyles of the rich and beautiful.

2767. A Man Betrayed (Republic; 1937). *Cast:* Lloyd Hughes, Carleton Young, Edward Nugent, Smiley Burnette. *D:* John H. Auer.

B melodrama.

2768. The Man Called Back (Tiffany; 1932). *Cast:* Conrad Nagel, Doris Kenyon, Reginald Owen, John T. Murray, Alan Mowbray, Gilbert Emery, Mae Busch, Mona Maris. *D:* Robert Florey; *St:* Andrew Soutar.

"Poverty row" drama.

2769. The Man from Arizona (Monogram; 1932). *Cast:* Rex Bell, Charles King, Theodore Lorch, George Nash, Naomi Judge, John Elliott, Nat Carr, Lex Lindsay, James Marcus, Henry Sedley, John Beck, Hank Bell, George Cooper, Bob McKenzie. *D:* Harry Fraser; *P:* Trem Carr; *St & Sc:* Wellyn Totman. (0:58)

Rex Bell western with a formula plot.

2770. The Man from Blankley's (WB; 1930). *Cast:* John Barrymore, Loretta Young, Emily Fitzroy, Louise Carver, May Milloy, Dale Fuller, Edgar Norton, William Austin, Albert Gran, Fanny Brice, Angella Mawby, D'Arcy Corrigan, Tiny Jones, Diana Hope, Charles Fallon, Yorke Sherwood, Dick

Henderson. *D:* Alfred E. Green; *Sc:* Harvey Thew, Joseph Jackson. (1:07)

Hit comedy of its day of a drunk who goes to the wrong party. Based on the play by F. Anstey, it was voted one of the "10 Best" films of the year by the National Board of Review. Previously filmed as a silent.

2771. The Man from Death Valley (Monogram; 1931). *Cast:* Tom Tyler, Betty Mack, John Oscar, Si Jenks, Gino Corrado, Stanley Blystone, Hank Bell. *D:* Lloyd Nosler; *St:* Nosler, George Arthur Durlam; *Sc:* Durlam. (1:02)

Tom Tyler western of a cowboy who brings a corrupt sheriff to justice.

2772. The Man from Guntown (Puritan; 1935). *Cast:* Tim McCoy, Billie Seward, Rex Lease, Jack Clifford, Wheeler Oakman, Jack Rockwell, Bob McKenzie, George Chesebro, Ella McKenzie, Horace B. Carpenter, Hank Bell, George Pierce. *D:* Ford Beebe; *Sc:* Beebe, Thomas H. Ince, Jr. (1:00)

Tim McCoy western of a man wrongly accused of a crime who escapes jail to find the guilty party.

2773. The Man from Hell (Willis Kent; 1933). *Cast:* Reb Russell, Ann D'Arcy, Fred Kohler, George Hayes, Jack Rockwell, Yakima Canutt, Slim Whitaker, Roy D'Arcy, Tracy Layne, Mary Gordon, Tommy Bupp, Charles K. French, Murdock MacQuarrie. *D:* Lewis D. Collins; *P:* Willis Kent; *Sc:* Melville Shyer. (0:58)

Reb Russell western of a man who gets out of Yuma Prison to find out who framed him.

2774. The Man from Hell's Edges (Sono Art-World Wide; 1932). *Cast:* Bob Steele, Nancy Drexel, Julian Rivero, Robert Homans, George Hayes, Pee Wee Holmes, Earl Dwire, Dick Dickinson, Perry Murdock, Blackie Whiteford. *D:* Robert N. Bradbury; *P:* Trem Carr; *Sc:* Bradbury. (1:00)

Bob Steele western of a prison escapee who saves the life of a sheriff and becomes his deputy.

2775. The Man from Monterey (WB/Vitagraph; 1933). *Cast:* John Wayne, Ruth Hall, Luis Alberni, Donald Reed, Nena Quartero, Francis Ford, Lafe McKee, Lillian Leighton, Slim Whitaker. *D:* Mack V. Wright; *P:* Leon Schlesinger; *As.P.:* Sid Rogell; *Sc:* Lesley Mason. (0:57)

John Wayne western involving some dirty dealing to ranchers who received their land through a Spanish grant. A remake of *The Canyon of Adventure* (First National; 1928) with Ken Maynard.

2776. The Man from Montreal (Universal; 1939–40). *Cast:* Andy Devine, Richard Arlen, Anne Gwynne, Lane Chandler, Joseph Sawyer, Jerry Marlowe, Kay Sutton, Reed Hadley, Addison Richards, Tom Whitten, Don Brodie, Karl Hackett, Pat Flaherty, Eddy Waller, William Royle, Eddie Conrad. *D:* Christy Cabanne; *P:* Ben Pivar; *Sc:* Owen Francis. (1:00)

B quickie of a fur trapper who must prove himself innocent of theft.

2777. The Man from Music Mountain (Republic; 1938). *Cast:* Gene Autry, Smiley Burnette, Carol Hughes, Sally Payne, Ivan Miller, Edward Cassidy, Lew Kelly, Howard Chase, Albert Terry, Frankie Marvin, Earl Dwire, Lloyd Ingraham, Lillian Drew, Al Taylor, Joe Yrigoyen, Polly Jenkins & Her Plowboys, Champion. *D:* Joe Kane; *As.P.:* Charles E. Ford; *St:* Bernard McConville; *Sc:* Luci Ward, Betty Burbridge. (0:54) (video)

Gene Autry western with songs which is no relation to the 1943 Roy Rogers' western of the same name for this studio.

2778. The Man from New Mexico (Monogram; 1932). *Cast:* Tom Tyler, Caryl Lincoln, Jack Richardson,

Robert Walker, Frank Ball, Lewis Sargent, Blackie Whiteford, Slim Whitaker, Lafe McKee, Frederick Ryter, Jack Long, William Nolte, Lee Timm, C.H. "Fargo" Bussey. *D:* John P. McCarthy; *P:* Trem Carr; *Sc:* Harry O. Hoyt. (0:54)

Tom Tyler western of a rancher who is beset by cattle rustlers. Based on the story "Frag Branded" by Frederick Ryter.

2779. The Man from Sundown (Columbia; 1939). *Cast:* Charles Starrett, Iris Meredith, Richard Fiske, Sons of the Pioneers with Bob Nolan and Pat Brady, Jack Rockwell, Alan Bridge, Dick Botiller, Robert Fiske, Ed Peil, Sr., Edmund Cobb, Art Mix, Kit Guard, Forrest H. Dillon, Clem Horton, Al Haskell, Edward LeSaint, Tex Cooper, George Chesebro, Oscar Gahan, Frank Ellis. *D:* Sam Nelson; *Sc:* Paul Franklin. (0:58)

Charles Starrett western of a Texas Ranger investigating the murder of a rancher who was to testify against members of an outlaw gang.

2780. The Man from Texas (Monogram; 1939). *Cast:* Tex Ritter, Ruth Rogers, Hal Price, Charles B. Wood, Charles King, Kenne Duncan, Vic Demourelle, Jr., Roy Barcroft, Frank Wayne, Tom London, Nelson McDowell, Sherry Tansey, Chick Hannon, White Flash the horse. *D:* Al Herman; *P:* Edward Finney (Boots and Saddles Prods.); *Sc:* Robert Emmett (Tansey). (0:56) (video)

In this Tex Ritter western with musical interludes, a railroad agent and reformed outlaw get the goods on a greedy land grabber.

The Man from the Folies Bergere (G.B. title) *see* **Folies Bergere**

2781. The Man from Tumbleweeds (Columbia; 1939–40). *Cast:* Bill Elliott, Dub Taylor, Iris Meredith, Raphael (Ray) Bennett, Francis Walker, Ernie Adams, Al Hill, Stanley Brown (later Brad Taylor), Richard Fiske, Edward J. LeSaint, Don Beddoe, Eddie Laughton, John Tyrell, Edward Cecil, Jack Lowe, Bruce Bennett, George Chesebro, Hank Bell. *D:* Joseph H. Lewis; *P:* Leon Barsha; *Sc:* Charles Francis Royal. (0:59)

A western with Bill Elliott as "Wild Bill Saunders" in a story of paroled prisoners cleaning up the lawless element in a western town.

2782. The Man from Utah (Monogram-Lone Star; 1934). *Cast:* John Wayne, Polly Ann Young, George Hayes, Yakima Canutt, Edward Peil, Anita Compillo, Lafe McKee, George Cleveland, Earl Dwire, Artie Ortego. *D:* Robert N. Bradbury; *P:* Paul Malvern; *Supervisor:* Trem Carr; *St & Sc:* Lindsley Parsons. (0:55)

John Wayne western of outlaws who are using a rodeo as a front for their illegal activities.

2783. A Man from Wyoming (Paramount; 1930). *Cast:* Gary Cooper, June Collyer, Regis Toomey, E.H. Calvert, Morgan Farley, Edgar Dearing, Mary Foy, Emile Chautard, Ben Hall. *D:* Rowland V. Lee; *Sc:* John Weaver, Albert Shelby LeVino. (1:10)

A romantic war story of an American doughboy and a girl of loose morals. A remake of *Civilian Clothes* (Paramount; 1920) with Thomas Meighan and Martha Mansfield.

2784. The Man from Yesterday (Paramount; 1932). *Cast:* Claudette Colbert, Clive Brook, Charles Boyer, Andy Devine, Alan Mowbray, Christian Rub, Yola D'Avril, Boyd Irwin, George Davis, Emile Chautard, Ronnie Cosbey, Donald Stuart, Reginald Pasch, Barry Winton. *D:* Berthold Viertel; *Sc:* Oliver H.P. Garrett. (1:11)

Another variation on the "Enoch Arden" theme as a wife who thinks her husband killed in World War I, takes up with another only to find her husband is still alive.

2785. Man Hunt (RKO/King Motion Pictures; 1933). *Cast:* James (Junior) Durkin, Charlotte Henry, Mrs. Wallace (Dorothy) Reid, Arthur Vinton, Edward J. LeSaint, Richard Carle, Carl Gross, Jr. *D:* Irving Cummings; *P:* J.G. Bachmann; *St & Sc:* Leonard Praskins, Sam Mintz. (1:03)

A youth who yearns to be a private detective, gets his chance after some diamonds are stolen.

2786. Man Hunt (WB; 1936). *Cast:* Ricardo Cortez, Charles "Chic" Sale, Marguerite Churchill, William Gargan, Richard (Dick) Purcell, Maude Eburne, Olin Howland, Addison Richards, Kenneth Harlan, George E. Stone, Don Barclay, Larry Kent. *D:* William Clemens (directorial debut); *P:* Bryan Foy; *St:* Earl Felton; *Sc:* Roy Chanslor.

B comedy-melodrama of an old man who catches a criminal.

2787. The Man Hunter (WB; 1930). *Cast:* Rin-Tin-Tin, Nora Lane, Charles Delaney, Pat Hartigan, Christiane Yves, Floyd Shackleford, John Loder. *D:* D. Ross Lederman; *St:* Lillian (Lillie) Hayward; *Sc:* James A. Starr.

Hit low-budget action-adventure of a canine who helps save a girl's ivory and rubber company.

2788. The Man I Killed (Paramount; 1932). *Cast:* Lionel Barrymore, Nancy Carroll, Phillips Holmes, ZaSu Pitts, Lucien Littlefield, Emma Dunn, Tom Douglas, Louise Carter, Julia Swayne Gordon, Tully Marshall, Joan Standing, Reginald Pasch, Marvin Stephens, George Bickel, Lillian Elliott, Frank Sheridan, Rodney McLennon. *D:* Ernst Lubitsch; *Sc:* Ernest Vajda, Samson Raphaelson. (1:17) (title change: *Broken Lullaby*)

Flop drama of a French soldier who kills a German soldier in the war and feels guilty, subsequently falling for the dead soldier's girl. Based on the play "L'Homme que J'ai Tue" by Maurice Rostand.

2789. The Man I Love (Paramount; 1929). *Cast:* Richard Arlen, Mary Brian, Olga Baclanova, Jack Oakie, Harry Green, Leslie Fenton, Pat O'Malley. *D:* William Wellman; *P:* David O. Selznick; *St & Sc:* Herman J. Mankiewicz.

Low-budget romance of a young boxer pursued by a wealthy society woman, despite the fact he loves another.

2790. The Man I Marry (Universal; 1936). *Cast:* Michael Whalen, Peggy Shannon, Doris Nolan, Charles "Chic" Sale, Skeets Gallagher, Marjorie Gateson, Arthur Aylesworth, Cliff Edwards, Rollo Lloyd, Lew Kelly, Harry Barris, Harry Hayden, Gerald Oliver Smith. *D:* Ralph Murphy; *P:* Val Paul; *St:* M. Coates Webster; *Sc:* Harry Clork. (1:15)

B drama of a playwright who is torn between his mother, his girl and his career as a writer.

2791. The Man in Blue (Universal; 1937). *Cast:* Robert Wilcox, Nan Grey, Richard Carle, Edward Ellis, Milburn Stone, George Cleveland, Ralph Morgan, Mary Gordon, Florence Bates (a former attorney in her film debut), Billy Burrud, Alma Kruger, Selmer Jackson, Frederick Burton, Herbert Corthell, Aggie Herring. *D:* Milton Carruth; *P:* Kubec Glasmon; *St:* Glasmon; *Sc:* Lester Cole. (1:04)

B melodrama of a young bank teller who falls under the influence of his criminal father.

2792. The Man in Possession (MGM; 1931). *Cast:* Robert Montgomery, Charlotte Greenwood, C. Aubrey Smith, Irene Purcell, Reginald Owen, Beryl Mercer, Alan Mowbray, Maude Eburne, Forrester Harvey, Yorke Sherwood. *D:* Sam Wood; *Sc:* Sarah Y. Mason; *Additional Dialogue:* P.G. Wodehouse. (1:24)

Hit comedy of mistaken identity, based on the play by H.M. Harwood. Remade as *Personal Property* (q.v.).

The Man in Possession (1937) (G.B. title) *see* **Personal Property**

2793. The Man in the Iron Mask (United Artists; 1939). *Cast:* Louis Hayward (dual role as King Louis XIV and Philippe of Gascony), Joan Bennett (Maria Theresa), Warren William (D'Artagnan), Joseph Schildkraut (Fouquet), Walter Kingsford (Colbert), Alan Hale (Porthos), Miles Mander (Aramis), Bert Roach, Montagu Love, Doris Kenyon (final film — ret. as Queen Anne), Marion Martin, Albert Dekker (King Louis XIII), Nigel de Brulier (Cardinal Richelieu), William Royle (commandant of the Bastille), Boyd Irwin (Lord High Constable of France), Howard Brooks (cardinal), Reginald Barlow (Jean Paul), Lane Chandler (captain of Fouquet's guards), Wyndham Standing (doctor), Dorothy Vaughan (midwife), Sheila Darcy (Maria Theresa's maid), Robert Milasch (torturer), D'Arcy Corrigan (tortured prisoner), Harry Woods (1st officer), Peter Cushing (2nd officer), Emmett King (king's chamberlain), St. Brendan Choir, Dwight Frye, Fred Cavens. *D:* James Whale; *P:* Edward Small; *Adaptation:* George Bruce; *Original Music Score:* (A.A.N.) Lud Gluskin & Lucien Moraweck. (1:59) (video)

Alexandre Dumas' classic novel of two brothers, one king of France, the other kept prisoner in an iron mask. A remake of *The Iron Mask* (q.v.). *Prisoner in the Iron Mask* came out of Italy in 1962 while the story was remade in the U.S.A. in 1977 as a TV movie, and as *The Fifth Musketeer* (Austria; 1979). Computer-colored prints produced in the late 1980s.

Man Killer *see* **Private Detective 62**

The Man Maker (G.B. title) *see* **$20 a Week**

2794. Man of Action (Columbia; 1933). *Cast:* Tim McCoy, Caryl Lincoln, Julian Rivero, Wheeler Oakman, Walter Brennan, Joseph Girard, Stanley Blystone, Lafe McKee, Charles K. French, Ted Adams. *D:* George Melford; *Sc:* Robert Quigley. (1:00)

Tim McCoy western of a Texas Ranger and his saddle pal who investigate a bank robbery and find more dirty dealings.

2795. Man of Conquest (Republic; 1939). *Cast:* Richard Dix (Sam Houston), Joan Fontaine, Gail Patrick, Edward Ellis (Andrew Jackson), Victor Jory (Col. William B. Travis), George "Gabby" Hayes, Robert Barrat, Ralph Morgan (Stephen Austin), Robert Armstrong, C. Henry Gordon (General Santa Anna), Janet Beecher, Max Terhune, Leon Ames, Kathleen Lockhart, Ferris Taylor, George (Montgomery) Letz, Guy Wilkerson, Charles Stevens, Hal Taliaferro, Lane Chandler, Edmund Cobb, Ethan Laidlaw, Tex Cooper, Billy Benedict, Ernie Adams, Carlo Strinati, Pedro de Cordoba. *D:* George Nicholls, Jr.; *P:* Sol C. Siegel; *St:* Wells Root, Harold Shumate; *Sc:* Root, Edward E. Paramore, Jr., Jan Fortune; *Art-Set Decoration:* (A.A.N.) John Victor MacKay; *Music:* (A.A.N.) Victor Young; *Sound Recording:* (A.A.N.) Charles Lootens. (1:45)

Filmed biography of famed Texan, Sam Houston with a large scale recreation of the Texans' final battle to hold the Alamo.

2796. Man of Iron (WB/F.N.; 1935). *Cast:* Barton MacLane (starring debut), Dorothy Peterson, Mary Astor, Joseph Crehan, Craig Reynolds, Joseph King, John Qualen, Joseph Sawyer, Gordon "Bill" Elliott, John Eldredge, Edward Keane, Ian MacLaren, Florence Fair. *D:* William McGann; *P:* Bryan Foy; *St:* Dawn Powell; *Sc:* William Wister Haines.

B melodrama of an iron mill foreman who seeks to be a member of society.

2797. A Man of Sentiment (Chesterfield; 1933). *Cast:* William Bakewell, Marian Marsh, Owen Moore, Edmund Breese. *D:* Richard Thorpe.

"Poverty row" drama.

2798. Man of the Forest (Paramount; 1933). *Cast:* Randolph Scott, Buster Crabbe, Verna Hillie, Harry Carey, Guinn Williams, Barton MacLane, Noah Beery, Vince Barnett, Tempe Pigott, Blanche Frederici, Tom Kennedy, Frank McGlynn, Jr., Lew Kelly, Duke Lee, Merrill McCormack, Tom London. *D:* Henry Hathaway; *Sc:* Jack Cunningham, Harold Shumate. (Re-release title: *Challenge of the Frontier*) (1:02)

B actioner of a man wrongly accused of murder who escapes with the help of his pet mountain lion and later proves his innocence. Based on a novel by Zane Grey, it was previously filmed in 1921, with a Paramount remake following in 1926 with Jack Holt and Georgia Hale.

Man of the Frontier *see* **Red River Valley**

2799. Man of the People (MGM; 1937). *Cast:* Joseph Calleia, Florence Rice, Thomas Mitchell, Ted Healy, Catherine Doucet, Edward Nugent, Noel Madison, Soledad Jiminez, William Ricciardi, Donald Briggs, Paul Stanton, James Barnes, Robert Emmett Keane. *D:* Edwin L. Marin; *P:* Lucien Hubbard; *St & Sc:* Frank Dolan.

B drama of an immigrant lawyer who works his way up, all the while being involved in corruption.

2800. Man of the World (Paramount; 1931). *Cast:* Carole Lombard, William Powell, Wynne Gibson, Guy Kibbee, George Chandler, Lawrence Gray, Tom Ricketts, Maude Truax, Tom Costello, André Cheron. *D:* Richard Wallace; *Sc:* Herman J. Mankiewicz. (1:11)

The romance of a girl and a con artist.

2801. Man of Two Worlds (RKO; 1934). *Cast:* Francis Lederer (American debut as Aigo), Henry Stephenson, Elissa Landi, Walter Byron, J. Farrell MacDonald, Steffi Duna, Sarah Padden, Forrester Harvey, Christian Rub, Ivan Simpson, Lumsden Hare, Emile Chautard, Gertrude Wise. *D:* J. Walter Ruben; *P:* Pandro S. Berman; *Sc:* Ainsworth Morgan, Howard J. Green. (1:36)

An Eskimo from Greenland is introduced to "civilized society" and falls for an upper crust society girl. Based on the novel by Ainsworth Morgan, the film became a debit for the studio.

2802. The Man on the Flying Trapeze (Paramount; 1935). *Cast:* W.C. Fields, Kathleen Howard, Mary Brian, Grady Sutton, Vera Lewis, Lucien Littlefield, Walter Brennan, Oscar Apfel, Joseph Sawyer, Pat O'Malley, James Burke, Arthur Aylesworth, Tammany Young, Harry Ekezian, David Clyde, Lew Kelly, Tor Johnson. *D:* Clyde Bruckman (final film — ret.); *P:* William LeBaron; *St:* Charles Bogle (Fields), Sam Hardy; *Sc:* Ray Harris, Hardy, Jack Cunningham, Bobby Vernon. (G.B. title: *The Memory Expert*) (1:05)

Classic domestic comedy farce which is another Field's field-day.

2803. Man-Proof (MGM; 1937–38). *Cast:* Myrna Loy, Franchot Tone, Walter Pidgeon, Rosalind Russell, Nana Bryant, Ruth Hussey, Rita Johnson, Leonard Penn, John Miljan, Oscar O'Shea, Joyce Compton, William Stack, Dan Tobey, Jack Norton. *D:* Richard Thorpe; *P:* Louis D. Lighton; *Sc:* Vincent Lawrence, Waldemar Young, George Oppenheimer. (1:14)

Comedy of girls on the prowl for romance. Based on the novel "The Four Marys" by Fanny Heaslip Lea.

2804. The Man They Could Not Hang (Columbia; 1939). *Cast:* Boris

Karloff, Lorna Gray (later known as "Karin Booth"), Robert Wilcox, Roger Pryor, Don Beddoe, Byron Foulger, Ann Doran, James Craig, Dick Curtis. *D:* Nick Grinde; *Sc:* Karl Brown. (1:12) (video)

B horror film of a man brought back to life by his assistant after being hanged for murder. This was the first in a series of films with Karloff in which he played a mad doctor.

2805. Man to Man (WB; 1930). *Cast:* Phillips Holmes, Grant Mitchell, Lucille Powers, Barbara Weeks, Charles Sellon, Dwight Frye, Robert Emmett O'Connor, George F. Marion, Otis Harlan, Russell Simpson, James Hall, Paul Nicholson, Bill Banker. *D:* Allan Dwan; *St:* Ben Ames Williams; *Sc:* Joseph Jackson.

Low-budget melodrama of a young man forced to leave college after finding that his father is in prison for murder.

2806. A Man to Remember (RKO; 1938). *Cast:* Edward Ellis (Dr. Abbott), Anne Shirley, Lee Bowman, William Henry, Granville Bates, Dickie Jones, Gilbert Emery, John Wray, Harlan Briggs, Frank M. Thomas, Carol Leete, Joseph de Stephani, Charles Halton. *D:* Garson Kanin (directorial debut); *P:* Robert Sisk; *Sc:* Dalton Trumbo. (1:20)

Critically acclaimed small town drama of various people who remember a doctor and his deeds while attending his funeral. A surprise box office hit, it was a remake of *One Man's Journey* (q.v.). Based on the short story "The Failure" by Katharine Haviland-Taylor.

2807. The Man Trailer (Columbia; 1934). *Cast:* Buck Jones, Cecilia Parker, Arthur Vinton, Clarence Geldert, Steve Clark, Charles West, Tom Forman, Lew Meehan, Dick Botiller, Artie Ortego. *D:* Lambert Hillyer; *Sc:* Hillyer. (0:59)

Buck Jones western of a man on the run for a murder he didn't commit, who is blackmailed after becoming the town

sheriff. A remake of *Texas Gunfighter* (q.v.).

2808. Man Trouble (Fox; 1930). *Cast:* Dorothy Mackaill, Kenneth MacKenna, Sharon Lynn, Milton Sills, Oscar Apfel, Roscoe Karns, Paul Fix, Edythe Chapman. *D:* Berthold Viertel.

Light romantic comedy.

2809. Man Wanted (WB; 1932). *Cast:* Kay Francis, David Manners, Claire Dodd, Andy Devine, Una Merkel, Kenneth Thomson, Guy Kibbee, Edward Van Sloan, Robert Greig, Frank (Junior) Coghlan, Charlotte Merriam. *D:* William Dieterle; *St:* Robert Lord; *Adaptation:* Charles Kenyon. (1:00)

Marital comedy of a bored wife who becomes infatuated with her male secretary.

2810. The Man Who Broke the Bank at Monte Carlo (Fox; 1935). *Cast:* Ronald Colman, Joan Bennett, Colin Clive, Nigel Bruce, Montagu Love, Ferdinand Gottschalk, Frank Reicher, E.E. Clive, John Carradine (nee: John Peter Richmond), Lynn Bari, Lionel Pape. *D:* Stephen Roberts; *P:* Nunnally Johnson; *St:* Ilya Surgutchoff; *Sc:* Johnson, Howard Ellis Smith. (1:07)

A poor cab driver hits it big at the Monte Carlo casino. Based on a popular song of the time.

2811. The Man Who Came Back (Fox; 1930–31). *Cast:* Janet Gaynor, Charles Farrell, Kenneth MacKenna, William Holden, Mary Forbes, Peter Gawthorne, Henry Hull, Leslie Fenton, William Worthington, Ullrich Haupt. *D:* Raoul Walsh; *P:* Joseph Urban; *Sc:* Edwin J. Burke (based on the novel by John Fleming Wilson and the play by Jules Eckert Goodman). (1:14)

Hit romantic drama of a man, forced to evaluate his lifestyle after discovering that his girl friend is a drug addict. One of the 15 top grossing films of 1930–31. Previously filmed in 1924 by this studio with George O'Brien and Dorothy Mackaill.

2812. The Man Who Cried Wolf (Universal; 1937). *Cast:* Lewis Stone, Tom Brown, Barbara Read, Marjorie Main, Forrester Harvey, Robert Gleckler, Jameson Thomas, Jason Robards. *D:* Lewis R. Foster; *P:* E.M. Asher; *Sc:* Charles Grayson, Sy Bartlett. (1:06)
B drama of an actor who confesses to murders he didn't commit, while actually planning one of his own.

The Man Who Dared (1932) (G.B. title) *see* **Behind the Mask**

2813. The Man Who Dared (Fox; 1933). *Cast:* Preston Foster, Zita Johann, Joan Marsh, Frank Sheridan, Douglass Dumbrille, Leon (Ames) Waycoff, June (Lang) Vlasek, Matt McHugh, Leonid Snegoff, Clifford Jones, Jay Ward, Douglas Cosgrove, Irene Biller. *D:* Hamilton MacFadden; *St & Sc:* Dudley Nichols, Lamar Trotti. (1:15)
The story of the life of Mayor Anton Cermak of Chicago, killed by a bullet supposedly intended for Franklin D. Roosevelt in early 1933. Fact based.

2814. The Man Who Dared (WB; 1939). *Cast:* Charley Grapewin, Henry O'Neill, Dickie Jones, Jane Bryan, Elizabeth Risdon, James McCallion, Emmett Vogan. *D:* Crane Wilbur; *As.P.:* Bryan Foy; *St:* Lucien Hubbard; *Sc:* Lee Katz. (1:00)
A family witnesses a murder and their young son is kidnapped to prevent them from talking to the police in this B drama. A remake of *Star Witness* (q.v.), this version had the working title of "I Am Not Afraid."

2815. The Man Who Found Himself (RKO; 1937). *Cast:* John Beal, Joan Fontaine, Philip Huston, Jane Walsh, George Irving, Jimmy Conlin, Frank M. Thomas, Diana Gibson,

Dwight Frye, Edward Van Sloan, Billy Gilbert. *D:* Lew Landers; *P:* Cliff Reid; *Sc:* J. Robert Bren, Edmund L. Hartmann, Gladys (G.V.) Atwater, Thomas Lennon. (1:07)
B drama of a young surgeon who redeems himself by performance of an emergency operation. Based on the story "Wings of Mercy" by Alice F. Curtis.

2816. The Man Who Lived Twice (Columbia; 1936). *Cast:* Ralph Bellamy, Marian Marsh, Isabel Jewell, Thurston Hall, Nana Bryant, Ward Bond, Ann Doran, Willard Robertson. *D:* Harry Lachman; *P:* Ben Pivar; *St:* Tom Van Dycke, Henry Altimus; *Sc:* Fred Niblo, Jr., Van Dycke, Arthur Strawn. (1:13)
Following brain surgery, a killer undergoes a personality change. A B melodrama remade as *Man in the Dark* (Columbia; 1953).

2817. The Man Who Played God (WB; 1932). *Cast:* George Arliss (Montgomery Royale), Violet Heming (Mildred Miller), Bette Davis (Grace Blair—a role that made audiences take notice of Ms. Davis), Ivan Simpson (Battle), Andre Luguet (King), Louise Closser Hale (Florence Royale), Donald Cook (Harold Van Adam), Hedda Hopper (Alice Chittendon), Charles E. Evans (doctor), Oscar Apfel (lip reader), William Janney (boy in the park), Grace Durkin (girl in the park), Paul Porcasi (French concert manager), Ray Milland (Eddie), Dorothy Libaire (Jenny), Russell Hopton (reporter), Murray Kinnell (king's aide), Harry Stubbs (Chittendon), Wade Boteler (detective), Alexander Ikonikoff, Paul Panzer, Michael Visaroff, Fred Howard. *D:* John G. Adolfi; *Sc:* Julien Josephson, Maude Howell. (G.B. title: *The Silent Voice*) (1:23)
Drama of a pianist who is going deaf and the woman who sticks with him through thick and thin. A remake of the 1922 United Artists release of the same name with Arliss. One of the 15 top

grossing films of 1932, it was based on the story by Gouverneur Morris and the play adapted from it titled "The Silent Voice" by Jules Eckert Goodman. Remade in 1955 as *Sincerely Yours* by Warners.

2818. The Man Who Reclaimed His Head (Universal; 1934–35). *Cast:* Claude Rains, Joan Bennett, Lionel Atwill, Baby Jane (later Juanita Quigley), Henry O'Neill, Lawrence Grant, Wallace Ford, Henry Armetta, Gilbert Emery, Edward Van Sloan, Bessie Barriscale, Rollo Lloyd, Ferdinand Gottschalk, Hugh O'Connell. *D:* Edward Ludwig; *As.P.:* Henry Henigson; *Sc:* Jean Bart, Samuel Ornitz. (1:22)

Offbeat melodrama told in flashbacks of a man's reactions to various people when he finds he has been used by them. Based on the play by Jean Bart, it was remade as *Strange Confession* (Universal; 1945).

The Man with the Electric Voice (G.B. title) *see* **Fifteen Wives**

2819. The Man with Two Faces (WB/F.N.; 1934). *Cast:* Edward G. Robinson, Mary Astor, Ricardo Cortez, Mae Clarke, Louis Calhern, Arthur Byron, John Eldredge, David Landau, Emily Fitzroy, Henry O'Neill, Arthur Aylesworth, Margaret Dale, Virginia Sale, Bud Flanagan (Dennis O'Keefe). *D:* Archie Mayo; *P:* Robert Lord; *Sc:* Tom Reed, Niven Busch. (1:12)

Melodrama of an actor who goes after the man driving his sister to insanity. Based on the play "The Dark Tower" by George S. Kaufman and Alexander Woollcott.

2820. A Man's Castle (Columbia; 1933). *Cast:* Spencer Tracy, Loretta Young, Glenda Farrell, Walter Connolly, Marjorie Rambeau, Arthur Hohl, Dickie Moore. *D:* Frank Borzage; *Adaptation & Sc:* Jo Swerling. (1:15)

Based on the play by Lawrence Hazard, this drama deals with various down and outs who reside in a riverfront shanty town. TV prints may have some original footage missing.

2821. Man's Country (Monogram; 1938). *Cast:* Jack Randall, Marjorie Reynolds, Walter Long, Ralph Peters, Forrest Taylor, David Sharpe, Harry Harvey, Charles King, Bud Osborne, Dave O'Brien, Sherry Tansey, Ernie Adams. *D:* Robert Hill; *P:* Robert Tansey; *Sc:* Robert Emmett (Tansey). (0:53)

Jack Randall formula western.

2822. A Man's Game (Columbia; 1934). *Cast:* Tim McCoy, Evalyn Knapp, Ward Bond, Wade Boteler. *D:* D. Ross Lederman.

Low-budget action melodrama.

Man's Heritage (G.B. title) *see* **The Spirit of Culver**

2823. A Man's Land (Allied; 1932). *Cast:* Hoot Gibson, Marion Shilling, "Skeeter" Bill Robbins, Alan Bridge, Charles King, Ethel Wales, Robert Ellis, Hal Burney, William Nye, Merrill McCormack, Slim Whitaker. *D:* Phil Rosen; *P:* M.H. Hoffman, Jr.; *Sc:* Adele Buffington. (1:05)

Hoot Gibson western which involves a girl who wants to turn her spread into a dude ranch, but has her efforts hampered by cattle rustlers.

2824. Mandalay (WB/F.N.; 1933–34). *Cast:* Kay Francis (in a role originally intended for Ruth Chatterton), Ricardo Cortez, Warner Oland, Lyle Talbot, Ruth Donnelly, Lucien Littlefield, Reginald Owen, Etienne Girardot, David Torrence, Rafaela Ottiano, Halliwell Hobbes, Bodil Rosing, Herman Bing, Hobart Cavanaugh, Shirley Temple (unbilled bit). *D:* Michael Curtiz; *P:* Robert Presnell; *St:* Paul Hervey Fox; *Sc:* Austin Parker, Charles Kenyon. (1:05)

Hit B melodrama of gun-running and a woman with a past.

2825. The Mandarin Mystery (Republic; 1936). *Cast:* Eddie Quillan, Rita LaRoy, Charlotte Henry, Franklin Pangborn, Wade Boteler. *D:* Ralph Staub.

A low-budget "Ellery Queen" mystery based on the characters created by Manfred B. Lee and Frederick Dannay. Based on the book "The Chinese Orange Mystery."

Note: Another series of "Ellery Queen" mysteries was produced by Columbia between 1940 and 1942, four of which starred Ralph Bellamy and three starring William Gargan.

2826. Manhattan Butterfly (Imperial; 1935). *Cast:* William Bakewell, Dorothy Burgess, Kenneth Thomson, Carmelita Geraghty (her last film— ret.). *D:* Lewis D. Collins.

A low-budget independent romantic melodrama from "poverty row."

2827. Manhattan Love Song (Monogram; 1934). *Cast:* Robert Armstrong, Dixie Lee, Franklin Pangborn, Nydia Westman, Helen Flint, Cecil Cunningham, Harold Waldridge, Herman Bing, Harrison Greene, George Irving, Nick Copeland. *D:* Leonard Fields; *P:* Trem Carr; *Sc:* Fields, David Silverstein. (1:03)

B comedy-drama of financially depleted socialites whose domestics reside in their apartment because they are unable to pay their back wages. Based on the novel by Cornell Woolrich.

Manhattan Madness (G.B. title) *see* **Adventure in Manhattan**

Manhattan Mary *see* **Follow the Leader**

2828. Manhattan Melodrama (MGM; 1934). *Cast:* Clark Gable (Blackie Gallagher), William Powell (in his first film for this studio as Jim

Wade), Myrna Loy (Eleanor Packer), Leo Carrillo (Father Joe), Isabel Jewell (Annabelle), Nat Pendleton (Spud), George Sidney (Poppa Rosen), Thomas Jackson (Richard Snow), Muriel Evans (Tootsie Malone), Claudelle Kaye (Miss Adams), Frank Conroy (Blackie's attorney), Noel Madison (Mannie Arnold), Mickey Rooney (Blackie—age 12), Jimmy Butler (Jim—age 12), Samuel S. Hinds (prison warden), Wade Boteler (prison guard), Shirley Ross (singer at the Cotton Club), John Marston (Coates), Vernon Dent, Pat Moriarty, Leonid Kinskey, Edward Van Sloan, George Irving, Emmett Vogan, Lee Phelps, Sam McDaniel. *D:* W.S. Van Dyke; *P:* David O. Selznick; *Original Story:* (A.A.) Arthur Caesar; *Sc:* Oliver H.P. Garrett, Joseph L. Mankiewicz; *Song:* "The Bad in Every Man" by Richard Rodgers & Lorenz Hart (as introduced in this film, became better known at a later date as "Blue Moon"). (1:33)

Two friends orphaned by the burning of the excursion steamer "General Slocum" on the East River in 1904, grow up on opposite sides of the law. A big hit for the studio, it was reworked in 1942 as *Northwest Rangers* (MGM).

Note: Historically, this film is noted as the last one seen by public enemy #1, John Dillinger shortly before being shot to death by federal agents in front of Chicago's Biograph theater.

2829. Manhattan Merry-Go-Round (Republic; 1937). *Cast:* Phil Regan, Ann Dvorak, Leo Carrillo, James Gleason, Tamara Geva, Henry Armetta, Max Terhune, Smiley Burnette, Gene Autry, Cab Calloway & His Band, Jack Benny, Ted Lewis, Louis Prima & His Band, Joe DiMaggio, Eddie Kane, Gennaro Curci, Nellie V. Nichols, Rosalean, Kay Thompson & Her Radio Choir, Moroni Olsen, Selmer Jackson. *D:* Joseph Santley, Charles F. Reisner; *P:* Harry Sauber; *Sc:* Sauber; *St:* Frank Hummert; *Art-Set Decoration:* (A.A.N.) John Victor

MacKay. (G.B. title: *Manhattan Music Box*) (1:20) (video)

An A musical for this studio about a gangster who takes over a record company.

2830. Manhattan Moon (Universal; 1935). *Cast:* Ricardo Cortez, Dorothy Page, Jean Rogers, Henry Armetta. *D:* Stuart Walker (final film — ret.). (G.B. title: *Sing Me a Love Song*) (1:02)

B comedy with songs of a night club owner on the make for a singer in his club.

Manhattan Music Box (G.B. title) *see* **Manhattan Merry-Go-Round**

2831. Manhattan Parade (WB; 1931–32). *Cast:* Joe Smith, Charles Dale (better known as Smith & Dale as the producers), Winnie Lightner, Charles Butterworth, Luis Alberni (Russian director), Walter Miller, Greta Granstedt, Charles Middleton, Nat Pendleton, Bobby Watson, William Humphrey, Edward Van Sloan, Dickie Moore, Polly Walters, William Irving, Douglas Gerrard, Harold Waldridge, Frank Conroy, Ethel Griffies, Claire McDowell. *D:* Lloyd Bacon; *Sc:* Robert Lord, Houston Branch; *Songs:* Harold Arlen & others, include: "I Love a Parade," "Temporarily Blue," "I'm Happy When You're Jealous."

Two-color technicolor slapstick comedy with songs of two Broadway producers in conflict with their Russian director. Based on the play by Samuel Shipman.

2832. Manhattan Tower (Remington; 1932). *Cast:* James Hall, Mary Brian, Irene Rich, Nydia Westman. *D:* Frank Strayer.

"Poverty row" romance.

2833. Maniac (Hollywood Producers & Distributors; 1934). *Cast:* Bill Woods, Horace Carpenter, Ted Edwards, Thea Ramsey, Phyllis Diller (not "the"), Jennie Dark. *D:* Dwain Esper; *P:* Esper; *Sc:* Hildegarde Stadie (Mrs. Epser). (1:07) (video)

Ultra low-budget exploitation horror film (for adults only in its day) which goes out of its way to shock the viewing audience.

2834. Mannequin (MGM; 1937–38). *Cast:* Joan Crawford, Spencer Tracy, Alan Curtis, Ralph Morgan, Mary Philips, Oscar O'Shea, Elizabeth Risdon, Leo Gorcey, Paul Fix, Phillip Terry, George Chandler. *D:* Frank Borzage; *P:* Joseph L. Mankiewicz; *St:* Katherine Brush; *Sc:* Lawrence Hazard. (1:34) (video)

A rags-to-riches romance, a remake of the 1926 silent production with Dolores Costello.

2835. Manslaughter (Paramount; 1930). *Cast:* Claudette Colbert, Fredric March, Natalie Moorhead, Emma Dunn, Richard Tucker, Hilda Vaughn, Stanley Fields, Louise Beavers, George Pat Collins, Irving Mitchell, Gaylord (Steve) Pendleton, Ivan Simpson, Arnold Lucy. *D:* George Abbott; *Sc:* Abbott.

An updated talkie version of Cecil B. De Mille's 1922 silent classic which starred Leatrice Joy and Thomas Meighan of a woman who accidentally kills a man while behind the wheel of her car. Based on the book by Alice Duer Miller, filming took place at Paramount's Astoria Studio in Long Island, N.Y.

2836. Many a Slip (Universal; 1931). *Cast:* Lew Ayres, Joan Bennett, Ben Alexander, Slim Summerville, Virginia Sale, Roscoe Karns, J.C. Nugent. *D:* Vin Moore. (1:14)

A romantic comedy of supposed pregnancy. At the time of release, this film was considered detrimental to its star's popularity. Based on the play by Robert Riskin and Edith Fitzgerald.

2837. Many Happy Returns (Paramount; 1934). *Cast:* George Burns,

Gracie Allen, Joan Marsh, George Barbier, Ray Milland, Franklin Pangborn, William Demarest, Jack Mulhall, Kenneth Thomson, Johnny Arthur, Larry Adler, Morgan Wallace, Egon Brecher, John Kelly. *D:* Norman (Z.) McLeod; *St:* Lady Mary Cameron. (1:00)

B budget Burns and Allen farce with music by Guy Lombardo and His Royal Canadians, concerning another of Gracie's nitwit ideas.

March of the Wooden Soldiers *see* **Babes in Toyland**

2838. Marianne (MGM/Cosmopolitan; 1929). *Cast:* Marion Davies (talkie debut as Marianne), Lawrence Gray (Stagg), Cliff Edwards (Soapy), Benny Rubin (Sam), George Baxter (André), Scott Kolk (Lieut. Frane), Robert Edeson (general), Emile Chautard (Pere Joseph). *D:* Robert Z. Leonard; *P:* Marion Davies; *St:* Dale Van Every; *Dialogue:* Laurence Stallings, Gladys Unger; *Songs:* Roy Turk, Fred E. Ahlert; *Song Interpolations:* Jesse Greer, Raymond Klages, Nacio Herb Brown, Arthur Freed. (1:52)

Romantic comedy with songs of a company of doughboys billeted in the barn of a French girl following WWI, and the one she falls for.

2839. Marie Antionette (MGM; 1938). *Cast:* Norma Shearer (A.A.N. for B.A. and voted "Best Actress of the Year at the Venice Film Festival as Marie Anrionette), Tyrone Power (Count Axel de Fersen), John Barrymore (King Louis XV), Gladys George (Madame Du Barry), Robert Morley (A.A.N. for B.S.A. and an Acting Award from the National Board of Review in his film debut as King Louis XVI), Anita Louise (Princess DeLamballe), Joseph Schildkraut (Duke d'Orleans), Henry Stephenson (Count de Mercey), Cora Witherspoon (Countess de Noailles), Reginald Gardner (Artois), Peter Bull (Gamin), Albert Van Dekker (later as "Albert Dekker") (Provence), Barnett Parker (Prince DeRohan), Joseph Cal-

leia (Drouet), Henry Kolker (court aide), George Meeker (Robespierre), Marilyn Knowlden (Princess Theresa), Scotty Beckett (Dauphin), Alma Kruger (Maria Theresa), Henry Daniell (LaMotte), Ivan F. Simpson (Sauce), Leonard Penn (Toulan), George Zucco (governor of Conciergerie), Ian Wolfe (Herbert the jailer), John Burton (Lafayette), Mae Busch (Madame LaMotte), Cecil Cunningham (Madame DeLerchenfeld), Ruth Hussey (Madame LePolignac), Walter Walker (Benjamin Franklin), Claude King (Choisell), Herbert Rawlinson (Goguelot), Wade Crosby (Danton), George Houston (Marquis De St. Priest), Harry Davenport (de Cosse), Olaf Hytten (Boehmer the jeweler), Anthony Warde (Marat), Rafaela Ottiano (Louise), Robert Barrat, Horace McMahon, Holmes Herbert, Barry Fitzgerald, Victor Kilian. *D:* W.S. Van Dyke II; *P:* Hunt Stromberg; *Sc:* Claudine West, Donald Ogden Stewart, Ernest Vajda; *Art-Set Decoration:* (A.A.N.) Cedric Gibbons, William A. Horning, Edwin B. Willis; *Song:* "Amour Eternal Amour" by Bob Wright, Chet Forrest, Herbert Stothart; *Music:* (A.A.N.) Herbert Stothart. (2:29) (video)

The life and final days of King Louis XVI of France and his queen Marie Antionette are partially fictionalized historical drama with the full MGM treatment. The film partially based on the book by Stephen Zweig was in nomination for "Best Film" at the Venice Film Festival. On the "10 Best" list of *Film Daily* it placed #5.

2840. Marie Galante (Fox; 1934). *Cast:* Spencer Tracy, Ketti Gallian, Helen Morgan, Ned Sparks, Leslie Fenton, Jay C. Flippen (film debut), Sig Rumann, Stepin Fetchit, J. Carrol Naish, Arthur Byron, Frank Darien, Robert Lorraine, Tito Coral. *D:* Henry King; *P:* Winfield Sheehan; *St:* Jacques Deval; *Sc:* Samuel Hoffenstein (unc.), Reginald Berkeley, Seton I. Miller (unc.).

Romantic drama.

Marie Walewska (G.B. title) *see* Conquest (1937)

2841. Marihuana—The Devil's Weed (Road Show Productions; 1936–37). *Cast:* Harley Wood, Hugh McArthur, Pat Carlyle, Paul Ellis, Dorothy Dehr. *D:* Dwain Esper; *P:* Esper; *Sc:* Hildegarde Stadie (Mrs. Esper). (aka: *Marijuana* and *Marijuana, The Weed with Roots in Hell*) (0:58) (video)

Independent exploitive "warning" melodrama of the period centering on a woman who smokes the "devil's weed" and finds her life going downhill, eventually becoming a big-time dealer in drugs. A present day "camp" curiosity.

Marijuana *see* **Marihuana—The Devil's Weed**

Marijuana, the Weed with Roots in Hell *see* **Marihuana—The Devil's Weed**

2842. The Marines Are Coming (Mascot; 1934). *Cast:* William Haines (final film—ret.), Esther Ralston, Conrad Nagel, Armida, Edgar Kennedy, Hale Hamilton, George Regas, Broderick O'Farrell, Michael Visaroff, Del Henderson. *D:* David Howard; *St:* John Rathmell, Colbert Clark; *Sc:* James Gruen. (1:10)

A marine officer is kicked out of the corps and reenlists as a private.

2843. The Marines Are Here (Monogram; 1938). *Cast:* Gordon Oliver, June Travis, Ray Walker, Guinn Williams, Ronnie Cosbey, Billy Dooley, Pat Gleason, Edward Earle, Wade Boteler. *D:* Phil Rosen; *P:* Scott R. Dunlap; *St:* Edwin C. Parsons, Charles Logue; *Sc:* Jack Knapp, J. Benton Cheney. (1:00)

Following an attitude adjustment, a young marine comes through for his buddies when needed in this B production which *is not* a sequel to the preceding film.

The Marines Have Landed (G.B. title) *see* **The Leathernecks Have Landed**

2844. Mark of the Spur (Big 4; 1932). *Cast:* Bob Custer, Lillian Rich (final film—ret.), Lafe McKee, Franklyn Farnum, Bud Osborne, George Chesebro, Blackie Whiteford, Frank Ball. *D:* J.P. McGowan; *P:* John R. Freuler.

Bob Custer western.

2845. Mark of the Vampire (MGM; 1935). *Cast:* Lionel Barrymore, Elizabeth Allan, Bela Lugosi, Lionel Atwill, Jean Hersholt, Henry Wadsworth, Donald Meek, Jessie Ralph, Ivan Simpson, Franklyn Ardell, Leila Bennett, June Gittelson, Carol Borland, Holmes Herbert, Michael Visaroff. *D:* Tod Browning; *P:* E.J. Mannix; *St:* Bernard Schubert; *Sc:* Guy Endore, Schubert. (1:01) (video)

A police inspector and a vampire expert try to solve an unusual murder in this mystery-satire of horror films, previously filmed by the director in 1927 as *London After Midnight* with Lon Chaney.

2846. Marked Money (Pathé; 1928). *D:* Spencer Gordon Bennet.

Part-talkie melodrama originally released in 1928 with synchronised music and sound effects with a re-release in 1929 with passages of dialogue added.

2847. Marked Woman (WB/F.N.; 1937). *Cast:* Bette Davis (received a "Best Actress Award" at the Venice Film Festival for her role as Mary Dwight [Strauber] in combination with her role in *Kid Galahad* [q.v.]), Humphrey Bogart (David Graham), Jane Bryan (Betty Strauber), Eduardo Ciannelli (Johnny Vanning), Isabel Jewell (Emmy Lou Egan), Lola Lane (Gabby Marvin), Allen Jenkins (Louie), Rosalind Marquis (Florrie Liggett), Ben Welden (Charley Delaney), Henry O'Neill (D.A. Arthur Sheldon), Mayo Methot (Estelle Porter—in real-life the

3rd Mrs. Humphrey Bogart), John Litel (Gordon), Damian O'Flynn (Ralph Krawford), Robert Strange (George Beler), James "Archie" Robbins (bell captain), William B. Davidson (Bob Crandall), John Sheehan (Vincent, Sugar Daddy), Sam Wren (Mac), Kenneth Harlan (Eddie, Sugar Daddy), Guy Usher (Detective Ferguson), Ed Stanley (Detective Casey), Gordon Hart (judge), Arthur Aylesworth (Sheriff John Truble), Pierre Watkin (other judge), Raymond Hatton, Alan Davis, Allen Mathews, John Harron, Frank Faylen, Norman Willis, Ralph Dunn, Wilfred Lucas, Jack Norton, Carlyle Moore, Jr., Emmett Vogan, Jack Mower, Herman Marks (Little Joe). *D:* Lloyd Bacon; *As.P.:* Lou Edelman; *Sc:* Robert Rossen, Abem Finkel; *Song:* "My Silver Dollar Man" by Al Dubin & Harry Warren. (1:39) (video)

Fact based crime drama inspired by the trial of gangster Lucky Luciano as a woman's life is threatened after testifying against her boss, an underworld figure.

2848. The Marriage Bargain (Hollywood Exchange; 1935). *Cast:* Lon Chaney, Jr.

(No other information available)

2849. Marriage Forbidden (Grand National; 1938). *Cast:* Gretchen Thomas, Frank Melton, Arletta Duncan, Douglas Walton, Ferdinand Munier, Clarence Wilson, Pedro de Cordoba. *D:* Phil Goldstone; *P:* Goldstone; *Sc:* Upton Sinclair, Joseph Hoffman.

B production.

2850. Marriage Interlude (Xxxx Xxxx; 1931). (No information available)

2851. Marriage on Approval (Monarch; 1933). *Cast:* Barbara Kent, William Farnum, Clarence Geldert. *D:* Howard Higgin; *Sc:* Higgin (co-writer).

B romance.

2852. The Marriage Playground (Paramount; 1929). *Cast:* Kay Francis, Fredric March, Mary Brian, Lilyan Tashman, Huntley Gordon, Anita Louise, William Austin, David Newell, Seena Owen (final film as an actress), Jocelyn Lee, "Little Mitzi" Green (film debut), Philippe de Lacy, Maude Turner Gordon, Armand Kaliz, Joan Standing, Gordon DeMain, Donald Smith, Ruby Parsley, Billy Seay. *D:* Lothar Mendes; *Sc:* J. Walter Ruben, Doris Anderson. (1:10)

A romantic comedy of an American family in Europe. Based on the novel "The Children" by Edith Wharton.

The Marriage Symphony (G.B. title) *see* **Let's Try Again**

2853. Married Before Breakfast (MGM; 1937). *Cast:* Florence Rice, Robert Young, Hugh Marlowe, June Clayworth, Barnett Parker, Irene Franklin, Warren Hymer, Tom Kennedy, Mary Gordon, Jack Norton, Helen Flint, Edgar Dearing. *D:* Edwin L. Marin; *P:* Sam Zimbalist; *St:* Harry Ruskin; *Sc:* Everett Freeman, George Oppenheimer.

Offbeat B romantic comedy.

Married in Haste (G.B. title) *see* **Consolation Marriage**

2854. Married in Hollywood (Fox; 1929). *Cast:* J. Harold Murray, Norma Terris, John Garrick, Walter Catlett, Tom Patricola, Herman Bing, Douglas Gilmore, Jack Stambaugh, Lennox Pawle, Gloria Gray, Irene Palasty, Lelia Karnelly, Bert Sprotte, Paul Ralli, Evelyn Hall. *D:* Marcel Silver; *St:* Oskar Straus; *Sc:* Harlan Thompson.

Romantic comedy.

2855. Marry the Girl (WB; 1937). *Cast:* Hugh Herbert, Mary Boland, Carol Hughes, Mischa Auer, Frank McHugh, Allen Jenkins, Alan Mowbray, Tom Kennedy, Teddy Hart, Hugh O'Connell, Veda Ann Borg,

Arthur Aylesworth, Ann Doran, Dewey Robinson. *D:* William McGann; *P:* Harry Joe Brown; *St:* Edward Hope; *Sc:* Sig Herzig, Pat C. Flick, Tom Reed.

Screwball B comedy of match-making.

2856. Marrying Widows (Tower; 1934). *Cast:* Judith Allen, John Mack Brown, Minna Gombell. *D:* Sam Newfield.

"Poverty row" romance.

2857. Mars Attacks the World (Universal; 1938). *Cast:* Buster Crabbe, Jean Rogers, Charles Middleton, Frank Shannon, Donald Kerr, Beatrice Roberts, Wheeler Oakman, Kane Richmond, Montague Shaw. *D:* Ford Beebe, Robert F. Hill; *P:* Barney A. Sarecky; *St:* Alex Raymond; *Sc:* Wyndham Gittens, Norman S. Hall, Ray Trampe. (1:41) (video) (See also: *The Deadly Ray from Mars*)

Hit feature version of the serial "Flash Gordon's Trip to Mars."

2858. The Marshal of Mesa City (RKO; 1939–40). *Cast:* George O'Brien, Virginia Vale, Leon Ames, Henry Brandon, Harry Cording, Lloyd Ingraham, Slim Whitaker, Joe McGuinn, Mary Gordon, Frank Ellis, Carl Stockdale. *D:* David Howard; *P:* Bert Gilroy; *Sc:* Jack Lait, Jr. (1:02)

George O'Brien western with a "clean up the corrupt town" formula. A remake of *The Arizonian* (q.v.).

The Marx Brothers at the Circus *see* **At the Circus**

2859. Mary Burns, Fugitive (Paramount; 1935). *Cast:* Sylvia Sidney, Melvyn Douglas, Alan Baxter (film debut), Pert Kelton, Wallace Ford, Brian Donlevy, Esther Dale, Charles Waldron, Fuzzy Knight, Frank Sully, William Pawley, Ann Doran, Boothe Howard, Norman Willis, Frances Gregg, Ivan Miller, Kernan Cripps, William Ingersoll, Joe Twerp. *D:* William K. Howard; *P:* Walter Wanger; *St:* Gene Towne; *Sc:* Towne, Graham Baker, Louis Stevens. (1:24)

Hit melodrama of an innocent girl implicated in crime through her gangster boyfriend.

2860. Mary Jane's Pa (WB/F.N.; 1935). *Cast:* Guy Kibbee, Aline MacMahon, Tom Brown, Robert McWade, Nan Grey, Minor Watson, John Arledge, Carl Stockdale. *D:* William Keighley; *P:* Robert Presnell; *Sc:* Tom Reed, Peter Milne. (G.B. title: *Wanderlust*)

B comedy-drama of a man who leaves his family and responsibility behind only to return years later. Based on the play by Edith Ellis Furness and the novel derived from the play by Norman Way.

2861. Mary of Scotland (RKO; 1936). *Cast:* Katharine Hepburn (Mary Stuart), Fredric March (Earl of Bothwell), Florence Eldridge (Elizabeth I), Douglas Walton (Lord Darnley), John Carradine (David Rizzio), Moroni Olsen (John Knox), Alan Mowbray (Throckmorton), Donald Crisp (Huntley), Robert Barrat, Gavin Muir, Ian Keith, William Stack, Ralph Forbes, Frieda Inescort, David Torrence, Molly Lamont, Anita Colby, Jean Fenwick, Lionel Pape, Alec Craig, Mary Gordon, Monte Blue, Leonard Mudie, Brandon Hurst, Wilfred Lucas, D'Arcy Corrigan, Frank Baker, Cyril McLaglen, Doris Lloyd, Robert Warwick, Murray Kinnell, Lawrence Grant, Ivan Simpson, Nigel de Brulier, Barlowe Borland, Walter Byron, Wyndham Standing, Earle Foxe, Paul McAllister, Lionel Belmore, Gaston Glass, Neil Fitzgerald, Robert Watson. *D:* John Ford; *P:* Pandro S. Berman; *Sc:* Dudley Nichols. (2:03) (video)

A slice of royal English history set in the 16th-century as Mary Stuart of Scotland lays claim to the English throne and is eventually imprisoned and executed by order of Elizabeth I. Based on the play by Maxwell Anderson, this lavish production flopped at the box office.

2862. Mary Stevens, M.D. (WB; 1933). *Cast:* Kay Francis, Lyle Talbot, Una O'Connor, Glenda Farrell, Hobart Cavanaugh, Harold Huber, Thelma Todd, George Cooper. *D:* Lloyd Bacon; *P:* Hal Wallis; *St:* Virginia Kellogg; *Sc:* Rian James, Robert Lord.

Intense romantic drama of the trials and tribulations of a lady doctor.

2863. The Mask of Fu Manchu (MGM/Cosmopolitan; 1932). *Cast:* Boris Karloff (Dr. Fu Manchu), Lewis Stone (Nayland Smith), Karen Morley (Sheila), Charles Starrett (Terrence Granville), Myrna Loy (Fah Lo See), Jean Hersholt (Von Berg), Lawrence Grant (Sir Lionel Barton), David Torrence (McLeod). *D:* Charles Brabin, Charles Vidor (unc.); *Sc:* John Willard, Edgar Allan Woolf, Irene Kuhn. (1:12)

Lavishly produced thriller about an expedition to the tomb of Genghis Khan which is menaced by the infamous Dr. Fu Manchu. Based on the book by Sax Rohmer.

2864. Mason of the Mounted (Monogram; 1932). *Cast:* Bill Cody, Andy Shuford, Nancy Drexel, Jack Carlyle, Capt. Art Smith (Art Mix), John "Blackie" Whiteford, Nelson McDowell, James Marcus, Joe Dominguez, LeRoy Mason, Dick Dickinson, Frank Hall Crane, Jack Long, Earl Dwire, Gordon McGee. *D:* Harry Fraser; *P:* Trem Carr; *St & Sc:* Fraser. (0:58)

A Bill Cody northwestern of a Mountie out to get his man.

2865. Masquerade (Fox; 1929). *Cast:* Leila Hyams, Alan Birmingham, Clyde Cook, J. Farrell MacDonald. *D:* Russell J. Birdwell.

B romantic drama.

2866. The Masquerader (United Artists/Samuel Goldwyn; 1933). *Cast:* Ronald Colman (in a dual role — his final film for Goldwyn following a lawsuit), Elissa Landi, Halliwell Hobbes, Juliette Compton, Helen Jerome Eddy, David Torrence, Creighton Hale, Eric Wilton, Montague Shaw. *D:* Richard Wallace; *P:* Samuel Goldwyn; *Sc:* Howard Estabrook, Moss Hart. (1:17)

Drama of a man who impersonates his drug addicted cousin who is a member of the English Parliament. Based on the novel by Katherine Cecil Thurston and the play by John Hunter Booth, the film is a remake of the 1922 First National production with Guy Bates Post.

2867. Massacre (WB/F.N.; 1934). *Cast:* Richard Barthelmess, Ann Dvorak, Claire Dodd, Dudley Digges, Henry O'Neill, Clarence Muse, Robert Barrat, Arthur Hohl, Sidney Toler, Douglass Dumbrille, Charles Middleton, Tully Marshall, Wallis Clark, William V. Mong, DeWitt Jennings, Juliet Ware, James Eagles, Frank McGlynn, Sr., Agnes Narcha, Samuel S. Hinds, Philip Faversham, George Blackwood, Iron Eyes Cody (bit), Chief John Big Tree (bit). *D:* Alan Crosland; *P:* Robert Presnell; *St:* Robert Gessner; *Sc:* Ralph Block, Sheridan Gibney. (1:10)

A social commentary of an American Indian rodeo performer who returns to the reservation and battles against the exploitation of his people by whites.

2868. Master of Men (Columbia; 1933). *Cast:* Jack Holt, Fay Wray, Walter Connolly, Theodore von Eltz, Berton Churchill. *D:* Lambert Hillyer; *St:* Eugene Solow, Chester Erskine.

Low-budget romantic melodrama.

2869. Mata Hari (MGM; 1932). *Cast:* Greta Garbo (Mata Hari), Ramon Novarro (Lieut. Alexis Rosanoff), Lionel Barrymore (Gen. Serge Shubin), Lewis Stone (Andriani), C. Henry Gordon (Dubois), Karen Morley (Carlotta), Blanche Frederici (Sister Angelica),

Frank Reicher (cook-spy), Alec B. Francis (Major Caron), Edmund Breese (prison warden), Helen Jerome Eddy (Sister Genevieve), Sarah Padden (Sister Teresa), Harry Cording (Ivan), Gordon DeMain, Mischa Auer, Cecil Cunningham, Michael Visaroff, Roy Barcroft (film debut as an extra). *D:* George Fitzmaurice; *P:* Fitzmaurice; *Sc:* Benjamin Glazer, Doris Anderson, Leo Birinski, Gilbert Emery. (1:32)

Hit romantic story of the intrigues of the famous female spy of World War I. One of the 15 top grossing films of 1932. Another film of the same name was produced in 1985.

2870. The Match King (WB/ F.N.; 1932). *Cast:* Warren William (Paul Kroll), Lily Damita, Glenda Farrell, Harold Huber, Hardie Albright, John Wray, Claire Dodd, Spencer Charters, Alan Hale, Edmund Breese, Bodil Rosing, Alphonse Ethier. *D:* Howard Bretherton & William Keighley (in his directorial debut); *Sc:* Houston Branch, Sidney Sutherland. (1:20)

The wheeling and dealing in the affairs of a world famous manufacturer of safety matches. Loosely based on the life of Ivar Kreuger and the novel by Einar Thorvaldson.

2871. The Matrimonial Bed (WB; 1930). *Cast:* Frank Fay, Florence Eldridge, Lilyan Tashman, James Gleason, Beryl Mercer, Vivian Oakland, Arthur Edmund Carewe, Marion Byron, James Bradbury, Sr. *D:* Michael Curtiz; *Sc:* Harvey Thew, Seymour Hicks. (G.B. title: *A Matrimonial Problem*)

Comedy of a man with amnesia who is thought to be dead by his wife. Based on the French play by Yves Mirande and André Mouezy-Eon. Remade as *Kisses for Breakfast* (WB; 1941) with Dennis Morgan and Jane Wyatt.

A Matrimonial Problem (G.B. title) *see* **The Matrimonial Bed**

2872. Maybe It's Love (WB; 1930). *Cast:* Joan Bennett, Joe E. Brown, James Hall, Anders Randolf, Laura Lee, Stuart Erwin, George Bickel, Sumner Getchell, 1929 All-American Football Team. *D:* William Wellman; *Sc:* Joseph Jackson; *St:* Mark Canfield (Darryl F. Zanuck). (TV title: *Eleven Men and a Girl*)

College gridiron comedy with songs which was a hit for the studio.

2873. Maybe It's Love (WB/ F.N.; 1935). *Cast:* Ross Alexander, Gloria Stuart, Henry Travers, Frank McHugh, Ruth Donnelly, Helen Lowell, Joseph Cawthorn, Maude Eburne, J. Farrell MacDonald, Dorothy Dare, Philip Reed. *D:* William McGann; *P:* Harry Joe Brown; *Adaptation:* Lawrence Hazard; *Sc:* Jerry Wald, Harry Sauber.

Social drama of life among the impoverished of New York City. A remake of the 1929 part-talkie *Saturday's Children* (q.v.). Based on the 1926 play "Saturday's Children" by Maxwell Anderson, it was remade under that title in 1940.

2874. The Mayor of Hell (WB; 1933). *Cast:* James Cagney, Madge Evans, Frankie Darro, Allen Jenkins, Dudley Digges, Arthur Byron, Allen "Farina" Hoskins, Robert Barrat, Hobart Cavanaugh, Harold Huber, Dorothy Peterson, Mickey Bennett, George Offerman, Jr., Sidney Miller, Charles Cane, Edwin Maxwell. *D:* Archie Mayo; *St:* Islin Auster; *Sc:* Edward Chodorov. (1:20)

Offbeat melodrama of the new superintendent of a boys reformatory. Rehashed as *Crime School* (q.v.) and remade as *Hell's Kitchen* (q.v.).

2875. Maytime (MGM; 1937). *Cast:* Jeanette MacDonald (Marcia Mornay — Miss Morrison), Nelson Eddy (Paul Allison), John Barrymore (replacing Paul Lukas as Nicolai Nazaroff), Herman Bing (replacing Frank Morgan as Archipenko), Rafaela Ottiano (Ellen), Sig Rumann (Fanchon), Lynne Carver (film debut as Barbara),

Tom Brown (Kip), Charles Judels (Cabby), Guy Bates Post (Louis Napoleon), Anna Demetrio (Madame Fanchon), Walter Kingsford (Rudyard), Paul Porcasi (Trentini), Iphigenie Castiglioni (Empress Eugenie), Frank Puglia (orchestra conductor), Edgar Norton (secretary), Adia Kuznetzoff, Joan Le Sueur (film debut), Russell Hicks, Harry Davenport, Harry Hayden, Howard Hickman, Robert C. Fischer, Harlan Briggs, Frank Sheridan, Billy Gilbert, Ivan Lebedeff, Leonid Kinskey, Clarence Wilson, Maurice Cass, Douglas Wood, Bernard Suss, Henry Rocquemore, Alexander Schonberg, Mariska Aldrich, Don Cossack Chorus. *D:* Robert Z. Leonard; *P:* Leonard, Hunt Stromberg; *Sc:* Noel Langley; *Music:* (A.A.N.) Herbert Stothart: *Sound Recording:* (A.A.N.) Douglas Shearer; *Songs:* "Sweetheart (Will You Remember?)," "Maytime Finale" by Sigmund Romberg & Rida Johnson Young; "Virginia Ham and Eggs," "Vive L'Opera" by Herbert Stothart, Bob Wright & Chet Forrest; "The Student Drinking Song" by Stothart; "Carry Me Back to Old Virginny" by James A. Bland: "Czaritza" based on Tchiakovsky's Fifth Symphony with libretto by Wright & Forrest; "Reverie" based on Romberg airs, "Jump Jim Crow," "Dancing Will Keep You Young" and "Road to Paradise" by Young, Cyrus Wood & Romberg; "Maypole" by Ed Ward; and "Street Singer" by Wright, Forrest & Stothart. (2:12) (video)

The classic 1917 operetta by Rida Johnson Young and Sigmund Romberg of two singers who briefly meet and fall in love only to shortly thereafter go their separate ways. The film began production in technicolor with Edmund Goulding directing, only to cease production with the death of MGM production head Irving Thalberg. It later resumed production in black and white with various changes. One of the 38 top grossing films of 1936–37 and a major hit all over the world.

2876. McFadden's Flats (Paramount; 1935). *Cast:* Walter C. Kelly, Andy Clyde, Richard Cromwell, Phyllis Brooks, Jane Darwell, Betty Furness, Nella Walker, Mary Forbes, George Barbier, Frederick Burton, Anna Demetrio, Pat Moriarty, Howard Wilson, Jerry Mandy, Joe Barton, Esther Michaelson. *D:* Ralph Murphy; *P:* Charles R. Rogers; *St:* Gus Hill; *Sc:* Arthur Caesar, Edward Kaufman; *Adapt.:* Casey Robinson; *Additional Dial.:* Andy Rice.

Low-budget comedy, a remake of the 1927 silent production of the same name, of the offspring of two old men, forever at odds with each other, who fall in love.

2877. McKenna of the Mounted (Columbia; 1932). *Cast:* Buck Jones, Greta Granstedt, James Flavin, Walter McGrail, Niles Welch, Mitchell Lewis, Claude King, Glenn Strange, Bud Osborne, Edmund Cobb. *D:* D. Ross Lederman; *Sc:* Stuart Anthony. (1:06)

A Buck Jones actioner of the Royal Canadian Mounted Police.

2878. Me and My Gal (Fox; 1932). *Cast:* Spencer Tracy, Joan Bennett, George Walsh, Marion Burns, J. Farrell MacDonald, Noel Madison, Henry B. Walthall, George Chandler, Bert Hanlon, Adrian Morris. *D:* Raoul Walsh; *St:* Philip Klein; *Sc:* Arthur Kober, Barry Conners. (G.B. title: *Pier 13*) (1:19)

Comedy-melodrama of a cop and a waitress who get involved with gangsters. Remade in 1940 as *Pier 13* with Lloyd Nolan and Lynn Bari.

2879. The Meanest Gal in Town (RKO; 1934). *Cast:* ZaZu Pitts, Pert Kelton, Skeets Gallagher, El Brendel, James Gleason, Edward McWade, Arthur Hoyt, Morgan Wallace, Wallis Clark, John Peter Richmond (John Carradine). *D:* Russell Mack; *As.P.:* H.N. Swanson; *St:* Arthur T. Horman; *Sc:* Mack, Richard Schayer, H.W. Hanemann. (1:07)

A low-budget small town romantic comedy farce.

Medals (G.B. title) *see* **Seven Days Leave**

2880. The Medicine Man (Tiffany; 1930). *Cast:* Jack Benny, Betty Bronson, George E. Stone, Eva Novak, E. Alyn Warren, Billy Butts, Adolph Milar, Tommy Dugan. *D:* Scott Pembroke. (1:06) (video)
"Poverty row" melodrama.

2881. Meet Dr. Christian (RKO/Stephens-Lang; 1939). *Cast:* Jean Hersholt (who also appeared on the radio show as Dr. Christian), Dorothy Lovett (Nurse Judy), Robert Baldwin, Enid Bennett, Paul Harvey, Marcia Mae Jones, Jackie Moran, Frank (Junior) Coghlan, Maude Eburne, John Kelly, Patsy Lee Parsons, Sarah Edwards. *D:* Bernard Vorhaus; *P:* William Stephens; *St:* Harvey Gates; *Sc:* Gates, Ring Lardner, Jr., Ian McLellan Hunter. (1:03) (video)
Premiere entry in a series of six low-budget films of a country doctor who solves everybody's problems. A popular series of its day, followed in 1940 by *The Courageous Dr. Christian*. Based on the popular radio soap opera of the 1930s.

2882. Meet Nero Wolfe (Columbia; 1936). *Cast:* Edward Arnold, Lionel Stander, Joan Perry, Victor Jory, Nana Bryant, Walter Kingsford, Rita (Hayworth) Cansino, John Qualen, Dennie Moore, Boyd Irwin, Frank Conroy, Gene Morgan. *D:* Herbert Biberman; *P:* B.P. Schulberg; *Sc:* Howard J. Green, Bruce Manning, Joseph Anthony. (1:13)
Premiere film effort to bring Rex Stout's rotund detective to the screen. Based on Stout's "Fer de Lance," the low-budget film was a hit for the studio and dealt with a case of two seemingly unrelated murders.

2883. Meet the Baron (MGM; 1934). *Cast:* Jack Pearl (a popular radio star of the day portraying Baron Munchausen), Jimmy Durante, ZaSu Pitts, Ted Healy & His Stooges (Moe Howard, Jerry "Curly" Howard, Larry Fine), Edna May Oliver, Henry Kolker, William B. Davidson, Greta Meyer, Ben Bard, Fred "Snowflake" Toones. *D:* Walter Lang; *P:* David O. Selznick; *St:* Norman Krasna, Herman J. Mankiewicz; *Sc:* Allen Rivkin, P.J. Wolfson, Arthur Kober, William K. Wells; *Songs:* Jimmy McHugh & Dorothy Fields. (1:06)
A comedy with songs which the studio didn't find humorous after it flopped at the box office.

2884. Meet the Boyfriend (Republic; 1937). *Cast:* Carol Hughes, David Carlyle (Robert Paige), Gwili Andre, Warren Hymer, Smiley Burnette, Leonid Kinskey, Andrew Tombes, Selmer Jackson, Mary Gordon. *D:* Ralph Staub.
B romantic comedy.

2885. Meet the Girls (20th Century–Fox; 1938). *Cast:* Lynn Bari, June Lang, Erik Rhodes, Gene Lockhart, Robert Allen, Ruth Donnelly, Paul McVey, Wally Vernon, Jack Norton, Harlan Briggs, Constantine Romanoff, Emmett Vogan. *D:* Eugene Forde; *P:* Sol M. Wurtzel; *As.P.:* Howard Green; *Sc:* Marguerite Roberts.
B comedy, the first of two in the proposed "Big Town Girls" series of two chorus girls who lose their jobs and stowaway on a ship. Following the unpopular second entry in the series *Pardon Our Nerve* (q.v.), the series was discontinued.

2886. Meet the Mayor (Sterling/ Times Pictures; 1933–38). *Cast:* Frank Fay, Ruth Hall, Eddie Nugent, Nat Pendleton, George Meeker, Franklin Pangborn, Berton Churchill. *D:* Ralph Cedar; *P:* Frank Fay; *St:* Fay.
B comedy which was produced in 1933 with release held up until 1938.

2887. Meet the Missus (RKO; 1937). *Cast:* Victor Moore, Helen Broderick, Anne Shirley, Alan Bruce, Edward H. Robins, William Brisbane, Frank M. Thomas, Ray Mayer, Ada Leonard, George Irving, Alec Craig, Willie Best, Virginia Sale, Jack Norton. *D:* Joseph Santley; *P:* Albert Lewis; *St:* Jack Goodman, Albert Rice; *Sc:* Jack Townley, Bert Granet, Joel Sayre. (1:01)

B comedy spoof of a woman's passion for entering contests which confounds her loving husband until she becomes a finalist in the "Happy Noodles" contest.

2888. Meet the Wife (Columbia; 1931). *Cast:* Harry Myers, Laura La Plante, Lew Cody, Claud Allister. *D:* A. Leslie Pearce.

Low-budget comedy.

2889. Melody Cruise (RKO; 1933). *Cast:* Charles Ruggles, Phil Harris, Helen Mack, Greta Nissen, Chick Chandler, June Brewster, Shirley (Ross) Chambers, Florence Roberts, Marjorie Gateson, Betty Grable. *D:* Mark Sandrich (feature directorial debut); *As.P.:* Lou Brock; *Sc:* Sandrich, Ben Holmes; *Songs:* Will Jason, Val Burton. (1:16) (video)

Hit musical-comedy farce of a debonair ladies man and his various romantic escapades on a steamship bound for California from New York.

2890. Melody for Two (WB; 1937). *Cast:* Patricia Ellis, James Melton (final film), Marie Wilson, Fred Keating, Winifred Shaw (final film — ret.), Dick Purcell, Eddie "Rochester" Anderson, Gordon Hart, Harry Hayden, Craig Reynolds, Eddie Kane, Gordon (Bill) Elliott, Charles Foy, Donald O'Connor (film debut — bit). *D:* Louis King; *P:* Bryan Foy; *St:* Richard Macaulay; *Sc:* George Bricker, Luci Ward, Joe K. Watson; *Songs:* "September in the Rain" and the title song by Al Dubin & Harry Warren; "A Flat in Manhattan," "An Excuse for Dancing," & "Jose O'Neill the Cuban Heel" by M.K. Jerome & Jack Scholl.

B romance of a cranky bandleader who is bitten by the love bug and reforms.

2891. Melody in Spring (Paramount; 1934). *Cast:* Charles Ruggles, Lanny Ross, Ann Sothern, Mary Boland, Wade Boteler, George Meeker, Herman Bing, Norma Mitchell, Thomas Jackson, William Irving, Helen Lynd. *D:* Norman Z. McLeod; *St:* Frank Leon Smith; *Sc:* Benn Levy; *Songs:* Harlan Thompson, Lewis Gensler. (1:15)

A romantic comedy which was designed as a musical showcase for radio singer Lanny Ross.

2892. Melody Lane (Universal; 1929). *Cast:* Eddie Leonard, Josephine Dunn, Huntley Gordon, Jane LaVerne, George E. Stone. *D:* Robert F. Hill; *Sc:* Hill, J.G. Hawks; *Songs:* "Roly Poly Eyes" by Eddie Leonard; "The Song of the Islands" by Charles King; "Here I Am," "There's Sugar Cane 'Round My Door" & "The Boogey Man Is Here" by Eddie Leonard, Grace & Jack Stern.

Romantic drama with songs of married vaudevillians who decide to go their separate ways. The first all-talkie musical by this studio, it is based on the play "The Understander" by Jo Swerling.

2893. The Melody Lingers On (United Artists/Reliance; 1935). *Cast:* Josephine Hutchinson, George Houston (film debut), Helen Westley, Laura Hope Crews, David Scott, Mona Barrie, William Harrigan, Walter Kingsford, Ferdinand Gottschalk, John Halliday, Grace Poggi, Marion Ballou, Frank Puglia, Francisco Maran, Gennaro Curci, Inez Palange, Eily Malyon. *D:* David Burton; *P:* Edward Small; *Sc:* Ralph Block, Philip Dunne.

A drama with operatic music of a piano virtuoso who has an illegitimate child after a fling with an Italian army officer. Based on the novel by Lowell Brentano.

2894. The Melody Man (Columbia; 1930). *Cast:* William Collier, Jr., Alice Day, Johnny Walker, John St. Polis. *D:* Roy William Neill.

Low-budget musical production based on a play by Herbert Fields and Richard Rodgers.

Melody of Life (G.B. title) *see* **Symphony of Six Million**

2895. Melody of Love (Universal; 1928). *Cast:* Walter Pidgeon, Mildred Harris, Jane Winton, Tommy Dugan, Jack Richardson, Victor Potel, Flynn O'Malley. *D:* A.B. Heath; *Sc:* Robert Arch. (aka: *Madelon*) (1:30 approx.)

Drama of a song writer who loses the use of one arm in World War I, only to regain it when he realizes the woman he really loves. Filmed in one week, this is notable as this studio's first all-talkie.

2896. Melody of the Plains (Spectrum; 1937). *Cast:* Fred Scott, Louise Small, Al St. John, Hal Price, Lew Meehan, Slim Whitaker, David Sharpe, Lafe McKee, Bud Jamison, Carl Mathews, George Fiske, George Morrell. *D:* Sam Newfield; *P:* Jed Buell; *Sc:* Bennett Cohen. (0:55)

Fred Scott western with songs of a cowboy who believes he killed the son of a rancher.

Melody of Youth (G.B. title) *see* **They Shall Have Music**

2897. Melody Trail (Republic; 1935). *Cast:* Gene Autry, Smiley Burnette, Ann Rutherford, Wade Boteler, Willy Costello, Alan Bridge, Fern Emmett, Marie Quillan, Gertrude Messinger, Tracy Layne, Abe Lefton, George DeNormand, Jane Barnes, Ione Reed, Maryan Downing, Buck the dog, Champion. *D:* Joseph Kane; *P:* Nat Levine; *St:* Betty Burbridge, Sherman Lowe; *Sc:* Lowe. (1:00) (video)

Gene Autry western with songs of a ranch that hires female ranchhands after the men quit.

The Memory Expert (G.B. title) *see* **The Man on the Flying Trapeze**

2898. Men Are Like That (Paramount; 1929–30). *Cast:* Hal Skelly, Doris Hill, Charles Sellon, Clara Blandick, Morgan Farley, Helene Chadwick, William Davidson, Eugene Pallette George Fawcett. *D:* Frank Tuttle; *Sc:* Marion Dix; *Adapt.:* Herman J. Mankiewicz.

Hit comedy of a neer-do-well. A remake of *The Show-Off* (Paramount; 1926), with Ford Sterling, it was based on the popular stage hit of that name of 1924 by George Kelly (an uncle to Grace Kelly—later Princess Grace of Monaco), adapted by him from an earlier novel by William Wolff. Twice remade as *The Show-Off* by MGM, in 1934 (q.v.) and 1946.

Men Are Like That (1931) (G.B. title) *see* **Arizona**

2899. Men Are Such Fools (RKO/Jefferson Pictures; 1932). *Cast:* Vivienne Osborne, Leo Carrillo, Earle Foxe, Una Merkel, Joseph Cawthorn, Tom Moore, J. Farrell MacDonald, Paul Hurst, Albert Conti, Lester Lee, Donald Briggs, Eddie Nugent. *D:* William Nigh; *P:* Joseph I. Schnitzer; *St:* Thomas Lloyd Lennon; *Sc:* Viola Brothers (Shore).

Independent romantic drama of expectation which ends in murder.

2900. Men Are Such Fools (WB; 1938). *Cast:* Wayne Morris, Priscilla Lane, Humphrey Bogart, Hugh Herbert, Johnnie Davis, Penny Singleton, Mona Barrie, Marcia Ralston, Gene Lockhart, Claud Allister, Carole Landis, Nedda Harrigan, Eric Stanley, Renie Riano. *D:* Busby Berkeley; *As.P.:* David Lewis; *Sc:* Norman Reilly Raine, Horace Jackson. (1:09)

A married woman wants to become a singer and leave her husband in this marital drama based on the Saturday Evening Post story by Faith Baldwin.

2901. Men Call It Love (MGM; 1931). *Cast:* Adolphe Menjou, Leila Hyams, Mary Duncan, Hedda Hopper, Norman Foster, Robert Emmett Keane, Harry Northrup. *D:* Edgar Selwyn; *St:* Vincent Lawrence; *Sc:* Doris Anderson.

Low-budget romantic comedy.

2902. Men in Exile (WB/F.N.; 1937). *Cast:* Dick Purcell, June Travis, Alan Baxter, Margaret Irving, Victor Varconi, Olin Howland, Veda Ann Borg. *D:* John Farrow (directorial debut); *P:* Bryan Foy; *St:* Marie Baumer, Houston Branch; *Sc:* Roy Chanslor.

B action melodrama of an island dictator who combats gun-runners in his domain.

2903. Men in Her Life (Columbia; 1931). *Cast:* Lois Moran, Charles Bickford, Gilbert Roland, Victor Varconi, Donald Dillaway, Oscar Apfel, Barbara Weeks, Adrienne D'Ambricourt, Wilson Benge, Hooper Atchley. *D:* William Beaudine; *St:* Warner Fabian; *Sc:* Fabian, Robert Riskin; *Adapt. & Dial.:* Robert Riskin; *Cont.:* Dorothy Howell.

Low-budget romantic comedy.

2904. Men in White (MGM; 1934). *Cast:* Clark Gable, Myrna Loy, Jean Hersholt, Elizabeth Allan, Otto Kruger, Wallace Ford, C. Henry Gordon, Henry B. Walthall, Samuel S. Hinds, Berton Churchill, Russell Hardie, Russell Hopton, Frank Puglia, Donald Douglas, Leo Chalzel. *D:* Richard Boleslawski; *P:* Monta Bell; *Sc:* Waldemar Young. (1:20)

Hit hospital drama of its day. Based on the play by Sidney Kingsley.

2905. Men Must Fight (MGM; 1933). *Cast:* Diana Wynyard, Lewis Stone, Phillips Holmes, May Robson, Ruth Selwyn, Robert Young, Robert Greig, Hedda Hopper, Donald Dillaway, Mary Carlisle, Luis Alberni. *D:* Edgar Selwyn; *Sc:* C. Gardner Sullivan. (1:13)

Pacifism vs. patriotism in a futuristic look at 1940, as war comes to the United States, climaxing with an air attack on New York City. Based on the play by S.K. Lauren and Reginald Lawrence.

2906. Men of Action (Ambassador; 1935). *Cast:* Frankie Darro, Roy (LeRoy) Mason, Barbara Worth, Roger Williams, Arthur Hoyt, John Ince. *D:* Xxxx Xxxx; *P:* Maurice Conn; *St:* Peter B. Kyne.

Low-budget juvenile actioner.

2907. Men of America (RKO; 1932). *Cast:* Bill Boyd, Charles "Chic" Sale, Dorothy Wilson, Ralph Ince, Henry Armetta, Alphonse Ethier, Theresa Maxwell Conover, Eugene Strong, Fatty Layman, Fred Lindstrand, Frank Mills. *D:* Ralph Ince; *As.P.:* Pandro S. Berman; *St:* Humphrey Pearson, Henry McCarty; *Sc:* Samuel Ornitz, Jack Jungmeyer. (G.B. title: *The Great Decision*) (0:57)

Modern low-budget western of small-towners who are forced to defend their homes against a group of wanted criminals.

2908. Men of Chance (RKO; 1931–32). *Cast:* Ricardo Cortez, Mary Astor, Ralph Ince, John Halliday, Kitty Kelly, James Donlan, George Davis. *D:* George Archainbaud; *As.P.:* Pandro S. Berman; *St:* Louis Weitzenkorn; *Sc:* Louis Stevens, Wallace Smith. (1:07)

B melodrama of a gambler and his girl who become victims of their own under-handedness.

Men of Steel (G.B. title) *see* **Bill Cracks Down**

2909. Men of the Hour (Columbia; 1935). *Cast:* Richard Cromwell, Wallace Ford, Wesley Barry, Charles C. Wilson. *D:* Lambert Hillyer.

Low-budget story of news photographers.

2910. Men of the Night (Columbia; 1934). *Cast:* Bruce Cabot, Judith

Allen, Ward Bond, Matthew Betz, Lucille Ball (bit). *D:* Lambert Hillyer; *St & Sc:* Hillyer.

B melodrama.

2911. Men of the North (MGM/Hal Roach; 1930). *Cast:* Gilbert Roland, Barbara Leonard, Nena Quartero, Arnold Korff, Robert Elliott. *D:* Hal Roach; *P:* Roach; *Sc:* Richard Schayer, Willard Mack. (1:01)

Northwest Mounted Police adventure which was originally filmed in five languages, English, German, French, Spanish and Italian.

2912. Men of the Plains (Colony; 1936). *Cast:* Rex Bell, Joan Barclay, George Ball, Charles King, Forrest Taylor, Roger Williams, Ed Cassidy, Lafe McKee, Jack Cowell. *D:* Bob Hill; *P:* Max & Arthur Alexander; *Sc:* Robert Emmett. (1:03)

Rex Bell western of a government agent sent to investigate the theft of some gold shipments.

2913. Men of the Sky (WB/F.N.; 1931). *Cast:* Irene Delroy, Jack Whiting, John St. Polis, Frank McHugh, Edwin Maxwell, Otto Matiesen, Lotti Loder, John Loder. *D:* Alfred E. Green; *Sc:* Jerome Kern, Otto Harbach; *Songs:* Kern & Harbach include "Every Little While," "Boys March," "Stolen Dreams" & "You Ought to See Sweet Marguerite."

World War musical-drama of the love affair of an American flyer and a female spy which ends tragically.

2914. Men on Call (Fox; 1931). *Cast:* Edmund Lowe, Mae Clarke, Warren Hymer, Sharon Lynn, William Harrigan. *D:* John G. Blystone.

Low-budget service drama.

Men on Her Mind (G.B. title) *see* **The Girl from 10th Avenue**

Men with Steel Faces *see* **Radio Ranch**

2915. Men with Wings (Paramount; 1938). *Cast:* Fred MacMurray, Ray Milland, Louise Campbell, Andy Devine, Walter Abel, Lynne Overman, Porter Hall, Virginia Weidler, Donald O'Connor, Evelyn Keyes, Willard Robertson, Joan (Leslie) Brodel, Billy Cook, Richard Stanley (Dennis Morgan), James Burke, Marilyn Knowlden, Juanita Quigley, Russ Clark, Dorothy Tennant. *D:* William Wellman; *P:* Wellman; *Sc:* Robert Carson. (1:46)

Technicolor aviation drama.

2916. Men Without Law (Columbia; 1930). *Cast:* Buck Jones, Tom Carr, Carmelita Geraghty, Lydia Knott, Harry Woods, Fred Burns, Fred Kelsey, Syd Saylor, Lafe McKee, Ben Corbett, Art Mix. *D:* Louis King; *P:* Sol Lesser; *Sc:* Dorothy Howell. (1:00)

Buck Jones western with musical interludes of a World War I vet who returns to find things are different than when he left.

2917. Men Without Names (Paramount; 1935). *Cast:* Fred MacMurray, Madge Evans, Lynne Overman, Dean Jagger, Herbert Rawlinson, John Wray, Grant Mitchell, Elizabeth Patterson, Paul Fix, Leslie Fenton, J.C. Nugent, Hilda Vaughn, Frank Shannon, Harry Tyler, Helen Shipman, George Lloyd, Clyde Dilson. *D:* Ralph Murphy; *P:* Albert Lewis; *St:* Dale Van Every; *Sc:* Kubec Glasmon, Howard Green, Marguerite Roberts.

B crime melodrama of government agents on the trail of the bad guys.

2918. Men Without Women (Fox; 1930). *Cast:* Kenneth MacKenna, Frank Albertson, Paul Page, Pat Somerset, Stuart Erwin, Warren Hymer, John Wayne, J. Farrell MacDonald, Roy Stewart, Robert Parrish, Ben Hendricks, (Jr.), Warner Richmond, Walter McGrail, Charles Gerrard, George LeGuere, Harry Tenbrook. *D:* John Ford; *Sc:* Dudley Nichols. (1:17)

When a submarine sinks to the bottom of the ocean, her crew members are trapped inside. This film drama based on the story "Submarine" by James Kevin McGuinness and John Ford was voted one of the year's "10 Best" films of the National Board of Review.

Men Women Love (G.B. title) *see* **Salvation Nell**

2919. Menace (Paramount; 1934). *Cast:* Paul Cavanagh, Gertrude Michael, Henrietta Crosman, John Lodge, Ray Milland, Berton Churchill, Halliwell Hobbes, Robert Allen, Montagu Love, Desmond Roberts, Forrester Harvey, Gwenllian Gill, Arletta Duncan, Doris Llewellyn. *D:* Ralph Murphy; *St:* Philip MacDonald; *Sc:* Chandler Sprague, Anthony Veiller. (0:58)
B thriller of a killer stalking residents of an old dark house.

2920. The Menace (Columbia; 1932). *Cast:* H.B. Warner, Bette Davis, Walter Byron, Natalie Moorhead, William B. Davidson, Crauford Kent, Halliwell Hobbes, Charles Gerrard, Murray Kinnell. *D:* Roy William Neill. (1:04)
A man seeks vengeance on his stepmother after she frames him for his father's murder. Based on a story by Edgar Wallace.

2921. Mercy Plane (Producer's Distributing Corporation; 1939). *Cast:* James Dunn, Frances Gifford, Matty Fain, William Pawley, Harry Harvey, Sr., Forbes Murray, Edwin Miller, Duke York. *D:* Richard Harlan (his only film as director); *P:* Ben Judell; *Sc:* William Lively. (G.B. title: *Wonder Plane*) (1:12)
Low-budget drama of the invention of a new kind of flying machine.

2922. Merely Mary Ann (Fox; 1931). *Cast:* Janet Gaynor, Charles Farrell, Beryl Mercer, J.M. Kerrigan, G.P. Huntley, Jr., Arnold Lucy, Lorna Balfour, Thomas Whiteley. *D:* Henry King; *Sc:* Jules Furthman.

Romantic comedy-drama, a remake of the 1916 production from this studio by director John Adolfi. Based on the play by Israel Zangwill.

Merrily We Go To ____ (G.B. title) *see* **Merrily We Go to Hell**

2923. Merrily We Go to Hell (Paramount; 1932). *Cast:* Sylvia Sidney, Fredric March, Adrienne Allen (American debut), Richard "Skeets" Gallagher, Florence Britton, Esther Howard, Kent Taylor, Milla Davenport, Mildred Boyd, Cary Grant (bit), George Irving, Leonard Carey, Robert Greig, Rev. Neal Dodd. *D:* Dorothy Arzner; *Sc:* Edwin Justus Mayer. (G.B. title: *Merrily We Go To ____*) (1:18)
After their marriage, a woman discovers the fact that her husband is an alcoholic. Based on the novel "I, Jerry Take Thee, Joan" by Cleo Lucas.

2924. Merrily We Live (MGM/Hal Roach; 1938). *Cast:* Constance Bennett, Brian Aherne, Alan Mowbray, Billie Burke (A.A.N. for B.S.A.), Bonita Granville, Patsy Kelly, Ann Dvorak, Tom Brown, Marjorie Rambeau, Clarence Kolb, Philip Reed, Willie Best, Paul Everton, Sidney Bracey, Marjorie Kane. *D:* Norman Z. McLeod; *As.P.:* Milton H. Bren; *Sc:* Eddie Moran, Jack Jevne; *Cinematographer:* (A.A.N.) Norbert Brodine; *A.D.:* (A.A.N.) Charles D. Hall; *Title Song:* (A.A.N. for Best Song) Phil Craig, Arthur Quenzer; *Sound Recording:* (A.A.N.) Elmer Raguse. (1:30)
Another of those classic screwball comedies of the late 1930s as a famous writer, posing as a tramp is hired as a domestic in a nutty household.

2925. The Merry Frinks (WB/F.N.; 1934). *Cast:* Aline MacMahon (Mrs. Frink), Hugh Herbert, Guy Kibbee, Allen Jenkins, Helen Lowell, Joan Wheeler, Frankie Darro, Ivan Lebedeff, James Burke, Harold Huber, Louise Beavers. *D:* Alfred E. Green; *P:* Robert

Lord; *Sc:* Gene Markey, Kathryn Scola. (G.B. title: *The Happy Family*)

Low-budget comedy-drama of the Frink family, whose members only concerns are themselves—that is of course except Mrs. Frink.

Merry-Go-Round *see* **Afraid to Talk**

2926. Merry-Go-Round of 1938 (Universal; 1937). *Cast:* Jimmy Savo, Bert Lahr, Mischa Auer, Billy House, Alice Brady, Joy Hodges, Louise Fazenda, Dave Appollon & His Orchestra, Hattie McDaniel, Charles Williams, John King, Barbara Read, Howard Cantonwine. *D:* Irving Cummings; *P:* Charles R. Rogers; *St:* Monte Brice, Harry Myers; *Sc:* Brice, Dorian A. Otvos; *Songs:* "The Woodman's Song" by E.Y. Harburg-Harold Arlen (sung by Lahr); "River, Stay 'way from My Door" by Mort Dixon-Harry Woods (sung by Savo); "I'm in My Glory," "More Power to You," and "You're My Dish" by Harold Adamson-Jimmy McHugh. (1:22)

The sentimental musical story of members of a vaudevillian comedy troupe who adopt a little girl.

2927. The Merry Widow (MGM; 1934). *Cast:* Maurice Chevalier (Captain Danilo), Jeanette MacDonald (Sonia), Una Merkel (Queen Dolores), Edward Everett Horton (Ambassador Popoff), George Barbier (King Achmed), Herman Bing (Zizipoff), Donald Meek (valet), Sterling Holloway (Mischke), Minna Gombell (Marcelle), Henry Armetta (Turk), Akim Tamiroff (Maxim's manager), Ruth Channing (Lulu), Leonid Kinskey, Richard Carle, Ivan Lebedeff, Billy Gilbert, Jason Robards, Katherine Burke (Virginia Field), Arthur Housman, Shirley (Ross) Chambers. *D:* Ernst Lubitsch; *P:* Irving Thalberg; *Sc:* Samson Raphaelson, Ernest Vajda; *Interior Decoration:* (A.A.) Cedric Gibbons, Gabriel Scognamillo, Frederic Hope; *Songs:* Gus Kahn, Richard Rodgers, Lorenz Hart. (1:39) (video)

A lavishly produced film version of the Franz Lehar operetta "Die lustige Witwe" by Victor Leon and Leo Stein which Lehar adapted from the play "L'Attache de' ambassade" by Henry Meilhac. The extravagant production set in 1885 in the mythical kingdom of Marshovia, caused the film to flop at the box office, as did this studio's earlier 1925 (Metro-Goldwyn) silent version by director Erich Von Stroheim. Remade in 1952.

2928. The Merry Wives of Reno (WB; 1934). *Cast:* Margaret Lindsay, Donald Woods, Guy Kibbee, Glenda Farrell, Hugh Herbert, Ruth Donnelly, Frank McHugh, Hobart Cavanaugh, Roscoe Ates, Louise Beavers. *D:* H. Bruce Humberstone; *P:* Robert Lord; *Sc:* Lord; *Additional Dialogue:* Joe Traub.

Romantic comedy.

2929. Mesquite Buckaroo (Metropolitan; 1939). *Cast:* Bob Steele, Carolyn (Clarene) Curtis, Frank LaRue, Charles King, Ted Adams, Joe Whitehead, Ed Brady, Snub Pollard, Carleton Young, John Elliott, Gordon Roberts, Juanita Fletcher, Jimmy Aubrey. *D:* Harry S. Webb; *Sc:* George Plympton. (0:55)

Bob Steele western with a rodeo theme and much stock footage.

2930. A Message to Garcia (20th Century-Fox; 1936). *Cast:* Wallace Beery, John Boles, Barbara Stanwyck, Alan Hale, Herbert Mundin, Martin Garralaga, Enrique Acosta, Jose Luis Tortosa, Juan Torena, Mona Barrie, Warren Hymer, Frederick Vogeding, Sam Appel, Iris Adrian, Yorke Sherwood, Davison Clark, Lon Chaney, Jr., Del Henderson, Rita (Hayworth) Cansino, Philip Morris, John Carradine (voice only), Blanca Vischer, Octavio Giraud, Pat Moriarty, Lucio Villegas. *D:* George Marshall; *P:* Raymond Griffith; *St:* Elbert Hubbard; *Sc:* W.P. Lipscomb, Gene Fowler. (1:25)

A fictionalized account of a historical incident which occurred during the Spanish American War. Based on the book by Andrew S. Rowan.

2931. Metropolitan (20th Century-Fox; 1935). *Cast:* Lawrence Tibbett, Alice Brady, Virginia Bruce, Cesar Romero, Thurston Hall, Luis Alberni, Kenny Baker, Walter Brennan, Ruth Donnelly, Jessie Ralph, Christian Rub, Jane Darwell, George F. Marion, Franklyn Ardell, Adrian Rosley. *D:* Richard Boleslawski; *P:* Darryl F. Zanuck; *Sc:* Bess Meredyth, George Marion, Jr. (1:19)

A spoiled prima donna quits the Metropolitan Opera after an argument with the owner and goes on to form her own opera company in this box office disappointment.

2932. Mexicali Kid (Monogram; 1938). *Cast:* Jack Randall, Wesley Barry (Mexicali Kid), Eleanor Stewart, Ed Cassidy, Bud Osborne, George Chesebro, Ernie Adams, William von Brincken, Frank LaRue, Sherry Tansey. *D:* Wallace Fox; *P:* Robert Tansey; *Sc:* Robert Emmett (Tansey). (0:51)

Jack Randall western of a cowboy and a reformed outlaw who join together to save a girl's ranch.

2933. Mexicali Rose (Columbia; 1929-30). (G.B. title: *The Girl from Mexico*)

Low-budget production, notable as Barbara Stanwyck's second Hollywood film, her first being 1929's *The Locked Door,* a silent for U.A. which was based on Channing Pollock's play "The Sign on the Door." Also starring in "Rose" was William Janney with direction by Erle C. Kenton.

Note: Stanwyck's film debut was in 1927's *Broadway Nights,* a silent feature which she made in New York City before going to Hollywood.

2934. Mexicali Rose (Republic; 1939). *Cast:* Gene Autry, Smiley Burnette, Luana Walters, Noah Beery, William Farnum, William Royle, LeRoy Mason, Wally Albright, Kathryn Frye, Roy Barcroft, Dick Botiller, Fred "Snowflake" Toones, Champion. *D:* George Sherman; *P:* Harry Grey; *St:* Luci Ward, Connie Lee; *Sc:* Gerald Geraghty; *Title Song:* Jack Tenney. (1:00)

Gene Autry western with renditions of "You're the Only Star in My Blue Heaven," "El Rancho Grande" and the title song.

2935. Michael O'Halloran (Republic; 1937). *Cast:* Warren Hull, Jackie Moran, Wynne Gibson, Sidney Blackmer, Vera Gordon. *D:* Karl Brown.

B rural drama, based on the 1915 novel by Gene Stratton-Porter. Remade in 1948 by Windsor for Monogram release.

Michael Strogoff (G.B. title) *see* **The Soldier and the Lady**

2936. Mickey the Kid (Republic; 1939). *Cast:* Ralph Byrd, Tommy Ryan, June Storey, Bruce Cabot, ZaSu Pitts, John Qualen, Scotty Beckett, Jessie Ralph, James Flavin, J. Farrell MacDonald, Archie Twitchell, Robert Elliott. *D:* Arthur Lubin; *St:* Alice Altschuler; *Sc:* Gordon Kahn, Doris Malloy.

Low-budget juvenile drama.

2937. Midnight (Universal/All Star; 1934). *Cast:* Sidney Fox, O.P. Heggie, Henry Hull, Humphrey Bogart, Margaret Wycherly, Lynne Overman (film debut), Richard Whorf (film debut), Cora Witherspoon, Henry O'Neill, Helen Flint, Katherine Wilson, Moffat Johnson, Granville Bates. *D:* Chester Erskine; *P:* Erskine: *Sc:* Erskine. (Re-release & home video title: *Call It Murder*) (1:20) (video)

A woman is sent to the electric chair and afterwards problems arise in this melodrama based on the play by Paul and Claire Sifton.

2938. Midnight (Paramount; 1939). *Cast:* Claudette Colbert, Don Ameche, John Barrymore, Francis Lederer, Mary Astor, Hedda Hopper, Elaine Barrie, Rex O'Malley, Monty Woolley, Armand Kaliz, Nestor Paiva, Ferdinand Munier, Lionel Pape, Gennaro Curci. *D:* Mitchell Leisen (who also directed the remake); *P:* Arthur Hornblow, Jr.; *St:* Edwin Justus Mayer, Franz Schulz; *Sc:* Charles Brackett, Billy Wilder. (1:35)

Hit sophisticated comedy of a poor girl hired by a man to impersonate a wealthy lady of royalty in order to draw the attentions of a gigolo away from his wife. Remade as *Masquerade in Mexico* (Paramount; 1945).

2939. Midnight Alibi (WB/F.N.; 1934). *Cast:* Richard Barthelmess (dual role), Ann Dvorak, Helen Chandler, Helen Lowell, Henry O'Neill, Robert Barrat, Robert McWade, Purnell Pratt, Harry Tyler, Paul Hurst, Arthur Aylesworth, Vincent Sherman, Boothe Howard, Eric Wilton. *D:* Alan Crosland; *Sc:* Warren Duff. (0:59)

Melodrama of a gambler on the lam from gangsters who is befriended by an elderly recluse. Based on the story "The Old Doll's House" by Damon Runyon.

2940. Midnight Club (Paramount; 1933). *Cast:* Clive Brook, George Raft, Helen Vinson, Guy Standing, Alison Skipworth, Ethel Griffies, Alan Mowbray, Richard Carlyle, Teru Shimada, Ferdinand Gottschalk, Billy Bevan. *D:* Alexander Hall, George Somnes; *St:* E. Phillips Oppenheim.

Low-budget melodrama of a gang of crooks who utilize doubles of themselves to form an alibi while they commit a robbery.

2941. Midnight Court (WB; 1936–37). *Cast:* John Litel, Ann Dvorak, Carlyle Moore, Jr., Joseph Crehan, William B. Davidson, Stanley Fields, Walter Miller, John J. Sheehan, Gordon (Bill) Elliott, Gordon Hart, Harrison Greene, Charles Foy, Eddie Foster, Lyle Moraine, George Offerman, Jr., Joan Woodbury. *D:* Frank McDonald; *P:* Bryan Foy; *St & Sc:* Don Ryan, Ken Gamet. (1:05)

B melodrama of a district attorney who is on the mob's payroll.

2942. Midnight Daddies (Mack Sennett; 1929–30). *Cast:* Andy Clyde, Rosemary Theby, Alma Bennett. *D:* Mack Sennett; *P:* Sennett; *Co-Sc:* Harry McCoy.

The first of two slapstick talkie features by Sennett.

2943. Midnight Intruder (Universal; 1938). *Cast:* Louis Hayward, Barbara Read, Eric Linden, Joseph Crehan, J.C. Nugent, Selmer Jackson. *D:* Arthur Lubin; *P:* Trem Carr. (1:06)

B melodrama of impersonation and murder.

2944. The Midnight Lady (Chesterfield; 1932). *Cast:* Lina Basquette, Claudia Dell, John Darrow, Donald Keith, Montagu Love, Lucy Beaumont, Louise Beavers, Brandon Hurst, Theodore von Eltz, B. Wayne Lamont, Sarah Padden. *D:* Richard Thorpe; *St & Sc:* Edward T. Lowe. (G.B. title: *Dream Mother*)

"Poverty row" drama.

2945. Midnight Madonna (Paramount; 1937). *Cast:* Warren William, Mady Correll, Frank Reicher, Joseph Sawyer, Jack Clifford, Irene Franklin, Joseph Crehan, Robert Baldwin, May Wallace. *D:* James Flood; *P:* Emanuel Cohen; *St:* David Boehm; *Sc:* Gladys Lehman, Doris Malloy.

B soaper of the custody fight over a child.

2946. Midnight Mary (MGM; 1933). *Cast:* Loretta Young, Franchot Tone, Ricardo Cortez, Una Merkel, Andy Devine, Harold Huber, Warren

Hymer, Halliwell Hobbes, Sandy Roth, Charley Grapewin, Martha Sleeper, Ivan Simpson, Frank Conroy. *D:* William A. Wellman; *St:* Anita Loos; *Sc:* Gene Markey, Kathryn Scola. (unc.). (1:16)

Hit drama of a girl who looks back on the events in her life that put her on trial.

2947. Midnight Morals (Mayfair; 1932). *Cast:* Rex Lease, Alberta Vaughn, Charles Delaney, DeWitt Jennings. *D:* E. Mason Hopper.

"Poverty row" drama.

2948. Midnight Mystery (RKO; 1930). *Cast:* Betty Compson, Lowell Sherman, Raymond Hatton, Hugh Trevor, June Clyde, Ivan Lebedeff, Rita LaRoy, Marcelle Corday, Sidney D'Albrook, William P. Burt, Alice Joyce (final film—ret.). *D:* George B. Seitz; *As.P.:* Bertram Millhauser; *Sc:* Beulah Marie Dix. (1:09)

A house party in a castle on a remote island off the coast of Maine is stalked by a murderer. Based on the play "Hawk Island" by Howard Irving Young.

2949. The Midnight Patrol (Monogram; 1932). *Cast:* Regis Toomey, Betty Bronson, Edwina Booth, Mary Nolan (final film—ret.), Earle Foxe, Robert Elliott, Mack Swain (final film—d. 1935), Snub Pollard, Mischa Auer, Tod Sloan, Jim Jeffries, Ray Cooke, Eddie Kane, William Norton Bailey, Jack Mower, Barry Oliver, Wilfred Lucas, J.C. Fowler. *D:* Christy Cabanne; *St:* Arthur Hoerl; *Sc:* George Jeske, Barry Barringer, C. Harrington. (1:07)

Low-budget mystery melodrama of a reporter assigned to scoop a murder.

2950. The Midnight Phantom (Reliable; 1935). *Cast:* Reginald Denny. (No other information available)

2951. The Midnight Special (Chesterfield; 1930). *Cast:* Glenn Tryon, Merna Kennedy. *D:* Duke Worne; *Sc:* Arthur Hoerl.

"Poverty row" melodrama.

2952. Midnight Taxi (WB; 1928). *Cast:* Helene Costello, Myrna Loy, Antonio Moreno, Robert Agnew, William Russell, Tommy Dugan, Paul Kruger, Jack Santoro. *D:* John G. Adolfi; *St:* Gregory Rogers (Darryl F. Zanuck); *Sc:* Freddie Foy.

Part-talkie melodrama of bootlegging. Remade in 1937 (see below).

2953. Midnight Taxi (20th Century–Fox; 1937). *Cast:* Brian Donlevy, Frances Drake, Alan Dinehart, Sig Rumann, Gilbert Roland, Harold Huber, Lon Chaney, Jr. *D:* Eugene Forde; *Sc:* Lou Breslow, John Patrick. (1:13)

B melodrama of a G-man who goes after a gang of counterfeiters. A remake of the preceding film, it is based on a short story by Borden Chase.

2954. Midnight Warning (Mayfair; 1933). *Cast:* Lloyd Whitlock, Claudia Dell, Lloyd Ingraham. *D:* Spencer Gordon Bennet.

"Poverty row" melodrama.

2955. Midshipman Jack (RKO; 1933). *Cast:* Bruce Cabot (Jack), Betty Furness, Frank Albertson, John Darrow, Arthur Lake, Florence Lake (Arthur's real-life sister), Purnell Pratt, Margaret Seddon. *D:* Christy Cabanne; *As.P.:* Glendon Allvine; *Sc:* Frank "Spig" Wead, F. McGrew Willis. (1:11)

Drama of a young man who learns responsibility while attending the Naval Academy at Annapolis. Filmed on location. Remade as *Annapolis Salute* (RKO; 1937) (q.v.).

2956. Midstream (Tiffany; 1929). *Cast:* Ricardo Cortez, Montagu Love, Claire Windsor. *D:* James Flood.

"Poverty row" part-talkie melodrama.

2957. A Midsummer Night's Dream (WB; 1935). *Cast:* James Cagney (Bottom), Dick Powell (Lysander), Joe E. Brown (Flute), Jean Muir (Helena), Hugh Herbert (Snout), Ian Hunter

(Theseus), Olivia de Havilland (in her film debut as Hermia), Anita Louise (Titania), Mickey Rooney (Puck), Frank McHugh (Quince), Victor Jory (Oberon), Arthur Treacher (Ninny's Tomb), Ross Alexander (Demetrius), Grant Mitchell (Egeus), Nini Theilade (first fairy), Verree Teasdale (Hippolyta, Queen of the Amazons), Dewey Robinson (Snug), Hobart Cavanaugh (Philostrate), Otis Harlan (Starveling), Billy Barty (Mustardseed). *D:* Max Reinhardt (his only American film), William Dieterle; *P:* Reinhardt; *Supervisor:* Henry Blanke; *Sc:* Charles Kenyon, Mary McCall, Jr.; *Cinematographers:* (A.A.) Hal Mohr (the only Oscar ever awarded on a write-in vote) *Choreographer:* Bronislawa Nijinska (Nijinsky); *Editor:* (A.A.) Ralph Dawson. (Original running time — 2:12) (video & current prints — 1:57)

Classic filming of William Shakespeare's comedy-fantasy play. One of the 12 top grossing films of 1935, it received an A.A.N. for "Best Picture" as well as placing #10 on the "10 Best" list of *Film Daily.* Remade in 1966 with the New York Ballet company and again in Great Britain in 1968 by the Royal Shakespeare Company.

Mightier Than the Sword (G.B. title) *see* **A Girl with Ideas**

2958. The Mighty (Paramount; 1929). *Cast:* George Bancroft, Esther Ralston, Warner Oland, Raymond Hatton, Dorothy Revier, O.P. Heggie, Charles Sellon, Morgan Farley, E.H. Calvert, John Cromwell (bit). *D:* John Cromwell; *St:* Robert N. Lee; *Sc:* Grover Jones, William Slavens McNutt, Nellie Revell.

After serving his country in World War I, a former criminal joins law enforcement.

2959. The Mighty Barnum (United Artists/20th Century; 1934). *Cast:* Wallace Beery (Phineas T. Bar-

num), Adolphe Menjou (Bailey Walsh), Virginia Bruce (Jenny Lind), Janet Beecher (Mrs. Barnum), Rochelle Hudson, Herman Bing, May Boley, Lucille La Verne, George Brasno (Colonel Tom Thumb), Olive Brasno (Lavinia Thumb), Ian Wolfe, Tammany Young, John Hyams, Richard Brasno, R.E. "Tex" Madsen (Cardiff giant), Davison Clark (Horace Greeley), George MacQuarrie (Daniel Webster), Charles Judels, Christian Rub. *D:* Walter Lang; *P:* Darryl F. Zanuck, William Goetz, Raymond Griffith; *Sc:* Gene Fowler, Bess Meredyth (from their play). (1:27)

A filmed biography of the famed showman which plays with the facts. The same subject matter was also handled in the 1986 TV movie *Barnum,* wherein it was debunked that the showman ever coined the phrase "There's a sucker born every minute."

2960. The Mighty Treve (Universal; 1937). *Cast:* Noah Beery, Jr., Tuffy the dog (Treve), Samuel S. Hinds, Barbara Read, Hobart Cavanaugh, Frank Reicher, Edmund Cobb. *D:* Lewis D. Collins; *P:* Val Paul. (1:08)

B family film of a boy and his dog on a western ranch.

2961. Mile a Minute Love (Ace; 1937). *Cast:* William Bakewell, Wilfred Lucas, Duncan Renaldo. *D:* Elmer Clifton.

Low-budget independent production.

2962. The Milky Way (Paramount/Harold Lloyd; 1936). *Cast:* Harold Lloyd, Adolphe Menjou, Verree Teasdale, Helen Mack, William Gargan, George Barbier, Dorothy Wilson, Lionel Stander, Marjorie Gateson, Milburn Stone, Charles (Lane) Levison, Bull Anderson, Jim Marples, Larry McGrath. *D:* Leo McCarey; *P:* E. Lloyd Sheldon; *Sc:* Grover Jones, Frank Butler, Richard Connell. (1:23) (video)

Critically acclaimed hit comedy of a mild-mannered milkman who turns prizefighter with the underhandedness of a fight promoter. Based on the play by Lynn Root and Harry Clork. Remade as *The Kid from Brooklyn* (Samuel Goldwyn; 1946).

2963. Millie (RKO; 1931). *Cast:* Helen Twelvetrees, Robert Ames, John Halliday, Anita Louise, Lilyan Tashman, Joan Blondell, Edmund Breese, James Hall, Frank McHugh, Otis Harlan, Franklin Parker, Charlotte Walker, Charles Delaney, Louise Beavers, Carmelita Geraghty, Harry Stubbs, Harvey Clark, Geneva Mitchell, Marie Astaire, Aggie Herring. *D:* John Francis Dillon; *P:* Charles R. Rogers; *Sc:* Charles Kenyon. (1:25)

A naive country girl is led astray by love in the big city, eventually leading to murder. Based on the novel by Donald Henderson Clarke.

2964. Million Dollar Baby (Monogram; 1934). *Cast:* Ray Walker, Arline Judge, Jimmy Fay, George E. Stone, Eddie Kane, Willard Robertson, Ralf Harolde, Lee Shumway, Edward Peil, Sr., Paul Porcasi, Wilbur Mack, Jeanette Loff, Arthur Stone, Harry Holman, Connor twins. *D:* Joseph Santley; *P:* Ben Verschleiser; *St:* Santley; *Sc:* Santley, John W. Krafft. (1:05)

B comedy-drama of two vaudevillians who dress their son as a girl in order to enter a contest that if the boy would win, he would become "another Shirley Temple."

2965. The Million Dollar Collar (WB; 1929). *Cast:* Rin-Tin-Tin (in his 17th feature film), Evelyn Pierce, Matty Kemp, Tommy Dugan, Allan Cavan, Philo McCullough, Grover Liggon. *D:* D. Ross Lederman; *St & Sc:* Robert Lord.

Hit low-budget part-talkie canine adventure of a dog with an expensive necklace hidden inside his collar.

Remade in 1964 as a "Wonderful World of Disney" presentation.

2966. Million Dollar Haul (First Division; 1935). *Cast:* William Farnum, Reed Howes, Tarzan the dog. *D:* Xxxx Xxxx.

B action melodrama.

2967. Million Dollar Legs (Paramount; 1932). *Cast:* W.C. Fields, Jack Oakie, Susan Fleming, Andy Clyde, Lyda Roberti, Ben Turpin, Dickie Moore, Billy Gilbert, Hugh Herbert, George Barbier, Syd Saylor, Hank Mann, Teddy Hart, Vernon Dent, Ben Taggart, John Sinclair, Sam Adams, Chick Collins. *D:* Edward Cline; *P:* Herman J. Mankiewicz; *St:* Joseph L. Mankiewicz; *Sc:* J.L. Mankiewicz, Harry Myers, Nick Barrows.

Classic comedy of the president of a small mythical country named Klopstokia who decides to enter his country in the Olympics.

2968. Million Dollar Legs (Paramount; 1939). *Cast:* Betty Grable, John Hartley, Donald O'Connor, Jackie Coogan, Buster Crabbe, Peter Lind Hayes, Thurston Hall, Richard Denning, William Tracy, Byron Foulger, Billy Gilbert, Joyce Mathews. *D:* Nick Grinde; *Sc:* Lewis Foster, Richard English. (1:05)

B college comedy with a race horse, the center of attention.

2969. Million Dollar Racket (Victory; 1937). *Cast:* Herman Brix (Bruce Bennett), Jimmy Aubrey. *D:* Robert F. Hill; *P:* Sam Katzman.

Low-budget independent crime melodrama.

2970. Million Dollar Ransom (Universal; 1934). *Cast:* Phillips Holmes, Edward Arnold, Mary Carlisle, Marjorie Gateson, Andy Devine, Winifred Shaw, Robert Gleckler, Jane Darwell, Jay C. Flippen, Henry Kolker, Spencer Charters, Joyce Compton,

Bradley Page, Charles Coleman, Huey White, Edgar Norton. *D:* Murray Roth; *St:* Damon Runyon. (1:10)

Drama of a bootlegger who gets out of prison after serving his time, only to find that prohibition has ended and he has to seek another line of work.

2971. A Million to One (Puritan; 1937). *Cast:* Herman Brix (Bruce Bennett), Joan Fontaine, Monte Blue, Kenneth Harlan, Suzanne Kaaren, Reed Howes. *D:* Lynn Shores. (1:00) (video)

B drama which deals with a potential Olympic athlete and his ups and downs.

2972. The Millionaire (WB; 1931). *Cast:* George Arliss (who also starred in the '22 production), Evalyn Knapp, Florence Arliss, David Manners, Noah Beery, J. Farrell MacDonald, James Cagney, Bramwell Fletcher, Charley Grapewin, Tully Marshall, J.C. Nugent, Ivan Simpson, Ethel Griffies. *D:* John Adolfi; *Sc:* Maude T. Howell, Julien Josephson; *Dial.:* Booth Tarkington. (1:20)

A millionaire industrialist retires, but circumstances prevent him from taking it easy. A hit film of its day, it was based on a story by Earl Derr Biggers. A remake of *The Ruling Passion* (United Artists; 1922). Remade as *That Way with Women* (WB; 1947).

2973. The Millionaire Kid (Reliable; 1936). *Cast:* Betty Compson, Bryant Washburn, Creighton Hale. *D:* Bernard B. Ray.

The Millionaire Playboy (G.B. title) *see* **Park Avenue Logger**

2974. Millions in the Air (Paramount; 1935). *Cast:* John Howard, Wendy Barrie, Willie Howard, Eleanore Whitney, Robert Cummings, Joan Davis (feature film debut), Catherine Doucet, Benny Baker, Billy Gilbert, Halliwell Hobbes, Paul Fix, Samuel S. Hinds, Inez Courtney, Alden (Stephen) Chase, Dave Chasen, Ralph Spence,

Bennie Bartlett. *D:* Ray McCarey; *P:* Harold Hurley; *St:* Jane Storm; *Sc:* Sig Herzig.

B comedy of a radio amateur show and the daughter of the sponsor who becomes a contestant and wins.

2975. Mills of the Gods (Columbia; 1935). *Cast:* Fay Wray, Raymond Walburn, May Robson, Frank Reicher, Victor Jory, Edward Van Sloan, Samuel S. Hinds, Willard Robertson, James Millican. *D:* Roy William Neill.

Low-budget drama.

2976. Min and Bill (MGM; 1930). *Cast:* Marie Dressler (A.A. for B.A. 1930–31 as Min Divot), Wallace Beery (Bill), Dorothy Jordan (Nancy Smith), Marjorie Rambeau (Bella Pringle), Donald Dillaway (film debut as Dick Cameron), DeWitt Jennings, Russell Hopton, Frank McGlynn, Greta Gould, Jack Pennick, Henry Rocquemore, Hank Bell, Miss Vanessi. *D:* George Hill; *Sc:* Frances Marion, Marion Jackson. (1:09) (video)

Sentimental comedy of a couple who reside on the waterfront and want to find a better home for her daughter. Based on the book "Dark Star" by Lorna Moon, it was the studio's biggest moneymaker of the year with a $2,000,000 gross, as well as one of the 15 top grossing films of 1930–31. *Film Daily* placed it at #5 on their "10 Best" list.

2977. The Mind Reader (WB/F.N.; 1933). *Cast:* Constance Cummings, Warren William, Allen Jenkins, Natalie Moorhead, Mayo Methot, Clara Blandick, Clarence Muse, Donald Dillaway, Harry Beresford, Ruthelma Stevens, Earle Foxe, Robert Greig, Harry Stubbs. *D:* Roy Del Ruth; *P:* Hal Wallis; *Sc:* Wilson Mizner, Robert Lord. (1:09)

B drama of a phony clairvoyant. Based on the play by Vivian Cosby.

2978. Mind Your Own Business (Paramount; 1936). *Cast:* Charles Ruggles, Alice Brady, Lyle Talbot, Jack

LaRue, Frankie Darro, Gene Lockhart, William Demarest, Lloyd Crane (Jon Hall), Benny Baker. *D:* Norman Z. McLeod; *P:* Emanuel Cohen.

Low-budget comedy of a kidnapped couple who are rescued by a troop of boy scouts.

2979. The Mine with the Iron Door (Columbia; 1936). *Cast:* Richard Arlen, Cecilia Parker, Henry B. Walthall, Stanley Fields, Horace Murphy, Spencer Charters, Charles H. Wilson, Barbara Bedford. *D:* David Howard; *P:* Sol Lesser; *Sc:* Don Swift, Dan Jarrett. (1:10)

Western story of a hidden gold mine. Based on the 1923 novel by Harold Bell Wright, it is a remake of the 1924 Principal production.

Miracle in the Sand *see* **Three Godfathers**

2980. The Miracle Man (Paramount; 1932). *Cast:* Chester Morris, Sylvia Sidney, Irving Pichel, John Wray, Robert (Bobby) Coogan, Hobart Bosworth, Boris Karloff, Ned Sparks, Virginia Bruce, Lloyd Hughes, Jackie Searle, Florine McKinney, Frank Darien, Lew Kelly. *D:* Norman Z. McLeod; *Sc:* Waldemar Young, Samuel Hoffenstein. (1:25)

Offbeat drama of lawless element that is reformed by a faith healer. Based on a play by George M. Cohan and Frank L. Packard, this is a remake of the 1919 Paramount-Artclass production which starred Lon Chaney.

The Miracle of Life (G.B. title) *see* **Our Daily Bread**

2981. Miracle on Main Street (Columbia/Grand National; 1939–40). *Cast:* Margo, Walter Abel, Jane Darwell, Lyle Talbot, William Collier, Sr. *D:* Steve Sekely; *P:* Jack H. Skirball (for Grand National). (1:08)

Low-budget drama of a down-and-out dancer who finds an abandoned baby on Christmas Eve. Released by Columbia after Grand National closed its doors.

2982. The Miracle Rider (Mascot; 1935). *Cast:* Tom Mix, Joan Gale, Charles Middleton, Jason Robards, Robert Kortman, Edward Hearn, Edward Earle, Tom London, Niles Welch, Edmund Cobb, Ernie Adams, Max Wagner, Charles King, George Chesebro, Jack Rockwell, Robert Frazer, Stanley Price, George Burton, Wally Wales (Hal Taliaferro), Jay Wilsey (nee: Buffalo Bill, Jr.), Dick Curtis, Frank Ellis, Dick Alexander, Earl Dwire, Lafe McKee, Hank Bell, Pat O'Malley, Charles "Slim" Whitaker, Art Ardigan, Chief Big Tree, Forrest Taylor, Fred Burns, Black Hawk, Chief Standing Bear, Tony, Jr. (Mix's horse). *D:* Armand Schaefer, B. Reeves Eason; *P:* Nat Levine; *Supervisor:* Victor Zobel; *St:* Barney Sarecky, Wellyn Totman, Gerald Geraghty, Maurice Geraghty; *Sc:* John Rathmell. (video — original serial only)

Feature version of this studio's 15 chapter serial which marked the final film appearance of famed cowboy star Tom Mix. The story concerns a gang of crooks preying on Indian superstition to get the redman's land.

2983. The Miracle Woman (Columbia; 1931–32). *Cast:* Barbara Stanwyck, Sam Hardy, David Manners, Beryl Mercer, Russell Hopton, Charles Middleton, Thelma Hill, Eddie Boland, Aileen Carlyle. *D:* Frank Capra; *P:* Harry Cohn; *Sc:* Jo Swerling. (1:30)

Drama of a female evangelist, patterned loosely after Aimee Semple Macpherson. Based on the play "Bless You Sister" by Robert Riskin and John Meehan.

2984. Miracles for Sale (MGM; 1939). *Cast:* Robert Young, Florence Rice, Henry Hull, Frank Craven, Lee Bowman, William Demarest, Astrid

Allwyn, Charley Grapewin, Harry Davenport, Frederick Worlock, Gloria Holden, Richard Loo, Cliff Clark. *D:* Tod Browning (final film as director); *Sc:* James Edward Grant, Marion Parsonnet, Harry Ruskin. (1:11)

B murder-mystery set within the confines of a group of stage musicians. Based on the novel "Death from a Top Hat" by Clayton Rawson.

2985. Misbehaving Ladies (WB/ F.N.; 1931). *Cast:* Ben Lyon, Lila Lee, Louise Fazenda, Julia Swayne Gordon, Virginia Grey, Lucien Littlefield, Emily Fitzroy, Martha Mattox, Oscar Apfel. *D:* William Beaudine; *St:* Juliet Wilbur Tompkins; *Sc:* Julien Josephson. (G.B. title: *Once There Was a Princess*)

An American girl marries into a royal family, returning to her homeland after her husband dies. A low-budget comedy.

2986. The Misleading Lady (Paramount; 1932). *Cast:* Claudette Colbert, Edmund Lowe, Stuart Erwin, William Gargan (film debut), Selena Royle (film debut), Will Geer (film debut), Robert Strange, Edgar Nelson, Harry Ellerbee, George Meeker, Nina Walker, Fred Stewart, Curtis Cooksey, Donald MacBride. *D:* Stuart Walker; *St & Sc:* Charles W. Goddard, Paul Dickey.

Romantic comedy of an actress seeking a role as a vamp. Filmed at Astoria Studios in Long Island, N.Y.

2987. Miss Fane's Baby Is Stolen (Paramount; 1933-34). *Cast:* Dorothea Wieck (American finale), Alice Brady, Baby LeRoy, Georgie "Spanky" McFarland, William Frawley, George Barbier, Alan Hale, Jack LaRue, Dorothy Burgess, Florence Roberts, Edwin Maxwell, Charles Wilson. *D:* Alexander Hall; *Adaptation:* Jane Storm; *St:* Rupert Hughes; *Sc:* Adela Rogers St. John. (G.B. title: *Kidnapped*)

Suspense drama of an actress whose baby disappears.

2988. Miss Pacific Fleet (WB; 1935). *Cast:* Glenda Farrell, Joan Blondell, Hugh Herbert, Allen Jenkins, Warren Hull, Guinn Williams, Eddie Acuff, Paul Fix, Mary Doran, Douglas Fowley, Ed Gargan, Jack Norton, Anita Kerry. *D:* Ray Enright; *P:* Earl Baldwin; *St:* Frederick Hazlitt Brennan; *Sc:* Lucille Newmark, Peter Milne, Patsy Flick. (1:16)

Comedy of two showgirls who are stranded without funds and their attempts to get home.

2989. Miss Pinkerton (WB/ F.N.; 1932). *Cast:* Joan Blondell, George Brent, John Wray, Ruth Hall, C. Henry Gordon, Mae Madison, Elizabeth Patterson, Holmes Herbert, Lucien Littlefield, Allan Lane, Blanche Frederici, Mary Doran, Donald Dillaway, Luana Walters, Eulalie Jensen, Treva Lawler. *D:* Lloyd Bacon; *Sc:* Lillie Hayward, Niven Busch. (1:06)

B mystery-comedy of a nurse who turns to sleuthing. Based on the magazine serial and book by Mary Roberts Rinehart. Remade as *The Nurse's Secret* (WB; 1946).

2990. Missing Daughters (Columbia; 1939). *Cast:* Rochelle Hudson, Richard Arlen, Marian Marsh, Dick Wessel, Isabel Jewell, Claire Rochelle, Don Beddoe, Wade Boteler, Eddie Kane, Edward Raquello. *D:* C.C. Coleman, Jr.; *Sc:* Michael Simmons, George Bricker.

Low-budget exploitation melodrama.

2991. Missing Evidence (Universal; 1939). *Cast:* Preston Foster, Irene Hervey, Inez Courtney, Chick Chandler, Noel Madison, Cliff Clark, Tom Dugan, Joseph Downing, Ray Walker, Oscar O'Shea. *D:* Phil Rosen; *P:* Rosen; *St:* Dorrell & Stuart McGowan; *Sc:* Arthur T. Horman. (1:04)

B crime melodrama of a bogus sweepstakes operation.

2992. Missing Girls (Chesterfield; 1936). *Cast:* Roger Pryor, Muriel

Evans, Ann Doran, Sidney Blackmer, Noel Madison, Wallis Clark, George Cooper, Dewey Robinson. *D:* Phil Rosen; *P:* George R. Batcheller; *Sc:* John W. Krafft, Martin Mooney.

"Poverty row" mystery-drama.

2993. The Missing Guest (Universal; 1938). *Cast:* Paul Kelly, Constance Moore, William Lundigan, Edwin Stanley, Selmer Jackson, Billy Wayne, George Cooper, Harlan Briggs, Florence Wix, P.J. Kelly. *D:* John Rawlins; *P:* Barney A. Sarecky; *Sc:* Charles Martin, Paul Perez. (1:08)

B remake of *The Secret of the Blue Room* (q.v.), of murder in an old dark house. Based on a story by Erich Phillipi, it was remade as *Murder in the Blue Room* (Universal; 1944).

2994. Missing Witnesses (WB/ F.N.; 1937). *Cast:* Dick Purcell, Jean Dale (film debut), John Litel, Raymond Hatton, Sheila Bromley, William Haade, Harland Tucker, Ben Welden, Veda Ann Borg, John Harron, Louis Natheaux, Jack Mower, Earl Gunn, Michael Mark. *D:* William Clemens; *P:* Bryan Foy; *Sc:* Kenneth Gamet, Don Ryan.

B crime melodrama involving a protection racket.

2995. Mississippi (Paramount; 1935). *Cast:* Bing Crosby, W.C. Fields, Joan Bennett, Gail Patrick, Queenie Smith, John Miljan, Claude Gillingwater, Fred Kohler, Mahlon Hamilton, Jack Mulhall, Elizabeth Patterson, J.P. McGowan, Harry Myers, Jean Rouverol, Ann Sheridan, Charles King (1894–1944 in his final film, retiring to the stage), Stanley Andrews, James Burke, Paul Hurst, King Baggot, Harry Beresford, Forrest Taylor, Theresa Maxwell Conover, Matthew Betz, Libby Taylor, Edward Pawley, Jules Cowles, Bruce Covington, Bud Flanagan (Dennis O'Keefe). *D:* A. Edward Sutherland; *P:* Arthur Hornblow, Jr.; *Sc:* Herbert Fields, Claude Binyon,

Jack Cunningham, Francis Martin, Dore Schary (unc.); *Songs Include:* "Soon," "Down by the River" & "It's Easy to Remember (So Hard to Forget)" by Richard Rodgers, Lorenz Hart. (1:20)

Hit musical-comedy set aboard a riverboat of which W.C. Fields is the captain. Based on the story "Magnolia" by Booth Tarkington, it was first filmed as *The Fighting Coward* (Paramount; 1924) with Cullen Landis, Mary Astor and Ernest Torrence. Remade in 1929 as *River of Romance* (q.v.).

2996. The Mississippi Gambler (Universal; 1929). *Cast:* Joseph Schildkraut, Joan Bennett, Alec B. Francis, Carmelita Geraghty, Otis Harlan, William Welsh. *D:* Reginald Barker; *St:* Karl Brown, Leonard Fields; *Sc:* Edward T. Lowe, Jr., Winifred Reeve, H.H. Van Loan, Dudley Early.

A gambler is redeemed by love. Remade in 1953.

2997. Mister Antonio (Tiffany; 1929). *Cast:* Leo Carrillo (film debut), Virginia Valli, Frank Reicher, Gareth Hughes. *D:* James Flood, Frank Reicher.

Early "poverty row" talkie.

2998. Mr. Boggs Steps Out (Grand National; 1938). *Cast:* Stuart Erwin, Helen Chandler, Harry Tyler, Milburn Stone, Nora Cecil, Wilson Benge, Walter Byron, Spencer Charters, Betty Mack, Toby Wing. *D:* Gordon Wiles; *P:* Ben Pivar; *Sc:* Richard English. (1:08)

Comedy of a country boy who buys an old barrel factory. Based on *The Saturday Evening Post* story titled "Face the Facts" by Clarence Budington Kelland, the two working titles were "Face the Facts" and "Mr. Boggs Buys a Barrel."

2999. Mr. Broadway (Broadway-Hollywood Productions; 1933). *Cast:* Bert Lahr, Tom Moore, Jack Benny, Dita Parlo, Lupe Velez, Maxie Rosenbloom, Ed Sullivan, Josephine Dunn (final film — ret.), William Desmond, Benny Fields. *D:* Edgar G. Ulmer, Johnny Walker (only film as a director). Independent musical-comedy.

3000. Mr. Chump (WB; 1938). *Cast:* Johnnie "Scat" Davis, Lola Lane, Penny Singleton, Donald Briggs, Chester Clute, Sidney Bracey, Clem Bevans. *D:* William Clemens; *As.P.:* Bryan Foy; *Sc:* George Bricker; *Song:* "As Long as You Live (You'll Be Dead If You Die)" by Davis.

B comedy of a trumpet player who instead of working for a living would rather "make the big deal."

3001. Mr. Cinderella (MGM/ Hal Roach; 1936). *Cast:* Jack Haley, Betty Furness, Raymond Walburn, Robert McWade, Kathleen Lockhart, Edward Brophy, Monroe Owsley, Rosina Lawrence, Tom Dugan, Iris Adrian, Arthur Treacher, Toby Wing, Arthur Aylesworth. *D:* Edward Sedgwick; *P:* Hal Roach; *Sc:* Richard Flournoy, Arthur V. Jones; *St:* Jack Jevne.

Comedy of a poor barber who poses as a millionaire.

3002. Mr. Deeds Goes to Town (Columbia; 1936). *Cast:* Gary Cooper (A.A.N. for B.A. — his first — as Longfellow Deeds), Jean Arthur (Babe Bennett), George Bancroft (MacWade), Lionel Stander (Cornelius Cobb), Douglass Dumbrille (John Cedar), Raymond Walburn (Walter), H.B. Warner (Judge Walker), Mayo Methot (Mrs. Semple), Walter Catlett (Morrow), Margaret Matzenauer (Madame Pomponi), Ruth Donnelly (Mabel Dawson), Muriel Evans (Theresa), Warren Hymer (bodyguard), Spencer Charters (Mal), Emma Dunn (Mrs. Meredith), Wyrley Birch (psychiatrist), Arthur Hoyt (Budington), Stanley Andrews (James Cedar), Pierre Watkin (Arthur Cedar), John Wray (disgruntled farmer), Christian Rub (Swenson), Jameson Thomas (Mr. Semple), Russell

Hicks (Doctor Malcolm), Gustav von Seyffertitz (Dr. Frazier), Edward LeSaint (Dr. Fosdick), Charles (Lane) Levison (Hallor), Irving Bacon (Frank), George Cooper (Bob), Gene Morgan (waiter), Barnett Parker (butler), Margaret Seddon (Jane Faulkner), Margaret McWade (Amy Faulkner), Harry C. Bradley (Anderson), Ed Gargan (2nd bodyguard), Edwin Maxwell (Douglas), Paul Hurst (first deputy), Paul Porcasi (Italian), Franklin Pangborn (tailor), George F. Hayes (farmer's spokesman), Billy Bevan (cabby), Bud Flanagan (Dennis O'Keefe as a reporter), George Meeker (Brookfield), Dale Van Sickel (lawyer), Eddie Kane, Jay Eaton, Lee Shumway, James Millican. *D:* (A.A. — his second) Frank Capra; *P:* Capra; *Sc:* (A.A.N. Robert Riskin; *Sound Recording:* (A.A.N.) John Livadary, Edward Bernds. (1:55)

Classic story of a simple man who inherits $20,000,000 and has his plain existence turned upside down. This production which premiered in New York City on April 16th was voted "Best Film of the Year" by the National Board of Review and the New York Film Critics. It also received an A.A.N. for "Best Picture" and was in nomination at the Venice Film Festival, while placing #2 and #3 respectively on the "10 Best" lists of *Film Daily* and the *New York Times*. Based on the story "Opera Hat" by Clarence Budington Kelland it became one of the 25 top grossing films of 1935-36.

3003. Mr. Dodd Takes the Air (WB; 1937). *Cast:* Kenny Baker, Jane Wyman (in her starring debut), Alice Brady, Gertrude Michael, Frank Reicher, Luis Alberni, Henry O'Neill, Harry Davenport, John Eldredge, Ferris Taylor, Frank Faylen, Linda Perry, DeWolf (William) Hopper. *D:* Alfred E. Green; *P:* Mervyn LeRoy; *St:* Clarence Budington Kelland; *Sc:* William Wister Haines, Elaine Ryan; *Songs Include:* "Am I in Love?" "If I Were a Little Pond Lily," "The Girl You Used to Be," "Here Comes the Sandman" & "Remember Me?" (which received an A.A.N. for "Best Song") for Al Dubin & Harry Warren. (1:18)

Musical-comedy of a small town boy who gains fame as a crooner. A box office flop.

3004. Mr. Doodle Kicks Off (RKO; 1938). *Cast:* Joe Penner, June Travis, Ben Alexander, William B. Davidson, Frank M. Thomas, Richard Lane, Billy Gilbert, Jack Carson, Alan Bruce, George Irving, Pierre Watkin, Wesley Barry, Robert Parrish. *D:* Leslie Goodwins; *P:* Robert Sisk; *St:* Mark Kelly; *Sc:* Bert Granet; *Songs:* Hal Raynor. (1:16)

B college comedy of a wealthy man who wants his son to become a star gridiron player.

3005. Mr. Dynamite (Universal; 1935). *Cast:* Edmund Lowe, Esther Ralston, Jean Dixon, Victor Varconi, Minor Watson, Joyce Compton, Verna Hillie, Jameson Thomas, Bradley Page, Greta Meyer, George Pat Collins, Robert Gleckler, James Burtis, Matt McHugh. *D:* Alan Crosland; *P:* E.M. Asher; *Sc:* Harry Clork, Doris Malloy. (1:12)

B mystery-thriller based on a short story by Dashiell Hammett.

Mr. Faintheart (G.B. title) *see* **$10 Raise**

3006. Mr. Lemon of Orange (Fox; 1931). *Cast:* El Brendel, Fifi D'Orsay, William Collier, Sr., Nat Pendleton, Joan Castle, Donald Dillaway, Ruth Warren, Eddie Gribbon. *D:* John G. Blystone; *St:* Jack Hayes; *Dial.:* Eddie Cantor, Edwin Burke.

Low-budget comedy.

3007. Mr. Moto in Danger Island (20th Century–Fox; 1939). *Cast:* Peter Lorre, Jean Hersholt, Amanda Duff, Warren Hymer, Richard Lane, Leon Ames, Douglass Dumbrille, Robert Lowery, Victor Varconi, Ward Bond, Harold Huber. *D:* Herbert I. Leeds; *P:* Sol M. Wurtzel; *As.P.:* John Stone; *St:* John Reinhardt, George Bricker; *Sc:* Peter Milne. (G.B. title: *Mr. Moto on Danger Island*) (aka: *Danger Island*) (1:03)

Entry in the popular series of the Japanese detective created by John P. Marquand. A remake of *Murder in Trinidad* (q.v.), which was based on the novel of that name by John W. Vandercook. Remade as *The Caribbean Mystery* (20th Century–Fox; 1945).

Mr. Moto on Danger Island (G.B. title) *see* **Mr. Moto in Danger Island**

3008. Mr. Moto Takes a Chance (20th Century–Fox; 1938). *Cast:* Peter Lorre, Rochelle Hudson, J. Edward Bromberg, Robert Kent, Chick Chandler, George Regas, Fredrik Vogeding. *D:* Norman Foster; *P:* Sol M. Wurtzel; *St:* Foster, Willis Cooper; *Sc:* John Patrick, Lou Breslow. (1:03)

In this entry in the series Mr. Moto (Lorre) is in Indochina posing as an archeologist. Based on the character created by John P. Marquand.

3009. Mr. Moto Takes a Vacation (20th Century–Fox; 1939). *Cast:* Peter Lorre, Joseph Schildkraut, Lionel Atwill, Virginia Field, Iva Stewart, Victor Varconi, John Davidson, John King, Willie Best, Morgan Wallace, John Bleifer, Honorable Wu, Harry Strang, Anthony Warde. *D:* Norman Foster; *P:* Sol M. Wurtzel; *St:* Foster; *Sc:* Foster, Philip MacDonald. (1:01)

In this entry, the last of the eight films in the series, the Japanese detective (the creation of John P. Marquand) is guarding a precious crown enroute to San Francisco.

3010. Mr. Moto's Gamble (20th Century–Fox; 1938). *Cast:* Peter Lorre, Keye Luke, Dick Baldwin, Lynn Bari, Douglas Fowley, Maxie Rosenbloom, Lon Chaney, Jr., George E. Stone,

Harold Huber, Ward Bond, Bernard Nedell, Cliff Clark, Mike Mazurki, Paul Fix, Pierre Watkin, John Hamilton, Jayne Regan, Edward Marr, Russ Clark, Charles Williams. *D:* James Tinling; *P:* Sol M. Wurtzel; *Sc:* Charles Belden, Jerry Cady. (1:12)

Moto investigates the murder of a boxer in this entry which was originally a "Charlie Chan" script, adapted for the Moto series following the death of Warner Oland. Based on the character created by John P. Marquand.

3011. Mr. Moto's Last Warning (20th Century–Fox; 1939). *Cast:* Peter Lorre, Virginia Field, Ricardo Cortez, John Carradine, George Sanders, Joan Carol, Robert Coote, E.E. Clive, Holmes Herbert, Leyland Hodgson, John Davidson. *D:* Norman Foster; *P:* Sol M. Wurtzel; *Sc:* Foster, Philip MacDonald. (1:11) (video)

Terrorists are out to destroy a fleet of French ships in this entry, but the Japanese sleuth puts the crimps to their plans. Based on the character created by John P. Marquand.

3012. Mr. Robinson Crusoe (United Artists; 1932). *Cast:* Douglas Fairbanks, Maria Alba, William Farnum, Earle Browne. *D:* A. Edward Sutherland; *P:* Douglas Fairbanks; *St:* Elton Thomas (Fairbanks); *Adaptation:* Thomas Geraghty. (1:16) (video)

A playboy takes a bet that he can survive on a deserted island for a year. This comic vehicle which was also released in a silent version was a box office flop.

3013. Mr. Skitch (Fox; 1933). *Cast:* Will Rogers, ZaSu Pitts, Rochelle Hudson, Florence Desmond, Charles Starrett, Eugene Pallette, Harry Green. *D:* James Cruze; *St:* Anne Cameron (based on her novel "Green Dice"); *Sc:* Sonya Levien, Ralph Spence. (1:10)

Hit Will Rogers comedy of a family on a motor-trip to California.

3014. Mr. Smith Goes to Washington (Columbia; 1939). *Cast:* James Stewart (A.A.N. for B.A. as well as being voted "Best Actor of the Year" by the New York Film Critics for his portrayal of Jefferson Smith), Jean Arthur (Saunders), Claude Rains (A.A.N. for B.S.A. as Senator Joseph Paine), Edward Arnold (Jim Taylor), Guy Kibbee (Governor Hopper), Thomas Mitchell (Diz Moore), Eugene Pallette (Chick McGann), Beulah Bondi (Ma Smith), Harry Carey (A.A.N. for B.S.A. as the Senate president), H.B. Warner (Senate majority leader), Astrid Allwyn (Susan Paine), Ruth Donnelly (Mrs. Hopper), Grant Mitchell (Senator MacPherson), Porter Hall (Senator Monroe), Pierre Watkin (Senator Barnes), Charles Lane (Nosey), William Demarest (Bill Griffith), Dick Elliott (Carl Cook), Billy Watson, Delmer Watson, Harry Watson, Garry Watson, John Russell & Baby Dumpling (Larry Simms) (as the Hopper boys), Jack Carson (Sweeney), Joe King (Summers), Paul Stanton (Flood), Russell Simpson (Allen), Stanley Andrews (Senator Hodges), Walter Soderling (Senator Pickett), Frank Jaquet (Senator Byron), Ferris Taylor (Senator Carlisle), Carl Stockdale (Senator Burdette), Alan Bridge (Senator Dwight), Edmund Cobb (Senator Gower), Frederick Burton (Senator Dearhorn), H.V. Kaltenborn (broadcaster), Kenneth Carpenter (announcer), Vera Lewis (Mrs. Edwards), Dora Clement (Mrs. McGann), Laura Treadwell (Mrs. Taylor), Ann Doran (Paine's secretary), James Millican, Mary Gordon, Louis Jean Heydt, Dub Taylor, Byron Foulger, Lloyd Whitlock, Maurice Costello, Allan Cavan. *D:* (A.A.N.) Frank Capra; *P:* (A.A.N. for "Best Picture") Capra; *Original Story:* (A.A.) Lewis R. Foster; *Sc:* (A.A.N.) Sidney Buchman; *Art-Set Decoration:* (A.A.N.) Lionel Banks; *Music:* (A.A.N.) Dimitri Tiomkin; *Editors:* (A.A.N.) Gene Havlick, Al Clark; *Sound Recording:* (A.A.N.) John Livadary. (2:09) (video)

One of the all-time favorite classics of the 1930s, the story of a naive small town man who becomes a U.S. senator and ultimately a dupe for a corrupt political machine. A film with a message (and a hint of expose), it was panned and condemned when it opened in Washington, D.C., but was well received throughout the rest of the country. It became one of the 21 top grossing films of 1939–40, making the studio's initial investment of $1,500,000 worthwhile. Eleven Academy Award nominations garnered only one Oscar. *Film Daily* placed it at #2 on their "10 Best" list, while the National Board of Review and the *New York Times* both placed it at #8 on their respective lists. The New York Film Critics had it in nomination for "Best Film of the Year," with the final vote going to *Wuthering Heights* (q.v.).

3015. Mr. Wong, Detective (Monogram; 1938). *Cast:* Boris Karloff (Mr. Wong), Grant Withers, Maxine Jennings, Evelyn Brent, Lucien Prival, John St. Polis, William Gould, Hooper Atchley, John Hamilton, Frank Bruno, Lee Tong Foo, George Lloyd, Tchin, Wilbur Mack, Grace Wood. *D:* William Nigh; *P:* William T. Lackey; *Sc:* Houston Branch. (1:09) (video)

Premiere entry in the low-budget detective series featuring the character of Mr. James Lee Wong, as created by Hugh Wiley. Wong investigates the death of three business partners who died separately under similar circumstances.

Note: Remade as *Docks of New Orleans* (Monogram; 1948) a "Charlie Chan" mystery with Roland Winters.

3016. Mr. Wong in Chinatown (Monogram; 1939). *Cast:* Boris Karloff (James Lee Wong), Grant Withers, Marjorie Reynolds, Peter George Lynn, William Royle, Huntley Gordon, James Flavin, Lotus Long, Richard Loo, Bessie Loo, Lee Tong Foo, Little Angelo (Angelo Rossitto), Guy Usher. *D:* William Nigh; *P:* Scott R. Dunlap; *Sc:* W. Scott Darling. (1:10) (video)

Third entry in the series as Wong

investigates the murder of a Chinese princess. Based on the character created by Hugh Wiley.

Note: Remade as *The Chinese Ring* (Monogram; 1947) a "Charlie Chan" mystery with Roland Winters.

3017. Mrs. Wiggs of the Cabbage Patch (Paramount; 1934). *Cast:* Pauline Lord (film debut as Mrs. Wiggs), W.C. Fields (Mr. Stubbins), ZaSu Pitts (Miss Hazy), Evelyn Venable (Lucy Olcott), Kent Taylor (Bob Redding), Donald Meek (Mr. Wiggs), Jimmy Butler (Billy Wiggs), George Breakston (Jimmy Wiggs), Virginia Weidler (Europena Wiggs), Carmencita Johnson (Asia Wiggs), Edith Fellows (Australia Wiggs), Charles Middleton (Mr. Bagby), George Reed (Julius), Mildred Gover (Priscilla), Arthur Housman (Dick Harris), Walter Walker (Dr. Barton), Sam Flint, Clara Lou (Ann) Sheridan, James Robinson. *D:* Norman Taurog; *P:* Douglas MacLean; *Sc:* William Slavens McNutt, Jane Storm. (1:20) (video)

Hit comedy-drama of a poor woman with five children who awaits the return of her husband who went to the gold fields to seek his fortune. Based on the popular 1901 novel by Alice Hegan Rice, which was adapted to the Broadway stage in 1904 by Anne Crawford Flexner. First filmed (Paramount; 1919) with Mary Carr. Remade (Paramount; 1942) with Fay Bainter.

3018. Mixed Doubles (Xxxx Xxxx; 1930). (No information available)

3019. M'liss (RKO; 1936). *Cast:* Anne Shirley, John Beal, Guy Kibbee, Douglass Dumbrille, Moroni Olsen, Arthur Hoyt, Margaret Armstrong, William (Billy) Benedict, Frank M. Thomas, Ray Mayer, Barbara Pepper, James Bush, Esther Howard. *D:* George Nicholls, Jr.; *As.P.:* Robert Sisk; *Sc:* Dorothy Yost. (1:06) (video)

The adventures of a girl growing up and falling in love amidst the rowdy atmosphere of the California gold rush. Based on the story by Bret Harte, the film is a remake of a 1918 production for Paramount with Mary Pickford and Thomas Meighan, and another *The Girl Who Ran Wild* (Universal; 1922) with Gladys Walton, Marc Robbins and Vernon Steele.

3020. Moby Dick (WB/Vitaphone; 1930). *Cast:* John Barrymore (Captain Ahab), Joan Bennett (Faith), Walter Long (Stubbs), Nigel de Brulier (Elijah), Noble Johnson (Queequeg), Lloyd Hughes (Derek), May Boley (Whale Oil Rosie), Virginia Sale, John Ince, Jack Curtis, Tom O'Brien (Starbuck), Virginia Weidler (film debut—bit), William Walling. *D:* Lloyd Bacon; *Adaptation:* Oliver H.P. Garrett; *Sc:* J. Grubb Alexander. (1:10)

Herman Melville's classic of Captain Ahab and his quest for the great white whale, with an added romantic angle. A remake of *The Sea Beast* (WB; 1925-26), a silent with John Barrymore and Dolores Costello. Remade in 1956 without the love story.

3021. A Modern Hero (WB; 1934). *Cast:* Richard Barthelmess, Jean Muir, Marjorie Rambeau, Verree Teasdale, Florence Eldridge, Dorothy Burgess, Hobart Cavanaugh, William Janney, Arthur Hohl, Theodore Newton, J.M. Kerrigan, Maidel Turner, Mickey Rentschler, Richard Tucker, Judith Vosselli. *D:* G.W. Pabst (the famed German director on his only American film); *P:* James Seymour; *Sc:* Gene Markey, Kathryn Scola. (1:11)

Drama of what happens to a businessman when the 1929 stock market crashes. Based on the novel by Louis Bromfield.

3022. Modern Love (Universal; 1929). *Cast:* Kathryn Crawford, Charlie Chase, Jean Hersholt, Edward Martindel. *D:* A.B. Heath.

Part-talkie of a woman who must choose between love and a career.

Modern Madness (G.B. title) *see* **The Big Noise**

A Modern Miracle (G.B. title) *see* **The Story of Alexander Graham Bell**

3023. Modern Times (United Artists; 1936). *Cast:* Charles Chaplin, Paulette Goddard (in her starring debut), Henry Bergman, Chester Conklin, Stanley Sandford, Lloyd Ingraham, Wilfred Lucas, Hank Mann, Henry Blystone, Allan Garcia, Louis Natheaux, Gloria DeHaven (film debut as an extra). *D:* Charles Chaplin; *P:* Chaplin; *St & Sc:* Chaplin (who also wrote the music score). (1:29) (video)

Charlie Chaplin's last pantomimic film (actually a part-talkie) and his final portrayal of "The Little Tramp." Charlie attacks the machine age with a passion, making way for a finale that is considered by critics and film buffs alike as a classic in itself. The National Board of Review placed it at #3 on their "10 Best" list of the year. One of the 25 top grossing films of 1935-36.

3024. Molly and Me (Tiffany; 1929). *Cast:* Joe E. Brown, Belle Bennett. *D:* Albert Ray.

Part-talkie "poverty row" romantic comedy.

3025. Money Means Nothing (Monogram; 1934). *Cast:* Wallace Ford, Gloria Shea, Edgar Kennedy, Maidel Turner, Betty Blythe, Eddie Tamblyn, Vivian Oakland, Richard Tucker, Tenen Holtz, Ann Brody, Olaf Hytten. *D:* Christy Cabanne; *P:* Ben Verschleiser; *Sc:* Frances Hyland. (1:10)

B marital drama of a rich girl who marries a poor boy and sticks with him through thick and thin. Based on the play "Cost of Living" by William Anthony McGuire.

3026. Money to Burn (Republic; 1939). *Cast:* James Gleason, Lucile Gleason, Russell Gleason, Harry Davenport, Tommy Ryan. *D:* Gus Meins.

The 5th entry in the low-budget "Higgins Family" comedy series.

3027. Monkey Business (Paramount; 1931). *Cast:* Groucho Marx, Harpo Marx, Chico Marx, Zeppo Marx, Thelma Todd, Ruth Hall, Rockliffe Fellowes, Harry Woods, Tom Kennedy, Douglass Dumbrille, Cecil Cunningham, Maxine Castle, Otto Fries, Ben Taggart, Evelyn Pierce. *D:* Norman Z. McLeod; *P:* Herman J. Mankiewicz; *St:* Roland Pertwee, S.J. Perelman, Will B. Johnstone; *Sc:* Arthur Sheekman. (1:17) (video)

More Marxian lunacy as the foursome stowaway on a luxury liner. This was the first of their films to have an original story line (not based on another medium) and also the first of their films to be shot in Hollywood.

3028. The Monkey's Paw (RKO; 1933). *Cast:* Ivan Simpson (father), Louise Carter (mother), C. Aubrey Smith (Sgt. Major Morris), Bramwell Fletcher (son), Betty Lawford, Winter Hall, Herbert Bunston, Nena Quartero, LeRoy Mason, J.M. Kerrigan, Nigel de Brulier. *D:* Wesley Ruggles; *As.P.:* Pandro S. Berman; *Sc:* Graham John.

Based on the famous story by W.W. Jacobs and the stage play adaptation by Louis N. Parker, this horror tale deals with a dried monkey's paw brought from India which carries with it three wishes. The story's original shock ending is altered in this film version. The age of television brought a number of productions of the original story for that medium.

3029. Monster of the Deep (Xxxx Xxxx; 1933). *P:* Harold Austin. Documentary.

The Monster Show *see* **Freaks**

The Monster Walked (G.B. title) *see* **The Monster Walks**

3030. The Monster Walks (Mayfair; 1932). *Cast:* Rex Lease, Vera Reynolds, Mischa Auer, Sleep 'n' Eat (Willie Best), Sheldon Lewis, Sidney Bracey. *D:* Frank Strayer; *P:* Cliff Broughton; *Sc:* Robert Ellis. (G.B. title: *The Monster Walked*) (1:03) (video)

"Poverty row" horror thriller set in an old dark house of a madman in a wheelchair, and an ape suspected of murder.

3031. The Montana Kid (Monogram; 1931). *Cast:* Bill Cody, Andy Shuford, Doris Hill, William L. Thorne, G.D. Wood (Gordon DeMain), John Elliott, Paul Panzer. *D:* Harry Fraser; *P:* Trem Carr; *St:* Fraser; *Sc:* George Arthur Durlam. (1:00)

Bill Cody western of a cowboy who comes to the aid of a boy whose father was murdered.

3032. Montana Moon (MGM; 1930). *Cast:* John Mack Brown, Joan Crawford (who reportedly despised her connection with this film), Ricardo Cortez, Lloyd Ingraham, Cliff Edwards, Dorothy Sebastian, Benny Rubin, Karl Dane. *D:* Malcolm St. Clair; *Sc:* Sylvia Thalberg, Frank Butler; *Dialogue:* Joe Farnham; *Songs:* Nacio Herb Brown, Arthur Freed. (1:28)

A modern day western with songs of a girl who leaves New York City and goes west to her father's ranch where she finds romance. A box office dud.

3033. Montana Rider (Sono Art-World Wide; 1930). George Duryea (Tom Keene) "poverty row" western.

3034. Monte Carlo (Paramount; 1930). *Cast:* Jack Buchanan (in his last American film until 1953), Jeanette MacDonald, ZaSu Pitts, Claud Allister, Tyler Brooke, Lionel Belmore, Albert Conti, Edgar Norton, Donald Novis, David Percy, John Roche. *D:* Ernst Lubitsch; *P:* Lubitsch; *Sc:* Ernest Vajda, Vincent Lawrence; *Other Songs:* Leo Robin & Richard Whiting. (1:34)

A box office flop, this musical-comedy set among the European elite is based on "Monsieur Beaucaire" by Booth Tarkington and the play "The Blue Coast" by Hans Mueller. Notable is the finale song "Beyond the Blue Horizon" by Leo Robin and Richard Whiting which became a big hit, and somewhat of an American standard.

3035. Monte Carlo Nights (Monogram; 1934). *Cast:* John Darrow, Mary Brian, Kate Campbell, Robert Frazer, Yola D'Avril, Astrid Allwyn, George Hayes, Bill Van Every, Carl Stockdale, George Cleveland. *D:* William Nigh; *P:* Paul Malvern; *Sc:* Norman Houston.

B mystery-melodrama of a man wrongfully imprisoned for murder who escapes to set the record straight. Suggested by the story "Numbers of Death" by E. Phillips Oppenheim, the film had the working title of "Numbers of Monte Carlo."

3036. Moon Over Harlem (Meteor Productions; 1939). *Cast:* Herb Jeffreys, Mantan Moreland. *D:* Edgar G. Ulmer.

Independent low-budget romance which catered to the black audiences of the day.

3037. The Moon's Our Home (Paramount; 1936). *Cast:* Margaret Sullavan, Henry Fonda, Charles Butterworth, Beulah Bondi, Henrietta Crosman, Walter Brennan, Dorothy Stickney, Brandon Hurst, Lucien Littlefield, Margaret Hamilton, Spencer Charters, Margaret Fielding, John Spacey, Jack Norton. *D:* William A. Seiter; *P:* Walter Wanger; *Sc:* Isabel Dawn, Boyce DeGaw, Dorothy Parker, Alan Campbell. (1:16) (video)

Comedy of marital discord. Based on the *Cosmopolitan* magazine serial by Faith Baldwin.

Moonlight and Melody (G.B. title) *see* **Moonlight and Pretzels**

3038. Moonlight and Pretzels (Universal; 1933). *Cast:* Leo Carrillo, Mary Brian, Roger Pryor (feature film debut), Lillian Miles, Bobby Watson, William Frawley, Herbert Rawlinson, Jack Denny and his orchestra (unbilled), Bernice Claire, Alexander Gray, Richard Keene, Mary Lange. *D:* Karl Freund; *St:* Monte Brice, Arthur Jarrett; *Sc:* Brice, Sig Herzig; *Songs:* E.Y. Harburg, Sammy Fain, Jay Gorney, Herman Hupfeld. (G.B. title: *Moonlight and Melody*)

Depression-era B musical-comedy of the "puttin' on a show" variety.

3039. Moonlight Murder (MGM; 1936). *Cast:* H.B. Warner, Katherine Alexander, Leo Carrillo, Benita Hume, Madge Evans, Chester Morris, Frank McHugh, Grant Mitchell, J. Carrol Naish, Duncan Renaldo, Charles Trowbridge, Leonard Ceeley, Pedro de Cordoba. *D:* Edwin L. Marin; *P:* Lucien Hubbard; *As.P.:* Marin; *Sc:* Florence Ryerson, Edgar Allan Woolf; *St:* Robert T. Shannon, Albert J. Cohen.

B mystery-melodrama with an opera background.

3040. Moonlight on the Prairie (WB; 1935). *Cast:* Dick Foran, Sheila Mannors, George E. Stone, Robert Barrat, Dickie Jones, Gordon (Bill) Elliott, Joe Sawyer, Joe King, Glenn Strange. *D:* D. Ross Lederman; *P:* Bryan Foy; *Sc:* William Jacobs; *Songs:* "Covered Wagon Days," title song by M.K. Jerome, Joan Jasmyn, Vernon Spencer & Bob Nolan. (1:03)

Dick Foran western (his first for this studio as a singing cowboy). A cowboy helps a woman save her ranch.

3041. Moonlight on the Range (Spectrum; 1937). *Cast:* Fred Scott, Lois January, Al St. John, Dick Curtis, Frank LaRue, Jimmy Aubrey, Oscar Gahan, Carl Mathews, Wade Walker, William McCall, Shorty Miller, Jack Evans, Rudy Sooter, Lew Meehan, Ed Cassidy, George Morrell. *D:* Sam

Newfield; *P:* Jed Buell; *Sc:* Fred Myton. (1:00)

Fred Scott western with songs of a cowboy out to apprehend his look-a-like half brother, a cattle rustler.

Moonlight Over Texas (G.B. title) *see* **Starlight Over Texas**

3042. The Moonstone (Monogram; 1934). *Cast:* David Manners, Phyllis Barry, Gustav von Seyffertitz, Jameson Thomas, Herbert Bunston, Evelyn Bostock, John Davidson, Elspeth Dudgeon, Claude King, Olaf Hytten, Charles Irwin, Fred Walton. *D:* Reginald Barker; *P:* Paul Malvern; *Sc:* Adele Buffington. (1:02)

B mystery based on the novel by Wilkie Collins involving the theft of a fabulous diamond.

3043. Morals for Women (Tiffany; 1931). *Cast:* Lina Basquette, June Clyde, David Rollins, Natalie Moorhead, Virginia Lee Corbin, John Holland, Emma Dunn. *D:* Mort Blumenstock; *St & Sc:* Frances Hyland.

Low-budget production.

More Than a Kiss (G.B. title) *see* **Don't Bet on Women**

3044. More Than a Secretary (Columbia; 1936). *Cast:* Jean Arthur, George Brent, Ruth Donnelly, Lionel Stander, Reginald Denny, Dorothea Kent, Charles Halton, Geraldine Hall. *D:* Alfred E. Green; *St:* Ethel Hill, Aben Kandel & Matt Taylor, "Safari in Manhattan"; *Sc:* Dale Van Every, Lynn Starling. (1:17)

B romantic comedy of a secretary in love with her boss.

3045. Mormon Conquest (Art Mix; 1938). *D:* Victor Adamson (Denver Dixon).

B western.

(No other information available)

3046. Morning Glory (RKO; 1933). *Cast:* Katharine Hepburn (A.A. for B.A.—her first—as Eva Lovelace),

Adolphe Menjou (Louis Easton), Douglas Fairbanks, Jr. (Joseph Sheridan), Mary Duncan (Rita Vernon), C. Aubrey Smith (Robert Harley Hedges), Don Alvarado (Pepe Velez), Richard Carle (Henry Lawrence), Tyler Brooke (Charles Van Dusen), Frederick Santley (Will Seymour), Geneva Mitchell (Gwendolyn Hall), Theresa Harris. *D:* Lowell Sherman; *As.P.:* Pandro S. Berman; *Sc:* Howard J. Green. (1:14) (video)

A New York City actress suffers many disappointments in her bid to become a popular stage star. Based on the play by Zoe Akins. Remade as *Stage Struck* (Buena Vista/RKO; 1957).

3047. Morocco (Paramount; 1930). *Cast:* Gary Cooper (Tom Brown), Marlene Dietrich (A.A.N. for B.A. in her American film debut as Amy Jolly), Adolphe Menjou (Labessier), Ullrich Haupt (Adjutant Caesar), Juliette Compton (Anna Dolores), Francis McDonald (Sergeant Barney Tatoche), Albert Conti (Colonel Quinnevieres), Eve Southern (Madame Caesar), Michael Visaroff (Barratire), Paul Porcasi (Lo Tinto), Theresa Harris (camp follower). *D:* (A.A.N.) Josef von Sternberg; *P:* von Sternberg; *Adaptation & Sc:* Jules Furthman; *Cinematographer:* (A.A.N.) Lee Garmes; *Art-Set Decoration:* (A.A.N.) Hans Dreier. (1:32) (video)

A cabaret singer dangles many male admirers on a string until she meets the one who turns the tables on her. This film was voted one of the year's "10 Best" by the National Board of Review, as well as being one of the 15 top grossing films of 1930–31. Based on the play "Amy Jolly, die Frau aus Marrakesch" by Benno Vigny.

3048. The Most Dangerous Game (RKO; 1932). *Cast:* Joel McCrea, Fay Wray, Leslie Banks (Count Zaroff), Robert Armstrong, Noble Johnson, Steve Clemente, Dutch Hendrian, Larry "Buster" Crabbe (film debut). *D:* Ernest B. Schoedsack, Irving Pichel (directorial debut); *As.P.:* Merian C.

Cooper; *Sc:* James A. Creelman. (G.B. title: *The Hounds of Zaroff*) (1:03) (video)

A hit in its day and based on the famous short story by Richard Connell, this melodramatic thriller tells of a madman stalking shipwreck victims on a remote island as though they were animal prey. The film uses some of the sets used for *King Kong* (q.v.). Remade as *A Game of Death* (RKO; 1945) and *Run for the Sun* (United Artists; 1957).

3049. A Most Immoral Lady (WB/F.N.; 1929). *Cast:* Leatrice Joy, Sidney Blackmer, Walter Pidgeon, Montagu Love, Josephine Dunn, Robert Edeson, Donald Reed. *D:* John Griffith Wray; *Sc:* Forrest Halsey.

Melodrama of a woman and her husband who extort money from millionaires by blackmail and victimization. Based on the play by Townsend Martin.

3050. Most Precious Thing in Life (Columbia; 1934). *Cast:* Jean Arthur, Richard Cromwell, Donald Cook, Ben Alexander, Anita Louise, Samuel S. Hinds, Mary Forbes, Ward Bond, Jane Darwell, Dutch Hendrian. *D:* Lambert Hillyer.

Mother-love drama of a woman and her child.

3051. The Moth (Marcy Exchange; 1934). *Cast:* Sally O'Neil, Paul Page, Wilfred Lucas. *D:* Fred Newmeyer, Jr.

(No other information available)

3052. Mother and Son (Monogram; 1931). *Cast:* Clara Kimball Young (Faro Lil), Bruce Warren, G.D. Wood (Gordon DeMain), Mildred Golden, John Elliott. *D:* John P. McCarthy; *P:* Trem Carr; *St & Sc:* Wellyn Totman. (1:00)

Low-budget drama of a son's objections to his mother returning to her former profession of running a gambling house.

3053. Mother Carey's Chickens (RKO; 1938). *Cast:* Anne Shirley, Ruby Keeler (in a role intended for Katharine Hepburn — whose refusal to do the film got her fired from RKO), James Ellison, Fay Bainter (Mother Carey), Walter Brennan, Donnie Dunagan, Frank Albertson, Alma Kruger, Jackie Moran, Margaret Hamilton, Virginia Weidler, Ralph Morgan, Phyllis Kennedy, Lucille Ward. *D:* Rowland V. Lee; *P:* Pandro S. Berman; *Sc:* S.K. Lauren, Gertrude Purcell. (1:22)

Sentimental drama of a large family which was based on the 1911 novel by Kate Douglas Wiggin. The film which was a hit for the studio, won the "Minister of Popular Culture Award" at the Venice Film Festival. The novel was also adapted to the stage by Wiggin and Rachel Crothers and was remade as *Summer Magic* (Walt Disney; 1963).

3054. Mother Knows Best (Fox; 1928). *Cast:* Madge Bellamy, Louise Dresser, Barry Norton, Stuart Erwin (film debut), Dawn O'Day (Anne Shirley), Lucien Littlefield. *D:* John G. Blystone.

Part-talkie drama of a girl dominated by her mother.

3055. Mother Machree (Fox; 1928). *Cast:* Victor McLaglen, Belle Bennett, Philippe deLacy, Ethel Clayton, Pat Somerset, Constance Howard, Rodney Hildebrand, Joyce Wiard, Robert Parrish (film debut), Ted McNamara, John Wayne (unbilled extra). *D:* John Ford; *St:* Rida Johnson Young; *Song:* "Mother Machree" by S.L. Rothafel, Erno Rapee.

Sentimental drama, a part-talkie with synchronized music score, sound effects and a vocalized song.

3056. Mother's Cry (WB/F.N.; 1930-31). *Cast:* Dorothy Peterson, Helen Chandler, David Manners, Evalyn Knapp, Edward Woods, Pat O'Malley, Reginald Pasch, Sidney Blackmer, Claire McDowell, Boris Karloff, Charles Hill Mailes. *D:* Hobart Henley; *P:* Robert North; *Sc:* Lenore J. Coffee.

Drama of a woman who raises her

four children and the eventual outcome of each child over a period of thirty years. Based on the novel by Helen Grace Carlisle.

3057. Mother's Millions (Universal; 1931). *Cast:* May Robson, Edmund Breese, Lawrence Gray, Frances Dade, James Hall, William L. Thorne, Leah Winslow, Elinor Flynn, Lillian Harmer. *D:* James Flood; *St:* Howard McKent Barnes. (Originally known as *She-Wolf of Wall Street*) (aka: *She-Wolf*) (1:25)

Drama of a ruthless lady financier who goes after her late husband's business competition, only to find her family is becoming adversely affected.

3058. Motive for Revenge (Majestic; 1935). *Cast:* Donald Cook, Irene Hervey. *D:* Burt Lynwood; *Sc:* Stuart Anthony.

"Poverty row" drama.

3059. Motor Madness (Columbia; 1937). *Cast:* Ralph Byrd, Marc Lawrence, Joseph Sawyer. *D:* D. Ross Lederman.

B action melodrama.

3060. Moulin Rouge (United Artists/20th Century; 1933–34). *Cast:* Constance Bennett (dual role), Franchot Tone, Tullio Carminati, Helen Westley (film debut), Andrew Tombes, Hobart Cavanaugh, Russ Columbo, Boswell Sisters (featuring Connee), Fuzzy Knight, Russ Brown, Ivan Lebedeff, Lucille Ball (bit), Georges Renavent. *D:* Sidney Lanfield; *P:* Darryl F. Zanuck, William Goetz, Raymond Griffith; *St:* Nunnally Johnson; *Sc:* Johnson, Henry Lehrman; *Songs:* Al Dubin, Harry Warren. (1:09)

Musical of a woman who impersonates her sister in order to save her marriage and career. Based on the play "Lyon de Bri."

3061. Mountain Justice (Universal; 1930). *Cast:* Ken Maynard, Kathryn Crawford, Paul Hurst, Richard Carlisle,

Otis Harlan, Gilbert "Pee Wee" Holmes, Les Bates, Edgar "Blue" Washington, Fred Burns. *D:* Harry Joe Brown; *P:* Maynard; *Sc:* Bennett Cohen, Lesley Mason. (Original title: *Kettle Creek*) (1:04)

Ken Maynard western of a cowboy who heads into the Kentucky hills to find who killed his father.

3062. Mountain Justice (WB/F.N.; 1937). *Cast:* George Brent, Josephine Hutchinson, Robert Barrat, Guy Kibbee, Margaret Hamilton, Mona Barrie, Robert McWade, Fuzzy Knight, Minerva Urecal, Harry Davenport, Marcia Mae Jones, Guy Wilkerson, Edward Pawley, Granville Bates, Sybil Harris. *D:* Michael Curtiz; *P:* Lou Edelman; *Sc:* Norman Reilly Raine, Luci Ward.

B rural drama of a woman who is forced to kill her crude insensitive father.

3063. Mountain Music (Paramount; 1937). *Cast:* Martha Raye, "Bazooka" Bob Burns, John Howard, George Hayes, Wally Vernon, Spencer Charters, Ward Bond, Rita LaRoy, Fuzzy Knight, Rufe Davis, Arthur Hohl, Olin Howland, Terry Walker, Jan Duggan, Miranda Giles, Terry Ray (Ellen Drew), Georgia Simmons, Charles Timblin. *D:* Robert Florey; *P:* Benjamin Glazer; *St:* MacKinlay Kantor; *Sc:* Charles Lederer, John C. Moffitt, Duke Atteberry, Russel Crouse.

This rustic B comedy with songs of romance in the backwoods was one of the 38 top grossing films of 1936–37.

3064. Mountain Rhythm (Republic; 1939). *Cast:* Gene Autry, Smiley Burnette, June Storey, Maude Eburne, Ferris Taylor, Walter Fenner, Jack Pennick, Hooper Atchley, Bernard Suss, Ed Cassidy, Jack Ingram, Tom London, Roger Williams, Frankie Marvin, Champion. *D:* B. Reeves Eason; *P:* Harry Grey; *St:* Connie Lee; *Sc:* Gerald Geraghty. (1:01)

Gene Autry western with songs.

3065. Mounted Fury (Sono Art-World Wide; 1931). *Cast:* John Bowers (silent screen star in his final film — d. 1936 by drowning), Blanche Mehaffey, Frank Rice, Lina Basquette, Robert Ellis, George Regas, John Ince. *D:* Stuart Paton; *Sc:* Betty Burbridge. (1:03)

Low-budget "poverty row" action adventure of a Mountie out to get his man.

3066. The Mounted Stranger (Universal; 1930). *Cast:* Hoot Gibson, Louise Lorraine, Fred Burns, Buddy Hunter, Francis Ford, Milton Brown, Jim Corey, Walter Patterson, Francelia Billington. *D:* Arthur Rosson; *Sc:* Rosson. (1:05)

Hoot Gibson western of a boy who sees his father murdered and grows up to apprehend the killer. A remake of *Ridin' Kid from Powder River* (Universal; 1924) with Gibson and Gladys Hulette, and based on the pulp story of that name by H.H. Knibbs.

3067. The Mouthpiece (WB; 1932). *Cast:* Warren William, Sidney Fox, Mae Madison, Aline MacMahon, John Wray, J. Carrol Naish, Noel Francis, Guy Kibbee, Jack LaRue (film debut), Berton Churchill, Paulette Goddard (bit), Morgan Wallace, Polly Walters, Emerson Treacy, Walter Walker. *D:* Elliott Nugent, James Flood; *P:* Lucien Hubbard; *Sc:* Joseph Jackson, Earl Baldwin. (1:30)

Fact-based story of attorney William Fallon, an up-and-coming D.A. who changes horses in midstream and becomes a defense attorney. The *New York Times* voted it #6 on their "10 Best" list of the year. Remade as *The Man Who Talked Too Much* (WB; 1940) and as *Illegal* (WB; 1955).

3068. Movie Crazy (Paramount/Harold Lloyd; 1932). *Cast:* Harold Lloyd, Constance Cummings, Kenneth Thomson, Sydney Jarvis, Eddie Fetherston, Mary Doran, Grady Sutton, DeWitt Jennings, Robert McWade, Arthur Housman. *D:* Clyde Bruckman; *P:* Harold Lloyd; *St:* Agnes Christine Johnston, John Grey, Felix Adler; *Sc:* Lloyd, Vincent Lawrence. (1:22)

One of Lloyd's early talkies, as a naive young man goes to Hollywood with the idea of becoming a movie star.

Movie Struck *see* **Pick a Star**

Movietone Follies of 1929 (G.B. title) *see* **Fox Movietone Follies of 1929**

3069. The Mummy (Universal; 1932). *Cast:* Boris Karloff (Im-ho-tep), Zita Johann (Helen Grosvenor), David Manners, Arthur Byron, Edward Van Sloan, Bramwell Fletcher, Henry Victor, Leonard Mudie, Arnold Gray, Eddie Kane, Noble Johnson, Kathryn Byron, Tony Marlow, James Crane. *D:* Karl Freund (directorial debut); *P:* Stanley Bergerman; *St:* Richard Schayer, Nina Wilcox Putnam; *Sc:* John L. Balderston. (1:12) (video)

Classic horror film of the mummy of the Egyptian Prince Im-ho-tep being brought back to life and pursuing the girl he believes to be the reincarnation of an ancient love. A big hit for Universal, which had nothing to do with the later low-budget series of the 1940s by this studio except inspiration and stock footage. Remade in Great Britain in 1959.

3070. Mummy's Boys (RKO; 1936). *Cast:* Bert Wheeler, Robert Woolsey, Barbara Pepper, Frank M. Thomas, Moroni Olsen, Willie Best, Francis McDonald, Frank Lackteen, Charles Coleman, Mitchell Lewis, Frederick Burton. *D:* Fred Guiol; *P.:* Lee Marcus; *St:* Lew Lipton, Jack Townley; *Sc:* Townley, Philip G. Epstein, Charles Roberts. (1:08)

The zany duo of Wheeler and Woolsey get involved in the search for an ancient Egyptian treasure in this low-budget comedy.

3071. Murder at Dawn (Big 4 Film Corp.; 1932). *Cast:* Jack Mulhall, Josephine Dunn, Mischa Auer, Crauford Kent. *D:* Richard Thorpe; *P:* John R. Freuler. (G.B. title: *The Death Ray*)

Low-budget independent melodrama.

3072. Murder at Glen Athol (Invincible; 1935–36). *Cast:* Iris Adrian, Irene Ware, John Miljan, Noel Madison, Barry Norton, Betty Blythe, Robert Frazer, Oscar Apfel. *D:* Frank Strayer. (G.B. title: *The Criminal Within*)

"Poverty row" murder-mystery.

3073. Murder at Midnight (Tiffany; 1931). *Cast:* Alice White, Robert Ellis, Aileen Pringle, Leslie Fenton, William Humphrey, Kenneth Thomson, Tyrell Davis, Aileen Carlisle, Hale Hamilton, Brandon Hurst, Clara Blandick, Robert Elliott. *D:* Frank Strayer; *St:* W. Scott Darling, Frank R. Strayer; *Dial.:* W. Scott Darling.

"Poverty row" mystery-thriller.

3074. Murder at the Vanities (Paramount; 1934). *Cast:* Jack Oakie, Kitty Carlisle, Victor McLaglen, Carl Brisson, Gail Patrick, Dorothy Stickney, Gertrude Michael, Jessie Ralph, Donald Meek, Toby Wing, Duke Ellington, Charles Middleton, Colin Tapley, Barbara Fritchie, Otto Hoffman, Beryl Wallace, Charles McAvoy, Clara Lou (Ann) Sheridan. *D:* Mitchell Leisen; *P:* E. Lloyd Sheldon; *St:* Earl Carroll, Rufus King; *Sc:* Carey Wilson, Joseph Gollomb, Sam Hellman; *Songs Include:* "Cocktails for Two" by Sam Coslow & Arthur Johnston, as well as a musical number titled "Sweet Marijuana." (1:29) (video)

Murder strikes backstage at the opening of Earl Carroll's Vanities (a musical revue of bygone days). A musical-comedy murder-mystery.

3075. Murder by an Aristocrat (WB/F.N.; 1936). *Cast:* Lyle Talbot, Marguerite Churchill, William Davidson, Claire Dodd, Virginia Brissac, John Eldredge, Gordon (Bill) Elliott, Stuart Holmes, Joseph Crehan, Florence Fair, Mary Treen, Milton Kibbee, Lottie Williams, Henry Otho. *D:* Frank McDonald; *P:* Bryan Foy; *Sc:* Luci Ward, Roy Chanslor.

B murder-mystery of blackmail and murder within a wealthy family. Based on the book by Mignon Eberhart.

3076. Murder by Television (Cameo/Imperial Distributors; 1935). *Cast:* Bela Lugosi (dual role), June Collyer, Huntley Gordon, George Meeker, Claire McDowell, Henry Mowbray. *D:* Clifford Sanforth; *As.P:* Edward M. Spitz; *Sc:* Joseph O'Donnell. (1:00) (video)

Low-budget independent murder melodrama involving the murder of the inventor of a television set.

3077. Murder by the Clock (Paramount; 1931). *Cast:* William "Stage" Boyd, Lilyan Tashman, Regis Toomey, Irving Pichel, Blanche Frederici, Sally O'Neil, Walter McGrail, Lester Vail, Willard Robertson, Frederick Sullivan, Frank Sheridan, Harry Burgess, Lenita Lane, Martha Mattox, John Rogers. *D:* Edward Sloman; *Sc:* Henry Myers, Rufus King, Charles Beahan (based on King's book and Beahan's stage adaptation). (1:16)

Offbeat B mystery of a woman who is buried in a tomb from which she can escape in case she is buried alive. The subject matter of the film fell in disfavor with British audiences, forcing its withdrawal from circulation in that country.

3078. Murder Goes to College (Paramount; 1937). *Cast:* Lynne Overman (Hank Hyer), Roscoe Karns, Marsha Hunt, Buster Crabbe, Astrid Allwyn, Terry Ray (Ellen Drew). *D:* Charles Reisner; *P:* Harold Hurley.

Premiere entry in a proposed low budget series, based on a series of mysteries by Kurt Steel. The second entry in the series, *Partners in Crime* (q.v.) flopped and the series was dropped.

3079. Murder in Greenwich Village (Columbia; 1937). *Cast:* Richard Arlen, Fay Wray, Raymond Walburn, Marc Lawrence, Wyn Cahoon, Scott Colton, Thurston Hall, George McKay, Marjorie Reynolds, Gene Morgan, Mary Russell, Barry Macollum, Leon Ames. *D:* Albert S. Rogell; *St:* Robert T. Shannon; *Sc:* Michael Simmons. (1:08)

B mystery-comedy.

3080. Murder in the Air (Xxxx Xxxx; 1935). (No information available)

Murder in the Big House (G.B. title) *see* **Jailbreak**

3081. Murder in the Clouds (WB/F.N.; 1934). *Cast:* Ann Dvorak, Lyle Talbot, Gordon Westcott, Robert Light, George Cooper, Charles Wilson, Wheeler Oakman, Henry O'Neill, Arthur Pierson, Lester Vail, Russell Hicks, Edward McWade, Clay Clement, Eddie Shubert, Nick Copeland, Gordon (Bill) Elliott. *D:* D. Ross Lederman; *P:* Sam Bischoff; *St & Sc:* Dore Schary, Roy Chanslor. (1:00)

A scientist who has drawn up plans for a new type of explosive is abducted in this B actioner.

3082. Murder in the Fleet (MGM; 1935). *Cast:* Robert Taylor, Jean Parker, Jean Hersholt, Ted Healy, Una Merkel, Nat Pendleton, Raymond Hatton, Donald Cook, Mischa Auer, Mary Doran, Ward Bond, Robert Livingston, Arthur Byron, Edward Norris, Frank Shields. *D:* Edward Sedgwick; *P:* Lucien Hubbard; *Sc:* Sedgwick, Frank "Spig" Wead, Joe Sherman. (1:10)

B comedy-melodrama of murder and sabotage aboard a U.S. naval cruiser.

3083. Murder in the Museum (Willis Kent; 1933). *Cast:* Henry B. Walthall, John Harron. *D:* Melville Shyer; *Sc:* E.B. Crosswhite.

"Poverty row" crime drama.

3084. Murder in the Private Car (MGM; 1934). *Cast:* Russell Hardie, Mary Carlisle, Charles Ruggles, John Harron, Una Merkel, Porter Hall, Akim Tamiroff, Sterling Holloway, Berton Churchill, Willard Robertson. *D:* Harry Beaumont; *P:* Lucien Hubbard; *Sc:* Ralph Spence, Al Boasberg, Edgar Allan Woolf, Harvey Thew. (G.B. title: *Murder on the Runaway Train*) (0:52)

B mystery-comedy aptly described by its two titles.

3085. Murder in Trinidad (Fox; 1934). *Cast:* Heather Angel, Nigel Bruce, Victor Jory, J. Carrol Naish, John Davidson, Douglas Walton, Pat Somerset, Murray Kinnell, Francis Ford, Claude King, Noble Johnson. *D:* Louis King.

Low-budget murder-mystery based on the novel by John W. Vandercook. Remade as *Mr. Moto in Danger Island* (q.v.).

3086. The Murder Man (MGM; 1935). *Cast:* Spencer Tracy, Virginia Bruce, Lionel Atwill, Harvey Stephens, Robert Barrat, James Stewart (film debut as Shorty), William Collier, Sr., Bobby Watson, William Demarest, John Sheehan, Lucien Littlefield, George Chandler, Fuzzy Knight, Louise Henry, Robert Warwick, Joe Irving, Ralph Bushman, Stanley Andrews. *D:* Tim Whelan (American directorial debut); *P:* Harry Rapf; *St:* Whelan, Guy Bolton; *Sc:* Whelan, John C. Higgins. (1:11)

B newspaper melodrama.

3087. The Murder of Dr. Harrigan (WB/F.N.; 1936). *Cast:* Ricardo Cortez, Kay Linaker, Mary Astor, Joseph Crehan, Frank Reicher, Anita Kerry, Philip Reed, John Eldredge, Johnny Arthur, Mary Treen, Robert Strange, Don Barclay, Joan Blair. *D:* Frank McDonald; *P:* Bryan Foy; *Sc:* Peter Milne, Sy Bartlett, Charles Belden.

B murder-mystery set in a hospital. Based on the book by Mignon G. Eberhart.

3088. Murder on a Bridal Path (RKO; 1936). *Cast:* Helen Broderick (Miss Hildegarde Withers — replacing Edna May Oliver who initiated the role in the first three films), James Gleason (Inspector Piper), Leslie Fenton, Louise Latimer, Owen Davis, Jr., John Arledge, John Carroll, Sheila Terry, Christian Rub, Willie Best, John Miltern, Spencer Charters, James Donlan, Gustav von Seyffertitz, Frank Reicher, Harry Jans. *D:* Edward Killy, William Hamilton; *As.P.:* William Sistrom; *Sc:* Edmund North, Dorothy Yost, Thomas Lennon, James Gow. (1:06)

Fourth entry in the Hildegarde Withers-Oscar Piper mystery-comedy series as old maid school teacher, Miss Withers solves a murder in Central Park with the help of her cranky police inspector friend. Based on the novel by Stuart Palmer.

3089. Murder on a Honeymoon (RKO; 1935). *Cast:* Edna May Oliver (Hildegarde Withers), James Gleason (Oscar Piper), Lola Lane, George Meeker, Dorothy Libaire, Harry Ellerbee, Chick Chandler, Sleep 'n' Eat (Willie Best), Leo G. Carroll, DeWitt Jennings, Spencer Charters, Arthur Hoyt, Matt McHugh, Morgan Wallace, Brooks Benedict, Rollo Lloyd. *D:* Lloyd Corrigan; *P:* Kenneth McGowan; *Sc:* Robert Benchley, Seton I. Miller. (1:13)

The 3rd entry in the Withers-Piper mystery-comedy series as old maid schoolteacher Hildegarde Withers takes to sleuthing a murder aboard a plane bound for Catalina Island. Based on the novel "The Puzzle of the Pepper Tree" by Stuart Palmer.

3090. Murder on the Blackboard (RKO; 1934). *Cast:* Edna May Oliver (Miss Withers), James Gleason (Inspector Piper), Bruce Cabot, Gertrude Michael, Regis Toomey, Edgar Kennedy, Tully Marshall, Jackie Searle, Frederik Vogeding, Barbara Fritchie, Gustav von Seyffertitz, Tom Herbert, Jed Prouty. *D:* George Archainbaud; *As.P.:* Kenneth Macgowan; *Sc:* Willis Goldbeck. (1:11)

Second entry in the Withers-Piper series as Miss Withers sleuths the murder of a music teacher in her school with musical notes on the blackboard as the main clue. Based on the novel by Stuart Palmer.

3091. Murder on the Campus (Chesterfield; 1934). *Cast:* J. Farrell MacDonald, Edward Van Sloan, Dewey Robinson. *D:* Richard Thorpe. (G.B. title: *On the Stroke of Nine*)

"Poverty row" mystery.

3092. The Murder on the Roof (Columbia; 1930). *Cast:* Virginia Brown Faire, Dorothy Revier, Raymond Hatton, Fred Kelsey. *D:* George B. Seitz; *Sc:* F. Hugh Herbert.

"Poverty row" mystery.

Murder on the Runaway Train (G.B. title) *see* **Murder in the Private Car**

3093. Murder Will Out (WB/F.N.; 1930). *Cast:* Jack Mulhall, Lila Lee, Malcolm McGregor, Hedda Hopper, Alec B. Francis, Noah Beery, Claud Allisten. *D:* Clarence Badger; *St:* Murray Leinster, Will Jenkins; *Sc:* J. Grubb Alexander.

B espionage melodrama.

3094. Murder with Pictures (Paramount; 1936). *Cast:* Lew Ayres, Gail Patrick, Paul Kelly, Onslow Stevens, Joyce Compton, Benny Baker, Joseph Sawyer, Anthony Nace, Terry Ray (Ellen Drew). *D:* Charles Barton; *P:* A.M. Botsford; *Sc:* John C. Moffitt, Sidney Salkow.

B melodrama of a girl framed for murder and proven innocent by a news photographer.

3095. Murders in the Rue Morgue (Universal; 1932). *Cast:* Bela Lugosi (Dr. Mirakle), Sidney Fox, Leon (Ames) Waycoff (film debut), Bert

Roach, Brandon Hurst, Arlene Francis (film debut), Betty Ross Clarke, Noble Johnson, D'Arcy Corrigan. *D:* Robert Florey; *P:* Carl Laemmle, Jr.; *Adaptation:* Florey; *Sc:* Tom Reed, Dale Van Every; *Additional Dialogue:* John Huston. (1:32) (video)

An offbeat horror film of its time as a series of mysterious murders baffle the police. Loosely based on the Edgar Allan Poe story of the same name. The same story also served as a basis for *Phantom of the Rue Morgue* (WB; 1954), *Murders in the Rue Morgue* (American International; 1971) and *The Murders in the Rue Morgue,* a 1986 TV movie which closely followed the original Poe story.

3096. Murders in the Zoo (Paramount; 1933). *Cast:* Lionel Atwill, Charles Ruggles, Kathleen Burke, Randolph Scott, Gail Patrick, John Lodge, Edward McWade, Jane Darwell. *D:* A. Edward Sutherland; *St:* Philip Wylie; *Sc:* Wylie, Seton I. Miller. (1:04)

Horror thriller of a jealous zookeeper who disposes of any man he believes to be interested in his wife. This precode production shocked audiences of its day with scenes that never would have made it past the 1934 film code.

3097. Music for Madame (RKO; 1937). *Cast:* Nino Martini, Joan Fontaine, Alan Mowbray, Billy Gilbert, Alan Hale, Grant Mitchell, Erik Rhodes, Lee Patrick, Romo Vincent, Jack Carson, Frank Conroy, Bradley Page, Ada Leonard, Alan Bruce, Barbara Pepper, Edward H. Robins, George Shelley, Milburn Stone, Ward Bond. *D:* John G. Blystone; *P:* Jesse L. Lasky, Jr.; *St:* Robert Harari; *Sc:* Harari, Gertrude Purcell; *Songs:* title song, Herb Magidson, Allie Wrubel; "I Want the World to Know" & "Bambina" by Rudolf Friml, Gus Kahn; "King of the Road" by Nathaniel Shilkret, Edward Cherkose. (1:21)

Musical-comedy of an Italian opera singer, used as a pawn by crooks after arriving in Hollywood. Notable is Nino Martini's rendering of "Vesti La Giubba" from Ruggiero Leoncavallo's "Pagliacci" (1892). A box office flop.

3098. The Music Goes 'Round (Columbia; 1936). *Cast:* Harry Richman, Rochelle Hudson, Walter Connolly, Herman Bing, Lionel Stander, Victor Kilian, Douglass Dumbrille, Michael Bartlett, Gene Morgan, Henry Mollison, Edward Farley, Irving Bacon, Michael Riley, Wyrley Birch, Dora Early, Jack Pennick. *D:* Victor Schertzinger; *St:* Sidney Buchman; *Sc:* Jo Swerling; *Songs:* Schertzinger, Harry Akst, Lew Brown.

Musical.

3099. Music in the Air (Fox; 1934). *Cast:* Gloria Swanson, John Boles, Douglass Montgomery, June Lang, Al Shean, Reginald Owen, Joseph Cawthorn, Hobart Bosworth, Sara Haden, Jed Prouty, Fuzzy Knight, Christian Rub, Marjorie Main, Roger Imhof. *D:* Joe May; *Sc:* Howard Young, Billy Wilder. (1:25)

Musical centered around a couple's marital difficulties. Based on the play by Jerome Kern and Oscar Hammerstein II.

3100. Music Is Magic (Fox; 1935). *Cast:* Alice Faye, Bebe Daniels, Ray Walker, Frank Mitchell, Jack Durant, Hattie McDaniel, Andrew Tombes, Charles C. Wilson, Lynn Bari. *D:* George Marshall; *Sc:* Edward Eliscu, Lou Breslow; *Songs:* Oscar Levant, Sidney Clare. (1:07)

B musical of a has-been star.

3101. Muss 'Em Up (RKO; 1936). *Cast:* Preston Foster (Tip O'Neil), Margaret Callahan, Alan Mowbray, John Carroll, Ralph Morgan, Maxie Rosenbloom, Guinn Williams, Molly Lamont, Florine McKinney, Robert Middlemass, Noel Madison, Maxine Jennings, Harold Huber, Clarence Muse, Paul Porcasi, Ward Bond, John Adair, Willie Best. *D:* Charles Vidor; *P:*

Pandro S. Berman; *Sc:* Erwin Gelsey. (G.B. title: *The House of Fate*) (1:08)

B mystery-melodrama involving a kidnapping plot and murder. Based on the novel by James Edward Grant.

3102. Mussolini Speaks (Columbia; 1933). Feature length documentary narrated by Lowell Thomas detailing the early activities and accomplishments of "Il Duce" prior to his fascist dictatorship. This film was a pet project of Columbia Studios top man, Harry Cohn and was a hugh box office hit, grossing a million dollars at the box office.

3103. Mutiny Ahead (Majestic; 1935). *Cast:* Neil Hamilton, Leon Ames. *D:* Tommy Atkins.

(No other information available)

3104. Mutiny in the Big House (Monogram; 1939). *Cast:* Charles Bickford, Barton MacLane, Dennis Moore, Pat Moriarty, William Royle, George Cleveland, Charles Foy, Russell Hopton, Jeffrey Sayre, Eddie Foster, Jack Daley, Dave O'Brien, Wheeler Oakman, Charles King, Nigel de Brulier, Merrill McCormack. *D:* William Nigh; *P:* Grant Withers; *St:* Martin Mooney; *Sc:* Robert D. Andrews. (1:23)

Hit prison melodrama of a young man sent up for forging a check to pay his mother's medical expenses and a prison chaplain who takes the boy under his wing. Based on an actual incident.

3105. Mutiny on the Blackhawk (Universal; 1939). *Cast:* Richard Arlen, Constance Moore, Andy Devine, Mala, Noah Beery, Guinn Williams, Mabel Albertson, Thurston Hall, Byron Foulger, Paul Fix, Eddy Waller, Charles Trowbridge, Bill Moore, Mamo Clark, Richard Lane, William Moore, Francisco Maran, Sandra Kane. *D:* Christy Cabanne; *P:* Ben Pivar; *Sc:* Michael L. Simmons. (1:06)

B action-adventure of slave-running which uses much stock footage from *Sutter's Gold* (q.v.).

3106. Mutiny on the Bounty (MGM; 1935). *Cast:* Charles Laughton (A.A.N. for B.A. and "Best Actor of the Year" by the New York Film Critics as Captain Bligh — combined with his performance in *Ruggles of Red Gap* [q.v.]), Clark Gable (A.A.N. for B.A. as Fletcher Christian), Franchot Tone (A.A.N. for B.A. as Roger Byam), Herbert Mundin (Smith), Eddie Quillan (Ellison), Dudley Digges (Bacchus), Donald Crisp (Burkitt), Henry Stephenson (Sir Joseph Banks), Mamo Clark (Maimiti), Marie (Movita) Castenada (Tehani), Spring Byington (Mrs. Byam), Francis Lister (Captain Nelson), Ian Wolfe (Maggs), Ivan Simpson (Morgan), DeWitt Jennings (Fryer), Vernon Downing (Hayward), Stanley Fields (Muspratt), Wallis Clark (Morrison), Dick Winslow (Tinkler), Robert Livingston (Young), Douglas Walton (Stewart), Byron Russell (Quintal), Percy Waram (Coleman), David Torrence (Lord Hood), John Harrington (Mr. Purcell), Marion Clayton (Mary Ellison), Hal LeSueur (Millard), William Bainbridge (Hitihiti), David Thursby (McIntosh), Crauford Kent (Lieut. Edwards), Pat Flaherty (Churchill), Alec Craig (McCoy), Charles Irwin (Byrne), John Powers (Hillebrandt), King Mojave (Richard Skinner), Harold Entwistle (Captain Colpoys), Will Stanton (Portsmouth Joe), Lionel Belmore (innkeeper), Doris Lloyd (Cockney Moll), Mary Gordon (peddler), William Stack (judge advocate), Harry Cording (soldier), Eric Wilton, David Niven (film debut — extra). *D:* (A.A.N.) Frank Lloyd; *As.P.:* (A.A. for Best Picture) Albert Lewin; *Sc:* (A.A.N.) Talbot Jennings, Jules Furthman, Carey Wilson; *Music:* (A.A.N.) Herbert Stothart; *Editor:* (A.A.N.) Margaret Booth; *Song:* "Love Song of Tahiti" by Gus Kahn, Bronislau Kaper & Walter Jurmann. (2:12) (video)

Based on an actual incident published in a 1932 book by Charles Nordhoff and James Norman Hall, this action drama details the mutiny of sailors against a tyrannical sea captain. The film, a classic, was three years in the making at a cost of $2,000,000 and became the highest grossing film of 1935 despite only being released on November 8th. *Film Daily* voted it "Best Film of the Year" (1936) while the National Board of Review designated it as one of the year's "10 Best." Filmed on authentic locations, it was remade by the studio in 1962. The mutiny itself inspired two other film versions not based on the Nordhoff-Hall book, namely: *In the Wake of the Bounty* (Australia; 1933) which marked the film debut of Errol Flynn, and 1984's *The Bounty* with Mel Gibson. A low-budget quickie *The Women of Pitcairn Island* (20th Century–Fox; 1957) purported to tell of what became of the mutineers on their island hideaway.

3107. My American Wife (Paramount; 1936). *Cast:* Ann Sothern, Francis Lederer, Billie Burke, Fred Stone, Grant Mitchell, Billy Gilbert, Hal K. Dawson, Adrian Morris, Terry Ray (Ellen Drew). *D:* Harold Young; *P:* Albert Lewis; *St:* Elmer Davis; *Sc:* Edith Fitzgerald, Virginia Van Upp.

Comedy-satire on snobbery. Filmed before by this studio in 1923 with Gloria Swanson and Antonio Moreno.

3108. My Bill (WB/F.N.; 1938). *Cast:* Kay Francis, Bonita Granville, Anita Louise, Bobby Jordan, Dickie Moore, John Litel, John Ridgely, Sidney Bracey, Maurice Murphy, Helena Phillips Evans, Jan Holm, Bernice Pilot. *D:* John Farrow; *As.P.:* Bryan Foy; *Sc:* Vincent Sherman, Robertson White. (1:04)

B drama of a poverty ridden widow with four children to support. A remake of *Courage* (q.v.) and based on the play of that name by Tom Barry.

3109. My Dear Miss Aldrich (MGM; 1937). *Cast:* Maureen O'Sulli-

van (owner), Walter Pidgeon (editor), Edna May Oliver, Rita Johnson, Janet Beecher, Paul Harvey, Walter Kingsford, Guinn Williams, J. Farrell MacDonald, Robert Greig, Leonid Kinskey, Jack Norton. *D:* George B. Seitz; *P:* J.J. Cohn; *Sc:* Herman J. Mankiewicz. (1:13)

B comedy of the clashes between the owner and the editor of a newspaper.

3110. My Lips Betray (Fox; 1933). *Cast:* John Boles, Lillian Harvey, El Brendel, Maude Eburne, Henry Stephenson, Herman Bing, Irene Browne. *D:* John G. Blystone; *St:* Attila Orbok; *Sc:* Hans Kräly, Jane Storm.

Romantic comedy.

3111. My Little Chickadee (Universal; 1939–40). *Cast:* Mae West (Flower Belle Lee), W.C. Fields (Cuthbert J. Twillie), Joseph Calleia, Dick Foran, Ruth Donnelly, Margaret Hamilton, Donald Meek, Lloyd Ingraham, Addison Richards, George Melford, Fuzzy Knight, Willard Robertson, George Moran. *D:* Edward Cline; *P:* Lester Cowan; *Sc:* West & Fields; *Song:* "Willie of the Valley" by Milton Drake & Ben Oakland. (1:23) (video)

Western-comedy notable only for putting together the clashing egos of Mae West and W.C. Fields. Stories abound of what went on behind the scenes during filming.

My Love for Yours *see* **Honeymoon in Bali**

3112. My Lucky Star (20th Century-Fox; 1938). *Cast:* Sonja Henie, Richard Greene, Joan Davis, Cesar Romero, Buddy Ebsen, Arthur Treacher, Billy Gilbert, George Barbier, Louise Hovick (Gypsy Rose Lee), Elisha Cook, Jr., Paul Hurst, Patricia Wilder. *D:* Roy Del Ruth; *As.P.:* Harry Joe Brown; *St:* Karl Tunberg, Don Ettlinger; *Sc:* Jack Yellen, Harry Tugend; *Songs:* Mack Gordon, Harry Revel. (1:24)

Musical-comedy with an ice skating background.

3113. My Man (WB; 1928). *Cast:* Fanny Brice (film debut), Richard Tucker, Ann Brody, Edna Murphy, Guinn Williams, Andre de Segurola, Arthur Hoyt, Billy Seay, Clarissa Selwynne. *D:* Archie L. Mayo; *St:* Mark Canfield (Darryl F. Zanuck); *Sc:* Robert Lord, Joseph Jackson; *Title Song:* (from the 1921 Ziegfeld Follies) by Channing Pollock & Maurice Yvain; "I'd Rather Be Blue (With You Than Happy with Somebody Else)" by Billy Rose & Fred Fisher; "Second Hand Rose" by Grant Clarke & James Hanley; "If You Want a Rainbow You Must Have the Rain" by Billy Rose, Mort Dixon & Oscar Levant; "I'm an Indian" by Blanche Merrill & Leo Edwards; & "I Was a Florodora Baby" by Ballard MacDonald & Harry Carroll. (1:25 approx.)

Part-talkie musical drama of the trials and tribulations endured by a young woman on the way to becoming a Broadway star. No relation to the 1924 Vitagraph release of the same name with Patsy Ruth Miller. Premiering December 21, 1928, the film became a big box office hit.

3114. My Man Godfrey (Universal; 1936). *Cast:* William Powell (A.A.N. for B.A. as Godfrey), Carole Lombard (A.A.N. for B.A. as Irene Bullock), Alice Brady (A.A.N. for B.S.A. as Angelica Bullock), Eugene Pallette (Alexander Bullock), Gail Patrick (Cornelia Bullock), Alan Mowbray (Tommy Gray), Mischa Auer (A.A.N. for B.S.A. as Carlo), Jean Rogers, Jean Dixon (Molly), Robert Light (George), Pat Flaherty (Mike), Robert Perry (hobo), Franklin Pangborn (scorekeeper), Selmer Jackson (Blake), Grady Sutton (Van Rumple), Reginald Mason (mayor), Ernie Adams, Phyllis Crane, Jack Chefe, Eddie Fetherston, Edward Gargan, Jean Rogers, James Flavin, Art Singley, Jane Wyman (film debut), Bess Flowers (known affectionately in Hollywood as "Queen of the Extras"). *D:* (A.A.N.) Gregory La Cava; *P:* La Cava; *Sc:* (A.A.N.) Eric Hatch, Morrie Ryskind, La Cava. (1:32) (video)

Classic screwball comedy set in the depression of an eccentric family that acquires a butler on a scavenger hunt (from the city dump no less). Based on the novel by Eric Hatch, it became one of the 38 top grossing films of 1936–37.

3115. My Marriage (20th Century-Fox; 1935–36). *Cast:* Claire Trevor, Paul Kelly, Kent Taylor, Pauline Frederick, Noel Madison, Lynn Bari, Helen Wood, Thomas Beck. *D:* George Archainbaud; *P:* Sol M. Wurtzel; *Sc:* Frances Hyland.

B production.

3116. My Old Kentucky Home (Monogram-Crescent Pictures; 1938). *Cast:* Evelyn Venable, Grant Richards, Clara Blandick, Bernadene Hayes, J. Farrell MacDonald, Mildred Gover, Margaret Marquis, Cornelius Keefe, Kitty McHugh, Raquel Davido, Paul White, Hall Johnson Choir. *D:* Lambert Hillyer; *P:* E.B. Derr; *Original Story & Sc:* John T. Neville. (1:12)

In this B production set in the 19th-century, a southern boy, engaged to a southern girl becomes infatuated with a Yankee actress. The film is no relation to the 1922 silent film with Monte Blue.

My Old Man's a Fireman (G.B. title) *see* **The Chief**

3117. My Pal, the King (Universal; 1932). *Cast:* Tom Mix, Mickey Rooney (King of Alvonia), Noel Francis, James Kirkwood (prime minister), Stuart Holmes, Paul Hurst, Finis Barton, Jim Thorpe, Clarissa Selwynne, Wallis Clark, Ferdinand Schumann-Heink, Christian Frank, Tony (Mix's horse). *D:* Kurt Neumann; *St:* Richard Schayer; *Sc:* Jack Natteford, Tom J. Crizer. (1:03)

Offbeat Tom Mix western of a cowboy in a traveling wild west show who shows a boy monarch the ways of the west and then saves him from a scheming prime minister.

3118. My Past (WB; 1931). *Cast:* Ben Lyon, Bebe Daniels, Lewis Stone, Joan Blondell, Natalie Moorhead, Virginia Sale, Daisy Belmore. *D:* Roy Del Ruth; *Sc:* Charles Kenyon. (G.B. title: *Ex-Mistress*)

Romantic drama based on a best seller novel titled "Ex-Mistress" by Dora Macy.

3119. My Second Wife (20th Century–Fox; 1936). *Cast:* Michael Whalen, Gloria Stuart. *D:* Eugene Forde; *Sc:* Don Ettlinger.

(No other information available)

3120. My Sin (Paramount; 1931). *Cast:* Tallulah Bankhead, Fredric March, Harry Davenport, Scott Kolk, Anne Sutherland, Eric Blore, Margaret Adams, Jay Fassett, Lily Cahill. *D:* George Abbott; *St:* Frederick Jackson; *Sc:* Abbott, Owen Davis, Adelaide Heilbron. (1:19)

Drama of a woman who killed her husband, defended by a boozing lawyer. A box office flop.

3121. My Son Is a Criminal (Columbia; 1939). *Cast:* Alan Baxter, Jacqueline Wells (Julie Bishop), Gordon Oliver, Willard Robertson, Joseph King, Eddie Laughton, John Tyrrell. *D:* C.C. Coleman, Jr.; *Sc:* Arthur T. Horman.

B crime drama.

3122. My Weakness (Fox; 1933). *Cast:* Lew Ayres, Lillian Harvey (American debut), Harry Langdon (cupid), Henry Travers, Charles Butterworth, Susan Fleming, Sid Silvers, Irene Ware, Barbara Weeks, Adrian Rosley, Irene Bentley, Mary Howard. *D:* David Butler; *St:* B.G. DeSylva; *Sc:* Butler.

Romantic comedy.

3123. My Wife's Relatives (Republic; 1939). *Cast:* James Gleason, Lucile Gleason, Russell Gleason, Harry Davenport, Lynn Roberts, Tommy Ryan, Marjorie Gateson, Maude Eburne. *D:* Gus Meins.

Hit 2nd entry in the "Higgins Family" low-budget comedy series. Pop Higgins loses his job at a candy factory and decides to start his own candy business.

3124. My Woman (Columbia; 1933). *Cast:* Helen Twelvetrees, Victor Jory, Wallace Ford, Warren Hymer, Hobart Cavanaugh, Boothe Howard, Edwin Stanley, Lorin Raker, Harry Holman, Ralph Freud, William Jeffrey, Lester Crawford, Mary Gordon, Claire Dodd. *D:* Victor Schertzinger; *St:* Brian Marlow.

Low-budget drama.

3125. Myrt and Marge (Universal; 1933). *Cast:* Myrtle Vail (Myrt), Donna Damerel (Vail's real life daughter as Marge), Ray Hedge (Clarence), Eddie Foy, Jr. (Eddie Hanley), Ted Healy (Mike Mullins), Howard, Fine & Howard (The Three Stooges, Moe, Larry & Curley), Thomas Jackson (Mr. Jackson), Trixie Friganza (Marge's mother), J. Farrell MacDonald, Grace Hayes, Culenette Ballet, Ray Hedge. *D:* Al Boasberg: *P:* Foy Productions, Ltd.; *St:* Beatrice Banyard; *Songs:* M.K. Jerome, Joan Jasmyn. (G.B. title: *Laughter in the Air*) (1:05)

Backstage B musical comedy-drama, starring the popular radio duo of bygone days.

3126. The Mysterious Avenger (Columbia; 1936). *Cast:* Charles Starrett, Joan Perry, Charles Locher (Jon Hall), Wheeler Oakman, Edward J. LeSaint, Lafe McKee, Hal Price, George Chesebro, Jack Rockwell, Edmund Cobb, Dick Botiller, Sons of the Pioneers with Dick Weston (Roy

Rogers). *D:* David Selman; *St:* Peter B. Kyne; *Sc:* Ford Beebe. (1:00)

Charles Starrett western (his second for this studio), dealing with rival cattle ranchers.

3127. Mysterious Crossing (Universal; 1936). *Cast:* James Dunn, Jean Rogers, Andy Devine, J. Farrell MacDonald, John Eldredge, Hobart Cavanaugh, Clarence Muse, Herbert Rawlinson. *D:* Arthur Lubin; *P:* Val Paul; *St:* Fred MacIsaacs; *Sc:* John Grey, Jefferson Parker. (0:56)

B mystery-comedy of a reporter who gets involved in murder and finds romance to boot.

3128. The Mysterious Dr. Fu Manchu (Paramount; 1929). *Cast:* Warner Oland, Jean Arthur, Neil Hamilton, O.P. Heggie, William Austin, Claude King, Tully Marshall, Evelyn Selbie. *D:* Rowland V. Lee; *Sc:* Florence Ryerson, Lloyd Corrigan.

Hit melodramatic thriller of an oriental seeking revenge on some British officers responsible for the deaths of his wife and child. Based on the character created by Sax Rohmer.

3129. The Mysterious Island (MGM; 1929). *Cast:* Lionel Barrymore (Dakkar), Lloyd Hughes (Nikolai), Jane Daly (nee: Jacqueline Gadsden as Sonia), Montagu Love (Falon), Harry Gribbon (Mikhail), Snitz Edwards (Anton), Gibson Gowland (Dmitry), Dolores Brinkman (Teresa). *D:* Lucien Hubbard, Maurice Tourneur (unc.), Benjamin Christensen (unc.); *Sc:* Hubbard. (1:33)

Part-talkie science fiction, based on a story by Jules Verne of a submersible craft which discovers an undersea kingdom. Originally photographed in 2-color technicolor, the special effects were engineered by James Basevi, Louis H. Tolhurst and Irving G. Reis. Remade in Great Britain in 1969 as *Captain Nemo and the Underwater City,* with release by MGM.

3130. The Mysterious Miss X (Republic; 1939). *Cast:* Lynn Roberts, Michael Whalen, Chick Chandler, Wade Boteler, Charles Irwin. *D:* Gus Meins.

B mystery-comedy.

3131. The Mysterious Mr. Moto (of Devil's Island) (20th Century–Fox; 1938). *Cast:* Peter Lorre (Mr. Moto), Henry Wilcoxon, Mary Maguire, Erik Rhodes, Leon Ames, Harold Huber, Forrester Harvey, Lester Matthews, Lee Shumway, Frederick Vogeding, John Rogers, Karen Sorrell. *D:* Norman Foster; *Sc:* Foster, Philip MacDonald. (1:03)

The Japanese detective pursues a gang of assassins in this hit entry in the low-budget series, based on the character created by J.P. Marquand.

The Mysterious Mr. Sheffield (G.B. title) *see* **Law of the .45s**

3132. The Mysterious Mr. Wong (Monogram; 1935). *Cast:* Bela Lugosi (Mr. Wong), Wallace Ford, Arline Judge, Fred Warren, Lotus Long, Robert Emmett O'Connor, Edward Peil, Luke Chan, Lee Shumway, Etta Lee, Ernest F. Young, Theodore Lorch, James B. Leong, Chester Gan. *D:* William Nigh; *P:* George Yohalem; *Adaptation:* Nina Howatt; *Sc:* Lew Levenson; *Additional Dialogue:* James Herbuveaux. (1:08)

B mystery-melodrama of a diabolical oriental who is determined to own 12 coins which legend says belonged to the Chinese philosopher Confucius and hold the secret to power. Based on the novel "The 12 Coins of Confucius" by Harry Stephen Keeler.

3133. The Mysterious Rider (Paramount; 1933). *Cast:* Kent Taylor, Gail Patrick, Irving Pichel, Warren Hymer, Berton Churchill, E.H. Calvert, Cora Sue Collins, Fred Burns, Clarence H. Wilson. *D:* Fred Allen; *Sc:* Harvey Gates, Robert N. Lee. (1:01)

B western of homesteaders fighting for their land against a large rancher. A remake of the 1927 silent production by this studio with Jack Holt and Betty Jewel, it was based on a book by Zane Grey. Remade in 1938 (see below).

3134. The Mysterious Rider (Paramount; 1938). *Cast:* Douglass Dumbrille, Sidney Toler, Russell Hayden, Monte Blue, Glenn Strange, Stanley Andrews. *D:* Lesley Selander; *P:* Harry Sherman; *Sc:* Maurice Geraghty. (1:18)

A B remake of the preceding film.

The Mysterious Stranger (G.B. title) *see* **Western Gold**

3135. Mystery House (WB/F.N.; 1938). *Cast:* Dick Purcell, Ann Sheridan, Anne Nagel, Roy Barcroft, Trevor Bardette, Anthony Averill, Ben Welden, Sheila Bromley, DeWolf (William) Hopper, Dennie Moore, Hugh O'Connell, Anderson Lawler, Elspeth Dudgeon. *D:* Noel Smith; *P:* Bryan Foy; *Sc:* Sherman Lowe, Robertson White.

B murder-mystery based on the book by Mignon G. Eberhart.

3136. Mystery Liner (Monogram; 1934). *Cast:* Noah Beery, Astrid Allwyn, Cornelius Keefe, Gustav von Seyffertitz, Edwin Maxwell, Ralph Lewis, Boothe Howard, John Maurice Sullivan, Gordon DeMain, Zeffie Tilbury, Howard Hickman, Jerry Stewart, George Hayes, George Cleveland, Olaf Hytten, Ray Brown, George Nash. *D:* William Nigh; *P:* Paul Malvern; *Sc:* Wellyn Totman. (G.B. title: *The Ghost of Mr. Holling*) (1:02)

Low-budget espionage melodrama which was based on the novel "The Ghost of John Holling" by Edgar Wallace which appeared in serialized form in *The Saturday Evening Post.*

3137. The Mystery Man (Monogram; 1935). *Cast:* Robert Armstrong,

Maxine Doyle, Henry Kolker, LeRoy Mason, James Burke, Guy Usher, James Burtis, Monty Collins, Sam Lufkin, Otto Fries, Norman Houston, Del Henderson. *D:* Ray McCarey; *P:* Trem Carr; *St:* Tate Finn; *Sc:* John W. Krafft, Rollo Lloyd. (1:05)

B mystery-melodrama of a man who pawns a gun, only to later find it was used in a murder and he is the chief suspect. Remade as *Man from Headquarters* (Monogram; 1942).

The Mystery of Diamond Island (G.B. title) *see* **Rip Roaring Riley**

3138. The Mystery of Edwin Drood (Universal; 1935). *Cast:* Claude Rains (John Jasper), Douglass Montgomery (Neville Landless), Heather Angel (Rosa Bud), David Manners (Edwin Drood), E.E. Clive (Thomas Sapsea), Valerie Hobson (Helena Landless), Walter Kingsford (Hiram Grewgious), Forrester Harvey (Durdles), Francis L. Sullivan (Mr. Crisparkle), Will Geer, Ethel Griffies, Zeffie Tilbury, George Ernest, Veda Buckland. *D:* Stuart Walker; *Adaptation:* Bradley King, Leopold Atlas; *Sc:* John L. Balderston, Gladys Unger. (1:27) (video)

Suspense thriller of a multiple murderer. Based on the unfinished work of Charles Dickens it was also adapted for the stage as a Broadway musical in 1985.

3139. The Mystery of Life (Universal; 1931). *Produced by:* Classic Productions, an independent company.

Documentary feature on the theories put forth by Charles Darwin as explained and demonstrated by attorney Clarence Darrow (five years after the Scopes trial) and Dr. H.M. Parshley.

3140. The Mystery of Mr. Wong (Monogram; 1939). *Cast:* Boris Karloff (James Lee Wong), Grant Withers, Dorothy Tree, Craig Reynolds, Lotus Long, Morgan Wallace, Holmes

Herbert, Ivan Lebedeff, Hooper Atchley, Bruce Wong, Lee Tong Foo, Chester Gan. *D:* William Nigh; *P:* William T. Lackey; *Sc:* W. Scott Darling. (1:08) (video)

In this the second entry in the low-budget series, the oriental criminologist investigates the murder of a curio collector. Based on the character created by Hugh Wiley, which appeared in a series in *Collier's* magazine.

3141. The Mystery of Mr. X (MGM; 1934). *Cast:* Robert Montgomery, Elizabeth Allan, Lewis Stone, Ralph Forbes, Henry Stephenson, Forrester Harvey, Alec B. Francis, Leonard Mudie, Ivan Simpson. *D:* Edgar Selwyn; *P:* Lawrence Weingarten; *Sc:* Philip MacDonald, Howard Emmett Rogers, Monckton Hoffe. (1:24)

Hit drama of a jewel thief who reforms in order to find the killer of several London policemen. Based on a novel by Philip MacDonald. Remade as *The Hour of 13* (MGM; 1952) a British production.

3142. The Mystery of the Hooded Horsemen (Grand National; 1937). *Cast:* Tex Ritter, Iris Meredith, Horace Murphy, Snub Pollard, Charles King, Heber Snow (Hank Worden), Earl Dwire, Forrest Taylor, Joseph Girard, Lafe McKee, Oscar Gahan, Jack C. Smith, Chick Hannon, Tex Palmer, Lynton Brent, Ray Whitley & His Range Busters (the Phelps Bros., Ken Card), White Flash the horse. *D:* Ray Taylor; *P:* Edward Finney (Boots & Saddles Prods.); *St & Sc:* Edmund Kelso. (1:00) (video)

Tex Ritter western with songs of a cowboy who saves his niece's mine.

3143. The Mystery of the Wax Museum (WB; 1933). *Cast:* Lionel Atwill, Fay Wray, Glenda Farrell, Allen Vincent, Frank McHugh, Arthur Edmund Carewe, Gavin Gordon, Holmes Herbert, Edwin Maxwell, Thomas Jackson, DeWitt Jennings, Pat O'Malley, Bull Anderson, Monica Banister. *D:* Michael Curtiz; *Supervisor:* Henry Blanke; *Sc:* Don Mullaly, Carl Erickson (based on the play by Charles S. Belden). (1:17) (video)

A madman after being burned in a fire creates wax museum exhibits with human bodies. Photographed in the 2-color technicolor process, this was the first horror film with a contemporary urban setting and a big hit for the studio. This film was believed to have no existing copies until one was "found" in the 1960s. Remade as *House of Wax* (WB; 1953), probably one of the best known films utilizing the unpopular process of 3-D.

3144. The Mystery of the White Room (Universal; 1939). *Cast:* Bruce Cabot, Helen Mack, Constance Worth, Joan Woodbury, Mabel Todd, Tom Dugan, Holmes Herbert, Frank Reicher, Roland Drew. *D:* Otis Garrett; *P:* Irving Starr. (0:59)

B entry in the "Crime Club" series of murder in a hospital operating room.

3145. Mystery Plane (Monogram; 1939). *Cast:* John Trent (Tommy), Marjorie Reynolds (Betty Lou), Milburn Stone (Skeeter), Jason Robards (Paul), Peter George Lynn, Lucien Littlefield, Polly Ann Young, Tommy Bupp, Betsy Gay, Sayre Dearing, John Peters. *D:* George Waggner; *P:* Paul Malvern; *Sc:* Paul Schofield, Joseph West (Waggner). (Re-release title: *Sky Pilot*) (1:00)

Premiere entry (of 4) in the "Tailspin Tommy" series as Tommy and his friends develop an invention that is sought by a foreign power. A low-budget adventure which was based on comic-strip characters created by Hal Forrest and first filmed by Universal as a silent serial.

3146. Mystery Ranch (Fox; 1932). *Cast:* George O'Brien, Cecilia Parker, Charles Middleton, Roy Stewart, Charles King, George Chesebro, Charles Stevens, Forrester Harvey,

Virginia Herdman, Noble Johnson, Russ Powell, Betty Francisco. *D:* David Howard; *St:* Stewart Edward White; *Sc:* Al Cohn. (1:05)

George O'Brien western of a cowboy who comes to the aid of a girl kidnapped by a ruthless rancher.

3147. Mystery Ranch (Reliable; 1934). *Cast:* Tom Tyler, Roberta Gale, Jack (Perrin) Gable, Louise Gabo, Frank Hall Crane, Jimmy Aubrey, Charles King, Tom London, Lafe McKee, George Chesebro, Ray Corrigan (film debut). *D:* Ray Bernard (Bernard B. Ray); *P:* Harry S. Webb; *Sc:* Carl Krusada, Rose Gordon. (0:56)

Tom Tyler comedy western of a mystery writer who goes to a ranch to write, but finds all sorts of screwy goings on and some gold thieves to boot. The film sounds as though it may have been inspired by *Seven Keys to Baldpate* (q.v.).

3148. Mystery Range (Victory; 1937). *Cast:* Tom Tyler, Jerry Bergh, Milburn Morante, Lafe McKee, Roger Williams, Richard Alexander, Jim Corey, Slim Whitaker, Steve Clark. *D:* Robert Hill; *P:* Sam Katzman; *Sc:* Basil Dickey. (0:55)

Tom Tyler horse opera of a special agent investigating a plot to swindle a girl out of her ranch.

3149. Mystery Ship (RKO-Pathé; 1931). (No information available)

3150. The Mystery Train (Standard-Continental; 1931). *Cast:* Hedda Hopper, Bryant Washburn. *D:* Phil Whitman; *Sc:* Hampton Del Ruth.

"Poverty row" railroad drama.

3151. Mystery Woman (Fox; 1935). *Cast:* Rod La Rocque, Mona Barrie, Gilbert Roland, John Halliday, Mischa Auer, William Faversham, Arno Frey, Billy Bevan, Howard Lang, George Barraud. *D:* Eugene Forde; *P:* John Stone; *St:* Dudley Nichols, Edward E. Paramore, Jr.; *Sc:* Philip MacDonald.

B mystery melodrama.

3152. The Mystic Circle Murder (Merit; 1939). *Cast:* Betty Compson, Robert Fiske, Mme. Harry Houdini. *D:* Frank O'Connor; *Sc:* Charles Condon, Don Gallaher.

"Poverty row" mystery.

3153. Nagana (Universal; 1933). *Cast:* Melvyn Douglas, Tala Birell, Onslow Stevens, Paul Lukas, Everett Brown, Frank Lackteen, Noble Johnson, Dr. Billie McClain, William Dunn, Mike Morita. *D:* Ernst L. Frank; *St:* Lester Cohen; *Sc:* Dal Van Every, Don Ryan. (1:02)

B jungle adventure of a doctor in search of a cure for sleeping sickness.

3154. Name the Woman (Columbia; 1934). *Cast:* Richard Cromwell, Arline Judge, Rita LaRoy, Crane Wilbur, Bradley Page, Stanley Fields. *D:* Albert Rogell.

B drama.

3155. Nana (United Artists/Samuel Goldwyn; 1934). *Cast:* Anna Sten (American debut), Lionel Atwill, Phillips Holmes, Richard Bennett, Muriel Kirkland, Mae Clarke, Reginald Owen, Jessie Ralph, Lawrence Grant, Barry Norton, Taylor Holmes, Charles Middleton, Eily Malyon. *D:* Dorothy Arzner; *P:* Samuel Goldwyn; *Sc:* Willard Mack, Harry Wagstaff Gribble. (G.B. title: *Lady of the Boulevards*) (1:27)

Romantic drama of a high-living woman. Set in the late 19th-century, it was based on a book by Emile Zola and was Samuel Goldwyn's first attempt at making Anna Sten the new Garbo. Previously filmed in France in 1926 and remade in that country in 1954. A box office flop.

3156. Nancy Drew and the Hidden Staircase (WB; 1939). *Cast:* Bonita Granville (Nancy Drew), Frank Thomas, Jr. (Ted Nickerson), John litel (Carson Drew), Frank Orth (Capt. Tweedy), Renie Riano, Vera Lewis, Louise Carter, William Gould, George Guhl, John Ridgely, DeWolf (William)

Hopper, Creighton Hale, Frank Mayo, Frederic Tozere, Don Rowan, Dick Elliott. *D:* William Clemens; *As.P.:* Bryan Foy; *Sc:* Kenneth Gamet. (0:59)

Fourth and final film in this series as Nancy solves a mystery in an old house owned by two spinsters. Based on the book by Edward Stratemeyer & Harriet Evans (Carolyn Keene).

3157. Nancy Drew — Detective (WB; 1938). *Cast:* Bonita Granville (Nancy), John Litel (Carson Drew), Frank Thomas, Jr. (Ted Nickerson), Frank Orth (Capt. Tweedy), James Stephenson, Helena Phillips Evans, Renie Riano, Charles Trowbridge, Dick Purcell, Ed Keane, Mae Busch. *D:* William Clemens; *As.P.:* Bryan Foy; *Sc:* Kenneth Gamet. (1:00)

Premiere entry in this series of B films of a small town teen and the mysteries she solves. Based on the series of books written by the father and daughter team of Edward Stratemeyer and Harriet Evans (Carolyn Keene). The story involves the disappearance of an elderly woman after she bequeaths a large sum of money to a girls school.

3158. Nancy Drew — Reporter (WB; 1939). *Cast:* Bonita Granville (Nancy), John Litel (Carson Drew), Frank Thomas, Jr. (Ted Nickerson), Frank Orth (Capt. Tweedy), Mary Lee, Dickie Jones, Renie Riano, Betty Amann, Larry Williams, Thomas Jackson, Olin Howland, Sheila Bromley, Vera Lewis, Louise Carter, Charles Halton, Joan (Leslie) Brodel. *D:* William Clemens; *As.P.:* Bryan Foy; *St & Sc:* Kenneth Gamet. (1:08)

Nancy proves a woman innocent of murder in this second entry in the series based on characters created by Edward Stratemeyer and Harriet Evans (Carolyn Keene).

3159. Nancy Drew — Trouble Shooter (WB; 1939). *Cast:* Bonita Granville (Nancy), Frank Thomas, Jr. (Ted), John Litel (Carson Drew), Aldrich Bowker, Renie Riano, Charlotte

Wynters, Edgar Edwards, Willie Best, Roger Imhof, Erville Alderson, John Harron, Cliff Saum, Tom Wilson. *D:* William Clemens; *As.P.:* Bryan Foy; *Sc:* Kenneth Gamet. (1:09)

Third entry in this popular B series as Nancy and Ted uncover the truth about a murder.

3160. Nancy Steele Is Missing (20th Century–Fox; 1937). *Cast:* Victor McLaglen, Peter Lorre, June Lang, Walter Connolly, Jane Darwell, John Carradine, Robert Kent, Kane Richmond, Mary Gordon, George Chandler, Stanley Andrews, Joan Davis, Granville Bates, Frank Conroy, Margaret Fielding, Shirley Deane. *D:* George Marshall; *P:* Nunnally Johnson; *Sc:* Gene Fowler, Hal Long. (1:25)

Melodrama of a girl who is passed off as a long ago kidnapped heir to a fortune. Based on the novel by C.F. Coe.

3161. Narcotic (Dwain Esper; 1937). *D:* Dwain Esper; *P:* Esper.

Obscure exploitive independent melodrama of a doctor who becomes addicted to opium and wins a free trip down the path of self destruction.

3162. The Narrow Corner (WB; 1933). *Cast:* Douglas Fairbanks, Jr., Ralph Bellamy, Patricia Ellis, Dudley Digges, Arthur Hohl, Sidney Toler, Willie Fung, Reginald Owen, Henry Kolker, William V. Mong. *D:* Alfred E. Green; *P:* Hal Wallis; *Sc:* Robert Presnell. (1:11)

B drama of a kidnapped man who is taken to an East Indian island to keep him quiet. Based on the novel by Somerset Maugham. Remade as *Isle of Fury* (q.v.).

3163. Nation Aflame (Treasure Productions; 1937). *Cast:* Noel Madison, Lila Lee, Lee Shumway, Lee Phelps, Snub Pollard, Carl Stockdale. *D:* Victor Halperin; *P:* Halperin, Edward Halperin; *Sc:* Oliver Drake.

Low-budget independent drama of a Klan-like terrorist organization.

Similar in story line to *Legion of Terror*
(q.v.) and the hit *Black Legion* (q.v.).
Based on a story by Thomas Dixon
(whose writing was also the basis for the
story of *Birth of a Nation* in 1915).

A Natural Born Salesman (G.B.
title) *see* **Earthworm Tractors**

Nature's Mistakes *see* **Freaks**

3164. Naughty But Nice (WB;
1939). *Cast:* Dick Powell, Ann Sheridan,
Gale Page, Ronald Reagan, ZaSu Pitts,
Jerry Colonna, Helen Broderick, Allen
Jenkins, Hobart Cavanaugh, John
Ridgely, Maxie Rosenbloom, Grady
Sutton, Halliwell Hobbes, Vera Lewis,
Elizabeth Dunne, National Jitterbig
Champions. *D:* Ray Enright; *As.P.:*
Sam Bischoff; *Sc:* Jerry Wald, Richard
Macaulay. (1:30)
   A stuffy music professor writes a
popular song (by accident) and finds his
life turned upside down. The songs in
this film by Johnny Mercer and Harry
Warren are all adaptations of the
classical works of Wagner, Lizst,
Mozart and Bach. A remake of the 1927
First National production with Coleen
Moore and Donald Reed.

3165. The Naughty Flirt (WB/
F.N.; 1931). *Cast:* Alice White, Paul
Page, Douglas Gilmore, Myrna Loy,
Robert Agnew, George Irving. *D:* Ed-
ward Cline; *St:* Frederick Bowen; *Sc:*
Richard Weil, Earl Baldwin.
   B drama of a girl's fickle romantic
notions.

3166. Naughty Marietta (MGM;
1935). *Cast:* Jeanette MacDonald
(Princess Marie – Marietta), Nelson
Eddy (Capt. Warrington), Frank Mor-
gan (Governor d'Annard), Elsa Lan-
chester (Madame d'Annard), Douglass
Dumbrille (Uncle), Joseph Cawthorn
(Herr Schuman), Cecilia Parker (Julie),
Walter Kingsford (Don Carlos), Greta
Meyer (Frau Schuman), Akim Tamiroff
(Rudolpho), Harold Huber (Abe), Ed-
ward Brophy (Zeke), Walter Long
(pirate leader), Olive Carey (Madame

Renavent), William Desmond (gen-
darme chief), Cora Sue Collins (Felice),
Guy Usher (ship's captain), Edward
Keane (Major Bonnell), Marjorie Main,
Mary Doran, Patrícia Farley, Jean
Chatburn, Jane Barnes, Kay English,
Jane Mercer, Linda Parker, Dr. Ed-
ouard Lippe (Eddy's real life singing
coach), Louis Mercier, Robert McKen-
zie, Ben Hall, Harry Tenbrook, Ralph
Brooks, Edward Norris, Richard
Powell, Wilfred Lucas, Arthur Belasco,
Tex Driscoll, Edmund Cobb, Edward
Hearn, Charles Dunbar, Frank Hag-
ney, Ed Brady. *D:* W.S. Van Dyke II;
P: (A.A.N. for Best Picture) Hunt
Stromberg; *Sc:* Frances Goodrich,
Albert Hackett, John Lee Mahin; *Songs:*
"I'm Falling in Love with Someone,"
"Chansonette," "The Owl and the Bob-
cat," "Antoinette and Anatole," "Live for
Today," "Tramp, Tramp, Tramp Along
the Highway," "Dance of the Marion-
ettes," "Italian Street Song," "'Neath the
Southern Moon," "Ah, Sweet Mystery
of Life" and "Student's Song" by Victor
Herbert (music), Rida Johnson Young
(lyrics), Gus Kahn (additional lyrics);
Sound Recording: (A.A.) Douglas
Shearer. (1:46) (video)
   An European princess flees to
America to escape an arranged marriage
in this, the first pairing of the singing
duo of Jeanette MacDonald and Nelson
Eddy. Based on the 1910 operetta by Victor Herbert and Rida Johnson Young,
the film received *Photoplay's* Gold Medal
Award, while placing #4 on the "10 Best"
list of *Film Daily*.

3167. Navy Blue and Gold
(MGM; 1937). *Cast:* Robert Young,
James Stewart, Tom Brown, Florence
Rice, Lionel Barrymore, Billie Burke,
Paul Kelly, Samuel S. Hinds, John
Shelton, Frank Albertson, Barnett
Parker, Phillip Terry (film debut),
Stanley Morner (Dennis Morgan),
Minor Watson, Robert Middlemass,
Charles Waldron, Pat Flaherty, Matt
McHugh. *D:* Sam Wood; *P:* Sam Zim-
balist; *Sc:* George Bruce. (1:34)

A hit comedy-drama set at Annapolis Naval Academy.

3168. Navy Blues (MGM; 1929–30). *Cast:* William Haines, Anita Page, Karl Dane, J.C. Nugent, Edythe Chapman, Wade Boteler. *D:* Clarence Brown; *St:* Raymond Schrock; *Sc:* J.C. Nugent, Elliott Nugent; *Dial.:* J.C. Nugent, Elliott Nugent, W.L. River; *Adapt.:* Dale Van Every.

Early talkie romantic comedy of a sailor and a dance hall honey.

3169. Navy Blues (Republic; 1937). *Cast:* Dick Purcell, Carleton Young, Mary Brian, Warren Hymer, Joseph Sawyer, Lucile Gleason, Horace MacMahon. *D:* Ralph Staub.

B production.

3170. Navy Born (Republic; 1936). *Cast:* William Gargan, Claire Dodd. *D:* Nate Watt; *Sc:* Albert DeMond, Olive Cooper.

"Poverty row" adventure.

3171. Navy Secrets (Monogram; 1939). *Cast:* Grant Withers, Fay Wray, Craig Reynolds, Dewey Robinson, Andre Cheron, Robert Frazer, George Sorel, William von Brincken, Joseph Crehan, Duke York, Arthur Housman, Joseph Girard. *D:* Howard Bretherton; *P:* William T. Lackey; *Sc:* Harvey Gates. (1:02)

B espionage melodrama based on the story by Steve Fisher which appeared in *Cosmopolitan* magazine.

3172. Navy Spy (Grand National/Condor; 1937). *Cast:* Conrad Nagel, Eleanor Hunt, Judith Allen, Jack Doyle, Phil Dunham, Don Barclay, Howard Lang, Crauford Kent. *D:* Crane Wilbur, Joseph H. Lewis (directorial debut); *P:* George A. Hirliman; *Sc:* Wilbur. (0:58)

B espionage melodrama.

3173. Navy Wife (Fox; 1935). *Cast:* Claire Trevor, Ben Lyon, Ralph Bellamy, Warren Hymer, Jane Darwell. *D:* Allan Dwan; *Sc:* Sonya Levien.

Minor romantic production which was known under the working title of "Beauty's Daughter."

3174. Near the Rainbow's End (Tiffany; 1930). *Cast:* Bob Steele, Louise Lorraine, Al Ferguson, Lafe McKee, Alfred Hewston. *D:* J.P. McGowan; *P:* Trem Carr; *Sc:* Sally Winters, Charles A. Post. (1:00)

Bob Steele western which was his first talkie as well as his first for this "poverty row" studio. The son of a cattleman is blamed when a sheepman is murdered.

3175. Near the Trail's End (Tiffany; 1931). *Cast:* Bob Steele, Marion Shockley, Hooper Atchley, Si Jenks, Jay Morley, Murdock McQuarrie, Henry Rocquemore, Fred Burns, Artie Ortego. *D:* Wallace Fox; *P:* Trem Carr; *Sc:* George Arthur Durlam. (0:55)

Bob Steele western of a cowboy who helps a girl who witnessed a double murder.

3176. 'Neath the Arizona Skies (Monogram-Lone Star; 1934). *Cast:* John Wayne, Sheila Terry, Shirley Jane Rickert (Shirley Jane Rickey), Jack Rockwell, Yakima Canutt, Weston Edwards, Buffalo Bill, Jr., Phil Keefer, Earl Dwire, George Hayes, Frank Hall Crane, Artie Ortego, Tex Phelps, Eddie Parker. *D:* Harry Fraser; *P:* Paul Malvern; *Supervisor:* Trem Carr; *St:* Burl R. Tuttle; *Sc:* Tuttle. (0:52)

John Wayne western of a cowboy who protects a young Indian girl, heiress to a fortune in oil.

3177. 'Neath Western Skies (Syndicate; 1930). *Cast:* Tom Tyler, Lotus Thompson, Harry Woods, J.P. McGowan, Hank Bell, Bobby Dunn, Alfred Hewston, Barney Furey. *D:* J.P. McGowan; *Sc:* Sally Winters. (1:00)

Tom Tyler western of outlaws out to sabotage an oil drilling operation.

3178. Neck and Neck (Sono Art-World Wide; 1931). *Cast:* Glenn Tryon,

Vera Reynolds, Lafe McKee, Stepin Fetchit, Walter Brennan. *D:* Richard Thorpe.

"Poverty row" race track drama.

3179. Neighbor's Wives (Fanchon Royer; 1933). *Cast:* Tom Moore, Dorothy Mackaill. *D:* B. Reeves Eason.

3180. Nevada (Paramount; 1935). *Cast:* Larry "Buster" Crabbe (Jim "Nevada" Lacy), Kathleen Burke, Glenn (Leif) Erickson, Raymond Hatton, Monte Blue, William Desmond, Syd Saylor, William Duncan, Richard Carle, Stanley Andrews, Frank Sheridan, Jack Kennedy, Henry Rocquemore, Frank Rice, Barney Furey, William L. Thorne. *D:* Charles Barton; *P:* Harold Hurley; *Sc:* Garnett Weston, Stuart Anthony. (1:10)

B western based on the Zane Grey book of the same name. A remake of the 1927 silent by this studio with Gary Cooper and Thelma Todd. Remade in 1944 by RKO. A story with the familiar premise of a cowboy seeking the party, guilty of a murder he is accused of committing.

3181. Nevada Buckaroo (Tiffany; 1931). *Cast:* Bob Steele, Dorothy Dix, George Hayes, Ed Brady, Glen Cavender, Billy Engle, Artie Ortego. *D:* John P. McCarthy; *Sc:* Wellyn Totman. (0:59)

Bob Steele western of a cowboy attempting to go straight for the love of a girl after living a life of lawlessness.

3182. Never Say Die (Paramount; 1939). *Cast:* Bob Hope, Martha Raye, Andy Devine, Gale Sondergaard, Alan Mowbray, Sig Rumann, Monty Woolley, Ernest Cossart, Christian Rub, Frances Arms, Paul Harvey, Ivan Simpson, Victor Kilian, Hans Conried, Frank Reicher. *D:* Elliott Nugent; *P:* Paul Jones; *Sc:* Don Hartman, Frank Butler, Preston Sturges. (1:20)

Comedy of a hypochondriac who thinks he is dying and gets married only to find—you guessed it! Based on the hit Broadway play of 1912 by William Collier, Sr., and William Post which was previously filmed in 1924.

3183. Never the Twain Shall Meet (MGM; 1931). *Cast:* Leslie Howard, Conchita Montenegro (starring debut), Karen Morley, C. Aubrey Smith, Clyde Cook, Hale Hamilton, Bob Gilbert, Mitchell Lewis, Joan Standing, Eulalie Jensen. *D:* W.S. Van Dyke; *Sc:* Ruth Cummings, Edwin Justus Mayer, John Lynch; *Song:* "Islands of Love" by Arthur Freed. (A Cosmopolitan Production) (1:20)

The romance of a lawyer and a native girl from the South Seas. Based on the novel by Peter B. Kyne, it was previously filmed by this studio in 1925 with Bert Lytell and Anita Stewart.

3184. Never Too Late (Reliable; 1935). *Cast:* Richard Talmadge.

B melodrama.

(No other information available)

The New Adventures of Dr. Fu Manchu *see* **The Return of Dr. Fu Manchu**

3185. The New Adventures of Get-Rich-Quick Wallingford (MGM; 1931). *Cast:* William Haines, Jimmy Durante (his first for MGM), Leila Hyams, Guy Kibbee, Ernest Torrence, Clara Blandick, Walter Walker, Hale Hamilton, Henry Armetta, Robert McWade. *D:* Sam Wood; *Sc:* Charles MacArthur. (G.B. title: *Get-Rich-Quick Wallingford*) (1:16)

A hit low-budget comedy of its day. Based on the novel by G.R. Chester.

The New Adventures of Tarzan *see* **Tarzan's New Adventure**

The New Deal *see* **Looking Forward**

3186. New Faces of 1937 (RKO; 1937). *Cast:* Milton Berle, Joe Penner, Parkyakarkus, Harriet Hilliard (Nelson), Jerome Cowan, Richard Lane, William Brady, Thelma Leeds, Tommy

Mack, Bert Gordon, Lorraine Krueger, Ann Miller (bit), Four Playboys, Hillary Brooke (film debut), Rio Brothers, Loria Brothers, Brian Sisters, Three Chocolateers, Frances Gifford, Dewey Robinson, George Rosener, Dudley Clements, Harry Bernard, Patricia Wilder, William Corson, Harry C. Bradley. *D:* Leigh Jason; *P:* Edward Small; *St:* George Bradshaw; *Adaptation:* Harold Kusell, Harry Clork, Howard J. Green; *Sc:* Nat Perrin, Irving S. Brecher, Philip G. Epstein, David Freedman; *Songs:* Charles Henderson, Walter Bullock, Harold Spina, Joe Penner, Hal Raynor, Lew Brown, Sammy Fain. (1:40)

A comedy with various musical acts of a producer who deliberately produces theatrical bombs, which is what this film was at the box office.

3187. The New Frontier (Republic; 1935). *Cast:* John Wayne, Muriel Evans, Alan Bridge, Warner Richmond, Murdock McQuarrie, Alan Cavan, Sam Flint, Mary MacLaren, Glenn Strange, Hooper Atchley, Earl Dwire, Jack Kirk, Frank Ball, Sherry Tansey. *D:* Carl L. Pierson; *Sc:* Robert Emmett (Tansey). (0:55) (video)

John Wayne oater of a wagonmaster who takes over the job as marshal of a wide open town after hearing news of the murder of his father.

3188. The New Frontier (Republic; 1938–39). *Cast:* Ray Corrigan (Tucson Smith), John Wayne (Stony Brooke), Raymond Hatton (Rusty Joslin), Phyllis Isley (later Jennifer Jones in her film debut), Eddy Waller, LeRoy Mason, Dave O'Brien, Sammy McKim, Harrison Greene, Reginald Barlow, Burr Caruth, Hal Price, Jack Ingram, Bud Osborne, Slim Whitaker. *D:* George Sherman; *P:* William Berke; *Sc:* Betty Burbridge, Luci Ward. (TV & video title: *Frontier Horizon*) (0:55)

"Three Mesquiteers" western with the trio trying to convince settlers to move on to new lands, not knowing the land is worthless. The last film in the series for Wayne and Corrigan.

3189. New Moon (MGM; 1930). *Cast:* Lawrence Tibbett, Grace Moore, Adolphe Menjou, Roland Young, John Carroll, Gus Shy. *D:* Jack Conway; *St:* Frank Mandel, Lawrence Schwab; *Adapt.:* Sylvia Thalberg, Frank Butler; *Dial.:* Cyril Hume. (TV title: *Parisian Belle*)

An operetta by Oscar Hammerstein II and Sigmund Romberg which is set in early Louisiana. Originally produced on the stage in 1928 it retained many memorable songs, including: "Stout-Hearted Men," "One Kiss," "Lover Come Back to Me," and "Softly as in a Morning Sunrise," but was a financial flop for the studio. The 1940 remake with Jeanette MacDonald and Nelson Eddy did become a hit for the studio though.

3190. New Morals for Old (MGM; 1932). *Cast:* Robert Young, Margaret Perry, Lewis Stone, Laura Hope Crews, Myrna Loy, David Newell, Jean Hersholt, Elizabeth Patterson, Donald Cook, Ruth Selwyn, Kathryn Crawford, Louise Closser Hale, Mitchell Lewis, Lillian Harmer. *D:* Charles Brabin; *Sc:* Zelda Sears, Wanda Tuchock, John Van Druten.

Based on the British play "After All" by John Van Druten, this drama with a middle-class American setting tells the tale of a brother and sister who refuse the advice of their parents.

3191. The New Movietone Follies of 1930 (Fox; 1930). *Cast:* William Collier, Jr., El Brendel, Yola D'Avril, Noel Francis, Miriam Seegar, Huntley Gordon, J.M. Kerrigan, Marjorie White, Betty Grable, Paul Nicholson, Frank Richardson. *D:* Ben Stoloff; *Sc:* William K. Wells.

Musical-comedy. A follow-up to *The Fox Movietone Follies of 1929* (q.v.).

3192. New Orleans (Tiffany; 1929). *Cast:* Ricardo Cortez, Alma Bennett, William Collier, Jr. *D:* Reginald Barker.

Early part-talkie melodrama from "poverty row."

3193. New York Nights (United Artists/Art Cinema; 1929). *Cast:* Norma Talmadge (talkie debut), Gilbert Roland, John Wray, Lilyan Tashman, Mary Doran, Roscoe Karns. *D:* Lewis Milestone; *As.P.:* John W. Considine, Jr.; *Sc:* Jules Furthman.

Drama of a musical-comedy star, her alcoholic composer husband, with the triangle completed by a notorious gangster. Based on the play by Hugh Stanislaus Stange.

3194. Newly Rich (Paramount; 1931). *Cast:* Edna May Oliver, Jackie Searle, Mitzi Green, Virginia Hammond, Del Henderson, George Regas, Noah Young, Ben Hall, Bruce Line, Harold Goldstein, General Targart. *D:* Norman Taurog; *Sc:* Joseph L. Mankiewicz (co-writer). (aka: *Forbidden Adventure*)

Low-budget comedy of two Hollywood child stars on the loose in London.

3195. News Is Made at Night (20th Century–Fox; 1939). *Cast:* Preston Foster, Lynn Bari, Eddie Collins, Russell Gleason, George Barbier, Charles Halton, Paul Fix, Charles Lane, Paul Guilfoyle, Betty Compson, Minor Watson, Richard Lane. *D:* Alfred Werker; *Sc:* John (Francis) Larkin. (1:12)

B newspaper comedy-drama of an editor who goes one step too far in boosting his sagging circulation.

3196. Newsboys' Home (Universal; 1938). *Cast:* Jackie Cooper, Edmund Lowe, Wendy Barrie, Edward Norris, Joseph Crehan, Samuel S. Hinds, Elisha Cook, Jr., Hally Chester, Harris Berger, Billy Benedict, David Gorcey, Charles Duncan, Horace MacMahon. *D:* Harold Young; *P:* Kenneth Goldsmith; *St:* Charles Grayson, Gordon Kahn; *Sc:* Gordon Kahn. (1:13)

B feature of some newsboys who are caught in the middle of a newspaper war. A "Little Tough Guys" series entry.

3197. The Next Time I Marry (RKO; 1938). *Cast:* Lucille Ball, Lee Bowman, James Ellison, Granville Bates, Mantan Moreland, Elliott Sullivan, Murray Alper. *D:* Garson Kanin; *St:* Thames Williamson; *Sc:* John Twist, Helen Meinardi; *P:* Cliff Reid. (1:05)

B comedy of a girl who must marry someone she doesn't want in order to collect an inheritance.

3198. The Next Time We Love (Universal; 1936). *Cast:* Margaret Sullavan, James Stewart, Ray Milland, Grant Mitchell, Robert McWade, Anna Demetrio, Florence Roberts, Hattie McDaniel, Christian Rub, Leonid Kinskey, Ronnie Cosbey, Nat Carr, Gottlieb Huber, Charles Fallon. *D:* Edward H. Griffith; *P:* Paul Kohner; *Sc:* Melville Baker, Preston Sturges (unc.). (G.B. title: *Next Time We Live*) (1:25)

Triangular romantic drama in the love vs. career formula. Based on the novel "Say Goodbye Again" by Ursula Parrott.

3199. Nice Women (Universal; 1932). *Cast:* Sidney Fox, Russell Gleason, Lucile Webster Gleason, Alan Mowbray, Carmel Myers, Frances Dee, James Durkin, Leonard Carey, Florence Enright, Patsy O'Byrne, Kenneth Seiling, Jo Wallace. *D:* Edwin H. Knopf (final film as director until 1951); *St:* William A. Grew. (1:10)

Low-budget drama of a mother who interferes with her daughter's romantic affair when the chance comes along to marry the girl to a millionaire.

3200. Nick Carter—Master Detective (MGM; 1939). *Cast:* Walter Pidgeon (Nick Carter), Rita Johnson, Henry Hull, Stanley Ridges, Donald Meek, Addison Richards, Henry Victor, Milburn Stone, Martin Kosleck, Frank Faylen, Sterling Holloway, Wally Maher, Edgar Dearing. *D:* Jacques Tourneur; *P:* Lucien Hubbard; *St:* Bertram Millhauser, Harold Buckley; *Sc:* Millhauser. (0:59)

B detective melodrama, the premiere entry in a short series of films which were based on a series of paperback novels.

3201. Night After Night (Paramount; 1932). *Cast:* George Raft, Constance Cummings, Mae West (film debut), Wynne Gibson, Roscoe Karns, Louis Calhern, Alison Skipworth, Bradley Page, Mary Boland, Harry Wallace, Al Hill, Marty Martyn, Bud Flanagan (Dennis O'Keefe). *D:* Archie Mayo; *P:* William LeBaron; *Sc:* Vincent Lawrence, Kathryn Scola. (1:10)

Low-budget romantic drama with a night club setting. The film is notable as the film debut of Mae West, wherein she replies "Goodness had nothing to do with It, dearie" in response to a hatcheck girl's remark "Goodness, what diamonds!" Based on the novel "Single Night" by Louis Bromfield.

3202. Night Alarm (Majestic; 1934). *Cast:* Bruce Cabot, H.B. Warner, Judith Allen, Fuzzy Knight, Betty Blythe. *D:* Spencer Gordon Bennet.

"Poverty row" melodrama.

3203. The Night Angel (Paramount; 1931). *Cast:* Fredric March, Nancy Carroll (in a role originally intended for Marlene Dietrich), Alan Hale, Alison Skipworth, Katherine Emmett, Phoebe Foster, Clarence Derwent, Hubert Druce, Cora Witherspoon (film debut), Francis Pierlot, Doris Rankin, Francine Dowd, Charles Howard, Otis Sheridan, Lewis Walker. *D:* Edmund Goulding; *Sc:* Goulding. (1:15)

The dramatic trials and tribulations of a lawyer who falls for the daughter of a madam he has sent to prison for murder. A box office megabomb.

3204. A Night at the Opera (MGM; 1935). *Cast:* Groucho Marx (Otis B. Driftwood), Chico Marx (Fiorello), Harpo Marx (Tomasso), Kitty Carlisle (Rosa), Allan Jones (Ricardo), Siegfried (Sig) Rumann (Gottlieb), Margaret Dumont (Mrs. Claypool), Walter Woolf King (Rudolfo Lasspari), Edward Keane (captain), Robert Emmett O'Connor (Detective Henderson), Gino Corrado (steward), Purnell Pratt (mayor), Frank Yaconelli (engineer), Claude Peyton (police captain), Luther Hoobyar (Ruiz), Rita and Rubin (dancers), Rodolfo Hoyos (Count di Luna), Olga Dane (Azucena), James J. Wolf (Ferrando), Inez Palange (maid), Jonathan Hale (stage manager), Leo White, Jay Eaton & Rolfe Sedan (three bearded aviators), Alan Bridge (immigration inspector), Lorraine Bridges (Louisa), Billy Gilbert, Sam Marx, Otto Fries, William Gould, Wilbur Mack, George Irving, George Guhl, Harry Tyler, Selmer Jackson, Harry Allen, Phillips Smalley (final film — d. 1939). *D:* Sam Wood; *P:* Irving Thalberg; *St:* James Kevin McGuinness; *Sc:* Morrie Ryskind, George S. Kaufman; *Songs:* "Cosi-Cosa" by Bronislau Kaper, Walter Jurmann & Ned Washington, "Alone" by Nacio Herb Brown & Arthur Freed. (video) (1:32)

Classic Marx Brothers comedy which is their sixth film venture, their first without brother Zeppo and their first for this studio. Lunacy abounds as the brothers enter the world of grand opera. Before the final destruction scene at the opera house, there is the famed crowded stateroom sequence and the "Sanity Claus" sequence. One of the 25 top grossing films of 1935–36.

3205. A Night at the Ritz (WB; 1935). *Cast:* William Gargan, Erik Rhodes, Patricia Ellis, Dorothy Tree, Allen Jenkins, Paul Porcasi, Berton Churchill, Bodil Rosing, Gordon Westcott, Arthur Hoyt, Mary Treen, William Davidson, Mary Russell. *D:* William McGann; *St:* Robert T. Shannon; *Sc:* A.J. Cohen, Shannon, Manuel Seff. (1:00)

B comedy of a renowned chef who

doesn't know the first thing about cooking. A box office hit.

3206. Night Beat (Action Pictures; 1931). *Cast:* Jack Mulhall, Patsy Ruth Miller. *D:* George B. Seitz.
Low-budget independent melodrama.

3207. Night Cargo (Marcy; 1936). *Cast:* Jacqueline Wells (Julie Bishop), Lloyd Hughes, Walter Miller. *D:* Charles Hutchison; *Sc:* Sherman L. Lowe.
(No information available)

Night Club (G.B. title) *see* **Gigolette**

Night Club Hostess (G.B. title) *see* **Unmarried**

3208. The Night Club Lady (Columbia; 1932). *Cast:* Adolphe Menjou, Greta Granstedt, Skeets Gallagher, Nat Pendleton, Blanche Frederici, George Humbert, Teru Shimada, Lee Phelps, William von Brincken, Gerald Fielding, Edward Brady, Ruthelma Stevens, Niles Welch. *D:* Irving Cummings; *St:* Anthony Abbot; *Sc:* Robert Riskin.
Low-budget comedy-melodrama.

3209. Night Club Scandal (Paramount; 1937). *Cast:* John Barrymore, Lynne Overman, Charles Bickford, Louise Campbell, Elizabeth Patterson, Harvey Stephens, Cecil Cunningham, Evelyn Brent, J. Carrol Naish, Richard Cramer, Lee Shumway, George Guhl, John Sheehan, Frank O'Connor, Leonard Willey, Barlowe Borland. *D:* Ralph Murphy; *Sc:* Lillie Hayward. (1:10)
B melodrama of a man who kills his wife and frames her lover. A remake of *Guilty as Hell* (q.v.). Based on the play "Riddle Me This" by Daniel N. Rubin.

3210. Night Court (MGM; 1932). *Cast:* Phillips Holmes, Walter Huston, Anita Page, Lewis Stone, Mary Carlisle, John Miljan, Jean Hersholt, Tully Marshall, Noel Francis, Warner Richmond, Eily Malyon. *D:* W.S. Van

Dyke; *Play:* Mark Hellinger, Charles Beahan; *Sc:* Bayard Veiller, Lenore Coffee. (G.B. title: *Justice for Sale*) (1:30)
Hit melodrama of a girl who is set up by a corrupt judge and charged with prostitution.

3211. Night Flight (MGM; 1933). *Cast:* John Barrymore, Helen Hayes, Lionel Barrymore, Clark Gable, Robert Montgomery, Myrna Loy, William Gargan, C. Henry Gordon, Leslie Fenton, Harry Beresford, Ralf Harolde, Frank Conroy. *D:* Clarence Brown; *P:* David O. Selznick; *St:* Antoine de St. Exupery; *Sc:* Oliver H.P. Garrett. (1:24)
In South America, an airline company continues to make night flights even after a series of accidents indicate that the flights should be discontinued. The final film to star the Barrymore brothers together.

3212. The Night Hawk (Republic; 1938). *Cast:* Bob Livingston, June Travis, Paul Fix, Robert Armstrong, Ben Welden, Billy Burrud (final film—ret. at age 13), Paul McVey, Dwight Frye. *D:* Sidney Salkow.
B actioner.

A Night in Cairo (G.B. title) *see* **The Barbarian**

3213. The Nights Is Ours (Xxxx Xxxx; 1933). (No information available)

3214. The Night Is Young (MGM; 1934). *Cast:* Evelyn Laye (her last of two American films), Ramon Novarro, Una Merkel, Edward Everett Horton, Rosalind Russell, Charles Butterworth, Herman Bing, Henry Stephenson, Donald Cook. *D:* Dudley Murphy; *P:* Harry Rapf; *St:* Vicki Baum; *Sc:* Edgar Allan Woolf, Franz Schulz; *Songs:* "When I Grow Too Old to Dream," the title song & others with music by Sigmund Romberg & libretto by Oscar Hammerstein II. (1:22)
A romantic musical set amidst European royalty. As with many films in this genre, it was a box office flop.

3215. Night Key (Universal; 1937). *Cast:* Boris Karloff, Jean Rogers, Warren Hull, Samuel S. Hinds, Alan Baxter, Ward Bond, Edwin Maxwell, Roy Barcroft, Hobart Cavanaugh, David Oliver, Frank Reicher. *D:* Lloyd Corrigan; *P:* Robert Presnell; *St:* William Pierce; *Sc:* Tristram Tupper, John C. Moffit. (1:07).

B melodrama of an inventor who gets involved with crooks over his new burglar alarm system.

3216. Night Life in Reno (Supreme/Artclass; 1931). *Cast:* Virginia Valli, Jameson Thomas, Carmelita Geraghty, Clarence Wilson, Arthur Housman. *D:* Ray Cannon.

Low-budget production.

3217. The Night Life of the Gods (Universal; 1934). *Cast:* Alan Mowbray, Florine McKinney, Richard Carle, Peggy Shannon, William "Stage" Boyd, Robert Warwick (Neptune), Gilbert Emery, Phillips Smalley, Douglas Fowley, Henry Armetta, Wesley Barry, Irene Ware, Ann Doran, Ferdinand Gottschalk, Theresa Maxwell Conover, Pat DeCicco, Paul Kaye, George Hassell, Marda Deering. *D:* Lowell Sherman (final film — d. 1934); *Sc:* Barry Trivers. (1:14)

Offbeat comedy-fantasy of an inventor who turns statues into people and people into statues. Based on the popular novel by Thorne Smith (who also created "Topper").

3218. The Night Mayor (Columbia; 1932). *Cast:* Lee Tracy, Evalyn Knapp, Warren Hymer, Eugene Pallette, Vince Barnett, Astrid Allwyn, Wallis Clark, Emmett Corrigan, Wade Boteler, Donald Dillaway, Harold Minjir, Tom O'Brien, Gloria Shea. *D:* Ben Stoloff; *St:* Samuel Marx; *Sc:* Gertrude Purcell.

"Poverty row" drama.

3219. Night Must Fall (MGM; 1937). *Cast:* Robert Montgomery (A.A.N. for B.A. and an Acting Award from the National Board of Review for his portrayal of Danny), Rosalind Russell (Olivia), (Dame) May Whitty (A.A.N. for B.S.A. and an Acting Award from the National Board of Review for her portrayal of Mrs. Bramson), Alan Marshal (Justin), Merle Tottenham (Dora), Kathleen Harrison (Mrs. Terence), Matthew Boulton (Belsize), Eily Malyon (nurse), E.E. Clive (guide), Beryl Mercer (saleslady), Winifred Harris (Mrs. Laurie). *D:* Richard Thorpe; *P:* Hunt Stromberg: *Sc:* John Van Druten (based on the suspenseful stage play by Emlyn Williams). (1:57)

The psychological study of a psychotic killer who carries a head around in a hatbox. Reportedly Louis B. Mayer, head of MGM denounced this film as "sick" on its release but changed his mind when the favorable reviews started coming in as well as the big bucks. Remade in Great Britain in 1964 for MGM release. The National Board of Review voted it the "Best Picture of the Year."

3220. Night Nurse (WB; 1931). *Cast:* Barbara Stanwyck, Ben Lyon, Joan Blondell, Clark Gable (in a role originally slated for James Cagney), Charles Winninger, Vera Lewis, Blanche Frederici, Charlotte Merriam, Ralf Harolde, Allan Lane, Edward Nugent, Walter McGrail, Betty Jane Graham, Betty May. *D:* William A. Wellman; *Sc:* Oliver H.P. Garrett, Charles Kenyon. (1:12)

Critically acclaimed melodrama which was a hit in its day of a private nurse who uncovers a sinister plot directed at members of the household in which she is employed. Based on the novel by Dora Macy.

3221. The Night of June 13th (Paramount; 1932). *Cast:* Gene Raymond, Frances Dee, Clive Brook, Lila Lee, Mary Boland, Adrianne Allen, Charles Ruggles, Charley Grapewin, Helen Jerome Eddy, Helen Ware, Richard Carle, Arthur Hohl, Edward Le-

Saint, Billy Butts. *D:* Stephen Roberts; *P:* Louis D. Lighton; *St:* Vera Caspary; *Sc:* Agnes Brand Leahy, Brian Marlow, William Slavens McNutt.

Drama set in the suburbs of a city of four couples who are implicated in the purported murder of a woman.

3222. A Night of Mystery (Paramount; 1937). *Cast:* Grant Richards (Philo Vance), Roscoe Karns, Ruth Coleman, Helen Burgess (final film—d. during production, of pneumonia), Terry Ray (Ellen Drew), Eduardo Ciannelli, Colin Tapley, Elizabeth Patterson. *D:* E.A. Dupont.

A Philo Vance murder-mystery set in an old house. A remake of *The Greene Murder Case* (q.v.), and based on the book of that name by S.S. Van Dine.

3223. The Night of Nights (Paramount; 1939). *Cast:* Pat O'Brien, Olympe Bradna, Reginald Gardiner, Roland Young, George E. Stone, Mary Gordon, Pat O'Malley, Aileen Pringle (final film—ret.), Murray Alper, Oscar O'Shea, Ron Randell, Frank Shannon, Frank Sully, Charles Miller, Russell Powell, Laura Treadwell, Dink Templeton. *D:* Lewis Milestone; *P:* George M. Arthur; *St:* Donald Ogden Stewart; *Sc:* Stewart. (1:26)

Melodrama of a Broadway playwright whose talents are no longer required due to his drinking problem.

3224. Night of Terror (Columbia; 1933). *Cast:* Wallace Ford, Sally Blane, Tully Marshall, Bela Lugosi, Edwin Maxwell, Bryant Washburn, George Meeker. *D:* Ben Stoloff; *Sc:* Beatrice Van, William Jacobs, Lester Nielson. (aka: *He Lived to Kill*) (1:00)

Low-budget thriller of a maniacal killer who is stalking the grounds of a large estate.

3225. Night Parade (RKO; 1929). *Cast:* Hugh Trevor, Aileen Pringle, Robert Ellis, Ann Pennington, Lloyd Ingraham, Dorothy Gulliver, Lee Shumway, Heinie Conklin, Charles

Sullivan. *D:* Malcolm St. Clair; *As.P.:* Louis Sarecky; *Sc:* James Gruen, George O'Hara. (G.B. title: *Sporting Life*) (1:14)

A boxer is framed by racketeers. Based on a play by Edward E. Paramore, Jr., Hyatt Daab and George Abbott.

3226. Night Ride (Universal; 1930). *Cast:* Joseph Schildkraut, Edward G. Robinson, Barbara Kent, Harry Stubbs, DeWitt Jennings, George Ovey, Ralph Welles, Hal Price. *D:* John S. Robertson; *St:* Henry La Cossitt; *Sc:* Edward T. Lowe, Jr. (1:10)

Low-budget melodrama of a gangster's clash with a newsman over some printed stories about him.

3227. The Night Rider (Artclass; 1932). *Cast:* Harry Carey, Elinor Fair, George F. Hayes, Julian Rivero, Jack Weatherby, Nadja, Tom London, Robert Kortman, Walter Shumway. *D:* William Nigh; *As.P.:* George M. Merrick; *St & Sc:* Harry C. Crist (Harry Fraser). (0:53)

Harry Carey western of a lawman who poses as a gunman to get the bad guys.

3228. The Night Riders (Republic; 1939). *Cast:* Ray Corrigan (Tucson Smith), John Wayne (Stony Brooke), Max Terhune (Lullaby), Doreen McKay, Tom Tyler, Ruth Rogers, George Douglas, Kermit Maynard, Sammy McKim, Ethan Laidlaw, Walter Willis, Ed Peil, Tom London, Jack Ingram, Yakima Canutt, William Nestell, Glenn Strange, David Sharpe, Bud Osborne, Lee Shumway, Cactus Mack, Hal Price, Hank Worden, Roger Williams, Olin Francis, Francis Walker, Hugh Prosser, Jack Kirk. *D:* George Sherman; *P:* William Berke; *Sc:* Stanley Roberts, Betty Burbridge. (0:56) (video)

"Three Mesquiteers" western with the trio donning hoods to thwart attempts of a man attempting to control rangeland.

3229. Night Spot (RKO; 1938). *Cast:* Allan Lane, Joan Woodbury, Parkyakarkus, Gordon Jones, Lee Patrick, Bradley Page, Jack Carson, Frank M. Thomas, Joseph Crehan, Crawford Weaver, Cecil Kellaway, Rollo Lloyd. *D:* Christy Cabanne; *P:* Robert Sisk; *St:* Anne Jordan; *Sc:* Lionel Houser; *Song:* Sam H. Stept, Herman Ruby. (1:00)

B crime drama of a night club singer and a rookie cop on the trail of a gang who heisted some jewels.

3230. Night Waitress (RKO; 1936). *Cast:* Margot Grahame, Gordon Jones, Jack Arnold (Vinton Haworth), Marc Lawrence, Billy Gilbert, Otto Yamaoka, Donald "Red" Barry (film debut), Paul Stanton, Arthur Loft, Walter Miller, Anthony Quinn, Frank Faylen, Willie Best. *D:* Lew Landers; *As.P.:* Joseph Henry Steele; *St:* Golda Draper; *Sc:* Marcus Goodrich. (0:57)

B crime drama of a female ex-con working as a waitress in a waterfront cafe.

3231. Night Work (Sono Art-World Wide; 1930). *Cast:* Nora Lane, Eddie Quillan, George Duryea (Tom Keene), Vince Barnett, Ruth Hiatt, Ben Bard, Kit Guard, Arthur Hoyt, Georgia Caine. *D:* Russell Mack.

"Poverty row" melodrama.

3232. Night Work (Paramount; 1939). *Cast:* Mary Boland, Charles Ruggles, Donald O'Connor, William Frawley, Joyce Mathews, William Haade, Clem Bevans. *D:* George Archainbaud.

B comedy of the new manager of an apartment complex and his multitude of problems with his tenants.

3233. Night World (Universal; 1932). *Cast:* Lew Ayres (Michael Rand), Mae Clarke (Ruth Taylor), Boris Karloff (Happy MacDonald), Russell Hopton (Klauss), Dorothy Revier (Mrs. MacDonald), George Raft (Ed Powell), Bert Roach (Tommy), Hedda Hopper (Mrs. Rand), Clarence Muse (doorman), Gene Morgan (Joe), Huntley Gordon (Jim), Dorothy Peterson (Edith Blair), Arletta Duncan (cigarette girl), Robert Emmett O'Connor (Officer Ryan), Eddie Phillips, Sam Blum, Paisley Noon, Tom Tamarez. *D:* Hobart Henley; *P:* Carl Laemmle, Jr.; *As.P.:* E.M. Asher; *St:* P.J. Wolfson, Allen Rivkin; *Sc:* Richard Schayer; *Choreography:* Busby Berkeley. (1:00)

B drama of 12 hours in the lives of assorted patrons of a night spot known as "Happy's Club." In his book on TV movies, Leonard Maltin acclaimed the re-emergence of this long unseen low-budget film on cable TV.

Nightstick *see* **Alibi**

3234. Ninotchka (MGM; 1939). *Cast:* Greta Garbo (A.A.N. for B.A. and an Acting Award from the National Board of Review as Ninotchka), Melvyn Douglas (Count Leon), Ina Claire (Grand Duchess Swana), Sig Rumann (Iranoff), Felix Bressart (Buljanoff), Alexander Granach (Kopalski), Bela Lugosi (Commissar Razinin), Richard Carle (Gaston), Gregory Gaye (Count Rakonin), Edwin Maxwell (Mercier), Rolfe Sedan (hotel manager), George Tobias (Russian visa official), Dorothy Adams (Jacqueline the maid), Lawrence Grant (General Savitsky), Charles Judels (Pere Mathieu, cafe owner), Mary Forbes (Lady Lavenham), Tamara Shayne (Anna), Paul Weigel (Vladimir), Florence Shirley (Marianne), Frank Reicher, Edwin Stanley, Marek Windheim, Peggy Moran, Alexander Schonberg, George Davis, Armand Kaliz, Wolfgang Zilzer, William Irving, Bess Flowers, Elizabeth Williams, Harry Semels, Jody Gilbert. *D:* Ernst Lubitsch; *As.P.:* (A.A.N. for Best Picture) Lubitsch; *St:* (A.A.N.) Melchior Lengyel; *Sc:* (A.A.N.) Billy Wilder, Charles Brackett, Walter Reisch. (1:50) (video)

Classic comedy of a female Russian

agent who goes to Paris on a mission concerning some expensive jewels and finds herself hopelessly falling in love. This was Garbo's first comedy and thus promoted as "Garbo Laughs." One of the 21 top grossing films of 1939–40, *Film Daily* placed it at #3 on their "10 Best" list (of 1940), while the National Board of Review and the *New York Times* placed it at #4 and #9 respectively on their same lists of 1939. Remade as *The Iron Petticoat* (MGM; 1956), a British production. It was also the basis for the hit Broadway musical "Silk Stockings" and the 1957 film derived from it, also an MGM release.

3235. The Ninth Guest (Columbia; 1934). *Cast:* Donald Cook, Genevieve Tobin, Hardie Albright, Vince Barnett, Edwin Maxwell, Samuel S. Hinds, Helen Flint, Sidney Bracey, Nella Walker. *D:* Roy William Neill; *St:* Owen Davis; *Sc:* Garnett Weston.

Low-budget murder-mystery.

3236. The Nitwits (RKO; 1935). *Cast:* Bert Wheeler, Robert Woolsey, Fred Keating, Betty Grable, Evelyn Brent, Erik Rhodes, Hale Hamilton, Charles Wilson, Arthur Aylesworth, Willie Best, Lew Kelly, Arthur Treacher, Joey Ray. *D:* George Stevens; *As.P.:* Lee Marcus; *St:* Stuart Palmer; *Sc:* Fred Guiol, Al Boasberg; *Songs:* "Music in My Heart" by Dorothy Fields & Jimmy McHugh; "You Opened My Eyes" by L. Wolfe Gilbert & Felix Bernard. (1:21)

A slapstick farce of two cigar store owners (Wheeler & Woolsey) who get mixed up in murder. A hit for the studio.

3237. Nix on Dames (Fox; 1929). *Cast:* Mae Clarke, Robert Ames, William Harrigan, Frederick Graham, Ben Hall, Billy Colvin, Louise Beavers, George MacFarlane, Marshall Ruth, Grace Wallace, Hugh McCormack, Camillo Rovello. *D:* Donald Gallaher; *St & Sc:* Maude Fulton.

Low-budget romantic comedy.

3238. No Defense (WB; 1929). *Cast:* Monte Blue, May McAvoy, Kathryn Carver, William Desmond, Lee Moran, William Tooker. *D:* Lloyd Bacon; *Sc:* Robert Lord.

Drama of a man who takes the blame for another when a bridge they are working on collapses.

3239. No Greater Glory (Columbia; 1934). *Cast:* Jackie Searle, Lois Wilson, Ralph Morgan, Frankie Darro, Samuel S. Hinds, Frank Reicher, Donald Haines, Jimmy Butler, Wesley Giraud, Beaudine Anderson, Bruce Line, Tom Ricketts, Christian Rub, Julius Molnar, Egon Brecher. *D:* Frank Borzage; *Sc:* Jo Swerling.

Somewhat of an antiwar allegory about a neighborhood gang that is forced to defend its playground against the takeover by a rival gang. Voted one of the year's "10 Best" by the National Board of Review.

3240. No Greater Love (Columbia; 1932). *Cast:* Hobart Bosworth, Richard Bennett, Dickie Moore, Tom McGuire, Alec B. Francis, Mischa Auer, Martha Mattox, Betty Jane Graham, Helen Jerome Eddy. *D:* Lewis Seiler; *St:* Isadore Bernstein. (G.B. title: *Divine Love*)

"Poverty row" romantic drama.

3241. No Limit (Paramount; 1931). *Cast:* Clara Bow, Norman Foster, Stuart Erwin, Dixie Lee, Harry Green, Mischa Auer. *D:* Frank Tuttle; *St:* George Marion, Jr.

Low-budget romantic comedy of a New York theatre usherette who is put in charge of a gambling operation. A box office flop.

3242. No Living Witness (Mayfair; 1932). *Cast:* Carmel Myers, Barbara Kent, Gilbert Roland, Noah Beery, Dorothy Revier, J. Carrol Naish, John Ince. *D:* E. Mason Hopper.

"Poverty row" melodrama.

3243. No Man of Her Own (Paramount; 1932). *Cast:* Carole Lombard, Clark Gable, Dorothy Mackaill, Grant Mitchell, George Barbier, Tommy Conlin, Elizabeth Patterson, Lilliam Harmer, J. Farrell MacDonald, Charley Grapewin, Frank McGlynn, Paul Ellis, Walter Walker. *D:* Wesley Ruggles; *P:* Albert Lewis; *St:* Edmund Goulding, Benjamin Glazer; *Sc:* Maurine Watkins, Milton H. Gropper. (1:25) (video)

Comedy-drama of a gambler who marries a girl and gradually begins his reformation.

3244. No Man's Range (Supreme; 1935). *Cast:* Bob Steele, Roberta Gale, Buck Connors, Steve Clark, Charles French, Jack Rockwell, Roger Williams, Earl Dwire. *D:* Robert N. Bradbury; *P:* A.W. Hackel; *St:* Forbes Parkhill; *Sc:* Parkhill. (0:55)

Bob Steele western of a drifter and his partner who save a girl's ranch.

3245. No Marriage Ties (RKO; 1933). *Cast:* Richard Dix, Elizabeth Allan, Doris Kenyon, Alan Dinehart, David Landau, Hobart Cavanaugh, Hilda Vaughn, Charles Wilson. *D:* J. Walter Ruben; *As.P.:* William Goetz; *Sc:* Sam Mintz, H.W. Hanemann, Arthur Caesar. (1:13)

Low-budget drama of a newspaperman who changes his profession to advertising. Based on the play "Ad Man" by Arch Gaffney and Charles W. Curran.

3246. No More Ladies (MGM; 1935). *Cast:* Joan Crawford, Robert Montgomery, Franchot Tone, Charles Ruggles, Edna May Oliver, Gail Patrick, Reginald Denny, Arthur Treacher, Vivienne Osborne, Joan (Fontaine) Burfield (film debut), Fred Kohler, Jr., David Horsley, Jean Chatburn. *D:* Edward H. Griffith; *P:* Irving Thalberg (unc.); *Sc:* Donald Ogden Stewart, Horace Jackson. (1:19)

Sophisticated comedy of a society girl who marries a playboy with the intention of changing his womanizing ways. Based on the hit play by A.E. Thomas.

3247. No More Orchids (Columbia; 1932). *Cast:* Carole Lombard, Lyle Talbot, Walter Connolly, Jameson Thomas, Louise Closser Hale, C. Aubrey Smith, Sidney Bracey, Charles Hill Mailes, Allen Vincent, Edward LeSaint, Harold Minjir, William V. Mong, Ruthelma Stevens, William Worthington, Broderick O'Farrell, Belle Johnstone, Arthur Housman. *D:* Walter Lang; *St:* Grace Perkins; *Sc:* Gertrude Purcell.

Romantic comedy of a woman who chooses love over money.

3248. No More Women (Paramount; 1934). *Cast:* Victor McLaglen, Edmund Lowe, Sally Blane, Minna Gombell, Alphonse Ethier, Tom Dugan, Harold Huber, Christian Rub, J.P. McGowan, Frank Moran, William Franey. *D:* Albert Rogell; *St:* John Mikale Strong; *Sc:* Delmer Daves, Lou Breslow. (1:17)

"Flagg & Quirt" type comedy of the romantic rivalry between two deep sea divers over the lady owner of their boat and salvage operation.

3249. No, No, Nanette (WB/F.N.; 1930). *Cast:* Bernice Claire, Lucien Littlefield, Alexander Gray, Lilyan Tashman, Bert Roach, ZaSu Pitts, Louise Fazenda, Mildred Harris, Jocelyn Lee, Henry Stockbridge. *D:* Clarence Badger; *Sc:* Howard Emmett Rogers; *Songs Include:* "I Want to Be Happy" & "Tea for Two" by Vincent Youmans & Irving Caesar; *Title Song:* Youmans & Otto Harbach, "As Long as I'm With You," "King of the Air," & "Dancing to Heaven." (1:30 approx.)

Early talkie version of the hit Broadway musical of the comic dilemma of a married Bible manufacturer. The film includes a 2-color technicolor sequence, and was remade by RKO in

1940. The musical was by Otto Harbach and Frank Mandel.

3250. No One Man (Paramount; 1932). *Cast:* Carole Lombard, Ricardo Cortez, Paul Lukas, George Barbier, Jane Darwell, Arthur Pierson, Frances Moffett. *D:* Lloyd Corrigan; *St:* Rupert Hughes; *Adaptation & Dialogue:* Sidney Buchman, Agnes Brand Leahy. (1:13)

Triangular romantic drama of a high-living divorcee and her fickleness regarding men.

3251. No Other Woman (RKO; 1933). *Cast:* Irene Dunne, Charles Bickford, Gwili Andre, Eric Linden, Christian Rub, Leila Bennett, J. Carrol Naish, Buster Miles, Hilda Vaughn, Frederick Burton, Edwin Stanley, Brooks Benedict, Joseph Bernard. *D:* J. Walter Ruben; *P:* David O. Selznick; *St:* Owen Francis; *Sc:* Wanda Tuchock, Bernard Schubert. (0:59)

Marital drama of a man who pays the consequences after betraying his wife. Based on the play "Just a Woman" by Eugene Walter, this is a partial remake of First National's silent feature (1925) of that name with Conway Tearle and Claire Windsor.

3252. No Place to Go (WB/F.N.; 1939). *Cast:* Dennis Morgan, Gloria Dickson, Dennie Moore, Fred Stone, Sonny Bupp, Aldrich Bowker, Charles Halton, Georgia Caine, Frank Faylen. *D:* Terry Morse; *As.P.:* Bryan Foy; *Sc:* Lee Katz, Lawrence Kimble, Fred Niblo, Jr. (based on the play by Edna Ferber and George S. Kaufman).

A B remake of *The Expert* (q.v.) of a man who brings his elderly father to live with him.

3253. No Ransom (Liberty; 1935). *Cast:* Edward Nugent, Phillips Holmes, Leila Hyams, Hedda Hopper, Vince Barnett, Fritzi Ridgeway, Arthur Hoyt. *D:* Fred Newmeyer; *P:* M.H. Hoffman, Jr. (G.B. title: *Bonds of Honor*)

Low-budget independent melodrama.

3254. No Sleep on the Deep (Xxxx Xxxx; 1934). *D:* Charles Lamont; *P:* Educational Prods.

(No other information available)

3255. No Time to Marry (Columbia; 1938). *Cast:* Richard Arlen, Mary Astor, Lionel Stander, Virginia Dale, Thurston Hall, Paul Hurst, Marjorie Gateson, Arthur Loft, George Humbert, Matt McHugh, Jay Adler. *D:* Harry Lachman; *P:* Nat Perrin; *St:* Paul Gallico; *Sc:* Paul Jarrico.

B romantic comedy focused around the newspaper business.

3256. Noah's Ark (WB/Vitaphone; 1928–29). *Cast:* Dolores Costello (Marie-Miriam), George O'Brien (Travis — Japheth), Noah Beery (Russian Officer — Nephilim), Guinn "Big Boy" Williams (Al — Ham), Louise Fazenda (tavern maid), Paul McAllister (Noah), Myrna Loy (slave girl), Anders Randolf, Armand Kaliz, William V. Mong, Malcolm White (Shem), Nigel de Brulier, Noble Johnson, Otto Hoffman. *D:* Michael Curtiz; *St:* Darryl Francis Zanuck; *Sc:* Anthony Coldeway; *Song:* "Heart o' Mine" by Billy Rose, Louis Silvers; *Titles:* DeLeon Anthony. (Original running time: 2:15) (Silent version: 1:15) (Restored version: 1:40).

Part-talkie story of Noah and the flood parallelled with a World War I love story. A lavish production which employed no trick photography in the flood sequences, which reportedly took the lives of several extras during filming. Following initial release, the talkie sequences were deleted leaving an all silent film which ran (1:15). The film has recently been partially restored with some talkie sequences by Turner Entertainment.

3257. Nobody's Baby (MGM; 1936–37). *Cast:* Patsy Kelly, Lynne Overman, Lyda Roberti (final film — d. 1938), Robert Armstrong, Don Alvarado, Chill Wills & the Avalon Boys, Ottola Nesmith, Tom Dugan, Herbert Rawlinson, Rosina Lawrence,

Florence Roberts, Si Wills, Dora Clement, Laura Treadwell. *D:* Gus Meins; *P:* Hal Roach; *St & Sc:* Harold Law, Hal Yates, Pat C. Flick.

Slapstick comedy set in a maternity hospital.

3258. Nobody's Fool (Universal; 1936). *Cast:* Edward Everett Horton, Glenda Farrell, Cesar Romero, Frank Conroy, Florence Roberts, Warren Hymer, Pierre Watkin, Clay Clement, Ivan Miller, Henry Hunter, Bud Flanagan (Dennis O'Keefe). *D:* Arthur Greville Collins, Irving Cummings; *P:* Irving Starr; *St:* Frank Mitchell Dazey, Agnes Christine Johnston; *Sc:* Ralph Block, Ben Markson. (1:04)

B comedy of a small town man who outwits some big-city real estate swindlers.

3259. Noisy Neighbors (Pathé; 1929). *Cast:* Alberta Vaughn, Eddie Quillan, Theodore Roberts, Billy Gilbert. *D:* Charles Reisner.

Early talkie comedy.

3260. North of Arizona (Reliable; 1935). *Cast:* Jack Perrin, Blanche Mehaffey, Lane Chandler, Alan Bridge, Murdock MacQuarrie, George Chesebro, Budd Buster, Artie Ortego, Frank Ellis, Blackie Whiteford, Starlight the horse. *D:* Harry S. Webb; *P:* Bernard B. Ray; *Sc:* Carl Krusada. (1:00)

Jack Perrin western of a cowboy who joins an outlaw gang in an attempt to thwart their cheating of the local Indians.

3261. North of Nome (Columbia; 1936). *Cast:* Jack Holt, Evelyn Venable, Guinn Williams, John Miljan, Roger Imhoff, Dorothy Appleby, Paul Hurst, Frank McGlynn, George Cleveland, Ben Hendricks, Jr. *D:* William Nigh; *Sc:* Albert DeMond. (1:02)

B action drama of a man on the lam from the law who comes upon a shipwreck and helps the survivors.

3262. North of Shanghai (Columbia; 1939). *Cast:* James Craig, Betty Furness (final film—ret.), Morgan Conway, Joseph Downing, Keye Luke. *D:* D. Ross Lederman.

B espionage melodrama.

3263. North of the Rio Grande (Paramount; 1937). *Cast:* Bill Boyd (Cassidy), Russell Hayden (Lucky), George Hayes (Windy), Stephen Morris (Morris Ankrum), Bernadene Hayes, John Rutherford, Lorraine Randall, Walter Long, Lee Colt (later Lee J. Cobb—in his film debut), John Beach, Al Ferguson, Lafe McKee. *D:* Nate Watt; *P:* Harry M. Sherman; *Sc:* Joseph O'Donnell. (1:05)

Number 11 in the "Hopalong Cassidy" series with Cassidy posing as an outlaw in order to find the killer of his brother.

3264. North of the Yukon (Columbia; 1939). *Cast:* Charles Starrett, Linda Winters (Dorothy Comingore), Sons of the Pioneers with Pat Brady & Bob Nolan, Lane Chandler, Paul Sutton, Robert Fiske, Vernon Steele, Edmund Cobb, Tom London, Kenne Duncan, Hal Taliaferro, Richard Botiller, Harry Cording, Ed Brady. *D:* Sam Nelson; *Sc:* Bennett Cohen. (0:59)

Charles Starrett northwoods adventure of two Mounties searching for the fur thieves who murdered a trader.

3265. Northern Frontier (Ambassador; 1934–35). *Cast:* Kermit Maynard, Eleanor Hunt, J. Farrell MacDonald, LeRoy Mason, Charles King, Ben Hendricks, Jr., Nelson McDowell, Russell Hopton, Walter Brennan, Gertrude Astor, Dick Curtis, Kernan Cripps, Jack Chisholm, Lloyd Ingraham, Lafe McKee, Tyrone Power (Jr.), Artie Ortego. *D:* Sam Newfield; *P:* Maurice Conn; *Sc:* Barry Barringer. (0:57)

Kermit Maynard Mountie actioner of fur thieves and counterfeiting.

3266. Northwest Passage (Part I: Roger's Rangers) (MGM; 1939–40).

Cast: Spencer Tracy (Major Robert Rogers), Robert Young (Langdon Towne), Walter Brennan (Hunk Marriner), Nat Pendleton (Cap Huff), Ruth Hussey (Elizabeth Browne), Robert Barrat (Humphrey Towne), Regis Toomey (Webster), Truman Bradley (Capt. Ogden), Lumsden Hare (General Amherst), Montagu Love (Wiseman Claggett), Douglas Walton (Lieut. Avery), Donald MacBride (Sgt. McNott), Addison Richards (Lieut. Crofton), Louis Hector (Reverend Browne), Isabel Jewell (Jennie Coit), Hugh Sothern (Jesse Beacham), Lester Matthews (Sam Livermore), Andrew Pena (Konkapot), Don Castle (Richard Towne), Rand Brooks (Eben Towne), Kent Rogers (Odiorne Towne), Verna Felton (Mrs. Towne), Richard Cramer (Sheriff Packer), Ray Teal (Bradley McNeil), Edward Gargan (Captain Butterfield), John Merton (Lieut. Dunbar), Gibson Gowland (MacPherson), Frank Hagney (Capt. Grant), Gwendolyn Logan (Mrs. Brown), Addie McPhail (Jane Browne), Helen MacKellar (Sarah Hadden), Arthur Aylesworth (innkeeper), Tom London (ranger), Eddie Parker (ranger), Ted Oliver (Farrington), Lawrence Porter (Billy, the Indian boy), Tony Guerrero (Capt. Jacobs), Ferdinand Munier (Stoodley), George Eldredge (McMullen), Robert St. Angelo (Solomon), Denis Green (Capt. Williams), Peter George Lynn (Turner), Frederick Worlock (Sir William Johnson), Hank Worden (ranger). *D:* King Vidor; *P:* Hunt Stromberg; *Sc:* Talbot Jennings, Laurence Stallings. (2:06) (video)

Technicolor frontier saga which covers the first part of the book by Kenneth Roberts of which the second part (which actually deals with the discovery of the Canadian Northwest Passage) was never filmed. Filmed on location in Idaho, it became one of the 21 top grossing films of 1939–40, as well as placing #8 on the "10 Best" list of *Film Daily* in 1940.

Note: The book and film were also the basis for a TV series.

3267. Not Damaged (Fox; 1930). *Cast:* Walter Byron, Lois Moran, Inez Courtney, George Corcoran. *D:* Chandler Sprague; *St:* Richard Connell; *Sc:* Frank Gay.

Low-budget romantic melodrama.

Not Exactly Gentlemen *see* **Three Rogues**

3268. Not Quite Decent (Fox; 1929). *Cast:* Louise Dresser, Allan Lane (film debut), June Collyer, Marjorie Beebe, Jack Kenney, Ben Hewlett, Paul Nicholson, Oscar Apfel. *D:* Irving Cummings; *St:* Wallace Smith.

Part-talkie comedy.

3269. Not So Dumb (MGM; 1929). *Cast:* Marion Davies, Raymond Hackett, Elliott Nugent, Julia Faye, Franklin Pangborn, Sally Starr, John Miljan, Dorothy Jordan, George Davis, William Holden. *D:* King Vidor; *Sc:* Wanda Tuchock; *Dialogue:* Edwin Justus Mayer. (G.B. title: *Rosalie*)

Hit comedy of a girl who throws a party with the intent of furthering her boyfriend's career. A remake of *Dulcy* (First National; 1923) with Constance Talmadge and Johnny Harron. Based on the play of that name by Marc Connelly and George S. Kaufman. Remade as *Dulcy* (MGM; 1940) with Ann Sothern.

3270. Nothing But the Truth (Paramount; 1929). *Cast:* Richard Dix (talkie debut), Wynne Gibson (film debut), Berton Churchill, Ned Sparks, Helen Kane, Preston Foster (film debut), Madeline Gray, Louis John Bartels, Nancy Ryan, Dorothy Hall. *D:* Victor Schertzinger; *Sc:* John McGowan; *Song:* "Do Something" by Bud Green & Sammy Stept.

Hit comedy of a man who bets he can go for 24 hours without telling a lie. Based on the 1914 novel by Frederic Isham and the 1916 stage adaptation by

James Montgomery. Previously filmed (Metro; 1920) with Taylor Holmes. Remade in 1941 with Bob Hope.

3271. Nothing Sacred (United Artists; 1937). *Cast:* Carole Lombard (Hazel Flagg), Fredric March, Walter Connolly, Charles Winninger, Sig Rumann, Frank Fay, Troy Brown, Margaret Hamilton, Hedda Hopper, Hattie McDaniel, Maxie Rosenbloom, Monty Woolley, Olin Howland, John Qualen, Aileen Pringle, Ernest Whitman, George Chandler, Claire DuBrey, Charles Richman. *D:* William A. Wellman; *P:* David O. Selznick; *St:* "Letter to the Editor" by James H. Street; *Sc:* Ben Hecht, Ring Lardner, Jr. (unc.), George Oppenheimer (unc.). (1:15) (video)

Classic technicolor comedy of a girl who is given the royal treatment by the city of New York when it is believed she is dying of radium poisoning. In 1953 the screenplay was adapted for the stage musical "Hazel Flagg" which in turn became the basis for the 1954 Paramount film *Living It Up.*

3272. A Notorious Affair (WB/ F.N. — Vitaphone; 1930). *Cast:* Billie Dove, Basil Rathbone, Kay Francis, Montagu Love, Kenneth Thomson, Philip Strange, Malcolm Waite. *D:* Lloyd Bacon; *Sc:* J. Grubb Alexander. (1:06)

Romantic drama of the wife of a married violinist who finds her husband is having an affair and decides to have one of her own. Based on the play "Fame" by Audrey and Waverly Carter.

3273. Notorious But Nice (Chesterfield; 1933). *Cast:* Robert Ellis, Marian Marsh, Betty Compson, J. Carrol Naish, Rochelle Hudson, Robert Frazer, John St. Polis, Louise Beavers, Wilfred Lucas, Dewey Robinson. *D:* Richard Thorpe.

Low-budget romantic melodrama from "poverty row."

3274. A Notorious Gentleman (Universal; 1935). *Cast:* Charles Bickford, Helen Vinson, Onslow Stevens, Dudley Digges, Sidney Blackmer, John Darrow, John Larkin, Evelyn Selbie, Alice Ardell. *D:* Edward Laemmle; *St:* Colin Clements, Florence Ryerson; *Sc:* Leopold Atlas, Robert Tasker. (1:15)

B melodrama of murder and deception which ends in a courtroom trial.

3275. The Notorious Sophie Lang (Paramount; 1934). *Cast:* Gertrude Michael (Sophie Lang), Paul Cavanagh, Alison Skipworth, Leon Errol, Arthur Hoyt, Jack Mulhall, Arthur Byron, Joseph (Sawyer) Sauers, Ferdinand Gottschalk, Del Henderson, Ben Taggart, Adrian Rosley, Edward McWade, Norman Ainsley, Lucio Villegas, Stanhope Wheatcroft, Madame Jacoby. *D:* Ralph Murphy; *Sc:* Anthony Veiller. (1:04)

B crime melodrama of a female jewel thief, the first in a series of three films. Based on the character created by Frederick Irving Anderson.

3276. Now and Forever (Paramount; 1934). *Cast:* Gary Cooper, Carole Lombard, Shirley Temple, Sir Guy Standing, Charlotte Granville, Gilbert Emery, Henry Kolker, Harry Stubbs, Jameson Thomas, Akim Tamiroff, Richard Loo, Egon Brecher, Tetsu Komai. *D:* Henry Hathaway; *P:* Louis D. Lighton; *St:* Jack Kirkland, Melville Baker; *Sc:* Vincent Lawrence, Sylvia Thalberg. (1:22)

Comedy-drama of a jewel thief, his daughter and his girl friend.

3277. Now I'll Tell (Fox; 1934). *Cast:* Spencer Tracy, Helen Twelvetrees, Hobart Cavanaugh, Alice Faye, G.P. Huntley, Jr., Leon (Ames) Waycoff, Shirley Temple, Henry O'Neill, Vince Barnett, James Donlan, Clarence Wilson, Ray Cooke, Ronnie Cosbey, Robert Gleckler, Frank Marlowe, Barbara Weeks, Theodore Newton, Jack Norton. *D:* Edwin Burke; *P:* Winfield

Sheehan; *St:* Mrs. Arnold Rothstein; *Sc:* Edwin Burke. (G.B. title: *When New York Sleeps*) (1:12)

The story of Arnold Rothstein, a gambler and crime boss of the 1920s. The story is relayed in flashbacks by his widow.

3278. Now or Never (Ajax; 1935). *Cast:* Richard Talmadge, Janet Chandler, Robert Walker, Eddie Davis. *D:* B.B. Ray; *Sc:* C.C. Church; *P:* Bernard B. Ray; *As.P.:* Harry S. Webb.

Low-budget crime melodrama. Talmadge plays two parts in this "poverty row" drama.

3279. The Nuisance (MGM; 1933). *Cast:* Lee Tracy, Madge Evans, Frank Morgan, Charles Butterworth, John Miljan, Virginia Cherrill, Syd Saylor, Herman Bing, Samuel S. Hinds, Greta Meyer, David Landau, Nat Pendleton. *D:* Jack Conway; *As.P.:* Lawrence Weingarten; *St:* Howard Emmett Rogers, Chandler Sprague; *Sc:* Sam & Bella Spewack. (G.B. title: *Accidents Wanted*) (1:22)

A box office hit was this B drama of an ambulance chaser who must use his legal skills against a street-car company. Remade as *The Chaser* (q.v.).

3280. Numbered Men (WB/ F.N.; 1930). *Cast:* Conrad Nagel, Raymond Hackett, Bernice Claire, Tully Marshall, Ralph Ince, Fred Howard, William Holden, Karl Dane, Blanche Frederici, George Cooper, Maurice Black, Ivan Linow. *D:* Mervyn LeRoy; *Sc:* Al Cohn, Henry McCarty.

An early prison melodrama, filmed on location at San Quentin, California. Based on the play "Jailbreak" by Dwight Taylor.

3281. Numbered Woman (Monogram; 1938). *Cast:* Sally Blane, Lloyd Hughes, Mayo Methot, Clay Clement, J. Farrell MacDonald, John Arledge, Ward Bond, Morgan Wallace, Mary MacLaren, Gordon Hart, Robert Fiske, Ralph Dunn, Oscar O'Shea, Mary Lou Lender, Howard Hickman, Kathryn Sheldon. *D:* Karl Brown; *P:* E.B. Derr; *Sc:* John T. Neville. (1:03)

B melodrama of a nurse who sets out to prove her brother innocent of wrong-doing.

3282. Nurse Edith Cavell (RKO/ Imperadio; 1939). *Cast:* Anna Neagle (American debut as Edith Cavell), Edna May Oliver, George Sanders, ZaSu Pitts, May Robson, H.B. Warner, Robert Coote, Martin Kosleck, Halliwell Hobbes, Sophie Stewart, Gilbert Emery, Mary Howard, Fritz Leiber, Gustav von Seyffertitz (final film—d. 1943), Gui Ignon, Lionel Royce, Jimmy Butler, Rex Downing, Henry Brandon, Ernst Deutsch, Will Kaufman, Bodil Rosing, Bert Roach, William Edmunds, Richard Deane, Lucien Prival. *D:* Herbert Wilcox; *P:* Wilcox; *Sc:* Michael Hogan; *Original Music Score:* (A.A.N.) Anthony Collins. (1:35) (video)

Dramatic story of the famed World War I nurse who aided the wounded on the battlefields of Europe. Based on the novel "Dawn," by Reginald Berkeley, and previously filmed before in Great Britain in 1930 under that name.

3283. Nurse from Brooklyn (Universal; 1938). *Cast:* Sally Eilers, Paul Kelly, Larry Blake, Morgan Conway, Maurice Murphy, David Oliver, Lucile Gleason. *D:* S. Sylvan Simon; *P:* Edmund Grainger; *St:* Steve Fisher; *Sc:* Roy Chanslor. (1:05)

B romantic melodrama of a cop wounded in the line of duty who is blamed for the death of a woman's brother in the same gun battle.

3284. The Nut Farm (Monogram; 1935). *Cast:* Wallace Ford, Florence Roberts, Oscar Apfel (Bob Bent), Betty Alden (Helen Bent), Bradley Page, Joan Gale, Spencer Charters, Lorin Raker, Arnold Gray, Arthur Hoyt, Syd Saylor, Stanley Blystone, John Ince, Hank Mann, Lona Andre. *D:* Melville Brown; *P:* William

T. Lackey; *Sc:* George Waggner (based on the play by John C. Brownell). (1:05)

B comedy of a man who sells his grocery store with the intent of buying a nut farm, but plans change when his wife becomes involved with a swindler.

3285. O'Malley of the Mounted (20th Century–Fox; 1936). *Cast:* George O'Brien, Irene Ware, Stanley Fields, Charles King, Richard Cramer, Olin Francis, Crauford Kent, Tom London, Victor Potel, Reginald Barlow, James Bush. *D:* David Howard; *Sc:* Dan Jarrett, Frank Howard Clark. (0:59)

George O'Brien action-adventure of a Mountie who goes undercover to capture a gang. A liberal remake of a 1921 William S. Hart film of the same name.

O'Riley's Luck (G.B. title) *see* **Rose Bowl**

3286. O'Shaughnessy's Boy (MGM; 1935). *Cast:* Wallace Beery, Jackie Cooper, Leona Maricle, Sara Haden, Spanky McFarland, Henry Stephenson, Oscar Apfel, Willard Robertson, Clarence Muse, Wade Boteler, Granville Bates, Ben Hendricks, Jr., Jack Daley. *D:* Richard Boleslawski; *P:* Philip Goldstone; *Sc:* Leonard Praskins, Otis Garrett, Wanda Tuchock. (1:28)

A sentimental story, typical of its stars of a man's search for his son, taken by the boy's mother years before. A dud at the box office.

3287. Obey the Law (Columbia; 1933). *Cast:* Leo Carrillo, Lois Wilson, Dickie Moore, Henry Clive, Gino Corrado, Eddie Garr, Ward Bond. *D:* Ben Stoloff; *St:* Harry Sauber; *Sc:* Arthur Caesar.

Low-budget crime melodrama.

3288. Of Human Bondage (RKO; 1934). *Cast:* Leslie Howard (Philip Carey), Bette Davis (Mildred Rogers), Alan Hale (Emil Miller), Kay Johnson (Norah), Frances Dee (Sally Athelny), Reginald Denny (Griffiths), Reginald Owen (Athelny), Reginald Sheffield (Dunsford), Desmond Roberts (Dr. Jacobs), Tempe Pigott (landlady), Ethel Griffies, John Peter Richmond (John Carradine). *D:* John Cromwell: *P:* Pandro S. Berman; *Sc:* Lester Cohen. (1:23) (video)

Known as the film which gave Ms. Davis her Hollywood star, this critically acclaimed box office flop is a drama of a doctor who becomes infatuated with a crude low-life waitress. Based on the novel by W. Somerset Maugham, it was remade (WB; 1946) and again in Great Britain (MGM; 1964).

3289. Of Human Hearts (MGM; 1938). *Cast:* Walter Huston, James Stewart, Beulah Bondi (A.A.N. for B.S.A.), Gene Reynolds, Guy Kibbee, Charles Coburn, John Carradine (Abe Lincoln), Ann Rutherford, Gene Lockhart, Charley Grapewin, Esther Dale, Clem Bevans, Sterling Holloway, Robert McWade (final film — d. 1938), Ted Healy, Leatrice Joy Gilbert, Ward Bond, Frank Reicher, Charles Peck, Arthur Aylesworth, Leona Roberts, Minor Watson. *D:* Clarence Brown; *P:* John W. Considine, Jr.; *Sc:* Bradbury Foote. (1:40)

A sentimental drama of a backwoods family during the Civil War. Based on the novel "Benefits Forgot" by Honoré Morrow, the film placed #7 on the "10 Best" list of the National Board of Review, but flopped at the box office.

3290. Of Mice and Men (United Artists; 1939). *Cast:* Burgess Meredith (George), Betty Field (Acting Award from the National Board of Review for her portrayal of Mae), Lon Chaney, Jr. (Lenny), Charles Bickford (Slim), Bob Steele (Curley), Roman Bohnen (Candy), Noah Beery, Jr. (Whit), Oscar O'Shea (Jackson), Granville Bates (Carlson), Leigh Whipper (Crooks), Leona Roberts (Aunt Clara), Helen Lynd (Susie), Eddie Dunn (bus driver), Howard Mitchell (sheriff), Henrietta Kaye, Barbara Pepper, John Beach, Carl Pitti, Whitney De Rahm, Baldy

Cooke, Jack Lawrence, Charles Watt. *D:* Lewis Milestone; *P:* (A.A.N. for Best Picture) Milestone; *As.P.:* Frank Ross (for Hal Roach); *Sc:* Eugene Solow; *Original Music Score:* (A.A.N.) Aaron Copland; *Sound Recording:* (A.A.N.) Elmer Raguse. (1:47)

Classic drama based on the novel and play by John Steinbeck of two men, one feeble-minded, and the other his protector who work on a ranch and dream of a future idyllic life. On the "10 Best" list of the National Board of Review of 1940 it placed #3. Remade in 1981 as a TV movie.

3291. Off the Record (WB; 1939). *Cast:* Pat O'Brien, Joan Blondell, Morgan Conway, Bobby Jordan, Alan Baxter, William Davidson, Clay Clement, Emory Parnell, Ralph Morgan, Mary Gordon, Pierre Watkin, Addison Richards, Selmer Jackson, Douglas Wood, Armand Kaliz, Joseph King. *D:* James Flood; *As.P.:* Sam Bischoff; *St:* Saul Elkins, Sally Sandlin; *Sc:* Niven Busch, Lawrence Kimble, Earl Baldwin. (G.B. title: *Unfit to Print*)

A juvenile is sent to a reformatory after an investigation into a slot-machine racket.

3292. Off to the Races (20th Century–Fox; 1937). *Cast:* Jed Prouty, Spring Byington, Florence Roberts, Shirley Deane, Kenneth Howell, George Ernest, Billy Mahan, June Carlson, Slim Summerville, Russell Gleason, Ann Gillis, Chick Chandler, Ruth Gillette, Fred "Snowflake" Toones. *D:* Frank Strayer; *St & Sc:* Robert Ellis, Helen Logan.

This was the 4th entry in the "Jones Family" comedy series.

3293. The Office Scandal (Pathé; 1929). *Cast:* Phyllis Haver, Raymond Hatton, Leslie Fenton, Margaret Livingston. *D:* Paul L. Stein.

Low-budget part-talkie comedy.

3294. The Office Wife (WB; 1930). *Cast:* Dorothy Mackaill, Lewis Stone, Natalie Moorhead, Joan Blondell, Hobart Bosworth, Blanche Frederici, Brooks Benedict, Dale Fuller, Walter Merrill. *D:* Lloyd Bacon; *St:* Faith Baldwin; *Sc:* Charles Kenyon.

B drama of an office girl's affair with her much older boss.

3295. Officer O'Brien (Pathé; 1930). *Cast:* William "Hopalong Cassidy" Boyd, Russell Gleason, Dorothy Sebastian, Ernest Torrence, Clyde Cook, Paul Hurst, Ralf Harolde, Arthur Housman. *D:* Tay Garnett; *St & Sc:* Tom Buckingham.

Police drama.

3296. Officer 13 (First Division; 1933). *Cast:* Monte Blue, Lloyd Ingraham, Lila Lee, Robert Ellis, Charles Delaney, Jackie Searle, Florence Roberts, Joseph Girard. *D:* George Melford.

Low-budget independent melodrama.

3297. Oh, Doctor! (Universal; 1937). *Cast:* Edward Everett Horton, Eve Arden, Drue (Leyton) Leighton, Jessie Royce Landis, Ed Brophy, Thurston Hall, William Demarest, Minerva Urecal, William Hall. *D:* Edmund Grainger, Ray McCarey; *P:* Grainger; *St:* Harry Leon Wilson; *Sc:* Harry Clork, Brown Holmes. (1:07)

B comedy of a hypochondriac who worries that he will die before collecting his due inheritance. A remake of the 1925 silent production of this studio with Reginald Denny and Mary Astor.

3298. Oh, For a Man! (Fox; 1930). *Cast:* Jeanette MacDonald, Reginald Denny, Alison Skipworth, Warren Hymer, Bela Lugosi, Mary Gordon. *D:* Hamilton MacFadden (directorial debut).

Low-budget comedy.

3299. Oh! Sailor, Behave! (WB; 1930). *Cast:* Ole Olsen, Chic Johnson, Charles King, Irene Delroy, Lotti Loder, Noah Beery, Lowell Sherman,

Vivian Oakland, Lawrence Grant, Gino Corrado. *D:* Archie Mayo; *Sc:* Joseph Jackson, Sid Silvers; *Song:* "The Laughing Song" by Olsen & Johnson; *Other Songs:* "Love Comes in the Moonlight," "Leave a Little Smile," "Tell Us Which One Do You Love" & "Highway to Heaven" by Al Dubin & Joe Burke.

Low-budget musical-comedy of two American sailors in Italy on the trail of a thief with a wooden leg. Based on the Broadway play by Elmer Rice.

3300. Oh, Susanna! (Republic; 1936). *Cast:* Gene Autry, Smiley Burnette, Frances Grant, Earle Hodgins, Donald Kirke, Boothe Howard, Champion the horse, Clara Kimball Young, Ed Peil, Sr., Frankie Marvin, Carl Stockdale, Fred "Snowflake" Toones, Gerald Roscoe, Roger Gray, Fred Burns, Earl Dwire, Light Crust Doughboys, Walter James, Lew Meehan. *D:* Joseph Kane; *P:* Nat Levine; *Supervisor:* Armand Schaefer; *St & Sc:* Oliver Drake; *Songs:* Sam H. Stept, Drake, Autry, Burnette. (0:56)

Gene Autry western with songs.

3301. Oil for the Lamps of China (WB; 1935). *Cast:* Pat O'Brien (Stephen Chase), Josephine Hutchinson (Hester), Jean Muir (Alice), Lyle Talbot (Jim), Arthur Byron (No. 1 boss), John Eldredge (Don), Donald Crisp (McCarger), Willie Fung (Kim), Tetsu Komai (Ho), Henry O'Neill, Ronnie Cosbey, William Davidson, George Meeker, Joseph Crehan, Christian Rub, Willard Robertson, Edward McWade, Florence Fair, Keye Luke. *D:* Mervyn LeRoy; *P:* Robert Lord; *Sc:* Laird Doyle. (1:38)

Drama of an oil representative in the orient and his various problems. This box office flop was a Cosmopolitan production based on the novel by Alice Tisdale Hobart. Remade as *Law of the Tropics* (WB; 1941).

3302. The Oil Raider (Mayfair; 1934). *Cast:* Buster Crabbe, Gloria Shea, George Irving, Max Wagner, Emmett Vogan, Harold Minjir, Tom London, Wally Wales (Hal Taliaferro). *D:* Spencer Gordon Bennet; *P:* Lester Scott, Jr.; *Sc:* George Morgan, Homer King Gordon. (0:59)

"Poverty row" melodrama of skullduggery in the oil fields.

3303. Okay, America (Universal; 1932). *Cast:* Lew Ayres, Maureen O'Sullivan, Louis Calhern, Walter Catlett, Edward Arnold, Berton Churchill, Onslow Stevens, Margaret Lindsay (film debut), Henry Armetta, Akim Tamiroff (film debut), Nance O'Neil, Frank Sheridan, Frederick Burton, Wallis Clark, Emerson Treacy, Ruth Lyons, Frank Darien, Rollo Lloyd, Charles Dow Clark. *D:* Tay Garnett; *Sc:* William Anthony McGuire. (G.B. title: *Penalty of Fame*) (1:20)

Melodrama of a corrupt reporter who pays a penalty after saving a politician's daughter from kidnappers. Remade as *Risky Business* (q.v.).

3304. Oklahoma Cyclone (Tiffany; 1930). *Cast:* Bob Steele, Nita Ray, Al St. John, Charles L. King, Slim Whitaker, Shorty Hendrix, Emilio Fernandez, Hector Sarno, Fred Burns, John Ince, Cliff Lyons. *D:* John P. McCarthy; *P:* Trem Carr; *Sc:* Ford Beebe. (1:00)

Bob Steele western of a man who joins a gang of outlaws in search of his father.

3305. Oklahoma Frontier (Universal; 1939). *Cast:* Johnny Mack Brown, Bob Baker, Fuzzy Knight, Anne Gwynne, Charles King, Robert Cummings, James Blaine, Lane Chandler, Anthony Warde, Robert Kortman, Harry Tenbrook, Horace Murphy, George Chesebro, Joe de la Cruz, Lloyd Ingraham. *D:* Ford Beebe; *Sc:* Beebe. (0:59)

Johnny Mack Brown western of the Oklahoma land rush.

3306. Oklahoma Jim (Monogram; 1931). *Cast:* Bill Cody, Marion Burns, Andy Shuford, William Desmond, Si Jenks, Franklyn Farnum, John Elliott, Ed Brady, G.D. Wood (Gordon DeMain), Iron Eyes Cody, J.W. Cody, Ann Ross, Artie Ortego, White Eagle. *D:* Harry Fraser; *P:* Trem Carr; *St:* Fraser; *Sc:* George Arthur Durlam. (0:53)

Bill Cody western of a cowboy who comes to the aid of a woman faced with losing her trading post.

3307. The Oklahoma Kid (WB; 1939). *Cast:* James Cagney (who also sings "Rockabye Baby" in Spanish & "I Don't Want to Play in Your Yard"), Humphrey Bogart, Rosemary Lane, Donald Crisp, Harvey Stephens, Charles Middleton, Ward Bond, Edward Pawley, Trevor Bardette, John Miljan, Hugh Sothern, Lew Harvey, Clem Bevans, Joe Devlin, Arthur Aylesworth. *D:* Lloyd Bacon; *As.P.:* Sam Bischoff; *St:* Wally Klein, Edward E. Paramore; *Sc:* Warren Duff, Robert Buckner, Edward E. Paramore. (1:20) (video)

Hit western of a cowboy seeking vengeance on the ones responsible for lynching his father.

3308. Oklahoma Terror (Monogram; 1939). *Cast:* Jack Randall, Virginia Carroll, Al "Fuzzy" St. John, Davison Clark, Nolan Willis, Glenn Strange, Warren McCollum, Don Rowan, Brandon Beach, Tristram Coffin, Ralph Peters, Slim Whitaker, Rusty the Wonder Horse. *D:* Spencer Gordon Bennet; *P:* Lindsley Parsons; *St:* Parsons; *Sc:* Joseph West (George Waggner). (0:50)

Jack Randall western of a Union soldier who returns to the west after the war only to discover that his father has been murdered.

3309. The Old Barn Dance (Republic; 1938). *Cast:* Gene Autry, Smiley Burnette, Helen Valkis, Sammy McKim, Walt Shrum & His Colorado Hillbillies, Stafford Sisters, Maple City Four, Dick Weston (Roy Rogers), Ivan Miller, Earl Dwire, Hooper Atchley, Raphael (Ray) Bennett, Carleton Young, Frankie Marvin, Earle Hodgins, Gloria Rich, Champion the horse. *D:* Joseph Kane; *As.P.:* Sol C. Siegel; *Sc:* Bernard McConville, Charles Francis Royal; *Songs:* Autry, Burnette, Jack Lawrence, Peter Tinturin, Marvin, Colorado Hillbillies. (1:00) (video)

Gene Autry western with songs of a crooked tractor company fleecing some small farmers.

The Old Corral (Grand National; 1936) (G.B. title) *see* **Song of the Gringo**

3310. The Old Corral (Republic; 1936). *Cast:* Gene Autry, Hope (Irene) Manning, Smiley Burnette, Lon Chaney, Jr., Cornelius Keefe, Marc Kramer, Milburn Morante, Frankie Marvin, Abe Lefton, Buddy Roosevelt, Merrill McCormack, Lew Kelly, Oscar & Elmer (Ed Platt & Lou Fulton), Jack Ingram, Sons of the Pioneers with Bob Nolan & Dick Weston (Roy Rogers), Champion. *D:* Joseph Kane; *Sc:* Joseph Poland, Sherman Lowe. (0:56) (video)

A Gene Autry western with songs of some good guys after some bad guys from the east.

3311. The Old Dark House (Universal; 1932). *Cast:* Melvyn Douglas, Charles Laughton, Boris Karloff, Gloria Stuart, Raymond Massey (American debut), Ernest Thesiger (American debut), Eva Moore, Lillian Bond, Brember Wills, John Dudgeon. *D:* James Whale; *P:* Carl Laemmle, Jr.; *Sc:* Benn W. Levy; *Additional Dialogue:* R.C. Sherriff. (1:15)

A horror classic with comic overtones of motorists who are stranded on a stormy night at the decrepit old mansion of the Femm family. Within the mansion resides assorted looney and sinister types as well as a few who appear "normal." Based on the novel "Benighted" by

J.B. Priestley, the film remained unseen for many years until 1975 due to copyright problems with the novel. Remade in Great Britain in 1963.

3312. Old English (WB; 1930). *Cast:* George Arliss, Leon Janney, Doris Lloyd, Ivan Simpson, Reginald Sheffield, Harrington Reynolds, Ethel Griffies. *D:* Alfred E. Green; *Sc:* Maude Howell, Walter Anthony. (1:27)

The story of an aging financier seeking to provide for his grandchildren after his passing. Based on the play by John Galsworthy, it placed #10 on the "10 Best" list of *Film Daily.*

3313. The Old-Fashioned Way (Paramount; 1934). *Cast:* W.C. Fields, Judith Allen, Joe Morrison, Baby LeRoy, Jan Duggan, Jack Mulhall, Oscar Apfel, Nora Cecil, Del Henderson, Otis Harlan, Richard Carle, Clarence Wilson, Joe Mills, Emma Ray, Ruth Marion, Samuel Ethridge. *D:* William Beaudine; *P:* William LeBaron; *St:* Charles Bogle (Fields); *Sc:* Garnett Weston, Jack Cunningham. (1:14)

The comic adventures of a traveling theatrical troupe headed by "The Great McGonigle" that goes from town to town presenting the old time melodramatic play "The Drunkard."

Old Great Heart (G.B. title) *see* **Way Back Home**

3314. The Old Homestead (Liberty; 1935). *Cast:* Bob Nolan (film debut), Lawrence Gray, Mary Carlisle, Edward Nugent, Willard Robertson, Fuzzy Knight. *D:* William Nigh; *P:* M.H. Hoffman, Jr.

An independent musical western which is notable as the film debuts of the Sons of the Pioneers and Roy Rogers (listed under his real name Len [Leonard] Slye).

3315. Old Hutch (MGM; 1936). *Cast:* Wallace Beery, Eric Linden, Elizabeth Patterson, Cecilia Parker, Donald Meek, Virginia Grey, Robert McWade, James Burke, Frank Reicher, Caroline Perkins, Julia Perkins, Delmar Watson, Harry Watson, Stanley Morner (Dennis Morgan). *D:* J. Walter Ruben; *P:* Harry Rapf; *St:* Garret Smith; *Sc:* George Kelly. (1:20)

In this hit comedy, an indigent finds $100,000 in cash and encounters various difficulties in trying to spend it without raising anyone's suspicions. Based on the Broadway play by George Kelly, it was previously filmed as *Honest Hutch* (Fox; 1920) with Will Rogers.

3316. Old Louisiana (Crescent Pictures; 1937). *Cast:* Tom Keene, Rita (Hayworth) Cansino, Will Morgan, Robert Fiske, Budd Buster, Ray Bennett, Allan Cavan, Carlos de Valdez, Wally Albright, Ramsay Hill, J. Louis Johnson, Iron Eyes Cody. *D:* Irvin Willat; *P:* E.B. Derr; *Sc:* Mary Ireland. (1:00)

A low-budget historically based drama centered around the Louisiana Purchase.

3317. The Old Maid (WB/F.N.; 1939). *Cast:* Bette Davis (Charlotte Lovell), Miriam Hopkins (Delia Lovell), Jane Bryan (Tina), George Brent (Clem Spender), Donald Crisp (Doctor Lanskell), Louise Fazenda (in her final film before retiring as Dora), Jerome Cowan (Joe Ralston), James Stephenson (Jim Ralston), William Lundigan (Lanning Halsey), Cecilia Loftus (Grandmother Lovell), DeWolf (William) Hopper (John), Rand Brooks (Jim), Janet Shaw (Dee), Marlene Burnett (Tina the child), Frederick Burton (Mr. Halsey), Doris Lloyd. *D:* Edmund Goulding; *As.P.:* Henry Blanke; *Sc:* Casey Robinson. (1:35) (video)

A hit "woman's film" set in the era following the Civil War of emotional interchange between a woman, her illegitimate daughter and her sister. Based on the 1935 Pulitzer Prize winning play by Zoe Akins, which in turn was based on a novel by Edith Wharton. The film which placed #10 on the "10 Best" list of *Film Daily,* was also one of the 21 top grossing films of 1939–40.

Note: Actor Rod Cameron made his debut in this film, but wound up on the cutting room floor.

3318. Old Man Rhythm (RKO; 1935). *Cast:* Charles "Buddy" Rogers, George Barbier, Barbara Kent, Grace Bradley, Betty Grable, Eric Blore, Erik Rhodes, John Arledge, Johnny Mercer, Donald Meek, Evelyn Poe, Douglas Fowley, Lucille Ball (bit). *D:* Edward Ludwig; *As.P.:* Zion Myers; *St:* Lewis Gensler, Sig Herzig, Don Hartman; *Sc:* Herzig, Ernest Pagano; *Additional Dialogue:* H.W. Hanemann; *Songs:* Gensler, Johnny Mercer. (1:15)

Musical-comedy of a wealthy tycoon who enrolls at college to keep tabs on his son.

The Old School Tie (G.B. title) *see* **We Went to College**

3319. The Old Wyoming Trail (Columbia; 1937). *Cast:* Charles Starrett, Donald Grayson, Barbara Weeks, Sons of the Pioneers with Bob Nolan, Dick Curtis, Edward J. LeSaint, Guy Usher, George Chesebro, Art Mix, Slim Whitaker, Alma Chester, Ernie Adams, Dick Botiller, Frank Ellis, Joe Yrigoyen, Charles Brinley, Fred Burns, Si Jenks, Curley Dresden, Ray Whitley, Blackie Whiteford, Tom London, Art Dillard, Ray Jones, Jerome Ward, Tex Cooper. *D:* Folmar Blangsted; *Sc:* Ed Earl Repp. (0:56)

Charles Starrett western of a man out to swindle another on the cost of his property.

3320. Oliver Twist (Monogram; 1933). *Cast:* Dickie Moore (Oliver), Irving Pichel (Fagin), William "Stage" Boyd (Bill Sikes), Doris Lloyd (Nancy Sikes), Barbara Kent (Rose Maylie), Alec B. Francis (Mr. Brownlow), George K. Arthur (Toby Crackit), Lionel Belmore (Mr. Bumble), Clyde

Cook (Chitling), George Nash, Virginia Sale, Nelson McDowell, Tempe Pigott, Harry Holman, Sonny Ray, Bobby Nelson. *D:* William Cowen; *P:* I.E. Chadwick; *Supervisor:* Herbert Brenon; *Sc:* Elizabeth Meehan. (1:17) (video)

The first talkie version of the Charles Dickens' classic of a street waif who becomes involved with Fagin and his world of thievery. Previously filmed (Pathé; 1909), (Vitagraph; 1910), (Vitagraph; 1912) with Nat C. Gordon as "Fagin," (Lasky; 1916) with Marie Doro as "Oliver" and Tully Marshall as "Fagin," (First National; 1922) with Jackie Coogan as "Oliver" and Lon Chaney as "Fagin." Remade in Great Britain in 1948, in Great Britain in 1968 as the Academy Award winning musical *Oliver!,* and again in the United States as a 1982 TV movie.

3321. Olsen's Big Moment (Fox; 1933–34). *Cast:* El Brendel, John Arledge, Walter Catlett, Ethel Griffies. *D:* Malcolm St. Clair.

Low-budget comedy.

3322. On Again – Off Again (RKO; 1937). *Cast:* Bert Wheeler, Robert Woolsey, Marjorie Lord, Patricia Wilder, Esther Muir, Paul Harvey, Russell Hicks, George Meeker, Maxine Jennings, Kitty McHugh, Hal K. Dawson, Alec Hartford, Pat Flaherty. *D:* Edward Cline; *P:* Lee Marcus; *Sc:* Benny Rubin, Nat Perrin; *Songs:* Dave Dreyer, Herman Ruby. (1:08)

Comedy farce of quarreling partners who wager their pill business on a wrestling match, with the loser to become the other's valet. A remake of *A Pair of Sixes* (Essanay; 1918), which was based on the play of that name by Edward H. Peple. Also filmed as *Queen High* (q.v.).

3323. On Borrowed Time (MGM; 1939). *Cast:* Lionel Barrymore, Sir Cedric Hardwicke (Death – Mr. Brink), Beulah Bondi, Una Merkel, Bobs Watson, Nat Pendleton, Henry

Travers, Grant Mitchell, Eily Malyon, James Burke, Charles Waldron, Ian Wolfe, Phillip Terry, Truman Bradley, Hans Conried. *D:* Harold S. Bucquet; *P:* Sidney Franklin; *Sc:* Frank O'Neill, Alice D.G. (Duer) Miller, Claudine West. (1:38)

In this fantasy, Death comes to claim an elderly man, but the old coot isn't ready to go and with the help of his grandson traps his visitor in an apple tree. Based on the novel by Lawrence Edward Watkin and the play by Paul Osborn.

3324. On Dress Parade (WB; 1939–40). *Cast:* Billy Halop, Bobby Jordan, Huntz Hall, Gabriel Dell, Leo Gorcey, Selmer Jackson, John Litel, Bernard Punsley, Cissie Loftus, Aldrich Bowker, Frankie Thomas, Donald Douglas, Douglas Meins, William Gould. *D:* William Clemens; *As.P.:* Bryan Foy; *Sc:* Tom Reed, Charles Belden. (aka: *The Dead End Kids on Dress Parade*) (1:02)

B melodrama of a non-conformist cadet at a military school who eventually "sees the light." The final film of the "Dead End Kids" before they moved over to their "East Side Kids" series at Monogram. In 1946 they became the "Bowery Boys" for Monogram-Allied Artists.

3325/3326. On Probation (Peerless; 1935). *Cast:* Monte Blue.

(No other information available)

On Secret Service (G.B. title) *see* **Trailin' West**

3327. On Such a Night (Paramount; 1937). *Cast:* Karen Morley, Grant Richards, Roscoe Karns, Alan Mowbray, Eduardo Ciannelli, Eddie "Rochester" Anderson, Frank Reicher, Paul Fix, Philo McCullough, Milli Monti. *D:* E.A. Dupont; *P:* Emmanuel Cohen; *St:* Morley F. Cassidy, Salisbury

Field, John Klorer; *Sc:* William R. Lipman, Doris Malloy.

B drama of various people, one of which is a killer, trapped by rising flood waters.

3328. On the Avenue (20th Century–Fox; 1937). *Cast:* Dick Powell (Gary Blake), Madeleine Carroll (Mimi Caraway), Ritz Brothers (themselves), George Barbier (Commodore Caraway), Alice Faye (Mona Merrick), Alan Mowbray (Frederick Sims), Walter Catlett (Jake Dibble), Joan Davis (Miss Katz), Billy Gilbert (Joe Papaloupas), Cora Witherspoon (Aunt Fritz Peters), Sig Rumann (Herr Hanfstangel), E.E. Clive (Vince, the cabby), Stepin Fetchit (Herman), Douglas Fowley (Eddie Eads), Douglas Wood (Mr. Trivet), John Sheehan (stage manager), Paul Irving (Harry Morris), Harry Stubbs (Kelly), Ricardo Mandia (Luigi), Lynn Bari, Dewey Robinson, Edward Cooper, Paul Gerrits, Mary Jane Irving. *D:* Roy Del Ruth; *As.P.:* Gene Markey; *Sc:* Markey, William Conselman; *Songs:* "Slumming on Park Avenue," "I've Got My Love to Keep Me Warm," "This Year's Kisses," "You're Laughing at Me," "He Ain't Got Rhythm" and "The Girl on the Police Gazette" by Irving Berlin. (1:29) (video)

Musical romance, loosely remade as *Let's Make Love* (20th Century–Fox; 1960). One of the 38 top grossing films of 1936–37.

3329. On the Border (WB; 1930). *Cast:* Rin-Tin-Tin, Armida, John Litel (film debut), Philo McCullough, Bruce Covington, Walter Miller. *D:* William McGann (directorial debut); *Sc:* Lillie Hayward.

B action-adventure of border smugglers which is notable as the first all-talking, all-barking film of Rin-Tin-Tin. A box office hit as were all of Rinty's films.

3330. On the Great White Trail (Grand National; 1938). *Cast:* James

Newill (Renfrew "the singing Mountie"), Terry Walker, Robert Frazer, Richard Alexander, Richard Tucker, Robert Terry, Eddie Gribbon, Walter McGrail, Philo McCullough, Charles King, Juan Duval, Carl Mathews, Silver King the dog. *D:* Al Herman; *P:* Herman, Phil Krasne; *Sc:* Charles Logue. (aka: *Renfrew on the Great White Trail*). (0:59) (video)

A Mountie must arrest his girl's father in this action-adventure of "Renfrew of the Royal Mounted." Based on the writings of Laurie York Erskine.

3331. On the Level (Fox; 1930). *Cast:* Victor McLaglen, Lilyan Tashman, William Harrigan, Fifi D'Orsay, Arthur Stone, Lee Tracy, Leila McIntyre, Ben Hewlett, Mary McAllister, R.O. Pennell, Harry Tenbrook. *D:* Irving Cummings; *St:* William K. Wells, Andrew Bennison; *Sc:* Dudley Nichols, Wells, Bennison; *Dial.:* Bennison & Wells.

Romantic comedy.

On the Stroke of Nine (G.B. title) *see* **Murder on the Campus**

3332. On Trial (WB; 1928). *Cast:* Bert Lytell, Pauline Frederick, Lois Wilson, Holmes Herbert, Jason Robards, Richard Tucker, Franklin Pangborn, Fred Kelsey, Johnny Arthur, Edward Martindel, Edmund Breese, Vondell Darr. *D:* Archie L. Mayo; *Sc:* Robert Lord, Max Pollock.

Warners 4th all-talkie which premiered November 14, 1928, in New York City. Courtroom drama of a man on trial for the murder of his friend. Based on the play by Elmer Rice, it was remade in 1939 (see below).

3333. On Trial (WB; 1939). *Cast:* Margaret Lindsay, John Litel, Edward Norris, Janet Chapman, James Stephenson, Larry Williams, William Davidson, Gordon Hart, Nat Carr, Stuart Holmes, Sidney Bracey, Earl Dwire, Nedda Harrigan. *D:* Terry Morse; *As.P.:* Bryan Foy; *Sc:* Don Ryan.

B melodrama of a lawyer who takes on the case of a man who refuses to defend himself on murder charges. Based on the play by Elmer Rice, and a remake of the preceding film.

On Wings of Song (G.B. title) *see* **Love Me Forever**

3334. On with the Show (WB; 1929). *Cast:* Betty Compson, Joe E. Brown, Arthur Lake, Sally O'Neil, Ethel Waters (film debut), Louise Fazenda, Purnell Pratt, William Bakewell, Fairbanks Twins, Wheeler Oakman, Thomas Jefferson, Lee Moran, Harry Gribbon, Sam Hardy, Josephine Houston. *D:* Alan Crosland: *P:* Darryl Zanuck; *Sc:* Robert Lord; *Songs:* Grant Clarke & Harry Akst include: "In the Land of Let's Pretend," "Let Me Have My Dreams," "Welcome Home," "Don't It Mean a Thing to You?" "Lift the Juleps to Your Two Lips," title song & "Am I Blue?" & "Birmingham Bertha" (both sung by Ethel Waters). (1:38)

Backstage musical filmed in 2-color (prismatic color) technicolor and notable as the first all-color all-talkie. Based on the play "Shoestring" by Humphrey Pearson.

3335. On Your Back (Fox; 1930). *Cast:* Irene Rich, Raymond Hackett, H.B. Warner, Ilka Chase, Charlotte Henry, Rose Dione, Marion Shilling, Arthur Hoyt, Wheeler Oakman. *D:* Guthrie McClintic; *St:* Rita Weiman; *Sc:* Howard J. Green.

Romantic comedy.

3336. On Your Toes (WB; 1939). *Cast:* (Vera) Zorina, Eddie Albert, Alan Hale, Frank McHugh, James Gleason, Leonid Kinskey, Gloria Dickson, Donald O'Connor, Erik Rhodes (his final film—returning to his stage career), Queenie Smith, Paul Hurst, Berton Churchill, Marek Windheim, Sarita

Wooten, Alex Melesh. *D:* Ray Enright; *As.P.:* Robert Lord; *Adaptation:* Sig Herzig, Lawrence Riley; *Sc:* Jerry Wald, Richard Macaulay; *Songs:* "There's a Small Hotel," "Quiet Night" & the title song by Rodgers & Hart. (1:34)

Musical drama of backstage jealousies in a ballet company. Filmed before in 1927. Notable is Zorina's "Slaughter on 10th Avenue" ballet with choreography by George Balanchine. Based on the Broadway show by George Abbott with songs by Richard Rodgers and Lorenz Hart.

3337. Once a Doctor (WB/F.N.; 1937). *Cast:* Donald Woods, Gordon Oliver, Jean Muir, Henry Kolker, Gordon Hart, Ed Stanley, Louise Stanley, David Carlyle (Robert Paige), Houseley Stevenson. *D:* William Clemens; *P:* Bryan Foy; *St:* Frank Daugherty, Paul Perez; *Sc:* Robertson White, Ben Grauman Kohn.

B drama of a young doctor who places the blame on his brother when a patient dies.

3338. Once a Gentleman (Sono Art-World Wide; 1930). *Cast:* Edward Everett Horton, Lois Wilson, Francis X. Bushman, George Fawcett, King Baggot, Emerson Treacy, Cyril Chadwick. *D:* James Cruze; *St:* George F. Worts; *Sc:* Walter Woods.

"Poverty row" romantic comedy.

Once a Hero (G.B. title) *see* **It Happened in Hollywood**

3339. Once a Lady (Paramount; 1931). *Cast:* Ruth Chatterton, Ivor Novello (in his only American talkie), Jill Esmond, Bramwell Fletcher, Doris Lloyd, Theodore von Eltz, Geoffrey Kerr, Claude King, Ethel Griffies, Herbert Bunston, Lillian Rich, Stella Moore, Edith Kingdon, Gwendolyn Logan. *D:* Guthrie McClintic (better known as a theatrical director); *Sc:* Zoe Akins, Samuel Hoffenstein. (1:20)

A woman deserts her husband and daughter in this tear-jerker. A remake of *Three Sinners* (Paramount; 1928) with Pola Negri, and based on the German play of that name by Rudolf Bernauer and Rudolf Oesterreicher.

3340. Once a Sinner (Fox; 1931). *Cast:* Dorothy Mackaill, Joel McCrea, George Brent, Sally Blane, John Halliday, Ilka Chase, C. Henry Gordon, Sidney Blackmer, Clara Blandick, Theodore Lodi, Myra Hampton, Ninette Faro. *D:* Guthrie McClintic; *St & Sc:* George Middleton.

Marital drama of a woman with a past.

3341. Once in a Blue Moon (Paramount/Hecht-MacArthur; 1936). *Cast:* Jimmy Savo, Nikita Balieff, Cecilia Loftus, Howard daSilva (film debut), Hans Steinke, Edwina Armstrong, Whitney Bourne, Michael Dalmatoff, Sandor Szabo, J. Charles Gilbert, Jackie Borene. *As.P.:* Lee Garmes.

Russian aristocrats are fleeing the revolution in a circus wagon in this drama written, directed and produced by Ben Hecht and Charles MacArthur.

3342. Once in a Lifetime (Universal; 1932). *Cast:* Jack Oakie, Sidney Fox, Aline MacMahon, Russell Hopton, ZaSu Pitts, Louise Fazenda, Onslow Stevens, Gregory Ratoff, Robert McWade, Jobyna Howland, Claudia Morgan, Beverly Bayne, Mona Maris, Gregory Gaye, Carol Tevis, Johnny Morris, Alan Ladd (film debut—bit), Eddie Kane, Frank LaRue. *D:* Russell Mack; *P:* Carl Laemmle, Jr.; *Sc:* Seton I. Miller. (1:15)

Hollywood at the beginning of the talkie era is depicted in this hit comedy based on the hit Broadway play by George S. Kaufman and Moss Hart.

Once There Was a Princess (G.B. title) *see* **Misbehavin' Ladies**

3343. Once to Every Bachelor (Liberty; 1934). *Cast:* Neil Hamilton,

Marian Nixon. *D:* William Nigh; *P:* M.H. Hoffman, Jr. (G.B. title: *Once to Every Man*) (aka: (?) *The Fighting Heart*)

Once to Every Man (G.B. title) *see* **Once to Every Bachelor**

3344. Once to Every Woman (Columbia; 1934). *Cast:* Fay Wray, Mary Carlisle, Ralph Bellamy, Walter Connolly, Walter Byron, J. Farrell MacDonald, Ben Alexander, Jane Darwell, Rebecca Wassem, Mary Foy, Kathrin Clare Ward, Billie Seward, Edward LeSaint, Nora Cecil, Leila Bennett, Georgia Caine. *D:* Lambert Hillyer; *St:* A.J. Cronin; *Sc:* Jo Swerling. Romantic drama.

3345. One Dark Night (Sack Amusement; 1939). *Cast:* Mantan Moreland, Betty Treadville, Lawrence Criner. *D:* Leo C. Popkin; *P:* Harry M. Popkin.

(No other information available)

3346. One Exciting Adventure (Universal; 1934). *Cast:* Binnie Barnes, Neil Hamilton, Eugene Pallette, Grant Mitchell, Paul Cavanagh, Ferdinand Gottschalk, Jason Robards, Dick Winslow, William Worthington, Ann Doran. *D:* Ernst L. Frank; *Sc:* William Hurlbut, Samuel Ornitz; *Dial.:* Samuel Ornitz; *St:* Franz Schulz, Billy Wilder. (1:10)

B drama of a female kleptomaniac with a penchant for jewelry.

One Fatal Hour *see* **Two Against the World**

One for All (G.B. title) *see* **The President's Mystery**

3347/3348. One Frightened Night (Mascot; 1935). *Cast:* Wallace Ford, Mary Carlisle, Charley Grapewin, Evalyn Knapp, Arthur Hohl, Lucien Littlefield, Hedda Hopper, Regis Toomey, Fred Kelsey, Clarence Wilson, Rafaela Ottiano, Adrian Morris. *D:* Christy Cabanne; *St:* Stuart Palmer; *Sc:* Wellyn Totman. (1:06) (video)

B comic mystery-melodrama set in an old dark house.

3349. One Heavenly Night (United Artists/Samuel Goldwyn; 1931). *Cast:* Evelyn Laye (American debut), John Boles, Leon Errol, Lilyan Tashman, Hugh Cameron, Marian Lord, Luis Alberni, Lionel Belmore, Sidney Blackmer, Vince Barnett, Henry Victor, George Bickel. *D:* George Fitzmaurice; *P:* Samuel Goldwyn; *St:* Louis Bromfield; *Sc:* Sidney Howard. (1:22)

Mistaken identity is the premise in this romantic operetta set in Eastern Europe. A box office fizzle.

One Horse Town *see* **Small Town Girl**

3350. One Hour Late (Paramount; 1935). *Cast:* Helen Twelvetrees, Joe Morrison, Conrad Nagel, Ray Milland, Frank Mayo, George E. Stone, Gail Patrick, Arline Judge, Diana Lewis, Bradley Page, Eddie Phillips, Arthur Hoyt, John Gallaudet, Jack Norton. *D:* Ralph Murphy; *P:* Albert Lewis; *Sc:* Kathryn Scola, Paul Gerard Smith.

B drama of various people trapped in an elevator.

3351. One Hour to Live (Universal; 1939). *Cast:* Charles Bickford, Doris Nolan, John Litel, Samuel S. Hinds, Paul Guilfoyle, Emory Parnell, Olin Howland, Jack Carr. *D:* Harold Schuster; *P:* George Yohalem; *St & Sc:* Roy Chanslor. (0:59)

B crime melodrama.

3352. One Hour with You (Paramount; 1932). *Cast:* Maurice Chevalier (Dr. Andre Bertier), Jeanette MacDonald (Colette Bertier, a role originally intended for Carole Lombard), Genevieve Tobin (Mitzi Olivier), Roland Young (Professor Olivier), Charles Ruggles (Adolph), George Barbier (police chief), Josephine Dunn (Mlle. Martel), Richard Carle (detective), Charles Coleman (Marcel, the butler), Charles Judels, Barbara Leonard, Florinne McKinney (film debut), Donald Novis, Eric Wilton, George Davis, Gordon (Bill) Elliott, Robert Emmett Keane. *D:* Ernst Lubitsch & George Cukor (who walked out on directing the production and got credit as dialogue director); *P:* (A.A.N. for Best Picture) Lubitsch; *Sc:* Samson Raphaelson; *Songs:* title song, "Oh, That Mitzi," "We Will Always Be Sweethearts," "Three Times a Day," "What Would You Do?" by Leo Robin, Oscar Straus & Richard A. Whiting. (1:24)

A happily married couple encounter difficulties when a flirtatious female comes on the scene. A remake of Lubitsch's *The Marriage Circle* (WB; 1924). Based on the play "Only a Dream" by Lothar Schmidt, the film placed #7 on the "10 Best" list of the *New York Times*. It was also one of the 15 top grossing films of 1932.

3353. One Hundred Men and a Girl (Universal; 1937). *Cast:* Deanna Durbin (Patricia Cardwell), Leopold Stokowski (himself), Adolphe Menjou (John Cardwell), Alice Brady (Mrs. Frost), Eugene Pallette (John R. Frost), Mischa Auer (Michael Borodoff), Alma Kruger (Mrs. Tyler), Billy Gilbert (garage owner), Jed Prouty (Tommy Bitters), Jack (J. Scott) Smart (Marshall, the doorman), Jameson Thomas (Russell), Howard Hickman (Johnson), Frank Jenks (taxi driver), Christian Rub (Gustav Brandstetter), Gerald Oliver Smith (Stevens, the butler), Edwin Maxwell (Ira Westing), Jack Mulhall, James Bush, John Hamilton, Mary Forbes, Eric Wilton, Rolfe Sedan, Charles Coleman, Hooper Atchley, Leonid Kinskey. *D:* Henry Koster; *P:* (A.A.N. for Best Picture) Joe Pasternak, Charles R. Rogers; *Original Story:* (A.A.N.) Hans Kräly; *Sc:* Bruce Manning, Charles Kenyon, James Mulhauser; *Music:* (A.A.) Charles Previn; *Editor:* (A.A.N.) Bernard W. Burton; *Sound Recording:* (A.A.N.) Homer G. Tasker; *Songs:* "It's Raining Sunbeams"

by Sam Coslow, Frederick Hollander, "A Heart That's Free" by Alfred G. Robyn, Thomas T. Railey. (1:24)

Hit musical-comedy set during the depression of a girl who is trying to find work for her father and his musician friends. The film showcases various classical works including Liszt's "Hungarian Rhapsody #2," "The Drinking Song" from "La Traviata" (Verdi), "Alleluja" (Mozart), with other excerpts from Wagner's "Lohengrin" and Tchaikovsky's "Fifth Symphony" as well as two modern songs.

100% Pure (G.B. title) *see* **The Girl from Missouri**

3354. One Hysterical Night (Universal; 1930). *Cast:* Reginald Denny, Nora Lane, E.J. Ratcliffe, Fritz Feld, Slim Summerville, Peter Gawthorne. *D:* William James Craft. (1:15)

Screwball type comedy of a family heir who is committed to an asylum by greedy relatives who are after his fortune.

3355. One in a Million (Invincible; 1934). *Cast:* Dorothy Wilson, Charles Starrett, Guinn "Big Boy" Williams. *D:* Frank Strayer; *Sc:* Karl Brown, Robert Ellis.

(No other information available)

3356. One in a Million (20th Century–Fox; 1936). *Cast:* Sonja Henie (U.S. film debut as Greta Muller), Adolphe Menjou (Tad), Don Ameche (Bob), Ned Sparks (photographer), Jean Hersholt (Heinrich Muller), Ritz Brothers (themselves doing a spoof on horror films), Leah Ray (Leah), Arline Judge (Billie), Dixie Dunbar (Goldie), Borrah Minevich (Adolph), Montagu Love (Ratoffsky), Albert Conti (hotel manager), Julius Tannen (Chapelle), Shirley Deane, June Wilkins, Pauline Craig, June Gale, Bonnie Bannon, Lillian Porter, Diana Cook, Clarice Sherry, Margo Webster, Bess Flowers, Frederic Gierman, Egon Brecher, Paul McVey. *D:* Sidney Lanfield; *P:* Darryl F.

Zanuck; *As.P.:* Raymond Griffith; *Sc:* Leonard Praskins, Mark Kelly; *Choreographer:* (A.A.N.) Nick Castle for his "Skating Ensemble" number; *Songs:* title song, "Who's Afraid of Love?" "The Moonlight Waltz," "Lovely Lady in White" & "We're Back in Circulation Again" by Sidney D. Mitchell & Lew Pollack. (1:35)

Musical-comedy with an ice skating background which served as the American film debut of skater Sonja Henie. The film was one of the 38 top grossing films of 1936–37.

3357. One Is Guilty (Columbia; 1934). *Cast:* Ralph Bellamy, Warren Hymer, Rita LaRoy, J. Carrol Naish, Wheeler Oakman, Vincent Sherman, Willard Robertson. *D:* Lambert Hillyer.

B crime melodrama.

3358. One Mad Kiss (Fox; 1930). *Cast:* Don Jose Mojica, Mona Maris, Antonio Moreno, Tom Patricola. *D:* James Tinling, Marcel Silver; *St:* Adolph Paul; *Sc:* Dudley Nichols.

Romantic comedy.

3359. One-Man Justice (Columbia; 1937). *Cast:* Charles Starrett, Barbara Weeks, Hal Taliaferro, Jack Clifford, Alan Bridge, Walter Downing, Mary Gordon, Jack Lipson, Edmund Cobb, Dick Curtis, Maston Williams. *D:* Leon Barsha; *Sc:* Paul Perez. (0:59)

Charles Starrett western with the hero impersonating a man who has been dead for several years.

3360. One-Man Law (Columbia; 1931–32). *Cast:* Buck Jones, Shirley Grey, Robert Ellis, Murdock MacQuarrie, Harry Todd, Henry Sedley, Ernie Adams, Richard Alexander, Wesley Giraud, Edward J. LeSaint. *D:* Lambert Hillyer; *Sc:* Hillyer. (1:00)

Buck Jones western of a cowboy who becomes sheriff at the request of a crook who thinks he can control him.

3361. One Man's Journey (RKO; 1933). *Cast:* Lionel Barrymore

(Eli Watt), Joel McCrea, Frances Dee, Dorothy Jordan, James Bush, May Robson, David Landau, Buster Phelps, June Filmer, Oscar Apfel, Hale Hamilton, Samuel S. Hinds. *D:* John S. Robertson; *P:* Pandro S. Berman; *Sc:* Samuel Ornitz, Lester Cohen.

Critically acclaimed hit drama of a benevolent country doctor, remembered by many after his death. Based on the novel "Failure" by Katharine Haviland-Taylor, it was remade as *A Man to Remember* (q.v.).

3362. One Mile from Heaven (20th Century–Fox; 1937). *Cast:* Claire Trevor, Chick Chandler, Bill Robinson, Fredi Washington, Sally Blane, Eddie "Rochester" Anderson, Douglas Fowley, John Eldredge, Russell Hopton, Ray Walker, Ralf Harolde, Lon Chaney, Jr., Paul McVey, Joan Carol, Howard Hickman. *D:* Allan Dwan; *St:* Judge Ben Lindsey, Alfred Golden, Robin Harris; *Sc:* John Patrick, Lou Breslow.

B racial melodrama of a black woman who claims to be the mother of a white child.

3363. One More River (Universal; 1934). *Cast:* Colin Clive (Sir Gerald), Diana Wynyard (Clare), C. Aubrey Smith, Jane Wyatt (film debut as Dinny Cherrell), Lionel Atwill, Mrs. Patrick Campbell (Lady Mont), Reginald Denny, Frank Lawton (Tony Croom), Henry Stephenson, Alan Mowbray, E.E. Clive, Gilbert Emery, Kathleen Howard, Tempe Pigott, Robert Greig, J. Gunnis Davis. *D:* James Whale; *P:* Whale; *Sc:* R.C. Sherriff. (G.B. title: *Over the River*) (1:28)

A drama of marital infidelity and divorce. Based on the final novel of John Galsworthy (the 3rd book of the "Forsyte trilogy").

3364. One More Spring (Fox; 1935). *Cast:* Janet Gaynor, Warner Baxter, Walter Woolf King, Grant Mitchell, Jane Darwell, Roger Imhof, John Qualen, Astrid Allwyn, Nick (Dick)

Foran, Stepin Fetchit, Rosemary Ames, Jack Norton, Lee Kohlmar, Jayne Regan. *D:* Henry King; *P:* Winfield Sheehan; *Sc:* Edwin Burke. (1:27)

Depression-era comedy-drama of three down-and-outs who meet in Central Park in New York City. Based on the novel by Robert Nathan.

3365. One New York Night (MGM; 1935). *Cast:* Franchot Tone, Una Merkel, Steffi Duna, Conrad Nagel, Charles Starrett, Harold Huber, Harvey Stephens, Louise Henry. *D:* Jack Conway; *P:* Bernard B. Hyman; *Sc:* Frank Davis (based on the play by Edward Childs Carpenter). (G.B. title: *The Trunk Mystery*) (1:20)

A rural type gets more than he bargained for when he finds a body in the hotel room next to his while on a visit to New York City. A comedy-mystery which bombed at the box office.

3366. One Night at Susie's (WB/F.N.; 1930). *Cast:* Douglas Fairbanks, Jr., Billie Dove, Helen Ware, Tully Marshall, James Crane, John Loder, Claude Fleming. *D:* John Francis Dillon; *St:* Frederick Hazlitt Brennan; *Sc:* Kathryn Scola, Forrest Halsey.

B crime melodrama of a man who serves a prison sentence for a crime committed by his girl friend.

3367. One Night of Love (Columbia; 1934). *Cast:* Grace Moore (A.A.N. for B.A. and a gold medal from the Society of Arts and Science of New York — the first such award from this group to a film personality, for her performance as Mary), Tullio Carminati (Monteverdi), Lyle Talbot (Bill Houston), Mona Barrie (Lally), Nydia Westman (Muriel), Jessie Ralph (Angelina), Luis Alberni (Giovanni), Rosemary Glosz (Frappazini), Jane Darwell (Mary's mother), William Burress (Mary's father), Henry Armetta (cafe proprietor), Frederick Burton (impresario), Andres de Segurola (Caluppi), Sam Hayes, Reginald Barlow, Fredrik

Vogeding, Olaf Hytten, Arno Johnson, Herman Bing, Leo White, Edward Keane, Reginald Le Borg, Wilfred Lucas, Edmund Burns, Paul Ellis, Joseph Mack, Marion Lessing, Hans Joby, Rafael Storm, Victoria Stuart, John Ardizoni, Kurt Furberg, Spec O'Donnell, Michael Mark, Richard La Marr, Wadsworth Harris, Arthur Stuart Hull. *D:* (A.A.N.) Victor Schertzinger; *P:* Harry Cohn; *As.P.:* (A.A.N. for Best Picture) Everett Riskin; *St:* Dorothy Speare, Charles Beahan; *Sc:* S.K. Lauren, James Gow, Edmund North; *Title Song:* Victor Schertzinger, Gus Kahn; *Music:* (A.A.) Louis Silvers; *Editor:* (A.A.N.) Gene Milford; *Sound Recording:* (A.A.) Paul Neal. (1:22) (video)

The classic musical of an aspiring opera singer and her demanding teacher. One of the 15 top grossing films of 1934, the film placed #4 on the "10 Best" list of *Film Daily* and #7 on the same list of the *New York Times*.

3368. One Rainy Afternoon (United Artists; 1935–36). *Cast:* Francis Lederer, Ida Lupino, Roland Young, Hugh Herbert, Erik Rhodes, Mischa Auer, Donald Meek, Eily Malyon, Joseph Cawthorn, Countess Liev de Maigret, Iris Adrian, Billy Gilbert, Phyllis Barry, Ferdinand Munier, Murray Kinnell, Angie Norton, Georgia Caine. *D:* Rowland V. Lee; *P:* Mary Pickford, Jesse L. Lasky; *Sc:* Stephen Morehouse Avery, Maurice Hanline; *Song Lyrics:* "Secret Rendevous" by Preston Sturges. (1:19) (video)

Comedy of a misdirected kiss in a dark movie theater on "one rainy afternoon." Based on the play "Monsieur Sans-Gene" by Slovenskee Riga (Emeric) Pressburger and René Pujol.

3369. One Romantic Night (United Artists/Art Cinema; 1930). *Cast:* Lillian Gish (in her talkie debut), Rod La Rocque (Prince Albert), Marie Dressler, Conrad Nagel, Albert Conti, O.P. Heggie, Philippe De Lacey, Edgar Norton, Billie Bennett, Barbara

Leonard, Byron Sage. *D:* Paul Stein, George Fitzmaurice (unc.); *As.P.:* John W. Considine, Jr.; *Sc:* Melville Baker.

Ruritanian romantic comedy based on Ferenc Molnar's "The Swan" of a princess betrothed to a crown prince who loves another. Previously filmed as *The Swan* (Paramount; 1925) with Frances Howard. Remade under that title in 1956 by MGM with Grace Kelly.

3370. One Stolen Night (WB; 1929). *Cast:* William Collier, Jr., Betty Bronson, Harry Schultz, Mitchell Lewis, Harry Todd, Charles Hill Mailes, Nena Quartero, Otto Lederer. *D:* Scott R. Dunlap (his final film as director); *Sc:* Edward T. Lowe, Jr.

Part-talkie desert romance of a deserter who succumbs to the wiles of a girl with a vaudevillian whip act. Based on D.D. Calhoun's "The Arab," it was previously filmed by Vitagraph in 1923.

3371. One Sunday Afternoon (Paramount; 1932–33). *Cast:* Gary Cooper, Frances Fuller, Fay Wray, Neil Hamilton, Roscoe Karns, Jane Darwell, Clara Blandick, John Burtis, Jack Clifford, Sam Hardy, A.S. Byron, Harry Schultz. *D:* Stephen Roberts; *P:* Louis D. Lighton; *Sc:* William Slavens McNutt, Grover Jones. (1:33)

Comedy-drama set in 1910 Brooklyn, New York of a young dentist who takes his wife for granted. Based on the play by James Hagan it was remade as *The Strawberry Blonde* (WB; 1941) and the musical *One Sunday Afternoon* (WB; 1949).

3372. . . . one third of a nation. . . (Paramount/Federal Theater Project; 1939). *Cast:* Sylvia Sidney, Leif Erickson, Myron McCormick, Hiram Sherman, Sidney Lumet, Iris Adrian, Percy Waram, Byron Russell, Charles Dingle, Muriel Hutchison, Baruch Lumet, Horace Sinclair, Wayne Nunn, Hugh Cameron, Edmonia Nolley, Otto Hulett, Robert George, Julia Fassett. *D:* Dudley Murphy; *P:* Murphy; *As.P.:* Harold Orlob; *Sc:* Murphy, Oliver H.P. Garrett. (1:19) (video)

A social documentary on tenement life which was based on the play by Arthur Arent.

3373. $1,000 a Minute (Republic; 1935). *Cast:* Roger Pryor, Leila Hyams, George Hayes, William Austin, Edward Brophy, Edgar Kennedy, Herman Bing, Ian Wolfe, Franklin Pangborn, Sterling Holloway, Arthur Hoyt, Russell Hicks, Harry C. Bradley, Purnell Pratt, Morgan Wallace, Rolfe Sedan, Lee Phelps, Fern Malatesta, James Burtis, Claude King. *D:* Aubrey H. Scotto; *St:* Everett Freeman; *Sc:* Joseph Fields, Claire Church, Jack Natteford; *Sound Recording:* (A.A.N.) Republic Sound Department.

Musical-comedy.

3374. $1,000 a Touchdown (Paramount; 1939). *Cast:* Joe E. Brown, Martha Raye, Eric Blore, Susan Hayward, Charles Middleton, William Haade, Joyce Mathews, Tom Dugan, Syd Saylor, John Hartley, Matt McHugh. *D:* James Hogan; *P:* William Thomas; *St:* Delmer Daves; *Sc:* Daves.

B gridiron comedy of a couple who inherit a college and make a winning season for the football team.

3375. One-Way Passage (WB; 1932). *Cast:* William Powell (Dan Hardesty), Kay Francis (Joan Ames), Aline MacMahon (Countess Barilhaus—"Barrel House Betty"), Warren Hymer (Steve Burke), Frank McHugh (Skippy), Herbert Mundin (ship's steward), Frederick Burton (doctor), Roscoe Karns (ship's bartender), Douglas Gerrard (Sir Harold), Stanley Fields (ship's captain), Harry Seymour (ship's officer), Wilson Mizner, Heinie Conklin, Mike Donlin, Dewey Robinson, William Halligan, Willie Fung, Ruth Hall, Allan Lane. *D:* Tay Garnett; *P:* Robert Lord; *Original Story:* (A.A.) Robert Lord; *Sc:* Joseph Jackson, Wilson Mizner. (1:09)

Hit tear-jerker of the shipboard love affair between a man being sought for murder and a terminally ill woman. Location shooting was done aboard the S.S. Calawaii. Remade as *'Til We Meet Again* (WB; 1941).

3376. One-Way Ticket (Columbia; 1935). *Cast:* Peggy Conklin, Lloyd Nolan, Walter Connolly, Thurston Hall, Jack Clifford, Edith Fellows, Robert Middlemass, Gloria Shea, James Flavin, Nana Bryant, George McKay, Willie Fung. *D:* Herbert J. Biberman (directorial debut); *P:* B.P. Schulberg; *St:* Ethel Turner; *Sc:* Vincent Lawrence, Grover Jones, Oliver H.P. Garrett, Joseph Anthony.

Crime melodrama.

3377. The One-Way Trail (Columbia; 1931). *Cast:* Tim McCoy, Doris Hill, Polly Ann Young, Carroll Nye, Al Ferguson, Bud Osborne, Slim Whitaker, Herman Hack, Blackjack Ward. *D:* Ray Taylor; *Sc:* George H. Plympton. (1:00)

Tim McCoy western of a cowboy seeking revenge for the murder of his brother. McCoy's talking feature debut, as well as his first for this studio. Re-released theatrically in 1987, it has never been seen on TV.

3378. One Wild Night (20th Century–Fox; 1938). *Cast:* June Lang, Dick Baldwin, J. Edward Bromberg, Lyle Talbot, Sidney Toler, William Demarest, Andrew Tombes, Romaine Callender, Harlan Briggs, Jan Duggan. *D:* Eugene Forde; *P:* John Stone; *Sc:* Charles Belden, Jerry Cady.

B comedy.

3379. One Year Later (Alliance; 1933). *Cast:* Virginia True Boardman, Mary Brian, Lloyd Whitlock, Russell Hopton, Pauline Garon, John Ince, Jackie Searle, Myrtle Stedman, Tom London, Kit Guard. *D:* E. Mason Hopper.

"Poverty row" production.

3380. Only Angels Have Wings (Columbia; 1939). *Cast:* Cary Grant (Jeff Carter), Jean Arthur (Bonnie Lee), Richard Barthelmess (Bat MacPherson), Rita Hayworth (Judy MacPherson), Thomas Mitchell (Kid), Sig Rumann (Dutchy), John Carroll (Gent Shelton), Allyn Joslyn (Les Peters), Noah Beery, Jr. (Joe), Victor Kilian (Sparks), Donald Barry (Tex), Milissa Sierra (Lily), Lucio Villegas (Doc), Maciste, Pat Flaherty, Pedro Regas, James Millican, Pat West, Robert Sterling (film debut – bit). *D:* Howard Hawks; *P:* Hawks; *St:* Hawks; *Sc:* Jules Furthman; *Special Effects:* (A.A.N.) Roy Davidson & Edwin C. Hahn. (2:01) (video)

Hit action-adventure drama of pilots flying the mail to obscure points in South America.

3381. Only Eight Hours (MGM; 1934). *Cast:* Chester Morris, Robert Taylor (starring debut as Dr. Ellis), Virginia Bruce, Billie Burke, Raymond Walburn, Henry Kolker, Dorothy Peterson, William Henry, Mary Jo Matthews, Robert McWade, Donald Meek, Louise Henry, Johnny Hines, Addison Richards, Bobby Watson. *D:* George B. Seitz; *P:* Lucien Hubbard; *Sc:* Samuel Marx, Michael Fessier. (Retitled: *Society Doctor*) (1:03)

B hospital melodrama of a doctor with new operating innovations who comes up against the establishment's old order. Based on the play "The Harbor" by Theodore Reeves.

3382. Only Saps Work (Paramount; 1930). *Cast:* Leon Errol, Richard Arlen, Mary Brian, Stuart Erwin, Charley Grapewin, George Chandler, Fred Kelsey, Clarence Burton, Nora Cecil, George Pat Collins, Anderson Lawler, Jack Richardson, Clifford Dempsey, Charles Giblyn. *D:* Cyril Gardner, Edwin H. Knopf; *Sc:* Joseph L. Mankiewicz (co-writer).

A young man searching for independence becomes involved in crime in this B production. A remake of *Easy Come, Easy Go* (Paramount; 1928) with Richard Dix, which was based on the

Hit Broadway play of 1925 by Owen Davis.

3383. Only the Brave (Paramount; 1930). *Cast:* Gary Cooper, Mary Brian, Phillips Holmes, Virginia Bruce, E.H. Calvert, James Neill, Morgan Farley, Guy Oliver, John Elliott, Elda Voelkel, William LeMaire, Freeman S. Wood, Lalo Encinas, Clinton Rosemond. *D:* Frank Tuttle; *St:* Keene Thompson; *Sc:* Edward E. Paramore, Jr.; *Adapt.:* Agnes Brand Leahy; *Dial.:* Paramore. (1:11)

Civil War melodrama of a Union spy caught by the confederates and sentenced to a firing squad.

3384/3385. Only Yesterday (Universal; 1933). *Cast:* Margaret Sullavan (film debut), John Boles, Billie Burke, Edna May Oliver, Reginald Denny, Benita Hume, George Meeker, Onslow Stevens, June Clyde, Walter Catlett, Jane Darwell, Marie Prevost, Jimmy Butler, Jason Robards, Joyce Compton, Berton Churchill, Ruth Clifford, Barry Norton, Arthur Hoyt, Grady Sutton, Franklin Pangborn, Natalie Moorhead, Vivian Oakland, Tommy Conlin, Oscar Apfel, Dorothy Christy, Julia Faye, Crauford Kent. *D:* John M. Stahl; *P:* Carl Laemmle, Jr.; *Sc:* William Hurlbut, George O'Neill, Arthur Richman. (1:45)

Hit drama of an unwed mother and her problems between World War I and the depression. Based around a popular American history book by Frederick Lewis Allen.

3386. Open Road (Xxxx Xxxx; 1932). (No information available)

3387. Operator 13 (MGM/Cosmopolitan; 1933). *Cast:* Marion Davies, Gary Cooper, Jean Parker, Katherine Alexander, Ted Healy, Russell Hardie, Henry Wadsworth, Douglass Dumbrille, Willard Robertson, Fuzzy Knight, Sidney Toler, Robert Mc-

Wade, Marjorie Gateson, Wade Boteler, Walter Long, Mills Brothers (singing "Roll, Jordan, Roll" & "Sleepy Head"), Sam McDaniel, Mae Clarke, Henry B. Walthall, Ned Sparks, Samuel S. Hinds, Douglas Fowley, Larry Adler, Buddy Roosevelt, Hattie McDaniel (sister of the aforementioned Sam), Sterling Holloway. *D:* Richard Boleslawski; *P:* Lucien Hubbard; *St:* Robert W. Chambers; *Sc:* Harvey Thew, Zelda Sears, Eve Greene; *Cinematographer:* (A.A.N.) George Folsey; *Songs:* Walter Donaldson, Gus Kahn. (G.B. title: *Spy 13*) (1:26)

Lavishly produced Civil War melodrama of an actress who becomes a Union spy. This may have been one of the films that Irving Thalberg was referring to in 1936 when he said to Louis B. Mayer, regarding the proposed filming of *Gone with the Wind* (q.v.)—"Forget it Louis, no Civil War picture ever made a nickel." A box office dud.

The Optimist (G.B. title) *see* **The Big Shot** (1931)

3388. Orchids to You (Fox; 1934–35). *Cast:* John Boles, Jean Muir, Margaret Dumont, Arthur Lake, Charles Butterworth, Sidney Toler, Spring Byington, Arthur Treacher, John Qualen, Harvey Stephens, Patricia Farr, Ruthelma Stevens. *D:* William A. Seiter; *P:* Robert T. Kane; *St:* Robert Dillon, Gordon Rigby; *Sc:* Bartlett Cormack, William Hurlbut, Glenn Tryon, Howard Estabrook.

Romantic comedy.

3389. The Oregon Trail (Republic; 1936). *Cast:* John Wayne, Ann Rutherford, Yakima Canutt, Ben Hendricks, Jr., Joseph Girard, Frank Rice (final film—d. 1936), E.H. Calvert, Harry Harvey, Jack Rutherford, Edward LeSaint, Gino Corrado, Roland Ray, Fern Emmett. *D:* Scott Pembroke; *Sc:* Jack Natteford, Lindsley Parsons, Robert Emmett (Tansey). (0:59)

John Wayne oater of a cowboy seeking the killer of his father.

3390. Orient Express (Fox; 1934). *Cast:* Norman Foster, Heather Angel, Dorothy Burgess, Ralph Morgan, Herbert Mundin, Una O'Connor, Irene Ware, Roy D'Arcy, William Irving. *D:* Paul Martin. (G.B. title: *Stamboul Train*)

Low-budget mystery based on a writing by Graham Greene.

3391. Orphan of the Pecos (Victory; 1937). *Cast:* Tom Tyler, Jeanne Martel, Howard Bryant, Forrest Taylor, Lafe McKee, Slim Whitaker, Theodore Lorch, John Elliott. *D:* Sam Katzman; *P:* Katzman; *Sc:* Basil Dickey. (0:57)

Tom Tyler western of a cowboy out to find the killer of his friend and also protect the man's daughter.

Orphan of the Ring (G.B. title) *see* **The Kid from Kokomo**

3392. Orphans of the Street (Republic; 1937–38). *Cast:* Bob Livingston, Ralph Morgan, Harry Davenport, Sidney Blackmer, Victor Kilian, Hobart Cavanaugh, Ian Wolfe. *D:* John H. Auer.

B melodrama.

3393. Other Men's Women (WB; 1931). *Cast:* Grant Withers, Mary Astor, James Cagney, Joan Blondell, Regis Toomey, Louise Brooks, Walter Long, J. Farrell MacDonald. *D:* William A. Wellman; *St:* Maude Fulton; *Sc:* William K. Wells. (1:10)

Triangular romantic drama set on the railroad of which the original working title was "The Steele Highway."

Other People's Business *see* **Way Back Home**

3394. The Other Tomorrow (WB/F.N.; 1930). *Cast:* Billie Dove, Grant Withers, Kenneth Thomson, Frank Sheridan, Otto Hoffman, William Granger. *D:* Lloyd Bacon; *St:* Octavus Roy Cohen; *Sc:* Fred Myton, James A. Starr.

Drama of an unhappily married woman who resumes a relationship with her first love.

3395. Ouanga (Xxxx Xxxx; 1934–35). *Cast:* Fredi Washington, Sheldon Leonard (black actor). *D:* George Terwilliger. (Remade in 1939 as *Pocomania* [q.v.])

Independently produced tale of Haitian voodoo, filmed on location with an all black cast.

3396. Our Betters (RKO; 1933). *Cast:* Constance Bennett, Violet Kemble-Cooper, Phoebe Foster, Charles Starrett, Anita Louise, Gilbert Roland, Minor Watson, Hugh Sinclair, Alan Mowbray, Harold Entwistle, Grant Mitchell, Finis Barton, Virginia Howell, Walter Walker, Tyrrell Davis. *D:* George Cukor; *P:* David O. Selznick; *Sc:* Jane Murfin, Harry Wagstaff Gribble. (1:24)

An heiress gets revenge on her money-grubbing husband in this drawing room comedy-drama. Based on a play by W. Somerset Maugham, it was a box office flop.

3397. Our Blushing Brides (MGM; 1930). *Cast:* Joan Crawford, Anita Page, Dorothy Sebastian, Robert Montgomery, Raymond Hackett, John Miljan, Hedda Hopper, Edward Brophy, Albert Conti, Mary Doran, Martha Sleeper, Robert Emmett O'Connor, Gwen Lee, Claire Dodd, Louise Beavers. *D:* Harry Beaumont; *P:* Hunt Stromberg; *Sc:* Bess Meredyth, John Howard Lawson. (1:14)

Romantic drama of three friends in search of rich husbands. This is the third in what might be called a trilogy of films begun with *Our Dancing Daughters* (MGM; 1928), followed by *Our Modern Maidens* (MGM; 1929), both of which starred Ms. Crawford.

3398. Our Daily Bread (United Artists/King Vidor; 1934). *Cast:* Karen Morley, Tom Keene, John Qualen, Barbara Pepper, Addison Richards,

Harry Holman, Guinn Williams, Henry Hall, Lynton Brent, Harry C. Bradley, Harry Semels, Ray Spiker, Alex Schumberg, Lionel Baachus, Sidney Miller, Buddy Ray, Si Clogg, Bob Reeves, Bill Engle, Harris Gordon, Captain Anderson, Frank Hammond, Frank Minor. *D:* King Vidor; *P:* Vidor; *St:* Vidor; *Sc:* Elizabeth Hill, Joseph L. Mankiewicz. (G.B. title: *The Miracle of Life*) (1:14) (video)

One of the few films made about the depression during the depression, this is considered a classic in some circles, particularly by the back-to-the-landers of the late 1960s and early 1970s. The story concerns various homeless people who band together to form a communal farm. A sequel to Vidor's *The Crowd* (MGM; 1928), the film placed #10 on the "10 Best" list of the *New York Times,* but bombed at the box office.

3399. Our Leading Citizen (Paramount; 1939). *Cast:* Charles Bickford, Bob Burns, Gene Lockhart, Elizabeth Patterson, Susan Hayward, Clarence Kolb, Monte Blue, Paul Guilfoyle, Fay Helm, Olaf Hytten, Otto Hoffman, Harry C. Bradley, Gus Glassmire, Jim Kelso, Phil Dunham, Joseph Allen, Jr., Thomas Louden, Hattie Noel, Kathryn Sheldon, Frances Morris. *D:* Alfred Santell; *P:* George M. Arthur; *St:* Irvin S. Cobb; *Sc:* John C. Moffitt.

B comedy-drama of a lawyer's dealings with a former partner.

3400. Our Little Girl (Fox; 1935). *Cast:* Shirley Temple, Joel McCrea, Rosemary Ames, Lyle Talbot, Erin O'Brien-Moore, J. Farrell MacDonald, Warren Hymer, Leonard Carey, Margaret Armstrong, Rita Owin, Poodles Hanneford, Jack Baxley. *D:* John Robertson (his final film before retiring); *P:* Edward Butcher; *Sc:* Stephen Morehouse Avery, Allen Rivkin, Jack Yellen. (1:03 (video)

Sentimental drama of a little girl who reunites her estranged parents.

Based on the story "Heaven's Gate" by Florence Leighton Pfalzgraf. Computer-colored in 1988.

3401. Our Neighbors, the Carters (Paramount; 1939). *Cast:* Frank Craven, Genevieve Tobin, Edmund Lowe, Fay Bainter, Thurston Hall, Frank Reicher, Edward McWade, Grace Hayle, Janet Waldo, John Conte, Gloria Carter, Scotty Beckett, Olaf Hytten, Edward Marr, Judy King, Bennie Bartlett, Wanda Kay, Frances Morris, Norman Phillips, Jr., Betty Farrington, Martha Mears, Frank O'Connor, Patsy Mace. *D:* Ralph Murphy; *P:* Charles R. Rogers; *St:* Renaud Hoffman; *Sc:* S.K. Lauren. (1:25)

Hit upbeat film of it's day of an impoverished druggist in a small town.

3402. Our Relations (Hal Roach/Stan Laurel Productions; 1936). *Cast:* Stan Laurel, Oliver Hardy, James Finlayson, Alan Hale, Sidney Toler, Daphne Pollard, Betty Healy, Iris Adrian, Noel Madison, Ralf Harolde, Arthur Housman, Lona Andre, Charlie Hall, "Tiny" Sandford. *D:* Harry Lachman; *Sc:* Richard Connell, Felix Adler, Charles Rogers, Jack Jevne. (1:14) (video)

Considered by many as one of the best Laurel and Hardy features, as Stan and Ollie meet up with their long-lost twin brothers. Based on "The Money Box" by W.W. Jacobs.

3403. Out All Night (Universal; 1933). *Cast:* Slim Summerville, ZaSu Pitts, Laura Hope Crews, Shirley Grey, Alexander Carr, Shirley Temple (in her 3rd feature), Rollo Lloyd. *D:* Sam Taylor; *P:* Carl Laemmle, Jr.; *St:* Tim Whelan; *Sc:* William Anthony McGuire. (1:08)

Low-budget comedy of a man, dominated by his mother, who marries against her wishes.

3404. Out for Murder (Xxxx Xxxx; 1938). (No information available)

3405. Out of Singapore (Goldsmith/William Steiner; 1932). *Cast:* Noah Beery, Dorothy Burgess, Montagu Love. *D:* Charles Hutchison; *Sc:* John S. Natteford.

(No other information available)

3406. Out West with the Hardys (MGM; 1938). *Cast:* Lewis Stone (Judge Hardy), Mickey Rooney (Andy Hardy), Fay Holden (Mrs. Hardy), Cecilia Parker (Marian Hardy), Ann Rutherford (Polly Benedict), Don Castle (Dennis Hunt), Sara Haden (Aunt Milly), Virginia Weidler, Gordon Jones, Ralph Morgan, Nana Bryant, Tom Neal (film debut), Anthony Allan (John Hubbard). *D:* George B. Seitz; *Sc:* Kay Van Riper, Agnes Christine Johnston, William Ludwig. (1:24)

The title tells all in the 5th entry in the hit family series of which this one was one of the 16 top grossing films of 1938–39. Based on the characters created by Aurania Rouverol.

3407. Outcast (Paramount; 1937). *Cast:* Warren William, Karen Morley, John Wray, Lewis Stone, Jackie Moran, Harry Woods, Matthew Betz, Christian Rub. *D:* Robert Florey; *P:* Emmanuel Cohen; *St:* Frank R. Adams; *Sc:* Dore Schary, Doris Malloy.

Mob violence ensues after a doctor is accused of murder.

3408. Outcast Lady (MGM; 1934). *Cast:* Constance Bennett, Hugh Williams, Herbert Marshall, Mrs. Patrick Campbell, Elizabeth Allan, Leo G. Carroll, Robert Lorraine, Henry Stephenson, Ralph Forbes, Alec B. Francis (final film—d. 1934), Lumsden Hare. *D:* Robert Z. Leonard; *Sc:* Zoe Akins. (G.B. title: *A Woman of the World*) (1:19)

A fickle woman goes from man to man in search of love and happiness. Based on the novel "The Green Hat" by Michael Arlen, the film is a remake of *A Woman of Affairs* (MGM; 1928) with Greta Garbo.

3409. The Outcasts of Poker Flat (RKO; 1937). *Cast:* Preston Foster (John Oakhurst), Jean Muir, Al St. John (Uncle Billy), Van Heflin, Virginia Weidler (Luck), Margaret Irving (Duchess), Billy Gilbert, Richard Lane, Monte Blue, Frank M. Thomas, Si Jenks, Dick Elliott, Bradley Page, Dudley Clements. *D:* Christy Cabanne; *P:* Robert Sisk; *Sc:* John Twist, Harry Segall. (1:08)

A low-budget western based on the story by Bret Harte, with elements from another of his stories, "The Luck of Roaring Camp." The story concerns a group of people considered undesirables, run out of a western mining town and subsequently trapped in a snowbound mountain cabin. Previously filmed by John Ford (Universal; 1919) with Harry Carey. Filmed again, (20th Century–Fox; 1952).

3410. The Outer Gate (Monogram; 1937). *Cast:* Ben Alexander, Ralph Morgan, Kay Linaker, Edward Acuff, Charles Brokaw. *D:* Ray Cannon; *P:* I.E. Chadwick; *St:* Laurie Brazee, Octavus Roy Cohen; *Sc:* Brazee. (aka: *Behind Prison Bars*) (1:02)

B melodrama of a bookkeeper, wrongfully imprisoned for theft, who vows revenge on the man who put him there.

3411. The Outlaw Deputy (Puritan; 1935). *Cast:* Tim McCoy, Nora Lane, Bud Osborne, George Offerman, Jr., Si Jenks, Joseph Girard, Hooper Atchley, Dick Botiller, Charles Brinley, Jack Montgomery, Jim Corey, Hank Bell, Eddie Gribbon, Tex Cooper. *D:* Otto Brower; *Sc:* Del Andrews. (0:56)

Tim McCoy western, his first for this indie company of a cowboy out to get revenge for the murder of his friend.

3412. Outlaw Express (Universal; 1938). *Cast:* Bob Baker, Fuzzy Knight, Cecilia Callejo, Carleton Young, Don Barclay, LeRoy Mason, Forrest Taylor, Nina Campana, Martin Garralaga, Carlyle Moore, Jr., Jack Kirk, Ed Cassidy, Chief Many Treaties, Jack Ingram, Julian Rivero. *D:* George

Waggner; *P:* Trem Carr; *Sc:* Norton S. Parker. (0:56)

Bob Baker horse opera with songs of a cavalry officer out to get those responsible for killing Pony Express riders.

3413. Outlaw Justice (Majestic; 1932-33). *Cast:* Jack Hoxie, Dorothy Gulliver, Donald Keith, Chris-Pin Martin, Charles King, Kermit Maynard, Jack Rockwell, Walter Shumway, Tom London, Jack Trent. *D:* Armand L. Schaefer; *P:* Max & Arthur Alexander; *Sc:* Oliver Drake. (1:01)

Jack Hoxie "poverty row" western (his first talkie) of a cowboy posing as an outlaw in order to bring in the bad guys.

3414. The Outlaw Tamer (Empire/Kinematrade; 1934-35). *Cast:* Lane Chandler, Janet Morgan (Blanche Mehaffey), Charles "Slim" Whitaker, Ben Corbett, George F. Hayes, J.P. McGowan, Tex Palmer, Herman Hack. *D:* J.P. McGowan; *Sc:* John Wesley Patterson. (1:00)

Lane Chandler indie western of a cowboy seeking a murderer.

Note: Chandler's final starring series western.

3415. Outlaw's Paradise (Victory; 1939). *Cast:* Tim McCoy (in a dual role), Joan Barclay, Ben Corbett, Ted Adams, Forrest Taylor, Bob Terry, Don Gallagher, Dave O'Brien, Jack Mulhall, Carl Mathews, George Morrell, Jack C. Smith. *D:* Sam Newfield; *P:* Sam Katzman; *Sc:* Basil Dickey. (1:02)

Tim McCoy as "Lightnin' Bill Carson," with the hero posing as a look-a-like outlaw.

3416. Outlawed Guns (Universal; 1935). *Cast:* Buck Jones, Ruth Channing, Frank McGlynn, Roy D'Arcy, Joseph Girard, Pat (J.) O'Brien, Joan Gale, Charles King, Jack Rockwell, Lee Shumway, Monte Montague, Robert Walker, Carl Stockdale, Jack Montgomery, Cliff Lyons. *D:* Ray Taylor; *Sc:* Jack (John) T. Neville. (1:02)

Buck Jones shoot-'em-up of a cowboy out to save his brother, a member of an outlaw gang.

3417. Outlaws' Highway (Trop Productions; 1934). *Cast:* John King, Bonita Baker, Tom London. *D:* Bob Hill; *P:* J.D. Trop; *Sc:* Myron Dattlebaum.

(No other information available)

3418. Outlaws of Sonora (Republic; 1938). *Cast:* Bob Livingston (in a dual role as Stony Brooke and the killer), Ray Corrigan (Tucson Smith), Max Terhune (Lullaby Joslin), Jack Mulhall, Jean Joyce, Stelita Peluffe, Otis Harlan, Tom London, Gloria Rich, Ralph Peters, George Chesebro, Frank LaRue, Jack Ingram, Merrill McCormack, Curley Dresden, George Cleveland, Earl Dwire, Jack Kirk, Jim Corey, Edwin Mordant. *D:* George Sherman; *Sc:* Betty Burbridge, Edmund Kelso. (0:56)

"Three Mesquiteers" western, the 14th entry in the series with the trio on the trail of a killer who looks like Stony.

3419. Outlaws of the Orient (Columbia; 1937). *Cast:* Jack Holt, Mae Clarke, Ray Walker, James Bush, Harold Huber, Bernice Roberts, Harry Worth, Joseph Crehan. *D:* Ernest B. Schoedsack; *St:* Ralph Graves; *Sc:* Paul Franklin, Charles Francis Royal.

B action melodrama.

3420. Outlaws of the Prairie (Columbia; 1937). *Cast:* Charles Starrett, Donald Grayson, Iris Meredith, Sons of the Pioneers with Bob Nolan, Edward LeSaint, Dick Curtis, Hank Bell, Norman Willis, Edmund Cobb, Art Mix, Steve Clark, Earle Hodgins, Frank Shannon, Richard Alexander, Fred Burns, Jack Rockwell, George Chesebro, Jack Kirk, Frank Ellis, Charles LeMoyne, Curley Dresden, Frank McCarroll, Vernon Dent, George Morrell. *D:* Sam Nelson (directorial debut); *Sc:* Ed Earl Repp. (0:59)

Charles Starrett western of a cowboy on the trail of the man who branded him as a child after killing his father.

3421. Outlaws of the Range (Spectrum; 1936). *Cast:* Bill Cody, Catherine Cotter, Bill Cody, Jr., William McCall, Gordon Griffith, Dick Strong, Wally West. *D:* Al Herman; *Sc:* Zara Tazil. (1:00)

Bill Cody indie oater of cattle rustling.

3422. Outpost of the Mounties (Columbia; 1939). *Cast:* Charles Starrett, Iris Meredith, Sons of the Pioneers with Bob Nolan & Pat Brady, Stanley Brown, Kenneth MacDonald, Edmund Cobb, Lane Chandler, Dick Curtis, Albert Morin, Hal Taliaferro, Pat O'Hara. *D:* C.C. Coleman, Jr.; *Sc:* Charles Francis Royal. (1:03)

Charles Starrett action-adventure of a Mountie who believes he has arrested the wrong man.

3423. Outside of Paradise (Republic; 1938). *Cast:* Phil Regan, Penny Singleton, Peter Lind Hayes (film debut), Leonid Kinskey, Mary Forbes. *D:* John H. Auer.

B musical.

3424. Outside the Law (Universal; 1930). *Cast:* Edward G. Robinson, Owen Moore, Mary Nolan, Edwin Sturgis, John George, DeWitt Jennings, Delmar Watson, Barbara Pepper, Rockliffe Fellowes, Sidney Bracey, Frankie Burke. *D:* Tod Browning; *Sc:* Browning, Garrett Fort. (1:10)

Melodrama of an underworld double-cross. A remake of Tod Browning's 1921 production for this studio with Lon Chaney.

3425. Outside the Law (Columbia; 1938). *D:* Lewis D. Collins.

(No other information available)

3426. Outside These Walls (Columbia; 1939). *Cast:* Michael Whalen, Dolores Costello, Virginia Weidler. *D:* Raymond B. McCarey; *Sc:* Harold Buchman.

"B" prison drama.

3427. Outward Bound (WB; 1930). *Cast:* Leslie Howard (American & talkie debut as Tom Prior), Douglas Fairbanks, Jr. (Henry), Helen Chandler (Ann), Alec B. Francis (Scrubby), Lyonel Watts (repeating his stage role as Reverend William Duke), Beryl Mercer (repeating her stage role as Mrs. Midget), Alison Skipworth (Mrs. Cliveden-Banks), Montagu Love (Mr. Lingley), Dudley Digges (examiner), Walter Kingsford (policeman), Laddie the dog. *D:* Robert Milton (who also directed the stage production); *Sc:* J. Grubb Alexander. (1:23)

An offbeat fantasy-drama of two people who attempt suicide and find themselves in a "netherworld" aboard an ocean liner. Based on the 1923 play by Sutton Vane, it was voted #6 on the "10 Best" list of the *New York Times,* while being voted one of the year's "10 Best" by the National Board of Review. Remade as *Between Two Worlds* (WB; 1944), as well as a variation remake *The Flight That Disappeared* (United Artists; 1961).

3428. Over the Goal (WB/F.N.; 1937). *Cast:* June Travis, William Hopper, Mabel Todd, Willard Parker, Gordon Oliver, William Harrigan, Johnnie "Scat" Davis (film debut), Raymond Hatton, Hattie McDaniel, Eddie "Rochester" Anderson, Herbert Rawlinson, Douglas Wood, Eric Stanley, University of Southern California football squad. *D:* Noel Smith; *P:* Bryan Foy; *Sc:* Anthony Coldeway, William Jacobs; *Songs:* "Scattin' with My Bear" & "As Easy as Rolling Off a Log" by M.K. Jerome, Jack Scholl.

B football story.

3429. Over the Hill (Fox; 1931). *Cast:* Mae Marsh, James Kirkwood, James Dunn, Sally Eilers, Joan Peers, Olin Howland, William Pawley, Edward Crandall, Eula Guy, Claire Maynard. *D:* Henry King; *Sc:* Jules Furthman, Tom Barry.

Romantic comedy, a remake of *Over the Hill to the Poorhouse* (Fox; 1920) and adapted from the work of that name by Will Carleton.

Over the River (G.B. title) *see* **One More River**

3430. Over the Wall (WB; 1938). *Cast:* Dick Foran, Dick Purcell, June Travis, John Litel, Tommy Bupp, George E. Stone, Veda Ann Borg, Ward Bond, John Hamilton, Raymond Hatton, Eddie Chandler, Alan Davis, Mabel Hart. *D:* Frank McDonald; *As.P.:* Bryan Foy; *St:* Warden Lewis E. Lawes; *Sc:* Crane Wilbur, George Bricker; *Songs:* "Little White House on the Hill," "One More Tomorrow" & "Have You Met My Lulu" by M.K. Jerome, Jack Scholl.

B prison drama of an innocently imprisoned man who becomes a singer. A remake of *Weary River* (q.v.).

3431. Overland Bound (Presidio Pictures; 1929). *Cast:* Leo Maloney (final film—d. 1929), Jack Perrin, Allene Ray, Wally Wales (Hal Taliaferro), Bullet the dog, Flash the horse. *D:* Leo Maloney; *P:* Maloney; *St:* Ford Beebe, Joseph Kane; *Sc:* Ford Beebe.

A low-budget all-talkie indie western, the second all-talkie film of that genre following *In Old Arizona* (q.v.) and preceding *The Virginian* (q.v.).

3432. The Overland Express (Columbia/Coronet; 1937–38). *Cast:* Buck Jones, Marjorie Reynolds, Carlyle Moore, Jr., Maston Williams, William Arnold, Lew Kelly, Bud Osborne, Ben Taggart, Ben Corbett, Blackie Whiteford, Gene Alsace (Rocky Camron), Bob Woodward. *D:* Drew Eberson; *Sc:* Monroe Shaff. (0:56)

Buck Jones horse opera with a tale of the forming of the Pony Express.

3433. Overland Mail (Monogram; 1939). *Cast:* Jack Randall, Vince Barnett, Jean Joyce, Tristram Coffin, Glenn Strange, George Cleveland, Dennis Moore, Merrill McCormack, Joe Garcia, Maxine Leslie, James Sheridan

(Sherry Tansey), Hal Price, Harry Semels, Rusty the Wonder Horse. *D:* Robert Hill; *P:* Robert Tansey; *St & Sc:* Robert Emmett (Tansey). (0:51)

Jack Randall western involving counterfeiting and the murder of an Indian.

3434. Overland Stage Raiders (Republic; 1938). *Cast:* Ray Corrigan (Tucson Smith), John Wayne (Stony Brooke), Max Terhune (Lullaby Joslin), Louise Brooks (final film—ret.), Anthony Marsh, Ralph Bowman (John Archer), Gordon Hart, Olin Francis, Roy James, Fern Emmett, Henry Otho, George Sherwood, Archie Hall, Yakima Canutt, Frank LaRue, Milton Kibbee, Jack Kirk, Bud Osborne, Slim Whitaker, Dirk Thane, Bud McClure, John Beach, Tommy Coats, Curley Dresden, George Plues, Edwin Gaffney. *D:* George Sherman; *P:* William Berke; *Sc:* Luci Ward. (0:55)

The "Three Mesquiteers" in the 18th entry in their series, investigating the theft of aerial gold shipments.

3435. The Pace That Kills (Willis Kent; 1936). *Cast:* Noel Madison, Lois January. *D:* William A. O'Connor.

Low-budget anti-drug exploitation melodrama.

3436. Pacific Liner (RKO; 1938–39). *Cast:* Victor McLaglen (Crusher McKay), Chester Morris, Wendy Barrie, Alan Hale, Allan Lane, Barry Fitzgerald, Halliwell Hobbes, Cyrus W. Kendall, Paul Guilfoyle, Emory Parnell, John Wray, Adia Kuznetzoff, John Bleifer. *D:* Lew Landers; *P:* Robert Sisk; *St:* Anthony Coldeway, Henry Roberts Symonds; *Sc:* John Twist; *Original Music Score:* (A.A.N.) Russell Bennett. (1:16)

An epidemic of cholera breaks out on the S.S. Arcturus, bringing about a mutiny. A box office winner.

3437. Pack Up Your Troubles (MGM/Hal Roach; 1932). *Cast:* Stan Laurel, Oliver Hardy, Mary Carr, Jacquie Lyn, Donald Dillaway, James Finlayson, Charles Middleton, Dick Cramer, Muriel Evans, Tom Kennedy, Billy Gilbert, Grady Sutton, Richard Tucker, Mary Gordon, E.H. Calvert, Adele Watson, Montague Shaw. *D:* George Marshall, Ray McCarey; *P:* Hal Roach; *Sc:* H.M. Walker. (1:08) (video)

Laurel and Hardy as two doughboys who try to find relatives of an orphaned little girl after World War I. This was the comedy team's second feature and a box office hit.

3438. Pack Up Your Troubles (20th Century–Fox; 1939). *Cast:* Jane Withers, Ritz Brothers, Lynn Bari, Joseph Schildkraut, Stanley Fields, Leon Ames, Fritz Leiber, Henry Victor, Adrienne D'Ambricourt, Lionel Royce, William von Brincken, Georges Renavent, Robert Emmett Keane. *D:* H. Bruce Humberstone; *P:* Sol M. Wurtzel: *Sc:* Lou Breslow, Owen Francis. (G.B. title: *We're in the Army Now*) (1:15)

A hit World War I comedy of its day.

3439. Paddy O'Day (20th Century–Fox; 1935). *Cast:* Jane Withers, Pinky Tomlin, Jane Darwell, Rita (Hayworth) Cansino, Francis Ford, Vera Lewis, George Givot, Louise Carter, Michael Visaroff, Nina Visaroff. *D:* Lewis Seiler; *P:* Sol M. Wurtzel; *Sc:* Lou Breslow, Edward Eliscu; *Songs:* Harry Akst, Sidney Clare. (1:13)

Hit comedy-drama of a little girl who comes to America, only to learn that her mother has died.

3440. Paddy the Next Best Thing (Fox; 1933). *Cast:* Janet Gaynor, Warner Baxter, Walter Connolly, Harvey Stephens, Margaret Lindsay, Claire McDowell, Roger Imhof, J.M. Kerrigan, Fiske O'Hara, Trevor Bland, Mary McCormick, Merle Tottenham. *D:* Harry Lachman; *Sc:* Edwin Burke. (1:15)

New York based romantic comedy of an Irish tomboy. Based on the play by Gertrude Page, it was previously filmed in Great Britain in 1923.

3441. Pagan Lady (Columbia; 1931). *Cast:* Conrad Nagel, Evelyn Brent, Charles Bickford, Roland Young, Leslie Fenton, Lucile Gleason, Gwen Lee, Wallace MacDonald, William Farnum. *D:* John Francis Dillon; *St.* William DuBois; *Sc:* Benjamin Glazer.

Low-budget romantic drama.

3442. Page Miss Glory (WB/ Cosmopolitan; 1935). *Cast:* Marion Davies, Dick Powell, Pat O'Brien, Frank McHugh, Mary Astor, Lyle Talbot, Patsy Kelly, Allen Jenkins, Barton MacLane, Berton Churchill, Joseph Cawthorn, Lionel Stander, Hobart Cavanaugh, Helen Lowell, Mary Treen, Al Shean, Jack Norton. *D:* Mervyn LeRoy; *P:* Robert Lord; *Sc:* Lord, Delmer Daves; *Title Song:* Al Dubin & Harry Warren. (1:30)

Hit comedy of a con artist who wins a beauty contest with a composite photo of a non-existent beauty. Based on the play by Joseph Schrank and Philip Dunning.

3443. Paid (MGM; 1930–31). *Cast:* Joan Crawford, Kent Douglass (Douglass Montgomery in his film debut), Robert Armstrong, Marie Prevost, John Miljan, Polly Moran, William Bakewell, Purnell Pratt, Gwen Lee, Ed Brophy, George Cooper, Hale Hamilton, Tyrrell Davis, Isabel Withers. *D:* Sam Wood; *Sc:* Charles MacArthur, Lucien Hubbard. (G.B. title: *Within the Law*) (1:20)

Hit drama of a woman who seeks to pay back the persons responsible for sending her to prison. Based on the play "Within the Law" by Bayard Veiller. Previously filmed under the original title, (Vitagraph; 1917) with Alice Joyce, (First National; 1923) with Norma Talmadge. Remade in 1939 as *Within the Law* (q.v.).

3444. Paid to Dance (Columbia; 1937). *Cast:* Don Terry, Jacqueline Wells (Julie Bishop), Rita Hayworth, Ralph Byrd, Thurston Hall, Paul Fix, Horace MacMahon, Louise Stanley, Arthur Loft, Ann Doran, Al Herman, Paul Stanton, Beatrice Curtis, Beatrice Blinn, Jane Hamilton, Bess Flowers. *D:* C.C. Coleman, Jr.; *St:* Leslie White; *Sc:* Robert E. Kent.

B melodrama of the dance hall rackets.

3445. Paid to Love (Xxxx Xxxx; 1931). (No information available)

3446. The Painted Angel (WB; 1929). *Cast:* Billie Dove, Edmund Lowe, George MacFarlane, Cissy Fitzgerald, J. Farrell MacDonald, Norman Selby. *D:* Millard Webb; *St:* Fannie Hurst; *Sc:* Forrest Halsey; *Songs:* "Help Yourself to Love," "Bride Without a Groom," "Only the Girl," "Everybody's Darling" & "That Thing" by Herman Ruby & M.K. Jerome.

Lavishly produced romantic musical drama of a singer who becomes popular as a New York night club singer.

3447. The Painted Desert (RKO-Pathé; 1930–31). *Cast:* Bill Boyd, Helen Twelvetrees, William Farnum, J. Farrell MacDonald, Clark Gable (talkie debut), Charles Sellon, Hugh Adams, Wade Boteler, Will Walling, Edmund Breese, Guy Edward Hearn, William LeMaire, Richard Cramer. *D:* Howard Higgin; *St & Sc:* Higgin, Tom Buckingham; *P:* E.B. Derr. (1:15) (video)

Western of two prospectors who find an abandoned child. Loosely remade in 1938 (see below).

3448. The Painted Desert (RKO; 1938). *Cast:* George O'Brien, Laraine (Day) Johnson, Ray Whitley, Stanley Fields, Maude Allen, Fred Kohler, Sr. (final film—d. 1938), Lloyd Ingraham, Harry Cording, Max Wagner, Lee Shumway, William V. Mong, Lew Kelly. *D:* David Howard; *P:* Bert Gilroy; *St:* Jack Cunningham; *Sc:* Oliver Drake, John Rathmell; *Songs:* Oliver Drake, Ray Whitley. (0:59)

George O'Brien western of tungsten miners vs. a greedy banker who is after their claim. A loose remake of the preceding film.

3449. Painted Faces (Tiffany-Stahl; 1929–30). *Cast:* Joe E. Brown, Helen Foster, Dorothy Gulliver. *D:* Albert S. Rogell.

"Poverty row" comedy.

3450. The Painted Trail (Monogram; 1938). *Cast:* Tom Keene, Eleanor Stewart, LeRoy Mason, Walter Long, Jimmy Eagles, Forrest Taylor, Harry Harvey, Ernie Adams, Bud Osborne, Glenn Strange, Frank Campeau (final film—ret.), Bob Kortman, Richard Cramer, Tom London. *D:* Robert Hill; *P:* Robert Tansey; *Sc:* Robert Emmett (Tansey). (0:50)

Tom Keene western of a U.S. Marshal who goes undercover to infiltrate a gang of cattle rustlers.

3451. The Painted Veil (MGM; 1934). *Cast:* Greta Garbo, Herbert Marshall, George Brent, Warner Oland, Jean Hersholt, Katherine Alexander, Bodil Rosing, Cecilia Parker, Soo Yong, Forrester Harvey, Beulah Bondi, Ethel Griffies, Keye Luke (film debut). *D:* Richard Boleslawski; *P:* Hunt Stromberg; *Sc:* John Meehan, Salka Viertel, Edith Fitzgerald. (1:24)

A drama of love, marriage and infidelity in the orient which is based on the novel by W. Somerset Maugham. The Chinese fantasy sequence was conceived by Stowitts and staged by Chester Hale. Remade as *The Seventh Sin* (MGM; 1957).

3452. The Painted Woman (Fox; 1932). *Cast:* Spencer Tracy, Peggy Shannon, William "Stage" Boyd, Irving Pichel, Wade Boteler, Stanley Fields, Chris-Pin Martin, Dewey Robinson, Murray Kinnell, Paul Porcasi, Laska Winter, Raul Roulien, Jack Kennedy. *D:* John G. Blystone; *Sc:* Guy Bolton, A.C. Kennedy.

The romance of a loose woman and a pearl trader.

3453. The Pal from Texas (Metropolitan; 1939). *Cast:* Bob Steele, Claire Rochelle, Jack Perrin, Josef Swickard, Ted Adams, Betty Mack, Carleton Young, Jack Ingram, Robert Walker. *D:* Harry S. Webb; *Sc:* Carl Krusada. (0:55)

Bob Steele oater of a man with a gold mine, the crook who is after it and the cowboy who comes to the rescue.

3454. Palm Springs (Paramount; 1936). *Cast:* Frances Langford, Sir Guy Standing, Smith Ballew, David Niven, Ernest Cossart, Spring Byington, E.E. Clive, Nell Craig, Grady Sutton, Sterling Holloway, Ann Doran. *D:* Aubrey Scotto; *P:* Walter Wanger; *Sc:* Joseph Fields; *Songs:* Ralph Rainger, Leo Robin. (G.B. title: *Palm Springs Affair*) (1:14)

Romantic comedy of an Englishman who becomes a gambler.

Palm Springs Affair (G.B. title) *see* **Palm Springs**

3455. Palmy Days (United Artists/Samuel Goldwyn; 1931). *Cast:* Eddie Cantor, Charlotte Greenwood, Barbara Weeks, Spencer Charters, Paul Page, Charles Middleton, George Raft, Harry Woods, Frances Dean (Betty Grable—bit), Goldwyn Girls, Walter Catlett. *D:* A. Edward Sutherland; *P:* Samuel Goldwyn; *Sc:* Keene Thompson; *St & Dialogue:* Eddie Cantor, Morrie Ryskind, David Freedman; *Choreography:* Busby Berkeley; *Songs:* Con Conrad, Harry Akst. (1:17)

A hit romantic comedy involving some crooked fortune tellers.

3456. Palooka (United Artists/Reliance; 1934). *Cast:* Jimmy Durante (Knobby Walsh), Lupe Velez (Nina Madero), Stuart Erwin (Joe Palooka), Marjorie Rambeau (Mayme Palooka), Robert Armstrong (Pete Palooka), William Cagney (Al McSwatt), Mary Carlisle (Anne), Tom Dugan (Whitey), Thelma Todd, Louise Beavers, Fred "Snowflake" Toones, Guinn Williams, Franklyn Ardell. *D:* Benjamin Stoloff; *P:* Edward Small; *Sc:* Jack Jevne, Gertrude Purcell, Arthur Kober, Ben Ryan, Murray Roth. (G.B. title: *The Great Schnozzle*) (aka: *Joe Palooka*) (1:26) (video)

Comedy with music set in and around the boxing ring. Based on the comic strip characters created by Ham Fisher. Durante does a rendition of his famous "Inka-Dinka-Doo." In the 1940s a low-budget series with Joe Kirkwood was produced by Monogram, followed in the 1950s with a TV series (also with Kirkwood).

3457. Pals of the Range (Superior; 1935). *Cast:* Rex Lease, Frances (Morris) Wright, Art Mix, George Chesebro, Yakima Canutt, Blackie Whiteford, Bill Patton, Milburn Morante, Artie Ortego, Bud Osborne, Ben Corbett, Tom Forman, Joey Ray, George Morrell. *D:* Elmer Clifton; *P:* Louis Weiss; *Sc:* Clifton, George Merrick. (0:55)

Rex Lease western of a rancher accused of stealing cattle who escapes from jail.

3458. Pals of the Saddle (Republic; 1938). *Cast:* Ray Corrigan (Tucson Smith), John Wayne (in his first "Mesquiteers" film, replacing Bob Livingston as Stony Brooke), Max Terhune (Lullaby Joslin), Doreen McKay, George Douglas, Josef (Joe) Forte, Frank Milan, Ted Adams, Harry Depp, Dave Weber, Don Orlando, Jack Kirk, Charles Knight, Monte Montague, Olin Francis, Curley Dresden, Art Dillard. *D:* George Sherman; *P:* William Berke; *Sc:* Stanley Roberts, Betty Burbridge. (0:55)

Seventeenth "Three Mesquiteers" entry with the trio in pursuit of enemy agents with the help of a government woman.

3459. Panama Flo (RKO-Pathé; 1932). *Cast:* Helen Twelvetrees, Charles Bickford, Robert Armstrong, Marjorie

Peterson, Maude Eburne, Paul Hurst, Reina Velez, Hans Joby, Ernie Adams. *D:* Ralph Murphy; *As.P.:* Harry Joe Brown; *St:* Garrett Fort; *Sc:* Fort. (1:10)

After falling ill in Panama, a woman is taken to the home of a man who is much feared by the locals. A romantic drama which was remade as *Panama Lady* (q.v.).

3460. Panama Lady (RKO; 1939). *Cast:* Lucille Ball, Allan Lane, Steffi Duna, Evelyn Brent, Donald Briggs, Bernadene Hayes, Abner Biberman, William Pawley, Earle Hodgins. *D:* Jack Hively; *P:* Cliff Reid; *St:* Garrett Fort; *Sc:* Michael Kanin. (1:05) (video)

B remake of *Panama Flo* (q.v.), as a woman is blackmailed into becoming a housekeeper for a prospector with a jealous local girl friend.

3461. Panama Patrol (Grand National/Fine Arts; 1939). *Cast:* Leon Ames, Charlotte Wynters, Adrienne Ames, Donald Barry, Weldon Heyburn, Abner Biberman, Sidney Miller, John (Jack) Smart, Hugh McArthur, William von Brincken, Frank Darien, Paul McVey, Gerald Mohr. *D:* Charles Lamont; *P:* Franklyn Warner; *Sc:* Arthur Hoerl. (1:09)

Code experts bring some enemy agents to justice in this B sequel to *Cipher Bureau* (q.v.). Based on characters created by Arthur Hoerl & Monroe Shaff.

3462. Panamint's Bad Man (20th Century–Fox/Principal; 1938). *Cast:* Smith Ballew, Evelyn Daw, Noah Beery, Stanley Fields, Harry Woods, Pat (J.) O'Brien, Armand Wright. *D:* Ray Taylor; *P:* Sol Lesser; *Sc:* Luci Ward, Charles A. Powell. (1:00)

Smith Ballew in his final series western of a marshal going undercover as an outlaw to get the bad guys.

3463. Panic on the Air (Columbia; 1936). *Cast:* Lew Ayres, Florence Rice, Berton Churchill, James Millican,

Benny Baker, Charles C. Wilson, Murray Alper, Edwin Maxwell, Gene Morgan, Eddie Lee. *D:* D. Ross Lederman; *Sc:* Harold Shumate. (G.B. title: *Trapped by the Wireless*)

B melodrama.

Panic on the Air (G.B. title) *see* **You May Be Next** (1936)

3464. Parachute Jumper (WB; 1933). *Cast:* Douglas Fairbanks, Jr., Bette Davis, Frank McHugh, Claire Dodd, Leo Carrillo, Harold Huber, Thomas E. Jackson, Sheila Terry, Leon (Ames) Waycoff, Walter Brennan, Nat Pendleton, George Pat Collins, Ferdinand Munier, Harold Healy. *D:* Alfred E. Green; *P:* Ray Griffith; *Sc:* John Francis Larkin. (1:05)

B melodrama of flyers who become involved with criminal element. Based on the story "Some Call It Love" by Rian James.

3465. Paradise Canyon (Monogram-Lone Star; 1935). *Cast:* John Wayne, Marion Burns, Earle Hodgins, Yakima Canutt, Reed Howes, Perry Murdock, John Goodrich, Gino Corrado, Gordon Clifford, Tex Palmer, Herman Hack, Earl Dwire. *D:* Carl Pierson; *P:* Paul Malvern; *Supervisor:* Trem Carr; *St:* Lindsley Parsons; *Sc:* Robert Emmett (Tansey). (0:52) (video)

John Wayne western involving a gang of counterfeiters.

3466. Paradise Express (Republic; 1937). *Cast:* Grant Withers, Dorothy Appleby, Arthur Loft, Harry Davenport, George Cleveland, Guy Wilkerson, Maude Eburne, Arthur Hoyt. *D:* Joseph Kane.

B action-drama which involves the railroad and a trucking company.

3467. Paradise for Three (MGM; 1937–38). *Cast:* Robert Young, Frank Morgan, Mary Astor, Edna May Oliver, Florence Rice, Reginald Owen,

Henry Hull, Sig Rumann, Herman Bing, Walter Kingsford. *D:* Edward Buzzell; *P:* Sam Zimbalist; *Sc:* George Oppenheimer, Harry Ruskin. (G.B. title: *Romance for Three*) (1:18)

Based on the novel "Three Men in the Snow" by Erich Kaestner, this romantic comedy is set in Germany.

3468. Paradise Island (Tiffany; 1930). *Cast:* Kenneth Harlan, Marceline Day, Tom Santschi, Paul Hurst, Gladden James. *D:* Bert Glennon.

"Poverty row" romantic drama.

3469. Paradise Isle (Monogram; 1937). *Cast:* Movita, Warren Hull, George Piltz, William Davidson, John St. Polis, Russell Simpson, Kenneth Harlan, Pierre Watkin. *D:* Arthur Greville Collins; *P:* Mrs. Dorothy Reid; *Sc:* Marion Orth. (1941 re-release title: *Siren of the South Seas*) (1:13)

Following a shipwreck a blind artist is nursed back to health by an island beauty. Based on the *Cosmopolitan* magazine story "The Belled Palm" by Allan Vaughan Ellston.

3470. Paramount on Parade (Paramount; 1930). *Cast:* Iris Adrian (film debut as the dancer with Chevalier), Richard Arlen, Jean Arthur, Mischa Auer (guest), William Austin, George Bancroft, Clara Bow, Evelyn Brent, Mary Brian, Clive Brook (Sherlock Holmes), Virginia Bruce, Nancy Carroll, Ruth Chatterton, Maurice Chevalier, Gary Cooper, Cecil Cunningham (hostess), Leon Errol, Stuart Erwin, Henry Fink (guest), Kay Francis, Richard "Skeets" Gallagher, Edmund Goulding (himself), Harry Green, Mitzi Green, Robert Greig (Egyptian), James Hall, Phillips Holmes, Helen Kane, Dennis King, Abe Lyman and his band, Fredric March, Nino Martini, Mitzi Mayfair, Marion Morgan Dancers, David Newell, Zelma O'Neal, Jack Oakie (M.C.), Warner Oland (Dr. Fu Manchu), Eugene Pallette (Sgt. Heath),

Joan Peers, Jack Pennick (soldier), William Powell (Philo Vance), Charles "Buddy" Rogers, Lillian Roth, Rolfe Sedan (bench sitter), Stanley Smith, Fay Wray. *D:* Dorothy Arzner, Otto Brower, Edmund Goulding, Victor Heerman, Edwin H. Knopf, Rowland V. Lee, Ernst Lubitsch, Lothar Mendes, Victor Schertzinger, A. Edward Sutherland, Frank Tuttle; *P:* Albert Kaufman; *Production Supervisor:* Elsie Janis; *Songs:* title song, "I'm True to the Navy Now," "Anytime Is the Time to Fall in Love," & "What Did Cleopatra Say?" by Elsie Janis & Jack King; "Sweeping the Clouds Away" by Sam Coslow; "All I Want Is Just One Girl," by Leo Robin & Richard A. Whiting; "Dancing to Save Your Soul," "I'm in Training for You" & "Drink to the Girl of My Dreams" by L. Wolfe Gilbert & Abel Baer; "Come Back to Sorrento" by Leo Robin & Ernesto De Curtis; "My Marine" by Ray Egan & Whiting; "We're the Masters of Ceremony" by Ballard MacDonald & Dave Dreyer & "I'm Isadore the Toreador" by David Franklin. (1:42)

This studio's all-star revue of 1930 featuring twenty variety acts, seven of which are in 2-color technicolor, with the color segments missing from some TV prints.

3471. Pardon My Gun (Pathé; 1930). *Cast:* Sally Starr, George Duryea (Tom Keene), Lee Moran, Robert Edeson, Frank MacFarlane, Tom MacFarlane, Ethan Laidlaw, Lew Meehan, Harry Woods, Harry Watson, Ida May Chadwick, Al Norman. *D:* Robert De Lacy; *Sc:* Hugh Cummings. (1:10)

A light western romance with musical interludes.

3472. Pardon Our Nerve (20th Century–Fox; 1938–39). *Cast:* Lynn Bari, June Gale, Guinn Williams, Michael Whalen, Ed Brophy, John Miljan, Tom Kennedy, Ward Bond. *D:* H. Bruce Humberstone; *P:* Sol M. Wurtzel; *Sc:* Robert Ellis, Helen Logan.

B comedy, the 2nd and last entry in the "Big Town Girls" series, which has them involved as fight promoters for a dim-wit boxer.

3473. Pardon Us (MGM/Hal Roach; 1931). *Cast:* Stan Laurel, Oliver Hardy, Wilfred Lucas, James Finlayson, Walter Long, June Marlowe, Charlie Hall. *D:* James Parrott; *P:* Hal Roach, Parrott; *Sc:* H.M. Walker. (G.B. title: *Jailbirds*) (0:55) (video)

Laurel and Hardy in their first feature film, a box office hit which is a spoof on prison films. There are many musical numbers and the film utilizes left-over sets from *The Big House* (q.v.).

3474. Parents on Trial (Columbia; 1939). *Cast:* Johnny Downs, Jean Parker, Noah Beery, Jr., Richard Fiske, Linda Terry, Virginia Brissac, Nana Bryant, Mary Gordon. *D:* Sam Nelson; *Sc:* Gladys Atwater, J. Robert Bren, Lambert Hillyer.

Low-budget exploitation melodrama.

3475. Paris (WB/F.N./Vitaphone; 1929). *Cast:* Irene Bordoni (talkie debut recreating her stage role), Jack Buchanan (a British song-and-dance man in his talkie debut), Louise Closser Hale, Jason Robards, ZaSu Pitts, Margaret Fielding. *D:* Clarence Badger; *P:* Robert North; *St:* Martin Brown; *Adaptation:* Hope Loring; *Songs:* title song, "I Wonder What Is Really on His Mind," "I'm a Little Negative," "Somebody Mighty Like You" & "My Lover" by Al Bryan & Ed Ward. (1:28)

A lavish production musical, based on the stage musical by Cole Porter, Martin Brown and E. Ray Goetz, but without Porter's musical score. Several sequences were in 2-color technicolor in this story of a woman who flies to Paris to stop her son's marriage. A remake of the 1925 silent production.

3476. Paris Bound (Pathé; 1929). *Cast:* Fredric March, Ann Harding (film debut), Leslie Fenton, Ilka Chase (film debut), Hallam Cooley, George Irving, Frank Reicher, Juliette Crosby, Charlotte Walker, Carmelita Geraghty. *D:* Edward H. Griffith; *St:* Philip Barry; *Sc:* Frank Reicher; *Adapt.:* Horace Jackson; *Dial.:* Frank Reicher.

Romantic comedy.

3477. Paris Honeymoon (Paramount; 1939). *Cast:* Bing Crosby, Shirley Ross, Edward Everett Horton, Franciska Gaal, Akim Tamiroff, Ben Blue, Rafaela Ottiano, Raymond Hatton, Victor Kilian, Gregory Gaye, Konstantin Shayne, Keith Kenneth, Michael Visaroff, Alex Melesh. *D:* Frank Tuttle; *P:* Harlan Thompson; *St:* Angela Sherwood; *Sc:* Frank Butler, Don Hartman; *Songs:* Ralph Rainger, Leo Robin. (1:32)

Romantic musical of a Texas millionaire and his infatuation with an European countess.

3478. Paris in Spring (Paramount; 1935). *Cast:* Mary Ellis, Tullio Carminati, Lynne Overman, Ida Lupino, Jessie Ralph, Jack Mulhall, Akim Tamiroff, Joseph North, Arthur Housman, James Blakely, Hugh Enfield (aka: Craig Reynolds). *D:* Lewis Milestone; *P:* Benjamin Glazer; *Sc:* Samuel Hoffenstein, Franz Schultz, Keene Thompson (based on the play by Dwight Taylor). (G.B. title: *Paris Love Song*) (1:21)

The romance of two people who meet on the Eiffel Tower, after both have gone there to commit suicide.

3479. Paris Interlude (MGM; 1934). *Cast:* Madge Evans, Otto Kruger, Una Merkel, Robert Young, George Meeker, Edward Brophy, Richard Tucker, Ted Healy, Bert Roach, Louise Henry. *D:* Edwin L. Marin; *P:* Lucien Hubbard; *Sc:* Wells Root.

B romantic drama involving three American journalists in France. Based on a play by Laura and S.J. Perelman.

Paris Love Song (G.B. title) *see* **Paris in Spring**

3480. A Parisian Romance (Allied; 1932). *Cast:* Lew Cody, Joyce Compton, Marion Shilling, Gilbert Roland, Yola D'Avril, Helen Jerome Eddy. *D:* Chester M. Franklin; *P:* M.H. Hoffman, Jr.

Low-budget romance based on the classic writing of Feuillet.

3481. Park Avenue Logger (RKO; 1937). *Cast:* George O'Brien, Beatrice Roberts, Ward Bond, Lloyd Ingraham, Willard Robertson, Bert Hanlon, Gertrude Short, George Rosener, Robert Emmett O'Connor. *D:* David Howard; *P:* George A. Hirliman; *As.P.:* Leonard Goldstein; *Sc:* Dan Jarrett, Ewing Scott. (G.B. title: *Millionaire Playboy*) (TV title: *Tall Timber[s]*) (1:07)

Melodramatic actioner of the son of a wealthy New Yorker who is sent to a rugged lumber camp where he uncovers corruption and of course, falls in love. Based on a story by Bruce Hutchison which appeared in the *Saturday Evening Post*.

3482. Parlor, Bedroom and Bath (MGM; 1931). *Cast:* Buster Keaton (Reginald Irving), Reginald Denny (Jeffrey Haywood), Charlotte Greenwood (Polly Hathaway), Dorothy Christy (Angelica Embrey), Cliff Edwards (bell hop), Joan Peers (Nita Leslie), Sally Eilers (Virginia Embrey), Natalie Moorhead (Leila Crofton), Edward Brophy (detective), Walter Merrill (Frederick Leslie), Sidney Bracey (butler). *D:* Edward Sedgwick; *P:* Keaton; *Sc:* Richard Schayer; *Additional Dialogue:* Robert Hopkins. (G.B. title: *A Romeo in Pyjamas*) (1:12) (video)

Domestic comedy which was filmed on location at Buster Keaton's home in Beverly Hills. Filmed before (Metro; 1920), it was based on a 1920 play of the same name by Charles W. Bell and Mark Swan. The Metro production starred Eugene Pallette.

3483. Parnell (MGM; 1937). *Cast:* Clark Gable (Parnell), Myrna Loy (Katie O'Shea), Edmund Gwenn, Edna May Oliver, Alan Marshal, Donald Crisp, Billie Burke, Berton Churchill, Donald Meek, Montagu Love, George Zucco, Halliwell Hobbes, J. Farrell MacDonald, Neil Fitzgerald, Brandon Tynan, Phyllis Coghlan, Byron Russell. *D:* John M. Stahl; *P:* Stahl; *Sc:* John Van Druten, S.N. Behrman. (1:59)

Lavishly produced biography of the "King of Ireland" of the late 1800s whose career as a politician went downhill after a scandal broke. Based on the play by Elsie T. Schauffler, the film was a financial disaster for the studio.

3484. Parole! (Universal; 1936). *Cast:* Henry Hunter, Ann Preston, Grant Mitchell, Alan Baxter, Noah Beery, Jr., Berton Churchill, Billy Gilbert, Alan Hale, Frank McGlynn, Selmer Jackson, Christian Rub, Charles Richman, Frank Mills, Wallis Clark, Edward Keane, Jack Kennedy, Douglas Wood, John Miltern, Bernadene Hayes, Clifford Jones, Selmer Jackson, Anthony Quinn (film debut—bit). *D:* Louis Friedlander (Lew Landers); *P:* Robert Presnell; *St & Sc:* Joel Sayre, Horace McCoy, Kubec Glasmon. (1:07)

B drama of a man paroled from prison who must cope with readjustment to society.

3485. Parole Girl (Columbia; 1933). *Cast:* Mae Clarke, Ralph Bellamy, Marie Prevost, Ferdinand Gottschalk, Sam Godfrey, Lee Phelps, Hale Hamilton, Ernest Wood, John Paul Jones. *D:* Edward Cline; *St & Sc:* Norman Krasna. (1:13)

B melodrama.

3486. Parole Racket (Columbia; 1937). *Cast:* Paul Kelly, Rosalind Keith, Francis McDonald, Montague Shaw, Leona Maricle, John Spacey, Bud Flanagan (Dennis O'Keefe). *D:* C.C. Coleman, Jr.; *Sc:* Harold Shumate.

B crime melodrama.

3487. Paroled from the Big House (Syndicate; 1938). *Cast:* Milburn Stone, Jean Carmen, Richard Adams, Gwen Lee. *D:* Elmer Clifton; *Sc:* George Plympton.

(No other information available)

3488. Paroled to Die (Republic-Supreme; 1938). *Cast:* Bob Steele, Kathleen Eliot, Karl Hackett, Horace Murphy, Steve Clark, Budd Buster, Sherry Tansey, Frank Ball, Jack C. Smith, Horace B. Carpenter. *D:* Sam Newfield; *P:* A.W. Hackel; *Sc:* George Plympton. (0:55) (video)

Bob Steele western of a rancher blamed for robbery and murder committed by another.

Part-Time Wife *see* **The Shepper-Newfounder**

3489. Partners (RKO-Pathé; 1932). *Cast:* Tom Keene, Nancy Drexel, Bobby Nelson, Lee Shumway, Otis Harlan, Victor Potel, Billy Franey, Carlton King, Ben Corbett, Fred Burns. *D:* Fred Allen; *St:* Donald W. Lee; *Sc:* Lee. (0:58)

Tom Keene western of a cowboy who undertakes the responsibility of caring for an orphan.

3490. Partners in Crime (Paramount; 1937). *Cast:* Lynne Overman, Roscoe Karns, Inez Courtney, Charles Halton, Anthony Quinn. *D:* Ralph Murphy; *P:* Harold Hurley.

B mystery fare which is the second and last entry in a proposed series, this one involving politics and extortion. Preceded by *Murder Goes to College* (q.v.).

3491. Partners of the Plains (Paramount; 1938). *Cast:* Bill Boyd (Hoppy), Russell Hayden (Lucky), Harvey Clark, Gwen Gaze, Hilda Plowright, John Warburton, Alan Bridge, Earle Hodgins, Al Hill, John Beach, Jim Corey. *D:* Lesley Selander; *P:* Harry M. Sherman; *Sc:* Harrison Jacobs. (1:10)

Fifteenth entry in the "Hopalong Cassidy" series with the Bar 20 boys helping a woman rancher plagued with cattle rustlers.

3492. Partners of the Trail (Monogram; 1931). *Cast:* Tom Tyler, Betty Mack, Reginald Sheffield, Lafe McKee, Margarite McWade, Horace B. Carpenter, Pat Rooney. *D:* Wallace Fox; *P:* Trem Carr; *St:* Will Beale; *Sc:* George Arthur Durlam. (1:03)

Tom Tyler western of a man wrongly accused of murder. Remade as *West of the Divide* (q.v.).

3493. Party Girl (Tiffany; 1930). *Cast:* Douglas Fairbanks, Jr., Marie Prevost, Jeanette Loff, Lucien Prival, Sidney D'Albrook, Almeda Fowler, John St. Polis, Charles Giblyn, Harry Northrup, Florence Dudley, Judith Barrie. *Directed, produced & written by:* Victor & Edward Halperin; *St:* Edwin Balmer; *Co-Sc:* Monte Katterjohn, George Draney.

"Poverty row" drama, considered controversial in its day.

3494. Party Husband (WB/F.N.; 1931). *Cast:* James Rennie, Dorothy Mackaill, Mary Doran, Dorothy Peterson, Paul Porcasi, Donald Cook, Joe Donahue, Barbara Weeks, Louise Beavers, Gilbert Emery. *D:* Clarence Badger; *St:* Geoffrey Barnes; *Sc:* Charles Kenyon.

A marriage is on the rocks in this low-budget drama.

3495. Party Wire (Columbia; 1935). *Cast:* Jean Arthur, Victor Jory, Lyle Talbot, Robert Allen, Charley Grapewin, Maude Eburne, Clara Blandick. *D:* Erle C. Kenton; *Sc:* John Howard Lawson (co-writer). (1:12)

B small town romance.

3496. The Party's Over (Columbia; 1934). *Cast:* Stuart Erwin, Ann Sothern, William Bakewell, Patsy Kelly, Chick Chandler, Henry Travers, Arline Judge, Catherine Doucet. *D:* Walter Lang.

Romantic comedy, based on a play by Daniel Kusell.

3497. Passion Flower (MGM; 1930). *Cast:* Kay Johnson, Kay Francis, Charles Bickford, Lewis Stone, ZaSu Pitts, Dickie Moore, Winter Hall, Ray Milland (bit). *D:* William De Mille; *Sc:* Martin Flavin, Laurence Johnson, Edith Fitzgerald.

Based on the novel by Kathleen Norris, this marital drama tells the story of a poor man who cannot support his wife's expensive tastes. A remake of the 1921 First National production with Norma Talmadge and Harrison Ford.

3498. The Passionate Plumber (MGM; 1932). *Cast:* Buster Keaton (Elmer E. Tuttle), Jimmy Durante (Julius J. McCracken), Polly Moran (Albine), Irene Purcell (Patricia), Gilbert Roland (Tony Lagorce), Mona Maris (Nina), Maude Eburne (Aunt Charlotte), Henry Armetta (bouncer), Paul Porcasi (Paul Le Maire), Jean Del Val (chauffeur), August Tollaire (General Bouschay). *D:* Edward Sedgwick; *P:* Keaton; *Adaptation:* Laurence Johnson; *Dialogue:* Ralph Spence. (1:13)

Romantic comedy, based on the play "Her Cardboard Lover" by French playwright Jacques Deval. Previously filmed in 1928 with Marion Davies under the play's original title. Remade in 1942 under that title with Norma Shearer.

3499. Passport Husband (20th Century–Fox; 1938). *Cast:* Joan Woodbury, Stuart Erwin, Paul McVey, Pauline Moore, Lon Chaney, Jr., Edward Brophy, Harold Huber, Joseph Sawyer, Douglas Fowley, Robert Lowery. *D:* James Tinling; *P:* Sol M. Wurtzel; *St:* Hilda Stone; *Sc:* Robert Chapin, Karen DeWolf.

B comedy.

Passport to Fame (G.B. title) *see* **The Whole Town's Talking**

3500. A Passport to Hell (Fox; 1932). *Cast:* Elissa Landi, Paul Lukas,

Warner Oland, Alexander Kirkland, Donald Crisp, Earle Foxe, Yola D'Avril, Ivan Simpson, William von Brincken, Anders Van Haden, Eva Dennison, Vera Morrison, Bert Sprotte. *D:* Frank Lloyd; *St:* Harry Hervey; *Sc:* Bradley King, Leon Gordon. (G.B. title: *Burnt Offering*)

Drama of a romantic triangle which was a flop for the studio.

3501. Passport to Paradise (Mayfair; 1932). *Cast:* Jack Mulhall, John Ince. *D:* George B. Seitz; *Sc:* Seitz.

"Poverty row" production.

3502/3503. The Past of Mary Holmes (RKO; 1933). *Cast:* Helen Mac-Kellar, Eric Linden, Jean Arthur, Richard "Skeets" Gallagher, Ivan Simpson, Clay Clement, J. Carrol Naish, Roscoe Ates, Rochelle Hudson, Jane Darwell, Franklin Parker, John Sheehan, Edward Nugent. *D:* Harlan Thompson, Slavko Vorkapich (better known later in the decade for his cinematic montages); *As.P.:* Bartlett Cormack; *Sc:* Marion Dix, Edward Doherty.

To get publicity for herself, a woman points to her son as the one responsible for a local murder. A remake of *The Goose Woman* (Universal; 1925) with Jack Pickford and Louise Dresser, based on the novel of that name by Rex Beach.

3504. The Patient in Room 18 (WB/F.N.; 1938). *Cast:* Ann Sheridan, Patric Knowles, Eric Stanley, John Ridgely, Rosella Towne, Harland Tucker, Cliff Clark, Jean Benedict, DeWolf (William) Hopper, Edward McWade, Charles Trowbridge, Frank Orth, Ralph Sandford, Edward Raquello. *D:* Crane Wilbur, Bobby Connolly; *As.P.:* Bryan Foy; *Sc:* Eugene Solow, Robertson White. (1:00)

B mystery of murder and theft in a hospital. Based on the novel by Mignon G. Eberhart.

3505. The Patriot (Paramount 1928). *Cast:* Emil Jannings (Czar Paul

I), Lewis Stone (A.A.N. for B.A.), Florence Vidor, Neil Hamilton (Crown Prince Alexander), Vera Voronina, Harry Cording. *D:* (A.A.N.) Ernst Lubitsch; *Sc:* (A.A.) Hans Kräly; *Art-Set Decoration:* (A.A.N.) Hans Dreier. (1:50 approx.)

Part-talkie drama of the madness of Russia's Czar Paul I, son of Catharine the Great. Filmed as a silent with synchronized music, sound effects and a few passages of garbled dialogue added for release. The film received an A.A.N. for "Best Picture" (1927–28), was voted "Best Picture of the Year" by *Film Daily,* while placing #6 on the "10 Best" list of the *New York Times.* Critics in some circles objected to this film because of sequences considered to be sexually suggestive. Based on the play by Alfred Neumann.

3506. The Pay-Off (RKO; 1930). *Cast:* Lowell Sherman, Marian Nixon, Hugh Trevor, William Janney, George F. Marion, Helene Millard, Walter McGrail, Robert McWade, Alan Roscoe. *D:* Lowell Sherman; *As.P.:* Henry Hobart; *Sc:* Jane Murfin. (G.B. title: *The Losing Game*) (1:10)

B melodrama of a young couple who become involved with a big city crime boss. Based on the play by Samuel Shipman and John B. Hymer, it was remade as *Law of the Underworld* (q.v.).

3507. The Pay-Off (WB/F.N.; 1935). *Cast:* James Dunn, Patricia Ellis, Claire Dodd, Alan Dinehart, Joseph Crehan, Frankie Darro, Andre Beranger, Al Hill, Claire Dodd, Frank Sheridan, Eddie Shubert. *D:* Robert Florey; *P:* Bryan Foy; *Sc:* George Bricker, Joel Sayre.

B newspaper drama of a sportswriter whose life starts to head downhill.

3508. Paying the Penalty (Xxxx Xxxx; 1931). (No information available)

3509. Payment Deferred (MGM; 1932). *Cast:* Charles Laughton (repeating his stage role), Maureen O'Sullivan,

Dorothy Peterson, Verree Teasdale, Ray Milland, Billy Bevan, Neil Hamilton, William Stack. *D:* Lothar Mendes; *P:* Mendes; *Sc:* Claudine West, Ernest Vajda. (1:22)

A shy man finds himself involved in murder. Based on the play by Jeffrey Dell, the film was voted one of the year's "10 Best" by the National Board of Review. A box office flop.

3509a. Peach-O-Reno (RKO; 1931). *Cast:* Bert Wheeler, Robert Woolsey, Dorothy Lee, Zelma O'Neal, Joseph Cawthorn, Cora Witherspoon, Sam Hardy, Mitchell Harris, Arthur Hoyt, Joseph Whittel. *D:* William A. Seiter; *P:* William LeBaron; *Sc:* Ralph Spence, Tim Whelan, Eddie Welch.

B comedy in which Wheeler and Woolsey run a combination gambling-divorce service and encounter trouble in the form of a gambler who wants info on his wife's divorce.

3510. Peacock Alley (Tiffany; 1930). *Cast:* Mae Murray (talkie debut), Phillips Smalley, Jason Robards, Arthur Hoyt, E.H. Calvert, Billy Bevan. *D:* Marcel De Sano.

"Poverty row" romantic drama based on a stage play and previously filmed in 1922 with Monte Blue.

3511. Peck's Bad Boy (Fox; 1934). *Cast:* Jackie Cooper, Thomas Meighan, Jackie Searle, Dorothy Peterson, O.P. Heggie, Billy Gilbert, Harvey Clark, Lawrence Wheat, Charles Evans, Gertrude Howard, Katherine (K.T.) Stevens (film debut). *D:* Edward Cline; *P:* Sol Lesser; *Sc:* Bernard Schubert, Marguerite Roberts. (1:10)

Classic juvenile family type story of a little boy who personifies the word "brat." A remake of the First National production of 1921 with Jackie Coogan, it was based on the story by G.W. Peck which was also adapted to a popular stage play in the early part of this century.

3512. Peck's Bad Boy with the Circus (RKO/Principal; 1938). *Cast:*

Tommy Kelly, Edgar Kennedy, Ann Gillis, Billy Gilbert, Benita Hume, Spanky McFarland, Grant Mitchell, Louise Beavers, Nana Bryant, William Demarest, Wade Boteler, Harry Stubbs, Fay Helm, Mickey Rentschler. *D:* Edward F. Cline; *P:* Sol Lesser; *As.P.:* Leonard Fields; *Sc:* Al Martin, Robert Neville, David Boehm. (1:18) (video)

The further adventures of the bratty kid and his friends as the circus comes to town. Based on the character created by G.W. Peck.

3513. The Pecos Kid (Ajax; 1935). *Cast:* Fred Kohler, Jr., Ruth Findlay, Roger Williams, Ed Cassidy, Wally Wales (Hal Taliaferro), Earl (Dwire) Dwyer, Francis Walker. *D:* William Berke; *P:* William Berke; *St:* Allen Hall; *Sc:* Henry Hess. (0:57)

Fred Kohler, Jr., western, one of two starring features.

3514. Peg o' My Heart (MGM; 1933). *Cast:* Marion Davies, Onslow Stevens, Alan Mowbray, Robert Greig, Irene Browne, J. Farrell MacDonald, Juliette Compton, Doris Lloyd, Billy Bevan, Nora Cecil, Tyrrell Davis, Geoffrey Gill, Mutt the dog. *D:* Robert Z. Leonard; *P:* Leonard; *Adaptation:* Frances Marion. (1:29)

B romantic drama of an obnoxious Irish girl and her effects on the residents of a staid and stuffy English manor. The film, a big hit for the studio was based on the hit play by J. Hartley Manners, which was previously filmed in 1922–23 by King Vidor for Metro with Laurette Taylor recreating her stage role.

3515. The Penal Code (Monarch; 1932–33). *Cast:* Robert Ellis, Jean Porter, John Ince. *D:* George Melford; *P:* John R. Freuler.

"Poverty row" melodrama.

Penalty of Fame (G.B. title) *see* **Okay, America**

3516. Penguin Pool Murder (RKO; 1932). *Cast:* Edna May Oliver

(Miss Hildegarde Withers), James Gleason (Inspector Oscar Piper), Mae Clarke, Robert Armstrong, Donald Cook, Edgar Kennedy, Clarence H. Wilson, James Donlan, Gustav von Seyffertitz, Guy Usher, William LeMaire, Joe Hermano, Rochelle Hudson, Wilfred North. *D:* George Archainbaud; *As.P.:* Kenneth MacGowan; *Sc:* Willis Goldbeck. (G.B. title: *The Penguin Pool Mystery*) (1:10)

B comedy-mystery set in an aquarium with old maid school teacher/amateur sleuth Hildegarde Withers the constant bane to Inspector Oscar Piper as he investigates two murders. The premiere entry in a series of six films featuring the two characters. Gleason appeared in all six, while Oliver played Withers three times, was replaced by ZaSu Pitts in #'s 4 and 5 and Helen Broderick in #6. A box office hit, it was based on the novel by Stuart Palmer and a story by Lowell Brentano.

The Penguin Pool Mystery (G.B. title) *see* **Penguin Pool Murder**

3517. Penitentiary (Columbia; 1938). *Cast:* Walter Connolly, John Howard, Jean Parker, Edward Van Sloan, Marjorie Main, Ann Doran, Paul Fix, Thurston Hall, Ward Bond, Marc Lawrence, Dick Curtis, Charles Halton, Arthur Hohl, Robert Barrat, Dick Elliott. *D:* John Brahm; *St:* Martin Flavin; *Sc:* Seton I. Miller, Fred Niblo, Jr.

A remake of *The Criminal Code* (q.v.) is this B prison melodrama, remade again in 1950 as *Convicted.*

3518. Pennies from Heaven (Columbia; 1936). *Cast:* Bing Crosby, Edith Fellows, Madge Evans, Donald Meek, Louis Armstrong and his band (in their feature film debut), Stanley Andrews, Harry Tyler, Tom Dugan, John Gallaudet, Charles Wilson, Tom Ricketts, William Stack. *D:* Norman Z. McLeod; *P:* Emmanuel Cohen; *Sc:* Jo Swerling, Katherine Leslie Moore, William Rankin; *Title Song:* (A.A.N. for Best

Song) Arthur Johnston & Johnny Burke. (1:21)

Basically a Bing Crosby vehicle dealing with an orphaned girl and her grandfather. No relation to the 1981 film of the same name.

3519. Penrod and His Twin Brother (WB; 1938). *Cast:* Billy & Bobby Mauch (twins), Frank Craven, Spring Byington, Charles Halton, Claudia Coleman, Jackie Morrow, Philip Hurlic, Charles Foy, Eddie Collins, Bennie Bartlett, Bernice Pilot, Charles Jordan, Jerry Madden, Max Wagner, Jack Mower, John Pirrone. *D:* William McGann; *As.P.:* Bryan Foy; *Sc:* William Jacobs, Hugh Cummings. (1:03)

B Americana of a small town boy accused of something he didn't do. Based on the characters created by Booth Tarkington. A follow-up to *Penrod and Sam* (1937) (q.v.).

3520. Penrod and Sam (WB/F.N.; 1931). *Cast:* Leon Janney, Junior (Frank) Coghlan, Dorothy Peterson, Matt Moore, Nestor Aber, Wade Boteler, Johnny Arthur, ZaSu Pitts, Charles Sellon, Helen Beaudine, Elizabeth Patterson, James Robinson, Robert Dandridge, Betty Jane Graham, Margaret Marquis, Billy Lord. *D:* William Beaudine (who also directed the '23 version); *Sc:* Waldemar Young.

Juvenile family adventure of a boy who becomes involved with bank robbers. A remake of the 1923 production by First National with Ben Alexander, which was a follow-up to *Penrod* (First National; 1922) with Wesley Barry which was based on Booth Tarkington's 1914 story. Remade in 1937 (see below).

3521. Penrod and Sam (WB/F.N.; 1937). *Cast:* Billy Mauch, Frank Craven, Spring Byington, Craig Reynolds, Bernice Pilot, Harry Watson, Jackie Morrow, Charles Halton, Philip Hurlic, Alan Davis, Jerry Madden, Billy Lechner, Si Wills, Billy Wolfstone. *D:* William McGann; *P:* Bryan Foy; *Sc:* Lillie Hayward, Hugh Cummings. (1:04)

B remake of the preceding film, which was followed by two sequels (q.v.).

3522. Penrod's Double Trouble (WB/F.N.; 1938). *Cast:* Billy & Bobby Mauch, Dick Purcell, Gene Lockhart, Hugh O'Connell, Philip Hurlic, Charles Halton. *D:* Lewis Seiler; *As.P.:* Bryan Foy; *Sc:* Ernest Booth, Crane Wilbur. (1:01)

The further adventures of Booth Tarkington's characters in a juvenile melodrama involving Penrod's kidnapping. A follow-up to *Penrod and His Twin Brother* (q.v.).

3523. Penthouse (MGM; 1933). *Cast:* Warner Baxter, Myrna Loy, C. Henry Gordon, Charles Butterworth, Nat Pendleton, Phillips Holmes, Mae Clarke, George E. Stone, Raymond Hatton, Robert Emmett O'Connor, Martha Sleeper, Samuel S. Hinds, Arthur Belasco. *D:* W.S. Van Dyke; *P:* Hunt Stromberg; *Sc:* Frances Goodrich, Albert Hackett; *St:* Arthur Somers Roche. (G.B. title: *Crooks in Clover*) (1:30)

Comedy-melodrama of a criminal lawyer who is trying to extricate himself from a murder charge. Remade as *Society Lawyer* (q.v.).

3524. Penthouse Party (Liberty; 1936). *Cast:* Reginald Denny. *D:* William Nigh; *P:* M.H. Hoffman, Jr.

3525. People Will Talk (Paramount; 1935). *Cast:* Mary Boland, Charles Ruggles, Leila Hyams, Dean Jagger, Ruthelma Stevens, Hans Steinke, Margaret Hamilton, Edward Brophy, Jack Mulhall, John Rogers, Constantine Romanoff. *D:* Alfred Santell; *P:* Douglas MacLean; *St:* Sophie Kerr (Richardson); *Sc:* Herbert Fields. (1:07)

B domestic comedy of small town gossip.

3526. The People's Enemy (RKO/Select; 1935). *Cast:* Preston Foster (Vince), Melvyn Douglas, Lila Lee, William Collier, Jr. (final film —

retired), Shirley Grey, Roscoe Ates, Sybil Elaine, Herbert Rawlinson, Charles Coburn. *D:* Crane Wilbur; *As.P.:* Burt Kelly (for Select Productions); *St:* Edward Dean Sullivan; *Sc:* Sullivan, Gordon Kahn.

Independent melodrama of a ruthless gangland character.

3527. Pepper (20th Century-Fox; 1936). *Cast:* Jane Withers, Irvin S. Cobb, Slim Summerville, Ivan Lebedeff, Dean Jagger, Romaine Callender, Muriel Robert, Tommy Bupp. *D:* James Tinling; *Sc:* Lamar Trotti.

B juvenile comedy-drama.

3528. The Perfect Clue (Majestic; 1935). *Cast:* David Manners, Skeets Gallagher, Betty Blythe, Pat O'Malley, Jack Richardson, Charles C. Wilson, Frank Darien, William P. Carleton, Ernie Adams, Ralf Harolde, Robert Gleckler, Dorothy Libaire. *D:* Robert Vignola; *Sc:* Albert DeMond.

B mystery from "poverty row."

3529. The Perfect Crime (Film Booking Office; 1928). *Cast:* Clive Brook, Irene Rich, Tully Marshall, Edmund Breese. *D:* Bert Glennon.

Part-talkie melodrama with synchronized music and songs. Remade as *The Crime Doctor* (q.v.). Based on the story "The Big Bow Mystery" by Israel Zangwill.

3530. The Perfect Gentleman (MGM; 1935). *Cast:* Cicely Courtneidge (British actress in her only American film), Frank Morgan, Heather Angel, Herbert Mundin, Henry Stephenson, Una O'Connor, Forrester Harvey, Mary Forbes, Doris Lloyd, Brenda Forbes, Edward Cooper. *D:* Tim Whelan; *P:* Harry Rapf; *Sc:* Edward Childs Carpenter. (G.B. title: *The Imperfect Lady*) (1:13)

Comedy-drama of a fading actress who is assisted in a comeback by a ne'er-do-well. A financial disaster for the studio.

3531. The Perfect Specimen (WB/F.N.; 1937). *Cast:* Errol Flynn, Joan Blondell, Hugh Herbert, Edward Everett Horton, Dick Foran, May Robson, Beverly Roberts, Allen Jenkins, Harry Davenport, Dennie Moore, Hugh O'Connell, Tim Henning. *D:* Michael Curtiz; *Supervisor:* Harry Joe Brown; *Sc:* Norman Reilly Raine, Lawrence Riley, Brewster Morse, Fritz Falkenstein. (1:38)

Comedy of a man who must finally face the outside world after being sheltered by a doting protective grandmother. Based on a story by Samuel Hopkins Adams which appeared in Cosmopolitan magazine.

The Perfect Weekend (G.B. title) *see* **The St. Louis Kid**

Perilous Journey (G.B. title) *see* **Bad Boy** (1939)

3532. Perils from the Planet Mongo (Universal; 1936). *Cast:* Buster Crabbe, Jean Rogers, Frank Shannon, Charles Middleton, Priscilla Lawson, John Lipson. *D:* Frederick Stephani. (1:31)

The feature version of the second "Flash Gordon" serial in 13 chapters and the most expensive serial produced to date, coming in at $350,000.

3533. Personal Maid (Paramount; 1931). *Cast:* Nancy Carroll, Gene Raymond (film debut), Pat O'Brien, Mary Boland, Donald Meek, George Fawcett (final film — ret.), Hugh O'Connell, Charlotte Wynters, Jessie Busley, Ernest Lawford. *D:* Monta Bell, Lothar Mendes; *St:* Grace Perkins.

The complications of a romance between a domestic and her employer's son.

3534. The Personal Maid's Secret (WB; 1935). *Cast:* Ruth Donnelly, Warren Hull, Margaret Lindsay, Anita Louise, Arthur Treacher, Gordon (Bill) Elliott, Henry O'Neill, Frank Albertson, Bud Flanagan (Dennis O'Keefe).

A family maid solves everyone's problems in this B comedy.

3535. Personal Property (MGM; 1937). *Cast:* Jean Harlow, Robert Taylor, Reginald Owen, Una O'Connor, Cora Witherspoon, Henrietta Crosman (final film), E.E. Clive, Barnett Parker, Forrester Harvey, Marla Shelton, Lionel Braham. *D:* W.S. Van Dyke II; *P:* John W. Considine, Jr.; *Sc:* Ernest Vajda, Hugh Mills. (G.B. title: *The Man in Possession*) (1:24)

A hit romantic comedy, based on the play "The Man in Possession" by H.M. Harwood. A remake of the 1931 film of that title (q.v.).

3536. Personal Secretary (Universal; 1938). *Cast:* William Gargan, Joy Hodges, Andy Devine, Kay Linaker, Ruth Donnelly, Samuel S. Hinds, Selmer Jackson, Florence Roberts, Jack Carr, Louise Stanley. *D:* Otis Garrett; *P:* Max H. Golden; *Sc:* Betty Laidlaw, Robert Lively, Charles Grayson. (1:03)

B drama of rival news columnists working to prove a woman innocent of murder.

3537. Personality (Columbia; 1930). *Cast:* Vivian Oakland, Johnny Arthur, Blanche Frederici. *D:* Victor Heerman.

Low-budget comedy.

3538. The Personality Kid (WB; 1934). *Cast:* Pat O'Brien, Glenda Farrell, Claire Dodd, Henry O'Neill, Robert Gleckler, Jackie Fields, Thomas Jackson, Arthur Vinton, Clarence Muse, Mushy Callahan, Marvin Shechter, George Cooper, George Pat Collins, Clay Clement, Pudgie White. *D:* Alan Crosland; *P:* Robert Presnell; *St:* Gene Towne, C. Graham Baker; *Adaptation:* David Boehm; *Sc:* F. Hugh Herbert, Erwin Gelsey.

B drama of a successful boxer whose exalted opinion of himself creates problems in his marriage and career.

3539. Persons in Hiding (Paramount; 1939). *Cast:* Patricia Morison (film debut), J. Carrol Naish, Lynne Overman, William Henry, Helen Twelvetrees, William Frawley, John Eldredge, William Collier, Sr., Judith Barrett, Richard Denning, Janet Waldo, Richard Carle, May Boley, Leona Roberts, Richard Stanley (Dennis Morgan), Dorothy Howe (Virginia Vale). *D:* Louis King; *P:* Edward T. Lowe; *Sc:* Horace McCoy, William Lipman. (1:10)

Melodrama which is loosely based on the story of Clyde Barrow and Bonnie Parker. Partially based on the popular book by J. Edgar Hoover (ghost written by Courtney Riley Cooper).

3540. Peter Ibbetson (Paramount; 1935). *Cast:* Gary Cooper, Ann Harding, Ida Lupino, John Halliday, Virginia Weidler, Dickie Moore, Doris Lloyd, Douglass Dumbrille, Gilbert Emery, Donald Meek, Constance Collier, Leonid Kinskey, Christian Rub, Colin Tapley, Elsa Buchanan, Theresa Maxwell Conover, Adrienne D'Ambricourt, Clive Morgan, Elsa Prescott, Ambrose Barker, Blanche Craig, Marcelle Corday, Thomas Monk. *D:* Henry Hathaway; *P:* Louis D. Lighton; *Adaptation:* Constance Collier; *Sc:* Vincent Lawrence, Waldemar Young; *Additional Dialogue:* Edwin Justus Mayer, John Meehan; *Music:* (A.A.N.) Ernest Toch. (1:25)

Offbeat romantic drama of lovers separated in childhood who are drawn together by fate as adults, forming an eternal bond. A remake of *Forever* (Paramount; 1921, known in Europe as *Peter Ibbetson*) with Wallace Reid and Elsie Ferguson. Based on the novel by George du Maurier and the 1917 play by John Nathaniel Raphael.

3541. The Petrified Forest (WB/ F.N.; 1936). *Cast:* Leslie Howard (recreating his stage role as Alan Squier), Bette Davis (Gabrielle "Gabby" Maple), Humphrey Bogart (recreating his stage role as Duke Mantee), Genevieve Tobin (Mrs. Chisholm), Dick Foran (Boze Hertzlinger), Charley

Grapewin (Gramps), Joe Sawyer (Jackie), Paul Harvey (Mr. Chisholm), Porter Hall (Jason Maple), Eddie Acuff (lineman), Adrian Morris (Ruby), Nina Campana (Paula), Slim Thompson (Slim), John Alexander (Joseph, the chauffeur), Arthur Aylesworth (commander of the Black Horse Troopers), George Guhl (trooper), Constance Bergen (Duke's girl), James Farley (sheriff), Jack Cheatham (deputy), Gus Leonard (postman), Francis Shide (second lineman). *D:* Archie Mayo; *P:* Henry Blanke; *Sc:* Charles Kenyon, Delmer Daves. (1:23) (video)

Classic drama of escaped hoodlum Duke Mantee who holds various people hostage at a roadside eatery in the Arizona desert. Based on the Broadway play by Robert E. Sherwood, it was remade by this studio in 1945 as *Escape in the Desert.*

3542. Petticoat Fever (MGM; 1936). *Cast:* Robert Montgomery, Myrna Loy, Reginald Owen, Winifred Shotter, Irving Bacon, Forrester Harvey, George Hassell, Otto Yamaoka, Iris Yamaoka, Bo Ching. *D:* George Fitzmaurice; *P:* Frank Davis; *Sc:* Harold Goldman. (1:20)

Offbeat romantic comedy of an engaged couple who crashland their plane in Labrador and encounter a man who hasn't seen a woman for years. Based on the Broadway play by Mark Reed.

3543. The Phantom (Xxxx Xxxx; 1931). *Cast:* Guinn Williams, Allene Ray.

(No other information available)

3544. The Phantom Broadcast (Monogram; 1933). *Cast:* Ralph Forbes, Vivienne Osborne, Gail Patrick, Paul Page, Guinn Williams, Arnold Gray, Rockliffe Fellowes, Harland Tucker, Pauline Garon, George Nash, Mary MacLaren, Carl Miller, Althea Henley, George Hayes. *D:* Phil Rosen; *P:* William T. Lackey; *St & Sc:* Tristram Tupper. (G.B. title: *Phantom of the Air*) (Working title: "False Fronts") (1:08)

"Poverty row" mystery involving the murder of a popular radio crooner and a well kept secret.

3545. Phantom Cowboy (Awyon; 1935). *D:* Robert J. Horner; *P:* Horner.

B western starring Ted Wells, a former silent western star for Universal.

3546. The Phantom Creeps (Universal; 1939). *Cast:* Bela Lugosi (Dr. Zorka), Robert Kent, Dorothy Arnold, Edwin Stanley, Edward Van Sloan, Regis Toomey, Lee J. Cobb, Roy Barcroft. *D:* Ford Beebe, Saul Goodkind; *As.P.:* Henry McRae; *Sc:* George Plympton, Basil Dickey, Mildred Parrish. (1:15) (video)

A mad scientist uses an assortment of bizarre inventions in his attempt to rule the world. The feature-version of the 12-chapter serial of the same name.

The Phantom Empire *see* **Radio Ranch**

3547. The Phantom Express (Majestic; 1932). *Cast:* William Collier, Jr., Sally Blane, J. Farrell MacDonald, Hobart Bosworth, Axel Axelson, Lina Basquette, Eddie Phillips, Claire McDowell, Jack Hoxie, Robert Ellis, Tom O'Brien, Jack Pennick. *D:* Emory Johnson; *Sc:* Johnson. (1:06) (video)

"Poverty row" action melodrama about the attempts to sabotage a railroad.

3548. Phantom Gold (Columbia; 1938). *Cast:* Jack Luden, Beth Marion, Barry Downing, Charles "Slim" Whitaker, Tuffy the dog, Buzz Barton, Hal Taliaferro, Art Davis, Jimmy Robinson, Jack Ingram, Marin Sais. *D:* Joseph Levering; *Sc:* Nate Gatzert. (0:56)

Jack Luden western of two cowboys who get involved with a hidden gold mine.

3549. The Phantom in the House (Syndicate-Continental Talking

Pictures; 1929). *Cast:* Ricardo Cortez, Henry B. Walthall, Nancy Welford. *D:* Phil Rosen; *P:* Trem Carr.

Low-budget mystery-melodrama.

3550. The Phantom of Crestwood (RKO; 1932). *Cast:* Ricardo Cortez, Karen Morley, H.B. Warner, Anita Louise, Pauline Frederick, Robert McWade, Sam Hardy, Skeets Gallagher, Robert Elliott, Ivan Simpson, Mary Duncan, Tom Douglas, Aileen Pringle, George E. Stone, Matty Kemp, Hilda Vaughn. *D:* J. Walter Ruben; *As.P.:* Merian C. Cooper; *St:* Bartlett Cormack, Ruben; *Sc:* Cormack. (1:17)

Hit mystery with comic overtones of a lady blackmailer who gets her victims together for a mass scheme, only to become the victim of a mysterious killer.

3551. The Phantom of Paris (MGM; 1931). *Cast:* John Gilbert (Chéri-Bibi), Leila Hyams (Cecile), Lewis Stone (Costaud), Jean Hersholt (Herman), C. Aubrey Smith (Bourrelier), Natalie Moorhead (Vera), Ian Keith (Marquis DuTouchais), Alfred Hickman (Dr. Gorin). *D:* John S. Robertson; *Sc:* Bess Meredyth; *Dialogue:* John Meehan, Edwin Justus Mayer. (1:13)

Mystery of a magician who is accused of murder. Based on Gaston LeRoux's "Chéri-Bibi."

3552. The Phantom of Santa Fe (Burroughs-Tarzan; 1936). *Cast:* Norman Kerry, Nena Quartero, Frank Mayo, Monte Montague, Tom O'Brien, Carmelita Geraghty, Jack Mower, Frank Ellis, Merrill McCormack. *D:* Jacques Jaccard; *Sc:* Charles Francis Royal. (1:27)

B color independent western of a cowboy who disguises himself as a character known as "The Hawk" in order to get the bad guy. Originally filmed in 1931 as "The Hawk," and later redone in this format.

Phantom of the Air (G.B. title) *see* **The Phantom Broadcast**

3553. Phantom of the Desert (Syndicate; 1930). *Cast:* Jack Perrin, Eva Novak, Josef Swickard, Lila Eccles, Ben Corbett, Edward Earle, Pete Morrison, Robert Walker. *D:* Harry S. Webb; *Sc:* Carl Krusada. (0:55)

Jack Perrin western of two cowboys investigating horses apparently being rustled by a wild stallion.

3554. Phantom of the Range (Victory; 1936–37). *Cast:* Tom Tyler, Beth Marion, Sammy Cohen, Forrest Taylor, Soledad Jimenez, Charles King, John Elliott, Richard Cramer. *D:* Robert Hill; *P:* Sam Katzman; *Sc:* Basil Dickey. (0:58)

Tom Tyler oater involving a search for a hidden treasure.

3555. Phantom Patrol (Ambassador; 1935–36). *Cast:* Kermit Maynard, Joan Barclay, Dick Curtis, George Cleveland, Harry Worth, Paul Fix, Julian Rivero, Roger Williams, Eddie Phillips, Lester Dorr. *D:* Charles Hutchison; *P:* Maurice Conn; *Sc:* Stephen Norris. (1:00) (video)

Kermit Maynard action adventure as a Mountie poses as an American writer in order to bring in a gang of crooks.

3556. The Phantom President (Paramount; 1932). *Cast:* George M. Cohan (talkie debut in a dual role), Claudette Colbert, Jimmy Durante, Sidney Toler, George Barbier, Jameson Thomas, Paul Hurst, Alan Mowbray (George Washington), Eleanor Boardman, Charles Middleton, Louise Mackintosh, Julius McVicker. *D:* Norman Taurog; *Sc:* Walter De Leon, Harlan Thompson; *Music & Songs:* Richard Rodgers, Lorenz Hart. (1:20)

Political musical of mistaken identity. Based on the novel by George F. Worts, it was a box office flop.

3557. Phantom Ranger (Monogram; 1938). *Cast:* Tim McCoy, Suzanne Kaaren, John St. Polis, Karl

Hackett, Charles King, Tom London, John Merton, Richard Cramer, Herbert Holcombe, Harry Strang, Wally West, Horace B. Carpenter, Sherry Tansey, George Morrell, Herman Hack. *D:* Sam Newfield; *P:* Maurice Conn; *St:* Stanley Roberts, Joseph O'Donnell; *Sc:* O'Donnell. (0:54)

Tim McCoy western with a gang of counterfeiters working the area.

3558. Phantom Shadows (Xxxx Xxxx; 1936). (No information available)

3559. The Phantom Stage (Universal; 1939). *Cast:* Bob Baker, Marjorie Reynolds, George Cleveland, Forrest Taylor, Reed Howes, Tex Palmer, Murdock MacQuarrie, Glenn Strange, Jack Kirk, Ernie Adams, Dick Rush, Apache the horse. *D:* George Waggner; *P:* Trem Carr; *Sc:* Joseph West (Waggner). (0:58) (video)

Bob Baker western with songs of two men coming to the aid of a girl whose stageline is being robbed of its gold shipments.

3560. The Phantom Thunderbolt (World Wide/KBS Productions; 1933). *Cast:* Ken Maynard, Frances Dade, Frank Rice, Robert Kortman, William Gould, Frank Beal, Harry Holman, Wilfred Lucas, William Robyns, Nelson McDowell, Lew Meehan. *D:* Alan James (aka: Alvin J. Neitz); *Sc:* James. (1:03) (video)

Ken Maynard western of townsmen who hire "The Thunderbolt Kid" to stop a gang that is preventing the railroad from coming through.

3561. Piccadilly Jim (MGM; 1936). *Cast:* Robert Montgomery (Jim Crocker), Frank Morgan (Mr. Crocker), Madge Evans (Ann Chester), Eric Blore (Bayliss), Billie Burke (Eugenia), Robert Benchley (Macon), Ralph Forbes (Lord Priory), Cora Witherspoon (Nesta Pett), Tommy Bupp (Ogden Pett), Aileen Pringle (Paducah), Grant Mitchell (Herbert Pett), E.E. Clive (editor), Grayce Hampton (Mrs. Brede), Billy Bevan (taxi driver), Stanley Morner (later Dennis Morgan). *D:* Robert Z. Leonard; *P:* Leonard, Harry Rapf; *Sc:* Charles Brackett, Edwin Knopf. (1:40)

Hit comedy of a man's romantic affair and his son who has to stick his nose in. Based on the novel by P.G. Wodehouse.

3562. Pick a Star (MGM/Hal Roach; 1937). *Cast:* Patsy Kelly, Rosina Lawrence, Jack Haley, Mischa Auer, Stan Laurel, Oliver Hardy, Charles Halton, Lyda Roberti, Tom Dugan, James Finlayson, Joyce Compton, Walter Long, Johnny Arthur, Mary Gordon, Jack Norton, Wesley Barry, Leila McIntyre, Cully Richards, John Hyams, Sam Adams, Benny Burt. *D:* Edward Sedgwick; *P:* Hal Roach; *St:* Thomas J. Dugan, Arthur Vernon Jones; *Sc:* Richard Flournoy, Jones, Dugan. (Retitled: *Movie Struck*) (1:10) (video)

Musical-comedy of a girl reaching for stardom in Hollywood.

3563. Pick-Up (Paramount; 1933). *Cast:* Sylvia Sidney, George Raft, Lillian Bond, William Harrigan, Gail Patrick, Oscar Apfel, Charles Middleton, Louise Beavers, Eddie Clayton, Dorothy Layton, Alice Adair, Florence Dudley, George Meeker, Clarence Wilson. *D:* Marion Gering; *P:* B.P. Schulberg; *St:* Vina Delmar; *Sc:* S.K. Lauren, Agnes Brand Leahy. (1:20)

B drama of an escaped convict who finds his wife is having an affair.

3564. Picture Brides (First Division; 1933). *Cast:* Dorothy Mackaill, Alan Hale, Jimmy Aubrey. *D:* Phil Rosen.

Low-budget independent production.

3565. The Picture Snatcher (WB; 1933). *Cast:* James Cagney (Danny Kean), Ralph Bellamy, Patricia Ellis, Alice White, Ralf Harolde,

Robert Emmett O'Connor, Robert Barrat, Hobart Cavanaugh, Sterling Holloway, George Pat Collins, Barb Rogers, Tom Wilson, Reneé Whitney, Jill Dennett, Alice Jans. *D:* Lloyd Bacon; *P:* Ray Griffith; *St:* Danny Ahearn; *Sc:* P.J. Wolfson, Allen Rivkin. (1:17)

Comedy-melodrama of a photog with daring-do, out to make a name for himself. Based on a true story, it was remade as *Escape from Crime* (WB; 1942).

Pier 13 (G.B. title) *see* **Me and My Gal**

3566. Pigskin Parade (20th Century-Fox; 1936). *Cast:* Stuart Erwin (A.A.N. for B.A. as Amos Dodd), Patsy Kelly (Bessie Winters), Jack Haley (Winston "Slug" Winters), Johnny Downs (Chip Carson), Betty Grable (Laura Watson), Arline Judge (Sally Saxon), Dixie Dunbar (Ginger Jones), Judy Garland (feature film debut as Sairy Dodd), Tony Martin (Tommy Barker), Fred Kohler, Jr. (Biff Bentley), Elisha Cook, Jr. (Herbert Terwilliger Van Dyck), Eddie Nugent (Sparks), Grady Sutton (Mortimer Higgins), Julius Tannen (Doctor Burke), Yacht Club Boys (themselves), Sam Hayes (radio announcer playing himself), Maurice Cass (Prof. Tutweiler), Jack Best (Prof. McCormick), Douglas Wood (Prof. Dutton), Charles Croker-King (Prof. Pillsbury), Robert McClung, George Herbert, Jack Murphy, Pat Flaherty, David Sharpe, Si Jenks, John Dilson, Jack Stoney, George Y. Harvey, Lynn Bari, Ben Hall, Charles Wilson, George Offerman, Jr., Alan Ladd, Edward LeSaint. *D:* David Butler; *As.P.:* Bogart Rogers; *St:* Arthur Sheekman, Nat Perrin, Mark Kelly; *Sc:* Harry Tugend, Jack Yellen, William Conselman; *Songs:* "It's Love I'm After," "The Balboa," "You're Slightly Terrific," "You Do the Darndest Things, Baby," "T.S.U. Alma Mater," "Hold That Bulldog" and "The Texas Tornado" by Sidney Mitchell & Lew Pollack; "We'd Rather Be in College," &

"Down with Everything" by The Yacht Club Boys. (G.B. title: *The Harmony Parade*) (1:33)

Hit musical-comedy with a football theme. One of the 38 top grossing films of 1936–37.

3567. Pilgrimage (Fox; 1933). *Cast:* Henrietta Crosman, Heather Angel (American debut), Norman Foster, Marion Nixon, Lucille La Verne, Hedda Hopper, Charley Grapewin, Robert Warwick, Francis Ford, Maurice Murphy, Jay Ward, Louise Carter, Frances Rich. *D:* John Ford; *Sc:* Barry Connors, Philip Klein; *Dialogue:* Dudley Nichols. (1:35)

Sentimental drama of a mother who interferes with her son's romance. Based on the story "Gold Star Mothers" by I.A.R. (Ida) Wylie.

3568. Pinto Rustlers (Reliable; 1936). *Cast:* Tom Tyler, George Walsh, Al St. John, Catherine Cotter, Earl Dwire, William Gould, George Chesebro, Bud Osborne, Roger Williams, Murdock MacQuarrie, Charles King, Charles "Slim" Whitaker, Milburn Morante, Sherry Tansey. *D:* Henri Samuels (Harry S. Webb); *P:* Bernard B. Ray; *Sc:* Robert Tansey. (0:56)

Tom Tyler western of a man out to get the outlaw gang that killed his father.

The Pioneer Builders *see* **The Conquerors**

3569. Pioneer Trail (Columbia; 1938). *Cast:* Jack Luden, Joan Barclay, Hal Taliaferro, Tuffy the dog, Marin Sais, Slim Whitaker, Leon Beaumont, Eva McKenzie, Hal Price, Dick Botiller, Tom London, Bud Osborne, Robert McKenzie. *D:* Joseph Levering; *Sc:* Nate Gatzert. (0:54)

Jack Luden western of a cattle drive and cattle rustling.

3570. Pioneers of the Frontier (Columbia; 1939–40). *Cast:* Bill Elliott, Dub Taylor (Cannonball), Linda Winters (Dorothy Comingore), Dick Curtis, Lafe McKee, Stanley Brown, Richard Fiske, Carl Stockdale, Ralph McCullough, Al Bridge, Edmund Cobb, George Chesebro, Lynton Brent, Ralph Peters, Jack Kirk. *D:* Sam Nelson; *P:* Leon Barsha; *Sc:* Fred Myton. (0:58)

Bill Elliott in a "Wild Bill Saunders" western of a gunman who kills a landowner and attempts to take over his ranch.

3571. Pioneers of the West (Republic; 1939–40). *Cast:* Bob Livingston (Stony Brooke), Raymond Hatton (Rusty Joslin), Duncan Renaldo (Rico), Noah Beery, Beatrice Roberts, Lane Chandler, George Cleveland, Hal Taliaferro, Yakima Canutt, John Dilson, Earl Askam, Joe McGuinn, Ray Jones, Artie Ortego, Chuck Baldra. *D:* Lester Orlebeck; *P:* Harry Grey; *Sc:* Jack Natteford, Karen deWolf, Gerald Geraghty. (0:56)

The "Three Mesquiteers" in their 28th feature film in a story of a wagon train heading west through Indian territory.

3572. Pirates of the Skies (Universal; 1939). *Cast:* Kent Taylor, Rochelle Hudson, Samuel S. Hinds, Horace MacMahon, Henry Brandon. *D:* Joseph A. McDonough; *P:* Barney A. Sarecky. (1:01)

B action melodrama of an air policeman, whose wife doesn't like his kind of work.

3573. The Plain-Clothes Man (Columbia; 1931–32). *Cast:* Jack Holt, Walter Connolly (in his film debut).

(No other information available)

3574. The Plainsman (Paramount; 1936). *Cast:* Gary Cooper (Wild Bill Hickok), Jean Arthur (Calamity Jane), James Ellison (Buffalo Bill Cody), Charles Bickford (John Latimer), Porter Hall (Jack McCall), Helen Burgess (Louisa Cody), Paul Harvey (Yellow Hand), Victor Varconi (Painted Horse), John Miljan (George A. Custer), Frank McGlynn (Abraham Lincoln), Granville Bates (Van Ellyn), Purnell Pratt (Capt. Wood), Fred Kohler (Jake), George Hayes (Breezy), Patrick Moriarty (Sgt. McGinnis), Charles Judels (Tony, the barber), Harry Woods (quartermaster sergeant), George MacQuarrie (General Merritt), John Hyams (Schuyler Colfax), Edwin Maxwell (Secretary of War, Stanton), Charlie Stevens (Injun Charley), William Royle (Corp. Brannigan), Fuzzy Knight (Dave, the miner), Leila McIntyre (Mary Todd Lincoln), Harry Stubbs (John F. Usher), Davison Clark (James Speed), Charles W. Herzinger (William H. Seward), William Humphries (Hugh McCulloch), Sidney Jarvis (Gideon Wells), Wadsworth Harris (William Dennison), Frank Albertson (young trooper of the 7th Cavalry), Anthony Quinn (Northern Cheyenne Indian), Francis McDonald (riverboat gambler), George Ernest, Bruce Warren, Arthur Aylesworth, Douglas Wood, George Cleveland, Lona Andre, Irving Bacon, Francis Ford, Hank Worden, Bud Flanagan (Dennis O'Keefe), Noble Johnson, Jonathan Hale, Bud Osborne, Robert Wilbur. *D:* Cecil B. De Mille; *P:* De Mille; *Adaptation:* Jeanie MacPherson; *Sc:* Waldemar Young, Lynn Riggs, Harold Lamb. (1:53) (video)

Lavishly produced de Mille saga based on historical characters, facts along with the usual smattering of fictionalization of the facts. Based on "Wild Bill Hickok" by Frank J. Wilstach, as well as various stories by Grover Jones and Courtney Ryley Cooper. A big money-maker for the studio, being one of the 38 top grossing films of 1936–37. Loosely remade in 1966 as a theatrical production which wound up as a TV movie instead.

Planet Outlaws *see* **Destination Saturn**

3575. Platinum Blonde (Columbia; 1931). *Cast:* Loretta Young, Jean

Harlow, Robert Williams (final film — d. 1932), Reginald Owen, Louise Closser Hale, Halliwell Hobbes, Donald Dillaway, Walter Catlett, Claud Allister, Edmund Breese. *D:* Frank Capra; *Sc:* Jo Swerling, Robert Riskin. (1:30)

A romantic comedy of a reporter who marries a rich society girl. The film which made Jean Harlow a star. Based on a story by Harry E. Chandlee and Douglas W. Churchill.

3576. Playboy of Paris (Paramount; 1930). *Cast:* Maurice Chevalier, Frances Dee, O.P. Heggie, Dorothy Christy, Stuart Erwin, Eugene Pallette, William Davidson, Tyler Brooke, Edmund Breese, Frank Elliott, Cecil Cunningham, Charles Giblyn. *D:* Ludwig Berger.

Romantic comedy with songs of two women after the same man. A remake of *Le Petit Cafe* (1920).

3577. Play Girl (WB; 1932). *Cast:* Loretta Young, Norman Foster, Dorothy Burgess, Winnie Lightner, Guy Kibbee, Noel Madison, Polly Walters, James Ellison (film debut), Edward Van Sloan, Elizabeth Patterson, Nat Pendleton, Mae Madison, Reneé Whitney, Charles Coleman, Adrienne Dore, Harold Waldridge, Aileen Carlyle. *D:* Ray Enright; *Sc:* Maurine Watkins.

A depression-era marital drama of a working girl who marries a gambler.

3578. Playing Around (WB/F.N.; 1930). *Cast:* Alice White, William Bakewell, Chester Morris, Marion Byron, Maurice Black, Lionel Belmore, Helen Werle, Shep Camp, Ann Brody, Richard Carlyle, Nellie V. Nichols. *D:* Mervyn LeRoy; *St:* Vina Delmar; *Sc:* Adele Commandini, Frances Nordstrom; *Songs:* "That's the Lowdown on the Lowdown," "We Learn About Love Everyday," "You're My Captain Kidd" & title song by Sam Stept & Bud Green.

A girl makes a misguided romantic decision in this melodrama with music.

Playing the Game (G.B. title) *see* **Touchdown!**

3579. Playthings of Hollywood (Xxxx Xxxx; 1931). (No information available)

3580. Pleasure (Supreme/Artclass; 1931–32). *Cast:* Conway Tearle, Carmel Myers, Frances Dade, Roscoe Karns. *D:* Otto Brower.

"Poverty row" drama.

3581. Pleasure Crazed (Fox; 1929). *Cast:* Dorothy Burgess, Marguerite Churchill, Kenneth MacKenna, Rex Bell, Henry Kolker, Charlotte Merriam. *D:* Donald Gallagher.

Low-budget comedy.

3582. Pleasure Cruise (Fox; 1933). *Cast:* Roland Young, Genevieve Tobin, Ralph Forbes, Una O'Connor, Minna Gombell, Herbert Mundin, Robert Greig, Arthur Hoyt, Theodore von Eltz, Frank Atkinson. *D:* Frank Tuttle; *Sc:* Guy Bolton; *St:* Austen Allen. (1:12)

A husband and wife decide to take separate vacations in this marital comedy.

The Plot Thickens (G.B. title) *see* **Here Comes Cookie**

3583. The Plot Thickens (RKO; 1936). *Cast:* ZaSu Pitts (Hildegarde Withers), James Gleason (Oscar Piper), Owen Davis, Jr., Louise Latimer, Arthur Aylesworth, Paul Fix, Richard Tucker, Barbara Barondess, James Donlan, Agnes Anderson, Oscar Apfel. *D:* Ben Holmes; *As.P.:* William Sistrom; *St:* Stuart Palmer; *Sc:* Jack Townley, Clarence Upson Young. (G.B. title: *The Swinging Pearl Mystery*) (1:09)

Sleuthing old maid school teacher Hildegarde Withers solves another murder-mystery with the help of police inspector Oscar Piper in this B entry in a series of six films.

3584. The Plough and the Stars (RKO; 1936). *Cast:* Barbara Stanwyck,

Preston Foster, Barry Fitzgerald (American debut), Denis O'Dea, Eileen Crowe, F.J. McCormick, Una O'Connor, Arthur Shields (film debut), J.M. Kerrigan, Moroni Olsen, Bonita Granville, Mary Gordon, Doris Lloyd, Erin O'Brien-Moore, Cyril McLaglen, Neil Fitzgerald, Brandon Hurst. *D:* John Ford, George Nicholls, Jr. (unc.); *As.P.:* Cliff Reid, Robert Sisk; *Sc:* Dudley Nichols. (1:18)

A domestic drama which is set in Ireland's 1916 revolutionary period. Based on the 1926 play by Sean O'Casey, the film was a financial deficit for the studio.

Pluck of the Irish (G.B. title) *see* **Great Guy**

3585. The Plutocrat (Xxxx Xxxx; 1931). *Cast:* Will Rogers, Jetta Goudal, Joel McCrea. *D:* David Butler.

Alternate title for "Business and Pleasure."

3586. The Pocatello Kid (Tiffany; 1931). *Cast:* Ken Maynard (in a dual role), Marceline Day, Richard Cramer, Charles King, Lafe McKee, Lew Meehan, Jack Rockwell, Bert Lindley, Bud Osborne, Bob Reeves, Jack Ward. *D:* Phil Rosen; *P:* Phil Goldstone (for Amity productions); *Sc:* W. Scott Darling. (1:01) (video)

Ken Maynard western of a cowboy who takes the place of his twin brother, a corrupt lawman he believes he has killed.

3587. Pocomania (Lenwal; 1939). *Cast:* Nina Mae McKinney, Jack Carter, Ida James, Hamtree Harrington. *D:* Arthur Leonard; *P:* Leonard; *Sc:* George Terwilliger. (aka: *Devil's Daughter*)

A tale of voodoo filmed on location in Jamaica with an all black cast. A remake of *Ouanga* (q.v.).

3588. Pointed Heels (Paramount; 1929). *Cast:* William Powell, Fay Wray, Phillips Holmes, Helen Kane, Skeets Gallagher, Eugene Pallette,

Adrienne Dore. *D:* A. Edward Sutherland; *St:* Charles Brackett; *Sc:* Florence Ryerson, John V.A. Weaver. (1:01)

Bootleg liquor figures prominently in making a show a hit in this romantic backstage musical-drama with a ballet sequence filmed in 2-color technicolor.

3589. Police Call (Showmen's Pictures; 1933). *Cast:* Nick Stuart, Roberta Gale, Robert Ellis, Merna Kennedy, Eddie Phillips, Mary Carr, Ralph Freud, Walter McGrail, Harry Myers, Warner Richmond. *D:* Philip H. Whitman.

Low-budget independent crime melodrama.

3590. Police Car 17 (Columbia; 1933). *Cast:* Tim McCoy, Evalyn Knapp, Harold Huber, Ward Bond. *D:* Lambert Hillyer; *St:* Norman Keen.

Low-budget crime melodrama.

3591. Police Court (Monogram; 1932). *Cast:* Henry B. Walthall, Al St. John, Leon Janney, Aileen Pringle, King Baggot, Lionel Belmore, Edmund Breese, Walter James. *D:* Louis King; *P:* I.E. Chadwick; *St & Sc:* Stuart Anthony. (aka: *Fame Street*) (1:03)

"Poverty row" drama of a once great actor, now an alcoholic who is given support by his loving son.

3592. Politics (MGM; 1931). *Cast:* Marie Dressler, Polly Moran, Karen Morley, William Bakewell, John Miljan, Joan Marsh, Kane Richmond, Mary Alden, Roscoe Ates, Tom McGuire. *D:* Charles Reisner; *St:* Zelda Sears, Malcolm Stuart Boylan; *Sc:* Sears, Boylan; *Adapt.:* Wells Root; *Dial.:* Robert E. Hopkins.

A hit comedy, the 5th production to star the popular comedy duo of Marie Dressler and Polly Moran, with Dressler running for mayor in an attempt to clean up her town's corruption. One of the 15 top grossing films of 1930–31.

3593. Polly of the Circus (MGM; 1931–32). *Cast:* Marion Davies,

Clark Gable, Raymond Hatton, C. Aubrey Smith, David Landau, Maude Eburne, Ruth Selwyn, Guinn Williams, Ray Milland, Little Billy, Lillian Elliott, Clark Marshall. *D:* Alfred Santell; *P:* Marion Davies; *Sc:* Carey Wilson, Laurence Johnson. (1:10)

Flop romantic drama of a circus trapeze artist who falls for a minister. A remake of the 1917 Samuel Goldwyn production (Goldwyn's first), based on the play by Margaret Mayo.

3594. Polo Joe (WB; 1936). *Cast:* Joe E. Brown (his last film for this studio), Carol Hughes, Richard "Skeets" Gallagher, Joseph King, George E. Stone, Fay Holden, Gordon (Bill) Elliott, Olive Tell, Charles Foy, Frank Orth, John Kelly, David Newell, Milton Kibbee. *D:* William McGann; *P:* Bryan Foy; *Sc:* Peter Milne, Hugh Cummings. (1:02)

B comedy of a guy who learns to play polo to impress his highbrow girl friend.

3595. Poor Little Rich Girl (20th Century–Fox; 1936). *Cast:* Shirley Temple, Jack Haley, Alice Faye, Gloria Stuart, Michael Whalen, Jane Darwell, Sara Haden, Claude Gillingwater, Henry Armetta, Billy Gilbert, John Wray, John Kelly, Charles Coleman, Paul Stanton, Mathilde Comont. *D:* Irving Cummings; *P:* Darryl F. Zanuck; *St:* Eleanor Gates, Ralph Spence; *Sc:* Harry Tugend, Gladys Lehman, Sam Hellman; *Songs:* Mack Gordon, Harry Revel. (1:12) (video)

Popular musical of a little girl who runs away from home and joins a vaudeville troupe. A remake of Mary Pickford's film of the same name (Paramount-Artclass; 1917). Computer-colored prints were produced in 1988.

3596. The Poor Millionaire (Biltmore; 1929–30). *Cast:* Richard Talmadge. *D:* George Melford; *Sc:* Henry Lehrman.

Low-budget comedy.

3597. The Poor Rich (Universal; 1934). *Cast:* Edna May Oliver, Edward Everett Horton, Grant Mitchell, Leila Hyams, Andy Devine, E.E. Clive, Henry Armetta, Una O'Connor, Ward Bond, Sidney Bracy, Thelma Todd, John Miljan, Jack Clifford. *D:* Edward Sedgwick. (1:16)

B comedy of a couple who feign a wealthy lifestyle to gain acceptance of rich friends.

3598. Poppy (Paramount; 1936). *Cast:* W.C. Fields (recreating his stage role as Eustace McGargle), Rochelle Hudson, Richard Cromwell, Catherine Doucet, Lynne Overman, Granville Bates, Maude Eburne, Rosalind Keith, Tom Kennedy, Helen Holmes, Bill Wolfe, Ralph Remley, Adrian Morris, Dewey Robinson. *D:* A. Edward Sutherland; *P:* William LeBaron; *As.P.:* Paul M. Jones; *Sc:* Waldemar Young, Virginia Van Upp. (1:14)

Hit comedy of a father's attempts to find a place for his daughter with the society crowd. First filmed as *Poppy* (Select; 1917) with Norma Talmadge and Eugene O'Brien. Remade as *Sally of the Sawdust* (D.W. Griffith; 1925) with W.C. Fields and Carol Dempster, the title of the play on which it is based by Dorothy Donnelly.

3599. Port of Hate (Metropolitan/Times; 1939). *Cast:* Polly Ann Young, Kenneth Harlan, Monte Blue. *D:* Harry S. Webb.

"Poverty row" drama.

3600. Port of Lost Dreams (Chesterfield; 1934). *Cast:* Bill Boyd, Lola Lane, Robert Elliott, Lafe McKee, Harold Huber, Charles Wilson. *D:* Frank Strayer.

"Poverty row" melodrama.

3601. Port of Missing Girls (Monogram; 1938). *Cast:* Judith Allen, Milburn Stone, Harry Carey, Betty Compson, Matty Fain, Jane Jones, George Cleveland, William Costello, Sandra Karina, Lyle Moraine, Louis

Vincent. *D:* Karl Brown; *P:* Lon Young; *Sc:* Brown. (1:05)

B melodrama of a night club entertainer who flees to the Orient when she is wrongfully implicated in a gangland murder. A remake of a 1928 silent production.

3602. Port of Seven Seas (MGM; 1938). *Cast:* Wallace Beery, Maureen O'Sullivan, Frank Morgan, John Beal, Jessie Ralph, Cora Witherspoon, Etienne Girardot, E. Alyn Warren. *D:* James Whale; *P:* Henry Henigson; *Sc:* Preston Sturges. (1:21)

Romance set on the Marseilles waterfront. Based on Marcel Pagnol's "Marius" trilogy, which was filmed again later in France as a three feature trilogy *(Marius, Fanny* and *Cesar)* and again in the U.S. in 1960 as *Fanny.*

3603. Portia on Trial (Republic; 1937). *Cast:* Heather Angel, Chick Chandler, Barbara Pepper, Frieda Inescort, Walter Abel, Leo Gorcey, Neil Hamilton, Hobart Bosworth, Ruth Donnelly, George Cooper, Paul Stanton, John Kelly, Anthony Marsh, Clarence Kolb, Ian MacLaren. *D:* George Nicholls, Jr.; *P:* Albert E. LeVoy; *St:* Faith Baldwin; *Sc:* Samuel Ornitz; *Music:* (A.A.N.) Alberto Colombo. (G.B. title: *The Trial of Portia Merriman*)

B courtroom drama.

3604. Possessed (MGM; 1931). *Cast:* Joan Crawford, Clark Gable, Wallace Ford, Skeets Gallagher, Frank Conroy, Marjorie White, John Miljan, Clara Blandick. *D:* Clarence Brown; *Sc:* Lenore Coffee. (1:12) (video)

Hit romantic melodrama of the depression era which was considered to be sexually explicit in 1931. Based on the play "The Mirage" by Edgar Selwyn.

3605. The Postal Inspector (Universal; 1936). *Cast:* Patricia Ellis, Ricardo Cortez, Bela Lugosi, Michael Loring, Billy Burrud, Hattie McDaniel. *D:* Otto Brower; *P:* Robert Presnell; *St:* Presnell, Horace McCoy. (0:58)

B melodrama of a mail theft and acts of mail fraud.

3606. Powdersmoke Range (RKO; 1935). *Cast:* Harry Carey (Tucson Smith), Hoot Gibson (Stony Brooke), Guinn Williams (Lullaby Joslin), Bob Steele, Tom Tyler, Sam Hardy, William Farnum, Boots Mallory, Franklyn Farnum, William Desmond, Buddy Roosevelt, Buffalo Bill, Jr. (final film—retired), Buzz Barton, Wally Wales (Hal Taliaferro), Art Mix, Ray Mayer, Adrian Morris, Ethan Laidlaw, Frank Rice. *D:* Wallace Fox; *As.P.:* Cliff Reid; *Sc:* Adele Buffington (who typed out many a western screenplay in her Hollywood career). (1:11) (video)

Considered a minor classic among western film buffs, this oater is based on William Colt MacDonald's 1934 book of the same name which introduces the characters "The Three Mesquiteers," but has nothing to do with the later series by Republic. A basic "clean up the town" plot, the film is particularly notable for its large cast of horse opera stars.

3607. The Power and the Glory (Fox; 1933). *Cast:* Spencer Tracy, Colleen Moore, Ralph Morgan, Helen Vinson, J. Farrell MacDonald, Clifford Jones, Bill O'Brien, Cullen Johnston, Sarah Padden. *D:* William K. Howard; *P:* Jesse L. Lasky; *St & Sc:* Preston Sturges. (1:16)

Drama of a business tycoon's rise to power and his final corruption by greed. Told in flashbacks, some consider it not unlike *Citizen Kane* (RKO; 1941).

3608. Prairie Justice (Universal; 1938). *Cast:* Bob Baker, Dorothy Fay, Hal Taliaferro, Jack Rockwell, Carleton Young, Jack Kirk, Forrest Taylor, Glenn Strange, Tex Palmer, Slim Whitaker, Murdock MacQuarrie. *D:* George Waggner; *P:* Trem Carr; *Sc:* Joseph West (Waggner). (0:58)

Bob Baker western with songs.

3609. Prairie Moon (Republic; 1938). *Cast:* Gene Autry, Shirley Deane, Smiley Burnette, Tommy Ryan, Tom London, William Pawley, Warner Richmond, Walter Tetley, David Gorcey, Stanley Andrews, Peter Potter, Bud Osborne, Ray Bennett, Jack Rockwell, Hal Price, Merrill McCormack, Lew Meehan, Jack Kirk, Champion. *D:* Ralph Staub; *P:* Harry Grey; *Sc:* Betty Burbridge, Stanley Roberts; *Songs Include:* "In the Jailhouse Now" by Jimmie Rodgers. (0:58) (video)

Gene Autry western with songs and a story of cattle rustling.

Prairie Sundown (G.B. title) *see* **Sundown on the Prairie**

3610. Prairie Thunder (WB/ F.N.; 1937). *Cast:* Dick Foran, Ellen Clancy (Janet Shaw), Wilfred Lucas, Frank Orth, Frank Ellis, Yakima Canutt, George Chesebro, John Harron, Albert J. Smith, "Slim" Whitaker, J.P. McGowan, Jack Mower, Henry Otho, Paul Panzer, Smoke the Wonder Horse. *D:* B. Reeves Eason; *P:* Bryan Foy; *Sc:* Ed Earl Repp. (0:54)

Dick Foran western of a cavalry scout who looks into sabotaged telegraph lines supposedly destroyed by Indians.

3611. The Prescott Kid (Columbia; 1934). *Cast:* Tim McCoy, Sheila Mannors, Alden Chase (later known as Stephen Chase), Hooper Atchley, Joseph (Sawyer) Sauers, Albert J. Smith, Ernie Adams, Charles King, Slim Whitaker, Bud Osborne, Walter Brennan. *D:* David Selman; *Sc:* Ford Beebe. (1:00)

Tim McCoy oater of a cowboy mistaken for the newly expected marshal.

3612. Prescription for Romance (Universal; 1937). *Cast:* Kent Taylor, Wendy Barrie, Mischa Auer, Frank Jenks, George Cleveland, Gregory Gaye, Frank Reicher, Samuel S. Hinds, William Lundigan. *D:* S. Sylvan Simon; *P:* Edmund Grainger. (1:10)

Set in Hungary, this B romance follows a detective on the trail of an embezzler.

Present Arms (G.B. title) *see* **Leathernecking**

3613. The President Vanishes (Paramount; 1934). *Cast:* Edward Arnold, Paul Kelly, Rosalind Russell, Sidney Blackmer, Walter Kingsford, Peggy Conklin, Osgood Perkins, Janet Beecher, Charley Grapewin, Arthur Byron, Edward Ellis, Andy Devine, Robert McWade, Jason Robards, J. Carrol Naish, Tom Dugan, DeWitt Jennings, Charles Richman, Douglas Wood. *D:* William A. Wellman; *P:* Walter Wanger; *Sc:* Lynn Starling, Carey Wilson, Cedric Worth. (G.B. title: *The Strange Conspiracy*)

A political mystery-comedy of a United States president who fakes his own kidnapping to prove a point. The film based on an anonymous novel was a box office flop.

3614. The President's Mystery (Republic; 1936). *Cast:* Henry Wilcoxon, Betty Furness, Evelyn Brent, Sidney Blackmer, Wade Boteler, Arthur Aylesworth, Guy Usher, Mel Ruick, Si Jenks, Barnett Parker. *D:* Phil Rosen; *P:* Nat Levine; *St:* Anthony Abbot, Samuel Hopkins Adams, Rupert Hughes, Rita Weiman, S.S. Van Dine, John Erskine; *Sc:* Nathanael West, Lester Cole. (G.B. title: *One for All*)

Hit low-budget mystery which was based on a popular novel inspired by U.S. president Franklin D. Roosevelt.

3615. Prestige (RKO-Pathé; 1932). *Cast:* Ann Harding, Adolphe Menjou, Melvyn Douglas, Ian MacLaren, Guy Bates Post, Rollo Lloyd, Clarence Muse, Tetsu Komai, Creighton Hale, Carmelita Geraghty. *D:* Tay Garnett; *As.P.:* Harry Joe Brown; *Adaptation:* Garnett, Rollo Lloyd; *Sc:* Francis Edwards Faragoh; *Song:* Harold Lewis, Bernie Grossman. (1:11)

A jungle melodrama set in a

Malayan penal colony. Based on the novel "Lips of Steel" by Harry Hervey.

3616. The Preview Murder Mystery (Paramount; 1936). *Cast:* Reginald Denny, Frances Drake, Gail Patrick, Rod La Rocque, Bryant Washburn, Jack Mulhall, Franklyn Farnum, Ian Keith, Conway Tearle, Chester Conklin, Henry Kleinbach (Henry Brandon), Thomas Jackson, Jack Raymond, Lee Shumway, Jack Norton, Eddie Dunn. *D:* Robert Florey; *P:* Harold Hurley; *St:* Garnett Weston; *Sc:* Robert Yost, Brian Marlow.

Two murders on a Hollywood sound stage form the plot of this B mystery.

3617. Pride of the Blue Grass (WB; 1939). *Cast:* Edith Fellows, James McCallion, Granville Bates, Sam McDaniel, Arthur Loft. *D:* William McGann; *As.P.:* Bryan Foy; *Sc:* Vincent Sherman.

B horse racing drama involving a juvenile and a blind race horse.

3618. Pride of the Legion (Mascot; 1932–33). *Cast:* Victor Jory (film debut), Rin-Tin-Tin, Jr., Barbara Kent, J. Farrell MacDonald, Sally Blane, Glenn Tryon, Lucien Littlefield, Matt Moore, Ralph Ince, Jason Robards, Douglass Dumbrille. *D:* Ford Beebe; *St:* Peter B. Kyne; *Adaptation:* Beebe. (G.B. & Re-release title: *The Big Pay Off*) (1:10)

A cop accused of cowardice redeems himself in this B melodrama.

3619. Pride of the Marines (Columbia; 1936). *Cast:* Charles Bickford, Florence Rice, Robert Allen, Billy Burrud (film debut), Thurston Hall, Joe Sawyer, Ward Bond, George McKay. *D:* D. Ross Lederman; *St:* Gerald Beaumont; *Sc:* Harold Shumate.

B action drama.

3620. Pride of the Navy (Republic; 1939). *Cast:* James Dunn, Rochelle Hudson, Joseph Crehan, Horace MacMahon. *D:* Charles Lamont.

B romantic military service story of torpedo boats.

3621. Pride of the West (Paramount; 1938). *Cast:* William Boyd (Cassidy), Russell Hayden (Lucky), George Hayes (Windy), Charlotte Field, Earle Hodgins, Billy King, Kenneth Harlan, Glenn Strange, James Craig, Bruce Mitchell. *D:* Lesley Selander; *P:* Harry M. Sherman; *Sc:* Nate Watt. (0:56)

"Hopalong Cassidy" western, 17th entry in the series with the Bar 20 boys going up against a crooked land agent.

3622. The Prince and the Pauper (WB; 1937). *Cast:* Errol Flynn, Billy & Bobby Mauch (real life twins), Claude Rains (Earl of Hertford), Alan Hale, Montagu Love (Henry VIII), Henry Stephenson (Duke of Norfolk), Lester Matthews, Barton MacLane, Eric Portman, Lionel Pape, Halliwell Hobbes, Fritz Leiber, Phyllis Barry, Leonard Willey, Robert Warwick, Murray Kinnell, Ian Wolfe, Holmes Herbert, Ivan Simpson, Harry Cording, Mary Field, Elspeth Dudgeon, Helen Valkis, Robert Adair, St. Luke's Choristers. *D:* William Keighley; *P:* Robert Lord; *Sc:* Laird Doyle. (2:00) (video)

Mark Twain's classic of two boys (who would pass for twins), one a street urchin, the other a prince who exchange positions in life. Previous versions: (Biograph; 1909) with Miss Cecil Spooner, (Famous Players; 1915) with Marguerite Clark and Edwin Mordante, and one in 1922. Remade in 1977 (U.S. title: *Crossed Swords*), as well as 2-part Disney production for TV in 1962. Computer-colored by Turner Entertainment in 1987.

3623. The Prince of Diamonds (Columbia; 1930). *Cast:* Ian Keith, Aileen Pringle, Claude King, Fritzi Ridgeway, Gilbert Emery, Tom Ricketts. *D:* Karl Brown, A.H. Van Buren.

"Poverty row" romantic comedy.

3624. The Princess and the Plumber (Fox; 1930). *Cast:* Charles Farrell, Maureen O'Sullivan, Louise Closser Hale, Lucien Prival, H.B. Warner, Murray Kinnell, Arnold Lucy, Bert Roach. *D:* Alexander Korda; *St:* Alice Duer Miller; *Sc:* Howard Green.
Low-budget romantic comedy.

3625. The Princess Comes Across (Paramount; 1936). *Cast:* Carole Lombard, Fred MacMurray (in a role originally scheduled for George Raft), Alison Skipworth, Douglass Dumbrille, William Frawley, Porter Hall, Sig Rumann, George Barbier, Lumsden Hare, Mischa Auer, Tetsu Komai, Milburn Stone, Bradley Page. *D:* William K. Howard; *P:* Arthur Hornblow, Jr.; *Sc:* Frank Butler, Don Hartman, Walter De Leon, Francis Martin, Claude Binyon, J.B. Priestley. (1:16)
A girl posing as royalty on an ocean voyage gets involved in murder. This romantic mystery-comedy was based on two novels, one by Louis Lucien Rogger, the other by Philip MacDonald.

3626. Princess O'Hara (Universal; 1935). *Cast:* Chester Morris, Jean Parker, Leon Errol, Vince Barnett, Verna Hillie, Clara Blandick, Henry Armetta, Tom Dugan, Clifford Jones, Anne Howard, Dorothy Gray, Ralph Remley, Jimmy Fay, Pepi Sinoff. *D:* David Burton; *St:* Damon Runyon; *Sc:* Harry Clork, Doris Malloy. (1:14)
B comedy of a gang of hoods who are protecting a girl. Remade in 1943 as *It Ain't Hay.*

3627. Prison Break (Universal; 1938). *Cast:* Barton MacLane, Glenda Farrell, Constance Moore, Paul Hurst, Ward Bond, Edward Pawley, Edmund MacDonald, Victor Kilian, Glenn Strange, Frank Darien, John Russell. *D:* Arthur Lubin; *P:* Trem Carr; *Sc:* Norton S. Parker, Dorothy Reid. (1:12)
B drama of a fisherman sent to prison for a murder he didn't commit who must deal with rigid parole restrictions when he is finally released. Based on the story "Walls of San Quentin" by Norton S. Parker.

3628. Prison Farm (Paramount; 1938). *Cast:* Lloyd Nolan, John Howard, Shirley Ross, Marjorie Main, J. Carrol Naish, Porter Hall, Anna Q. Nilsson, Esther Dale, Mae Busch, May Boley, Ruth Warren, Philip Warren, John Hart, Virginia Dabney, Howard Mitchell, Gloria Williams, Diane Wood, Robert Brister, William Holden (film debut as an extra). *D:* Louis King; *P:* Stuart Walker; *St:* Edwin Wastrate; *Sc:* Robert Yost, Eddie Welch, Stuart Anthony. (1:09)
B melodrama of a co-ed prison farm.

3629. Prison Nurse (Republic; 1938). *Cast:* Marian Marsh, Henry Wilcoxon, John Arledge, Frank Reicher, Ben Welden, Fred Kohler, Jr., Minerva Urecal, Selmer Jackson, Ray Mayer, Norman Willis, Addison Richards, Bernadene Hayes. *D:* James Cruze; *St:* Dr. Louis Berg, Adele Buffington; *Sc:* Earl Felton, Sidney Salkow.
Title tells all in this B production.

3630. Prison Shadows (Victory; 1936). *Cast:* Eddie Nugent, Forrest Taylor. *D:* Robert F. Hill; *P:* Sam Katzman.
Independent B melodrama.

3631. Prison Train (Equity; 1938). *Cast:* Peter Potter, Linda Winters (Dorothy Comingore), Fred Keating, Franklyn Farnum, Clarence Muse, Nestor Paiva, Sam Bernard, Kit Guard. *D:* Gordon Wiles; *P:* Bennie F. Zeidman. (aka: *People's Enemy*) (1:24) (video)
Indie B melodrama of gangsters who are attempting to rub out one of their own who is en route to prison via rail.

3632. The Prisoner of Shark Island (20th Century–Fox; 1936). *Cast:* Warner Baxter (Dr. Mudd), Gloria Stuart (Peggy Mudd), Claude Gillingwater, Sr. (Colonel Dyer), Joyce Kay (Marth Mudd), John Carradine (Sgt. Rankin), Harry Carey (commandant),

Ernest Whitman (Buck), Arthur Byron (Erickson, final film—ret.), O.P. Heggie (Dr. McIntire, final film—d. 1936), Frank McGlynn, Sr. (Abraham Lincoln), Douglas Wood (General Ewing), Fred Kohler, Jr. (Sgt. Cooper), Paul Fix (David Herold), Francis McDonald (John Wilkes Booth), John McGuire (Lovett), Paul McVey (Hunter), Francis Ford (O'Toole), Frank Shannon (Judge Advocate Holt), Lloyd Whitlock (Major Rathbone), Leila McIntyre (Mrs. Lincoln), Murdock MacQuarrie (Spangler), Cecil Weston (Mrs. Surratt), Cyril Thornton (Maurice O'Laughlin), Beulah Hall Jones (Blanche), J.M. Kerrigan (Judge Maiben), Etta McDaniel (Rosabelle), Arthur Loft, Maurice Murphy, Ronald (Jack) Pennick, Paul Stanton, Merrill McCormack, James Marcus, Jan Duggan, Dick Elliott, Robert Dudley, Duke Lee, Wilfred Lucas, Robert E. Homans, Bud Geary, J.P. McGowan, Harry Strang. *D:* John Ford; *P:* Darryl F. Zanuck; *As.P.:* Nunnally Johnson; *Sc:* Johnson. (1:35) (video)

Fact-based story of Dr. Samuel Mudd who unknowingly set the broken leg of John Wilkes Booth following the assassination of Abraham Lincoln and was subsequently sentenced to life in prison. The film placed #9 on the "10 Best" list of the National Board of Review. It was reworked in 1952 as *Hellgate,* with the same story appearing as a 1980 TV movie entitled *The Ordeal of Dr. Mudd.*

3633. The Prisoner of Zenda (United Artists/Selznick International; 1937). *Cast:* Ronald Colman (in a dual role as Rudolph Rassendyl & King Rudolf V), Madeleine Carroll (Princess Flavia), Douglas Fairbanks, Jr. (Rupert of Hentzau), Mary Astor (Antionette De Mauban), C. Aubrey Smith (Colonel Zapt), Raymond Massey (Black Michael), David Niven (Capt. Fritz von Tarlenheim), Montagu Love (Detchard), Byron Foulger (Johann), William von Brincken (Kraftstein), Phillip Sleeman (Lauengram), Ralph Faulkner (Bersonin), Alexander D'Arcy (De Gauiet), Torben Meyer (Michael's butler), Lawrence Grant (Marshal Strakencz), Howard Lang (Josef), Emmett King (Lord High Chamberlain Von Haugwitz), Florence Roberts (Duenna), Eleanor Wesselhoeft (cook), Ian MacLaren (cardinal), Ben Webster, Evelyn Beresford, Boyd Irwin, Charles K. French, Al Shean, Charles Halton, Otto Fries, Spencer Charters, Russ Powell, Francis Ford, D'Arcy Corrigan, Vladimir Sokoloff. *D:* John Cromwell, W.S. Van Dyke; *P:* David O. Selznick; *Adaptation:* Wells Root; *Sc:* John Balderston, Donald Ogden Stewart; *Art-Set Decoration:* (A.A.N.) Lyle Wheeler; *Music:* (A.A.N.) Alfred Newman. (1:41) (video)

Classic adventure of a commoner who stands in for his look-alike cousin, the King. Partially filmed in sepiatones, it was based on the 1894 novel by Anthony J. Hope (Sir Anthony Hope Hawkins) and the play adapted from it by Edward Rose. Previously filmed: (Famous Players; 1913) with James K. Hackett and Beatrice Beckly, (Metro; 1922) with Ramon Novarro, with remakes (MGM; 1952) and (Universal; 1979).

3634. Prisoners (WB/F.N.; 1929). *Cast:* Corinne Griffith, Ian Keith, Otto Matiesen, Julanne Johnston, Baron von Hesse, Bela Lugosi. *D:* William A. Seiter: *St:* Ferenc Molnar; *Sc:* Forrest Halsey.

Part-talkie drama of an Austrian cabaret singer sentenced to prison when her lawyer lover is unable to get her off, but finds him waiting when her sentence is up.

Private Affairs (G.B. title) *see* **Public Stenographer**

3635. Private Detective (WB/F.N.; 1939). *Cast:* Jane Wyman, Dick Foran, Gloria Dickson, Maxie Rosenbloom, John Ridgely, Morgan Conway, John Eldredge. *D:* Noel Smith; *As.P.:* Bryan Foy; *St:* Kay Krausse; *Sc:* Earle Snell, Raymond Schrock.

B melodrama of a female private dick working with a rival homicide investigator to solve a murder.

3636. Private Detective 62 (WB; 1933). *Cast:* William Powell, Margaret Lindsay, Arthur Hohl, Ruth Donnelly, Natalie Moorhead, Arthur Byron, Gordon Westcott, James Bell, Hobart Cavanaugh, Irving Bacon, Sheila Terry. *D:* Michael Curtiz; *P:* Hal Wallis; *St:* Raoul Whitfield; *Sc:* Rian James. (Retitled: *Man Killer*) (1:07)

A detective falls for the woman he is hired to investigate in this low-budget production.

3637. Private Jones (Universal; 1933). *Cast:* Lee Tracy, Donald Cook, Gloria Stuart, Walter Catlett, Berton Churchill, Richard Cramer, Russell Gleason, Ethel Clayton, Frank McHugh, Hans von Twardowsky, Richard Carle, Al Hill, Shirley Grey, Roland Varno. *D:* Russell Mack; *St:* Richard Schayer; *Sc:* Prescott Chaplin, William N. Robson.

World War I comedy of a draftee with numerous problems.

3638. Private Lives (MGM; 1931). *Cast:* Norma Shearer (Amanda Paynne), Robert Montgomery, Una Merkel, Reginald Denny, Jean Hersholt, George Davis. *D:* Sidney Franklin; *P:* Irving Thalberg; *Sc:* Claudine West, Hans Kräly, Richard Schayer. (1:24)

Comedy of a married couple who are constantly at each other's throats. Based on Noel Coward's 1930 play, it placed #9 on the "10 Best" list of the *New York Times*.

3639. The Private Lives of Elizabeth and Essex (WB; 1939). *Cast:* Bette Davis (Queen Elizabeth I), Errol Flynn (Earl of Essex), Olivia de Havilland (Lady Penelope Gray), Donald Crisp (Francis Bacon), Alan Hale (Earl of Tyrone), Vincent Price (Sir Walter Raleigh), Robert Warwick, Henry Daniell, Henry Stephenson, Nanette (Fabray) Fabares. *D:* Michael Curtiz; *As.P.:* Robert Lord; *Sc:* Norman Reilly Raine, Aeneas MacKenzie; *Cinematographers:* (A.A.N.) Sol Polito & W. Howard Greene (for color cinematography); *Art-Set Decoration:* (A.A.N.) Anton Grot; *Music:* (A.A.N.) Erich Wolfgang Korngold; *Sound Recording:* (A.A.N.) Nathan Levinson; *Special Effects:* (A.A.N.) Byron Haskin & Nathan Levinson. (Re-release title: *Elizabeth the Queen*) (1:46) (video)

Lavishly produced technicolor historical drama, based on the play "Elizabeth the Queen" by Maxwell Anderson. Fact blends with fiction.

3640. Private Number (20th Century–Fox; 1936). *Cast:* Loretta Young, Robert Taylor, Patsy Kelly, Basil Rathbone, Marjorie Gateson, Paul Harvey, Joe Lewis, Monroe Owsley, John Miljan, Kane Richmond, Jane Darwell, Paul Stanton, Billy Bevan. *D:* Roy Del Ruth; *P:* Raymond Griffith; *Sc:* Gene Markey, William Conselman. (G.B. title: *Secret Interlude*) (1:20)

A man from a wealthy family keeps his marriage to a household domestic a secret to keep from embarrassing them. Based on the novel "Common Clay" by Cleves Kinkead it was previously filmed twice under that title (Pathé; 1919) with Fannie Ward and W.E. Lawrence and 1933 (q.v.).

3640a. A Private Scandal (Headline; 1931). *Cast:* Marian Nixon, Lloyd Hughes, Walter Hiers, Lucile Powers, Theodore en Eltz, Fletcher Norton, Eddie Phillips, George Wells, Fred "Snowflake" Toones. *D:* Charles Hutchison; *St:* John Francis Natteford.

"Poverty row" crime drama.

3641. Private Scandal (Paramount; 1934). *Cast:* Phillips Holmes, Mary Brian, ZaSu Pitts, Ned Sparks, Lew Cody, John Qualen, Olive Tell, Rollo Lloyd, June Brewster, Harold Waldridge, Charles Sellon. *D:* Ralph Murphy; *St:* Vera Caspary, Bruce Manning.

B mystery of a supposed suicide which turns out to be murder.

3642. Private Worlds (Paramount; 1935). *Cast:* Claudette Colbert (A.A.N. for B.A.), Charles Boyer, Joel McCrea, Joan Bennett, Helen Vinson, Esther Dale, Jean Rouverol, Samuel S. Hinds, Guinn Williams, Theodore von Eltz, Maurice Murphy, Harry C. Bradley, Eleanore King, Julian Madison, Monte Vandergrift, Arnold Gray, Nick Shaid, Dora Clement, Sam Godfrey, Bess Flowers. *D:* Gregory La Cava; *P:* Walter Wanger; *Sc:* La Cava, Lynn Starling. (1:24)

An offbeat drama of a mental institution, its staff and its patients. Based on a popular novel of the day by Phyllis Bottome.

3643. The Prizefighter and the Lady (MGM; 1933). *Cast:* Myrna Loy, Max Baer (film debut), Otto Kruger, Walter Huston, Jack Dempsey, Primo Carnera, Jess Willard, James J. Jeffries, Vince Barnett, Robert McWade, Muriel Evans, Jean Howard. *D:* W.S. Van Dyke; *P:* Van Dyke; *As.P.:* Hunt Stromberg; *Original Story:* (A.A.N.) Frances Marion; *Sc:* John Meehan, John Lee Mahin. (G.B. title: *Every Woman's Man*) (1:42)

Drama of a boxer who falls for the moll of a local gangster.

3644. Probation (Chesterfield; 1932). *Cast:* Sally Blane, J. Farrell MacDonald, Roy Stewart, Frances Dean (Betty Grable), Clara Kimball Young. *D:* Richard Thorpe.

"Poverty row" melodrama.

3645. The Prodigal (MGM; 1931). *Cast:* Lawrence Tibbett, Esther Ralston, Roland Young, Cliff Edwards, Hedda Hopper, Purnell B. Pratt, Stepin Fetchit, Theodore von Eltz, John Larkin, Gertrude Howard, Emma Dunn, Wally Albright, Jr., Suzanne Ransom, Louis John Bartels. *D:* Harry Pollard; *Sc:* Bess Meredyth, Wells Root; *Song:* "Without a Song" by Vincent Youmans; *Other Songs:* Herbert Stothart, Jacques Wolfe, Howard Johnson. (Retitled: *The Southerner*) (1:16)

Drama of a man who returns to his southern family after a life on the road. A box office flop.

3646. The Prodigal Son (Universal; 1935). *Cast:* Luis Trenker, Maria Andergast, Marion Marsh. *D:* Luis Trenker. (1:00)

A German-American co-production of the dilemma suffered by a German immigrant to the United States while in New York City.

3647. Professional Soldier (20th Century–Fox; 1935). *Cast:* Victor McLaglen, Freddie Bartholomew, Gloria Stuart, Constance Collier, Michael Whalen (film debut), Dixie Dunbar, Lester Matthews, C. Henry Gordon, Pedro de Cordoba. *D:* Tay Garnett; *P:* Darryl F. Zanuck; *Sc:* Gene Fowler, Howard Ellis Smith. (1:15)

A friendship develops between a man and the young prince he has kidnapped. Based on a story by Damon Runyon.

3648. Professional Sweetheart (RKO; 1933). *Cast:* Ginger Rogers (Glory Eden), Norman Foster (Jim Davey), ZaSu Pitts, Frank McHugh, Allen Jenkins, Gregory Ratoff, Franklin Pangborn, Lucien Littlefield, Edgar Kennedy, Frank Darien, Betty Furness, Sterling Holloway. *D:* William A. Seiter; *As.P.:* H.N. Swanson; *Sc:* Maurine Watkins; *Song:* "My Imaginary Sweetheart" by Harry Akst, Edward Eliscu. (G.B. title: *Imaginary Sweetheart*) (1:13)

A satirical romance of a city girl who marries a country boy from the Kentucky hills as a publicity stunt for a radio sponsor.

3649. Professor Beware (Paramount; 1938). *Cast:* Harold Lloyd, Phyllis Welch, Raymond Walburn, William Frawley, Lionel Stander, Thurston Hall, Cora Witherspoon, Etienne Girardot, Sterling Holloway,

Spencer Charters, Montagu Love, Leonid Kinskey, Guinn Williams, Christian Rub, Charles Lane, Ward Bond, George Humbert, Mary Lou Lender. *D:* Elliott Nugent; *St:* Crampton Harris, Francis M. Cockrell, Marian B. Cockrell; *Sc:* Delmer Daves; *Adapt.:* Jack Cunningham, Clyde Bruckman. (1:27)

Comedy of an Egyptologist's cross country chase in pursuit of a rare tablet. Notable as Lloyd's last film for this studio, as well as his last film until 1947.

3650. Prosperity (MGM; 1932). *Cast:* Marie Dressler, Polly Moran, Anita Page, Norman Foster, Henry Armetta, John Miljan, Jacquie Lyn, Wallace Ford, John Roche, Frank Darien, Jerry Tucker, Charles Giblyn. *D:* Sam Wood; *P:* Arthur Hornblow, Jr.; *St:* Sylvia Thalberg, Frank Butler; *Sc:* Eve Greene, Zelda Sears, Butler. (1:30)

Hit depression-era comedy with the comedy duo of Marie Dressler and Polly Moran as mothers and mothers-in-law of a young married couple. The final film to pair Dressler and Moran.

The Public Be Hanged (G.B. title) *see* **The World Gone Mad**

3651. Public Cowboy No. 1 (Republic; 1937). *Cast:* Gene Autry, Smiley Burnette, Ann Rutherford, William Farnum, Arthur Loft, Frankie Marvin, House Peters, Jr., James C. Morton, Maston Williams, Frank LaRue, Milburn Morante, King Mojave, Hal Price, Jack Ingram, Ray Bennett. *D:* Joe Kane; *P:* Armand Schaefer; *St:* Bernard McConville; *Sc:* Oliver Drake; *Songs:* Felix Bernard, Paul Francis Webster, Oliver Drake, Fleming Allan, includes the sentimental "Old Buckaroo." (0:59)

Gene Autry western with songs of modern day cattle rustlers who use trucks and radios.

3652. The Public Defender (RKO; 1931). *Cast:* Richard Dix, Shirley Grey, Alan Roscoe, Boris Karloff, Paul Hurst, Purnell Pratt, Frank Sheridan,

Carl Gerard, Nella Walker, Ruth Weston, Edmund Breese, Robert Emmett O'Connor, Phillips Smalley, William Halligan. *D:* J. Walter Ruben; *As.P.:* Louis Sarecky; *Sc:* Bernard Schubert. (1:10)

Hit crime melodrama of a man who poses as a crook to get the goods on those involved in bank larceny. Based on the book "The Splendid Crime" by George Goodchild.

3653. The Public Enemy (WB/ Vitaphone; 1931). *Cast:* James Cagney (Tom Powers), Edward Woods (Matt Doyle), Donald Cook (Mike Powers), Joan Blondell (Mamie), Jean Harlow (Gwen Allen), Mae Clarke (Kitty), Beryl Mercer (Mrs. Powers), Mia Marvin (Jane), Leslie Fenton (Nails Nathan), Robert Emmett O'Connor (Paddy Ryan), Murray Kinnell (Putty Nose), Ben Hendricks, Jr. (Bugs Moran), Rita Flynn (Molly), Clark Burroughs (Dutch), Snitz Edwards (Hack), Frankie Darro (Matt as a boy), Lee Phelps (Steve, the bartender), Frank (Junior) Coghlan (Tommy as a boy), Dorothy Gee (Nails' girl friend), Robert E. Homans (Officer Pat Burke), Purnell Pratt (Officer Powers), Adele Watson (Mrs. Doyle), Ben Hendricks III (Bugs as a boy), Eddie Kane (Joe, the headwaiter), Charles Sullivan (Mug), Sam McDaniel, George Daly, Helen Parrish, Dorothy Gray, Nanci Price, Douglas Gerrard, William H. Strauss. *D:* William A. Wellman; *P:* Kubec Glasmon; *Adaptation:* Harvey Thew. (G.B. title: *Enemies of the Public*) (1:24) (video)

One of the classics of the genre and the era, this crime melodrama ruthlessly tells of the rise and fall of two bootleggers in the kingdom of organized crime. The scene in this film where Cagney shoves a grapefruit half into the kisser of Mae Clarke is a classic in it's own right. When this film originally started production Cagney had the role of "Matt Doyle" and Woods had the role of "Tom Powers," but studio heads insisted the actors reverse their roles. The original story

"Beer and Blood" by John Bright and Kubec Glasmon received an A.A.N. The film had an original running time of 1:36, but had about 12 minutes of footage cut for release.

3654. Public Enemy No. 1 (Xxxx Xxxx; 1937). (No information available)

3655. Public Enemy's Wife (WB; 1935–36). *Cast:* Pat O'Brien, Margaret Lindsay, Cesar Romero, Robert Armstrong, Dick Foran, Dick Purcell, Joseph King, Addison Richards, Hal K. Dawson, Selmer Jackson, Alan Bridge, William Pawley, Harry Hayden. *D:* Nick Grinde; *P:* Sam Bischoff; *St:* David O. Selznick, P.J. Wolfson; *Sc:* Abem Finkel, Harold Buckley. (G.B. title: *G-Man's Wife*)

Gangster melodrama which was remade as *Bullets for O'Hara* (WB; 1941) with Roger Pryor and Joan Perry.

3656. Public Hero No. 1 (MGM; 1935). *Cast:* Lionel Barrymore, Jean Arthur, Chester Morris, Joseph Calleia, Paul Kelly, Lewis Stone, Paul Hurst, George E. Stone, Sam Baker, Selmer Jackson, Cora Sue Collins, Lillian Harmer, John Kelly, Lawrence Wheat. *D:* J. Walter Ruben; *P:* Lucien Hubbard; *St:* Wells Root, Ruben; *Sc:* Root. (1:29)

Hit crime melodrama with the good guys out to get the notorious "Purple Gang." Remade as *The Getaway* (MGM; 1941).

3657. The Public Menace (Columbia; 1935). *Cast:* Jean Arthur, George Murphy, Victor Kilian, Thurston Hall, Douglass Dumbrille, Bradley Page, Charles Wilson. *D:* Erle C. Kenton.

B gangster melodrama.

3658. Public Opinion (Chesterfield; 1935). *Cast:* Richard Carlyle, Lois Wilson, Robert Frazer, Florence Roberts, Crane Wilbur, Andres De Segurola. *D:* Frank Strayer.

Low-budget melodrama.

3659. Public Stenographer (Marcy Exchange; 1933). *Cast:* William Collier, Jr., Lola Lane, Duncan Renaldo, Jason Robards, Al St. John. *D:* Lewis D. Collins; *Sc:* Collins, Joe Connell (co-writer). (G.B. title: *Private Affairs*)

Romantic comedy of the independent low-budget variety.

3660. Public Wedding (WB; 1937). *Cast:* Jane Wyman, William Hopper, Dick Purcell, Berton Churchill, James Robbins, Marie Wilson, Veda Ann Borg, Frank Faylen, Raymond Hatton. *D:* Nick Grinde; *P:* Bryan Foy; *Sc:* Roy Chanslor, Houston Branch.

Much to the chagrin of those involved, a publicity stunt wedding winds up as the real thing in this B comedy.

3661. The Pueblo Terror (Cosmos; 1930–31). *Cast:* Buffalo Bill, Jr., Yakima Canutt, Wanda Hawley, Art Mix. *D:* Alvin J. Neitz (aka: Alan James).

Buffalo Bill, Jr., western.

3662. The Purchase Price (WB; 1932). *Cast:* Barbara Stanwyck, George Brent, Lyle Talbot, Hardie Albright, David Landau, Murray Kinnell, Leila Bennett, Snub Pollard, Clarence Wilson, Adele Watson, Victor Potel, Lucille Ward, Dawn O'Day (Anne Shirley). *D:* William A. Wellman; *St:* Arthur Stringer; *Sc:* Robert Lord. (1:07)

A city girl goes west as a mail-order bride in order to escape her gangster boyfriend in this B marital drama.

3663. The Purple Vigilantes (Republic; 1938). *Cast:* Ray Corrigan (Tucson Smith), Bob Livingston (Stony Brooke), Max Terhune (Lullaby), Joan Barclay, Earle Hodgins, Earl Dwire, Jack Perrin, Francis Sayles, George Chesebro, Robert Fiske, William Gould, Ernie Adams, Harry Strang, Ed Cassidy, Frank O'Connor. *D:* George Sherman; *Sc:* Betty Burbridge, Oliver Drake. (0:58) (video)

Twelfth entry in the "Three Mesquiteers" series as the trio go up against a gang of outlaws terrorizing a town by posing as vigilantes.

3664. Pursued (Fox; 1934). *Cast:* Victor Jory, Russell Hardie, Rosemary Ames, Pert Kelton, George Irving. *D:* Louis King; *Sc:* Lester Cole, Stuart Anthony.
(No other information available)

3665. Pursuit (MGM; 1935). *Cast:* Chester Morris, Sally Eilers, Scotty Beckett, Henry Travers, Dorothy Peterson, C. Henry Gordon, Minor Watson, Harold Huber, Dewey Robinson. *D:* Edwin L. Marin; *P:* Lucien Hubbard; *Sc:* Wells Root.
B chase thriller of a flyer and a lady detective who are hired to get a young boy out of the country. Based on the novel by L.G. Blochman.

3666. The Pursuit of Happiness (Paramount; 1934). *Cast:* Joan Bennett, Francis Lederer, Charles Ruggles, Mary Boland, Walter Kingsford (film debut), Minor Watson, Holmes Herbert, Barbara Barondess, Henry Mowbray, Colin Tapley, Boyd Irwin, Ed Peil, Burr Caruth, John Marston, Adrian Morris, Bert Sprotte, Ricca Allen, George Billings, Duke York, Jules Cowles, Paul Kruger, Reginald Pasch, Winter Hall, Harry Schultz. *D:* Alexander Hall; *P:* Arthur Hornblow, Jr.; *Sc:* Stephen Morehouse Avery, Jack Cunningham, J.P. McEvoy, Virginia Van Upp. (1:15)
Colonial costume comedy centered around the affair of a Puritan girl and a Hessian soldier and the curious old custom of bundling. Based on the play by Lawrence Langner and Armina Marshall, the film flopped.

3667. Put on the Spot (Victory; 1936). *Cast:* Nick Stuart, Edward Nugent, George Walsh, Fuzzy Knight, Don Alvarado, Forrest Taylor, George Cleveland. *D:* Robert Hill; *P:* Sam Katzman. (G.B. title: *Framed*)
B indie actioner.

3668. Puttin' on the Ritz (United Artists/Art Cinema; 1930). *Cast:* Harry Richman (feature film debut), Joan Bennett, James Gleason, Aileen Pringle, Lilyan Tashman, Purnell Pratt, George Irving, Richard Tucker, Eddie Kane, Sidney Franklin. *D:* Edward H. Sloman; *P:* John W. Considine, Jr.; *St:* Considine; *Sc:* Considine, William K. Wells; *Songs:* including the title song: Irving Berlin. (1:30)
Melodrama with music of a has-been vaudevillian who makes a comeback and starts to hit the bottle. The "Alice in Wonderland" sequence is in 2-color technicolor.

3669. Quality Street (RKO; 1937). *Cast:* Katharine Hepburn, Franchot Tone, Fay Bainter, Eric Blore, Cora Witherspoon, Estelle Winwood (American debut), William Bakewell, Joan Fontaine, Florence Lake, Clifford Severn, Sherwood Bailey, Roland Varno, Helena Grant. *D:* George Stevens; *P:* Pandro S. Berman; *Sc:* Mortimer Offner, Allan Scott; *Music:* (A.A.N.) Roy Webb. (1:24) (video)
Costume romance set in early 19th-century England of a woman who pretends to be her niece to win back an old love. A remake of the 1927 MGM production with Marion Davies. Based on the play by Sir James M. Barrie, the film was a box office flop.

3670. Queen Christina (MGM; 1933). *Cast:* Greta Garbo, John Gilbert (replacing Laurence Olivier at Garbo's request), Ian Keith, Lewis Stone, Elizabeth Young, C. Aubrey Smith, Reginald Owen, Georges Renavent, David Torrence, Gustav von Seyffertitz, Ferdinand Munier, Henry Stephenson, Edward Norris (film debut), Lawrence Grant, Akim Tamiroff, Cora Sue Collins. *D:* Rouben Mamoulian; *P:* Walter Wanger; *St:* Salka Viertel, Margaret F. Levin; *Sc:* Viertel, H.M. Harwood, Ben Hecht (unc.); *Dialogue:* S.N. Behrman. (1:37) (video)
A lavishly produced costume

drama of the 17th-century Swedish queen who gave up her throne in favor of her lover. The film was in nomination at the Venice Film Festival of 1934, and was a big hit in the United States and abroad, being one of the 15 top grossing films of 1934.

3671. Queen High (Paramount; 1930). *Cast:* Charles Ruggles, Frank Morgan, Ginger Rogers, Stanley Smith, Tom Brown, Theresa Maxwell Conover, Betty Garde, Nina Olivette, Helen Carrington, Rudolph Cameron. *D:* Fred Newmeyer.

Musical-comedy of partners in a garter business who make a bet, with the loser becoming the servant of the other. A remake of *A Pair of Sixes* (Essanay; 1918). Remade as *On Again — Off Again* (q.v.). Based on the 1926 Broadway musical "Queen High," which in turn was based on the play "A Pair of Sixes" by Edward H. Peple. Filmed at Paramount's Astoria Studios in Long Island, N.Y.

3672. Queen of Main Street (Xxxx Xxxx; 1930). (No information available)

3673. Queen of Scandal (Xxxx Xxxx; 1930). (No information available)

3674. Queen of the Jungle (Screen Attractions Corp.; 1935). *Cast:* Mary Kornman, Reed Howes, Dickie Jones, Marilyn Spinner, Lafe McKee. *D:* Robert Hill. (1:27) (video)

Feature version of the independent 12-chapter serial of the same name, which centers around a little girl stranded in the jungle who survives and grows up to become the heroine of this melodrama.

3675. Queen of the Night Clubs (WB; 1929). *Cast:* Texas Guinan (Texas Malone), Lila Lee, Jack Norworth, John Davidson, William Davidson, John Miljan, Eddie Foy, Jr. (film debut), Charlotte Merriam, George Raft (film debut), James T. Mack, Arthur Housman, Jimmy Phillips, Lee Shumway, Agnes Franey. *D:* Bryan Foy; *Sc:* Addison Burkhart, Murray Roth.

Melodrama of a popular night club entertainer who falls victim to jealous rivals.

The Queen's Husband (G.B. title) *see* **The Royal Bed**

3676. Quick Millions (Fox; 1931). *Cast:* Spencer Tracy (Bugs Raymond), Marguerite Churchill (Dorothy Stone), Sally Eilers (Daisy de Lisle), Robert "Bazooka Bob" Burns (film debut as Arkansas Smith), John Wray (Kenneth Stone), George Raft (Jimmy Kirk), Warner Richmond (Nails Markey), John Swor (contractor). *D:* Rowland Brown (former writer in his directorial debut); *St:* Brown, Courtney Terrett; *Dialogue:* Terrett, Brown, John Wray. (1:09)

Hit melodrama of a truck driver who becomes a kingpin in the rackets. Voted one of the year's "10 Best" films by the National Board of Review.

3677. Quick Millions (20th Century–Fox; 1939). *Cast:* Jed Prouty, Spring Byington, Florence Roberts, June Carlson, Kenneth Howell, George Ernest, Billy Mahan, Helen Ericson, Eddie Collins, Horace MacMahon, Paul Hurst. *D:* Mal St. Clair; *Sc:* Buster Keaton (co-writer).

The 13th entry in the "Jones Family" comedy series.

3678. Quick Money (RKO; 1937). *Cast:* Fred Stone, Gordon Jones, Dorothy Moore, Berton Churchill, Paul Guilfoyle, Jack Carson, Harlan Briggs, Dorothy Vaughan, Sherwood Bailey, Frank M. Thomas, Kathryn Sheldon, Dick Elliott, James Farley, Hattie McDaniel, Fuzzy Knight, William Franey. *D:* Edward Killy; *St:* Arthur T. Horman; *Sc:* Horman, Franklin Coen, Bert Granet. (0:59)

B comedy-drama of a small town mayor whose opponents want him out of the way.

3679. Quick-Trigger Law (Columbia; 1938). *Cast:* Charles Starrett, Iris Meredith, Dick Curtis, Donald Grayson, Sons of the Pioneers with Bob Nolan. *D:* Sam Nelson.

Charles Starrett western.

3680. Quick-Trigger Lee (Big 4; 1931). *Cast:* Bob Custer, Richard Carlyle. *D:* J.P. McGowan; *P:* John R. Freuler.

Bob Custer western.

3681. The Quitter (Chesterfield; 1934). *Cast:* William Bakewell, Barbara Bedford, Mary Kornman, Glen Boles, Hale Hamilton, Lafe McKee, Emma Dunn, Barbara Weeks, Jane Keckley, Aggie Herring. *D:* Richard Thorpe; *St & Sc:* Robert Ellis.

"Poverty row" drama.

3682. RaceTrack (Sono Art-World Wide; 1932–33). *Cast:* Leo Carrillo, Kay Hammond, Lee Moran, Frank (Junior) Coghlan, Wilfred Lucas, Huntley Gordon, Joseph Girard. *D:* James Cruze; *St:* Wells Root, J. Walter Ruben; *Sc:* Walter Lang, Douglas Doty.

Sentimental horse racing drama from "poverty row."

3683. Racing Blood (Ambassador; 1936). *Cast:* Frankie Darro, Kane Richmond, Matthew Betz, Arthur Housman. *D:* Rex Hale; *P:* Maurice Conn.

Indie B drama set at the race track.

3684. Racing Lady (RKO; 1937). *Cast:* Ann Dvorak, Smith Ballew, Harry Carey, Berton Churchill, Willie Best, Frank M. Thomas, Ray Mayer, Hattie McDaniel, Harry Jans, Lew Payton, Harland Tucker, Alex Hill. *D:* Wallace Fox; *Sc:* Dorothy Yost, Thomas Lennon, Cortland Fitzsimmons.

B production of a horse trainer who takes a job with an auto manufacturer. Based on two separate stories, one by Damon Runyon, the other by J. Robert Bren and Norman Houston.

3685. Racing Luck (Republic; 1935). *Cast:* Bill Boyd, Barbara Worth, Esther Muir. *D:* Sam Newfield.

Low-budget production.

Racing Luck (WB/F.N.; 1935) (G.B. title) *see* **Red Hot Tires**

3686. Racing Strain (Irving/Maxim; 1932). *Cast:* J. Farrell MacDonald, Wally Reid, Jr., Dickie Moore. *D:* Jerome Storm.

"Poverty row" air drama.

3687. Racing Youth (Universal; 1932). *Cast:* Frank Albertson, June Clyde, Slim Summerville, Louise Fazenda, Arthur Stuart Hull. *D:* Vin Moore. (1:02)

Programmer of auto racing.

3688. Racket Busters (WB/Cosmopolitan; 1938). *Cast:* George Brent, Humphrey Bogart, Gloria Dickson, Allen Jenkins, Walter Abel, Penny Singleton, Henry O'Neill, Don Rowan, Anthony Averill, Fay Helm, Norman Willis, Oscar O'Shea, Elliott Sullivan. *D:* Lloyd Bacon; *P:* Sam Bischoff; *Sc:* Robert Rossen, Leonardo Bercovici. (1:11)

Crime melodrama involving the trucking business.

3689. The Racketeer (Pathé; 1929–30). *Cast:* Robert Armstrong, Carole Lombard, Roland Drew, Jeanette Loff, John Loder, Paul Hurst, Al Hill, Hedda Hopper, Kit Guard. *D:* Howard Higgin; *St & Sc:* Paul Gangelin. (G.B. title: *Love's Conquest*) (1:08) (video)

Low-budget drama of a gangster torn between romance and the mob.

Racketeer Roundup *see* **Gunners and Guns**

3690. Racketeers in Exile (Columbia; 1937). *Cast:* George Bancroft, Wynne Gibson, Evelyn Venable, Marc Lawrence, Richard Carle, Jack Clifford, Garry Owen, John Gallaudet, Jonathan Hale, George McKay. *D:* Erle C. Kenton; *St:* Harry Sauber; *Sc:* Sauber, Robert T. Shannon.

B crime melodrama.

3691. Racketeers of the Range (RKO; 1939). *Cast:* George O'Brien, Chill Wills, Marjorie Reynolds, Gay Seabrook, Robert Fiske, John Dilson, Monte Montague, Bud Osborne, Ben Corbett, Ray Whitley, Cactus Mack, Frankie Marvin, Mary Gordon. *D:* D. Ross Lederman; *P:* Bert Gilroy; *St:* Bernard McConville; *Sc:* Oliver Drake; *Songs:* Ray Whitley, Fred Rose. (1:02) (video)

Modern George O'Brien western of a cattle rancher who tries to prevent a meat packing plant from selling out to a competitor.

3692. Rackety Rax (Fox; 1932). *Cast:* Ben Lyon, Victor McLaglen, Greta Nissen, Allen Jenkins, Vince Barnett, Marjorie Beebe, Stanley Fields, Joe Brown, Nell O'Day, Ward Bond, Arthur Pierson, Ivan Linow, John Keyes, Esther Howard, Eric Mayne. *D:* Alfred L. Werker; *St:* Joel Sayre; *Sc:* Ben Markson, Lou Breslow.

College gridiron story.

3693. Radio City Revels (RKO; 1937). *Cast:* Robert "Bazooka Bob" Burns, Ann Miller, Kenny Baker, Jack Oakie, Milton Berle, Helen Broderick, Victor Moore, Jane Froman, Buster West, Melissa Mason, Richard Lane, Marilyn Vernon, Hal Kemp & His Orchestra. *D:* Ben Stoloff, Joseph Santley (musical numbers only); *P:* Edward Kaufman; *St:* Matt Brooks; *Sc:* Eddie Davis, Brooks, Anthony Veiller, Mortimer Offner; *Choreography:* Hermes Pan; *Songs:* Herb Magidson, Allie Wrubel. (1:30)

Flop musical of a songwriter who composes music and lyrics from his dreams.

The Radio Murder Mystery (G.B. title) *see* **Love Is on the Air**

3694. Radio Patrol (Universal; 1932). *Cast:* Robert Armstrong, Lila Lee, Russell Hopton, Andy Devine, June Clyde, Sidney Toler, Onslow Stevens, Harry Woods, Joseph Girard, John L. Johnson. *D:* Edward L. Cahn; *St & Sc:* Tom Reed. (1:05)

Low-budget crime melodrama of a married cop and his pregnant wife.

3695. Radio Ranch (Republic-Mascot; 1935–40). *Cast:* Gene Autry (in his starring debut), Frankie Darro, Lester (Smiley) Burnette, Betsy King Ross, Dorothy Christy, Wheeler Oakman, Charles K. French, Warner Richmond, William Moore, J. Frank Glendon, Ed Peil, Sr., Jack Carlyle, Wally Wales (Hal Taliaferro), Jay Wilsey (Buffalo Bill, Jr.), Fred Burns, Stanley Blystone, Dick (Richard) Talmadge, Frank Ellis. *D:* Otto Brower, B. Reeves Eason; *P:* Nat Levine; *St:* Wallace MacDonald, Gerald Geraghty, Hy Freedman, Maurice Geraghty; *Sc:* Armand Schaefer, John Rathmell, Maurice Geraghty (unc.). (G.B. title: *Couldn't Possibly Happen*) (aka: *The Phantom Empire*) (Re-release title: *Men with Steel Faces*). (Feature running time: 1:20 and/or 1:30) (video: available on feature length & full 12-chapter serial)

Feature version of the 12-chapter Mascot serial "The Phantom Empire" with a dude rancher battling crooks and discovering a futuristic underground kingdom. The feature version of the serial was edited in 1935, but sat unreleased until 1940.

The Radio Star (G.B. title) *see* **The Loudspeaker**

3696. Raffles (United Artists/ Samuel Goldwyn; 1930). *Cast:* Ronald Colman (Raffles), Kay Francis (Gwen), David Torrence (Inspector MacKenzie), Bramwell Fletcher, Frances Dade,

Alison Skipworth, Frederick Kerr, John Rogers, Wilson Benge. *D:* Harry D'Abbadie D'Arrast, George Fitzmaurice; *P:* Sam Goldwyn; *Sc:* Sidney Howard; *Sound Recording:* (A.A.N.) Oscar Lagerstrom. (1:20)

The much filmed story of a gentleman thief who keeps Scotland Yard baffled, while carrying on a front of champion cricketer and man-about-town. Based on the turn-of-the-century novel by E.W. Hornung titled "Raffles, the Amateur Cracksman" and the play adapted from it. Three previous filmings include (Vitagraph; 1905) with J. Barney Sherry (a one-reeler), an independent production of 1917 with John Barrymore and (Universal; 1925) with House Peters, all of which were released with the title *Raffles, the Amateur Cracksman.* Remade by Goldwyn (see below).

3697. Raffles (United Artists/ Samuel Goldwyn; 1939–40). *Cast:* David Niven (Raffles), Olivia de Havilland (Gwen), Douglas Walton (Bunny), Dame May Whitty (Lady Melrose), Dudley Digges (Inspector MacKenzie), Lionel Pape (Lord Melrose), E.E. Clive, Peter Godfrey, Margaret Seddon, Gilbert Emery, Hilda Plowright, James Finlayson, George Cathrey. *D:* Sam Wood; *P:* Sam Goldwyn; *Sc:* John Van Druten, Sidney Howard. (1:12)

A remake of the above feature.

3698. Rafter Romance (RKO; 1933). *Cast:* Ginger Rogers, Norman Foster, Robert Benchley, Laura Hope Crews, Guinn Williams, George Sidney, Sidney Miller. *D:* William A. Seiter; *As.P.:* Kenneth MacGowan; *St:* John Wells; *Adaptation:* Glenn Tryon; *Sc:* Sam Mintz, H.W. Hanemann.

Romantic comedy of two people who share an apartment, but have never met each other there. Remade as *Living on Love* (q.v.).

3699. The Rage of Paris (Universal; 1938). *Cast:* Danielle Darrieux (American debut as Nicole de Cor-

tillon), Douglas Fairbanks, Jr., Louis Hayward, Mischa Auer, Helen Broderick, Harry Davenport, Samuel S. Hinds, Nella Walker, Charles Coleman, Mary Martin (film debut in an unbilled bit). *D:* Henry Koster; *P:* B.G. "Buddy" DeSylva; *Sc:* Bruce Manning, Felix Jackson. (1:18) (video)

Hit comedy of con-men who team up with a girl to find her a rich husband.

3700. Rain (United Artists/Art Cinema; 1932). *Cast:* Joan Crawford (Sadie Thompson), Walter Huston (Rev. Alfred Davidson), William Gargan (Sgt. O'Hara), Beulah Bondi (Mrs. Davidson), Guy Kibbee (Joe Horn), Walter Catlett (Quartermaster Bates), Matt Moore (Dr. MacPhail), Kendall Lee (Mrs. MacPhail), Ben Hendricks, Jr. (Griggs), Frederick Howard (Hodgson), Mary Shaw (Ameena). *D:* Lewis Milestone; *P:* Joseph M. Schenck, Milestone; *Sc:* Maxwell Anderson. (1:33) (video)

The famous South Sea island tale of a prostitute condemned and lusted after by a fundamentalist preacher of the hellfire and brimstone variety. This was sensationalism of its day and curiously a box office bomb. Based on a story by W. Somerset Maugham and the play adaptation by John Colton and Clemence Randolph. A remake of *Sadie Thompson* (United Artists; 1928) with Gloria Swanson. Remade as *Miss Sadie Thompson* (Columbia; 1953) in color and 3-D with Rita Hayworth.

Note: Shorter prints known to exist from a post-code re-release.

3701. Rain or Shine (Columbia; 1930). *Cast:* Joe Cook (repeating his stage role), Louise Fazenda, Joan Peers, Dave Chasen, Tom Howard, William Collier, Jr., Clarence Muse, Nora Lane, Alan Roscoe, Edward Martindel, Tyrell Davis. *D:* Frank Capra; *Sc:* James Gleason, Jo Swerling; *St:* James Gleason; *Dial. Cont.:* Dorothy Howell, Jo Swerling. (1:32)

A circus story, based on a play by James Gleason.

3702. The Rainbow Man (Paramount; 1929). *Cast:* Eddie Dowling, Marian Nixon, Frankie Darrow (Darro), Sam Hardy, George Hayes, Lloyd Ingraham, James Hanley. *D:* Fred Newmeyer.

Low-budget romantic drama of a song 'n' dance man who falls for the aunt of a young boy he adopts.

3704. Rainbow Over Broadway (Chesterfield; 1933). *Cast:* Joan Marsh, Frank Albertson. *D:* Richard Thorpe.

"Poverty row" romance.

3705. Rainbow Ranch (Monogram; 1933). *Cast:* Rex Bell, Cecilia Parker, Robert Kortman, Henry Hall, George Nash, Gordon DeMain, Phil Dunham, Jerry Storm, Stanley J. Sandford, Val Galbert, Jackie Hoefli. *D:* Harry Fraser; *P:* Trem Carr; *St & Sc:* Harry O. Jones (Fraser); *Dialogue:* Phil Dunham. (0:54)

Rex Bell western of an ex-navy man who returns to his ranch and finds he has to right some wrongs.

3706. The Rainbow Trail (Fox; 1931–32). *Cast:* George O'Brien, Cecilia Parker, Robert Frazer, James Kirkwood, Roscoe Ates, Edward Hearn, Ruth Donnelly, Landers Stevens, Niles Welch, William L. Thorne, Alice Ward, Laska Winter. *D:* David Howard.

Scenic western filmed in the Grand Canyon of Arizona, based on the Zane Grey novel and a sequel to *Riders of the Purple Sage* (q.v.). Filmed twice before by Fox, in 1918 with William Farnum and in 1925 with Tom Mix.

3707. Rainbow Valley (Monogram-Lone Star; 1935). *Cast:* John Wayne, Lucile Browne, LeRoy Mason, George Hayes, Buffalo Bill, Jr., Bert Dillard, Lloyd Ingraham, Lafe McKee, Fern Emmett, Henry Rocquemore, Eddie Parker, Herman Hack, Frank Ellis, Art Dillard, Frank Ball. *D:* Robert N. Bradbury; *P:* Paul Malvern; *Supervisor:* Trem Carr; *St & Sc:* Lindsley Parsons. (0:52)

John Wayne western involving the attempts to stop the construction of a road.

3708. Rainbow's End (First Division; 1935). *Cast:* Hoot Gibson, June Gale, Oscar Apfel, Warner Richmond, Buddy Roosevelt, Ada Ince, Stanley Blystone, Henry Rocquemore, John Elliott. *D:* Norman Spencer; *Sc:* Rollo Ward. (0:59)

Hoot Gibson modern comic western involving a crooked lawyer trying to get control of a ranch.

3709. The Rainmakers (RKO; 1935). *Cast:* Bert Wheeler, Robert Woolsey, Dorothy Lee, Berton Churchill, George Meeker, Frederic Roland, Edgar Dearing. *D:* Fred Guiol; *As.P.:* Lee Marcus; *St:* Guiol, Albert Treynor; *Sc:* Grant Garrett, Leslie Goodwins; *Song:* Louis Alter, Jack Scholl. (1:19)

California farmers in the midst of a drought, seek relief by hiring two rainmakers in this comedy farce.

3710. The Rains Came (20th Century–Fox; 1939). *Cast:* Myrna Loy (Lady Edwina Esketh), Tyrone Power (Major Rama Safti), George Brent (Tom Ransome), Brenda Joyce (film debut as Fern Simon), Nigel Bruce (Lord Albert Esketh), Maria Ouspenskaya (Maharani), Joseph Schildkraut (Mr. Bannerjee), Mary Nash (Miss MacDaid), Jane Darwell (Aunt Phoebe Smiley), Marjorie Rambeau (Mrs. Simon), Henry Travers (Rev. Homer Smiley), H.B. Warner (Maharajah), Laura Hope Crews (Lily Hoggett-Egburry), William Royle (Raschid Ali Khan), Montague Shaw (General Keith), Herbert Evans (Bates), Abner Biberman (John the Baptist), Harry Hayden (Elmer Simon), Mara Alexander (Mrs. Bannerjee), William Edmunds (Mr. Das), Frank Lackteen (engineer), George Regas (Rajput), Guy D'Ennery (Mr. Durga), Adele Labansat, Sonia Charsky, Rita Page, Rosina Galli, Connie Leon, Pedro

Regas, Lal Chand Mehra, Leyland Hodgson, Fern Emmett, Jamiel Hasson. *D:* Clarence Brown; *P:* Darryl F. Zanuck; *As.P.:* Harry Joe Brown; *Sc:* Philip Dunne, Julien Josephson; *Art-Set Decoration:* (A.A.N.) William Darling, George Dudley; *Original Music Score:* (A.A.N.) Alfred Newman; *Editor:* (A.A.N.) Barbara McLean; *Sound Recording:* (A.A.N.) E.H. Hansen; *Title Song:* Mack Gordon, Harry Revel; "Hindoo Song of Love" by Lal Chand Mehra. (1:43)

A romantic drama set in India of a native doctor's affair with the wife of a titled Englishman. Based on the novel by Louis Bromfield, this was the first film to win an Academy Award for special effects (Fred Sersen), depicting a devastating earthquake and flood following the breaking of a dam, all in the midst of a torrential downpour. Remade as *The Rains of Ranchipur* (20th Century-Fox; 1955). One of the 21 top grossing films of 1939-40.

Raising the Wind (G.B. title) *see* **The Big Race**

3711. Ramona (20th Century-Fox; 1936). *Cast:* Loretta Young, Don Ameche, Kent Taylor, Pauline Frederick, Jane Darwell, Katherine de Mille, Victor Kilian, John Carradine, J. Carrol Naish, Pedro de Cordoba, Charles Waldron, Claire DuBrey, Russell Simpson, William (Billy) Benedict, Robert Spindola, Chief Thundercloud, Charles Middleton. *D:* Henry King; *As.P.:* John Stone; *Sc:* Lamar Trotti (based on the 1884 novel by Helen Hunt Jackson); *Songs:* William Kernell. (1:30)

A technicolor romantic drama set in 1870 California. The film and the title song were both hits in their day. Previous versions: (Biograph; 1910) with Mary Pickford and Henry B. Walthall (a 1 reeler directed by D.W. Griffith), (W.H. Clune; 1916) with Adda Gleason and Monroe Salisbury (directed by Donald Crisp), and (United Artists/Inspiration; 1928) with Dolores Del Rio

and Warner Baxter (by director Edwin Carewe).

3712. The Rampant Age (Syndicate/Continental Talking Pictures; 1930). *Cast:* James Murray, Merna Kennedy, Yola D'Avril, Florence Turner. *D:* Phil Rosen.

Low-budget drama.

3713. Rancho Grande (Republic; 1939-40). *Cast:* Gene Autry, Smiley Burnette, June Storey, Mary Lee, Dick Hogan, Ellen Lowe, Roscoe Ates, Rex Lease, Ferris Taylor, Joe De Stefani, Ann Baldwin, Roy Barcroft, Brewer Kids, Pals of the Golden West, Champion. *D:* Frank McDonald; *P:* William Berke; *St:* Peter Milne, Connie Lee; *Sc:* Bradford Ropes, Milne, Betty Burbridge. (1:08)

A Gene Autry western with songs of a cowboy who helps three youngsters in danger of being taken for their inherited property.

3714. Randy Rides Alone (Monogram-Lone Star; 1934). *Cast:* John Wayne, Alberta Vaughn, George Hayes, Yakima Canutt, Earl Dwire, Tex Phelps, Artie Ortego, Tex Palmer, Mack V. Wright, Herman Hack. *D:* Harry Fraser; *P:* Paul Malvern; *Supervisor:* Trem Carr; *St & Sc:* Lindsley Parsons. (0:54) (video)

John Wayne in an offbeat western involving the apprehension of a gang responsible for a massacre.

Randy Strikes Oil (G.B. title) *see* **The Fighting Texans**

3715. Range Defenders (Republic; 1937). *Cast:* Bob Livingston (Stony Brooke), Ray Corrigan (Tucson Smith), Max Terhune (Lullaby Joslin), Eleanor Stewart, Harry Woods, Yakima Canutt, Earle Hodgins, Thomas Carr, John Merton, Harrison Greene, Horace B. Carpenter, Fred "Snowflake" Toones. *D:* Mack V. Wright; *Sc:* Joseph Poland. (0:54)

The 8th "Three Mesquiteers" entry with the trio attempting to find the reason Stony's brother was falsely accused of murder.

3716. Range Feud (Columbia; 1931). *Cast:* Buck Jones, Susan Fleming, John Wayne, William Walling, Harry Woods, Wallace MacDonald, Frank Austin, Glenn Strange, Lew Meehan, Jim Corey, Bob Reeves, Frank Ellis. *D:* D. Ross Lederman; *Sc:* George Plympton. (1:04)

Buck Jones western of a feud between two ranchers which has been instigated by a third party. A loose remake of *The Dawn Trail* (q.v.).

3717. Range Law (Tiffany; 1931). *Cast:* Ken Maynard, Frances Dade, Lafe McKee, Frank Mayo, Charles King, Jack Rockwell, Tom London, William Duncan, Aileen Manning. *D:* Phil Rosen; *P:* Phil Goldstone (Amity Productions); *Sc:* Earle Snell. (1:00)

Ken Maynard western of a man falsely accused of a crime who is broken out of jail by friends.

3718. Range Riders (Superior; 1934). *Cast:* Buddy Roosevelt, Barbara Starr, Merrill McCormack, Horace B. Carpenter, Herman Hack, Lew Meehan, Denver Dixon. *D:* Victor Adamson (Denver Dixon); *P:* California Motion Picture Enterprises (Denver Dixon); *Sc:* L.V. Jefferson. (0:45)

Buddy Roosevelt western of a lawman in disguise to capture outlaws.

3719. Range War (Paramount; 1939). *Cast:* William Boyd (Hoppy), Russell Hayden (Lucky), Britt Wood (Speedy), Willard Robertson, Matt Moore, Pedro de Cordoba, Betty Moran, Kenneth Harlan, Eddie Dean, Earle Hodgins, Glenn Strange, Jason Robards, George Chesebro, Raphael (Ray) Bennett, Stanley Price. *D:* Lesley Selander; *P:* Harry M. Sherman; *Sc:* Sam Robins. (1:04)

"Hopalong Cassidy" western (the 23rd) in a story involving a railroad (utilizing left-over sets from *Union Pacific*— q.v.).

3720. Range Warfare (Willis Kent; 1935). *Cast:* Reb Russell, Lucille Lund, Wally Wales (Hal Taliaferro), Lafe McKee, Roger Williams, Bart Carre. *D:* S. Roy Luby; *P:* Willis Kent; *Sc:* E.B. Mann. (Re-release title: *Vengeance*) (0:55)

Reb Russell western.

3721. Ranger Courage (Columbia; 1937). *Cast:* Bob Allen, Martha Tibbetts, Walter Miller, Buzz Henry, Bud Osborne, Bob Kortman, Harry Strang, William Gould, Franklyn Farnum, Buffalo Bill, Jr., Horace Murphy, Gene Alsace (Rocky Camron). *D:* Spencer Gordon Bennet; *Sc:* Nate Gatzert. (0:58)

Bob Allen western of a ranger who comes to the aid of a besieged wagon train.

3722. Ranger of the Law (American; 1935). *Cast:* Buffalo Bill, Jr., Jeanee (Genee) Boutell, George Chesebro, Jack Long, Ben Corbett, Boris Bullock, Frank Clark, Duke Lee, Lake Reynolds. *D:* R.J. Renroh (Robert J. Horner); *P:* Horner; *Sc:* Royal Hampton. (0:50)

Buffalo Bill, Jr., western of a rodeo performer who helps a girl save her ranch. Much stock footage.

3723. The Ranger's Code (Monogram; 1933). *Cast:* Bob Steele, Doris Hill, George Hayes, George Nash, Ernie Adams, Ed Brady, Hal Price, Dick Dickinson, Frank Ball. *D:* Robert N. Bradbury; *P:* Paul Malvern; *Supervisor:* Trem Carr; *St:* John T. Neville; *Sc:* Harry (Fraser) O. Jones. (0:59)

Bob Steele western of a Texas Ranger who must do his duty and bring in the brother of his girl friend.

3724. The Ranger's Roundup (Spectrum; 1937–38). *Cast:* Fred Scott, Al St. John, Christine McIntyre, Earle

Hodgins, Steve Ryan, Karl Hackett, Robert Owen, Syd Chatan, Carl Mathews, Richard Cramer, Jimmy Aubrey, Lew Porter, Cactus Mack, Chick Hannon, Steve Clark, Milburn Morante. *D:* Sam Newfield; *P:* Stan Laurel Productions, Jed Buell; *Sc:* George Plympton. (0:57)

Fred Scott western with songs (including "The Terror of Termite Valley"), involving a ranger working undercover.

3725. The Rangers Step In (Columbia; 1937). *Cast:* Bob Allen, Eleanor Stewart, Hal Taliaferro, John Merton, Jay Wilsey (Buffalo Bill, Jr.), Jack Rockwell, Lafe McKee, Jack Ingram, Robert Kortman, Billy Townsend, Lew Meehan, Ray Jones. *D:* Spencer Gordon Bennet; *Sc:* Nate Gatzert. (0:58)

Bob Allen western (his final in the "Ranger" series) of a family feud retriggered by a third party and a ranger who is called in to stop it.

3726. Rango (Paramount; 1931). *Cast:* Claude King, Douglas Scott, Ali, Bin, Rango the orangutan, Tua the orangutan. *D:* Ernest B. Schoedsack; *P:* Schoedsack.

Documentary feature of a family's dilemma while living in the Malaysian jungle. Voted one of the "10 Best" films of the year by the National Board of Review.

The Rare Book Murder *see* **Fast Company** (1938)

3727. Rascals (20th Century–Fox; 1938). *Cast:* Jane Withers, Rochelle Hudson, Robert Wilcox, Katherine Alexander, Steffi Duna, Howard Hickman, Frank Reicher, Kathleen Burke, Paul Stanton, Robert Gleckler, Borrah Minevitch & His Harmonica Gang, Frank Puglia, Eddie Dunn, Edward Cooper, Myra Marsh, Chester Clute. *D:* H. Bruce Humberstone; *P:* John Stone; *Sc:* Robert Ellis, Helen Logan; *Songs:* Harry Akst, Sidney Clare.

B comedy-drama set in the world of gypsies. A box office hit.

3728. Rasputin and the Empress (MGM; 1932). *Cast:* John Barrymore (Prince Paul Chegodieff—fictional character created to depict the real Prince Yousoupoff), Ethel Barrymore (talkie debut as Czarina Alexandra), Lionel Barrymore (Rasputin), Ralph Morgan (Czar Nicholas II), Diana Wynyard (film debut as Natasha—fictional character created to depict Princess Yousoupoff), Tad Alexander (Czarovich Alexis), C. Henry Gordon (Grand Duke Igor—fictional character), Edward Arnold (Dr. Remezoff—fictional character), Jean Parker (Princess Maria), Dawn O'Day (Anne Shirley as Princess Anastasia), Gustav von Seyffertitz (Dr. Wolfe), Frank Shannon (Professor Propotkin), Sarah Padden, Henry Kolker, Frank Reicher, Hooper Atchley, Leo White, Lucien Littlefield, Maurice Black, Dave O'Brien, Mischa Auer, Charlotte Henry, Nigel de Brulier. *D:* Richard Boleslawsky (replacing Charles Brabin); *P:* Bernard Hyman; *Original Story:* (A.A.N.) Charles MacArthur; *Sc:* MacArthur. (G.B. title: *Rasputin the Mad Monk*) (2:03)

Historically based drama of the monk Rasputin and his influence on the royal family of Czarist Russia. A notable film in that it is the only film in which the three Barrymore siblings appeared together. Following the release of this production, a major lawsuit was filed against MGM by the Prince and Princess Yousoupoff which they won, claiming the rape of the princess depicted in the film was false, though Yousoupoff himself is credited with the killing of Rasputin. Actual film footage of the era is utilized in the film which placed #10 on the "10 Best" list of *Film Daily,* as well as being one of the 11 top grossing films of 1933.

Rasputin the Mad Monk (G.B. title) *see* **Rasputin and the Empress**

3729. The Raven (Universal; 1935). *Cast:* Bela Lugosi (Dr. Vollin), Boris Karloff (Bateman), Irene Ware, Samuel S. Hinds, Lester Matthews, Spencer Charters, Ian Wolfe, Inez Courtney, Maidel Turner, Arthur Hoyt. *D:* Louis Friedlander (Lew Landers); *Sc:* David Boehm, Dore Schary (unc.), Guy Endore (unc.). (1:01) (video)

A horror film of a doctor who is obsessed with the writings of Edgar Allan Poe and his experiments on a gangster who is on the lam from the law. The film is no relation to Poe's poem of the same name.

3730. Raw Timber (Crescent Pictures; 1937). *Cast:* Tom Keene, Peggy Keys, Robert Fiske, Budd Buster, Lee Phelps, John Rutherford, Raphael (Ray) Bennett, Slim Whitaker, Bart Carre. *D:* Ray Taylor; *P:* E.B. Derr; *Sc:* Bennett Cohen, John Thomas Neville. (1:03)

B melodrama of a ruthless lumber baron and the murder he commits to cover his dirty dealings.

3731. Rawhide (20th Century-Fox/Principal; 1938). *Cast:* Smith Ballew, Lou Gehrig (better known as the first baseman of the New York Yankees who died in 1940), Evalyn Knapp, Lafe McKee, Carl Stockdale, Cyrus Kendall, Slim Whitaker, Arthur Loft, Si Jenks, Lee Shumway, Dick Curtis, Cliff Parkinson, Harry Tenbrook, Ed Cassidy, Tom Forman (final film – d. 1938), Cecil Kellogg. *D:* Ray Taylor; *P:* Sol Lesser; *St:* Dan Jarrett; *Sc:* Jarrett, Jack Natteford. (0:58) (video)

Smith Ballew western of a singing cowboy who helps a rancher.

3732. Rawhide Mail (Reliable/William Steiner; 1934). *Cast:* Jack Perrin, Jimmy Aubrey, George Chesebro, Richard Cramer. *D:* Bernard B. Ray.

A Jack Perrin horse opera.

3733. Rawhide Romance (Superior; 1934). *Cast:* Buffalo Bill, Jr., Genee Boutell, Lafe McKee, Si Jenks, Bart Carre, Boris Bullock, Jack Evans, Marin Sais, Clyde McClary. *D:* Victor Adamson (Denver Dixon); *P:* Dixon; *Sc:* L.V. Jefferson. (0:47)

Buffalo Bill, Jr., western of a cowboy, a girl and some outlaws.

3734. The Rawhide Terror (Security; 1934). *Cast:* Art Mix (better known as a supporting actor in B westerns in his starring debut), William Desmond, Edmund Cobb, William Barrymore (Boris Bullock), Frances Morris, Bill Patton, Tommy Bupp, Herman Hack, George Holt, George Gyton, Ed Carey, Ernest Scott, Fred Parker, Denver Dixon. *D:* Jack Nelson, Bruce Mitchell; *P:* Victor Adamson (Denver Dixon); *Sc:* Nelson. (0:52)

B western of a lawman out to bring in a notorious outlaw who turns out to be the lawman's long-lost brother.

3735. Reaching for the Moon (United Artists/Art Cinema; 1930–31). *Cast:* Douglas Fairbanks, Bebe Daniels, Edward Everett Horton, Claude Allister, Jack Mulhall, Helen Jerome Eddy, Bing Crosby (singing an Irving Berlin song), June MacCloy, Walter Walker, Bud Flanagan (Dennis O'Keefe in his film debut – bit). *D:* Edmund Goulding; *P:* Joseph M. Schenck (for Art Cinema Associates, Inc.); *St:* Irving Berlin; *Sc:* Goulding; *Additional Dialogue:* Elsie Janis. (1:30) (video – 1:02)

Shipboard comedy of a girl-shy businessman and the effects that a certain alcoholic drink has on him. This film is no relation to Fairbanks 1917 film of the same name.

3736. Ready for Love (Paramount; 1934). *Cast:* Ida Lupino, Richard Arlen, Marjorie Rambeau, Beulah Bondi, Henry Travers, Esther Howard, Louise Carter. *D:* Marion Gering.

B drama of a girl whose reputation is maligned by a bunch of small town gossips, eventually putting her life in peril.

3737. Ready, Willing and Able (WB; 1937). *Cast:* Ruby Keeler, Lee Dixon, Allen Jenkins, Louise Fazenda, Carol Hughes, Ross Alexander (final film — suicide, 1937), Winifred Shaw, Teddy Hart, E.E. Clive, Jane Wyman, Hugh O'Connell, Charles Halton, Montague Shaw, Adrian Rosley. *D:* Ray Enright; *P:* Sam Bischoff; *St:* Richard Macaulay; *Sc:* Sig Herzig, Jerry Wald, Warren Duff; *Songs:* Johnny Mercer, Richard Whiting. (1:35)

Romantic musical, notable for the production number "Too Marvelous for Words" by dance director Bobby Connolly which features a giant typewriter and received an A.A.N. for it's originality.

3738. The Real Glory (United Artists/Samuel Goldwyn; 1939). *Cast:* Gary Cooper, David Niven, Broderick Crawford, Andrea Leeds, Reginald Owen, Kay Johnson, Russell Hicks, Vladimir Sokoloff, Henry Kolker, Tetsu Komai (Alipang), Benny Inocencio, Rudy Robles, Roy Gordon. *D:* Henry Hathaway; *P:* Sam Goldwyn; *As.P.:* Robert Riskin; *Sc:* Jo Swerling, Robert N. Presnell. (1:36)

Action-adventure set in 1906 in the Philippines after the Spanish-American War. Based on the novel by Charles L. Clifford.

3739. Rebecca of Sunnybrook Farm (Fox; 1932). *Cast:* Marian Nixon (Rebecca), Ralph Bellamy, Charlotte Henry, Louise Closser Hale, Mae Marsh, Alan Hale, Alphonse Ethier, Sarah Padden, Eula Guy, Tommy Conlon, Wally Albright, Ronald Harris, Lucille Ward, Claire McDowell, Willis Marks. *D:* Alfred Santell; *St:* Charlotte Thompson; *Sc:* Sonya Levien, S.N. Behrman.

The famous children's classic, based on the 1903 book by Kate Douglas Wiggin. Filmed before (Artclass; 1917) with Mary Pickford.

3740. Rebecca of Sunnybrook Farm (20th Century–Fox; 1938). *Cast:* Shirley Temple, Randolph Scott, Jack Haley, Gloria Stuart, Phyllis Brooks, Helen Westley, Slim Summerville, Bill Robinson, Dixie Dunbar, Paul Harvey, J. Edward Bromberg, Carroll Nye, Franklin Pangborn, William Demarest, Paul Hurst, Eily Malyon, Clarence Wilson, Ruth Gillette, Raymond Scott, Peters Sisters, Gary Breckner, Sam Hayes, Mary McCarty, William Wagner. *D:* Allan Dwan; *P:* Raymond Griffith; *Sc:* Karl Tunberg, Don Ettlinger. (1:20) (video)

A vehicle for Shirley Temple which has little to do with the famous children's book by Kate Douglas Wiggin. Notable for Shirley's rendering of "On the Good Ship Lollipop" and her dance with Bill Robinson to "March of the Wooden Soldiers." Computer-colored prints produced in 1986.

3741. Rebellion (Crescent Pictures; 1936). *Cast:* Tom Keene, Rita (Hayworth) Cansino, Duncan Renaldo, William Royle, Gino Corrado, Jack Ingram, Roger Gray, Bob McKenzie, Allan Cavan, Lita Cortez, Theodore Lorch, Merrill McCormack. *D:* Lynn Shores; *P:* E.B. Derr; *Sc:* John Thomas Neville. (Re-release title: *Lady from Frisco*) (G.B. title: *Treason*) (1:02)

Historically based melodrama of an army officer sent by President Zachary Taylor to California to investigate the harrassment of Spanish land owners.

3742. Rebellious Daughters (Progressive Pictures; 1938–39). *Cast:* Paul Lukas, Sheila Bromley, Marjorie Reynolds, Monte Blue, Verna Hillie, Irene Franklin. *D:* Jean Yarbrough.

B independent melodrama.

3743. Rebound (RKO-Pathé; 1931). *Cast:* Ina Claire (Sara), Robert Ames (Bill Truesdale), Myrna Loy (Evie), Robert Williams (Johnnie Coles), Hale Hamilton, Hedda Hopper, Walter Walker, Louise Closser Hale,

Leigh Allen, Alan Hale. *D:* Edward H. Griffith; *As.P.:* Harry Joe Brown; *Sc:* Horace Jackson. (1:31)

Triangular romantic comedy which is based on the hit Broadway play by Donald Ogden Stewart. A box office flop.

3744. Recaptured Love (WB; 1930). *Cast:* John Halliday, Belle Bennett, Dorothy Burgess, James (Junior) Durkin (film debut), Richard Tucker, George Bickel, Brooks Benedict, Sisters "G," Louise Beavers. *D:* John Adolfi; *Sc:* Charles Kenyon.

Early talkie example of a mid-life crisis drama. A man divorces his wife to marry a cabaret tootsie, only to afterwards realize his error. Based on a play by Basil Woon.

3745. Reception (Xxxx Xxxx; 1933). (No information available)

3746. Reckless (MGM; 1935). *Cast:* Jean Harlow, William Powell, Franchot Tone, May Robson, Ted Healy, Nat Pendleton, Rosalind Russell, Henry Stephenson, Man Mountain Dean (better known as a professional wrestler), James Ellison, Leon (Ames) Waycoff, Allan Jones (film debut), Mickey Rooney, Nina Mae McKinney, Akim Tamiroff, Charles Middleton, Paul Fix, Louise Henry, Carl Randall, Allen "Farina" Hoskins, Robert Light. *D:* Victor Fleming; *P:* David O. Selznick; *St:* Oliver Jeffries (Selznick); *Sc:* P.J. Wolfson; *Title Song:* Jerome Kern. (1:36)

Romantic melodrama set in the world of the theatre. Based on episodes in the life of actress Libby Holman following the suicide of her husband. A double was used for Harlow's song and dance numbers.

3747. The Reckless Hour (WB/ F.N.; 1931). *Cast:* Conrad Nagel, Dorothy Mackaill, Joan Blondell, Walter Byron, H.B. Warner, Robert Allen, Joe Donahue, Ivan Simpson, Dorothy Peterson, Claude King, Helen Ware, Mae Madison, William (Billy) House. *D:* John Francis Dillon; *St:* Arthur Richman; *Sc:* Florence Ryerson, Robert Lord.

A girl model falls for a lying, cheating no-good-nik in this low-budget melodrama.

3748. Reckless Living (Universal; 1931). *Cast:* Norman Foster, Mae Clarke, Ricardo Cortez, Marie Prevost, Slim Summerville, Robert Emmett O'Connor, Thomas Jackson, Louise Beavers, Matt McHugh, Perry Ivins, Louis Natheaux, Murray Kinnell, Brooks Benedict. *D:* Cyril Gardner; *Adaptation:* Gardner, Tom Reed; *Sc:* Courtney Terrett. (1:06)

B melodrama involving the owners of a speakeasy who wants to go straight, but are thwarted in their efforts by the husband's race track betting. Remade in 1938 (see below). Based on the story "Twenty Grand" by Eve K. Flint and Martha Madison and the play "The Up and Up" by Flint.

3749. Reckless Living (Universal; 1938). *Cast:* Robert Wilcox, Nan Grey, Louise Beavers, Eddie "Rochester" Anderson, Harry Davenport. *D:* Frank McDonald; *P:* Val Paul; *Sc:* Charles Grayson. (1:05)

B drama of a race track gambler which is a remake of the preceding film.

3750. Reckless Ranger (Columbia; 1937). *Cast:* Bob Allen, Louise Small, Mary MacLaren, Harry Woods, Jack Perrin, Buddy Cox, Jack Rockwell, Slim Whitaker, Roger Williams, Lafe McKee, Hal Taliaferro. *D:* Spencer Gordon Bennet; *St:* J.A. Duffy, Joseph Levering; *Sc:* Nate Gatzert. (0:56)

Bob Allen western in the "Ranger" series of a range feud involving cattlemen and sheepmen.

3751. The Reckless Rider (Willis Kent; 1931). *D:* Armand Schaefer; *P:* Willis Kent.

Lane Chandler indie western, one

of a series of eight films. A remake of *When the Law Rides* (Film Booking Office; 1928) with Tom Tyler. Remade as *Gun Law* (q.v.).

3752. Reckless Roads (Majestic; 1935). *Cast:* Judith Allen, Regis Toomey, Lloyd Hughes, Ben Alexander. *D:* Burt P. Lynwood; *Sc:* Betty Burbridge.
(No other information available)

3753. Reckless Romance (Columbia; 1932). *Cast:* Charles "Buck" Jones in a non-western.
(No other information available)

3754. The Reckless Way (Liberty; 1936). *Cast:* Marian Nixon, Kane Richmond. *D:* Xxxx Xxxx; *P:* C.C. Burr.
A girl seeks to make it big in Hollywood in this low-budget melodrama.

3755. The Reckoning (Monogram/Peerless; 1932). *Cast:* Sally Blane, James Murray, Edmund Breese, Thomas Jackson, Bryant Washburn, Pat O'Malley, Richard Tucker. *D:* Dwight Cummings; *St:* Harry Fraser; *Sc:* Leon Lee. (1:03)
Two young lovers are ensnared in the web of a vicious gangster.

3756. Red Blood of Courage (Ambassador; 1935). *Cast:* Kermit Maynard, Ann Sheridan, Reginald Barlow, Charles King, Ben Hendricks, Jr., George Regas, Nat Carr. *D:* Jack (John) English; *P:* Maurice Conn; *Sc:* Barry Barringer. (0:55) (video)
Kermit Maynard Mountie actioner involving kidnapping and impersonation.

3757. Red Dust (MGM; 1932). *Cast:* Clark Gable (Dennis Carson), Jean Harlow (Vantine), Mary Astor (Barbara Willis), Gene Raymond (Gary Willis), Donald Crisp (Guidon), Tully Marshall (McQuarg), Forrester Harvey (Limey), Willie Fung (Hoy). *D:* Victor Fleming; *P:* Hunt Stromberg; *Sc:* John Lee Mahin. (1:26) (video)

Classic torrid romantic drama of a love triangle on an Indochinese rubber plantation. Comic overtones abound in this prime example of what Hollywood could get away with in its days before the censorship code went into effect in 1934. Based on the story "Congo Landing" by Wilson Collison, the film was a bonanza for the studio. Loosely remade as *Congo Maisie* (q.v.), followed by *Mogambo* (MGM; 1953) a remake which also starred Gable. Footage from *Red Dust* was later used in *Bombshell* (q.v.).

3758. Red Fork Range (Big 4; 1931). *Cast:* Wally Wales (aka: Hal Taliaferro), Ruth Mix, Al Ferguson, Clifford Lyons, Bud Osborne, Lafe McKee, Jim Corey, Chief Big Tree, Will Armstrong, George Gerwin. *D:* Alvin J. Neitz (Alan James): *P:* John R. Freuler; *Sc:* Neitz. (1:00)
Wally Wales (Hal Taliaferro) western involving an outlaw gang interfering with a stagecoach race.

3759. The Red Haired Alibi (Tower; 1932). *Cast:* Merna Kennedy, Grant Withers, Arthur Hoyt, Theodore von Eltz, Purnell Pratt, Huntley Gordon, Fred Kelsey, Paul Porcasi, Marion Lessing, John Vosburgh, Shirley Temple (feature film debut). *D:* Christy Cabanne; *St:* Wilson Collison.
A "poverty row" melodrama which is notable as the feature film debut of Shirley Temple at age four.

3760. Red-Headed Woman (MGM; 1932). *Cast:* Jean Harlow (Lil Andrews), Chester Morris, Lewis Stone, Leila Hyams, Una Merkel, May Robson, Henry Stephenson, Charles Boyer, Harvey Clark, Luis Alberni. *D:* Jack Conway; *P:* Albert Lewin; *Sc:* Anita Loos. (1:19)
Romantic drama of a tart's efforts to snag her boss's married son. Another early example of a film which suffered censorship problems. Based on the novel by Katharine Brush which appeared in serialized form in *The Saturday Evening Post*.

3761. Red Hot Rhythm (Pathé; 1929). *Cast:* Alan Hale, Kathryn Crawford, Josephine Dunn, Ilka Chase. *D:* Leo McCarey.

Low-budget musical romance with some scenes in 2-color technicolor.

3762. Red Hot Speed (Universal; 1929). *Cast:* Alice Day, Reginald Denny, Charles Byer, Thomas Ricketts, Hector V. Sarno, DeWitt Jennings, Fritzi Ridgeway. *D:* Joseph E. Henabery; *Sc:* Gladys Lehman, Matt Taylor, Albert DeMond, Faith Thomas. (1:10 approx.)

Part-talkie romantic comedy of a girl caught for speeding who attempts to hide the fact from her father, a newspaper publisher currently on an anti-speeding campaign in his paper.

3763. Red Hot Tires (WB/F.N.; 1935). *Cast:* Lyle Talbot, Mary Astor, Roscoe Karns, Frankie Darro, Mary Treen, Henry Kolker, Bradley Page, John Elliott, Eddie Sturgis. *D:* D. Ross Lederman; *P:* Sam Bischoff; *St:* Tristram Tupper; *Sc:* Tupper, Dore Schary. (G.B. title: *Racing Luck*)

A man is accused of murder after an auto race in this B melodrama. No relation to this studio's 1925 silent comedy of the same name.

3764. Red Lights Ahead (Chesterfield; 1936). *Cast:* Paula Stone, Ben Alexander, Lucile Gleason, Sam Flint, Ann Doran. *D:* Roland D. Reed.

"Poverty row" comedy.

3765. Red Morning (RKO; 1934). *Cast:* Steffi Duna, Regis Toomey, Raymond Hatton, Mitchell Lewis, Charles Middleton, George Lewis, Francis McDonald, Arthur "Pat" West, Brandon Hurst, Willie Fung, Olaf Hytten, Alphonse Ethier, Lionel Belmore, James Marcus. *D:* Wallace Fox; *As.P.:* Cliff Reid; *Sc:* Fox, John Twist. (1:03)

Low-budget adventure of a girl and her father who face danger from headhunters following a shipboard mutiny. This film includes footage from an unfinished production by Merian C. Cooper on New Guinea.

3766. Red River Range (Republic; 1938). *Cast:* Ray Corrigan (Tucson Smith), John Wayne (Stony Brooke), Max Terhune (Lullaby), Polly Moran, Lorna Gray (Adrian Booth), Kirby Grant, Sammy McKim, William Royle, Perry Ivins, Stanley Blystone, Lenore Bushman, Roger Williams, Fred "Snowflake" Toones, Burr Caruth, Ed Cassidy, Bob McKenzie, Theodore Lorch. *D:* George Sherman; *P:* William Berke; *Sc:* Stanley Roberts, Betty Burbridge, Luci Ward. (0:56)

"Three Mesquiteers" (#20) western of modern day cattle rustling.

3767. Red River Valley (Republic; 1936). *Cast:* Gene Autry, Smiley Burnette, Frances Grant, Boothe Howard, Jack Kennedy, Sam Flint, George Chesebro, Charles King, Eugene Jackson, Edward Hearn, Frank LaRue, Ken Cooper, Frankie Marvin, Earl Dwire, Cap Anderson, Monty Cass, John Wilson, Lloyd Ingraham, Hank Bell, George Morrell, Champion. *D:* B. Reeves Eason; *P:* Nat Levine; *Supervisor:* Armand Schaefer; *St & Sc:* Dorrell and Stuart McGowan; *Songs:* Autry, Burnette, Sam H. Stept. (Retitled: *Man of the Frontier*—which is also the home-video title) (1:00) (video)

Gene Autry western with songs, of a banker who goes to lengths to halt construction of a dam. This film is no relation to the 1941 feature of the same name by this studio with Roy Rogers.

3768. The Red Rope (Republic-Supreme; 1937). *Cast:* Bob Steele, Lois January, Horace Murphy, Ed Cassidy, Bobby Nelson, Charles King, Lew Meehan, Frank Ball, Karl Hackett, Jack Rockwell. *D:* S. Roy Luby; *P:* A.W. Hackel; *St:* Johnston McCulley; *Sc:* George Plympton. (1:00)

Bob Steele western of a cowboy who assists a young couple who plan to marry.

3769. Red Salute (United Artists/ Reliance; 1935). *Cast:* Barbara Stanwyck, Robert Young, Hardie Albright, Cliff Edwards, Ruth Donnelly, Gordon Jones, Edward McWade, Henry Otho. *D:* Sidney Lanfield; *P:* Edward Small; *St:* Humphrey Pearson; *Sc:* Pearson, Manuel Seff. (1:18)

An offbeat cross-country romantic comedy which stirred controversy upon release due to the fact that communism as a political force is used in the story. The title was also objected to bringing about the use of two alternate titles, namely: *Her Unlisted Man* and *Runaway Daughter.*

3770. Redemption (MGM; 1930). *Cast:* John Gilbert, Renee Adoree, Conrad Nagel, Eleanor Boardman, Claire McDowell, Agostino Borgato, Charles Quartermaine, George Spelvin, Nigel de Brulier, Mack Swain. *D:* Fred Niblo; *P:* Niblo; *Sc:* Dorothy Farnum, Edwin Justus Mayer (based on the play by Arthur Hopkins). (1:04)

Drama of a gypsy thought to be dead who returns to his wife only to find that things are no longer the same. Based on Leo Tolstoy's 1911 novel "The Living Corpse," this is a remake of a 1928 silent German-Russian co-production. A red ink entry for the studio.

3771. Redhead (Monogram; 1934). *Cast:* Bruce Cabot, Grace Bradley, Regis Toomey, Berton Churchill, George Humbert, Rita Campagna, LeRoy Mason, Monte Carter, Jack Mack, Edwin J. Brady, Bess Stafford, Addison Page. *D:* Melville Brown; *Supervisor:* Dorothy Reid (widow of silent screen actor Wallace Reid); *Sc:* Betty Burbridge; *Additional Dialogue:* Jesse Lasky, Jr. (1:16)

Comedy-drama of a night club entertainer who stikes a bargain with the wealthy father of her playboy husband. Based on the novel by Vera Brown, it was remade by this studio in 1941.

3772. Redheads on Parade (Fox; 1935). *Cast:* John Boles, Dixie Lee, Ray-

mond Walburn, William Austin, Herman Bing, Lynn Bari. *D:* Norman Z. McLeod.

Low-budget musical.

3773. Reducing (MGM; 1931). *Cast:* Marie Dressler, Polly Moran, William Collier, Jr., Anita Page, Sally Eilers, William Bakewell, Lucien Littlefield, Roscoe Ates, Jay Ward, Billy Naylor. *D:* Charles Reisner.

Slapstick comedy set in a reducing salon, starring the popular comedy team of Dressler and Moran. One of the 15 top grossing films of 1930–31.

Reefer Madness *see* **The Burning Question**

3774. Reform Girl (Tower; 1933). *Cast:* Robert Ellis, Dorothy Peterson, Noel Francis, Richard "Skeets" Gallagher. *D:* Sam Newfield.

"Poverty row" melodrama.

3775. Reform School (Million Dollar Productions; 1939). *Cast:* Louise Beavers.

(No other information available)

3776. Reformatory (Columbia; 1938). *Cast:* Jack Holt, Frankie Darro, Charlotte Wynters, Sheila Bromley, Lloyd Ingraham, Grant Mitchell, Tommy Bupp, Paul Everton, Ward Bond, Joe Caits. *D:* Lewis D. Collins; *St & Sc:* Gordon Rigby.

Title tells all in this low-budget production.

3777. Registered Nurse (WB/ F.N.; 1934). *Cast:* Bebe Daniels, Lyle Talbot, John Halliday, Irene Franklin, Sidney Toler, Gordon Westcott, Minna Gombell, Mayo Methot, Beulah Bondi, Louise Beavers, Dorothy Burgess, Vince Barnett, Bud Flanagan (Dennis O'Keefe). *D:* Robert Florey; *Supervisor:* Sam Bischoff; *Sc:* Lillie Hayward, Peter Milne.

Romantic drama of two doctors in love with the same nurse. Based on the play by Florence Johns and Wilton Lackaye, Jr.

Registered Woman (G.B. title) *see* **A Woman of Experience**

3778. Religious Racketeer (Xxxx Xxxx; 1938). (No information available)

3779. Remember? (MGM; 1939). *Cast:* Robert Taylor, Greer Garson, Lew Ayres, Billie Burke, Reginald Owen, George Barbier, Henry Travers, Richard Carle, Laura Hope Crews, Halliwell Hobbes, Sig Rumann, Sara Haden, Paul Hurst. *D:* Norman Z. McLeod; *P:* Milton H. Bren; *St:* Corey Ford; *Sc:* McLeod, Ford. (1:23)

Comedy of a feudin' and fightin' married couple who take a magic potion, forget all that's gone before and fall in love all over again.

3780. Remember Last Night? (Universal; 1935). *Cast:* Robert Young, Constance Cummings, Edward Arnold, George Meeker, Sally Eilers, Louise Henry, Arthur Treacher, Robert Armstrong, Reginald Denny, Edward Brophy, Jack LaRue, Gustav von Seyffertitz, Gregory Ratoff, Monroe Owsley, E.E. Clive, Rafaela Ottiano, Frank Reicher. *D:* James Whale; *P:* Carl Laemmle, Jr.; *Sc:* Harry Clork, Dan Totheroh, Doris Malloy. (1:21)

Offbeat comedy-mystery of a wealthy socialite couple who awaken one morning after a wild drunken party to find murder in their midst. Based on the novel "The Hangover Murders" by Adam Hobhouse.

Remember the Alamo *see* **Heroes of the Alamo**

3781. Remote Control (MGM; 1930). *Cast:* William Haines, Charles King, Eileen Percy, John Miljan, J.C. Nugent, Mary Doran, Polly Moran, Edward Nugent, Ed Brophy, Wilbur Mack, Warner Richmond. *D:* Nick Grinde, Mal St. Clair (with some scenes by Edward Sedgwick); *Sc:* Frank Butler & others.

B comedy of a radio announcer who puts the crimps to a shady radio personality.

3782. Rendevous (MGM; 1935). *Cast:* William Powell, Rosalind Russell (in a role planned for Myrna Loy), Binnie Barnes, Lionel Atwill, Cesar Romero, Samuel S. Hinds, Henry Stephenson, Frank Reicher, Charley Grapewin, Milburn Stone, Leonard Mudie, Howard Hickman, Charles Trowbridge, Margaret Dumont, Sterling Holloway. *D:* William K. Howard; *P:* Lawrence Weingarten; *Adaptation:* Sam & Bella Spewack; *Sc:* P.J. Wolfson, George Oppenheimer. (1:31)

World War I home-front comedy-drama of a clerk who gets involved in an enemy spy plot. Based on the novel "Black Chamber" by Major Herbert Yardley. Remade as *Pacific Rendevous* (MGM; 1942).

3783. Rendevous at Midnight (Universal; 1935). *Cast:* Ralph Bellamy, Valerie Hobson, Catherine Doucet, Irene Ware, Helen Jerome Eddy, Kathlyn Williams, Edgar Kennedy. *D:* Christy Cabanne. (1:04)

A B who-dun-it set in city politics.

3784. The Renegade Ranger (RKO; 1939). *Cast:* George O'Brien, Rita Hayworth, Tim Holt, Ray Whitley, Lucio Villegas, William Royle, Cecilia Callejo, Neal Hart, Monte Montague, Robert Kortman, Charles Stevens, Tom London, James (Jim) Mason. *D:* David Howard; *P:* Bert Gilroy; *St:* Bennett Cohen; *Sc:* Oliver Drake; *Songs:* Albert Hay Malotte, Willie Phelps. (0:59) (video)

George O'Brien western of a Texas Ranger who sets out to bring in a wanted female outlaw. A remake of *Come On, Danger* (q.v.). Remade as *Come On, Danger* (RKO; 1942) with Tim Holt.

3785. The Renegade Trail (Paramount; 1939). *Cast:* William Boyd

(Hoppy), Russell Hayden (Lucky), George Hayes (Windy), Charlotte Wynters, Russell Hopton, Sonny Bupp, Jack Rockwell, Roy Barcroft, John Merton, Eddie Dean, Robert Kortman, King's Men. *D:* Lesley Selander; *P:* Harry M. Sherman; *Sc:* John Rathmell, Harrison Jacobs. (1:01) (video)

Number 26 in the "Hopalong Cassidy" series as the Bar 20 boys help a woman and her son plagued by cattle rustlers.

3786. Renegades (Fox; 1930). *Cast:* Warner Baxter, Myrna Loy, Noah Beery, Bela Lugosi, Gregory Gaye, George Cooper, C. Henry Gordon, Noble Johnson, Colin Chase. *D:* Victor Fleming; *Sc:* Jules Furthman. (1:24)

A tale of the French Foreign Legion. Based on the novel "Le Renegat" by André Armandy.

3787. Renegades of the West (RKO; 1932–33). *Cast:* Tom Keene, Betty Furness, Roscoe Ates, James (Jim) Mason, Carl Miller, Max Wagner, Rockliffe Fellowes, Roland Southern, Jules Cowles, Joseph Girard, Jack Pennick. *D:* Casey Robinson; *As.P.:* B.F. Zeidman; *Sc:* Albert LeVino. (0:55)

Tom Keene horse opera of cattle rustling, murder and revenge. A remake of *The Miracle Baby* (Film Booking Office; 1923) with Harry Carey.

3788. Renfrew of the Royal Mounted (Grand National; 1937). *Cast:* James Newill (in his starring debut as Renfrew), Carol Hughes, William Royle, Herbert Corthell, Kenneth Harlan, Dickie Jones, Chief Thundercloud, William Austin, Lightning the Wonder Dog, Donald Reed, Bob Terry, William Gould, David Barclay (Dave O'Brien), Dwight Frye. *D:* Al Herman; *P:* Phil Krasne, Herman; *Sc:* Charles Logue. (0:57)

Premiere entry in a series of action-adventure dramas set in the wilds of Canada. In this entry, Sergeant Renfrew, the singing Mountie tracks down the killers of a fellow Mountie. Includes the song "Mounted Men." Suggested by a series of books by Laurie York Erskine and a popular radio show of the 1930s.

Renfrew of the Great White Trail
see **On the Great White Trail**

3789. Reno (Sono Art-World Wide; 1930). *Cast:* Kenneth Thomson, Doris Lloyd, Ruth Roland (former silent screen serial queen), Montagu Love, Douglas Scott, Sam Hardy, Alyce McCormick, Edward Hearn, Judith Vosselli, Emmett King. *D:* George J. Crone; *Songs:* Leslie Barton (Sam Coslow).

"Poverty row" drama based on a story by Cornelius Vanderbilt, Jr. Filmed before in 1923 for Goldwyn by director Rupert Hughes with George Walsh.

3790. Reno (RKO; 1939). *Cast:* Richard Dix, Gail Patrick, Anita Louise, Paul Cavanagh, Laura Hope Crews, Louis Jean Heydt, Hobart Cavanaugh, Charles Halton, Astrid Allwyn, Joyce Compton, Frank Faylen, William Haade, Carole Landis. *D:* John Farrow; *P:* Robert Sisk; *St:* Ellis St. Joseph; *Sc:* John Twist. (1:13)

Retrospective drama of how a lawyer brought the town of Reno, Nevada, from a mining town to the country's best known haven for those marrieds intent on dissolving their marriage ties.

3791. Reported Missing (Universal; 1937). *Cast:* Jean Rogers, William Gargan, Dick Purcell, Joe Sawyer, Hobart Cavanaugh, Jack Carson, Robert Spencer, Michael Fitzmaurice, Billy Wayne. *D:* Milton Carruth; *P:* E.M. Asher; *St:* Verne Whitehead; *Sc:* Jerome Chodorov, Joseph Fields. (1:04)

B action-drama of an ex-pilot out to apprehend a plane saboteur.

Reprieved (G.B. title) *see* **Sing Sing Nights**

Reputation (G.B. title) *see* **Lady with a Past**

3792. Rescue Squad (Empire; 1935). *Cast:* Ralph Forbes, Sheila Terry, Verna Hillie, Jimmy Aubrey. *D:* Spencer Gordon Bennet.
Independent B melodrama.

The Rest Cure *see* **We're in the Legion Now**

3793. Resurrection (Universal; 1931). *Cast:* Lupe Velez (Katusha), John Boles (Prince Dimitri Nekhludoff), Nance O'Neil (Princess Marya), William Keighley (Mayor Schoenblock), Rose Tapley (Princess Sophya), Grace Cunard, George Irving, Mary Forman, Michael Mark, Edward Cecil, Dorothy Flood, Sylva Nadina. *D:* Edwin Carewe (who also directed the '27 version); *Sc:* Finis Fox. (1:21)
A much filmed romantic drama of a Russian prince and a peasant girl. Based on the 1889–1900 novel by Leo Tolstoy. First filmed in 1907 with later productions (Biograph; 1909) with Florence Lawrence and Arthur Johnson, as well as 1909, 1912, 1915, 1918 and (United Artists; 1927) with Dolores Del Rio and Rod La Rocque. Remade as *We Live Again* (q.v.) and again in 1961 in Russia.

3794. The Return of Casey Jones (Monogram; 1933). *Cast:* Charles Starrett, Ruth Hall, Robert Elliott, George Hayes, Jackie Searle, George Walsh, Margaret Seddon, G.D. Wood (Gordon DeMain), George Nash, Anne Howard. *D:* John P. McCarthy; *P:* I.E. Chadwick; *Sc:* McCarthy, Harry O. Jones (Harry Fraser)—based on the novelette "Railroad Stories" by John Johns). (G.B. title: *Train 2419*) (1:03)
Low-budget actioner of the legendary railroad engineer.

3795. The Return of Chandu (Principal; 1934). *Cast:* Bela Lugosi (Chandu), Maria Alba (Princess Nadji), Clara Kimball Young, Iron Eyes Cody, Lucien Prival, Phyllis Ludwig, Bryant Washburn. *D:* Ray Taylor; *P:* Sol Lesser; *Sc:* Barry Barringer. (See also: *Chandu on Magic Island*) (1:19) (video— available in feature version & full serial)
Feature version of the first four chapters of the serial of the same name as an occult magician goes to a mysterious island to rescue a princess from an evil sorceress who reigns over a cult of cat-worshippers.

3796. The Return of Dr. Fu Manchu (Paramount; 1930). *Cast:* Warner Oland, Jean Arthur, Neil Hamilton, O.P. Heggie, William Austin, Shayle Gardner, Evelyn Hall. *D:* Rowland V. Lee; *Sc:* Lloyd Corrigan, Florence Ryerson. (aka: *The New Adventures of Dr. Fu Manchu*)
The second entry in a series of three films by this studio of the evil oriental, who in this one is out to do in the family of his adopted daughter's boyfriend. See also: *The Mysterious Dr. Fu Manchu* (q.v.) and *Daughter of the Dragon* (q.v.). Based on the characters created by Sax Rohmer.

3797. The Return of Doctor X (WB; 1939). *Cast:* Wayne Morris, Rosemary Lane, Humphrey Bogart (Doctor X—Marshall Quesne), Dennis Morgan, John Litel, Lya Lys, Huntz Hall, John Ridgely, Glenn Langan (film debut—better known as *The Amazing Colossal Man* [American International; 1957]), Ian Wolfe, DeWolf (William) Hopper, Arthur Aylesworth, Howard Hickman, Vera Lewis, Charles Wilson, Jack Mower. *D:* Vincent Sherman (directorial debut); *As.P.:* Bryan Foy; *Sc:* Lee Katz. (1:02)
B horror film with the curiosity of Bogart as the undead villain. Based on the novel "The Doctor's Secret" by William J. Makin, the film is *not* a sequel to *Doctor X* (q.v.).

3798. The Return of Jimmy Valentine (Republic; 1936). *Cast:* Roger Pryor, Charlotte Henry, Lois Wilson, Robert Warwick, J. Carrol Naish, Edgar Kennedy, Lane Chandler, George Chesebro, Wade Boteler, Charles C. Wilson, Dewey Robinson. *D:* Lewis Collins; *Sc:* Olive Cooper (co-writer).

B crime melodrama of a newspaper's efforts to track down a retired cracksman, thus setting off a series of murders. Remade as *The Affairs of Jimmy Valentine* (Republic; 1942). A hit for the studio.

3799. The Return of Peter Grimm (RKO; 1935). *Cast:* Lionel Barrymore (Peter Grimm), Helen Mack, Edward Ellis, Donald Meek, George Breakston, Allen Vincent, James Bush, Lucien Littlefield, Ethel Griffies, Ray Mayer, Greta Meyer. *D:* George Nicholls, Jr.; *P:* Kenneth MacGowan (his last for RKO); *Sc:* Francis Edwards Faragoh. (1:23)

Offbeat drama of the spirit of a deceased man who returns to correct a mistake he made before his death. Based on the play by David Belasco, it was previously filmed in 1925 by Fox with Alec B. Francis and Janet Gaynor.

3800. The Return of Sherlock Holmes (Paramount; 1929). *Cast:* Cive Brook, H. Reeves-Smith, Harry T. Morey, Betty Lawford, Phillips Holmes, Charles Hay, Hubert Druce, Arthur Mack, Donald Crisp. *D:* Basil Dean.

Low-budget mystery-melodrama which has Holmes vs. Professor Moriarty on an ocean voyage. Based on the characters created by Sir Arthur Conan Doyle.

3801. The Return of Sophie Lang (Paramount; 1936). *Cast:* Gertrude Michael (Sophie Lang), Sir Guy Standing, Ray Milland, Elizabeth Patterson, Colin Tapley, Paul Harvey, Ted Oliver, Don Rowan, Garry Owen, Purnell Pratt, James Blaine, Terry Ray (Ellen Drew). *D:* George Archainbaud; *P:* A.M. Botsford; *St:* Frederick Irving Anderson; *Sc:* Patterson McNutt, Brian Marlow. (1:0)

The second entry in a B series of three films of a lady jewel thief who is trying to go straight.

3802. The Return of the Cisco Kid (20th Century–Fox; 1939). *Cast:* Warner Baxter (Kid), Cesar Romero, Lynn Bari, Chris-Pin Martin, C. Henry Gordon, Kane Richmond, Henry Hull, Robert Barrat, Ward Bond, Victor Kilian, Eddie (Eddy) Waller, Arthur Aylesworth, Adrian Morris, Harry Strang, Ruth Gillette, Paul Burns, Ralph Dunn. *D:* Herbert I. Leeds; *As.P.:* Kenneth MacGowan; *Sc:* Milton Sperling.

B western which is a delayed sequel to *The Cisco Kid* (q.v.). Followed by *Cisco Kid and the Lady* (q.v.).

3803. The Return of the Terror (WB/F.N.; 1934). *Cast:* John Halliday, Mary Astor, Lyle Talbot, Frank McHugh, Irving Pichel, J. Carrol Naish, Frank Reicher, Reneé Whitney (Virginia Mayo), George E. Stone, Charley Grapewin, Maude Eburne, George Cooper. *D:* Howard Bretherton; *Supervisor:* Sam Bischoff; *Sc:* Eugene Solow, Peter Milne. (1:05)

B mystery-thriller of a man who escapes prosecution for murder by feigning insanity. The title is from a book by Edgar Wallace and the film is a loose remake of *The Terror* (q.v).

Re-Union (G.B. title) *see* **In Love with Life**

3804. Reunion (20th Century–Fox; 1936). *Cast:* Dionne Quintuplets (Annette, Cecile, Emilie, Marie & Yvonne), Jean Hersholt, Rochelle Hudson, J. Edward Bromberg, Dorothy Peterson, Tom Moore, Helen Vinson, Slim Summerville, Esther Ralston, Sara Haden, Maude Eburne, Hattie McDaniel, John Qualen, Robert Kent, Montagu Love, George Chandler, Julius Tannen, George Ernest, Katherine Alexander. *D:* Norman Taurog; *St:* Bruce Gould; *Sc:* Sonya Levien, Gladys Lehman, Sam Hellman. (G.B. title: *Hearts in Reunion*)

Hit sequel to the popular *The Country Doctor* (q.v.), relaying a story centered around the Dionne quintuplets. Followed by *Five of a Kind* (q.v.).

3805. Reunion in Vienna (MGM; 1933). *Cast:* John Barrymore, Diana Wynyard, Frank Morgan, May Robson, Eduardo Ciannelli (film debut), Una Merkel, Henry Travers (film debut), Nella Walker, Stephen Morris (Morris Ankrum — film debut), Bodil Rosing, Herbert Evans, Bela Loblov, Morris Nussbaum. *D:* Sidney Franklin; *Sc:* Ernest Vajda, Claudine West; *Cinematographer:* (A.A.N.) George J. Folsey. (1:40)

Sophisticated romantic comedy of an exiled nobleman's attempts to regain his now married ex-girlfriend. Based on the play by Robert E. Sherwood, it received the #2 position on the "10 Best" list of the *New York Times.* A box office flop.

3806. Revenge at Monte Carlo (Mayfair; 1933). *Cast:* Lloyd Whitlock, June Collyer, Dorothy Gulliver, Wheeler Oakman, Edward Earle, Lloyd Ingraham, Clarence Geldert. *D:* B. Reeves Eason.

"Poverty row" melodrama.

3807/3808. The Revenge Rider (Columbia; 1935). *Cast:* Tim McCoy, Robert Allen, Billie Seward, Edward Earle, Frank Sheridan, Jack Clifford, Jack Mower, George Pierce, Joseph (Sawyer) Sauers, Allan Sears, Harry Semels, Lafe McKee, Charles King, Tom London. *D:* David Selman; *Sc:* Ford Beebe. (1:00)

Tim McCoy shoot-'em-up of a man who returns to his home town to find that his brother, the sheriff has been murdered. Remade as *Riders of Black River* (q.v.).

3809. Revolt of the Zombies (Academy Pictures; 1936). *Cast:* Dean Jagger, Dorothy Stone, Roy D'Arcy, Robert Noland, George Cleveland, Carl Stockdale, Teru Shimada, William Crowell, Fred Warren. *D:* Victor Halperin; *P:* Edward Halperin; *Sc:* Howard Higgin, Rollo Lloyd, Victor Halperin. (1:05) (video)

Independent B horror film of dead Cambodian soldiers who are re-animated to become the titled terrors.

Rhuma *see* **Rumba**

3810. Rhythm in the Clouds (Republic; 1937). *Cast:* Patricia Ellis, Warren Hull, Joyce Compton. *D:* John H. Auer.

3811. Rhythm of the Saddle (Republic; 1938). *Cast:* Gene Autry, Smiley Burnette, Pert Kelton, Peggy Moran, LeRoy Mason, Arthur Loft, Ethan Laidlaw, Walter De Palma, Archie Hall, Eddie Hart, Eddie Acuff, Douglas Wright, Kelsey Sheldon, Lola Monte, Alan Gregg, Rudy Sooter, James (Jim) Mason, Jack Kirk, Emmett Vogan, Roger Williams, Tom London, Curley Dresden, William Norton Bailey, Champion. *D:* George Sherman; *P:* Harry Grey; *Sc:* Paul Franklin. (0:58)

A Gene Autry western with songs and a rodeo plot.

Rhythm on the Ranch (G.B. title) *see* **Rootin' Tootin' Rhythm**

3812. Rhythm on the Range (Paramount; 1936). *Cast:* Bing Crosby (Jeff Larrabee), Martha Raye (feature film debut as Emma), Frances Farmer (Doris Halliday), Robert "Bazooka Bob" Burns (Buck Burns), Lucile Webster Gleason (Penelope Ryland), Samuel S.

Hinds (Robert Halliday), George E. Stone (Shorty), Warren Hymer (Big Brain), Martha Sleeper (Constance), Leonid Kinskey (Mischa), Clem Bevans (Gila Bend), Charles Williams (Gopher), James Burke (Wabash), Beau Baldwin (Cuddles), Billy Bletcher (other Shorty), Syd Saylor (Gus), Sons of the Pioneers with Dick Weston (Roy Rogers), Emmett Vogan, Eddy Waller, Bud Flanagan (Dennis O'Keefe), Herbert Ashley, Duke York, James Blaine, James "Slim" Thompson, Edward Le-Saint, Jim Toney, Robert E. Homans, Sam McDaniel, Oscar Smith, Charles E. Arnt, Harry C. Bradley, Bob McKenzie, Otto Yamaoka, Heinie Conklin, Irving Bacon, Frank Dawson, Terry Ray (Ellen Drew). *D:* Norman Taurog; *P:* Benjamin Glazer; *St:* Mervin J. Houser; *Sc:* Sidney Salkow, John C. Moffitt, Walter de Leon, Francis Martin; *Songs:* "I Can't Escape from You" by Leo Robin, Richard A. Whiting; "I'm an Old Cowhand (from the Rio Grande)" by Johnny Mercer; "If You Can't Sing It You'll Have to Swing It (Mr. Paganini)" by Sam Coslow (and sung by Ms. Raye); "The House Jack Built for Jill" by Leo Robin, Frederick Hollander; "Drink It Down" by Leo Robin, Ralph Rainger; "Hang Up My Saddle" & the title song by Walter Bullock, Richard A. Whiting; "Memories" by Richard A. Whiting, Frederick Hollander; "Roundup Lullaby" by Bager Clark, Gertrude Ross; & "Empty Saddles" by Billy Hill, J. Keirn Brennan. (1:27)

A musical-comedy with a western setting which became one of the 25 top grossing films of 1935–36. Remade as *Pardners* (Paramount; 1956).

Rhythm on the River (G.B. title) *see* **Freshman Love**

Rhythm Romance *see* **Some Like It Hot**

3813. The Rich Are Always With Us (WB/F.N.; 1932). *Cast:* Miss

Ruth Chatterton, George Brent, John Miljan, Bette Davis, Adrienne Dore, Robert Warwick, Mae Madison, Berton Churchill, Virginia Hammond, Eula Guy, Walter Walker. *D:* Alfred E. Green; *P:* Sam Bischoff; *Sc:* Austin Parker. (1:13)

Comedy-drama of a woman who following her divorce, still loves her husband. Based on the novel by E. Pettit.

3814. Rich Man, Poor Girl (MGM; 1938). *Cast:* Robert Young, Lew Ayres, Ruth Hussey, Lana Turner, Guy Kibbee, Sarah Padden, Rita Johnson, Don Castle, Gordon Jones, Virginia Grey, Marie Blake. *D:* Reinhold Schunzel; *P:* Edward Chodorov; *Sc:* Joseph Fields, Jerome Chodorov. (1:05)

A comedy-drama, aptly described by the title and based on the play "White Collars" by Edith Ellis which was adapted from a story by Edgar Franklin. A remake of *The Idle Rich* (q.v.).

3815. Rich Man's Folly (Paramount; 1931). *Cast:* George Bancroft, Frances Dee, Robert Ames, Juliette Compton, Dorothy Peterson, Gilbert Emery, David Durand, Guy Oliver, George MacFarlane, Dawn O'Day (Anne Shirley), William Arnold. *D:* John Cromwell; *Sc:* Grover Jones, Edward E. Paramore, Jr. (1:20)

A man shows minimal interest in rearing his children. Based on the 1848 novel "Dombey and Son" by Charles Dickens.

3816. Rich People (Pathé; 1930). *Cast:* Constance Bennett, Mahlon Hamilton, Regis Toomey, John Loder, Ilka Chase, Polly Ann Young. *D:* Edward H. Griffith.

This is cinematic proof that money can't buy happiness.

3817. The Richest Girl in the World (RKO; 1934). *Cast:* Miriam Hopkins, Joel McCrea, Fay Wray, Henry Stephenson, Reginald Denny,

Beryl Mercer, George Meeker, Wade Boteler, Herbert Bunston, Burr McIntosh, Edgar Norton, Frederic Howard. *D:* William A. Seiter, Glenn Tryon (unc.); *P:* Pandro S. Berman; *St:* Norman Krasna; *Sc:* Krasna, Tryon (unc.). (1:16)

A hit comedy of a wealthy woman in search of a man who is interested in her instead of her millions. Remade as *Bride by Mistake* (RKO; 1944).

The Richest Man in the World (G.B. title) *see* **Sins of the Children**

3818. Riddle Ranch (Beaumont; 1935). *Cast:* Black King the horse, David Worth, June Marlowe, Baby Charlene Barry, Julian Rivero, Richard Cramer, Fred "Snowflake" Toones, Budd Buster, Art Felix, Henry Sylvester, Ray Gallagher, Ace Cain. *D:* Charles Hutchison; *P:* Mitchell Leichter; *Sc:* L.V. Jefferson. (1:03)

B western horse story of a Mexican outlaw who wants a rancher's prize stallion. The second of two "horse operas" featuring the equine star "Black King." See also: *Gunners and Guns* (q.v.).

3819. Ride a Crooked Mile (Paramount; 1938). *Cast:* Akim Tamiroff, Frances Farmer, Leif Erickson, Lynne Overman, John Miljan, Nestor Paiva (film debut), J.M. Kerrigan, Eva Novak, Ethel Clayton, Vladimir Sokoloff, Dewey Robinson, John Bleifer, James Flavin, Michael Mark, William Newell, Fred "Snowflake" Toones, Leonid Snegoff, Alex Woloshin, Michael Dido, Wade Crosby. *D:* Alfred E. Green; *P:* Jeff Lazarus; *St & Sc:* Ferdinand Reyher, John C. Moffitt. (G.B. title: *Escape from Yesterday*) (1:18)

Offbeat B western melodrama of a Russian Cossack who comes to America and becomes a cattle rustler.

3820. Ride 'em Cowboy (Universal; 1936). *Cast:* Buck Jones, Luana Walters, George Cooper, William Law-

rence, J.P. McGowan, Joseph Girard, Donald Kirke, Charles LeMoyne, Edmund Cobb, Lester Dorr. *D:* Lesley Selander (feature directorial debut); *P:* Jones; *Sc:* Frances Guihan. (TV title: *Cowboy Roundup*) (0:59)

Offbeat Buck Jones western of a cowboy who takes up auto racing to save his girl and her father from impending bankruptcy. Based on an original story by Jones.

3821. Ride 'em Cowgirl (Grand National/Coronado Pictures; 1939). *Cast:* Dorothy Page, Milton Frome, Vince Barnett, Lynn Mayberry, Joseph Girard, Frank Ellis, Harrington Reynolds, Merrill McCormack, Fred Berhle, Pat Henning, Edward Gordon, Fred Cordova, Lester Dorr, Walter Patterson, Snowey the horse. *D:* Samuel Diege; *P:* George A. Hirliman, Arthur Dreifuss; *St & Sc:* Arthur Hoerl. (0:52) (video)

Dorothy Page western of a girl's father who is framed in an attempt to get his ranch. Ms. Page was the only member of the fair sex to ever have her own B series of westerns, ending with the third production when Grand National closed its doors in 1939.

3822. Ride Him Cowboy (WB/Vitagraph; 1932). *Cast:* John Wayne, Ruth Hall, Henry B. Walthall, Harry Gribbon, Otis Harlan, Frank Hagney, Charles Sellon, Lafe McKee, Ben Corbett, Glenn Strange, Fred Burns, Duke the horse. *D:* Fred Allen; *St:* Kenneth Perkins; *Sc:* Scott Mason. (G.B. title: *The Hawk*) (0:56)

John Wayne (in his first series western) in a story involving a wild horse named "Duke" blamed for killing a rancher. A remake of *The Unknown Cavalier* (First National; 1926) with Ken Maynard.

3823. Ride, Ranger, Ride (Republic; 1936). *Cast:* Gene Autry, Smiley Burnette, Kay Hughes, Monte Blue, Max Terhune (film debut), George J.

Lewis, Robert E. Homans, Chief Thundercloud, Frankie Marvin, Iron Eyes Cody, Sunny Chorre, Bud Pope, Nelson McDowell, Shooting Star, Arthur Singley, Tennessee Ramblers, Greg Whitespear, Robert Thomas, Champion. *D:* Joe Kane; *P:* Nat Levine; *As.P.:* Armand Schaefer; *St:* Karen DeWolf, Bernard McConville; *Sc:* Dorrell & Stuart McGowan; *Songs:* Sam H. Stept, Sidney D. Mitchell, Sons of the Pioneers, Smiley Burnette. (1:03) (video)

Gene Autry western with songs of a Texas Ranger caught between Indians and the cavalry.

3824. Rider of Death Valley (Universal; 1932). *Cast:* Tom Mix, Tony, Lois Wilson, Fred Kohler, Otis Harlan, Forrest Stanley, Willard Robertson, Edith Fellows, Mae Busch, Max Asher, Edmund Cobb, Pete Morrison, Francis Ford, Richard Cramer, Bob McKenzie, Lloyd Whitlock, Iron Eyes Cody. *D:* Albert S. Rogell; *Sc:* Jack Cunningham. (TV title: *Riders of the Desert*) (1:05)

A Tom Mix western, his second of nine features for this studio. The story of a cowboy who helps a girl whose brother was killed while protecting their gold mine. The film had the original working title of "Destry of Death Valley." Remade in 1941 as a serial.

3825. Rider of the Law (Supreme; 1935). *Cast:* Bob Steele, Gertrude Messinger, Si Jenks, Earl Dwire, Forrest Taylor, Lloyd Ingraham, John Elliott, Sherry Tansey, Tex Palmer, Chuck Baldra. *D:* Robert N. Bradbury; *P:* A.W. Hackel; *Sc:* Jack Natteford. (0:56)

Bob Steele western of a government agent in disguise to capture a gang of outlaws.

3826. Rider of the Plains (Syndicate; 1931). *Cast:* Tom Tyler, Andy Shuford, Lillian Bond, Alan Bridge, Gordon DeMain, Jack Perrin, Slim

Whitaker, Ted Adams, Fern Emmett. *D:* J.P. McCarthy; *Sc:* Wellyn Totman. (0:57)

Tom Tyler western of an outlaw, reformed by the love of a girl and the friendship of a young boy.

3827. Riders of Black River (Columbia; 1939). *Cast:* Charles Starrett, Iris Meredith, Sons of the Pioneers with Bob Nolan & Pat Brady, Dick Curtis, Edmund Cobb, Stanley Brown, Francis Sayles, George Chesebro, Forrest Taylor, Olin Francis, Lew Meehan, Maston Williams. *D:* Norman Deming; *Sc:* Bennett Cohen. (0:59)

Charles Starrett western of a former ranger who intends to marry, but finds the girl's brother is involved with an outlaw gang. A remake of *The Revenge Rider* (q.v.).

3828. Riders of Destiny (Monogram-Lone Star; 1933). *Cast:* John Wayne (Singin' Sandy Saunders), Cecilia Parker, George Hayes, Forrest Taylor, Al St. John, Charles "Heinie" Conklin, Earl Dwire, Lafe McKee, Horace B. Carpenter, Yakima Canutt, Hal Price, Si Jenks, Duke the horse. *D:* Robert N. Bradbury; *P:* Paul Malvern; *Supervisor:* Trem Carr; *St:* Bradbury; *Sc:* Bradbury. (0:58) (video)

John Wayne western dealing with the settling of water rights for ranchers.

3829. Riders of the Black Hills (Republic; 1938). *Cast:* Bob Livingston (Stony Brooke), Ray Corrigan (Tucson Smith), Max Terhune (Lullaby), Ann Evers, Roscoe Ates, Maude Eburne, Johnny Lang Fitzgerald, Frank Melton, Jack Ingram, John P. Wade, Fred "Snowflake" Toones, Monte Montague, Jack O'Shea, Art Dillard. *D:* George Sherman; *Sc:* Betty Burbridge; *St:* Bernard McConville. (0:55)

A "Three Mesquiteers" western, the 15th entry in the hit series, this one involving a kidnapped race horse.

3830. Riders of the Cactus (Big 4; 1931). *Cast:* Wally Wales, Buzz Barton, Lorraine LaVal, Fred Church, Ed Cartwright, Don Wilson. *D:* David Kirkland; *P:* John R. Freuler; *Sc:* Kirkland. (1:00)

Wally Wales (Hal Taliaferro) western of a search for buried treasure.

3831. Riders of the Dawn (Monogram; 1937). *Cast:* Jack Randall (real-life brother of Bob Livingston), Peggy Keyes, Warner Richmond, George Cooper, James Sheridan (Sherry Tansey), Earl Dwire, Lloyd Ingraham, Ed Brady, Yakima Canutt, Steve Clark, Frank Hagney, Ella McKenzie, Ed Coxen, Chick Hannon, Tim Davis, Jim Corey, Oscar Gahan, Forrest Taylor, Tex Cooper. *D:* Robert N. Bradbury; *P:* Bradbury; *Supervisor:* Scott R. Dunlap; *Sc:* Robert Emmett (Tansey). (0:53)

Jack Randall's (nee: Addison Randall) premiere entry as a western cowboy hero. A marshal helps a town which is the target of a gang of outlaws. No relation to the 1945 Jimmy Wakely western of the same name by this studio.

3832. Riders of the Desert (Sono Art-World Wide; 1932). *Cast:* Bob Steele, Gertrude Messinger, George Hayes, Al St. John, Horace B. Carpenter, Louise Carter, Joe Dominguez, Greg Whitespear, John Elliott, Earl Dwire. *D:* Robert N. Bradbury; *Sc:* Wellyn Totman. (0:57)

Bob Steele "poverty row" western of an Arizona Ranger on the trail of some bad guys.

Riders of the Desert (Universal; 1932) *see* **The Rider of Death Valley**

3833. Riders of the Frontier (Monogram; 1939). *Cast:* Tex Ritter, Jack Rutherford, Hal Taliaferro (Wally Wales), Jean Joyce, Marin Sais, Mantan Moreland, Olin Francis, Roy Barcroft, Merrill McCormack, Maxine Leslie, Nolan Willis, Nelson McDowell, Charles King, Forrest Taylor, Robert Frazer, White Flash the horse. *D:* Spen-

cer Gordon Bennet; *P:* Edward Finney (for Boots & Saddles Productions); *Sc:* Jesse Duffy, Joseph Levering. (G.B. title: *Ridin' the Frontier*) (0:58)

Tex Ritter western with musical interludes of undercover work to expose a vicious gang.

3834. Riders of the Golden Gulch (West Coast; 1932). *Cast:* Buffalo Bill, Jr., Yakima Canutt, Mary Dunn, Peter Morrison, Edmund Cobb. *D:* Clifford Smith; *Sc:* Yakima Canutt. (0:52)

Buffalo Bill, Jr., western.

3835. Riders of the North (Syndicate; 1931). *Cast:* Bob Custer, Blanche Mehaffey, Frank Rice, Eddie Dunn, George Regas, Buddy Shaw, William Walling. *D:* J.P. McGowan; *Sc:* George Arthur Durlam. (0:59)

Bob Custer northwoods adventure of a Mountie after some bad guys.

3836. Riders of the Purple Sage (Fox; 1931). *Cast:* George O'Brien, Marguerite Churchill, Noah Beery, Yvonne Pelletier, James Todd, Stanley Fields, Lester Dorr, Frank McGlynn, Sr., Shirley Nails. *D:* Hamilton MacFadden; *Sc:* John F. Goodrich, Philip Klein, Barry Connors. (0:58)

George O'Brien western based on one of Zane Grey's better known novels, originally published in 1912. A cowboy kills the man who kidnapped his sister, becomes an outcast and eventually saves a girl and her ranch from outlaws. Two previous filmings include (Fox; 1918) with William Farnum and (Fox; 1925) with Tom Mix. Remade (20th Century–Fox; 1941) with George Montgomery. Followed by a sequel, *The Rainbow Trail* (q.v.).

3837. Riders of the Rockies (Grand National; 1937). *Cast:* Tex Ritter, Louise Stanley, Snub Pollard, Horace Murphy, Charles King, Yakima Canutt, Earl Dwire, Martin Garralaga, Jack Rockwell, Pard Lopez, Heber

Snow (Hank Worden), Tex Palmer, Clyde McClary, Tex Ritter's Texas Tornadoes, White Flash the horse. *D:* Robert N. Bradbury; *P:* Edward F. Finney (for Boots & Saddles Productions); *Sc:* Robert Emmett (Tansey), Norman Leslie. (0:59) (video — 0:56)

Tex Ritter western with songs of a ranger who goes undercover within a gang of cattle rustlers.

3838. Riders of the Sage (Metropolitan; 1939). *Cast:* Bob Steele, Claire Rochelle, Ralph Hoopes, James Whitehead, Earl Douglas, Ted Adams, Dave O'Brien, Frank LaRue, Bruce Dane, Jerry Sheldon, Reed Howes, Bud Osborne, Gordon Roberts (Carlton Young). *D:* Harry S. Webb; *Sc:* Carl Krusada. (0:55) (video)

Bob Steele range saga of a feud between cattlemen and sheepmen.

3839. Riders of the Whistling Skull (Republic; 1937). *Cast:* Bob Livingston (Stony Brooke), Ray Corrigan (Tucson Smith), Max Terhune (Lullaby Joslin), Mary Russell, Yakima Canutt, Fern Emmett, Roger Williams, C. Montague Shaw, John Ward, George Godfrey, Frank Ellis, Earle Ross, John Van Pelt, Ed Peil, Chief Thundercloud, Jack Kirk, Iron Eyes Cody, Tom Steele, Wally West, Tracy Layne, Ken Cooper. *D:* Mack V. Wright; *P:* Nat Levine; *Sc:* Oliver Drake. (0:58) (video)

The 4th "Three Mesquiteers" entry and one of the most popular at the box office. The trio find a lost city and a hidden treasure in this offbeat series entry. Based on William Colt MacDonald's 1934 novel "The Singing Scorpion."

3840. The Ridin' Fool (Tiffany; 1931). *Cast:* Bob Steele, Frances Morris, Ted Adams, Florence Turner, Alan Bridge, Eddie Fetherston, Jack Henderson, Gordon DeMain, Josephine Velez, Fern Emmett, Artie Ortego. *D:* John P. McCarthy; *P:* Trem Carr; *Sc:* Wellyn Totman. (0:58)

Bob Steele oater of romantic rivalry between a cowboy and the gambler he saved from hanging, when they both fall for the same girl.

3841. Ridin' for Justice (Columbia; 1931–32). *Cast:* Buck Jones, Mary Doran, Walter Miller. *D:* D. Ross Lederman.

Buck Jones western.

3842. Ridin' Law (Big 4/Biltmore; 1930). *Cast:* Jack Perrin, Reneé Borden, Yakima Canutt, Jack Mower, Ben Corbett, Robert Walker, Pete Morrison, Fern Emmett, Olive Young. *D:* Harry S. Webb; *P:* John R. Freuler; *Sc:* Carl Krusada. (0:55)

Jack Perrin western of a man searching in Mexico for the killer of his father.

3843. Ridin' On (Reliable; 1935–36). *Cast:* Tom Tyler, Geraine Greear (Joan Barclay), Rex Lease, John Elliott, Earl Dwire, Robert McKenzie, Roger Williams, Slim Whitaker, Jimmy Aubrey, Francis Walker, Wally West, Richard Cramer. *D:* Bernard B. Ray; *P:* Harry S. Webb; *Sc:* John Thomas Neville. (1:00)

Tom Tyler western of a family feud on the range.

Ridin' the Frontier (G.B. title) *see* **Riders of the Frontier**

3844. Ridin' the Lone Trail (Republic-Supreme; 1937). *Cast:* Bob Steele, Claire Rochelle, Charles King, Ernie Adams, Lew Meehan, Julian Rivero, Steve Clark, Hal Price, Frank Ball, Jack Kirk. *D:* Sam Newfield; *Sc:* E.B. Mann. (0:56)

Bob Steele western of an outlaw gang, their nefarious deeds and a cowboy and a sheriff who attempt to stop them.

Ridin' the Range *see* **Home on the Prairie**

3845. Ridin' the Trail (Spectrum/Arthur Ziehm; 1939–42). *Cast:*

Fred Scott, Iris Lancaster, Harry Harvey, Jack Ingram, John Ward, Bud Osborne, Carl Mathews, Gene Howard, Ray Lenhart, Buddy Kelly, Elias Gamboa, Denver Dixon. *D:* Raymond K. Johnson; *P:* C.C. Burr; *Sc:* Phil Dunham. (0:57)

The final Fred Scott western produced by Spectrum, but unreleased until 1942. A tale of a masked avenger.

3846. Ridin' Thru (Reliable; 1934). *Cast:* Tom Tyler, Ruth Hiatt, Lafe McKee, Philo McCullough, Ben Corbett, Lew Meehan, Bud Osborne, Colin Chase, Jayne Regan, Buck Morgan. *D:* Harry S. Webb; *P:* Bernard B. Ray; *Sc:* Rose Gordon, Carl Krusada. (0:55)

Tom Tyler oater of cattle thievery.

3847. The Riding Avenger (Diversion; 1936). *Cast:* Hoot Gibson, Ruth Mix, June Gale, Buzz Barton, Stanley Blystone, Roger Williams, Slim Whitaker, Francis Walker, Budd Buster, Blackie Whiteford, Jack Evans. *D:* Harry Fraser; *Sc:* Norman Houston. (0:58)

Hoot Gibson western of a marshal appointed by the state governor to bring in some rustlers.

3848. Riding on Air (RKO-Loew; 1937). *Cast:* Joe E. Brown, Florence Rice, Guy Kibbee, Vinton Haworth, Anthony Nace, Harlan Briggs, Andrew Tombes, Clem Bevans, Harry C. Bradley, Bud Flanagan (Dennis O'Keefe). *D:* Edward Sedgwick; *St:* Richard Macaulay (based on a series in the *Saturday Evening Post*); *Sc:* Macaulay, Richard Flournoy. (1:11) (video—0:58)

Successful low-budget romantic comedy of an invention which is able to control planes in flight (remote control?). An independent production of David L. Loew.

3849. Riding Speed (Superior; 1934). *Cast:* Buffalo Bill, Jr., Joile Benet, Bud Osborne, Lafe McKee, Clyde McClary, Allen Holbrook, Ernest Scott, Denver Dixon. *D:* Jay Wilsey (Buffalo Bill, Jr.); *P:* Victor Adamson (Denver Dixon); *Sc:* Delores Booth (Mrs. Dixon). (0:50)

Buffalo Bill, Jr., western of a cowboy combating border smugglers.

3850. Riding the Lonesome Trail (Reliable; 1934). Tom Tyler horse opera produced and directed by Bernard (B.B.) Ray and Harry S. Webb.

3851. The Riding Tornado (Columbia; 1932). *Cast:* Tim McCoy, Shirley Grey, Wallace MacDonald, Wheeler Oakman, Russell Simpson, Montagu Love, Lafe McKee, Art Mix, Vernon Dent, Bud Osborne, Hank Bell, Silver Tip Baker, Tex Palmer, Artie Ortego. *D:* D. Ross Lederman; *Sc:* Kurt Kempler. (0:59)

Tim McCoy western of cattle rustlers.

3852. Riding Wild (Columbia; 1935). *Cast:* Tim McCoy, Billie Seward, Niles Welch, Edward J. LeSaint, Richard Alexander, Richard Botiller, Eddie (Edmund) Cobb, Jack Rockwell, Bud Osborne, Wally West, Al Haskell, Si Jenks, Lafe McKee. *D:* David Selman; *St:* Ford Beebe; *Sc:* Beebe. (0:57)

Tim McCoy (in a dual role) western of a range war between cattlemen and nestors. McCoy's final film for this studio.

3853. Riffraff (MGM; 1935). *Cast:* Jean Harlow, Spencer Tracy, Joseph Calleia, Una Merkel, Mickey Rooney, Victor Kilian, J. Farrell MacDonald, Vince Barnett, William Newell, Rafaela Ottiano, Helene Costello (final film), Paul Hurst, George Givot, Roger Imhof, Juanita Quigley (nee: Baby Jane), Arthur Housman. *D:* J. Walter Ruben; *As.P.:* David Lewis; *St:* Frances Marion; *Sc:* Marion, H.W. Hanemann, Anita Loos. (1:29)

Comedy-drama of a waterfront

tuna cannery and a young couple who wind up on the wrong side of the law.

3854. The Right of Way (WB/ F.N.; 1931). *Cast:* Conrad Nagel, Loretta Young, Fred Kohler, William Janney, Snitz Edwards, George Pearce, Halliwell Hobbes, Olive Tell, Yola D'Avril, Brandon Hurst. *D:* Frank Lloyd; *P:* Lloyd; *Sc:* Francis Edwards Faragoh.

Drama of what happens after a lawyer loses his memory. Based on the novel by Sir Gilbert Parker, the film was a box office failure.

3855. The Right to Live (WB; 1935). *Cast:* George Brent, Colin Clive, Josephine Hutchinson, Peggy Wood, C. Aubrey Smith, Leo G. Carroll, Halliwell Hobbes, Henrietta Crosman, Phyllis Coghlan. *D:* William Keighley; *P:* James Seymour; *Sc:* Ralph Block. (G.B. title: *The Sacred Flame*) (1:15)

Drama of the death of a crippled war veteran via euthanasia. Based on the play "The Sacred Flame" by W. Somerset Maugham, it was previously filmed under that title by this studio in 1929 (q.v.).

3856. The Right to Love (Paramount; 1930). *Cast:* Ruth Chatterton (in a dual role as mother and daughter), Paul Lukas, David Manners, Oscar Apfel, Irving Pichel, George Baxter, Robert Parrish, Veda Buckland. *D:* Richard Wallace; *Sc:* Zoe Akins (based on the 1928 novel "Brook Evans" by Susan Glaspell); *Cinematographer:* (A.A.N.) Charles Lang.

A popular drama of it's day, especially with the female audience of a young woman who leaves home and family to become a missionary in China after learning that she is illegitimate.

3857. The Right to Romance (RKO; 1933). *Cast:* Ann Harding, Robert Young, Nils Asther, Sari Maritza, Irving Pichel, Helen Freeman, Alden Chase (Stephen), Delmar Watson, Louise Carter, Bramwell Fletcher, Patricia O'Brien, Howard Hickman, Thelma Hardwicke. *D:* Alfred Santell; *As.P.:* Myles Connolly; *St:* Connolly; *Sc:* Sidney Buchman, Henry McCarty. (1:07)

A female plastic surgeon favors her profession over romantic involvement. Primarily a "woman's film" of its day.

3858. Ring Around the Moon (Chesterfield; 1936). *Cast:* Donald Cook, Barbara Bedford, Erin O'Brien-Moore, Carl Stockdale, John Qualen, Douglas Fowley, Ann Doran. *D:* Charles Lamont.

"Poverty row" romance.

Ring Up the Curtain (G.B. title) *see* **Broadway to Hollywood**

3859. Rio (Universal; 1939). *Cast:* Basil Rathbone, Victor McLaglen, Sigrid Gurie, Robert Cummings, Leo Carrillo, Billy Gilbert, Irving Bacon, Irving Pichel, Maurice Moscovich, Samuel S. Hinds, Ferike Boros. *D:* John Brahm; *St:* Jean Negulesco; *Sc:* Stephen Morehouse Avery, Edwin Justus Mayer, Frank Partos, Aben Kandel. (1:17)

A prisoner on Devil's Island suspects his wife of having an affair and escapes to ease his mind by finding out the truth.

3860. Rio Grande (Columbia; 1938-39). *Cast:* Charles Starrett, Ann Doran, Sons of the Pioneers with Bob Nolan & Pat Brady, Dick Curtis, Hal Taliaferro (Wally Wales), Stanley Brown, Hank Bell, Forrest Taylor, Harry Strang, Edward J. LeSaint, Ed Peil, Sr., Ted Mapes, Art Mix, Lee Prather, Fred Burns, George Morrell, John Tyrell. *D:* Sam Nelson; *Sc:* Charles Francis Royal. (0:58)

A Charles Starrett western of land grabbers that are after a girl's ranch.

3861. Rio Grande Ranger (Columbia; 1936). *Cast:* Bob Allen, Hal

Taliaferro (Wally Wales), Iris Meredith, Paul Sutton, Buzz Henry, John Elliott, Tom London, Jack Rockwell, Slim Whitaker, Dick Botiller, Art Mix, Frank Ellis, Jack Ingram, Al Taylor, Jim Corey, Henry Hall, Jack C. Smith, Ed Cassidy, Ray Jones. *D:* Spencer Gordon Bennet; *Sc:* Nate Gatzert. (0:54)

Bob Allen western of two rangers assigned to get some outlaws in a border town.

3862. Rio Grande Romance (Victory; 1936). *Cast:* Edward Nugent, Maxine Doyle, Fuzzy Knight, Nick Stuart, Don Alvarado, George Walsh, Forrest Taylor, Lucille Lund, Ernie Adams, George Cleveland, Joyce Kay. *D:* Robert Hill; *P:* Sam Katzman; *Sc:* Al Martin. (1:10)

B crime melodrama of an FBI agent after some crooks.

3863. Rio Rattler (Reliable; 1935). *Cast:* Tom Tyler, Marion Shilling, Eddie Gribbon. *D:* Franklin Shamray (B.B. Ray); *P:* William Steiner; *Sc:* Carl Krusada.

A Tom Tyler western.

3864. Rio Rita (RKO; 1929). *Cast:* Bebe Daniels (talkie debut as Rita Ferguson), John Boles (Captain Jim Stewart), Bert Wheeler (feature talkie debut as Chick Bean), Robert Woolsey (film debut as Lovett), Georges Renavent (General Ravinoff), Dorothy Lee (Dolly), Don Alvarado (Roberto Ferguson), Helen Kaiser (Mrs. Bean), Fred Burns (Wilkins), Eva Rosita (Carmen), Sam Nelson (McGinn), Sam Blum (cafe owner), Nick de Ruiz (Padrone), Stanley "Tiny" Sandford (Davalos). *D:* Luther Reed; *P:* William LeBaron; *Adaptation:* Reed; *Dialogue:* Russell Mack; *Songs:* title song, "The Ranger Song," "Sweetheart, We Need Each Other," "If You're in Love You'll Waltz," "The Kinkajou," "Following the Sun Around" & "You're Always in My Arms (But Only in My Dreams)" by Harry Tierney & Joe McCarthy; & "Long Before You Came Along" by E.Y. Harburg & Harold Arlen. (2:15)

A big budget musical-comedy with the final ballroom scene in 2-color technicolor. Filmed as a stage play, it was based on the long running Broadway hit by Guy Bolton and Fred Thompson, by producer Florenz Ziegfeld. It placed #4 on the "10 Best" list of *Film Daily* and was remade by MGM in 1942.

3865. Riot Squad (Mayfair; 1933). *Cast:* Madge Bellamy, Addison Richards (film debut), Kit Guard. *D:* Harry S. Webb.

"Poverty row" melodrama.

3866. Rip Roarin' Buckaroo (Victory; 1936). *Cast:* Tom Tyler, Beth Marion, Sammy Cohen, Charles King, Forrest Taylor, Richard Cramer, John Elliott. *D:* Robert Hill; *P:* Sam Katzman; *Sc:* William Buchanan. (0:51)

Tom Tyler vehicle of an eastern boxer framed in a crooked match who goes west to get those responsible.

3867. Rip Roaring Riley (Puritan; 1935). *Cast:* Grant Withers, Lloyd Hughes, Kit Guard. *D:* Elmer Clifton. (G.B. title: *The Mystery of Diamond Island*)

Independent B adventure-melodrama.

3868. Riptide (MGM; 1934). *Cast:* Norma Shearer, Robert Montgomery, Herbert Marshall, Mrs. Patrick Campbell (American debut), Lilyan Tashman (final film — d. 1934 at the age of 35), Skeets Gallagher, Ralph Forbes, Helen Jerome Eddy, George K. Arthur, Halliwell Hobbes, C. Aubrey Smith, Arthur Treacher, E.E. Clive, Arthur Jarrett, Earl Oxford. *D:* Edmund Goulding; *Sc:* Goulding. (1:30)

Drama of a married woman who finds herself drifting back into an affair with her old flame. Loosely based on "The Green Hat" by Michael Arlen. One of the 15 top grossing films of 1934.

The Rise of Helga (G.B. title) *see* **Susan Lenox, Her Fall and Rise**

3869. Risky Business (Universal; 1939). *Cast:* George Murphy, El Brendel, Dorothea Kent, Eduardo Ciannelli, Leon Ames, Frances Robinson, Grant Richards, Mary Forbes, Charles Trowbridge, Pierre Watkin, Arthur Loft, Richard Tucker. *D:* Arthur Lubin; *P:* Burt Kelly; *St:* William Anthony McGuire; *Sc:* Charles Grayson. (1:10)

B melodrama of a reporter who uncovers a kidnap plot and what he does about it. A remake of *Okay, America* (q.v.).

3870. The River (Fox; 1928). *Cast:* Charles Farrell, Mary Duncan, Ivan Linow, Margaret Mann, Bert Woodruff. *D:* Frank Borzage (his first talkie).

Part-talkie outdoor drama of man against the elements.

River of Destiny *see* **Forlorn River**

River of Missing Men *see* **Trapped by G-Men**

3871. The River of Romance (Paramount; 1929). *Cast:* Charles "Buddy" Rogers, Wallace Beery, Mary Brian, June Collyer, Henry B. Walthall, Fred Kohler, Natalie Kingston, Anderson Lawler, Mrs. George Fawcett, Walter McGrail, George Reed. *D:* Richard Wallace; *Sc:* Ethel Doherty, Dan Totheroh, John V.A. Weaver.

Romantic drama on a riverboat. Based on Booth Tarkington's play "Magnolia," the film is a remake of *The Fighting Coward* (Paramount; 1924) with Cullen Landis. Remade as *Mississippi* (q.v.).

3872. The River Pirate (Fox; 1928). *Cast:* Victor McLaglen, Lois Moran, Donald Crisp, Nick Stuart, Earle Foxe, Robert Perry. *D:* William K. Howard.

Part-talkie melodrama.

3873. The River Woman (Lumas Film Corp./Gotham Productions; 1928).

Cast: Lionel Barrymore, Jacqueline Logan, Sheldon Lewis. *D:* Joseph Henabery.

Part-talkie romantic melodrama with a rustic setting and sound by the Bristolphone disk system.

3874. River's End (WB; 1930). *Cast:* Charles Bickford (in a dual role), Evalyn Knapp, J. Farrell MacDonald, ZaSu Pitts, David Torrence, Frank (Junior) Coghlan, Tom Santschi, Walter McGrail, Tom London. *D:* Michael Curtiz; *Sc:* Charles Kenyon. (1:14)

A Mountie dies in pursuit of his man, who then impersonates the Mountie. Based on the story by James Oliver Curwood, the film is a remake of *The River's End* (Associated Producers; 1920) with Lewis Stone and directed by Marshal Neilan. Remade in 1940 by this studio as *River's End* with Dennis Morgan. A box office hit.

3875. The Road Back (Universal; 1937). *Cast:* Richard Cromwell, John King (Ernst), Slim Summerville (Tjaden), Andy Devine (Willy), Noah Beery, Jr. (Wessling), Barbara Read, Louise Fazenda, Lionel Atwill, John Emery (film debut), Etienne Girardot, Greta Gynt, Spring Byington, Laura Hope Crews, Robert Warwick, William Davidson, Dwight Frye, Samuel S. Hinds, Arthur Hohl, Frank Reicher, Charles Halton, Jean Rouverol, Al Shean, Maurice Murphy, Henry Hunter, Larry Blake, Renee Garrick. *D:* James Whale; *P:* Whale, Charles R. Rogers, Edmund Grainger; *Sc:* R.C. Sherriff, Charles Kenyon. (1:43)

Soldiers return home to the difficulties of post World War I Germany in this sequel to the classic *All Quiet on the Western Front* (q.v.). Based on the novel by Erich Maria Remarque it was one of the 38 top grossing films of 1936–37.

3876. Road Demon (20th Century–Fox; 1938). *Cast:* Henry Arthur, Joan Valerie, Henry Armetta (Poppa Gambini), Inez Palange (Momma

Gambini), Bill Robinson, Johnny Pironne, Eleanor Virzie, Betty Greco, Lon Chaney, Jr. *D:* Otto Brower; *P:* Sol M. Wurtzel.

B auto racing drama which is the second entry in the short-lived "Gambini" series. See also: *Speed to Burn* (q.v.) and *Winner Take All* (q.v.).

3877. Road Gang (WB/F.N.; 1936). *Cast:* Donald Woods, Kay Linaker, Carlyle Moore, Jr., Marc Lawrence, Henry O'Neill, Joseph King, Addison Richards, Edward Van Sloan, Charles Middleton, Joseph Crehan, Harry Cording, Eddie Schubert, Olin Howland. *D:* Louis King; *P:* Bryan Foy; *St:* Abem Finkel, Harold Buckley; *Sc:* Dalton Trumbo (debut as a screenwriter). (G.B. title: *Injustice*)

B melodrama of southern prison camps and chain gangs.

The Road Show (G.B. title) *see* **Chasing Rainbows**

3878. The Road to Glory (20th Century–Fox; 1936). *Cast:* Fredric March, Warner Baxter, Lionel Barrymore, June Lang, Gregory Ratoff, Victor Kilian, John Qualen, Julius Tannen, Leonid Kinskey, Paul Fix, Theodore von Eltz, Paul Stanton, Jacques Vanaire, Edythe Raynore, George Warrington. *D:* Howard Hawks; *P:* Darryl F. Zanuck; *As.P.:* Nunnally Johnson; *St:* Joel Sayre; *Sc:* Sayre, William Faulkner. (1:42)

World War I drama of French soldiers at the front. The 1926 silent film of the same name by Howard Hawks is no relation to this film.

3879. The Road to Paradise (WB/F.N.; 1930–31). *Cast:* Loretta Young (in a dual role), Jack Mulhall, Raymond Hatton, Kathlyn Williams, Dot Farley, George Barraud, Fred Kelsey, Ben Hendricks, Jr., Purnell Pratt, Georgette Rhodes, Winter Hall. *D:* William Beaudine; *Sc:* F. Hugh Herbert.

Drama of twin sisters separated since childhood who meet during the robbery of the one sister's home. Based on the play by Zelda Sears and Dodson Mitchell.

3880. The Road to Reno (Paramount; 1931). *Cast:* Charles "Buddy" Rogers, Peggy Shannon, Lilyan Tashman, William "Stage" Boyd, Skeets Gallagher, Claire Dodd, Wynne Gibson, Charles D. Brown, Kent Taylor (film debut), Tom Douglas, Renie Riano, Judith Wood, Leni Stengel, Emile Chautard. *D:* Richard Wallace; *St:* Virginia Kellogg; *Songs:* Jimmy McHugh, Harold Adamson.

A woman falls for a man who in turn has designs on the woman's daughter.

3881. The Road to Reno (Universal; 1938). *Cast:* Randolph Scott, Hope Hampton, Alan Marshal, Glenda Farrell, Helen Broderick, Charles Murphy, David Oliver, Ted Osborne, Samuel S. Hinds, Spencer Charters, Mira McKinney. *D:* S. Sylvan Simon; *P:* Edmund Grainger; *St:* Charles Kenyon, F. Hugh Herbert; *Sc:* Roy Chanslor, Adele Commandini; *Dialogue:* Brian Marlowe. (1:12)

Comedy of a woman who goes to Reno seeking a divorce, even though she still loves her husband, but has promised to marry another. Based on the story "Puritan at Large" by Ida (I.A.R.) Wylie.

3882. The Road to Ruin (True Life Photoplays; 1934). *Cast:* Helen Foster, Richard Tucker, Paul Page, Virginia True Boardman, Glen Boles, Nell O'Day. *D:* Mrs. Wallace (Dorothy) Reid, Melville Shyer; *St:* Reid; *Sc:* Reid (co-writer).

Low-budget independently produced exploitive "sex" film of a girl on the down-road of life.

3883. The Road to Singapore (WB; 1931). *Cast:* William Powell, Doris

Kenyon, Marian Marsh, Louis Calhern, Alison Skipworth, Lumsden Hare, Tyrrell Davis, A.E. Anson, Amar N. Sharma, Arthur Clayton, Margaret Martin, Ethel Griffies, Douglas Gerrard, H. Reynolds. *D:* Alfred E. Green; *Sc:* J. Grubb Alexander. (1:10)

Torrid romantic drama with songs of adultery in the orient. Based on a story by Denise Robins and a play by Roland Pertwee.

3884. The Roadhouse Murder (RKO; 1932). *Cast:* Eric Linden, Dorothy Jordan, Purnell Pratt, Roscoe Ates, David Landau, Bruce Cabot, Phyllis Clare, Gustav von Seyffertitz, Roscoe Karns, William Morris, Frank Sheridan, Carl Gerard. *D:* J. Walter Ruben; *As.P.:* Willis Goldbeck; *Sc:* Ruben, Gene Fowler. (1:13)

Low-budget mystery set at "The Lame Dog Inn" on a stormy night, of a reporter who is accused of several murders. Based on the novel by Maurice Level.

3885/3886. Roadhouse Nights (Paramount; 1930). *Cast:* Helen Morgan, Charles Ruggles, Fred Kohler, Fuller Mellish, Jr., Joseph King, Leo Donnelly, Tammany Young, Jimmy Durante (film debut), Lou Clayton, Eddie Jackson. *D:* Hobart Henley; *Sc:* Garrett Fort. (1:11)

Low-budget crime melodrama of a reporter who exposes the owner of a pouplar night spot as a notorious gangland figure. The film is notable as the film debut of Jimmy Durante, as part of the comedy trio of Durante, Lou Clayton and Eddie Jackson, popular entertainers of their day. Filmed at Astoria Studios in Long Island, N.Y., and based on a story by Ben Hecht.

3887. Roamin' Wild (Reliable; 1936). *Cast:* Tom Tyler, Carol Wyndham, Max Davidson, Al Ferguson, George Chesebro, Fred Parker, Bud Osborne, Slim Whitaker, Earl Dwire,

Wally West, Lafe McKee, Sherry Tansey, Frank Ellis, John Elliott. *D:* Bernard B. Ray; *P:* Harry S. Webb; *Sc:* Robert Emmett (Tansey). (0:58)

Tom Tyler shoot-'em-up of a U.S. marshal investigating lawless element posing as government men and cheating miners out of their labors.

3888. The Roaming Cowboy (Spectrum; 1937). *Cast:* Fred Scott, Al St. John, Lois January, Forrest Taylor, Buddy Cox, Roger Williams, Art Miles, George Morrell, George Chesebro, Carl Mathews, Richard Cramer, Oscar Gahan, Lew Meehan. *D:* Robert Hill; *P:* Jed Buell; *Sc:* Fred Myton. (1:00)

Fred Scott western with musical interludes of several Stephen Foster songs. The story of a range war.

3889. Roaming Lady (Columbia; 1936). *Cast:* Ralph Bellamy, Fay Wray, Paul Guilfoyle, Thurston Hall. *D:* Albert Rogell.

B production.

3890. Roar of the Dragon (RKO; 1932). *Cast:* Richard Dix, Gwili Andre (film debut), ZaSu Pitts, Edward Everett Horton, C. Henry Gordon, Arline Judge, Dudley Digges, Arthur Stone, William Orlamond, Toshi Mori, Will Stanton, Jimmy Wang. *D:* Wesley Ruggles; *P:* Merian C. Cooper; *St:* Cooper, Jane Bigelow; *Sc:* Howard Estabrook. (1:08)

During a Manchurian civil war, a river pilot endeavors to protect his passengers who are seeking refuge in a local hotel. Based on the book "A Passage to Hong Kong" by George Kibbe Turner, the film failed to generate a profit.

3891. Roarin' Guns (Puritan; 1936). *Cast:* Tim McCoy, Rosalinda Price, Wheeler Oakman, Karl Hackett, John Elliott, Tommy Bupp, Jack Rockwell, Lew Meehan, Rex Lease, Frank Ellis, Ed Cassidy, Artie Ortego,

Richard Alexander, Tex Phelps, Al Taylor. *D:* Sam Newfield; *Sc:* Joseph O'Donnell. (1:06) (video)

Tim McCoy western of a range war.

3892. Roarin' Lead (Republic; 1936). *Cast:* Bob Livingston (Stony Brooke), Ray Corrigan (Tucson Smith), Max Terhune (Lullaby Joslin), Christine Maple, Hooper Atchley, Yakima Canutt, George Chesebro, Grace Kern, Tommy Bupp, George Plues, Harry Tenbrook, Newt Kirby, Pascale Perry, Baby Jane Keckley. *D:* Mack V. Wright, Sam Newfield; *Sc:* Oliver Drake, Jack Natteford. (0:54)

The 3rd "Three Mesquiteers" entry with the trio opposing a gang of outlaws terrorizing the area like a military unit.

Roaring Mountain *see* **Thunder Mountain**

3893. Roaring Ranch (Universal; 1930). *Cast:* Hoot Gibson, Sally Eilers (later Mrs. Hoot Gibson), Wheeler Oakman, Bobby Nelson, Frank Clark, Leo White. *D:* B. Reeves Eason; *Sc:* Eason. (1:08)

Hoot Gibson range adventure of romantic rivalry for the hand of a girl.

Roaring River *see* **Wyoming Whirlwind**

3894. Roaring Roads (Marcy; 1935). *Cast:* David Sharpe, Gertrude Messinger, Jack Mulhall. *D:* William Berke.

(No other information available)

3895. Roaring Six-Guns (Ambassador; 1937). *Cast:* Kermit Maynard, Mary Hayes, Sam Flint, John Merton, Budd Buster, Ed Cassidy, Robert Fiske, Curley Dresden, Dick Moorehead, Slim Whitaker, Earle Hodgins, Rene Stone. *D:* J.P. McGowan (final film — retired, after directing many a B western in the silent and early talkie era); *P:* Maurice Conn; *Sc:* Arthur Everett. (0:55) (video)

Kermit Maynard western of a rancher trying to get the title to his neighbor's ranch.

Roaring Timber (U.A.; 1936) *see* **Come and Get It**

3896. Roaring Timber (Columbia; 1937). *Cast:* Jack Holt, Grace Bradley, Ruth Donnelly, J. Farrell MacDonald, Raymond Hatton, Willard Robertson, Fred Kohler, Jr., Charles Wilson, Tom London, Philip Ahn, Ben Hendricks, Jr., Ernest Wood. *D:* Phil Rosen; *St:* Robert James Cosgriff; *Sc:* Paul Franklin. (1:05)

Attempts are made to prevent the filling of a lumber contract in this B action-adventure.

3897. The Roaring Twenties (WB; 1939). *Cast:* James Cagney (received an Acting Award from the National Board of Review for his portrayal of Eddie Bartlett), Humphrey Bogart (George Hally), Jeffrey Lynn (Lloyd Hart), Priscilla Lane (Jean Sherman), Gladys George (Panama Smith), Frank McHugh (Danny Green), Joseph Sawyer (Sgt. Pete Jones), Paul Kelly (Nick Brown), Elizabeth Risdon (Mrs. Sherman), Ed Keane (Pete Henderson), Abner Biberman (Lefty), George Humbert (Luigi), Clay Clement (Bramfield), Don Thaddeus Kerr (Bobby Hart), Vera Lewis (Mrs. Gray), Joseph Crehan (Fletcher), Paul Phillips (Mike), Ray Cooke, Dick Wessel, Murray Alper, Norman Willis, Robert Elliott, John Hamilton, Eddy Chandler, Elliott Sullivan, Arthur Loft, Pat O'Malley, Al Hill, Raymond Bailey, Lew Harvey, Joe Devlin, Jeffrey Sayre, George Meeker, Jack Norton, Bert Hanlon, Alan Bridge, Fred Graham, James Blaine, Lottie Williams, Harry C. Bradley, Emory Parnell, John Ridgely, Ben Welden, Max Wagner. *D:* Raoul Walsh; *P:* Hal B. Wallis; *As.P.:* Sam Bischoff; *Sc:* Jerry Wald, Robert Rossen, Richard Macaulay; *Narrator:* John Deering. (1:44) (video — original b/w & computer-colored)

Prohibition era gangster film of a bootlegger's rise to power. Cagney's final role as a gangster until 1949. Based on a story by Mark Hellinger, the film was voted #9 on the "10 Best" list of the National Board of Review. Computer-colored by Turner Entertainment in 1987.

3898. Robber's Roost (Fox; 1933). *Cast:* George O'Brien, Maureen O'Sullivan, Walter McGrail, Reginald Owen, Doris Lloyd, Maude Eburne, William Pawley, Ted Oliver, Frank Rice, Bill Nestell, "Pee Wee" Holmes, Clifford Santley, Vinegar Roan. *D:* Louis King; *Sc:* Dudley Nichols.

George O'Brien western of rustled cattle, based on a book by Zane Grey.

3899. Roberta (RKO; 1935). *Cast:* Irene Dunne (Stephanie), Fred Astaire (Huck Haines), Ginger Rogers (Lizzie Gatz—Countess Tanka Scharwenka), Randolph Scott (John Kent), Helen Westley (Aunt Millie—"Roberta"), Claire Dodd (Sophie Tearle), Victor Varconi (Ladislaw), Luis Alberni (Alexander Voyda), Ferdinand Munier (Lord Henry Delves), Torben Meyer (Albert), Bodil Rosing (Fernando), Adrian Rosley (professor), "Candy" Candido, Muzzy Marcelino, Gene Sheldon, Howard Lally, William Carey, Paul McLarind, Hal Bown, Charles Sharpe, Ivan Dow, Phil Cuthbert, Delmon Davis & William Dunn (orchestra members), Lucille Ball (in her first RKO film), Mike Tellegen & Sam Savitsky (Cossacks), Zena Savine, Jane Hamilton, Kay Sutton, Margaret McChrystal, Maxine Jennings, Virginia Reid (later: Lynne Carver), Lorna Low, Lorraine DeSart, Wanda Perry, Diane Cook, Virginia Carroll, Betty Dumbries, Donna Roberts, Mary Forbes, William B. Davidson, Judith Vosselli, Rita Gould. *D:* William A. Seiter; *P:* Pandro S. Berman; *Sc:* Jane Murfin, Sam Mintz, Allan Scott; *Additional Dialogue:* Glenn Tryon; *Songs:* "Lovely to Look At" (A.A.N. for Best Song) Jerome Kern, Dorothy Fields & Jimmy McHugh; "Smoke Gets in Your Eyes," "Yesterdays" & "Let's Begin" by Otto Harbach & Jerome Kern; "I'll Be Hard to Handle" by Harbach, Kern & Bernard Dougall; "I Won't Dance" by Oscar Hammerstein II, Fields, McHugh & Kern & "The Touch of Your Hand." (1:45) (video—1:25)

Hit musical with a technicolor sequence which became one of the 12 top grossing films of 1935. Based on the book "Gowns by Roberta" by Alice Duer Miller and the 1933 Broadway success adapted from it by Otto Harbach & Jerome Kern. The film placed #9 on the "10 Best" list of *Film Daily* and was remade as *Lovely to Look At* (MGM; 1952).

3900. Robin Hood of El Dorado (MGM; 1936). *Cast:* Warner Baxter, Bruce Cabot, Margo, Eric Linden, Ann Loring, J. Carrol Naish, Edgar Kennedy, Harvey Stephens, Paul Hurst, Harry Woods, Francis McDonald, Carlos de Valdez, Kay Hughes, Soledad Jimenez, Charles Trowbridge, George Regas, Boothe Howard, Ralph Remley. *D:* William Wellman; *P:* John W. Considine, Jr.; *St:* Walter Noble Burns; *Sc:* Wellman, Melvin Levy, Joseph Calleia. (1:26)

The story of western outlaw Joaquin Murietta from the early 19th-century. Loosely based on fact, the story was similarly told in *The Gay Defender* (Paramount; 1928) with Richard Dix and Thelma Todd.

3901. Robinson Crusoe on Mystery Island (Republic; 1936). *Cast:* Mala, Buck, Rex, Mamo Clark, Herbert Rawlinson, George Cleveland. *D:* Ray Taylor, Mack V. Wright. (G.B. title: *S.O.S. Clipper Island*) (1:40)

Set in the south seas, this is the feature version of this studio's serial "Robinson Crusoe on Clipper Island."

3902. Rockabye (RKO-Pathé; 1932). *Cast:* Constance Bennett, Joel McCrea (replacing Phillips Holmes), Jobyna Howland, Paul Lukas, June Filmer, Walter Pidgeon, Virginia Hammond, J.M. Kerrigan, Walter Catlett, Clara Blandick, Laura Hope Crews, Charles Middleton, Sterling Holloway. *D:* George Cukor (replacing George Fitzmaurice); *P:* David O. Selznick; *Sc:* Jane Murfin; *Songs:* Edward Eliscu, Harry Akst, Jeanne Borlini, Nacio Herb Brown. (1:08)

This, the final film to be released by this studio under the Pathé label is a drama of a stage actress' efforts to adopt a child. Based on the play by Lucia Bronder.

3903. Rocky Mountain Mystery (Paramount; 1935). *Cast:* Randolph Scott, Ann Sheridan, Kathleen Burke, Charles "Chic" Sale, Mrs. Leslie Carter, George Marion, James C. Eagles, Howard Wilson, Willie Fung, Florence Roberts. *D:* Charles Barton; *P:* Harold Hurley; *Sc:* Edward E. Paramore, Jr., Ethel Doherty. (aka: *The Fighting Westerner*) (1:03)

B western involving murder at a radium mine. Loosely based on Zane Grey's "Golden Dreams." A remake of *The Vanishing Pioneer* (Paramount; 1928) with Jack Holt and Sally Blane. "The Vanishing Pioneer" was also the working title for this version.

3904. Rocky Rhodes (Universal; 1934). *Cast:* Buck Jones, Stanley Fields, Sheila Terry, Walter Miller, Alf P. James, Paul Fix, Lydia Knott, Jack Rockwell, Lee Shumway, Carl Stockdale, Monte Montague, Bud Osborne, Harry Semels. *D:* Al Raboch; *Sc:* Edward Churchill. (1:04)

Buck Jones western (his first for this studio) of a cowboy and a city gangster who team up to thwart land grabbers.

3905. Rodeo Kissin' (Sono Art-World Wide; 1930). *Cast:* George Duryea (later Tom Keene).

"Poverty row" light western romance.

(No other information available)

3906. Rogue of the Range (Supreme; 1936). *Cast:* Johnny Mack Brown, Lois January, Phyllis Hume, Alden (Stephen) Chase, George Ball,

Jack Rockwell, Lloyd Ingraham, Horace Murphy, Frank Ball, Fred Hoose, Forrest Taylor, George Morrell, Slim Whitaker, Blackie Whiteford, Tex Palmer, Horace B. Carpenter, Max Davidson, Art Dillard. *D:* S. Roy Luby; *P:* A.W. Hackel; *Sc:* Earle Snell. (1:00)

Johnny Mack Brown western of an agent undercover to roundup a gang, who finds romance with a saloon girl.

3907. Rogue of the Rio Grande (Sono Art-World Wide; 1930). *Cast:* Jose Bohr, Myrna Loy, Raymond Hatton, Carmelita Geraghty, Walter Miller, Gene Morgan, William P. Burt, Florence Dudley. *D:* Spencer Gordon Bennet; *Sc:* Oliver Drake. (1:10) (video)

A south-of-the-border romance from "poverty row."

3908. The Rogue Song (MGM; 1929–30). *Cast:* Lawrence Tibbett (receiving an A.A.N. for B.A. in his film debut, 1929–30), Catherine Dale Owen, Florence Lake, Judith Vosselli, John Carroll, Nance O'Neil, Stan Laurel, Oliver Hardy, Ullrich Haupt, Lionel Belmore, Kate Price, Wallace MacDonald, Elsa Alsen, H.A. Morgan, James Bradbury, Jr., Burr McIntosh. *D:* Lionel Barrymore, Hal Roach; *P:* Barrymore; *St:* A.W. Willner; *Sc:* Frances Marion, John Colton.

This was originally billed upon release as "The First De-Luxe Screen Operetta." In 2-color technicolor it tells the story of a Russian Robin Hood type and is loosely based on the operetta "Gypsy Love" by Franz Lehar and Robert Bodansky.

3909. The Rogue's Tavern (Puritan; 1936). *Cast:* Jack Mulhall, Joan Woodbury, Wallace Ford. *D:* Robert F. Hill.

Independent B melodrama.

3910. Roll Along, Cowboy (20th Century–Fox/Principal; 1937). *Cast:* Smith Ballew, Cecilia Parker, Stanley Fields, Gordon (Bill) Elliott, Wally

Albright, Jr., Ruth Robinson, Frank Milan, Monte Montague, Bud Osborne, Budd Buster, Harry Bernard, Buster Fite & His Six Saddle Tramps. *D:* Gus Meins; *P:* Sol Lesser; *Sc:* Dan Jarrett. (0:57)

Smith Ballew western (his 2nd in the series) with musical interludes. A remake of *The Dude Ranger* (q.v.), and based on the Zane Grey book of that title.

Roll Covered Wagon (G.B. title) *see* **Roll, Wagons, Roll**

3911. Roll, Wagons, Roll (Monogram; 1939). *Cast:* Tex Ritter, Nelson McDowell, Muriel Evans, Nolan Willis, Steve Clark, Tom London, Reed Howes, Frank Ellis, Kenne Duncan, Frank LaRue, Chick Hannon, White Flash the horse. *D:* Al Herman; *P:* Edward Finney; *St & Sc:* Victor Adamson (Denver Dixon), Edmund Kelso, Roger Merton. (G.B. title: *Roll Covered Wagon*) (0:55)

Tex Ritter western of a wagon train headed for Oregon (with musical interludes).

3912. Rollin' Plains (Grand National; 1938). *Cast:* Tex Ritter, Horace Murphy (Ananias), Snub Pollard (Pee Wee), Harriet Bennett, Hobart Bosworth, Ed Cassidy, Karl Hackett, Charles King, Beverly Hill Billies, Ernie Adams, Lynton Brent, Horace B. Carpenter, Hank Worden, Augie Gomez, Oscar Gahan, Rudy Sooter, Carl Mathews, George Morrell, White Flash the horse. *D:* Al Herman; *P:* Edward Finney, Al Lane; *St:* Jacques & Ciela Jacquard; *Sc:* Lindsley Parsons, Edmund Kelso. (0:57)

Tex Ritter western with musical interludes of a cattlemen-sheepmen dispute. To give an indication of how limited the budgets could be on these series B westerns, the final reel of this film is identical to the one in *Sing, Cowboy, Sing* (q.v.) produced the preceding year by this studio.

Rollin' West (G.B. title) *see* **Rollin' Westward**

3913. Rollin' Westward (Monogram; 1939). *Cast:* Tex Ritter, Dorothy Fay (later Mrs. Tex Ritter), Horace Murphy, Charles "Slim" Whitaker, Herbert Corthell, Harry Harvey, Charles King, Sr., Hank Worden, Dave O'Brien, Tom London, Estrelita Novarro, White Flash the horse. *D:* Al Herman; *P:* Edward Finney; *Sc:* Fred Myton. (G.B. title: *Rollin' West*) (0:55)

Tex Ritter western with songs of a cowboy who puts the crimps to some landgrabbers.

3914. Rolling Caravans (Columbia; 1938). *Cast:* John (Jack) Luden, Eleanor Stewart, Harry Woods, Slim Whitaker, Lafe McKee, Buzz Barton, Tuffy the dog, Bud Osborne, Richard Cramer, Jack Rockwell, Franklyn Farnum, Cactus Mack, Tex Palmer, Sherry Tansey, Oscar Gahan, Curley Dresden, Francis Walker, Horace Murphy. *D:* Joseph Levering; *Sc:* Nate Gatzert. (0:55)

John (Jack) Luden horse opera of a landrush.

3915. Roman Scandals (United Artists/Samuel Goldwyn; 1933). *Cast:* Eddie Cantor (Eddie), Gloria Stuart (Princess Sylvia), Ruth Etting (Olga), Edward Arnold (Emperor Valerius), David Manners (Josephus), Alan Mowbray (Major-domo), Verree Teasdale (Empress Agrippa), Jack Rutherford (Manius), Grace Poggi (slave dancer), Willard Robertson (Warren F. Cooper), Harry Holman (mayor of West Rome), Lee Kohlmar (storekeeper), Stanley Fields (slave auctioneer), Charles C. Wilson (Police Chief Pratt), Clarence Wilson (Buggs), Charles Arnt (Caius the food tester), Frank Hagney (Lucius), Billy Barty (Little Eddie), Abbottiers (including: Florence Wilson, Rose Kirsner, Genevieve Irwin, Dolly Bell), Stanley Andrews, Stanley Blystone, Harry Cording, Lane Chandler,

William Wagner, Louise Carver, Francis Ford, Leo Willis, Duke York, Michael Mark, Paul Porcasi, Dick Alexander, John Ince, Jane Darwell, Iris Shunn, Aileen Riggin; Katharine Mauk, Lucille Ball, Barbara Pepper, Vivian Keefer, Theo Plane, Rosalie Fromson, Mary Lange (slave girls). *D:* Frank Tuttle, Ralph Cedar (chariot sequence only); *P:* Sam Goldwyn; *St:* George S. Kaufman, Robert E. Sherwood; *Adaptation:* William Anthony McGuire; *Sc, Additional Dialogue:* George Oppenheimer, Arthur Sheekman, Nat Perrin; *Choreography:* Busby Berkeley; *Songs:* "Rome Wasn't Built in a Day," "Build a Little Home," "Keep Young and Beautiful" & "No More Love" by Al Dubin & Harry Warren; "Tax on Love" by L. Wolfe Gilbert & Warren. (1:32) (video)

Musical-comedy with a lavish production involving a young man who dreams himself back to ancient Rome. One of the 15 top grossing films of 1934, the pre-code dialogue is peppered with many innuendos.

3916. Romance (MGM; 1930). *Cast:* Greta Garbo (A.A.N. for B.A., 1929–30 as Rita Cavallini), Lewis Stone (Cornelius Van Tuyl), Gavin Gordon (Tom Armstrong), Elliott Nugent (Harry), Florence Lake (Susan Van Tuyl), Clara Blandick (Miss Armstrong), Henry Armetta (Beppo), Mathilde Comont (Vannucci), Countess De Liguoro (Nina). *D:* (A.A.N., 1929–30) Clarence Brown; *P:* Brown; *Sc:* Bess Meredyth, Edwin Justus Mayer. (1:16)

Lavishly produced costume drama involving an affair between an opera singer and a man of the cloth. Based on the play by Edward (E. Lloyd) Sheldon, it was voted one of the year's "10 Best" films by the National Board of Review.

Romance for Three (G.B. title) *see* **Paradise for Three**

3917. Romance in Manhattan (RKO; 1934). *Cast:* Francis Lederer,

Ginger Rogers, Arthur Hohl, J. Farrell MacDonald, Sidney Toler, Eily Malyon, Donald Meek, Jimmy Butler, Helen Ware, Lillian Harmer, Oscar Apfel, Reginald Barlow. *D:* Stephen Roberts; *P:* Pandro S. Berman; *Sc:* Jane Murfin, Edward Kaufman. (1:18)

An illegal immigrant from Czechoslovakia is befriended by a New York chorus girl and romance ensues. Based on the play by Norman Krasna and Don Hartman.

3918. Romance in the Dark (Paramount; 1938). *Cast:* Gladys Swarthout, John Boles, John Barrymore, Fritz Feld, Claire Dodd, Curt Bois, Esther Muir, Ferdinand Gottschalk, Torben Meyer, Carlos de Valdez, Fortunio Bonanova, Meg Randall. *D:* H.C. Potter; *P:* Harlan Thompson; *Sc:* Frank Partos, Ann Morrison Chapin. (1:18)

This romantic musical-comedy is based on the play "The Yellow Nightingale" by Hermann Bahr.

3919. Romance in the Rain (Universal; 1934). *Cast:* Roger Pryor, Esther Ralston, Victor Moore, Heather Angel, Ruth Donnelly, Paul Kaye, Guinn Williams, Henry Armetta, Clara Kimball Young, King Baggot, Yellow Horse, Christian Rub, David Worth. *D:* Stuart Walker; *St:* Sig Herzig, Jay Gorney; *Sc:* Barry Trivers; *Add'l Dial.:* Gladys Unger, John V.A. Weaver. (1:10)

A publicity campaign is put into motion to promote a newly published book entitled "Livid Love Tales" in this B comedy.

Romance Is Sacred (G.B. title) *see* **The King and the Chorus Girl**

3920. Romance of the Limberlost (Monogram; 1938). *Cast:* Jean Parker, Eric Linden, Marjorie Main, Betty Blythe, Edward Pawley, Hollis Jewell, George Cleveland, Sarah Padden, Guy Usher, Jack Kennedy, Jean O'Neill. *D:* William Nigh; *Sc:* Marion Orth. (1:21)

Rural drama of a girl who loves a young man, but her aunt wishes her to marry a wealthy widower. Based on the story "Her Father's Daughter" by Gene Stratton-Porter.

3921. Romance of the Redwoods (Columbia; 1939). *Cast:* Charles Bickford, Jean Parker, Alan Bridge, Gordon Oliver, Lloyd Hughes, Pat O'Malley, Marc Lawrence, Ann Shoemaker, Don Beddoe, Ann Doran. *D:* Charles Vidor; *Sc:* Michael L. Simmons (1:07)

B romantic actioner set in a lumber camp. Based on a story by Jack London. Previously filmed by Paramount in 1917 with Mary Pickford.

3922. Romance of the Rio Grande (Fox; 1929). *Cast:* Warner Baxter, Mary Duncan, Antonio Moreno, Mona Maris, Robert Edeson, Merrill McCormack, Charles Byer, Soledad Jimenez, Albert Roccardi, Major Coleman. *D:* Alfred Santell; *St:* Katherine Fullerton Gerould.

South-of-the-border story much in the spirit of *In Old Arizona* (q.v.) and made to capitalize on that film's success. Remade in 1940.

3923. Romance of the Rockies (Monogram; 1937). *Cast:* Tom Keene, Beryl Wallace, Don Orlando, Bill Cody, Jr., Franklyn Farnum, Earl Dwire, Russell Paul, Steve Clark, Jim Corey, Tex Palmer, Jack C. Smith, Blackie Whiteford, Frank Ellis. *D:* Robert N. Bradbury; *P:* Bradbury; *Sc:* Robert Emmett (Tansey). (0:53)

Tom Keene western of a country doctor who comes to the rescue when ranchers' water rights are threatened.

3924. Romance on the Run (20th Century–Fox; 1938). *Cast:* Donald Woods, Patricia Ellis, Craig Reynolds, Grace Bradley, William Demarest, Andrew Tombes, Edward Brophy. *D:* Gus Meins.

B romantic comedy.

3925. Romance Rides the Range (Spectrum; 1936). *Cast:* Fred Scott, Marion Shilling, Cliff Nazarro, Buzz Barton, Robert Kortman, Theodore Lorch, Frank Yaconelli, Bill Steele, Allen Greer. *D:* Harry Fraser; *P:* Jed Buell; *Sc:* Tom Gibson. (0:59)

Fred Scott in his singing western debut, billed as "the silvery-voiced buckaroo" (his first series western for this indie company). A cowboy saves a girl and her brother from swindlers.

The Romantic Age (G.B. title) *see* **Sisters Under the Skin**

3926. Romeo and Juliet (MGM; 1936). *Cast:* Norma Shearer (A.A.N. for B.A. as Juliet), Leslie Howard (Romeo), Edna May Oliver (Juliet's nurse), John Barrymore (Mercutio), C. Aubrey Smith (Lord Capulet), Basil Rathbone (A.A.N. for B.S.A. as Tybalt), Andy Devine (Peter), Reginald Denny (Benvolio), Henry Kolker (Friar Lawrence), Robert Warwick (Lord Montague), Violet Kemble-Cooper (Lady Capulet), Ralph Forbes (Paris), Maurice Murphy (Balthasar), Conway Tearle (Prince of Verona, final film — d. 1938), Virginia Hammond (Lady Montague), Vernon Downing (Samson Capulet), Ian Wolfe (apothecary), Anthony Kemble-Cooper (Gregory Capulet), Howard Wilson (Abraham Montague), Anthony March (Mercutio's page), Carlyle Blackwell, Jr. (Tybalt's page), John Bryan (Friar John), Katherine de Mille (Rosalind), Wallis Clark, Dean Richmond Bentor, Lita Chevret, Jeanne Hart, Dorothy Granger, Harold Entwistle, Charles Bancroft, Jose Rubio, Lon McCallister (film debut — bit). *D:* George Cukor; *P:* (A.A.N. for Best Picture) Irving Thalberg; *Sc:* Talbot Jennings; *Art-Set Decoration:* (A.A.N.) Cedric Gibbons, Frederic Hope, Edwin B. Willis, Oliver Messel. (2:07)

William Shakespeare's famous romance of the star-crossed lovers. Critically acclaimed in most circles, it found disfavor with Shakespeare purists. A "prestige" film from MGM and a financial disaster, despite being one of the 38 top grossing films of 1936–37. On the "10 Best" lists of the *New York Times, Film Daily* and the National Board of Review, it placed #5, #6 (in 1937) and #8 (1936) respectively. Previous versions: (Vitagraph; 1908) with Paul Panzer and Florence Lawrence, (Biograph; 1914), (Metro; 1916) with Francis X. Bushman and Beverly Bayne, (Fox; 1916) with Harry Hilliard and Theda Bara. Later versions (Great Britain; 1954), (U.S.S.R.; 1955) a ballet, (Great Britain; 1966) a ballet and the lavishly produced British-Italian co-production of 1968.

A Romeo in Pyjamas (G.B. title) *see* **Parlor, Bedroom and Bath**

3927. The Rookie Cop (RKO; 1939). *Cast:* Tim Holt, Virginia Weidler, Ace the Wonder Dog, Janet Shaw, Frank M. Thomas, Robert Emmett Keane, Monte Montague, Don Brodie, Ralf Harolde, Muriel Evans. *D:* David Howard; *P:* Bert Gilroy; *St:* Guy K. Austin, Earl Johnson; *Sc:* Jo Pagano, Morton Grant. (1:00)

B juvenile drama of a rookie policeman, his police dog and the little girl who lives next door.

3928. Room Service (RKO; 1938). *Cast:* Groucho Marx, Harpo Marx, Chico Marx, Frank Albertson, Lucille Ball, Donald MacBride (film debut), Ann Miller, Philip Loeb, Charles Halton, Cliff Dunstan, Philip Wood, Alexander Asro. *D:* William A. Seiter; *P:* Pandro S. Berman; *Sc:* Morrie Ryskind. (1:18) (video)

Based on the hit Broadway play by John Murray and Allan Boretz, this Marx Brothers romp deals with some broke theatrical producers, who while trying to get backing for their play, are also trying to keep from getting kicked out of their hotel room. A box office flop that was remade as *Step Lively* (RKO;

1944). Computer-colored prints have been produced.

3929. Rootin' Tootin' Rhythm (Republic; 1937). *Cast:* Gene Autry, Smiley Burnette, Armida, Monte Blue, Al Clauser & His Oklahoma Outlaws, Hal Taliaferro, Ann Pendleton, Max Hoffman, Jr., Charles King, Frankie Marvin, Nina Campana, Charles Meyers, Karl Hackett, Henry Hall, Curley Dresden, Art Davis, Champion. *D:* Mack V. Wright; *As.P.:* Armand Schaefer; *St:* Johnston McCulley; *Sc:* Jack Natteford: *Songs:* Autry, Fleming Allen, Al Clauser, Tex Hoepner, Jack Natteford. (G.B. title: *Rhythm on the Ranch*). (1:00) (video—0:55)

Gene Autry western with songs, including the title song and "Mexicali Rose," in a story of a range feud.

Rosalie (MGM; 1929) (G.B. title) *see* **Not So Dumb**

3930. Rosalie (MGM; 1937). *Cast:* Nelson Eddy, Eleanor Powell, Frank Morgan (recreating his stage role), Edna May Oliver, Ray Bolger, Ilona Massey (American debut), Reginald Owen, Billy Gilbert, Jerry Colonna, George Zucco, William Demarest, Janet Beecher, Virginia Grey, Clay Clement, Tom Rutherford, Oscar O'Shea, Roy Barcroft. *D:* W.S. Van Dyke; *P:* William Anthony McGuire; *Sc:* McGuire; *Songs:* Cole Porter (the score being different from that which accompanied the stage production). (2:02) (video)

An ultra-lavish romantic musical set at West Point which boasts a cast of over 2,000 actors, singers, dancers and extras. Based on the Broadway play by William Anthony McGuire and Guy Bolton, it became one of the 15 top grossing films of 1937–38. In 1930 this studio started to produce a version of the play with Marion Davies, but scrapped it before completion.

3931. Rose Bowl (Paramount; 1936). *Cast:* Tom Brown, Buster

Crabbe, Eleanore Whitney, William Frawley, Nydia Westman, Benny Baker, Priscilla Lawson, Terry Ray (Ellen Drew). *D:* Charles Barton; *P:* A.M. Botsford; *St:* Francis Wallace; *Sc:* Marguerite Roberts. (G.B. title: *O'Riley's Luck*)

B romantic gridiron story.

3932. Rose-Marie (MGM; 1936). *Cast:* Jeanette MacDonald (Marie de Flor), Nelson Eddy (Sgt. Bruce), James Stewart (John Flower), Reginald Owen (Myerson), Allan Jones (Romeo), Gilda Gray (Belle), George Regas (Boniface), Una O'Connor (Anna), David Niven (Teddy), Dorothy Gray (Edith), James Conlin (Joe), Herman Bing (Mr. Daniells), Lucien Littlefield (storekeeper), Robert Greig (cafe manager), Alan Mowbray (premier), Mary Anita Loos (corn queen), Aileen Carlyle (Susan), Halliwell Hobbes (Mr. Gordon), Paul Porcasi (Emil), Milton Owen (stage manager), Leonard Carey (Louis), Edgar Dearing, Pat West, David Clyde, Russell Hicks, Rolfe Sedan, Jack Pennick, David Robel, Rinaldo Alacorn, Bert Lindley. *D:* W.S. Van Dyke II; *P:* Hunt Stromberg; *Sc:* Frances Goodrich, Albert Hackett, Alice Duer Miller; *Opera Sequences:* William Von Wymetal; *Totem Pole Dance Staged by:* Chester Hale; *Songs:* "Rose-Marie," "Song of the Mounties," "Lak Jeem," "Indian Love Call," "Totem Tom Tom" by Otto Harbach, Oscar Hammerstein II & Rudolf Friml; "Just for You" by Gus Kahn, Herbert Stothart & Friml; "Pardon Me Madam" by Kahn, Stothart; "Dinah" by Sam Lewis, Joe Young & Harry Akst, & "Some of These Days" by Shelton Brooks. (TV title: *Indian Love Call*) (1:53) (video—1:50)

A Canadian Mountie is out to get his man, who happens to be the brother of the girl he has fallen for. Based on the play by Otto A. Harbach and Oscar Hammerstein II, which was scored by Herbert Stothart and Rudolph Friml. A big hit for the studio, being one of the 25 top grossing films of 1935-36. Previous

version by this studio: a 1927-28 silent which starred Joan Crawford and House Peters. Remade in 1954.

3933. Rose of the Rancho (Paramount; 1935-36). *Cast:* Gladys Swarthout (film debut), John Boles, Willie Howard, Charles Bickford, H.B. Warner, Grace Bradley, Don Alvarado, Herb Williams, Charlotte Granville, Benny Baker, Pedro de Cordoba, Minor Watson, Louise Carter, Russell Hopton, Harry Woods, Arthur Aylesworth, Gino Corrado. *D:* Marion Gering; *P:* William LeBaron; *St:* Richard Walton Tully; *Sc:* Frank Partos, Arthur Sheekman, Charles Brackett, Nat Perrin. (1:25)

A musical romance with a latin setting which was based on the 1906 play by David Belasco. A remake of *The Rose of the Rancho* (Lasky; 1914) with Bessie Barriscale and Monroe Salisbury.

3934. Rose of the Rio Grande (Monogram; 1938). *Cast:* Movita, John Carroll, Antonio Moreno, Don Alvarado, Lina Basquette, Duncan Renaldo, George Cleveland, Gino Corrado, Martin Garralaga, Rosa Turich. *D:* William Nigh; *P:* George E. Kann; *St:* Johnston McCulley; *Sc:* Ralph Bettinson. (1:00)

B south-of-the-border romantic type western involving a wealthy man who assumes another identity. A remake of the 1930 silent Syndicate production of the same name with Tom Tyler.

3935. Rose of Washington Square (20th Century–Fox; 1939). *Cast:* Alice Faye, Tyrone Power, Al Jolson, Hobart Cavanaugh, William Frawley, Joyce Compton, Horace MacMahon, Louise Prima & His Band, Moroni Olsen, E.E. Clive, John Hamilton, Ben Welden, Charles Lane, Paul Burns, Hal K. Dawson, Charles Wilson, Paul Stanton. *D:* Gregory Ratoff; *P:* Nunnally Johnson; *Sc:* Johnson. (1:26) (video)

Romantic musical of a singer on the way up who is married to a man on the way down. The story is based on events in the life of Fanny Brice with the same story being told in the Broadway hit "Funny Girl" and the 1968 film adapted from it.

3936. Rough Riders Roundup (Republic; 1939). *Cast:* Roy Rogers, Lynn Roberts, Raymond Hatton, Eddie Acuff, William Pawley, Dorothy Sebastian, Jack Rockwell, Robert Wilke, Jack Kirk, Fred Kelsey, George Chesebro, Jim Corey, Al Haskell. *D:* Joseph Kane; *Sc:* Jack Natteford. (0:58) (video)

A Roy Rogers western involving the reunion of the Rough Riders to preserve law and order.

3937. Rough Riding Ranger (Superior; 1935). *Cast:* Rex Lease, Janet Chandler, Bobby Nelson, Yakima Canutt, Mabel Strickland, Sunday "The Knowing One," David Horsley, George Chesebro, Robert Walker. *D:* Elmer Clifton; *P:* George Merrick; *St:* Clifton, Merrick; *Sc:* Clifton. (0:56)

Rex Lease western with comic overtones of a ranger who investigates a series of threatening letters received by various people.

3938. Rough Riding Rhythm (Ambassador; 1937). *Cast:* Kermit Maynard, Beryl Wallace, Ralph Peters (Scrubby), Olin Francis, Betty Mack, Curley Dresden, Cliff Parkinson, Dave O'Brien, Newt Kirby, J.P. McGowan. *D:* J.P. McGowan; *P:* Maurice Conn; *Sc:* Arthur Everett. (0:57)

Kermit Maynard western of two pals out to get a gang leader who killed the sister of the one and also shot the sheriff.

3939. Rough Romance (Fox; 1930). *Cast:* George O'Brien, Helen Chandler, Antonio Moreno, Roy Stewart, Harry Cording, David Hartford, Eddie Borden, Noel Francis, Frank Lanning, John Wayne. *D:* A.F. Erickson; *St:* Kenneth B. Clarke; *Sc:* Elliott Lester, Donald Davis. (0:55)

George O'Brien action drama with musical interludes and set in the big timber country.

3940. Rough Waters (WB; 1930). *Cast:* Rin-Tin-Tin, Lane Chandler, Jobyna Ralston, Edmund Breese, Walter Miller, Richard Alexander. *D:* John Daumery; *Sc:* James A. Starr.

A Rin-Tin-Tin adventure (his 19th starring feature film), with Rinty apprehending some payroll robbers. This was the popular canine's final feature film and also his final appearance for this studio. Had it not been for the immense popularity of the low-budget features of this canine star, the Warner Brothers studio would probably have gone under in the latter days of the silent era. His heroic exploits appealed to adults as well as children and likely equaled the popularity of the B westerns of the day. To give an idea of Rinty's popularity, it might be noted that on the voting of the first Academy Awards, Rin-Tin-Tin won hands down the vote for "Best Actor," but was disqualified, the award eventually going to Emil Jannings. Following this feature, Rinty made two 12-chapter serials for Mascot, namely: "The Lone Defender" (1930) and "The Lightning Warrior" in 1931. He died August 10, 1932, at the age of 13-years.

3941. Roundup Time in Texas (Republic; 1937). *Cast:* Gene Autry, Smiley Burnette, Maxine Doyle, Cabin Kids, LeRoy Mason, Earle Hodgins, Buddy Williams, Dick Wessel, Cornie Anderson, Frankie Marvin, Ken Cooper, Elmer Fain, Al Ferguson, Slim Whitaker, Al Knight, Carleton Young, Jim Corey, Jack C. Smith, Jack Kirk, George Morrell, Champion. *D:* Joseph Kane; *P:* Nat Levine; *As.P.:* Armand Schaefer; *Sc:* Oliver Drake; *Songs:* Autry, Burnette, Sam H. Stept, Sidney Mitchell, Ned Washington, Sam Lewis, Joe Young, Harry Akst, Vincent & Howard, Andy Razof. (0:58) (video)

Offbeat Gene Autry western set in Africa.

3942. Rovin' Tumbleweeds (Republic; 1939). *Cast:* Gene Autry, Smiley Burnette, Mary Carlisle, Douglass Dumbrille, William Farnum, Lee "Lasses" White, Ralph Peters, Gordon Hart, Victor Potel, Sammy McKim, Jack Ingram, Reginald Barlow, Eddie Kane, Horace Murphy, Dave Sharpe, Jack Kirk, Rose Plummer, Bob Burns, Art Mix, Chuck Morrison, Pals of the Golden West, Horace Carpenter, Frank Ellis, Fred Burns, Ed Cassidy, Forrest Taylor, Tom Chatterton, Maurice Costello, Guy Usher. *D:* George Sherman; *P:* William Berke; *Sc:* Betty Burbridge, Dorrell & Stuart McGowan. (1:04)

Gene Autry western with songs, including "Back in the Saddle Again."

3943. The Royal Bed (RKO; 1931). *Cast:* Mary Astor, Lowell Sherman, Nance O'Neil, Anthony Bushell, Robert Warwick, Hugh Trevor, J. Carrol Naish, Gilbert Emery, Alan Roscoe, Frederic Burt, Desmond Roberts. *D:* Lowell Sherman; *P:* William LeBaron; *Supervisor:* Henry Hobart; *Sc:* J. Walter Ruben. (G.B. title: *The Queen's Husband*) (1:14)

Sophisticated Ruritanian comedy of the separate lives of European royalty. Based on the play "The Queen's Husband" by Robert E. Sherwood.

3944. The Royal Family of Broadway (Paramount; 1930). *Cast:* Fredric March (A.A.N. for B.A., 1930–31), Ina Claire, Mary Brian, Henrietta Crosman, Charles Starrett, Arnold Korff, Frank Conroy (film debut), Murray Alper, Wesley Stark, Herschel Mayall, Royal G. Stout, Elsie Edmond. *D:* George Cukor, Cyril Gardner; *Sc:* Herman J. Mankiewicz, Gertrude Purcell. (1:22)

A theatrical family (Barrymore style) is torn between their careers and living a "normal life." Filmed at Astoria Studios in Long Island, N.Y., it was based on the popular 1927 New York play by Edna Ferber and George S. Kaufman.

3945. A Royal Romance (Columbia; 1930). *Cast:* William Collier, Jr., Pauline Starke, Clarence Muse, Eugenie Besserer, Ann Brody. *D:* Erle C. Kenton.

Low-budget production aptly described by the title.

3946. Ruggles of Red Gap (Paramount; 1935). *Cast:* Charles Laughton (received "Best Actor" Award for his performance as Ruggles along with his performance as "Captain Bligh" in *Mutiny on the Bounty* [q.v.] by the New York Film Critics), Charles Ruggles (Egbert Floud), Roland Young (Van Bassingwell), Mary Boland (Effie Floud), ZaSu Pitts (Mrs. Judson), Leila Hyams (Nell Kenner), Maude Eburne (Ma Pettingill), Lucien Littlefield (Charles Belknap-Jackson), Del Henderson (Sam), James Burke (Jeff Tuttle), Clarence Hummel Wilson (Jake Henshaw), Leota Lorraine (Mrs. Belknap-Jackson), Brenda Fowler (Judy Ballard), Baby Ricardo Lord Cezon (Baby Judson), Augusta Anderson (Mrs. Wallaby), Sarah Edwards (Mrs. Myron Carey), George Burton (Hank), Frank Rice (Buck), William J. Welsh (Eddie), Lee Kohlmar (Red Gap jailer), Alice Ardell (Lisette), Rolfe Sedan (barber), Jack Norton (barfly), Genaro Spagnoli (Frank), Rafael Storm, Victor Potel, Harry Bernard, Jim Welch, Libby Taylor, Willie Fung, Armand Kaliz, Harry Bowen, Henry Rocquemore, Heinie Conklin, Edward Le Saint, Charles Fallon, Albert Petit, Carrie Daumery, Isabelle La Mal, Ernest S. (Ernie) Adams, Frank O'Connor. *D:* Leo McCarey; *P:* (A.A.N. for Best Picture) Arthur Hornblow, Jr.; *Sc:* Harlan Thompson, Walter De Leon, Humphrey Pearson; *Songs:* Ralph Rainger, Sam Coslow. (1:32) (video)

Classic comedy of an Englishman who loses his butler in a poker game to a westerner in the United States. Based on the novel by Harry Leon Wilson it placed #2 on the "10 Best" list of the *New York Times,* as well as being voted one of the "10 Best" films of the year by the National Board of Review. Other versions: (Essanay; 1918) with Lawrence D'Orsay and Taylor Holmes, (Paramount; 1923) with Edward Everett Horton and Louise Dresser and *Fancy Pants* (Paramount; 1950) with Bob Hope and Lucille Ball. It also placed #6 on the "10 Best" list of *Film Daily*.

3947. Rulers of the Sea (Paramount; 1939). *Cast:* Douglas Fairbanks, Jr., Margaret Lockwood (in her second and last American film), Will Fyffe, George Bancroft, Montagu Love, Mary Gordon, Alan Ladd, Neil Fitzgerald, Lester Matthews, Ivan Simpson, Lawrence Grant, David Torrence (final film—d. 1942), George Melford, Wyndham Standing, Olaf Hytten, Lionel Pape, Vaughan Glaser, Mike Driscoll, David Clyde. *D:* Frank Lloyd; *P:* Lloyd; *St & Sc:* Frank Cavett, Richard Collins, Talbot Jennings. (1:36)

Action-drama of the first steamship voyage across the Atlantic Ocean.

3948. The Ruling Voice (WB/F.N.; 1931). *Cast:* Loretta Young, Walter Huston, David Manners, Doris Kenyon, John Halliday, Dudley Digges, Willard Robertson, Gilbert Emery, Nat Pendleton, Douglas Scott. *D:* Rowland V. Lee; *St:* Roland V. & Donald Lee; *Adaptation:* Robert Lord; *Sc:* Byron Morgan.

Hit gangster drama of its day.

3949. Rumba (Paramount; 1935). *Cast:* Carole Lombard, George Raft, Margo, Lynne Overman, Gail Patrick, Monroe Owsley, Iris Adrian, Samuel S. Hinds, Jameson Thomas, Akim Tamiroff, Clara Lou (Ann) Sheridan, Virginia Hammond. *D:* Marion Gering; *P:* William LeBaron; *St:* Seena Owen, Guy Endore; *Sc:* Howard J. Green, Harry Ruskin, Frank Partos. (aka: *Rhumba*) (1:17)

Romantic drama which followed in the footsteps of the 1934 hit *Bolero* (q.v.), in an attempt to capitalize on that film's

popularity. As in *Bolero,* Veloz and Yolanda doubled for much of the actual dancing. A box office flop.

3950. The Runaround (RKO; 1931). *Cast:* Mary Brian, Geoffrey Kerr, Joseph Cawthorn, Marie Prevost, Johnny Hines. *D:* William James Craft; *As.P.:* Louis Sarecky; *St:* Zandah Owen; *Sc:* Alfred Jackson, Barney Sarecky. (G.B. title: *Waiting for the Bride*)

Comedy-drama filmed in 2-color technicolor of a dancer trying to preserve her virtue. A box office loser.

3951. The Runaway Bride (RKO; 1930). *Cast:* Mary Astor, Lloyd Hughes, David Newell, Paul Hurst, Natalie Moorhead, Edgar Norton, Francis McDonald, Maurice Black, Harry Tenbrook. *D:* Donald Crisp; *As.P.:* William Sistrom; *Sc:* Jane Murfin. (1:09)

Melodrama of blackmail, kidnapping and murder. Based on the play by Lolita Ann Westman and H.H. Van Loan, the film showed no profit.

Runaway Daughter *see* **Red Salute**

3952. Rustlers' Paradise (Ajax; 1935). *Cast:* Harry Carey, Gertrude Messinger, Edmund Cobb, Carmen Bailey, Theodore Lorch, Slim Whitaker, Roger Williams, Allen Greer, Chuck Morrison, Chief Thundercloud. *D:* Harry Fraser; *P:* William Berke; *Sc:* Weston Edwards. (1:01)

Harry Carey western (one in a series of six for this company) of a man's search for his wife and daughter who had been kidnapped by outlaws years earlier.

3953. Rustlers' Roundup (Universal; 1933). *Cast:* Tom Mix, Diane Sinclair, Douglass Dumbrille, Roy Stewart, Noah "Pidge" Beery, Jr., Frank Lackteen, William Desmond, Bud Osborne, Nelson McDowell, Tony, Jr., the horse. *D:* Henry MacRae. (1:00)

Tom Mix western of a rancher who comes to the aid of a girl whose father has been murdered. This was Mix's final feature film as he was severely injured in a fall during production. His final film appearance was in a 1935 Mascot serial in 15-chapters titled "The Miracle Rider" (also released in feature-length — q.v.). Mix was killed October 12, 1940, when he crashed his Cord roadster on an Arizona highway to avoid hitting a work crew. On the spot where he died, the Arizona Highway Commission erected an inscribed monument of a riderless horse to his memory.

3954. Rustlers' Valley (Paramount; 1937). *Cast:* William Boyd (Hoppy), Russell Hayden (Lucky), George Hayes (Windy), John St. Polis, Lee Colt (Lee J. Cobb), Stephen Morris (Morris Ankrum), Muriel Evans, Ted Adams, Al Ferguson, John Beach, Oscar Apfel, Bernadene Hayes. *D:* Nate Watt; *P:* Harry M. Sherman; *Sc:* Harry O. Hoyt. (1:00) (video)
The 12th entry in the "Hopalong Cassidy" series as the Bar 20 boys put the crimps to a crooked lawyer.

3955. Rusty Rides Alone (Columbia; 1933). *Cast:* Tim McCoy, Barbara Weeks, Dorothy Burgess, Wheeler Oakman, Edmund Cobb, Ed Burns, Rockliffe Fellowes, Clarence Geldert, Silver King the dog. *D:* D. Ross Lederman; *Sc:* Robert Quigley. (0:58)
Tim McCoy range saga of a cowboy who attempts to stop a ruthless sheepman, bent on driving cattlemen from the range.

S.O.S. Clipper Island (G.B. title) *see* **Robinson Crusoe on Mystery Island**

3956. S.O.S. Coast Guard (Republic; 1937–42). *Cast:* Ralph Byrd, Bela Lugosi, Louis Jean Heydt, Roy Barcroft, George Chesebro. *D:* William Witney, Alan James (aka: Alvin J. Neitz); *Supervisor:* Nat Levine.

Feature version edited down in 1942 of a 1937 serial.

3957. S.O.S. Iceberg (Universal; 1933). *Cast:* Rod La Rocque, Leni Riefenstahl, Gibson Gowland, Ernst Udet, Walter Rimi. *D:* Tay Garnett, Dr. Arnold Fanck; *Sc:* Fanck (co-writer). (1:16)
A German-American co-produced adventure melodrama of an expedition to Greenland to rescue a group of lost explorers.

3958. S.O.S. Tidal Wave (Republic; 1939). *Cast:* Ralph Byrd, Kay Sutton, Donald Barry, Marc Lawrence, Ferris Taylor, George Barbier, Raymond Bailey, Frank Jenks, Dorothy Lee, Oscar O'Shea, Mickey Kuhn. *D:* John H. Auer; *St:* James R. Webb; *Sc:* Maxwell Shane, Gordon Kahn. (G.B. title: *Tidal Wave*)
B production of a man who perpetrates a hoax on some people.

3959. Sabotage (Republic; 1939). *Cast:* Arleen Whelan, Charley Grapewin, Horace MacMahon, Lucien Littlefield, Maude Eburne, Donald Douglas, Dorothy Peterson, Frank Darien, Wade Boteler, J.M. Kerrigan, Paul Guilfoyle, Gordon Oliver, Joseph Sawyer, John Russell, Charles Halton. *D:* Harold Young; *Sc:* Alice Altschuler, Lionel Houser. (G.B. title: *Spies at Work*)
B espionage melodrama.

3960. The Sacred Flame (WB; 1929). *Cast:* Conrad Nagel, Lila Lee, Pauline Frederick, William Courtenay, Walter Byron, Alec B. Francis, Dale Fuller. *D:* Archie Mayo; *Sc:* Harvey Thew.
Marital drama of a paralyzed war hero and his wife. Based on the play by W. Somerset Maugham, it was remade as *The Right to Live* (q.v.).

The Sacred Flame (WB; 1935) (G.B. title) *see* **The Right to Live**

3961. Saddle Aces (Resolute; 1935). *Cast:* Rex Bell, Ruth Mix, Buzz Barton, Stanley Blystone, Earl Dwire, Chuck Morrison, Mary MacLaren, John Elliott, Roger Williams, Chief Thundercloud. *D:* Harry Fraser; *Sc:* Harry P. Crist (Fraser). (0:56)

Rex Bell indie western (one of a series of four) of two cowpokes sent up for crimes they didn't commit who escape from a prison train to get the guilty party.

3962. The Saddle Buster (RKO-Pathé; 1932). *Cast:* Tom Keene, Helen Foster, Marie Quillan, Robert Frazer, Richard Carlyle, Fred Burns, Charles Quigley, Harry Bowen, Slim Whitaker. *D:* Fred Allen; *P:* Charles R. Rogers; *St:* Cherry Wilson; *Sc:* Oliver Drake. (1:00)

Offbeat Tom Keene western of rodeo bronc riders.

3963. Sadie McKee (MGM; 1934). *Cast:* Joan Crawford (Sadie), Franchot Tone (Michael), Gene Raymond (Tommy), Edward Arnold (Brennan), Esther Ralston (Dolly), Jean Dixon, Earl Oxford, Akim Tamiroff, Leo G. Carroll, Gene Austin, Zelda Sears, Minerva Urecal, Ethel Griffies, Samuel S. Hinds, Helen Ware, "Candy" & Coco, Helen Freeman. *D:* Clarence Brown; *P:* Lawrence Weingarten; *St:* Vina Delmar; *Sc:* John Meehan; *Song:* "All I Do Is Dream of You" by Nacio Herb Brown, Arthur Freed (vocalized by Gene Raymond). (1:30)

Romantic comedy-drama of a factory girl and the three men in her life.

3964. Safe in Hell (WB/F.N.; 1931). *Cast:* Dorothy Mackaill, Donald Cook, Ralf Harolde, John Wray, Ivan Simpson, Victor Varconi, Morgan Wallace, Nina Mae McKinney, Charles Middleton, Clarence Muse, Gustav von Seyffertitz, Noble Johnson, Cecil Cunningham, George F. Marion. *D:* William A. Wellman; *Adaptation:* Joseph Jackson, Maude Fulton (of a play by Houston Branch). (G.B. title: *The Lost Lady*) (1:09)

After she believes she killed a man, a girl flees to a remote tropical island where wanted fugitives hang out, in this low-budget melodrama.

3965. Safety in Numbers (Paramount; 1930). *Cast:* Charles "Buddy" Rogers, Kathryn Crawford, Josephine Dunn, Carole Lombard, Roscoe Karns, Francis McDonald, Geneva Mitchell, Virginia Bruce, Richard Tucker, Lawrence Grant, Louise Beavers. *D:* Victor Schertzinger; *St:* Percy Heath, George Marion, Jr.; *Sc:* Marion Dix; *Songs:* Richard A. Whiting, Marion.

Comedy with musical interludes involving the uncle of a young heir who hires three chorus girls to protect the young man from golddiggers.

3966. Safety in Numbers (20th Century–Fox; 1938). *Cast:* Jed Prouty, Spring Byington, Florence Roberts, June Carlson, Kenneth Howell, George Ernest, Billy Mahan, Shirley Deane, Russell Gleason, Paul McVey, Marvin Stephens, Helen Freeman, Iva Stewart. *D:* Mal St. Clair; *Sc:* Karen DeWolf, Robert Chapin, Joseph Hoffman.

The 10th entry in the low-budget "Jones Family" comedy series.

3967. Saga of Death Valley (Republic; 1939). *Cast:* Roy Rogers, Donald Barry, George "Gabby" Hayes, Frank M. Thomas, Doris Day (not the singer), Hal Taliaferro, Jack Ingram, Lew Kelly, Jimmy Wakely, Ed Brady. *D:* Joseph Kane; *P:* Kane; *Sc:* Stuart Anthony, Karen DeWolf. (0:56) (video)

Roy Rogers western of two brothers, orphaned when young who grow up on different sides of the law.

Sage of the West *see* **When a Man's a Man**

3968. The Sagebrush Family Trails West (Producers Distributing Corp.; 1939). *Cast:* Bobby Clark, Earle

Hodgins, Nina Guilbert, Joyce Bryant, Minerva Urecal, Archie Hall, Kenneth (Kenne) Duncan, Forrest Taylor, Carl Mathews, Wally West, Byron Vance, Augie Gomez. *D:* Peter Stewart (Sam Newfield); *P:* Sig Neufeld (brother to Sam Newfield); *St & Sc:* William Lively. (1:00)

Low-budget family oriented western of a traveling medicine show and their star attraction, a juvenile trick roper (Clark).

3969. Sagebrush Politics (Art Mix Productions; 1930). *Cast:* Art Mix, Lillian Bond, Tom Forman. *D:* Denver Dixon; *P:* Art Mix (Dixon).

Part-talkie B western.

3970. Sagebrush Trail (Monogram-Lone Star; 1933). *Cast:* John Wayne, Lane Chandler, Nancy Shubert, Wally Wales (Hal Taliaferro), Yakima Canutt, Henry Hall, William Dyer, Earl Dwire, Art Mix, Hank Bell, Slim Whitaker, Robert Burns, Hal Price. *D:* Armand Schaefer; *P:* Paul Malvern; *Supervisor:* Trem Carr; *St & Sc:* Lindsley Parsons. (0:58) (video)

John Wayne western of a cowboy who escapes prison after being wrongfully accused of murder.

3971. Sagebrush Troubedor (Republic; 1935). *Cast:* Gene Autry, Barbara Pepper, Smiley Burnette, Fred Kelsey, J. Frank Glendon, Hooper Atchley, Julian Rivero, Denny Meadows (Dennis Moore), Tom London, Wes Warner, Frankie Marvin, Bud Pope, Tommy Gene Fairey, Champion. *D:* Joseph Kane; *P:* Nat Levine; *Supervisor:* Armand Schaefer; *St:* Oliver Drake; *Sc:* Drake, Joseph Poland; *Songs:* Autry, Burnette. (0:54)

Gene Autry western with songs of circumstances surrounding the murder of an elderly rancher.

3972. Sailor Be Good (RKO/Jefferson; 1933). *Cast:* Jack Oakie (Jonesy), Vivienne Osborne (Red),

Gertrude Michael, George E. Stone, Lincoln Stedman, Max Hoffman, Jr., Huntley Gordon, Gertrude Sutton, Charles Coleman, Crauford Kent. *D:* James Cruze; *P:* Joseph I. Schnitzer, Samuel Zierler (for Jefferson Pictures Corporation); *St:* Viola Brothers Shore; *Sc:* Shore, Ethel Doherty, Ralph Spence.

Independent comedy of a boxing sailor who joins society by marrying a debutante.

3973. Sailor's Holiday (Pathé; 1929). *Cast:* Sally Eilers, Alan Hale, Mary Carr, Charles Clary, George Cooper. *D:* Fred Newmeyer.

Low-budget romantic comedy.

3974. Sailor's Luck (Fox; 1933). *Cast:* James Dunn, Sally Eilers, Sammy Cohen, Victor Jory, Frank Morgan, Lucien Littlefield, Esther Muir, Will Stanton, Curley Wright, Jerry Mandy, Buster Phelps, Frank Atkinson. *D:* Raoul Walsh; *St & Sc:* Marguerite Roberts, Charlotte Miller. (1:18)

Romantic comedy of sailors on shore leave.

3975. The Saint in New York (RKO; 1938). *Cast:* Louis Hayward (Simon Templar), Kay Sutton, Sig Rumann, Jonathan Hale, Frederick Burton, Jack Carson, Paul Guilfoyle, Ben Welden, Charles Halton, Cliff Bragdon, Paul Fix. *D:* Ben Holmes; *P:* William Sistrom; *Sc:* Mortimer Offner, Charles Kaufman. (1:12) (video)

Hit crime melodrama, based on the book by Leslie Charteris. This box office hit was the first film to feature the title character. Followed by *The Saint Strikes Back* (q.v.).

3976. St. Louis Blues (Paramount; 1939). *Cast:* Dorothy Lamour, Lloyd Nolan (in a role originally intended for George Raft), Tito Guizar, Jerome Cowan, Jessie Ralph, William Frawley, King's Men, Matty Malneck & His Orchestra, Maxine Sullivan, Hall

Johnson Choir, Mary Parker, Cliff Nazarro, Emory Parnell, Sterling Holloway, Victor Kilian, Virginia Howell, Walter Soderling, Grafton Lynn, Jon Dodson, Rad Robinson. *D:* Raoul Walsh; *P:* Jeff Lazarus; *St:* Eleanore Griffin, William Rankin; *Sc:* John C. Moffitt, Malcolm Stuart Boylan, Frederick Hazlitt Brennan; *Other Songs:* Loesser, Burton Lane, Sam Coslow. (TV title: *Best of the Blues*) (1:32)

Hit musical of an actress who trades in her career to join a riverboat. This film produced the hit song "I Go for That" by Frank Loesser and Matty Malneck (vocalized by Lamour).

3977. The St. Louis Kid (WB; 1934). *Cast:* James Cagney (Eddie Kennedy), Patricia Ellis, Allen Jenkins (Buck), Robert Barrat (Farmer Benson), Hobart Cavanaugh, Spencer Charters, Addison Richards, Dorothy Dare, Arthur Aylesworth, Charles Wilson, Ruth Robinson, Eddie Shubert, Gertrude Short, Harry Woods. *D:* Ray Enright; *P:* Sam Bischoff; *St:* Frederick Hazlitt Brennan; *Sc:* Seton I. Miller, Warren Duff. (G.B. title: *A Perfect Weekend*) (1:06)

Low-budget comedy of labor disputes among milk producers.

3978. St. Louis Woman (Showman's Pictures; 1935). *Cast:* Johnny Mack Brown, Jeanett Loff, Earle Foxe. *D:* Albert Ray; *St:* Elwood Ullman; *Sc:* Jack Natteford.

(No other information available)

3979. The Saint Strikes Back (RKO; 1939). *Cast:* George Sanders (replacing Louis Hayward as Simon Templar), Wendy Barrie, Jonathan Hale, Jerome Cowan, Neil Hamilton, Barry Fitzgerald, Robert Elliott, Russell Hopton, Edward Gargan, Robert Strange, Gilbert Emery, James Burke, Nella Walker, Willie Best. *D:* John Farrow; *P:* Robert Sisk; *Sc:* John Twist. (1:04) (video)

The 2nd entry in this popular series. Simon Templar is called in to solve a series of unusual murders. Based on the novel "Angels of Doom" by Leslie Charteris. Followed by *The Saint in London* (1939) an RKO British import.

3980. Sal of Singapore (Pathé; 1929). *Cast:* Phyllis Haver, Alan Hale, Noble Johnson, Dan Wolheim, Jules Cowles, Pat Harmon. *D:* Howard Higgin; *St:* Dale Collins; *Sc:* Elliott Clawson, Higgin; *Titles:* Edwin Justus Mayer.

Part-talkie romantic melodrama.

3981. Saleslady (Monogram; 1938). *Cast:* Anne Nagel, Weldon Heyburn, Harry Davenport, Harry Hayden, Ruth Fallows, Kenneth Harlan, Doris Rankin, John St. Polis. *D:* Arthur Greville Collins; *P:* Ken Goldsmith; *St:* "Nothing Down" by Kubec Glasmon; *Sc:* Marion Orth. (1:05)

B drama of an heiress who feigns poverty when she marries a poor sales clerk.

3982. Sally (WB/F.N. — Vitaphone; 1929). *Cast:* Marilyn Miller (film debut), Alexander Gray, Joe E. Brown, Pert Kelton (film debut), T. Roy Barnes, Ford Sterling, Maude Turner Gordon, E.J. Ratcliffe, Nora Lane, Jack Duffy. *D:* John Francis Dillon; *Sc:* Waldemar Young; *Art-Set Decoration:* (A.A.N.) Jack Okey. (1:30 approx.)

Technicolor musical-comedy of a waitress who makes it big on the Great White Way. Based on the 1920 play by Guy Bolton and Jerome Kern, this 2-color technicolor feature was an attempt to capitalize on Marilyn Miller's stage success. The film which placed #10 on the "10 Best" list of the *New York Times* was previously filmed by First National in 1925 with Colleen Moore.

3983. Sally, Irene and Mary (20th Century–Fox; 1938). *Cast:* Alice Faye, Tony Martin, Fred Allen, Jimmy Durante, Joan Davis, Marjorie Weaver, Gregory Ratoff, Louise Hovick (Gypsy Rose Lee), Eddie Collins, Andrew Tombes, Mary Treen, Charles Wilson, Brian Sisters, Raymond Scott quintet,

Barnett Parker. *D:* William A. Seiter; *P:* Gene Markey; *St:* Karl Tunberg, Don Ettlinger; *Sc:* Harry Tugend, Jack Yellen. (1:12)

Romantic musical-comedy previously filmed (Metro-Goldwyn; 1925) with Joan Crawford, Constance Bennett and Sally O'Neil.

3984. Sally of the Subway (Mayfair; 1932). *Cast:* Jack Mulhall, Dorothy Revier, Craufurd Kent. *D:* George B. Seitz; *St & Sc:* Seitz.

"Poverty row" feature.

Salomy Jane (G.B. title) *see* **Wild Girl**

3985. Salute (Fox; 1929). *Cast:* George O'Brien, Helen Chandler, John Breeden, Frank Albertson, Stepin Fetchit, Joyce Compton, Rex Bell, Clifford Dempsey, David Butler, Lumsden Hare, William Janney, Ward Bond (film debut — bit), John Wayne (bit). *D:* John Ford; *St:* John Stone, Tristram Tupper; *Sc:* James K. McGuinness.

College football story with some location shooting at West Point.

Salute to Romance (G.B. title) *see* **Annapolis Salute**

3986. Salvation Nell (Tiffany; 1931). *Cast:* Helen Chandler, Ralph Graves, Sally O'Neil, Jason Robards, Charlotte Walker, Matthew Betz, Rose Dione, DeWitt Jennings, Wally Albright. *D:* James Cruze; *St & Sc:* E. Lloyd (Edward) Sheldon; *Cont.:* Walter Woods; *Dial.:* Selma Stein. (G.B. title: *Men Women Love*)

"Poverty row" melodrama based on the 1908 play by Edward Sheldon and previously filmed in the silent era.

The Samaritan (G.B. title) *see* **Soul of the Slums**

3987. San Francisco (MGM; 1936). *Cast:* Clark Gable (Blackie Norton), Jeanette MacDonald (Mary Blake), Spencer Tracy (A.A.N. for B.A. as Father Tim Mullin), Jack Holt (Jack Burley), Ted Healy (Mat), Margaret Irving (Della), Jessie Ralph (Mrs. Burley), Shirley Ross (Trixie), Harold Huber (Babe), Edgar Kennedy (sheriff), Al Shean (professor), William Ricciardi (Signor Baldini), Kenneth Harlan (Chick), Roger Imhof (Alaska), Charles Judels (Tony), Russell Simpson (Red Kelly), Bert Roach (Freddie Duane), Warren Hymer (Hazeltine), Adrienne d'Ambricourt (Madame Albani), Jack Baxley (Kinko), Chester Gan (Jowl Lee), Frank Mayo, Tom Dugan, Nigel de Brulier, Mae Digges, Tudor Williams, Tandy MacKenzie, Nyas Berry, Tom Mahoney, Gertrude Astor, Jason Robards, Vernon Dent, Anthony Jowitt, Carl Stockdale, Richard Carle, Oscar Apfel, Frank Sheridan, Ralph Lewis, Jack Kennedy, Don Rowan, Cyrus Kendall, Robert J. Wilke (film debut), Paul Hurst. *D:* (A.A.N.) W.S. Van Dyke II; *P:* (A.A.N. for Best Picture) John Emerson, Bernard H. Hyman; *Original Story:* (A.A.N.) Robert Hopkins; *Sc:* Anita Loos; *Assistant Director:* (A.A.N.) Joseph Newman; *Sound Recording:* (A.A.) Douglas Shearer; *Special Earthquake Effects:* A. Arnold Gillespie, James Basevi (unc.); *Songs:* "San Francisco" by Gus Kahn, Bronislau Kaper, Walter Jurmann, "The One Love" by Kahn, Kaper & Jurmann; "Would You?" by Nacio Herb Brown, Arthur Freed. (1:55) (video)

Classic romantic drama set in and around the city's Barbary Coast in the period following the turn-of-the-century, as a roguish club owner makes a play for his star attraction, much to the disapproval of his boyhood friend, a local priest. The film climaxes with the great earthquake of April 18, 1906. The studio's biggest money-maker of the year, being one of the 25 top grossing films of 1935–36. It received *"Photoplay's* Gold Medal Award" and placed #4 on the "10 Best" list of *Film Daily.* Computer-colored by Turner Entertainment in 1987.

3988. San Quentin (WB/F.N.; 1937). *Cast:* Pat O'Brien, Humphrey

Bogart, Ann Sheridan, Barton Mac-Lane, Joseph Sawyer, Veda Ann Borg, Marc Lawrence, Raymond Hatton, Frank Faylen, Garry Owen. *D:* Lloyd Bacon; *P:* Sam Bischoff; *St:* Robert Tasker, John Bright; *Sc:* Peter Milne, Humphrey Cobb, Seton I. Miller (unc.); *Song:* "How Could You" by Al Dubin & Harry Warren. (1:10)

Hit prison melodrama.

3989. Sandflow (Universal; 1937). *Cast:* Buck Jones, Lita Chevret, Robert Kortman, Arthur Aylesworth, Robert Terry, Enrique DeRosas, Josef Swickard, Harold Hodge, Lee Phelps, Tom Chatterton, Arthur Van Slyke, Malcolm Graham, Ben Corbett. *D:* Lesley Selander; *Sc:* Frances Guihan. (0:58)

Buck Jones oater of a cowboy out to prove his brother innocent of murder.

Sandy *see* **Unexpected Father**

3990. Sandy of the Mounted (Xxxx Xxxx; 1934). *Cast:* Kermit Maynard.

(No other information available)

Sandy Takes a Bow (G.B. title) *see* **Unexpected Father**

3991. Santa Fe Bound (Reliable; 1936). *Cast:* Tom Tyler, Jeanne Martel, Richard Cramer, Charles King, Slim Whitaker, Ed Cassidy, Lafe McKee, Wally West, Dorothy Woods, Earl Dwire, Ray Henderson. *D:* Henri Samuels (Harry S. Webb); *P:* Bernard B. Ray; *Sc:* Carl Krusada. (0:56) (video)

Tom Tyler western of a cowboy wrongly accused of killing an elderly rancher. Tyler's final film for this independent company.

3992. Santa Fe Rides (Reliable; 1937). *Cast:* Bob Custer (his final film—ret.), Eleanor Stewart, David Sharpe, Ed Cassidy, Roger Williams, Slim Whitaker, Lafe McKee, Snub Pollard, Nelson McDowell, John Elliott, Singin'

Cowboys (Lloyd Perryman, Rudy Sooter, Curley Hoag). *D:* Raymond Samuels (Bernard B. Ray); *P:* Harry S. Webb; *Sc:* Pliny Goodfriend. (0:58)

Bob Custer western of a musical group who has false accusations made against them when they try to get a radio contract.

3993. Santa Fe Stampede (Republic; 1938). *Cast:* John Wayne (Stony Brooke), Ray Corrigan (Tucson Smith), Max Terhune (Lullaby), June Martel, William Farnum, LeRoy Mason, Martin Spellman, Genee Hall, Walter Wills, Ferris Taylor, Tom London, Dick Rush, James F. Cassidy, Curley Dresden, Charles King, Bill Wolfe. *D:* George Sherman; *P:* William Berke; *Sc:* Luci Ward, Betty Burbridge. (0:56)

A "Three Mesquiteers" western, #19 in the series with the trio proving Stony innocent of murder.

3994. The Santa Fe Trail (Paramount; 1930). *Cast:* Richard Arlen, Rosita Moreno, James (Junior) Durkin, Mitzi Green, Eugene Pallette, Luis Alberni, Hooper Atchley, Lee Shumway, Chief Yowlachie, Jack Byron, Blue Cloud, Chief Standing Bear. *D:* Otto Brower, Edwin H. Knopf; *St:* Hal G. Evarts; *Sc:* Sam Mintz, Edward E. Paramore, Jr. (1:20) (video)

Western of complications that are encountered while trail-herding a flock of sheep across the prairie.

3995. The Sap (WB; 1929). *Cast:* Edward Everett Horton, Patsy Ruth Miller, Edna Murphy, Franklin Pangborn, Alan Hale, Russell Simpson, Jerry Mandy. *D:* Archie L. Mayo; *Sc:* Robert Lord.

An impractical dreamer gets a chance to redeem himself in this comedy based on a play by William Grew which was previously filmed by this studio in 1926 with Kenneth Harlan.

The Sap Abroad (G.B. title) *see* **The Sap from Syracuse**

3996. The Sap from Syracuse (Paramount; 1930). *Cast:* Jack Oakie, Ginger Rogers, Verree Teasdale, George Barbier, Granville Bates, Betty Starbuck, Jack Daley, Walter Fenner, Bernard Jukes, J. Malcolm Dunn. *D:* A. Edward Sutherland; *Sc:* Joseph L. Mankiewicz (unc.), Gertrude Purcell; *Songs:* Johnny Green-E.Y. Harburg. (G.B. title: *The Sap Abroad*)

Shipboard musical-comedy of romance and mistaken identity. Filmed at Astoria Studios in Long Island, N.Y.

3997. Sarah and Son (Paramount; 1930). *Cast:* Ruth Chatterton (A.A.N. for B.A.), Fredric March, Doris Lloyd, Philippe de Lacy, Fuller Mellish, Jr., Gilbert Emery, William Stack. *D:* Dorothy Arzner; *P:* David O. Selznick; *Sc:* Zoë Akins. (1:16)

Hit tear-jerker of its day of a woman's search for her son, taken from her years before. Based on the novel by Timothy Shea.

3998. Saratoga (MGM; 1937). *Cast:* Clark Gable (Duke Bradley), Jean Harlow (final film — d. 1936 as Carol Clayton), Lionel Barrymore (Grandpa Clayton), Frank Morgan (Jesse Kiffmeyer), Walter Pidgeon (Hartley Madison), Una Merkel (Fritzi O'Malley), Cliff Edwards (Tip O'Brien), George Zucco (Dr. Bierd), Jonathan Hale (Frank Clayton), Hattie McDaniel (Rosetta), Frankie Darro (Dixie Gordon), Henry Stone (Hard Riding Hurley), Margaret Hamilton (Maizie), Carl Stockdale (Boswell), Ruth Gillette (Mrs. Hurley), Charles Foy (valet), Robert Emmett Keane (auctioneer), Edgar Dearing (trainer), Frank McGlynn, Sr. (Kenyon), Walter Robbins (Limpy), Sam Flint (judge), Harrison Greene, Pat West, Forbes Murray, Herbert Ashley, Si Jenks, George Chandler, Mel Ruick, Charles R. Moore, Patsy O'Connor, Fred "Snowflake" Toones, Edward (Bud) Flanagan (Dennis O'Keefe), Hooper Atchley, Drew Demarest, Bert Roach, Irene Franklin, Ernie Stanton, Hank Mann, John "Skins" Miller. *D:* Jack Conway; *P:* Bernard H. Hyman; *As.P.:* John Emerson; *St & Sc:* Anita Loos, Robert Hopkins; *Songs:* "The Horse with the Dreamy Eyes" & the title song by Walter Donaldson, Bob Wright & Chet Forrest. (1:34)

Hit race track drama which is chiefly notable as the final film of Jean Harlow who died before production was completed. Look-a-like Mary Dees completed the film.

3999. Satan Met a Lady (WB; 1936). *Cast:* Bette Davis, Warren William (Ted Shayne), Alison Skipworth (Madame Barrabbas), Arthur Treacher, Winifred Shaw, Marie Wilson, Porter Hall, Olin Howland, Charles Wilson, Barbara Blane, Maynard Holmes. *D:* William Dieterle; *P:* Henry Blanke; *Sc:* Brown Holmes. (1:15)

A re-working of Dashiell Hammett's "The Maltese Falcon" with comic overtones. Other versions: *The Maltese Falcon* (q.v.) and *The Maltese Falcon* (WB; 1941).

4000. The Saturday Night Kid (Paramount; 1929). *Cast:* Clara Bow, Jean Arthur, James Hall, Edna May Oliver (talkie debut), Charles Sellon, Ethel Wales, Frank Ross, Irving Bacon, Ernie Adams, Hyman Meyer, Jean Harlow (film debut — bit). *D:* A. Edward Sutherland; *Sc:* Ethel Doherty, Lloyd Corrigan, Edward E. Paramore, Jr., Joseph L. Mankiewicz (unc.).

Hit romantic comedy of two sisters out to snag the same man. Based on the popular Broadway comedy by John V.A. Weaver and George Abbott titled "Love 'em and Leave 'em" which was adapted from Weaver's novel. A remake of *Love 'em and Leave 'em* (Paramount; 1926) with Louise Brooks and Evelyn Brent.

4001. Saturday's Children (WB/F.N.; 1929). *Cast:* Corinne Griffith, Grant Withers, Albert Conti, Alma Tell, Lucien Littlefield, Charles Lane,

Ann Schaefer, Marcia Harris. *D:* Gregory La Cava; *P:* Walter Morosco; *Sc:* Forrest Halsey.

Part-talkie marital comedy based on Maxwell Anderson's play. Remade as *Maybe It's Love* (1935) (q.v.) and *Saturday's Children* (WB; 1940).

4002. Saturday's Heroes (RKO; 1937). *Cast:* Van Heflin, Marion Marsh, Richard Lane, Alan Bruce, Minor Watson, Frank Jenks, Al St. John, Willie Best, Walter Miller, Crawford Weaver, George Irving, Dick Hogan, Charles Trowbridge. *D:* Edward Killy; *P:* Robert Sisk; *St:* George Templeton; *Sc:* Paul Yawitz, Charles Kaufman, David Silverstein. (1:00)

College football story of a player who speaks out on the exploitation of athletes.

4003. Saturday's Millions (Universal; 1933). *Cast:* Robert Young, John Mack Brown, Leila Hyams, Andy Devine, Grant Mitchell, Mary Carlisle, Joseph (Sawyer) Sauers, Mary Doran, Paul Porcasi, Richard Tucker, Paul Hurst, Lucille Lund, Herbert Corthell, William Kent. *D:* Edward Sedgwick; *St:* Lucian Cary; *Sc:* Dale Van Every. (1:17)

Gridiron drama of a star player and his attitude problem.

4004. The Savage Girl (Monarch; 1932–33). *Cast:* Rochelle Hudson, Walter Byron, Harry Myers. *D:* Harry Fraser; *P:* John R. Freuler.

Low-budget romantic indie.

4005. Say It in French (Paramount; 1938). *Cast:* Ray Milland, Olympe Bradna, Irene Hervey, Janet Beecher, Holmes Herbert, Mary Carlisle, Walter Kingsford, Mona Barrie, William Collier, Sr., Erik Rhodes, Billy Lee, Gertrude Sutton, G.P. Huntley, Jr., Byron Foulger. *D:* Andrew L. Stone; *P:* Stone; *St:* Jacques Deval; *Sc:* Frederick Jackson. (1:10)

To get help for his debt-ridden father, a man seeks help from his wife and ex-girl friend.

4006. Say It with Songs (WB; 1929). *Cast:* Al Jolson, Marion Nixon, Davey Lee, Holmes Herbert, Fred Kohler, John Bowers, Kenneth Thomson. *D:* Lloyd Bacon; *St:* Darryl Zanuck, Harvey Gates; *Sc:* Joseph Jackson; *Songs:* "Little Pal," "Why Can't You," "Used to You," "Seventh Heaven," "Back in Your Own Back Yard" & "One Sweet Kiss" by Buddy DeSylva, Lew Brown & Ray Henderson. (1:29)

A man is sent to prison for killing a man who was flirting with his wife. A dramatic weeper which was an attempt to capitalize on the success of *The Jazz Singer* (q.v.) and *The Singing Fool* (q.v.). Audiences wouldn't buy it and the film flopped miserably.

4007. Scandal for Sale (Universal; 1932). *Cast:* Charles Bickford, Rose Hobart, Claudia Dell, Pat O'Brien, Berton Churchill (Bunnyweather), J. Farrell MacDonald, Harry Beresford, Glenda Farrell, Heinrich von Twardofsky (Hans von Twardowsky), Jack Richardson, James Farley, Lew Kelly, Buster Phelps, Mitchell Harris, Mary Jane Graham, Angie Norton, Paul Nicholson. *D:* Russell Mack; *St:* Emile Gauvreau; *Sc:* Ralph Graves. (1:15)

A newspaper's star reporter dies during a promotional gimmick to increase the paper's circulation.

4008. Scandal Sheet (Paramount; 1931). *Cast:* George Bancroft, Kay Francis, Regis Toomey, Clive Brook, Lucien Littlefield, Jackie Searle, Gilbert Emery, Mary Foy, Harry Beresford. *D:* John Cromwell; *St:* Oliver H.P. Garrett; *Sc:* Vincent Lawrence, Max Marcin. (1:17)

Newspaper drama of a romantic triangle.

4009. Scandal Sheet (Columbia; 1938). *Cast:* Otto Kruger, Ona Munson, Edward Norris. *D:* Nick Grinde; *Sc:* Joseph Carole. (1:07)

B newspaper drama of a ruthless tycoon.

4010. Scandal Street (Paramount; 1938). *Cast:* Lew Ayres, Louise Campbell, Roscoe Karns, Porter Hall, Edgar Kennedy, Virginia Weidler, Elizabeth Patterson, Cecil Cunningham, Lucien Littlefield, Louise Beavers, Jan Duggan, Lois Kent, Esther Howard, Carl "Alfalfa" Switzer, Laraine (Day) Johnson, George Offerman. *D:* James Hogan; *Sc:* Bertram Millhauser, Eddie Welch. (1:02)

Offbeat B mystery of a small town girl accused of murder.

Scared *see* **Whistling in the Dark**

4011. Scareheads (Capital; 1931). *Cast:* Richard Talmadge, Gareth Hughes (final film — ret.), King Baggot, Joseph Girard. *D:* Noel (Smith) Mason.

A "poverty row" production from Capital Film Exchange.

4012. Scarface (United Artists; 1930–32). *Cast:* Paul Muni (Tony Camonte), Ann Dvorak (Cesca Camonte), George Raft (Guido Rinaldo), Boris Karloff (Gaffney), Karen Morley (Poppy), Osgood Perkins (Johnny Lovo), C. Henry Gordon (Ben Guarino), Vince Barnett (Angelo), Inez Palange (Mrs. Camonte), Henry Armetta (Pietro), Harry J. Vejar ("Big Louie" Costillo), Edwin Maxwell (Chief of Detectives), Bert Starkey (Epstein), Purnell Pratt (Garston), Tully Marshall (managing editor), Paul Fix, Hank Mann, Harry Tenbrook, Charles Sullivan, Maurice Black. *D:* Howard Hawks; *P:* Howard Hughes, Hawks; *Sc:* Ben Hecht, W.R. Burnett, Seton I. Miller, John Lee Mahin, Fred Pasley. (G.B. title: *The Shame of a Nation*) (1:39) (video — 1:33)

Classic gangster film, originally completed in 1930 with release held up until 1932 because of censorship problems. Supposedly based on actual incidents in the life of mobster Al Capone, the film was voted one of the year's "10

Best" by the National Board of Review while placing #10 on the "10 Best" list of *Film Daily*. On release in 1932, the film had the subtitle "Shame of the Nation" and surprisingly was a loser at the box office, something not unusual for many of the films considered "classics" of yesteryear. Based on the novel by Armitage Trail, it was updated and remade in 1983 with a Florida setting and a drug-dealing theme.

4013. The Scarlet Brand (Big 4; 1932). *Cast:* Bob Custer, Fred Burns. *D:* J.P. McGowan; *P:* John R. Freuler.

Bob Custer western.

4014. Scarlet Dawn (WB; 1932). *Cast:* Douglas Fairbanks, Jr., Nancy Carroll, Lilyan Tashman, Guy Kibbee, Sheila Terry, Frank Reicher, Mischa Auer, Mae Busch, Earle Foxe, Yola D'Avril, Ivan Linow, Arnold Korff, Richard Alexander, Alphonse Kohlmar, Dewey Robinson, John Marston, William Ricciardi, Lee Kohlmar, Maurice Black, Hadji Ali, Betty Gillette. *D:* William Dieterle; *P:* Hal B. Wallis; *Sc:* Niven Busch, Erwin Gelsey, Fairbanks. (1:16) (aka: *Revolt*)

A drama set during the Russian Revolution of 1917, based on the novel "Revolt" by Mary McCall, Jr., the film which was considered sexually explicit in its day, was a box office flop.

4015. The Scarlet Empress (Paramount; 1934). *Cast:* Marlene Dietrich (Catherine the Great), John Lodge (Count Alexei), Sam Jaffe (film debut), Louise Dresser, C. Aubrey Smith, Gavin Gordon, Jameson Thomas, Edward Van Sloan, Jane Darwell, Olive Tell, Maria Sieber (Marlene Dietrich's real-life daughter), James Burke, Harry Woods, Erville Alderson, Marie Wells, Ruthelma Stevens. *D:* Josef von Sternberg; *Sc:* Manuel Komroff. (1:49)

Lavishly produced costumer and now considered a classic of the Russian empress, Catherine the Great. A financial disaster at the box office when originally released.

4016. The Scarlet Letter (Majestic; 1934). *Cast:* Colleen Moore (in her final film before retiring as Hester Prynne), Hardie Albright (minister), Henry B. Walthall (repeating his role in the '26 version as Roger Chillingworth), Cora Sue Collins (Hester's daughter), Virginia Howell, Alan Hale, Betty Blythe, Flora Finch. *D:* Robert G. Vignola; *P:* Larry Darmour; *Sc:* Leonard Fields, David Silverstein. (1:09) (video)

For a "poverty row" feature, this is a fairly lavish production of Nathaniel Hawthorne's classic novel of Hester Prynne who is branded an adulteress after having an affair which produces a child, with the truth becoming known that the affair was with the local minister. Previous versions filmed in the U.S.: 1910, 1911, 1913, (Fox; 1917) with Mary Martin and Stuart Holmes, (MGM; 1926) with Lillian Gish and Lars Hanson. Remade in 1979 as a TV movie.

4017. Scarlet Pages (WB/F.N.; 1930). *Cast:* Elsie Ferguson (recreating her stage role in her final film before retiring from the silver screen), Marion Nixon, John Halliday, Grant Withers, Helen Ferguson (no relation to Elsie, but also a silent screen star in her final film before retiring from films), DeWitt Jennings, Charlotte Walker, Wilbur Mack, Daisy Belmore. *D:* Ray Enright; *Sc:* Maude Fulton, Walter Anthony.

Melodramatic tear-jerker of a lady lawyer who finds that the woman she is defending on murder charges is her own daughter. Based on the play by Samuel Shipman and John B. Hymer, the film was a flop.

4018. Scarlet River (RKO; 1933). *Cast:* Tom Keene, Dorothy Wilson, Creighton (Lon) Chaney, (Jr.), Betty Furness, Roscoe Ates, Edgar Kennedy, Billy Butts, Hooper Atchley, Jack Raymond, James (Jim) Mason, Yakima Canutt. *D:* Otto Brower; *As.P.:* David Lewis; *Sc:* Harold Shumate. (1:00)

Offbeat western of a film company making a western at the Scarlet River Ranch, where the film's hero becomes a real-life hero by saving the ranch from the clutches of it's evil foreman, intent on getting the property for himself. The film features cameo appearances by Joel McCrea, Myrna Loy, Bruce Cabot and Paul Hurst.

4019. A Scarlet Weekend (Maxim; 1932). *Cast:* Dorothy Revier, Charles K. French. *D:* George Melford.

Low-budget independent production.

4020/4021. School for Girls (Liberty; 1934). *Cast:* Helen Foster, Sidney Fox (final film—ret.), Paul Kelly, Lois Wilson, Lona Andre, Russell Hopton, William Farnum, Harry Woods, Anna Q. Nilsson, George Cleveland, Myrtle Stedman, Charles Ray (formerly a very popular silent screen star), Fred Kelsey, Dawn O'Day (Anne Shirley). *D:* William Nigh; *P:* M.H. Hoffman, Jr.

Title tells all in this low-budget independent production.

The Schoolmaster (G.B. title) *see* **The Hoosier Schoolmaster**

4022. Scotland Yard (Fox; 1930). *Cast:* Joan Bennett, Edmund Lowe (in a dual role), Donald Crisp, David Torrence, J. Carrol Naish, Halliwell Hobbes, Georges Renavent, Barbara Leonard, Lumsden Hare. *D:* William K. Howard. (G.B. title: *Detective Clive Bart*)

Crime melodrama.

4023. The Scoundrel (Paramount; 1935). *Cast:* Noel Coward (in his starring film debut), Julie Haydon, Stanley Ridges, Martha Sleeper, Ernest Cossart, Eduardo Ciannelli, Alexander Woollcott, Lionel Stander (feature film debut), Harry Davenport, Everley Gregg, O.Z. Whitehead, Hope Williams, Rosita Moreno, Frank Conlan, Carl Schmidt, Richard Bond, Isabelle Foster, Raymond Bramley, Uhei Hasegawa, Miss Shushinka, William Ricciardi, Helen Strickland. *D:* Ben Hecht, Charles MacArthur; *P:* Hecht & MacArthur; *As.P.:* Lee Garmes; *Original Story:* (A.A.) Hecht (& Rose Caylor); *Sc:* (A.A.N.) Hecht & MacArthur. (1:18)

Original supernatural-fantasy drama of a published writer who manages to mess up the lives of various people—and then he gets his! Based on the play "All He Ever Loved" by Ben Hecht and Rose Caylor, production was engineered at Astoria Studios in Long Island, N.Y. The *New York Times* placed it at #6 on their "10 Best" list of the year, but the film showed no profit.

Scouts of the Air (G.B. title) *see* **Danger Flight**

4024. A Scream in the Night (Commodore; 1935–43). A low-budget adventure set in the orient, starring Lon Chaney, Jr., in a dual role. Apparently completed by Commodore in 1935 with release (Astor) held up until 1943.

4025a. Sea Devils (Continental; 1931). *Cast:* Walter Long, Edmund Burns, Molly O'Day. *D:* Joseph Levering.

"Poverty row" adventure.

4025. The Sea Bat (MGM; 1930). *Cast:* Charles Bickford, Raquel Torres, Nils Asther, George F. Marion, John Miljan, Boris Karloff, Gibson Gowland, Edmund Breese, Mathilde Comont, Mack Swain. *D:* Wesley Ruggles; *St:* Dorothy Yost; *Sc:* Bess Meredyth, John Howard Lawson. (1:09)

Action-adventure set on a West Indies island where sponge fishermen are menaced by a giant manta ray. Likely the *Jaws* (Universal; 1975) of its day, the film was a box office hit.

4026. Sea Devils (RKO; 1937). *Cast:* Victor McLaglen, Preston Foster, Ida Lupino, Donald Woods, Helen Flint, Gordon Jones, Pierre Watkin, Murray Alper, Billy Gilbert, Barbara Pepper, Dwight Frye. *D:* Ben Stoloff; *P:* Edward Small; *Sc:* Frank Wead, John Twist, P.J. Wolfson. (1:28) (video)

A friendly rivalry exists between two U.S. Coast Guardsmen. The film, dedicated to the officers and men of the United States Coast Guard was a box office success.

4027. Sea Fury (H.H. Rosenfield; 1929). *Cast:* Mildred Harris, James Hallet. *D:* George Melford; *P:* Tom White.

Part-talkie indie action-adventure.

4028. The Sea Ghost (Peerless; 1931). *Cast:* Laura La Plante, Alan Hale, Clarence Wilson. *D:* William Nigh; *Sc:* Nigh, Jo Von Ronbeo.

"Poverty row" melodrama.

4029. The Sea God (Paramount; 1930). *Cast:* Richard Arlen, Fay Wray, Eugene Pallette, Ivan Simpson, Robert Gleckler, Maurice Black, Robert Perry, Fred Wallace. *D:* George Abbott; *St:* John Russell.

A deep sea diver searching for pearls emerges from the sea before superstitious island natives who take him for a god.

4030. Sea Legs (Paramount; 1930). *Cast:* Jack Oakie, Lillian Roth, Harry Green, Eugene Pallette, Tom Ricketts, Charles Sellon, Jean Del Val, Andre Cheron. *D:* Victor Heerman (his final film before becoming a screenwriter); *St:* George Marion, Jr.

B comedy of misunderstandings involving a shanghaied sailor.

4031. Sea Racketeers (Republic; 1937). *Cast:* Lane Chandler, J. Carrol Naish, Jeanne Madden, Joyce Compson, Dorothy McNulty (Penny Singleton), Syd Saylor, Warren Hymer, Weldon Heyburn, Charles Trowbridge, Bryant Washburn, Molly O'Day, Edmund Burns, Molly O'Day. *D:* Hamilton MacFadden; *St & Sc:* Dorrell & Stuart McGowan.

B crime melodrama.

4032. The Sea Spoilers (Universal; 1936). *Cast:* John Wayne, Nan Grey, William Bakewell, Fuzzy Knight, Russell Hicks, Ethan Laidlaw. *D:* Frank Strayer; *P:* Trem Carr; *St:* Dorrell & Stuart McGowan; *Sc:* George Waggner. (1:02)

B actioner of the U.S. Coast Guard going after seal poachers.

4033. The Sea Wolf (Fox; 1930). *Cast:* Raymond Hackett, Jane Keith, Milton Sills (in his talkie debut & also his final film — d. 1930), Nat Pendleton, Alice White, Mitchell Harris, John Rogers. *D:* Alfred Santell; *Sc:* Ralph Block; *Dial:* S.N. Behrman.

The fourth filming of Jack London's novel of a brutal ship's captain. Previous versions: (Bosworth; 1913) with Hobart Bosworth and Herbert Rawlinson, (Paramount; 1920) with Noah Beery, Tom Forman and Mabel Julienne Scott and (Producers Distributing Corp.; 1925–26) with Ralph Ince, Theodore von Eltz and Claire Adams. Later versions include: (WB; 1941) with John Garfield, Edward G. Robinson and Ida Lupino, *Barricade*(WB; 1949–50) using a western format, *Wolf Larsen* (Allied Artists; 1958) and *Wolf Larsen* (Italy; 1975) with the alternate title *Wolf of the Seven Seas.*

Sealed Lips (G.B. title) *see* **After Tonight**

4034. Search for Beauty (Paramount; 1934). *Cast:* Larry "Buster" Crabbe, Ida Lupino (American film debut), Robert Armstrong, Gertrude Michael, James Gleason, Roscoe Karns, Toby Wing, Colin Tapley, Frank McGlynn, Verna Hillie, James B. Kenton, Clara Lou (Ann) Sheridan (film debut — bit). *D:* Erle C. Kenton; *Sc:* Frank Butler, Claude Binyon; *St:* Maurine Watkins, David Boehm (from play by E. Grey & Paul R. Milton).

At a health farm peopled by beautiful bodies, two Olympic swimmers are deceived by some crooked promoters.

4035. The Seas Beneath (Fox; 1931). *Cast:* George O'Brien, John Loder, Mona Maris, William Collier, Sr., Warren Hymer, Nat Pendleton, Francis Ford, Henry Victor, Ferdinand Schumann-Heink, Walter C. Kelly, Gaylord (Steve) Pendleton, Walter McGrail, Larry Kent, Marion Lessing. *D:* John Ford; *St:* James Parker, Jr.; *Sc:* Dudley Nichols.

World War I actioner.

4036. Second Choice (WB; 1930). *Cast:* Dolores Costello, Jack Mulhall, Chester Morris, Edna Murphy, Charlotte Merriam, Edward Martindel, Ethlyne Clair, Louise Beavers, Sally Blane. *D:* H.P. (Howard) Bretherton; *St:* Elizabeth Alexander; *Sc:* Joseph Jackson.

Low-budget romantic drama of jilted lovers who find each other.

4037. Second Fiddle (20th Century-Fox; 1939). *Cast:* Sonja Henie, Tyrone Power, Rudy Vallee, Edna May Oliver, Lyle Talbot, Edward Nugent, Mary Healy, Charles Lane, Minerva Urecal, Maurice Cass, George Chandler, Stewart Reburn. *D:* Sidney Lanfield; *P:* Darryl F. Zanuck; *As.P.:* Gene Markey; *Sc:* Harry Tugend; *Songs:* Irving Berlin, include (A.A.N. for Best Song) "I Poured My Heart Into a Song."

Romantic musical.

4038. The Second Floor Mystery (WB; 1930). *Cast:* Grant Withers, Loretta Young, H.B. Warner, Claude King, John Loder, Claire McDowell, Judith Vosselli, Crauford Kent, Sidney Bracy. *D:* Roy Del Ruth; *Sc:* Joseph Jackson. (G.B. title: *The Second Story Murder*)

Comic murder-mystery set in England of two lovers who communicate through the personal column in the newspaper. Based on a story by Earl

Derr Biggers, the film is a remake of *The Man Upstairs* (WB; 1926) with Monte Blue and Dorothy Devore. Remade as *Passage from Hong Kong* (WB; 1941).

4039. Second Hand Wife (Fox; 1933). *Cast:* Sally Eilers, Ralph Bellamy, Helen Vinson, Victor Jory, Nella Walker, Esther Howard, Clay Clement, Effie Ellsler, Karol Kay, Ara Haswell. *D:* Hamilton MacFadden; *St:* Kathleen Norris; *Adaptation:* MacFadden. (G.B. title: *The Illegal Divorce*)

Low-budget romantic comedy.

4040. Second Honeymoon (Syndicate-Continental Talking Pictures; 1930). *Cast:* Josephine Dunn, Edward Earle. *D:* Phil Rosen.

Light low-budget romance from "poverty row."

4041. Second Honeymoon (20th Century-Fox; 1937). *Cast:* Tyrone Power, Loretta Young, Stuart Erwin, Claire Trevor, Marjorie Weaver, Lyle Talbot, J. Edward Bromberg, Paul Hurst, Lon Chaney, Jr., Jayne Regan, Mary Treen, Hal K. Dawson. *D:* Walter Lang; *P:* Raymond Griffith; *Sc:* Kathryn Scola, Darrell Ware. (1:19)

Comedy of a man who is romancing his ex-wife with the intention of marrying her again. Based on a story by Philip Wylie.

The Second Story Murder (G.B. title) *see* **The Second Floor Mystery**

4042. Second Wife (RKO; 1929–30). *Cast:* Conrad Nagel, Lila Lee, Hugh Huntley, Mary Carr, Freddie Burke Frederick. *D:* Russell Mack (directorial debut); *As.P.:* Myles Connolly; *Sc:* Bert Glennon, F. Hugh Herbert. (1:08)

Domestic drama of a father's dilemma with his seven-year old son after he remarries. Based on the play "All the King's Men" by Fulton Oursler, it was remade in 1936 (see below).

4043. Second Wife (RKO; 1936). *Cast:* Gertrude Michael, Walter Abel, Erik Rhodes, Emma Dunn, Lee Van Atta, Brenda Fowler, Frank Reicher, George Breakston, Ward Bond, Florence Fair. *D:* Edward Killy; *As.P.:* Lee Marcus; *Sc:* Thomas Lennon. (0:59)

B remake of the preceding film.

4044. The Secret Bride (WB; 1935). *Cast:* Barbara Stanwyck, Warren William, Glenda Farrell, Grant Mitchell, Arthur Aylesworth, Vince Barnett, Samuel S. Hinds, Willard Robertson. *D:* William Dieterle; *P:* Henry Blanke; *Sc:* Tom Buckingham, F. Hugh Herbert, Mary McCall, Jr. (1:03)

A district attorney is secretly married to the daughter of a crooked politician he is trying to convict. A low-budget melodrama based on the play "Concealment" by Leonard Ide.

4045. The Secret Call (Paramount; 1931). *Cast:* Richard Arlen, Peggy Shannon (in a role intended for Clara Bow who was replaced due to a nervous breakdown), Claire Dodd, Ned Sparks, Selmer Jackson, Larry Steers, Harry Beresford, Charles Trowbridge, Patricia Farr, Frances Moffett, Jane Keith, Elaine Parker. *D:* Stuart Walker (in his directorial debut); *St:* William de Mille.

Melodrama of a telephone operator who destroys the career of the man who caused the death of her father. Previously filmed in 1915 as *The Woman* and *The Telephone Girl* (Paramount; 1927) with Madge Bellamy.

Secret Interlude (G.B. title) *see* **Private Number**

4046. The Secret Menace (Cardinal/Imperial; 1931). *Cast:* Glenn Tryon, Arthur Stone, Virginia Brown Faire, Margaret Mann. *D:* Richard C. Kahn; *Sc:* B. Wayne Lamont.

"Poverty row" western.

4047. The Secret of Dr. Kildare (MGM; 1939). *Cast:* Lew Ayres (Dr. Kildare), Lionel Barrymore (Dr. Gillespie), Lionel Atwill, Helen Gilbert, Laraine Day, Sara Haden, Walter Kingsford, Nat Pendleton, Samuel S. Hinds (Mr. Kildare), Emma Dunn (Mrs. Kildare), Grant Mitchell, Martha O'Driscoll, Alma Kruger, Marie Blake, Robert Kent, Byron Foulger, Nell Craig, George Reed, Frank Orth. *D:* Harold S. Bucquet; *P:* Lou Ostrow (unc.); *Sc:* Willis Goldbeck, Harry Ruskin. (1:24)

The third entry in this hit low-budget series involving young Dr. Kildare and old Dr. Gillespie.

4048. The Secret of Madame Blanche (MGM; 1933). *Cast:* Irene Dunne, Phillips Holmes, Lionel Atwill, Douglas Walton, Jean Parker, Una Merkel, C. Henry Gordon, Mitchell Lewis. *D:* Charles Brabin; *Sc:* Frances Goodrich, Albert Hackett. (1:25)

Tear-jerker with shades of *Madame X* (q.v.) as a woman takes the blame for a murder committed by her son. Set in France.

4049. Secret of the Blue Room (Universal; 1933). *Cast:* Lionel Atwill, Gloria Stuart, Paul Lukas, Edward Arnold, Onslow Stevens, Robert Barrat, William Janney, Elizabeth Patterson, Muriel Kirkland, Russell Hopton, James Durkin, Anders Van Haden. *D:* Kurt Neumann; *St:* Erich Phillipi; *Sc:* William Hurlbut. (1:06)

B murder-mystery involving the three suitors of an heiress who volunteer to spend a night in a room of Castle Heldorf where a number of murders have previously been committed. This box office hit had two remakes, *The Missing Guest* (q.v.) and *Murder in the Blue Room* (Universal; 1944).

4050. Secret of the Chateau (Universal; 1934). *Cast:* Jack LaRue, Claire Dodd, Alice White, Osgood Perkins, George E. Stone, Clark Williams, William Faversham, Ferdinand Gottschalk, DeWitt Jennings, Helen Ware, Frank Reicher, Pat

Flaherty. *D:* Richard Thorpe; *St:* Lawrence G. Blochman; *Sc:* co-written by Harry Behn. (1:05)

B mystery of various people who gather at a chateau, each with the intent of stealing a valuable Gutenberg Bible.

4051. Secret Patrol (Columbia; 1936). *Cast:* Charles Starrett, Finis Barton, J.P. McGowan, Henry Mollison, LeStrange Millman, James McGrath, Arthur Kerr, Reginald Hincks, Ted Mapes. *D:* David Selman (replacing Ford Beebe); *St:* Ford Beebe; *Sc:* J.P. McGowan, Robert Watson. (1:00)

Charles Starrett Mountie actioner which was filmed on location in Canada.

4052. Secret Service (RKO; 1931). *Cast:* Richard Dix, Shirley Grey, William Post, Jr., Gavin Gordon, Nance O'Neil, Harold Kinney, Florence Lake, Frederick Burton, Clarence Muse, Fred Warren, Eugene Jackson. *D:* J. Walter Ruben; *As.P.:* Louis Sarecky; *Sc:* Bernard Schubert. (1:08)

Civil War drama of the romance and the hazards encountered by a Union spy posing as a Confederate officer. A remake of *Secret Service* (Paramount; 1919) with Robert Warwick and Wanda Hawley. Based on an old play by William Gillette.

4053. Secret Service of the Air (WB; 1939). *Cast:* Ronald Reagan (Bancroft), John Litel (Saxby), Ila Rhodes, James Stephenson, Eddie Foy, Jr. (Gabby), Rosella Towne, John Ridgely, Anthony Averill, Bernard Nedell, Frank M. Thomas, Joe Cunningham, Morgan Conway, John Harron, Herbert Rawlinson, Larry Williams, Raymond Bailey. *D:* Noel Smith; *As.P.:* Bryan Foy; *Sc:* Raymond Schrock. (1:01)

B melodrama which was the premiere entry in a series of four films with Ronald Reagan as Lt. Brass Bancroft, a U.S. pilot working for the secret service. Based on factual material compiled by W.H. Moran, ex-chief of the U.S. Secret Service. Followed by *Code of the Secret Service* (q.v.).

4054. Secret Sinners (Mayfair; 1933). *Cast:* Nick Stuart, Jack Mulhall, Sue Carol, Cecilia Parker. *D:* Wesley Ford; *Sc:* F. McGrew Willis.
(No other information available)

4055. The Secret Six (MGM; 1931). *Cast:* Wallace Beery (Louis "Slaughterhouse" Scorpio), Lewis Stone, Clark Gable, Jean Harlow, John Mack Brown, Ralph Bellamy (film debut), Marjorie Rambeau, John Miljan, Paul Hurst, Theodore von Eltz, Tom London, DeWitt Jennings, Murray Kinnell, Fletcher Norton, Louis Natheaux, Frank McGlynn. *D:* George Hill; *Sc:* Frances Marion. (1:23)
A gangster drama which tried to capitalize on *The Big House* (q.v.).

4056. Secret Valley (20th Century–Fox/Principal; 1936). *Cast:* Richard Arlen, Virginia Grey, Jack Mulhall, Syd Saylor, Russell Hicks, Norman Willis, Willie Fung, Maude Allen. *D:* Howard Bretherton; *P:* Sol Lesser; *Sc:* Earle Snell, Dan Jarrett, Paul Franklin. (1:00)
B western of a farmer who opts to raise horses and finds a gang of outlaws are now interested in the fruits of his labors. Based on the novel by Harold Bell Wright.

4057. Secret Witness (Columbia; 1931). *Cast:* June Clyde, William Collier, Jr., Una Merkel, Nat Pendleton, ZaSu Pitts, Paul Hurst, Clyde Cook, Clarence Muse, Virginia Brown-Faire, Greta Granstedt, Rita LaRoy, Hooper Atchley, Purnell Pratt, Ralf Harolde. *D:* Thornton Freeland; *Play:* Sam Spewack. (aka: *Terror by Night*)
Low-budget independent murder-mystery.

4058. Secrets (United Artists; 1933). *Cast:* Mary Pickford, Leslie Howard, C. Aubrey Smith, Blanche Frederici, Doris Lloyd, Ned Sparks, Herbert Evans, Allan Sears, Mona Maris, Huntley Gordon, Virginia Grey, Bessie Barriscale, Ethel Clayton. *D:* Frank Borzage (who also directed the '24 version); *P:* Pickford; *Sc:* Frances Marion (who also wrote the '24 version).
Domestic drama of a 50-year marriage. Notable as the 194th and final film of actress Mary Pickford before retiring from the silver screen. In later years she worked on other films behind the camera. Based on the play by Rudolf Besier and May Edginton, the film is a remake, previously filmed by First National in 1924 with Norma Talmadge and Eugene O'Brien. A box office flop.

4059. Secrets of a Model (JDK Productions; 1939). *Cast:* Sharon Lee (later Cheryl Walker). *D:* Sam Newfield; *P:* J.D. Kendis; *Sc:* Arthur St. Claire, Sherman Lowe.
Low-budget indie exploitation film of a naive country girl who goes to the city with the intent of becoming a fashion model, but finds things don't go the way she expected.

4060. Secrets of a Nurse (Universal; 1938). *Cast:* Edmund Lowe, Helen Mack, Dick Foran, Leon Ames, Horace MacMahon, Paul Hurst, Clarence Muse, Samuel S. Hinds, George Chandler, Frances Robinson, David Oliver, Virginia Brissac, Clyde Dilson, Dorothy Arnold, Stanley Hughes. *D:* Arthur Lubin; *P:* Burt Kelly; *St:* Quentin Reynolds; *Sc:* Lester Cole, Thomas Lennon. (1:15)
When an ex-fighter is framed for murder, his girlfriend, a nurse helps him prove his innocence in this B melodrama.

4061. Secrets of a Secretary (Paramount; 1931). *Cast:* Claudette Colbert, Herbert Marshall, George Metaxa, Mary Boland, Berton Churchill, Porter Hall (film debut), Betty Garde, Millard Mitchell (film debut), Betty Lawford, Hugh O'Connell, Averell Harris. *D:* George Abbott; *St:* Charles Brackett; *Sc:* Dwight Taylor, Abbott. (1:11)
Filmed at Astoria Studios in Long Island, N.Y., this is a marital drama of

a woman who finds that her husband is a blackmailer.

4062. Secrets of an Actress (WB; 1938). *Cast:* Kay Francis, George Brent, Ian Hunter, Gloria Dickson, Isabel Jeans, Penny Singleton, Herbert Rawlinson, Dennie Moore, John Ridgely, Selmer Jackson, Emmett Vogan, James B. Carson. *D:* William Keighley; *As.P.:* David Lewis; *Sc:* Julius J. Epstein, Milton Krims, Rowland Leigh. (1:11)

B drama of marital infidelity.

Secrets of Chinatown (G.B. title) *see* **The Secrets of Wu Sin**

4063. Secrets of Chinatown (Northern Films; 1935). *Cast:* Nick Stuart, Lucille Browne. *D:* Fred Newmeyer; *Sc:* Guy Morton.

(No other information available)

4064. Secrets of Hollywood (Xxxx Xxxx; 1933). *Cast:* Wally Wales (Hal Taliaferro).

(No other information available)

4065. Secrets of the French Police (RKO; 1932). *Cast:* Gwili Andre, Gregory Ratoff, Murray Kinnell, Frank Morgan, John Warburton, Rochelle Hudson, Christian Rub, Arnold Korff, Kendall Lee, Lucien Prival, Guido Trento, Julia Swayne Gordon. *D:* (A.) Edward Sutherland; *P:* David O. Selznick; *Sc:* Sam Ornitz, Robert Tasker. (0:58)

A hypnotist tries to pass a girl off as the only surviving daughter of Czar Nicholas II, resulting in murder and suicide. A low-budget thriller based on a series of magazine articles by H. Ashton-Wolfe.

4066. The Secrets of Wu Sin (Chesterfield; 1933). *Cast:* Grant Withers, Lois Wilson, Richard Loo, Dorothy Revier. *D:* Richard Thorpe (who also edited). (G.B. title: *Secrets of Chinatown*)

"Poverty row" melodrama.

4067. See America Thirst (Universal; 1930). *Cast:* Harry Langdon, Slim Summerville, Bessie Love, Mitchell Lewis, Matthew Betz, Stanley Fields, Tom Kennedy, LeRoy Mason, Lloyd Whitlock, Dick Alexander, Lew Hearn. *D:* William James Craft; *Adaptation:* C. Jerome Horwin; *St:* Edward I. Luddy, Vin Moore; *Sc:* Henry La Cossitt. (1:15)

Low-budget comedy of two tramps who are mistaken for wanted gangsters.

4068. Seed (Universal; 1931). *Cast:* John Boles, Lois Wilson, Genevieve Tobin, ZaSu Pitts, Raymond Hackett, Bette Davis, Frances Dade, Richard Tucker, Dickie Moore, Cox Twins, Dick Winslow, Helen Parrish, Bill Willis, Jack Willis. *D:* John M. Stahl; *Sc:* Gladys Lehman (based on the novel by Charles G. Norris). (1:36)

A man deserts his wife and kids for another woman in this triangular soap-drama.

4069. Self Defense (Monogram; 1932). *Cast:* Pauline Frederick (Katy Devoux), Claire Windsor, Theodore von Eltz, Barbara Kent, Robert Elliott, Henry B. Walthall, Jameson Thomas, George Hackathorne, Willie Fung, Lafe McKee, Si Jenks, George Hayes. *D:* Phil Rosen; *P:* William T. Lackey; *Sc:* Tristram Tupper. (1:08)

"Poverty row" drama of the proprietor of a gambling house who turns her establishment into a respectable hotel when she learns her daughter is coming for a visit. Based on the story "The Just Judge" by Peter B. Kyne, the film had the working title of "My Mother."

4070. Senor Americano (Universal; 1929). *Cast:* Ken Maynard, Kathryn Crawford, Gino Corrado, J.P. McGowan, Frank Yaconelli. *D:* Harry Joe Brown.

Part-talkie Ken Maynard western with musical interludes.

4071. Sensation Hunters (Monogram; 1933). *Cast:* Preston Foster,

Arline Judge, Marion Burns, Juanita Hansen, Creighton Hale, Cyril Chadwick, Nella Walker, Harold Minjir, Finis Barton. *D:* Charles Vidor; *P:* Robert Welsh; *St:* Whitman Chambers; *Sc:* Paul Schofield, Albert E. DeMond. (1:14)

B melodrama of an innocent young girl who learns the ropes after taking a job at a cabaret in Panama.

4072. Sequoia (MGM; 1934). *Cast:* Jean Parker, Russell Hardie, Samuel S. Hinds, Paul Hurst, Ben Hall, Willie Fung, Harry Lowe, Jr., Malibu the deer, Gato the puma. *D:* Chester M. Franklin; *P:* John W. Considine, Jr.; *Sc:* Anne Cunningham, Sam Armstrong, Carey Wilson, C. Gardiner Sullivan (unc.). (Re-release title: *Malibu*) (1:13)

Offbeat outdoor drama set in the high Sierras of a girl who becomes the protector of the wild animals, namely a fawn and a young puma. Based on the book "Malibu" by Vance Joseph Hoyt, the film was over a year in production. The *New York Times* placed it at #9 on their "10 Best" list of 1935.

Serenade *see* **Broadway Serenade**

Serenade of the West (G.B. title) *see* **Git Along Little Dogies**

4073. Sergeant Madden (MGM; 1939). *Cast:* Wallace Beery, Tom Brown, Alan Curtis, Laraine Day (her first film for this studio), Fay Holden, Marc Lawrence, Marion Martin, Etta McDaniel, David Gorcey, Horace MacMahon, Dickie Jones, Ben Welden, Charles Trowbridge, Neil Fitzgerald, Drew Roddy, Donald Haines, John Kelly. *D:* Josef Von Sternberg; *P:* J. Walter Ruben; *Sc:* Wells Root. (1:30)

Crime melodrama of a policeman's son who is alienated by his father. Based on the story "A Gun in His Hand" by William A. Ullman, Jr., the film is notable as not being a typical film of its director, Von Sternberg.

4074. Sergeant Murphy (WB; 1938). *Cast:* Ronald Reagan (in a role originally scheduled for James Cagney), Mary Maguire, Donald Crisp, Ben Hendricks, Jr., William Davidson, Max Hoffman, Jr., Edmund Cobb, Sam McDaniel. *D:* B. Reeves Eason; *P:* Bryan Foy; *St:* Sy Bartlett; *Sc:* William Jacobs. (0:57)

B story of a soldier and his love for a horse. Based on a true story, it might be noted that Sergeant Murphy is the name of the horse.

4075. Servant's Entrance (Fox; 1934). *Cast:* Janet Gaynor, Lew Ayres, Walter Connolly, G.P. Huntley, Jr., Sig Rumann, Louise Dresser, Astrid Allwyn, Ned Sparks, Catherine Doucet, John Qualen, Greta Meyer, Harold Minjir, Ann Doran, Josephine Whittell, Buster Phelps, Ruth Marion, Ann Gibbons, Jerry Stewart. *D:* Frank Lloyd; *Sc:* Samson Raphaelson. (1:28)

Comedy-drama of the romance between a maid and a chauffeur, both employed in the same household. Based on the novel by Sigrid Boo.

Service (G.B. title) *see* **Looking Forward**

4076. Service de Luxe (Universal; 1938). *Cast:* Constance Bennett, Vincent Price (film debut), Charles Ruggles, Helen Broderick, Mischa Auer, Halliwell Hobbes, Frank (Junior) Coghlan, Joy Hodges, Frances Robinson, Lionel Belmore, Ben Hall, Chester Clute, Raymond Parker. *D:* Rowland V. Lee; *P:* Lee; *As.P.:* Edmund Grainger; *St:* Vera Caspary, B ice Man. ng; *Sc:* Gertrude Purcell, Leonard Spigelgass. (1:25)

Screwball comedy of a woman who avoids the love bug in favor of her business, then she falls for a hick.

4077. Seven Days Leave (Paramount; 1929). *Cast:* Gary Cooper, Beryl Mercer, Daisy Belmore, Nora Cecil, Tempe Pigott, Arthur Hoyt, Basil Rad-ford, Arthur Metcalfe. *D:* Richard Wallace, John Cromwell; *P:* Louis D. Lighton; *Sc:* John Farrow, Dan Totheroh. (G.B. title: *Medals*) (1:23)

Sentimental melodrama of an old charwoman who takes in a soldier. Based on the play "The Old Lady Shows Her Medals" by J.M. Barrie.

4078. Seven Faces (Fox; 1929). *Cast:* Paul Muni, Marguerite Churchill, Gustav von Seyffertitz, Eugenie Besserer, Russell Gleason, Lester Lonergan, Walka Stenermann, Walter Brown Rogers. *D:* Berthold Viertel; *St:* Richard Connell.

Offbeat early talkie with Paul Muni playing seven different roles, including Napoleon Bonaparte, Don Juan and Franz Schubert.

4079. Seven Footprints to Satan (WB/F.N.; 1929). *Cast:* Thelma Todd, Creighton Hale, Sheldon Lewis, Ivan Christy, William V. Mong, Sojin, Cissy Fitzgerald, Laska Winter, DeWitt Jennings. *D:* Benjamin Christensen; *St:* Abraham Merritt; *Sc:* Richard Bee.

Part-talkie old house thriller with a twist.

4080. Seven Keys to Baldpate (RKO; 1929). *Cast:* Richard Dix (in his first of many films for RKO), Miriam Seegar, Margaret Livingston, Lucien Littlefield, Joseph Allen, Nella Walker, Alan Roscoe, DeWitt Jennings, Crauford Kent, Harvey Clark, Edith Yorke, Carleton Macy. *D:* Reginald Barker; *As.P.:* Louis Sarecky; *Sc:* Jane Murfin.

Much filmed mystery comedy of a writer who goes to a "deserted" inn to finish his novel within a 24-hour deadline. Based on the novel by Earl Derr Biggers and the play by George M. Cohan, two silent filmings include (Artcraft; 1917) with George M. Cohan and Anna Q. Nilsson and (Paramount; 1925) with Douglas MacLean and Edith Roberts. Remade in 1935 (see below),

(RKO; 1947) and (Great Britain; 1983) as *House of Long Shadows*.

4081. Seven Keys to Baldpate (RKO; 1935). *Cast:* Gene Raymond, Margaret Callahan, Eric Blore, Grant Mitchell, Moroni Olsen, Henry Travers, Erin O'Brien-Moore, Ray Mayer, Beverly Bayne, Walter Brennan, Murray Alper, Erville Alderson, Emma Dunn, Harry Beresford, Monte Vandegrift. *D:* William Hamilton, Edward Killy, Glenn Tryon (unc.); *As.P.:* William Sistrom; *Sc:* Anthony Veiller, Wallace Smith, Jane Murfin (unc.); *Additional Dialogue:* Glenn Tryon. (1:08)

Remake of the preceding film.

4082. Seventh Heaven (20th Century–Fox; 1937). *Cast:* James Stewart, Simone Simon, Jean Hersholt, Gale Sondergaard, Gregory Ratoff, J. Edward Bromberg, John Qualen, Victor Kilian, Sig Rumann, Mady Christians, Henry Armetta, Rafaela Ottiano, Georges Renavent, Rollo Lloyd, Thomas Beck. *D:* Henry King; *As.P.:* Raymond Griffith; *P:* Darryl F. Zanuck; *Sc:* Melville Baker. (1:42)

A remake of the famed 1927 silent tear-jerker with Janet Gaynor and Charles Farrell of the romance of a sewer worker and a street girl, their marriage and what happens when he goes off to war. Based on a play by Austin Strong, this remake didn't come near the success of the now classic silent version.

4083. 70,000 Witnesses (Paramount; 1932). *Cast:* Phillips Holmes, Dorothy Jordan, John Mack Brown, Charles Ruggles, Lew Cody, Guinn Williams, J. Farrell MacDonald, Walter Hiers, Reed Howes, Paul Page, Kenneth Thomson, David Landau, George Rosener. *D:* Ralph Murphy; *St:* Cortland Fitzsimmons.

B melodrama of a murder that occurs during the deciding play of a football game.

Sex Madness *see* **They Must Be Told!**

4084. Sh! the Octopus (WB/
F.N.; 1937). *Cast:* Hugh Herbert, Allen
Jenkins, Marcia Ralston, John El-
dredge, George Rosener, Brandon
Tynan, Elspeth Dudgeon, Margaret Ir-
ving, Eric Stanley. *D:* William Mc-
Gann; *P:* Bryan Foy; *Sc:* George
Bricker.

B mystery-comedy of two scatter-
brained detectives investigating strange
goings on at an old lighthouse. Based on
the play by Ralph Murphy and Donald
Gallagher.

4085. The Shadow (Columbia;
1937). *Cast:* Charles Quigley, Rita Hay-
worth, Dick Curtis, Kane Richmond,
Marc Lawrence, Russell Hopton,
Dwight Frye, Dorothy Revier, Marjorie
Main, John Ince, Vernon Dent, Arthur
Loft, William Irving, Ann Doran, Ed-
die Fetherston, Donald Kirke, Bess
Flowers, Sally St. Clair, Sue St. Clair.
D: C.C. Coleman, Jr.; *St:* Milton
Raison; *Sc:* Arthur T. Horman. (G.B.
title: *The Circus Shadow*)

B murder-mystery set within a
circus.

4086. The Shadow Laughs (Invincible; 1933). *Cast:* Rose Hobart, Hal
Skelly (final film—d. 1934), Cesar Romero (film debut). *D:* Arthur Hoerl.

Low-budget mystery-comedy.

4087. Shadow of Chinatown
(Victory; 1936). *Cast:* Herman Brix
(Bruce Bennett), Bela Lugosi, Luana
Walters. *D:* Robert F. Hill; *P:* Sam
Katzman; *Sc:* Isador Bernstein, Basil
Dickey. (aka: *Yellow Phantom*)

Feature version of the 15-chapter
independent serial of the same name. A
Chinatown dragon lady hires an arch
criminal to do away with white tourists
in that section of the city.

4088. Shadow of Doubt (MGM;
1935). *Cast:* Virginia Bruce, Ricardo
Cortez, Constance Collier, Isabel
Jewell, Bradley Page, Betty Furness,
Regis Toomey, Arthur Byron, Edward

Brophy, Paul Hurst, Richard Tucker,
Samuel S. Hinds, Ivan Simpson, Bernard Siegel. *D:* George B. Seitz; *P:* Lucien Hubbard; *Sc:* Wells Root. (1:15)

B melodrama of an actress accused
of killing a notorious playboy. Based on
the novel by Arthur Somers Roche.

**4089. The Shadow of Silk Len-
nox** (Commodore; 1935). *Cast:* Lon
Chaney, Jr.

(No other information available)

4090. Shadow of the Law (Para-
mount; 1930). *Cast:* William Powell,
Regis Toomey, Natalie Moorhead, Paul
Hurst, Marion Shilling, Richard
Tucker, Walter James, Frederic Burt.
D: Louis Gasnier, Max Marcin; *Sc:*
John Farrow.

Drama of an accused man who
must clear his name and reputation.
Based on the novel "The Quarry" by
John A. Moroso. A remake of *The City
of Silent Men* (Paramount; 1921) with
Thomas Meighan and Lois Wilson.

4091. Shadow Ranch (Columbia;
1930). *Cast:* Buck Jones, Marguerite de
la Motte, Kate Price, Al Smith, Frank
Rice, Slim Whitaker, Ben Wilson,
Robert McKenzie, Fred Burns, Lafe
McKee, Frank Ellis, Hank Bell. *D:*
Louis King; *P:* Sol Lesser; *Sc:* Frank
Howard Clark. (0:55)

Buck Jones western of a cowboy who
saves a woman's ranch from a schemer.
Remade as *Sunset Trail* (q.v.).

4092. The Shadow Strikes
(Grand National; 1937). *Cast:* Rod La
Rocque, Lynn Anders, James Blakely,
John St. Polis, Walter McGrail, Bill
Kellogg, Cyrus Kendall, Kenneth Har-
lan, Norman Ainsley, Wilson Benge,
John Carnavale. *D:* Lynn Shores; *P:*
Max & Arthur Alexander; *Adaptation:* Al
Martin & Rex Taylor; *Sc:* Al Martin.
(Working title: "The Shadow") (aka:
Womantrap) (1:01) (video)

"The Shadow" (Lamont Cranston)
poses as an attorney while investigating

some murders at an old mansion. Loosely based on "The Ghost of the Manor" by Maxwell Grant (Walter B. Gibson) which appeared in "The Shadow" magazine.

4093. Shadows of Sing Sing (Columbia; 1933). *Cast:* Bruce Cabot, Mary Brian, Harry Woods, Bradley Page, Grant Mitchell, Fred Kelsey, Dewey Robinson, Claire DuBrey. *D:* Phil Rosen; *St:* Kathryn Scola, Doris Malloy; *Sc:* Albert De Mond.

B prison melodrama.

Shadows of Singapore (G.B. title) *see* **Malay Nights**

4094. Shadows of the Orient (Monogram; 1937). *Cast:* Esther Ralston, Regis Toomey, J. Farrell MacDonald, Sidney Blackmer, Oscar Apfel, Eddie Fetherston, Kit Guard, Matty Fain, James B. Leong. *D:* Burt Lynwood; *P:* Larry Darmour; *St:* L.E. (Lou) Heifetz; *Sc:* Charles Francis Royal. (1:09)

"Poverty row" melodrama of a woman who unknowingly becomes involved with the smuggling of Chinese aliens.

4095. Shadows Over Shanghai (Grand National/Fine Arts; 1938). *Cast:* James Dunn, Linda Gray, Ralph Morgan, Robert Barrat, Billy Bevan, William Haade, Richard Loo, Edward Woods, Paul Sutton, Edwin Mordant, Chester Gan, Victor Wong, Edward Keane, Victor Sen Yung. *D:* Charles Lamont; *P:* Franklyn Warner; *St:* Richard B. Sale; *Sc:* Joseph Hoffman. (1:05)

Hit B espionage caper of an American photographer who unknowingly gets involved with secret agents in search of an amulet.

4096. Shakedown (Columbia; 1936). *Cast:* Lew Ayres, Joan Perry, Victor Kilian, Thurston Hall, John Gallaudet, Gene Morgan, Henry Mollison,

George McKay. *D:* David Selman; *St:* Harry Shipman; *Sc:* Grace Neville.

"Poverty row" crime melodrama.

4097. Shall We Dance (RKO; 1937). *Cast:* Fred Astaire (Petrov — Pete Peters), Ginger Rogers (Linda Keene), Eric Blore (Cecil Flintridge), Edward Everett Horton (Jeffrey Baird), Ann Shoemaker (Mrs. Fitzgerald), Jerome Cowan (Arthur Miller), Harriet Hoctor (herself), Ketti Gallian (Lady Tarrington), William Brisbane (James Montgomery), Ben Alexander (bandleader), Emma Young (Tai), Sherwood Bailey, Pete Theodore, Marek Windheim, Rolfe Sedan, Charles Coleman, Frank Moran. *D:* Mark Sandrich; *P:* Pandro S. Berman; *St:* "Watch Your Step" by Lee Loeb & Harold Buchman; *Adaptation:* P.J. Wolfson; *Sc:* Allan Scott, Ernest Pagano; *Choreography:* Hermes Pan, Fred Astaire; *Songs:* "I've Got Beginner's Luck," "They All Laughed," "Let's Call the Whole Thing Off," "They Can't Take That Away from Me" (which received an A.A.N. for Best Song), "Slap That Bass," "Wake Up Brother and Dance" & the title song, all by George & Ira Gershwin. (1:56) (video)

Hit musical-comedy of various misunderstandings that present themselves as a Russian ballet dancer and an American ballroom dancer meet on board a ship bound for the U.S.A. The plot gimmick in this the 7th teaming of Astaire-Rogers comes when they have to pretend they are married. This film was in nomination for "Best Film" at the Venice Film Festival, as well as being one of the 38 top grossing films of 1936–37.

The Shame of a Nation (G.B. title) *see* **Scarface**

4098. Shanghai (Paramount; 1935). *Cast:* Loretta Young, Charles Boyer, Warner Oland, Alison Skipworth, Fred Keating, Charley Grapewin, Walter Kingsford, Keye Luke, Olive Tell, Willie Fung, Josephine

Whittell, Libby Taylor, Arnold Korff. *D:* James Flood; *P:* Walter Wanger; *St:* Lynn Starling, Gene Towne; *Sc:* Starling, Towne, Graham Baker. (1:17)

Romantic drama of an American woman who falls for a man who is oriental-caucasian mix.

4099. Shanghai Express (Paramount; 1932). *Cast:* Marlene Dietrich (Shanghai Lily — Madeline), Anna May Wong (Hui Fei), Clive Brook (Captain Donald Harvey), Warner Oland (Henry Chang), Eugene Pallette (Sam Salt), Louise Closser Hale (Mrs. Haggerty), Lawrence Grant (Reverend Carmichael), Gustav von Seyffertitz (Eric Baum), Emile Chautard (Major Lenard), Claude King (Albright), Neshida Minoru (Chinese spy), Willie Fung (engineer), Leonard Carey (minister), Forrester Harvey (ticket agent), James Leong, Miki Morita. *D:* (A.A.N.) Josef von Sternberg; *St:* Harry Hervey; *Sc:* Jules Furthman; *Cinematographer:* (A.A.) Lee Garmes. (1:20)

Classic drama of the events that occur aboard a train while it passes through China which is in the throes of a civil war. The film which received an A.A.N. for Best Picture was one of the 15 top grossing films of 1932, grossing over $3,000,000 for the studio. Remade as *Night Plane from Chungking* (Paramount; 1942) and *Peking Express* (Paramount; 1951).

4100. Shanghai Lady (Universal; 1929). *Cast:* Mary Nolan, Wheeler Oakman, James Murray, Yola D'Avril, Lydia Yeamans Titus, Mona Rico, James B. Leong, Irma Lowe. *D:* John S. Robertson; *St:* Daisy H. Andrews; *Orig. play by:* John Colton.

Low-budget romance of misunderstandings via mistaken identities.

4101. Shanghai Madness (Fox; 1933). *Cast:* Spencer Tracy, Fay Wray, Ralph Morgan, Eugene Pallette, Herbert Mundin, Albert Conti, Arthur Hoyt, Maude Eburne, Reginald Mason. *D:* John G. Blystone; *St:* Frederick Hazlitt Brennan.

Melodrama of a naval officer who opens fire on some Chinese communists.

4102. Shanghaied Love (Columbia; 1931). *Cast:* Sally Blane, Richard Cromwell, Noah Beery, Sidney Bracy. *D:* George B. Seitz.

Low-budget romantic drama.

4103. The Shannons of Broadway (Universal; 1929). *Cast:* James Gleason, Lucile Webster Gleason, Mary Philbin (final film — ret.), John Breeden, Tom Santschi, Harry Tyler, Gladys Crolius, Slim Summerville, Walter Brennan, Charley Grapewin (film debut), Tom Kennedy. *D:* Emmett J. Flynn (final film — ret.); *Sc:* James Gleason, Agnes Christine Johnston.

A vaudeville couple buy an old hotel, only to find the connecting property which they also have title to is sought by an airplane company. Based on the 1928 Broadway play by James Gleason. Remade as *Goodbye Broadway* (q.v.).

4104. Sharad of Atlantis (Republic; 1936). *Cast:* Ray "Crash" Corrigan, Lois Wilde, Monte Blue, William Farnum (Sharad), Boothe Howard, Lon Chaney, Jr., Lee Van Atta, Smiley Burnette, C. Montague Shaw. *D:* B. Reeves Eason, Joseph Kane; *P:* Nat Levine; *Sc:* John Rathmell, Maurice Geraghty, Oliver Drake. (1:40) (video — full serial only)

Feature version of the 12-chapter serial "Undersea Kingdom," a fantasy adventure dealing with the uncovering of a technologically advanced civilization under the sea.

4105. Sharpshooters (20th Century-Fox; 1938). *Cast:* Brian Donlevy, Wally Vernon, Lynn Bari, Douglass Dumbrille, John King, Sidney Blackmer, Frank Puglia, C. Henry Gordon, Martin Spellman, Romaine Callender, Hamilton MacFadden. *D:* James Tinling; *P:* Sol M. Wurtzel; *St:* Maurice Rapf, Lester Ziffren; *Sc:* Robert Ellis, Helen Logan.

Premiere entry in the short-lived "Camera Daredevils" series with the heroes attempting to prevent the assassination of a crown prince in a Ruritanian kingdom. See also: *Chasing Danger.*

4106. She (RKO; 1935). *Cast:* Helen Gahagan (in her only film as Hash-a-Mo-Tep—She Who Must Be Obeyed), Randolph Scott (Leo Vincey), Helen Mack (Tanya Dugmore), Nigel Bruce (Archibald Holly), Gustav von Seyffertitz (Billali), Lumsden Hare (Dugmore), Samuel S. Hinds (John Vincey), Noble Johnson (Amahagger Chief), Jim Thorpe (captain of the guards). *D:* Irving Pichel, Lansing C. Holden; *P:* Merian C. Cooper; *Sc:* Ruth Rose; *Additional Dialogue:* Dudley Nichols. (1:35—with most TV prints running 1:29)

Lavishly produced fantasy-adventure of an expedition to the Kingdom of Kor which is ruled by a mystical woman who is the keeper of the "Flame of Eternal Life." Based on the 1887 novel by H. Rider Haggard, it was previously filmed in 1912 with Marguerite Snow, in 1917, and a British silent (Artlee; 1926) with Betty Blythe and Carlyle Blackwell. Remade in Great Britain in 1965 and again in a 1982 Italian production which was not released until 1985. This film premiered at Radio City Music Hall in New York City on July 25, 1935, and was a box office flop. See also: *Last Days of Pompeii* (q.v.).

4107. She Asked for It (Paramount; 1937). *Cast:* William Gargan, Vivienne Osborne, Roland Drew, Joyce Compton. *D:* Erle C. Kenton; *P:* B.P. Schulberg.

B of a writer of mystery stories who finds those responsible for the murder of his uncle.

4108. She Couldn't Say No (WB; 1930). *Cast:* Winnie Lightner, Chester Morris, Sally Eilers, Louise Beavers, Tully Marshall, Johnny Arthur. *D:* Lloyd Bacon; *Adaptation:* Harvey Thew;

Sc: Arthur Caesar, Robert Lord; *Songs:* Al Dubin, Joe Burke.

Comedy-drama with music of an entertainer and the gangster who sponsors her. Based on the play by Benjamin M. Kaye. Remade in 1940.

4109. She Couldn't Take It (Columbia; 1935). *Cast:* George Raft, Joan Bennett, Walter Connolly, Billie Burke, Lloyd Nolan, Wallace Ford, Alan Mowbray, Franklin Pangborn, Donald Meek, William Tannen, James Blakely. *D:* Tay Garnett; *P:* B.P. Schulberg; *St:* Graham Baker, Gene Towne; *Sc:* Oliver H.P. Garrett. (G.B. title: *Woman Tamer*)

Comedy of a man who hires his ex-prison cellmate to straighten out his family.

4110. She Done Him Wrong (Paramount; 1933). *Cast:* Mae West (Lady Lou), Cary Grant (Capt. Cummings), Gilbert Roland (Serge Stanieff), Noah Beery (Gus Jordan), Rochelle Hudson (Sally Glynn), Rafaela Ottiano (Russian Rosie), Louise Beavers (Pearl), Owen Moore (Chick Clark), David Landau (Dan Flynn), Dewey Robinson (Spider Kane), Grace LaRue (Frances), Robert E. Homans (Doheney), Fuzzy Knight (Rag Time Kelly), Tom Kennedy (Big Bill), Tammany Young (Chuck Connors), Harry Wallace (Steak McGarry), James C. Eagles (Pete), Arthur Housman (barfly), Wade Boteler (Pal), Aggie Herring (Mrs. Flaherty), Lee Kohlmar (Jacobson), Tom McGuire (Mike), Al Hill (other barfly), Michael Mark (janitor), Mary Gordon (cleaning woman), Heinie Conklin (street cleaner), Jack Carr, Frank Moran, Ernie S. Adams. *D:* Lowell Sherman; *P:* William LeBaron; *Sc:* West, Harvey Thew, John Bright; *Songs:* "I Like a Man Who Takes His Time" & "I Wonder Where My Easy Rider's Gone" by Ralph Rainger & Leo Robin & the traditional "Frankie and Johnny." (1:06) (video)

Classic Mae West outing as she

recreates her famous 1928 stage role of "Diamond Lil," which she also authored. The pre-code spicy dialogue was also co-scripted by West. The film received an A.A.N. for "Best Picture," placed #7 on the "10 Best" list of *Film Daily,* while being voted one of the year's "10 Best" by the National Board of Review. The film which premiered January 27, 1933, was a major box office hit, bringing in a whopping $2,500,000 profit for the studio. There is also Mae's legendary proposition "Come up and see me some-time."

4111. She Gets Her Man (Universal; 1935). *Cast:* ZaSu Pitts, Helen Twelvetrees, Lucien Littlefield, Ward Bond, Warren Hymer, Edward Brophy, John Carradine, Jack Norton. *D:* William Nigh. (1:06)
B rural comedy of a waitress who stops a bank robbery and of the press agent who promotes her.

4112. She Goes to War (United Artists/Inspiration; 1929). *Cast:* Eleanor Boardman, John Holland, Al St. John, Alma Rubens (final film—d. 1931), Edmund Burns, Margaret Seddon, Evelyn Hall, Yola D'Avril, Eulalie Jensen, Glen Walters, Dina Smirnova. *D:* Henry King; *P:* King; *St:* Rupert Hughes; *Dialogue & Titles:* John Monk Saunders.
Part-talkie romantic comedy.

4113. She Got What She Wanted (Tiffany; 1930). *Cast:* Lee Tracy, Betty Compson, Alan Hale, Fred Kelsey, Gaston Glass. *D:* James Cruze; *P:* Cruze (co-producer).
Low-budget romance.

4114. She Had to Choose (Majestic; 1934). *Cast:* Buster Crabbe, Isabel Jewell, Sally Blane, Arthur Stone. *D:* Ralph Cedar.
"Poverty row" romantic comedy with a Hollywood setting.

4115. She Had to Eat (20th Century–Fox; 1937). *Cast:* Rochelle Hudson, Jack Haley, Eugene Pallette, Arthur Treacher, John Qualen, Douglas Fowley, Franklin Pangborn, Tom Kennedy, Tom Dugan, Maurice Cass, Wallis Clark, Lelah Tyler. *D:* Mal St. Clair; *St:* James Edward Grant, M.M. Musselman; *Sc:* Samuel G. Engel.
B romantic comedy.

4116/4117. She Had to Say Yes (WB/F.N.; 1933). *Cast:* Loretta Young, Regis Toomey, Lyle Talbot, Winnie Lightner, Hugh Herbert, Ferdinand Gottschalk, Wallace Ford. *D:* Busby Berkeley; *P:* Henry Blanke; *St:* John Francis Larkin; *Sc:* Rian James, Don Mullaly.
Romantic comedy of a secretary who entertains some out-of-town buyers after hours. A financial disappointment for the studio.

4118. She Learned About Sailors (Fox; 1934). *Cast:* Alice Faye, Lew Ayres, Harry Green, Frank Mitchell, Jack Durant, James Dunn. *D:* George Marshall; *P:* John Stone; *St:* Randall Faye. (1:16)
Romantic comedy which is much described by the titled implications.

4119. She Loved a Fireman (WB/F.N.; 1937). *Cast:* Dick Foran, Ann Sheridan, Robert Armstrong, Hugh O'Connell, Veda Ann Borg, Eddie Chandler, Eddie Acuff, Lane Chandler, Anne Nagel, Minerva Urecal, Ted Oliver, Pat Flaherty, May Beatty. *D:* John Farrow; *P:* Bryan Foy; *Sc:* Morton Grant, Carlton Sand. (0:56)
B romance which is aptly described by the title.

4120. She Loves Me Not (Paramount; 1934). *Cast:* Bing Crosby (Paul Lawton), Miriam Hopkins (Curly Flagg), Kitty Carlisle (Midge Mercer),

Lynne Overman (Gus McNeal), Henry Stephenson (Dean Mercer), George Barbier (J. Thorval Jones), Edward Nugent (Buzz Jones), Warren Hymer (Mugg Schnitzel), Judith Allen (Frances Arbuthnot), Ralf Harolde (J.B.), Henry Kolker (Charles M. Lawton), Vince Barnett (Baldy O'Hara), Franklyn Ardell (Arkle), Maude Turner Gordon (Mrs. Arbuthnot), Margaret Armstrong (Martha), Matt McHugh (Andy), Polly Walters. *D:* Elliott Nugent; *P:* Benjamin Glazer; *Sc:* Glazer; *Songs:* "Love in Bloom" (A.A.N. for Best Song) Ralph Rainger & Leo Robin; "After All, You're All I'm After" by Edward Heyman & Arthur Schwartz; "Straight from the Shoulder (Right from the Heart)," "I'm Hummin', I'm Whistlin', I'm Singin'" & "Put a Little Rhythm in Everything You Do" by Mack Gordon & Harry Revel. (1:23)

Comedy of a female night club performer who flees from a murder scene and hides out in a men's college dorm. Based on the novel by Edward Hope and the play adaptation by Howard Lindsay. *True to the Army* (1942) was a partial remake, with a full remake emerging in 1955 from Fox as *How to Be Very, Very Popular.* One of the 15 top grossing films of 1934.

4121. She Made Her Bed (Paramount; 1934). *D:* Richard Arlen, Sally Eilers, Robert Armstrong, Grace Bradley, Roscoe Ates, Charley Grapewin. *D:* Ralph Murphy; *Sc:* Casey Robinson (co-writer).

B melodrama involving the problems encountered in the life of a fairgrounds owner. Based on the novel by James M. Cain.

4122. She Married a Cop (Republic; 1939). *Cast:* Phil Regan, Jean Parker, Peggy Ryan, Jerome Cowan, Benny Baker, Horace MacMahon, Mary Gordon. *D:* Sidney Salkow; *Music:* (A.A.N.) Cy Feuer.

B romantic musical-comedy.

4123. She Married an Artist (Columbia; 1938). *Cast:* John Boles, Frances Drake, Albert Dekker, Jacqueline Wells (Julie Bishop), Franklin Pangborn, Ann Doran, Alexander D'Arcy, Marek Windheim, Luli Deste, Helen Westley. *D:* Marion Gering; *St:* Avery Strakosch; *Sc:* Delmer Daves, Gladys Lehman. (1:18)

B romance of an artist and his jealous wife.

4124. She Married Her Boss (Columbia; 1935). *Cast:* Claudette Colbert, Melvyn Douglas, Raymond Walburn, Edith Fellows, Jean Dixon, Michael Bartlett, Katherine Alexander, Clara Kimball Young. *D:* Gregory La Cava; *St:* Thyra Samter Winslow; *Sc:* Sidney Buchman. (1:30)

Hit romantic comedy aptly described by the title which became one of the 12 top grossing films of 1935.

4125. She Wanted a Millionaire (Fox; 1932). *Cast:* Joan Bennett, Spencer Tracy, Una Merkel, James Kirkwood, Dorothy Peterson, Donald Dillaway, Douglas Cosgrove, Tetsu Komai, Lucille La Verne. *D:* John G. Blystone; *St:* Sonya Levien; *Sc:* William Anthony McGuire.

Romantic comedy.

4126. She Was a Lady (Fox; 1934). *Cast:* Helen Twelvetrees, Donald Woods, Ralph Morgan, Jackie Searle, Doris Lloyd, Monroe Owsley. *D:* Hamilton MacFadden; *St:* Elisabeth Cobb.

Romance.

She-Wolf *see* **Mother's Millions**

She-Wolf of Wall Street *see* **Mother's Millions**

4127. She's Dangerous (Universal; 1937). *Cast:* Tala Birell, Walter Pidgeon, Walter Brennan, Cesar Romero, Warren Hymer, Samuel S.

Hinds, Grady Sutton, Franklin Pangborn. *D:* Lewis R. Foster, Milton Carruth; *P:* E.M. Asher; *St:* Murray Roth, Ben Ryan; *Sc:* Lionel Houser, Albert R. Perkins.

B melodrama of a female detective out to get her man.

4128. She's Got Everything (RKO; 1937). *Cast:* Gene Raymond, Ann Sothern, Victor Moore, Helen Broderick, Billy Gilbert, Parkyakarkus, Jack Carson, William Brisbane, Herbert Clifton, Alan Bruce, Solly Ward, Alec Craig, Fred Santley, Richard Tucker, George Irving. *D:* Joseph Santley; *P:* Albert Lewis; *Sc:* Harry Segall, Maxwell Shane; *Song:* Leon & Otis Rene. (G.B. title: *She's Got That Swing*) (1:12)

B romantic comedy of a coffee tycoon who comes to question the intentions of his girl friend.

She's Got That Swing (G.B. title) *see* **She's Got Everything**

4129. She's My Everything (Xxxx Xxxx; 1938). *Cast:* Harriet Hilliard (Nelson).

(No other information available)

4130. She's My Weakness (RKO; 1930). *Cast:* Sue Carol, Arthur Lake, William Collier, Sr., Lucien Littlefield, Alan Bunce, Helen Ware, Emily Fitzroy, Walter B. Gilbert. *D:* Melville Brown; *As.P.:* Henry Hobart; *Sc:* J. Walter Ruben; *St:* Howard Lindsay, Bertrand Robinson. (1:13)

Low-budget comedy of a father who attempts to guide his daughter in the choice of a suitor. Based on the play "Tommy" by Bertrand Robinson and Howard Lindsay.

4131. She's No Lady (Paramount; 1937). *Cast:* Ann Dvorak, John Trent, Guinn Williams, Paul Hurst, Aileen Pringle, Thomas Jackson, William Royle. *D:* Charles Vidor; *P:* B.P. Schulberg; *St:* James Edward Grant; *Sc:* Frank Partos, George Bruce.

B melodrama on the expose of a fake jewel robbery.

4132. Sheer Luck (Hollywood; 1930). *Cast:* Nick Stuart, Reed Howes, Jobyna Ralston (final film – ret.), Philo McCullough. *D:* Bruce Mitchell. (0:48)

4133. The Sheik Steps Out (Republic; 1937). *Cast:* Ramon Novarro, Lola Lane, Gene Lockhart, Kathleen Burke, Stanley Fields, Robert Coote, Billy Bevan, Leonid Kinskey. *D:* Irving Pichel; *P:* Herman Schlom; *Sc:* Adele Buffington, Gordon Kahn. (1:08)

Comedy spoof of a sheik experiencing life in a big American city.

4134. The Shepper-Newfounder (Fox; 1930). *Cast:* Leila Hyams, Edmund Lowe, Walter McGrail, George Corcoran, Sam Lufkin, Bodil Rosing, Tommy Clifford, Louis Payne. *D:* Leo McCarey; *St:* Stewart Edward White; *Sc:* McCarey, Raymond L. Schrock. (Re-release title: *Part-Time Wife*)

Marital comedy.

4135. The Sheriff's Secret (Cosmos; 1931). *Cast:* Jack Perrin, Jimmy Aubrey, George Chesebro. *D:* James Hogan; *St & Sc:* Hogan.

Jack Perrin western.

4136. Sherlock Holmes (Fox; 1932). *Cast:* Clive Brook (Sherlock Holmes), Reginald Owen (Dr. Watson), Ernest Torrence (Professor Moriarty), Miriam Jordan, Alan Mowbray, Herbert Mundin, Stanley Fields, Brandon Hurst, Montague Shaw, Arnold Lucy, Lucien Prival, Claude King, Edward Dillon, Robert Graves, Jr., Roy D'Arcy, Howard Leeds. *D:* William K. Howard; *Sc:* Bertram Millhauser (which *is not* based on the old play of the same name by William Gillette). (1:08)

Early American production of Sir Arthur Conan Doyle's famous London sleuth battling wits with his #1 adversary, Professor Moriarty.

Sherlock Holmes (20th Century–Fox; 1939) (G.B. title) *see* The Adventures of Sherlock Holmes

4137. Shine on, Harvest Moon (Republic; 1938). *Cast:* Roy Rogers, Mary Hart (Lynn Roberts), William Farnum, Lulu Belle & Scotty (Wiseman), Stanley Andrews, Frank Jacquet, Chester Gunnels, Matty Roubert, Pat Henning, Jack Rockwell, Joe Whitehead, David Sharpe. *D:* Joseph Kane; *Sc:* Jack Natteford. (1:00) (video)

Roy Rogers western with songs of a cowboy who clears an old man's reputation.

4138. The Shining Hour (MGM; 1938). *Cast:* Joan Crawford, Melvyn Douglas, Margaret Sullavan, Robert Young, Fay Bainter, Allyn Joslyn, Hattie McDaniel, Frank Albertson, Oscar O'Shea, Harry Barris. *D:* Frank Borzage; *P:* Joseph L. Mankiewicz; *Sc:* Jane Murfin, Ogden Nash. (1:20)

Hatred and jealousy expressed from various family members interferes with the happiness of a young married couple. This drama based on the hit play by Keith Winter was a failure as a screen effort.

4139. Ship Cafe (Paramount; 1935). *Cast:* Carl Brisson, Mady Christians, Arline Judge, Grant Withers, Inez Courtney, William Frawley, Harry Woods, Jack Norton. *D:* Robert Florey; *P:* Harold Hurley.

B romance of a ship's stoker and a countess whose influence inspires him to take up singing as a profession.

4140. The Ship from Shanghai (MGM; 1929–30). *Cast:* Louis Wolheim, Conrad Nagel, Holmes Herbert, Kay Johnson, Carmel Myers, Zeffie Tilbury, Ivan Linow, Jack McDonald. *D:* Charles Brabin; *Sc:* John Howard Lawson (based on the novel "Ordeal" by Dale Collins). (1:06)

After a ship is damaged in a storm, the passengers fall victim to a mutiny headed by a disgruntled steward.

4141. Ship of Wanted Men (Showmen's Pictures; 1933). *Cast:* Dorothy Sebastian, Leon (Ames) Waycoff, Jason Robards. *D:* Lewis Collins; *P:* Sam Katzman, Collins.

"Poverty row" melodrama.

4142. Shipmates (MGM; 1931). *Cast:* Robert Montgomery, Dorothy Jordan, Ernest Torrence, Joan Marsh, Hobart Bosworth, Gavin Gordon, Cliff Edwards, Eddie Nugent, Hedda Hopper, E. Alyn Warren, William Worthington. *D:* Harry Pollard; *Sc:* Delmer Daves, Lou Edelman, Raymond Schrock, Frank Wead.

Naval drama of a sailor and his clash with a chief petty officer.

4143. Shipmates Forever (WB/F.N.; 1935). *Cast:* Dick Powell, Ruby Keeler, Lewis Stone, Ross Alexander, Eddie Acuff, Dick Foran, John Arledge, Robert Light, Mary Treen, Harry Seymour, Frederick Burton, Carlyle Moore, Jr., Bud Flanagan (Dennis O'Keefe), Martha Merrill. *D:* Frank Borzage; *P:* Lou Edelman; *St:* Delmer Daves; *Sc:* Daves; *Songs:* "Don't Give Up the Ship," "I'd Rather Listen to Your Eyes," "All Aboard the Navy," "I'd Love to Take Orders from You" & "Do I Love My Teacher" by Al Dubin & Harry Warren. (Original running time: 2:04, now: 1:48)

A musical which revolves around the differing opinions between a father and son as to the latter's career, military or show business. Dedicated to the officers and midshipmen of the U.S. Naval Academy, this Cosmopolitan production was later edited down and re-released.

4144. Ships of Hate (Monogram; 1931). *Cast:* Lloyd Hughes, Dorothy Sebastian, Charles Middleton, Lloyd

Whitlock, Ted Adams, Constantine Romanoff, Gordon DeMain, Jean Mason. *D:* John P. McCarthy; *P:* Trem Carr; *St & Sc:* Wellyn Totman. (1:03)

"Poverty row" drama of a cruel ship's captain.

4145. Shock (Monogram; 1934). *Cast:* Ralph Forbes, Gwenllian Gill, Monroe Owsley, Reginald Sharland, Douglas Walton, Alex Courtney, David Jack Holt (son of Jack Holt), Billy Bevan, Clyde Cook, Mary Forbes, Charles Coleman, Colin Campbell, David Dunbar, Montague Shaw, Eric Snowden, Olaf Hytten, Harry Holden. *D:* Roy J. Pomeroy; *St:* Pomeroy; *Sc:* Madeline Ruthven. (1:09)

"Poverty row" romantic drama of a British officer who after marrying, is sent to the front where he suffers shell-shock.

4146. Shoot the Works (Paramount; 1934). *Cast:* Jack Oakie, Dorothy Dell (final film — d. 1934 in a car crash at the age of 18-years, cutting short a promising career), Ben Bernie (band leader in his film debut), Arline Judge, Alison Skipworth, Paul Cavanagh, Roscoe Karns, William Frawley, Lew Cody (final film — d. 1934), Clara Lou (Ann) Sheridan. *D:* Wesley Ruggles; *Sc:* Howard J. Green. (G.B. title: *Thank Your Stars*)

Carnival based romance with songs which was based on the flop Broadway play "The Great Magoo" by Ben Hecht and Gene Fowler. Remade as *Some Like It Hot* (q.v.).

4147. Shooting Straight (RKO; 1930). *Cast:* Richard Dix, Mary Lawlor, James Neill, Matthew Betz, George Cooper, William Janney, Robert Emmett O'Connor, Dick Curtis. *D:* George Archainbaud; *As.P.:* Barney Sarecky; *Sc:* Wallace Smith, J. Walter Ruben.

A gambler takes it on the lam after he believes, he has committed murder.

4148. Shop Angel (Tower; 1932). *Cast:* Marion Shilling, Holmes Herbert,

Anthony Bushell, Walter Byron, Dorothy Christy, Creighton Hale, Hank Mann. *D:* E. Mason Hopper. (1:06) (video)

"Poverty row" melodrama of a store buyer who gets involved in vice and crime.

4149. The Shop Around the Corner (MGM; 1939-40). *Cast:* James Stewart, Margaret Sullavan, Frank Morgan, Joseph Schildkraut, Sara Haden, Felix Bressart, William Tracy, Inez Courtney, Edwin Maxwell. *D:* Ernst Lubitsch; *P:* Lubitsch; *Sc:* Samson Raphaelson. (1:38) (video)

Period romance of two people who work together without the knowledge that they are pen pals. Set in Budapest, Hungary, this box office hit was based on a play by Nikolaus Laszlo. Remade as *In the Good Old Summertime* (MGM; 1949) and later became known as the Broadway musical "She Loves Me."

4150. Shopworn (Columbia; 1932). *Cast:* Barbara Stanwyck, Regis Toomey, ZaSu Pitts, Lucien Littlefield, Clara Blandick, Oscar Apfel, Albert Conti, Maude Turner Gordon, Wallis Clark, Robert Alden. *D:* Nick Grinde; *St:* Sarah Y. Mason; *Dialogue:* Robert Riskin, Jo Swerling. (1:12)

Drama of a common working girl who proves she can be somebody.

4151. The Shopworn Angel (Paramount; 1929). *Cast:* Gary Cooper (Pvt. Pettigrew), Nancy Carroll (in her talkie debut), Paul Lukas, Roscoe Karns, Emmett King, Mildred Washington. *D:* Richard Wallace; *P:* Louis D. Lighton; *Sc:* Howard Estabrook, Albert LeVino; *Song:* "A Precious Little Thing Called Love" by Lou Davis & J.F. Coots.

Part-talkie romantic drama of a soldier and the "lady" he meets and falls for. A remake of *Pettigrew's Girl* (Paramount; 1919) with Ethel Clayton and Monte Blue which was based on the play "Private Pettigrew's Girl" by Dana

Burnet. Remade as *Shopworn Angel* (see below).

4152. Shopworn Angel (MGM; 1938). *Cast:* Margaret Sullavan, James Stewart, Walter Pidgeon, Hattie McDaniel, Sam Levene, Nat Pendleton, Alan Curtis, Charles D. Brown, Eleanor Lynn. *D:* H.C. Potter; *P:* Joseph L. Mankiewicz; *Sc:* Waldo Salt. (1:25)

Romantic drama, a remake of the preceding film of a soldier who falls for a girl with intentions toward another who has money. Remade as *That Kind of Woman* (Paramount; 1959).

4153. A Shot in the Dark (Chesterfield; 1935). *Cast:* Charles Starrett, Edward Van Sloan, Marion Shilling, Helen Jerome Eddy, Herbert Bunston, Jane Keckley, Ralph Brooks, George Morell, Broderick O'Farrell, Eddie Tamblyn, Julian Madison, Robert McKenzie, Robert Warwick, John Davidson. *D:* Charles Lamont; *St:* Clifford Orr; *Sc:* Charles Belden.

"Poverty row" mystery.

4154. Shotgun Pass (Columbia; 1931). *Cast:* Tim McCoy, Virginia Lee Corbin, Frank Rice, Dick Stewart, Joe Marba, Monte Vandergrift, Ben Corbett, Albert J. Smith, Archie Ricks. *D:* J.P. McGowan; *Sc:* Robert Quigley. (1:00)

Tim McCoy horse opera of a cowboy with a herd of horses to fill an army contract, not given permission to travel through a pass controlled by two brothers.

4155. Should a Girl Marry? (Rayart; 1929). *Cast:* Helen Foster, Donald Keith, Andy Clyde. *D:* Scott Pembroke; *P:* Trem Carr.

Part-talkie melodrama of a girl's dilemma when it is found that she was born in prison. Remade in 1939 (see below).

4156. Should a Girl Marry? (Monogram; 1939). *Cast:* Anne Nagel, Warren Hull, Mayo Methot, Lester Matthews, Sarah Padden, Robert Elliott, Weldon Heyburn. *D:* Lambert Hillyer; *Sc:* Gayl Newbury, David Silverstein. (1:01)

A girl is victimized by blackmailers when it is learned she was born in prison of an inmate mother. A remake of the preceding film which was known prior to release as "Girl from Nowhere."

4157. Should Husbands Work? (Republic; 1939). *Cast:* James Gleason, Lucile Gleason, Russell Gleason, Harry Davenport, Tommy Ryan, Marie Wilson, Berton Churchill, Mary Forbes, Arthur Hoyt. *D:* Gus Meins.

Hit B entry in the "Higgins Family" comedy series.

4158. Should Ladies Behave? (MGM; 1933). *Cast:* Alice Brady, Lionel Barrymore, Conway Tearle, Katherine Alexander (film debut), Halliwell Hobbes, Mary Carlisle, William Janney. *D:* Harry Beaumont; *P:* Lawrence Weingarten; *Sc:* Sam & Bella Spewack. (1:30)

Based on the Broadway play "The Vinegar Tree" by Paul Osborn, this romantic comedy tells the story of a girl who falls for her aunt's boyfriend.

4159. Show Boat (Universal; 1929). *Cast:* Laura La Plante (Magnolia), Joseph Schildkraut (Gaylord Ravenal), Emily Fitzroy (Parthenia Hawks), Otis Harlan (Cap'n Andy), Alma Rubens (Julie), Elsie Bartlett, Jack McDonald, Stepin Fetchit, Neely Edwards, Theodore Lorch, Jane La Verne, Gertrude Howard, Max Asher, George Chesebro; and the combined voices of Jules Bledsoe, Claude Collins, the Billbrew Chorus, the Silverstone Quartet and the Four Emperors of Harmony singing offscreen. *D:* Harry Pollard; *P:* Carl Laemmle; *Sc:* Charles Kenyon; *Songs:* "Look Down That Lonesome Road" by Gene Austin & Nathaniel Shilkret; "Here Comes That Show Boat" by Maceo Pinkard, Billy

Rose; "Love Sings a Song in My Heart" by Joseph Cherniavsky & Clarence J. Marks; "Coon, Coon, Coon" by Gene Jefferson & Leo Friedmann; "Down South" by Sigmund Spaeth & William H. Myddleton & the traditional "Deep River" & "I've Got Shoes."

Based on an Edna Ferber novel, this part-talkie musical set at the turn-of-the-century tells of various people who live and work on a Mississippi River show boat. Originally filmed as a silent with sound, songs and dialogue added later. The film has a prologue introduced by Florenz Ziegfeld and Carl Laemmle with filmed extracts from the Broadway show with Helen Morgan singing "Bill" and "Can't Help Lovin' Dat Man," Jules Bledsoe singing "Ol' Man River" as well as Tess Gardella and the Jubilee Singers singing "C'mon Folks" and "Hey Feller." Remade by this studio in 1936 (see below).

4160. Show Boat (Universal; 1935–36). *Cast:* Irene Dunne (Magnolia Hawks Ravenal), Allan Jones (Gaylord Ravenal), Helen Morgan (recreating her stage role as Julie LaVerne), Charles Winninger (Captain Andy Hawks, recreating his stage role), Paul Robeson (Joe), Hattie McDaniel (Queenie), Clarence Muse (Sam), Helen Westley (Parthenia Hawks), Donald Cook (Steve), Queenie Smith (Ellie May Schultz), Sammy White (Frank Schultz), J. Farrell MacDonald (Windy), Arthur Hohl (Pete), Charles Middleton (Vallon), Francis X. Mahoney (Rubberface), Sunnie O'Dea (grownup Kim), Marilyn Knowlden (child Kim), Patricia Barry (Baby Kim), Harry Barris (Jake), Charles Wilson (Jim Green), Stanley Fields (Zebe), Stanley J. "Tiny" Sandford (backwoodsman), May Beatty (landlady), Bobs Watson (lost child), Jane Keckley (Mrs. Ewing), E.E. Clive (Englishman), Helen Jerome Eddy (reporter), Donald Briggs (press agent), LeRoy Prinz (dance director), Theodore Lorch ("Simon Legree"), Dorothy Granger, Reneé Whitney, Barbara Pepper, Arthur Housman, Patti Patterson, Eddie Anderson, Flora Finch, Helen Hayward, Elspeth Dudgeon. *D:* James Whale; *P:* Carl Laemmle, Jr.; *Sc:* Oscar Hammerstein II; *Songs:* "Bill" (sung by Helen Morgan), "Ol' Man River" (sung by Robeson), "Make Believe," "Can't Help Lovin' Dat Man," "Ah Still Suits Me," "Gallavantin' Around," "I Have the Room Above Her," "You Are Love" & "Why Do I Love You?" (music only) by Jerome Kern & Oscar Hammerstein II; "Goodbye My Lady Love" by Joe Howard; "At a Georgia Camp Meeting" by Kerry Mills; "After the Ball" by Charles K. Harris & "The Washington Post March" by John Philip Sousa. (1:50) (video)

The famous Broadway musical which opened originally in 1927 by Jerome Kern and Oscar Hammerstein II, brought to the silver screen for the second time. Taken from the novel by Edna Ferber, the film was in nomination at the Venice Film Festival. A hit for the studio, the property was sold to MGM who remade it in 1951.

4161. Show Folks (Pathé; 1928). *Cast:* Carol Lombard, Eddie Quillan, Robert Armstrong, Lina Basquette, Bessie Barriscale. *D:* Paul Stein.

Part-talkie comedy-drama released in 1928 as a silent with synchronized music and sound effects and re-released in 1929 with some passages of dialogue.

4162. Show Girl in Hollywood (WB/F.N.; 1930). *Cast:* Alice White, Jack Mulhall, Blanche Sweet, Ford Sterling, John Miljan, Herman Bing, Virginia Sale, Lee Shumway. *D:* Mervyn LeRoy; *P:* Robert Lord; *Sc:* Harvey Thew, James A. Starr; *Songs:* "Hang on to the Rainbow," "I've Got My Eye on You" (not to be confused with the Cole Porter song of the same name) & "There's a Tear for Every Smile in Hollywood" by Bud Green & Sammy Stept. (1:20)

Following her discovery, a girl is

groomed to be a glamorous film star. Based on the novel "Hollywood Girl" by J.P. McEvoy, the film includes a 2-color technicolor sequence.

4163. The Show of Shows (WB; 1929). "Prologue": Frank Fay, William Courtenay, H.B. Warner, Hobart Bosworth. "Military Parade": Monte Blue, Pasadena's American Legion Fife & Drum Corps & 300 dancing girls. "Florodora": Marian Nixon, Sally O'Neil, Myrna Loy, Patsy Ruth Miller, Lila Lee, Alice Day, Ben Turpin, Heinie Conklin, Lupino Lane, Lee Moran, Bert Roach, Lloyd Hamilton. "Skull and Crossbones": introduced by Frank Fay, Chester Morris, Sojin, Jack Mulhall, Ted Lewis & His Band & Ted Williams Adagio Dancers, with Wheeler Oakman, Tully Marshall, Bull Montana, J. Farrell MacDonald, Noah Beery, Kalla Pasha, Anders Randolf, Philo McCullough, Otto Matiesen, Jack Curtis, Johnny Arthur, Carmel Myers, Ruth Clifford, Sally Eilers, Viola Dana, Shirley Mason, Ethylyne Clair, Frances Lee, Julanne Johnston, Marcelle. "Eiffel Tower": Georges Carpentier, Patsy Ruth Miller, Alice White & a chorus of 75. "Recitations": Beatrice Lillie, Louise Fazenda, Lloyd Hamilton & Frank Fay. "Eight Sister Acts": introduced by Richard Barthelmess; Helene Costello, Sally O'Neil, Molly O'Day, Dolores Costello, Alice Day, Marceline Day, Sally Blane, Loretta Young, Lola & Armida, Marion Byron & Harriet Lake (Ann Sothern), Ada Mae Vaughn, Alberta Vaughn, Shirley Mason, Viola Dana. "Singin' in the Bathtub": Winnie Lightner, Bull Montana & a male chorus of 50. "Irene Bordoni": Eddie Ward, Louis Silvers, Ray Perkins, Harry Akst, Michael Cleary, Norman Spencer, Dave Silverman, Joe Burke, M.K. Jerome, Lester Stevens. "Chinese Fantasy": introduced by Rin-Tin-Tin; Nick Lucas, Myrna Loy, Jack Haskell Girls. "Bicycle Built for Two": introduced by Frank Fay & Sid Silvers; Douglas Fairbanks, Jr., Chester Conklin Grant Withers, William Collier, Jr., Jack Mulhall, Chester Morris, William Bakewell, Lois Wilson, Gertrude Olmstead, Pauline Garon, Sally Eilers, Edna Murphy, Jacqueline Logan. "Black and White": Frank Fay, Sid Silvers, Louise Fazenda & 75 dancing girls. "Your Love Is All That I Crave": Frank Fay & Harry Akst. "King Richard III": John Barrymore (in his talkie debut), Anthony Bushell, E.J. Ratcliffe, Reginald Sharland. "Mexican Moonshine": Frank Fay, Monte Blue, Albert Gran, Noah Beery, Lloyd Hamilton, Tully Marshall, Kalla Pasha, Lee Moran. "Lady Luck": Betty Compson, Alexander Gray & a chorus, followed by an all-star finale. *D:* John Adolfi; *P:* Darryl F. Zanuck; *Songs:* "Military March," "What's Become of the Floradora Boys" & "Lady Luck" by Ray Perkins; "Motion Picture Pirates" by M.K. Jerome; "If I Could Learn to Love" by M.K. Jerome & Harry Ruby; "Ping Pongo" by Al Dubin & Joe Burke; "Dear Little Pup," "The Only Song I Know" by J. Keirn Brennan & Ray Perkins; "Your Mother and Mine" by Joe Goodwin & Gus Edwards; "Meet My Sister" by Brennan & Perkins; "Singin' in the Bath-Tub" by Ned Washington, Herb Magidson & Michael Cleary; "Believe Me" by Eddie Ward; "Just an Hour of Love" by Al Bryan & Ward; "Li-Po-Li" by Bryan & Ward; "Rockabye Your Baby with a Dixie Melody" by Joe Young, Sam Lewis & Jean Schwartz; "If Your Best Friend Won't Tell You" by Al Dubin & Joe Burke; "Jumping Jack" by Herman Ruby & Rube Bloom; "Your Love Is All That I Crave" by Dubin, Perry Bradford & Jimmy Johnson; "Stars" & "You Were Meant for Me" by Arthur Freed & Nacio Herb Brown. (2:08)

An all-star variety show of musical and comedy acts with some 2-color technicolor sequences.

Note: The film debut of Harriett Lake (Ann Sothern); the final film of actresses Viola Dale, Shirley Mason and Gertrude Olmstead.

4164. The Show-Off (MGM; 1934). *Cast:* Spencer Tracy, Madge Evans, Clara Blandick, Henry Wadsworth, Grant Mitchell, Lois Wilson, Alan Edwards, Claude Gillingwater. *D:* Charles Riesner; *P:* Lucien Hubbard; *Sc:* Herman J. Mankiewicz. (1:20)

Comedy-drama of a woman whose family begins to take a dislike to her new husband. Based on the popular Broadway play by George Kelly, it's previous filmings include (Paramount; 1926) and as *Men Are Like That* (q.v.). Remade in 1946.

4165. Show Them No Mercy (20th Century–Fox; 1935). *Cast:* Rochelle Hudson, Cesar Romero, Bruce Cabot, Edward Norris, Edward Brophy, Warren Hymer, Herbert Rawlinson, Billy Benedict, Charles C. Wilson, William Davidson, Robert Gleckler, Paul McVey, Edythe Elliott, Frank Conroy, Boothe Howard. *D:* George Marshall; *P:* Darryl F. Zanuck; *As.P.:* Raymond Griffith; *Sc:* Kubec Glasmon, Henry Lehrman. (G.B. title: *Tainted Money*) (1:16)

Kidnappers hold a young family hostage as government men try to rescue them. Remade as the western *Rawhide* (20th Century–Fox; 1950–51) with Tyrone Power and Susan Hayward.

4166. A Shreik in the Night (Allied; 1933). *Cast:* Ginger Rogers, Lyle Talbot, Arthur Hoyt, Purnell Pratt, Harvey Clark, Lillian Harmer, Louise Beavers, Maurice Black. *D:* Albert Ray; *P:* M.H. Hoffman, Jr.; *St:* Kurt Kempler; *Sc:* Frances Hyland. (1:07) (video)

Murder-mystery set in an apartment house.

4167. Side Show (WB; 1931). *Cast:* Winnie Lightner, Charles Butterworth, Evalyn Knapp, Donald Cook, Guy Kibbee, Matthew Betz, Fred Kelsey, Tom Ricketts, Louise Carver, Luis Alberni, Edward Morgan, Otto Hoffman, Ann Magruder. *D:* Roy Del Ruth; *St:* William K. Wells, Ray Enright; *Sc:* Arthur Caesar, Enright. (1:00)

B comedy of a carnival girl who plays the roles of various side show characters.

4168. Side Street (RKO; 1929). *Cast:* Tom Moore, Matt Moore, Owen Moore, Frank Sheridan, Emma Dunn, Kathryn Perry (Mrs. Owen Moore), Charles Byer, Walter McNamara, Arthur Housman, Mildred Harris (the first wife of Charlie Chaplin), Irving Bacon, Edwin August, Charles (Heinie) Conkin. *D/St:* Malcolm St. Clair; *P:* William LeBaron; *Adaptation:* John Russell; *Sc:* Russell, St. Clair, O'Hara. (G.B. title: *The Three Brothers*) (1:18)

Melodrama of the three O'Farrell brothers, one a cop, one a surgeon and the other a gangster. The first film to star the Moore brothers in one feature.

4169. Side Streets (WB/F.N.; 1934). *Cast:* Paul Kelly, Aline MacMahon, Ann Dvorak, Mayo Methot, Helen Lowell, Dorothy Tree, Henry O'Neill, Dorothy Peterson, Reneé Whitney. *D:* Alfred E. Green; *P:* Sam Bischoff; *St:* Ann Garrick, Ethel Hill; *Sc:* Manuel Seff. (G.B. title: *A Woman in Her Thirties*)

Drama of a down-and-out sailor and his marriage to a lonely woman.

4170. Sidewalks of New York (MGM; 1931). *Cast:* Buster Keaton, Anita Page, Cliff Edwards, Frank Rowan, Norman Phillips, Jr., Syd Saylor, Oscar Apfel. *D:* Jules White, Zion Myers; *P:* Lawrence Weingarten; *Sc:* George Landy, Paul Gerard Smith, Eric Hatch, Robert E. Hopkins. (1:13)

A romantic comedy which is set among the tenements of New York City. Notable as one of Buster Keaton's early talkie films which set his popularity on a decline.

4171. The Sign of the Cross (Paramount; 1932). *Cast:* Fredric March

(Marcus Superbus), Elissa Landi (Mercia), Charles Laughton (Nero), Claudette Colbert (Poppaea), Ian Keith (Tigellinus), Vivian Tobin (Dacia), Nat Pendleton (Strabo), Harry Beresford (Flavius), Ferdinand Gottschalk (Glabrio), Arthur Hohl (Titus), Joyzelle Joyner (Ancaria), Tommy Conlon (Stephan), Clarence Burton (Servillus), William V. Mong (Licinius), Harold Healy (Tibul), Richard Alexander (Viturius), Robert Manning (Philodemus), Charles Middleton (Tyros), Joe Bonomo (mute giant), Kent Taylor, John Peter Richmond (John Carradine), Lane Chandler, Ethel Wales, Angelo Rossito, Lionel Belmore, Aline MacMahon, Clarence Burton, James Millican (film debut), Rex Ingram. *D:* Cecil B. De Mille; *P:* De Mille; *Sc:* Waldemar Young, Sidney Buchman, Dudley Nichols (unbilled); *Cinematographer:* (A.A.N.) Karl Struss. (2:03)

A lavishly produced classic of ancient Rome, the mad emperor Nero and the rise of christianity. Based on a popular old stage play by Wilson Barrett, the film is a remake of a 1914 production by Lasky with William Farnum and Rosina Henley. A success at the box office the film was re-released in 1944 with some original footage edited out and a 9 minute prologue written by Dudley Nichols added.

4172. Silence (Paramount; 1931). *Cast:* Clive Brook, Marjorie Rambeau, Peggy Shannon, Charles Starrett, John Wray, Wade Boteler, Charles Trowbridge, Ben Taggart, Willard Robertson, Paul Nicholson, Frank Sheridan, John Craig, John Maurice Sullivan. *D:* Louis Gasnier, Max Marcin; *St & Sc:* Marcin.

Drama of a man who takes the blame for a murder committed by his out-of-wedlock daughter.

4173. The Silent Code (Stage and Screen Prods./International; 1935). *Cast:* Kane Richmond, Blanche Mehaffey, J.P. McGowan, Joseph Gi-

rard, Barney Furey, Pat Harmon, Benny Corbett, Carl Mathews, Ed Coxen, Bud Osborne, Ted Mapes, Wolfgang (Rex, King of Dogs). *D:* Stuart Paton; *St:* George Morgan; *Sc:* Morgan. (0:55)

B actioner of a Mountie accused of murder.

4174. The Silent Enemy (Paramount; 1930). *Cast:* Chief Akawanush, Cheeka, Chief Long Lance, Chief Yellow Robe, Spotted Elk. *D:* H.P. Carver; *P:* W. Douglas Burden & William C. Chanler. (1:50) (video)

A part-talkie documentary of the Ojibwa Indian tribe which lives in Canada. The footage of this little known film was originally photographed in the 1920s and has recently been restored by film historians and archivists.

4175. Silent Men (Columbia; 1933). *Cast:* Tim McCoy, Florence Britton, Wheeler Oakman, J. Carrol Naish, Matthew Betz, Lloyd Ingraham, William V. Mong, Walter Brennan, Steve Clark, Syd Saylor, Joseph Conrad. *D:* D. Ross Lederman; *Sc:* Jack Cunningham, Stuart Anthony, Gerald Geraghty. (1:00)

Tim McCoy western of an agent for a group of cattlemen who is suspected of being a gang leader when it is found he was in prison.

4176. Silent Valley (Reliable; 1935). *Cast:* Tom Tyler, Nancy DeShon, Alan Bridge, Wally Wales (Hal Taliaferro), Charles King, Charles "Slim" Whitaker, Murdock MacQuarrie, Art Miles, Jimmy Aubrey, Frank Ellis. *D:* Bernard B. Ray; *P:* Harry S. Webb; *Sc:* Rose Gordon, Carl Krusada. (0:56)

A Tom Tyler western with a cattle rustling theme.

The Silent Voice (G.B. title) *see* **The Man Who Played God**

4177. Silent Witness (Fox; 1932). *Cast:* Lionel Atwill, Helen Mack, Weldon Heyburn, Greta Nissen, Bramwell Fletcher, Alan Mowbray, Billy Bevan, Mary Forbes, Herbert Mundin (American film debut), Montague Shaw, Wyndham Standing, Eric Wilton, Lowden Adams. *D:* Marcel Varnel (directorial debut), R.L. Hough. (1:13)

In this courtroom drama based on the play by Jack de Leon and Jack ⌐elestin, a man confesses to a murder to protect his son.

4178. The Silk Express (WB; 1933). *Cast:* Neil Hamilton, Sheila Terry, Guy Kibbee, Dudley Digges, Allen Jenkins, Arthur Byron, Harold Huber, Arthur Hohl, Robert Barrat, Edward Van Sloan, Douglass Dumbrille, George Pat Collins, Ivan Simpson, Vernon Steele. *D:* Ray Enright; *P:* Henry Blanke; *Sc:* Houston Branch, Ben Markson.

B melodrama of murder aboard a train bound from Seattle to New York with a load of silk.

4179. The Silk Hat Kid (Fox; 1935). *Cast:* Lew Ayres, Mae Clarke, Paul Kelly, William Harrigan, Vince Barnett, Warren Hymer, Billy Benedict, John Qualen, Billy Lee, Ralf Harolde. *D:* H. Bruce Humberstone; *P:* Joseph Engel; *St:* Gerald Beaumont; *Sc:* Edward Eliscu, Dore Schary, Lou Breslow.

Comedy.

4180. Silk Stockings (Xxxx Xxxx; 1932). *Cast:* Fifi D'Orsay.

(No other information available)

4181. Silks and Saddles (Treo; 1938). *Cast:* Herman Brix (Bruce Bennett), Fuzzy Knight, Toby Wing. *D:* Xxxx Xxxx.

B horse racing drama, a remake of a 1927 film.

4182. Silly Billies (RKO; 1936). *Cast:* Bert Wheeler, Robert Woolsey, Dorothy Lee, Harry Woods, Ethan Laidlaw, Chief Thunderbird, Delmar Watson, Richard Alexander. *D:* Fred Guiol; *As.P.:* Lee Marcus; *St:* Thomas Lennon, Fred Guiol; *Sc:* Al Boasberg, Jack Townley; *Song:* "Tumble on Tumbleweed" by Dave Dreyer & Jack Scholl. (1:04)

The popularity of the comedy team of Wheeler and Woolsey was on a decline with this zany comedy of two dentists who set up their practice in the old west.

4183. The Silver Bullet (Reliable; 1935). *Cast:* Tom Tyler, Jayne Regan, Lafe McKee, Charles King, George Chesebro, Slim Whitaker, Franklyn Farnum, Lew Meehan, Blackie Whiteford, Nelson McDowell, Robert Brower. *D:* Bernard B. Ray; *P:* Ray; *As.P.:* Harry S. Webb; *Sc:* Rose Gordon, Carl Krusada. (0:53)

Tom Tyler western which has nothing to do with "The Lone Ranger" or werewolves. One of many indie westerns Tyler did for this company.

4184. The Silver Cord (RKO; 1933). *Cast:* Irene Dunne, Joel McCrea, Laura Hope Crews, Frances Dee, Eric Linden, Helen Cromwell, Gustav von Seyffertitz, Reginald Pasch, Perry Ivins. *D:* John Cromwell; *P:* Pandro S. Berman; *Sc:* Jane Murfin. (1:15)

In this drama, based on the play by Sidney Howard, a possessive mother manipulates the lives of her sons.

4185. Silver Dollar (WB/F.N.; 1932). *Cast:* Edward G. Robinson (Yates Martin), Bebe Daniels (Lilly Owens), Aline MacMahon (Sarah Martin), Robert Warwick, Joybyna Howland, Russell Simpson, DeWitt Jennings, Leon (Ames) Waycoff, Herman Bing, Charles Middleton, Berton Churchill, Lee Kohlmar, Wade Boteler, Theresa Maxwell Conover, Niles Welch, David Durand, John Marston, Walter Brown Rogers, Harry Holman, Emmett Corrigan, Virginia Edwards. *D:* Alfred E. Green; *St:* David Karsner; *Sc:* Harvey Thew, Carl Erickson. (1:23)

The founding of Denver, Colorado by silver baron H.A.W. Tabor is the basis for this fictionalized historical 19th-century drama.

4186. The Silver Horde (RKO; 1930). *Cast:* Joel McCrea (Boyd), Jean Arthur (Mildred Wayland), Evelyn Brent (Cherry Malotte), Louis Wolheim, Raymond Hatton, Blanche Sweet (popular silent screen actress in her last film appearance until 1959), Purnell Pratt, William Davidson, Ivan Linow, Gavin Gordon. *D:* George Archainbaud; *As.P.:* William Sistrom; *Sc:* Wallace Smith. (1:15)

Adventure-drama of the salmon fishing industry of Seattle, Washington, and the men who work within it. Based on a story by Rex Beach. Previous filming: (Samuel Goldwyn; 1920) with Myrtle Stedman and Curtis Cooksey.

4187. The Silver Lining (United Artists/Patrician; 1932). *Cast:* Maureen O'Sullivan, Betty Compson, John Warburton, Montagu Love, Mary Doran, Wally Albright, John Holland, Cornelius Keefe. *D:* Alan Crosland; *P:* Walter Camp; *St:* Hal Conklin; *Sc:* Gertrude Orr.

Drama of a woman who comes into wealth collecting rents from slum tenements which she refuses to repair or renovate.

4188. Silver on the Sage (Paramount; 1939). *Cast:* Bill Boyd (Hoppy), Russell Hayden (Lucky), George "Gabby" Hayes (Windy), Stanley Ridges, Ruth Rogers, Frederick Burton, Jack Rockwell, Roy Barcroft, Ed Cassidy, Sherry Tansey, Bruce Mitchell, Jim Corey, Will Wright, George Morrell, Frank O'Connor, Buzz Barton, Herman Hack, Dick Dickinson, Hank Bell. *D:* Lesley Selander; *P:* Harry M. Sherman; *Sc:* Maurice Geraghty. (1:06) (video)

Number 25 in the "Hopalong Cassidy" series with Lucky being accused of murder.

4189. Silver Spurs (Universal; 1936). *Cast:* Buck Jones, Muriel Evans, J.P. McGowan, George Hayes, Denny Meadows, Beth Marion, Robert Frazer, Bruce Lane, Charles K. French, William Lawrence, Earl Askam, Kernan Cripps. *D:* Ray Taylor; *P: Jones; Sc:* Joseph Poland. (1:01)

Buck Jones western of cattle rustling.

4190. The Silver Streak (RKO; 1934). *Cast:* Sally Blane, Charles Starrett, William Farnum, Hardie Albright, Irving Pichel, Arthur Lake, Theodore von Eltz, Guinn Williams, Edgar Kennedy, Doris Dawson, Dick Curtis, James Bradbury, Sr., Harry Allen. *D:* Tommy Atkins; *As.P.:* Glendon Allvine; *St:* Roger Whately; *Sc:* Whately, H.W. Hanemann, Jack O'Donnell. (1:12) (video)

Hit railroad drama involving the transportation of iron lungs for a polio epidemic via a young engineer's revolutionary transportation invention called "The Burlington Zephyr."

4191. The Silver Trail (Reliable; 1937). *Cast:* Rin-Tin-Tin, Jr., Rex Lease (in his final starring film), Mary Russell, Ed Cassidy, Roger Williams, Steve Clark, Tom London, Oscar Gahan, Sherry Tansey. *D:* Raymond Samuels (Bernard B. Ray); *P:* Harry S. Webb; *Sc:* Bennett Cohen, Forrest Sheldon. (0:58)

B western adventure of a man and a dog who investigate the murders of some silver miners.

Sin Flood (G.B. title) *see* **The Way to All Men**

The Sin of Lena Rivers *see* **Lena Rivers**

4192. The Sin of Madelon Claudet (MGM; 1931). *Cast:* Helen Hayes (in her feature talkie debut, receiving an

A.A. for B.A., 1931-32 as Madelon Claudet), Lewis Stone (Carlo Boretti), Neil Hamilton (Larry), Robert Young (Jacques), Cliff Edwards (Victor), Jean Hersholt (Doctor Dulac), Marie Prevost (Rosalie), Karen Morley (Alice), Charles Winninger (photographer), Alan Hale (Hubert), Halliwell Hobbes (Roget), Lennox Pawle (St. Jacques), Russell Powell (Claudet), Frankie Darro (Larry as a boy). *D:* Edgar Selwyn; *Sc:* Charles MacArthur. (G.B. title: *The Lullaby*) (1:14) (video)

In this hit tear-jerker a woman devotes her life to her illegitimate son, eventually sending him to medical school on money she earned as a prostitute. Based on the 1924 Broadway play "The Lullaby" by Edward Knoblock. The Venice Film Festival of 1932 voted it "the film eliciting the greatest emotional response," while *Film Daily* placed it at #10 on their "10 Best" list.

4193. The Sin of Nora Moran (Majestic; 1933). *Cast:* Zita Johann, Paul Cavanagh, Alan Dinehart, Henry B. Walthall, John Miljan, Cora Sue Collins, Claire DuBrey, Sarah Padden. *D:* Phil Goldstone; *St:* Willis Maxwell Goodhue. (Retitled: *Voice from the Grave*)

"Poverty row" melodrama of illicit love which ends in tragedy.

4194. The Sin Ship (RKO; 1930-31). *Cast:* Louis Wolheim, Mary Astor, Hugh Herbert, Ian Keith, Alan Roscoe, Russell Powell. *D:* Louis Wolheim (his only film as director); *As.P.:* Myles Connolly; *St:* Keene Thompson, Agnes Brand Leahy; *Sc:* Hugh Herbert. (1:04)

In this melodrama a gruff sea captain is smitten with a beautiful lady passenger with a shady past.

4195. Sin Takes a Holiday (RKO-Pathé; 1930-31). *Cast:* Constance Bennett, Kenneth MacKenna, Basil Rathbone, Rita LaRoy, Louis John Bartels, John Roche, ZaSu Pitts, Kendall Lee, Murrell Finley, Helen John-

son, Fred Walton. *D:* Paul L. Stein; *P:* E.B. Derr; *St:* Robert Milton, Dorothy Cairns; *Sc:* Horace Jackson. (1:20)

A domestic comedy-drama concerning a marriage of convenience and what it evolves into.

4196. Sin's Pay Day (Mayfair; 1932). *Cast:* Lloyd Whitlock, Dorothy Revier, Mickey (Rooney) McGuire. *D:* George B. Seitz. (Re-release title: *Slums of New York*)

"Poverty row" drama of urban living.

4197. Sing and Be Happy (20th Century-Fox; 1937). *Cast:* Tony Martin, Dixie Dunbar, Allan Lane, Chick Chandler, Lynn Bari, Berton Churchill, Leah Ray, Andrew Tombes, Helen Westley, Frank McGlynn, Joan Davis. *D:* James Tinling; *Sc:* Lou Breslow, John Patrick, Ben Markson; *Songs:* Harry Akst, Sidney Clare.

B budget musical which was designed as a showcase for singer, Tony Martin.

4198. Sing and Like It (RKO; 1934). *Cast:* Nat Pendleton, ZaSu Pitts, Pert Kelton, Ned Sparks, Edward Everett Horton, Richard Carle, John Qualen, Matt McHugh, Stanley Fields, Joseph (Sawyer) Sauers, William M. Griffith, Grace Hayle, Roy D'Arcy, Florence Roberts. *D:* William A. Seiter; *As.P.:* Howard J. Green; *St:* Aben Kandel; *Sc:* Marion Dix, Laird Doyle; *Song:* Dave Dreyer, Roy Turk. (1:12)

B comedy of a gangster who takes a hapless girl and turns her into a singer.

4199. Sing, Baby, Sing (20th Century-Fox; 1936). *Cast:* Alice Faye, Adolphe Menjou, Gregory Ratoff, Ted Healy, Ritz Brothers (feature film debut), Patsy Kelly, Tony Martin, Montagu Love, Dixie Dunbar, Michael Whalen, Virginia Field (American film

debut), Lynn Bari, Douglas Fowley, Paul McVey, Paul Stanton, Cully Richards, Carol Tevis. *D:* Sidney Lanfield; *P:* Darryl F. Zanuck; *St:* Milton Sperling, Jack Yellen; *Sc:* Sperling, Yellen, Harry Tugend. (1:27)
Musical-comedy.

4200. Sing, Cowboy, Sing (Grand National; 1937). *Cast:* Tex Ritter, Louise Stanley, Al St. John, Karl Hackett, Charles King, Bob McKenzie, Budd Buster, Horace Murphy, Snub Pollard, Heber Snow (Hank Worden), Chick Hannon, Tex Palmer, Jack C. Smith, Oscar Gahan, Herman Hack, Milburn Morante, Chester Conklin, Tex Ritter's Texas Tornadoes. *D:* Robert N. Bradbury; *P:* Edward Finney (Boots & Saddles Prods.); *Sc:* Robert Emmett (Tansey). (0:59)
Tex Ritter western with songs of two cowboys posing as entertainers to find out who killed a shipping franchiser.
Note: The final reel of this film was reused the following year in another Ritter western entitled: *Rollin' Plains* (q.v.).

Sing Me a Love Song (1935) (G.B. title) *see* **Manhattan Moon**

4201. Sing Me a Love Song (WB/F.N.; 1936–37). *Cast:* James Melton, Patricia Ellis, Hugh Herbert, ZaSu Pitts, Allen Jenkins, Ann Sheridan, Dennis Moore, Nat Pendleton, Walter Catlett, Hobart Cavanaugh, Charles Halton, Robert Emmett O'Connor, Charles Richman, Adrian Rosley, Georgia Caine, Linda Perry, Granville Bates, George Sorel, Harry Hollingsworth, George Guhl. *D:* Ray Enright; *P:* Sam Bischoff; *St:* Harry Sauber; *Sc:* Sig Herzig, Jerry Wald; *Songs:* "Your Eyes Have Told Me So" by Gus Kahn, Walter Blaufuss & Egbert Van Alstyne; "Summer Night," "The Little House That Love Built," "That's the Least You Can Do for a Lady" by Al

Dubin & Harry Warren. (G.B. title: *Come Up Smiling*)
B romantic musical of a store owner who goes incognito as an employee in his own store.

4202. Sing Sing Nights (Monogram; 1934). *Cast:* Conway Tearle, Hardie Albright, Boots Mallory, Mary Doran, Ferdinand Gottschalk, Berton Churchill, Jameson Thomas, Lotus Long, Henry Kolker, Richard Tucker, George Baxter. *D:* Lewis D. Collins; *P:* Paul Malvern; *Sc:* Marion Orth; *Additional Dialogue:* Charles Logue. (G.B. title: *Reprieved*) (1:00)
Based on the novel by Harry Stephen Keeler, three accused murderers get a chance to relate their side of the story in this "poverty row" production.

Sing, Sinner, Sing (G.B. title) *see* **Clip Joint**

4203. Sing While You're Able (Ambassador/Melody Pictures; 1937). *Cast:* Lane Chandler, Toby Wing, Pinky Tomlin. *D:* Marshall Neilan; *P:* Maurice Conn.
(No other information available)

4204. Sing, You Sinners (Paramount; 1938). *Cast:* Bing Crosby (Joe Beebe), Fred MacMurray (David Beebe), Donald O'Connor (Mike Beebe), Elizabeth Patterson (Mrs. Beebe), Ellen Drew (Martha), John Gallaudet (Harry Ringmer), William Haade (Pete), Paul White (Filter), Irving Bacon, Tom Dugan, Herbert Corthell. *D:* Wesley Ruggles; *P:* Ruggles; *Sc:* Claude Binyon. (1:28)
Hit musical drama of a man who lives his life with no responsibility. It was in nomination for "Best Film of the Year" by the New York Film Critics. The National Board of Review placed it at #5 on their "10 Best" list.

The Singer of Seville (G.B. title) *see* **Call of the Flesh**

4205. The Singing Buckaroo (Spectrum; 1937). *Cast:* Fred Scott, William Faversham, Victoria Vinton, Cliff Nazarro, Howard Hill, Roger Williams, Dick Curtis, Rosa Caprino. *D:* Tom Gibson; *P:* Jed Buell, George Callaghan; *Sc:* Gibson. (0:50) (video)

Fred Scott, "the silvery-voiced buckaroo" western with songs of a cowboy who comes to the aid of a girl being harrassed by the bad guys.

4206. The Singing Cowboy (Republic; 1936). *Cast:* Gene Autry, Smiley Burnette, Lois Wilde, Creighton (Lon) Chaney, (Jr.), John Van Pelt, Ann Gillis, Earle Hodgins, Ken Cooper, Harrison Greene, Wes Warner, Jack Rockwell, Tracy Layne, Fred "Snowflake" Toones, Champion. *D:* Mack V. Wright; *P:* Nat Levine; *St:* Tom Gibson; *Sc:* Dorrell & Stuart McGowan. (0:56)

Gene Autry musical oater of a western caravan that broadcasts radio shows to raise money for a little girl's operation.

4207. The Singing Cowgirl (Grand National; 1939). *Cast:* Dorothy Page, David "Tex" O'Brien, Vince Barnett, Warner Richmond, Dorothy Short, Ed Peil, Dix Davis, Stanley Price, Paul Barrett, Lloyd Ingraham, Ethan Allen, Ed Gordon, Merrill McCormack. *D:* Samuel Diege; *P:* George A. Hirliman (a Coronado Picture); *Sc:* Arthur Hoerl. (0:59) (video)

Dorothy Page western of a lady rancher who takes in a young boy whose parents were killed. The third and final entry in Page's series.

4208. The Singing Fool (WB/Vitaphone; 1928). *Cast:* Al Jolson (Al Stone), Josephine Dunn (Molly Winton), Davey Lee (Sonny Boy), Betty Bronson (Grace), Reed Howes (John Perry), Edward Martindel (Marcus), Arthur Housman (Blackie Joe), Robert Emmett O'Connor (cafe manager). *D:* Lloyd Bacon; *Play:* Leslie S. Barrows; *Sc:* C. Graham Baker; *Dialogue & Titles:* Joseph Jackson; *Other Songs:* "It All Depends on You," & "I'm Sittin' on Top of the World" by Buddy DeSylva, Lew Brown & Ray Henderson; "There's a Rainbow 'Round My Shoulder," "Keep Smilin' at Trouble," "Golden Gate" & "The Spaniard Who Blighted My Life" by Billy Rose, Al Jolson & Dave Dreyer with "Vesti la giubba" from Leoncavallo's "I Pagliacci" as background music. (1:50)

Hit part-talkie tear-jerker of a singing waiter who yearns to become a songwriter, dealing with the proverbial trials and tribulations and a family tragedy. The film which had the working title of "Sonny Boy," grossed over $4,000,000 at the box office. The song "Sonny Boy" by DeSylva, Brown and Henderson, sung by Jolson following the death of his son, had audiences tears flowing in the aisles, and afterwards became the first song to sell over 1,000,000 copies (over 3,000,000 in all). Curiously enough, the trio wrote the song as a joke, never realizing it's emotional impact on audiences of the day. Premiere: September 19, 1928, at the Winter Garden in New York City.

4209. The Singing Kid (WB/F.N.; 1936). *Cast:* Al Jolson, Sybil Jason, Allen Jenkins, Edward Everett Horton, Beverly Roberts (film debut), Lyle Talbot, Claire Dodd, Winifred Shaw, Yacht Club Boys, Cab Calloway & His Band, Grady Sutton, Hattie McDaniel, William Davidson, Paula Stone, Kay Hughes, Edward Keane, Tom Manning, Frank Mitchell, John Hale, Jack Durant. *D:* William Keighley; *P:* Robert Lord; *St:* Lord; *Sc:* Warren Duff, Pat C. Flick; *Songs:* "You Gotta Have That Hi-Di-Ho in Your Soul" by Irving Mills & Cab Calloway; "My How This Country Has Changed," "You're the Cure for What Ails Me," "Here's Looking at You" & "Save Me Sister" by E.Y. Harburg & Harold Arlen. (1:23)

Hit musical of a self-centered entertainer.

4210. The Singing Marine (WB; 1937). *Cast:* Dick Powell, Doris Weston, Jane Darwell, Hugh Herbert, Lee Dixon, Allen Jenkins, Jane Wyman, Veda Ann Borg, Eddie Acuff, Berton Churchill, Guinn Williams, Larry Adler, Richard Loo, Ward Bond, Henry O'Neill, Addison Richards, Marcia Ralston, James Robbins, Rose King. *D:* Ray Enright; *St & Sc:* Delmer Daves; *Choreography:* Busby Berkeley; *Songs:* Al Dubin & Harry Warren include: "The Song of the Marines" (which upon release of the film was adopted by the U.S. Marine Corps as its official song), "I Know Now, 'Cause My Baby Says It's So," "Night Over Shanghai" (lyrics by Johnny Mercer), "The Lady Who Couldn't Be Kissed," & "You Can't Run Away from Love Tonight." (1:47) Musical in which the title tells all.

The Singing Musketeer (G.B. title) *see* **The Three Musketeers** (1939)

4211. The Singing Outlaw (Universal; 1938). *Cast:* Bob Baker, Fuzzy Knight, Joan Barclay, Harry Woods, Carl Stockdale, LeRoy Mason, Ralph Lewis, Glenn Strange, Georgia O'Dell, Jack Kirk, Ed Peil, Sr., Jack Rockwell, Bob McKenzie, Budd Buster, Lafe McKee, Hank Worden, Art Mix, Chick Hannon, Jack Montgomery, Herman Hack, Curley Gibson, Francis Walker. *D:* Joseph H. Lewis; *P:* Trem Carr; *Sc:* Harry O. Hoyt. (0:56)
Bob Baker western with songs of a rodeo performer who gets involved in murder.

4212. The Singing Vagabond (Republic; 1935). *Cast:* Gene Autry, Ann Rutherford, Smiley Burnette, Barbara Pepper, Niles Welch, Grace Goodall, Allan Sears, Warner Richmond, Henry Rocquemore, June Thompson, Elaine Shepard, Bob Burns, Tom Brower, Ray (Corrigan) Bernard, Charles King, Marion O'Connell, Frank LaRue, Robinson Neeman, George (Montgomery) Letz, Chief Thundercloud, Chief John Big Tree, Marie Quillan, Edmund Cobb, Champion. *D:* Carl Pierson; *P:* Nat Levine; *Supervisor:* Armand Schaefer; *St:* Oliver Drake; *Sc:* Drake, Betty Burbridge; *Songs:* Autry, Burnette, Drake, Herbert Myers. (0:54)
Gene Autry western (his second feature) with songs, involving a traveling show. Set in 1860.

4213. Single-Handed Sanders (Monogram; 1932). *Cast:* Tom Tyler, Margaret Morris, Robert Manning, G.D. Wood (Gordon DeMain), John Elliott, Hank Bell, Loie Bridge, Fred "Snowflake" Toones. *D:* Lloyd Nosler; *P:* Trem Carr; *Sc:* Charles A. Post. (1:01)
Tom Tyler western of townsmen fighting a corrupt politician.

4214. The Single Sin (Tiffany; 1931). *Cast:* Holmes Herbert, Kay Johnson, Bert Lytell, Geneva Mitchell, Paul Hurst, Matthew Betz, Lillian Elliott, Robert Emmett O'Connor. *D:* William Nigh; *St:* A.P. Younger.
"Poverty row" melodrama of a woman with a past who is trying to maintain a normal life.

4215. Sinister Hands (Willis Kent; 1932). *Cast:* Jack Mulhall, Phyllis Barrington, Crauford Kent, Mischa Auer, Bess Flowers. *D:* Armand L. Schaefer; *Sc:* Norton S. Parker, Oliver Drake.

4216. Sinner Take All (MGM; 1936–37). *Cast:* Bruce Cabot, Charley Grapewin, Vivienne Osborne, Stanley Ridges, Dorothy Kilgallen, Margaret Lindsay, Joseph Calleia, George Zucco, Edward Pawley, Theodore von Eltz, Eadie Adams, George Lynn. *D:* Errol Taggart; *P:* Lucien Hubbard, Samuel Marx; *Sc:* Walter Wise, Leonard Lee.
Offbeat B murder-mystery which was based on the novel "Murder for a Wanton" by Whitman Chambers.

4217. Sinner's Holiday (WB; 1930). *Cast:* Grant Withers, Evalyn

602 Sound Films, 1927-1939

Knapp, James Cagney (film debut recreating his stage role), Joan Blondell (film debut recreating her stage role), Lucille La Verne, Warren Hymer, Noel Madison (film debut), Hank Mann, Otto Hoffman, Purnell Pratt. *D:* John Adolfi; *Sc:* Harvey Thew, George Rosener. (1:00)

Low-budget romantic melodrama set at Coney Island, N.Y. Based on the unsuccessful play "Penny Arcade" by Marie Baumer.

4218. Sinners in Paradise (Universal; 1938). *Cast:* John Boles, Bruce Cabot, Madge Evans, Marion Martin, Gene Lockhart, Nana Bryant, Milburn Stone, Donald Barry, Charlotte Wynters, Willie Fung, Morgan Conway, Dwight Frye. *D:* James Whale; *P:* Kenneth Goldsmith; *St:* Harold Buckley; *Sc:* Buckley, Lester Cole, Louis Stevens. (1:05)

B drama of various passengers who survive a plane crash on a South Sea island.

4219. Sinners in the Sun (Paramount; 1932). *Cast:* Carole Lombard, Chester Morris, Alison Skipworth, Cary Grant, Adrienne Ames, Walter Byron, Rita LaRoy, Ida Lewis, Kent Taylor, Zita Moulton, Reginald Barlow, Veda Buckland, Frances Moffett, Russ Clark, Luke Cosgrave, Pierre de Ramey. *D:* Alexander Hall; *St:* Mildred Cram; *Sc:* Waldemar H. Young, Samuel Hoffenstein. (1:10)

Low-budget triangular romantic drama.

4220. Sins of Man (20th Century-Fox; 1936). *Cast:* Jean Hersholt, J. Edward Bromberg, Maxine Reiner, Edward Van Sloan, Don Ameche (feature film debut), Fritz Leiber, Gregory Ratoff, Francis Ford, Fred Kohler, Jr., DeWitt Jennings, Egon Brecher, Christian Rub, Ann Shoemaker, Adrian Rosley, Mickey Rentschler, Paul Stanton, Gene Reynolds, Ruth Robinson, John Miltern. *D:* Gregory Ratoff (directorial debut), Otto Brower; *P:* Darryl F.

Zanuck; *As.P.:* Kenneth MacGowan; *St:* Joseph Roth; *Sc:* Samuel G. Engel.

Low-budget drama.

4221. Sins of the Children (MGM; 1930). *Cast:* Louis Mann, Leila Hyams, Elliott Nugent, Robert Montgomery, Mary Doran, Clara Blandick, Robert McWade, Francis X. Bushman, Jr., Henry Armetta. *D:* Sam Wood; *Sc:* Elliott & J.C. Nugent. (G.B. title: *The Richest Man in the World*)

Low-budget production of an immigrant barber who sacrifices all for his children — with varied returns from each. Based on the play "Father's Day" by Elliott and J.C. Nugent, this film is a sequel to *Father's Day* (MGM; 1929) which also starred Mann, Hyams and Montgomery.

Sins of the Children (1937) *see* **In His Steps**

Siren of the South Seas *see* **Paradise Isle**

4222. Sister to Judas (Mayfair; 1933). *Cast:* Claire Windsor, John Harron, Holmes Herbert, Wilfred Lucas, Lee Moran. *D:* E. Mason Hopper.

"Poverty row" i am. of a woman's wickedness.

4223. The Sisters (WB; 1938). *Cast:* Errol Flynn (Frank Medlin), Bette Davis (Louise Elliott, a role intended for Kay Francis), Anita Louise (Helen Elliott), Ian Hunter (William Benson), Donald Crisp (Tim Hazleton), Beulah Bondi (Rose Elliott), Alan Hale (Sam Johnson), Dick Foran (Tom Knivel), Henry Travers (Ned Elliott), Patric Knowles (Norman French), Lee Patrick (Flora Gibbon), Jane Bryan (Grace Elliott), Laura Hope Crews (Flora's mother), Janet Shaw (Stella Johnson), Ruth Garland (Laura Bennett), Harry Davenport (Doc Moore), John Warburton (Anthony Bittick), Paul Harvey (Caleb Ammon), Mayo Methot (blonde at the prizefight), Irving Bacon (Robert Forbes), Arthur Hoyt (Tom Selig),

Susan Hayward (bit). *D:* Anatole Litvak; *As.P.:* David Lewis; *Sc:* Milton Krims. (1:38)

The story of three sisters and their marriages is told in this romantic-marital drama set in San Francisco after the turn-of-the-century. Based on the novel by Myron Brinig, the earthquake of 1906 is depicted in a climactic sequence.

4224. Sisters Under the Skin (Columbia; 1934). *Cast:* Frank Morgan, Elissa Landi, Joseph Schildkraut, Doris Lloyd, Samuel S. Hinds, Robert Graves, Shirley Grey, Howard Hickman, Montague Shaw, Arthur S. Hull, Clara Blandick, Selmer Jackson. *D:* David Burton; *St:* S.K. Lauren; *Sc:* Jo Swerling. (G.B. title: *The Romantic Age*)

Romantic drama of a girl and her protector.

4225. Sit Tight (WB; 1931). *Cast:* Joe E. Brown, Winnie Lightner, Claudia Dell, Don George, Lotti Loder, Hobart Bosworth, Snitz Edwards, Frank Hagney, Paul Gregory. *D:* Lloyd Bacon; *Sc:* Rex Taylor, William K. Wells.

Joe E. Brown B comedy with a focus on the professional wrestling game.

4226. Sitting on the Moon (Republic; 1936). *Cast:* Roger Pryor, Grace Bradley, Pert Kelton, Joyce Compton, William Janney, George Cooper. *D:* Ralph B. Staub (directorial debut).

B musical of young lovers being blackmailed by a devious female.

4227. Sitting Pretty (Paramount; 1933). *Cast:* Jack Oakie, Jack Haley, Ginger Rogers, Thelma Todd, Gregory Ratoff, Lew Cody, Harry Revel (bit), Mack Gordon (bit), Hale Hamilton, Jerry Tucker, Walter Walker, Kenneth Thomson. *D:* Harry Joe Brown; *P:* Charles R. Rogers; *St:* Nina Wilcox Putnam; *Sc:* Jack McGowan, S.J. Perelman, Lou Breslow; *Songs:* Gordon & Revel. (1:25)

Hit musical-comedy about two songwriters in Hollywood. The finale song "Did You Ever See a Dream Walking?" by Mack Gordon & Harry Revel became a big hit.

4228. Six-Cylinder Love (Fox; 1931). *Cast:* Spencer Tracy, Sidney Fox, Una Merkel, William Collier, Sr., Edward Everett Horton, El Brendel, Louise Beavers, Bert Roach, Ruth Warren, William Holden, Lorin Raker. *D:* Thornton Freeland; *St:* William Anthony McGuire.

A domestic drama which is a remake of the 1923 production of the same name by this studio with Florence Eldridge and Ernest Truex.

4229. 6-Day Bike Rider (WB/F.N.; 1934). *Cast:* Joe E. Brown, Maxine Doyle, Frank McHugh, Gordon Westcott, Arthur Aylesworth, Lottie Williams, Dorothy Christy, Lloyd Neal, William Granger, Harry Seymour. *D:* Lloyd Bacon; *P:* Sam Bischoff; *St & Sc:* Earl Baldwin. (1:09)

Joe E. Brown B comedy of a neer-do-well who enters a grueling bike marathon to impress his girl friend.

4230. Six-Gun Justice (Spectrum; 1935). *Cast:* Roger Williams, Bill Cody, Wally Wales (Hal Taliaferro), Ethel Jackson, Budd Buster. *P:* Robert Hill; *Sc:* Oliver Drake.

(No other information available)

(May be an Ajax production)

4231. Six-Gun Rhythm (Grand National/Arcadia; 1939). *Cast:* Tex Fletcher, Joan Barclay, Ralph Peters, Reed Howes, Malcolm "Bud" McTaggart, Ted Adams, Walter Shumway, Slim Hacker, Art Felix, Art Davis, Robert Frazer, Frank Ellis, Carl Mathews, Kit Guard, Sherry Tansey, Jack O'Shea, Joe Pazen, Cliff Parkinson, Jack McHugh, Adrian Hughes, Wade Walker. *D:* Sam Newfield; *P:* Newfield; *Sc:* Fred Myton. (0:55) (video)

A solo attempt to establish radio singer Tex Fletcher as a singing cowboy in a series. This story of a football star who returns to Texas to find lawlessness abounding became the only Fletcher feature before the studio closed its doors.

4232. Six-Gun Trail (Victory; 1938). *Cast:* Tim McCoy, Nora Lane, Alden (Stephen) Chase, Ben Corbett, Karl Hackett, Donald Gallagher, Kenne Duncan, Ted Adams, Sherry Tansey, Bob Terry, Jimmy Aubrey, George Morrell. *D:* Sam Newfield; *P:* Sam Katzman; *Sc:* Joseph O'Donnell. (1:00)

Tim McCoy western of a government man posing as an oriental to investigate the selling of stolen gems.

4233. Six Hours to Live (Fox; 1932). *Cast:* Warner Baxter, John Boles, Miriam Jordan (film debut), Irene Ware, George F. Marion, Beryl Mercer, Halliwell Hobbes, Dewey Robinson, Edward McWade, John Davidson, Edwin Maxwell. *D:* William Dieterle; *St:* Gordon Morris, Barteaux; *Sc:* Bradley King. (1:18)

Offbeat production of a murdered diplomat who is brought back to life for six hours in an attempt to find his killer.

4234. Six of a Kind (Paramount; 1934). *Cast:* W.C. Fields, George Burns, Gracie Allen, Charles Ruggles, Mary Boland, Alison Skipworth, Walter Long, Bradley Page, Verna Hillie, James Burke, Leo Willis, Tammany Young, Alf P. James, Dick Rush, Lew Kelly, William J. Kelly. *D:* Leo McCarey; *St:* Keene Thompson, Douglas MacLean; *Sc:* Walter de Leon, Harry Ruskin. (1:09)

A successful comedy of the adventures and misadventures of various people motoring across the United States who unknowingly have stolen money hidden in their car. An all-star comedy cast.

4235. Six-Shootin' Sheriff (Grand National; 1938). *Cast:* Ken Maynard, Marjorie Reynolds, Jane Keckley, Bob Terry, Harry Harvey, Sr., Walter Long, Earl Dwire, Lafe McKee, Tom London, Warner Richmond, Ben Corbett, Richard Alexander, Glenn Strange, Bud Osborne, Roger Williams, Milburn Morante, Ed Peil, Sr., Carl Mathews, Herb Holcombe, Tarzan the horse. *D:* Harry Fraser; *P:* Max & Arthur Alexander; *Sc:* Weston Edwards (Fraser). (0:59) (video)

Ken Maynard western of an outlaw who is made sheriff of a town, without the residents knowing his past.

4236. Sixteen Fathoms Deep (Monogram; 1933–34). *Cast:* Sally O'Neil, Creighton (Lon) Chaney, (Jr.) (who also appeared in the '48 vesrion), George Regas, Maurice Black, Jack Kennedy, Lloyd Ingraham, George Nash, Robert Kortman, Si Jenks, Richard Alexander, Constantine Romanoff, Russell Simpson, Philip Kieffer, Jean Gehring, Raul Figarola. *D:* Armand Schaefer; *Sc:* A.B. Barringer, Norman Houston. (0:57) (video)

"Poverty row" action-drama of a sponge diver and the opposition he meets when he attempts to purchase his own boat. Based on the story of the same name by Eustace L. Adams which appeared in *American Magazine,* it was previously filmed in the silent era. Remade by this studio in color in 1948.

4237. 6,000 Enemies (MGM; 1939). *Cast:* Walter Pidgeon, Rita Johnson, Paul Kelly, Guinn Williams, Nat Pendleton, Raymond Hatton, Tom Neal, Grant Mitchell, Harold Huber, John Arledge, Esther Dale, Horace MacMahon, Arthur Aylesworth, Willie Fung, Lionel Royce, Helena Phillips Evans, J.M. Kerrigan, Adrian Morris. *D:* George B. Seitz; *P:* Lucien Hubbard; *St:* Wilmon Menard, Leo L. Stanley; *Sc:* Bertram Millhauser.

B prison drama.

4238. Skin Deep (WB; 1929). *Cast:* Monte Blue, Betty Compson, Davey Lee, Alice Day, Tully Marshall, John Bowers, George E. Stone, John Davidson. *D:* Ray Enright; *St:* Mark Edmund Jones; *Sc:* Gordon Rigby; *Song:* Sidney Mitchell, Archie Gottler, Con Conrad.

Melodrama of a woman who gets her husband committed to prison, then helps to get him out, etc.

4239. Skinner Steps Out (Universal; 1929). *Cast:* Glenn Tryon, Merna Kennedy, E.J. Ratcliffe, Burr McIntosh, Lloyd Whitlock. *D:* William James Craft. (1:10)

A man lies to his wife and tells her he got a raise in pay, rather than confronting her with the truth. Filmed twice before as *Skinner's Dress Suit* by (Essanay; 1917) with Bryant Washburn and Hazel Daly and (Universal; 1925-26) with Reginald Denny and Laura La Plante. Based on the story "Skinner's Dress Suit" by Henry Irving Dodge.

4240. Skippy (Paramount; 1931). *Cast:* Jackie Cooper (A.A.N. for B.A. and the film which made him a top box office draw as a child star), Robert Coogan (kid brother of Jackie Coogan in his film debut as Sooky), Mitzi Green (Eloise), Jackie Searle (Sidney), Willard Robertson (Dr. Skinner), Enid Bennett (Mrs. Skinner), Donald Haines (Harley Nubbins), Helen Jerome Eddy (Mrs. Wayne), Guy Oliver (old meany who runs the dog pound), Jack Clifford. *D:* (A.A.) Norman Taurog; *P:* (A.A.N. for Best Pictures, 1930-31) Louis D. Lighton; *Adaptation:* Sam Mintz; *Sc:* (A.A.N.) Joseph L. Mankiewicz, Norman Z. McLeod; *Additional Dialogue:* Don Marquis. (1:28)

Family style comedy-drama of a little boy who takes extreme measures to get his best friend's dog out of the pound before.... A big money-maker for the studio, it was based on the comic strip characters of Percy Crosby. *Film Daily* placed it at #3 on their "10 Best" list, while the *New York Times* placed it at #8 on theirs.

Note: *Sooky* (q.v.), a sequel, followed later in the year.

4241. Skull and Crown (Reliable; 1935). *Cast:* Rin-Tin-Tin, Jr., Regis Toomey, Jack Mulhall, Molly O'Day, James Murray (final film—d.

1936 by drowning, age 35), Lois January, Jack Mower, Tom London, Robert Walker, John Elliott. *D:* Elmer Clifton; *P:* Bernard B. Ray, Harry S. Webb; *Sc:* Bennett Cohen, Carl Krusada. (1:00)

A canine western adventure of a dog and a lawman out to capture border smugglers.

4242. Sky Bride (Paramount; 1932). *Cast:* Richard Arlen, Jack Oakie, Virginia Bruce, Randolph Scott, Tom Douglas, Charles Starrett, Robert Coogan, Frances Dee, Louise Closser Hale, Harold Goodwin. *D:* Stephen Roberts (in his feature directorial debut); *St:* Waldemar Young; *Sc:* Joseph L. Mankiewicz, Agnes Brand Leahy, Grover Jones.

B action drama of a daredevil flyer who loses his nerve.

4243. Sky Devils (United Artists/Caddo; 1931-32). *Cast:* Spencer Tracy, William "Stage" Boyd, Ann Dvorak, George Cooper, Billy Bevan, Yola D'Avril, Forrester Harvey, Willard Robertson, Jerry Miley, John Miljan, Paul Fix. *D:* A. Edward Sutherland; *P:* Howard Hughes; *St:* Joseph Moncure March; *Sc:* March, Sutherland, Robert Benchley; *Choreography:* Busby Berkeley. (1:29)

Comedy of two draft dodgers in World War I. The film uses leftover footage from *Hell's Angels* (q.v.).

4244. Sky Giant (RKO; 1938). *Cast:* Richard Dix, Chester Morris, Joan Fontaine, Harry Carey, Paul Guilfoyle, Robert Strange, Max Hoffman, Jr., Vicki Lester, James Bush, Edward Marr, William Corson, Harry Campbell. *D:* Lew Landers; *P:* Robert Sisk; *St & Sc:* Lionel Houser. (1:20)

Drama localed at an army flying school and the conflict between two men over a girl.

4245. The Sky Hawk (Fox; 1929). *Cast:* Helen Chandler, John Garrick, Billy Bevan, Joyce Compton, Gilbert Emery, Percy Challenger, Lumsden Hare, Lennox Pawle, Daphne Pollard. *D:* John G. Blystone; *St:* Llewellyn Hughes.

Romantic drama which placed #8 on the "10 Best" list of the *New York Times.*

4246. The Sky Parade (Paramount; 1936). *Cast:* Jimmie Allen, William Gargan, Katherine de Mille, Kent Taylor, Colin Tapley, Grant Withers, Billy Lee, Georges Renavent, Bennie Bartlett, Syd Saylor, Keith Daniels, Robert Fiske, Edgar Dearing. *D:* Otho Lovering; *P:* Harold Hurley; *St:* Robert M. Burtt, Willfred G. Moore; *Sc:* Byron Morgan, Brian Marlow, Arthur Beckhard.

Some ex-flyers invent an automatic pilot for commercial airplanes in this B drama.

4247. Sky Patrol (Monogram; 1939). *Cast:* John Trent (Tommy), Marjorie Reynolds (Betty Lou), Milburn Stone (Skeeter), Jason Robards (Paul), Jackie Coogan, Boyd Irwin, Bryant Washburn, LeRoy Mason, John Peters, Johnny Day, Dickie Jones. *D:* Howard Bretherton; *P:* Paul Malvern; *Sc:* Joseph West (George Waggner), Norton S. Parker. (1:01)

B aerial adventure about apprehending some gun smugglers in this the 3rd of 4 entries in the "Tailspin Tommy" series. Based on the popular comic strip characters created by Hal Forrest.

Sky Pilot *see* **Mystery Plane**

4248. Sky Racket (Victory; 1937). *Cast:* Herman Brix (Bruce Bennett). *D:* Robert Hill; *P:* Sam Katzman.

Low-budget indie crime actioner.

4249. Sky Raiders (Columbia; 1931). *Cast:* Lloyd Hughes, Marceline Day, Wheeler Oakman, Kit Guard. *D:* Christy Cabanne.

Low-budget action melodrama.

4250. The Sky Spider (Action Pictures; 1931). *Cast:* Glenn Tryon, Blanche Mehaffey, Philo McCullough,

Pat O'Malley, John Trent, Jay Hunt, George Chesebro, Joseph Girard. *D:* Richard Thorpe.

Low-budget indie melodrama.

4251. Skybound (Puritan; 1935). *Cast:* Grant Withers, Lona Andre, Lloyd Hughes, Edward Nugent. *D:* Raymond K. Johnson.

4252. Skyline (Fox; 1931). *Cast:* Thomas Meighan, Hardie Albright, Maureen O'Sullivan, Myrna Loy, Stanley Fields, Dorothy Peterson, Robert McWade, Donald Dillaway, Jack Kennedy, Alice Ward. *D:* Sam Taylor; *St:* Felix Reisenberg; *Sc:* Dudley Nichols, Kenyon Nicholson, William Anthony McGuire.

Drama of the construction industry.

4253. Skyscraper Souls (MGM; 1932). *Cast:* Warren William, Maureen O'Sullivan, Verree Teasdale, Gregory Ratoff, Jean Hersholt, Norman Foster, Anita Page, George Barbier, Wallace Ford, Hedda Hopper, Helen Coburn, John Marston. *D:* Edgar Selwyn; *Sc:* C.G. Sullivan, Elmer Harris. (1:40)

Dramatic study of a ruthless businessman and the various individuals who work for and around him. Based on the novel by Faith Baldwin.

4254. Slander House (Progressive Pictures; 1938). *Cast:* Craig Reynolds, Adrienne Ames, Esther Ralston, George Meeker, Pert Kelton. *D:* Charles Lamont; *Sc:* Gertrude Orr, John W. Krafft.

"Poverty row" comedy.

4255. Slave Ship (20th Century–Fox; 1937). *Cast:* Wallace Beery, Warner Baxter, Elizabeth Allan, Mickey Rooney, George Sanders, Jane Darwell, Joseph Schildkraut, Arthur Hohl, Minna Gombell, Billy Bevan, Francis Ford, Edwin Maxwell, J. Farrell MacDonald, Paul Hurst, Holmes Herbert, J.P. McGowan, Dorothy Christy, DeWitt Jennings (film finale—d. 1937), Miles Mander, Charles Middleton, Arthur Aylesworth, Jane Jones. *D:* Tay Garnett; *P:* Nunnally Johnson; *St:* William Faulkner; *Sc:* Sam Hellman, Lamar Trotti, Gladys Lehman. (1:30)

Hit action drama of mutiny and rebellion aboard a slave ship. Based on the novel by George S. King.

One of the 38 top grossing films of 1936–37.

4256. Sleepers East (Fox; 1933–34). *Cast:* Mona Barrie (film debut), J. Carrol Naish, Wynne Gibson. *D:* Kenneth MacKenna.

Low-budget mystery of murder aboard an east-bound train. Based on the book by Frederick Nebel, it was remade as *Sleepers West* (20th Century–Fox; 1941).

4257. Slide, Kelly, Slide (Xxxx Xxxx; 1935). *Cast:* Marie Wilson.

Filmed before in 1927 by MGM with William Haines.

(No other information available)

4258. A Slight Case of Murder (WB; 1938). *Cast:* Edward G. Robinson, Jane Bryan, Allen Jenkins, Ruth Donnelly, Willard Parker, John Litel, Edward Brophy, Harold Huber, Eric Stanley, Paul Harvey, Bobby Jordan, Joe Downing, Margaret Hamilton, George E. Stone, Bert Hanlon, Jean Benedict, Harry Seymour, Betty Compson, Joe Caits, George Lloyd, John Harmon, Duke York, Pat Daly, Harry Tenbrook. *D:* Lloyd Bacon; *As.P.:* Sam Bischoff; *Sc:* Earl Baldwin, Joseph Schrank. (1:25)

A bootlegger finds that his troubles have just begun when prohibition ends. This comedy was based on an unsuccessful play by Damon Runyon and Howard Lindsay. The *New York Times* placed it at #5 on their "10 Best" list of the year. Remade as *Stop, You're Killing Me* (WB; 1952).

4259. Slightly Honorable (United Artists/Walter Wanger; 1939–40). *Cast:* Pat O'Brien, Edward Arnold, Broderick Crawford, Eve Arden, Claire Dodd, Ruth Terry, Bernard Nedell, Alan Dinehart, Douglass Dumbrille, Ernest Truex, Evelyn Keyes, Phyllis Brooks, Janet Beecher, Addison Richards, Douglas Fowley, Willie Best. *D:* Tay Garnett; *P:* Wanger, Garnett; *Sc:* Ken Englund. (1:25) (video)

Hit comedy-drama of an attorney who is framed for two murders. Based on the novel "Send Another Coffin" by F.G. Presnell.

4260. Slightly Married (Chesterfield; 1932). *Cast:* Robert Ellis, Evalyn Knapp, Walter Byron, Jason Robards, Marie Prevost. *D:* Richard Thorpe.

"Poverty row" romance.

4261. Slightly Scarlet (Paramount; 1930). *Cast:* Evelyn Brent, Clive Brook, Paul Lukas, Eugene Pallette, Helen Ware, Henry Wadsworth, Virginia Bruce, Paul Lukas, Eugene Pallette, Helen Ware, Henry Wadsworth, Virginia Bruce, Claud Allister, Morgan Farley. *D:* Louis J. Gasnier, Edwin H. Knopf; *Sc:* Joseph L. Mankiewicz, Howard Estabrook.

In France, a wealthy American woman falls for a mysterious Englishman while also becoming involved with a jewel thief. A remake of *Blackbirds* (1915).

4262. Slim (WB; 1937). *Cast:* Henry Fonda (Slim), Pat O'Brien, Margaret Lindsay, Stuart Erwin, J. Farrell MacDonald, Jane Wyman, John Litel, Dick Purcell, Craig Reynolds, Joe Sawyer, Max Wagner, Ben Hendricks, Jr., Dick Wessel, Maidel Turner, Carlyle Moore, Jr., Henry Otho, James Robbins, Alonzo Price, Harland Tucker. *D:* Ray Enright; *Supervisor:* Sam Bischoff; *Sc:* William Wister Haines, Delmer Daves (unc.). (1:20)

Romantic adventure of linemen who work on high tension wires. Based on the novel by William Wister Haines.

Slums of New York *see* **Sin's Pay Day**

4263. Small Town Boy (Grand National; 1937). *Cast:* Stuart Erwin, Joyce Compton, Erville Alderson, Dorothy Appleby, Jed Prouty, Clara Blandick, James Blakely, Clarence Wilson, Paul Hurst, Eddie Kane, Victor Potel, George Chandler, Eddy Waller. *D:* Glenn Tryon; *P:* Zion Myers; *Sc:* Tryon. (1:03)

B comedy of what happens when a young man finds a thousand dollar bill. Based on the story "The Thousand Dollar Bill" by Manuel Komroff, which was also the working title of the film prior to release.

4264. Small Town Girl (MGM; 1936). *Cast:* Janet Gaynor, Robert Taylor, James Stewart, Binnie Barnes, Lewis Stone, Frank Craven, Elizabeth Patterson, Andy Devine, Isabel Jewell, Charley Grapewin, Agnes Ayres, Robert Greig, Edgar Kennedy, Douglas Fowley, Paul Hurst, Edward Norris, Willie Fung, Nella Walker. *D:* William A. Wellman; *P:* Hunt Stromberg; *Sc:* John Lee Mahin, Edith Fitzgerald. (Retitled: *One Horse Town*) (1:47)

In this comedy a girl gets a man to agree to marry her when he's drunk and then tries to do the same thing after he sobers up. Based on the novel by Ben Ames Williams.

Small Town Lawyer (G.B. title) *see* **Main Street Lawyer**

4265. Smart Blonde (WB; 1936–37). *Cast:* Glenda Farrell (Torchy Blane), Barton MacLane (Steve McBride), David Carlyle (Robert Paige), Winifred Shaw, Joseph Crehan, Craig Reynolds, Tom Kennedy, Jane Wyman, Frank Faylen, Addison Richards, Max Wagner, Charlotte Wynters, John Sheehan, George Lloyd. *D:* Frank McDonald; *P:* Bryan Foy; *Sc:* Don Ryan, Kenneth Gamet; *Song:* "Why Do I Have to Sing a Torch Song?" by M.K. Jerome, Jack Scholl. (0:59)

Premiere entry in the "Torchy Blane" series of a girl reporter and her tough police inspector buddy. In this one, the duo investigate the murder of a night club owner. Based on the characters created by Frederick Nebel in a series of short stories. The entire series ran for nine films.

4266. Smart Girl (Paramount; 1935). *Cast:* Ida Lupino, Kent Taylor, Gail Patrick, Sidney Blackmer, Charles C. Wilson. *D:* Aubrey H. Scotto; *P:* Walter Wanger.

B melodrama of a man who marries one girl while being loved by her sister, who comes to the rescue when wifie gets hubby in trouble.

4267. Smart Money (WB; 1931). *Cast:* Edward G. Robinson, James Cagney, Evalyn Knapp, Margaret Livingston, Noel Francis, Ralf Harolde, Boris Karloff, Morgan Wallace, Billy House, Paul Porcasi, John Larkin, Polly Walters, Maurice Black, Mae Madison, Walter Percival, Clark Burroughs. *D;* Alfred E. Green; *St:* (A.A.N.) Lucien Hubbard, Joseph Jackson; *Sc:* Jackson, Kubec Glasmon, John Bright, Hubbard. (1:30)

Hit drama of a barber who makes it as a big-time gambler. Notable as the only film ever to star Cagney and Robinson together.

4268. Smart Woman (RKO; 1931). *Cast:* Robert Ames (final film — d. 1931), Mary Astor, Noel Francis, John Halliday, Edward Everett Horton, Ruth Weston, Gladys Gale, Alfred Cross, Lillian Harmer, Charles Wilson, Pearl Varvell, Gordon (Bill) Elliott. *D:* Gregory La Cava; *As.P.:* Bertram Millhauser; *Sc:* Salisbury Field. (1:08)

B marital comedy of a wife's attempts to dissuade the advances of two designing women on her husband. Based on the play "Nancy's Private Affair" by Myron C. Fagan.

4269. The Smartest Girl in Town (RKO; 1936). *Cast:* Gene Raymond, Ann Sothern, Helen Broderick,

Eric Blore, Erik Rhodes, Harry Jans, Frank Jenks, Alan Curtis, Edward Price, Rolfe Sedan, John Shelton (film debut—bit). *D:* Joseph Santley; *P:* Edward Kaufman; *St:* Muriel Scheck, H.S. Kraft; *Sc:* Viola Brothers Shore. (0:58) (video)

B comedy of the romance between a rich playboy and a model with the inevitable comic misunderstandings.

4270. Smarty (WB; 1934). *Cast:* Warren William, Joan Blondell, Edward Everett Horton, Frank McHugh, Claire Dodd, Joan Wheeler, Virginia Sale, Leonard Carey, Bud Flanagan (Dennis O'Keefe). *D:* Robert Florey; *P:* Robert Presnell; *Sc:* F. Hugh Herbert, Carl Erickson. (G.B. title: *Hit Me Again*)

B comedy-drama of a fluctuating marriage. Based on the play by F. Hugh Herbert.

4271. Smashing the Money Ring (WB; 1939). *Cast:* Ronald Reagan (Bancroft), Eddie Foy, Jr., Margot Stevenson, Joe Downing, Charles D. Brown, Elliott Sullivan, Joe King (Saxby), Charles Wilson, John Ridgely, William Davidson, John Hamilton, Sidney Bracy, Jack Wise, Jack Mower, Don Turner. *D:* Terry Morse; *As.P.:* Bryan Foy; *St:* Jonathan Finn; *Sc:* Anthony Coldeway, Raymond L. Schrock. (0:57)

Third entry in the "Brass Bancroft" B series with Brass getting himself committed to prison in order to investigate counterfeiting. Followed in 1940 by *Murder in the Air.*

4272. Smashing the Rackets (RKO; 1938). *Cast:* Chester Morris (Jim Conway), Frances Mercer, Rita Johnson, Bruce Cabot, Edward Pawley, Joseph de Stefani, Donald Douglas, Kay Sutton, Ben Welden, Paul Fix, Edward (Eddie) Acuff, George Irving, George Lloyd, Walter Miller, Frank O'Connor, Theodore von Eltz. *D:* Lew Landers; *P:* B.P. Fineman; *Sc:* Lionel Houser. (1:09)

Inspired by the career of New York D.A. Thomas E. Dewey, this fact based melodrama tells of a crusading assistant D.A. out to clear the city of the gangster element. Suggested by a series of articles by Forrest Davis in *The Saturday Evening Post.*

4273. Smashing the Spy Ring (Columbia; 1938). *Cast:* Ralph Bellamy, Fay Wray, Warren Hull, Ann Doran. *D:* Christy Cabanne.

Title tells all in this B melodrama.

4274. Smilin' Through (MGM; 1932). *Cast:* Norma Shearer (Kathleen), Fredric March (Kenneth Wayne), Leslie Howard (John Carteret), O.P. Heggie (Doctor Owen), Beryl Mercer (Mrs. Crouch), Ralph Forbes (Willie Ainley), Margaret Seddon (Ellen), Forrester Harvey (orderly), Cora Sue Collins (Kathleen as a child), Norman Foster, David Torrence. *D:* Sidney Franklin (who also directed the '22 version); *P:* Irving Thalberg (A.A.N. for Best Picture); *Sc:* Ernest Vajda, Claudine West; *Dialogue:* Donald Ogden Stewart, James Bernard Fagan. (1:37)

A giant box office hit which tells of several people who review their lives following the murder of a bride on her wedding day by a rejected suitor. A remake of the 1922 First National release with Norma Talmadge, Harrison Ford and Wyndham Standing. Remade by MGM in 1941. Based on the stage play by Jane Cowl and Jane Murfin. The recipient of "*Photoplay's* Gold Medal Award," it also placed #5 on the "10 Best" list of *Film Daily.*

4275. Smiling Faces (Xxxx Xxxx; 1932). *Cast:* Dorothy Stone, Fred Stone, Isabel D'Madigan, Doris Patston, Ray Romain, Tom Romain, Adora Andrews, Charles Collins, Rex Coover, Boyd Davis, Ed Garvey, Hope Emerson (film debut & only film until 1948), Carl Duart, Bradford Hatton, Harold Offer, Roy Royston, Barbara Williams, Ali Youssoff, Merriel Abbott Dancers. *D:* Xxxx Xxxx; *St:* Harry Clork.

4276. Smiling Irish Eyes (WB/ F.N.; 1929). *Cast:* Colleen Moore (her first all-talkie), James Hall, Claude Gillingwater, Robert E. Homans, Aggie Herring, Betty Francisco, George Hayes, Edward Earle, Julanne Johnston, Madam Bosocki, Fred Kelsey, Tom O'Brien, Ann Schaefer, Robert Emmett O'Connor. *D:* William A. Seiter; *Sc:* Tom Geraghty; *Songs:* Herman Ruby, Norman Spencer.

Musical of an Irish songwriter who heads for Broadway.

4277. The Smiling Lieutenant (Paramount; 1931). *Cast:* Maurice Chevalier (Lieut. Niki), Claudette Colbert (Franzi), Miriam Hopkins (Princess Anna), Charles Ruggles (Max), George Barbier (King Adolph), Hugh O'Connell (orderly), Elizabeth Patterson (Baroness von Schwedel), Granville Bates (bill collector), Robert Strange (adjutant von Rockoff), Janet Reade (Lily), Con MacSunday (emperor), Harry C. Bradley (Count von Halden), Werner Saxtorph (Joseph), Karl Stall (master of ceremonies). *D:* Ernest Lubitsch; *P:* (A.A.N. for Best Picture) Lubitsch; *Sc:* Lubitsch, Ernest Vajda, Samson Raphaelson; *Songs:* "One More Hour of Love," "Breakfast Table Love," "Toujours L'Amour in the Army," "While Hearts Are Singing," & "Jazz Up Your Lingerie" by Oscar Straus & Clifford Grey. (1:42)

Romantic musical-comedy which was based on the novel "Nux Der Prinzgemahl" by Hans Muller and the operetta "A Waltz Dream" by Leopold Jacobson and Felix Doermann. Filmed at Astoria Studios in Long Island, N.Y., the film placed #3 on the *New York Times* "10 Best" list of the year.

4278. The Smiling Vagabond (Xxxx Xxxx; 1935). *Cast:* Charles King. (No other information available)

4279. Smoke Lightning (Fox; 1933). *Cast:* George O'Brien, Nell O'Day, Betsy King Ross, Frank Atkin-

son, Virginia Sale, Douglass Dumbrille, Morgan Wallace, Clarence Wilson, Fred Wilson, George Burton. *D:* David Howard; *Sc:* Gordon Rigby, Sidney Mitchell. (1:03)

George O'Brien western of a cowboy protecting a little girl from her greedy uncle. Based on the novel "Canyon Walls" by Zane Grey.

4280. Smoke Tree Range (Universal; 1937). *Cast:* Buck Jones, Muriel Evans, John Elliott, Edmund Cobb, Robert Kortman, Donald Kirke, Ted Adams, Ben Hall, Dickie Jones, Charles King, Earle Hodgins, Lee Phelps, Mabel Colcord, Eddie Phillips, Bob McKenzie, Slim Whitaker. *D:* Lesley Selander; *P:* Jones; *Sc:* Arthur Henry Gordon. (0:59)

Buck Jones oater of a cowboy protecting a girl's ranch from rustlers.

4281. Smokey Smith (Supreme; 1935). *Cast:* Bob Steele, Mary Kornman, George Hayes, Warner Richmond, Earl Dwire, Tex Phelps, Archie Ricks, Horace B. Carpenter. *D:* Robert N. Bradbury; *P:* A.W. Hackel; *Sc:* Bradbury. (0:58)

Bob Steele western of a man out to avenge the murder of his parents.

4282. Smoking Guns (Universal; 1933–34). *Cast:* Ken Maynard, Gloria O'Shea, Jack Rockwell, Walter Miller, William Gould, Harold Goodwin, Robert Kortman, Edward Coxen, Etta McDaniel, Edgar "Blue" Washington, Slim Whitaker, Bob Reeves, Jim Corey, Wally Wales (Hal Taliaferro), Fred Mackaye, Martin Turner, Edmund Cobb, Hank Bell, Horace B. Carpenter, Blackjack Ward, Roy Bucko, Buck Bucko, Bud McClure, Ben Corbett, Cliff Lyons. *D:* Alan James (aka: Alvin J. Neitz); *Sc:* Maynard. (1:02)

Ken Maynard (in his final film for this studio) western with an offbeat story of assumed identity.

4283. Smoky (Fox; 1933). *Cast:* Victor Jory, Irene Manning, LeRoy

Mason, Hank Mann, Frank Campeau, Leonid Snegoff, Will James. *D:* Eugene Forde; *P:* Sol M. Wurtzel; *Sc:* Stuart Anthony, Paul Perez. (1:09)

A cowboy tames a wild stallion in this B western based on the novel by Will James. Remade in 1946 and again in 1966.

4284. Smoky Trails (Metropolitan; 1939). *Cast:* Bob Steele, Jean Carmen, Murdock MacQuarrie, Jimmy Aubrey, Ted Adams, Frank LaRue, George Chesebro, Frank Wayne, Bob Terry, Bruce Dane, Carleton Young. *D:* Bernard B. Ray; *P:* Harry S. Webb; *Sc:* George Plympton. (0:55)

Bob Steele western of a cowboy after an outlaw gang.

4285. Smooth Guy (Xxxx Xxxx; 1933). *Cast:* Evalyn Knapp.

(No other information available)

4286. Smuggled Cargo (Republic; 1939). *Cast:* Barry Mackay, Rochelle Hudson, Ralph Morgan. *D:* John H. Auer (who also co-produced).

B drama of California orange growers.

4287. Snow White and the Seven Dwarfs (RKO/Walt Disney; 1937). *Character Voices:* Adriana Caselotti (Snow White), Harry Stockwell (prince), Lucille La Verne (queen), Moroni Olsen (magic mirror), Roy Atwell (Doc), Pinto Colvig (Grumpy & Sleepy), Otis Harlan (Happy), Billy Gilbert (Sneezy), Scotty Mattraw (Bashful). *Supervising Director:* David Hand; *P:* Walt Disney; *Sequence Directors:* Perce Pearce, Larry Morey, William Cottrell, Wilfred Jackson, Ben Sharpsteen; *Writers:* Dorothy Ann Blank, Richard Creedon, Merrill de Maris, Otto Englander, Earl Hurd, Dick Richard, Ted Sears, Webb Smith; *Musical Score:* (A.A.N. – 1937) Frank Churchill, Leigh Harline, Paul J. Smith; *Songs:* "Heigh Ho," "Just Whistle While You Work," "Some Day My Prince Will Come," "Snow White," "I'm Wishing," "With a Smile and a Song," "One Song," "The Washing Song," "Isn't This a Silly Song?" "Buddle-Uddle-Um-Dum," "Music in Your Soup" & "You're Never Too Old to Be Young" by Larry Morey & Frank Churchill. (1:22)

Another genuine Hollywood classic is this the first all color animated feature film to be produced by the Walt Disney Studios, premiering December 21, 1937, at the Carthay Circle Theater in Los Angeles. Time seems to have no effect on this film which was proven by the fact of a re-release in its 50th year of 1987, reaping another box office bonanza. The production took the combined efforts of 750 people (including 570 artists) and three years to complete. *Film Daily* and the *New York Times* both voted it "Best Film of the Year" in 1938, while the National Board of Review placed it at #2 on their "10 Best" list of the same year. Also in 1938 it received the "International Art Festival Prize" at the Venice Film Festival, a "Special Award" from the New York Film Critics, while the Motion Picture Academy of Arts and Sciences awarded the film and Disney studios eight Oscars (1 large – 7 miniature) for the "new innovation in screen entertainment." One of the 15 top grossing films of 1937–38. A silent production *Snow White* (Paramount-Artclass; 1916), one of the first productions of that studio with Marguerite Clark was admitted by Walt Disney to be the model for this animated production. Based on the Brothers Grimm fairy tale "Little Snow White," adapted to the stage in 1912 by Winthrop Ames and also starring Miss Clark.

Note 1: Marge Belcher (later Marge Champion) was the real-life model for the animated "Snow White."

Note 2: *Snow White and the Seven Dwarfs* is often erroneously referred to as the first animated feature film, which it was not, this honor going to *The Sinking of the Lusitania* (1918) by Winsor McCay cartoonist for the *New York Herald* whose

1909 creation "Gertie the Dinosaur" became the first animated film in the United States to be exhibited theatrically.

4288. Snowed Under (WB/F.N.; 1936). *Cast:* George Brent, Genevieve Tobin, Glenda Farrell, Patricia Ellis, Porter Hall, Frank McHugh, Helen Lowell, John Eldredge. *D:* Ray Enright; *P:* Harry Joe Brown; *St:* Lawrence Saunders; *Sc:* F. Hugh Herbert, Brown Holmes, Edward Chodorov (unc.).

A playwright seeking peace and solitude in the country, finds everything but in this comedy as two ex-wives and a potential new wife descend on him.

4289. So Big (WB; 1932). *Cast:* Barbara Stanwyck (Selina Peake), Dickie Moore, Guy Kibbee, Bette Davis, Mae Madison, George Brent, Hardie Albright, Robert Warwick, Dawn O'Day (Anne Shirley), Alan Hale, Elizabeth Patterson, Willard Robertson, Rita LaRoy, Arthur Stone, Dick Winslow, Blanche Frederici, Dorothy Peterson, Eulalie Jensen, Earle Foxe, Harry Holman, Harry Beresford. *D:* William Wellman; *P:* Lucien Hubbard; *Sc:* J. Grubb Alexander, Robert Lord. (1:22)

An acclaimed rural drama of a school teacher who must raise her son following the death of her husband. Based on the best selling Pulitzer Prize winning novel by Edna Ferber. A remake of the 1925 First National production with Colleen Moore and Joseph DeGrasse. Remade in 1953 with Jane Wyman.

4290. So Long, Letty (WB; 1929). *Cast:* Charlotte Greenwood (recreating her stage role as the ousted wife), Bert Roach (husband), Patsy Ruth Miller (replacement wife), Claude Gillingwater (uncle), Grant Withers, Marion Byron, Hallam Cooley, Helen Foster, Harry Gribbon. *D:* Lloyd Bacon; *Sc:* Robert Lord, Arthur Caesar; *Songs:* "One Sweet Little Yes," "Clown-ing," "Beauty Shop," "Am I Blue?" "Let Me Have My Dreams," "My Strongest Weakness Is You," title song by Earl Carroll and "Down Among the Sugar Cane" by Charles Tobias & Grant Clarke.

Musical-comedy of a man with an eccentric wife who learns his rich uncle is coming to town and gets a more conventional woman to pose as his wife in order to impress the uncle. A remake of the 1920 independent production with Colleen Moore and T. Roy Barnes by director Al Christie. Based on the play by Elmer Harris.

4291. So Red the Rose (Paramount; 1935). *Cast:* Margaret Sullavan (Valette Bedford), Walter Connolly, Randolph Scott, Elizabeth Patterson, Janet Beecher, Robert Cummings, Dickie Moore, Johnny Downs, George Reed, Charles Starrett, Daniel Haynes, Clarence Muse, Warner Richmond, Arthur Stone, Alfred Delcambre, Harry Ellerbee. *D:* King Vidor; *P:* Douglas MacLean; *Sc:* Maxwell Anderson, Edwin Justus Mayer, Laurence Stallings, Virginia Van Upp (unc.), Frank Partos (unc.). (1:22)

Domestic drama set at the time of the American Civil War. Based on the novel by Stark Young, the film was a box office flop.

4292. So This Is Africa! (Columbia; 1933). *Cast:* Bert Wheeler, Robert Woolsey, Raquel Torres, Esther Muir, Berton Churchill, Henry Armetta. *D:* Edward Cline; *St:* Norman Krasna; *Adaptation:* Krasna.

Wheeler and Woolsey comedy of two goofs on safari. This was the team's first and only assignment away from their home studio of RKO.

4293. So This Is College (MGM; 1929). *Cast:* Sally Starr, Elliott Nugent, Robert Montgomery (starring debut), Cliff Edwards, Polly Moran, Joel McCrea (talkie debut), Ann Brody, Phyllis Crane, Lee Shumway, Oscar Rudolph, Dorothy Dehn, Max Davidson. *D:* Sam Wood; *Sc:* Delmer Daves, Al Boasberg, Joe Farnham.

Romantic college comedy with songs.

4294. So This Is London (Fox; 1930). *Cast:* Will Rogers, Irene Rich, Maureen O'Sullivan, Frank Albertson, Bramwell Fletcher, Mary Forbes, Dorothy Christy (film debut), Lumsden Hare, Martha Lee Sparks, Ellen Woodston. *D:* John G. Blystone; *St:* Arthur Goodrich; *Sc:* Sonya Levien.

Hit comedy set aboard a ship bound for England.

4295. So This Is Mexico? (Xxxx Xxxx; 1930). *Cast:* Rex Lease.

(No other information available)

4296. Soak the Rich (Paramount; 1935–36). *Cast:* Walter Connolly, Mary Taylor, John Howard, Alice Duer Miller, Ilka Chase, Lionel Stander, Percy Kilbride, Francis Compton, Joseph Sweeney, John W. Call, Abner Biberman (film debut), Eddie Phillips, George Watts, Isabelle Foster, Allan Ross MacDougall, Robert Wallsten, Ed Garvey, Con MacSunday. *D:* Ben Hecht, Charles MacArthur; *P:* Hecht & MacArthur; *Sc:* Hecht & MacArthur. (1:27)

Comedy-drama of the daughter of a wealthy businessman who is kidnapped while at college, only to fall for her kidnapper. Based on the play by Ben Hecht and Charles MacArthur.

4297. Sob Sister (Fox; 1931). *Cast:* James Dunn, Molly O'Day, Minna Gombell, Linda Watkins (film debut), George E. Stone, Charles Middleton, Harold Waldridge, Maurice Black, Wally Albright, Edward Dillon, Lex Lindsay, Harry Beresford, Neal Burns, Ernest Wood, Sarah Padden, Clifford Dempsey, George Byron, Howard Phillips. *D:* Alfred Santell; *St:* Mildred Gilman. (G.B. title: *The Blonde Reporter*)

Newspaper comedy-drama.

4298. Social Error (Ajax; 1935). *Cast:* Roger Williams, Gertrude Messinger. *P:* William Berke.

(No other information available)

4299. The Social Lion (Paramount; 1930). *Cast:* Jack Oakie, Mary Brian, Olive Borden, Richard "Skeets" Gallagher, E.H. Calvert, Charles Sellon, Jack Byron, Cyril Ring, James Gibson, Henry Rocquemore, William Bechtel. *D:* A. Edward Sutherland; *St:* Octavius Roy Cohen; *Sc:* Agnes Brand Leahy; *Adapt./Dial.:* Joseph L. Mankiewicz.

B romantic comedy of a prizefighter involved with a society girl who tries to change him.

4300. Social Register (Columbia; 1934–35). *Cast:* Colleen Moore, Pauline Frederick, Ross Alexander, Charles Winninger, Margaret Livingston (film finale—ret.), Robert Allen, Robert Benchley. *D:* Marshall Neilan; *Play:* Anita Loos, John Emerson; *Sc:* James Ashmore Creelman, Grace Perkins, Clara Beranger.

B romantic drama.

Society Doctor *see* **Only Eight Hours**

4301. Society Fever (Chesterfield; 1935). *Cast:* Sheila Terry, Grant Withers, Lois Wilson, Guinn Williams, Lois January, Reginald Sheffield, Lloyd Hughes, Hedda Hopper. *D:* Frank Strayer.

"Poverty row" comedy.

4302. Society Girl (Fox; 1932). *Cast:* Spencer Tracy, Peggy Shannon, James Dunn, Marjorie Gateson, Walter Byron, Bert Hanlon, Eula Guy Todd. *D:* Sidney Lanfield; *St:* John Larkin, Jr.; *Adapt.:* Charles Beahan; *Dial.:* Elmer Harris.

Low-budget romantic comedy.

4303. Society Lawyer (MGM; 1939). *Cast:* Walter Pidgeon, Virginia Bruce, Leo Carrillo, Eduardo Ciannelli, Frances Mercer, Paul Guilfoyle, Lee

Bowman, Ann Morriss, Joseph Crehan, Herbert Mundin (final film — killed in a 1939 auto crash), Edward Brophy, Ian Wolfe, Clarence Kolb, Pierre Watkin, Frances Mercer. *D:* Edwin L. Marin; *P:* John W. Considine, Jr.; *St:* Arthur Somers Roche; *Sc:* Hugo Butler, Leon Gordon.

Comedy drama of a lawyer who goes after a big-time racketeer. A B remake of *Penthouse* (q.v.).

4304. Society Smugglers (Universal; 1938). *Cast:* Irene Hervey, Preston Foster, Milburn Stone, Frank Reicher, Fred Keating, Frances Robinson, Jack Norton. *D:* Joe May; *P:* Kenneth Goldsmith. (1:10)

B crime melodrama of a gang of diamond smugglers.

4305. The Soldier and the Lady (RKO; 1937). *Cast:* Anton Walbrook (American debut as Michael Strogoff), Elizabeth Allan, Akim Tamiroff, Margot Grahame, Fay Bainter, Eric Blore, Edward Brophy, Paul Guilfoyle, William Stack, Paul Harvey, Michael Visaroff, Oscar Apfel, Margaret Armstrong. *D:* George Nicholls, Jr.; *P:* Pandro S. Berman; *Sc:* Anthony Veiller, Mortimer Offner, Anne Morrison Chapin. (G.B. title: *Michael Strogoff*) (1:25)

Costume drama of Alexander II's 19th-century czarist Russia at the time of the Tartar invasion. Based on the book "Michael Strogoff" by Jules Verne, it was filmed previously in the U.S. as *Michael Strogoff* (Lubin; 1914) with Jacob Adler. Many other versions of the story have been filmed abroad. The exterior shots were borrowed from a 1936 German-French co-production by producer Joseph Ermolieff titled *Courier to the Tsar*.

A Soldier's Pay (G.B. title) *see* **A Soldier's Plaything**

4306. A Soldier's Plaything (WB; 1930–31). *Cast:* Harry Langdon, Ben Lyon, Lotti Loder, Fred Kohler,

Noah Beery, Jean Hersholt, Lee Moran, Otto Matiesen, Cameron Prud'Homme, Frank Campeau, Marie Astaire. *D:* Michael Curtiz; *St:* Vina Delmar; *Sc:* Perry Vekroff, Arthur Caesar. (G.B. title: *A Soldier's Pay*)

Comedy-drama of two American doughboys in France following World War I.

4307. Soldiers and Women (Columbia; 1930). *Cast:* Grant Withers, Aileen Pringle, Emmett Corrigan, Walter McGrail, Sam Nelson, Blanche Frederici, William Colvin, Helen Johnson (later Judith Wood), Raymond Largay, Wade Boteler. *D:* Edward Sloman.

"Poverty row" production.

4308. Soldiers of the Storm (Columbia; 1933). *Cast:* Robert Ellis, Anita Page, Henry Wadsworth, Wheeler Oakman, Barbara Weeks, Regis Toomey, Barbara Barondess, George Cooper, Arthur Wanzer, Dewey Robinson. *D:* D. Ross Lederman; *St:* Thomas Burtis.

Low-budget drama.

4309. The Solitaire Man (MGM; 1933). *Cast:* Herbert Marshall, Elizabeth Allan, Mary Boland, Lionel Atwill, May Robson, Ralph Forbes, Lucile Gleason, Robert McWade. *D:* Jack Conway; *Sc:* James Kevin McGuinness. (1:08)

B production comedy of a number of crooks and their double-crossing antics aboard a flight from Paris to London. Based on the play by Bella and Sam Spewack.

4310. Some Blondes Are Dangerous (Universal; 1937). *Cast:* Noah Beery, Jr., Nan Grey, Dorothea Kent, William Gargan, Roland Drew, Edwin Stanley, Polly Rowles, Lew Kelly, John Butler, Walter Friedman, Eddie Roberts, Joe Smallwood. *D:* Milton Carruth; *P:* E.M. Asher; *St:* W.R. Burnett; *Sc:* Lester Cole. (1:05)

B boxing drama, a remake of *The Iron Man* (q.v.). Based on the novel "The Iron Man" by W.R. Burnett, it was remade under that title in 1951.

4311. Some Like It Hot (Paramount; 1939). *Cast:* Bob Hope, Shirley Ross, Una Merkel, Gene Krupa, Richard Denning, Frank Sully, Byron Foulger, Clarence Wilson, Jack Smart, Bernadene Hayes, Dudley Dickerson, Pat West, Eddie Kane, Lillian Fitzgerald, Rufe Davis, Harry Barris, Sam Ash, Wayne "Tiny" Whitt, Harry Bailey, Jack Chapin. *D:* George Archainbaud; *P:* William Thomas; *Sc:* Lewis R. Foster; *Play by:* Ben Hecht, Gene Fowler. (1:05)

B romantic comedy of a sideshow owner's attempts to get funding when his money runs out. Based on the play "The Great McGoo," the film is a remake of *Shoot the Works* (q.v.).

4312. Something to Sing About (Grand National; 1937). *Cast:* James Cagney (in one of two films for this studio after walking out on his contract with the brothers Warner), Evelyn Daw, William Frawley, Mona Barrie, Gene Lockhart, James Newill (film debut), Harry Barris, Cully Richards, "Candy" Candido, William Davidson, Richard Tucker, Marek Windheim, Johnny Arthur, Dwight Frye, Philip Ahn. *D:* Victor Schertzinger; *P:* Zion Myers; *St:* Schertzinger; *Sc:* Austin Parker; *Music & Lyrics:* (A.A.N.) Schertzinger & music department head, Constantin Bakaleinikoff. (1:33) (video—b/w & computer-colored)

Musical-drama of a bandleader who heads for Hollywood. A box office flop on original release, it was edited down to (1:22) and re-released in 1947 by Screencraft Pictures as *The Battling Hoofer*.

4313. Somewhere in Sonora (WB; 1933). *Cast:* John Wayne, Henry B. Walthall, Shirley Palmer, Paul Fix, Ann Fay, Billy Franey, Ralph Lewis, Frank Rice, J.P. McGowan, Charles

"Slim" Whitaker. *D:* Mack V. Wright; *St:* Will L. Comfort; *Sc:* Joe Roach. (0:57)

John Wayne western of a cowboy giving aid to a man in search of his son who was taken by outlaws. A remake of the 1927 First National production with Ken Maynard.

4314. A Son Comes Home (Paramount; 1936). *Cast:* Donald Woods, Mary Boland, Wallace Ford, Julie Haydon, Charles Middleton, Gertrude W. Hoffman, Ann Evers, Roger Imhof, Thomas Jackson, Lee Kohlmar, Herbert Rawlinson, Eleanor Wesselhoeft, Anthony Nace, Robert Middlemass. *D:* E.A. Dupont; *P:* Albert Lewis; *St:* Harry Hervey; *Sc:* Sylvia Thalberg.

B dilemma drama of a woman's adopted son who is accused of a murder that was committed by her biological son.

4315. The Son-Daughter (MGM; 1932). *Cast:* Ramon Novarro, Helen Hayes, Lewis Stone, Warner Oland, Ralph Morgan, H.B. Warner, Louise Closser Hale. *D:* Clarence Brown; *Sc:* Claudine West, Leon Gordon, John Goodrich. (1:19)

Based on an old play by David Belasco and George M. Scarborough, this romantic drama is set amidst warring tong factions in San Francisco's Chinatown. A box office bomb.

4316. Son of a Sailor (WB/F.N.; 1933). *Cast:* Joe E. Brown (Handsome Callahan), Thelma Todd, Jean Muir, Frank McHugh, John Mack Brown, Sheila Terry, Samuel S. Hinds, Merna Kennedy, Joseph (Sawyer) Sauers, Kenneth Thomson, Arthur Vinton, Clay Clement, Purnell Pratt, Garry Owen, John Marston, George Blackwood. *D:* Lloyd Bacon; *P:* James Seymour; *Sc:* Al Cohn, Paul Gerard Smith, Ernest Pagano, H.M. Walker. (1:13)

Hit Joe E. Brown comedy involving military espionage and purloined secret plans.

4317. The Son of Frankenstein (Universal; 1939). *Cast:* Basil Rathbone, Boris Karloff, Bela Lugosi, Lionel Atwill, Josephine Hutchinson, Donnie Dunagan, Emma Dunn, Edgar Norton, Lionel Belmore, Gustav von Seyffertitz, Ward Bond, Dwight Frye, Lawrence Grant. *D:* Rowland V. Lee; *P:* Lee; *Sc:* Willis Cooper. (1:39) (video)

This follow-up to *The Bride of Frankenstein* (q.v.) has Victor Frankenstein's son (Rathbone) returning in an effort to vindicate the family name. A lavishly produced hit horror film of its day that saw Karloff giving his final performance as the monster. Followed in 1942 by *The Ghost of Frankenstein*.

4318. Son of India (MGM; 1931). *Cast:* Ramon Novarro (Karim), Conrad Nagel (William Darsay), Marjorie Rambeau (Mrs. Darsay), Madge Evans (Janice), C. Aubrey Smith (Dr. Wallace), Mitchell Lewis (Hamid), John Miljan (Juggat), Nigel de Brulier (Rao Rama). *D:* Jacques Feyder; *Sc:* Ernest Vajda; *Additional Dialogue:* Claudine West, John Meehan. (1:11)

An exotic romantic adventure as the son of the local Rajah falls for an American girl. The rage for "latin lover types" never carried over from the silent era into the sound era and this flopped at the box office as did most of Novarro's talkies. Based on the book "Mr. Isaacs" by F. Marion Crawford.

4319. The Son of Kong (RKO; 1933). *Cast:* Robert Armstrong (Carl Denham), Helen Mack (Hilda Peterson), Victor Wong (Charlie the cook), Frank Reicher (Capt. Englehorn), John Marston (Helstrom), Lee Kohlmar (Mickey), Edwin J. (Ed) Brady (Red), Clarence Wilson (Peterson), Kathrin Clare Ward (Mrs. Hudson), Gertrude Short (girl reporter), Gertrude Sutton (servant girl), James Leong (Chinese trader), Noble Johnson (native chief), Steve Clemente (witch king), Frank O'Connor (process server). *D:* Ernest B.

Schoedsack; *As.P.:* Archie Marshek; *Sc:* Ruth Rose. (1:10) (video)

This sequel to RKO's box office bonanza of the Year, *King Kong* (q.v.) was a rush-job production to capitalize on the big ape's popularity and has Carl Denham fleeing his creditors and the law, returning to Skull Island in search of hidden treasure. Upon arriving, Denham and his party soon discover the albino son of the "Eighth Wonder of the World." One of the 15 top grossing films of 1934. Willis O'Brien's special effects are played more for comedy than for serious adventure.

4320. Son of Oklahoma (Sono Art-World Wide/KBS Prods.; 1932). *Cast:* Bob Steele, Josie Sedgwick, Julian Rivero, Carmen LaRoux, Earl Dwire, Robert E. Homans, Henry Rocquemore. *D:* Robert N. Bradbury; *P:* Trem Carr; *Sc:* Burl Tuttle. (0:57)

Bob Steele western of a man brought up by outlaws who attempts to find his parents.

Son of Russia *see* **The Guardsman**

4321. Son of the Border (RKO; 1933). *Cast:* Tom Keene, Edgar Kennedy, Julie Haydon, David Durand, Creighton (Lon) Chaney, (Jr.), Al Bridge, Charles King, Claudia Coleman. *D:* Lloyd Nosler; *As.P.:* David Lewis; *St:* Wellyn Totman; *Sc:* Totman. (0:55)

Tom Keene western of a lawman who accidentally kills his friend in the line of duty and proceeds to adopt the man's younger brother.

4322. Son of the Gods (WB; 1930). *Cast:* Richard Barthelmess, Constance Bennett, Dorothy Mathews, Dickie Moore, Barbara Leonard, Jimmy Eagles, Frank Albertson, Geneva Mitchell, Claude King, E. Alyn Warren, Anders Randolf, Ivan Christie, King Hoo Chang. *D:* Frank Lloyd; *P:* Lloyd; *Sc:* Bradley King; *Song:* "Pretty

Like You" by Ben Ryan & Sol Vidinsky. (1:22)

Believing he has oriental blood, a young man heads for Europe to attend college and escape prejudice. The film which has 2-color technicolor sequences was based on a novel by Rex Beach.

4323. A Son of the Plains (Syndicate; 1931). *Cast:* Bob Custer, Doris Phillips, J.P. McGowan, Edward Hearn, Gordon DeMain, Al St. John. *D:* Robert N. Bradbury; *Sc:* Bradbury. (0:59)

Bob Custer western of a lawman's dilemma when torn between a girl and his duty.

4324. The Song and Dance Man (20th Century–Fox; 1936). *Cast:* Paul Kelly, Claire Trevor, Michael Whalen, Ruth Donnelly, James Burke, Margaret Dumont, Lester Matthews, Irene Franklin, Billy Bevan, Lynn Bari, Ralf Harolde, Gloria Roy, Helen Troy. *D:* Allan Dwan; *P:* Sol M. Wurtzel; *Sc:* Maude Fulton. (1:12)

B drama of a down-and-out vaudevillian. Based on the play by George M. Cohan and filmed previously 1925–26 by Paramount with Tom Moore.

4325. Song o' My Heart (Fox; 1930). *Cast:* John McCormack, Alice Joyce, John Garrick, J.M. Kerrigan, Maureen O'Sullivan (film debut), J. Farrell MacDonald, Andres de Segurola, Effie Ellsler, Edward Martindel, Tommy Clifford, Edwin Schneider. *D:* Frank Borzage; *St:* Tom Barry; *Sc:* Sonya Levien.

A film to showcase the talents of famed baritone John McCormack.

4326. A Song of Kentucky (Fox; 1929). *Cast:* Lois Moran, Joseph Wagstaff, Dorothy Burgess, Herman Bing. *D:* Lewis Seiler.

Romantic drama.

4327. Song of Love (Columbia; 1929). *Cast:* Belle Baker, Ralph Graves, David Durand, Eunice Quedens (Eve Arden—film debut), Arthur Housman. *D:* Erle C. Kenton; *P:* Edward Small; *Sc:* Henry McCarty, Dorothy Howell, Howard Green; *Song:* "I'm Somebody's Baby Now."

Early "poverty row" musical.

4328. The Song of Songs (Paramount; 1933). *Cast:* Marlene Dietrich, Brian Aherne (American debut), Lionel Atwill, Alison Skipworth, Hardie Albright, Helen Freeman. *D:* Rouben Mamoulian; *P:* Mamoulian; *Sc:* Samuel Hoffenstein, Leo Birinski. (1:29)

Drama of a girl who instead of marrying the honest man she loves and loves her, goes to the altar with a wealthy no-good-nik. Set in 19th-century Germany, this film was based on the novel "Das hohe Lied" by Herman Sudermann and the play adapted from it by Edward (E. Lloyd) Sheldon. First filmed as *The Song of Songs* (Paramount; 1918), with Elsie Ferguson and Crauford Kent with *Lily of the Valley* (Paramount; 1924) with Pola Negri and Ben Lyon being its remake.

4329. Song of the Buckaroo (Monogram; 1938–39). *Cast:* Tex Ritter, Jinx Falkenburg, Mary Ruth, Frank LaRue, Tom London, Snub Pollard (Pee Wee), Horace Murphy (Ananias), Dave O'Brien, Dorothy Fay (later Mrs. Tex Ritter), George Chesebro, Ernie Adams, Bob Terry, Charles King, White Flash the horse. *D:* Al Herman; *P:* Edward Finney (for Boots & Saddles Prods.); *St & Sc:* John Rathmell. (0:58)

Tex Ritter western with songs of an outlaw who assumes the identity of a dead man and becomes elected mayor of a western town. Prior to release the film was known as "Little Tenderfoot."

4330. Song of the Caballero (Universal; 1930). *Cast:* Ken Maynard, Doris Hill, Francis Ford, Gino Corrado, Evelyn Sherman, Frank Rice, Josef Swickard, William Irving, Joyzelle Joyner. *D:* Harry Joe Brown; *P:* Maynard; *Sc:* Bennett Cohen, Lesley Mason. (1:10)

Ken Maynard western set in Mexico of a man out to get the goods on his rich uncle.

4331. Song of the City (MGM; 1937). *Cast:* Margaret Lindsay, Jeffrey Dean (Dean Jagger), Marla Shelton, Nat Pendleton, J. Carrol Naish, Stanley Morner (Dennis Morgan), Charles Judels, Edward Norris, Eugene Pallette. *D:* Errol Taggart; *P:* Lucien Hubbard, Michael Fessier; *Sc:* Fessier.

B melodrama set along the waterfront of San Francisco with a shipboard fire as its climax.

Song of the Damned *see* **Escape from Devil's Island**

4332. Song of the Eagle (Paramount; 1933). *Cast:* Richard Arlen, Charles Bickford, Mary Brian, Louise Dresser, Jean Hersholt, Andy Devine, George E. Stone, Julie Haydon, Harry Walker, George Hoffman, Gene Morgan, Bert Sprotte. *D:* Ralph Murphy; *P:* Charles R. Rogers; *St:* Gene Towne, Graham Baker; *Adaptation:* Casey Robinson, Willard Mack; *St:* Towne, Baker. (G.B. title: *The Beer Baron*)

B melodrama set at the end of prohibition as bootleggers try to get into the legal production of alcoholic beverages.

4333. Song of the Flame (WB/F.N.; 1930). *Cast:* Alexander Gray, Bernice Claire, Noah Beery, Alice Gentle, Ivan Linow, Bert Roach, Shep Camp, Janina Smolinska. *D:* Alan Crosland; *Adaptation:* Gordon Rigby; *Sound Recording:* (A.A.N.) George Groves; *Songs:* "Cossack Love Song," "One Little Drink," title song, "Petrograd," "Liberty Song," "The Goose Hangs High," "Passing Fancy" & "When Love Calls" by George Gershwin, Herbert Stothart, Harry Akst, Grant Clarke, Edward Ward.

A lavishly produced 2-color technicolor operetta of the Russian Revolution. Based on the play and music of Oscar Hammerstein II, Otto Harbach, George Gershwin and Herbert Stothart.

4334. Song of the Gringo (Grand National; 1936). *Cast:* Tex Ritter, Joan Woodbury, Monte Blue, Fuzzy Knight, Richard (Ted) Adams, Warner Richmond, Al Jennings, Martin Garralaga, William Desmond, Glenn Strange, Budd Buster, Ethan Laidlaw, Murdock MacQuarrie, Charles "Slim" Whitaker, Ed Cassidy, Earl Dwire, Jack Kirk, Bob Burns, Forrest Taylor, Robert Fiske, Rosa Rey, Jose Pacheco & His Continental Orchestra, White Flash the horse. *D:* John P. McCarthy; *P:* Edward Finney (for Boots & Saddles Prods.); *St:* McCarthy, Robert Emmett (Tansey); *Sc:* McCarthy, Emmett, Al Jennings. (G.B. title: *The Old Corral*) (1:02) (video)

Tex Ritter in his film debut of a deputy sheriff who goes after claim jumpers.

4335. Song of the Saddle (WB/F.N.; 1936). *Cast:* Dick Foran, Alma Lloyd, Charles Middleton, Addison Richards, Jim Farley, Monte Montague, Myrtle Stedman, Victor Potel, Bud Osborne, Kenneth Harlan, William Desmond, Bonita Granville, Julian Rivero, Eddie Shubert, George Ernest, Pat West. *D:* Louis King; *P:* Bryan Foy; *St & Sc:* William Jacobs; *Songs:* "Underneath a Western Sky" & "Vengeance" by M.K. Jerome, Jack Scholl & Ted Fio Rito. (0:58)

Dick Foran series western of a singing cowboy searching for those responsible for killing his father.

4336. Song of the Trail (Ambassador; 1936). *Cast:* Kermit Maynard, Evelyn Brent, Fuzzy Knight, George Hayes, Antoinette Lees (Andrea Leeds), Wheeler Oakman, Lee Shumway, Roger Williams, Ray Gallagher, Charles McMurphy, Bob McKenzie, Lynette London, Horace Murphy, Frank McCarroll, Artie Ortego. *D:* Russell Hopton; *P:* Maurice Conn; *Sc:* George Sayre, Barry Barringer. (1:05) (video)

Kermit Maynard western of a

rodeo performer's efforts to thwart the theft of his girl's father's mine.

4337. Song of the West (WB; 1930). *Cast:* John Boles, Vivienne Segal (film debut), Joe E. Brown, Edward Martindel, Eddie Gribbon, Marie Wells, Sam Hardy, Marion Byron. *D:* Ray Enright; *Sc:* Harvey Thew; *Songs include:* "The Bride Was Dressed in White," & "Hay Straw" by Oscar Hammerstein II & Vincent Youmans; "Come Back to Me" by Grant Clarke & Harry Akst.

Two color technicolor romantic western operetta which was based on the play "Rainbow" by Oscar Hammerstein II and Laurence Stallings.

4338. Songs and Bullets (Spectrum; 1938). *Cast:* Fred Scott, Al St. John, Alice Ardell, Karl Hackett, Charles King, Frank LaRue, Richard Cramer, Carl Mathews, Budd Buster, Jimmy Aubrey, Lew Porter, Sherry Tansey. *D:* Sam Newfield; *P:* Stan Laurel Productions, Jed Buell; *Sc:* Joseph O'Donnell, George Plympton; *Songs:* Don & June Swander. (0:58)

A Fred Scott singing western of a lawman and his partner out to clean up a lawless town.

4339. Songs and Saddles (Colony; 1938). *Cast:* Gene Austin, Joan Brooks, Lynne Barkeley, Henry Rocquemore, Walter Willis, Charles King, John Merton, Ben Corbett, Karl Hackett, Ted Claire, Bob Terry, John Elliott, Lloyd Ingraham, Russell "Candy" Hall & Otto "Coco" Heimel, Darryl Harper. *D:* Harry Fraser; *P:* Max & Arthur Alexander; *Sc:* Wayne Carter. (1:05)

B western which was an attempt to establish piano player-songwriter Gene Austin as a singing cowboy. The story involving a musical troupe captured by outlaws was a flop.

4340. Sonny Boy (WB; 1929). *Cast:* Gertrude Olmstead, Master Davey Lee, Betty Bronson, Edward

Everett Horton, John T. Murray, Tommy Dugan, Jed Prouty, Edmund Breese, Al Jolson (cameo). *D:* Archie Mayo; *St:* Leon Zuardo; *Sc:* C. Graham Baker, Leon Zuardo.

Part-talkie marital drama of a pending divorce and the abduction of a young boy by his mother and aunt who fear loss of custody.

4341. Sons o' Guns (WB; 1935). *Cast:* Joe E. Brown, Joan Blondell, Eric Blore, Winifred Shaw, Robert Barrat, Beverly Roberts, Craig Reynolds, G.P. Huntley, Jr., Mischa Auer. *D:* Lloyd Bacon; *P:* Harry Joe Brown; *Sc:* Julius J. Epstein, Jerry Wald; *Songs:* "In the Arms of an Army Man" & "For a Brick and a Quarter a Day" by Al Dubin & Harry Warren. (1:22)

Hit Joe E. Brown comedy of accidental military enlistment which was based on a play by Fred Thompson and Jack Donahue.

4342. Sons of Steel (Chesterfield; 1935). *Cast:* Charles Starrett, Polly Ann Young, Barbara Bedford, William Bakewell, Aileen Pringle, Walter Walker, Holmes Herbert, Richard Carlyle, Lloyd Ingraham, Florence Roberts, Tom Ricketts. *D:* Charles Lamont; *P:* George R. Batcheller; *St & Sc:* Charles Belden.

"Poverty row" drama.

4343. Sons of the Desert (MGM/ Hal Roach; 1933). *Cast:* Stan Laurel, Oliver Hardy, Charley Chase, Mae Busch, Dorothy Christy, Lucien Littlefield, Billy Gilbert (voice only), John Elliott, Charles Hall, John Merton, Stanley Blystone, Hal Roach (bit). *D:* William A. Seiter; *P:* Hal Roach; *Sc:* Frank Craven, Byron Morgan. (G.B. title: *Fraternally Yours*) (1:08) (video)

This classic Laurel and Hardy romp is considered one of their best feature films by many and in it they are plotting and scheming against their wives in an attempt to attend a fraternal convention. One of the 15 top grossing films of 1934, it was based on two silent comedy shorts, namely: "Ambrose's First Falsehood" (Keystone; 1914) and "We Faw Down" (MGM/Hal Roach; 1928), one of the comedy team's own shorts.

4344. Sons of the Legion (Paramount; 1938). *Cast:* Lynne Overman, Evelyn Keyes, Donald O'Connor, William Frawley, Elizabeth Patterson, Edward Pawley, Bennie Bartlett, Richard Tucker, Lucille Ward, Wally Albright, Billy Cook, Billy Lee, Ronnie Paige. *D:* James Hogan; *P:* Stuart Walker; *St:* Robert F. McGowan; *Sc:* Lewis R. Foster, Lillie Hayward, McGowan.

B comedy of two siblings out to clear their father's name.

4345/4346. Sons of the Saddle (Universal; 1930). *Cast:* Ken Maynard, Doris Hill, Joseph Girard, Francis Ford, Carroll Nye, Harry Todd. *D:* Harry Joe Brown; *P:* Maynard; *Sc:* Bennett Cohen, Lesley Mason. (1:16)

Ken Maynard western of a ranch foreman who saves his employer's ranch.

4347. Sooky (Paramount; 1931). *Cast:* Jackie Cooper (Skippy), Robert Coogan (Sooky), Jackie Searle (Sidney), Helen Jerome Eddy (Mrs. Wayne), Willard Robertson (Dr. Skinner), Enid Bennett (Mrs. Skinner), Leigh Allen, Guy Oliver, Harry Beresford, Oscar Apfel, Gertrude Sutton. *D:* Norman Taurog; *P:* Louis D. Lighton; *Sc:* Joseph L. Mankiewicz, Sam Mintz, Norman Z. McLeod. (1:25)

A sentimental comedy-drama which followed in the successful footsteps of *Skippy* (q.v.), and how two boys deal with the impending death of the one lad's mother. Based on the book "Dear Sooky" by Percy Crosby.

4348. Sophie Lang Goes West (Paramount; 1937). *Cast:* Gertrude Michael (Sophie), Buster Crabbe, Robert Cummings, Lee Bowman, C. Henry Gordon, Guy Usher, Rafael Corio (Rafael Storm), Archie Twitchell, Barlowe Borland, Nick Lukats, Fred Miller, Sandra Storme, Herbert Ransom. *D:* Charles Reisner; *P:* A.M. Botsford; *St:* Frederick Irving Anderson; *Sc:* Brian Marlow, Robert Wyler, Doris Anderson.

The third and final entry in a moderately popular B series involving a lady jewel thief who goes straight. Set aboard a train bound for California.

4349. The Sophomore (Pathé; 1929). *Cast:* Eddie Quillan, Sally O'Neil, Stanley Smith, Stuart Erwin, Jeanette Loff, Russell Gleason, Brooks Benedict, Spec O'Donnell, Sarah Padden, Lew Ayres (film debut—bit), Grady Sutton (bit). *D:* Leo McCarey; *St:* Corey Ford, T.H. Wenning.

College comedy.

4350. Sorority House (RKO; 1939). *Cast:* Anne Shirley, James Ellison, Barbara Read, J.M. Kerrigan, Adele Pearce, Helen Wood, Doris Jordan, June Storey, Elizabeth Risdon, Margaret Armstrong, Chill Wills, Selmer Jackson, Dick Hogan, Veronica Lake (Constance Keane). *D:* John Farrow; *P:* Robert Sisk; *Sc:* Dalton Trumbo. (G.B. title: *That Girl from College*) (1:04)

B drama of sorority house snobbery. Based on the story "Chi House" by Mary Coyle Chase.

4351. The Soul Kiss (Xxxx Xxxx; 1930). *Cast:* Jobyna Howland, Gilbert Emery. (alt. title: *A Lady's Morals*)

(No other information available)

4352. Soul of the Slums (Action Pictures; 1931). *Cast:* William Collier, Jr., Walter Long. *D:* Frank Strayer. (G.B. title: *The Samaritan*)

Low-budget melodrama.

4353. Souls at Sea (Paramount; 1937). *Cast:* Gary Cooper, George Raft, Frances Dee, Olympe Bradna, Henry Wilcoxon, Harry Carey, Robert Cummings, Joseph Schildkraut, George Zucco, Virginia Weidler, Fay Holden, Paul Fix, Porter Hall, Robert Barrat, Gilbert Emery, Monte Blue, Alan Ladd, Lucien Littlefield, Tully Marshall, Charles Middleton. *D:* Henry Hathaway; *P:* Grover Jones; *St:* Ted Lesser; *Sc:* Dale Van Every, Grover Jones; *Art-Set Decoration:* (A.A.N.) Hans Dreier, Roland Anderson; *Music:* (A.A.N.) W. Franke Harling, Milan Roder & musical director, Borris Morros; *Assistant Director:* (A.A.N.) Hal Walker. (1:32)

This hit drama tells of the after effects of a sea disaster.

4354. Soup to Nuts (Fox; 1930). *Cast:* Ted Healy, Moe Howard, Shemp Howard, Larry Fine, Freddie "Pansy" Sanborn (fourth stooge who only appeared in this film), Charles Winningham, Hallam Cooley. *D:* Ben Stoloff; *St:* Rube Goldberg.

Low-budget comedy notable as the film debuts of Ted Healy and his Stooges (debuting here as "The Racketeers").

4355. South of Arizona (Columbia; 1938). *Cast:* Charles Starrett, Iris Meredith, Sons of the Pioneers with Bob Nolan & Pat Brady, Dick Curtis, Robert Fiske, Edmund Cobb, Art Mix, Richard Botiller, Lafe McKee, Ed Coxen, Hank Bell, Hal Taliaferro, John Tyrell, Merrill McCormack. *D:* Sam Nelson; *Sc:* Bennett Cohen. (0:55)

Charles Starrett western of cattle rustling.

4356. South of Santa Fe (Sono Art-World Wide/KBS Prods.; 1932). *Cast:* Bob Steele, Janis Elliott, Chris-Pin Martin, Jack Clifford, Eddie Dunn, Bob Burns, Allan Garcia, Hank Bell. *D:* Bert Glennon (final film as director—returned to cinematography); *P:* Trem Carr; *Sc:* George Arthur Durlam. (1:00)

Bob Steele western of a cowboy combating a band of border outlaws. Steele's first for the "poverty row" studio.

4357. South of the Border (Republic; 1939). *Cast:* Gene Autry, Smiley Burnette, June Storey, Lupita Tovar, Mary Lee (film debut), Duncan Renaldo, Frank Reicher, Alan Edwards, Claire DuBrey, Dick Botiller, William Farnum, Selmer Jackson, Sheila Darcy, Rex Lease, Charles King, Reed Howes, Checkerboard Band, Slim Whitaker, Hal Price, Jack O'Shea, Julian Rivero, Curley Dresden, Champion. *D:* George Sherman; *P:* William Berke; *St:* Dorrell & Stuart McGowan; *Sc:* Betty Burbridge, Gerald Geraghty. (1:11) (video)

This offbeat Gene Autry western of government men attempting to quell a rebellion which was instigated by a foreign power was a huge hit at the box office.

4358. South of the Rio Grande (Columbia; 1932). *Cast:* Buck Jones, Mona Maris, George J. Lewis, Doris Hill, Philo McCullough, Paul Fix, Charles Requa, James Durkin, Harry Semels, Charles Stevens. *D:* Lambert Hillyer; *St:* Harold Shumate; *Adapt.:* Milton Krims. (1:00)

In this Buck Jones western, the title tells all.

4359. South Sea Rose (Fox; 1929). *Cast:* Charles Bickford (film debut), Lenore Ulric, Kenneth MacKenna, Roscoe Ates (film debut), Elizabeth Patterson, J. Farrell MacDonald, Daphne Pollard, Charlotte Walker, George MacFarlane, Ilka Chase, Ben Hall, Emile Chautard, Tom Patricola. *D:* Allan Dwan; *St:* Tom Cushing; *Sc:* Sonya Levien.

Romantic melodrama.

The Southerner *see* **The Prodigal**

4360. Southward Ho! (Republic; 1939). *Cast:* Roy Rogers, George "Gabby" Hayes (his first film as Roy's sidekick), Mary Hart (Lynn Roberts), Wade Boteler, Arthur Loft, Lane Chandler, Tom London, Nicodemus Stewart. *D:* Joseph Kane; *P:* Kane; *St:* John Rathmell, Jack Natteford; *Sc:* Gerald Geraghty. (0:57)

Roy Rogers western with a Civil War theme.

4361. Spaceship to the Unknown (Universal; 1936). *Cast:* Buster Crabbe (Flash Gordon), Jean Rogers (Dale Arden), Frank Shannon (Dr. Arkoff), Charles Middleton (Ming), Priscilla Lawson, John Lipson, Richard Alexander, James Pierce. *D:* Frederick Stephani. (aka: *Rocketship* & *Perils from the Planet Mongo*) (1:37) (video)

Feature version of the first "Flash Gordon" serial (the most expensive ever made at a cost of $350,000) as Flash, Dale and Dr. Arkoff head for the planet Mongo to combat the evil forces of Ming the Merciless. Followed in 1938 by the serial "Flash Gordon's Trip to Mars" which became known in it's feature version as *Mars Attacks the World* (q.v.) and *The Deadly Ray from Mars* (q.v.).

4362. The Spanish Cape Mystery (Republic; 1935). *Cast:* Donald Cook (Ellery Queen), Helen Twelvetrees, Berton Churchill, Barbara Bedford, George Cleveland, Richard Cramer, Betty Blythe. *D:* Lewis Collins.

Low-budget mystery, notable as the first film featuring the character of "Ellery Queen." Based on the characters created by Manfred B. Lee and Frederic Dannay.

Spats to Spurs (G.B. title) *see* **Henry Goes Arizona**

4363. Spawn of the North (Paramount; 1938). *Cast:* Henry Fonda, George Raft, Dorothy Lamour, Louise Platt, John Barrymore, Akim Tamiroff, Lynne Overman, Duncan Renaldo, Fuzzy Knight, Vladimir Sokoloff, John Wray, Lee Shumway, Frank Puglia, Monte Blue, Henry Brandon, Robert Middlemass, Alex Woloshin. *D:* Henry

Hathaway; *P:* Albert Lewin; *St:* Barrett Willoughby; *Sc:* Jules Furthman, Talbot Jennings; *Songs:* Burton Lane-Frank Loesser; *Special Effects:* (A.A. — special placque) Gordon Jennings & staff; *Sound Effects:* (A.A. — special placque) Loren Ryder & staff. (1:50)

Hit action drama of Canadian salmon fishermen battling Russian salmon piracy in their waters. Most of the exteriors were shot on location in Alaska, with "special" Academy Awards (placques) given for sound reproduction and special effects. Remade as *Alaska Seas* (Paramount; 1954).

4364. Speak Easily (MGM; 1932). *Cast:* Buster Keaton, Jimmy Durante, Hedda Hopper, Ruth Selwyn, Thelma Todd, Sidney Toler, Henry Armetta, Edward Brophy, ZaSu Pitts, Lawrence Grant, William Pawley. *D:* Edward Sedgwick; *P:* Lawrence Weingarten; *Sc:* Ralph Spence, Laurence E. Johnson (based on the novel "Footlights" by Clarence Budington Kelland). (1:23)

A college professor suddenly finds himself the owner of a Broadway show in this comedy.

4365. Special Agent (WB/Cosmopolitan; 1935). *Cast:* Bette Davis, George Brent, Ricardo Cortez, Jack LaRue, Henry O'Neill, Robert Strange, Joseph Crehan, J. Carrol Naish, Joseph Sawyer (nee Joseph Sauers), William Davidson, Robert Barrat, Joseph King, John Alexander (film debut), Charles Middleton. *D:* William Keighley; *St:* Martin Mooney; *Sc:* Abem Finkel, Laird Doyle. (1:16)

Crime melodrama.

4366. Special Inspector (Syndicate; 1939). *Cast:* Rita Hayworth, Charles Quigley, George McKay, Edgar Edwards, Eddie Laughton, Bob Rideout, Grant MacDonald, Bill Irving, Virginia Coomb, Fred Bass, Vincent McKenna, Don Douglas. *D:* Leon Barsha; *P:* Kenneth J. Bishop.

A murdered trucker's sisters teams with a Treasury man to try to stop fur smugglers who are killing truckers and transporting furs across the border.

4367. Special Investigator (RKO; 1936). *Cast:* Richard Dix, Margaret Callahan, Erik Rhodes, Owen Davis, Jr., Ray Mayer, Harry Jans, Joseph Sawyer, J. Carrol Naish, Sheila Terry, J.M. Kerrigan, Jed Prouty, Russell Hicks, Ethan Laidlaw, Si Jenks. *D:* Louis King; *As.P.:* Cliff Reid; *Sc:* Louis Stevens, Thomas Lennon, Ferdinand Reyher. (1:01)

B melodrama of a criminal lawyer who heads out west to find those who killed his brother. Based on the novel by Erle Stanley Gardner.

4368. Speed (MGM; 1936). *Cast:* James Stewart, Wendy Barrie, Weldon Heyburn, Una Merkel, Ted Healy, Ralph Morgan, Patricia Wilder. *D:* Edwin L. Marin; *P:* Lucien Hubbard; *St:* Lawrence (Larry) Bachmann, Milton Krims; *Sc:* Michael Fessier. (1:10)

B auto racing drama.

Speed Brent Wins (G.B. title) *see* **Breed of the Border**

4369. Speed Demon (Columbia; 1932). *Cast:* Robert Ellis, Joan Marsh, Fuzzy Knight, William Collier, Jr., Ethan Laidlaw, Wheeler Oakman, Wade Boteler. *D:* D. Ross Lederman.

Low-budget auto racing drama.

4370. Speed Limited (Regent; 1936–40). *Cast:* Ralph Graves, Claudia Dell. *D:* Al Herman; *Sc:* Graves.

Crime melodrama produced in 1936 with release held up till 1940.

4371. Speed Madness (Capital Films; 1931). *Cast:* Richard Talmadge, Donald Keith, Matthew Betz, Nancy Drexel, Lucien Littlefield. *D:* George Crone; *Sc:* Charles R. Condon.

(No other information available)

4372. Speed Reporter (Xxxx Xxxx; 1936). *Cast:* Richard Talmadge, Luana Walters, Richard Cramer, Bob Walker. *D:* Bernard B. Ray; *P:* Ray; *Sc:* Rose Gordon.

(No other information available)

4373. Speed to Burn (20th Century–Fox; 1938). *Cast:* Michael Whalen, Lynn Bari, Charles D. Brown, Henry Armetta (Poppa Gambini), Inez Palange (Momma Gambini), Chick Chandler, Johnny Pirrone, Eleanor Firzie, Betty Greco, Sidney Blackmer, Lon Chaney, Jr., Marvin Stephens. *D:* Otto Brower; *P:* Sol M. Wurtzel; *As.P.:* Jerry Hoffman; *St:* Edwin Dial Torgerson; *Sc:* Robert Ellis, Helen Logan.

Premiere entry in the B "Gambini" series. An auto racing comedy-melodrama. Followed by *Road Demon* (q.v.).

4374. Speed to Spare (Columbia; 1936). *Cast:* Eddie Nugent, Charles Quigley, Dorothy Wilson, Gordon (Bill) Elliott. *D:* Lambert Hillyer; *Sc:* Bert Granet, Hillyer.

B auto racing actioner.

4375. Speed Wings (Columbia; 1934). *Cast:* Tim McCoy, Evalyn Knapp, Vincent Sherman. *D:* Otto Brower; *Sc:* Horace McCoy.

B aerial action adventure.

The Spellbinder (Pathé; 1929) (G.B. title) *see* **The Spieler**

4376. The Spellbinder (RKO; 1939). *Cast:* Lee Tracy, Barbara Read, Patric Knowles, Allan Lane, Linda Hayes, Morgan Conway, Robert Emmett Keane, Roy Gordon, Robert Strange, Elliott Sullivan, Leonid Kinskey, Virginia Weidler. *D:* Jack Hively; *P:* Cliff Reid; *St:* Joseph Anthony; *Sc:* Joseph A. Fields, Thomas Lennon. (1:09)

A criminal lawyer who defends men he knows to be guilty, finds himself tried for murder in this B courtroom drama.

4377. Spendthrift (Paramount; 1936). *Cast:* Henry Fonda, Pat Paterson, Mary Brian, George Barbier, Edward Brophy, Halliwell Hobbes, Clarence Muse, J.M. Kerrigan, Greta Meyer,

Jerry Mandy, June Brewster, Miki Morita. *D:* Raoul Walsh; *P:* Walter Wanger; *Sc:* Walsh, Bert Hanlon. (1:20)

Romantic comedy of a penniless millionaire playboy.

4378. The Sphinx (Monogram; 1933). *Cast:* Lionel Atwill (in a dual role), Sheila Terry, Theodore Newton, Paul Hurst, Luis Alberni, Robert Ellis, Lucien Prival, Paul Fix, Lillian Leighton, George Hayes, Hooper Atchley, Wilfred Lucas. *D:* Phil Rosen; *Supervisor:* Sid Rogell; *St:* Albert E. DeMond; *Sc:* DeMond. (1:04)

"Poverty row mystery involving twin brothers, one a mute, the other a homicidal maniac. Remade as *The Phantom Killer* (Monogram; 1942).

4379. The Spieler (Pathé; 1929). *Cast:* Alan Hale, Reneé Adoree, Clyde Cook, Fred Kohler, Lloyd Ingraham, Fred Warren, Billy Latimer, Kewpie Morgan, Jimmie Quinn. *D:* Tay Garnett; *P:* Ralph Block; *St:* Hal Conklin. (G.B. title: *The Spellbinder*)

Part-talkie melodrama.

Spies at Work (G.B. title) *see* **Sabotage**

4380/4381. The Spider (Fox; 1931). *Cast:* Edmund Lowe, El Brendel, Warren Hymer, Lois Moran, Manya Roberti, George E. Stone, William Pawley, Ruth Donnelly, Purnell Pratt, Earle Foxe, Jesse DeVorska, Kendall McComas, Howard Phillips. *D:* Kenneth MacKenna, William Cameron Menzies; *St & Sc:* Lowell Brentano, Fulton Oursler; *Cont./Dial.:* Barry Conners, Philp Klein.

Melodrama. Remade by 20th Century-Fox in 1946.

4382. The Spirit of Culver (Universal; 1939). *Cast:* Jackie Cooper, Freddie Bartholomew, Tim Holt, Andy Devine, Gene Reynolds, Jackie Moran, Henry Hull, Kathryn Kane, Walter Tetley, Milburn Stone, Robert Keith. *D:* Joseph Santley; *P:* Burt Kelly; *St:* George Green, Tom Buckingham, Clarence Marks; *Sc:* Nathanael West, Whitney Bolton. (G.B. titles: *Two Smart Boys* and *Man's Heritage*) (1:29)

A story of life in a boys military school, and a remake of *Tom Brown of Culver* (q.v.). A box office hit.

4383. The Spirit of Notre Dame (Universal; 1931). *Cast:* Lew Ayres, Andy Devine, J. Farrell MacDonald, William Bakewell, Sally Blane, Nat Pendleton, Harry Barris, Notre Dame's "Four Horsemen": Harry Stuhldreher (quarterback), Jim Crowley (halfback), Don Miller (halfback), Elmer Layden (fullback), Adam Walsh, Moon Mullins, Bucky O'Connor, John Law, Art McManmon, Frank Carideo, Al Howard, John O'Brien. *D:* Russell Mack; *P:* Carl Laemmle, Jr.; *St:* Richard Schayer, Dale Van Every; *Sc:* Van Every, Frank "Spig" Wead. (G.B. title: *Vigour of Youth*) (1:20)

Gridiron drama with the proverbial "big game" finale. The film was dedicated to Knute Rockne (the famed Notre Dame football coach who passed away in 1931).

4384. The Spirit of the West (Allied; 1932). *Cast:* Hoot Gibson, Doris Hill, Hooper Atchley, Alan Bridge, Walter Perry, George Mendoza, Lafe McKee, Charles Brinley, Ralph "Tiny" Sandford. *D:* Otto Brower; *P:* M.H. Hoffman, Jr.; *St:* Jack Natteford; *Sc:* Philip Graham White. (1:00) (video)

Hoot Gibson comic western of a rodeo performer who pretends to be a dumb cluck in order to get the goods on the bad guys.

4385. Spirit of Youth (Grand National/Globe Pictures Corp.; 1938). *Cast:* Joe Louis, Clarence Muse, Edna Mae Harris, Mae Turner, Mantan Moreland, Cleo Desmond, Clarence Brooks, Anthony Scott, Janette O'Dell. *D:* Harry Fraser; *P:* Lew Golder; *Sc:* Arthur Hoerl. (1:06)

In this low-budget drama, a black boxer makes it big in the fight game.

4386. Splendor (United Artists/ Samuel Goldwyn; 1935). *Cast:* Joel McCrea, Miriam Hopkins, Helen Westley, Katherine Alexander, Paul Cavanagh, Billie Burke, David Niven, Arthur Treacher, Ruth Weston, Ivan Simpson, Torben Meyer, Ben Alexander, Reginald Sheffield. *D:* Elliott Nugent; *P:* Sam Goldwyn; *Sc:* Rachel Crothers. (1:17)

Based on the play by Rachel Crothers, this domestic drama tells of the son of a socially prominent family who chooses to marry outside his "class."

4387. The Spoilers (Paramount; 1930). *Cast:* Gary Cooper, Kay Johnson, Betty Compson, William "Stage" Boyd, Harry Green, Slim Summerville, Oscar Apfel, Lloyd Ingraham, George Irving, James Kirkwood, Knute Erickson. *D:* Edwin Carewe, David Burton; *P:* Carewe; *Sc:* Bartlett Cormack, Agnes Brand Leahy. (1:24)

Based on the popular and much filmed book by Rex Beach, this adventure-romance set in the Klondike tells the story of a man fighting to save his gold mine from two schemers intent on claiming it for themselves. Previous versions: (Selig-Polyscope; 1913–14) with William Farnum and Tom Santschi, (First National/Samuel Goldwyn; 1923) with Milton Sills and Noah Beery, followed by two remakes, (Universal; 1942) and (Universal; 1955). The film is best remembered for its violent climactic fight scene.

4388. Spoilers of the Range (Columbia; 1939). *Cast:* Charles Starrett, Iris Meredith, Sons of the Pioneers with Bob Nolan and Pat Brady, Dick Curtis, Kenneth MacDonald, Edward LeSaint, Hank Bell, Forbes Murray, Art Mix, Edmund Cobb, Ed Peil, Sr., Charles Brinley, Horace B. Carpenter, Ethan Laidlaw, Carl Sepulveda, Joe Weaver. *D:* C.C. Coleman, Jr.; *Sc:* Paul Franklin. (0:58)

Charles Starrett western of outlaws attempting to prevent cattlemen from getting their cattle to market.

Sport of a Nation (G.B. title) *see* **The All-American**

4389. The Sport Parade (RKO; 1932). *Cast:* Joel McCrea, Marian Marsh, William Gargan, Robert Benchley (feature film debut), Walter Catlett, Richard "Skeets" Gallagher, Clarence H. Wilson, Ivan Linow. *D:* Dudley Murphy; *P:* David O. Selznick; *Sc:* Corey Ford, Francis Cockrell. (1:05)

After leaving college, an athlete is exploited by a crooked manager in this low-budget sports drama. Based on material supplied by Jerry Horwin.

4390. Sporting Blood (MGM; 1931). *Cast:* Clark Gable, Ernest Torrence, Madge Evans, Lew Cody, Marie Prevost, J. Farrell MacDonald, Hallam Cooley, Oscar Apfel, Eugene Jackson, John Larkin, Harry Holman. *D:* Charles Brabin; *Sc:* Wanda Tuchock, Willard Mack. (1:22)

Hit drama of a race horse and its various owners. Remade in 1940 by this studio.

4391. Sporting Chance (Peerless; 1931). *Cast:* James Hall, Claudia Dell, William Collier, Jr., Mahlon Hamilton, Eugene Jackson, Joseph Levering, Henry Rocquemore, Hedwig Reicher. *D:* Al Herman; *St:* King Baggot.

Low-budget production.

Sporting Life (G.B. title) *see* **Night Parade**

Sporting Widow (G.B. title) *see* **Madame Racketeer**

4392. The Spreading Dawn (Xxxx Xxxx; 1929). (No information available)

4393. Spring Is Here (WB/F.N.; 1930). *Cast:* Bernice Claire, Lawrence Gray, Alexander Gray, Wilbur Mack, Louise Fazenda, Ford Sterling, Frank Albertson, Irving Bacon. *D:* John Francis Dillon; *Sc:* James A. Starr; *Songs:*

"Have a Little Faith in Me," "Cryin' for the Carolines," "What's the Big Idea?" & "Bad Baby" by Sam Lewis, Joe Young & Harry Warren; "Who Wrote That Song" by Dick Jacobs.

Romantic musical of a girl who has to deal with an unwanted suitor, chosen by her father. Based on the Broadway musical book by Owen Davis.

4394. Spring Madness (MGM; 1938). *Cast:* Maureen O'Sullivan, Lew Ayres, Ruth Hussey, Burgess Meredith, Ann Morriss, Joyce Compton, Jacqueline Wells (Julie Bishop), Frank Albertson, Marjorie Gateson, Sterling Holloway, Truman Bradley, Willie Best, Dick Baldwin, Renie Riano. *D:* S. Sylvan Simon; *P:* Edward Chodorov; *St:* Eleanor Golden, Eloise Barrangon; *Sc:* Chodorov. (1:20)

A college romance based on the play "Spring Dance" by Philip Barry.

4395. Spring Tonic (Fox; 1935). *Cast:* Lew Ayres, Claire Trevor, Jack Haley, ZaSu Pitts, Sig Rumann, Walter Woolf King, Lynn Bari. *D:* Clyde Bruckman; *Sc:* Patterson McNutt, H.W. Hanemann.

Romantic comedy, based on the play "Man-Eating Tiger" by Ben Hecht and Rose Caylor.

4396. Springtime for Henry (Fox; 1934). *Cast:* Nancy Carroll, Otto Kruger, Herbert Mundin, Nigel Bruce, Heather Angel, Arthur Hoyt. *D:* Frank Tuttle.

Low-budget comedy.

4397. Springtime in the Rockies (Republic; 1937). *Cast:* Gene Autry, Smiley Burnette, Polly Rowles, Ula Love, Ruth Bacon, Jane Hunt, George Chesebro, Alan Bridge, Tom London, Edward Hearn, Frankie Marvin, William Hale, Edmund Cobb, Fred Burns, Art Davis, George (Montgomery) Letz, Jimmy's Saddle Pals (featuring Jimmy Wakely), Lew Meehan, Jack Kirk, Frank Ellis, Robert Dudley, Jack Rockwell, Champion. *D:* Joseph Kane; *P:* Sol C. Siegel; *Sc:* Betty Burbridge, Gilbert Wright. (1:00) (video)

Gene Autry 'raising sheep in cattle country' western with songs. Remade as *Utah* (Republic; 1945) with Roy Rogers.

4398. Spurs (Universal; 1930). *Cast:* Hoot Gibson, Helen Wright, Buddy Hunter, Robert E. Homans, Pee Wee Holmes, Philo McCullough, Pete Morrison. *D:* B. Reeves "Breezy" Eason; *Sc:* Eason. (0:59)

Hoot Gibson western of a cowboy seeking the killer of a young boy's brother.

4399. The Spy (Fox; 1931). *Cast:* Neil Hamilton, Kay Johnson, John Halliday, Henry Kolker, Rita Johnson. *D:* Berthold Viertel; *Sc:* Ernest Pascal.

Melodrama.

4400. The Spy Ring (Universal; 1938). *Cast:* Jane Wyman, William Hall, Esther Ralston, Ben Alexander, Leon Ames, Glenn Strange, Jack Mulhall, Egon Brecher, Robert Warwick, Paul Sutton, LeRoy Mason, Don Barclay, Philip Trent. *D:* Joseph H. Lewis; *P:* Trem Carr; *Sc:* George Waggner. (aka: *International Spy*) (1:00)

The title tells all in this B production of espionage discovered on an army base.

Spy 13 (G.B. title) *see* **Operator 13**

4401. Squadron of Honor (Columbia; 1938). *Cast:* Don Terry, Marc Lawrence, Thurston Hall. *D:* C.C. Coleman, Jr.; *Sc:* Michael Simmons.

(No other information available)

4402. The Squall (WB/F.N.; 1929). *Cast:* Myrna Loy, Alice Joyce, Loretta Young (talkie debut), Richard Tucker, Carroll Nye, ZaSu Pitts, Harry Cording, Nicholas Soussanin, Knute Erickson, George Hackathorne. *D:* Alexander Korda (talkie debut); *Sc:* Bradley King; *Song:* "Gypsy Charmer" by Harry Akst, Grant Clarke. (1:45)

Critically panned drama of a gypsy girl who invades a farmhouse, creating havoc among the residents. Based on the play by Jean Bart.

4403. Square Shooter (Columbia; 1935). *Cast:* Tim McCoy, Jacqueline Wells (Julie Bishop), Wheeler Oakman, J. Farrell MacDonald, Charles Middleton, Steve Clark, Erville Alderson, John Darrow, Eddie Chandler, William V. Mong, Ernie Adams, Bud Osborne, Art Mix. *D:* David Selman; *Sc:* Harold Shumate. (0:57)

Tim McCoy western of a man released from prison after five years, after being falsely accused of killing his uncle.

4404. Square Shoulders (Pathé; 1929). *Cast:* Louis Wolheim, Anita Louise, Frank (Junior) Coghlan. *D:* E. Mason Hopper.

Low-budget part-talkie.

4405. The Squaw Man (MGM; 1931). *Cast:* Warner Baxter, Lupe Velez, Charles Bickford, Eleanor Boardman, Roland Young, Paul Cavanagh, Raymond Hatton, Dickie Moore, Lillian Bond, Julia Faye, Mitchell Lewis, C. Aubrey Smith, J. Farrell MacDonald, Chris-Pin Martin, Victor Potel, Frank Rice, Desmond Roberts, Edwin S. Brady, Luke Cosgrave, Harry Northrup, Frank Hagney, Eva Dennison, Winifred Kingston, Rodd Redwing. *D:* Cecil B. DeMille; *P:* DeMille; *Sc:* Lucien Hubbard, Lenore Coffee; *Dialogue:* Elsie Janis. (G.B. title: *The White Man*) (1:46)

An Englishman leaves his home country and heads for the American west to clear his name. Based on the popular 1905 melodramatic play by Edwin Milton Royle, it was first filmed in 1913–14 (Lasky), historically significant as the first feature length film made in the area now known as Hollywood. It starred Dustin Farnum and Winifred Kingston, with direction by Oscar Apfel and Cecil B. De Mille, and was a huge box office hit. Remade (Paramount; 1918) with Elliott Dexter, Katherine MacDonald, Jack Holt and Ann Little. This first talkie version was a box office flop, and de Mille's last film for this studio before moving over to Paramount.

4406. The Squawk (Xxxx Xxxx; 1931). *Cast:* Nena Quartero.
(No other information available)

4407. The Squealer (Columbia; 1930). *Cast:* Jack Holt, Dorothy Revier, Robert Ellis, ZaSu Pitts, Matthew Betz, Matt Moore, Davey Lee, Arthur Housman. *D:* Harry Joe Brown; *Sc:* Dorothy Howell; *Cont.:* Casey Robinson; *Dial.:* Jo Swerling.

"Poverty row" crime melodrama.

4408. Stablemates (MGM; 1938). *Cast:* Mickey Rooney, Wallace Beery, Margaret Hamilton, Minor Watson, Arthur Hohl, Marjorie Gateson, Oscar O'Shea. *D:* Sam Wood; *P:* Harry Rapf; *St:* Reginald Owen, Wilhelm (William) Thiele; *Sc:* Richard Maibaum, Leonard Praskins. (1:29)

A hit sentimental comedy-drama (with the emphasis on sentimental) of a young jockey and his beloved race horse.

4409. The Stadium Murders (Republic; 1938). *Cast:* Lynn Roberts, Neil Hamilton, Evelyn Venable, Lucien Littlefield, Reed Hadley, Barbara Pepper, William Haade, Pat Flaherty, Jimmy Wallington, Smiley Burnette, Dan Tobey, Al Bayne, James Spottswood, Charles Williams. *D:* David Howard; *St:* Stuart Palmer. (alt. title: *Hollywood Stadium Mystery*)

B mystery set around the murder of a boxer in view of a packed house.

4410. Stage Door (RKO; 1937). *Cast:* Katharine Hepburn (Terry Randall-Sims), Ginger Rogers (Joan Maitland), Adolphe Menjou (Anthony Powell), Lucille Ball (Judy Canfield), Gail Patrick (Linda Shaw), Constance Collier (Catherine Luther), Andrea Leeds (A.A.N. for B.S.A. as Kaye Hamilton), Samuel S. Hinds (Henry Sims), Jack Carson (Milbank), William Corson (Bill), Franklin Pangborn (Harcourt), Pierre Watkin (Richard Carmichael), Grady Sutton (Butcher), Frank Reicher (stage director), Phyllis Kennedy (Hattie), Eve Arden (Eve), Ann Miller (Annie), Jane Rhodes (Ann Braddock), Margaret Early (Mary), Jean Rouverol (Dizzy), Elizabeth Dunne (Mrs. Orcutt), Norma Drury (Olga Brent), Peggy O'Donnell (Susan), Harriett Brandon (Madeline), Katherine Alexander, Ralph Forbes, Mary Forbes, Huntley Gordon, Jack Rice, Lynton Brent, Theodore von Eltz, Bob Perry, Harry Strang, Larry Steers. *D:* (A.A.N.) Gregory La Cava (who also received the "Best Director Award" from the New York Film Critics); *P.:* (A.A.N. for "Best Picture") Pandro S. Berman; *Sc:* (A.A.N.) Morrie Ryskind, Anthony Veiller; *Song:* "Put Your Heart Into Your Feet and Dance" by Hal Borne, Mort Green. (1:32) (video)

Classic and critically acclaimed comedy-drama of a hotel for aspiring actresses who each have their own story to tell. The *New York Times* placed it at #3 on their "10 Best" list, the National Board of Review at #10 on theirs, with *Film Daily* placing it at #7 on theirs. Based on the hit play by Edna Ferber and George S. Kaufman, the film was also a major box office hit.

4411. Stage Mother (MGM; 1933). *Cast:* Alice Brady, Maureen O'Sullivan, Franchot Tone, Ted Healy, Phillips Holmes, Ben Alexander, C. Henry Gordon, Alan Edwards. *D:* Charles Brabin; *P:* Hunt Stromberg; *St:* Bradford Ropes; *Sc:* Ropes, John Meehan. (1:27)

Backstage B drama of a vaudevillian who seeks to make a star of her daughter.

4412. Stage Struck (WB/F.N.; 1936). *Cast:* Dick Powell, Joan Blondell, Jeanne Madden, Warren William, Frank McHugh, Yacht Club Boys, Carol Hughes, Hobart Cavanaugh, Craig Reynolds, Andrew Tombes, Spring Byington, Jane Wyman, Johnny Arthur, Iris Adrian, Mary Gordon, Thomas Pogue, Lulu McConnell. *D:* Busby Berkeley; *P:* Robert Lord; *St:* Lord; *Sc:* Tom Buckingham, Pat C. Flick; *Choreography:* Berkeley; *Songs:* "In Your Own Quiet Way," "Fancy Meeting You," "You're Kinda Grandish" & "The New Parade" by E.Y. Harburg & Harold Arlen. (1:26) (video)

Another of those "puttin' on a show' musicals.

4413. Stagecoach (United Artists/ Walter Wanger; 1939). *Cast:* John Wayne (The Ringo Kid), Claire Trevor (Dallas), Thomas Mitchell (A.A. for B.S.A. as well as an Acting Award from the National Board of Review for his portrayal of Dr. Josiah Boone), Andy Devine (Buck the stage driver), John Carradine (Hatfield), Donald Meek (Mr. Peacock the whiskey drummer), George Bancroft (Curley Wilcox), Louise Platt (Mrs. Lucy Mallory), Berton Churchill (Gatewood the banker), Francis Ford (Sgt. Billy Pickett), Elvira Rios (Yakeema), Tim Holt (Lieut. Blanchard), Chris-Pin Martin (Chris), Marga Ann Daighton (Mrs. Pickett), Tom Tyler (Luke Plummer), Cornelius Keefe (Capt. Whitney), Louis Mason (sheriff), Walter McGrail (Capt. Sickle), Chief Big Tree (Cheyenne scout), Yakima Canutt (cavalry scout), Florence Lake (Nancy Whitney), Paul McVey (express agent), Brenda Fowler (Mrs. Gatewood), Chief White Horse (Indian leader), Bryant Washburn (Capt. Simmons), Duke Lee (sheriff of Lordsburg), Joe Rickson (Ike Plummer), Harry Tenbrook (telegraph operator), Kent Odell (Billy, Jr.), William Hopper (cavalry sergeant), Jack Pennick (Jerry the bartender), Nora Cecil (landlady), Ed Brady (saloon-keeper), Vester Pegg (Hank Plummer), Robert E. Homans (Ed the editor), Mary Kathleen Walker (Lucy's baby—actual 2½ day-old infant), Buddy Roosevelt, Bill Cody, Si Jenks, Jim Mason, Franklyn Farnum, Merrill McCormack, Artie Ortego, Theodore Lorch, J.P.

McGowan, John Eckert, Jack Mohr. *D:* (A.A.N.) "Best Director of the Year" by the New York Film Critics, John Ford; *P:* (A.A.N. for "Best Picture") Walter Wanger; *Sc:* Dudley Nichols; *Black & White Cinematography:* (A.A.N.) Bert Glennon & Ray Binger; *Art-Set Decoration:* (A.A.N.) Alexander Toluboff; *Musical Score:* (A.A.) Richard Hageman, W. Franke Harling, John Leipold, Leo Shuken, Louis Gruenberg; *Editors:* (A.A.N.) Dorothy Spencer, Otho Lovering. (1:39) (video)

Classic western of various people traveling via stagecoach through dangerous Indian territory. Filmed in Monument Valley, Utah, this critically acclaimed film was based on the story "Stage to Lordsburg" by Ernest Haycox which appeared in *Collier's* magazine. The *New York Times* placed it at #2 on their "10 Best" list, while the National Board of Review placed it at #3 on their same list. Remade in 1966 and again in 1986 as a TV movie. One of the 16 top grossing films of 1938–39.

4414. Stagecoach Days (Columbia; 1938). *Cast:* Jack Luden, Eleanor Stewart, Harry Woods, Tuffy the dog, Hal Taliaferro, Slim Whitaker, Lafe McKee, Jack Ingram, Dick Botiller, Bob Kortman, Tom London, Blackjack Ward. *D:* Joseph Levering; *Sc:* Nate Gatzert. (0:58)

Jack Luden western of a stagecoach race to win a mail contract.

4415. Stairs of Sand (Paramount; 1929). *Cast:* Wallace Beery, Phillips Holmes, Jean Arthur. *D:* Otto Brower.

An eastern tenderfoot tries to deal with the rowdy old wild west. Based on the novel of the same name by Zane Grey. Remade as *Arizona Mahoney* (q.v.).

4416. Stamboul Quest (MGM; 1934). *Cast:* Myrna Loy, George Brent, Lionel Atwill, C. Henry Gordon, Mischa Auer, Douglass Dumbrille, Leo G. Carroll, Virginia Weidler, Joseph

(Sawyer) Sauers, Rudolf Amendt. *D:* Sam Wood; *P:* Walter Wanger; *Sc:* Herman J. Mankiewicz. (1:28)

Fact based romantic intrigue set in World War I Turkey of a female spy who falls for an American medical student. A similar variation on the story was filmed in France in 1936 titled *Mademoiselle Docteur* and in 1968 as an Italian-Yugoslavian co-production titled *Fraulein Doktor.*

Stamboul Train (G.B. title) *see* **Orient Express**

4417. Stampede (Columbia; 1936). *Cast:* Charles Starrett, Finis Barton, J.P. McGowan, LeStrange Millman, Reginald Hincks, James McGrath, Arthur Kerr, Michael Heppell, Ted Mapes, Jack Atkinson. *D:* Ford Beebe; *Sc:* Robert Watson. (0:58)

Charles Starrett western involving a greedy rancher who wants his neighbor's ranch.

4418. Stand-In (United Artists/ Walter Wanger; 1937). *Cast:* Leslie Howard, Joan Blondell, Humphrey Bogart, Alan Mowbray, Marla Shelton, C. Henry Gordon, Jack Carson, Tully Marshall, Charles Middleton, J.C. Nugent, William V. Mong. *D:* Tay Garnett; *P:* Walter Wanger; *Sc:* Gene Towne, Graham Baker. (1:31) (video)

Hit Hollywood satire of a banker sent to the American film capitol to find out why a studio is on the brink of bankruptcy. Based on a story by Clarence Budington Kelland, this film's "right on" approach is reputed to have ruffled the feathers of many a Hollywood film mogul.

4419. Stand Up and Cheer (Fox; 1934). *Cast:* Warner Baxter, Madge Evans, Sylvia Froos, John Boles, James Dunn, "Aunt Jemima," Arthur Byron, Shirley Temple, Ralph Morgan, Nick (Dick) Foran (film debut), Nigel Bruce, Mitchell & Durant, John "Skins" Miller, Stepin Fetchit, Frank Melton, Lila Lee,

George K. Arthur, Anne Nagel, Lynn Bari, Jimmy Dallas. *D:* Hamilton MacFadden; *P:* Winfield Sheehan; *As.P.:* Lew Brown; *St:* Brown; *Dialogue:* Brown, Ralph Spence. (1:20) (video)

This musical deals with the U.S. Government's forming of a special commission to uplift the spirits of depression conscious Americans. Based on an idea by Will Rogers and Philip Klein, this is the film that brought Shirley Temple to the public's attention as she sings and dances to "Baby Take a Bow," written by Jay Gorney and Lew Brown. Computer-colored in 1989.

4420. Stand Up and Fight (MGM; 1939). *Cast:* Wallace Beery, Robert Taylor, Florence Rice, Helen Broderick, Clinton Rosemond, Charles Bickford, Charley Grapewin, Barton MacLane, Selmer Jackson, John Qualen, Jonathan Hale, Robert Gleckler, Cyrus Kendall, Clem Bevans, Claudia Morgan, Robert Middlemass, Paul Everton. *D:* W.S. Van Dyke II; *P:* Mervyn LeRoy; *St:* Forbes Parkhill; *Sc:* Jane Murfin, James M. Cain, Harvey Ferguson. (1:45)

Western of the conflict between a railroad and a stagecoach line.

4421. Stanley and Livingstone (20th Century–Fox; 1939). *Cast:* Spencer Tracy (Stanley), Nancy Kelly (Eve), Cedric Hardwicke (Dr. Livingstone), Walter Brennan (Jeff Slocum), Charles Coburn (Lord Tyce), Henry Hull (Bennett), Henry Travers (John Kingsley), Miles Mander (John Gresham), Holmes Herbert (Frederick Holcomb), Paul Harvey (Colonel Grimes), David Torrence (Mr. Cranston), Montague Shaw (Sir Oliver French), Brandon Hurst (Sir Henry Forrester), Hassan Said (Hassan), Russell Hicks (commissioner), Frank Dae (other commissioner), Clarence Derwent (Sir Francis Vane), Joseph Crehan (Morehead), Robert Middlemass (Carmichael), William Williams (Mace), Ernest Baskett (Zucco), William Dunn (Chuma), Emmett Smith (Susi), Jack Clisby (Mombay), Everett Brown (Bongo), Frank Jaquet, Emmett Vogan, James McNamara, Dick Stanley, Thomas A. Coleman, William E. "Red" Blair, Frank Orth, Billy Watson, Harry Harvey, Vernon Dent, Paul Stanton. *D:* Henry King; *As.P.:* Kenneth MacGowan; *St:* Hal Long, Sam Hellman; *Sc:* Philip Dunne, Julien Josephson. (1:41) (video)

A lavish production in the well known story of a reporter who goes to Africa in search of a missing missionary. "Dr. Livingstone, I presume." *Film Daily* placed it at #9 on their "10 Best" list.

4422. Star for a Night (20th Century–Fox; 1936). *Cast:* J. Edward Bromberg, Claire Trevor, Chick Chandler, Arline Judge, Evelyn Venable, Dickie Moore, Astrid Allwyn, Jane Darwell, Joyce Compton, Hattie McDaniel, Frank Reicher, Dean Jagger, Adrienne Marden, Susan Fleming, Karen Michaelis. *D:* Lewis Seiler; *Songs:* Harry Akst, Sidney Claire.

B romantic drama.

4423. A Star Is Born (United Artists/Selznick International; 1937). *Cast:* Fredric March (A.A.N. for B.A. as Alfred Hinkel—"Norman Maine"), Janet Gaynor (A.A.N. for B.A. as Esther Blodgett—"Vicki Lester"), Adolphe Menjou (Oliver Niles), May Robson (Granny), Lionel Stander (Libby), Andy Devine (Danny McGuire), Franklin Pangborn (Billy Moon), Owen Moore (final film—d. 1939 as Casey Burke), Elizabeth Jenns (Anita Regis), J.C. Nugent (Theodore Blodgett), Clara Blandick (Aunt Mattie), A.W. Sweatt (Alex), Edgar Kennedy (Pop Randall), Pat Flaherty (Cuddles), Dr. Leonard Walker (conductor at the Hollywood Bowl), Marshall Neilan (Bert the director), Jed Prouty (Artie Carver), Vince Barnett (Bernie the photographer), Peggy Wood (Central Casting's receptionist), Clarence Wilson (justice of the peace), Jonathan Hale (night court judge), Adrian Rosley

(Harris the makeup man), Arthur Hoyt (Ward the makeup man), Edwin Maxwell (voice coach), Guinn Williams (posture coach), Trixie Friganza (waitress), Paul Stanton (speaker at the Academy Award ceremony), Charles Williams, Robert Emmett O'Connor, Olin Howland, Carleton Griffin, Claude King, Eddie Kane, Bud Flanagan (Dennis O'Keefe), Francis Ford, Kenneth Howell, Chris-Pin Martin, Carole Landis, Lana Turner (film debut—bit), Fred "Snowflake Toones. *D:* (A.A.N.) William A. Wellman; *P:* (A.A.N. for "Best Picture") David O. Selznick; *St:* (A.A.) Wellman, Robert Carson; *Sc:* (A.A.N.) Carson, Alan Campbell, Dorothy Parker, Ring Lardner, Jr. (unc.), Budd Schulberg (unc.); *Cinematographer:* (A.A.—special plaque) W. Howard Greene; *Assistant Director:* (A.A.N.) Eric Stacey. (1:51) (video)

Classic drama filmed in technicolor of an actress' rise to fame while her once famous husband hits the bottle and the skids. The story was inspired by the film *What Price Hollywood?* (q.v.) and events in the life of actor John Bowers who committed suicide in 1936 by drowning. *Film Daily*, the *New York Times* and the National Board of Review respectively placed it at #5, #7 and #9 on their lists of "10 Best" films of the year. It became one of the 38 top grossing films of 1936–37 and was also in nomination at the Venice Film Festival. Remade in 1954 as a musical drama with Judy Garland and again in 1977 with a rock music background.

4424. The Star Maker (Paramount; 1939). *Cast:* Bing Crosby (Larry Earl), Louise Campbell, Linda Ware, Laura Hope Crews, Ned Sparks, Janet Waldo, Ethel Griffies, Walter Damrosch, Billy Gilbert, Thurston Hall, Darryl Hickman, Sig Arno (German actor in his American debut), Frank Faylen, Emory Parnell, Ottola Nesmith, Ben Welden, Earl Dwire. *D:* Roy Del Ruth; *P:* Charles R. Rogers; *St:* Arthur Caesar, William Pierce; *Sc:* Caesar,

Frank Butler, Don Hartman; *Songs:* "An Apple for the Teacher" (which became a big hit) & "A Man and His Dreams" by James V. Monaco & Johnny Burke. (1:34)

Musical, based on the life of vaudeville impresario Gus Edwards, who specialized in children's acts. If no one is familiar with Edwards himself, his famous theme song "School Days" should spark some nostalgic memories.

4425. Star of Midnight (RKO; 1935). *Cast:* William Powell, Ginger Rogers, Paul Kelly, Gene Lockhart, Ralph Morgan, Leslie Fenton, J. Farrell MacDonald, Francis McDonald, Vivian Oakland, Frank Reicher, Robert Emmett O'Connor, Russell Hopton, Paul Hurst. *D:* Stephen Roberts; *P:* Pandro S. Berman; *Sc:* Howard J. Green, Anthony Veiller, Edward Kaufman. (1:30) (video)

Hit mystery-comedy of a lawyer in search of what really happened to a theatrical star that he is accused of murdering. Based on the novel by Arthur Somers Roche.

4426. The Star Packer (Monogram-Lone Star; 1934). *Cast:* John Wayne, Verna Hillie, George Hayes, Yakima Canutt, Earl Dwire, Eddie Parker, George Cleveland, Tom Lingham, Artie Ortego, Tex Palmer, Davie Aldrich, Glenn Strange, Billy Franey. *D:* Robert N. Bradbury; *P:* Paul Malvern; *Supervisor:* Trem Carr; *St & Sc:* Bradbury. (G.B. title: *He Wore a Star*) (0:54) (video)

John Wayne western of a U.S. marshal who takes over the job of a murdered sheriff and brings the outlaws to justice.

4427. Star Reporter (Monogram; 1939). *Cast:* Warren Hull, Marsha Hunt, Morgan Wallace, Virginia Howell, Clay Clement, Wallis Clark, Paul Fix, Joseph Crehan, Eddie Kane. *D:* Howard Bretherton; *P:* E.B. Derr; *Sc:* John T. Neville. (1:02)

"Poverty row" newspaper melodrama of a publisher's attempts to get a murder confession from a man, who unknown to him is his father.

4428. The Star Witness (WB; 1931). *Cast:* Charles "Chic" Sale, Walter Huston, Frances Starr, Grant Mitchell, Sally Blane, Ralph Ince, Edward J. Nugent, Dickie Moore, Nat Pendleton, George Ernest, Russell Hopton, Tom Dugan, Robert Elliott. *D:* William A. Wellman; *St:* (A.A.N.) Lucien Hubbard; *Sc:* Hubbard. (1:08)

Low-budget melodrama of an elderly man who witnesses a crime only to later find himself threatened by the perpetrators. Remade as *The Man Who Dared* (q.v.).

4429. Stark Mad (WB; 1929). *Cast:* Louise Fazenda, H.B. Warner, Jacqueline Logan, Claude Gillingwater, Warner Richmond, John Miljan, Andre Beranger, Lionel Belmore, Irving Bacon. *D:* Lloyd Bacon; *St:* Jerome Kingston; *Sc:* Harvey Gates.

Melodrama of people on a yachting expedition who discover their captain is a dangerous criminal.

4430. Starlight Over Texas (Monogram; 1938). *Cast:* Tex Ritter, Carmen LaRoux, Snub Pollard (Pee Wee), Salvatore Damino, Horace Murphy (Ananias), Karl Hackett, Charles King, Martin Garralaga, George Chesebro, Carlos Villarias, Ed Cassidy, Jerry Gomez, Sherry Tansey, Bob Terry, Horace B. Carpenter, Dave O'Brien, Denver Dixon, Chick Hannon, Tex Palmer, Rosa Turich, Fred Velasco, Stelita, Carmen Alvarez, Eduardo Chaves, Northwesterners (Merle Scobee, Ray Scobee, Shorty Brier, Buck Rasch, Chuck Davis), White Flash the horse. *D:* Al Herman; *P:* Edward Finney; *St:* Harry MacPherson; *Sc:* Jack Rathmell. (G.B. title: *Moonlight Over Texas*) (0:58)

Tex Ritter "poverty row" western with musical interludes. Ritter's first for this studio after leaving Grand National. Tex has to deal with some Mexican banditos.

4431. Stars Over Arizona (Monogram; 1937). *Cast:* Jack Randall, Kathleen Eliot, Horace Murphy, Warner Richmond, Tom Herbert, Hal Price, Earl Dwire, Chick Hannon, Charles Romas, Shuma Shermatova, Jack Rockwell, Forrest Taylor, Bob McKenzie, Tex Palmer, Sherry Tansey. *D:* Robert N. Bradbury; *P:* Bradbury; *Supervisor:* Scott R. Dunlap; *Sc:* Robert Emmett (Tansey), Ernie S. Adams. (1:02)

Jack Randall western of a cowboy and his partner who rid a town of an outlaw gang.

4432. Stars Over Broadway (WB; 1935). *Cast:* James Melton (operatic tenor in his film debut), Jane Froman (film debut), Pat O'Brien, Jean Muir, Frank McHugh, Marie Wilson, Frank Fay, E.E. Clive, Phil Regan, George Chandler, William Ricciardi, Eddie Conrad. *D:* William Keighley; *P:* Sam Bischoff; *St:* Mildred Cram; *Sc:* Jerry Wald, Pat C. Flick, Julius J. Epstein; *Songs:* "Broadway Cinderella," "Where Am I?" "At Your Service Madam," "You Let Me Down," "Over Yonder Moon" & "September in the Rain" (music only) by Al Dubin & Harry Warren; "Carry Me Back to the Lone Prairie" Carson J. Robinson; & opera extracts from "Aida" & "Martha." (1:29)

Musical of a hotel employee who hits it big as a radio star.

4433. Start Cheering (Columbia; 1938). *Cast:* Charles Starrett (in his final non-western role with singing voice dubbed by Robert Paige), Jimmy Durante, Walter Connolly, Joan Perry, Gertrude Niesen, Hal LeRoy, Three Stooges (Larry Fine, Moe Howard, Curley Howard), Broderick Crawford, Raymond Walburn, Virginia Dale (film debut), Ernest Truex, Minerva Urecal, Arthur Hoyt, Chaz Chase, Ann Doran,

Romo Vincent, Howard Hickman, Johnny Green & orchestra, Louis Prima & band, Arthur Loft, Gene Morgan, Dr. Craig E. Earle, Nick Lukats, Louise Stanley, Jimmy Wallington. *D:* Albert S. Rogell; *St:* Corey Ford; *Sc:* Eugene Solow, Richard E. Wormser, Philip Rapp. (1:18)

Collegiate musical-comedy.

4434. State Fair (Fox; 1933). *Cast:* Will Rogers (Abel Frake), Janet Gaynor (Margy Frake), Lew Ayres (Pat Gilbert), Sally Eilers (Emily Joyce), Norman Foster (Wayne Frake), Louise Dresser (Melissa Frake), Victor Jory (barker), Frank Craven (storekeeper), Frank Melton (Harry Ware), John Sheehan (barker at the aerial act), Doro Merande (lady at the food contest), Harry Holman & Hobart Cavanaugh (hog judges), Erville Alderson (hog owner). *D:* Henry King; *P:* Winfield Sheehan; *Adaptation & Sc:* (A.A.N.) Paul Green & Sonya Levien. (1:20)

Critically acclaimed Americana, based on the novel by Phil Stong, which tells of a rural family getting ready for and attending the annual state fair. Voted one of the "10 Best" films of the year by the National Board of Review. *Film Daily* and the *New York Times* voted it #5 and #4 respectively on their lists of "10 Best" films. One of the 11 top grossing films of the year, it was remade in 1945 (20th Century–Fox) as a technicolor musical (TV title: *It Happened One Spring*) and again by Fox in 1962 (also a musical).

4435. State Police (Universal; 1938). *Cast:* John King, William Lundigan, Constance Moore, Larry Blake, J. Farrell MacDonald, Eddy Waller, Sam Flint. *D:* John Rawlins (directorial debut); *P:* Trem Carr. (1:01)

Title implies all in this B crime actioner set in a coal-mining town.

4436. State Street Sadie (WB; 1928). *Cast:* Conrad Nagel, Myrna Loy, William Russell, George E. Stone, Pat Hartigan. *D:* Archie L. Mayo; *St:*

Melville Crossman (Darryl Zanuck); *Sc:* Edward T. Lowe, Jr. (G.B. title: *The Girl from State Street*)

Part-talkie crime melodrama which was a minor box office success, premiering September 2, 1928, at New York's lavish Mark Strand Theater.

4437. State Trooper (Columbia; 1933). *Cast:* Evalyn Knapp, Regis Toomey, Eddie Chandler, Matthew Betz, Don Chapman, Raymond Hatton, Lew Kelly, Walter McGrail, Edwin Maxwell, Barbara Weeks. *D:* D. Ross Lederman; *St:* Lambert Hillyer; *Sc:* Stuart Anthony.

B crime melodrama.

4438. State's Attorney (RKO; 1932). *Cast:* John Barrymore, Helen Twelvetrees, Jill Esmond, William "Stage" Boyd, Mary Duncan, C. Henry Gordon, Oscar Apfel, Ralph Ince, Albert Conti, Frederick Burton, Paul Hurst, Nat Pendleton, Raul Roulien, Leon (Ames) Waycoff. *D:* George Archainbaud; *As. P.:* James Kevin McGuinness; *St:* Louis Stevens; *Sc:* Rowland Brown, Gene Fowler. (G.B. title: *Cardigan's Last Case*) (1:19) (video)

Critically acclaimed drama of an attorney who has aspirations to be state governor. Remade as *Criminal Lawyer* (q.v.).

4439. Steady Company (Universal; 1932). *Cast:* June Clyde, Norman Foster, ZaSu Pitts, J. Farrell MacDonald, Henry Armetta. *D:* Edward (Ludwig) Luddy (directorial debut). (1:05)

Programmer boxing drama.

4440. Steamboat 'Round the Bend (Fox; 1935). *Cast:* Will Rogers (Dr. John Pearly), Anne Shirley (Fleety Belle), Eugene Pallette (Sheriff Rufe Jetters), Irvin S. Cobb (Captain Eli), John McGuire (Duke), Berton Churchill (New Moses), Francis Ford (Efe), Roger Imhof (Pappy), Raymond Hatton (Matt Abel), Hobart Bosworth (chaplain), Stepin Fetchit (Jonah), Fred Kohler, Jr.

(Popkins), William (Billy) Benedict (Breck), Lois Verner (Addie May), John Lester Johnson (Uncle Jeff), Pardner Jones (New Elijah), Charles Middleton (Fleety Belle's father), Ben Hall (Fleety Belle's brother), Hobart Cavanaugh, Si Jenks, Louis Mason, Robert E. Homans, Del Henderson, Otto Richards, John Wallace, Jack Pennick, Captain Anderson, Grace Goodall, Ferdinand Munier (governor), D'Arcy Corrigan (hangman), James Marcus (warden), Luke Cosgrave, Heinie Conklin. *D:* John Ford; *P:* Sol M. Wurtzel; *Sc:* Dudley Nichols, Lamar Trotti. (1:36)

Based on the novel by Ben Lucien Burman, this hit 19th-century Americana is set aboard a Mississippi riverboat. The next to last film of Will Rogers, released after his death in 1935 to become one of the 12 top grossing films of the year for the beloved humorist-actor.

The Steel Highway *see* **Other Men's Women**

4441. Stella Dallas (United Artists/Samuel Goldwyn; 1937). *Cast:* Barbara Stanwyck (A.A.N. for B.A. as Stella Dallas, a role originally intended for Ruth Chatterton), John Boles (Stephen Dallas), Anne Shirley (A.A.N. for B.S.A. as Laurel Dallas), Barbara O'Neil (Helen Morrison), Alan Hale (Ed Munn), Tim Holt (Richard Grosvenor III), Marjorie Main (Mrs. Martin), Dickie Jones, Ann Shoemaker, Laraine (Day) Johnson (film debut—bit), Nella Walker, George Walcott, Gertrude Short, Mary Hart (Lynn Roberts), Jimmy Butler, Edmund Elton, Jack Egger, Bruce Satterlee. *D:* King Vidor; *P:* Sam Goldwyn; *Sc:* Victor Heerman, Sarah Y. Mason. (1:51) (video)

This classic tearjerker of an uncultured but loving mother who sacrifices all for her daughter was one of the box office smash hits of the year. Based on the novel by Olive Higgins Prouty, the wedding scene is probably best remem-

bered as it was in the 1925 silent version (also by Goldwyn with a U.A. release) with Belle Bennett and Ronald Colman, of which this is a remake. Remade in 1990 as *Stella.*

4442. Step Lively, Jeeves! (20th Century–Fox; 1937). *Cast:* Arthur Treacher, Patricia Ellis, Robert Kent, Franklin Pangborn, George Givot, George Cooper, Arthur Housman, Helen Flint, John Harrington, Max Wagner. *D:* Eugene Forde; *St:* Frances Hyland; *Sc:* Lynn Root, Frank Fenton.

Low-budget comedy sequel to the hit comedy *Thank You, Jeeves* (q.v.) which was based on characters created by P.G. Wodehouse.

4443. Stepdaughters (Xxxx Xxxx; 1931). *Cast:* Ethel Griffies. (No other information available)

Stepping Into Society (G.B. title) *see* **Doughnuts and Society**

4444. Stepping Out (MGM; 1931). *Cast:* Lillian Bond, Charlotte Greenwood, Reginald Denny, Leila Hyams, Cliff Edwards, Merna Kennedy, Charley Chase, Kane Richmond (feature film debut). *D:* Charles Reisner; *Sc:* Elmer Harris, Robert Hopkins.

B slapstick farce of marital confusions at a posh Mexican resort.

4445. Stepping Sisters (Fox; 1932). *Cast:* Stanley Smith, Barbara Weeks, Louise Dresser, Jobyna Howland, Robert Greig, Minna Gombell, Julanne Johnston, William Collier, Sr., Mary Forbes, Howard Phillips, Ferdinand Munier. *D:* Seymour Felix (more notable as a choreographer, directing the last of two films); *St:* Howard Warren Comstock.

Low-budget romantic comedy.

4446. Stingaree (RKO; 1934). *Cast:* Richard Dix (Stingaree), Irene Dunne, Mary Boland, Conway Tearle, Andy Devine, Henry Stephenson, Una

O'Connor, Reginald Owen, Snub Pollard, George Barraud, Billy Bevan, Robert Greig. *D:* William A. Wellman; *As.P.:* David Lewis; *Adaptation:* Leonard Spigelgass, Lynn Riggs; *Sc:* Becky Gardiner. (1:16)

Lavishly produced romantic actioner set in the Australia of the 1880s as a band of outlaws pursue a rancher's daughter. Based on stories by E.W. Hornung, the studio was attempting to recapture the popularity of its two stars from *Cimarron* (q.v.). Previously filmed as the silent cliff-hanger "The Adventures of Stingaree" (Kalem; 1915).

4447. The Stoker (Allied; 1932). *Cast:* Monte Blue, Dorothy Burgess, Noah Beery, Chris-Pin Martin, Clarence Geldert, Natalie Morehead. *D:* Chester M. Franklin; *P:* M.H. Hoffman, Jr.; *St:* Peter B. Kyne.

Indie melodrama with a B production.

4448. Stolen Harmony (Paramount; 1935). *Cast:* George Raft, Ben Bernie & His Band, Grace Bradley, Lloyd Nolan (film debut), Iris Adrian, Jack Norton, Roscoe Karns, Leslie Fenton, William Pawley, Charles Arnt, Cully Richards, Ralf Harolde, Goodee Montgomery, Paul Gerrits, Christian Rub. *D:* Alfred Werker; *P:* Albert Lewis; *St:* Leon Gordon; *Sc:* Gordon, Harry Ruskin.

B musical melodrama involving urban gangsters.

4449. Stolen Heaven (Paramount; 1931). *Cast:* Nancy Carroll, Phillips Holmes, Louis Calhern, Guy Kibbee (film debut), Joseph Crehan (film debut), Horace Murphy, Joan Carr, Dagmar Oakland, Joan Kenyon, Buford Armitage, G. Albert Smith, Edward Keane. *D:* George Abbott; *St:* Dana Burnet; *Sc:* Abbott, George Hill.

Hit low-budget romantic melodrama of a street girl and a thief.

4450. Stolen Heaven (Paramount; 1938). *Cast:* Gene Raymond,

Olympe Bradna, Glenda Farrell, Lewis Stone, Porter Hall, Douglass Dumbrille, Joe Sawyer, Esther Dale, Charles Halton, Charles Judels, Bert Roach, Rolfe Sedan. *D:* Andrew L. Stone; *P:* Stone; *St:* Stone; *Sc:* Eve Greene, Frederick Jackson. (1:28)

No relation to the preceding film is this production of jewel thieves who pose as musicians to escape the law.

4451. Stolen Holiday (WB/F.N.; 1936–37). *Cast:* Claude Rains, Kay Francis, Ian Hunter, Alison Skipworth, Charles Halton, Kathleen Howard, Alexander D'Arcy, Walter Kingsford, Frank Reicher, Frank Conroy, Egon Brecher, Robert Strange, Betty Lawford, Wedgewood Nowell. *D:* Michael Curtiz; *P:* Harry Joe Brown; *St:* Virginia Kellogg, Warren Duff; *Sc:* Casey Robinson. (1:22)

A fortune hunter and a model marry in this romantic drama based on the career of Alexander Stavisky.

4452. Stolen Kisses (WB; 1929). *Cast:* Claude Gillingwater, May McAvoy, Hallam Cooley, Edna Murphy, Reed Howes, Arthur Hoyt, Agnes Franey, Phyllis Crane. *D:* Ray Enright; *St:* Franz Suppe; *Sc:* Edward T. Lowe, Jr., James A. Starr.

Part-talkie comedy of an old man who wants a grandchild from his son and daughter-in-law.

4453. Stolen Sweets (Chesterfield; 1934). *Cast:* Sally Blane, Charles Starrett, Polly Ann Young, Jameson Thomas, Tom Ricketts. *D:* Richard Thorpe.

"Poverty row" romance.

4454. Stone of Silver Creek (Universal; 1934–35). *Cast:* Buck Jones, Noel Francis, Niles Welch, Murdock MacQuarrie, Marion Shilling, Peggy Campbell, Rodney Hildebrand, Grady Sutton, Bob McKenzie, Lew Meehan, Harry Semels, Frank Rice, Kernan

Cripps. *D:* Nick Grinde; *Sc:* Earle Snell. (1:03)

Buck Jones offbeat western of the proprietor of a gambling house who learns of a scheme to rob him.

4455. Stop, Look and Love (20th Century-Fox; 1939). *Cast:* William Frawley (in a rare lead role), Minna Gombell, Jean Rogers, Cora Sue Collins, Jay Ward, Eddie Collins, Robert Kellard, Roger McGee, Lillian Porter. *D:* Otto Brower; *Sc:* Sada Cowan, Harry Tarshis. (0:57)

Programmer domestic comedy based on the play "The Family Upstairs" by Harry Delf. A remake of *Harmony at Home* (q.v.).

4456. The Storm (Universal; 1930). *Cast:* William "Stage" Boyd, Paul Cavanagh, Lupe Velez, Alphonse Ethier, John Huston, Frank Reicher, Tom London. *D:* William Wyler; *Adaptation:* Charles A. Logue; *Sc:* Wells Root. (1:20)

Triangular drama of two men and a beautiful girl stranded in a mountain cabin during a blizzard. Based on the play "Men Without Skirts" by Langdon McCormick, it was previously filmed by this studio in 1922 with House Peters, Virginia Valli and Matt Moore.

4457. The Storm (Universal; 1938). *Cast:* Charles Bickford, Barton MacLane, Preston Foster, Tom Brown, Nan Grey, Andy Devine, Jack Mulhall, Milburn Stone, Frank Reicher, Samuel S. Hinds, Joe Sawyer, Florence Roberts, Frank Jenks, Marion Martin, Dorothy Arnold, Stanley Hughes, Helen Gilliland. *D:* Harold Young; *P:* Kenneth Goldsmith; *St:* Hugh King, Daniel Moore; *Sc:* Moore, Theodore Reeves, King. (1:18)

No relation to the preceding film is this action drama of seafarers trying to survive a violent tropical typhoon.

4458. Storm at Daybreak (MGM; 1932-33). *Cast:* Walter Huston, Kay Francis, Nils Asther, Phillips Holmes, Jean Parker, Eugene Pallette, C. Henry Gordon, Frank Conroy, Louise Closser Hale, Mischa Auer, Akim Tamiroff, Richard Cramer. *D:* Richard Boleslawski; *P:* Lucien Hubbard; *Sc:* Bertram Millhauser; *Songs:* Gus Kahn. (1:20)

Lavishly produced film which relates the events leading up to the assassination of Archduke Ferdinand and his wife at Sarajevo prior to World War I. Based on the play by Sandor Hunyady.

4459. Storm Over Bengal (Republic; 1938). *Cast:* Richard Cromwell, Rochelle Hudson, Patric Knowles, Claud Allister, Colin Tapley, Edward Van Sloan, Gilbert Emery, Douglass Dumbrille, Halliwell Hobbes, Clyde Cook, John Burton, Douglas Walton. *D:* Sidney Salkow; *Sc:* Garrett Fort.

Action-adventure.

4460. Storm Over the Andes (Universal; 1935). *Cast:* Jack Holt, Antonio Moreno, Mona Barrie, Grant Withers, Gene Lockhart. *D:* Christy Cabanne; *P:* Ben Pivar; *Sc:* Frank Wead (co-writer). (1:22)

Action-adventure of rivalry between air pilots in Bolivia.

4461. Stormy (Universal; 1935). *Cast:* Noah Beery, Jr., Jean Rogers, J. Farrell MacDonald, Raymond Hatton, Walter Miller, Fred Kohler, James P. Burtis, Arizona Wranglers, Bud Osborne, James Phillips, Kenny Cooper, Jack Sanders, Cecil Kellogg, Jack Shannon, Wilfred Lucas, Robert E. Homans, Sam McDaniel, Edmund Cobb, Charles Murphy, Shirley Marks, James Welch, Chester Gan, William Welsh, Jack Leonard, Monte Montague, W.H. Davis, Rex the horse. *D:* Louis Friedlander (Lew Landers); *Sc:* George Plympton, Ben Grauman Kohn. (1:07)

Family entertainment of a youth who saves a herd of wild horses.

4462. Stormy Trails (Colony; 1936-37). *Cast:* Rex Bell, Robert

Hodges, Lois Wilde, Lane Chandler, Earl Dwire, Lloyd Ingraham, Karl Hackett, Earle Ross, Murdock MacQuarrie, Jimmy Aubrey, Roger Williams, George Morrell. *D:* Sam Newfield; *P:* Max & Arthur Alexander; *Sc:* Phil Dunham. (0:59)

Rex Bell western of two brothers who own a mortgaged ranch with gold deposits.

4463. The Story of Alexander Graham Bell (20th Century-Fox/Cosmopolitan; 1939). *Cast:* Don Ameche (A.G. Bell), Loretta Young (Mrs. Bell), Henry Fonda (Thomas Watson), Charles Coburn, Gene Lockhart, Spring Byington, Sally Blane, Polly Ann Young, Georgianna Young, Bobs Watson, Harry Davenport, Russell Hicks, Elizabeth Patterson, Claire DuBrey, Jan Duggan, Ralph Remley, Paul Stanton, Charles Trowbridge, Harry Tyler. *D:* Irving Cummings; *As.P.:* Kenneth MacGowan; *St:* Ray Harris; *Sc:* Lamar Trotti. (G.B. title: *The Modern Miracle*) (1:37)

Hit production of events in the life of the man who invented the telephone in the latter part of the 19th-century.

4464. The Story of Louis Pasteur (WB; 1936). *Cast:* Paul Muni (A.A. for B.A., as well as being voted "Best Actor" at the Venice Film Festival for his portrayal of Pasteur), Josephine Hutchinson (Marie Pasteur), Anita Louise (Annette Pasteur), Donald Woods (Jean Martel), Fritz Leiber (Dr. Charbonnet), Henry O'Neill (Roux), Porter Hall (Dr. Rosignol), Raymond Brown (Dr. Radisse), Akim Tamiroff (Dr. Zaranoff), Halliwell Hobbes (Dr. Lister),Frank Reicher (Dr. Pheiffer), Dickie Moore (Phillip Meister), Ruth Robinson (Mrs. Meister), Walter Kingsford (Napoleon III), Iphigenie Castiglioni (Empress Eugenie), Herbert Heywood (Boncourt), Herbert Corthell (President Thiers), Frank Mayo (President Carnot), Lottie Williams (Cecile), William Burress, Robert Strange, Niles Welch,

Mabel Colcord, Leonard Mudie, Brenda Fowler, Eric Mayne, Alphonse Ethier, Edward Van Sloan, George Andre Beranger, Otto Hoffman, Montague Shaw, Tempe Pigott, Richard Alexander, Baron Hesse, Wheaton Chambers, Fred Walton, Leonid Snegoff, Wilfred Lucas, Gordon (Bill) Elliott, Jack Santoro, Ferdinand Schumann-Heink. *D:* William Dieterle; *P:* (A.A.N. for Best Picture) Henry Blanke; *Original Story:* (A.A.) Pierre Collings, Sheridan Gibney; *Sc:* (A.A.) Collings & Gibney. (1:27) (video)

A critically acclaimed biography of the man, his life and his discoveries. The National Board of Review voted it the #2 position on their "10 Best" list, *Film Daily,* #6 on theirs, while the *New York Times* gave it a #8 placement. A Cosmopolitan production, it was one of the 25 top grossing films of 1935–36.

Note: A curious side-note to this production is the fact that the Brothers Warner did not want Muni in the film.

4465. The Story of Temple Drake (Paramount; 1933). *Cast:* Miriam Hopkins, Jack LaRue, William Gargan, William Collier, Jr., Irving Pichel, Guy Standing (film debut), Elizabeth Patterson, Florence Eldridge, John Peter Richmond (John Carradine), Jobyna Howland, Hattie McDaniel, Henry Hall (film debut), Grady Sutton, Kent Taylor, Oscar Apfel, James Eagles, James (Jim) Mason, Harlan Knight. *D:* Stephen Roberts; *Sc:* Oliver H.P. Garrett. (1:11)

Hit pre-code drama of a girl with loose morals who is kidnapped, sexually assaulted and then willingly falls in with her abductors. Based on William Faulkner's torrid best selling "Sanctuary," this film shocked audiences of its day with its frank style. Remade as *Sanctuary* (20th Century-Fox; 1961).

4466. The Story of Vernon and Irene Castle (RKO; 1939). *Cast:* Fred Astaire (Vernon Castle), Ginger Rogers (Irene Castle), Edna May Oliver,

Walter Brennan, Lew Fields (himself), Etienne Girardot, Donald MacBride, Victor Varconi, Janet Beecher, Frank Faylen, Leonid Kinskey, Clarence Derwent, Robert Strange, Rolfe Sedan, Sonny Lamont. *D:* H.C. Potter; *P:* George Haight; *Adaptation:* Oscar Hammerstein II, Dorothy Yost; *Sc:* Richard Sherman; *Choreography:* Hermes Pan, Astaire; *Song:* "Only When You're in My Arms" by Con Conrad, Harry Ruby & Bert Kalmar. (1:33) (video)

A retelling of events in the lives of the famous man and wife team who set the stage for ballroom dancing following the turn-of-the-century, until he was killed in a flying accident in World War I. Based on Irene's book "My Husband" and another work by her, the film features many popular songs of the era and is notable as the final Astaire-Rogers vehicle for this studio. It also flopped at the box office.

4467. Stowaway (20th Century–Fox; 1936). *Cast:* Shirley Temple, Robert Young, Alice Faye, Eugene Pallette, Helen Westley, Arthur Treacher, J. Edward Bromberg, Astrid Allwyn, Allan Lane, Helen Jerome Eddy, Leon Ames, William Stack, Paul McVey, Willie Fung, Philip Ahn, Julius Tannen, Jayne Regan. *D:* William A. Seiter; *P:* Earl Carroll, Harold Wilson; *Sc:* William Conselman, Arthur Sheekman, Nat Perrin; *Songs:* Mack Gordon, Harry Revel. (1:26) (video)

Popular romantic musical with Shirley Temple as the stowaway on a cruise ship who gets involved in everybody's lives. Computer-colored prints produced in the 1980s.

Note: If you ever wanted to hear Shirley sing in Chinese.

4468. The Stowaway (Universal; 1932). *Cast:* Fay Wray, Leon (Ames) Waycoff, Montagu Love, Lee Moran, Roscoe Karns, James Gordon. *D:* Phil Whitman. (1:00)

A girl with a past that she would sooner forget, hides out on a ship, only to be discovered by crew members in this B drama.

4469. Straight from the Heart (Universal; 1935). *Cast:* Mary Astor, Roger Pryor, Baby Jane (later Juanita Quigley), Carol Coombe, Warren Hymer, Andy Devine, Henry Armetta, Grant Mitchell, Willard Robertson, Douglas Fowley, Virginia Hammond, Frank Reicher, Louise Carter, Helen Parrish. *D:* Scott R. Beal; *Sc:* Doris Anderson. (1:10)

Tear-jerker of a phony paternity suit brought on the local mayor by a political opponent.

4470. Straight from the Shoulder (Paramount; 1936). *Cast:* Ralph Bellamy, David Holt, Katherine Locke, Onslow Stevens, Noel Madison, Paul Fix, Andy Clyde. *D:* Stuart Heisler (directorial debut); *P:* A.M. Botsford.

A man and his son are forced into hiding after witnessing a gangland killing in this B.

4471. Straight Is the Way (MGM; 1934). *Cast:* Franchot Tone, Gladys George (Broadway actress in her talkie debut), Karen Morley, May Robson, Jack LaRue, Nat Pendleton, C. Henry Gordon, William Bakewell, Raymond Hatton, John Qualen. *D:* George Abbott, Paul Sloane; *P:* Lucien Hubbard; *Sc:* Bernard Schubert.

Crime drama, a remake of *Four Walls* (MGM; 1928) with John Gilbert and Joan Crawford. Based on the hit Broadway play of that name by George Abbott and Dana Burnet.

4472. Straight, Place and Show (20th Century–Fox; 1938–39). *Cast:* Ritz Brothers (Al, Harry and Jim), Ethel Merman, Richard Arlen, Phyllis Brooks, George Barbier, Sidney Blackmer, Ivan Lebedeff, Ben Welden, Stanley Fields, Lon Chaney, Jr., Edward Greene, Rafael Storm, Will Stanton, Gregory Gaye, Tiny Roebuck, Pat McKee. *D:* David Butler; *P:* Darryl F.

Zanuck; *Play:* Damon Runyon, Irving Caesar; *Sc:* M.M. Musselman, Allen Rivkin. (G.B. title: *They're Off*) (1:06)

A zany low-budget comedy which might be more aptly titled "The Ritz Brothers at the Races."

4473. Straight-Shooter (Victory; 1939). *Cast:* Tim McCoy, Ben Corbett (Magpie), Julie Sheldon, Forrest Taylor, Carl Mathews, Ted Adams, Reed Howes, Budd Buster, Wally West, Jack Ingram. *D:* Sam Newfield; *P:* Sam Katzman; *Sc:* Basil Dickey, Joseph O'Donnell. (1:00)

Tim McCoy in a "Lightnin' Bill Carson" western (his last for this indie company) of a lawman who poses as a rancher attempting to purchase a property where some outlaw loot is supposed to be hidden.

4474. Straightaway (Columbia; 1933). *Cast:* Tim McCoy, Sue Carol, Ward Bond, Samuel S. Hinds, Lafe McKee. *D:* Otto Brower.

Low-budget auto racing melodrama.

4475. Stranded (WB; 1935). *Cast:* Kay Francis, George Brent, Patricia Ellis, Donald Woods, Robert Barrat, Barton MacLane, June Travis (film debut), Frankie Darro, Richard Loo, Henry O'Neill, Ann Shoemaker, Mary Forbes, Joseph Crehan, Eily Malyon, Shirley Grey, William Harrigan. *D:* Frank Borzage; *P:* Sam Bischoff; *Sc:* Delmer Daves. (1:16)

B melodrama of a worker for traveler's aid and her romance with a construction worker. Based on the novel "The Lady with a Badge" by Frank Wead and Ferdinand Reyher.

Stranded in Paris (G.B. title) *see* **Artists and Models Abroad**

4476. Strange Adventure (Monogram; 1932). *Cast:* Regis Toomey, June Clyde, Lucille La Verne, William V. Mong, Jason Robards, Eddie Phillips, Dwight Frye, Isabelle Vecki, Alan Roscoe, Nadine Dore, Fred "Snowflake" Toones, William J. Humphrey, Harry Myers, Eddy Chandler. *D:* Phil Whitman, Hampton Del Ruth; *P:* I.E. Chadwick; *St:* Arthur Hoerl; *Sc:* Lee Chadwick; *Dialogue:* Hampton Del Ruth. (aka: *The Wayne Murder Case*) (1:00)

A man dies while reading his will to his heirs in this "poverty row" mystery-melodrama.

4477. Strange Cargo (Pathé-Cargo; 1929). *Cast:* Lee Patrick (film debut), June Nash, Russell Gleason, Ned Sparks, Warner Richmond, Charles Hamilton, Claude King, Otto Matiesen, Harry Allen, Josephine Brown, Cosmo Kyrle Bellew, Frank Reicher, Andre Beranger. *D:* Benjamin Glazer, Arthur Gregor; *P:* Glazer; *St:* Glazer, Melchior Lengyel; *Sc:* Horace Jackson.

Melodrama.

4478. The Strange Case of Clara Deane (Paramount; 1932). *Cast:* Wynne Gibson, Pat O'Brien, Frances Dee, Russell Gleason, Louise Carter, Dudley Digges, Cora Sue Collins, Arthur Pierson, George Barbier, Lee Kohlmar, Florence Britton. *D:* Louis Gasnier, Max Marcin; *St:* Arthur M. Brilant.

B drama of an adopted girl who unknowingly meets her biological mother.

4479. The Strange Case of Dr. Meade (Columbia; 1939). *Cast:* Beverly Roberts, Jack Holt, Noah Beery, Jr., John Qualen, Charles Middleton. *D:* Lewis D. Collins; *Sc:* Gordon Rigby.

(No other information available)

The Strange Conspiracy (G.B. title) *see* **The President Vanishes**

4480. Strange Faces (Universal; 1938). *Cast:* Dorothea Kent, Frank Jenks, Andy Devine, Leon Ames, Charles Middleton, Jack Norton. *D:* Errol Taggart; *P:* Burt Kelly. (1:05)

When two reporters are after the same story, one is framed by the other.

4481. Strange Interlude (MGM; 1932). *Cast:* Norma Shearer, Clark Gable, May Robson, Maureen O'Sullivan, Robert Young, Ralph Morgan, Henry B. Walthall, Mary Alden, Alexander Kirkland, Tad Alexander. *D:* Robert Z. Leonard; *P:* Leonard; *Sc:* Bess Meredyth, C. Gardiner Sullivan. (G.B. title: *Strange Interval*) (1:50)

Hit drama of two people who age without resolving their problems, though their inner thoughts are revealed to the audience. The film was based on a five hour play by Eugene O'Neill and was in nomination at the Venice Film Festival.

Strange Interval (G.B. title) *see* **Strange Interlude**

4482. Strange Justice (RKO/ King Motion Pictures; 1932). *Cast:* Marian Marsh, Reginald Denny, Richard Bennett, Norman Foster, Irving Pichel, Nydia Westman (film debut), Thomas E. Jackson, Larry Steers, Walter Brennan. *D:* Victor Schertzinger; *P:* J.G. Bachmann; *Sc:* William A. Drake. (1:22)

Independently produced drama of two young people who are innocently involved in theft and murder.

Strange Laws (G.B. title) *see* **The Cherokee Strip**

4483. The Strange Love of Molly Louvain (WB/F.N.; 1932). *Cast:* Ann Dvorak, Richard Cromwell, Lee Tracy, Leslie Fenton, Guy Kibbee, Evalyn Knapp, Frank McHugh, Richard Cramer, Claire McDowell, Mary Doran, Louise Beavers, Hank Mann, Charles Middleton, Ben Alexander, Donald Dillaway, C. Henry Gordon, Harold Waldridge, Willard Robertson, Harry Beresford, William Burress, Maurice Black. *D:* Michael Curtiz; *Sc:* Erwin Gelsey, Brown Holmes. (1:14)

Based on the play by Maurine Watkins, this was a hit melodrama of its day of a woman with an illegitimate child and the various men who seek her affections.

4484. Strange People (Chesterfield; 1933). *Cast:* John Darrow, Gloria Shea, Wilfred Lucas, Michael Visaroff, Mary Foy, Hale Hamilton, Lew Kelly, Jane Keckley, Frank H. LaRue, Walter Brennan, Stanley Blystone, Jerry Mandy, Jack Pennick. *D:* Richard Thorpe; *St & Sc:* Jack Townley.

"Poverty row" melodrama.

4485. Strange Wives (Universal; 1935). *Cast:* Roger Pryor, Esther Ralston, June Clayworth, Hugh O'Connell, Cesar Romero, Ralph Forbes, Leslie Fenton, Francis L. Sullivan. *D:* Richard Thorpe. (1:13)

Low-budget drama of a man who marries a Russian girl, only to find their married life is full of surprises.

4486. The Stranger from Arizona (Columbia/Coronet; 1938). *Cast:* Buck Jones, Dorothy Fay, Hank Mann, Roy Barcroft, Bob Terry, Hank Worden, Horace Murphy, Dot Farley, Budd Buster, Stanley Blystone, Ralph Peters. *D:* Elmer Clifton; *P:* Monroe Shaff; *Sc:* Shaff. (1:00)

Buck Jones oater of a railroad detective, undercover to expose the baddies.

4487. The Stranger from Texas (Columbia; 1939). *Cast:* Charles Starrett, Lorna Gray (Adrian Booth), Sons of the Pioneers with Bob Nolan & Pat Brady, Richard Fiske, Dick Curtis, Alan Bridge, Edmund Cobb, Jack Rockwell, Hal Taliaferro, Edward LeSaint, Art Mix, George Chesebro. *D:* Sam Nelson; *Sc:* Paul Franklin. (0:54)

Charles Starrett western of cattle rustling. A remake of *The Mysterious Avenger* (q.v.).

4488. Stranger in Town (WB; 1932). *Cast:* David Manners, Ann Dvorak, Charles "Chic" Sale, Noah Beery, Maude Eburne, Lyle Talbot, John Larkin, Raymond Hatton, Jessie Arnold. *D:* Erle C. Kenton; *Sc:* Carl Erickson, Harvey Thew.

Low-budget comedy-drama set in a small town.

4489. Strangers All (RKO; 1935). *Cast:* May Robson, Preston Foster, William Bakewell, James Bush, Florine McKinney, Samuel S. Hinds, Clifford Jones, Suzanne Kaaren, Leon Ames (nee: Leon Waycoff), Reginald Barlow, Paul Stanton, Virginia Reed (Lynne Carver). *D:* Charles Vidor; *As.P.:* Cliff Reid; *Sc:* Milton Krims. (1:10)

Domestic comedy-drama of a family of five who live together, but know very little about each other. Based on a play by Marie M. Bercovici.

4490. Strangers in Love (Paramount; 1932). *Cast:* Kay Francis, Fredric March (in a dual role), Stuart Erwin, Juliette Compton, Sidney Toler, George Barbier, Lucien Littlefield, Earle Foxe, Gertrude Howard, Ben Taggart, Leslie Palmer, John Maurice Sullivan. *D:* Lothar Mendes; *Sc:* Grover Jones, William Slavens McNutt. (1:16)

Twin brothers change places in this comedy-drama based on a popular novel called "The Shorn Lamb" by William J. Locke.

4491. Strangers May Kiss (MGM; 1931). *Cast:* Norma Shearer, Robert Montgomery, Neil Hamilton, Marjorie Rambeau, Irene Rich, Jed Prouty, Henry Armetta, Conchita Montenegro (American debut), Hale Hamilton, Albert Conti, Kane Richmond, George Davis. *D:* George Fitzmaurice; *Sc:* John Meehan. (1:25)

Romantic drama based on the novel by Ursula Parrott. One of the 15 top grossing films of 1930–31.

4492. Strangers of the Evening (World Wide/Tiffany; 1932). *Cast:* Miriam Seegar, Mahlon Hamilton, ZaSu Pitts, Eugene Pallette, William Scott, Theodore von Eltz, Alan Roscoe, Charles Williams, James Burtis, Lucien Littlefield, Warner Richmond, Francis Sayles, Harold Waldridge. *D:* H. Bruce

Humberstone (directorial debut); *St:* Tiffany Thayer.

"Poverty row" mystery-comedy. Produced by Tiffany studios and released by World Wide.

4493. The Stranger's Return (MGM; 1933). *Cast:* Lionel Barrymore, Miriam Hopkins, Franchot Tone, Beulah Bondi, Stuart Erwin, Irene Hervey, Grant Mitchell, Joseph (Sawyer) Sauers, Aileen Carlyle, Tad Alexander. *D:* King Vidor; *P:* Vidor, Lucien Hubbard; *Sc:* Stong, Brown Holmes. (1:29)

Romantic drama of a woman who leaves her husband and the city and goes to reside on her grandfather's farm where she finds a new way of life. Based on the novel by Phil Stong, this film was not popular with depression-era audiences.

4494. The Strawberry Roan (Universal; 1933). *Cast:* Ken Maynard, Ruth Hall, Frank Yaconelli, Harold Goodwin, Charles King, William Desmond, James Marcus, Jack Rockwell, Bill Patton, Ben Corbett, Robert Walker, Bud McClure, Art Mix. *D:* Alan James (aka: Alvin J. Neitz); *Sc:* Nate Gatzert; *Title Song:* Curley Fletcher. (G.B. title: *Flying Fury*) (0:59)

Ken Maynard western with musical interludes of the capture and taming of a wild horse. Maynard named this as his personal favorite of all the westerns he made over the years. No relation to the 1948 Gene Autry film of the same name.

4495. Streamline Express (Mascot; 1935). *Cast:* Evelyn Venable, Victor Jory, Esther Ralston, Erin O'Brien-Moore, Ralph Forbes, Sidney Blackmer, Vince Barnett, Clay Clement, Robert Watson, Lee Moran, Syd Saylor, Libby Taylor, Edward Hearn, Allan Cavan, Joseph Girard, Tommy Bupp, Harvey Thew, Smiley Burnette, Wade Boteler. *D:* Leonard Fields; *P:* George Yohalem; *St:* Wellyn Totman; *Sc:* Fields, David Silverstein, Olive Cooper. (1:11)

Comedy of a Broadway producer in pursuit of his star actress who has walked out on him. Based on the play "Napoleon of Broadway" by Charles Bruce Millholland, it was previously filmed as *Twentieth Century* (q.v.).

4496. Street Angel (Fox; 1928). *Cast:* Janet Gaynor (A.A. for B.A. combined with *Seventh Heaven* and *Sunrise* [Fox; 1927] — 1927-28), Charles Farrell, Alberto Rabagliati, Gino Conti, Guido Trento, Henry Armetta, Natalie Kingston. *D:* Frank Borzage; *Sc:* Marion Orth; *Cinematographers:* (A.A.N.) Ernest Palmer, Paul Ivano; *Art-Set Decoration:* (A.A.N.) Harry Oliver; *Song:* "Angela Mia" by Erno Rapee. (1:41)

Part-talkie romance of an Italian girl and a painter. A film which capitalized on the popularity of *Seventh Heaven* (Fox; 1927) which also paired the stars. Basically a silent with synchronized music, sound effects, titles and a vocalized song. Based on the play "Lady Cristilinda" by Monckton Hoffe, the film placed #2 on the "10 Best" list of the *New York Times,* while *Film Daily* placed it at #5 on their same list.

4497. Street Girl (RKO; 1929). *Cast:* Betty Compson, John Harron, Ivan Lebedeff, Jack Oakie, Ned Sparks, Guy Buccola, Joseph Cawthorn, Doris Eaton, Gus Arnheim & His Ambassadors, Henry Armetta, Russ Columbo, Eddie Kane. *D:* Wesley Ruggles; *As.P.:* Louis Sarecky; *St:* W. Carey Wonderly; *Sc:* Jane Murfin; *Songs:* Oscar Levant, Sidney Clare. (1:31)

Romantic musical notable as the first production of RKO-Radio, but their second release. A big box office hit.

Note: Loosely remade as *That Girl from Paris* (q.v.) and in 1942 by this studio as *Four Jacks and a Jill.*

4498. Street of Chance (Paramount; 1930). *Cast:* William Powell, Kay Francis, Jean Arthur, Regis Toomey, Brooks Benedict, Joan Standing, Maurice Black, Betty Francisco,

John Risso. *D:* John Cromwell; *P:* David O. Selznick; *St:* Oliver H.P. Garrett; *Sc:* (A.A.N.) Howard Estabrook.

Drama of a gambler who risks everything to shield his brother. The original story was inspired by the life of New York gambler, Arnold Rothstein. Voted one of the year's "10 Best" films by the National Board of Review.

4499. Street of Missing Men (Republic; 1939). *Cast:* Charles Bickford, Ralph Graves, Mabel Todd, Guinn Williams, Harry Carey, John Gallaudet, Regis Toomey, Nana Bryant, Tommy Ryan. *D:* Sidney Salkow; *St:* William Rankin, Eleanore Griffin; *Sc:* Frank Dolan, Leonard Lee.

B crime melodrama.

Street of Missing Women *see* **Cafe Hostess**

4500. Street of Women (WB; 1932). *Cast:* Kay Francis, Roland Young, Gloria Stuart (film debut), Alan Dinehart, Marjorie Gateson, Allen Vincent, Louise Beavers, Adrienne Dore. *D:* Archie Mayo; *Sc:* Mary McCall, Jr.

Low-budget drama of the crisscross relationships of various people.

4501. Street Scene (United Artists/Samuel Goldwyn; 1931). *Cast:* Sylvia Sidney (Rose Maurrant), William Collier, Jr. (Sam Kaplan), Max Montor (repeating his stage role as Abe Kaplan), David Landau (repeating his stage role as Frank Maurrant), Estelle Taylor (Anna Maurrant), Beulah Bondi (film debut, repeating her stage role as Emma Jones), Russell Hopton (Steve Sankey), John M. Qualen (film debut, repeating his stage role as Karl Olsen), Greta Granstedt (Mae Jones), Matt McHugh (repeating his stage role as Vincent Jones), Tom H. Manning (repeating his stage role as George Jones), Adele Watson (Olga Olsen), Anna Kostant (repeating her stage role as Shirley Kaplan), George Humbert (repeating his stage role as Filippo Fiorentino),

Eleanor Wesselhoeft (film debut, repeating her stage role as Greta Fioentino), Allen Fox (Dick McGann), Nora Cecil (Alice Simpson), Louis Natheaux (Harry Easter), Lambert Rogers (Willie Maurrant), Virginia Davis (Mary Hildebrand), Helen Lovett (Laura Hildebrand), Kenneth Selling (Charlie Hildebrand), Conway Washburn (repeating his stage role as Dan Buchanan), Howard Russell (Dr. John Wilson), Richard Powell (Officer Harry Murphy), Walter James (Marshal James Henry), Harry Wallace (Fred Cullen), Monte Carter, Walter Miller, Jane Mercer, Margaret Robertson. *D:* King Vidor; *P:* Sam Goldwyn; *Adaptation & Sc:* Elmer Rice. (1:20) (video)

Based on the hit Pulitzer Prize winning (1928–29) play by Elmer Rice which ran for over two years on the stage, this drama of life on the streets and in the tenements of New York City was considered heavy stuff in its day. *Film Daily* placed it at #2 on their list of "10 Best" films of the year.

4502/4503. Streets of New York (Monogram; 1939). *Cast:* Jackie Cooper, Dick Purcell, Marjorie Reynolds, Martin Spellman, Sidney Miller, Buddy Pepper, Bobby Stone, David Durand, William Tucker, Robert Tucker, Kent Rogers, George Cleveland. *D:* William Nigh; *P:* William T. Lackey; *St & Sc:* Robert D. Andrews. (aka: *The Abe Lincoln of Ninth Avenue*) (1:13) (video)

A young street hustler yearns to be an attorney in this B drama.

Strictly Confidential (G.B. title) *see* **Broadway Bill**

4504. Strictly Dishonorable (Universal; 1931). *Cast:* Paul Lukas (Gus), Sidney Fox, Lewis Stone, George Meeker, William Ricciardi, Sidney Toler, Natalie Moorhead, Carlo Schipa, Samuel Bonello, Joe Torilla. *D:* John M. Stahl; *Sc:* Gladys Lehman. (1:10)

Successful at the box office was this romance of a naive young girl and a worldly opera singer. Based on the hit comedy play by Preston Sturges, it was remade by MGM in 1951.

4505. Strictly Dynamite (RKO; 1934). *Cast:* James (Jimmy) Durante, Lupe Velez, Norman Foster, Marian Nixon, William Gargan, Eugene Pallette, Sterling Holloway, Minna Gombell, Leila Bennett, Franklin Pangborn, Mills Brothers, Jackie Searle, Berton Churchill, Irene Franklin. *D:* Elliott Nugent; *As.P.:* H.N. Swanson; *St:* Robert T. Colwell, Robert A. Simon; *Sc:* Maurine Watkins, Ralph Spence, Milton Raison, Jack Harvey; *Add'l Dial.:* Milton Raison, Jack Harvey; *Songs:* Harold Adamson, Burton Lane, Irving Kahal, Sammy Fain, Jimmy Durante. (1:14)

Musical-comedy of a young poet who becomes a gag writer for a radio comic.

4506. Strictly Modern (WB/F.N.; 1930). *Cast:* Dorothy Mackaill, Julanne Johnston, Sidney Blackmer, Warner Richmond, Mickey Bennett, Kathrin Clare Ward. *D:* William A. Seiter; *Sc:* Ray Harris, Gene Towne, J. Morris.

Low-budget romance of a lady writer who knowingly gets involved with the man who left her cousin standing at the altar. Based on the play by Hubert Henry Davies.

4507. Strictly Personal (Paramount; 1933). *Cast:* Marjorie Rambeau, Eddie Quillan, Dorothy Burgess, Louis Calhern, Dorothy Jordan, Hugh Herbert, Olive Tell, Helen Jerome Eddy, Thomas Jackson, Charles Sellon, Rollo Lloyd, Gay Seabrook, Harvey Clark, Ben Hall, Hazel Jones. *D:* Ralph Murphy; *P:* Charles R. Rogers; *St:* Robert T. Shannon, Wilson Mizner; *Sc:* Willard Mack, Beatrice Banyard; *Add'l Dial.:* Casey Robinson.

B drama of some crooks who take control of a lonely hearts club.

4508. Strictly Unconventional (MGM; 1930). *Cast:* Catherine Dale Owen, Tyrrell Davis, Lewis Stone, Paul Cavanagh, Mary Forbes, Alison Skipworth, Ernest Torrence. *D:* David Burton; *Sc:* Frank Butler, Sylvia Thalberg.

A remake of *The Circle* (MGM; 1925) with Eleanor Boardman and Malcolm McGregor, by director Frank Borzage. Based on Somerset Maugham's 1921 hit play of that name, it is a tale of marital infidelity through two generations.

4509/4510. Strike Me Pink (United Artists/Samuel Goldwyn; 1936). *Cast:* Eddie Cantor, Sally Eilers, Ethel Merman, William Frawley, Parkyakarkus (Harry Parks), Brian Donlevy, Jack LaRue, Edward Brophy, Gordon Jones, Sunnie O'Dea, Rita Rio (Dona Drake), Charles Wilson, Stanley Blystone, Helen Lowell, Duke York, Don Brodie, Sidney Fields, Charles McAvoy, Goldwyn Girls. *D:* Norman Taurog; *P:* Sam Goldwyn; *St:* Clarence Budington Kelland; *Sc:* Frank Butler, Philip Rapp, Walter de Leon, Francis Martin; *Songs:* Harold Arlen, Lew Brown. (1:40)

Hit musical-comedy of an amusement park owner and his harassment by racketeers.

4511. Stronger Than Desire (MGM; 1939). *Cast:* Virginia Bruce, Walter Pidgeon, Ann Dvorak (Mrs. Leslie Fenton), Lee Bowman, Rita Johnson, Ilka Chase, Tom Neal, Donald Douglas, Thomas Jackson, Ann (E.) Todd (film debut), Richard Lane, Paul Stanton, Ferike Boros. *D:* Leslie Fenton; *P:* John W. Considine, Jr.; *Sc:* David Hertz, William Ludwig.

Domestic drama of a lawyer who is unaware that his wife is guilty of a crime. A remake of *Evelyn Prentice* (q.v.), the name of the novel by W.E. Woodward upon which it is based.

4512. The Struggle (United Artists; 1931). *Cast:* Hal Skelly, Zita Johann, Charlotte Wynters, Jackson Halliday, Edna Hagan, Helen Mack, Charles Richman, Scott Moore, Evelyn Baldwin, Claude Cooper, Dave Manley, Arthur Lipson. *D:* Griffith; *P:* Griffith; *Sc:* Anita Loos, John Emerson, Griffith (unc.). (1:28)

This melodrama was an indictment against bootleg liquor and was the final film to be directed by famed silent director David Wark (D.W.) Griffith. Based on a popular melodramatic stageplay by Emile Zola, titled "The Drunkard," the film was not favored by the movie going public.

Note: For the only other all-talkie directed by Griffith, see: *Abraham Lincoln* (q.v.).

4513. Student Tour (MGM; 1934). *Cast:* Jimmy Durante, Charles Butterworth, Maxine Doyle, Phil Regan, Florine McKinney, Betty Grable, Herman Brix (Bruce Bennett in his film debut), Nelson Eddy, Monte Blue, Mary Anita Loos, Fay McKenzie, Mischa Auer, Bobby Gordon, Minerva Urecal, Douglas Fowley, Arthur Treacher, Pauline Brooks, Florence & Alvarez, Dewey Robinson. *D:* Charles F. Reisner; *P:* Monta Bell; *St:* Samuel Marx, George Seaton; *Sc:* Philip Dunne, Ralph Spence; *Songs:* Nacio Herb Brown, Arthur Freed. (1:27)

Flop musical-comedy of students from a college who go on a world tour.

4514. The Studio Murder Mystery (Paramount; 1929). *Cast:* Neil Hamilton, Warner Oland, Fredric March, Florence Eldridge, Doris Hill, Chester Conklin, Mischa Auer, Lane Chandler, E.H. Calvert, Gardner James, Donald MacKenzie, Guy Oliver. *D:* Frank Tuttle; *Sc:* Tuttle. (1:02)

Low-budget backstage Hollywood

comedy-mystery based on a magazine serial by the Edingtons.

Studio Romance (G.B. title) *see* **Talent Scout**

4515. A Study in Scarlet (World Wide/KBS Prods.; 1933). *Cast:* Reginald Owen (Holmes), Alan Dinehart (Merrydew), Alan Mowbray (Inspector La Strade), Anna May Wong, June Clyde, John Warburton, Warburton Gamble (Watson), Doris Lloyd, Billy Bevan, Halliwell Hobbes, J.M. Kerrigan, Hobart Cavanaugh, Leila Bennett, Wyndham Standing, Tetsu Komai, Tempe Pigott, Cecil Reynolds. *D:* Edwin L. Marin; *Sc:* Robert Florey; *Cont. & Dial.:* Reginald Owen. (1:10) (video)

"Poverty row" mystery featuring the characters of Sherlock Holmes and Dr. Watson, but is only remotely related to Sir Arthur Conan Doyle's story of the same name.

4516. Stunt Pilot (Monogram; 1939). *Cast:* John Trent (Tommy), Marjorie Reynolds (Betty Lou), Milburn Stone (Skeeter), Jason Robards (Paul), Pat O'Malley, George Meeker, Wesley Barry, George Cleveland, Johnny Day, Charles Morton, Mary Field, Buddy Cox. *D:* George Waggner; *P:* Paul Malvern; *Sc:* W. Scott Darling, Joseph West (Waggner). (1:02) (video)

During the filming of a movie, a real murder is committed aboard an airplane. This was the 2nd entry (of 4) in the "Tailspin Tommy" series, based on comic strip characters created by Hal Forrest which also appeared in silent films and serials.

4517. Submarine D-1 (WB/F.N.; 1937). *Cast:* Pat O'Brien, George Brent, Wayne Morris, Frank McHugh, Doris Weston, Henry O'Neill, Dennie Moore, Veda Ann Borg, Broderick Crawford, Regis Toomey, John Ridgely (film debut), Don Defore, Owen King, Jerry Fletcher, Wally Maher. *D:* Lloyd Bacon; *P:* Lou Edelman; *Sc:* Frank Wead, Warren Duff, Lawrence Kimble. (1:38)

Adventure drama set in the titled submergible craft.

4518. Submarine Patrol (20th Century–Fox; 1938). *Cast:* Richard Greene, Nancy Kelly, Preston Foster, George Bancroft, Slim Summerville, John Carradine, Robert Lowery, Maxie Rosenbloom, Victor Varconi, Douglas Fowley, J. Farrell MacDonald, Moroni Olsen, George E. Stone, Henry Armetta, Ward Bond, Elisha Cook, Jr., E.E. Clive, Warren Hymer, Lon Chaney, Jr., Dick Hogan, Charles Trowbridge, Charles Tannen, Joan Valerie, Jack Pennick, Harry Strang. *D:* John Ford; *P:* Darryl F. Zanuck; *St:* Ray Millholland, Jack Yellen; *Sc:* James Darrell Ware, Jack Yellen. (1:35) (video)

World War I action drama.

4519. Subway Express (Columbia; 1931). *Cast:* Jack Holt, Aileen Pringle, Jason Robards, Alan Roscoe, John Kelly, Harry Semels, Maston Williams, Robert St. Angelo, Lillian Leighton, James Goss, Fred Kelsey, Sidney Bracy, Selmer Jackson, Mary Gordon. *D:* Fred Newmeyer.

"Poverty row" action drama.

4520. Success at Any Price (RKO; 1934). *Cast:* Douglas Fairbanks, Jr., Genevieve Tobin, Frank Morgan, Colleen Moore, Edward Everett Horton, Nydia Westman, Allen Vincent, Henry Kolker, Spencer Charters. *D:* J. Walter Ruben; *As.P.:* H.N. Swanson; *Sc:* Howard J. Green, Lawson. (1:14)

Rags-to-riches drama of a man, born and raised in the slums who achieves success in the world of business. Based on the play "Success Story" by John Howard Lawson.

4521. A Successful Calamity (WB; 1931). *Cast:* George Arliss, Mary Astor, Evalyn Knapp, Grant Mitchell, William Janney, Hardie Albright, Randolph Scott, David Torrence, Richard Tucker, Leon (Ames) Waycoff, Harold Minjir, Fortunio Bonanova, Barbara

Leonard, Nola Luxford. *D:* John Adolfi; *Sc:* Maude Howell, Julien Josephson, Austin Parker. (1:15)

Comedy of a millionaire who feigns bankruptcy to test members of his family. Based on the 1917 play by Clare Kummer.

4522. A Successful Failure (Monogram; 1934). *Cast:* William Collier, Sr., Lucile Gleason, Russell Hopton, Gloria Shea, William Janney, Jameson Thomas, George Breakston, Richard Tucker, Clarence Wilson, Francis McDonald. *D:* Arthur Lubin; *St:* Michael Kane; *Sc:* Marion Orth. (1:02)

"Poverty row" comedy of a newsman who loses his job, only to find success on the radio.

4523. Such Men Are Dangerous (Fox; 1930). *Cast:* Warner Baxter, Catherine Dale Owen, Hedda Hopper, Albert Conti, Bela Lugosi, Claud Allister. *D:* Melville Burke, Kenneth Hawks; *St:* Elinor Glyn; *Adaptation & Sc:* Ernest Vajda.

Melodrama.

Such Things Happen (G.B. title) *see* **Love Is a Racket**

4524. Such Women Are Dangerous (Fox; 1934). *Cast:* Warner Baxter, Rochelle Hudson, Rosemary Ames, Mona Barrie, Henrietta Crosman, Herbert Mundin, Lily (Lillian) D. Stuart. *D:* James Flood; *St:* Vera Caspary.

Drama of a young girl who falls for an older man.

4525. Sucker Money (Progressive; 1933). *Cast:* Melville Shyer, Mischa Auer, Phyllis Barrington, Earl McCarthy, Ralph Lewis, Mae Busch, Fletcher Norton. *D:* Dorothy Reid, Melville Shyer. (G.B. title: *Victims of the Beyond*) (1:02) (video)

Low-budget crime drama involving a phony mystic.

4526. Sudden Bill Dorn (Universal; 1937). *Cast:* Buck Jones, Evelyn Brent, Noel Francis, Frank McGlynn, Harold Hodge, Ted Adams, William Lawrence, Lee Phelps, Carlos Valdez, Tom Chatterton, Ezra Paulette, Red Hightower, Charles LeMoyne, Adolph Milar. *D:* Ray Taylor; *P:* Jones; *Sc:* Frances Guihan. (1:00)

Buck Jones western of a lawless boomtown. Jones' final film for this studio.

4527. Sudden Money (Paramount; 1939). *Cast:* Charles Ruggles, Marjorie Rambeau, Billy Lee, Charles Halton, Charley Grapewin, Broderick Crawford, Dick Elliott, Joyce Mathews. *D:* Nick Grinde; *Sc:* Lewis R. Foster.

B comedy of what happens when a family wins the sweepstakes.

4528. Sued for Libel (RKO; 1939). *Cast:* Kent Taylor, Linda Hayes, Lilian Bond, Morgan Conway, Richard Lane, Roger Pryor, Thurston Hall, Emory Parnell, Roy Gordon, Keye Luke, Edward Earle, Jack Arnold (aka: Vinton Haworth), Leona Roberts, Solly Ward. *D:* Leslie Goodwins; *P:* Cliff Reid; *St:* Wolfe Kaufman; *Sc:* Jerry Cady. (1:05)

B mystery of a man suing a news broadcaster for libel. The man is murdered and guess who's the chief suspect?

4529. Suez (20th Century–Fox; 1938). *Cast:* Tyrone Power (Ferdinand de Lesseps), Loretta Young (Countess Eugenie De Montijo), Annabella (Toni Pellerin), J. Edward Bromberg (Prince Said), Joseph Schildkraut (Viscomte René De Latour), Henry Stephenson (Count Mathieu de Lesseps), Sidney Blackmer (Marquis Du Brey), Miles Mander (Benjamin Disraeli), Victor Varconi (Victor Hugo), Maurice Moscovich, Sig Rumann, Nigel Bruce, George Zucco, Leon Ames, Rafaela Ottiano, Frank Reicher, Albert Conti, Georges Renavent, Marcelle Corday, Carlos de Valdez, Jacques Lory. *D:* Allan Dwan; *P:* Darryl F. Zanuck;

As.P.: Gene Markey; *St:* Sam Duncan; *Sc:* Philip Dunne, Julien Josephson; *Cinematographer:* (A.A.N.) Peverell Marley; *Original Music Score:* (A.A.N.) Louis Silvers; *Sound Recording:* (A.A.N.) Edmund Hansen. (1:44)

Lavishly produced story of Ferdinand de Lesseps, the Frenchman who built the Suez Canal, relating more fiction than fact. Fred Sersen created the special effects for the violent desert storm which climaxes the film. Publicity was sparked for the film when descendants of de Lesseps filed suit against Zanuck's studio.

The Suicide Club (G.B. title) *see* **Trouble for Two**

4530. Suicide Fleet (RKO-Pathé; 1931). *Cast:* William "Hopalong Cassidy" Boyd (Baltimore Clark), Robert Armstrong (Dutch Herman), Ginger Rogers (Sally), James Gleason (Skeets), Harry Bannister, Frank Reicher, Ben Alexander, Henry Victor, Hans Joby. *D:* Albert S. Rogell; *As.P.:* Harry Joe Brown; *St:* "Mystery Ship" by Commander Herbert A. Jones, U.S.N.; *Sc:* Lew Lipton; *Dialogue:* F. McGrew Willis. (1:27)

Three naval buddies from Coney Island, N.Y., vie for the hand of the same girl during World War I.

4531. The Sun Never Sets (Universal; 1939). *Cast:* Douglas Fairbanks, Jr., Basil Rathbone, Virginia Field, Barbara O'Neil, Lionel Atwill (Zurof), C. Aubrey Smith, Melville Cooper, Mary Forbes, Cecil Kellaway, Holmes Herbert, Sidney Bracey, John Burton, Arthur Mullinor. *D:* Rowland V. Lee; *P:* Lee; *St:* Jerry Horwin, Arthur Fitz-Richards; *Sc:* W.P. Lipscomb. (1:38)

Action-drama set in the African British colonial service as two brothers attempt to prevent the outbreak of a local war.

4532. Sundown on the Prairie (Monogram; 1939). *Cast:* Tex Ritter, Dorothy Fay (later Mrs. Tex Ritter),

Horace Murphy, Karl Hackett, Charles King, Hank Worden, Frank Ellis, Wally West, Ernie Adams, Frank LaRue, Ed Peil, Sr., Musical Tornadoes featuring Juanita Street, White Flash the horse. *D:* Al Herman; *P:* Edward Finney (for Boots & Saddles Productions); *Sc:* William Nolte, Edmond Kelso. (G.B. title: *Prairie Sundown*) (0:58)

Tex Ritter western with songs of a ranger who goes after some border smugglers.

4533. The Sundown Rider (Columbia; 1933). *Cast:* Buck Jones, Barbara Weeks, Wheeler Oakman, Pat O'Malley, Niles Welch, Frank LaRue, Bradley Page, Ward Bond, Ed Brady, Harry Todd. *D:* Lambert Hillyer; *Sc:* Hillyer. (0:56)

Buck Jones horse opera of a cowboy accused of rustling who finds crooks are after a girl's ranch.

4534. Sundown Saunders (Supreme; 1936). *Cast:* Bob Steele, Catherine Cotter, Earl Dwire, Ed Cassidy, Jack Rockwell, Milburn Morante, Frank Ball, Charles King, Hal Price, Horace Murphy, Edmund Cobb, Robert McKenzie, Jack Kirk, Herman Hack. *D:* Robert N. Bradbury; *P:* A.W. Hackel; *Sc:* Bradbury. (1:04)

Bob Steele western of a cowboy who acquires a ranch after winning a horse race, but guess what? The bad guys want it.

4535. Sundown Trail (RKO-Pathé; 1931). *Cast:* Tom Keene, Marion Shilling, Nick Stuart, Hooper Atchley, Stanley Blystone, Alma Chester, William Welsh, Murdock MacQuarrie, Louise Beavers. *D:* Robert F. Hill; *P:* Fred Allen; *St & Sc:* Hill; *Song:* Hill, Arthur Lange. (0:51)

Tom Keene (nee: George Duryea) in his first series western for this studio, involving a girl who goes west to claim the ranch left to her by her father.

4536. Sunny (WB/F.N.; 1930). *Cast:* Marilyn Miller (Sunny), Lawrence Gray, Joe Donahue, Mackenzie Ward, O.P. Heggie, Barbara Bedford, Clyde Cook, Inez Courtney, Judith Vosselli, Ben Hendricks, Jr. *D:* William A. Seiter; *Sc:* Humphrey Pearson, Henry McCarthy; *Choreographer:* Theodore Kosloff; *Songs:* Harbach, Hammerstein II & Kern. (1:21)

Hit romantic musical of a girl disguised as a boy who stows away on a ship, only to be discovered after the ship sails. Based on the hit Broadway musical by Otto Harbach, Oscar Hammerstein II and Jerome Kern, the film was also a runaway hit at the box office, due largely to the casting of Ms. Miller, who recreates her stage success. Remade by RKO in 1941 with Anna Neagle.

4537. Sunny Side Up (Fox; 1929). *Cast:* Janet Gaynor, Charles Farrell, El Brendel, Marjorie White, Joe E. Brown, Frank Richardson, Jackie Cooper, Sharon Lynn, Mary Gordon, Mary Forbes, Alan Paull, Peter Gawthorne. *D:* David Butler; *St:* B.G. DeSylva, Ray Henderson; *Sc:* Lew Brown, Butler; *Songs Include:* "I'm a Dreamer," title song, "If I Had a Talking Picture of You" & "Turn on the Heat," the last being an offbeat production number by choreographer Seymour Felix, making his debut as a film choreographer. (1:55) (video)

Hit musical of its day with the popular duo of Gaynor and Farrell in a romance of a poor tenement girl who falls for a wealthy man.

4538. Sunny Skies (Tiffany; 1930). *Cast:* Benny Rubin, Rex Lease, Marceline Day, Wesley Barry, Greta Granstedt, Harry Lee, Marjorie Kane. *D:* Norman Taurog; *St:* A.P. Young.

"Poverty row" college comedy.

4539. Sunrise Trail (Tiffany; 1931). *Cast:* Bob Steele, Blanche Mehaffey, Jack Clifford, Richard Alexander, Eddie Dunn, Fred Burns, Germaine DeNeel. *D:* John P. McCarthy; *P:* Trem Carr; *Sc:* Wellyn Totman. (1:05)

Bob Steele western of cattle rustling.

4540. The Sunset Murder Case (Grand National; 1941). *Cast:* Sally Rand, Reed Hadley, Sugar Kane, Henry King & His Orchestra. *D:* Louis J. Gasnier; *P:* George A. Hirliman; *Sc:* Arthur Hoerl, Paul Franklin. (aka: *The Sunset Strip Case*) (G.B. title: *High Explosive*) (0:57)

An exotic dancer seeks the killer of her father in this B mystery-melodrama based on the story "Murder on Sunset Boulevard" by Harold Joyce.

4541. Sunset of Power (Universal; 1936). *Cast:* Buck Jones, Dorothy Dix, Charles Middleton, Donald Kirk, Charles King, Ben Corbett, William Lawrence, Nina Campana, Joe de la Cruz, Alan Sears, Murdock MacQuarrie, Glenn Strange, Monte Vandergrift, Eumenco Blanco. *D:* Ray Taylor; *Sc:* Earle Snell. (1:06)

Buck Jones western of a ranch foreman out to find who is rustling his boss' cattle.

4542. Sunset Pass (Paramount; 1933). *Cast:* Randolph Scott, Tom Keene, Kathleen Burke, Harry Carey, Noah Beery, Leila Bennett, Fuzzy Knight, Kent Taylor, George Barbier, Patricia Farley, Charles Middleton, Vince Barnett, Christian J. Frank, Tom London, Frank Beal, Alan Bridge, Robert Kortman, Jim Mason, Nelson McDowell. *D:* Henry Hathaway; *Sc:* Jack Cunningham, Gerald Geraghty. (1:04)

Western with a "get-the-train-robbers" theme. Based on the novel by Zane Grey, the film is a remake of the 1929 production by this studio with Jack Holt and Nora Lane. Remade by RKO in 1946.

4543. Sunset Range (First Division; 1935). *Cast:* Hoot Gibson, Mary

Doran, James Eagles, Walter McGrail, Ralph Lewis, John Elliott, Eddie Lee, Kitty McHugh, Lee Fong, Martha Sleeper, Fred Gilman. *D:* Ray McCarey; *Sc:* Paul Schofield. (0:59)

Hoot Gibson comic western with a modern setting, of crooks after a girl's ranch.

The Sunset Strip Case *see* **The Sunset Murder Case**

4544. The Sunset Trail (Tiffany; 1931–32). *Cast:* Ken Maynard, Ruth Hiatt, Frank Rice, Philo McCullough, Buddy Hunter, Richard Alexander, Slim Whitaker, Frank Ellis, Jack Rockwell, Lew Meehan, Bud Osborne, Bud McClure. *D:* B. Reeves Eason; *P:* Phil Goldstone (for Amity Productions); *Sc:* Bennett Cohen. (1:02) (video)

Ken Maynard "poverty row" western of two cowpokes in love with the same girl.

4545. Sunset Trail (Paramount; 1938). *Cast:* William Boyd (Hoppy), Russell Hayden (Lucky), George "Gabby" Hayes (Windy), Charlotte Wynters, Jane (Jan) Clayton, Robert Fiske, Maurice Cass, Kathryn Sheldon, Kenneth Harlan, Anthony Nace, Alphonse Ethier, Glenn Strange, Tom London, Jack Rockwell. *D:* Lesley Selander; *P:* Harry M. Sherman; *Sc:* Norman Houston. (1:00)

The 19th entry in the "Hopalong Cassidy" series as the Bar 20 boys come to the aid of a woman and her daughter who own a dude ranch that the bad guys want.

4546. Super-Sleuth (RKO; 1937). *Cast:* Jack Oakie, Ann Sothern, Edgar Kennedy, Eduardo Ciannelli, Joan Woodbury, Bradley Page, Alan Bruce, Paul Guilfoyle, Willie Best, William Corson, Alec Craig, Richard Lane, Paul Hurst, George Rosener, Fred Kelsey, Robert Emmett O'Connor, Philip Morris, Dick Rush. *D:* Ben Stoloff; *P:* Edward Small; *Sc:* Gertrude Purcell, Ernest Pagano. (1:10)

A successful B comedy of a movie detective attempting to solve a real murder. Based on a play by Harry Segall, it was loosely remade as *Genius at Work* (RKO; 1946).

4547. Supernatural (Paramount; 1933). *Cast:* Carole Lombard, H.B. Warner, Randolph Scott, Vivienne Osborne, Alan Dinehart, Beryl Mercer, William Farnum. *D:* Victor Halperin; *P:* Edward Halperin; *St:* Garnett Weston; *Sc:* Harvey Thew, Brian Marlow. (1:00)

Released at a time when spiritualism was popular in the U.S. and Europe, this thriller tells of an innocent girl whose body is taken over by the discarnate spirit of a deceased murderess. Latter-day re-release give the film a PG rating by the M.P.A.A.

4548. Superspeed (Columbia; 1935). *Cast:* Mary Carlisle, Norman Foster, Florine McKinney, Charley Grapewin, Florence Rice. *D:* Lambert Hillyer.

B action drama.

4549. Surrender (Fox; 1931). *Cast:* Warner Baxter, Leila Hyams, C. Aubrey Smith, Ralph Bellamy, Alexander Kirkland, Andre Beranger, Virginia Weidler (film debut), Tom Ricketts, Joseph (Sawyer) Sauers (feature film debut), William Frawley (film debut), Bodil Rosing, Bert Hanlon, Albert Burke, Frank Swales, Howard Phillips, Jack Conrad. *D:* William K. Howard; *Sc:* Sonya Levien, S.N. Behrman.

A romantic comedy which was voted one of the year's "10 Best" films by the National Board of Review.

4550. Surrendered Dawn (Xxxx Xxxx; 1932). *Cast:* Josephine Dunn. (No other information available)

Surrounded by Women *see* **Between Two Women**

4551. Susan Lenox: Her Fall and Rise (MGM; 1931). *Cast:* Greta

Garbo, Clark Gable (in a role originally intended for John Gilbert), Jean Hersholt, John Miljan, Alan Hale, Hale Hamilton, Hilda Vaughn, Russell Simpson, Cecil Cunningham, Ian Keith, Helene Millard, Theodore von Eltz. *D:* Robert Z. Leonard; *P:* Paul Bern (better known as the man who committed suicide shortly after marrying Jean Harlow); *Adaptation:* Wanda Tuchock; *Dialogue:* Zelda Sears, Leon Gordon. (G.B. title: *The Rise of Helga*) (1:16)

Based on the novel by David Graham Phillips, this romantic drama tells of a girl who flees to the city to escape a marriage arranged by her father. Notable as the only film to star Garbo and Gable together.

4552. Susannah of the Mounties (20th Century–Fox; 1939). *Cast:* Shirley Temple, Randolph Scott, Margaret Lockwood (British actress in her American debut), J. Farrell Mac-Donald, Moroni Olsen, Victor Jory, Maurice Moscovich, Lester Matthews, Chief Big Tree, Herbert Evans, Charles Irwin, Leyland Hodgson, John Sutton, Martin Good Rider. *D:* William A. Seiter; *P:* Kenneth MacGowan; *Orig. Book:* Muriel Denison; *St:* Fidel La-Barba, Walter Ferris; *Sc:* Robert Ellis, Helen Logan. (1:17) (video)

Romantic actioner of a little girl orphaned in an attack on a wagon train who is cared for by some Canadian Mounties. Computer-colored prints produced in 1988.

4553. Sutter's Gold (Universal; 1936). *Cast:* Edward Arnold, Lee Tracy, Binnie Barnes, Katherine Alexander, Addison Richards, Montagu Love, Harry Carey, John Miljan, Billy Gilbert, Bryant Washburn, Robert Warwick, Russell Hopton, Frank Reicher, Jim Thorpe, Ronnie Cosbey, Allen Vincent, Gaston Glass, Joanne Smith, Aura DeSilva. *D:* James Cruze; *P:* Carl Laemmle, Jr.; *As.P.:* Edmund Grainger; *St:* Bruno Frank; *Sc:* Jack Kirkland, Walter Woods, George O'Neil. (1:34)

This box office disaster on the life of Johan (John) Sutter and the gold strike at Sutter's Mill in 19th-century California went way over budget and was the contributing factor in the ousting of Carl Laemmle, Jr., from Universal and finished the career of James Cruze as a top director. Based on the novel by Blaise Cendrars.

Note: Footage from this film was reused in the low-budget production, *Mutiny on the Blackhawk* (q.v.).

4554. Suzy (MGM; 1936). *Cast:* Jean Harlow, Franchot Tone, Cary Grant, Lewis Stone, Benita Hume, Reginald Mason, Inez Courtney, David Clyde, Greta Meyer, George Spelvin, Christian Rub, Una O'Connor, Theodore von Eltz, Stanley Morner (Dennis Morgan, film debut — bit). *D:* George Fitzmaurice; *P:* Maurice Revnes; *Sc:* Dorothy Parker, Alan Campbell, Horace Jackson, Lenore Coffee; *Song:* (A.A.N.) "Did I Remember?" by Walter Donaldson & Harold Adamson. (1:39)

This World War I spy drama is based on the novel by Herbert Gorman.

4555. Svengali (WB; 1931). *Cast:* John Barrymore (Svengali), Marian Marsh (Trilby), Donald Crisp, Bramwell Fletcher (Billee), Carmel Myers, Luis Alberni, Lumsden Hare, Paul Porcasi, Adrienne D'Ambricourt, Ferike Boros. *D:* Archie Mayo; *Sc:* J. Grubb Alexander; *Cinematographer:* (A.A.N.) Barney "Chick" McGill; *Art-Set Decoration:* (A.A.N.) Anton Grot. (1:21) (video)

Classic story of hypnotist Svengali and the girl Trilby who becomes a famous singer while under his spell. Previous filmings: *Trilby* (World; 1915) by director Maurice Tournour with Wilton Lackaye and Clara Kimball Young, *Trilby* (First National; 1923) by director James Young with Arthur Edmund Carewe and Andree Lafayette. Remade in Great Britain in 1955 as *Svengali* and again in 1983 in the U.S.A.

as a TV movie. Based on the novel "Trilby" by George Louis du Maurier, the 1931 version is noted for its bizarre surrealistic sets.

Note: The box office popularity of this film spawned a follow-up later in the year titled *The Mad Genius* (q.v.).

4556. Swanee River (Sono Art–World Wide; 1930–31). *Cast:* Grant Withers, Thelma Todd, Philo McCullough. *D:* Raymond Cannon; *Sc:* Barbara Chambers Woods; *Adapt.:* Arthur Hoerl.

(No other information available)

4557. Swanee River (20th Century–Fox; 1939). *Cast:* Don Ameche (Stephen Collins Foster), Andrea Leeds (Jane Foster), Al Jolson (E.P. Christy of the "Christy Minstrels"), Felix Bressart (Henry Kleber), Richard Clarke (Tom Harper), Chick Chandler (Bones), Russell Hicks (Andrew McDowell), George Reed (Old Joe), Diane Fisher (Marion Foster), George Breakston (Ambrose), Hall Johnson Choir (themselves), Al Herman (Mr. Tambo), Charles Trowbridge (Mr. Foster), George Meeker (Henry Foster), Leona Roberts (Mrs. Foster), Charles Tannen (Morrison Foster), Clara Blandick (Mrs. Griffin), Nella Walker (Mrs. McDowell), Ann Rowan (Georgia Caine), Charles Halton, Harry Hayden. *D:* Sidney Lanfield; *As.P.:* Kenneth MacGowan; *Sc:* John Taintor Foote, Philip Dunne; *Music:* (A.A.N.) Louis Silvers. (1:24) (video)

A lavishly produced technicolor "Hollywood" biography of 19th-century songwriter Stephen Foster.

4558. Sweepings (RKO; 1933). *Cast:* Lionel Barrymore, Eric Linden, William Gargan, Gloria Stuart, Alan Dinehart, Gregory Ratoff, Helen Mack, Lucien Littlefield, George Meeker, Ninetta (Nan) Sunderland, Esther Muir, Ivan Lebedeff, Chick Chandler. *D:* John Cromwell; *As.P.:* Pandro S. Berman; *Sc:* Lester Cohen. (1:20)

Following the Chicago fire of 1871,

a man creates a prosperous department store empire. Based on the novel of the same name by Lester Cohen, it was remade as *Three Sons* (q.v.). A box office hit.

4559. Sweepstakes (RKO-Pathé; 1931). *Cast:* Eddie Quillan, James Gleason, Marian Nixon, Lew Cody, Paul Hurst, Frederick Burton, Billy Sullivan, Lillian Leighton, King Baggot, Thomas Jackson. *D:* Albert S. Rogell; *As.P.:* Harry Joe Brown; *St:* Lew Lipton; *Sc:* Lipton, Ralph F. Murphy; *Song:* Ted Snyder, Mort Harris. (1:17)

Comedy of a jockey who wins races by chanting to his horse.

4560. Sweepstake Annie (Liberty; 1934–35). *Cast:* Tom Brown, Marian Nixon, Dorothy Peterson, Ivan Lebedeff, Inez Courtney, Lucien Littlefield, William Janney. *D:* William Nigh; *P:* M.H. Hoffman, Jr. (G.B. title: *Annie Doesn't Live Here Anymore*)

Light low-budget comedy.

4561. Sweepstakes Winner (WB/F.N.; 1939). *Cast:* Marie Wilson, Allen Jenkins, Johnnie "Scat" Davis, Charles Foy, Jerry Colonna, Vera Lewis, Sidney Bracy. *D:* William McGann; *As.P.:* Bryan Foy; *St:* Albert DeMond, Hugh Cummings; *Sc:* DeMond, John Krafft. (0:59)

B comedy of a woman who supplies a meal to a person who returns payment by giving her a sweepstakes ticket which turns out to be a winner.

4562. Sweet Adeline (WB; 1935). *Cast:* Irene Dunne, Donald Woods, Hugh Herbert, Ned Sparks, Winifred Shaw, Louis Calhern, Joseph Cawthorn, Nydia Westman, Noah Beery, Dorothy Dare, Jack Mulhall, Phil Regan. *D:* Mervyn LeRoy; *P:* Edward Chodorov; *Sc:* Erwin S. Gelsey; *Songs:* "Here Am I," "Why Was I Born?" "Don't Ever Leave Me," "Twas Not So Long Ago," "We Were So Very Young" & "Out of the Blue" by Jerome Kern & Oscar Hammerstein II. (1:27)

This "Gay 90s" musical was based on the Broadway play by Jerome Kern, Oscar Hammerstein II, Harry Armstrong, and Dick Gerard.

Sweet Aloes (G.B. title) *see* **Give Me Your Heart**

4563. Sweet Kitty Bellairs (WB; 1930). *Cast:* Claudia Dell (film debut), Ernest Torrence, Walter Pidgeon, Perry Askam, June Collyer, Lionel Belmore, Arthur Edmund Carewe, Flora Finch. *D:* Alfred E. Green; *Sc:* J. Grubb Alexander.

A 2-color technicolor romantic drama set in merry olde England of the love affair between a girl and a highwayman. Based on the old stage play by David Belasco, which was adapted from the novel by Agnes and Egerton Castle. Previously filmed by Lasky Feature Plays in 1916 with Mae Murray, Tom Forman and Belle Bennett.

4564. Sweet Mama (WB/F.N.; 1930). *Cast:* Alice White, Richard Cramer, David Manners, Rita Flynn, Kenneth Thomson, Lee Shumway, Lew Harvey, Lee Moran, Robert Elliott. *D:* Edward Cline; *Sc:* Frederick Hazlitt Brennan, Earl Baldwin. (G.B. title: *Conflict*)

Low-budget crime melodrama of a girl out to round up a gang of crooks.

4565. Sweet Music (WB; 1934–35). *Cast:* Rudy Vallee, Ann Dvorak, Ned Sparks, Helen Morgan, Allen Jenkins, Alice White, Robert Armstrong, Philip Reed, Joseph Cawthorn, Henry O'Neill, Clay Clement, Al Shean, Addison Richards, Jack Norton, Russell Hicks. *D:* Alfred E. Green; *P:* Sam Bischoff; *St:* Jerry Wald; *Sc:* Wald, Carl Erickson, Warren Duff; *Choreography:* Bobby Connolly; *Title Song:* Al Dubin, Harry Warren; *Other Songs, Including:* "Good Green Acres of Home," "Ev'ry Day," "Fare Thee Well, Annabelle," "I See Two Lovers" & "There's a Different You" by Irving

Kahal & Sammy Fain, Mort Dixon & Allie Wrubel. (1:40)

Musical-comedy.

4566. Sweet Surrender (Universal; 1935). *Cast:* Frank Parker, Tamara (film debut in a dual role), Helen Lynd, Russ Brown, Arthur Pierson. *D:* Monte Brice; *P:* Carl Laemmle, Jr.; *St:* Herbert Fields; *Adaptation:* Charles Beahan; *Sc:* John V.A. Weaver; *Songs:* "Love Makes the World Go Round," "Take This Ring" & "I'm So Happy I Could Cry" by Edward Heyman, Dana Suesse, James Henley & Arthur Swanstrom. (1:20)

Musical-drama set aboard a ship bound for Europe.

4567. The Sweetheart of Sigma Chi (Monogram; 1933). *Cast:* Mary Carlisle, Buster Crabbe, Charles Starrett, Florence Lake, Eddie Tamblyn, Sally Starr, Mary Blackford, Tom Dugan, Burr McIntosh, Major Goodsell, Grady Sutton, Purnell Pratt, Franklin Parker, Ted Fiorito & His Orchestra, Glenn (Leif) Erickson (film debut — bit). *D:* Edwin L. Marin; *P:* William T. Lackey; *St:* George Waggner; *Sc:* Luther Reed, Albert E. DeMond. (G.B. title: *Girl of My Dreams*) (1:16)

"Poverty row" college comedy of a campus flirt who finally meets her match in a star athlete. Remade as *Sweetheart of Sigma Chi* (Monogram; 1946).

4568. Sweetheart of the Navy (Grand National; 1937). *Cast:* Eric Linden, Cecilia Parker, Roger Imhof, Bernadene Hayes, Jason Robards, Cully Richards, Etta McDaniel, Don Barclay, Reed Howes, Eddy Waller. *D:* Duncan Mansfield; *P:* B.F. (Bennie) Zeidman; *St:* Garrett Graham, Jay Strauss; *Sc:* Carroll Graham. (1:01)

B romantic drama of a naive young sailor who falls for a dance hall singer.

4569. Sweethearts (MGM; 1938). *Cast:* Jeanette MacDonald (Gwen Marlowe), Nelson Eddy (Ernest Lane), Frank

Morgan (Felix Lehman), Florence Rice (Kay Jordan), Ray Bolger (Fred), Mischa Auer (Leo Kronk), Herman Bing (Oscar Engel), Fay Holden (Hannah), Betty Jaynes (Una Wilson), Douglas McPhail (Harvey Horton), Reginald Gardiner (Norman Trumpett), Allyn Joslyn (Dink Rogers), Raymond Walburn (Orlando Lane), Terry Kilburn (Gwen's brother), Lucile Watson (Mrs. Marlowe), Philip Loeb (Samuel Silver), Kathleen Lockhart (Aunt Amelia), Gene Lockhart (Augustus), Berton Churchill (Sheridan Lane), Olin Howland (Appleby), Gerald Hamer (Harry), Charles Sullivan (Tommy the fighter), Dalies Frantz, Lester Dorr, Irving Bacon, Marvin Jones, Dorothy Gray, Maude Turner Gordon, Emory Parnell, Jac George, Mira McKinney, Barbara Pepper, Grace Hayle. *D:* W.S. Van Dyke II; *P:* Hunt Stromberg; *St:* Fred de Gresac, Harry B. Smith, Robert B. Smith; *Sc:* Dorothy Parker, Alan Campbell; *Cinematographers:* (A.A. — special plaques) Oliver T. Marsh, Allen Davey; *Musical Director:* (A.A.N.) Herbert Stothart; *Sound Recording:* (A.A.N.) Douglas Shearer; *Songs:* "Every Lover Must Meet His Fate," "Angelus," "The Game of Love," "Grandmother," "Iron, Iron, Iron," "Mademoiselle on Parade," "Pretty as a Picture," "Summer Serenade," "Sweethearts," "Waiting for the Bride" & "Wooden Shoes" by Chet Forrest, Bob Wright & Victor Herbert. (2:00) (video)

Musical of married stage performers who are manipulated by their manager to the point of marital disharmony. Notable as the first full-technicolor production from this studio. It received *"Photoplay's* Gold Medal Award" and was one of the 16 top grossing films of 1938–39.

4570. Sweethearts and Wives (WB/F.N.; 1930). *Cast:* Clive Brook, Billie Dove, Sidney Blackmer, Leila Hyams, Crauford Kent, John Loder. *D:* Clarence Badger; *Sc:* Forrest Halsey.

Mystery-comedy involving a stolen necklace, based on the play "Other Men's Wives" by Walter Hackett.

4571. Sweethearts on Parade (Columbia; 1930). *Cast:* Lloyd Hughes, Alice White, Kenneth Thomson, Marie Prevost, Wilbur Mack. *D:* Marshall Neilan; *P:* Al Christie.

Romantic comedy from "poverty row."

4572. Sweetie (Paramount; 1929). *Cast:* Nancy Carroll, Stanley Smith, Jack Oakie, Helen Kane, Stuart Erwin, William Austin, Wallace MacDonald, Aileen Manning, Charles Sellon. *D:* Frank Tuttle; *Sc:* Lloyd Corrigan, George Marion, Jr.; *Songs:* Richard A. Whiting, Al Lewis, Abner Silver & Al Sherman.

Collegiate musical based on an old play titled "The Charm School" which has been the basis for many other films, including *Someone to Love* (Paramount; 1928) with Charles "Buddy" Rogers and the earlier *The Charm School* (Paramount; 1921) with Wallace Reid. Based on the story by Alice Duer Miller which she adapted with Robert Milton to the stage in 1920 as "The Charm School."

4573. The Swellhead (Tiffany; 1930). *Cast:* James Gleason, Johnnie Walker, Paul Hurst, Wallace Ford (feature film debut), Natalie Kingston, Bessie Love. *D:* James Flood; *Sc:* James Gleason (co-writer). (G.B. title: *Counted Out*)

"Poverty row" boxing tale of a fighter who gets too big for his britches. Filmed before in 1927 and remade in 1935 (see below).

4574. Swellhead (Columbia; 1935). *Cast:* Wallace Ford, Barbara Kent, J. Farrell MacDonald, Dickie Moore. *D:* Ben Stoloff; *St:* Gerald Beaumont; *Sc:* William Jacobs.

A remake of the preceding film.

Swift Vengeance (G.B. title) *see* **The Rookie Cop**

4575. Swifty (Diversion; 1935). *Cast:* Hoot Gibson, June Gale, George Hayes, Wally Wales (Hal Taliaferro), Ralph Lewis, Robert Kortman, William Gould, Lafe McKee, Art Mix, Duke Lee, Starlight the horse. *D:* Alan James (aka: Alvin J. Neitz); *Sc:* Bennett Cohen. (1:02)

Hoot Gibson western of a drifter wrongly accused of murdering a rancher.

4576. Swing High (Pathé; 1930). *Cast:* Helen Twelvetrees, Fred Scott, Dorothy Burgess, Nick Stuart, Sally Starr, Bryant Washburn, George Fawcett, Stepin Fetchit, Ben Turpin, Mickey Bennett, Robert Edeson, John Sheehan, Daphne Pollard, William Langan, Little Billy. *D:* Joseph Santley; *Sc:* Santley (co-writer).

Romantic musical.

4577. Swing High, Swing Low (Paramount; 1937). *Cast:* Carole Lombard (Maggie King), Fred MacMurray (Skid Johnson), Charles Butterworth (Harry), Jean Dixon (Ella), Dorothy Lamour (Anita Alvarez), Harvey Stephens (Harvey Dexter), Cecil Cunningham (Murphy), Charles Arnt (Georgie), Franklin Pangborn (Henri), Anthony Quinn (The Don), Charles Judels (Tony), Ralph Remley (Musselwhite), Bud Flanagan (Dennis O'Keefe as the pursuer), Harry Semels (chief of police), Ricardo Mandia, Enrique DeRosas, Charles Stevens, Chris-Pin Martin, Nick Lukats, Lee Bowman, Darby Jones, Eumenio Blanco, George W. Jimenez, Gino Corrado, George Sorel, Esther Howard, Richard Kipling, Spencer Chan, Donald Kerr, P.E. "Tiny" Newland, Will Wright. *D:* Mitchell Leisen; *P:* Arthur Hornblow, Jr.; *Sc:* Virginia Van Upp, Oscar Hammerstein II; *Songs:* "Panamania," title song by Burton Lane, Ralph Freed; "I Hear a Call to Arms" by Sam Coslow & Al Siegel; "If It Isn't Pain, Then It Isn't Love" by Ralph Rainger, Leo Robin; & "Spring Is in the Air" by Ralph Freed & Charles Kisco. (1:37) (video)

A comedy-drama which tells the story of a musician, his rise to success and eventual decline. Based on the play "Burlesque" by George Manker Watters and Arthur Hopkins. A remake of *The Dance of Life* (q.v.). Remade as *When My Baby Smiles at Me* (20th Century–Fox; 1948). One of the 38 top grossing films of 1936–37.

Swing It, Buddy (G.B. title) *see* **Swing It, Professor**

4578. Swing It, Professor (Ambassador; 1937). *Cast:* Milburn Stone, Paula Stone, George Cleveland. *D:* Marshall Neilan; *P:* Maurice Conn. (G.B. title: *Swing It, Buddy*)

Independent B musical-comedy.

4579. Swing It, Sailor (Grand National; 1937). *Cast:* Wallace Ford, Isabel Jewell, Ray Mayer, Mary Treen, Cully Richards, Rex Lease, Tom Kennedy, Alexander Leftwich, Max Hoffman, Jr. *D:* Raymond Cannon; *P:* David Diamond; *St:* Diamond, Clarence Marks; *Sc:* Diamond, Marks. (Working Title: "He Wanted to Marry") (0:57) (video)

B romantic comedy of two sailors who squabble over the same girl.

4580. Swing, Sister, Swing (Universal; 1938). *Cast:* Ken Murray, Johnny Downs, Kathryn Kane, Eddie Quillan, Ted Weems & His Orchestra, Edna Sedgwick, Ernest Truex, Nana Bryant, Clara Blandick. *D:* Joseph Santley; *As.P.:* Burt Kelly; *Sc:* Charles Grayson; *Songs:* Frank Skinner, Charles Henderson. (1:12)

Low-budget fad musical which capitalizes on the new jitterbug craze and introduces a new dance called "The Baltimore Bubble."

Swing, Teacher, Swing (G.B. title) *see* **College Swing**

4581. Swing That Cheer (Universal; 1938). *Cast:* Tom Brown, Robert

Wilcox, Constant Moore, Andy Devine, Ernest Truex, Samuel S. Hinds, Doodles Weaver, David Oliver, Margaret Early, Stanley Hughes, Raymond Parker. *D:* Harold Schuster; *P:* Max H. Golden; *St:* Thomas Ahearn, F. Maury Grossman. (1:10)

College gridiron story in a B production.

4582. Swing Time (RKO; 1936). *Cast:* Fred Astaire (John "Lucky" Garnett), Ginger Rogers (Penelope "Penny" Carrol), Victor Moore (Pop — Ed), Helen Broderick (Mabel Anderson), Eric Blore (Gordon), Betty Furness (Margaret Watson), George Metaxa (Ricardo Romero), Edgar Dearing (policeman), Pierre Watkin (Al Simpson), Abe Reynolds (Schmidt), Gerald Hamer (Eric), Frank Jenks (Red), Ferdinand Munier (minister), Harry Bowen, Harry Bernard, Ted O'Shea, Donald Kerr, Frank Edmunds, Bill Brand, Olin Francis, Ralph Byrd, Floyd Shackleford, Joey Ray, Jack Good, Jack Rice. *D:* George Stevens; *P:* Pandro S. Berman; *Sc:* Howard Lindsay, Allan Scott; *Choreography:* (A.A.N.) Hermes Pan for the "Bojangles of Harlem" number, a tribute to dancer Bill Robinson; *Songs:* "The Way You Look Tonight" (A.A. for Best Song), "A Fine Romance," "The Waltz in Swing Time," "Never Gonna Dance," "Pick Yourself Up" & "Bojangles..." by Jerome Kern & Dorothy Fields. (1:43) (video)

This musical-comedy was the sixth teaming of Astaire and Rogers, based on the story "Portrait of John Garnett" by Erwin Gelsey. One of the 38 top grossing films of 1936–37.

4583. Swing Your Lady (WB; 1937–38). *Cast:* Humphrey Bogart, Frank McHugh, Penny Singleton, Louise Fazenda, Nat Pendleton, The Weaver Brothers & Elviry (film debuts), Allen Jenkins, Ronald Reagan, Olin Howland, Hugh O'Connell, Tommy Bupp, Sonny Bupp, Sue Moore, Joan Howard, Daniel Boone Savage, Sammy

White. *D:* Ray Enright; *P:* Sam Bischoff; *Sc:* Joseph Schrank, Maurice Leo; *Songs:* "Mountain Swingaroo," "Hillbilly from Tenth Avenue," "The Old Apple Tree," title song, & "Dig Me a Grave in Old Missouri" by M.K. Jerome & Jack Scholl. (1:17)

A wrestling promoter takes a backwoods hick and turns him into a star grappler. This comedy was based on the story "Toehold on Artemus" by H.R. Marsh and the play adapted from it by John Kenyon Nicholson and Charles Robinson.

Note 1. Bogart maintained that this was the worst film he ever made.

Note 2. The Weavers (Leon, Frank and June) later had a low-budget series for Republic Studios, which ran into the early 1940s — see index for early entries in the series.

The Swinging Pearl Mystery (G.B. title) *see* **The Plot Thickens** (1936)

4584. Swiss Miss (MGM/Hal Roach; 1938). *Cast:* Stan Laurel, Oliver Hardy, Walter Woolf King, Della Lind, Eric Blore, Adia Kuznetzoff, Charles Judels, Eddie Kane, George Sorel, Ludovico Tomarchio, Jean DeBriac, Charles Gemora, Anita Garvin. *D:* John G. Blystone; *P:* Hal Roach; *St:* Jean Negulesco, Charles Rogers; *Sc:* James Parrott, Felix Adler, Charles Melson. (1:13) (video)

Produced as a comic opera, this Laurel and Hardy star opus tells of the misadventures of two mousetrip salesmen in Switzerland.

4585. Sworn Enemy (MGM; 1936). *Cast:* Robert Young, Joseph Calleia, Florence Rice, Lewis Stone, Nat Pendleton, Harvey Stephens, Leslie Fenton, Anthony Quinn, Samuel S. Hinds, Bud Flanagan (Dennis O'Keefe), John Wray, Robert Gleckler, Cyrus Kendall, Edward Pawley. *D:* Edwin L. Marin; *P:* Lucien Hubbard; *St:* Richard E. Wormser; *Sc:* Wells Root.

B crime melodrama.

4586. Sylvia Scarlett (RKO; 1935). *Cast:* Katharine Hepburn, Cary Grant, Brian Aherne, Edmund Gwenn, Natalie Paley, Lennox Pawle, Dennie Moore, E.E. Clive. *D:* George Cukor; *P:* Pandro S. Berman; *Sc:* Gladys Unger, John Collier, Mortimer Offner. (1:34) (video)

Comedy-drama of a girl disguised as a boy escaping to France with her father via a traveling show. Based on the novel by Compton MacKenzie, this was the first film to pair Hepburn and Grant. The audiences of the day strongly disapproved of this film and it showed flop returns, but in recent years has acquired a cult following, possibly indicating it was a film ahead of its time.

4587. Symphony of Living (Chesterfield; 1935). *Cast:* Evelyn Brent, John Harron, Ferdinand Schumann-Heink. *D:* Frank Strayer.

"Poverty row" romantic comedy-drama.

4588. Symphony of Six Million (RKO; 1932). *Cast:* Ricardo Cortez, Irene Dunne, Anna Appel, Gregory Ratoff (film debut), Noel Madison, Lita Chevret, John St. Polis, Julie Haydon, Helen Freeman, Josephine Whittell, Oscar Apfel, Eddie Phillips. *D:* Gregory La Cava; *As.P.:* Pandro S. Berman; *Sc:* J. Walter Ruben, Bernard Schubert; *Additional Dialogue:* James Seymour. (G.B. title: *Melody of Life*) (1:34)

In this drama, based on the novel by Fannie Hurst, a young doctor leaves a poor paying ghetto practice for another on Park Avenue in New York.

4589. Syncopation (RKO; 1929). *Cast:* Barbara Bennett (sister of Constance & Joan, daughter of Richard Bennett & wife of Morton Downey, Sr.), Bobby (Robert) Watson, Fred Waring & His Pennsylvanians, Morton Downey (Sr.), Verree Teasdale, Osgood Perkins, Dorothy Lee, Mackenzie Ward. *D:* Bert Glennon; *P:* Robert Kane; *Adaptation:* Frances Agnew; *Dialogue:* Gene Markey; *Songs:* Leo Robin, Richard Myers, Herman Ruby, Bud Green, Sammy Stept.

Romantic musical of a dance team. Based on the novel by Gene Markey, filming was done in New York City. This was the second production of RKO-Radio pictures, but the first film to be released by them for circulation. A box office hit.

4590. Tail Spin! (20th Century-Fox; 1938). *Cast:* Alice Faye, Constance Bennett, Joan Davis, Nancy Kelly, Charles Farrell, Jane Wyman, Kane Richmond, Wally Vernon, Harry Davenport, Milburn Stone, Edward Norris, Robert Allen, Robert Lowery, Ralph Dunn, Eddie Dunn, Mary Gordon, J. Anthony Hughes, Emmett Vogan, Edward Marr, Joan Valerie, Billy Wayne. *D:* Roy Del Ruth; *P:* Harry Joe Brown; *St & Sc:* Frank Wead. (1:23)

The lives and loves of female flyers is the focus of this drama.

4591. A Tailor Made Man (MGM; 1931). *Cast:* William Haines, Dorothy Jordan, Joseph Cawthorn, William Austin, Marjorie Rambeau, Ian Keith, Hedda Hopper, Hale Hamilton, Martha Sleeper, Joan Marsh, Henry Armetta, Walter Walker, Forrester Harvey. *D:* Sam Wood; *Sc:* Edgar Allan Woolf.

A naive tailor believes that some fancy duds will get him accepted into society. Previously filmed by Charles Ray for U.A. release in 1922 starring Ray and Ethel Grandin.

Tainted Money (G.B. title) *see* **Show Them No Mercy**

4592. Take a Chance (Paramount; 1933). *Cast:* James Dunn, Cliff Edwards, June Knight, Charles "Buddy" Rogers, Lillian Roth, Dorothy Lee, Lillian Bond, Lona Andre, Robert Gleckler, Marjorie Main, Charles Richman. *D:* Laurence Schwab, Monte Brice; *Sc:* Brice, Schwab; *Songs Include:*

"It's Only a Paper Moon" by Harold Arlen, E.Y. Harburg & Billy Rose; "Eadie Was a Lady" by B.G. DeSylva, Nacio Herb Brown & Richard A. Whiting. (1:24)

The film version of the 1932–33 Broadway show based on the play "Humpty Dumpty" by Vincent Youmans of a group of carnival people out to hit the big time. Filmed at Astoria Studios in Long Island, N.Y.

4593. Take the Heir (Screenstory; 1930). *Cast:* Edward Everett Horton, Dorothy Devore, Edythe Chapman. *D:* Lloyd Ingraham (final film as director).

Low-budget independent comedy.

4594. Take the Stand (Liberty; 1934). *Cast:* Sheila Terry, Thelma Todd, Russell Hopton, Leslie Fenton, Gail Patrick, Berton Churchill, Jason Robards, Paul Hurst, Vince Barnett, Bradley Page, Oscar Apfel. *D:* Phil Rosen; *P:* M.H. Hoffman, Jr. (G.B. title: *The Great Radio Mystery*)

Low-budget mystery-comedy.

4595. A Tale of Two Cities (MGM; 1935). *Cast:* Ronald Colman (Sydney Carton), Elizabeth Allan (Lucie Manette), Edna May Oliver (Miss Pross), Reginald Owen (Mr. Stryver), Blanche Yurka (film debut as Madame DeFarge), Basil Rathbone (Marquis St. Evremonde), Donald Woods (Charles Darnay), Fritz Leiber (Gaspard), Henry B. Walthall (Dr. Manette), Walter Catlett (Barsad), H.B. Warner (Gabelle), Mitchell Lewis (Ernest DeFarge), Claude Gillingwater (Jarvis Lorry), Billy Bevan (Jerry Cruncher), Fay Chaldecott (Lucie the daughter), Eily Malyon (Mrs. Cruncher), Lucille La Verne (LaVengeance), Isabel Jewell (seamstress), John Davidson (Morveau), Tom Ricketts (Tellson, Jr.), Donald Haines (Jerry Cruncher, Jr.), E.E. Clive (judge in Old Bailey), Lawrence Grant (prosecuting attorney in Old Bailey), Tully Marshall (wood-cutter), Ed Peil, Sr. (Cartwright), Boyd Irwin, Sr. (aristocrat), Ralf Harolde (prosecutor), Richard Alexander (executioner), Cyril McLaglen (headsman), Barlowe Borland (Jacques, #116), Edward Hearn, Frank Mayo, Nigel de Brulier, Walter Kingsford, Rolfe Sedan, Robert Warwick, Dale Fuller, Montague Shaw, Chappell Dossett, Tempe Pigott, Forrester Harvey, Jimmy Aubrey, Billy House. *D:* Jack Conway; *P:* (A.A.N. for Best Picture — 1936) David O. Selznick; *Sc:* W.P. Lipscomb, S.N. Behrman; *Ed:* (A.A.N.) Conrad A. Nervig. (2:06) (video — 2:01)

Classic version of Charles Dickens much read tale of the French Revolution of the 1780s with an ultra-lavish production utilizing 17,000 extras. Faithful to the original work. Previous versions include two one reelers, one of which was in 1910, (Vitagraph; 1911) with Maurice Costello, Norma Talmadge and Florence Turner in three reels, (Fox; 1917) with William Farnum, Jewel Carmen and Josef Swickard by director Frank Lloyd in seven reels, and a British production by Herbert Wilcox titled *The Only Way* (U.A.; 1926). Remade in Great Britain in 1958 and again in the U.S.A. in 1980 as a TV movie. The '35 version placed #7 on *Film Daily's* "10 Best" list of 1936, while the film also became one of the 25 top grossing films of 1935–36. Computer-colored by Turner Entertainment in 1990.

4596. Talent Scout (WB/F.N.; 1937). *Cast:* Jeanne Madden, Donald Woods, Fred Lawrence, Rosalind Marquis, Charles Halton, Joseph Crehan, Allen Jenkins, Frank Faylen, Al Herman, Mary Treen, Helen Valkis, Teddy Hart, John Pearson. *D:* William Clemens; *P:* Bryan Foy; *Sc:* George Bilson, William Jacobs; *Songs:* "In the Silent Picture Days," "I Am the Singer, You Are the Song," "Born to Love" & "I Was Wrong" by M.K. Jerome & Jack Scholl. (G.B. title: *Studio Romance*) (1:02)

B musical of a girl singer's rise to fame.

4597. The Talk of Hollywood (Sono Art—World Wide/Prudence; 1929). *Cast:* Nat Carr, Fay Marbe (Adore Renee), Hope Sutherland. *D:* Mark Sandrich; *St:* Sandrich.

An early "poverty row" talkie.

Tall Timber *see* **Park Avenue Logger**

4598. The Taming of the Shrew (United Artists; 1929). *Cast:* Douglas Fairbanks (Petruchio), Mary Pickford (Katharine), Edwin Maxwell (Baptista), Dorothy Jordan (Bianca), Clyde Cook (Grumio), Geoffrey Wardwell (Hortensio), Joseph Cawthorn (Gremio). *D:* Sam Taylor; *P:* Fairbanks/Pickford; *Additional Dialogue:* Taylor. (1:08) (video)

Shakespeare's comedy of the roguish Petruchio's marriage to and taming of Baptista's shrewish daughter, Katharine. Notable as the only film to pair Fairbanks and his then wife Pickford. A wide-screen version was released in 1967. The *New York Times* placed it at #5 on their "10 Best" list of the year.

4599. The Taming of the West (Columbia; 1939). *Cast:* Bill Elliott (his first as Saunders), Iris Meredith, Dub Taylor (Cannonball), Dick Curtis, James Craig, Stanley Brown, Kenneth MacDonald, Victor Wong, Charles King, Ethan Allen, Lane Chandler, Jack Kirk, George Morrell, Art Mix, Don Beddoe, Richard Fiske, Bob Woodward, John Tyrell, Hank Bell. *D:* Norman Deming; *P:* Leon Barsha; *Sc:* Robert Lee Johnson, Charles Francis Royal; *St:* Johnson. (0:55)

Bill Elliott western of lawman "Wild Bill Saunders" cleaning up a lawless town after a girl's sister is killed by outlaws.

4600. Taming the Wild (Victory; 1936). *Cast:* Rod La Rocque, Maxine Doyle, Barbara Pepper, Bryant Washburn. *D:* Robert F. Hill; *St:* Peter B. Kyne; *Sc:* Al Martin.

(No other information available)

4601. Tampico (Columbia; 1933). *Cast:* Jack Holt, Raquel Torres. (alt. title: *The Woman I Stole*)

(No other information available)

4602. Tangled Destinies (Mayfair; 1932). *Cast:* Glenn Tryon, Lloyd Whitlock, Doris Hill, Vera Reynolds, Sidney Bracy. *D:* Frank Strayer.

"Poverty row" melodrama.

4603. Tangled Fortunes (Big 4; 1932). *Cast:* Buzz Barton, Francis X. Bushman, Jr., Edmund Cobb. *D:* J.P. McGowan; *P:* John R. Freuler.

Buzz Barton juvenile western, the third in a series of three films.

4604. Tango (Invincible; 1936). *Cast:* Marian Nixon, Chick Chandler, Warren Hymer, Marie Prevost, Herman Bing, Franklin Pangborn. *D:* Phil Rosen.

A "poverty row" drama which may or may not have been inspired by *Bolero* (q.v.) and *Rumba* (q.v.).

4605. Tanned Legs (RKO; 1929). *Cast:* Arthur Lake, June Clyde (film debut), Nella Walker, Albert Gran, Sally Blane, Edmund Burns, Dorothy Revier, Ann Pennington, Allen Kearns, Lincoln Stedman, Grady Sutton, Lloyd Hamilton. *D:* Marshall Neilan; *As.P.:* Louis Sarecky; *Sc:* Tom Geraghty; *Songs:* Oscar Levant, Sidney Clare. (1:07)

Low-budget comedy-drama with music and a seaside locale.

4606. Tarnished Angel (RKO; 1938). *Cast:* Sally Eilers, Lee Bowman, Ann Miller, Alma Kruger, Paul Guilfoyle, Jonathan Hale, Jack Arnold (aka: Vinton Haworth), Cecil Kellaway, Janet Dempsey, Hamilton MacFadden, Byron Foulger. *D:* Leslie Goodwins; *P:* B.P. Fineman; *St:* Saul Elkins; *Sc:* Jo Pagano; *Song:* Lew Brown, Sammy Fain. (1:08)

B melodrama of a cabaret singer who becomes an evangelist, while some believe she is in league with crooks.

4607. Tarnished Lady (Paramount; 1931). *Cast:* Tallulah Bankhead, Clive Brook, Phoebe Foster, Osgood Perkins, Elizabeth Patterson, Alexander Kirkland, Berton Churchill, Eric Blore, Cora Witherspoon. *D:* George Cukor (solo directorial debut); *P:* Walter Wanger; *Sc:* Donald Ogden Stewart. (1:23)

A woman marries a man for his money and then falls in love with him. Based on a story by Donald Ogden Stewart, this was a production from Paramount's Astoria Studios in Long Island, N.Y.

4608. Tarzan and His Mate (MGM; 1934). *Cast:* Johnny Weissmuller, Maureen O'Sullivan, Neil Hamilton, Paul Cavanagh, Forrester Harvey, Desmond Roberts, Nathan Curry, William Stack & more bellowing elephants, roaring lions & screeching simians (humans in costume & real) than you are likely to see in any other film. *D:* Cedric Gibbons (better known as MGM's head art director), Jack Conway; *P:* Bernard Hyman; *Sc:* Howard Emmett Rogers, Leon Gordon. (1:33)

Johnny Weissmuller in his second outing as Edgar Rice Burroughs' jungle hero. In this box office hit, Tarzan finds he has a romantic rival for the affections of Jane. Considered by many Tarzan buffs as one of the best in the series (if not the best).

4609. Tarzan and the Green Goddess (Principal-New Realm Productions; 1938). *Cast:* Herman Brix (Bruce Bennett), Ula Holt, Frank Baker, Don Castello, Lew Sargent. *D:* Edward Kull; *Sc:* Charles Francis Royal. (1:12) (video)

For the most part this is a reworking of footage from the serial "The New Adventures of Tarzan" produced in 1935 in 12-chapters with new footage added in the attempt to disguise it as a new feature. See also: *Tarzan's New Adventures.*

4610. Tarzan Escapes (MGM; 1936). *Cast:* Johnny Weissmuller, Maureen O'Sullivan, John Buckler, Benita Hume, William Henry, Herbert Mundin, E.E. Clive, Darby Jones. *D:* Richard Thorpe; *P:* Sam Zimbalist (debut film as a producer); *Sc:* Karl Brown, Cyril Hume. (1:35)

Tarzan is taken captive by a hunter who intends to put him on display in England. The third feature for Weissmuller in the title role was a box office hit.

4611. Tarzan Finds a Son (MGM; 1939). *Cast:* Johnny Weissmuller, Maureen O'Sullivan, Johnny Sheffield (film debut as Boy), Ian Hunter, Frieda Inescort, Laraine Day, Henry Wilcoxon, Henry Stephenson, Morton Lowry. *D:* Richard Thorpe; *P:* Sam Zambalist; *Sc:* Cyril Hume. (1:22)

A little boy, the sole survivor of a plane crash is found and adopted by Tarzan and Jane, but relatives come in search of him with the intent of getting their hands on a large inheritance. The fourth entry in the series with Weissmuller and a box office hit.

4612. Tarzan, the Ape Man (MGM; 1932). *Cast:* Johnny Weissmuller (starring debut as Tarzan), Maureen O'Sullivan (Jane Parker), C. Aubrey Smith (James Parker), Neil Hamilton (Harry Holt), Doris Lloyd (Mrs. Cutten), Forrester Harvey (Beamish), Ivory Williams (Riano). *D:* W.S. Van Dyke; *Adaptation:* Cyril Hume; *Dialogue:* Ivor Novello. (1:39) (video)

Premiere entry in this studio's series starring ex–Olympic swimmer Johnny Weissmuller as Edgar Rice Burroughs' jungle hero. In this entry, a safari in search of ivory gets the jungle man to lead them to the elephant's graveyard. A tremendous box office success and one of the 15 top grossing films of 1932 (a $2,000,000 gross on an original $450,000 production). The National Board of Review voted it one of the "10 Best" films of the year. Remade in 1959 as a low budget quickie and again in the infamous 1981 production which received much publicity. Computer-colored by Turner Entertainment in 1990.

Note: The film utilizes left-over footage from *Trader Horn* (q.v.).

4613. Tarzan the Fearless (Principal-Wardour Productions; 1933). *Cast:* Buster Crabbe (another ex–Olympic swimmer in his only film as Tarzan), Jacqueline Wells (Julie Bishop), Edward Woods, Philo McCullough, E. Alyn Warren, Mischa Auer, Matthew Betz, Frank Lackteen. *D:* Robert F. Hill; *P:* Sol Lesser; *St:* Edgar Rice Burroughs; *Sc:* Basil Dickey, George H. Plympton. (1:25) (video)

Feature version of the first four chapters of the serial of the same name in 12-chapters.

4614. Tarzan's New Adventures (Burroughs-Tarzan; 1935). *Cast:* Herman Brix (Bruce Bennett as Tarzan), Ula Holt, Don Castello, Frank Baker, Lewis Sargent, Dale Walsh, Harry Ernest, W.F. McGaugh, Merrill McCormack. *D:* Edward Kull; *P:* George W. Stout, Ben S. Cohen, Ashton Dearholt, Edgar Rice Burroughs; *Sc:* Charles Francis Royal. (1:15)

The feature version of the 12-chapter serial "The New Adventures of Tarzan" which was released as a serial and a feature simultaneously. The production suffered many setbacks while on location in Guatamala.

Note: See also: *Tarzan and the Green Goddess*

4615. Tarzan's Revenge (20th Century–Fox; 1938). *Cast:* Glenn Morris (former Olympic athlete in his only film as Tarzan), Eleanor Holm (also a former Olympic athlete), C. Henry Gordon, George Barbier, Joseph Sawyer, Hedda Hopper, George Meeker, John L. Johnson. *D:* D. Ross Lederman; *P:* Sol Lesser; *Sc:* Robert Lee Johnston, Jay Vann. (1:10)

The jungle man helps a girl being pursued by an evil king.

4616. Taxi! (WB; 1932). *Cast:* James Cagney, Loretta Young, George E. Stone, Guy Kibbee, David Landau, Dorothy Burgess, Leila Bennett, Nat Pendleton, Matt McHugh, Ray Cooke, Berton Churchill, George Raft, George MacFarlane, Polly Walters. *D:* Roy Del Ruth; *P:* Robert Lord; *Sc:* Kubec Glasmon, John Bright. (1:10)

Hit comedy-melodrama involving a war which breaks out among big city cab drivers. Based on the play "The Blind Spot" by John Kenyon Nicholson.

4617. Taxi 13 (Film Booking Office; 1928–29). *Cast:* Chester Conklin, Ethel Wales, Martha Sleeper. *D:* Marshall Neilan.

Low-budget part-talkie comedy.

4618. Telegraph Trail (WB/ Vitagraph; 1933). *Cast:* John Wayne, Frank McHugh, Marceline Day, Otis Harlan, Albert J. Smith, Yakima Canutt, Lafe McKee, Clarence Geldert, Duke the horse. *D:* Tenny Wright; *P:* Sid Rogel; *St & Sc:* Kurt Kempler. (0:54)

John Wayne western of men trying to get supply wagons to the men stringing the first telegraph lines across the country.

4619. Telephone Operator (Monogram; 1937). *Cast:* Judith Allen, Grant Withers, Warren Hymer, Alice White, Pat Flaherty, Greta Granstedt, William Haade. *D:* Scott Pembroke; *P:* Lon Young; *St:* John Krafft; *Sc:* W. Scott Darling. (1:02)

"Poverty row" drama of a telephone operator who becomes a heroine during a flood.

4620. Television Spy (Paramount; 1938–39). *Cast:* William Henry, Judith Barrett, Richard Denning, Anthony Quinn, William Collier, Sr., John Eldredge, Minor Watson, Byron Foulger. *D:* Edward Dmytryk; *P:* Edward T. Lowe.

B melodrama, aptly described by the title as a young man's invention is stolen.

4621. Tell No Tales (MGM; 1938–39). *Cast:* Melvyn Douglas, Louise Platt, Gene Lockhart, Douglass Dumbrille, Zeffie Tilbury, Halliwell Hobbes, Sara Haden, Florence George, Esther Dale, Hobart Cavanaugh, Oscar O'Shea, Mantan Moreland, Ian Wolfe, Mary Gordon, Joseph Crehan, Jean Fenwick, Harlan Briggs, Theresa Harris, Tom Collins. *D:* Leslie Fenton (feature directorial debut); *P:* Edward Chodorov; *St:* Pauline London, Alfred Taylor; *Sc:* Lionel Houser. (1:08)

B newspaper melodrama of an editor who will go to any lengths to keep his paper from going under.

Tell Your Children *see* **The Burning Question**

4622. Temple Tower (Fox; 1930). *Cast:* Kenneth MacKenna (Drummond), Marceline Day, Henry B. Walthall, Peter Gawthorne, Ivan Linow, Cyril Chadwick. *D:* Donald Gallaher.

Low-budget mystery melodrama featuring the character of "Bulldog Drummond." Based on the story of the same name by "Sapper." This film was not part of a series, as was its remake *Bulldog Drummond's Secret Police* (q.v.).

Note: No copies of this film are known to exist.

4623. Temptation (Xxxx Xxxx; 1930). *D:* E. Mason Hopper; *Sc:* Leonard Praskins.

(No other information available)

4624. Temptation (Micheaux; 1936). Low-budget independent feature, produced, directed and written by Oscar Micheaux.

4625. Ten Cents a Dance (Columbia; 1931). *Cast:* Barbara Stanwyck, Ricardo Cortez, Monroe Owsley, Sally Blane, Blanche Frederici, Olive Tell, Martha Sleeper, Phyllis Crane. *D:* Lionel Barrymore; *St & Sc:* Jo Swerling. (1:20)

Romantic drama of a taxi dancer who discovers she is married to a no-good-nik.

4626. $10 Raise (Fox; 1935). *Cast:* Edward Everett Horton, Karen Morley, Berton Churchill, William (Billy) Benedict (film debut). *D:* George Marshall; *St:* Peter B. Kyne. (G.B. title: *Mr. Faintheart*)

B domestic comedy which was previously filmed in 1921.

4627. Ten Minutes to Kill (Micheaux; 1933). Low-budget independent melodrama produced, directed and written by Oscar Micheaux.

4628. Ten Minutes to Live (Micheaux; 1932). Low-budget independent melodrama produced, directed and written by Oscar Micheaux.

4629. Ten Nights in a Barroom (Road Show Productions; 1931). *Cast:* William Farnum, Tom Santschi, Phyllis Barrington, Rosemary Theby, Robert Frazer, Thomas Jefferson, Lionel Belmore, John Darrow, Patty Lou Lynd. *D:* William O'Connor.

Independent melodrama most notable for a fight scene between stars William Farnum and Tom Santschi, similar in intensity to the one they did back in the 1914 version of *The Spoilers.*

4630. The Tenderfoot (WB; 1932). *Cast:* Joe E. Brown, Ginger Rogers, Lew Cody, Robert Greig, Ralph Ince, Marion Byron, Spencer Charters, Douglas Gerrard, George Chandler, Allan Lane, Richard Cramer, Wilfred Lucas, Herman Bing, Lee Kohlmar, Vivian Oakland, Harry Seymour, Jill Dennett, Mae Madison. *D:* Ray Enright; *Adaptation:* Earl Baldwin, Monty Banks, Arthur Caesar. (1:10)

Hit comedy of a Texan who heads for Broadway to become the financial backer of a show. Based on the play "The Butter and Egg Man" by George S. Kaufman; story by Richard Carle. A remake of *The Butter and Egg Man* (1928). Remade as *Dance, Charlie, Dance* (q.v.), and again in 1940 as *An Angel from Texas.*

4631. A Tenderfoot Goes West (Hoffberg; 1937). *Cast:* Jack LaRue, Virginia Carroll, Russell Gleason, Ralph Byrd, Chris-Pin Martin, John Merton, Si Jenks, Joseph Girard, John Ince, Ray Turner, Glenn Strange, Addison (Jack) Randall. *D:* Maurice O'Neill. (1:05)

Indie western comedy of an outlaw who saves an eastern tenderfoot from a lynch mob.

4632. Tenderloin (WB/Vitaphone; 1928). *Cast:* Dolores Costello, Conrad Nagel, John Miljan, Mitchell Lewis, George E. Stone, Dan Wolheim, Pat Hartigan, Fred Kelsey, Dorothy Vernon, Evelyn Pierce. *D:* Michael Curtiz; *St:* Melville Crossman (Darryl Zanuck); *Sc:* Edward T. Lowe, Jr. (1:28)

Part-talkie melodrama of a dancer, accused by the underworld of stealing a large amount of money.

4633. Tenth Avenue Kid (Republic; 1938). *Cast:* Bruce Cabot, Tommy Ryan, Beverly Roberts, Horace MacMahon, Jay Novello (film debut), Charles Wilson, Ralph Dunn, Paul Bryar, Ben Welden, Julian Petruzzi, Walter Sande, Byron Foulger, Billy Wayne. *D:* Bernard Vorhaus; *P:* Harry Grey; *St:* Gordon Kahn; *Sc:* Adele Buffington, Kahn.

Melodrama.

4634. The Terror (WB/Vitaphone; 1928). *Cast:* May McAvoy, Louise Fazenda, Edward Everett Horton, Alec B. Francis, Frank Austin, John Miljan, Holmes Herbert, Otto

Hoffman. *D:* Roy Del Ruth; *Play & Story:* Edgar Wallace; *Sc:* Harvey Gates. (1:22)

Thriller of an organ playing maniac terrorizing the residents of a British hotel. A box office hit, no titles appear on screen, but are instead read by Conrad Nagel, combined with sound effects. This was Warners second all-talkie, premiering on August 15, 1928. Remade in Great Britain in 1938.

4635. Terror Aboard (Paramount; 1933). *Cast:* Charles Ruggles, Verree Teasdale, Neil Hamilton, John Halliday, Shirley Grey, Jack LaRue, Thomas Jackson, Paul Hurst, Wynne Gibson, Leon Janney, Stanley Fields. *D:* Paul Sloane; *P:* William LeBaron; *Sc:* Harvey Thew, Manuel Seff. (1:10)

B murder-mystery set aboard a cruise ship.

Terror by Night *see* **The Secret Witness**

4636. Terror of the Plains (Reliable; 1934). *Cast:* Tom Tyler, Roberta Gale, Charles "Slim" Whitaker. *Produced & directed:* Bernard B. Ray & Harry Webb.

Tom Tyler western.

4637. The Terror of Tiny Town (Columbia/Astor; 1938). *Cast:* Billy Curtis, Yvonne Moray, Little Billy, John Bambury, Bill Platt, Joseph Herbert, Charles Becker, Nita Krebs, George Ministeri. *D:* Sam Newfield; *P:* Jed Buell — Sol Lesser; *As. P.:* Abe Meyer, Bert Sternbach; *Sc:* Fred Myton, Clarence Markes; *Songs:* Lew Porter, Phil Stern. (1:03) (video)

An exploitive musical-western with good guys, bad guys and dance hall girls, all played by little people who ride ponys. A formula plot, but a novelty never-the-less.

4638. Terror Trail (Universal; 1933). *Cast:* Tom Mix, Tony, Jr., Naomi Judge, Arthur Rankin, Raymond Hatton, John St. Polis, Francis McDonald, Robert Kortman, Francis Brownlee, Harry Tenbrook, Lafe McKee, Hank Bell, Leonard Trainer, W.J. Holmes, Jay Wilsey (Buffalo Bill, Jr.), Jim Corey. *D:* Armand L. Schaefer; *St:* Grant Taylor; *Sc:* Jack Cunningham. (0:58)

Tom Mix western of a cowboy out to retrieve his horse which was stolen by outlaws.

4639. Tess of the Storm Country (Fox; 1932). *Cast:* Janet Gaynor, Charles Farrell, Dudley Digges, June Clyde, George Meeker, Claude Gillingwater, Louise Carter, Edward Pawley, DeWitt Jennings, Matty Kemp, Sarah Padden. *D:* Alfred Santell; *Sc:* S.N. Behrman, Sonya Levien, Rupert Hughes (based on the novel by Grace Miller White). (1:20)

The romance of the daughter of a sea captain after emigrating to America. Previous versions: (Famous Players; 1914) with Mary Pickford and Harold Lockwood, (United Artists; 1922) with Mary Pickford and Lloyd Hughes. Remade in 1960.

4640. The Test (Reliable; 1935). *Cast:* Rin-Tin-Tin, Jr., Grant Withers, Grace Ford, Monte Blue, Lafayette (Lafe) McKee, James (Jimmy) Aubrey, Dorothy Vernon, Artie Ortego, Jack Evans, Tom London, Nanette the dog. *D:* Bernard B. Ray; *P:* Harry S. Webb; *Sc:* L.V. Jefferson. (0:55)

Northwoods B adventure of romantic rivalry between two fur trappers.

4641. Test Pilot (MGM; 1938). *Cast:* Clark Gable (Jim Lane), Myrna Loy (Ann Barton), Spencer Tracy (Gunner Sloane), Lionel Barrymore (Howard B. Drake), Samuel S. Hinds (General Ross), Marjorie Main (landlady), Arthur Aylesworth (Frank Barton), Gloria Holden (Mrs. Benson), Louis Jean Heydt (Benson), Virginia Grey (Sarah), Priscilla Lawson (Mabel),

Ted Pearson (Joe), Claudia Coleman (Mrs. Barton), Gregory Gaye (Grant), Dudley Clements (Mr. Brown), Henry Rocquemore (fat man), Dorothy Vaughan (fat woman), Byron Foulger (designer), Roger Converse (advertising man), Frank Jaquet (motor expert), Phillip Terry (photographer), Garry Owen (pilot), Robert Fiske (attendant), Billy Engle, Brent Sargent, Mary Howard, Gladden James, Douglas McPhail, Don Douglas, Richard Tucker, Forbes Murray, James Flavin, Hooper Atchley, Ray Walker, Dick Winslow, Frank Sully, Fay Holden, Syd Saylor, Tom O'Grady. *D:* Victor Fleming; *P:* (A.A.N. for "Best Picture") Louis D. Lighton; *St:* (A.A.N.) Frank "Spig" Wead; *Sc:* Waldemar Young, Vincent Lawrence; *Editor:* (A.A.N.) Tom Held. (1:58)

A critically acclaimed comedy-drama of daredevil pilots who fly the latest in aeronautical technology (ala 1938). One of the 15 top grossing films of 1937–38, the film was in nomination for "Best Picture" at the Venice Film Festival.

4642. Tex Rides with the Boy Scouts (Grand National; 1937). *Cast:* Tex Ritter, Marjorie Reynolds, Horace Murphy (Ananias), Snub Pollard (Pee Wee), Tommy Bupp, Charles King, Forrest Taylor, Karl Hackett, Lynton Brent, Ed Cassidy, Heber Snow (Hank Worden), Philip Ahn, Timmy Davis, Beverly Hillbillies, White Flash the horse. *D:* Ray Taylor; *P:* Edward Finney (for Boots & Saddles Productions); *St:* Lindsley Parsons, Edmond Kelso; *Sc:* Kelso. (1:06)

Offbeat Tex Ritter western with songs of a geologist who is aided by a troop of boy scouts in capturing train robbers. The film is dedicated to the Boy Scouts of America.

4643. Tex Takes a Holiday (First Division; 1932). *Cast:* Wallace MacDonald, Virginia Brown Faire, George Chesebro, Ben Corbett, Jack Perrin,

James Dillon, Claude Peyton, Sheldon Lewis, George Gerwing. *D:* Alvin J. Neitz (Alan James); *Sc:* Robert Walker. (1:00)

Color B western of a stranger in town who is suspected of committing a series of crimes. Filmed in a 2-color process called "natural color."

4644. The Texan (Paramount; 1930). *Cast:* Gary Cooper, Fay Wray, Emma Dunn, Oscar Apfel, Donald Reed, Enrique Acosta, James Marcus, Soledad Jiminez, Veda Buckland, Cesar Vanoni, Edwin J. Brady, Romualdo Tirado, Russ Columbo. *D:* John Cromwell; *P:* David O. Selznick, Hector Turnbull; *Sc:* Daniel Nathan Rubin. (1:19)

Western of an outlaw who tries to rectify errors from his past by posing as a wealthy woman's long-lost son. Based on the story "A Double-Eyed Deceiver" by O'Henry (William Sidney Porter), it was remade as *The Llano Kid* (q.v.).

4645. The Texan (Principal; 1932). *Cast:* Buffalo Bill, Jr., Lucille Browne, Bobby Nelson, Lafe McKee, Jack Mower, Art Mix, Yakima Canutt. *D:* Cliff Smith; *P:* Sol Lesser. (1:04)

B western of a fugitive from the law and two crooks who bilk townspeople of their money in a rigged horse race.

4646. The Texans (Paramount; 1938). *Cast:* Randolph Scott, Joan Bennett, May Robson, Walter Brennan, Robert Cummings, Raymond Hatton, Robert Barrat, Francis Ford, Harvey Stephens, Otis Harlan, Chris-Pin Martin, William Haade, Clarence H. Wilson, John Qualen, Richard Tucker, Anna Demetrio, Archie Twitchell, Jack Moore. *D:* James Hogan; *P:* Lucien Hubbard; *Sc:* Paul Sloane, Bertram Millhauser, William Wister Haines. (1:32)

There's trouble in Texas following the American Civil War. A remake of *North of 36* (Paramount; 1924) with Jack Holt, Lois Wilson and Ernest Torrence

(which followed in the tracks of the success generated by *The Covered Wagon* (Paramount; 1923), both of which were based on books by Emerson Hough.

4647. Texas Bad Man (Universal; 1932). *Cast:* Tom Mix, Tony, Lucille Powers, Fred Kohler, Willard Robertson, Theodore Lorch, Edward J. LeSaint, Franklyn Farnum, Lynton Brent, Joseph Girard, Francis Sayles, Richard Alexander, C.E. Anderson, Buck Moulton, James Burtis, Slim Cole, Boothe Howard, George Magrill, Bud Osborne, Buck Bucko. *D:* Edward Laemmle; *Sc:* Jack Cunningham. (1:03)

Tom Mix western of a U.S. marshal who goes undercover to capture a wanted killer. The third of nine talking features with Mix for this studio.

4648. Texas Buddies (World Wide/Tiffany; 1932). *Cast:* Bob Steele, Nancy Drexel, Francis McDonald, Harry Semels, George Hayes, Billy Dyer, Dick Dickinson, Earl Dwire. *D:* Robert N. Bradbury; *Sc:* Bradbury. (0:57)

Bob Steele western of a Texan who returns from the great war (WWI) and tries to set his life in order. A production of Tiffany with release by World Wide.

4649. Texas Cyclone (Columbia; 1932). *Cast:* Tim McCoy, Shirley Grey, Wheeler Oakman, John Wayne, Wallace MacDonald, James Farley, Harry Cording, Vernon Dent, Walter Brennan, Mary Gordon. *D:* D. Ross Lederman; *Sc:* Randall Faye. (1:03)

Tim McCoy oater of a cowboy who is mistaken for another.

Texas Desperadoes *see* **Drift Fence**

4650. Texas Gun-Fighter (Tiffany; 1932). *Cast:* Ken Maynard, Sheila Mannors, Harry Woods, Bob Fleming, Jim Mason, Edgar Lewis, Lloyd Ingraham, Frank Ellis, Jack Rockwell, Bob Burns, Blackjack Ward, Bud Mc-

Clure. *D:* Phil Rosen; *P:* Phil Goldstone (Amity Prods.); *Sc:* Bennett Cohen. (1:03)

Ken Maynard western of an outlaw who wants to go straight, but his cohorts have other ideas. A remake of *The Lone Rider* (q.v.).

4651. Texas Jack (Reliable; 1932). *Cast:* Jack Perrin, Jayne Regan, Nelson McDowell, Robert Walker, Lew Meehan, Cope Borden, Blackie Whiteford, Oscar Gahan, Budd Buster, Jim Oates, Steve Clark. *D:* Bernard B. Ray; *P:* Harry S. Webb; *Sc:* Carl Krusada. (0:52)

Jack Perrin western of a cowboy seeking the party responsible for instigating his sister's suicide.

Texas Legionnaires *see* **Come On, Rangers**

4652. Texas Pioneers (Monogram; 1932). *Cast:* Bill Cody, Andy Shuford, LeRoy Mason, Sheila Mannors, John Elliott, Frank Lackteen, Harry Allen, Chief Standing Bear, Iron Eyes Cody, Ann Ross. *D:* Harry Fraser; *P:* Trem Carr; *St:* Fraser; *Sc:* Wellyn Totman, Fraser. (0:58) (video)

Bill Cody western of an army officer who goes undercover to expose a gang running guns to the Indians.

4653. The Texas Rambler (Spectrum; 1935). *Cast:* Bill Cody, Catherine Cotter, Earle Hodgins, Stuart James, Mildred Rogers, Budd Buster, Ace Cain, Roger Williams, Buck Morgan, Colin Chase, Allen Greer. *D:* Robert Hill; *Sc:* Oliver Drake. (0:59)

Bill Cody western of attempts to thwart the kidnapping of a girl.

4654. The Texas Ranger (Columbia; 1931). *Cast:* Buck Jones, Carmelita Geraghty, Harry Woods, Ed Brady, Billy Bletcher, Nelson McDowell, Harry Todd, Budd Fine, Ed Peil, Sr., Blackie Whiteford, Lew Meehan, Bert Woodruff. *D:* D. Ross Lederman; *Sc:* Forrest Sheldon. (1:00)

Buck Jones horse opera of a Texas Ranger sent to investigate a range feud.

4655. The Texas Rangers (Paramount; 1936). *Cast:* Fred MacMurray, Jack Oakie, Jean Parker, Lloyd Nolan, Edward Ellis, Bennie Bartlett, Elena Martinez, George Hayes, Jed Prouty, Frank Shannon, Charles Middleton, Jack Luden. *D:* King Vidor; *P:* Vidor; *St:* Vidor, Elizabeth Hill; *Sc:* Louis Stevens; *Sound Recording:* (A.A.N.) Franklin Hansen. (1:35)

Hit western of three friends who rode the range together who go their separate ways, two to become Texas Rangers, the other a wanted outlaw. Followed in 1940 by a sequel, *The Texas Rangers Ride Again.* Remade in 1949 as *Streets of Laredo.*

4656. Texas Renegades (Producers Distributing Corp.; 1939–40). *Cast:* Tim McCoy, Nora Lane, Harry Harvey, Sr., Kenne Duncan, Lee Prather, Earl Gunn, Hal Price, Joe McGuinn, Raphael (Ray) Bennett, Ed Cassidy. *D:* Peter Stewart (Sam Newfield); *P:* Sigmund Neufeld; *Sc:* Joseph O'Donnell. (0:59)

Tim McCoy western of a lawman, undercover to get the goods on a gang of outlaws. The film had the working title of "Swift Justice."

Texas Serenade (G.B. title) *see* **The Old Corral** (Republic; 1936)

4657. Texas Stampede (Columbia; 1939). *Cast:* Charles Starrett, Iris Meredith, Sons of the Pioneers with Bob Nolan & Pat Brady, Fred Kohler, Jr., Lee Prather, Ray Bennett, Edmund Cobb, Hank Bell, Blackjack Ward, Edward Hearn, Ernie Adams, Ed Coxen, Charles Brinley. *D:* Sam Nelson; *Sc:* Charles Francis Royal. (0:59)

Charles Starrett western of cattlemen vs. sheepmen. A remake of *The Dawn Trail* (q.v.).

4658. Texas Terror (Monogram-Lone Star; 1935). *Cast:* John Wayne,

Lucille Browne, LeRoy Mason, George Hayes, Buffalo Bill, Jr., Bert Dillard, Yakima Canutt, Bobby Nelson, Fern Emmett, John Ince, Henry Rocquemore, Jack Duffy, Lloyd Ingraham, Hooper Atchley. *D:* Robert N. Bradbury; *P:* Paul Malvern; *Supervisor:* Trem Carr; *St:* Bradbury; *Sc:* Bradbury. (0:58) (video)

John Wayne western of a lawman accused of killing his friend.

4659. Texas Tornado (Willis Kent; 1932). *Cast:* Lane Chandler, Doris Hill, Buddy Roosevelt, Yakima Canutt, Roberta Gale, Ben Corbett, Bart Carre, Fred Burns, J. Frank Glendon, Edward Hearn, Mike Brand, Wes Warner, Pat Healy. *D:* Oliver Drake; *P:* Willis Kent; *Sc:* Drake. (0:55)

Lane Chandler western of a Texas Ranger who goes after outlaws who have taken a girl and killed her father.

4660. Texas Trail (Paramount; 1937). *Cast:* William Boyd (Hoppy), George Hayes (Windy), Russell Hayden (Lucky), Judith Allen, Billy King, Alexander Cross, Karl Hackett, Robert Kortman, Jack Rockwell, John Beach, Ray Bennett, Earle Hodgins, Ben Corbett, Philo McCullough, John Judd, Clyde Kinney, Leo McMahon. *D:* David Selman; *P:* Harry M. Sherman; *Sc:* Joseph O'Donnell. (0:58)

The 14th "Hopalong Cassidy" western with the Bar 20 boys getting a government contract to deliver 500 horses for the Spanish-American War, combating outlaws who also want the herd.

4661. Texas Wildcats (Victory; 1939). *Cast:* Tim McCoy, Joan Barclay, Ted Adams, Forrest Taylor, Dave O'Brien, Frank Ellis, Carl Mathews, Bob Terry, Reed Howes, Slim Whitaker, George Morrell, Avando Reynaldo. *D:* Sam Newfield; *P:* Sam Katzman; *Sc:* George Plympton. (0:57)

Tim McCoy in a "Lightnin' Bill Carson" western, as the lawman dons a disguise to apprehend the bad guy.

4662. Thank You, Jeeves (20th Century–Fox; 1936). *Cast:* Arthur Treacher (Jeeves), David Niven (in his starring debut), Virginia Field, Lester Matthews, Colin Tapley, Willie Best, Gene Reynolds, Douglas Walton, John Spacey, Ernie Stanton. *D:* Arthur Greville Collins; *P:* Sol M. Wurtzel; *St:* P.G. Wodehouse; *Sc:* Joseph Hoffman, Stephen Gross. (Retitled: *Thank You, Mr. Jeeves*) (1:08)

Hit low-budget comedy of a man-servant who keeps his employer out of trouble. Followed by a sequel: *Step Lively, Jeeves* (q.v.).

Thank You Mr. Jeeves *see* **Thank You, Jeeves**

4663. Thank You, Mr. Moto (20th Century–Fox; 1937). *Cast:* Peter Lorre (Moto), Pauline Frederick (in her final film), Sidney Blackmer, Sig Rumann, John Carradine, Nedda Harrigan, Philip Ahn, Richard Loo, William von Brincken, John Bleifer, Jayne Regan, Thomas Beck. *D:* Norman Foster; *P:* Sol M. Wurtzel; *Sc:* Foster, Willis Cooper. (1:08)

The Japanese sleuth, based on the character created by John P. Marquand, encounters murder while on a hunt for a hidden scroll. An entry in the B series of eight films.

Thank Your Stars (G.B. title) *see* **Shoot the Works**

4664. Thanks a Million (20th Century–Fox; 1935). *Cast:* Dick Powell (Eric Land), Ann Dvorak (Sally Mason), Fred Allen (film debut as Ned Lyman), Patsy Kelly (Phoebe Mason), Alan Dinehart (Mr. Kruger), Margaret Irving (Mrs. Kruger), Paul Whiteman & His Band, Yacht Club Boys (featuring Charles Adler, James V. Kern, Billy Mann & George Kelly), Benny Baker (Tammany), David Rubinoff (orchestra leader), Phil Baker (sequence with beetle and bottle), Charles Richman (governor—opposition party), Andrew

Tombes (Mr. Grass), Raymond Walburn (Judge Culliman), Paul Harvey (Maxwell), Edwin Maxwell (Casey), Russell Hicks (Mr. Bradley), Yorke Sherwood (Mr. Hartford), Ramona, Herbert Ashley, Harry Dunkinson, Walter Downing, Ralph Lewis, Frank Darien, Ricca K. Allen, Wally Maher, Si Jenks, Olaf Hytten, Harry Stubbs, Walter Walker, Stanhope Wheatcroft, Charles C. Wilson, Harry C. Bradley, Lynn Bari, Frank Faylen (film debut—bit). *D:* Roy Del Ruth; *P:* Darryl F. Zanuck; *St:* Melville Crossman (Darryl F. Zanuck); *Sc:* Nunnally Johnson, Harry Tugend; *Sound Recording:* (A.A.N.) E.H. Hansen; *Songs:* title song, "Sing, Brother, Sing," "New O'leans," "Sugar Baby," "Sittin' on a Hilltop," "A Pocketful of Sunshine" by Gus Kahn, Arthur Johnston; "What a Beautiful Night" by Bert Kalmar & Harry Ruby. (1:27) (video)

Musical-comedy of a singer who decides to run for state governor. Remade as *If I'm Lucky* (20th Century-Fox; 1946). One of the 25 top grossing films of 1935–36.

4665. Thanks for Everything (20th Century-Fox; 1938). *Cast:* Adolphe Menjou, Jack Haley, Jack Oakie, Arleen Whelan, Tony Martin, Binnie Barnes, George Barbier, Warren Hymer, Paul Hurst, Charles Lane, Edgar Dearing, Charles Trowbridge, Gregory Gaye, Jan Duggan, Andrew Tombes, Gary Breckner, Frank Sully, Renie Riano, James Flavin. *D:* William A. Seiter; *P:* Darryl F. Zanuck; *Sc:* Harry Tugend, Art Arthur, Curtis Kenyon; *Orig. St:* Gilbert Wright. (1:10)

Comedy satire of the advertising world.

4666. Thanks for Listening (Ambassador; 1937). *Cast:* Pinky Tomlin, Maxine Doyle, Aileen Pringle, Henry Rocquemore. *D:* Marshall Neilan; *P:* Maurice Conn; *Sc:* John B. Clymer.

(No other information available)

4667. Thanks for the Memory (Paramount; 1938). *Cast:* Bob Hope, Shirley Ross, Laura Hope Crews, Roscoe Karns, Otto Kruger, Charles Butterworth, William Collier, Sr., Emma Dunn, Hedda Hopper, Patricia Wilder, Jack Norton, Eddie "Rochester" Anderson, Vernon Dent, Johnnie Morris, Jack Chapin, Pat West, Barney Dean. *D:* George Archainbaud; *P:* Mel Shauer; *Sc:* Lynn Starling; *Song:* "Two Sleepy People" by Hoagy Carmichael, Frank Loesser. (1:15)

Hit domestic comedy of a novelist and his marriage. A remake of *Up Pops the Devil* (q.v.). Based on the play of that name by Frances Goodrich and Albert Hackett.

4668. That Certain Age (Universal; 1938). *Cast:* Deanna Durbin, Melvyn Douglas, Jackie Cooper, Irene Rich, Nancy Carroll, John Halliday, Jackie Searle, Juanita Quigley, Charles Coleman, Peggy Stewart, Grant Mitchell. *D:* Edward Ludwig; *P:* Joe Pasternak; *St:* F. Hugh Herbert; *Sc:* Bruce Manning, Billy Wilder, Charles Brackett; *Sound Recording:* (A.A.N.) Bernard B. Brown; *Title Song:* "You're as Pretty as a Picture," "Be a Good Scout" & "My Own" (A.A.N. for Best Song) Harold Adamson & Jimmy McHugh; selection from "Romeo and Juliet" by Gounod & one from "Les Filles DeCadiz" by de Musset-Delibes. (1:35)

Deanna Durbin romantic musical-comedy of a girl who becomes infatuated with her parents' house guest. One of the 16 top grossing films of 1938–39.

4669. That Certain Woman (WB/F.N.; 1937). *Cast:* Bette Davis, Henry Fonda, Anita Louise, Ian Hunter, Donald Crisp, Minor Watson, Katherine Alexander, Mary Philips, Sidney Toler, Richard Lee, Frank Faylen, Ben Welden, Herbert Rawlinson, Hugh O'Connell, Charles Trowbridge, Norman Willis, Willard Parker (film debut—bit), Tim Henning, Dwane Day. *D:* Edmund Goulding; *P:* Robert Lord; *Sc:* Goulding. (1:33)

Melodrama of a gangster's widow and her search for love. A remake of *The Tresspasser* (q.v.).

That Girl from College (G.B. title) *see* **Sorority House**

4670. That Girl from Paris (RKO; 1936). *Cast:* Lily Pons, Jack Oakie, Gene Raymond, Herman Bing, Mischa Auer, Frank Jenks, Lucille Ball, Vinton Haworth (Jack Arnold), Patricia Wilder, Gregory Gaye, Willard Robertson, Rafaela Ottiano, Ferdinand Gottschalk, Harry Jans, Landers Stevens. *D:* Leigh Jason; *P:* Pandro S. Berman; *St:* Jane Murfin; *Sc:* P.J. Wolfson, Dorothy Yost; *Songs:* Arthur Schwartz, Edward Heyman; *Sound Recording:* (A.A.N.) John O. Aalberg. (1:45) (video)

Hit musical of a singer who flees her French wedding, joins a band and comes to America. Inspired by a story by J. Carey Wonderly, this is a loose remake of *Street Girl* (q.v.). Remade in 1942 as *Four Jacks and a Jill*. One of the musical interludes is "Tarantella" by Panofka.

4671. That I May Live (20th Century-Fox; 1937). *Cast:* Robert Kent, Rochelle Hudson, J. Edward Bromberg, Billy Benedict, George Cooper, Fred Kelsey, Lon Chaney, Jr., DeWitt Jennings, Frank Conroy. *D:* Allan Dwan; *P:* Sol M. Wurtzel; *Sc:* William Conselman, Ben Markson.

B drama.

4672. That Man's Here Again (WB/F.N.; 1937). *Cast:* Hugh Herbert, Tom Brown, Mary Maguire, Joseph King, Teddy Hart, Arthur Aylesworth, Al Herman, Tetsu Komai, Dorothy Vaughan. *D:* Louis King; *P:* Bryan Foy; *Adaptation:* Dalton Trumbo, Abem Finkel, Harold Buckley; *Sc:* Lillie Hayward.

B production of a blackmailing matchmaker. A remake of *Young Nowheres* (q.v.), the title of the play by Ida (I.A.R.) Wylie on which it is based.

That Navy Spirit (G.B. title) *see* **Hold 'em Navy**

4673. That's Gratitude (Columbia; 1934). *Cast:* Frank Craven, Mary Carlisle, Franklin Pangborn. *D:* Frank Craven (only film as a director).

Low-budget comedy, based on an original play by Frank Craven.

4674. That's My Boy (Columbia; 1932). *Cast:* Richard Cromwell, Dorothy Jordan, Joan Marsh, Douglass Dumbrille, Mae Marsh, Otis Harlan, Arthur Stone, Larry "Buster" Crabbe, Sumner Getchell, Lucien Littlefield, Dutch Hendrian, Russ Saunders, Elbridge Anderson. *D:* Roy William Neill; *St:* Francis Wallace; *Sc:* Norman Krasna.

Low-budget comedy.

4675. That's My Story (Universal; 1937). *Cast:* Claudia Morgan, William Lundigan, Eddie Garr, Ralph Morgan, Hobart Cavanaugh. *D:* Sidney Salkow; *P:* Robert Presnell. (1:03)

B production of two reporters who get themselves jailed with the intent of interviewing a gangster's girl friend.

4676. That's Right — You're Wrong (RKO; 1939). *Cast:* Adolphe Menjou, Kay Kyser (film debut), Lucille Ball, Dennis O'Keefe, May Robson, Edward Everett Horton, Hobart Cavanaugh, Ish Kabibble (film debut), Ginny Simms (film debut), Roscoe Karns, Moroni Olsen, Sheilah Graham, Hedda Hopper, Harry Babbitt (film debut), Sully Mason (film debut), Dorothy Lovett, Lillian West, Denis Tankard, Horace MacMahon. *D:* David Butler; *P:* Butler; *St:* Butler, William Conselman; *Sc:* Conselman, James V. Kern. (1:35)

Hit musical-comedy which cashed in on the popularity of Kay Kyser's radio show "The Kollege of Musical Knowledge."

Theatre Royale (G.B. title) *see* **The Royal Family of Broadway**

4677. Their Big Moment (RKO; 1934). *Cast:* ZaSu Pitts, Slim Summerville, William Gaxton, Bruce Cabot, Kay Johnson, Julie Haydon, Ralph Morgan, Huntley Gordon, Tamara Geva. *D:* James Cruze; *As.P.:* Cliff Reid; *Sc:* Marion Dix, Arthur Caesar. (G.B. title: *Afterwards*) (1:08)

Comedy-mystery of a faked seance which turns out to be the real thing and uncovers a murderer. A B production based on the play by Walter Hackett.

4678. Their Mad Moment (Fox; 1931). *Cast:* Dorothy Mackaill, Warner Baxter, ZaSu Pitts, Mary Doran, Leon Janney, John St. Polis. *D:* Hamilton MacFadden, Chandler Sprague.

Romantic comedy.

4679. Their Own Desire (MGM; 1929-30). *Cast:* Robert Montgomery (who gained box office popularity from this film), Norma Shearer (A.A.N. for B.A.—1929-30), Helene Millard, Belle Bennett, Lewis Stone, Henry Herbert, Cecil Cunningham, June Nash. *D:* E. Mason Hopper; *St:* Sarita Fuller; *Sc:* Frances Marion, J.G. Forbes.

Sophisticated romantic drama of a guy, his girl and their romance—and his mother, her father and their romance.

4680. Theodora Goes Wild (Columbia; 1936). *Cast:* Irene Dunne (A.A.N. for B.A.), Melvyn Douglas, Thomas Mitchell, Thurston Hall, Rosalind Keith, Spring Byington, Robert Greig, Henry Kolker, Elizabeth Risdon, Margaret McWade, Leona Maricle, Bud Flanagan (Dennis O'Keefe). *D:* Richard Boleslawski; *P:* Everett Riskin; *Sc:* Sidney Buchman; *Editor:* (A.A.N.) Otto Meyer. (1:34)

Hit comedy-farce about a small town lady who writes a scandalous novel and the romance that ensues. The film was in nomination at the Venice Film Festival of 1937. Based on a story by Mary McCarthy which was previously filmed in 1926.

4681. There Goes My Girl (RKO; 1937). *Cast:* Gene Raymond,

Ann Sothern, Gordon Jones, Richard Lane, Frank Jenks, Bradley Page, Joan Woodbury, Marla Shelton, Alec Craig, Joseph Crehan, William Corson, Maxine Jennings, Clyde Dilson, Charles Coleman, Roy James, Harry Worth. *D:* Ben Holmes; *P:* William Sistrom; *St:* George Beck; *Sc:* Harry Segall. (1:14)

B mystery-comedy of the rivalry between two news reporters when a murder story breaks.

4682. There Goes My Heart (United Artists/Hal Roach; 1938). *Cast:* Fredric March, Virginia Bruce, Patsy Kelly, Alan Mowbray, Nancy Carroll, Eugene Pallette, Claude Gillingwater, Harry Langdon, Arthur Lake, Etienne Girardot, Robert Armstrong, Marjorie Main, J. Farrell MacDonald, Irving Pichel. *D:* Norman Z. McLeod; *P:* Milton H. Bren; *St:* Ed Sullivan; *Sc:* Jack Jevne, Eddie Moran; *Music:* (A.A.N.) Marvin Hatley. (1:22)

A hit romantic comedy of a runaway heiress which was the first Hal Roach production to be released by United Artists.

4683. There Goes the Groom (RKO; 1937). *Cast:* Ann Sothern, Burgess Meredith, Mary Boland, Onslow Stevens, Louise Henry, William Brisbane, Roger Imhof, Sumner Getchell, George Irving, Leona Roberts, Adrian Morris. *D:* Joseph Santley; *P:* Albert Lewis; *St:* David Garth; *Sc:* S.K. Lauren, Dorothy Yost, Harold Kusell. (1:05)

B comedy of a man, newly wealthy, who finds himself targeted by a family out to get their mitts on his money.

4684. There's Always a Woman (Columbia; 1938). *Cast:* Joan Blondell, Melvyn Douglas, Mary Astor, Frances Drake, Jerome Cowan, Robert Paige, Thurston Hall, Pierre Watkin, Lester Matthews, Rita Hayworth, Walter Kingsford. *D:* Alexander Hall; *St:* Wilson Collison; *Sc:* Morris Ryskind, Gladys Lehman. (1:22)

Mystery-comedy of a D.A. and his sleuthing wife who try to solve the same crime without the help of each other. Followed by a sequel: *There's That Woman Again.*

4685. There's Always Tomorrow (Universal; 1934). *Cast:* Frank Morgan (Joseph White), Lois Wilson (Mrs. White), Binnie Barnes (English actress in her American debut), Helen Parrish, Louise Latimer, Elizabeth Young, Alan Hale, Dick Winslow, Pierre Watkin, Robert Taylor, Maurice Murphy, Margaret Hamilton. *D:* Edward Sloman; *Sc:* William Hurlbut. (1:24)

A man becomes fed up with the fact that his children constantly take advantage of him. Based on the novel by Ursula Parrott, it was remade in 1956 with Barbara Stanwyck and Fred MacMurray.

4686. There's That Woman Again (Columbia; 1938). *Cast:* Melvyn Douglas, Virginia Bruce, Margaret Lindsay, Stanley Ridges, Gordon Oliver, Tom Dugan, Don Beddoe (film debut), Marc Lawrence, Mantan Moreland. *D:* Alexander Hall; *P:* B.B. Kahane; *St:* Gladys Lehman; *Sc:* Philip G. Epstein, James Edward Grant, Ken Englund. (G.B. title: *What a Woman!*) (1:15)

Comedy of a D.A. and his troublesome wife — a follow-up to the hit *There's Always a Woman* (q.v.).

4687. These Glamour Girls (MGM; 1939). *Cast:* Lana Turner (starring debut), Lew Ayres, Richard Carlson, Anita Louise, Marsha Hunt, Mary Beth Hughes, Ann Rutherford, Jane Bryan, Tom Brown, Owen Davis, Jr., Peter Lind Hayes, Sumner Getchell, Ernest Truex, Tom Collins, Mary Forbes, Don Castle, Henry Kolker. *D:* S. Sylvan Simon; *P:* Sam Zimbalist; *St:* Jane Hall; *Sc:* Hall, Marion Parsonnet. (1:20)

The romance of a simple girl who shows up a bunch of college snobs.

4688. These Thirty Years (Industrial/Caravel; 1934). *Cast:* Robert T. Haines, Frances Lee, K. Elmo Lowe, Donald MacDonald, David Morris, Helen Wynn, Robert Strange. *D:* David Pincus; *St:* James Ashmore Creelman.

4689. These Three (United Artists/Samuel Goldwyn; 1936). *Cast:* Miriam Hopkins (who also appeared in a supporting role in the remake), Merle Oberon, Joel McCrea, Catherine Doucet, Alma Kruger (film debut), Marcia Mae Jones, Margaret Hamilton, Walter Brennan, Bonita Granville (A.A.N. for B.S.A.), Marie Louise Cooper, Carmencita Johnson. *D:* William Wyler; *P:* Sam Goldwyn; *Sc:* Lillian Hellman. (1:32) (video)

A reworking — to get past the censors — of Lillian Hellman's play "The Children's Hour," about two women who run a private girls school and the student who maliciously slanders them. Hellman wrote the screenplay herself, working around the original theme which dealt with lesbianism. One of the 25 top grossing films of 1935–36, it placed #9 on the list of "10 Best" films of the *New York Times,* while being in nomination for "Best Picture" by the New York Film Critics. Remade in 1962 under the original title with the lesbian theme intact.

4690/4691. They All Come Out (MGM; 1939). *Cast:* Tom Neal, Rita Johnson, Bernard Nedell, George Tobias, Ed Gargan, Addison Richards, John Gallaudet, Frank M. Thomas, Ann Shoemaker, Roy Barcroft, Charles Lane, Paul Fix. *D:* Jacques Tourneur (son of director Maurice Tourneur in his American feature directorial debut); *P:* Jack Chertok; *Sc:* John C. Higgins.

B drama of a young couple whose criminal tendencies are overcome by prison rehab. This was originally intended as an entry in this studio's "Crime Does Not Pay" series of shorts, but was expanded to feature length.

4692. They Asked for It (Universal; 1939). *Cast:* William Lundigan, Joy Hodges, Michael Whalen, Lyle Talbot, Isabel Jewell, Thomas Beck, Charles Halton, Edward McWade, James Bush. *D:* Frank McDonald; *P:* Max Gordon; *St:* Lester Fuller; *Sc:* Arthur T. Horman. (1:01)

Offbeat B melodrama of what happened when the editor of the local newspaper found the town drunk dead.

4693. They Call It Sin (WB/F.N.; 1932). *Cast:* Loretta Young, David Manners, George Brent, Louis Calhern, Una Merkel, Elizabeth Patterson, Helen Vinson, Nella Walker, Erville Alderson, Mike Marito. *D:* Thornton Freeland; *Sc:* Lillie Hayward, Howard J. Green. (G.B. title: *The Way of Life*) (1:15)

Based on the novel by Alberta Stedman Eagan, this romantic B drama deals with a woman and her many men.

4694. They Gave Him a Gun (MGM; 1937). *Cast:* Spencer Tracy (Fred), Franchot Tone (Jimmy), Gladys George (Rose Duffy), Edgar Dearing (Sgt. Meadowlark), Mary Lou Treen (Saxe), Cliff Edwards (Laro), Charles Trowbridge (judge), Horace MacMahon, Joseph Sawyer, George Chandler. *D:* W.S. Van Dyke II; *P:* Harry Rapf; *Sc:* Cyril Hume, Richard Maibaum, Maurice Rapf. (1:34)

Melodrama of a World War I veteran who turns to a life of crime due to a psychological imbalance. Based on the novel by William Joyce Cowen.

4695. They Had to See Paris (Fox; 1929). *Cast:* Will Rogers, Irene Rich, Edgar Kennedy, Fifi D'Orsay (film debut), Marguerite Churchill, Rex Bell, Ivan Lebedeff, Gregory Gaye, Bob Kerr, Marcia Manon, Andre Cheron, Marcelle Corday, Christiane Yves, Theodore Lodi. *D:* Frank Borzage; *St:* Homer Croy; *Sc:* Sonya Levien.

A wealthy man takes his family to Paris in this hit comedy which was voted #7 on the *New York Times'* list of "10 Best" films of the year. Followed in 1932 by a sequel, *Down to Earth* (q.v.).

4696. They Just Had to Get Married (Universal; 1932–33). *Cast:* ZaSu Pitts, Slim Summerville, Roland Young, Verree Teasdale, C. Aubrey Smith, Guy Kibbee, Henry Armetta, Cora Sue Collins, Elizabeth Patterson, Fifi D'Orsay, Vivian Oakland, Virginia Howell, David Landau, Louise Mackintosh, William Burress, Wallis Clark, Bertram Marburgh, David Lee Tillotson, Robert Greig. *D:* Edward Ludwig; *P:* Carl Laemmele, Jr.; *St:* Cyril Harcourt; *Sc:* Gladys Lehman, H.M. Walker (unc.), Preston Sturges. (1:05)

Hit B comedy of married domestics who become beneficiaries in a will.

4697. They Learned About Women (MGM; 1929–30). *Cast:* Gus Van, Joseph T. Schenck, Bessie Love, Mary Doran, Francis X. Bushman, Jr., J.C. Nugent, Benny Rubin. *D:* Sam Wood, Jack Conway; *Sc:* Sarah Y. Mason, Arthur Baer; *Songs:* Milton Ager, Jack Yellen.

A blend of baseball, romance and music which flopped at the box office. The story was reworked in 1949 and released as *Take Me Out to the Ball Game*.

Note: The stars of this vehicle were better known on the vaudeville circuit as "Van and Schenck," the latter dying shortly after this film was completed.

4698. They Made Her a Spy (RKO; 1939). *Cast:* Sally Eilers, Allan Lane, Fritz Leiber, Frank M. Thomas, Theodore von Eltz, Addison Richards, Larry Blake, Pierre Watkin, Louis Jean Heydt, Spencer Charters, Leona Roberts, Charles Halton, Alec Craig, Grady Sutton. *D:* Jack Hively (directorial debut); *P:* Robert Sisk; *St:* George

Bricker; *Sc:* Michael Kanin, Jo Pagano.
(1:20)

Melodrama of a girl who poses as a
spy to find those that killed her brother.

4699. They Made Me a Criminal
(WB; 1939). *Cast:* John Garfield, Claude
Rains, Ann Sheridan, May Robson,
Gloria Dickson, Billy Halop, Bobby Jor-
dan, Leo Gorcey, Huntz Hall, Gabriel
Dell, Bernard Punsley, Robert Gleck-
ler, John Ridgely, Barbara Pepper,
William Davidson, Ward Bond, Robert
Strange, Louis Jean Heydt, Frank
Riggi, Cliff Clark, Dick Wessel, Ray-
mond Brown, Sam Hayes, Clem Bev-
ans. *D:* Busby Berkeley; *As.P.:* Ben-
jamin Glazer; *Sc:* Sig Herzig. (1:32)
(video)

Hit melodrama of a man who flees
the law when he believes he has killed
another. A remake of *The Life of Jimmy
Dolan* (q.v.), it was based on the play of
that name by Bertram Millhauser and
Beulah Marie Dix.

4700. They Met in a Taxi (Co-
lumbia; 1936). *Cast:* Chester Morris,
Fay Wray, Raymond Walburn, Lionel
Stander, Ward Bond, Henry Mollison.
D: Alfred E. Green; *St:* Octavus Roy
Cohen; *Sc:* Howard J. Green.

B melodrama.

4701. They Must Be Told! (Film
Ventures, Inc.; 1934). *Cast:* Monica
Derry. *D:* Dwain Esper. (TV & video ti-
tle: *Sex Madness* — 0:50)

An actress can only find work in
porno films in this exploiter which pur-
ports to warn of the dangers of syphilis.
A low-budget indie.

4702. They Never Came Back
(Artclass; 1932). *Cast:* Dorothy Sebas-
tian, Regis Toomey, Gertrude Astor,
Earle Foxe, Greta Granstedt, Jack
Richardson, Edward Woods. *D:* Fred
Newmeyer; *St:* Arthur Hoerl.

"Poverty row" feature.

4703. They Shall Have Music
(United Artists/Samuel Goldwyn;
1939). *Cast:* Jascha Heifetz, Joel
McCrea, Andrea Leeds, Walter Bren-
nan, Gene Reynolds, Marjorie Main,
Porter Hall, Dolly Loehr (Diana Lynn,
film debut — bit), Terry Kilburn,
Tommy Kelly, Peter Meremblum Cali-
fornia Junior Symphony Orchestra,
Emory Parnell, Walter Tetley, John St.
Polis, Mary Ruth, Alexander Schon-
berg, Alfred Newman (bit), Chuck
Stubbs, Jacqueline Nash (aka: Gale
Sherwood). *D:* Archie Mayo; *P:* Sam
Goldwyn; *Sc:* Irmgard Von Cube &
John Howard Lawson. (G.B. title: *Mel-
ody of Youth*) (1:41) (video)

Sentimental story of a group of
children attempting to save a settlement
house by putting on a benefit. The
soundtrack features much classical
music.

4704. They Wanted to Marry
(RKO; 1937). *Cast:* Betty Furness, Gor-
don Jones, E.E. Clive, Patsy Lee Par-
sons, Henry Kolker, Frank M. Thomas,
William (Billy) Benedict, Diana Gibson,
Charles Wilson, Franklin Pangborn,
Ralph Byrd, Spencer Charters. *D:* Lew
Landers; *As.P.:* Zion Myers; *St:* Larry
Bachmann, Darwin L. Teilhet; *Sc:* Paul
Yawitz, Ethel Borden. (1:00)

B comedy-romance of a girl in pursuit of a daredevil journalist much to her
father's disapproval.

4705. They Won't Forget (WB/
F.N.; 1937). *Cast:* Claude Rains (An-
drew J. Griffin), Gloria Dickson (film
debut as Sybil Hale), Edward Norris
(Robert Hale), Otto Kruger (Gleason),
Allyn Joslyn (film debut as Bill Brock),
Elisha Cook, Jr. (Joe Turner), Lana
Turner (Mary Clay), Linda Perry (Imo-
gene Mayfield), Cy Kendall (Detective
Laneart), Clinton Rosemond (Tump
Redwine), E. Alyn Warren (Carlisle B.
Buxton), Elisabeth Risdon (Mrs. Hale),
Clifford Sourbier (Jim Timberlake),
Granville Bates (Detective Pindar), Ann
Shoemaker (Mrs. Mountford), Paul
Everton (Governor Mountford), Don-
ald Briggs (Harmon Drake), Sybil Har-
ris (Mrs. Clay), Eddie Acuff (Fred the

drugstore clerk), Frank Faylen (Bill Price), Raymond Brown (Foster), Leonard Mudie (Judge Moore), Trevor Bardette (Shattuck Clay), Elliott Sullivan (Luther Clay), Wilmer Hines (Ransome Clay), John Dilson (Briggs), Frank Rasmussen (Tucker), Harry Davenport, Harry Beresford, Edward McWade (three Confederate Civil War veterans), Adele St. Maur (Mrs. Timberlake), Claudia Coleman (Dolly Holly), Owen King (Flanigan), Robert Porterfield (Harrison the young juror), Psyche Nibert (Hazel), Howard Mitchell (police captain), Thomas Jackson (first detective), George Lloyd (second detective), Maidel Turner, John Ridgely, William Moore (later: Peter Potter), Eddie Foster, Jerry Fletcher, Irene Tedrow (film debut—unbilled bit). *D:* Mervyn LeRoy; *P:* LeRoy; *Sc:* Robert Rossen, Aben Kandel. (1:35) (video)

Classic and critically acclaimed drama of the murder of a high school girl (played by Lana Turner) and the train of events which follow. Based on the novel "Death in the Deep South" by Ward Greene, which was inspired by the real-life Leon M. Frank case of 1913, in which he was charged with the murder of teenager Mary Phagan and subsequently lynched. The real-life story of the incident was factually related in a 1988 two-part TV movie titled *The Murder of Mary Phagan.* Curiously this film received no Academy Award nominations, but the *New York Times* and the National Board of Review placed it respectively at #5 and #7 on their "10 Best" lists of the year.

They're Off (G.B. title) *see* **Straight, Place and Show**

4706. Thin Ice (20th Century–Fox; 1937). *Cast:* Sonja Henie, Tyrone Power, Arthur Treacher, Joan Davis, Alan Hale, Raymond Walburn, Sig Rumann, Melville Cooper, Maurice Cass, George Davis, Torben Meyer, Leah Ray. *D:* Sidney Lanfield; *As.P.:* Raymond Griffith; *Sc:* Boris Ingster,

Milton Sperling; *Choreographer:* (A.A.N.) Harry Losee for "The Prince Igor Suite" number. (1:18)

A prince falls for a commoner in this musical designed to showcase Henie's ice skating. Based on the novel "Der Komet" by Attila Orbok.

4707. The Thin Man (MGM; 1934). *Cast:* William Powell (A.A.N. for B.A. as Nick Charles), Myrna Loy (Nora Charles), Maureen O'Sullivan (Dorothy Wynant), Nat Pendleton (Guild), Asta the dog (Asta), Minna Gombell (Mimi), Porter Hall (MacCauley), Henry Wadsworth (Andrew), William Henry (Gilbert), Harold Huber (Nunheim), Cesar Romero (Chris), Natalie Moorhead (Julia), Edward Brophy (Morelli), Edward Ellis (Wynant), Cyril Thornton (Tanner), Douglas Fowley (taxi driver), Thomas Jackson (first reporter), Ruth Channing (Mrs. Jorgenson), Gertrude Short (Marion), Clay Clement (Quinn), Robert E. Homans (Bill), Raymond Brown (Dr. Walton), Sherry Hall (taxi driver), Walter Long (Stutsy), Bert Roach (Foster), Huey White (Tefler), Fred Malatesta (head waiter), Rolfe Sedan, Leo White, Kenneth Gibson, Tui Lorraine, Creighton Hale, Ben Taggart, Charles Williams, Garry Owen. *D:* (A.A.N.) W.S. Van Dyke II; *P:* (A.A.N. for Best Picture) Hunt Stromberg; *Sc:* (A.A.N.) Frances Goodrich & Albert Hackett. (1:33) (video)

The premiere entry in the sophisticated comedy-mystery series of husband and wife detective team, Nick and Nora Charles and their ever precocious dog, Asta. Based on the novel by Dashiel Hammett, the story concerns the murder of an inventor. This production was a box office gold mine for the studio, being voted one of the year's "10 Best" films by the National Board of Review. On the "10 Best" lists of the *New York Times* and *Film Daily,* it placed #4 and #6 respectively. Followed in 1936 by the second entry in the series of six films (which ran into the 1940s), *After the Thin Man.* A Cosmopolitan production.

4708. Think Fast, Mr. Moto (20th Century–Fox; 1937). *Cast:* Peter Lorre (Mr. Moto), Virginia Field, Thomas Beck, Sig Rumann, Murray Kinnell, Lotus Long, J. Carrol Naish, George Cooper, John Rogers, Fredrik Vogeding. *D:* Norman Foster; *P:* Sol M. Wurtzel; *Sc:* Foster, Howard Ellis Smith. (1:06)

Mr. Moto, a Japanese sleuth tracks a gang of smugglers operating between San Francisco and Shanghai. Based on the novel of the same name by John P. Marquand, the film became such a hit, that the studio decided to create a series.

4709. The Third Alarm (Tiffany; 1930). *Cast:* James Hall, Jean Hersholt, Anita Louise, Hobart Bosworth, Mary Doran, Dot Farley, Joseph Girard, Tom London, Paul Hurst. *D:* Emory Johnson.

"Poverty row" melodrama.

Note: Filmed before in 1923 with Johnny Walker.

4710. Thirteen Hours by Air (Paramount; 1936). *Cast:* Fred MacMurray, Joan Bennett, ZaSu Pitts, Alan Baxter, John Howard, Brian Donlevy, Fred Keating, Bennie Bartlett, Ruth Donnelly, Grace Bradley, Dean Jagger, Marie Prevost (final film—d. 1937), Jack Mulhall, Bud Flanagan (Dennis O'Keefe), Granville Bates, Bruce Warren, Clyde Dilson, Mildred Stone, Adrienne Marden. *D:* Mitchell Leisen; *P:* E. Lloyd Sheldon; *St:* Bogart Rogers, Frank Dazey; *Sc:* Rogers, (John) Kenyon Nicholson. (1:20)

A variety of characters are aboard a transcontinental flight when murder strikes. A hit mystery of its day.

4711. Thirteen Women (RKO; 1932). *Cast:* Ricardo Cortez (Sgt. Clive), Irene Dunne, (Laura Stanhope), Myrna Loy (Ursula Georgei), Jill Esmond (Jo), Florence Eldridge (Grace), C. Henry

Gordon (swami), Betty Furness (13th woman), Marjorie Gateson, Julie Haydon, Kay Johnson, Mary Duncan, Harriet Hagman, Kenneth Thomson, Blanche Frederici, Wally Albright, Edward Pawley, Elsie Prescott, Leon (Ames) Waycoff, Peg Entwistle (final film—d. 1932). *D:* George Archainbaud; *P:* David O. Selznick; *Sc:* Bartlett Cormack, Samuel Ornitz. (1:13)

A group of twelve women, former college sorority sisters are being murdered one at a time via mind suggestion. Based on the novel by Tiffany Thayer.

Note: Ms. Entwistle jumped to her death from the "H" of the landmark Hollywood sign shortly after the film was released to bad reviews.

4712. The Thirteenth Chair (MGM; 1929). *Cast:* Conrad Nagel (Richard Crosby), Leila Hyams (Helen "Nell" O'Neill), Margaret Wycherly (film debut recreating her stage role as the medium, Madame Rosalie LaGrange), Helene Millard (Mary Eastwood), Holmes Herbert (Sir Roscoe Crosby), Mary Forbes (Lady Crosby), Bela Lugosi (Inspector Delzante), John Davidson (Edward Wales), Charles Quartermaine (Dr. Philip Mason), Moon Carroll (Helen Trent), Cyril Chadwick (Brandon Trent), Bertram Johns (Howard Standish), Gretchen Holland (Grace Standish), Frank Leigh (Professor Feringeea), Clarence Geldert (Commissioner Grimshaw), Lal Chand Mehra (Chotee). *D:* Tod Browning; *Sc:* Elliott Clawson. (1:11)

A melodramatic thriller of spiritualism and murder. Based on the hit 1916 off Broadway stage play by Bayard Veiller, it was first filmed in 1919. Remade in 1937 (see below).

4713. The 13th Chair (MGM; 1936–37). *Cast:* Dame May Whitty (medium), Henry Daniell, Holmes Herbert (repeating his role in the '29 version), Elissa Landi, Ralph Forbes, Lewis Stone, Madge Evans, Charles

Trowbridge, Janet Beecher, Robert Coote (American debut), Heather Thatcher, Thomas Beck, Matthew Boulton, Inez Courtney. *D:* George B. Seitz; *P:* J.J. Cohn; *Sc:* Marion Parsonnet.

A medium, a seance and murder — a remake of the preceding film.

4714. The Thirteenth Guest (Monogram; 1932). *Cast:* Ginger Rogers, Lyle Talbot, J. Farrell Mac-Donald, James Eagles, Eddie Phillips, Erville Alderson, Craurord Kent, Frances Rich, Ethel Wales, Phillips Smalley, Paul Hurst, William Davidson, Tom London, Al Bridge, Adrienne Dore, Charles Meacham, Isabel LeMal, Robert Klein, Harry Tenbrook, John Ince, Allan Cavan, Henry Hall, Stanley J. "Tiny" Sandford, Kit Guard, Lynton Brent, Bobby Burns. *D:* Albert Ray; *P:* M.H. Hoffman, Jr.; *Adaptation:* Arthur Hoerl; *Additional Dialogue:* Armitage Trail; *Continuity:* Frances Hyland. (G.B. title: *Lady Beware*) (1:08) (video)

An old dark house mystery-comedy-thriller of a group of people assembled and terrorized by a mysterious killer. Based on the novel by Armitage Trail, this is probably one of the better known productions of this studio as it was re-released many times in the 1930s. Remade as *The Mystery of the 13th Guest* (Monogram; 1943).

4715. The Thirteenth Man (Monogram; 1937). *Cast:* Weldon Heyburn, Inez Courtney, Selmer Jackson, Milburn Stone, Matty Fain, Robert Homans, Eadie Adams, Grace Durkin, Sidney D'Albrook. *D:* William Nigh; *P:* Lon Young; *Sc:* John Krafft. (1:10)

B mystery involving the death of a district attorney via poison dart. This was the initial release of the newly organized Monogram Pictures after pulling out of a merger with Mascot Pictures to create Republic Pictures.

4716/4717. Thirty Day Princess (Paramount; 1934). *Cast:* Sylvia Sidney,

Cary Grant, Edward Arnold, Henry Stephenson, Vince Barnett, Edgar Norton, Lucien Littlefield, William Austin, George Baxter, Ray Walker. *D:* Marion Gering; *P:* B.P. Schulberg; *Sc:* Preston Sturges, Frank Partos, Edwin Justus Mayer, Sam Hellman. (1:14)

Comedy of a princess who falls ill while visiting the United States and the woman who is hired to impersonate her. Based on the novel by Clarence Budington Kelland.

Thirty Days *see* **Silver Lining**

4718. 36 Hours to Live (20th Century–Fox; 1936). *Cast:* Brian Donlevy, Gloria Stuart, Douglas Fowley, Warren Hymer, Isabel Jewell, Stepin Fetchit, Charles Lane, Romaine Callender, James Burke, Jonathan Hale, Gloria Mitzi, Julius Tannen, Lynn Bari. *D:* Eugene Forde; *Sc:* John Patrick, Lou Breslow. (Working Title: *36 Hours to Kill*)

B melodrama. Based on the story "Across the Aisle" by W.R. (William Riley) Burnett.

4719. This Day and Age (Paramount; 1933). *Cast:* Charles Bickford, Judith Allen (film debut), Richard Cromwell, Harry Green, Ben Alexander, Eddie Nugent, Bradley Page, George Barbier, Louise Carter, Samuel S. Hinds, Charles Middleton, John Peter Richmond (John Carradine), Fuzzy Knight, Billy Gilbert, Michael Stuart, Lester Arnold, Oscar Rudolph. *D:* Cecil B. De Mille; *P:* De Mille; *Sc:* Bartlett Cormack. (1:25)

An offbeat drama of a group of school boys who put a notorious gangster on trial and force him to confess to murder. This box office hit was a curiosity in its day, particularly due to its director.

4720. This Is America (Beekman Film Corp.; 1933). *Sc:* Gilbert Seldes. Documentary produced by Frederic Ullman, Jr.

(No other information available)

4721. This Is Heaven (United Artists/Samuel Goldwyn; 1929). *Cast:* Vilma Banky (talkie debut), James Hall, Lucien Littlefield, Fritzi Ridgeway, Richard Tucker. *D:* Alfred Santell; *P:* Sam Goldwyn; *St:* Arthur Mantell; *Sc:* Hope Loring.

Part-talkie romantic comedy of a Hungarian immigrant who falls for a chauffeur who later turns out to be a millionaire.

4722. This Is My Affair (20th Century–Fox; 1937). *Cast:* Robert Taylor, Barbara Stanwyck (who became Mrs. Robert Taylor in 1939), Victor McLaglen, Brian Donlevy, Sidney Blackmer, John Carradine, Sig Rumann, Alan Dinehart, Douglas Fowley, Marjorie Weaver, Robert McWade, J.C. Nugent, Paul Hurst, Frank Conroy, Willard Robertson, Lynn Bari, Mary Young, Douglas Wood. *D:* William A. Seiter; *P:* Kenneth MacGowan; *Sc:* Lamar Trotti, Allen Rivkin. (G.B. title: *His Affair*) (1:42)

Drama of a man who goes undercover to trap a gang on orders from President McKinley, but must prove he is not a member of the gang after McKinley is assassinated.

4723. This Is the Life (Fox; 1935). *Cast:* Jane Withers, Sally Blane, John McGuire, Sidney Toler, Selmer Jackson. *D:* Marshall Neilan.

B comedy.

4724. This Is the Night (Paramount; 1932). *Cast:* Lily Damita, Charles Ruggles, Roland Young, Thelma Todd, Cary Grant (film debut), Claire Dodd, Irving Bacon, Davison Clark. *D:* Frank Tuttle; *Sc:* George Marion, Jr., Benjamin Glazer; *Songs:* Ralph Rainger, Sam Coslow, Marion. (1:18)

Romantic comedy-farce set in Europe. Based on the Broadway play "Naughty Cinderella" by Avery Hopwood, which in turn was adapted from the French play "Pouche" by Rene Peter and Henri Falk.

4725. This Mad World (MGM; 1930). *Cast:* Kay Johnson, Basil Rathbone, Louise Dresser, Veda Buckland, Louis Natheaux. *D:* William de Mille; *Sc:* Clara Beranger, Arthur Caesar.

Flop drama of a spy whose identity is discovered while visiting his dying mother behind enemy lines.

4726. This Man Is Mine (RKO; 1934). *Cast:* Irene Dunne, Constance Cummings, Ralph Bellamy, Kay Johnson, Charles Starrett, Sidney Blackmer, Vivian Tobin, Louis Mason, Adda Gleason, Herbert Evans. *D:* John Cromwell; *As.P.:* Pandro S. Berman; *Sc:* Jane Murfin. (1:16)

Triangular romantic drama set among members of a posh country club. Based on the play "Love Flies in the Window" by Anne Morrison Chapin.

4727. This Marriage Business (RKO; 1938). *Cast:* Victor Moore, Allan Lane, Vicki Lester, Richard Lane, Cecil Kellaway, Jack Carson, Kay Sutton, Paul Guilfoyle, Jack Arnold (aka: Vinton Haworth), Frank M. Thomas, Leona Roberts, George Irving. *D:* Christy Cabanne; *P:* Cliff Reid; *St:* Mel Riddle, Alex Ruben; *Sc:* J. Robert Bren, Gladys Atwater. (1:10)

Comedy of a small town judge with a reputation for issuing licenses for marriages which succeed, who decides to run for mayor against a disreputable incumbent.

4728. This Modern Age (MGM; 1931). *Cast:* Joan Crawford, Pauline Frederick, Neil Hamilton, Monroe Owsley, Hobart Bosworth, Emma Dunn, Marjorie Rambeau, Albert Conti, Ann Dvorak, Marcelle Corday, Adrienne D'Ambricourt. *D:* Nick Grinde; *St:* Mildred Cram; *Sc:* Sylvia Thalberg, Frank Butler, John Meehan. (1:16)

The romance of a rich boy and a poor girl.

4729. This Reckless Age (Paramount; 1932). *Cast:* Frances Dee,

Charles "Buddy" Rogers, Peggy Shannon, Mary Carlisle, Richard Bennett, Frances Starr, Charles Ruggles, Grady Sutton, Leonard Carey, Allen Vincent, David Landau, Reginald Barlow, Harry Templeton, George Pearce. *D:* Frank Tuttle; *Adaptation:* Tuttle; *Sc:* Joseph L. Mankiewicz.

B domestic comedy-drama of sacrificing parents and their thankless offspring. A remake of *The Goose Hangs High* (Paramount; 1925) with Constance Bennett and Esther Ralston. Based on the play of that name by Lewis Beach.

4730. This Side of Heaven (MGM; 1934). *Cast:* Lionel Barrymore, Tom Brown, Mary Carlisle, Mae Clarke, Fay Bainter (film debut), Dickie Moore, Henry Wadsworth, Eddie Nugent, Una Merkel, Onslow Stevens, C. Henry Gordon. *D:* William K. Howard; *P:* John W. Considine, Jr.; *St:* Marjorie Bartholomew Paradis; *Sc:* Eve Greene, Zelda Sears, Florence Ryerson, Edgar Allan Woolf.

Hit domestic drama of its day of a man who is supported by his loving family when he is accused of embezzlement.

4731. This Sporting Age (Columbia; 1932). *Cast:* Jack Holt, Evalyn Knapp, Nora Lane, Walter Byron, Hardie Albright, J. Farrell MacDonald, Hal Price, Ruth Weston, Shirley Palmer. *D:* Andrew Bennison, A.F. Erickson; *St:* James Kevin McGuinness; *Sc:* Dudley Nichols.

Drama.

4732. This Thing Called Love (Pathé; 1929). *Cast:* Edmund Lowe, Constance Bennett (talkie debut), ZaSu Pitts, Roscoe Karns, Stuart Erwin, Carmelita Geraghty, Adele Watson, Wilson Benge, Ruth Taylor, John Roche. *D:* Paul Stein.

Romantic comedy with some scenes in 2-color technicolor.

4733. This Way Please (Paramount; 1937). *Cast:* Charles "Buddy"

Rogers, Betty Grable (starring debut), Mary Livingstone, Ned Sparks, Jim Jordan (Fibber McGee), Marian Jordan (Molly), Porter Hall, Lee Bowman, Rufe Davis, Wally Vernon, Cecil Cunningham, Romo Vincent, Akim Tamiroff, Joyce Mathews, Jerry Bergen, Terry Ray (Ellen Drew). *D:* Robert Florey; *P:* Mel Shauer; *St:* Maxwell Shane, William Thomas; *Sc:* Seena Owen, Grant Garrett, Howard J. Greene. (1:15)

Flop musical-comedy of the romance of a theater usherette and a movie idol.

Note: Grable's role originally intended for Shirley Ross.

4734. The Thoroughbred (Tiffany; 1930). *Cast:* Wesley Barry (formerly a child star of silents), Larry Steers, Pauline Garon. *D:* Richard Thorpe.

"Poverty row" race track drama.

4735. Thoroughbreds Don't Cry (MGM; 1937). *Cast:* Mickey Rooney, Judy Garland, Ronald Sinclair, Sophie Tucker, C. Aubrey Smith, Forrester Harvey, Charles D. Brown, Frankie Darro, Henry Kolker, Helen Troy. *D:* Alfred E. Green; *P:* Harry Rapf; *St:* J. Walter Ruben, Eleanore Griffin; *Sc:* Lawrence Hazard; *Songs:* Nacio Herb Brown, Arthur Freed. (1:20)

A horse racing story with musical interludes, notable as the first screen teaming of Mickey Rooney and Judy Garland.

4736. Those High Grey Walls (Columbia; 1939). *Cast:* Walter Connolly, Iris Meredith, Onslow Stevens, Paul Fix, Don Beddoe, Philip Van Zandt (film debut—bit), Oscar O'Shea, Nicholas Soussanin. *D:* Charles Vidor; *St:* William A. Ullman, Jr.; *Sc:* Gladys Lehman, Lewis Meltzer. (G.B. title: *The Gates of Alcatraz*)

As the title implies, a melodrama with a prison theme.

4737. Those Three French Girls (MGM; 1930). *Cast:* Fifi D'Orsay, Reginald Denny, George Grossmith, Cliff Edwards, Yola D'Avril, Sandra Ravel, Polly Moran, Edward Brophy, Peter Gawthorne. *D:* Harry Beaumont; *St:* Arthur Freed, Dale Van Every; *Sc:* Sylvia Thalberg, Frank Butler, P.G. Wodehouse.

Low-budget romantic comedy of three men who are thrown into jail with three French girls.

4738. Those We Love (Sono Art-World Wide; 1932). *Cast:* Kenneth MacKenna, Mary Astor, Lilyan Tashman, Earle Foxe. *D:* Robert Florey.

A triangular romantic drama from "poverty row."

4739. Those Who Dance (WB; 1930). *Cast:* Lila Lee, Monte Blue, Betty Compson, "Hoppy" William Boyd, William Janney, DeWitt Jennings, Wilfred Lucas, Gino Corrado, Cornelius Keefe. *D:* William Beaudine; *St:* George Kibbe Turner; *Sc:* Joseph Jackson.

A girl tries to prove her brother innocent of murder in this low-budget melodrama, a remake of a 1924 silent from First National.

4740. Thou Shalt Not Kill (Republic; 1939–40). *Cast:* Charles Bickford, Sheila Bromley, Leona Roberts, Charles Waldron, Emmett Vogan, George Chandler, Doris Day (not the singer), Edmund Elton, Elsie Prescott, Ethel May Halls. *D:* John H. Auer; *St:* George Carleton Brown; *Sc:* Robert Presnell.

B melodrama.

4741. Three Blind Mice (20th Century–Fox; 1938). *Cast:* Loretta Young, Joel McCrea, David Niven, Stuart Erwin, Marjorie Weaver, Pauline Moore, Binnie Barnes, Jane Darwell, Leonid Kinskey, Elisha Cook, Jr., Herbert Heywood. *D:* William A. Seiter; *P:* Darryl F. Zanuck; *As.P.:* Raymond Griffith; *St:* Stephen Powys; *Sc:* Brown Holmes, Lynn Starling. (1:15)

Hit romantic comedy of three girls who venture to the big city in search of rich husbands. A remake of *The Greeks Had a Word for Them* (q.v.) and based on the play of that name by Zoe Akins. Three remakes by 20th Century–Fox include: *Moon Over Miami* (1941), *Three Little Girls in Blue* (1946), and *How to Marry a Millionaire* (1953). Many other variations on the story have also been filmed over the years.

Three Broadway Girls *see* **The Greeks Had a Word for Them**

The Three Brothers (G.B. title) *see* **Side Street**

4742. Three Cheers for Love (Paramount; 1936). *Cast:* Robert Cummings, Eleanore Whitney, John Halliday, Olympe Bradna (film debut), Veda Ann Borg (film debut), Harry Davenport, William Frawley, Roscoe Karns, Elizabeth Patterson, Louis DaPron, Billy Lee, Si Wells. *D:* Ray McCarey; *P:* A.M. Botsford; *St:* George Marion, Jr.; *Sc:* Barry Trivers.

B comedy with music, set in a girls finishing school.

4743. Three Comrades (MGM; 1938). *Cast:* Robert Taylor (Erich Lohkamp), Margaret Sullavan (A.A.N. for B.A. and voted "Best Actress of the Year" by the New York Film Critics for her portrayal of Pat Hollmann), Franchot Tone (Otto Koster), Robert Young (Gottfried Lenz), Guy Kibbee (Alfons), Lionel Atwill (Franz Breuer), Henry Hull (Dr. Heinrich Becker), George Zucco (Dr. Plauten), Charley Grapewin (local doctor), Monty Woolley (Dr. Jaffe), Spencer Charters (Herr Schultz), Sarah Padden (Frau Schultz), George Offerman, Jr. (Adolph), Ferdinand Munier (Burgomaster), Leonard Penn (Tony), Priscilla Lawson (Frau Brunner), Esther Muir (Frau Schmidt), Claire McDowell (Frau Zalewska), Barbara Bedford (Rita), Mitchell Lewis (Boris), Morgan Wallace, Walter

(Bohn) Bonn, Edward McWade, Harvey Clark, Henry Brandon, Alva Kellogg, George Chandler, Ralph Bushman (Francis X. Bushman, Jr.), Norman Willis, Donald Haines, William Haade, Marjorie Main, Jessie Arnold, Roger Converse, Ricca Allen, E. Alyn Warren. *D:* Frank Borzage; *P:* Joseph L. Mankiewicz; *Sc:* F. Scott Fitzgerald (only film on which he worked that he ever received screen credit), Edward E. Paramore, Jr. (1:38)

Drama set in Germany in the days following World War I and the shared love of three friends for a woman who is dying of TB. Based on the bestseller by Erich Maria Remarque, the film was a box office hit, placing #6 on the "10 Best" list of the *New York Times* and #10 on the same list of the National Board of Review.

4744. Three-Cornered Moon (Paramount; 1933). *Cast:* Claudette Colbert, Richard Arlen, Mary Boland, Wallace Ford, Hardie Albright, Lyda Roberti, Tom Brown, William Bakewell, Joan Marsh, Clara Blandick, Joseph (Sawyer) Sauers, Leonid Kinskey. *D:* Elliott Nugent; *P:* B.P. Schulberg; *Sc:* S.K. Lauren, Ray Harris. (1:17)

Popular screwball-type comedy of one family's attempts at dealing with the depression. Based on the play by Gertrude Tonkonogy, the film was voted one of the year's "10 Best" by the National Board of Review.

4745. Three Faces East (WB; 1930). *Cast:* Constance Bennett, Erich Von Stroheim, William Courtenay, Anthony Bushell, Charlotte Walker, William Holden, Crauford Kent. *D:* Roy Del Ruth; *P:* Darryl F. Zanuck; *Sc:* Oliver H.P. Garrett, Arthur Caesar. (1:11)

This espionage melodrama is a remake of the 1926 production of the same name by Producers Distributing Corporation with Robert Ames, Jetta Goudal and Clive Brook. Based on the

play of that name by Anthony Paul Kelly, it was remade as *British Intelligence* (WB; 1940) with Boris Karloff.

4746. Three Girls Lost (Fox; 1931). *Cast:* Loretta Young, Joan Marsh, John Wayne, Joyce Compton, Paul Fix, Kathrin Clare Ward. *D:* Sidney Lanfield; *St:* Robert D. Andrews; *Sc:* Bradley King.

Low-budget romance.

4747. Three Godfathers (MGM; 1936). *Cast:* Chester Morris, Lewis Stone, Walter Brennan, Irene Hervey, Sidney Toler, Dorothy Tree, Roger Imhof, Willard Robertson, John Sheehan, Robert Livingston, Joseph Marievsky, Victor Potel, Helen Brown, Harvey Clark, Virginia Brissac, Jean Kirchner. *D:* Richard Boleslawski; *P:* Joseph L. Mankiewicz; *Sc:* Edward E. Paramore, Manuel Seff. (TV title: *Miracle in the Sand*) (1:22)

A much filmed western tale, based on a 1913 *Saturday Evening Post* story by Peter B. (Bernard) Kyne of three outlaws crossing the desert with a baby they adopt after the infant's mother dies. Previously filmed as *Three Godfathers* (Universal; 1916) with Harry Carey, *Marked Men* (Universal; 1919–20) also with Carey; *Hell's Heroes* (q.v.), with remakes *Three Godfathers* (MGM/Argosy; 1948) by director John Ford (who also directed the 1920 version), and a 1975 TV movie titled *The Godchild. Three Bad Men* (Fox; 1926) with George O'Brien and also directed by Ford, followed a similar story line with three outlaws who adopted a little girl after her father dies.

4748. 365 Nights in Hollywood (Fox; 1934). *Cast:* Alice Faye (in a role originally intended for Lilian Harvey), James Dunn, Frank Melton, John Bradford, Frank Mitchell, Jack Durant, John Qualen. *D:* George Marshall; *P:* Sol M. Wurtzel; *St:* James A. Starr; *Sc:* William Conselman, Henry Johnson.

Musical-comedy.

4749. Three Kids and a Queen (Universal; 1935). *Cast:* May Robson, Frankie Darro, William (Billy) Benedict, Henry Armetta, Billy Burrud, Charlotte Henry, Herman Bing, Lillian Harmer, John Miljan, Hedda Hopper, Lawrence Grant, Frank McHugh, Noel Madison, Hale Hamilton. *D:* Edward Ludwig; *St:* Harry Poppe, Chester Beecroft, Mary Marlind; *Sc:* Barry Trivers, Samuel Ornitz. (G.B. title: *The Baxter Millions*) (1:25)

A hit family oriented comedy-drama of an eccentric old lady who fakes her own kidnapping. Remade by this studio in 1946 as *Little Miss Big* with Fay Holden.

4750. Three Legionnaires (General Films; 1937). *Cast:* Lyle Talbot, Robert Armstrong, Fifi D'Orsay, Anne Nagel, Stanley Fields, Donald Meek, Leonid Snegoff, Maurice Black, Herbie Freeman. *D:* Hamilton MacFadden; *P:* Robert E. Walsh; *St:* George Waggner; *Sc:* Carl Harbaugh, Waggner.

Independent B desert drama.

4751. Three Live Ghosts (United Artists/Art Cinema; 1929). *Cast:* Robert Montgomery, Claud Allister, Charles McNaughton, Joan Bennett, Beryl Mercer, Harry Stubbs, Hilda Vaughn, Nancy Price, Arthur Clayton, Jack Cooper, Shayle Gardner. *D:* Thornton Freeland (directorial debut); *P:* Max Marcin; *Sc:* Helen Hallett; *Adapt. & Dial.:* Marcin.

Comedy of three soldiers reported killed in World War I, though actually held by the Germans, returning to their old "haunts." Based on the play by Frederic S. Isham, it was previously filmed in Great Britain in 1922 for Paramount release with Norman Kerry, Cyril Chadwick and Anna Q. Nilsson by director George Fitzmaurice. Remade in 1935 (see below).

4752. Three Live Ghosts (MGM; 1935). *Cast:* Richard Arlen, Cecilia Parker, Claud Allister, Charles McNaughton, Beryl Mercer, Dudley Digges, Robert Greig, Nydia Westman. *D:* H. Bruce Humberstone; *P:* John W. Considine, Jr.; *Sc:* C. Gardiner Sullivan.

Three soldiers return to London on Armistice Day to find themselves listed as killed in action. Based on the play by Frederic Isham, a remake of the preceding film.

4753. Three Loves Has Nancy (MGM; 1938). *Cast:* Janet Gaynor, Robert Montgomery, Franchot Tone, Guy Kibbee, Claire Dodd, Reginald Owen, Charley Grapewin, Emma Dunn, Cora Witherspoon, Grady Sutton, Lester Matthews, Grant Withers, Sarah Edwards. *D:* Richard Thorpe; *P:* Norman Krasna; *St:* Mortimer Braus, Lee Loeb; *Sc:* Bella & Sam Spewack, George Oppenheimer, David Hertz. (1:09)

Hit low-budget comedy of a bride, left standing at the altar, who intends to shop around before committing herself again.

4754. Three Married Men (Paramount; 1936). *Cast:* Lynne Overman, Roscoe Karns, William Frawley, Mary Brian, Cora Sue Collins, Donald Meek. *D:* Edward Buzzell; *P:* Arthur Hornblow, Jr.; *Sc:* Dorothy Parker, Alan Campbell.

B marital comedy of domestic difficulties.

Three Men and a Girl (G.B. title) *see* **Kentucky Moonshine**

4755. Three Men on a Horse (WB/F.N.; 1936). *Cast:* Frank McHugh, Sam Levene (film debut, repeating his stage role), Joan Blondell, Guy Kibbee, Carol Hughes, Teddy Hart, Allen Jenkins, Edgar Kennedy, Eddie "Rochester" Anderson, Harry Davenport, George Chandler, Paul Harvey, Margaret Irving, Eily Malyon, Charles Lane, Ottola Nesmith. *D:* Mervyn LeRoy; *P:* Sam Bischoff; *Sc:* Laird Doyle. (1:28)

Hit comedy of a shy and retiring man who has a knack for picking winning horses at the track. Based on the Broadway play by George Abbott and John Cecil Holm, the fun begins when the local mob finds out about the man and his "gift."

4756. The Three Mesquiteers (Republic; 1936). *Cast:* Robert Livingston (Stony Brooke), Ray Corrigan (Tucson Smith), Syd Saylor (replaced by Max Terhune after this feature as Lullaby Joslin), Kay Hughes, J.P. McGowan, Frank Yaconelli, Alan Bridge, Stanley Blystone, John Merton, Milburn Stone, Jean Marvey, Duke York, Allen Connor. *D:* Ray Taylor; *Sc:* Jack Natteford. (1:01)

Premiere feature in what was eventually to become a long-running series of 51 features for this studio which ran until 1943. Based on the novel by William Colt MacDonald, this entry deals with three returning war veterans who bring a gang of cattle rustlers to justice.

4757. The Three Musketeers (RKO; 1935). *Cast:* Walter Abel (starring debut as d'Artagnan), Paul Lukas (Athos), Heather Angel (Constance), Ian Keith (Rochefort), Moroni Olsen (Porthos), Onslow Stevens (Aramis), Rosamond Pinchot (Queen Anne), John M. Qualen (Planchet), Ralph Forbes (Duke of Buckingham), Nigel de Brulier (Cardinal Richelieu), Miles Mander (King Louis XIII), Murray Kinnell, Lumsden Hare, Stanley Blystone, Ralph Faulkner. *D:* Rowland V. Lee; *As.P.:* Cliff Reid; *Sc:* Lee, Dudley Nichols. (1:30) (video)

A straight-forward version of the 1844 Alexandre Dumas classic of court intrigue and swordplay in olde France. Other version: (Edison; 1911) with Sydney Booth (d'Artagnan), Herbert Delmar (Athos), Jack Cagnon (Porthos), Harold Shaw (Aramis), William Bechtel (Louis XIII), & Carey Lee (Milady de Winter); (Edward Laurillard; 1913); (C.V. Henkel; 1914); *D'Artagnan* (Triangle; 1916) — (aka: *The Three Musketeers*) by producer Thomas H.

Ince; (United Artists; 1921) with Douglas Fairbanks; 1939 (see below); (MGM; 1948) and (20th Century-Fox; 1973-74) a British production.

4758. The Three Musketeers (20th Century-Fox; 1939). *Cast:* Don Ameche (d'Artagnan), Ritz Brothers (Al, Harry & Jimmy), Lionel Atwill, Binnie Barnes, Joseph Schildkraut, Gloria Stuart, Miles Mander, Pauline Moore, John Carradine, John King, John Qualen, Douglass Dumbrille, Russell Hicks, Moroni Olsen, Lester Matthews, Gregory Gaye, Egon Brecher. *D:* Allan Dwan; *As.P.:* Raymond Griffith; *Sc:* M.M. Musselman, William A. Drake, Sam Hellman. (G.B. title: *The Singing Musketeer*) (1:13) (video)

A satirical musical version of the Dumas Classic with the Ritz Brothers as lackeys pretending to be the trio of famous swordsmen.

4759. Three of a Kind (Invincible; 1936). *Cast:* Evalyn Knapp, Chick Chandler, Berton Churchill, Billy Gilbert. *D:* Phil Rosen.

"Poverty row" comedy.

4760. Three on a Honeymoon (Fox; 1934). *Cast:* John Mack Brown, Sally Eilers, Irene Hervey, Henrietta Crosman, Winifred Shaw (film debut), ZaSu Pitts, Charles Starrett. *D:* James Tinling.

Romantic comedy.

4761. Three on a Match (WB/F.N.; 1932). *Cast:* Joan Blondell, Ann Dvorak, Bette Davis, Warren William, Lyle Talbot, Humphrey Bogart, Allen Jenkins, Edward Arnold, Virginia Davis, Dawn O'Day (Anne Shirley), Betty Carse, Glenda Farrell, Clara Blandick, Grant Mitchell, Frankie Darro, Patricia Ellis (film debut), Buster Phelps, John Marston. *D:* Mervyn LeRoy; *P:* Sam Bischoff; *St:* Kubec Glasmon, John Bright; *Sc:* Lucien Hubbard. (1:04)

Three childhood friends meet years

later in the big city. A low-budget melodrama remade as *Broadway Musketeers* (q.v.).

4762. Three on the Trail (Paramount; 1936). *Cast:* William Boyd (Hopalong Cassidy), James Ellison (Johnny Nelson), George Hayes (Windy Halliday), Muriel Evans, Claude King, William Duncan, Clara Kimball Young, Ernie Adams, Lew Meehan, John St. Polis, Ted Adams, Al Hill, Lita Cortez, Jack (John) Rutherford, Franklyn Farnum, Artie Ortego. *D:* Howard Bretherton; *P:* Harry M. Sherman; *Sc:* Doris Schroeder, Vernon Smith. (1:00)

The 5th entry in the "Hopalong Cassidy" series as the Bar 20 boys bring justice to the town by halting the nefarious activities of a saloon owner and an equally corrupt sheriff.

4763. Three Rogues (Fox; 1931). *Cast:* Victor McLaglen, Fay Wray, Lew Cody, Robert Warwick, Eddie Gribbon, David Worth, Joyce Compton, Louise Huntington, Franklyn Farnum, James Farley, Carol Wines. *D:* Ben Stoloff; *St:* "Over the Border" by Herman Whitaker; *Sc:* William Conselman, Dudley Nichols, Emmett Flynn. (Retitled: *Not Exactly Gentlemen*) (1:10)

Western of three rogues who kidnap a girl from a wagon train, intent on getting a map to a gold mine that her father has.

4764. The Three Sisters (Fox; 1930). *Cast:* Kenneth MacKenna, June Collyer, Joyce Compton, Herman Bing. *D:* Paul Sloane.

Low-budget romance.

4765. Three Smart Girls (Universal; 1936). *Cast:* Binnie Barnes (Donna Lyons), Alice Brady (Mrs. Lyons), Ray Milland (Lord Michael Stuart), Barbara Read (Kay Craig), Mischa Auer (Count Arisztid), Nan Grey (Joan Craig), Deanna Durbin (feature film debut as Penny Craig), Charles Winninger (Judson Craig),

Nella Walker (Dorothy Craig), Lucile Watson (Trudel), Hobart Cavanaugh (Wilbur Lamb), John King (Bill Evans), Ernest Cossart (Binns), Walter C. Miller, Bud Flanagan (Dennis O'Keefe), Franklin Pangborn. *D:* Henry Koster; *As.P:* (A.A.N. for Best Picture) Joe Pasternak; *Original Story:* (A.A.N.) Adele Comandini; *Sc:* Comandini, Austin Parker; *Songs:* "Someone to Care for Me" & "My Heart Is Singing" by Gus Kahn, Walter Jurmann, Bronislau Kaper; "Il Bacio" by Luigi Arditi & other various operatic selections; *Sound Recording:* (A.A.N.) Homer G. Tasker. (1:26)

Musical-comedy of three sisters who get their parents back together again after rescuing Dad from a scheming woman. A big box office hit which spawned two hit songs (see credits).

Note: American debut of director Koster.

4766. Three Smart Girls Grow Up (Universal; 1939). *Cast:* Deanna Durbin (Penny Craig), Charles Winninger (Judson Craig), Nan Grey (Joan Craig), Helen Parrish (Kay Craig), Robert Cummings (Harry Loren), William Lundigan (Richard Watkins), Ernest Cossart (Binns), Nella Walker (Dorothy Craig), Felix Bressart, Thurston Hall, Grady Sutton. *D:* Henry Koster; *P:* Joe Pasternak; *Sc:* Bruce Manning, Felix Jackson; *Songs:* "The Last Rose of Summer" by Thomas Moore & Richard Alfred Milliken; "Because" by Edward Teschemacher & Guy D'Hardelot (which became a hit). (1:27)

A musical-comedy sequel of the preceding film, made to capitalize on that film and Durbin's popularity. One of the 16 top grossing films of 1938–39.

Note: Universal was on the brink of bankruptcy in the late 1930s. The box office popularity of the Deanna Durbin musicals returned the studio to financial solvency.

4767. Three Sons (RKO; 1939). *Cast:* Edward Ellis (Daniel Pardway),

William Gargan, Kent Taylor, J. Edward Bromberg, Katherine Alexander, Virginia Vale (film debut), Robert Stanton (Kirby Grant—film debut), Dick Hogan, Grady Sutton, Adele Pearce, Alexander D'Arcy, Barbara Pepper. *D:* Jack Hively; *P:* Robert Sisk; *Sc:* John Twist. (1:12)

The story of a simple merchant named Daniel Pardway who becomes a department store tycoon, only to find that his sons are not interested in following in his tracks. A remake of *Sweepings* (q.v.) and based on the novel of that name by Lester Cohen.

Note: Vale and Grant won their debut roles in a talent search by Jesse L. Lasky (his "Gateway to Hollywood" promotion).

4768. Three Texas Steers (Republic; 1939). *Cast:* John Wayne (Stony Brooke), Ray Corrigan (Tucson Smith—and the gorilla), Max Terhune (in his final entry as Lullaby Joslin), Carole Landis, Ralph Graves, Roscoe Ates, Collette Lyons, Billy Curtis, David Sharpe, Ted Adams, Stanley Blystone, Ethan Laidlaw, Lew Kelly, Dave Willock, John Merton, Ted Mapes, Naba the gorilla. *D:* George Sherman; *P:* William Berke; *Sc:* Betty Burbridge, Stanley Roberts. (G.B. title: *Danger Rides the Range*) (0:57) (video)

The 22nd entry in the "Three Mesquiteers" series, this one with a circus setting.

4769. Three Who Loved (RKO; 1931). *Cast:* Betty Compson, Conrad Nagel, Robert Ames, Robert Emmett O'Connor, Bodil Rosing, Dickie Moore, Fred Santley. *D:* George Archainbaud; *As.P.:* Bertram Millhauser; *St:* Martin Flavin; *Sc:* Beulah Marie Dix. (1:18)

A romantic drama of a man's deception and betrayal.

4770. Three Wise Girls (Columbia; 1931–32). *Cast:* Jean Harlow, Mae Clarke, Walter Byron, Jameson Thomas, Marie Prevost, Andy Devine, Lucy Beaumont, Natalie Moorhead, Kathrin Clare Ward, Marcia Harris, Robert Dudley. *D:* William Beaudine; *Sc:* Agnes C. Johnston; *Dialogue:* Robert Riskin. (1:06)

Comedy-drama of a small town girl who goes to the big city where she learns how to survive in her new environment.

4771. Three Wise Guys (MGM; 1936). *Cast:* Robert Young, Betty Furness, Bruce Cabot, Raymond Walburn, Herman Bing, Harvey Stephens, Donald Meek, Thurston Hall, Armand Kaliz, Harry Tyler. *D:* George B. Seitz; *P:* Harry Rapf; *Sc:* Elmer Harris.

B comedy-drama based on the writings of Damon Runyon.

4772. The Thrill Hunter (Columbia; 1933). *Cast:* Buck Jones, Dorothy Revier, Edward J. LeSaint, Eddie Kane, Arthur Rankin, Robert Ellis, Frank LaRue, Harry Semels, Al Smith, John Ince, Alf James, Harry Todd, Willie Fung, Frank Ellis, Hank Bell, Jim Corey, Joe Ryan, Glenn Strange, Art Mix, Buddy Roosevelt, Buffalo Bill, Jr. *D:* George B. Seitz; *Sc:* Harry O. Hoyt. (0:58)

Buck Jones in a change-of-pace western of a cowboy who gets a job as a Hollywood stuntman to back up claims of his past deeds.

4773. The Thrill of a Lifetime (Paramount; 1937). *Cast:* Betty Grable, Leif Erickson, Judy Canova, Dorothy Lamour, Eleanore Whitney, Ben Blue, Franklin Pangborn, Tommy Wonder, Yacht Club Boys, Zeke & Anne. *D:* George Archainbaud; *P:* Fanchon Royer; *St & Sc:* Seena Owen, Grant Garrett, Paul Gerard Smith; *Songs:* Sam Coslow.

A secretary falls for her boss in this flop comedy with musical interludes including Dorothy Lamour singing the title song.

4774. The Thrill of Youth (Invincible; 1932). *Cast:* June Clyde,

Dorothy Peterson, Ethel Clayton, Tom Ricketts. *D:* Richard Thorpe.

"Poverty row" production.

4775. The Throwback (Universal; 1935). *Cast:* Buck Jones, Muriel Evans, George F. Hayes, Eddie Phillips, Paul Fix, Frank LaRue, Earl Pingree, Robert Walker, Charles K. French, Bryant Washburn, Allan Ransay, Margaret Davis, Bobby Nelson, Mickey Martin. *D:* Ray Taylor; *Sc:* Frances Guihan. (1:01)

Buck Jones horse opera of a cowboy who sets out to prove that his father was not a cattle rustler.

4776. Thru Different Eyes (Fox; 1929). *Cast:* Warner Baxter, Edmund Lowe, Mary Duncan, Sylvia Sidney (talkie debut), Stuart Erwin, Stepin Fetchit, Earle Foxe, Natalie Morehead, DeWitt Jennings, Purnell Pratt, Arthur Stone, Donald Gallagher, Selmer Jackson, Dolores Johnson, Florence Lake, Lola Salvi, George Lamont. *D:* John G. Blystone; *St:* Milton Herbert Gropper, Edna Sherry.

Romantic comedy.

4777. Thunder Afloat (MGM; 1939). *Cast:* Wallace Beery, Chester Morris, Virginia Grey, Douglass Dumbrille, Carl Esmond, Clem Bevans, Regis Toomey, Henry Victor, John Qualen, Jonathan Hale, Addison Richards, Phillip Terry, Leon Ames, Mitchell Lewis, Frank Faylen, Hans Joby, Henry Hunter. *D:* George B. Seitz; *P:* J. Walter Ruben; *St:* Ralph Wheelwright, Harvey Haislip; *Sc:* Wells Root, Harvey Haislip. (1:35)

Comedy-drama of the rivalry between two boat owners during World War I.

4778. Thunder Below (Paramount; 1932). *Cast:* Tallulah Bankhead, Charles Bickford, Paul Lukas, Eugene Pallette, James Finlayson, Edward Van Sloan, Enrique Acosta, Leslie Fenton, Ralph Forbes, Mona Rico, Gabry Rivas, Carlos Salazar. *D:* Richard

Wallace; *Adaptation:* Sidney Buchman, Josephine Lovett. (1:07)

Triangular romantic melodrama set in a tropic oil field. Based on the novel by Thomas Rourke.

4779. Thunder in the Desert (Republic-Supreme; 1937). *Cast:* Bob Steele, Don Barclay, Louise Stanley, Ed Brady, Charles King, Horace Murphy, Steve Clark, Lew Meehan, Ernie Adams, Budd Buster, Richard Cramer, Sherry Tansey. *D:* Sam Newfield; *P:* A.W. Hackel; *Sc:* George Plympton. (1:00)

Bob Steele western of two pals who thwart attempts by outlaws to gain control of a ranch belonging to the murdered uncle of one of them.

4780. Thunder in the Night (Fox; 1935). *Cast:* Karen Morley, Polly Ann Young, Gene Lockhart, Paul Cavanagh, Una O'Connor, Herman Bing, John Qualen. *D:* George Archainbaud.

Low-budget production.

4781. Thunder Mountain (20th Century–Fox; 1935). *Cast:* George O'Brien, Barbara Fritchie, Frances Grant, Morgan Wallace, George Hayes, Edward LeSaint, Dean Benton, William Norton Bailey. *D:* David Howard; *P:* Sol Lesser (Atherton Productions); *Sc:* Dan Jarrett, Don Swift. (TV title: *Roaring Mountain*) (1:08)

George O'Brien tale of the northwoods and a man who is cheated out of his part of a mining claim.

Thunder of the Gods (G.B. title) *see* **Son of the Gods**

4782. Thunder Over Mexico (Mexican Picture Trust; 1933). *D:* Sergei Eisenstein; *P:* Sol Lesser; *Associate Director:* Grigori Alexandrov; *Sc:* Eisenstein.

An independent feature film which is made up from footage of the "Maguey" episode of Russian director Sergei Eisenstein's unfinished masterpiece "Que Viva Mexico!" Filmed on location in Mexico in 1931–32 with financing by writer, Upton Sinclair. Indie producer Sol Lesser was the brains behind this film venture.

4783. Thunder Over Texas (Beacon; 1934). *Cast:* Guinn "Big Boy" Williams, Marion Shilling, Helen Westcott, Richard Botiller, Philo McCullough, Ben Corbett, Bob McKenzie, Victor Potel, Jack Kirk, Hank Bell, Claude Peyton, "Tiny" Skelton. *D:* John Warner (better known as Edgar G. Ulmer); *St:* Shirle Ulmer; *Sc:* Eddie Granemann. (1:01)

Guinn "Big Boy" Williams western with comic overtones of a cowboy who rescues a girl taken by outlaws who want some valuable maps owned by her father. This was the first in a series of six films by Williams for this indie company.

4784. Thunder Trail (Paramount; 1937). *Cast:* Gilbert Roland, Charles Bickford, Marsha Hunt, James Craig (film debut), J. Carrol Naish, Monte Blue, Gene Reynolds, William Duncan, Billy Lee, Barlowe Borland. *D:* Charles Barton; *Sc:* Robert Yost, Stuart Anthony. (0:58)

A man returns to his family after fifteen years in this western based on Zane Grey's "Arizona Ames."

4785. Thunderbolt (Paramount; 1929). *Cast:* George Bancroft (A.A.N. for B.A. –1928–29), Fay Wray, Richard Arlen, Fred Kohler, Tully Marshall, George Irving, Eugenie Besserer, E.H. Calvert, Mike Donlin, Robert Elliott, Phyllis Haver, William L. Thorne, James Spottiswood. *D:* Josef von Sternberg; *P:* B.P. Fineman; *St:* Jules Furthman, Charles Furthman; *Sc:* Jules Furthman; *Dialogue:* Herman J. Mankiewicz; *Songs:* Sam Coslow. (1:34)

Prison melodrama of a deathrow inmate facing execution who plots the murder of another inmate.

4786. Thunderbolt (Regal; 1935). *Cast:* Kane Richmond, Bobby Nelson, Lobo the dog, Fay McKenzie, Hank Bell, Frank Hagney, Lafe McKee, Barney Furey, Frank Ellis, George Morrell, Wally West, Jack Kirk, Blackie Whiteford, Bob Burns. *D:* Stuart Paton; *P:* Sherman S. Krellberg; *Sc:* Jack Jevne. (0:55)

B western adventure of a boy and his dog doing battle with an outlaw gang.

4787. The Thundering Herd (Paramount; 1932–33). *Cast:* Randolph Scott, Judith Allen (film debut), Noah Beery (Randall Jett, the same role he played in the silent version), Harry Carey, Monte Blue, Frank Rice, Raymond Hatton, Blanche Frederici, Buster Crabbe, Barton MacLane, Alan Bridge, Buck Connors, Dick Rush, Charles McMurphy. *D:* Henry Hathaway; *Sc:* Jack Cunningham, Mary Flannery. (Re-release title: *Buffalo Stampede*) (1:02) (video)

B western of prairie conflict between buffalo hunters and Indians and an unsuspecting wagon train that treks into the middle of it. Based on the novel by Zane Grey, it was previously filmed by this studio in 1925 with Jack Holt and Lois Wilson, with much of the footage in this version, drawn from the earlier silent version.

4788. The Thundering West (Columbia; 1939). *Cast:* Charles Starrett, Iris Meredith, Sons of the Pioneers with Bob Nolan & Pat Brady, Hal Taliaferro, Dick Curtis, Hank Bell, Edward LeSaint, Robert Fiske, Edmund Cobb, Slim Whitaker, Blackie Whiteford, Art Mix, Fred Burns, Ed Peil, Sr., Art Dillard, Steve Clark. *D:* Sam Nelson; *Sc:* Bennett Cohen. (0:58)

Charles Starrett western of an outlaw who becomes sheriff of a small town, only to have his past come back and haunt him. A remake of *The Man Trailer* (q.v.).

4789. Ticket to a Crime (Beacon; 1934). *Cast:* Ralph Graves, Lola Lane,

Lois Wilson, Edward Earle. *D:* Lewis D. Collins.

Low-budget melodrama.

4790. Ticket to Paradise (Republic; 1936). *Cast:* Roger Pryor, Wendy Barrie, Stanley Fields, Harry Woods, Claude Gillingwater, Theodore von Eltz, Andrew Tombes, John Sheehan, Bud Jamison, Charles Lane, E.E. Clive, Charles Wilson. *D:* Aubrey Scotto; *St:* David Silverstein; *Sc:* Jack Natteford, Nathanael West.

B romantic comedy.

Tidal Wave (G.B. title) *see* **S.O.S. Tidal Wave**

4791. Tiger Rose (WB; 1929). *Cast:* Monte Blue, Lupe Velez, Rin-Tin-Tin, Grant Withers, H.B. Warner, Gaston Glass, Bull Montana, Charles (Heinie) Conklin, Tully Marshall. *D:* George Fitzmaurice; *Sc:* Harvey Thew, L.G. (Gordon) Rigby; *Song:* "The Day You Fall in Love."

Outdoor romantic drama involving a Mountie, a half-caste girl and a no-account scoundrel. Based on the play by Willard Mack, it was previously filmed by this studio in 1923 with Lenore Ulric, Forrest Stanley and Theodore von Eltz.

4792. Tiger Shark (WB/F.N.; 1932). *Cast:* Edward G. Robinson (Mike Mascarena), Richard Arlen, Zita Johann, Leila Bennett, J. Carrol Naish, Vince Barnett, William Ricciardi. *D:* Howard Hawks; *Sc:* Wells Root. (1:20)

Filmed on location in Monterey, California, this is a romantic comedy of a tuna fisherman who marries a girl only to find that she is becoming more interested in his friend. Based on the novel "Tuna" by Houston Branch.

4793/4794. The Tiger's Son (Xxxx Xxxx; 1931). *Cast:* Frank Albertson.

(No other information available)

4795. 'Til We Meet Again (WB; 1939–40). *Cast:* Merle Oberon, George Brent, Frank McHugh (who also appeared in the original version), Pat O'Brien (who also appeared in the original version), Geraldine Fitzgerald, Eric Blore, Binnie Barnes, Henry O'Neill, George Reeves, Marjorie Gateson, Frank Wilcox. *D:* Edmund Goulding; *As.P.:* David Lewis; *St:* Robert Lord; *Sc:* Warren Duff. (1:39)

Drama of the romantic affair between a dying woman and a man who is about to be executed. A remake of *One Way Passage* (q.v.).

4796. Till We Meet Again (Paramount; 1936). *Cast:* Herbert Marshall, Gertrude Michael, Lionel Atwill, Rod La Rocque, Colin Tapley, Frank Reicher, Egon Brecher, Torben Meyer, Guy Bates Post, Vallejo Gantner, Julia Faye. *D:* Robert Florey; *P:* Albert Lewis; *Sc:* Edwin Justus Mayer, Franklin Coen, Brian Marlow. (1:27)

Espionage drama of ex-lovers who find themselves spying on opposite sides. Based on the play by Alfred Davis.

4797. Tillie and Gus (Paramount; 1933). *Cast:* W.C. Fields, Alison Skipworth, Baby LeRoy, Jacqueline Wells (Julie Bishop), Clifford Jones, Clarence Wilson, Barton MacLane, Edgar Kennedy, George Barbier, Robert McKenzie, Maston Williams. *D:* Francis Martin; *P:* Douglas MacLean; *St:* Rupert Hughes; *Sc:* Martin, Walter de Leon. (1:01)

Low-budget comedy of two middle-aged cardsharps who assist their nephew and niece. Notable as the first film to pair W.C. Fields and his precocious nemesis, Baby LeRoy.

4798. Timber Stampede (RKO; 1939). *Cast:* George O'Brien, Chill Wills, Marjorie Reynolds, Morgan Wallace, Robert Fiske, Guy Usher, Earle Dwire, Frank Hagney, Bob

Burns, Monte Montague, Bud Osborne. *D:* David Howard; *P:* Bert Gilbroy; *St:* Bernard McConville, Paul Franklin; *Sc:* Morton Grant. (0:59)

George O'Brien western (his first to flop at the box office of a cowboy and a newswoman who foil some land-grabbers.

4799. Timber Terrors (Empire/ Stage & Screen Attractions; 1935). *Cast:* John Preston, Tom London, Marla Bratton, "Captain" King of Dogs, "Dynamite" the Wonder Horse, William Desmond, James Sheridan (Sherry Tansey), "Tiny" Skelton, Fred Parker, Tex Jones. *D:* Robert Emmett (Tansey); *P:* Tansey; *Sc:* Tansey. (0:59)

The low-budget indie adventures of Morton of the Royal Canadian Mounted as he searches for the killer of his partner.

4800. Timber War (Ambassador; 1935). *Cast:* Kermit Maynard, Lawrence Gray, Lucille Lund, Robert Warwick, Lloyd Ingraham, Wheeler Oakman, Roger Williams, George Morrell, James Pierce, Patricia Royal. *D:* Sam Newfield; *P:* Maurice Conn; *Sc:* Joseph O'Donnell. (0:58)

A Canadian Mountie tries to show an eastern playboy the ropes in a rugged lumber camp. A low-budget independent melodrama.

4801. Time Out for Murder (20th Century–Fox; 1938). *Cast:* Michael Whalen, Chick Chandler, Jean Rogers, Gloria Stuart, Ruth Hussey, Jane Darwell, Lester Matthews, June Gale, Robert Kellard, Edward Marr, Douglas Fowley, Cliff Clark, Peter Lynn. *D:* H. Bruce Humberstone; *P:* Sol M. Wurtzel; *As.P.:* Howard Green; *St:* Irving Reis; *Sc:* Jerry Cady.

Premiere entry in a short series of three low-budget films titled "The Roving Reporters." In this entry which had the working title of "Merdian 7-1212," a

reporter and his cameraman investigate the murder of a wealthy woman. Followed by *While New York Sleeps* (q.v.).

4802. Time Out for Romance (20th Century–Fox; 1937). *Cast:* Claire Trevor, Michael Whalen, Chick Chandler, Douglas Fowley, Inez Courtney, Joan Davis, Lelah Tyler, William Demarest, Bennie Bartlett, Andrew Tombes, William Griffith, Fred Kelsey, George Chandler, Jack Norton. *D:* Mal St. Clair; *St:* William Rankin, Eleanore Griffin; *Sc:* John Patrick, Lou Breslow.

B romantic comedy.

4803. The Time, the Place and the Girl (WB; 1929). *Cast:* Grant Withers, Betty Compson, Bert Roach, John Davidson, Gertrude Olmstead, Vivian Oakland, Gretchen Hartman, James Kirkwood, Irene Haisman, Gerald King. *D:* Howard Bretherton; *Sc:* Robert Lord; *Songs Include:* "I Wonder Who's Kissing Her Now," "Collegiate," "Doin' the Raccoon," "Fashionette," "Jack and Jill," "How Many Times" & "If You Could Care."

Musical-comedy set around a college football team. Based on the play by W.M. Hough, Joseph E. Howard and Frank R. Adams, the film is no relation to the "puttin' on a show" musical of the same name (WB; 1946).

4804. Times Square Lady (MGM; 1935). *Cast:* Robert Taylor, Virginia Bruce, Pinky Tomlin, Helen Twelvetrees, Isabel Jewell, Nat Pendleton, Jack LaRue, Henry Kolker, Raymond Hatton, Russell Hopton, Fred Kohler, Robert Elliott, Ward Bond. *D:* George B. Seitz; *P:* Lucien Hubbard; *Sc:* Albert Cohen, Robert T. Shannon; *Songs:* "The Object of My Affections" & "What's the Reason I'm Not Pleasin' You?" by Pinky Tomlin. (1:06)

A girl inherits her father's business operations, finds shady dealings.

4805. Times Square Playboy (WB; 1936). *Cast:* Warren William, Gene Lockhart, June Travis, Kathleen Lockhart (Gene's wife), Barton Mac-Lane, Dick Purcell, Craig Reynolds, Granville Bates, Dorothy Vaughan. *D:* William McGann; *P:* Bryan Foy; *Sc:* Roy Chanslor; *Song:* "Lookin' for Trouble" by M.K. Jerome, Joan Jasmyn. (G.B. title: *His Best Man*)

B drama of a wealthy man who falls for a younger girl, then slowly begins to suspect she may be a gold digger. A remake of *The Home Towners* (q.v.) and based on the original play of that name by George M. Cohan. Remade as *Ladies Must Live* (WB; 1940) with Wayne Morris.

4806. Timothy's Quest (Paramount; 1936). *Cast:* Tom Keene, Eleanore Whitney, Dickie Moore, Virginia Weidler, Raymond Hatton, Elizabeth Patterson (who made her film debut in the '29 version), Samuel S. Hinds, Jack Clifford, Irene Franklin, J.M. Kerrigan, Sally Martin. *D:* Charles Barton; *P:* Harold Hurley.

B juvenile story of two children who run away from an orphanage. Based on the book by Kate Douglas Wiggin, it was previously filmed as a sound feature with titles in 1929 by Gotham productions.

4807. Tin Pants (Xxxx Xxxx; 1933). *Cast:* E.E. Clive.

(No other information available)

4808. The Tip-Off (RKO-Pathé; 1931). *Cast:* Eddie Quillan, Robert Armstrong, Ginger Rogers, Joan Peers, Ralf Harolde, Mike Donlin, Ernie Adams, Charles Sellon, Cupid Ainsworth, Jack Herrick. *D:* Albert S. Rogell; *As.P.:* Harry Joe Brown; *St:* George Kibbe Turner; *Sc:* Earl Baldwin. (G.B. title: *Looking for Trouble*) (1:10)

Melodrama of a man who falls for a gangster's girl.

4809. Tip-Off Girls (Paramount; 1938). *Cast:* Lloyd Nolan, Mary Car-lisle, Evelyn Brent, J. Carrol Naish, Buster Crabbe, Benny Baker, Roscoe Karns, Anthony Quinn, Joyce Mathews, Harvey Stephens, Archie Twitchell, Pierre Watkin, Gertrude Short, Barlowe Borland. *D:* Louis King; *P:* Edward T. Lowe; *Sc:* Stuart Anthony, Maxwell Shane, Robert Yost.

B crime meller about truck hijackers.

4810. Titans of the Deep (Grand National; 1938). *Cast:* Dr. William Beebe, Otis Barton, Joan Igou, Gloria Hollister, Jocelyn Crane, John Bee Van. *D:* Otis Barton; *P:* Barton; *St:* Lowell Thomas. (0:47) (shorter versions only run 0:38)

Documentary of marine life off the Bermuda coast.

4811. To Beat the Band (RKO; 1935). *Cast:* Hugh Herbert, Helen Broderick, Phyllis Brooks, Roger Pryor, Eric Blore, Fred Keating, Evelyn Poe, Ray Mayer, Johnny Mercer, Joy Hodges & the California Collegians, Sonny Lamont. *D:* Ben Stoloff; *As.P.:* Zion Myers; *St:* George Marion, Jr.; *Sc:* Rian James; *Songs:* Johnny Mercer, Matty Malneck. (1:07)

B musical-comedy of a man who must marry in three days in order to get his $59,000,000 inheritance.

4812. To Mary—With Love (20th Century-Fox; 1936). *Cast:* Warner Baxter, Myrna Loy, Ian Hunter, Claire Trevor, Jean Dixon, Pat Somerset, Franklin Pangborn, Paul Hurst, Tyler Brooke, Ruth Clifford, Arthur Aylesworth, Florence Lake, Helen Brown, Harold Foshay, Margaret Fielding, Edward Cooper, Wedgewood Nowell. *D:* John Cromwell; *St:* Richard Sherman; *Sc:* Sherman, Howard Ellis Smith. (1:27)

Comedy-drama of a couple and their stormy marriage.

4813. To the Last Man (Paramount; 1933). *Cast:* Randolph Scott, Esther Ralston, Noah Beery, Jack

LaRue, Larry "Buster" Crabbe, Fuzzy Knight, Barton MacLane, Gail Patrick, Egon Brecher, Muriel Kirkland, Eugenie Besserer (final film — d. 1934), James Eagles, Harlan Knight, Shirley Temple (in her second feature film), John Peter Richmond (John Carradine). *D:* Henry Hathaway; *Sc:* Jack Cunningham. (1:10)

Western of a family feud which started in the hills of Kentucky and moved west to Nevada. Based on the novel by Zane Grey, it was previously filmed by this studio in 1923 with Richard Dix and Lois Wilson.

4814. The Toast of New York (RKO; 1937). *Cast:* Edward Arnold (Jim Fisk), Cary Grant (Nick Boyd), Frances Farmer (Josie Mansfield), Jack Oakie (Luke), Donald Meek (Daniel Drew), Thelma Leeds (Fleurique), Clarence Kolb (Cornelius Vanderbilt), Billy Gilbert (photographer), Stanley Fields (top sergeant), George Irving (broker), Russell Hicks (lawyer), Dudley Clements (Collins), Lionel Belmore (president of the board), Robert McClung (bellhop), Robert Dudley (janitor), Dewey Robinson (Beef Dooley), Oscar Apfel (final film — d. 1938), Frank M. Thomas, Gavin Gordon, Joyce Compton, Virginia Carroll, Clem Bevans, Mary Gordon. *D:* Rowland V. Lee; *P:* Edward Small; *Sc:* Dudley Nichols, John Twist, Joel Sayre; *Songs:* Nathaniel Shilkret, Allie Wrubel, L. Wolfe Gilbert. (1:49) (video)

Fictional and non-fictional events in the life of 19th-century Wall Street tycoon, Jim Fisk. Based on "The Book of Daniel Drew" by Bouck White and "Robber Barons" by Matthew Josephson, this was a major box office flop for the studio, coming in at over a half-million dollar loss.

4815. Today (Majestic; 1930). *Cast:* Catherine Dale Owen, Conrad Nagel, Drew Demarest, Julia Swayne Gordon, Judith Vosselli, John Maurice Sullivan, Sarah Padden. *D:* William Nigh; *St:* Abraham Schomer, George Broadhurst; *Sc:* Seton I. Miller.

"Poverty row" drama.

4816. Today We Live (MGM; 1933). *Cast:* Joan Crawford (Diana Boyce-Smith), Gary Cooper (Richard Bogard), Robert Young (Claude), Franchot Tone (Ronnie), Roscoe Karns (McGinnis), Louise Closser Hale (Applegate), Rollo Lloyd (Major), Hilda Vaughn (Eleanor), Eily Malyon. *D:* Howard Hawks; *Co-director:* Richard Rosson; *P:* Hawks; *Sc:* Edith Fitzgerald, Dwight Taylor; *Dialogue:* William Faulkner. (1:53)

Romantic drama of the front during World War I. Based on William Faulkner's story "Turnabout," his first work written directly for the screen. A box office bomb.

4817. Together We Live (Columbia; 1935). *Cast:* William Bakewell, Sheila Mannors, Willard Mack, Ben Lyon, Esther Ralston, Hobart Bosworth. *D:* Willard Mack; *Sc:* Mack.

Low-budget romantic drama.

4818. Tol'able David (Columbia; 1930). *Cast:* Richard Cromwell (film debut as David Kinemon), Noah Beery (Luke), Helen Ware (Mrs. Kinemon), Joan Peers (Esther Hatburn), George Duryea (Tom Keene as Alan Kinemon), Henry B. Walthall (Amos Hatburn), John Peter Richmond (John Carradine in his film debut), Barbara Bedford, Richard Carlyle, Edmund Breese, James Bradbury, Sr., Harlan Knight. *D:* John G. Blystone; *P:* Harry Cohn; *St:* Joseph Hergesheimer; *Sc:* Benjamin Glazer, Edmund Goulding. (1:05)

Backwoods tale of a youth who must avenge the murder of his father and the crippling of his brother by a neighboring family. A remake of the highly successful 1921 First National feature with Richard Barthelemess, Ernest Torrence and Gladys Hulette, directed produced and written by Henry King (Inspiration).

Note: Voted one of the year's "10

Best" films by the National Board of Review.

4819. Toll of the Desert (Ajax; 1935). *Cast:* Fred Kohler, Jr. (in his starring debut), Betty Mack, Roger Williams, Fred Kohler, Sr., Earl Dwire, Tom London, Ted Adams, George Chesebro, John Elliott, Edward Cassidy, Blackie Whiteford. *D:* Lester Williams (William Berke); *P:* Berke; *St:* Allen Hall; *Sc:* Miller Easton. (0:56)

Indie western of an honest sheriff who hangs an outlaw, not knowing it is his father.

4820. Tom Brown of Culver (Universal; 1932). *Cast:* Tom Brown (Tom Brown), H.B. Warner, Richard Cromwell, Slim Summerville, Ben Alexander, Sidney Toler, Russell Hopton, Andy Devine, Betty Blythe, Tyrone Power, Jr. (in his film debut), Willard Robertson, Alan Ladd, Dick Winslow, Kit Guard, Norman Phillips, Jr. *D:* William Wyler; *St:* Dale Van Every, George Green; *Sc:* Tom Buckingham; *Additional Dialogue:* Clarence Marks. (1:22)

An American youth has a rough time adjusting to the strict discipline of the famous military academy. Remade as *The Spirit of Culver* (q.v.).

4821. Tom Sawyer (Paramount; 1930). *Cast:* Jackie Coogan (popular child star of the silent era, making his talkie debut as Tom Sawyer), Mitzi Green (Becky Thatcher), James (Junior) Durkin (Huck Finn), Jackie Searle (Sidney Sawyer), Clara Blandick (Aunt Polly), Charles Stevens (Injun Joe), Tully Marshall (Muff Potter), Jane Darwell (talkie debut as Widow Douglass, Lucien Littlefield, Mary Jane Irving, Dick Winslow, Ethel Wales, Charles Sellon, Lon Poff. *D:* John Cromwell; *P:* Louis D. Lighton; *Sc:* Grover Jones, William Slavens McNutt, Sam Mintz. (1:26)

The first talkie version of the famous Mark Twain classic and a big box office hit. Previously filmed as a Paramount-Artclass production in 1917 starring Jack Pickford (brother of Mary) and directed by William Desmond Taylor. Remade as *The Adventures of Tom Sawyer* (q.v.), followed in 1973 by two versions, one a threatrical musical version, the other a TV movie. The *New York Times* placed it at #7 on their "10 Best" list of the year. The studio utilized the main actors and characters the following year (1931) in their production of *Huckleberry Finn* (q.v.).

4822. Tom Sawyer, Detective (Paramount; 1938). *Cast:* Billy Cook (Tom Sawyer), Donald O'Connor (Huck Finn), Raymond Hatton, Porter Hall, Monte Blue, Clara Blandick, Clem Bevans, William Haade. *D:* Louis King; *P:* Edward T. Lowe. (1:08)

A low-budget juvenile mystery which utilizes Twain's characters. Tom and Huck Finn come to the aid of a minister accused of murder.

4823. Tomboy (Monogram; 1939–40). *Cast:* Marcia Mae Jones, Jackie Moran, Grant Withers, George Cleveland, Charlotte Wynters, Marvin Stephens, Clara Blandick, Gene Morgan. *D:* Robert McGowan; *P:* William T. Lackey; *Sc:* Dorothy Reid, Marion Orth. (1:10)

A tomboy comes to aid of a farm boy who lives with his cruel uncle in this sentimental B juvenile drama.

4824. Tombstone Canyon (World Wide; 1932). *Cast:* Ken Maynard, Cecilia Parker, Sheldon Lewis, Frank Brownlee, Bob Burns, George Gerring, Lafe McKee, Jack Clifford, Ed Peil, Sr., George Chesebro, Jack Kirk, Merrill McCormack, Bud McClure. *D:* Alan James (Alvin J. Neitz); *Sc:* Earle Snell, Claude Rister. (1:02)

Offbeat Ken Maynard mystery western of an area being terrorized by a disfigured madman.

4825. Tombstone Terror (Supreme; 1935). *Cast:* Bob Steele, Kay McCoy, John Elliott, George Hayes, Earl Dwire, Hortense Petro, Ann Howard, Frank McCarroll, Artie Ortego, George Morrell, Herman Hack, Nancy DeShon. *D:* Robert N. Bradbury; *P:* A.W. Hackel; *Sc:* Bradbury. (0:55)

Bob Steele western of a cowboy who is mistaken for another.

4826. Tomorrow and Tomorrow (Paramount; 1932). *Cast:* Ruth Chatterton, Paul Lukas, Robert Ames, Tad Alexander, Harold Minjir, Walter Walker, Winter Hall, Margaret Armstrong, Arthur Pierson. *D:* Richard Wallace; *Sc:* Josephine Lovett.

Based on a successful Broadway play by Philip Barry, this box office flop was a romantic drama involving infidelity.

Tomorrow at Midnight (G.B. title) *see* **For Love or Money**

4827. Tomorrow at Seven (RKO/Jefferson; 1933). *Cast:* Chester Morris, Vivienne Osborne, Allen Jenkins, Frank McHugh, Henry Stephenson, Grant Mitchell, Oscar Apfel, Cornelius Keefe, Edward LeSaint, Charles B. Middleton, Virginia Howell, Gus Robinson. *D:* Ray Enright; *P:* Joseph I. Schnitzer, Samuel Zierler; *St & Sc:* Ralph Spence. (1:02) (video)

Low-budget indie production of a murderer who after dispensing with his victims, leaves an Ace of Spades as a calling card. A production of Jefferson Pictures Corporation.

4828. Tomorrow's Children (Fox; 1934). *Cast:* Crane Wilbur, Sterling Holloway. *D:* Crane Wilbur; *P:* Bryan Foy; *Sc:* Wilbur. (G.B. title: *The Unborn*)

4829. Tomorrow's Youth (Monogram; 1935). *Cast:* Dickie Moore, John Miljan, Gloria Shea, Martha Sleeper,

Jane Darwell, Franklin Pangborn, Paul Hurst, Barbara Bedford, Harry C. Bradley, Niles Welch, Edward LeSaint. *D:* Charles Lamont; *P:* Trem Carr; *St & Sc:* Harry Sauber, Gene Whitney, Robert Meller. (1:03)

B drama of the effects on a young boy when his parents divorce.

4830. Tonight at Twelve (Universal; 1929). *Cast:* Robert Ellis, Madge Bellamy, Margaret Livingston, Hallam Cooley, Vera Reynolds. *D:* Harry A. Pollard. (1:14)

Low-budget drama of a young man's deception.

4831. Tonight Is Ours (Paramount; 1933). *Cast:* Fredric March, Claudette Colbert, Alison Skipworth, Paul Cavanagh, Arthur Byron, Ethel Griffies, Warburton Gamble, Clay Clement, Edwin Maxwell. *D:* Stuart Walker, Mitchell Leisen; *Sc:* Edwin Justus Mayer. (1:16)

The romance of a princess and a commoner. Based on the play "The Queen Was in the Parlor" by Noel Coward.

4832. Tonight or Never (United Artists/Samuel Goldwyn; 1931). *Cast:* Gloria Swanson (her last major film until 1950's *Sunset Boulevard*), Melvyn Douglas (film debut recreating his stage role), Ferdinand Gottschalk, Robert Greig, Alison Skipworth, Boris Karloff, Greta Meyer, J. Carrol Naish, Warburton Gamble. *D:* Mervyn LeRoy; *P:* Sam Goldwyn; *Sc:* Ernest Vajda. (1:20)

Lavishly produced comedy of romantic misunderstandings which was based on the play by Lili Hatvany.

4833. The Tonto Kid (Resolute; 1934). *Cast:* Rex Bell, Ruth Mix, Buzz Barton, Theodore Lorch, Joseph Girard, Barbara Roberts, Jack Rockwell, Murdock MacQuarrie, Bert Lindley, Jane Keckley, Stella Adams, Bud Pope. *D:* Harry Fraser; *Sc:* Harry P. Crist (Fraser). (1:01) (video)

Rex Bell western (the first in a series of four co-starring Mix and Barton), of a scheming lawyer.

4834. Too Busy to Work (Fox; 1932). *Cast:* Will Rogers (who also starred in the '19 version), Marian Nixon, Dick Powell, Douglas Cosgrove, Frederick Burton, Louise Beavers, Constantine Romanoff. *D:* John G. Blystone.

Comedy-drama of a carefree "man of the road," based on a story by Ben Ames Williams which appeared in the *Saturday Evening Post.* A remake of *Jubilo* (Fox; 1919).

4835. Too Busy to Work (20th Century–Fox; 1939). *Cast:* Jed Prouty, Spring Byington, Florence Roberts, June Carlson, Joan Davis, Kenneth Howell, George Ernest, Billy Mahan, Chick Chandler, Marjorie Gateson, Louise Beavers, Andrew Tombes, Fred Kelsey. *D:* Otto Brower.

The 15th entry in the "Jones Family" comedy series.

4836. Too Hot to Handle (MGM; 1938). *Cast:* Clark Gable, Myrna Loy, Walter Pidgeon, Leo Carrillo, Johnny Hines, Virginia Weidler, Marjorie Main, Walter Connolly, Gregory Gaye, Betty Ross Clarke, Henry Kolker, Frank Faylen, Richard Loo, Willie Fung, Patsy O'Connor. *D:* Jack Conway; *P:* Lawrence Weingarten; *St:* Len Hammond; *Sc:* John Lee Mahin, Laurence Stallings. (1:45) (video)

A box office hit was this romantic comedy of rival newsreel photographers.

4837. Too Many Cooks (RKO; 1931). *Cast:* Bert Wheeler, Dorothy Lee, Roscoe Ates, Robert McWade, Sharon Lynne, Florence Roberts, Hallam Cooley, Clifford Dempsey, Ruth Weston, George Chandler. *D:* William A. Seiter; *As.P.:* Douglas MacLean; *Sc:* Jane Murfin. (1:17)

We have Wheeler without Woolsey in this domestic comedy of a family of 13

(the Cook family) who constantly meddle in the relationship of a young couple. Based on a play by Frank Craven.

4838. Too Many Parents (Paramount; 1936). *Cast:* Frances Farmer (film debut), Lester Matthews, Billy Lee, Carl "Alfalfa" Switzer, Colin Tapley, Porter Hall, Henry Travers, Gene Reynolds, Jack Norton. *D:* Robert McGowan; *P:* A.M. Botsford.

In this B production, four students cause problems at a military school.

4839. Too Many Wives (RKO; 1937). *Cast:* Anne Shirley, John Morley, Gene Lockhart, Dudley Clements, Barbara Pepper, Frank Melton, Charles Coleman, Dot Farley, Jack Carson, George Irving. *D:* Ben Holmes; *P:* William Sistrom; *St:* "Satisfaction Guaranteed" by Richard English; *Sc:* Dorothy Yost, Lois Eby, John Grey. (1:01)

B romantic comedy of a newspaper office and its' fall guy.

Too Many Women (G.B. title) *see* **God's Gift to Women**

4840. Too Much Beef (First Division; 1936). *Cast:* Rex Bell, Connie Bergen, Forrest Taylor, Lloyd Ingraham, Jimmy Aubrey, Jack Cowell, Peggy O'Connell, Fred Burns, Horace Murphy, George Ball, Jack Kirk, Steve Clark, Denny Meadows (Dennis Moore), Frank Ellis. *D:* Robert Hill; *P:* Max & Arthur Alexander; *Sc:* Rock Hawley (Hill). (1:06)

Rex Bell western of crooks attempting to get their hands on a man's ranch after learning the railroad is going through it. Based on a story by William Colt MacDonald.

4841. Too Much Harmony (Paramount; 1933). *Cast:* Bing Crosby, Jack Oakie, Judith Allen, Lilyan Tashman, Ned Sparks, Grace Bradley, Skeets Gallagher, Harry Green, Kitty Kelly, Billy Bevan, Henry Armetta, Anna Demetrio, Evelyn Oakie, Shirley Grey, Bud

Flanagan (Dennis O'Keefe). *D:* A. Edward Sutherland; *P:* William LeBaron; *St:* Joseph L. Mankiewicz; *Sc:* Mankiewicz, Harry Ruskin; *Songs by:* Sam Coslow & Arthur Johnston, include: "Thanks" & "Black Moonlight." (1:16)

Backstage musical of a New York crooner. A box office hit.

4842. Too Tough to Kill (Columbia; 1935). *Cast:* Sally O'Neil, Johnny Arthur, Victor Jory, Ward Bond, James Millican, Thurston Hall, Dewey Robinson. *D:* D. Ross Lederman.

B melodrama.

4843. Too Young to Marry (WB; 1930-31). *Cast:* Grant Withers, Loretta Young, O.P. Heggie, Emma Dunn, Virginia Sale, Aileen Carlyle, J. Farrell MacDonald, Lloyd Neal, Richard Tucker, Tom Ricketts. *D:* Mervyn LeRoy; *Sc:* Francis Edward Faragoh. (aka: *Broken Dishes*)

Drama of a mother who objects to her daughter's marriage to an older man. Based on the Broadway play "Broken Dishes" by Martin Flavin. Remade as *Love Begins at Twenty* (q.v.) and *Calling All Husbands* (WB; 1940).

4844. Top Hat (RKO; 1935). *Cast:* Fred Astaire (Jerry Travers), Ginger Rogers (Dale Tremont), Edward Everett Horton (Horace Hardwicke), Helen Broderick (Madge Hardwicke), Eric Blore (Bates), Erik Rhodes (Alberto Beddini), Donald Meek (Curate), Florence Roberts (Curate's wife), Lucille Ball (flower clerk), Leonard Mudie (flower salesman), Edgar Norton, Gino Corrado, Peter Hobbes, Nick Thompson, Ben Holmes, Tom Costello, John Impolito, Genaro Spagnoli, Phyllis Coghlan, Charles Hall, Rita Rozelle. *D:* Mark Sandrich; *P:* Pandro S. Berman; *Sc:* Dwight Taylor, Allan Scott; *Art-Set Decoration:* (A.A.N.) Van Nest Polglase, Carroll Clark; *Choreographer:* (A.A.N.) Hermes Pan for the "Piccolino" & "Top Hat" numbers (with additional choreography by Astaire); *Songs by:* Irving Berlin, include: "Cheek to Cheek" (which received an A.A.N. for Best Song), "Top Hat," "Isn't It a Lovely Day (to Be Caught in the Rain)," "The Piccolino," "No Strings" & "Get Thee Behind Me Satan." (1:41) (video)

Classic musical starring the dance team of Astaire and Rogers in what many critics and fans consider as the "best" of their vehicles. The plot involves the proverbial mistaken identity which leads to multiple misunderstandings. Based on a play by Alexander Farago and Aladar Laszlo and the 1932 musical play "The Gay Divorce" by Dwight Taylor. The premiere of this film was held at Radio City Music Hall in New York City, placing #7 on the "10 Best" list of *Film Daily*. It became one of the 12 top grossing films of 1935.

Top of the Bill (G.B. title) *see* **Fanny Foley Herself**

4845. Top of the Town (Universal; 1937). *Cast:* Doris Nolan, George Murphy, Ella Logan, Hugh Herbert, Mischa Auer, Gerald Oliver Smith, Gregory Ratoff, Peggy Ryan (film debut at age 12), Jack Smart, Henry Armetta, Samuel S. Hinds, Richard Carle, May Robson, Ben Blue, Joyce Compton, Gertrude Niesen, Claude Gillingwater, Three Sailors (aka: Jason, Robson & Blue), Original California Collegians, Four Esquires, Bud Flanagan (Dennis O'Keefe). *D:* Ralph Murphy; *As.P.:* Lou Brock; *St:* Brock; *Sc:* Brown Holmes, Charles Grayson; *Songs Include:* "Where Are You?" "Blame It on the Rhumba," title song, "Fireman, Save My Child" & "I Feel a Foolish Feeling Coming On," all by Harold Adamson & Jimmy McHugh. (1:26)

Musical-comedy set in a modernistic rooftop night club.

4846. Top Speed (WB/F.N.; 1930). *Cast:* Joe E. Brown, Bernice Claire, Jack Whiting, Frank McHugh, Laura Lee, Edmund Breese, Wade

Boteler, Rita Flynn, Billy Bletcher. *D:* Mervyn LeRoy; *Sc:* Humphrey Pearson, Henry McCarty; *Songs:* "As Long as I Have You and You Have Me" by Al Dubin & Joe Burke; "Goodness Gracious," "I'll Know and She'll Know," "Keep Your Undershirt On," "What Would I Care" & "Sweeter Than You" by Bert Kalmar & Harry Ruby. (1:10)

B musical-comedy of a poor clerk who pretends to be a millionaire. Based on a play by Guy Bolton, Bert Kalmar and Harry Ruby.

4847. Topaze (RKO; 1933). *Cast:* John Barrymore, Myrna Loy, Albert Conti, Luis Alberni, Reginald Mason, Jobyna Howland, Jackie Searle, Frank Reicher. *D:* Harry D'Abbadie D'Arrast; *As.P.:* Kenneth MacGowan; *Sc:* Benn W. Levy, Ben Hecht (unc.), Charles Lederer (unc.). (1:18) (video)

An honest but naive schoolteacher unknowingly becomes involved in a crooked business scheme. Based on the play by Marcel Pagnol, it was voted "Best Film of the Year" by the National Board of Review. Remade in Great Britain in 1962 as *I Like Money.* Also filmed thrice in France, 1932, 1935 and 1952.

Note: An attempt by RKO to re-release this film in 1936 was blocked by the censors of the Hays Office.

4848. Topper (MGM/Hal Roach; 1937). *Cast:* Constance Bennett (Marion Kerby), Cary Grant (George Kerby), Roland Young (A.A.N. for B.S.A. as Cosmo Topper), Billie Burke (Clara Topper), Alan Mowbray (Wilkins), Hedda Hopper, Arthur Lake, Eugene Pallette, Virginia Sale, Theodore von Eltz, J. Farrell MacDonald, Doodles Weaver, Ward Bond, Elaine Shepard, Si Jenks, Three Hits and a Miss. *D:* Norman Z. McLeod; *P:* Milton Bren; *Sc:* Jack Jevne, Eric Hatch, Eddie Moran; *Song:* "Old Man Moon" by Hoagy Carmichael; *Sound Recording:* (A.A.N.) Elmer Raguse. (1:37) (video — b/w & computer-colored)

George and Marion Kerby, a free living couple, die in an auto accident and remain as spirits on earth to upset and set right the hum-drum life of banker Cosmo Topper. Based on the novel "The Jovial Ghosts" by Thorne Smith, this now classic comedy-fantasy was a huge box office hit. Computer-colored by the Hal Roach studios in 1983. Remade in 1979 as a TV movie. Followed in 1939 by the sequel *Topper Takes a Trip* (see below).

4849. Topper Takes a Trip (United Artists/Hal Roach; 1939). *Cast:* Constance Bennett (Marion Kerby), Roland Young (Cosmo Topper), Billie Burke (Mrs. Topper), Alan Mowbray (Wilkins), Verree Teasdale (Mrs. Parkhurst), Franklin Pangborn (hotel manager), Alexander D'Arcy (baron), Skippy the dog (Mr. Atlas), Paul Hurst, Spencer Charters, Irving Pichel, Eddy Conrad, Leon Belasco (film debut), Armand Kaliz, Georges Renavent, George Humbert, Paul Everton, Duke York & Cary Grant (in a flashback). *D:* Norman Z. McLeod; *P:* Milton H. Bren; *Sc:* Eddie Moran, Jack Jevne, Corey Ford. (1:25) (video — b/w & computer-colored)

Cosmo Topper's wife wants to divorce him and heads for the French Riviera. Cosmo follows her and the ghost of Marion Kerby follows him in this farcical comedy-fantasy based on the novel by Thorne Smith. A box office hit, which was followed in 1941 by the third and final entry in the series, *Topper Returns.* Computer-colored by the Hal Roach Studios in 1987.

Tops Is the Limit *see* **Anything Goes**

4850. Torch Singer (Paramount; 1933). *Cast:* Claudette Colbert (who does her own singing), Ricardo Cortez, David Manners, Lyda Roberti, Baby LeRoy, Cora Sue Collins, Florence Roberts, Ethel Griffies, Helen Jerome Eddy, Kathleen Burke, Charley Grapewin, Barton MacLane, Bud Flanagan (Dennis O'Keefe). *D:* Alexander Hall, George Somnes; *P:* Albert E. Lewis; *Sc:* Lenore Coffee, Lynn Starling; *Songs:* Ralph Rainger, Leo Robin. (G.B. title: *Broadway Singer*) (1:12)

A tawdry torch singer abandons her baby and then tries to find her years later. Based on the play "Mike" by Grace Perkins.

4851. Torchy Blane in Chinatown (WB; 1939). *Cast:* Glenda Farrell (Torchy Blane), Barton MacLane (Steve McBride), Henry O'Neill, Tom Kennedy, Patric Knowles, James Stephenson, Richard Bond. *D:* William Beaudine; *As.P.:* Bryan Foy; *St:* Will F. Jenkins, Murray Leinster; *Sc:* George Bricker. (0:59)

A series of murders involving jade curios is the plotline in this, the 7th entry in the hit low-budget series based on characters created by Frederick Nebel.

4852. Torchy Blane in Panama (WB; 1938). *Cast:* Lola Lane (replacing Glenda Farrell as Torchy Blane), Paul Kelly (replacing Barton MacLane as Steve McBride), Tom Kennedy, Anthony Averill, Betty Compson, Hugh O'Connell, John Ridgely, James Nolan, James Conlon, Larry Williams, Joe Cunningham. *D:* William Clemens; *As.P.:* Bryan Foy; *St:* Anthony Coldeway; *Sc:* George Bricker. (G.B. title: *Trouble in Panama*) (0:58)

A girl reporter seeks the killers of a bank teller in this, the 5th entry in the low-budget series created by Frederick Nebel in his short stories.

Torchy Blane the Adventurous Blonde *see* **The Adventurous Blonde**

4853. Torchy Gets Her Man (WB; 1938). *Cast:* Glenda Farrell (Torchy Blane), Barton MacLane (Steve McBride), Willard Robertson, Tom Kennedy, George Guhl, John Ridgely, Thomas Jackson, John Harron, Frank Reicher, Frank Shannon, Nat Carr, Edward Keane, Edward Raquello, Cliff Saum, Loia Cheaney,

Greta Meyer, Herbert Rawlinson, Joe Cunningham. *D:* William Beaudine; *As.P.:* Bryan Foy; *Sc:* Albert DeMond. (1:02)

Sixth entry in the series with the girl reporter out to capture a counterfeiter. Based on the characters created by Frederick Nebel.

4854. Torchy Plays with Dynamite (WB; 1939). *Cast:* Jane Wyman (replacing Glenda Farrell as Torchy Blane), Allen Jenkins (replacing Barton MacLane as Steve McBride), Tom Kennedy, Sheila Bromley, Joe Cunningham, John Ridgely, Nat Carr. *D:* Noel Smith; *As.P.:* Bryan Foy; *St:* Scott Littleton; *Sc:* Earle Snell, Charles Belden. (0:59)

The 9th and final entry in the B series as the girl reporter gets herself sent to prison to get information on a case. Based on characters created in the short stories of Frederick Nebel.

4855. Torchy Runs the Mayor (WB; 1939). *Cast:* Glenda Farrell (Torchy Blane), Barton MacLane (Steve McBride), Tom Kennedy, Frank Shannon, Irving Bacon, Jack Mower, John Miljan, Joe Cunningham, John Ridgely. *D:* Ray McCarey; *As.P.:* Bryan Foy; *Sc:* Earle Snell. (0:58)

When murder follows an investigation into political graft, the girl reporter investigates, in this the 8th entry in the series based on the characters created by Frederick Nebel. Based on an idea by Irving Rubine.

4856. The Torpedo of Doom (Republic; 1938). *Cast:* Herman Brix (Bruce Bennett), Lee Powell, Eleanor Stewart, Montagu Love, Hugh Sothern. *D:* William Witney, John English; *P:* Robert Beche; *Sc:* Barry Shipman, Franklyn Adreon, Ronald Davidson, Sol Shor. (1:40)

Feature version of the Republic serial "Fighting Devil Dogs" of a band of marines out to save the world.

4857. Torture Ship (Producers Pictures; 1939). *Cast:* Lyle Talbot, Jacqueline Wells (Julie Bishop), Irving Pichel, Sheila Bromley, Wheeler Oakman, Russell Hopton, Anthony Averill, Skelton Knaggs, Adia Kuznetzoff, Stanley Blystone, Leander DeCordova, Julian Madison, Eddie Holden. *D:* Victor Halperin; *P:* Ben Judell; *Sc:* George Wallace Sayre, Harvey Huntley. (1:02)

B melodrama of a mad doctor who performs experiments upon criminals aboard his ship. Suggested by the story "A Thousand Deaths" by Jack London.

4858. Touchdown! (Paramount; 1931). *Cast:* Richard Arlen, Peggy Shannon, Jack Oakie, Charles Starrett, Regis Toomey, Charles D. Brown, J. Farrell MacDonald, George Barbier. *D:* Norman Z. McLeod; *P:* Louis D. Lighton; *St:* Francis Wallace; *Sc:* William Slavens McNutt, Grover Jones, Joseph L. Mankiewicz (unc.). (G.B. title: *Playing the Game*)

Gridiron comedy-drama of a coach who'll stop at nothing to win.

4859. Touchdown Army (Paramount; 1938). *Cast:* John Howard, Mary Carlisle, Robert Cummings, William Frawley, Raymond Hatton, Grant Withers, Benny Baker, Owen Davis, Jr., Charles Anthony Hughes, Minor Watson, Harry Bailey, Chester Clute, Hamilton MacFadden, Sarah Edwards, Paul Everton. *D:* Kurt Neumann; *P:* Edward T. Lowe; *St & Sc:* Lloyd Corrigan, Erwin Gelsey. (G.B. title: *Generals of Tomorrow*)

B gridiron romantic comedy of two rival cadets with a climax at the famed Army-Navy game.

4860. Tough Guy (MGM; 1936). *Cast:* Jackie Cooper, Joseph Calleia, Rin-Tin-Tin, Jr., Harvey Stephens, Jean Hersholt, Mischa Auer, Robert Warwick, Edward Pawley, Dwight Frye. *D:* Chester M. Franklin (his final film as director); *P:* Harry Rapf; *St & Sc:* Florence Ryerson, Edgar Allan Woolf. (1:15)

B sentimental melodrama of a run-away rich kid and his pet German shepherd who become involved with a wanted gunman and find themselves pursued by both the gunman's gang and the police.

4861. Tough Kid (Monogram; 1938). *Cast:* Frankie Darro, Dick Purcell, Judith Allen, Lillian Elliott, Don Rowan, William Ruhl, Lew Kelly, Ralph Peters, Max Marx, Jean Joyce, Cliff Howell, Joe Lynch, Wilbur Mack, Joseph Girard. *D:* Howard Bretherton; *P:* Lindsley Parsons; *St:* Brenda Weisberg; *Sc:* Wellyn Totman. (G.B. title: *The Fifth Round*) (0:59)

B melodrama of a street kid who tries to keep his prizefighter brother from getting involved with racketeers.

4862. Tough to Handle (Ambassador; 1937). *Cast:* Frankie Darro, Kane Richmond, Lee Phelps. *D:* S. Roy Luby; *P:* Maurice Conn.

B indie melodrama.

4863. Tovarich (WB; 1937). *Cast:* Claudette Colbert, Charles Boyer, Basil Rathbone, Anita Louise, Melville Cooper, Maurice Murphy, Morris Carnovsky, Gregory Gaye, Montagu Love, Fritz Feld, Isabel Jeans (American debut), Curt Bois (American debut), Renie Riano, Victor Kilian, Heather Thatcher, Doris Lloyd, Christian Rub, Clifford Soubier, Grace Hayle. *D:* Anatole Litvak; *P:* Robert Lord; *Adaptation:* Robert E. Sherwood; *Sc:* Casey Robinson. (1:38)

Comedy of a royal couple who flee the Russian Revolution, taking refuge in Paris where they become domestics for a family of eccentrics. Based on an original play by Jacques Deval, the film was a box office hit.

4864. The Tower of London (Universal; 1939). *Cast:* Basil Rathbone (Richard III), Boris Karloff (Mord), Barbara O'Neil (Elizabeth I), Ian Hunter (Edward IV), Vincent Price (Duke of Clarence), Nan Grey (Lady

Alice Jane Barton), John Sutton (John Wyatt), Leo G. Carroll (Hastings), Miles Mander (Henry VI), Ernest Cossart (Tom Clink), John Rodion (Lord de Verez), Ronald Sinclair & Donnie Dunagan (young princes), Walter Tetley, Rose Hobart, Lionel Belmore, Ralph Forbes, G.P. Huntley, Jr., Georgia Caine, Francis Powers, John Herbert-Bond. *D:* Rowland V. Lee; *P:* Lee; *Sc:* Robert N. Lee. (1:32)

Historical dramatization of the rise of Richard III to the throne of England via the murders of the princes in the Tower and others. Remade in 1962 with Vincent Price.

4865. The Toy Wife (MGM; 1938). *Cast:* Luise Rainer, Melvyn Douglas, Robert Young, Barbara O'Neil, H.B. Warner, Alma Kruger, Walter Kingsford, Libby Taylor, Clarence Muse, Leonard Penn, Margaret Irving, Theresa Harris, Rafaela Ottiano, Clinton Rosemond, Alan Perl. *D:* Richard Thorpe; *P:* Merian C. Cooper; *Sc:* Zoe Akins. (G.B. title: *Frou Frou*) (1:35)

The romantic adventures of a southern belle in 19th-century Louisiana. Lavishly produced, but a box office flop.

4866. Tracy Rides (Reliable; 1934–35). *Cast:* Tom Tyler (his first for this company), Virginia Brown Faire, Edmund Cobb, Charles K. French, Carol Shandrew, Jimmy Aubrey, Lafe McKee, Art Dillard, Jack Evans. *D:* Harry S. Webb; *P:* Bernard B. Ray; *Sc:* Rose Gordon, Betty Burbridge. (0:59)

Tom Tyler western of a range war between cattlemen and sheepmen.

4867. Trade Winds (United Artists/Walter Wanger; 1938). *Cast:* Fredric March, Joan Bennett, Ralph Bellamy, Ann Sothern, Sidney Blackmer, Thomas Mitchell, Robert Elliott, Patricia Farr, Walter Byron (final film — ret.), Robert Emmett O'Connor, Phyllis Barry, Dorothy Tree, Joyce Compton, Lee Phelps, Linda Winters (Dorothy Comingore), Wilson Benge, Harry Paine, Wilma Francis. *D:* Tay Garnett; *P:* Walter Wanger; *St:* Garnett; *Sc:* Dorothy Parker, Alan Campbell, Frank R. Adams. (1:30)

Critically acclaimed comedy-drama of a detective chasing a girl around the world who is under suspicion of murder. A box office hit.

4868. Trader Horn (MGM; 1930–31). *Cast:* Harry Carey (Trader Horn), Edwina Booth (Nina Trend), Duncan Renaldo (Peru), Mutia Omoolu (Rencharo), Olive Fuller Golden (later Olive Carey (Edith Trend), C. Aubrey Smith (trader). *D:* W.S. Van Dyke; *Adaptation:* Dale Van Every, John Thomas Neville; *Sc:* Richard Schayer; *Dialogue:* Cyril Hume. (2:00)

The legendary jungle adventure which thrilled audiences of its' day is considered tame by today's standards. Filmed on location in various parts of Africa in 1929, it became one of the 15 top grossing films of 1930–31 and was remade by this studio in 1973. Based on the 1927 novel by Alfred Aloysius Horn and Ethelreda Lewis, it received an A.A.N. for "Best Picture" (1930–31).

4869. The Trail Beyond (Monogram-Lone Star; 1934). *Cast:* John Wayne, Verna Hillie, Noah Beery, Sr., Noah "Pidge" Beery, Jr., Iris Lancaster, Robert Frazer, Earl Dwire, Eddie Parker, Artie Ortego, James Marcus, Reed Howes. *D:* Robert N. Bradbury; *P:* Paul Malvern; *Supervisor:* Trem Carr; *Sc:* Lindsley Parsons. (0:55) (video)

John Wayne western of a lawman in search of a gold mine and a lost girl. Based on "The Wolf Hunters" by James Oliver Curwood.

4870. The Trail Drive (Universal; 1933). *Cast:* Ken Maynard, Cecilia Parker, William Gould, Lafe McKee, Robert Kortman, Alan Bridge, Frank Rice, Jack Rockwell, Slim Whitaker,

Fern Emmett, Frank Ellis, Hank Bell, Wally Wales (Hal Taliaferro), Ben Corbett. *D:* Alan James (aka: Alvin J. Neitz); *Sc:* James, Nate Gatzert; *Title Song:* Maynard. (1:05)

Ken Maynard range saga of a cattle drive.

4871. Trail Dust (Paramount; 1936). *Cast:* William Boyd (Hoppy), James Ellison (Johnny), George Hayes (Windy), Gwynne Shipman, Stephen Morris (Morris Ankrum), Britt Wood (Speedy), Dick Dickinson, Earl Askam, Ted Adams, Alan Bridge, John Beach, Al St. John, Harold Daniels, Kenneth Harlan, John Elliott, George Chesebro, Robert Drew. *D:* Nate Watt; *P:* Harry M. Sherman; *Sc:* Al Martin. (1:17)

Number 8 in the "Hopalong Cassidy" series, as the boys of Bar 20 go on a trail drive.

4872. Trail of Terror (Supreme; 1935). *Cast:* Bob Steele, Beth Marion, Forrest Taylor, Charles King, Lloyd Ingraham, Charles K. French, Richard Cramer. *D:* Robert N. Bradbury; *P:* A.W. Hackel; *Sc:* Bradbury. (0:59)

Bob Steele western of a government man posing as an escaped convict.

4873. Trail of the Hawk (Xxxx Xxxx; 1935). *Cast:* Yancey Lane, Lafe McKee, Otis Harlan. *D:* Edward Dmytryk (directorial debut); *P:* Herman Wohl. (aka: *The Hawk*)

Yancey Lane western. This independent production was a lone attempt to establish its' star in a series. The attempt failed.

4874. The Trail of the Lonesome Pine (Paramount; 1936). *Cast:* Sylvia Sidney, Henry Fonda, Fred MacMurray, Fred Stone, Fuzzy Knight, Beulah Bondi, Spanky McFarland, Nigel Bruce, Frank McGlynn, Sr., Robert Barrat, Alan Baxter, Samuel S. Hinds, Richard Carle, Henry Brandon, Charles Middleton, Ricca Allen, John Beck, Jim Welch, Margaret Armstrong, Hank Bell, William McCormick. *D:*

Henry Hathaway; *P:* Walter Wanger; *Sc:* Grover Jones, Horace McCoy, Harvey Thew. *Song:* "A Melody from the Sky" (A.A.N. for Best Song) Louis Alter & Sidney Mitchell. (1:42)

Classic technicolor western style drama of the effect the coming of the railroad has on two feuding families. Based on the novel by John Fox, Jr., it is notable as the first full technicolor feature to be shot outdoors. Previous versions: (Lasky Feature Plays; 1916) with Charlotte Walker and Earle Foxe; (Paramount; 1923) with Antonio Moreno, Mary Miles Minter and Ernest Torrence. The novel was also adapted for the stage.

4875. Trail of Vengeance (Republic-Supreme; 1937). *Cast:* Johnny Mack Brown, Iris Meredith, Warner Richmond, Earle Hodgins, Richard Cramer, Dick Curtis, Karl Hackett, Frank Ellis, Frank LaRue, Frank Ball, Lew Meehan, Horace Murphy, Steve Clark, Budd Buster, Jack Kirk, Tex Palmer, Jim Corey. *D:* Sam Newfield; *P:* A.W. Hackel; *Sc:* George Plympton, Fred Myton. (1:00)

Johnny Mack Brown western involving a range war.

Trail to Utah (G.B. title) *see* **Utah Trail**

4876. Trail's End (Beaumont; 1935). *Cast:* Conway Tearle, Claudia Dell, Baby Charlotte Barry, Fred Kohler, Ernie Adams, Pat Harmon, Victor Potel, Gaylord (Steve) Pendleton, Stanley Blystone, Jack Duffy. *D:* Al Herman; *Sc:* Jack Jevne. (0:57)

Conway Tearle series western of a man seeking revenge after being sent to prison on a frame-up.

4877. Trailing North (Monogram; 1933). *Cast:* Bob Steele, George Hayes, Doris Hill, Arthur Rankin, Fred Burns, Dick Dickinson, Norman Feusier. *D:* John P. McCarthy; *P:* Paul Malvern; *Supervisor:* Trem Carr; *St:* Harry

O. Jones (Harry Fraser); *Sc:* John Morgan. (0:57)

Bob Steele western of a Texas Ranger who rides north to join forces with some Canadian Mounties.

4878. Trailin' Trouble (Universal; 1930). *Cast:* Hoot Gibson, Margaret Quimby, Pete Morrison, Olive Young, William McCall, Robert Perry. *D:* Arthur Rosson; *Sc:* Rosson, Harold Tarshis. (0:57)

Hoot Gibson oater of a trail boss, accused of absconding with the money from the cattle sale.

4879. Trailin' Trouble (Grand National; 1937). *Cast:* Ken Maynard, Lona Andre, Roger Williams, Vince Barnett, Grace Woods, Fred Burns, Ed Cassidy, Phil Dunham, Horace B. Carpenter, Marin Sais, Tex Palmer, Tarzan the horse. *D:* Arthur Rosson; *P:* M.H. Hoffman, Jr.; *Sc:* Philip Graham White. (0:58) (video)

Ken Maynard western of a cowboy mistaken for an outlaw. A remake of *Hard Hombre* (q.v.).

4880. Trailin' West (WB/F.N.; 1936). *Cast:* Dick Foran, Paula Stone, Gordon (Bill) Elliott, Addison Richards, Robert Barrat, Joseph Crehan, Stuart Holmes, Glenn Strange. *D:* Noel Smith; *P:* Bryan Foy; *Sc:* Anthony Coldeway; *Songs:* "Moonlight Valley" & "Drums of Glory" by M.K. Jerome, Jack Scholl. (G.B. title: *On Secret Service*) (0:59)

Dick Foran western with songs of an undercover agent sent by President Lincoln to break up a gang of guerrillas.

4881. Trailing the Killer (World Wide; 1932). *Cast:* Francis McDonald, Heinie Conklin, Jose (Joe) de la Cruz, Caesar the dog, Peter Rigas. *D:* Herman C. Raymaker; *P:* B.F. Zeidman; *St & Sc:* Jackson Richards. (aka: *Call of the Wilderness*) (1:04)

Wilderness melodrama of a wolf dog accused of killing his owner. Filmed on location in Canada.

4882. Trails of Peril (Big 4; 1930). *Cast:* Wally Wales (Hal Taliaferro), Virginia Brown Faire, Frank Ellis, Lew Meehan, Jack Perrin, Joe Rickson, Buck Connors, Pete Morrison, Bobby Dunn, Hank Bell. *D:* Alvin J. Neitz (Alan James); *P:* John R. Freuler; *Sc:* Neitz. (0:55)

Wally Wales (Hal Taliaferro) western of a cowboy mistaken for an outlaw.

4883. Trails of the Wild (Ambassador; 1935). *Cast:* Kermit Maynard, Billie Seward, Fuzzy Knight, Monte Blue, Matthew Betz, Theodore von Eltz, Frank Rice, Robert Frazer, Wheeler Oakman, Roger Williams, Charles Delaney, Dick Curtis, John Elliott. *D:* Sam Newfield; *P:* Maurice Conn; *Sc:* Joseph O'Donnell. (1:00)

Kermit Maynard northwoods adventure of a Canadian Mountie in search of the killer of his friend. Based on "Caryl of the Mountains" by James Oliver Curwood.

Train 2419 (G.B. title) *see* **The Return of Casey Jones**

4884. The Traitor (Puritan; 1936). *Cast:* Tim McCoy, Frances Grant, Karl Hackett, Dick Curtis, Jack Rockwell, Pedro Regas, Wally Wales (Hal Taliaferro), Frank Melton, Richard Botiller, Edmund Cobb, Tina Menard, Soledad Jiminez, Frank McCarroll, J. Frank Glendon, Wally West. *D:* Sam Newfield; *Sc:* Joseph O'Donnell. (0:56) (video)

Tim McCoy western of a Texas Ranger going undercover to get the bad guys.

4885. Transatlantic (Fox; 1931). *Cast:* Edmund Lowe, Greta Nissen, Jean Hersholt, John Halliday, Myrna Loy, Lois Moran, Ruth Donnelly, Billy Bevan, Crauford Kent, Earle Foxe, Claude King, Goodee Montgomery, Jesse DeVorska, Rosalie Roy. *D:* William K. Howard; *Sc:* Lynn Starling;

St: Guy Bolton; *Art-Set Decoration:* (A.A.) Gordon Wiles.

Drama set aboard an ocean liner.

4886. Transatlantic Merry-Go-Round (United Artists/Reliance; 1934). *Cast:* Jack Benny, Nancy Carroll, Gene Raymond, Sydney Howard, Sidney Blackmer, Patsy Kelly, Mitzi Green, Robert Elliott, Boswell Sisters, Marjorie Weaver (film debut), Franklin Parker, Sid Silvers, Jimmy Grier & his orchestra, Ralph Morgan, Virginia Grey, Sam Hardy, William "Stage" Boyd, Carlyle Moore, Shirley Grey, Jean Sargent, Bud Flanagan (Dennis O'Keefe). *D:* Ben Stoloff; *P:* Edward Small; *St:* Leon Gordon; *Sc:* Joseph Moncure March, Harry W. Conn; *Song Lyrics:* Johnny Mercer. (1:32) (video)

Romantic comedy melodrama with songs of a radio troupe on an ocean voyage who encounter mystery aboard ship.

4887. Transgression (RKO; 1931). *Cast:* Kay Francis, Paul Cavanagh, Ricardo Cortez, Nance O'Neil, Doris Lloyd, John St. Polis, Ruth Weston, Adrienne D'Ambricourt, Wilfred Noy, Cissy Fitzgerald. *D:* Herbert Brenon; *P:* William LeBaron; *Adaptation:* Elizabeth Meehan; *Additional Dialogue:* Benn Levy. (1:09)

Marital drama of a woman who plays while hubby is away. Based on the novel by Kate Jordan, the film is a remake of *The Next Corner* (Paramount; 1924) with Dorothy Mackaill, Lon Chaney and Ricardo Cortez.

4888. Transient Lady (Universal; 1935). *Cast:* Clark Williams, Gene Raymond, Frances Drake, June Clayworth, John Carradine, Henry Hull, Douglas Fowley, Eddie Anderson, Clara Blandick, Frederick Burton, Helen Lowell, Clifford Jones. *D:* Edward Buzzell; *St:* Octavus Roy Cohen. (G.B. title: *False Witness*) (1:08)

Members of a traveling ice show find themselves involved in murder in this B mystery-melodrama.

4889. Transient Love (Xxxx Xxxx; 1934). *Cast:* Charles Starrett. (No other information available)

4890. Trapped (Xxxx Xxxx; 1930). *Cast:* Nena Quartero, Nick Stuart, Priscilla Dean. *D:* Bruce Mitchell; *Sc:* Jackson Parks, Edith Brown. (No other information available)

4891. Trapped (Columbia; 1937). *Cast:* Charles Starrett, Peggy Stratford, Robert Middlemass, Allan Sears, Ted Oliver, Lew Meehan, Edward J. LeSaint, Ed Peil, Sr., Jack Rockwell, Francis Sayles, Art Mix. *D:* Leon Barsha (directorial debut); *Sc:* John Rathmell. (0:55)

Charles Starrett western of a man who tries to unravel the mystery surrounding his brother's death.

4892. Trapped by G-Men (Columbia; 1937). *Cast:* Jack Holt, Wynne Gibson, Edward Brophy, Eleanor Stewart, Jack LaRue, William Bakewell, William Pawley, George Cleveland, Frank Darien, Robert Emmett O'Connor, Arthur Hohl, C. Henry Gordon, Charles Lane, Richard Tucker, Lucien Prival. *D:* Lewis Collins; *St:* Bernard McConville; *Sc:* Tom Kilpatrick. (aka: *River of Missing Men*)

B crime melodrama.

4893. Trapped by Television (Columbia; 1936). *Cast:* Mary Astor, Lyle Talbot, Nat Pendleton, Joyce Compton, Marc Lawrence, Thurston Hall, Robert Strange, Wyrley Birch, Henry Mollison. *D:* Del Lord; *St:* Al Martin, Sherman Lowe; *Sc:* Lee Loeb, Harold Buchman.

B melodrama with a curious plotline.

Trapped by the Wireless (G.B. title) *see* **Panic on the Air**

4894. Trapped in the Sky (Columbia; 1939). *Cast:* Jack Holt, Ralph Morgan, Sidney Blackmer, Katherine de Mille, Ivan Lebedeff, Holmes Herbert. *D:* Lewis D. Collins.

B melodrama.

4895. Trapped in Tiajuana (Mayfair; 1932). *Cast:* Duncan Renaldo, Edwina Booth.

"Poverty row" melodrama.

(No other information available)

4896. Traveling Husbands (RKO; 1931). *Cast:* Frank Albertson, Hugh Herbert, Evelyn Brent, Constance Cummings, Carl Miller, Spencer Charters, Dorothy Peterson, Gwen Lee, Frank McHugh, Stanley Fields, Rita LaRoy, Lucille Williams, Purnell Pratt, Tom Francis. *D:* Paul Sloane; *As.P.:* Myles Connolly; *St:* Humphrey Pearson; *Sc:* Pearson; *Song:* Pearson, Max Steiner. (1:14)

When traveling salesmen are away — they play, is the theme of this low-budget comedy.

4897. The Traveling Saleslady (WB/F.N.; 1935). *Cast:* Joan Blondell, Glenda Farrell, Hugh Herbert, William Gargan, Grant Mitchell, Al Shean, Ruth Donnelly, Carroll Nye, Hattie McDaniel, Johnny Arthur, Mary Treen, Selmer Jackson, Bert Roach. *D:* Ray Enright; *P:* Sam Bischoff; *St:* Frank Howard Clark; *Sc:* F. Hugh Herbert, Manuel Seff, Benny Rubin. (1:03)

The premise of this B comedy is liquor-flavored toothpaste.

4898. Treachery Rides the Range (WB; 1936). *Cast:* Dick Foran, Paula Stone, Monte Blue, Jim Thorpe, Craig Reynolds, Carlyle Moore, Jr., Monte Montague, Henry Otho, Don Barclay, Dick Botiller, Frank Bruno. *D:* Frank McDonald; *P:* Bryan Foy; *Sc:* William Jacobs; *Songs:* "Ridin' Home" & "Leather and Steel" by M.K. Jerome, Jack Scholl. (0:56)

Dick Foran western with songs of Indians being victimized by white traders.

4899. Treason (Columbia; 1932–33). *Cast:* Buck Jones, Shirley Grey, Robert Ellis, Edward LeSaint, Frank Lackteen, Frank Ellis, Art Mix, Edwin Stanley, T.C. Jacks, Charles Brinley, Charles Hill Mailes, Ivar McFadden. *D:* George B. Seitz; *Sc:* Gordon Battle. (0:57)

Buck Jones western of an army scout in 1870 who gets involved with a group of Confederate sympathizers to check out their activities.

4900. Treasure Island (MGM; 1934). *Cast:* Wallace Beery (Long John Silver), Jackie Cooper (Jim Hawkins), Lewis Stone, Lionel Barrymore, Otto Kruger, Douglass Dumbrille, Nigel Bruce, Charles "Chic" Sale, Dorothy Peterson, James Burke, William V. Mong, Edmund Breese, Charles McNaughton. *D:* Victor Fleming; *P:* Hunt Stromberg; *Sc:* John Lee Mahin. (1:45) (video — b/w & computer-colored)

Hit adaptation of the classic Robert Louis Stevenson novel of piracy and buried treasure. This lavish production was one of MGM's biggest hits of the year. It was filmed in 1918 by Fox with Francis Carpenter (Jim Hawkins) and Violet Rdcliffe (Long John Wilver). Previously filmed in 1920 by Paramount with Lon Chaney as Long John Silver and Shirley Mason as Jim. Remade in 1950 as a British production for Walt Disney studios, again in Great Britain in 1971, and the most recent being a 1990 adaptation by Turner Entertainment for TV. The '34 version was computer-colored by Turner Entertainment in 1989.

4901. The Trespasser (United Artists; 1929). *Cast:* Gloria Swanson (A.A.N. for B.A., 1929–30 in her talkie debut), Robert Ames, William Holden, Kay Hammond, Blanche Frederici, Purnell Pratt, Wally Albright, Henry Armetta, Stuart Erwin, Mary Forbes, Henry B. Walthall, Marcelle Corday. *D:* Edmund Goulding; *P:* Gloria Swanson; *Sc:* Laura Hope Crews, Swanson, Goulding.

Tear-jerker of a marriage broken up by the husband's wealthy father, leaving the wife to care for their child alone. Remade as *That Certain Woman* (q.v.).

4902. The Trial of Mary Dugan (MGM; 1929). *Cast:* Norma Shearer (talkie debut), Raymond Hackett (repeating his stage role), H.B. Warner, Lewis Stone, Lilyan Tashman, Olive Tell, Claud Allister, Mary Doran, Adrienne D'Ambricourt, DeWitt Jennings, Landers Stevens, Myra Hampton, Wilfred North, Charles Moore, Westcott Clarke. *D:* Bayard Veiller; *Sc:* Veiller, Becky Gardiner. (2:00)

Courtroom drama of a woman on trial for murder. Based on the play by Bayard Veiller, it was remade by this studio in 1940.

The Trial of Portia Merriman (G.B. title) *see* **Portia on Trial**

4903. The Trial of Vivienne Ware (Fox; 1932). *Cast:* Joan Bennett, Donald Cook, Lillian Bond, Richard "Skeets" Gallagher, Jameson Thomas, Noel Madison, ZaSu Pitts, Nora Lane, Maude Eburne, Herbert Mundin, Christian Rub (film debut), William Pawley, Ruth Selwyn, Ward Bond, Edward Dillon, Bert Hanlon, Howard Phillips, Mary Gordon, John Maurice Sullivan. *D:* William K. Howard; *St:* Kenneth M. Ellis.

Romantic melodrama.

4904. Trick for Trick (Fox; 1933). *Cast:* Ralph Morgan, Sally Blane, Victor Jory, Edward Van Sloan, Willard Robertson, Luis Alberni, Tom Dugan, Adrian Morris, James Burtis, John George. *D:* Hamilton MacFadden; *St:* Vivian Crosby, Harry Wagstaff Gribble, Shirley Warde.

Low-budget production.

4905. Trigger Fingers (Victory; 1939). *Cast:* Tim McCoy, Jill Martin, Joyce Bryant, Ben Corbett, Kenne Duncan, John Elliott, Ralph Peters, Forrest Taylor, Bud McTaggart, Ted Adams, Carl Mathews, Carleton Young. *D:* Sam Newfield; *P:* Sam Katzman; *Sc:* Basil Dickey. (1:00)

Tim McCoy western of a lawman donning a disguise.

4906. Trigger Pals (Grand National/Cinemart; 1939). *Cast:* Art Jarrett, Lee Powell, Al St. John, Dorothy Fay, Ted Adams, Nina Guilbert, Ernie Adams, Charles King, Stanley Blystone, Earl Douglas, Frank LaRue, Ethan Allen. *D:* Sam Newfield; *P:* Phil Krasne; *St:* George Plympton, Ted Richmond; *Sc:* Plympton. (0:56) (video)

A solo attempt to establish 1930s crooner Art Jarrett as a singing cowboy.

4907. Trigger Smith (Monogram; 1939). *Cast:* Jack Randall, Joyce Bryant, Frank Yaconelli, Forrest Taylor, Dennis Moore, Dave O'Brien, Sherry Tansey, Ed Cassidy, Jim Corey, Reed Howes, Warner Richmond, Milton Kibbee. *D:* Alan James (aka: Alvin J. Neitz); *P:* Robert Tansey; *Sc:* Robert Emmett (Tansey). (0:51)

Jack Randall western of a drifting cowboy who goes after those responsible for the murder of his brother.

4908. Trigger Tom (Reliable; 1935). *Cast:* Tom Tyler, Al St. John, Bernadene Hayes, William Gould, John Elliott, Jack Evans, Wally Wales (Hal Taliaferro), Bud Osborne, Lloyd Ingraham. *D:* Henri Samuels (Harry S. Webb); *P:* Bernard B. Ray; *Sc:* Tom Gibson. (0:57)

Tom Tyler oater of a cattle buyer who gets involved with an outlaw gang.

4909. Trigger Tricks (Universal; 1930). *Cast:* Hoot Gibson, Sally Eilers (later Mrs. Hoot Gibson), Robert Homans, Jack Richardson, Neal Hart, Monte Montague, Walter Perry, Max Asher. *D:* B. Reeves Eason; *Sc:* Eason. (1:00)

Hoot Gibson western of a range war.

4910. Trigger Trio (Republic; 1937). *Cast:* Ray Corrigan (Tucson Smith), Max Terhune (Lullaby Joslin), Ralph Byrd (Larry Brooke temporarily replacing Bob Livingston as "Stony" who was recuperating from injuries),

Sandra Corday, Hal Taliaferro (aka: Wally Wales), Robert Warwick, Cornelius Keefe, Sammy McKim, Willie Fung, Jack Ingram. *D:* William Witney (feature directorial debut); *Sc:* Joseph Poland, Oliver Drake. (1:00)

"Three Mesquiteers" (#10) western of a rancher who murders a range inspector to keep him from finding that the rancher's herd is diseased.

4911. A Trip to Paris (20th Century-Fox; 1938). *Cast:* Jed Prouty, Spring Byington, Florence Roberts, June Carlson, Russell Gleason, Kenneth Howell, George Ernest, Billy Mahan, Harold Huber, Leonid Kinskey, Shirley Deane, Clay Clement, Armand Kaliz, Joan Valerie, Nedda Harrigan, Marvin Stephens. *D:* Mal St. Clair; *Sc:* Robert Ellis, Helen Logan.

The 9th entry in the "Jones Family" B comedy series.

Triple Trouble (G.B. title) *see* **Kentucky Kernals**

4912. Troopers Three (Tiffany; 1930). *Cast:* Rex Lease, Dorothy Gulliver, Roscoe Karns, Slim Summerville, Tom London, Joseph Girard, Walter Perry. *D:* Norman Taurog, B. Reeves Eason; *Sc:* Arthur Guy Empey.

"Poverty row" comic actioner.

4913. Tropic Fury (Universal; 1939). *Cast:* Richard Arlen, Andy Devine, Beverly Roberts, Milburn Stone, Samuel S. Hinds, Lupita Tovar, Charles Trowbridge, Adia Kuznetzoff, Leonard Mudie, Noble Johnson, Louis Merrill, Frank Mitchell. *D:* Christy Cabanne; *P:* Ben Pivar; *St:* Pivar, Maurice Tombragel; *Sc:* Michael Simmons. (1:02)

B actioner with South American locales and much stock footage.

4914. Tropic Holiday (Paramount; 1938). *Cast:* Dorothy Lamour, Ray Milland, Martha Raye, "Bazooka" Bob Burns, Tito Guizar, Fortunio Bo-

nanova, Michael Visaroff, Frank Puglia, Pepito, Robert Maya, Dominguez Brothers, Roberto Soto, Jesus Topete, Elvira Rios. *D:* Theodore Reed; *P:* Arthur Hornblow, Jr.; *Sc:* Don Hartman, Frank Butler, John C. Moffett, Duke Attebury; *Music:* (A.A.N.) Boris Morros. (1:18)

A romantic musical set in Mexico.

4915. Trouble at Midnight (Universal; 1938). *Cast:* Noah Beery, Jr., Catherine (Kay) Hughes, Larry Blake, Bernadene Hayes, Louis Mason, Charles Halton, Earl Dwire, Frank Melton, George Humbert, Harlan Briggs, Edward Hearn, Henry Hunter, Virginia Sale, Harry C. Bradley. *D:* Ford Beebe; *P:* Barney A. Sarecky; *Sc:* Beebe, Maurice Geraghty. (1:08)

B melodrama of modern day cattle rustlers with trucks who set their sights on the bovine residents of a dairy farm.

4916. Trouble Buster (Majestic; 1933). *Cast:* Jack Hoxie, Roger Williams. *D:* Lewis D. Collins; *P:* Max & Arthur Alexander; *Sc:* Oliver Drake. (0:55)

Jack Hoxie "poverty row" western of a cowboy who helps a girl about to be cheated out of her land. Hoxie who was popular in a series of silent westerns was done in by his talkie efforts.

4917. Trouble for Two (MGM; 1936). *Cast:* Robert Montgomery, Rosalind Russell, Frank Morgan, Reginald Owen, Louis Hayward, E.E. Clive, Walter Kingsford, Ivan Simpson, Tom Moore, Robert Greig, Pedro de Cordoba, Leyland Hodgson, Guy Bates Post, David Jack Holt, Virginia Weidler. *D:* J. Walter Ruben; *P:* Louis D. Lighton; *Sc:* Manuel Seff, Edward E. Paramore, Jr. (G.B. title: *The Suicide Club*) (1:15)

A "black" comedy of two people in London who get involved with a "suicide club." Based on the story "The Suicide Club" by Robert Louis Stevenson. Filmed before in 1909 by D.W. Griffith as *The Suicide Club* (a non feature).

4918. Trouble in Morocco (Columbia; 1937). *Cast:* Jack Holt, Mae Clarke, Victor Varconi, Harold Huber, Paul Hurst, Bradley Page, Oscar Apfel, C. Henry Gordon. *D:* Ernest B. Schoedsack; *St:* J.D. Newsom; *Sc:* Paul Franklin.

Melodramatic B actioner.

Trouble in Panama (G.B. title) *see* **Torchy Blane in Panama**

4919. Trouble in Paradise (Paramount; 1932). *Cast:* Herbert Marshall (Gaston Monescu — LaValle), Miriam Hopkins (Lily Vautier), Kay Francis (Mariette Colet), Charles Ruggles (The Major), Edward Everett Horton (Francois Filiba), C. Aubrey Smith (Adolph Giron), Robert Greig (Jacques the butler), Nella Walker (Madame Bouchet), George Humbert, Rolfe Sedan, Leonid Kinskey (film debut), Luis Alberni, Hooper Atchley, Perry Ivins, Tyler Brooke, Larry Steers. *D:* Ernst Lubitsch; *P:* Lubitsch; *Adaptation:* Grover Jones; *Sc:* Samson Raphaelson; *Songs:* "Colet and Company" & title song by W. Franke Harling & Leo Robin. (1:23)

Classic sophisticated comedy with "the Lubitsch touch" of a pair of jewel thieves who pose as aristocracy so they can fleece the wealthy — then the man falls for one of his female victims. Based on the play "The Honest Finder" by Laszlo Aladar, the film was voted one of the year's "10 Best" by the National Board of Review. It also placed #2 on the "10 Best" list of the *New York Times.*

4920. Trouble in Sundown (RKO; 1939). *Cast:* George O'Brien, Rosalind Keith, Chill Wills, Howard Hickman, Ray Whitley, Ward Bond, Cyrus Kendall, Monte Montague, John Dilson, Otto Yamaoka. *D:* David Howard; *P:* Bert Gilroy; *St:* Charles Francis Royal; *Sc:* Oliver Drake, Dorrell & Stuart McGowan. (1:00)

George O'Brien western involving a search for some bank robbers.

4921. Trouble in Texas (Grand National; 1937). *Cast:* Tex Ritter, Rita (Hayworth) Cansino, Horace Murphy, Earl Dwire, Charles King, Yakima Canutt, Dick Palmer, Hal Price, Fred Parker, Tom Cooper, Milburn Morante, Jack C. Smith, George Morrell, Shorty Miller, Rudy Sooter, Chick Hannon, Glenn Strange, Oral Zumalt, Bob Crosby, Foxy Callahan, Harry Knight, Tex Sherman, Tex Ritter's Texas Tornadoes, White Flash the horse. *D:* Robert N. Bradbury; *P:* Edward Finney (Boots & Saddles Productions); *Sc:* Robert Emmett (Tansey). (0:53) (video)

Tex Ritter western with musical interludes and a rodeo setting.

4922/4923. Trouble Wagon (Xxxx Xxxx; 1938). *Sc:* Borden Chase. (No other information available)

4924. True Confession (Paramount; 1937). *Cast:* Carole Lombard, Fred MacMurray, John Barrymore, Una Merkel, Porter Hall, Edgar Kennedy, Lynne Overman, Fritz Feld, Irving Bacon, Hattie McDaniel, Byron Foulger, Tom Dugan, Garry Owen, Toby Wing, Richard Carle, John T. Murray, Bernard Suss. *D:* Wesley Ruggles; *P:* Albert Lewin; *Sc:* Claude Binyon. (1:25)

Hit comedy of the problems that arise when a girl confesses to a murder she didn't commit. Based on the play "Mon Crime" by Louis Verneuil and Georges Berr, it was remade in 1945 as *Cross My Heart.*

4925. True to the Navy (Paramount; 1930). *Cast:* Clara Bow, Fredric March, Harry Green, Rex Bell, Sam Hardy, Eddie Fetherston, Jed Prouty, Ray Cooke, Harry Sweet, Eddie Dunn, Adele Windsor. *D:* Frank Tuttle; *Sc:* Keene Thompson, Doris Anderson; *Dialogue:* Herman J. Mankiewicz. (1:11)

A low-budget romantic affair between a sailor and a soda fountain girl.

4926. The Trumpet Blows (Paramount; 1934). *Cast:* George Raft, Adolphe Menjou (dual role), Frances Drake, Sidney Toler, Francis McDonald, Katherine de Mille, Nydia Westman, Joyce Compton, Edward Ellis, Douglas Wood, Lillian Elliott, Morgan Wallace, Gertrude Norman, Hooper Atchley, Alan Bridge, Aleth "Speed" Hanson, Howard Brooks, E. Alyn Warren, Charles Stevens, Mischa Auer. *D:* Stephen Roberts; *Sc:* Bartlett Cormack, Wallace Smith, J. Parker Read, Jr.; *Songs:* Ralph Rainger, Leo Robin. (G.B. title: *The Trumpet Calls*) (1:12)

Melodrama of a bullfighter and his lawless twin brother.

The Trumpet Calls (G.B. title) *see* **The Trumpet Blows**

The Trunk Mystery (G.B. title) *see* **One New York Night**

Trust Your Wife (G.B. title) *see* **The Fall Guy**

4927. The Trusted Outlaw (Republic-Supreme; 1937). *Cast:* Bob Steele, Lois January, Joan Barclay, Charles King, Earl Dwire, Hal Price, Budd Buster, Richard Cramer, Frank Ball, George Morrell, Oscar Gahan, Chick Hannon, Sherry Tansey, Clyde McClary. *D:* Robert N. Bradbury; *P:* A.W. Hackel; *Sc:* George Plympton, Fred Myton. (1:00)

Bob Steele western of the only surviving member of a family of outlaws who has trouble keeping on the side of law and order when he makes the decision to change.

4928. The Truth About Youth (WB/F.N.; 1930). *Cast:* Loretta Young, David Manners, Conway Tearle, Myrna Loy, J. Farrell MacDonald, Harry Stubbs, Myrtle Stedman, Dorothy Mathews, Ray Hallor. *D:* William A. Seiter; *Sc:* W. Harrison Orkow.

Romantic drama of a young woman who is married to an older man. Based on the play "When We Were Twenty-One" by Henry V. Osmond.

4929. Tugboat Annie (MGM; 1933). *Cast:* Marie Dressler (Annie Brennan), Wallace Beery (Terry Brennan), Robert Young (Alec Brennan, the man), Maureen O'Sullivan (Pat Severn), Willard Robertson (Red Severn), Tammany Young (Shif'less), Frankie Darro (Alec Brennan, the youth), Paul Hurst (Sam), Jack Pennick (Pete), Oscar Apfel (Reynolds), Robert McWade (mayor of Secoma), Willie Fung (Chow, the cook), Guy Usher (auctioneer), Robert Barrat (first mate), Vince Barnett (cabby), Robert E. Homans, Hal Price, Christian Rub, Major Sam Harris. *D:* Mervyn LeRoy; *As.P.:* Harry Rapf; *Adaptation:* Zelda Sears, Eve Greene; *Additional Dialogue:* Norman Reilly Raine. (1:28)

A box office phenomenon was this comedy-drama of a salty old female tugboat captain, her boozing husband and their son. Marie Dressler and Wallace Beery were top box office draws for the studio in the early 1930s, proven by the fact that this feature became one of the 11 top grossing films of 1933. Based on the *Saturday Evening Post* stories by Norman Reilly Raine, this was followed in 1940 by *Tugboat Annie Sails Again* (W.B.) and *Captain Tugboat Annie* (Republic; 1945). The year 1958 saw the beginning of a TV series with Minerva Urecal and Walter Sande.

4930. Tugboat Princess (Columbia; 1936). *Cast:* Walter C. Kelly, Valerie Hobson, Edith Fellows, Lester Matthews, Clyde Cook. *D:* David Selman; *St:* Dalton Trumbo, Isador Bernstein; *Sc:* Robert Watson.

B comedy-drama.

4931. Tumblin' Tumbleweeds (Republic; 1935). *Cast:* Gene Autry,

Smiley Burnette, Lucille Browne, George Hayes, Norma Taylor, Edward Hearn, Jack Rockwell, George Chesebro, Frankie Marvin, Tom London, Charles "Slim" Whitaker, Cornelius Keefe, Cliff Lyons, Tracy Layne, Charles King. *D:* Joseph Kane (feature directorial debut); *P:* Nat Levine; *St:* Alan Ludwig; *Sc:* Ford Beebe. (0:57) or (1:01)

Gene Autry western of a medicine show singer who returns home to find the killer of his father. This is the film which started the "singing cowboy" trend in the series B westerns in the late 1930s, and was the starring feature debut of Autry. Of the songs within this film, Gene sings the sentimental "That Silver Haired Daddy of Mine" which gave him a gold record (the first ever, given to a recording star). The title song "Tumblin' Tumbleweeds" (written by Robert W. [Bob] Nolan) became a huge hit for the Sons of the Pioneers throughout the country. Another song, "Ridin' Down the Canyon" (written by Autry and Smiley Burnette) was also introduced in this film and became a nationwide hit and a popular favorite of western singers of the day. This was also the first feature film to be released by the Newly formed Republic Pictures (following a merger of Mascot and Monogram). Remade with Autry in 1940 as *Carolina Moon.*

4932. Turn Back the Clock (MGM; 1933). *Cast:* Lee Tracy, Mae Clarke, Otto Kruger, Peggy Shannon, C. Henry Gordon, George Barbier, Ted Healy & His Stooges, Clara Blandick. *D:* Edgar Selwyn; *St & Sc:* Selwyn, Ben Hecht. (1:17)

Low-budget comedy-drama with an interesting premise, of a man struck by a car who perceives his life differently than it really was while under the influence of ether.

4933. Turn Off the Moon (Paramount; 1937). *Cast:* Charles Ruggles, Kenny Baker, Eleanore Whitney, Johnny Downs, Marjorie Gateson, Richard Cramer, Ben Blue, Eddie Foy, Jr., Andrew Tombes, Franklin Pangborn, Grady Sutton, Romo Vincent, Charles Williams, Pat West, Terry Ray (Ellen Drew), Constance Bergen. *D:* Lewis Seiler; *P:* Fanchon Royer; *St:* Mildred Harrington; *Sc:* Marguerite Roberts, Paul Gerard Smith, Harlan Ware.

B musical-comedy of various romances which are further complicated by astrological influences.

4934. Twelve Crowded Hours (RKO; 1939). *Cast:* Richard Dix, Lucille Ball, Allan Lane, Donald MacBride, Cyrus W. Kendall, John Arledge, Granville Bates, Bradley Page, Dorothy Lee, Addison Richards, Murray Alper, John Gallaudet, Joseph de Stephani, Edmund Cobb. *D:* Lew Landers; *P:* Robert Sisk; *St:* Garrett Fort, Peter Ruric; *Sc:* John Twist. (1:04)

B melodrama of a reporter who in one night investigates a multiple murder and busts the local numbers racket.

4935. Twentieth Century (Columbia; 1934). *Cast:* John Barrymore (Oscar Jaffe), Carole Lombard (Lilly Garland—Mildred Plotka), Roscoe Karns (Owen O'Malley), Walter Connolly (Oliver Webb), Ralph Forbes (George Smith), Dale Fuller (Sadie), Etienne Girardot (Matthew J. Clark), Billie Seward (Anita), James P. Burtis (train conductor), Charles (Lane) Levison (Max Jacobs—Mandelbaum), Mary Jo Mathews (Emmy Lou), Edward Gargan (sheriff), Edgar Kennedy (McGonigle), Gigi Parrish (Schultz), Pat Flaherty (Flannigan), Herman Bing (first beard), Lee Kohlmar (second beard), Cliff Thompson (Lockwood), Howard Hickman (Dr. Johnson), George Reed (Uncle Remus), Fred Kelsey, Ky Robinson, Nick Copeland, Arnold Gray, James Burke, Anita Brown, Irene Thompson, Buddy Williams, Clarence Geldert, Lillian West, Fred "Snowflake" Toones, Gaylord (Steve) Pendleton, George Offerman,

Jr., Frank Marlowe, Lynton Brent, Harry Semels, King Mojave. *D:* Howard Hawks; *P:* Hawks; *Sc:* Ben Hecht, Charles MacArthur. (1:31) (video)

Classic screwball-type comedy of a Broadway producer who will do anything he has to in order to win back his star actress who has walked out on him and boarded the Twentieth Century. Based on the play by Ben Hecht and Charles MacArthur which they adapted from the play "Napoleon of Broadway" by Charles Bruce Millholland. A later adaptation became the Broadway musical "On the Twentieth Century." Remade as *Streamline Express* (q.v.).

4936. $20 a Week (Xxxx Xxxx; 1935). *Cast:* James Murray, Pauline Starke (final film — ret.), Dorothy Revier, William Worthington. *D:* Xxxx Xxxx; *St:* Edgar Franklin. (G.B. title: *The Man Maker*)

A low-budget comedy previously filmed in 1924 by director Harmon Weight with Ronald Colman.

4937. Twenty-Four Hours (Paramount; 1931). *Cast:* Clive Brook, Kay Francis, Miriam Hopkins, Regis Toomey, Charlotte Granville, George Barbier, Adrienne Ames (film debut), Minor Watson, Lucille La Verne, Thomas Jackson, Charles D. Brown, Wade Boteler, Robert Kortman, Malcolm Waite. *D:* Marion Gering; *Sc:* Louis Weitzenkorn. (G.B. title: *The House Between*)

Marital drama of an adulterous wife and her equally adulterous and alcoholic husband. Based on the novel by Louis Bromfield.

4938. Twenty Grand (Xxxx Xxxx; 1931). *Cast:* Russell Hopton. (No other information available)

4939. Twenty Million Sweetheart (WB/F.N.; 1934). *Cast:* Dick Powell, Ginger Rogers, Pat O'Brien, Four Mills Brothers, Allen Jenkins, Grant Mitchell, Ted Fio Rito & His Band, Radio Rogues, Henry O'Neill, Joseph Cawthorn, Charles Halton, Johnny Arthur, Joan Wheeler. *D:* Ray Enright; *P:* Samuel Bischoff; *St:* Paul Finder Moss, Jerry Wald; *Sc:* Warren Duff, Harry Sauber; *Songs:* "Fair and Warmer," "What Are Your Intentions" & "I'll String Along with You" by Al Dubin & Harry Warren. (1:29)

A romantic musical of a radio singer which was remade as *My Dream Is Yours* (WB; 1949).

4940. 20,000 Men a Year (20th Century–Fox; 1939). *Cast:* Randolph Scott, Preston Foster, Kane Richmond, Mary Healy, Paul Stanton, Sidney Miller, Harry Tyler, George Ernest, Jane Darwell, Maxie Rosenbloom, Tom Seidel, Douglas Wood, Robert Shaw, Sen Yung, Edwin Stanley. *D:* Alfred E. Green; *P:* Sol M. Wurtzel; *St:* Frank Wead; *Sc:* Lou Breslow, Owen Francis.

Low-budget drama with a military setting.

4941. 20,000 Years in Sing Sing (WB/F.N.; 1932–33). *Cast:* Spencer Tracy, Bette Davis, Arthur Byron, Lyle Talbot, Warren Hymer, Louis Calhern, Sheila Terry, Grant Mitchell, Edward J. McNamara, Roscoe Karns, Nella Walker, Harold Huber, Arthur Hoyt, Walter Byron, George Pat Collins, William LeMaire. *D:* Michael Curtiz; *P:* Robert Lord; *Supervisor:* Ray Griffith; *Adaptation:* Courtenay Terrett, Lord; *Sc:* Wilson Mizner, Brown Holmes. (1:18)

Prison based crime melodrama based on the book by Lewis E. Lawes, a prison warden. Remade as *Castle on the Hudson* (q.v.).

4942. 23½ Hours Leave (Grand National; 1937). *Cast:* James Ellison, Terry Walker, Morgan Hill, Arthur Lake, Paul Harvey, Wally Maher, Andy Andrews, Murray Alper, Pat Gleason, John Kelly, Ward Bond, Russell Hicks. *D:* John G. Blystone; *P:*

Douglas MacLean; *Sc:* Harry Ruskin, Henry McCarty. (1:12)

World War I army comedy, based on a story by Mary Roberts Rinehart, previously filmed in 1919 by Paramount with Douglas MacLean and Doris May.

Note: Rinehart's story originally appeared in the *Saturday Evening Post.*

4943. Twin Beds (WB/F.N.; 1929). *Cast:* Patsy Ruth Miller, Jack Mulhall, Armand Kaliz, Edythe Chapman, ZaSu Pitts, Alice Lake, Bert Roach, Gertrude Astor, Ben Hendricks, Jr., Nita Martan, Knute Erickson, Eddie Gribbon, Jocelyn Lee, Carl Levinus. *D:* Alfred Santell; *Sc:* F. McGrew Willis.

Comedy with a show biz setting, based on a play by Margaret Mayo and Salisbury Field. Previously filmed by First National in 1920 with Carter DeHaven and Flora Parker (Mrs. DeHaven).

4944. Twin Husbands (Chesterfield; 1934). *Cast:* John Miljan, Robert Elliott, Shirley Grey, Monroe Owsley, Hale Hamilton. *D:* Frank Strayer; *Sc:* Anthony Coldeway, Robert Ellis.

(No other information available)

4945. Twisted Rails (Xxxx Xxxx; 1933). *Cast:* Ellen Corby (film debut).

(No other information available)

4946. Two Against the World (WB; 1932). *Cast:* Constance Bennett, Neil Hamilton, Gavin Gordon, Allen Vincent, Helen Vinson, Alan Mowbray, Oscar Apfel, Roscoe Karns, Leila Bennett, Maude Truax, Bud Flanagan (Dennis O'Keefe). *D:* Archie Mayo; *Sc:* Sheridan Gibney.

A romance develops between an attorney and a woman accused of murder in this B drama. Based on a play by Marion Dix and Jerry Horwin.

4947. Two Against the World (WB/F.N.; 1936). *Cast:* Humphrey Bogart, Beverly Roberts, Linda Perry, Carlisle (Carlyle) Moore, Henry O'Neill, Helen McKellar, Claire Dodd, Hobart Cavanaugh, Harry Hayden, Robert Middlemass, Clay Clement, Douglas Wood, Virginia Brissac, Paula Stone, Bobby Gordon, Frank Orth, Howard Hickman, Ferdinand Schumann-Heink. *D:* William McGann; *P:* Bryan Foy; *Sc:* Michel Jacoby. (Retitled: *One Fatal Hour*) (G.B. title: *The Case of Mrs. Pembroke*) (1:04)

The digging up of an old murder story has tragic repercussions in this B melodrama. A remake of *Five Star Final* (q.v.), it was based on the play of that name by Louis Weitzenkorn.

4948. Two Alone (RKO; 1934). *Cast:* Jean Parker, Tom Brown, ZaSu Pitts, Arthur Byron, Beulah Bondi, Nydia Westman, Willard Robertson, Charley Grapewin, Emerson Treacy, Paul Nicholson. *D:* Elliott Nugent; *As.P.:* David Lewis; *Sc:* Josephine Lovett, Joseph Moncure March. (1:17)

Low-budget rural romantic drama of a mistreated hired girl who finds brief happiness with a young reformatory fugitive. Based on the play "Wild Birds" by Dan Totheroh.

4949. Two Bright Boys (Universal; 1939). *Cast:* Freddie Bartholomew, Jackie Cooper, Alan Dinehart, Melville Cooper, Dorothy Peterson, J.M. Kerrigan, Willard Robertson, Eddie Acuff, Eddy Waller. *D:* Joseph Santley; *P:* Burt Kelly; *St:* Val Burton, Edmund L. Hartmann; *Sc:* Burton, Hartmann. (1:05)

A youth inherits a choice piece of land and finds a wealthy oil man is out to get it from him in this B.

4950. Two-Fisted (Paramount; 1935). *Cast:* Lee Tracy, Grace Bradley, Kent Taylor, Gail Patrick, Roscoe Karns, Gordon Westcott (final film — d. 1935), Samuel S. Hinds, Akim Tamiroff, Florence Lake, Billy Lee, G.P. Huntley, Jr. *D:* James Cruze; *P:* Harold Hurley; *St:* Richard Taber, James Gleason.

B comedy farce of a boxer and his manager who takes jobs in the home of a millionaire as domestics. A remake of *Is Zat So?* (Fox; 1927) with George O'Brien, Douglas Fairbanks, Jr., and Edmund Lowe.

4951. Two-Fisted Gentleman (Columbia; 1936). *Cast:* James Dunn, June Clayworth, Thurston Hall, Paul Guilfoyle, Gene Morgan, Harry Tyler, George McKay. *D:* Gordon Wiles; *Sc:* Tom Van Dycke.

B comedy.

4952. Two-Fisted Justice (Monogram; 1931). *Cast:* Tom Tyler, Barbara Weeks, Bobby Nelson, Yakima Canutt, John Elliott, Kit Guard, G.D. Wood (Gordon DeMain), William Walling, Pedro Regas, Carl DeLoue, Joe Mills, Si Jenks. *D:* George Arthur Durlam; *St & Sc:* Durlam. (1:03)

Tom Tyler shoot-'em-up of a cowboy who brings an outlaw gang to justice.

4953. Two-Fisted Law (Columbia; 1932). *Cast:* Tim McCoy, Alice Day, Wheeler Oakman, Wallace MacDonald, John Wayne, Tully Marshall, Richard Alexander, Walter Brennan. *D:* D. Ross Lederman; *Sc:* Kurt Kempler. (1:04)

Tim McCoy western outing of a man cheated of his ranch who discovers gold and is determined to prevent the cheat from doing the same to a female rancher.

4954. Two-Fisted Sheriff (Columbia; 1937). *Cast:* Charles Starrett, Barbara Weeks, Bruce Lane, Ed Peil, Sr., Allan Sears, Ernie Adams, Walter Downing, Claire McDowell, Frank Ellis, George Chesebro, Robert Walker, Alan Bridge, Art Mix, Richard Botiller, George Morrell, Merrill McCormack, Edmund Cobb, Richard Cramer, Tex Cooper, Richard Alexander, Maston Williams, Ethan Laidlaw, Steve Clark, Fred Burns, Wally West. *D:* Leon Barsha; *Sc:* Paul Perez. (1:00)

Charles Starrett western of a sheriff who goes up against a crazed killer.

4955. Two for Tonight (Paramount; 1935). *Cast:* Bing Crosby, Joan Bennett, Mary Boland, Lynne Overman, Thelma Todd, James Blakeley, Douglas Fowley, Maurice Cass (film debut), Charles Arnt, Charles (Lane) Levison, Arthur Housman, John Gough, A.S. Byron. *D:* Frank Tuttle; *P:* Douglas MacLean; *Sc:* Jane Storm, George Marion, Jr. (1:01)

B musical-comedy of a songwriter with a deadline to complete a musical play. The score includes the song "Without a Word of Warning" which became a hit.

4956. Two-Gun Caballero (Imperial; 1931). *Cast:* Robert Frazer, Bobby Nelson, Al Ferguson. *D:* Jack Nelson; *Sc:* Nelson.

(No other information available)

4957. Two-Gun Justice (Monogram-Concord; 1938). *Cast:* Tim McCoy, Betty Compson, John Merton, Joan Barclay, Lane Chandler, Al Bridge, Tony Paton, Allan Cavan, Harry Strang, Earl Dwire, Olin Francis, Enid Parrish, Curley Dresden, Jack Ingram. *D:* Alan James (aka: Alvin J. Neitz); *P:* Maurice Conn; *St & Sc:* Fred Myton. (0:58)

Tim McCoy western of an ex-ranger assigned to go after some cattle rustlers.

4958. Two-Gun Law (Columbia; 1937). *Cast:* Charles Starrett, Peggy Stratford, Hank Bell, Edward J. LeSaint, Alan Bridge, Charles Middleton, Lee Prather, Dick Curtis, Art Mix, Victor Potel, George Chesebro, George Morrell, Tex Cooper. *D:* Leon Barsha; *Sc:* John Rathmell. (0:56)

Charles Starrett western of two men who overhear a conspiracy to rustle some cattle from the ranch they are trying to get jobs on. Re-released theatrically by the studio in 1987, the film has never been seen on TV.

4959. The Two-Gun Man (Tiffany; 1931). *Cast:* Ken Maynard, Lucille Powers, Nita Martin, Charles King, Lafe McKee, Tom London, Murdock MacQuarrie, Walter Perry, Will Stanton, William Jackie, Ethan Allen, Blackjack Ward, Jim Corey, Roy Bucko, Buck Bucko. *D:* Phil Rosen; *P:* Phil Goldstone (Amity); *Sc:* John (Jack) Natteford. (1:00) (video)

Ken Maynard shoot-'em-up of a cowboy who uncovers a plot to rustle cattle.

4960. Two-Gun Man from Harlem (Associated Features; 1938). *Cast:* Herb Jeffreys, Mantan Moreland. *D:* Richard C. Kahn; *P:* Jed Buell.

Novelty B western with an all black cast.

4961. Two-Gun Troubadour (Spectrum; 1939). *Cast:* Fred Scott, Claire Rochelle, Harry Harvey, John Merton, Buddy Lenhart, Carl Mathews, Harry Harvey, Jr., Gene Howard, Buddy Kelly, William Woods, Jack Ingram, Bud Osborne, John Ward, Cactus Mack. *D:* Raymond K. Johnson; *P:* C.C. Burr; *Sc:* Richard L. Bare, Phil Dunham. (0:58)

Fred Scott western with songs of a man's return to avenge the death of his father by his uncle.

4962. Two Heads on a Pillow (Liberty; 1934). *Cast:* Miriam Jordan (final film — ret.), Hardie Albright, Lona Andre, Mary Forbes, Claudia Dell, Betty Blythe, Henry Armetta. *D:* William Nigh; *P:* M.H. Hoffman, Jr.

Indie romantic comedy.

4963. Two in a Crowd (Universal; 1936). *Cast:* Joan Bennett, Joel McCrea, Alison Skipworth, Henry Armetta, Nat Pendleton, Reginald Denny, Andy Clyde, Donald Meek, Elisha Cook, Jr., John Hamilton, Eddie Anderson, Milburn Stone, Joe Sawyer, Paul Fix, Billy Burrud, Tyler Brooke, Jean Rogers, Matt McHugh, Bob Murphy, Bradley Page. *D:* Alfred E. Green;

P: Charles R. Rogers; *St:* Lewis R. Foster; *Sc:* Foster, Doris Malloy, Earle Snell. (1:22)

Romantic comedy of two people who each find one half of a $1000 bill on New Year's Eve.

Two in a Million (G.B. title) *see* **East of Fifth Avenue**

4964. Two in Revolt (RKO; 1936). *Cast:* John Arledge, Louise Latimer, Moroni Olsen, Warrior the horse, Lightning the dog, Harry Jans, Willie Best, Murray Alper, Ethan Laidlaw, Emmett Vogan, Max Wagner. *D:* Glenn Tryon; *As.P.:* Robert Sisk; *St:* Earl Johnson, Thomas Storey; *Sc:* Ferdinand Reyher, Frank Howard Clark, Jerry Hutchinson. (1:05)

Offbeat programmer of the friendship between a race horse and a police dog and a human romance between a horse trainer and the stable owner's daughter.

4965. Two in the Dark (RKO; 1936). *Cast:* Walter Abel, Margot Grahame, Wallace Ford, Gail Patrick, Alan Hale, Leslie Fenton, Eric Blore, Erin O'Brien-Moore, Erik Rhodes, J. Carrol Naish, Addison (Jack) Randall, Moroni Olsen, Ward Bond. *D:* Ben Stoloff; *As.P.:* Zion Myers; *Sc:* Seton I. Miller. (1:14)

B mystery of an amnesiac in search of his identity and the solution to a murder he thinks he may have committed. Remade as *Two O'Clock Courage* (RKO; 1945) and based on the novel of that name by Gelett Burgess.

4966. Two Kinds of Women (Paramount; 1931–32). *Cast:* Miriam Hopkins, Phillips Holmes, Wynne Gibson, Vivienne Osborne, Irving Pichel, Claire Dodd, Stuart Erwin, Adrienne Ames, Josephine Dunn, Kent Taylor, Stanley Fields, James Crane, Larry Steers, Terrance Ray, Edwin Maxwell, Robert Emmett O'Connor, June Nash. *D:* William C. de Mille; *Sc:* Benjamin Glazer.

In this triangular romantic drama a naive girl falls in with the wrong crowd in New York City. Based on the play "This Is New York" by Robert E. Sherwood.

4967. Two Minutes to Play (Victory; 1937). *Cast:* Edward Nugent, Jeanne Martel, Betty Compson, Berman Brix (Bruce Bennett), Grady Sutton, Duncan Renaldo, Forrest Taylor, Sam Flint. *D:* Robert F. Hill; *P:* Sam Katzman.

Independent gridiron actioner.

4968. Two Seconds (WB/F.N.; 1932). *Cast:* Edward G. Robinson, Vivienne Osborne, Guy Kibbee, Preston Foster, J. Carrol Naish, Frederick Burton, Harry Beresford, Dorothea Wolbert, Berton Churchill, William Janney, Edward McWade, Gladys Lloyd, Franklin Parker, Walter Walker, Otto Hoffman, Lew Brice, Helen Phillips, Fred Howard. *D:* Mervyn LeRoy; *Sc:* Harvey Thew. (1:08)

Offbeat melodrama of a man reliving his life in the two seconds it takes him to die in the electric chair. Based on the play by Elliott Lester, it was voted one of the year's "10 Best" films by the National Board of Review.

4969. Two Sinners (Republic; 1935). *Cast:* Otto Kruger, Martha Sleeper, Cora Sue Collins. *D:* Arthur Lubin.

B production.

Two Smart Boys (G.B. title) *see* **The Spirit of Culver**

4970. Two Thoroughbreds (RKO; 1939). *Cast:* Jimmy Lydon, Joan (Leslie) Brodel, Arthur Hohl, J.M. Kerrigan, Marjorie Main, Selmer Jackson, Spencer Charters, Paul Fix. *D:* Jack Hively; *P:* Cliff Reid; *St:* Joseph A. Fields; *Sc:* Fields, Jerry Cady. (1:00)

Programmer drama of a boy and his love for a horse.

4971. Two Weeks Off (WB/F.N.; 1929). *Cast:* Jack Mulhall, Dorothy Mackaill, Gertrude Astor, James Finlayson, Kate Price, Jed Prouty, Eddie Gribbon, Gertrude Messinger. *D:* William Beaudine; *St:* John Kenyon Nicholson, Thomas Barrows; *Sc:* F. McGrew Willis, Joseph Poland; *Song:* "Love Thrills" by Al Bryan, George W. Meyer.

Part-talkie comedy of mistaken identity.

4972. Two Wise Maids (Republic; 1937). *Cast:* Alison Skipworth, Polly Moran, Donald Cook, Hope (Irene) Manning, Lila Lee (final film—ret.), Jackie Searle, Luis Alberni, Maxie Rosenbloom, Marcia Mae Jones, Selmer Jackson. *D:* Phil Rosen.

B comedy-drama of the efforts to retire a veteran school teacher. A box office hit.

4973. Unashamed (MGM; 1932). *Cast:* Helen Twelvetrees, Robert Young, Lewis Stone, Jean Hersholt, John Miljan, Monroe Owsley, Robert Warwick, Gertrude Michael, Wilfred North, Tommy (Thomas) Jackson, Louise Beavers. *D:* Harry Beaumont; *Sc:* Bayard Veiller. (1:14)

Low-budget courtroom drama of a man who kills his sister's lover.

The Unborn (G.B. title) *see* **Tomorrow's Children**

4974. Uncertain Lady (Universal; 1934). *Cast:* Edward Everett Horton, Genevieve Tobin, Renee Gadd, George Meeker, Paul Cavanagh, Donald Reed, Arthur Hoyt, Dorothy Peterson. *D:* Karl Freund. (1:05)

Offbeat B comedy of a man who plans to leave his wife for another woman, but must find her another man for a replacement.

4975. Unconquered Bandit (Reliable; 1935). *Cast:* Tom Tyler, Lillian

Gilmore, Charles "Slim" Whitaker, William Gould, John Elliott, Earl Dwire, Joe (Jose) de la Cruz, George Chesebro, Lew Meehan, Wally Wales (Hal Taliaferro), George Hazel, Richard Alexander, Ben Corbett, Colin Chase. *D:* Harry S. Webb; *P:* Bernard B. Ray; *Sc:* Rose Gordon, Lou C. Borden. (0:57)

Tom Tyler western outing of a man out to avenge his father's murder.

Unconventional Linda (G.B. title) *see* **Holiday** (1938)

4976. Under a Texas Moon (WB; 1930). *Cast:* Frank Fay, Raquel Torres, Armida, Myrna Loy, Noah Beery, George E. Stone, Fred Kohler, Betty Boyd, Tully Marshall, Inez Gomez, Nena Quartero, George Cooper, Charles Sellon, Bruce Covington, Francisco Maran. *D:* Michael Curtiz; *St:* Stewart Edward White; *Sc:* Gordon Rigby; *Title Song:* Roy Perkins. (1:22)

Two-color technicolor romantic action adventure of a border outlaw.

4977. Under-Cover Man (Paramount; 1932). *Cast:* George Raft, Nancy Carroll, Roscoe Karns, Gregory Ratoff, Lew Cody, William Janney, George Davis, Paul Porcasi, David Landau, Leyland Hodgson. *D:* James Flood; *St:* John Wilstach. (1:10)

Low-budget melodrama of a man who is seeking the killer of his father.

4978. Under Cover Man (Republic-Supreme; 1936). *Cast:* Johnny Mack Brown, Suzanne Kaaren, Ted Adams, Frank Darien, Lloyd Ingraham, Horace Murphy, Dick Morehead, Ed Cassidy, Margaret Mann, Frank Ball, George Morrell. *D:* Albert Ray; *P:* A.W. Hackel; *Sc:* Andrew Bennison. (0:56) (video)

Johnny Mack Brown western of a Wells Fargo agent who thwarts some local villains.

4979. Under Cover of Night (MGM; 1936–37). *Cast:* Edmund Lowe, Henry Daniell, Florence Rice, Dean Jagger, Nat Pendleton, Sara Haden, Dorothy Peterson, Harry Davenport, Theodore von Eltz, Frank Reicher, Marla Shelton, Zeffie Tilbury. *D:* George B. Seitz; *P:* Lucien Hubbard; *As.P.:* Ned Marin; *Sc:* Bertram Millhauser.

B meller of a detective seeking the killer of three people at a university.

4980. Under Eighteen (WB; 1931–32). *Cast:* Marian Marsh, Warren William, Regis Toomey, Anita Page, Emma Dunn, Joyce Compton, J. Farrell MacDonald, Paul Porcasi, Judith Vosselli, Claire Dodd, Norman Foster, Maude Eburne, Murray Kinnell, Walter McGrail, Dorothy Appleby. *D:* Archie Mayo; *St:* Frank M. Dazey, Maude Fulton, Charles Kenyon; *Sc:* Fulton, Kenyon.

Drama of a poor girl who is put under pressure by a lecherous theatrical producer.

4981. Under Montana Skies (Tiffany/Amity; 1930). *Cast:* Kenneth Harlan, Dorothy Gulliver, Slim Summerville, Nita Martan, Christian Frank, Harry Todd, Ethel Wales, Lafe McKee, Charles King. *D:* Richard Thorpe; *Sc:* Bennett Cohen, James A. (Jimmy) Aubrey. (1:00)

A lawman has his hands full between a troupe of stranded showgirls and apprehending the bad guys.

4982. Under Pressure (Fox; 1935). *Cast:* Edmund Lowe, Victor McLaglen, Charles Bickford, Florence Rice, Marjorie Rambeau, Sig Rumann, George Walsh, Roger Imhof, Charles Richman, Jack Wallace, Robert T. Kane. *D:* Raoul Walsh; *Sc:* Borden Chase, Noel Pierce, Lester Cole, Philip Dunne (unc.).

Comedy-drama revolving around men who are building a tunnel. Based on an unpublished novel titled "Sand Hog" by Chase and Edward J. Doherty.

4983. The Under-Pup (Universal; 1939). *Cast:* Gloria Jean (film debut), Robert Cummings, Nan Grey, Beulah Bondi, Virginia Weidler, Margaret Lindsay, Raymond Walburn, C. Aubrey Smith, Billy Gilbert, Ann Gillis, Samuel S. Hinds, Frank Jenks, Paul Cavanagh, Cecil Kellaway, Doris Lloyd, Dickie Moore, Ernest Truex, Bill Lenhart, Shirley Mills. *D:* Richard Wallace; *P:* Joe Pasternak; *St:* I. (Ida) A.R. Wylie; *Sc:* Grover Jones. (Original running time: 1:28, now 1:21)

Low-budget musical comedy-drama of a slum girl who gets an invite to a summer camp for the daughters of the wealthy.

4984. Under Secret Orders (Progressive Pictures; 1933). *Cast:* Don Alvarado, Donald Dillaway, J. Farrell MacDonald, Lafe McKee, Matthew Betz. *D:* Sam Newfield.

Low-budget indie melodrama.

4985. Under Strange Flags (Crescent; 1937). *Cast:* Tom Keene, Lana (Luana) Walters, Budd Buster, Roy D'Arcy, Paul Sutton, Maurice Black, Paul Barrett, Donald Reed, Jane Wolfe. *D:* Irvin Willat; *P:* E.B. Derr; *Sc:* Mary Ireland. (1:01)

American silver miners in Mexico find their shipments being hijacked by the Mexican revolutionary, Pancho Villa.

4986. Under Suspicion (Fox; 1931). *Cast:* Lois Moran, George Brent (film debut), J. Harold Murray, J.M. Kerrigan. *D:* A.F. Erickson; *Sc:* Tom Barry.

4987. Under Suspicion (Columbia; 1937). *Cast:* Jack Holt, Esther Muir, Craig Reynolds, Lee Phelps, Katherine de Mille, Margaret Irving, Robert Emmett Keane, Purnell Pratt, Morgan Wallace, George Anderson, Rosalind Keith, Maurice Murphy, Clyde Dilson. *D:* Lewis D. Collins; *St:* Philip Wylie; *Sc:* Jefferson Parker, Joseph Hoffman.

B melodrama of a factory owner who is marked for murder when he decides to turn his operation over to his employees.

4988. Under Texas Skies (Syndicate; 1930). *Cast:* Bob Custer, Natalie Kingston, Bill Cody, Tom London, Lane Chandler, William McCall, Bob Roper, Joseph Marba. *D:* J.P. McGowan; *Sc:* George Arthur Durlam. (1:00)

Bob Custer western set on a woman's horse ranch.

4989. Under the Big Top (Monogram; 1938). *Cast:* Anne Nagel, Grant Richards, Jack LaRue, Marjorie Main, George Cleveland, Herbert Rawlinson, Fred "Snowflake" Toones, Rolfe Sedan, Harry Harvey, Charlene Wyatt, Speed Hansen. *D:* Karl Brown; *P:* William T. Lackey; *St:* Llewellyn Hughes; *Sc:* Marion Orth. (G.B. title: *The Circus Comes to Town*) (1:03)

B triangular romantic drama involving members of a circus trapeze act. Prior to release the film was known as "The Circus Comes to Town."

4990. Under the Pampas Moon (Fox; 1935). *Cast:* Warner Baxter, Ketti Gallian, Rita (Hayworth) Cansino, Jack LaRue, J. Carrol Naish, John Miljan, Lona Andre, Armida, Ann Codee, Chris-Pin Martin, Frank LaRue, Soledad Jiminez, Paul Porcasi, Max Wagner, Phillip Cooper, Veloz & Yolanda. *D:* James Tinling; *P:* B.G. DeSylva; *St:* Gordon Morris; *Sc:* Ernest Pascal, Bradley King; *Song Lyrics:* Paul Francis Webster. (1:18)

"Western" adventure set in the Argentine Pampas.

4991. Under the Tonto Rim (Paramount; 1933). *Cast:* Stuart Erwin, Verna Hillie, John Lodge, Fuzzy Knight, Raymond Hatton, George Barbier, Kent Taylor. *D:* Henry Hathaway; *Sc:* Jack Cunningham, Gerald Geraghty. (1:03)

B budget western based on a Zane

Grey novel of a naive cowboy who overcomes all obstacles to win the girl. A remake of the 1928 production by this studio with Richard Arlen. The title was again used in a 1947 Tim Holt western for RKO.

4992. Under Two Flags (20th Century-Fox; 1936). *Cast:* Ronald Colman, Claudette Colbert (Cigarette), Victor McLaglen, Rosalind Russell, Gregory Ratoff, J. Edward Bromberg (film debut), Nigel Bruce, Herbert Mundin, John Carradine, C. Henry Gordon, Onslow Stevens, Fritz Leiber, Francis McDonald, Frank Reicher, Marc Lawrence, Douglas Gerrard, William Ricciardi, Harry Semels, Nicholas Soussanin, Thomas Beck, Jack Pennick, Tor Johnson. *D:* Frank Lloyd; *As.P.:* Raymond Griffith; *Sc:* W.P. Lipscomb, Walter Ferris, Bess Meredyth. (Original running time – 1:51, now 1:45)

Romantic foreign legion adventure based on the novel by Ouida (Marie Louise de la Ramee). Filmed on location in the Arizona desert, the story details a man torn between two women who also becomes the victim of his envious commandant. First filmed by Fox in 1915 with a remake following in 1917 starring Theda Bara. It was followed in 1922 by a Universal production with Priscilla Dean, James Kirkwood and Stuart Holmes.

4993. Under Western Stars (Republic; 1938). *Cast:* Roy Rogers, Smiley Burnette, Carol Hughes, Tom Chatterton, Kenneth Harlan, Stephen Chase, Guy Usher, Robert Wilke, Dick Elliott, Jack Rockwell, Frankie Marvin, Maple City Four, Burr Caruth, Charles "Slim" Whitaker, Jean Fowler, Brandon Beach, Earl Dwire, Dora Clement. *D:* Joseph Kane; *P:* Sol C. Siegel; *St:* Dorrell & Stuart McGowan; *Sc:* Betty Burbridge, Dorrell & Stuart McGowan; *Songs:* "Dust" (A.A.N. for Best Song) Johnny Marvin; "Rogers for Con-

gressman" by Eddie Cherkose, Charles Rosoff; "Send My Mail to the County Jail," "When a Cowboy Sings a Song" & "Back to the Backwoods" by Jack Lawrence, Peter Tinturin. (1:05) (video)

Roy Rogers in his starring feature debut in a story of a congressman who attempts to get water to the dust bowl. This was originally scheduled by the studio as a Gene Autry feature.

4994/4995. Under Your Spell (20th Century-Fox; 1936). *Cast:* Lawrence Tibbett (final film – ret.), Wendy Barrie, Lupe Velez, Gregory Ratoff, Arthur Treacher, Claudia Coleman, Joyce Compton, Berton Churchill, Charles Richman, Gregory Gaye. *D:* Otto Preminger (American directorial debut); *St:* Sy Bartlett, Bernice Mason; *Sc:* Saul Elkins, Frances Hyland.

B musical.

4996. Undercover Agent (Monogram; 1939). *Cast:* Russell Gleason, Shirley Deane, J.M. Kerrigan, Maude Eburne, Oscar O'Shea, Selmer Jackson, Ralf Harolde, Ray Bennett, Ralph Sanford. *D:* Howard Bretherton; *P:* E.B. Derr; *St:* Martin Mooney; *Sc:* Milton Raison. (0:56)

B melodrama involving the counterfeiting of sweepstakes tickets.

4997. Undercover Doctor (Paramount; 1939). *Cast:* J. Carrol Naish, Lloyd Nolan, Broderick Crawford, Heather Angel, Raymond Hatton, Paul Fix, John Eldredge, Clem Bevans, Richard Carle, Janice Logan, George Meeker, Stanley Price, Philip Warren. *D:* Louis King; *P:* Edward T. Lowe; *Sc:* William R. Lipman, Horace McCoy.

B crime melodrama of a physician who consorts with gangsters. Partially based on the book "Persons in Hiding" by J. Edgar Hoover (ghostwritten by Courtney Riley Cooper).

4998. Undertow (Universal; 1930). *Cast:* John Mack Brown, Mary Nolan, Robert Ellis. *D:* Harry A. Pollard; *St:* Wilbur Daniel Steele. (1:00)
Low-budget drama set around a lighthouse and its' blind keeper.

4999. Underworld (Micheaux; 1936). *Produced, directed & written by:* Oscar Micheaux.
Low-budget indie.

5000. Underworld Terror (Xxxx Xxxx; 1936). *Cast:* Nick Stuart.
(No other information available)

5001. Unexpected Father (Universal; 1932). *Cast:* ZaSu Pitts, Slim Summerville, Cora Sue Collins, Claud Allister, Dorothy Christy, Alison Skipworth, Tom O'Brien. *D:* Thornton Freeland; *Sc:* Dale Van Every. (1:04)
A man marries a nursemaid in this B comedy after becoming guardian of an orphan.

5002. Unexpected Father (Universal; 1939). *Cast:* Baby Sandy (in her second film), Dennis O'Keefe, Shirley Ross, Mischa Auer, Mayo Methot, Joy Hodges, Anne Gwynne, Anne Nagel, Donald Briggs, Frank Reicher, Dorothy Arnold, Paul Guilfoyle, Jane Darwell, Edwin Stanley, Dorothy Vaughan, Richard Lane. *D:* Charles Lamont; *As.P.:* Kenneth Goldsmith; *St:* Leonard Spigelgass; *Sc:* Spigelgass, Charles Grayson. (G.B. title: *Sandy Takes a Bow*) (aka: *Sandy*) (1:18)
Similar story, but no relation to the above mentioned film is this comedy of a dancer who finds himself the adopted father of his late partner's baby girl.

5003/5004. Unfaithful (Paramount; 1931). *Cast:* Ruth Chatterton, Paul Lukas, Donald Cook, Juliette Compton, Paul Cavanagh, Syd Saylor, Jack Richardson, Bruce Warren, Donald MacKenzie, Arnold Lucy, Stella Moore, Leslie Palmer, Dennis D'Au-burn, Ambrose Barker, Eric Kalkhurst, Captain George Jackson. *D:* John Cromwell; *St:* John Van Druten.
Drama of a woman who saves the reputation of her sister-in-law while ruining her own.

Unfit to Print (G.B. title) *see* **Off the Record**

5005. The Unguarded Hour (MGM; 1936). *Cast:* Franchot Tone, Loretta Young, Roland Young, Henry Daniell, Jessie Ralph, Lewis Stone, Dudley Digges, E.E. Clive, Robert Greig, Aileen Pringle, John Buckler, Wallis Clark. *D:* Sam Wood; *P:* Lawrence Weingarten; *Sc:* Howard Emmett Rogers, Leon Gordon. (1:27)
An English barrister's wife has evidence that will free a man who was convicted of murder, but is unable to reveal it. A mystery-thriller which was a box office hit for the studio. Based on the play by Ladislaus Fodor and the English version of the play by Bernard Merivale.

5006. The Unholy Garden (United Artists/Samuel Goldwyn; 1931). *Cast:* Ronald Colman, Fay Wray, Estelle Taylor, Tully Marshall, Warren Hymer, Mischa Auer, Henry Armetta, Lawrence Grant, Ullrich Haupt, Kit Guard, Lucille La Verne, Morgan Wallace, Arnold Korff, Charles Hill Mailes, Nadja. *D:* George Fitzmaurice; *P:* Sam Goldwyn; *Sc:* Charles MacArthur, Ben Hecht. (1:15)
A bunch of crooks have gathered at a Sahara oasis in this romantic desert saga.

5007. Unholy Love (Allied; 1932). *Cast:* Joyce Compton, H.B. Warner, Lila Lee, Lyle Talbot, Jason Robards, Ivan Lebedeff, Richard Carlyle, Kathlyn Williams. *D:* Albert Ray; *P:* M.H. Hoffman, Jr. (G.B. title: *Deceit*)

Low-budget independent costume drama which was based on Flaubert's "Madame Bovary." Remade in France in 1934 and in the U.S.A. in 1949 (MGM) under that title.

5008. The Unholy Night (MGM; 1929). *Cast:* Ernest Torrence, Dorothy Sebastian, Roland Young, Natalie Moorhead, John Loder, Sidney Jarvis, Polly Moran, Boris Karloff, John Miljan, Richard Tucker, Sojin, George Cooper. *D:* Lionel Barrymore; *Sc:* Edwin Justus Mayer, Dorothy Farnum. (1:34)

Several members of a British regiment are murdered and the survivors gather at one member's home in an attempt to uncover the murderer in this mystery-melodrama. Based on a story by Ben Hecht.

5009. The Unholy Three (MGM; 1930). *Cast:* Lon Chaney (his only talkie film, repeating his role in the '25 version as Echo — d. 8/26/1930), Lila Lee (Rosie O'Grady), Elliott Nugent (Hector), Harry Earles (repeating his role in the '25 version as Tweedledee the midget), Ivan Linow (Hercules the strongman), John Miljan, Clarence Burton, Crauford Kent. *D:* Jack Conway; *Sc:* Elliott Nugent, J.C. Nugent. (1:12)

A ventriloquist, a midget and a strongman from a sideshow perpetrate a crime spree. A remake of the 1925 production for Metro-Goldwyn directed by Tod Browning. Based on the book by Clarence Aaron Robbins.

Uniform Lovers (G.B. title) *see* **Hold 'em Yale**

5010. Union Depot (WB; 1932). *Cast:* Douglas Fairbanks, Jr., Joan Blondell, Alan Hale, Frank McHugh, Guy Kibbee, David Landau, Mary Doran, Dickie Moore, Dorothy Christy, George Rosener, Frank (Junior) Cogh-

lan, Polly Walters, Virginia Sale, Adrienne Dore, Earle Foxe, Eulalie Jensen, George MacFarlane, Ruth Hall, Mae Madison. *D:* Alfred E. Green; *Sc:* (John) Kenyon Nicholson, Walter de Leon. (G.B. title: *Gentleman for a Day*) (1:08)

Drama of various individuals waiting at a railway station and how their lives intertwine. Based on the play by Gene Fowler, Douglas Durkin and Joe Laurie, Jr.

5011. Union Pacific (Paramount; 1939). *Cast:* Barbara Stanwyck (Mollie Monahan), Joel McCrea (Jeff Butler), Brian Donlevy (Sid Campeau), Robert Preston (Dick Allen), Akim Tamiroff (Fiesta), Anthony Quinn (Jack Cordray), Lynne Overman (Leach Overmile), Robert Barrat (Duke Ring), Evelyn Keyes (Mrs. Calvin), Regis Toomey (Paddy O'Rourke), Lon Chaney, Jr. (Dollarhide), Stanley Ridges (Casement), Henry Kolker (Asa M. Barrows), Francis McDonald (Grenville M. Dodge), Willard Robertson (Oakes Ames), Harold Goodwin (Calvin), Richard Lane (Sam Reed), William Haade (Dusky Clayton), J.M. Kerrigan (Monahan), Fuzzy Knight (Cookie), Harry Woods (Al Brett), Joseph Crehan (General Ulysses S. Grant), Julia Faye (Mame), Sheila Darcy (Rose), Joseph Sawyer (Shamus), Earl Askam (Bluett), John Marston (Dr. Durant), Byron Foulger (Andrew Whipple), Selmer Jackson (Jerome), Morgan Wallace (Senator Smith), Russell Hicks (Sergeant), May Beatty (Mrs. Hogan), Ernie Adams (General Sheridan), Guy Usher (Governor Stanford), William J. Worthington (Oliver Ames), James McNamara (Mr. Mills), Gus Glassmire (Governor Stafford), Stanley Andrews (Dr. Harkness), Paul Everton (Rev. Dr. Tadd), Jack Pennick (harmonica player), Ruth Warren, Hugh McDonald, Richard Robles, Evelyn Luckey, Calla Waltz, Richard Denning, Frank McGlynn, Sr., Monte Blue, Syd Saylor, Lane Chandler, William Pawley, Nestor Paiva, Emory Parnell, Blackie Whiteford, Francis Sayles. *D:* Cecil B. De Mille; *P:* De Mille; *Adaptation:* Jack Cunningham; *Sc:* Walter de Leon, C. Gardner Sullivan, Jesse Lasky, Jr.; *Special Effects:* (A.A.N.) Farciot Edouart, Gordon Jennings & Loren Ryder (for the train wreck sequence). (2:15) (video)

Another of the big productions of Hollywood's block-buster year of 1939 is this lavishly produced western action drama of the opening of the west to the railroad. Based on the story "Trouble Shooter" by Ernest Haycox, it became one of the 16 top grossing films of 1938–39.

5012. Unknown Blonde (Majestic; 1934). *Cast:* Edward Arnold, Dorothy Revier, Walter Catlett, Claude Gillingwater, Arletta Duncan, Clarence H. Wilson, Helen Jerome Eddy, John Miljan, Maidel Turner, Franklin Pangborn, Barbara Barondess, Arthur Hoyt, Barry Norton. *D:* Hobart Henley; *St:* Theodore D. Irwin.

"Poverty row" comedy.

5013. The Unknown Ranger (Columbia; 1936). *Cast:* Bob Allen, Martha Tibbetts, Harry Woods, Hal Taliaferro (Wally Wales), Buzzy (Buzz) Henry, Henry Hall, Edward Hearn, Robert Kortman, Lew Meehan, Art Mix, Bob McKenzie. *D:* Spencer Gordon Bennet; *Sc:* Nate Gatzert. (0:58)

Bob Allen western, the first in his series for this studio. A tale of horse thieves.

5014. Unknown Valley (Columbia; 1933). *Cast:* Buck Jones, Cecilia Parker, Bert Black, Carlotta Warwick, Arthur Wanzer, Wade Boteler, Frank McGlynn, Sr., Charles Thurston, Gaylord (Steve) Pendleton, Ward Bond, Frank Ellis, Alf James. *D:* Lambert Hillyer; *Sc:* Hillyer. (1:09)

Buck Jones offbeat western involving a religious sect.

5015. Unknown Woman (Columbia; 1935). *Cast:* Marian Marsh,

Richard Cromwell, Douglass Dumbrille, Henry Armetta, Crane Wilbur. *D:* Albert S. Rogell.

B melodrama.

5016. Unmarried (Paramount; 1939). *Cast:* Helen Twelvetrees, Charles "Buck" Jones, Donald O'Connor, Robert Armstrong, Sidney Blackmer, Buster Crabbe, William Haade, John Hartley. *D:* Kurt Neumann; *Sc:* Lillie Hayward, Brian Marlow; *St:* Grover Jones, William Slavens McNutt. (G.B. title: *Night Club Hostess*) (1:06)

Drama of an unmarried ex-boxer and his girl friend who raise an orphan boy who wants to be a boxer. A remake of *Lady and Gent* (q.v.) and a rare non-western role for Jones, of which this was his only film of 1939.

5017. Unmasked (Artclass; 1929). *Cast:* Robert Warwick, Milton Krims, Sam Ash, Susan Conroy. *D:* Edgar Lewis; *P:* The Weiss Brothers.

Low-budget melodrama.

5018/5019. Untamed (MGM; 1929). *Cast:* Robert Montgomery, Joan Crawford (all-talkie debut), Ernest Torrence, Holmes Herbert, John Miljan, Gwen Lee, Don Terry, Edward Nugent, Gertrude Astor, Wilson Benge, Grace Cunard, Lloyd Ingraham, Tom O'Brien, Milton Fahrney. *D:* Jack Conway; *St:* C.E. Scoggins; *Sc:* Sylvia Thalberg, Frank Butler, Willard Mack. (1:28)

Bingo, a spoiled oil heiress raised in the tropical wilds, falls for a poor boy.

Unwanted *see* **The Deceiver**

5020. The Unwelcome Stranger (Columbia; 1935). *Cast:* Jack Holt, Mona Barrie, Frankie Darro, Ralph Morgan, Jackie Searle, Bradley Page, Sam McDaniel. *D:* Phil Rosen.

B melodrama.

5021. The Unwritten Law (Majestic; 1932). *Cast:* Mary Brian, Theodore von Eltz, Wilfred Lucas, Richard "Skeets" Gallagher, Hedda Hopper, Mischa Auer, Greta Granstedt. *D:* Christy Cabanne.

"Poverty row" melodrama.

5022. Up for Murder (Universal; 1931). *Cast:* Lew Ayres, Genevieve Tobin, Frank McHugh, Purnell Pratt, Richard Tucker, Dorothy Peterson, Louise Beavers, Frederick Burt. *D:* Monta Bell; *Sc:* Bell. (1:08)

Low-budget melodrama of a triangular romance which ends in murder. A remake of *Man, Woman and Sin* (MGM; 1927) with John Gilbert and Jeanne Eagels.

5023. Up Pops the Devil (Paramount; 1931). *Cast:* Norman Foster, Carole Lombard, Stuart Erwin, Lilyan Tashman, Skeets Gallagher, Joyce Compton, Claire Dodd, Sleep 'n' Eat (Willie Best), Theodore von Eltz, Edward J. Nugent, Harry Beresford, Guy Oliver, Effie Ellsler, Matty Roubert, Eulalie Jensen, Pat Moriarity. *D:* A. Edward Sutherland; *Sc:* Eve Unsell, Arthur Kober.

Domestic comedy of a novelist and his problem marriage. Based on the play of that name by Frances Goodrich and Albert Hackett, it was remade as *Thanks for the Memory* (q.v.).

5024. Up the River (Fox; 1930). *Cast:* Spencer Tracy (feature film debut), Warren Hymer, Claire Luce, Humphrey Bogart (his 2nd feature), William Collier, Sr., Edythe Chapman, Sharon Lynne, Robert Parrish, Johnnie Walker, Gaylord (Steve) Pendleton, Noel Francis, Goodee Montgomery, Joan Marie Lawes, George MacFarlane. *D:* John Ford; *St & Sc:* Maurine Watkins. (1:32)

Comedy of an ex-con and his threatening predicament. Remade in 1938 (see below).

5025/5026. Up the River (20th Century–Fox; 1938). *Cast:* Tony Martin, Preston Foster, Bill Robinson, Phyllis Brooks, Sidney Toler, Arthur Treacher, Slim Summerville, Robert Allen, Jane Darwell, Dorothy Dearing, Eddie Collins. *D:* Alfred Werker; *P:* Sol M. Wurtzel; *St:* Maurine Watkins; *Sc:* John Patrick, Lou Breslow.

B remake of the preceding film.

Upper Underworld *see* **The Ruling Voice**

5027. Upperworld (WB; 1934). *Cast:* Warren William, Mary Astor, Ginger Rogers, Andy Devine, J. Carrol Naish, Henry O'Neill, Dickie Moore, Mickey Rooney, Sidney Toler, Theodore Newton, Robert Barrat, John Qualen, Ferdinand Gottschalk, Willard Robertson, Bud Flanagan (Dennis O'Keefe). *D:* Roy Del Ruth; *P:* Robert Lord; *St:* Ben Hecht; *Sc:* Ben Markson. (1:15)

Melodrama of a demanding society woman who drives her husband into the arms of another.

5028. Uptown New York (Sono Art-World Wide; 1932). *Cast:* Jack Oakie, Shirley Grey, Leon (Ames) Waycoff, George Cooper, Lee Moran, Raymond Hatton, Henry Armetta. *D:* Victor Schertzinger; *St:* Vina Delmar. (1:20) (video)

"Poverty row" tear jerker of the unrequited love between a married woman and a Jewish man.

5029. The Utah Kid (Tiffany; 1930). *Cast:* Rex Lease (starring debut), Dorothy Sebastian, Tom Santschi, Mary Carr, Walter Miller, Lafe McKee, Boris Karloff, Bud Osborne. *D:* Richard Thorpe; *Sc:* Frank Howard Clark. (1:00)

"Poverty row" western of an outlaw who defends the local school teacher, when she wanders into an outlaw hideout by mistake.

5030. Utah Trail (Grand National; 1938). *Cast:* Tex Ritter, Adele Pearce (later: Pamela Blake), Horace Murphy, Snub Pollard, Karl Hackett, Ed Cassidy, Charles King, Dave O'Brien, Bud Osborne, Lynton Brent, George Morrell, Horace B. Carpenter, Denver Dixon, Ray Jones, Oscar Gahan, Herman Hack, Chick Hannon, Sherry Tansey, Rudy Sooter & Tex Ritter's Texas Tornadoes, White Flash the horse. *D:* Albert (Al) Herman; *P:* Edward Finney (Boots & Saddles Productions); *St:* Edmund Kelso, Lindsley Parsons; *Sc:* Kelso. (0:56)

Tex Ritter western with an original story by Ritter of a ghost train. This was Ritter's final film for Grand National before moving over to a Monogram contract.

5031. Vacation from Love (MGM; 1938). *Cast:* Dennis O'Keefe, Florence Rice, June Knight, Edward Brophy, Reginald Owen, Truman Bradley, Herman Bing, George Zucco, J.M. Kerrigan, Paul Porcasi, Andrew Tombes, Armand Kaliz, Tom Rutherford. *D:* George Fitzmaurice; *P:* John W. Considine, Jr.; *Sc:* Harlan Ware, Patterson McNutt.

A musician and a socialite have a whirlwind romance in this B production.

5032. The Vagabond King (Paramount; 1930). *Cast:* Dennis King (film debut recreating his '25 stage role of Villon), Jeanette MacDonald (in her second film), Lillian Roth, Warner Oland, O.P. Heggie, Arthur Stone, Tom Ricketts, Lawford Davidson. *D:* Ludwig Berger; *Sc:* Herman J. Mankiewicz; *Art-Set Decoration:* (A.A.N.) Hans Dreier; *Notable Songs by:* Rudolf Friml & Brian Hooker, the duet "Only a Rose" & "Song of the Vagabonds"; *Other Songs:* Sam Coslow, Leo Robin.

This studio's first all-talkie in 2-color technicolor is the story of the poet-scoundrel Francois Villon. The novel "If I Were King" by R.H. Russell was dramatised in 1901 by Justin McCarthy. First filmed as *If I Were King* (Fox; 1920) with William Farnum and Betty Ross Clarke, then *The Beloved Rogue* (United Artists; 1928) with John Barrymore. Remade as *If I Were King* (1938) (q.v.) and again in 1956 as the musical *The Vagabond King*. In 1925 it became a smash musical on Broadway by Russell Janney, William Post and Brian Hooker with songs by Rudolf Friml and Hooker, the duet "Only a Rose" and "Song of the Vagabonds"; other songs: Sam Coslow, Leo Robin. Note: No copies of this production are known to exist.

5033. Vagabond Lady (MGM/Hal Roach; 1935). *Cast:* Robert Young, Evelyn Venable, Frank Craven, Reginald Denny, Berton Churchill, Forrester Harvey, Ferdinand Gottschalk. *D:* Sam Taylor; *P:* Taylor; *St:* Dan Crimmins; *Sc:* Frank Butler.

A drama involving a wealthy family.

5034. The Vagabond Lover (RKO; 1929). *Cast:* Rudy Vallee (film debut), Marie Dressler, Sally Blane, Nella Walker (film debut), Charles Sellon, Norman Peck, Eddie Nugent, Alan Roscoe, Danny O'Shea, Malcolm Waite, Vallee's Connecticutt Yankee Band. *D:* Marshall Neilan; *As.P.:* Louis Sarecky; *St:* James Ashmore Creelman; *Sc:* Creelman; *Songs:* "A Little Kiss Each Morning," "Heigh-Ho Everybody" by Harry Woods; "If You Were the Only Girl" by Clifford Grey, Nat D. Ayer; "I'll Be Reminded of You" by Ed Heyman, Ken Smith; "I Love You, Believe Me, I Love You" by Rubey Cowan, Phil Bartholomae, Phil Boutelje. (1:09) (video)

Hit musical-comedy of a crooner-orchestra leader who impersonates an impresario.

5035. The Valiant (Fox; 1929). *Cast:* Paul Muni (A.A.N. for B.A. in his film debut), Johnny Mack Brown, Marguerite Churchill (film debut), Don Terry, DeWitt Jennings, Henry Kolker,

Edith Yorke, Clifford Dempsey, George Pearce. *D:* William K. Howard (talkie directorial debut); *St:* Holworthy Hall, Robert Middlemass; *Sc:* (A.A.N.) Tom Barry, John Hunter Booth.

One man kills another, refusing to say why and taking the secret to the electric chair with him. Remade as *The Man Who Wouldn't Talk* (20th Century–Fox; 1940) with Lloyd Nolan.

5036. Valiant Is the Word for Carrie (Paramount; 1936). *Cast:* Gladys George (A.A.N. for B.A.), Arline Judge, John Howard, Dudley Digges, Harry Carey, Isabel Jewell, Jackie Moran, William Collier, Sr., Maude Eburne, Charlene Wyatt, Hattie McDaniel, John Wray, Lew Payton, Grady Sutton. *D:* Wesley Ruggles; *P:* Ruggles; *Sc:* Claude Binyon. (1:50)

Hit tear-jerker of a woman who devotes her life to two orphans. Based on the best seller by Barry Benefield.

5037. The Valley of Adventure (Xxxx Xxxx; 1932). *Cast:* Monte Blue. (No other information available)

5038. Valley of Terror (Ambassador; 1937). *Cast:* Kermit Maynard, Harley Wood, John Merton, Jack Ingram, Dick Curtis, Roger Williams, Hank Bell, Hal Price, Frank McCarroll, Slim Whitaker, George Morrell, Blackie Whiteford, Herman Hack, Jack Casey. *D:* Al Herman; *P:* Maurice Conn; *Sc:* Stanley Roberts. (0:59)

Kermit Maynard western involving a crook after the mineral deposits on a girl's ranch.

5039. Valley of the Giants (WB; 1938). *Cast:* Wayne Morris, Claire Trevor, Frank McHugh, Alan Hale, Donald Crisp, Charles Bickford, Jack LaRue, John Litel, Dick Purcell, El Brendel, Russell Simpson, Cyrus Kendall, Harry Cording, Wade Boteler, Helen MacKellar, Addison Richards, Jerry Colonna, Clem Bevans, George Cleveland. *D:* William Keighley; *As.P.:*

Louis F. Edelman; *Sc:* Seton I. Miller, Michael Fessier. (1:19)

Technicolor adventure set in the redwood forest of northern California. Based on the novel by Peter B. Kyne, it was first filmed by Paramount in 1919 with Wallace Reid and Grace Darmond by director James Cruze with a First National remake in 1927 with Milton Sills.

5040. Valley of the Lawless (Supreme; 1935–36). *Cast:* Johnny Mack Brown, Joyce Compton, George Hayes, Denny Meadows (Dennis Moore), Bobby Nelson, Frank Hagney, Charles King, Jack Rockwell, Frank Ball, Forrest Taylor, Ed Cassidy, Blackie Whiteford, Steve Clark, Horace Murphy, George Morrell, Bob McKenzie, Jack Evans. *D:* Robert N. Bradbury; *P:* A.W. Hackel; *St:* Charles Francis Royal; *Sc:* Royal, Bradbury. (0:59)

Johnny Mack Brown western of a man in search of a map that belonged to his grandfather before the old man was killed.

5041. Valley of Wanted Men (Ambassador; 1935). *Cast:* Frankie Darro, Grant Withers, Drue Leyton, (Le)Roy Mason, Russell Hopton, Walter Miller, Paul Fix, Fred "Snowflake" Toones, Alan Bridge, Slim Whitaker, Jack Rockwell, William Gould, Roger Williams. *D:* Alan James (aka: Alvin J. Neitz); *P:* Maurice Conn; *Sc:* Barry Barringer, Forrest Barnes. (G.B. title: *Wanted Men*) (1:02)

B budget western of a youth who lives in a valley where all the residents are wanted by the law.

5042. The Vampire Bat (Majestic; 1933). *Cast:* Lionel Atwill, Fay Wray, Melvyn Douglas, Maude Eburne, George E. Stone, Dwight Frye, Lionel Belmore, Stella Adams, William V. Mong, Harrison Greene, Robert Frazer, William Humphrey, Carl Stockdale, Fern Emmett, Paul Weigel. *D:* Frank Strayer; *P:* Phil Goldstone; *St & Sc:* Edward T. Lowe. (1:11) (video)

Hit "poverty row" horror thriller of

a mad doctor who begins a series of murders of the local townsfolk while searching for a blood substitute. Notable performances by Eburne and Frye.

The Vanishing Body *see* **The Black Cat**

Vanessa (G.B. title) *see* **Vanessa, Her Love Story**

5043. Vanessa, Her Love Story (MGM; 1935). *Cast:* Helen Hayes (in her last starring role until 1951 as Vanessa), Robert Montgomery (Benjie), May Robson, Otto Kruger, Lewis Stone, Henry Stephenson, Violet Kemble-Cooper, Jessie Ralph, George K. Arthur (final film — ret.), Donald Crisp, Henry Armetta, Arthur Treacher, Ethel Griffies, Mary Gordon, Crauford Kent, Howard Leeds, Elspeth Dudgeon. *D:* William K. Howard; *P:* David O. Selznick; *Sc:* Hugh Walpole, Lenore Coffee. (G.B. title: *Vanessa*) (1:16)

Romantic drama of a woman who falls for a dashing gypsy while married to an insane man. Based on the novel by Hugh Walpole.

5044. The Vanishing Frontier (Paramount; 1932). *Cast:* John Mack Brown, Evalyn Knapp, ZaSu Pitts, Raymond Hatton, J. Farrell MacDonald, Ben Alexander, Wallace MacDonald. *D:* Phil Rosen; *Sc:* Stuart Anthony. (1:05)

B budget western of early California homesteaders who are being harrassed by outlaws.

5045. Vanishing Men (Monogram; 1932). *Cast:* Tom Tyler, Adele Lacey, Raymond Keane, William L. Thorne, John Elliott, Robert Manning, Charles King, James Marcus, Dick Dickinson. *D:* Harry Fraser; *P:* Trem Carr; *St & Sc:* Wellyn Totman. (1:02)

Tom Tyler western.

5046. The Vanishing Riders (Spectrum; 1935). *Cast:* Bill Cody, Ethel Jackson, Bill Cody, Jr., Wally Wales (Hal Taliaferro), Budd Buster, Roger Williams, Milburn Morante, Donald Reed, Francis Walker, Buck Morgan, Bert Young, Bud Osborne, Colin Chase. *D:* Robert Hill; *Sc:* Oliver Drake. (0:58)

Bill Cody western of cattle rustling.

5047. Vanity Fair (Allied; 1932). *Cast:* Myrna Loy (Becky), Barbara Kent, Walter Byron, Anthony Bushell, Conway Tearle, Montagu Love, Mary Forbes, Billy Bevan. *D:* Chester M. Franklin; *P:* M.H. Hoffman, Jr.; *Sc:* F. Hugh Herbert. (1:18) (video)

Independent, loosely based adaptation of William Makepeace Thackeray's literary work of a self-centered girl. Previous versions: (Vitagraph; 1911) with John Bunny, Helen Gardner and Tefft Johnson, (Edison; 1915) with Mrs. Fiske and Richard Tucker, and (Sam Goldwyn; 1923) with Mabel Ballin. Remade in 1935 as *Becky Sharp* (q.v.).

5048. Vanity Street (Columbia; 1932). *Cast:* Helen Chandler, Charles Bickford, Raymond Hatton, Claudia Morgan, Arthur Hoyt, May Beatty, George Meeker, Mayo Methot, Ruth Channing, Eddie Boland, Ann Fay, Kathrin Clare Ward, Dolores Rey, Dutch Hendrian. *D:* Nick Grinde; *Sc:* Gertrude Purcell, Edward Barry Roberts.

Romantic drama.

5049. Varsity (Paramount; 1928). *Cast:* Charles "Buddy" Rogers, Mary Brian (talkie debut), Chester Conklin, Phillips Holmes (film debut), Robert Ellis, John Westwood. *D:* Frank Tuttle; *St/Dial:* Wells Root; *Sc:* Howard Estabrook; *Song:* "My Varsity Girl, I'll Cling to You" by Al Bryan & W. Franke Harling.

Part-talkie collegiate comedy-drama with passages of spoken dialogue and a vocalized song. A box office hit.

5050. Varsity Show (WB; 1937). *Cast:* Dick Powell, Priscilla Lane (film debut), Fred Waring & His Pennsylvanians, Walter Catlett, Ted Healy, Rosemary Lane (sister to Priscilla in her film debut), Buck & Bubbles, Sterling Holloway, Lee Dixon, Veda Ann Borg, Ben Welden, Edward Brophy, Halliwell Hobbes, Roy Atwell, Mabel Todd, Scotty Bates, Poley McClintock. *D:* William Keighley; *P:* Louis F. Edelman; *St:* Warren Duff, Sig Herzig; *Sc:* Duff, Richard Macaulay, Jerry Wald, Sig Herzig; *Choreographer:* (A.A.N.) Busby Berkeley for the "Finale" number which was a tribute to learning institutions everywhere; *Songs:* "Love Is on the Air Tonight," "Moonlight on the Campus," "Old King Cole," "Have You Got Any Castles Baby?" "We're Working Our Way Through College," "On with the Dance," "You've Got Something There" & "When Your College Days Are Gone" by Johnny Mercer & Richard A. Whiting. (Original running time: 2:00, now 1:20)

A Broadway producer stages a musical show at his college alma mater.

5051. Veiled Aristocrats (Micheaux; 1932). *Produced, directed & written by:* Oscar Micheaux.

Low-budget independent production.

Veneer *see* **Young Bride**

5052. Vengeance (Columbia; 1930). *Cast:* Jack Holt, Dorothy Revier, Ralph Graves. *D:* Archie Mayo; *Sc:* F. Hugh Herbert.

Low-budget melodrama from "poverty row."

Vengeance (1935) *see* **Range Warfare**

Vengeance (1937) (G.B. title) *see* **What Price Vengeance?**

5053. The Vengeance of Rannah (Reliable; 1936). *Cast:* Rin-Tin-Tin, Jr., Bob Custer, John Elliott, Victoria Vinton, Roger Williams, Ed Cassidy, Eddie

Phillips, Oscar Gahan, Wally West. *D:* Franklin Shamroy (Bernard B. Ray); *P:* Harry S. Webb; *Sc:* Joseph O'Donnell. (0:59)

B western of a dog that holds the clue to a stagecoach robbery and the murder of his owner.

5054. Venus Makes Trouble (Columbia; 1937). *Cast:* James Dunn, Patricia Ellis, Astrid Allwyn, Thurston Hall, Spencer Charters. *D:* Gordon Wiles.

B romantic comedy.

5055. A Very Honorable Guy (WB/F.N.; 1934). *Cast:* Joe E. Brown, Alice White, Alan Dinehart, Hobart Cavanaugh, Al Dubin (bit), Harry Warren (bit), Robert Barrat, Irene Franklin, Harold Huber, Joseph Cawthorn. *D:* Lloyd Bacon; *P:* Robert Lord; *Sc:* Earl Baldwin. (1:02)

Based on a story by Damon Runyon, this offbeat B comedy tells the tale of a gambler who sells his body to science to pay off a gambling debt.

5056. The Very Idea (RKO; 1929). *Cast:* Allen Kearns, Doris Eaton, Frank Craven (film debut), Hugh Trevor, Sally Blane, Olive Tell, Theodore von Eltz. *D:* Richard Rosson: *Dial.:* Frank Craven; *As.P.:* Myles Connolly; *Sc:* William LeBaron. (1:08)

Low-budget comedy of "surrogate parents." Based on a play by William LeBaron.

5057. Via Pony Express (Majestic; 1933). *Cast:* Jack Hoxie, Marceline Day, Lane Chandler, Doris Hill, Julian Rivero, Matthew Betz, Charles K. French, Yakima Canutt. *D:* Lewis D. Collins; *P:* Max & Arthur Alexander; *Sc:* Collins, Oliver Drake. (1:00)

Jack Hoxie western for "poverty row."

5058. Vice Squad (Paramount; 1931). *Cast:* Paul Lukas, Kay Francis, Helen Johnson (later: Judith Wood), Esther Howard, William Davidson,

George Pat Collins, Tom Wilson, Phil Tead, Rockliffe Fellowes, William Arnold, Monte Carter, Davison Clark. *D:* John Cromwell; *St & Sc:* Oliver H.P. Garrett. (1:20) (video)

There's corruption in the city vice squad in this crime melodrama.

5059. Victims of Persecution (Xxxx Xxxx; 1933). *Cast:* John Willard, Bud Pollard. *D:* Bud Pollard.

(No other information available)

Victims of the Beyond (G.B. title) *see* **Sucker Money**

5060. Viennese Nights (WB/ F.N.; 1930–31). *Cast:* Alexander Gray, Walter Pidgeon, Vivienne Segal, Bert Roach, Milton Douglas, Jean Hersholt, June Purcell, Alice Day, Bela Lugosi, Louise Fazenda. *D:* Alan Crosland; *Sc:* Oscar Hammerstein II, Sigmund Romberg; *Songs written especially for the screen:* "I Bring a Love Song," "I'm Lonely," "You Will Remember Vienna," "Here We Are," "Regimental March," "Yes, Yes, Yes" & the title song by Hammerstein II & Romberg.

Lavishly produced hit operetta in 2-color technicolor which spans a period of forty-years in the life of a composer.

Vigour of Youth (G.B. title) *see* **The Spirit of Notre Dame**

5061. The Viking (Ambassador; 1931). *Cast:* Charles Starrett, Louise Huntington, Arthur Vinton, Roy Stewart, Captain Bob Bartlett. *D:* George Melford; *P:* J.D. Williams, Varick Frissell.

A low-budget actioner filmed in the frozen north with many production problems.

5062. A Village Tale (RKO; 1935). *Cast:* Randolph Scott, Kay Johnson, Robert Barrat, Arthur Hohl, Janet Beecher, Edward Ellis, Guinn Williams, Donald Meek, Dorothy Burgess, Andy Clyde, DeWitt Jennings, Ray Mayer, T. Roy Barnes. *D:* John

Cromwell; *P:* David Hempstead; *Sc:* Allan Scott. (1:20)

Rural drama based on the novel by Phil Stong of a man who besides being dominated by his brother, has to contend with local gossip regarding his wife and another man.

5063. The Virginia Judge (Paramount; 1935). *Cast:* Walter C. Kelly, Robert Cummings (film debut), Marsha Hunt (film debut), Johnny Downs, Stepin Fetchit, Charles Middleton, Virginia Hammond, T. Roy Barnes, Willard Robertson, Sam McDaniel. *D:* Edward Sedgwick; *P:* Charles R. Rogers.

B rural drama of a lawyer who is taken under the wing of a kind-hearted judge.

5064. The Virginian (Paramount; 1929). *Cast:* Gary Cooper (talking debut delivering his famous line "Smile when you say that"), Richard Arlen, Walter Huston, Mary Brian, Chester Conklin, Eugene Pallette, E.H. Calvert, Helen Ware, Victor Potel, Tex Young, Charles Stevens. *D:* Victor Fleming; *P:* Louis D. Lighton; *Sc:* Edward E. Paramore, Jr., Howard Estabrook. (1:35) (video)

This, the 3rd all-talkie western to come out of Hollywood, based on the 1902 novel by Owen Wister placed #9 on the "10 Best" list of the *New York Times.* In 1907, the novel was also adapted to the stage. Previous versions: (Lasky Feature Plays; 1914) with Dustin Farnum, Winifred Kingston and Horace B. Carpenter with direction by Cecil B. De Mille, (Preferred Pictures; 1923) with Kenneth Harlan and Florence Vidor, both of which were based on the '07 stage adaptation by Wister and Kirk La Shelle.

Note: Remade by Paramount in 1946 with an adaptation to a TV series in the '60s.

5065. Virtue (Columbia; 1932). *Cast:* Pat O'Brien, Carole Lombard, Jack LaRue, Ward Bond, Shirley Grey.

D: Edward Buzzell; *St:* Ethel Hill; *Sc:* Robert Riskin.

Low-budget marital drama of a man, his wife and a woman with a "past."

5066. The Virtuous Husband (Universal; 1931). *Cast:* Elliott Nugent, Betty Compson, Jean Arthur, Alison Skipworth, Tully Marshall, J.C. Nugent, Eva McKenzie. *D:* Vin Moore; *Adaptation:* Edward (Ludwig) Luddy, Jerome Horwin; *Sc:* Dale Van Every (based on a story by Dorrance Davis). (G.B. title: *What Wives Don't Want*) (1:16)

Comedy of a young man who lives by written instructions from his deceased mother, creating numerous problems in his love-life.

5067/5068. The Virtuous Sin (Paramount; 1930). *Cast:* Kay Francis, Walter Huston, Kenneth MacKenna, Paul Cavanagh, Jobyna Howland, Oscar Apfel. *D:* George Cukor, Louis Gasnier; *Sc:* Martin Brown, Louise Long. (G.B. title: *Cast Iron*) (1:21)

Romantic drama with a wartime setting of a married woman's affair with an officer. Based on the novel by Lajos Zilahy.

5069. Viva Villa! (MGM; 1934). *Cast:* Wallace Beery (voted "Best Actor" at the Venice Film Festival for his portrayal of Pancho Villa), Leo Carrillo (Diego), Fay Wray (Teresa), Donald Cook (Don Felipe), Stuart Erwin (replacing Lee Tracy as Johnny Sykes — see note below), George E. Stone (Chavito), Henry B. Walthall (Madero), Katherine de Mille (Rosita), Joseph Schildkraut (General Pascal), Frank Puglia (Villa's father), Phillip Cooper (Villa as a child), David Durand (bugle boy), John Merkel (Pascal's aide), Adrian Rosley, Hector Sarno & Henry Armetta (Mendoza Brothers), Ralph Bushman (Francis X. Bushman, Jr., as Calloway), Charles Stevens, Steve Clemente, Pedro Regas, Carlos de Valdez, Charles Requa, Tom Ricketts, George Regas, Harry Cording, Sam Godfrey, Nigel de Brulier, Clarence Hummel Wilson, James Martin, Anita Gordiana, Francis McDonald, Harry Semels, Julian Rivero, Bob McKenzie, Paul Stanton, Dan Dix, Belle Mitchell, Mischa Auer, John Davidson, Brandon Hurst, Leonard Mudie, Herbert Prior, Emile Chautard, Arthur Treacher, William von Brincken, Andre Cheron, Michael Visaroff, Shirley Chambers, Arthur Thalasso, Chris-Pin Martin, Nick de Ruiz & cast of thousands of extras. *D:* Howard Hawks, Jack Conway; *P:* (A.A.N. for Best Picture) David O. Selznick; *Sc:* (A.A.N.) Ben Hecht, Howard Hawks (unc.); *Sound Recording:* (A.A.N.) Douglas Shearer; *Assistant Directors:* (A.A.) Art Rosson & John Walters. (1:55)

A fictionalized account of the famed Mexican revolutionary, Pancho Villa, loosely based on the book by Edgcumb Pinchon and O.B. Stade. This film is noted for having many production problems and setbacks, eventually leaving the Mexican locales to finish up shooting in Hollywood (see note below). Howard Hawks was the original director, eventually being replaced by Jack Conway. The film was a major box office success for the studio, being voted one of the year's "10 Best" by the National Board of Review and placing #7 on the "10 Best" list of *Film Daily*.

Note: Stuart Erwin replaced Lee Tracy who was fired by MGM. Tracy, while drunk, was reported to have "rained" on a passing Mexican military parade from his hotel balcony, causing the Mexican government to withdraw all cooperation and forcing the entire production company back to Hollywood to complete the film.

5070. Vivacious Lady (RKO; 1938). *Cast:* Ginger Rogers, James Stewart, James Ellison, Beulah Bondi, Charles Coburn, Frances Mercer, Phyllis Kennedy, Franklin Pangborn, Grady

Sutton, Willie Best, Jack Carson, Alec Craig. *D:* George Stevens; *P:* Stevens; *Supervisor:* Pandro S. Berman; *St:* I.A.R. (Ida) Wylie; *Sc:* P.J. Wolfson, Ernest Pagano; *Cinematographer:* (A.A.N.) Robert de Grasse; *Sound Recording:* (A.A.N.) James Wilkinson; *Song:* "You'll Be Reminded of Me" by George Jessel, Jack Meskill & Ted Shapiro. (1:30) (video)

A college professor from a conservative family marries a night club singer with the effect on his family being about the same as if he had committed murder. A hit screwball comedy of its' day.

Vogues *see* **Vogues of 1938**

5071. Vogues of 1938 (United Artists/Walter Wanger; 1937). *Cast:* Warner Baxter, Joan Bennett, Helen Vinson, Mischa Auer, Alan Mowbray, Jerome Cowan, Marjorie Gateson, Polly Rowles, Hedda Hopper, Alma Kruger, Roman Bohnen, Dorothy McNulty (Penny Singleton), Kay Aldridge, Marla Shelton, Judith Barrett. *D:* Irving Cummings; *P:* Walter Wanger; *Sc:* Bella & Samuel Spewack; *Art-Set Decoration:* (A.A.N.) Alexander Toluboff; *Song:* (A.A.N.) "That Old Feeling" (Best Song) by Sammy Fain & Lew Brown; *Other Songs:* Frank Loesser. (G.B. title: *All This and Glamour Too*) (TV title: *Vogues*) (1:48) (video)

Technicolor musical-comedy of a wealthy woman who decides to become a fashion model, causing problems with her fiance.

Voice from the Grave *see* **The Sin of Nora Moran**

5072. A Voice in the Night (Columbia; 1934). *Cast:* Tim McCoy, Kane Richmond, Ward Bond. *D:* C.C. Coleman, Jr.

Low-budget melodrama.

5073. The Voice of Bugle Ann (MGM; 1936). *Cast:* Lionel Barrymore, Maureen O'Sullivan, Eric Linden, Dudley Digges, Spring Byington, Charley Grapewin, Henry Wadsworth, William Newell, James Macklin, Jonathan Hale, Frederick Burton. *D:* Richard Thorpe; *P:* John W. Considine, Jr.; *Sc:* Harvey Gates, Samuel Hoffenstein. (1:10)

Sentimental rural drama of a man's vengeance on his neighbor who he believes killed his beloved hunting dog. Based on the popular novel by MacKinlay Kantor, the film was a box office hit.

The Voice of Scandal (G.B. title) *see* **Here Comes Carter!**

5074. Voice of the City (MGM; 1929). *Cast:* Willard Mack, Sylvia Field, John Miljan, Robert Ames, James Farley, Clark Marshall, Duane Thompson. *D:* Willard Mack; *Sc:* Mack.

Low-budget crime melodrama of a detective who pins a rap on a wanted gangster.

5075. The Voice Within (Tiffany; 1929). *Cast:* Walter Pidgeon, Eve Southern, Montagu Love. *D:* George Archainbaud.

Part-talkie production from "poverty row."

5076. Voltaire (WB; 1933). *Cast:* George Arliss (Francois Marie Arouet de Voltaire), Doris Kenyon (Madame de Pompadour), Reginald Owen (King Louis XV), Margaret Lindsay, Alan Mowbray, David Torrence, Douglass Dumbrille, Theodore Newton, Doris Lloyd, Gordon Westcott, Leonard Mudie, Ivan Simpson, Helena Phillips. *D:* John G. Adolfi (final film—d. 1933); *Supervisor:* Raymond Griffith; *Sc:* Paul Green, Maude T. Howell. (1:12)

The life and times of the 18th-century French writer. Based on the novel by George Gibbs and E. Lawrence Dudley.

5077. The Wagon Master (Universal; 1929). *Cast:* Ken Maynard, Edith Roberts (final film—ret.), Tom Santschi. *D:* Harry Joe Brown; *P:* Maynard.

Part-talkie Ken Maynard western of a cowboy helping miners about to be swindled.

5078. Wagon Trail (Ajax; 1935). *Cast:* Harry Carey, Edward Norris, Gertrude Messinger, Earl Dwire, Roger Williams, Chief Thundercloud, John Elliott, Chuck Morrison, Lew Meehan, Francis Walker, Silver Tip Baker, Allen Greer, Dick Botiller. *D:* Harry Fraser; *P:* William Berke; *Sc:* Monroe Talbot. (0:55)

Harry Carey western of a lawman who helps his son when he is accused of murder.

5079. Wagon Wheels (Paramount; 1934). *Cast:* Randolph Scott, Gail Patrick, Billy Lee, Monte Blue, Raymond Hatton, Jan Duggan, Olin Howland, J.P. McGowan, Leila Bennett, James Marcus, Helen Hunt, James B. "Pop" Kenton, Alfred del Cambre, John Marston, Sam McDaniel, Howard Wilson, Colin Tapley, Michael Visaroff, E. Alyn Warren, Pauline Moore, Earl Conert & the Singing Guardsmen, Jim Thorpe, Clara Lou (Ann) Sheridan. *D:* Charles T. Barton (directorial debut); *Sc:* Jack Cunningham, Charles Logue, Carl Buss. (0:57)

A remake of *Fighting Caravans* (q.v.) is the low-budget saga of a wagon train's trek westward and the obstacles it encounters. Based on Zane Grey's novel "Fighting Caravans," this remake utilizes footage from the earlier film.

5080. Waikiki Wedding (Paramount; 1937). *Cast:* Bing Crosby (Tony Marvin), Martha Raye (Myrtle Finch), Shirley Ross (Georgia Smith), "Bazooka" Bob Burns (Shad Buggle), Leif Erickson (Dr. Victor Quimby), Grady Sutton (Everett Todhunter), Anthony Quinn (Kimo), George Barbier (J.P. Todhunter), Granville Bates (Uncle Herman), Mitchell Lewis (Koalani), George Regas (Muamua), Prince Lei Lani (priest), Maurice Liu (Kaiaka), Raquel Echeverria (Mahina), Lotus Liu (Suki), Nalani de Clercq (Maile), Kuulei de Clercq (Lani), Spencer Charters (Frame), Alexander Leftwich (Harrison), Ralph Remley (Tomlin), Harry Stubbs (Keith), Pierre Watkin (John Durkin), Nick Lukats, Miri Rei, Augie Goupil, Iris Yamaoka, Jack Chapin, Pedro Regas, David Newell, Emma Dunn, Ray Kinney, Robert Emmett O'Connor, Lalo Encinas, Sojin, Jr. *D:* Frank Tuttle; *P:* Arthur Hornblow, Jr.; *St:* Frank Butler, Don Hartman; *Sc:* Butler, Hartman, Walter de Leon, Francis Martin; *Choreographer:* (A.A.N.) LeRoy Prinz for the "Luau" number; *Songs:* "Sweet Leilani" (A.A.N. for Best Song) Harry Owens; "Blue Hawaii," "In a Little Hula Heaven," "Sweet Is the Word for You," "Nani Ona Pua" & "Okolehao" by Ralph Rainger & Leo Robin. (1:29)

Hit musical-comedy set around a pineapple princess contest in Hawaii. One of the 38 top grossing films of 1936–37.

Waiting for the Bride (G.B. title) *see* **The Runaround**

5081. Wake Up and Dream (Universal; 1934). *Cast:* Russ Columbo (final film—d. 1934), Roger Pryor, June Knight, Catherine Doucet, Henry Armetta, Andy Devine, Spencer Charters, Winifred Shaw, Paul Porcasi, Jane Darwell, Arthur Hoyt, Maurice Black, Clarence H. Wilson, Philip Dakin. *D:* Kurt Neumann; *P:* B.F. Zeidman; *Sc:* Meehan, Jr.

B musical-comedy taken from a stage play by Curtis Kenyon and John Meehan, Jr.

5082. Wake Up and Live (20th Century-Fox; 1937). *Cast:* Alice Faye (Alice Huntley), Walter Winchell (himself), Ben Bernie & His Band (themselves), Jack Haley (Eddie Kane, singing voice dubbed by Buddy Clark), Patsy Kelly (Patsy Kane), Ned Sparks (Steve Cluskey), Grace Bradley (Jean Roberts), Walter Catlett (Gus Avery),

Joan Davis (Spanish dancer), Douglas Fowley (Herman), Miles Mander (James Stratton), Etienne Girardot (Waldo Peebles), Condos Brothers (themselves), Brewster Twins (themselves), Leah Ray (cafe singer), Paul Hurst (McCabe), George Givot (manager), Barnett Parker (Foster), Charles Williams (Alberts), Edward Gargan (Murphy), Robert Lowery (film debut as the chauffeur), Warren Hymer (first gunman), William Demarest, John Sheehan, George Chandler, Gary Breckner, Rosemary Glosz, Harry Tyler, Si Jenks, Andre Beranger, Ellen Prescott, Elyse Knox. *D:* Sidney Lanfield; *P:* Darryl F. Zanuck; *As.P.:* Kenneth MacGowan; *Sc:* Harry Tugend, Jack Yellen; *Songs:* title song, "There's a Lull in My Life," "It's Swell of You," "Oh, But I'm Happy," "I'm Bubbling Over," "Never in a Million Years," "I Love You Too Much, Muchacha," "Red Seal Malt" & "Bernie's Love Song" by Mack Gordon & Harry Revel. (1:31)

A musical satire on radio broadcasting which is highlighted by the rivalry between a bandleader and a news commentator. Based on the book by Dorothea Brande, this film became one of the 38 top grossing films of 1936–37.

5083. The Walking Dead (WB; 1936). *Cast:* Boris Karloff (John Ellman), Edmund Gwenn, Marguerite Churchill, Warren Hull, Barton MacLane, Henry O'Neill, Joseph King, Addison Richards, Paul Harvey, Robert Strange, Eddie Acuff, Kenneth Harlan, Miki Morita, Ruth Robinson, Gordon (Bill) Elliott. *D:* Michael Curtiz; *P:* Louis Edelman; *St:* Joseph Fields, Ewart Adamson; *Sc:* Adamson, Peter Milne, Robert Andrews, Lillie Hayward. (1:06) (video)

Horror tale of a man brought back from the dead after being executed for a murder he didn't commit.

Walking Down Broadway (1933) *see* **Hello, Sister**

5084. Walking Down Broadway (20th Century–Fox; 1938). *Cast:* Claire Trevor, Michael Whalen, Dixie Dunbar, Leah Ray, Lynn Bari, Leon Ames, Douglas Fowley, William (Billy) Benedict, Lon Chaney, Jr., Phyllis Brooks, Jayne Regan. *D:* Norman Foster; *P:* Sol M. Wurtzel; *Sc:* Robert Chapin, Karen DeWolf.

B musical romance of six showgirls.

5085. Walking on Air (RKO; 1936). *Cast:* Ann Sothern, Gene Raymond, Henry Stephenson, Jessie Ralph, Alan Curtis, Gordon Jones, Anita Colby, George Meeker, Patricia Wilder, Andre Beranger, Maxine Jennings, Arthur Hoyt, Charles Coleman. *D:* Joseph Santley; *P:* Edward Kaufman; *St:* Francis M. Cockrell; *Sc:* Rian James, Bert Kalmar, Harry Ruby, Viola Brothers Shore; *Songs:* Kalmar, Ruby, Sid Silvers. (1:10)

A romantic B comedy with music of a girl who goes to great lengths to marry the man she thinks she wants.

5086. Wall Street Cowboy (Republic; 1939). *Cast:* Roy Rogers, George "Gabby" Hayes, Raymond Hatton, Ann Baldwin, Pierre Watkin, Craig Reynolds, Louisiana Lou, Ivan Miller, Adrian Morris, Reginald Barlow, Jack Roper, Jack Ingram, Hugh Sothern, Paul Fix, George Chesebro, Fred Burns, Ted Mapes. *D:* Joe Kane; *As.P.:* Kane; *Sc:* Gerald Geraghty, Norman S. Hall. (1:06)

Roy Rogers western of a cowboy who seeks financial help in the east for his ranch. This was one of Roy's few box office flops.

5087. Wallaby Jim of the Islands (Grand National; 1937). *Cast:* George Houston, Ruth Coleman, Douglas Walton, William von Brincken, Mamo Clark, Colin Campbell, Syd Saylor, Juan Torena, Nick Thompson, Warner Richmond, Wilson Benge. *D:* Charles Lamont; *P:* Bud Barsky; *St:* Albert

Richard Wetjen; *Sc:* Bennett Cohen, Houston Branch. (1:01)
B adventure.

5088. Walls of Gold (Fox; 1933). *Cast:* Sally Eilers, Norman Foster, Ralph Morgan, Rosita Moreno, Rochelle Hudson, Frederic Santley, Mary Mason, Margaret Seddon. *D:* Kenneth MacKenna; *St:* Kathleen Norris. (1:14)
Low-budget romantic drama of conflicting relationships.

5089. Wanderer of the Wasteland (Paramount; 1935). *Cast:* Dean Jagger, Gail Patrick, Larry "Buster" Crabbe, Fuzzy Knight, Al St. John, Anna Q. Nilsson, Kenneth Harlan, Monte Blue, Raymond Hatton, Jim Thorpe, Glenn (Leif) Erickson (bit as a dead man). *D:* Otho Lovering; *P:* Harold Hurley; *Sc:* Stuart Anthony. (1:02)
B western of a cowboy in search of the party who killed his father. Based on the book by Zane Grey, it was previously filmed by this studio in 1924 with Jack Holt and Billie Dove. Remade in 1945 by RKO.

Wanderlust (G.B. title) *see* **Mary Jane's Pa**

5090. Wanted by the Police (Monogram; 1938). *Cast:* Frankie Darro, Evalyn Knapp, Robert Kent, Lillian Elliott, Matty Fain, Don Rowan, Sam Bernard, Mauritz Hugo, Thelma White, William Costello, Walter Merrill, Ralph Peters. *D:* Howard Bretherton; *P:* Lindsley Parsons; *St:* Don Mullahy, Renaud Hoffman; *Sc:* Wellyn Totman. (0:59)
"Poverty row" melodrama of a youth who gets a job at a garage to help his mother financially, but finds he has inadvertently become involved in a ring of car thieves.

5091. Wanted! Jane Turner (RKO; 1936). *Cast:* Lee Tracy, Gloria Stuart, Judith Blake (Jane Turner), Barbara Pepper (Jane Turner), Paul Guilfoyle, John McGuire, Frank M. Thomas, Patricia Wilder, Willard Robertson, Irene Franklin. *D:* Edward Killy; *P:* Cliff Reid; *St:* Julius Klein, John Twist, Edmund L. Hartmann; *Sc:* Twist. (1:04)
B melodrama of a mail truck robbery and the search by authorities for a girl named "Jane Turner." Naturally, they find a "Jane Turner" who had nothing to do with the robbery.

Wanted Men (G.B. title) *see* **Valley of Wanted Men**

5092. War Correspondent (Columbia; 1932). *Cast:* Jack Holt, Lila Lee, Ralph Graves, Richard Loo, Victor Wong, Tetsu Komai. *D:* Paul Sloane; *St:* Keene Thompson; *Sc:* Jo Swerling. (G.B. title: *Soldier of Fortune*)
"Poverty row" adventure drama.

War Lord *see* **West of Shanghai**

5093. War Nurse (MGM; 1930). *Cast:* Robert Montgomery, June Walker, Anita Page, Robert Ames, Marie Prevost, Hedda Hopper, ZaSu Pitts, Helen Jerome Eddy, Eddie Nugent, John Miljan, Michael Vavitch, Martha Sleeper. *D:* Edgar Selwyn; *Sc:* Becky Gardiner, Joe Farnham.
Based on an anonymous biography, this is a chronicle of American volunteer nurses in France during World War I.

5094. War of the Range (Monarch; 1933). *Cast:* Tom Tyler, Lane Chandler, Lafe McKee, Slim Whitaker, Ted Adams, Charles French. *D:* John P. McGowan; *P:* John R. Freuler.
Tom Tyler shoot-'em-up.

5095. The Warrior's Husband (Fox; 1933). *Cast:* David Manners, Elissa Landi, Marjorie Rambeau, Ernest Truex, Maude Eburne, Ferdinand Gottschalk, John Sheehan, Lionel Belmore, Claudia Coleman, Helen Ware, Helene Madison, Stanley "Tiny"

Sandford. *D:* Walter Lang; *St:* Julian Thompson; *Sc/Adapt./Dial.:* Ralph Spence; *Cont.:* Sonya Levien.

Based on a Broadway play, this is a modern version of "Lysistrata."

Washington Cowboy *see* **Rovin' Tumbleweeds**

5096. The Washington Masquerade (MGM; 1932). *Cast:* Lionel Barrymore (recreating his stage role), Karen Morley, Nils Asther, Diane Sinclair, Reginald Barlow, William Collier, Sr., William Morris, Rafaela Ottiano, C. Henry Gordon, Berton Churchill, Henry Kolker, Hattie McDaniel. *D:* Charles Brabin; *Sc:* John Meehan, Samuel Blythe. (G.B. title: *Mad Masquerade*) (1:32)

Political melodrama of a senator on the road to ruin because of his affair with a tart. Based on the play "The Claw" by Henry Bernstein, the film flopped at the box office, as did most films with a political theme.

5097. Washington Merry-Go-Round (Columbia; 1931–32). *Cast:* Lee Tracy, Constance Cummings, Walter Connolly, Alan Dinehart, Jane Darwell, J. Carrol Naish, Donald Cook, Arthur Hoyt, Arthur Vinton, Clarence Muse, Sam Godfrey, Clay Clement, Frank Sheridan, Ernest Woods. *D:* James Cruze; *P:* Walter Wanger; *Sc:* Jo Swerling. (G.B. title: *Invisible Power*) (1:19)

A naive congressman gets a seat in Washington and runs into political corruption. Shades of *Mr. Smith Goes to Washington* (q.v.).

5098. Water Rustlers (Grand National/Coronado; 1939). *Cast:* Dorothy Page, Dave "Tex" O'Brien, Vince Barnett, Ethan Allen, Leonard Trainer, Merrill McCormack, Stanley Price, Warner Richmond, Lloyd Ingraham. *D:* Samuel Diege; *P:* Don Lieberman; *Sc:* Arthur Hoerl. (0:54) (video)

Dorothy Page western with songs (#1 in a series of three films), involving a story of a lady rancher's dilemma with the local water rights.

5099. Waterfront (WB; 1939). *Cast:* Dennis Morgan, Gloria Dickson, Marie Wilson, Larry Williams, Sheila Bromley, Ward Bond, Aldrich Bowker, Frank Faylen, George Lloyd, Arthur Gardner. *D:* Terry Morse; *As.P.:* Bryan Foy; *Sc:* Arthur Ripley, Lee Katz.

B drama of a long-standing feud between two tough longshoremen. Based on a play of (John) Kenyon Nicholson, the film had little box office appeal.

5100. Waterfront Lady (Republic/Mascot; 1935). *Cast:* Ann Rutherford (feature film debut), Frank Albertson, J. Farrell MacDonald, Barbara Pepper, Grant Withers, Charles C. Wilson, Purnell Pratt, Jack LaRue, Ward Bond, Paul Porcasi, Mary Gordon, Mathilde Comont, Robert Emmett O'Connor, Clarence H. Wilson, Victor Potel, Wally Albright, Smiley Burnette. *D:* Joseph Santley; *P:* Colbert Clark; *St & Sc:* Wellyn Totman; *Additional Dialogue:* Joseph Fields. (1:10)

Romantic low-budget melodrama involving a shooting on a gambling ship.

5101. Waterloo Bridge (Universal; 1931). *Cast:* Mae Clarke, Kent Douglass (Douglass Montgomery), Doris Lloyd, Ethel Griffies, Enid Bennett, Frederick Kerr, Bette Davis, Rita Carlisle. *D:* James Whale; *P:* Carl Laemmle, Jr.; *Sc:* Tom Reed, Benn W. Levy. (1:12)

Drama of a dancer who hits the skids after her army officer husband is reported missing. A hit "woman's picture" of its day it was based on the popular play by Robert E. Sherwood. Remade in 1940 with Vivien Leigh and Robert Taylor and again in 1956 as *Gaby*.

5102. Way Back Home (RKO; 1931). *Cast:* Phillips Lord (from radio as Seth Parker), Effie L. Palmer (from radio as Ma Parker), Bennett Kilpack (from radio as Cephus), Bette Davis, Frank Albertson, Frankie Darro, Dorothy Peterson, Stanley Fields, Oscar Apfel, Sofia (Mrs. Phillips) M. Lord (from radio as Lizzie), Raymond Hunter. *D:* William A. Seiter; *Production Supervisor:* Pandro S. Berman; *Sc:* Jane Murfin. (G.B. title: *Old Great Heart*) (aka: *Other People's Business*) (1:21)

Drama of life and love in a rural American community. Based on the radio soap opera of the same name.

5103. Way Down East (Fox; 1935). *Cast:* Rochelle Hudson (in a role originally intended for Janet Gaynor), Henry Fonda, Slim Summerville, Edward Trevor, Russell Simpson, Margaret Hamilton, Andy Devine, Spring Byington, Sara Haden, Billy Benedict, Ann Doran, Clem Bevans (film debut), Harry C. Bradley, Vera Lewis, Al Lydell, Phil La Toska. *D:* Henry King; *P:* Winfield Sheehan; *Sc:* Howard Estabrook, William Hurlbut. (1:20)

The melodramatic plight of an unwed mother, based on the old stage melodrama by Lottie Blair Parker. Filmed before: (United Artists/D.W. Griffith; 1921) with Lillian Gish, Richard Barthelmess and Lowell Sherman, a mammoth box office hit of the silent era.

5104. Way Down South (RKO/ Principal; 1939). *Cast:* Bobby Breen, Alan Mowbray, Sally Blane, Ralph Morgan, Edwin Maxwell, Clarence Muse, Steffi Duna, Robert Greig, Charles Middleton, Lillian Yarbo, Stymie Beard (of "Our Gang" fame), Jack Carr, Marguerite Whitten, Hall Johnson Choir. *D:* Bernard Vorhaus; *P:* Sol Lesser; *St:* Clarence Muse, Langston Hughes; *Sc:* Muse, Hughes; *Songs:* Muse, Hughes. (1:01)

In pre–Civil War Louisiana, a young boy is about to be swindled of his inheritance in this costume musical drama.

5105. Way for a Sailor (MGM; 1930). *Cast:* John Gilbert, Wallace Beery, Leila Hyams, Jim Tully, Polly Moran, Doris Lloyd, Ray Milland (American debut—bit). *D:* Sam Wood; *Sc:* Laurence Stallings, W.L. River, Charles MacArthur, Al Boasberg. (1:23)

The adventures of a sailor and his pet seal. A box office flop which was based on the novel by Albert Richard Wetjen.

5106. The Way of All Men (WB/ F.N.; 1930). *Cast:* Douglas Fairbanks, Jr., Dorothy Revier, Noah Beery, Robert Edeson, Wade Boteler, Anders Randolf, William Courtenay, Ivan Simpson, Leon Janney. *D:* Frank Lloyd; *P:* Lloyd; *Sc:* Bradley King. (G.B. title: *Sin Flood*)

In this melodrama, various people are trapped in an underground cafe during a flood. A remake of *Sin Flood* (Sam Goldwyn; 1921) with Richard Dix, it was based on a play by Henning Berger.

The Way of Life (G.B. title) *see* **They Call It Sin**

5107. The Way of the West (Superior; 1934). *Cast:* Wally Wales (his final starring western role), Art Mix, William Desmond, Myrla Bratton, Bobby Nelson, Billy Patton, Fred Parker, Jim (James) Sheridan (later: Sherry Tansey), Tex Jones, Harry Berry, Helen Gibson, "Tiny" Skelton, Gene Raymond, James (Jimmy) Aubrey. *D:* Robert Emmett (Tansey); *P:* Emmett (Tansey); *Sc:* Barry Barringer, Al Lane. (0:51)

Wally Wales (Hal Taliaferro) western of a conflict between cattlemen and sheepmen.

5108. Way Out West (MGM; 1930). *Cast:* William Haines, Leila Hyams, Polly Moran, Cliff Edwards, Francis X. Bushman, Jr., Vera Marsh, Charles Middleton, Jack Pennick, Buddy Roosevelt, Jay Wilsey (Buffalo Bill, Jr.). *D:* Fred Niblo; *St & Sc:* Byron Morgan, Alfred Block; *Dialogue:* Joe Farnham. (1:10)

A hit modern-day western comedy

of a carnival huckster, forced to work on a ranch to repay the cowboys he cheated.

5109. Way Out West (MGM/Hal Roach; 1936–37). *Cast:* Stan Laurel, Oliver Hardy, Sharon Lynne (Lola Marcel), James Finlayson (Mickey Finn), Rosina Lawrence (Mary Roberts), Stanley Fields, Vivian Oakland, Chill Wills & the Avalon Boys, Mary Gordon. *D:* James W. Horne; *P:* Hal Roach; *As.P.:* Stan Laurel; *St:* Charles Rogers, Jack Jevne; *Sc:* Rogers, James Parrott, Felix Adler; *Music:* (A.A.N.) Marvin Hatley. (1:05) (video — b/w & computer-colored)

Classic Laurel & Hardy comedy that has them out west delivering a mine deed to the daughter of their deceased partner. Notable as one of the first feature films to undergo computer-coloring around 1983.

5110. The Way to Love (Paramount; 1933). *Cast:* Maurice Chevalier, Ann Dvorak (in a role originally intended for Carole Lombard, started by Sylvia Sidney with replacement of Dvorak when Sidney walked out on the production), Edward Everett Horton, Minna Gombell, Arthur Pierson, Nydia Westman, John Miljan, Blanche Frederici, Sidney Toler, Grace Bradley, George Regas, Douglass Dumbrille, Arthur Housman, Billy Bevan, Jason Robards. *D:* Norman Taurog; *P:* Benjamin Glazer; *Sc:* Gene Fowler, Glazer; *Additional Dialogue:* Claude Binyon, Frank Butler; *Songs:* Ralph Rainger, Leo Robin. (1:20)

Romantic musical with a Paris setting.

The Wayne Murder Case *see* **Strange Adventure**

5111. Wayward (Paramount; 1932). *Cast:* Nancy Carroll, Richard Arlen, Pauline Frederick, Donald Meek, John Litel, Margalo Gillmore, Dorothy Stickney, Gertrude Michael (film debut), Sidney Easton. *D:* Edward

Sloman; *Sc:* Gladys Unger, William Day.

Marital drama of a woman who marries a man dominated by his mother. Based on the novel by Mateel Howe Farnham.

5112. We Are Not Alone (WB/F.N.; 1939). *Cast:* Paul Muni, Jane Bryan (who received an Acting Award from the National Board of Review in 1940), Una O'Connor, Henry Daniell, Cecil Kellaway, Alan Napier (American debut), Billy Bevan, Holmes Herbert, Montagu Love, James Stephenson, Eily Malyon, Raymond Severn, Douglas Scott, May Beatty, Colin Kenny, Stanley Logan, Ethel Griffies, Crauford Kent. *D:* Edmund Goulding; *As.P.:* Henry Blanke; *Sc:* James Hilton, Milton Krims. (1:52)

Illicit love and murder combine in this drama based on a James Hilton novel. A box office flop.

5113. We Have Our Moments (Universal; 1937). *Cast:* James Dunn, Sally Eilers, Marjorie Gateson, Joyce Compton, Mischa Auer, David Niven, Warren Hymer, Franklin Pangborn, Thurston Hall, Grady Sutton, Virginia Sale. *D:* Alfred Werker; *P:* Edmund Grainger; *St:* Frederick Stephani, Charles Belden; *Sc:* Bruce Manning, Charles Grayson. (1:05)

While on a cruise to Europe, a teacher gets mixed up with crooks in this B comedy.

We Humans (G.B. title) *see* **Young America**

5114. We Live Again (United Artists/Samuel Goldwyn; 1934). *Cast:* Anna Sten (Katusha), Fredric March (Prince Dmitri), Jane Baxter, C. Aubrey Smith, Sam Jaffe, Ethel Griffies, Gwendolyn Logan, Jessie Ralph, Leonid Kinskey, Dale Fuller, Morgan Wallace, Crauford Kent, Davison Clark, Cecil Cunningham, Jessie Arnold, Fritzi Ridgeway, Mary Forbes, Michael Visaroff, Edgar Norton. *D:* Rouben

Mamoulian; *P:* Samuel Goldwyn; *Sc:* Preston Sturges, Maxwell Anderson, Leonard Praskins. (1:22)

Set in 1875 Russia, a young prince falls for a peasant girl in this romantic drama based on Leo Tolstoy's "Resurrection." See *Resurrection* (q.v.) for other filmed versions of this work. A box office flop.

We Three (G.B. title) *see* **Compromised**

5115. We Went to College (MGM; 1936). *Cast:* Charles Butterworth, Walter Abel, Hugh Herbert, Una Merkel, Edith Atwater, Walter Catlett, Charles Trowbridge, Tom Ricketts. *D:* Joseph Santley; *P:* Harry Rapf; *St:* George Oppenheimer, Finley Peter Dunne, Jr.; *Sc:* Richard Maibaum, Maurice Rapf. (G.B. title: *The Old School Tie*)

B comedy of a class reunion.

5116. We Who Are About to Die (RKO; 1936–37). *Cast:* Preston Foster, Ann Dvorak, John Beal, Ray Mayer, Gordon Jones, Russell Hopton, J. Carrol Naish, Paul Hurst, Frank Jenks, John Wray, Frank M. Thomas, Barnett Parker, Willie Fung, John Carroll, DeWitt Jennings, Landers Stevens, John "Skins" Miller, Howard Hickman, Robert Emmett O'Connor. *D:* Christy Cabanne; *P:* Edward Small; *Sc:* John Twist. (1:22)

Crime melodrama of a man, framed by payroll thieves and sent to prison. Based on factual incidents in the life of David Lamson who also wrote the novel.

5117. We're Going to Be Rich (20th Century–Fox; 1938). *Cast:* Gracie Fields, Victor McLaglen, Brian Donlevy, Coral Browne, Gus McNaughton, Ted Smith, Tom Payne, Charles Harrison, Don McCorkindale, Joe Mott. *D:* Monty Banks; *P:* Samuel G. Engel; *St:* James Edward Grant; *Sc:* Banks, Rohama Siegel, Sam Hellman. (1:20)

A British-American co-produced musical comedy-drama set in the South African gold fields of the 19th century.

We're in the Army Now (G.B. title) *see* **Pack Up Your Troubles** (1939)

5118. We're in the Legion Now (Grand National/Regal; 1936–37). *Cast:* Reginald Denny, Esther Ralston, Eleanor Hunt, Vince Barnett, Claudia Dell, Robert Frazer, Rudolph Amendt, Merrill McCormack, Frank Hoyt, Manuel Pelufo, Grace Cunard, Charles Moyer, Lou Hicks. *D:* Crane Wilbur; *P:* George A. Hirliman; *Sc:* Roger Whately; *Additional Dialogue:* Wilbur. (Original title: *The Rest Cure*) (1:10)

A low-budget comedy-adventure filmed in magnacolor. Based on the story "The Rest Cure" by J.D. Newsom.

5119. We're in the Money (WB; 1935). *Cast:* Joan Blondell, Glenda Farrell, Hugh Herbert, Man Mountain Dean, Ross Alexander, Hobart Cavanaugh, Phil Regan, Anita Kerry, Lionel Stander, Henry O'Neill, Joseph Crehan, Mayo Methot, Joseph King, Ed Gargan, Myron Cox, E.E. CLive. *D:* Ray Enright; *P:* Harry Joe Brown; *St:* George R. Bilson; *Adaptation:* Erwin Gelsey; *Sc:* F. Hugh Herbert, Brown Holmes; *Song:* "So Nice Seeing You Again" by Mort Dixon & Allie Wrubel. (1:04)

Low-budget comedy of two female process servers which flopped at the box office.

5120. We're Not Dressing (Paramount; 1934). *Cast:* Bing Crosby, Carole Lombard, George Burns, Gracie Allen, Ethel Merman, Leon Errol, Jay Henry, Ray Milland, Ben Hendricks, Jr., Ted Oliver, John Irwin, Charles Morris. *D:* Norman Taurog; *P:* Benjamin Glazer; *Adaptation:* Glazer; *Sc:* Horace Jackson, Francis Martin, George Marion, Jr.; *Songs:* Mack Gordon & Harry Revel of which "May I?" & "Good Night, Lovely Little Lady" became popular hits of the day.

Madcap musical-comedy of various people shipwrecked on a desert island. Based on the British play "The Admirable Crichton" by James M. Barrie (who became terminally ill shortly after seeing the film). *The Admirable Crichton* (Columbia; 1957), a British production released in the U.S. as *Paradise Lagoon,* was another version of the play.

5121. We're on the Jury (RKO; 1937). *Cast:* Helen Broderick, Victor Moore, Louise Latimer, Robert McWade, Philip Huston, Vinton Haworth, Maxine Jennings, Frank M. Thomas, Colleen Clare, Billy Gilbert, Charles Lane, Charles Middleton, Leonid Kinskey, Jonathan Hale, Hal K. Dawson, Jean Howard, Sarah Edwards. *D:* Ben Holmes; *As.P.:* Joseph Henry Steele; *Sc:* Franklin Coen. (1:21)

A remake of *Ladies of the Jury* (q.v.) is this B comedy of a small town jury sitting in on a murder case, and one particular female member who finds out the real killer. Based on the play by John Frederick Ballard.

5122. We're Only Human (RKO; 1935). *Cast:* Preston Foster, Jane Wyatt, James Gleason, Jane Darwell, Arthur Hohl, John Arledge, Moroni Olsen, Christian Rub, Mischa Auer, Harold Huber, Rafaela Ottiano, Charles Wilson. *D:* James Flood; *As.P.:* Edward Kaufman; *St:* Thomas Walsh; *Sc:* Rian James. (1:08)

B budget crime melodrama of a cop who goes after a gangster he allowed to escape.

5123. We're Rich Again (RKO; 1934). *Cast:* Reginald Denny, Joan Marsh, Edna May Oliver, Billie Burke, Grant Mitchell, Marian Nixon, Larry "Buster" Crabbe (whose only verbal utterance in the film is the climax), Gloria Shea, Edgar Kennedy, Otto Yamaoka, Lenita Lane, Dick Elliott, Andres de Segurola, Dave O'Brien (bit). *D:* William A. Seiter; *As.P.:* Glendon Allvine; *Sc:* Ray Harris; *Song:* Albert Hay Malotte. (1:12)

Depression-era comedy based on a play by Alden Nash of a once-wealthy family trying to keep up appearances.

5124. Weary River (WB/F.N.; 1929). *Cast:* Richard Barthelmess, Betty Compson, William Holden, Louis Natheaux, George E. Stone, Raymond Turner, Gladden James. *D:* (A.A.N.) Frank Lloyd; *Sc:* Bradley King, Tom Geraghty, Courtney Riley Cooper; *St:* Lewis E. Lawes.

Part-talkie melodrama of a hoodlum sent to prison where he discovers a talent for music and singing. Remade as *Over the Wall* (q.v.).

5125. The Wedding Night (United Artists/Samuel Goldwyn; 1935). *Cast:* Gary Cooper, Anna Sten, Ralph Bellamy, Walter Brennan, Helen Vinson, Sig Rumann, Esther Dale, Margaret Hamilton, George Meeker, Leonid Snegoff, Eleanor Wesselhoeft, Douglas Wood, Hedi Shope, Robert Louis Stevenson II, Otto Yamaoka, Agnes Anderson, Hilda Vaughn, Milla Davenport, Ed Ebele, Violet Axzelle. *D:* King Vidor (voted "Best Director" at the Venice Film Festival); *P:* Sam Goldwyn; *St:* Edwin Knopf; *Sc:* Edith Fitzgerald. (1:23)

This $2,000,000 production of romantic idealism was the third and final attempt by Goldwyn to make Anna Sten into another Garbo. A major flop.

5126. Wedding Present (Paramount; 1936). *Cast:* Cary Grant, Joan Bennett, George Bancroft, Conrad Nagel, Gene Lockhart, William Demarest, Edward Brophy, Lois Wilson, Inez Courtney, George Meeker, Walter Long, Charles Middleton, Heinie Conklin, Jack Mulhall, Purnell Pratt, Damon Ford. *D:* Richard Wallace; *P:* B.P. Schulberg; *St:* Paul Gallico; *Sc:* Joseph Anthony. (1:21)

Screwball-type comedy of two daffy newspaper reporters.

5127/5128. Wedding Rings (WB/F.N.; 1929). *Cast:* Lois Wilson, Olive

Borden, H.B. Warner, Kathlyn Williams, Aileen Manning, Hallam Cooley, James Ford. *D:* William Beaudine; *Sc:* Ray Harris; *Song:* "Love Will Last Forever If It's True" by Al Bryan & Ed Ward.

Romantic drama, a remake of *The Dark Swan* (WB; 1924) with Monte Blue, Helene Chadwick and Marie Prevost, and based on the novel of that name by Ernest Pascal.

5129. Wednesday's Child (RKO; 1934). *Cast:* Edward Arnold, Karen Morley, Frankie Thomas (film debut), Robert Shayne, Frank Conroy, Shirley Grey, Paul Stanton, David Durand, Richard Barbee, Tom Franklin (Frank M. Thomas), Mona Bruns, Elsa Janssen. *D:* John S. Robertson; *As. P.:* Kenneth MacGowan; *Sc:* Willis Goldbeck. (1:09)

Drama of a young boy who is forced to undergo emotional adjustment when his parents decide to divorce. Based on the play of that name by Leopold Atlas. Remade as *Child of Divorce* (RKO; 1946).

5130. Wee Willie Winkie (20th Century–Fox; 1936–37). *Cast:* Shirley Temple (Wee Willie Winkie), Victor McLaglen, C. Aubrey Smith, Cesar Romero, Constance Collier, Mary Forbes, June Lang, Michael Whalen, Clyde Cook, Gavin Muir, Lynn Bari, Lauri Beatty, Douglas Scott, Willie Fung, Brandon Hurst, Pat Somerset, Lionel Braham, Cyril McLaglen, Lionel Pape, Hector V. Sarno. *D:* John Ford; *As.P.:* Gene Markey; *Sc:* Ernest Pascal, Julien Josephson; *Art-Set Decoration:* (A.A.N.) William S. Darling, David Hall. (Original running time—1:39, now 1:15). (video)

The story of a British regiment in Indie and the little girl who shares their lives. Based on a tale by Rudyard Kipling which was adapted for Temple. The 2nd entry in Ford's "British in India" trilogy. See also: *The Black Watch* (q.v.)

and *Four Men and a Prayer* (q.v.). One of the 38 top grossing films of 1936–37, the film has been computer-colored.

5131/5132. Week-End Marriage (WB/F.N.; 1932). *Cast:* Loretta Young, Norman Foster, Aline MacMahon, George Brent, Vivienne Osborne, Roscoe Karns, Sheila Terry, Guy Kibbee, J. Carrol Naish, Grant Mitchell, J. Farrell MacDonald, Louise Carter, Richard Tucker, Harry Holman. *D:* Thornton Freeland; *St:* Faith Baldwin; *Sc:* Sheridan Gibney. (G.B. titles: *Working Wives* & *Weekend Lives*) (1:06)

Marital comedy-drama of a woman who goes to work when her husband loses his job.

Weekend Lives (G.B. title) *see* **Week-End Marriage**

5133. Weekends Only (Fox; 1932). *Cast:* Ben Lyon, Joan Bennett, John Halliday, John Elliott, Walter Byron, Halliwell Hobbes, Berton Churchill, Henry Armetta. *D:* Alan Crosland; *St:* Warner Fabian; *Sc:* William Conselman.

Romantic comedy.

5134. Welcome Danger (Paramount; 1929). *Cast:* Harold Lloyd (talkie debut), Barbara Kent, Noah Young, Charles Middleton, Edgar Kennedy, William Walling. *D:* Clyde Bruckman; *P:* Harold Lloyd; *Sc:* Bruckman, Lex Neal, Felix Adler, Paul Gerard Smith; *St:* Bruckman, Neal, Adler; *Dial.:* Smith. (1:50)

Hit comedy of a mild-mannered botanist who becomes involved with criminal element. Originally completed as a silent with titles, and then redone as a talkie prior to release.

5135/5136. Welcome Home (Fox; 1935). *Cast:* James Dunn, Arline Judge, Rosina Lawrence, Raymond Walburn, George Hayes, William Frawley, Arthur Hoyt, Charles Ray, Dave O'Brien. *D:* James Tinling.

B comedy.

5137. Wells Fargo (Paramount; 1937). *Cast:* Joel McCrea (Ramsay MacKay, his first western), Frances Dee (Justine Pryor), "Bazooka" Bob Burns (Hank York), Lloyd Nolan (Dal Slade), Ralph Morgan (Nicholas Pryor), Johnny Mack Brown (Talbot Carter), Porter Hall (James Oliver), Robert Cummings (Dan Trimball), Henry O'Neill (Henry Wells), Harry Davenport (Ingalls the banker), Mary Nash (Mrs. Pryor), Jack Clark (William Fargo), Clarence Kolb (John Butterfield), Granville Bates (Bradford the banker), Frank Conroy (Ward the banker), Brandon Tynan (Edwards the newspaper publisher), Peggy Stewart (Alice MacKay), Bernard Siegel (Pawnee), Stanley Fields (Abe), David Durand (Alex Trimball), Jane Dewey (Lucy Dorsett Trimball), Frank McGlynn (Lincoln), Scotty Beckett (young Nick), Jimmy Butler (Nick, Jr.), Dorothy Tennant (Mrs. Ward), Clare Verdera (Mrs. Edwards), Edward Earle (Padden), Henry Brandon (Larry), Harry B. Stafford (Dinsmore), Lucien Littlefield (San Francisco postmaster), Rebecca Wassem (Lola Montez), Ronnie Cosbey (Ramsay, Jr.), Paul Newlan (Zeke Martin), Erville Alderson (marshal), Louis Natheaux (Jonathan), Babs Nelson (Alice — age 6), Shirley Coates (Alice — age 10), Helen Dickson, Jerry Tucker, Sheila Darcy, Hal K. Dawson, Willie Fung. *D:* Frank Lloyd; *P:* Lloyd; *As.P.:* Howard Estabrook; *Sc:* Gerald Geraghty, Paul Schofield, Frederick Jackson; *Sound Recording:* (A.A.N.) Loren Ryder; *Song:* "Where I Ain't Been Before" by Burton Lane & Ralph Freed. (1:55)

Hit action filled western of the forming of the famous express line in the 19th-century. Based on the novel by Stuart N. Lake, it became one of the 15 top grossing films of 1937–38.

5138. Werewolf of London (Universal; 1935). *Cast:* Henry Hull (Wilfred Glendon), Warner Oland (Yogami), Valerie Hobson (Mrs. Glendon), Lester Matthews (American debut), Spring Byington, Lawrence Grant, Clark Williams, J.M. Kerrigan, Charlotte Granville, Ethel Griffies, Zeffie Tilbury, Jeanne Bartlett. *D:* Stuart Walker; *As.P.:* Robert Harris; *St:* Harris; *Adaptation:* Harris, Harvey Gates; *Sc:* John Colton. (1:15)

Hit horror film of a man who becomes afflicted with lycanthropy. This film has the distinction of being the first ever made about werewolves.

5139. West of Broadway (MGM; 1931). *Cast:* John Gilbert, Lois Moran, Ralph Bellamy, El Brendel, Madge Evans, Frank Conroy, Hedda Hopper, Gwen Lee, John Miljan, Kane Richmond, Richard Carlyle. *D:* Harry Beaumont; *St:* Bess Meredyth, Ralph Graves; *Sc:* Gene Markey.

Flop romantic drama of marriage on the rebound.

5140. West of Cheyenne (Syndicate; 1931). *Cast:* Tom Tyler (feature talkie debut), Harry Woods, Josephine Hill, Ben Corbett, Robert Walker, Fern Emmett. *D:* Harry S. Webb; *Sc:* Bennett Cohen, Oliver Drake. (0:56)

Tom Tyler western of a father and son accused of murder who have to clear themselves.

5141. West of Cheyenne (Columbia; 1938). *Cast:* Charles Starrett, Iris Meredith, Sons of the Pioneers with Bob Nolan & Pat Brady (in his film debut), Dick Curtis, Edward LeSaint, Edmund Cobb, Art Mix, John Tyrell, Ernie Adams, Jack Rockwell, Tex Cooper, Frank Ellis, George Chesebro, Ed Peil, Sr. *D:* Sam Nelson; *Sc:* Ed Earl Repp. (0:53)

Charles Starrett western of cattle rustlers.

5142. West of Nevada (Colony; 1936). *Cast:* Rex Bell, Al St. John, Joan Barclay, Steve Clark, George O'Dell, Richard Botiller, Frank McCarroll, Forrest Taylor, Bob Woodward. *D:* Robert Hill; *P:* Max & Arthur Alexander; *Sc:* Rock Hawley (Robert Hill). (0:59)

Rex Bell western of a state senator who sends his son to investigate the theft of gold from a mine on an Indian reservation.

5143. West of Rainbow's End (Monogram; 1938). *Cast:* Tim McCoy, Kathleen Eliot, Walter McGrail, Frank LaRue, George Chang, Mary Carr, Ed Coxen, George Cooper, Bob Kortman, Jimmy Aubrey, Reed Howes, Ray Jones, Sherry Tansey. *D:* Alan James; *P:* Maurice Conn; *St:* Robert Emmett (Tansey); *Sc:* Stanley Roberts, Gennaro Rea. (0:57)

Tim McCoy western (his first for this "poverty row" studio) of a retired railroad detective who gets the goods on some landgrabbers.

5144. West of Santa Fe (Columbia; 1938). *Cast:* Charles Starrett, Iris Meredith, Dick Curtis, Robert Fiske, Sons of the Pioneers with Bob Nolan & Pat Brady, LeRoy Mason, Edmund Cobb, Hank Bell, Dick Botiller, Edward Hearn, Edward LeSaint, Buck Connors, Bud Osborne, Clem Horton. *D:* Sam Nelson; *Sc:* Bennett Cohen. (1:00)

Charles Starrett shoot-'em-up of cattle rustlers who murder a rancher.

5145. West of Shanghai (WB/ F.N.; 1937). *Cast:* Boris Karloff, Beverly Roberts, Ricardo Cortez, Gordon Oliver, Vladimir Sokoloff, Sheila Bromley, Richard Loo, Selmer Jackson, Gordon Hart, James B. Leong, Maurice Liu, Tetsu Komai, Douglas Wood, Mia Ichioaka, Chester Gan, Luke Chan, Eddie Lee. *D:* John Farrow; *P:* Bryan Foy; *Sc:* Crane Wilbur. (aka: *War Lord*) (1:04)

Westerners in the Orient are saved by a Chinese war lord in this B melodrama. Previously filmed in 1923 by First National and 1930 (q.v.) as *The Bad Man,* both westerns based on the play of the name by Porter Emerson Browne and C.H. Towne. Remade in 1941 (MGM) as *The Bad Man* with Wallace Beery.

5146. West of Singapore (Monogram; 1932–33). *Cast:* Betty Compson, Weldon Heyburn, Margaret Lindsay, Noel Madison, Thomas Douglas, Clyde Cook, Harvey Clark, Ernie Adams. *D:* Al (Albert) Ray; *P:* M.H. Hoffman, Jr.; *St:* Houston Branch; *Sc:* Adele Buffington. (1:08)

"Poverty row" romantic drama set in the Orient.

West of the Badlands *see* **The Border Legion** (1939–40)

5147. West of the Divide (Monogram-Lone Star; 1933). *Cast:* John Wayne, Virginia Brown Faire, George Hayes, Lloyd Whitlock, Yakima Canutt, Billy O'Brien, Lafe McKee, Earl Dwire, Dick Dickinson, Blackie Whiteford, Tex Palmer, Artie Ortego, Horace B. Carpenter, Hal Price, Archie Ricks. *D:* Robert N. Bradbury; *P:* Paul Malvern; *Supervisor:* Trem Carr; *St & Sc:* Bradbury. (0:54) (video)

John Wayne oater of a cowboy who searches for his younger brother and the man who killed their father.

5148. West of the Pecos (RKO; 1934–35). *Cast:* Richard Dix, Martha Sleeper, Fred Kohler, Samuel S. Hinds, Maria Alba, Sleep 'n' Eat (Willie Best), Louise Beavers, Pedro Regas, G. Pat Collins, Russell Simpson, Maurice Black, George Cooper, Irving Bacon. *D:* Phil Rosen; *As.P.:* Cliff Reid; *Sc:* John Twist, Milton Krims. (1:06)

Western based on a book by Zane Grey. Remade by this studio in 1945.

5149. West of the Rockies (J. Charles Davis Productions; 1930). *Cast:* Art Mix, Horace B. Carpenter, George Edward Brown, Cliff Lyons, Bud Osborne. *D:* Horace B. Carpenter; *St:* Philip Schuyler.

(No other information available)

5150. West Point of the Air (MGM; 1935). *Cast:* Wallace Beery, Robert Young, Maureen O'Sullivan, Lewis Stone, James Gleason, Rosalind Russell, Russell Hardie, Robert Taylor, Henry Wadsworth, Robert Livingston, Richard Tucker, George Pat Collins, Frank Conroy, Ronnie Cosbey, Marilyn Spinner, Bobbie Caldwell. *D:* Richard Rosson; *P:* Monta Bell; *St:* James K. McGuinness, John Monk Saunders; *Sc:* Frank Wead, Arthur J. Beckhard. (1:40)

A military man forces his son to go through air cadet training against his will.

5151. Westbound Limited (Universal; 1937). *Cast:* Lyle Talbot, Polly Rowles, Frank Reicher, Henry Brandon. *D:* Ford Beebe; *P:* Henry MacRae, Ben Koenig; *Sc:* Maurice Geraghty. (1:16)

B drama of a trainman who must prove his innocence when blamed for a train wreck.

5152. Westbound Mail (Columbia; 1937). *Cast:* Charles Starrett, Rosalind Keith, Edward Keane, Arthur Stone, Ben Welden, Al Bridge, George Chesebro, Art Mix. *D:* Folmar Blangsted (directorial debut); *Sc:* Frances Guihan. (0:54)

Charles Starrett western of a government man investigating a situation of a woman's ranch with a vein of ore running into it.

5153. Westbound Stage (Monogram; 1939). *Cast:* Tex Ritter, Muriel Evans, Nelson McDowell, Nolan Willis, Steve Clark, Tom London, Reed Howes, Frank Ellis, Frank LaRue, Kenne Duncan, Hank Bell, Chester Gan, Phil Dunham, Chick Hannon. *D:* Spencer Gordon Bennet; *P:* Edward Finney (Boots & Saddles Prods.); *St:* John Foster; *Sc:* Robert Emmett (Tansey). (0:56)

Tex Ritter western with songs.

5154. Western Caravans (Columbia; 1939). *Cast:* Charles Starrett, Iris Meredith, Sons of the Pioneers with Bob Nolan and Pat Brady, Russell Simpson, Hal Taliaferro (Wally Wales), Dick Curtis, Sammy McKim, Hank Bell, Ethan Laidlaw, Edmund Cobb, Steve Clark, Herman Hack, Charles Brinley. *D:* Sam Nelson; *Sc:* Bennett Cohen. (0:58)

Charles Starrett western of impending conflict between ranchers and incoming nestors.

5155. The Western Code (Columbia; 1932). *Cast:* Tim McCoy, Nora Lane, Wheeler Oakman, Matthew Betz, Dwight Frye, Mischa Auer, Gordon DeMain, Bud Osborne, Cactus Mack, Chuck Baldra. *D:* J.P. McCarthy; *Sc:* Milton Krims. (1:00)

Tim McCoy oater of a girl's stepfather who is attempting to steal her ranch.

5156. Western Courage (Columbia; 1936). *Cast:* Ken Maynard, Geneva Mitchell, Charles French, Betty Blythe, Cornelius Keefe, Ward Bond, E.H. Calvert, Renee Whitney. *D:* Spencer Gordon Bennet; *Sc:* Nate Gatzert. (1:01)

Ken Maynard western of a dude ranch foreman who takes a shine to a spoiled rich female guest.

5157. Western Frontier (Columbia; 1935). *Cast:* Ken Maynard, Lucille Browne, Nora Lane, Robert Henry, Otis Harlan, Frank Yaconelli, Harold Goodwin, Frank Hagney, James Marcus, Gordon Griffith, Tom Harris, Nelson McDowell, Frank Ellis, Art Mix, Slim Whitaker, William Gould, Dick Curtis, Herman Hack, Horace B. Carpenter, Oscar Gahan, Budd Buster. *D:* Al Herman; *Sc:* Nate Gatzert. (0:56)

Ken Maynard western of a lawman who finds his long-lost sister is actually the head of a local gang of outlaws.

5158. Western Gold (20th Century–Fox/Principal; 1937). *Cast:* Smith Ballew, Heather Angel, LeRoy Mason, Ben Alexander, Paul Fix, Horace Murphy, Frank McGlynn, Bud Osborne, Al Bridge, Tom London, Howard Hickman. *D:* Howard Bretherton; *P:* Sol Lesser; *Sc:* Forrest Barnes. (G.B. title: *The Mysterious Stranger*) (1:00)

Smith Ballew singing cowboy western, his first for producer Sol Lesser.

5159. Western Jamboree (Republic; 1938). *Cast:* Gene Autry, Smiley Burnette, Jean Rouverol, Esther Muir, Joe Frisco, Frank Darien, Margaret Armstrong, Harry Holman, Edward Raquello, Bentley Hewlett, Kermit Maynard, George Walcott, Ray Teal (feature debut), Frank Ellis, Jack Perrin, Jack Ingram, Eddie Dean, Champion. *D:* Ralph Staub; *As.P.:* Harry Grey; *St:* Patricia Harper; *Sc:* Gerald Geraghty. (0:57)

Gene Autry western with songs and a story involving a helium gas deposit.

5160. Western Justice (Supreme; 1934–35). *Cast:* Bob Steele, Renee Borden, Julian Rivero, Arthur Loft, Lafe McKee, Nora Lane. *D:* Robert N. Bradbury; *P:* A.W. Hackel; *Supervisor:* Sam Katzman; *Sc:* Bradbury. (0:56)

Bob Steele western of mistaken identity and vengeance.

5161. Western Limited (Monogram; 1932). *Cast:* Estelle Taylor, Edmund Burns, Lucien Prival, Gertrude Astor, Eddie Kane, James Burtis, John Vosburgh, Mahlon Hamilton, Crauford Kent, Adaline Asbury, Arthur Millett, J.L. Palmer. *D:* Christy Cabanne; *P:* C.C. Burr; *St:* Evelyn Campbell; *Sc:* C.E. Roberts. (1:05)

"Poverty row" mystery-melodrama involving a jewel robbery.

5162. Western Racketeers (Aywon; 1935). *Cast:* Bill Cody, Edna Aslin,

Wally Wales (Hal Taliaferro), Ben Corbett, Budd Buster, George Chesebro, Bud Osborne. *D:* Robert J. Horner.

Bill Cody western.

5163. Western Trails (Universal; 1938). *Cast:* Bob Baker, Marjorie Reynolds, Fuzzy Knight, John Ridgely, Carlyle Moore, Wimpy the dog (Smokey), Apache the horse. *D:* George Waggner; *P:* Trem Carr; *Sc:* Joseph West (Waggner). (0:58)

Bob Baker western with songs of a man who seeks the murderer of his father after a stage hold-up.

5164. The Westerner (Columbia; 1934). *Cast:* Tim McCoy, Marion Shilling, Joseph (Sawyer) Sauers, Hooper Atchley, Edward Le Saint, John Dilson, Eddie (Edmund) Cobb, Albert J. Smith, Harry Todd, Bud Osborne, Slim Whitaker, Merrill McCormack, Art Mix, Lafe McKee, Hank Bell. *D:* David Selman; *Sc:* Harold Shumate. (0:58)

Tim McCoy western of cattle rustling.

5165. The Westland Case (Universal; 1937). *Cast:* Preston Foster (Bill Crane), Frank Jenks (Doc Williams), Carol Hughes, Barbara Pepper, Theodore von Eltz, Astrid Allwyn, Thomas E. Jackson, Selmer Jackson, Arthur Hoyt, Russell Hicks, Rollo Lloyd, George Meeker. *D:* Christy Cabanne; *P:* Larry Fox, Irving Starr; *Sc:* Robertson White. (1:02)

B murder-mystery, notable as the premiere entry in this studio's "Crime Club" series. Based on the book "Headed for a Hearse" by Jonathan Latimer.

5166. Westward Bound (Syndicate; 1930–31). *Cast:* Buffalo Bill, Jr., Allene Ray, Buddy Roosevelt, Ben Corbett, Yakima Canutt, Fern Emmett, Tom London, Robert Walker, Pete Morrison. *D:* Harry S. Webb; *Sc:* Carl Krusada. (1:00)

Buffalo Bill, Jr., western of a playboy sent west by his father to mend his ways.

5167. Westward Ho! (Republic-Lone Star; 1935). *Cast:* John Wayne, Sheila Mannors, Dickie Jones, Frank McGlynn, Jr., James Farley, Jack Curtis, Bradley Metcalfe, Jr., Mary MacLaren, Yakima Canutt, Hank Bell, Glenn Strange. *D:* Robert N. Bradbury; *P:* Paul Malvern; *Supervisor:* Trem Carr; *Sc:* Lindsley Parsons, Robert Emmett (Tansey), Harry Friedman. (0:55)

John Wayne western, his first to be released by Republic Pictures after it came into being from the merger of Mascot and Monogram. The story of a man who meets (unknowingly) his brother who he had been separated from since childhood.

5168. Westward Passage (RKO-Pathé; 1932). *Cast:* Ann Harding, Laurence Olivier, ZaSu Pitts, Irving Pichel, Juliette Compton, Irene Purcell, Bonita Granville (film debut), Don Alvarado, Florence Lake, Edgar Kennedy, Florence Roberts, Ethel Griffies, Emmett King. *D:* Robert Milton; *As.P.:* Harry Joe Brown; *Sc:* Bradley King, Humphrey Pearson. (1:13)

This box office flop is about a wife who divorces her selfish husband to marry another man. Based on the novel by Margaret Ayer Barnes.

5169. The Wet Parade (MGM; 1932). *Cast:* (in the south) Dorothy Jordan (Maggie May Chilcote), Lewis Stone (Roger Chilcote), Neil Hamilton (Roger Chilcote, Jr.), Emma Dunn (Mrs. Chilcote), Frederick Burton (Major Randolph), Reginald Barlow (Judge Brandon), John Larkin (Moses), Gertrude Howard (Angelina); (in the north) Robert Young (Kip Tarleton), Walter Huston (Pow Tarleton), Jimmy Durante (Abe Shilling), Wallace Ford (Jerry Tyler), Myrna Loy (Eileen Pinchon), Joan Marsh (Evelyn Fessenden), John Miljan (Major Doleshal), Clarence Muse (Taylor Tibbs), Clara Blandick (Mrs. Tarleton), Forrester Harvey (Mr. Fortesque), John Beck (Mr. Garrison), Eily Malyon (Mike's wife). *D:* Victor Fleming; *P:* Hunt Stromberg; *Sc:* John Lee Mahin, John Meehan (unc.). (2:00)

A real American curio is this social comment on prohibition, its beginnings and the mass corruption which followed. Based on the novel by Upton Sinclair.

5170. Wharf Angel (Paramount; 1934). *Cast:* Victor McLaglen, Dorothy Dell (feature film debut), Preston Foster, Alison Skipworth, David Landau, Mischa Auer, Alice Lake, Frank Sheridan, John Rogers, John Northpole, Alfred Delcambre. *D:* George Somnes, William Cameron Menzies; *P:* Albert E. Lewis.

B melodrama of a wanted man on the lam from the police.

5171. What a Life! (Paramount; 1939). *Cast:* Jackie Cooper, Betty Field (film debut, recreating her stage role), John Howard, Janice Logan, Vaughan Glaser, Lionel Stander, Hedda Hopper, Andrew Tombes, Dorothy Stickney, Janet Waldo, Arthur Aylesworth, Nora Cecil, Bennie Bartlett, Roberta Smith, Douglas Fahy, James Corner, Kay Stewart, Leonard Sues, Sidney Miller, George Guhl, Wilda Bennett, Betty McLaughlin. *D:* Jay Theodore Reed; *P:* Reed; *Sc:* Billy Wilder, Charles Brackett. (1:15)

This was the original film which spawned the popularity in the 1940s of the "Henry Aldrich" series. A teen comedy, based on Clifford Goldsmith's 1938 Broadway play, it also became a popular radio show.

5172. What a Man! (Sono Art-World Wide; 1930). *Cast:* Reginald Denny, Anita Louise, Miriam Seegar, Carlyle Moore, Lucille Ward, Greta Granstedt, Christiane Yves, Norma Drew, Harvey Clark. *D:* George J. Crone.

"Poverty row" romantic comedy.

5173. What a Widow! (United Artists; 1930). *Cast:* Gloria Swanson (Tamarind Brooks), Lew Cody, Margaret Livingston, Owen Moore, Nella

Walker, Gregory Gaye, Herbert Braggiotti, William Holden, James Gleason, Adrienne D'Ambricourt, Daphne Pollard. *D:* Allan Dwan; *P:* Dwan, Swanson; *St:* Josephine Lovett; *Sc:* James Gleason, James Seymour.

Flop comedy of a wealthy woman who keeps a variety of men on a string.

What a Woman! (G.B. title) *see* **There's That Woman Again**

5174. What Every Woman Knows (MGM; 1934). *Cast:* Helen Hayes, Brian Aherne, Madge Evans, Lucile Watson (film debut), Dudley Digges, Donald Crisp, Leo G. Carroll (film debut), Henry Stephenson, David Torrence, Donald Meek, William Stack, Boyd Irwin. *D:* Gregory La Cava; *P:* Irving Thalberg; *Sc:* Monckton Hoffe, John Meehan. (1:32)

Critically acclaimed comedy of a woman who is the brains behind her dimwit husband, a politician. Based on the play by James M. Barrie, the film is a remake of the 1921 Paramount silent with Lois Wilson and Conrad Nagel.

5175. What Men Want (Universal; 1930). *Cast:* Ben Lyon, Pauline Starke, Robert Ellis, Barbara Kent, Hallam Cooley, Carmelita Geraghty. *D:* Ernst Laemmle. (1:05)

B drama of fickle romantic affairs.

5176. What—No Beer? (MGM; 1933). *Cast:* Buster Keaton, Jimmy Durante, Roscoe Ates, Phyllis Barry, John Miljan, Henry Armetta, Edward Brophy, Charles Dunbar, Charles Giblyn. *D:* Edward Sedgwick; *St:* Robert E. Hopkins; *Sc:* Carey Wilson; *Additional Dialogue:* Jack Cluett. (1:06)

A prohibition comedy of bootleggers which was Buster Keaton's final starring role in an American feature film.

What Price Beauty? (G.B. title) *see* **False Faces**

5177. What Price Crime? (Beacon; 1935). *Cast:* Charles Starrett, Noel

Madison, Charles Delaney, Jack Mulhall, Lafe McKee. *D:* Albert Herman. B melodrama.

5178. What Price Decency? (Majestic; 1933). *Cast:* Dorothy Burgess, Walter Byron, Alan Hale, Harry Durant, V. Durant. *D:* Arthur Gregor; *St & Sc:* Gregor.

"Poverty row" production.

5179. What Price Hollywood? (RKO-Pathé; 1932). *Cast:* Constance Bennett (in a role originally intended for Clara Bow), Lowell Sherman, Neil Hamilton, Gregory Ratoff, Brooks Benedict, Eddie Anderson (film debut), Louise Beavers, Bryant Washburn. *D:* George Cukor; *As.P.:* Pandro S. Berman; *Original Story:* (A.A.N.) Adela Rogers St. John; *Adaptation:* Gene Fowler, Rowland Brown; *Sc:* Jane Murfin, Ben Markson. (1:28) (video)

A boozing film director makes a star out of a waitress from the Brown Derby restaurant while drinking himself to a tragic end. This film was the original inspiration for *A Star Is Born* (q.v.).

5180. What Price Innocence? (Columbia; 1933). *Cast:* Jean Parker, Minna Gombell, Ben Alexander, Louise Beavers, Betty Grable, Bryant Washburn, Beatrice Banyard, Willard Mack. *D:* Willard Mack (final film); *St & Sc:* Mack.

Exploitation melodrama of a girl who loses her innocence and eventually takes her own life when she is unable to live with the Stigma.

What Price Melody? (G.B. title) *see* **Lord Byron of Broadway**

5181. What Price Vengeance? (Rialto; 1937). *Cast:* Lyle Talbot, Wendy Barrie, Lucille Lund, Arthur Kerr, Bob Rideout, Eddie Acuff, Marc Lawrence, Reginald Hincks, Wally Albright, Lois Albright. *D:* Del Lord; *P:* Kenneth J. Bishop; *Sc:* J.P. McGowan. (G.B. title: *Vengeance*) (1:01) (video)

Independent B melodrama.

5182. What's Your Racket? (Mayfair; 1934). *Cast:* Noel Francis, J. Carrol Naish, Creighton Hale, Regis Toomey. *D:* Fred Guiol; *P:* Xxxx Shallenberger.

"Poverty row" feature.

5183. The Wheel of Life (Paramount; 1929). *Cast:* Richard Dix, Esther Ralston, O.P. Heggie, Myrtle Stedman, Larry Steers, Nigel de Brulier, Regis Toomey. *D:* Victor Schertzinger; *Sc:* John Farrow.

A triangular romance set in British colonial India. A remake of a 1916 silent.

5184. Wheels of Destiny (Universal; 1934). *Cast:* Ken Maynard, Frank Rice, Dorothy Dix, Philo McCullough, Freddy Sale, Jr., Jay Wilsey (Buffalo Bill, Jr.), John Big Tree, Jack Rockwell, Nelson McDowell. *D:* Alan James (aka: Alvin J. Neitz); *Sc:* Nate Gatzert; *Songs:* Maynard. (1:04)

Ken Maynard western of a wagon train trek which utilizes much silent footage.

5185. When a Feller Needs a Friend (MGM; 1932). *Cast:* Jackie Cooper, Charles "Chic" Sale, Dorothy Peterson, Ralph Graves, Helen Parrish, Dickie Moore, Oscar Apfel, Donald Haines, Andy Shuford, Gus Leonard. *D:* Harry Pollard; *St:* William Johnston; *Sc:* Sylvia Thalberg, Frank Butler. (G.B. title: *When a Fellow Needs a Friend*)

Sentimental comedy-drama of a crippled boy and his problems.

When a Fellow Needs a Friend (G.B. title) *see* **When a Feller Needs a Friend**

5186. When a Man Rides Alone (Monarch; 1933). *Cast:* Tom Tyler, Adele Lacey, Alan Bridge, Bob Burns, Frank Ball, Alma Chester, Duke Lee, Barney Furey, Lee Cordova, Jack Rockwell. *D:* J.P. McGowan; *P:* John R. Freuler; *Sc:* Oliver Drake. (1:00) (video)

Tom Tyler western of a bandit who steals a gold shipment and gives it to needy settlers.

5187. When a Man Sees Red (Universal; 1934). *Cast:* Buck Jones, Peggy Campbell, Syd Saylor, Dorothy Revier, LeRoy Mason, Jack Rockwell, Charles French. *D/Sc:* Alan James; *P:* Sol Lesser; *St:* Basil Dickey. (1:00)

Buck Jones western of what happens when a ranch foreman locks horns with the new female owner of the spread.

5188. When a Man's a Man (Fox; 1935). *Cast:* George O'Brien, Dorothy Wilson, Paul Kelly, Harry Woods, Jimmy Butler, Richard Carlyle, Edgar Norton, Clarence Wilson, Richard Carle. *D:* Edward F. Cline; *P:* Sol Lesser (Atherton Prods.). (TV title: *Saga of the West*) (1:10)

George O'Brien western of a cowboy who helps a lady rancher whose water supply has been cut off by outlaws. Based on the Harold Bell Wright novel, the film is a remake of a 1924 silent.

When Blonde Meets Blonde (G.B. title) *see* **Anybody's Blonde**

5189. When G-Men Step In (Columbia; 1938). *Cast:* Don Terry, Jacqueline Wells (Julie Bishop), Robert Paige, Paul Fix, Horace MacMahon, Edward Earle, Gene Morgan, Stanley Andrews, Huey White. *D:* C.C. Coleman, Jr.; *St:* Robert Chalmers Bennett, Arthur T. Horman; *Sc:* Arthur T. Horman.

B crime melodrama.

5190. When Ladies Meet (MGM; 1933). *Cast:* Ann Harding, Robert Montgomery, Myrna Loy, Alice Brady, Frank Morgan, Martin Burton, Luis Alberni. *D:* Harry Beaumont; *Sc:* John Meehan, Leon Gordon; *Art-Set Decoration:* (A.A.N.) Cedric Gibbons. (1:13)

Romantic comedy of a lady writer who falls for her publisher. Based on the play by Rachel Crothers, it was remade by this studio in 1941 with Joan Crawford and Robert Taylor.

5191. When Love Is Young (Universal; 1936). *Cast:* Virginia Bruce (Wanda Werner), Kent Taylor, Walter Brennan, William Tannen, Greta Meyer, Sterling Holloway, Jack Smart, Nydia Westman, Franklin Pangborn, Christian Rub, David Oliver, Laurie Douglas. *D:* Hal Mohr; *P:* Robert Presnell; *Sc:* Joseph Fields, Eve Greene; *Songs include:* title song & "Did Anyone Ever Tell You" by Harold Adamson & Jimmy McHugh. (1:15)

In college, Wanda Werner was voted "least likely to succeed," but returns to her alma mater years later a famous Broadway star. A romantic musical based on the story "Class Prophecy" by Eleanore Griffin.

When New York Sleeps (G.B. title) *see* **Now I'll Tell**

5192. When Strangers Marry (Columbia; 1933). *Cast:* Jack Holt, Lillian Bond, Charles Stevens, Paul Porcasi, Gustav von Seyffertitz, Barbara Barondess, Arthur Vinton, Rudolph Amendt, Harry Stubbs, Ward Bond. *D:* Clarence Badger; *St:* Maximilian Foster.

Low-budget romantic melodrama.

5193. When Strangers Meet (Liberty; 1934). *Cast:* Richard Cromwell, Sheila Terry, Julie Haydon, Arline Judge, Arthur Hoyt, Vera Gordon, Herman Bing, Charles Middleton, Maude Eburne. *D:* Christy Cabanne; *P:* M.H. Hoffman, Jr.

Independent low-budget drama.

When the West Was Young *see* **Heritage of the Desert**

5194. When Tomorrow Comes (Universal; 1939). *Cast:* Irene Dunne, Charles Boyer, Barbara O'Neil, Nydia Westman, Onslow Stevens, Fritz Feld, Nella Walker, Milton Parsons, Milburn Stone, Greta Meyer, Harry C. Bradley. *D:* John M. Stahl; *P:* Stahl; *Sc:* Dwight

Taylor; *Sound Recording:* (A.A.) Bernard B. Brown. (1:30)

A married man is in love with another woman in this romantic drama. Based on a book by James M. Cain it was remade twice as *Interlude,* in 1957 and again in Great Britain in 1968.

5195. When Were You Born? (WB/F.N.; 1938). *Cast:* Anna May Wong, Margaret Lindsay, Lola Lane, Anthony Averill, Charles Wilson, Manley P. Hall, Jeffrey Lynn (film debut), James Stephenson, Leonard Mudie, Eric Stanley, Maurice Cass, Jack Moore, Frank Jaquet. *D:* William McGann; *As.P.:* Bryan Foy; *St:* Manley P. Hall; *Sc:* Anthony Coldeway.

A hit B murder-mystery with an astrological theme. The opening of the film has metaphysicist Manley P. Hall giving a lecture on the twelve signs of the zodiac.

5196. When You're in Love (Columbia; 1937). *Cast:* Grace Moore, Cary Grant, Aline MacMahon, Thomas Mitchell, Emma Dunn, Henry Stephenson, Catherine Doucet, Luis Alberni, Gerald Oliver Smith, George Pearce, Frank Puglia, Billy Gilbert, Ann Doran, Louise Brooks (chorus bit). *D:* Robert Riskin (better known as a screenwriter in his only film as a director); *As.P.:* Everett Riskin; *Sc:* Robert Riskin; *Songs:* Jerome Kern & Dorothy Fields. (G.B. title: *For You Alone*) (1:44)

Romantic musical-comedy of an European opera singer who "marries" an American man to get into the United States. Based on an idea by Ethel Hill and Cedric Worth.

5197. When's Your Birthday? (RKO-Loew; 1937). *Cast:* Joe E. Brown, Marian Marsh, Edgar Kennedy, Margaret Hamilton, Frank Jenks, Minor Watson, Fred Keating, Maude Eburne, Don Rowan, Granville Bates, Charles Judels, Bull Montana, Suzanne Kaaren, Bud Flanagan (Dennis O'Keefe), Corky the dog. *D:* Harry Beaumont, Leon Schlesinger; *As.P.:* Robert Harris; *Sc:*

Harvey Gates, Malcolm Stuart Boylan, Samuel M. Pike, Harry Clork. (1:17)

Hit comedy of a pugilist who finds his good and bad days are governed by astrological planetary positions. An independent production of David L. Loew Productions, the film opens with a color cartoon sequence. Based on the play by Frank Ballard.

5198. Where Sinners Meet (RKO; 1934). *Cast:* Clive Brook, Diana Wynyard, Billie Burke, Reginald Owen, Alan Mowbray, Gilbert Emery, Phyllis Barry, Walter Armitage, Katherine Williams, Robert Adair, Vernon Steele. *D:* J. Walter Ruben; *As.P.:* David Lewis; *Sc:* H.W. Hanemann. (G.B. title: *The Dover Road*)

Following two marriages on the rocks, a man sets up a situation to show others intending to marry, what to expect. Based on the play "The Dover Road" by A.A. Milne, it was previously filmed in 1927 as *The Little Adventuress* by the deMille Corporation.

5198. Where the Buffalo Roam (Monogram; 1938). *Cast:* Tex Ritter, Dorothy Short, Horace Murphy, Snub Pollard, Dave O'Brien, Charles King, John Merton, Karl Hackett, Louise Massey's Westerners, Richard Alexander, Bob Terry, Blackie Whiteford, Denver Dixon, Ernie Adams, Hank Worden, Ed Cassidy, Curt Massey, White Flash the horse. *D:* Al Herman; *P:* Edward Finney (Boots & Saddles Prods.); *St & Sc:* Robert Emmett (Tansey). (1:01)

Tex Ritter western with songs and a story of the mass slaughter of the buffalo herds (with much stock footage).

5200. Where the West Begins (Monogram; 1938). *Cast:* Jack Randall, Luana Walters, Fuzzy Knight, Budd Buster, Arthur Housman, Richard Alexander, Ralph Peters, Joe Garcia, Ray Whitley & the Six Bar Cowboys (Ken Card & the Phelps Bros.). *D:* John P. McGowan; *P:* Maurice Conn (for Concord Prods.); *St:* Stanley Roberts; *Sc:* Roberts, Gennaro Rea. (0:54)

Jack Randall oater of a ranch foreman employed on a ranch where sulphur deposits become the target of swindlers.

5201. Where Trails Divide (Monogram; 1937). *Cast:* Tom Keene, Eleanor Stewart, Warner Richmond, David Sharpe, Lorraine Randall, Charles K. French, Richard Cramer, Steve Clark, Hal Price, James Sheridan (Sherry Tansey), Bud Osborne, Horace B. Carpenter, Wally West, James (Jim) Mason, Forrest Taylor, Oscar Gahan. *D:* Robert N. Bradbury; *P:* Bradbury; *St & Sc:* Emmett (Tansey). (0:59)

Tom Keene "poverty row" western with a "get the stagecoach robbers" theme.

5202. While New York Sleeps (20th Century–Fox; 1938–39). *Cast:* Michael Whalen, Chick Chandler, Jean Rogers, Sidney Blackmer, Marc Lawrence, William Demarest, Joan Woodbury, Harold Huber, Robert Middlemass, Minor Watson, Cliff Clark, June Gale, Robert Kellard. *D:* H. Bruce Humberstone; *P:* Sol M. Wurtzel; *St:* Lynn Root, Frank Fenton; *Sc:* Albert Ray, Frances Hyland.

The 2nd entry in the "Roving Reporters" B series by this studio.

5203. While Paris Sleeps (Fox; 1932). *Cast:* Victor McLaglen, Helen Mack, William Bakewell, Rita LaRoy, Dot Farley, Dewey Robinson. *D:* Allan Dwan.

Low-budget production, previously filmed in 1920 with release held up until 1923.

5204. While the Patient Slept (WB/F.N.; 1935). *Cast:* Guy Kibbee, Aline MacMahon, Lyle Talbot, Patricia Ellis, Allen Jenkins, Hobart Cavanaugh, Dorothy Tree, Henry O'Neill, Russell Hicks, Walter Walker, Brandon Hurst, Eddie Shubert, Helen Flint. *D:* Ray Enright; *P:* Harry Joe Brown; *Sc:* Eugene Solow, Robert N. Lee, Brown Holmes.

B murder-mystery set in an old dark house. Based on the book by Mignon Eberhart.

5205. Whipsaw (MGM; 1935). *Cast:* Myrna Loy (Vivian Palmer), Spencer Tracy (Ross McBride), Harvey Stephens (Ed Dexter), William Harrigan ("Doc" Evans), Clay Clement (Harry Ames), Robert Gleckler (Steve Arnold), Robert Warwick (Wadsworth), Georges Renavent (Monetta), Paul Stanton (Chief Hughes), Wade Boteler (Humphries), Don Rowan (Curley), John Qualen (Dobson), Irene Franklin (Mme. Marie), Lillian Leighton (Aunt Jane), J. Anthony Hughes (Bailey), William Ingersoll (Dr. Williams), Charles Irwin (Larry King), Halliwell Hobbes. *D:* Sam Wood; *P:* Harry Rapf; *St:* James Edward Grant; *Sc:* Howard Emmett Rogers. (1:23)

Romantic crime drama of a G-Man who gets the goods on a gang of jewel thieves by romancing a female member of the gang.

5206. Whirlpool (Columbia; 1933–34). *Cast:* Jack Holt, Jean Arthur, Lila Lee, Donald Cook, Allen Jenkins, John Miljan, Rita LaRoy, Willard Robertson, Ward Bond. *D:* Roy William Neill; *St:* Howard Emmett Rogers.

Melodrama of an ex-con who seeks to know the child he abandoned years before. (1:12)

5207. The Whirlwind (Columbia; 1933). *Cast:* Tim McCoy, Alice Dahl, Pat O'Malley, Matthew Betz, Joseph Girard, J. Carrol Naish, Lloyd Whitcomb, Stella Adams, William McCall, Theodore Lorch, Mary Gordon. *D:* D. Ross Lederman; *Sc:* Stuart Anthony. (1:00)

Tim McCoy western of a man who returns home to find things have changed.

5208. Whirlwind Horseman (Grand National; 1938). *Cast:* Ken Maynard, Joan Barclay, Dave O'Brien, Kenny Dix, Walter Shumway, Roger Williams, Budd Buster, Lew Meehan,

Joseph Girard, Bill Griffith, Glenn Strange, Tarzan the horse. *D:* Robert Hill; *P:* Max & Arthur Alexander; *Sc:* George Plympton. (0:58)

Ken Maynard horse opera of two men looking for a missing friend.

Whirlwind Rider *see* **Ranger of the Law**

5209. Whispering Enemies (Columbia; 1939). *Cast:* Jack Holt, Dolores Costello, Pert Kelton, Joseph Crehan. *D:* Lewis D. Collins.

B melodrama.

5210. Whispering Smith Speaks (20th Century–Fox; 1935). *Cast:* George O'Brien (Whispering Smith), Irene Ware, Kenneth Thomson, Maurice Cass, Victor Potel, Frank Sheridan, Maude Allen, Edward Keane, William V. Mong. *D:* David Howard; *P:* Sol Lesser (Atherton Prods.).

A comic action romance of a railroad detective. Based on a real-life character as related in a story by Frank H. Spearman. Previously filmed in 1916 and 1926. Remade as *Whispering Smith* (Paramount; 1948) with another version following in 1952.

5211. Whistlin' Dan (Tiffany; 1932). *Cast:* Ken Maynard, Joyzelle Joyner, Georges Renavent, Harlan E. Knight, Don Terry, Jack Rockwell, Lew Meehan, Bud McClure, Merrill McCormack, Jessie Arnold, Wally Wales (Hal Taliaferro), Frank Ellis, Hank Bell. *D:* Phil Rosen; *P:* Phil Goldstone (Amity Prods.); *Sc:* Stuart Anthony. (1:00) (video)

Ken Maynard western of a guy seeking revenge for the murder of his friend.

5212. Whistling Bullets (Ambassador; 1937). *Cast:* Kermit Maynard, Harlene (Harley) Wood, Jack Ingram, Maston Williams, Karl Hackett, Bruce Mitchell, Sherry Tansey, Cliff Parkinson. *D:* John English; *P:* Maurice Conn; *Sc:* Joseph O'Donnell. (0:58)

Kermit Maynard western of two rangers after some thieves who stole bonds.

5213. Whistling in the Dark

(MGM; 1932). *Cast:* Edward Arnold, Ernest Truex, Una Merkel, Nat Pendleton, John Miljan, Joseph Cawthorn, Marcelle Corday, Johnny Hines. *D:* Elliott Nugent; *Sc:* Nugent. (TV title: *Scared*)

Mystery-comedy of a criminal mastermind who kidnaps a detective with the intent of pinning the perfect crime on him. Based on the play by Laurence Gross and Edward Childs Carpenter, it was remade by this studio in 1941 with Red Skelton and was so popular that "The Fox" was reprised in two more sequels. This early version was also a box office hit.

5214. White Angel (WB/F.N.;

1935–36). *Cast:* Kay Francis (Florence Nightingale), Ian Hunter, Donald Woods, Nigel Bruce, Donald Crisp, Henry O'Neill, Billy Mauch, Halliwell Hobbes, Frank Conroy, Clyde Cook, Montagu Love, Charles Irwin, Barbara Leonard, Lillian Kemble-Cooper, Alma Lloyd, Tempe Pigott, Ferdinand Munier, Georgia Caine, George Kirby, Egon Brecher, Harry Allen, Charles Croker-King, Ara Gerald. *D:* William Dieterle; *P:* Henry Blanke; *St:* Michel Jacoby; *Sc:* Mordaunt Shairp. (1:15)

A fictionalized biopic of the famed English nurse, Florence Nightingale. Based on the biographical work by Lytton Strachey, the production was a box office flop.

5215. White Banners (WB;

1938). *Cast:* Claude Rains, Fay Bainter (A.A.N. for B.A.), Jackie Cooper, Bonita Granville, Henry O'Neill, James Stephenson, Kay Johnson, J. Farrell MacDonald, John Ridgely, Edward McWade, Edward Pawley, William Pawley, Mary Field. *D:* Edmund Goulding; *As.P.:* Henry Blanke; *Sc:* Lenore Coffee, Cameron Rogers, Abem

Finkel (based on the novel by Lloyd C. Douglas). (1:40)

A morality tale involving an iceless ice box and its inventor.

5216. White Bondage (WB;

1937). *Cast:* Jean Muir, Gordon Oliver, Howard Phillips, Joseph King, Virginia Brissac, Harry Davenport, Eddie "Rochester" Anderson, Trevor Bardette, Cyrus Kendall, Milton Kibbee, Addison Richards. *D:* Nick Grinde; *P:* Bryan Foy; *Sc:* Anthony Coldeway. (0:59)

B drama of the hardships endured by sharecroppers.

5217. White Cockatoo (WB;

1934). *Cast:* Jean Muir, Ricardo Cortez, Minna Gombell, Pauline Garon, Ruth Donnelly, Walter Kingsford, John Eldredge, Gordon Westcott, Addison Richards, Armand de Bordes. *D:* Alan Crosland; *P:* Henry Blanke; *Sc:* Lillie Hayward, Ben Markson.

Based on the novel by Mignon Eberhart, this B mystery-melodrama tells of various people after a huge fortune.

5218. White Eagle (Columbia;

1932). *Cast:* Buck Jones, Barbara Weeks, Robert Ellis, Frank Campeau, Jason Robards, Clarence Geldert, Jim Thorpe (famed American Indian football player in his film debut), Ward Bond, Robert Elliott, Robert Kortman, Jimmie House. *D:* Lambert Hillyer; *Sc:* Fred Myton. (1:07)

Buck Jones western with Jones in an offbeat role of an Indian chief. The film was remade in 1941 by this studio as a 15-chapter serial of the same name with Jones in the same role.

5219. White Fang (20th Century–Fox; 1936). *Cast:* Michael Whalen, Jean Muir, Charles Winninger, Slim Summerville, Jane Darwell, Thomas Beck, John Carradine, George Ducount, Lightning the Wonder Dog, Joe Herrick, Edward Thorpe, Steve Clemente, Marie Chorre, Jack Curtis, Ken

Evans, Robert St. Angelo, Nick de Ruiz, Desmond Gallagher, Walter James, Joe Brown, Jack Stoney, Ward Bond, William Wagner, Francis McDonald, Herbert Heywood. *D:* David Butler; *P:* Darryl F. Zanuck; *Sc:* Hal Long, Sam Duncan. (1:10)

Northwoods tale based on the 1906 book by Jack London. Previously filmed in 1925 and remade in a 1972 European co-production, followed by another from the Disney studios in 1991.

5220. White Heat (Pinnacle; 1934). *Cast:* Hardie Albright, Mona Maris, Naomi Childers, Robert Stevenson, David Newell, Virginia Cherrill, Nohili Naumu, Kamaunani Achi, Nani Palsa, Arthur Clayton, Whitney de Rahm, Peter Lee Hyun, Kolimau Kamai. *D:* Lois Weber (final film— ret.); *St:* James Bodrero.

Independent South Seas tale.

5221. White Hunter (20th Century-Fox; 1936). *Cast:* Warner Baxter, June Lang, Gail Patrick, Alison Skipworth, Forrester Harvey, Olaf Hytten, George Hassell, Wilfrid Lawson, Willie Fung, Ralph Cooper, Will Stanton, Ernest Whitman. *D:* Irving Cummings; *St:* Gene Markey; *Sc:* Sam Duncan, Kenneth Earl.

B romance.

5222. The White Legion (Grand National; 1936). *Cast:* Ian Keith, Tala Birell, Ferdinand Gottschalk, Rollo Lloyd, Lionel Pape, Teru Shimada, Suzanne Kaaren, Snub Pollard, Ferdinand Munier, Nigel de Brulier, Nina Campana, Warner Richmond, Harry Allen, Don Barclay, Robert Warwick, Edward Peil, Sr., Jason Robards. *D:* Karl Brown; *P:* Bennie F. Zeidman; *St & Sc:* Brown. (1:21)

Hit drama of the building of the Panama Canal and the workers who are plagued by yellow fever until a medical team shows up to battle the deadly killer.

5223. White Lies (Columbia; 1934). *Cast:* Walter Connolly, Irene

Hervey, Victor Jory, Fay Wray, William Demarest, Oscar Apfel. *D:* Leo Bulgakov.

"Poverty row" melodrama.

The White Man (G.B. title) *see* **The Squaw Man**

5224. The White Parade (Fox; 1934). *Cast:* John Boles, Dorothy Wilson, Loretta Young, Joyce Compton, Astrid Allwyn, Frank Melton, Sara Haden, Walter Johnson, Muriel Kirkland, Frank Conroy, June Gittelson, Jane Darwell. *D:* Irving Cummings; *P:* (A.A.N. for Best Picture) Jesse L. Lasky; *St:* Rian James; *Sc:* Jesse Lasky, Jr., Sonya Levien, Ernest Pascal, James.

Hospital drama.

5225. White Shadows in the South Seas (MGM; 1928). *Cast:* Monte Blue, Raquel Torres, Robert Anderson. *D:* W.S. Van Dyke; *P:* Hunt Stromberg; *St:* Frederick J. O'Brien; *Sc:* Jack Cunningham, Ray Doyle, John Colton; *Cinematographer:* (A.A.—1928-29) Clyde de Vinna. (1:28)

This part-talkie South Sea island romantic drama was MGM's first sound feature with synchronized music, sound effects, titles and some dialogue. It placed #5 on the "10 Best" list of the *New York Times*.

Note: Robert Flaherty co-directed and co-photographed without credit.

5226. White Shoulders (RKO; 1931). *Cast:* Jack Holt, Mary Astor, Ricardo Cortez, Kitty Kelly, Sidney Toler, Robert Keith, Nicholas Soussanin. *D:* Melville Brown; *As.P.:* Henry Hobart; *Sc:* Jane Murfin, J. Walter Ruben.

After marrying a millionaire, a fickle woman runs off with a scoundrel. A remake of *Recoil* (Samuel Goldwyn; 1924), it was based on the novel of that name by Rex Beach.

5227. The White Sister (MGM; 1933). *Cast:* Helen Hayes (Angela

Chiaromonte), Clark Gable (Giovanni Severi), Lewis Stone (Prince Chiaromonte), Louise Closser Hale (Mina), May Robson (Mother Superior), Edward Arnold (Father Saracinesca), Alan Edwards (Ernest Traversi), Nat Pendleton. *D:* Victor Fleming; *P:* Hunt Stromberg; *Novel:* F. Marion Crawford; *Play Adaptation:* Walter Hackett; *Sc:* Donald Ogden Stewart. (1:48)

Hit drama of a woman who joins a convent when she believes her lover was killed in the war. Previous versions: (Essanay; 1915) with Viola Allen and Richard Travers and (Inspiration; 1923) with Lillian Gish and Ronald Colman in his American debut, the 2nd also a major hit.

5228. White Woman (Paramount; 1933). *Cast:* Charles Laughton, Carole Lombard, Kent Taylor, Charles Bickford, Percy Kilbride (film debut), Charles Middleton, James Bell, Marc Lawrence (film debut), Claude King, Ethel Griffies. *D:* Stuart Walker; *St:* Norman Reilly Raine, Frank Butler; *Sc:* Samuel Hoffenstein, Jane Loring, Gladys Lehman. (1:08)

Romantic melodrama of an overseer of a plantation in the Malaysian jungle who marries a beautiful cabaret singer and returns with her. Based on the play "Hangman's Whip," the story was reworked in 1939 as *Island of Lost Men* (q.v.).

5229. White Zombie (United Artists/American Securities Corp.; 1932). *Cast:* Bela Lugosi (Murder Legendre), Madge Bellamy, John Harron, Joseph Cawthorn, Robert Frazer, Brandon Hurst, Clarence Muse, Dan Crimmins, John Peters, George Burr MacAnnan. *D:* Victor Halperin; *P:* Edward Halperin; *Sc:* Garnett Weston. (1:14) (video)

Offbeat horror thriller of a tropical sugar plantation and its owner who "employs" a crew of zombie laborers. Notable as the first film ever to feature zombies or "the walking dead."

5230. Who Killed Gail Preston? (Columbia; 1938). *Cast:* Don Terry, Rita Hayworth, Robert Paige, Wyn Cahoon, Gene Morgan, Marc Lawrence, Arthur Loft, Dwight Frye, James Millican, Eddie Fetherston, John Gallaudet, Mildred Gover, John Spacey. *D:* Leon Barsha; *Sc:* Robert E. Kent, Henry Taylor. (1:00)

As the title implies, a who-dun-it.

5231. The Whole Town's Talking (Columbia; 1935). *Cast:* Edward G. Robinson, Jean Arthur, Arthur Hohl, Wallace Ford, Edward Brophy, Arthur Byron, Donald Meek, Etienne Girardot, John Wray, J. Farrell MacDonald, Robert Parrish, Effie Ellsler. *D:* John Ford; *P:* Lester Cowan; *Sc:* Jo Swerling, Robert Riskin. (G.B. title: *Passport to Fame*) (1:35)

Based on the story "Jail Break" by W.R. Burnett, this is a comedy of a meek and mild clerk who just happens to be a dead-ringer for a notorious gangster.

5232. Whom the Gods Destroy (Columbia; 1934). *Cast:* Walter Connolly, Doris Kenyon, Robert Young, Hobart Bosworth, Scotty Beckett, Gilbert Emery, Charles Middleton, Akim Tamiroff, Maidel Turner, George Humbert, Rollo Lloyd, Hugh Huntley, Macon Jones. *D:* Walter Lang; *Sc:* Sidney Buchman.

A drama, based on the book by Albert Payson Terhune which was previously filmed in 1916.

5233. Whoopee! (United Artists/Samuel Goldwyn-Florenz Ziegfeld; 1930). *Cast:* Eddie Cantor (Henry Williams), Ethel Shutta (Mary Custer), Eleanor Hunt (Sally Morgan), Paul Gregory (Wanenis), John (Jack) Rutherford (Sheriff Bob Wells), Spencer Charters (Jerome Underwood), Chief Caupolican (Black Eagle), Albert Hackett (Chester Underwood), Will H. Philbrick (Andy McNabb), Walter Law (Judd Morgan), Marilyn Morgan (later

Marian Marsh, film debut as Harriett Underwood), Barbara Weeks (film debut), George Olsen Band, Virginia Bruce, Betty Grable (bit). *D:* Thornton Freeland; *P:* Sam Goldwyn, Flo Ziegfeld; *Sc:* William Conselman; *Art-Set Decoration:* (A.A.N.) Richard Day; *Songs:* "Making Whoopee," "A Girl Friend of a Boy Friend of Mine," "My Baby Just Cares for Me" & "Stetson" by Walter Donaldson & Gus Kahn; "I'll Still Belong to You" by Edward Eliscu & Nacio Herb Brown. (1:33) (video)

Filmed in 2-color technicolor, this was a hit musical of its day involving a hypochondriac who goes west. Based on the story "The Nervous Wreck" by Owen Davis and adapted to the Broadway stage by William Anthony McGuire, Walter Donaldson and Gus Kahn (with Ziegfeld as producer). A production cost of $1.3 million showed a profit of $1.5 million for its producers. Most members of the stage production appear in the film. Remade in 1944 (RKO) as *Up in Arms.*

5234. Why Bring That Up? (Paramount; 1929). *Cast:* George Moran, Charles Emmett Mack (better known as the comedy team in vaudeville of Moran & Mack), Evelyn Brent, Harry Green, Selmer Jackson, Eddie Kane, Helen Lynch, Bert Swor, Charles Hall, Freeman Wood, Monte Collins, Jr., Lawrence Leslie, Jack Luden, George Thompson. *D:* George Abbott; *St:* Octavus Roy Cohen.

Low-budget comedy of two blackface comedians who run afoul of a lady out to take them.

Why Change Your Husband? (G.B. title) *see* **Gold Dust Gertie**

5235. Why Leave Home? (Fox; 1929). *Cast:* Dixie Lee, Nick Stuart, Sue Carol, Walter Catlett, David Rollins, Richard Keene, Ilka Chase. *D:* Raymond Cannon.

Low-budget romantic comedy.

5236. Why Marry? (Xxxx Xxxx; 1930). *Cast:* Rex Lease.
Romantic comedy.
(No other information available)

5237. Wicked (Fox; 1931). *Cast:* Victor McLaglen, Elissa Landi, Mae Busch, Una Merkel, Irene Rich, Blanche Frederici, Theodore von Eltz, Alice Lake, Ruth Donnelly, Edmund Breese, Lucille Williams, Blanche Payson, Kathleen Kerrigan, Eileen Percy. *D:* Allan Dwan; *St:* Adela Rogers St. John; *Sc:* (John) Kenyon Nicholson, Kathryn Scola.
Drama.

5238. A Wicked Woman (MGM; 1934). *Cast:* Mady Christians, Charles Bickford, Betty Furness, William Henry, Jackie Searle, Robert Taylor (MGM feature debut), Paul Harvey, Jean Parker, Zelda Sears (final film as an actress), Sterling Holloway, Samuel S. Hinds, DeWitt Jennings, Marilyn Harris, George Billings, Betty Jane Graham. *D:* Charles Brabin (final film as director); *P:* Harry Rapf; *Sc:* Florence Ryerson, Zelda Sears. (1:11)

To protect herself and her kids, a woman kills her drunken husband. Based on the novel by Anne Austin.

5239. Wide Open (WB; 1930). *Cast:* Patsy Ruth Miller, Edward Everett Horton, T. Roy Barnes, Louise Beavers, Louise Fazenda, Edna Murphy, Vera Lewis, Vince Barnett (film debut), E.J. Ratcliffe, Irving Bacon. *D:* Archie Mayo; *St:* Edward Bateman Morris; *Sc:* James A. Starr, Arthur Caesar.

Low-budget comedy set in the business world.

5240. Wide Open Faces (Columbia; 1938). *Cast:* Joe E. Brown, Jane Wyman, Alison Skipworth (final film — ret.), Lyda Roberti (final film — d. 1938), Alan Baxter, Lucien Littlefield, Sidney Toler, Berton Churchill, Barbara Pepper, Edward Earle, Stanley Fields, Horace Murphy. *D:* Kurt Neumann; *P:*

David L. Loew; *St:* Richard Flournoy; *Sc:* Earle Snell, Joe Bigelow, Clarence Marks. (1:07)

A soda jerk innocently becomes involved with hoodlums in this low-budget comedy.

5241. The Widow from Chicago (WB/F.N.; 1930). *Cast:* Alice White, Neil Hamilton, Edward G. Robinson, Frank McHugh, Lee Shumway, E.H. Calvert, Harold Goodwin, Betty Francisco, Brooks Benedict. *D:* Edward Cline; *Sc:* Earl Baldwin. (1:04)

B melodrama of a girl out to avenge the death of her brother.

5242. The Widow from Monte Carlo (WB; 1935). *Cast:* Dolores Del Rio, Warren William, Louise Fazenda, Colin Clive, Mary Forbes, Viva Tattersall, Olin Howland, Warren Hymer, Herbert Mundin, Eily Malyon, E.E. Clive, Frederick Burton. *D:* Arthur Greville Collins; *P:* Bryan Foy; *Sc:* F. Hugh Herbert, Charles Belden, George Bricker.

B romantic comedy-drama set in the casino at Monte Carlo. Based on a play by Ian Hay and A.E.W. Mason.

5243/5244. The Widow in Scarlet (Mayfair; 1932). *Cast:* Glenn Tryon, Dorothy Revier, Lloyd Whitlock, Lloyd Ingraham, Kenneth Harlan, Myrtle Stedman. *D:* George B. Seitz.

"Poverty row" melodrama.

5245. Wife, Doctor and Nurse (20th Century–Fox; 1937). *Cast:* Loretta Young, Warner Baxter, Virginia Bruce, Jane Darwell, Sidney Blackmer, Minna Gombell, Maurice Cass, Elisha Cook, Jr., Lon Chaney, Jr., Gordon (Bill) Elliott, Paul Hurst, Lynn Bari, Brewster Twins, Margaret Irving, Claire DuBrey, George Ernest, Hal K. Dawson. *D:* Walter Lang; *P:* Raymond Griffith; *Sc:* Lamar Trotti, Kathryn Scola, Darrell Ware. (1:24)

Triangular romantic comedy.

5246/5247. Wife, Husband and Friend (20th Century–Fox; 1939). *Cast:* Loretta Young, Warner Baxter, Binnie Barnes, Cesar Romero, George Barbier, J. Edward Bromberg, Eugene Pallette, Helen Westley, Renie Riano, Helen Erickson, Kay Griffith, Edward Cooper, Iva Stewart, Henry Rosenthal, Dorothy Dearing. *D:* Gregory Ratoff; *P:* Nunnally Johnson; *Sc:* Johnson. (1:20)

Marital comedy of a husband who tries to prevent his wife from having a singing career. Based on a story by James M. Cain. Remade as *Everybody Does It* (20th Century–Fox; 1949).

5248. Wife vs. Secretary (MGM; 1936). *Cast:* Clark Gable, Myrna Loy, Jean Harlow, May Robson, George Barbier, James Stewart, Hobart Cavanaugh, Marjorie Gateson, Gilbert Emery, Tom Dugan, Gloria Holden (film debut), Holmes Herbert, Margaret Irving, Billy Newell. *D:* Clarence Brown; *P:* Hunt Stromberg; *Sc:* Norman Krasna, Alice Duer Miller, John Lee Mahin. (1:28)

A wife suspects her husband has something going with his secretary in this romantic comedy based on the novel by Faith Baldwin. A box office hit.

Note: The same year this film was released, Gable and Loy were voted "King" and "Queen" of Hollywood by the movie-going public.

5249. Wild and Woolly (20th Century–Fox; 1937). *Cast:* Jane Withers, Walter Brennan, Pauline Moore, Carl "Alfalfa" Switzer, Jackie Searle, Berton Churchill, Robert Wilcox, Douglas Scott, Douglas Fowley, Lon Chaney, Jr., Syd Saylor, Frank Melton, John Beck, Joseph E. Bernard, Sidney Fields, Fred Kelsey, Roger Gray, Eddy Waller, Josephine Drimmer, Alice Armand, Sidney Jarvis, Romaine Callender, Russ Clark, Vester Pegg, Alex Palasthy, Erville Alderson. *D:* Alfred L. Werker; *Sc:* Lynn Root, Frank Fenton. (1:04)

Jane Withers B comedy-western of crooks planning to pull off a bank job during a Pioneer Days celebration.

5250. Wild Boys of the Road (WB; 1933). *Cast:* Frankie Darro, Rochelle Hudson, Dorothy Coonan, Edwin (Eddie) Phillips, Arthur Hohl, Ann Hovey, Sterling Holloway, Claire McDowell, Robert Barrat, Grant Mitchell, Ward Bond, Alan Hale, Jr. (film debut), Charley Grapewin, Shirley Dunstead. *D:* William A. Wellman; *P:* Robert Presnell; *St:* Daniel Ahearn; *Sc:* Earl Baldwin. (G.B. title: *Dangerous Days*) (1:08)

Depression-era melodrama of unemployed youths, wandering around the country, making it any way they can. The film was socially oriented toward a problem in the country at the time of release, but was a box office flop.

5251. Wild Brian Kent (20th Century–Fox/Principal; 1936). *Cast:* Ralph Bellamy, Mae Clarke, Helen Lowell, Stanley Andrews, Lew Kelly, Eddie Chandler, Richard Alexander, Jack Duffy. *D:* Howard Bretherton; *P:* Sol Lesser; *Sc:* Earle Snell, Don Swift, James Gruen. (1:00)

A playboy out west learns a few things when he has to help a woman save her ranch from outlaws. Based on *The Re-creation of Brian Kent* by Harold Bell Wright, the title under which it was previously filmed in 1925 with Kenneth Harlan.

5252. Wild Cargo (RKO/Van Beuren; 1934). *D:* Armand Denis; *P:* Frank Buck & the Van Beuren Organization; *Dialogue & Narration:* Courtney Ryley Cooper; *Cinematographers:* Nicholas Cavaliere, Leroy G. Phelps.

Hit jungle documentary set in Ceylon, Malaya and northern India of famed hunter and adventurer Frank Buck, showing methods of trapping various animals. Notable footage shows

a fight between a python and a panther. Based on the book by Buck and Edward Anthony.

5253. Wild Company (Fox; 1930). *Cast:* H.B. Warner, Frank Albertson, Sharon Lynne, Joyce Compton, Kenneth Thomson, Claire McDowell, Bela Lugosi, Grady Sutton, Richard Keene, George Fawcett, Frances McCoy. *D:* Leo McCarey. (1:13)

A youth has to learn the hard way in this antique generation-gap melodrama.

5254. Wild Girl (Fox; 1932). *Cast:* Charles Farrell, Joan Bennett, Ralph Bellamy, Eugene Pallette, Louise Beavers, Mary Gordon. *D:* Raoul Walsh; *Sc:* Edwin Justus Mayer (co-writer). (G.B. title: *Salomy Jane*)

Frontier drama of pioneering. Filmed twice before as *Salomy Jane,* by (Alco; 1914) with House Peters, Beatriz Michelena and William Nigh and (Paramount; 1923) with Maurice Flynn, Jacqueline Logan and George Fawcett by director George Melford. Based on the novel "Salomy Jane" by Bret Harte.

5255. Wild Gold (Fox; 1934). *Cast:* John Boles, Claire Trevor, Harry Green, Roger Imhof, Monroe Owsley, Ruth Gillette, Winifred Shaw. *D:* George Marshall; *St:* Dudley Nichols, Lamar Trotti; *Sc:* Lester Cole, H. Johnson. (1:15)

Romantic melodrama of a triangular affair in a gold mining town. The flood climax is stock footage from Fox's 1926 production *The Johnstown Flood.*

5256. Wild Horse (Allied; 1931). *Cast:* Hoot Gibson, Alberta Vaughn, Edward Peil, Sr., Stepin Fetchit, Glenn Strange, Jack Rockwell, Edmund Cobb, "Skeeter" Bill Robbins, Neal Hart, George Bunny. *D:* Richard Thorpe, Sidney Algier; *P:* M.H.

Hoffman, Jr.; *Sc:* Jack Natteford. (1:17)

Hoot Gibson western of a man who is killed after capturing a wild horse, with the man's partner being blamed. Gibson named this film as his personal favorite of all the westerns he made.

5257. Wild Horse Canyon (Monogram; 1939). *Cast:* Jack Randall, Dorothy Short, Warner Richmond, Dennis Moore, Sherry Tansey, Frank Yaconelli, Ed Cassidy, Charles King, Walter Long, Earl Douglas, Rusty the horse. *D:* Robert F. Hill; *P:* Robert Tansey; *Sc:* Robert Emmett (Tansey). (0:56)

Jack Randall western of a cowboy who goes after those who killed his brother.

5258. Wild Horse Mesa (Paramount; 1932). *Cast:* Randolph Scott, Sally Blane, Fred Kohler, George Hayes, Charley Grapewin, Lucille La Verne, Buddy Roosevelt, Jim Thorpe, E.H. Calvert. *D:* Henry Hathaway (directorial debut); *Sc:* Harold Shumate, Frank Howard Clark. (1:01)

B western involving the catching of wild horses illegally. Based on the novel by Zane Grey, it was previously filmed by this studio in 1925 with Jack Holt and remade, (RKO; 1947) with Tim Holt (son of Jack Holt). This version (the '32) utilizes footage from the silent.

5259. Wild Horse Rodeo (Republic; 1937). *Cast:* Bob Livingston (Stony Brooke), Ray Corrigan (Tucson Smith), Max Terhune (Lullaby Joslin), June Martel, Walter Miller, Edmund Cobb, Jack Ingram, William Gould, Henry Isabell, Art Dillard, Fred "Snowflake" Toones, Ralph Robinson, Dick Weston (Roy Rogers), Jack Kirk. *D:* George Sherman (directorial debut— previously an assistant director); *Sc:* Betty Burbridge. (0:54)

The 11th "Three Mesquiteers" western with the trio capturing a wild horse for a small rodeo.

5260. Wild Horse Roundup (Ambassador; 1936). *Cast:* Kermit Maynard, Betty Lloyd, Dickie Jones, Budd Buster, Frank Hagney, John Merton, Roger Williams, Dick Curtis, Jack Ingram. *D:* Alan James (aka: Alvin J. Neitz); *P:* Maurice Conn; *Sc:* Joseph O'Donnell. (0:55)

Kermit Maynard oater of a cowboy who helps a girl, about to lose her ranch.

5261. Wild Money (Paramount; 1937). *Cast:* Edward Everett Horton, Louise Campbell (film debut), Lynne Overman, Porter Hall, Benny Baker. *D:* Louis King; *St:* Paul Gallico; *Sc:* Charles Brackett (co-writer, unc.).

B comedy of a small town newspaper.

5262. Wild Mustang (Ajax; 1935). *Cast:* Harry Carey, Barbara Fritchie, Del Gordon, Robert Kortman, Cathryn Johns, George Chesebro, Milburn Morante, Chuck Morrison, George Morrell, Dick Botiller. *D:* Harry Fraser; *P:* William Berke; *Sc:* Weston Edwards. (1:02)

Harry Carey western with Carey as "Wild Mustang Norton."

5263. The Wild Party (Paramount; 1929). *Cast:* Clara Bow (talkie debut), Fredric March, Shirley O'Hara, Marceline Day, Joyce Compton, Jack Oakie, Phillips Holmes, Jack Luden, Adrienne Dore, Alice Adair, Kay Bryant, Ben Hendricks, Jr., Renee Whitney, Marguerite Cramer, Amo Ingraham, Virginia Thomas, Jack Raymond, Jean Lorraine. *D:* Dorothy Arzner; *St:* Warner Fabian; *Sc:* E. Lloyd Sheldon; *P:* Sheldon. (1:16) (video)

Hit romance of a professor and a sexy student at an all-girl school.

5264. Wild West Whoopee (Cosmos; 1931). *Cast:* Jack Perrin, Josephine Hill, Buzz Barton, Fred Church, John Ince, George Chesebro, Horace B. Carpenter, Henry Rocquemore, Ben Corbett. *D:* Robert J. Horner; *P:* Horner; *Sc:* Horner. (0:57)

Jack Perrin indie western, with much stock footage, of a rodeo rider and a girl.

5265. Wildcat Saunders (Atlantic; 1936). *Cast:* Jack Perrin, Blanche Mehaffey, Roger Williams, William Gould, Fred "Snowflake" Toones, Tom London, Ed Cassidy, Earl Dwire, Bud Osborne, Dennis Moore, Jim Corey. *D:* Harry Fraser; *P:* William Berke; *Sc:* Monroe Talbot. (1:00)

Jack Perrin western of a boxer from the east who goes west and wouldn't you know it, he gets involved with outlaws.

5266. Wildcat Trooper (Ambassador; 1936). *Cast:* Kermit Maynard, Lois Wilde, Hobart Bosworth, Fuzzy Knight, Yakima Canutt, Eddie Phillips, John Merton, Roger Williams. *D:* Elmer Clifton; *P:* Maurice Conn; *Sc:* Joseph O'Donnell. (1:00)

Kermit Maynard northwoods adventure of a Mountie after a gang of crooks, headed by a doctor.

5267. The Wildcatter (Universal; 1937). *Cast:* Jean Rogers, Scott Colton, Jack Smart, Russell Hicks, Ward Bond, Hattie McDaniel. *D:* Lewis D. Collins; *P:* George Owen; *Sc:* Charles A. Logue. (0:58)

B action-drama of two men who embark on a wildcatting adventure in Texas.

5268. Wilderness Mail (Ambassador; 1935). *Cast:* Kermit Maynard, Doris Brooks, Fred Kohler, Paul Hurst, Dick Curtis, Syd Saylor, Nelson McDowell, Kernan Cripps. *D:* Forrest Sheldon; *P:* Maurice Conn; *Sc:* Bennett Cohen, Robert Dillon. (1:00)

Kermit Maynard (in a dual role as twin brothers) Mountie actioner.

William Fox Movietone Follies of 1929 *see* **Fox Movietone Follies of 1929**

5269. Windjammer (RKO; 1937). *Cast:* George O'Brien, Constance Worth, Gavin Gordon, William Hall, Brandon Evans, Stanley Blystone, Lal Chand Mehra, Ben Hendricks, Jr., Lee Shumway, Frank Hagney, Sam Flint. *D:* Ewing Scott; *P:* George A. Hirliman; *As.P.:* David Howard; *St:* Major Raoul Haig; *Sc:* Dan Jarrett, James Gruen. (0:59)

B indie adventure of a subpoena server posing as a playboy who gets involved with gun smugglers.

5270. Winds of the Wasteland (Republic; 1936). *Cast:* John Wayne, Phyllis Fraser, Yakima Canutt, Lane Chandler, Robert Kortman, Sam Flint, Merrill McCormack, Douglas Cosgrove, Lew Kelly. *D:* Mack V. Wright; *Sc:* Joseph Poland. (0:57) (video)

John Wayne western of competition for a stagecoach mail contract.

5271. Wine, Women and Horses (WB; 1937). *Cast:* Barton MacLane, Ann Sheridan, Dick Purcell, Peggy Bates, Stuart Holmes, Walter Cassell, James Robbins, Lottie Williams, Kenneth Harlan, Frank Faylen. *D:* Louis King; *P:* Bryan Foy; *Sc:* Roy Chanslor.

B drama of a compulsive gambler. A remake of *Dark Hazard* (q.v.), and based on the novel of that name by W.R. Burnett.

5272. Wine, Women and Song (Chadwick; 1933–34). *Cast:* Lew Cody, Gertrude Astor, Lilyan Tashman, Esther Muir, Marjorie (Reynolds) Moore (talkie debut), Paul Gregory, Bobbe Arnst, Jesse de Vorska, Matty Kemp, Robert (Bobby) Watson. *D:* Herbert Brenon (final American film); *St:* Leon d'Usseau.

Low-budget romantic musical.

5273. Wings in the Dark (Paramount; 1935). *Cast:* Cary Grant, Myrna Loy, Dean Jagger, Roscoe Karns, Hobart Cavanaugh, Bert Hanlon, Samuel S. Hinds, Russell Hopton, James Burtis, Lee Phelps, Arnold Korff, Matt McHugh. *D:* James Flood; *P:*

Arthur Hornblow, Jr.; *St:* Nell Shipman, Philip Hurn; *Sc:* Jack Kirkland, Frank Partos. (1:17)

The romance of a lady flier and a test pilot who falls victim to self-pity after being blinded in an accident.

5274. Wings of Adventure (Tiffany; 1930). *Cast:* Rex Lease, Armida, Clyde Cook. *D:* Richard Thorpe.

A high-flying actioner with Mexican locales from "poverty row."

5275. Wings of the Navy (WB; 1939). *Cast:* George Brent, John Payne, Olivia de Havilland, Frank McHugh, John Litel, Victor Jory, Henry O'Neill, John Ridgely, Regis Toomey, John Gallaudet, Mary Gordon, Alan Davis, Pierre Watkin, Max Hoffman, Jr., Larry Williams, Alberto Morin, Donald Douglas, Donald Briggs, Edgar Edwards. *D:* Lloyd Bacon; *As.P.:* Louis F. Edelman; *Sc:* Michael Fessier. (1:29)

A tale of two brothers in the Navy Air Corps. A Cosmopolitan production filmed on location in a semi-documentary style at the Pensacola Air Training Station with the cooperation of the U.S. government.

5276. Wings Over Africa (Fox; 1934). Feature-length documentary of the dark continent by famed explorers, Martin and Osa Johnson.

5277. Wings Over Honolulu (Universal; 1937). *Cast:* Ray Milland, Wendy Barrie, Kent Taylor, Polly Rowles, William Gargan, Joyce Compton, Louise Beavers, Samuel S. Hinds, Mary Philips, Clara Blandick, Milburn Stone, Margaret McWade. *D:* H.C. Potter; *P:* Charles R. Rogers; *St:* Mildred Cram; *Sc:* Isabel Dawn, Boyce DeGaw; *Cinematographer:* (A.A.N.) Joseph Valentine. (1:18)

Marital drama of a wife at odds with her husband over his career as a navy flyer.

Wings Over Wyoming *see* **Hollywood Cowboy**

5278. Winner Take All (WB; 1932). *Cast:* James Cagney, Marian Nixon, Guy Kibbee, Dickie Moore, Virginia Bruce, Alan Mowbray, Esther Howard, Clarence Muse, Clarence Wilson, Ralf Harolde, John Roche, Harvey Perry, Allan Lane, George Hayes, Julian Rivero, Renee Whitney, Clarence Wilson. *D:* Roy Del Ruth; *St:* Gerald Beaumont; *Sc:* Wilson Mizner, Robert Lord. (1:08)

Hit low-budget romance of a boxer who has many problems in his love-life.

5279. Winner Take All (20th Century–Fox; 1939). *Cast:* Tony Martin, Gloria Stuart, Henry Armetta (Poppa Gambini), Kane Richmond, Robert Allen, Joseph Calleia, Inez Palange (Momma Gambini), Johnny Pironne, Betty Greco, Eleanor Virzle. *D:* Otto Brower; *P:* Sol M. Wurtzel.

The third and final entry in the B budget "Gambini" series, this one with a prize-fighting theme. Filmed before by Fox in 1924 with Charles "Buck" Jones and Peggy Shaw.

Winning the West *see* **The Light of the Western Stars**

5280. The Winning Ticket (MGM; 1934). *Cast:* Leo Carrillo, Louise Fazenda, Irene Hervey, Luis Alberni, Ted Healy, Robert Livingston, James Ellison, Akim Tamiroff, Arthur Treacher, Purnell Pratt, Billy Watson, Betty Jane Graham, John Indrisano. *D:* Charles Riesner; *P:* Riesner, Jack Cummings; *St:* Robert Pirosh, George Seaton; *Sc:* Richard Schayer, Ralph Spence.

Low-budget comedy of an Italian barber who has the winning ticket to the Irish Sweepstakes, but can't find it.

5281. Winter Carnival (United Artists/Walter Wanger; 1939). *Cast:* Ann Sheridan, Richard Carlson, Helen Parrish, Virginia Gilmore (film debut), Robert Walker (film debut — bit), James

Corner, Joan (Leslie) Brodel, Peggy Moran, Morton Lowry, Robert Armstrong, Alan Baldwin, Marsha Hunt, Robert Allen, Emory Parnell, Jimmy Butler, McCash Twins, Benny Drohan, Kenneth Stevens, Martin Turner. *D:* Charles F. Riesner; *P:* Walter Wanger; *St:* Budd Schulberg, Maurice Rapf; *Sc:* Schulberg, Lester Cole, Maurice Rapf. (1:45)

Romantic comedy set at Dartmouth College on a holiday weekend.

5282. Winterset (RKO; 1936). *Cast:* Burgess Meredith (film debut, recreating his stage role of Mio), Margo (recreating her stage role of Miriamne), Eduardo Ciannelli (recreating his stage role of Trock), Paul Guilfoyle (film debut as Garth), John Carradine (Romagna), Edward Ellis (Judge Gaunt), Stanley Ridges (Shadow), Myron McCormick (film debut as Carr), Maurice Moscovich (film debut as Esdras), Helen Jerome Eddy (Mrs. Romagna), Fernanda Eliscu (Piny), George Humbert (Lucia), Murray Alper (Louie), Paul Fix (Joe), Arthur Loft (district attorney), Willard Robertson (policeman), Mischa Auer (radical), Alec Craig (hobo), Barbara Pepper, Alan Curtis, Otto Hoffman, Grace Hayle, Al Hill, Lucille Ball (bit). *D:* Alfred Santell; *P:* Pandro S. Berman; *Sc:* Anthony Veiller; *Cinematographer:* Peverell Marley (who received a prize for photography at the Venice Film Festival of 1937); *Art-Set Decoration:* (A.A.N.) Perry Ferguson; *Musical Director:* (A.A.N.) Nathaniel Shilkret. (1:18) (video)

A man pays with his life for a crime he didn't commit while his son searches out the guilty party in this critically acclaimed drama based on Maxwell Anderson's Broadway play. The film was in nomination for "Best Film" with the New York Film Critics. It placed #4 and #5 respectively on the "10 Best" lists of the *New York Times* and the National Board of Review of 1936, placing #9 on the "10 Best" list of *Film Daily* in 1937.

5283. Wise Girl (RKO; 1937). *Cast:* Miriam Hopkins, Ray Milland, Walter Abel, Guinn Williams, Henry Stephenson, Margaret Dumont, Ivan Lebedeff, Betty Philson, Marianna Strelby, Jean de Briac, Alec Craig, Rafael Storm, Gregory Gaye, Richard Lane, Tom Kennedy, Cecil Kellaway. *D:* Leigh Jason; *P:* Edward Kaufman; *St:* Allan Scott, Charles Norman; *Sc:* Scott. (1:10)

B screwball comedy of a rich girl pretending to be poor while living among the residents of Greenwich Village in New York.

5284. Wise Girls (MGM; 1929). *Cast:* Elliott Nugent, J.C. Nugent (Elliott's real-life father), Norma Lee, Roland Young, Clara Blandick (feature film debut). *D:* E. Mason Hopper; *Sc:* J.C. & Elliott Nugent.

Low-budget domestic comedy, based on the play "Kempy" by J.C. and Elliott Nugent. The first film by this studio not to be issued in a silent version with titles — for theaters not yet wired for sound.

5285. The Wiser Sex (Paramount; 1932). *Cast:* Claudette Colbert, Melvyn Douglas, Franchot Tone (film debut), Lilyan Tashman, Ross Alexander (film debut), Douglass Dumbrille, Victor Kilian, Granville Bates, Robert Fischer, Effie Shannon. *D:* Berthold Viertel.

Filmed at Astoria Studios in Long Island, N.Y., this comedy-drama of politics, racketeers and murder is based on a play by Clyde Fitch. Previously filmed as *The Woman in the Case* (Lasky Feature Plays; 1916) and *The Law and the Woman* (Paramount; 1922) with Betty Compson and William P. Carleton.

5286. The Witching Hour (Paramount; 1934). *Cast:* Sir Guy Standing, John Halliday, Judith Allen, Tom Brown, Selmer Jackson, William Frawley, Olive Tell, Richard Carle, John Larkin, Ferdinand Gottschalk, Purnell Pratt, Gertrude Michael, Ralf Harolde,

Frank Sheridan. *D:* Henry Hathaway; *P:* Bayard Veiller.

A melodrama of hypnotism, mental telepathy and murder which was based on the hit 1907 Broadway play by Augustus Thomas. Previous versions: (World-Selznick; 1916) with C. Aubrey Smith, Helen Arnold and Jack Sherrill; (Paramount/Famous Players-Lasky; 1921) with Elliott Nugent by director William Desmond Taylor.

5287. With Byrd at the South Pole (Paramount; 1930). *Cinematography:* (A.A.) Joseph Rucker & Willard Van Der Veer.

Narrated by Floyd Gibbons, this documentary of Commander Richard E. Byrd's Antarctic expedition was voted "Best Film of the Year" by the *New York Times,* while placing #7 on the "10 Best" list of *Film Daily.*

5288. With Love and Kisses (Ambassador; 1936). *Cast:* Pinky Tomlin, Toby Wing, Kane Richmond, Arthur Housman, Russell Hopton, Fuzzy Knight, Kenneth Thomson, Jack Ingram. *D:* Leslie Goodwins (feature directorial debut); *P:* Maurice Conn. (1:06)

B bovine comedy with music of a country boy who writes songs while in the company of his pet cow.

Within the Law (MGM; 1930–31) (G.B. title) *see* **Paid**

5289. Within the Law (MGM; 1939). *Cast:* Tom Neal, William Gargan, Samuel S. Hinds, Ruth Hussey, Paul Kelly, Rita Johnson, Sidney Blackmer, John King, Lynne Carver, Paul Cavanagh, Cliff Clark, Claude King, Donald Douglas, Ann Morriss, Jo Ann Sayers. *D:* Gustav Machaty (American directorial debut); *P:* Lou Ostrow; *Sc:* Charles Lederer, Edith Fitzgerald.

B melodrama of vengeance, based on the play by Bayard Veiller. Previous versions: (Vitagraph; 1917) with Alice Joyce and Walter McGrail; (First Na-

tional; 1923) with Norma Talmadge and Lew Cody and *Paid* (q.v.).

5290. Without Children (Liberty; 1935). *Cast:* Marguerite Churchill, Bruce Cabot, Joan Woodbury. (aka: *Penthouse Party*)

(No other information available)

5291. Without Consent (Xxxx Xxxx; 1932). *Cast:* Marion Marsh, Lyle Talbot.

(No other information available)

5292. Without Honors (Artclass; 1932). *Cast:* Harry Carey, Mae Busch, Gibson Gowland, George Hayes, Lafe McKee, Mary Jane Irving, Tom London, Ed Brady, Jack Richardson. *D:* William Nigh; *Sc:* Harry P. (Fraser) Crist. (1:02)

Harry Carey western of a man who joins the rangers after returning home to find his brother murdered.

5293. Without Orders (RKO; 1936). *Cast:* Sally Eilers, Robert Armstrong, Frances Sage, Vinton Haworth (Jack Arnold), Charley Grapewin, Ward Bond, Frank M. Thomas, May Boley, Arthur Loft, Walter Miller. *D:* Lew Landers; *As.P.:* Cliff Reid; *Sc:* J. Robert Bren, Edmund L. Hartmann. (1:04)

High-flying B actioner with two pilots in love with the same stewardess. Based on a story by Peter B. Kyne, the film climaxes with the stewardess bringing in the pilotless plane.

5294. Without Regret (Paramount; 1935). *Cast:* Elissa Landi, Paul Cavanagh, Kent Taylor, Frances Drake, Gilbert Emery, David Niven. *D:* Harold Young; *P:* B.P. Fineman; *Sc:* Charles Brackett (co-writer).

B marital drama of bigamy, blackmail and murder. A remake of *Interference* (q.v.).

Without Warning *see* **The Invisible Menace**

5295. The Witness Chair (RKO; 1934). *Cast:* Ann Harding, Walter Abel,

Douglass Dumbrille, Frances Sage, Moroni Olsen, Margaret Hamilton, Maxine Jennings, William (Billy) Benedict, Paul Harvey, Murray Kinnell, Charles Arnt, Frank Jenks, Edward LeSaint. *D:* George Nicholls, Jr.; *As.P.:* Cliff Reid; *St:* Rita Weiman; *Sc:* Rian James, Gertrude Purcell. (1:04)

Who killed embezzler, Stanley Whittaker? A B who-dun-it with a courtroom setting.

5296. The Witness Vanishes (Universal; 1939). *Cast:* Edmund Lowe, Wendy Barrie, Bruce Lester, J.M. Kerrigan, Forrester Harvey, Leyland Hodgson, Robert Noble, Vernon Steele, Reginald Barlow, Barlowe Borland, Denis Green. *D:* Otis Garrett; *P:* Irving Starr; *St:* James Ronald; *Sc:* Robertson White. (1:06)

"Crime Club" series B melodrama of an escapee from a mental asylum who begins murdering those who sent him there.

5297. Wives Never Know (Paramount; 1936). *Cast:* Charles Ruggles, Mary Boland, Adolphe Menjou, Vivienne Osborne, Fay Holden, Claude Gillingwater, Louise Beavers, Purnell Pratt, Constance Bergen, Arthur Housman, Terry Ray (Ellen Drew). *D:* Elliott Nugent; *P:* Harlan Thompson; *St:* Keene Thompson; *Sc:* Frederick Hazlitt Brennan, Edwin Justus Mayer (unc.). (1:15)

Low-budget romantic comedy of a long-married couple who arouse each other's jealousy to respark their love.

5298. Wives Under Suspicion (Universal; 1937). *Cast:* Warren William, Gail Patrick, Ralph Morgan, William Lundigan, Constance Moore, Milburn Stone, Samuel S. Hinds, Minerva Urecal, James Flavin, J. Anthony Hughes, Lillian Yarbo, Edwin Stanley. *D:* James Whale (who also directed the earlier version); *P:* Edmund Grainger; *Sc:* Myles Connolly. (1:08)

A D.A. suspects his wife is seeing another man in this B budgeter. A

remake of *The Kiss Before the Mirror* (q.v.), which was based on the play of that name by Ladislaus Fodor.

5299. The Wizard of Oz (MGM; 1939). *Cast:* Judy Garland (who received a special mini-statuette from the Motion Picture Academy of Arts and Sciences for her portrayal of the juvenile Dorothy), Frank Morgan (Professor Marvel — The Wizard, guard, coachman), Ray Bolger (Hunk — Scarecrow), Bert Lahr (Zeke — Cowardly Lion), Jack Haley (in a role originally intended for Buddy Ebsen as Hickory — Tinman), Billie Burke (Glinda), Margaret Hamilton (Miss Gulch — Wicked Witch of the West), Charley Grapewin (Uncle Henry), Clara Blandick (Auntie Em), Toto (Toto), Pat Walshe (Nikko), Jerry Marenghi (Jerry Maren — film debut), and the Singer Midgets. *D:* Victor Fleming (technicolor sequences), King Vidor (sepia sequences — unc.); *P:* (A.A.N. for Best Picture) Mervyn LeRoy; *Adaptation:* Noel Langley; *Sc:* Langley, Florence Ryerson, Edgar Allan Woolf; *Art-Set Decoration:* (A.A.N.) Cedric Gibbons, William A. Horning & Edwin B. Willis; *Choreographer:* Bobby Connolly; *Music:* (A.A.) Herbert Stothart; *Special Effects:* (A.A.N.) Arnold Gillespie & Douglas Shearer; *Songs:* Harold Arlen & E.Y. Harburg — "Over the Rainbow" (which received the A.A. for Best Song), "Follow the Yellow Brick Road," "If I Only Had a Brain," "We're Off to See the Wizard," "Merry Old Land of Oz," "Laugh a Day Away," "If I Were King," "Courage," "Welcome to Munchkinland," "If I Only Had a Heart," "Ding Dong, the Witch Is Dead" & "The Jitterbug" (deleted from the final print). (1:41) (video — original & 50th anniversary edition).

This classic fantasy was originally filmed with the Kansas locations in sepia tones and the Oz locations in technicolor. After a tornado, young Dorothy and her dog Toto awaken in the mystical land of Oz where they meet many unusual characters and have many adventures. Based on the 1900 novel by L. Frank Baum, the film was a financial flop on its initial release, possibly because many critics panned it. It did not show a profit for MGM (who still retains all rights to the film) until its first TV showing on the CBS network on November 3, 1956. The film originally premiered August 17, 1939, at Loew's Theater in New York City. On the 50th anniversary of the premiere in 1989, a special home-video cassette was released with original sepia tones restored and additional footage deleted from the final print in 1939 (including a crude home-movie of "The Jitterbug" dance number). First filmed by Selig in 1910 in one reel (approximate 10 minute running time), followed by (Chadwick; 1925) with Dorothy Dwan (Dorothy), Larry Semon (scarecrow), and Oliver Hardy (tinman), of which no known prints exist. "Wizard" placed #7 on the "10 Best" list of *Film Daily*.

5300. Wolf Call (Monogram; 1939). *Cast:* John Carroll, Movita, Polly Ann Young, Wheeler Oakman, Peter George Lynn, Guy Usher, Holmes Herbert, John Sheehan, Charles Irwin, Roger Williams, Pat O'Malley, Grey Shadow the dog. *D:* George Waggner; *P:* Paul Malvern; *Sc:* Joseph West (Waggner). (1:02)

A New York playboy ventures to the wilds of Canada to see his father, finds skullduggery. Based on the novel by Jack London.

5301. The Wolf of Wall Street (Paramount; 1929). *Cast:* George Bancroft, Nancy Carroll (talkie debut), Paul Lukas, Olga Baclanova. *D:* Rowland V. Lee.

Low-budget drama of a Wall Street financier who finds his wife has been unfaithful with his partner.

5302. Wolf Riders (Reliable; 1935). *Cast:* Jack Perrin, Lillian Gilmore, Lafe McKee, Nancy Deshon, George Chesebro, William Gould, Earl Dwire, Slim Whitaker, Budd Buster,

Frank Ellis, Robert Walker, George Morrell, Blackie Whiteford. *D:* Harry S. Webb; *P:* Bernard B. Ray; *Sc:* Carl Krusada. (0:56)

Jack Perrin western of an Indian agent protecting the local tribe against fur thieves.

5303. Wolves of the Sea (Guaranteed; 1938). *Cast:* Hobart Bosworth, Jeanne Carmen, Dirk Thane, Pat West, Warner Richmond, John Merton. *D:* Elmer Clifton; *P:* J.D. Kendis; *Sc:* Clifton (co-writer).

(No other information available)

5304. The Woman Accused (Paramount; 1933). *Cast:* Nancy Carroll, Cary Grant, John Halliday, Irving Pichel, Louis Calhern, Jack LaRue, John Lodge (film debut), Lona Andre, Frank Sheridan, Harry Holman, William J. Kelly, Norma Mitchell, Donald Stuart. *D:* Paul Sloane; *P:* Polan Banks; *Sc:* Bayard Veiller. (1:13)

A woman kills her ex-lover and takes it on the lam in this low-budget melodrama. Based on an experimental ten-chapter serial story in Liberty magazine of which ten different people each wrote one chapter. The serial writers were Rupert Hughes, Vicki Baum, Zane Grey, Vina Delmar, Irvin S. Cobb, Gertrude Atherton, J.P. McEvoy, Ursula Parrott, Polan Banks & Sophie Kerr.

5305. Woman Afraid (Xxxx Xxxx; 1934). *Cast:* Lucile Gleason.

(No other information available)

5306. Woman Against the World (Columbia; 1938). *Cast:* Ralph Forbes, Alice Moore, Edgar Edwards, Collette Lyons, Sylvia Welsh. *D:* David Selman; *Sc:* Edgar Edwards.

(No other information available)

5307. Woman Against Woman (MGM; 1938). *Cast:* Herbert Marshall, Mary Astor, Virginia Bruce, Janet Beecher, Marjorie Rambeau, Betty Ross Clark, Zeffie Tilbury, Sarah Padden, Dorothy Christy, Morgan Wallace, Juanita Quigley, Joseph Crehan. *D:* Robert B. Sinclair (directorial debut); *P:* Edward Chodorov; *Sc:* Chodorov.

B drama of a man and his bitchy wife. Based on Margaret Culkin Banning's "Enemy Territory."

5308. The Woman Between (RKO; 1931). *Cast:* Lily Damita, O.P. Heggie, Lester Vail, Miriam Seegar, Anita Louise, Ruth Weston, Lincoln Stedman, Blanche Frederici, William Morris, Halliwell Hobbes, George Chandler, Rolfe Sedan. *D:* Victor Schertzinger; *P:* William LeBaron; *Sc:* Howard Estabrook; *Song:* Schertzinger. (G.B. title: *Madame Julie*) (1:13)

After marrying an older man, a woman falls for his son. Based on a play by Irving Kaye Davis.

The Woman Between (G.B. title) *see* **The Woman I Love**

5309. Woman Chases Man (United Artists/Samuel Goldwyn; 1937). *Cast:* Miriam Hopkins, Joel McCrea, Charles Winninger, Erik Rhodes, Ella Logan, Broderick Crawford (film debut), Leona Maricle, Charles Halton, Roger Gray, William Jaffrey, George Chandler, Frances G. Ford (film debut), Richard Cramer, Alan Bridge, Walter Soderling, Jack Baxley, Al K. Hall, Monte Vandergrift. *D:* John G. Blystone, William Wyler (unc.), Gregory La Cava (unc.), Edward Ludwig (unc.); *P:* Sam Goldwyn; *St:* Lynn Root, Frank Fenton; *Sc:* (see note below). (1:11)

Screwball comedy involving a scheme to get a millionaire to invest in a building project. The film had many production problems which involved four directors, three of them uncredited.

Note: The reference works used on this film present contradictory screenplay credits. In "The United Artists Story" by Ronald Bergen, Dorothy Parker, Alan Campbell and Joe Bigelow are listed as screenwriters, while "Halliwell's Film Guide" by Leslie

Halliwell lists Joseph Anthony, Mannie Seff and David Hertz as the screenwriters with Sam and Bella Spewack, Dorothy Parker and Ben Hecht listed as uncredited screenwriters.

5310. A Woman Commands (RKO; 1932). *Cast:* Pola Negri (talking film debut), Basil Rathbone, Roland Young, H.B. Warner, Anthony Bushell, Reginald Owen, Frank Reicher, May Boley, George Baxter, David Newell, Roy Barcroft, Alan Baxter, Cleo Louise Borden. *D:* Paul L. Stein; *As.P.:* Harry Joe Brown; *St:* Thilde Forster; *Sc:* Horace Jackson; *Songs:* Nacio Herb Brown & Gordon Clifford includes: "Paradise" (sung by Negri). (1:25)

A lavishly produced romantic melodrama of royalty and commoners which was a box office flop. Based on the story of Queen Maria Draga of Serbia.

5311. Woman Condemned (Xxxx Xxxx; 1934). *Cast:* Claudia Dell, Lola Lane, Jason Robards, Tom O'Brien, Mischa Auer. *D:* Dorothy Reid; *Sc:* Reid (co-writer).

B melodrama.

5312. Woman Doctor (Republic; 1939). *Cast:* Henry Wilcoxon, Joan Howard, Frieda Inescort, Cora Sue Collins, Virginia Brissac, Gus Glassmire, Sybil Jason, Cora Witherspoon, Frank Reicher. *D:* Sidney Salkow; *St:* Alice Altschuler, Miriam Geiger; *Sc:* Joseph Moncure March.

Low-budget drama.

5313. The Woman from Monte Carlo (WB/F.N.; 1931). *Cast:* Lil Dagover (German actress in her American debut), Walter Huston, Warren William, Robert Warwick, John Wray, George E. Stone, Maude Eburne, Oscar Apfel, Ben Hendricks, Jr., Matt McHugh, Francis McDonald, T. Roy Barnes, Dewey Robinson, Jack Kennedy, John Rutherford, Robert (Bob) Rose, Frank Leigh, Clarence Muse. *D:* Michael Curtiz; *Sc:* Harvey Thew. (1:08)

In this box office flop, the wife of a navy man is suspected of being an adulteress. This melodrama is a remake of *The Night Watch* (WB/F.N.; 1928) and based on the play of that name by M. Claude Farrere (Claude Ferrer) and Lucienne Nepoty (Lucien Nepoty). The '28 version starred Paul Lukas and Billie Dove, with direction by Alexander Korda.

5314. Woman Hungry (WB/ F.N.; 1931). *Cast:* Lila Lee, Sidney Blackmer, Raymond Hatton, Fred Kohler, Kenneth Thomson, Olive Tell, David Newell, J. Farrell MacDonald, Tom Dugan, Blanche Frederici. *D:* Clarence Badger; *Sc:* Howard Estabrook. (G.B. title: *The Challenge*)

This melodrama filmed in 2-color technicolor tells the story of a New England girl, forced to marry a western outlaw. Previously filmed as *The Great Divide* (MGM; 1925) with Wallace Beery, Alice Terry and Conway Tearle by director Reginald Barker and again in 1929 under that title (q.v.). Based on the 1906 play "The Great Divide" by William Vaughn Moody. A box office loser.

5315. The Woman I Love (RKO; 1937). *Cast:* Paul Muni, Miriam Hopkins, Louis Hayward, Colin Clive (final film—d. 1937), Minor Watson, Elizabeth Risdon, Paul Guilfoyle, Mady Christians, Vince Barnett, Sterling Holloway, Wally Albright, Alec Craig, Owen Davis, Jr., Adrian Morris, Donald Barry, Joe Twerp, William Stelling. *D:* Anatole Litvak (American directorial debut); *P:* Albert Lewis; *Sc:* Ethel Borden. (G.B. title: *The Woman Between*) (1:25)

Romantic World War I melodrama of the Lafayette Escadrille and a pilot who is in love with his superior officer's wife. Based on the French novel *L'Equipage* by Joseph Kessel, and previously filmed under that title in France. A box office dud.

5316. The Woman I Stole (Columbia; 1933). *Cast:* Jack Holt, Fay Wray, Raquel Torres, Donald Cook, Noah Beery, Edwin Maxwell, Ferdinand Munier, Lee Phelps; *St:* Based on *Tampico* by Joseph Hergesheimer. *D:* Irving Cummings; *Adaptation:* Jo Swerling. Romantic melodrama.

5317. Woman in Distress (Columbia; 1937). *Cast:* Irene Hervey, May Robson, Douglass Dumbrille, Dean Jagger, Paul Fix. *D:* Lynn Shores. Melodrama.

A Woman in Her Thirties (G.B. title) *see* **Side Streets**

The Woman in His House (G.B. title) *see* **The Animal Kingdom**

5318. The Woman in Red (WB/ F.N.; 1935). *Cast:* Barbara Stanwyck, Gene Raymond, Genevieve Tobin, John Eldredge, Philip Reed, Dorothy Tree, Russell Hicks, Nella Walker, Claude Gillingwater, Doris Lloyd, Hale Hamilton, Edward Van Sloan, Brandon Hurst, Ann Shoemaker, Robert E. Homans, Arthur Treacher. *D:* Robert Florey; *P:* Harry Joe Brown; *Sc:* Mary McCall, Jr., Peter Milne; *Song:* "So Close to the Forest" by J. Young & L. Reginald. (1:08)

B drama of a woman's in-laws who are trying to disrupt her marriage. Based on the novel "North Shore" by Wallace Irwin.

5319. The Woman in Room 13 (Fox; 1932). *Cast:* Elissa Landi, Ralph Bellamy, Myrna Loy, Neil Hamilton, Charley Grapewin, Gilbert Roland, Walter Walker, Oscar Apfel. *D:* Henry King; *Sc:* Guy Bolton.

Marital drama of a concert singer who must choose between her career and her husband. Based on the play by Samuel Shipman, Max Marcin and Percival Wilde, it was previously filmed in 1920 with Marguerite Snow.

The Woman in the Case (G.B. title) *see* **Headline Woman**

5320. Woman in the Dark (RKO/Select; 1934). *Cast:* Ralph Bellamy, Fay Wray, Melvyn Douglas, Granville Bates, Roscoe Ates, Reed Brown, Jr., Ruth Gillette, Nell O'Day. *D:* Phil Rosen; *As.P.:* Burt Kelly; *Sc:* Sada Cowan, Marcy Klauber, Charles Williams.

A man serves a prison term for manslaughter, only to be released and find himself in more trouble. A B budget production based on a story by Dashiell Hammett and was independently produced by Select Productions.

5321. A Woman Is the Judge (Columbia; 1939). *Cast:* Rochelle Hudson, Otto Kruger, Beryl Mercer (final film—d. 1939), Frieda Inescort, Arthur Loft, Gordon Oliver, Walter Fenner, Ann Doran, Bentley Hewlett, John Dilson. *D:* Nick Grinde; *Sc:* Karl Brown. B production.

5322. A Woman of Experience (RKO-Pathé; 1931). *Cast:* Helen Twelvetrees, William Bakewell, Lew Cody, H.B. Warner, ZaSu Pitts, C. Henry Gordon, Nance O'Neil, Edward Earle, George Fawcett, Franklin Pangborn, Alfred Hickman, Bertha Mann, William Tooker, Max Walzman. *D:* Harry Joe Brown; *P:* Charles R. Rogers; *Sc:* John Farrow, Ralph F. Murphy. (G.B. title: *Registered Woman*) (1:11)

In World War I Vienna a girl falls for a naval officer while at the same time, baiting a spy. A romantic drama based on the play "The Registered Woman" by John Farrow.

A Woman of the World (G.B. title) *see* **Outcast Lady**

5323. Woman Pursued (Columbia; 1931). *Cast:* Betty Compson, Genevieve Tobin, Ivan Lebedeff, Rita LaRoy, Ilka Chase. *D:* Richard Boleslawski.

B melodrama.

5324. The Woman Racket (MGM; 1929–30). *Cast:* Blanche Sweet, Tom Moore, John Miljan, Robert Agnew, Sally Starr, Tom London. *D:* Robert Ober & Albert Kelley (their only film as directors); *Sc:* Albert LeVino. (G.B. title: *Lights and Shadows*)

A Broadway crime melodrama based on the play "Night Hostess" by Philip and Frances Dunning.

5325. A Woman Rebels (RKO; 1936). *Cast:* Katharine Hepburn (in a role originally intended for Ann Harding as Pamela Thistlewaite), Herbert Marshall, Elizabeth Allan, Donald Crisp, Doris Dudley, David Manners (final film—ret.), Van Heflin (film debut), Lucile Watson, Eily Malyon, Margaret Seddon, Molly Lamont, Lionel Pape, Constance Lupino, Inez Palange, Lillian Kemble-Cooper, Nick Thompson. *D:* Mark Sandrich; *P:* Pandro S. Berman; *Sc:* Anthony Veiller, Ernest Vajda. (1:28) (video)

In Victorian England a woman defies convention and fights for the rights of other women. A box office flop, the film was based on the novel "Portrait of a Rebel" by Netta Syrett.

Woman Tamer (G.B. title) *see* **She Couldn't Take It**

5326. Woman to Woman (Tiffany; 1929–30). *Cast:* Betty Compson, George Barraud, Reginald Sharland, Margaret Chambers, George Billings, Winter Hall. *D:* Victor Saville.

"Poverty row" romantic drama.

5327. Woman Trap (Paramount; 1929). *Cast:* Chester Morris, Evelyn Brent, Hal Skelly, Guy Oliver, Charles Giblyn, Effie Ellsler, William Davidson, Wilson Hummell, Virginia Bruce. *D:* William A. Wellman; *St:* Edwin Burke.

Low-budget melodrama of two brothers, one on the side of the law, the other not.

5328. Woman Trap (Paramount; 1936). *Cast:* Gertrude Michael, George

Murphy, Akim Tamiroff, Edward Brophy, Sidney Blackmer, Bradley Page, Roscoe Karns, Samuel S. Hinds, Arthur Aylesworth, Dean Jagger, Ralph Malone, David Haines. *D:* Harold Young; *P:* Harold Hurley; *St:* Charles Brackett; *Sc:* Brian Marlow, Eugene Walter.

B crime melodrama of a politician's daughter being held for ransom by a gangster.

5329. Woman Unafraid (Ken Goldsmith Prods.; 1934). *Cast:* Warren Hymer, Ruth Clifford, Richard "Skeets" Gallagher, Jason Robards, Eddie Phillips. *D:* William J. Cowen (third & final film of this director); *P:* Ken Goldsmith.

Low-budget indie melodrama.

5330. Woman Wanted (MGM; 1935). *Cast:* Maureen O'Sullivan, Joel McCrea, Lewis Stone, Louis Calhern, Edgar Kennedy, Adrienne Ames, Robert Greig, Noel Madison, Gertrude Short, Granville Bates. *D:* George B. Seitz; *P:* Philip Goldstone; *St:* Wilson Collison; *Sc:* Leonard Fields, David Silverstein. (1:08)

B melodrama of a man protecting a woman being sought by hoods and the police.

5331. The Woman Who Dared (Xxxx Xxxx; 1934). *Cast:* Lola Lane, Claudia Dell, Matthew Betz, Robert Elliott, Douglas Fowley, Paul Fix, Joseph Girard. *D:* Xxxx Xxxx.

Low-budget melodrama.

5332. The Woman Who Was Forgotten (Xxxx Xxxx; 1930). *Cast:* Belle Bennett, LeRoy Mason, Jack Mower. *D:* Richard Thomas; *Sc:* Albert LeVino.

(No other information available)

5333. Woman-Wise (20th Century-Fox; 1937). *Cast:* Michael Whalen, Rochelle Hudson, Astrid Allwyn, Chick Chandler, Douglas Fowley, Pat Flaherty, Thomas Beck, George Hassell.

D: Allan Dwan; *P:* Sol M. Wurtzel; *Sc:* Ben Markson.

B romantic comedy.

5334. A Woman's Man (Monogram; 1934). *Cast:* John Halliday, Marguerite de la Motte, Wallace Ford, Kitty Kelly, Jameson Thomas, Wallis Clark, Tom Dugan, Don Douglas, Leigh Allen, George Mayo, Harry Green, Jack Perry, Billee Van Every. *D:* Edward Ludwig; *P:* Ben Verschleiser; *St:* Adela Rogers St. John (which appeared in *Cosmopolitan* magazine); *Sc:* Frances Hyland.

The romance of a popular film star and a prize fighter is told in this low-budget comedy-drama from "poverty row."

Womantrap *see* **The Shadow Strikes**

5335. The Women (MGM; 1939). *Cast:* Norma Shearer (Mary Haines), Joan Crawford (Chrystal Allen), Rosalind Russell (Sylvia Fowler), Mary Boland (Countess [Flora] DeLave), Paulette Goddard (Miriam Aarons), Joan Fontaine (Peggy Day), Lucile Watson (Mrs. Morehead), Phyllis Povah (repeating her stage role as Edith Potter), Virginia Weidler (Little Mary), Marjorie Main (Lucy), Virginia Grey (Pat), Ruth Hussey (Miss Watts), Florence Nash (Nancy Blake), Muriel Hutchison (Jane), Margaret Dumont (Mrs. Wagstaff), Dennie Moore (Olga), Mary Cecil (Maggie), Esther Dale (Ingrid), Hedda Hopper (Dolly Dupuyster), Mildred Shay (Helene the French maid), Mary Beth Hughes (Miss Trimmerback), Marjorie Wood (Sadie), Cora Witherspoon (Mrs. Van Adams), Theresa Harris (Olive), Priscilla Lawson, Estelle Etterre, Ann Morriss, Virginia Howell, Barbara Jo Allen (Vera Vague), Aileen Pringle, Judith Allen, Mariska Aldrich, Flora Finch (final film — d. 1940), Mary Anderson, Dorothy Adams. *D:* George Cukor; *P:* Hunt Stromberg; *Sc:* Anita Loos, Jane Murfin. (2:12) (video)

A drama of the interconnecting lives of a group of women. Based on the hit Broadway play by Clare Boothe, the film with a technicolor fashion-show sequences was a major box office hit, being one of the 21 top grossing films of 1939–40. On the "10 Best" lists of *Film Daily* and the *New York Times*, it placed #6 and #7 respectively.

5336. Women Are Like That (WB; 1938). *Cast:* Kay Francis, Pat O'Brien, Ralph Forbes, Melville Cooper, Thurston Hall, Grant Mitchell, Gordon Oliver, John Eldredge, Joyce Compton, DeWolf (William) Hopper, Loia Cheaney, Herbert Rawlinson, Josephine Whittell, William Broadley, Georgia Caine, Sarah Edwards, Hugh O'Connell. *D:* Stanley Logan; *As.P.:* Robert Lord; *St:* Albert H.Z. Carr; *Sc:* Horace Jackson. (1:18)

In this marital comedy a wife insists on helping her husband save his failing business.

5337. Women Are Trouble (MGM; 1936). *Cast:* Stuart Erwin, Paul Kelly, Florence Rice, Margaret Irving, Cyrus Kendall, John Harrington, Harold Huber, Kitty McHugh, Raymond Hatton. *D:* Errol Taggart (directorial debut); *P:* Lucien Hubbard, Michael Fessier; *St:* George Harmon Coxe; *Sc:* Fessier. (0:57)

B comedy-melodrama of rival news reporters.

5338. Women Everywhere (Fox; 1930). *Cast:* J. Harold Murray, Fifi D'Orsay, Rose Dione, Clyde Cook, George Grossmith, Ralph Kellard. *D:* Alexander Korda; *St:* George Grossmith, Zoltan Korda; *Sc:* Harlan Thompson, Lajos Biro.

Romantic comedy.

5339. Women Go On Forever (Tiffany; 1931). *Cast:* Clara Kimball Young, Marian Nixon, Thomas Jackson, Maurice Black, Yola D'Avril, Paul Page, Maurice Murphy, Morgan Wallace, Eddie Lambert, Nellie V.

Nichols, Lorin Raker. *D:* Walter Lang; *St & Sc:* Daniel N. Rubin.

A sentimental drama from "poverty row."

5340. The Women in His Life (MGM; 1933). *Cast:* Otto Kruger, Una Merkel, Irene Hervey, Ben Lyon, Nat Pendleton, Roscoe Karns, Isabel Jewell, Raymond Hatton, Paul Hurst, Samuel S. Hinds. *D:* George B. Seitz; *P:* Lucien Hubbard; *Sc:* F. Hugh Herbert.

B melodrama of an attorney who defends his ex-wife's husband in a murder trial.

5341. Women in Prison (Columbia; 1938). *Cast:* Scott Colton, Mary Russell, John Tyrrell, Eddie Fetherston, Ann Doran, Thurston Hall, Margaret Armstrong, Wyn Cahoon, Sarah Padden, Arthur Loft, Bess Flowers. *D:* Lambert Hillyer; *St:* Mortimer Braus; *Sc:* Saul Elkins.

B melodrama aptly described by the title.

5342. Women in the Wind (WB; 1939). *Cast:* Kay Francis, William Gargan, Maxie Rosenbloom, Victor Jory, Eddie Foy, Jr., Eve Arden, Sheila Bromley, Rosella Towne, John Ridgely, Frank Faylen, Frankie Burke, Charles Anthony Hughes, John Dilson. *D:* John Farrow; *As.P.:* Bryan Foy; *Sc:* Lee Katz, Albert DeMond.

A B drama of lady flyers which was based on a novel by Francis Walton.

5343. Women Love Once (Paramount; 1931). *Cast:* Eleanor Boardman, Paul Lukas, Mischa Auer, Juliette Compton, Herman Bing, Claude King, Helen Johnson (Judith Wood), Marilyn Knowlden. *D:* Edward Goodman.

Low-budget tear-jerker of an estranged couple, reunited by the death of their child.

5344. The Women Men Marry (Headline Pictures; 1931). *Cast:* Randolph Scott (talkie debut), Sally Blane,

Kenneth Harlan, Jimmy Aubrey, Natalie Morehead, Crauford Kent, Jean Del Val. *D:* Charles Hutchison; *St & Sc:* Jack Natteford.

Low-budget indie romance.

5345. The Women Men Marry (MGM; 1937). *Cast:* Sidney Blackmer, George Murphy, Claire Dodd, Josephine Hutchinson, Cliff Edwards, John Wray, Peggy Ryan, Toby Wing, Leonard Penn, Helen Jerome Eddy. *D:* Errol Taggart; *P:* Michael Fessier; *Sc:* Donald Henderson Clarke, James Grant, Harry Ruskin.

B drama of an newspaper editor who is having an affair with the wife of his star reporter.

5346. Women Must Dress (Monogram; 1935). *Cast:* Minna Gombell, Gavin Gordon, Hardie Albright, Lenita Lane, Suzanne Kaaren, Robert Light, Zeffie Tilbury, Alan Edwards, Paul Ellis, Gerald Young, Anne Johnston, Nell Rhoades, Madelyn Earle, Harriet de Bussman, Anne Kasper, Sondra Broaux, Fay Hammar, Charles Locher (later: Jon Hall in his film debut). *D:* Reginald Barker; *P:* Mrs. Wallace (Dorothy) Reid; *St & Sc:* Reid & Edmund Joseph. (1:17)

In this "poverty row" drama, a woman becomes a partner in a women's clothing store after being dumped by her husband.

5347. Women of All Nations (Fox; 1931). *Cast:* Edmund Lowe, Victor McLaglen, Greta Nissen, El Brendel, Fifi D'Orsay, Bela Lugosi, Humphrey Bogart, Joyce Compton, T. Roy Barnes, Cecilia Parker (film debut— bit), Jesse DeVorska, Charles Judels, Marjorie White. *D:* Raoul Walsh; *Sc:* Barry Connors. (1:12)

Another romp with "Flagg & Quirt," the ever squabbling buddies from *What Price Glory?* (Fox; 1926). One of the many follow-ups of that hit silent film.

5348. Women of Glamour (Columbia; 1937). *Cast:* Virginia Bruce,

Melvyn Douglas, Pert Kelton, Reginald Denny, Thurston Hall, Mary Forbes, Leona Maricle. *D:* Gordon Wiles; *St:* Milton Herbert Gropper; *Sc:* Lynn Starling, Mary C. McCall, Jr.

Romantic drama of a golddigger who falls for a playboy. Previously filmed in 1926 and 1930 (q.v.) as *Ladies of Leisure.*

5349. Women They Talk About (WB; 1928). *Cast:* Irene Rich, Anders Randolf, William Collier, Jr., Audrey Ferris, Claude Gillingwater, Jack Sanforo, John Miljan. *D:* Lloyd Bacon; *St:* Anthony Coldeway; *Sc:* Robert Lord.

Part-talkie romantic comedy-melodrama of a successful business woman and her flapper daughter. This film premiered October 14, 1928, in New York City.

5350. Women Won't Tell (Chesterfield; 1933). *Cast:* Robert Ellis, Walter Long, Jane Darwell, Edmund Breese, Otis Harlan, William V. Mong, Tom Ricketts, Charles Hill Mailes, Dewey Robinson. *D:* Richard Thorpe.

"Poverty row" melodrama.

5351. Wonder Bar (WB/F.N.; 1934). *Cast:* Al Jolson (Al Wonder), Kay Francis (Liane Renaud), Ricardo Cortez (Harry), Dolores Del Rio (Inez), Dick Powell (Tommy), Louise Fazenda (Pansy Pratt), Guy B. Kibbee (Henry Simpson), Ruth Donnelly (Ella Simpson), Hugh Herbert (Corey Pratt), Robert Barrat (Captain Von Ferring), Fifi D'Orsay (Mitzi), Merna Kennedy (Claire), Henry Kolker (Mr. Renaud), Henry O'Neill (Richards), Kathryn Sergava (Ilka), Mia Ichioka (Gee-Gee), Eddie Kane (Frank), Hal LeRoy (himself), Harry Woods, Gordon DeMain, George Irving, Marie Moreau, Emile Chautard, Pauline Garon, Mahlon Norvell, Alphonse Martell, William Granger, Rolfe Sedan, Jane Darwell, Edward Keane, Demetrius Alexis, John Marlow, Billy Anderson, Bud Jamison, Dave O'Brien, Hobart Cavanaugh, Bud Flanagan (Dennis O'Keefe), Gino Corrado, Grace Hayle, Gordon (Bill) Elliott, Paul Power, Dick Good, Michael Dalmatoff, Renee Whitney, Amo Ingraham, Rosalie Roy, Lottie Williams, William Stack, Clay Clement, Gene Perry, Spencer Charters, Louis Ardizoni, Robert Graves, Alfred P. James. *D:* Lloyd Bacon; *P:* Robert Lord; *Sc:* Earl Baldwin; *Choreography:* Busby Berkeley; *Songs:* "At the Wonder Bar," "I'm Goin' to Heaven on a Mule," "Why Do I Dream Those Dreams?" "Don't Say Goodnight" (Valse Amoureuse), "Vive La France," "Fairer on the Riviera," "Tango Del Rio" & "Dark Eyes" (O Tchorniya) by Al Dubin & Harry Warren. (1:24) (video)

Romantic musical-drama set in a Paris night club. A popular film in its day, it became one of the 15 top grossing films of 1934. Based on the play by Geza Herczeg, Karl Farkas and Robert Katscher. The production number "Goin' to Heaven on a Mule" stirred some controversy upon release of the film.

Wonder Plane (G.B. title) *see* **Mercy Plane**

5352. Wonders of the Congo (Fox; 1931). A feature length documentary of and by famed American explorers, Martin and Osa Johnson and their explorations of the African Congo.

Wooden Soldiers *see* **Babes in Toyland**

5353. Words and Music (Fox; 1929). *Cast:* Lois Moran, Helen Twelvetrees, David Percy, Ward Bond, Elizabeth Patterson, Frank Albertson, Helen Parrish, Duke Morrison (John Wayne—bit), Frances Dee (film debut as an extra), Dorothy Jordan (film debut as a dancer—bit). *D:* James Tinling; *Songs include:* "Too Wonderful for Words."

Light romantic musical, a remake of the 1919 production of the same name.

5354. Working Girls (Paramount; 1931). *Cast:* Charles "Buddy" Rogers, Frances Dee, Paul Lukas,

Stuart Erwin, Claire Dodd, Alberta Vaughn, Mary Forbes, Dorothy Stickney. *D:* Dorothy Arzner.

Low-budget drama of small town girls who go to New York City in search of jobs and romance.

5355. The Working Man (WB; 1933). *Cast:* George Arliss, Bette Davis, Theodore Newton, J. Farrell MacDonald, Hardie Albright, Gordon Westcott, Edward Van Sloan, Douglas Dumbrille, Claire McDowell, Ruthelma Stevens, Charles Evans, Pat Wing, Gertrude Sutton, Edward Cooper. *D:* John Adolfi; *P:* Lucien Hubbard; *Sc:* Maude T. Howell, Charles Kenyon. (aka: *The Adopted Father*) (1:15)

A businessman gives up his business and goes on vacation where he winds up helping his former business rival. Based on the novel by Edgar Franklin.

Working Wives (G.B. title) *see* **Week-End Marriage**

5356. The World Accuses (Chesterfield; 1935). *Cast:* Russell Hopton, Barbara Bedford, Lloyd Ingraham, Robert Elliott, Vivian Tobin, Dickie Moore, Jane Keckley, Mary Carr, Bryant Washburn, Cora Sue Collins, Sarah Edwards, Robert Frazer, Paul Fix, Jameson Thomas. *D:* Charles Lamont; *St & Sc:* Charles Belden.

"Poverty row" melodrama.

5357. The World and the Flesh (Paramount; 1932). *Cast:* George Bancroft, Miriam Hopkins, Alan Mowbray, George E. Stone, T. Roy Barnes, Max Wagner, Ferike Boros, Oscar Apfel, Harry Cording, Emmett Corrigan, Mitchell Lewis. *D:* John Cromwell; *St:* Philip Zeska, Ernst Spitz. (1:15)

A soldier-of-fortune bargains to save the lives of some aristocrats who are caught in the Russian Revolution in this low-budget drama.

5358. The World Changes (WB/ F.N.; 1933). *Cast:* Paul Muni, Aline

MacMahon, Mary Astor, Donald Cook, Guy Kibbee, Patricia Ellis, Jean Muir (film debut), Margaret Lindsay, Alan Dinehart, Anna Q. Nilsson, Henry O'Neill, Sidney Toler, Douglass Dumbrille (Buffalo Bill), Mickey Rooney, Alan Mowbray, Oscar Apfel, Richard Quine (film debut), Willard Robertson, Samuel S. Hinds, William Janney, Jackie Searle, Theodore Newton, Gordon Westcott, William Burress. *D:* Mervyn LeRoy; *Supervisor:* Robert Lord; *St:* Sheridan Gibney; *Sc:* Edward Chodorov. (1:31)

Flop morality drama on the corruption that is brought about by the abuse of power.

5359. The World Gone Mad (Majestic; 1933). *Cast:* Pat O'Brien, Evelyn Brent, Neil Hamilton, Louis Calhern, Mary Brian, J. Carrol Naish, John St. Polis, Edward Van Sloan, Lloyd Ingraham, Richard Tucker, Inez Courtney, Max Davidson, Joseph Girard, Wallis Clark, Buster Phelps. *D:* Christy Cabanne; *Sc:* Edward T. Lowe. (G.B. title: *The Public Be Hanged*) (1:13) (video)

Hit action-packed crime melodrama from "poverty row."

5360. The World Moves On (Fox; 1934). *Cast:* Madeleine Carroll (American debut), Franchot Tone, Reginald Denny, Stepin Fetchit, Lumsden Hare, Louise Dresser, Raul Roulien, Sig Rumann, Barry Norton, Dudley Digges, Ferdinand Schumann-Heink, Ivan Simpson, Frank Melton, Walter McGrail, Marcelle Corday, Claude King, Brenda Fowler, Frank Moran, Georgette Rhodes. *D:* John Ford; *P:* Winfield Sheehan; *Sc:* Reginald C. Berkeley. (1:30)

Generational drama of a powerful Louisiana family through the 19th-century up to World War I. A box office flop.

5361. Worldly Goods (Syndicate-Continental Talking Pictures; 1930).

Cast: Merna Kennedy, James Kirkwood, Ferdinand Schumann-Heink. *D:* Phil Rosen.

A "poverty row" melodrama.

5362. The Worst Woman in Paris (Fox; 1933). *Cast:* Benita Hume, Adolphe Menjou, Harvey Stephens, Helen Chandler, Margaret Seddon, Maidel Turner, Adele St. Maur. *D:* Monta Bell; *P:* Bell; *Sc:* Bell. (1:18)

Drama of an American woman who walks out on her wealthy European husband and returns to the states where she falls for another man.

5363. The Wrecker (Columbia; 1933). *Cast:* Jack Holt, Genevieve Tobin, Sidney Blackmer, Clarence Muse, Ward Bond, Irene White, Russell Waddle. *D:* Albert Rogell; *St:* Rogell; *Adaptation & Sc:* Jo Swerling.

"Poverty row" romantic melodrama.

5364. The Wrong Road (Republic; 1937). *Cast:* Richard Cromwell, Helen Mack, Lionel Atwill, Horace MacMahon, Arthur Hoyt, Billy Bevan, Marjorie Main, Selmer Jackson. *D:* James Cruze.

B budget crime melodrama.

5365. Wuthering Heights (United Artists/Samuel Goldwyn; 1939). *Cast:* Merle Oberon (Cathy), Laurence Olivier (A.A.N. for B.A. and an Acting Award from the National Board of Review for his portrayal of Heathcliffe), David Niven (Edgar), Donald Crisp (Dr. Kenneth), Flora Robson (American debut as Ellen "Nellie" Dean), Hugh Williams (Hindley), Geraldine Fitzgerald (American debut which garnered her an A.A.N. for B.S.A. and an Acting Award from the National Board of Review in conjunction with her performance in *Dark Victory* [q.v.] as Isabella), Cecil Kellaway (Mr. Earnshaw), Leo G. Carroll (Joseph), Miles Mander (Lockwood), Cecil Humphreys (Judge Linton), Sarita Wooten (Cathy the child), Rex Downing (Heathcliffe the child), Douglas Scott (Hindley the child), Helena Grant (Miss Hudkins), Harold Entwistle (Beadle), Alice Ahlers (Frau Johann), Vernon Downing (Giles), Romaine Callender, Susanne Leach, Schuyler Standish, Tommy Martin, Diane Williams, Frank Benson, Philip Winter, Eric Wilton, William Stelling. *D:* (A.A.N.) William Wyler; *P:* (A.A.N. for Best Picture) Sam Goldwyn; *Sc:* (A.A.N.) Ben Hecht, Charles MacArthur; *Cinematography:* (A.A. black/white) Gregg Toland; *Art-Set Decoration:* (A.A.N.) James Basevi; *Music:* (A.A.N.) Alfred Newman (for his original score). (1:43) (video)

Critically acclaimed classic adaptation of the first half of Emily Brontë's novel of the tragic romance of Cathy and Heathcliffe. Voted "Best Film of the Year" by the New York Film Critics. It placed #2 on the "10 Best" list of the National Board of Review, #3 on the same list of the *New York Times,* followed by a #4 placement on the "10 Best" list of *Film Daily.* Filmed in Great Britain in 1920 as a silent, in Mexico in 1954 by Luis Bunuel and again in 1970 by American International in Great Britain.

5366. Wyoming Outlaw (Republic; 1939). *Cast:* John Wayne (Stony Brooke), Ray Corrigan (Tucson Smith), Raymond Hatton (Rusty Joslin), David Sharpe, Donald Barry, LeRoy Mason, Adele Pearce (later Pamela Blake), Yakima Canutt, Jack Ingram, Charles Middleton. *D:* George Sherman; *Supervisor:* William Berke; *Sc:* Betty Burbridge, Jack Natteford. (0:56)

The 23rd entry in the "Three Mesquiteers" series with an offbeat story of a modern day Robin Hood.

5367. Wyoming Whirlwind (Capital; 1932). *Cast:* Lane Chandler, Adele Tracy, Harry Todd, Alan Bridge, Yakima Canutt, Harry Semels, Loie Bridge, Bob Roper, Hank Bell, Ted Adams, Fred Burns, Raven the horse.

D: Armand L. Schaefer; *P:* Willis Kent; *Sc:* Wallace MacDonald. (TV title: *Roaring Rider*) (0:55)

Lane Chandler western of a mysterious highwayman known as "The Lone Wolf."

5368. X Marks the Spot (Tiffany; 1931). *Cast:* Wallace Ford (who also appeared in the '42 version), Sally Blane, Lew Cody, Fred Kohler, Mary Nolan, Richard Tucker, Helen Parrish, Joyce Coad, Virginia Lee Corbin. *D:* Erle C. Kenton; *St:* Warren Duff, Gordon Kahn; *Sc:* F. Hugh Herbert.

A comedy-mystery from "poverty row" which was remade in 1942.

5369. Yankee Don (Capital; 1931). *Cast:* Richard Talmadge, Lupita Tovar, Julian Rivero, Sam Appel, Gayne Whitman, Alma Real, Victor Stanford. *D:* Noel Mason (Smith); *P:* Richard Talmadge; *Sc:* Frances Jackson. (1:00)

"Poverty row" western of a resident of New York's Bowery who heads west to escape the law and winds up helping a Spanish land owner save his ranch from outlaws.

Years Without Days (G.B. title) *see* **Castle on the Hudson**

5370. Yellow Cargo (Grand National/Pacific Pictures; 1936). *Cast:* Conrad Nagel, Eleanor Hunt, Vince Barnett, Claudia Dell, Jack LaRue, Henry Strange, John Ivan, Vance Carroll, Crane Wilbur. *D:* Crane Wilbur; *P:* George A. Hirliman; *Sc:* Wilbur. (1:03)

B budget indie melodrama of government agents who go after a gang that is smuggling aliens into the country.

5371. Yellow Dust (RKO; 1936). *Cast:* Richard Dix, Leila Hyams (final film—ret.), Moroni Olsen, Jessie Ralph, Andy Clyde, Onslow Stevens, Victor Potel, Ethan Laidlaw, Ted Oliver. *D:* Wallace Fox; *As.P.:* Cliff Reid; *Sc:* John Twist, Cyril Hume. (1:09)

B western suggested by the play "Mother Lode" by Dan Totheroh and George O'Neil of two miners trying to stake a claim.

5372. Yellow Jack (MGM; 1938). *Cast:* Robert Montgomery, Virginia Bruce, Lewis Stone (Major Walter Reed), Andy Devine, Henry Hull (Dr. Jesse Lazear), Charles Coburn, Buddy Ebsen, Henry O'Neill, Janet Beecher, William Henry, Alan Curtis, Sam Levene, Stanley Ridges, Phillip Terry, Jonathan Hale. *D:* George B. Seitz; *P:* Jack Cummings; *Sc:* Edward Chodorov. (1:23)

In 1899 Cuba, Major Walter Reed attempts to find a cure for the dreaded yellow fever. Based on the play by Sidney Howard and Paul de Kruif.

The Yellow Passport (G.B. title) *see* **The Yellow Ticket**

The Yellow Phantom *see* **Shadow of Chinatown**

5373. The Yellow Ticket (Fox; 1931). *Cast:* Elissa Landi, Laurence Olivier (American debut), Lionel Barrymore, Walter Byron, Sarah Padden, Mischa Auer, Arnold Korff, Boris Karloff. *D:* Raoul Walsh; *P:* Walsh; *Sc:* Jules Furthman, Guy Bolton. (G.B. title: *The Yellow Passport*) (1:21)

Melodrama of pre-revolutionary Russia of a Jewish girl seeking a traveling ticket. Previously filmed as *The Yellow Passport* (World-Selznick; 1916) with Clara Kimball Young and Edwin August; followed by *The Yellow Ticket* (Fox; 1918) with Milton Sills and Warner Oland. Based on the play "The Yellow Passport" by Michael Morton. A box office flop.

5374. Yellowstone (Universal; 1936). *Cast:* Henry Hunter, Judith Barrett (film debut), Andy Devine, Ralph Morgan, Alan Hale, Claud Allister, Raymond Hatton, Paul Fix, Mary Gordon. *D:* Arthur Lubin; *P:* Val Paul; *Sc:*

Jefferson Parker, Stuart Palmer, Houston Branch. (1:03) (video)

B murder-mystery of assorted characters searching for buried loot in Yellowstone National Park.

5375. Yes, My Darling Daughter (WB/F.N.; 1939). *Cast:* Priscilla Lane, Jeffrey Lynn, Roland Young, Fay Bainter, May Robson, Genevieve Tobin, Ian Hunter, Robert Homans. *D:* William Keighley; *As.P.:* Benjamin Glazer; *Sc:* Casey Robinson. (1:26)

Based on the Broadway play by Mark Reed, this romantic comedy of eloping lovers was a hit for the studio.

5376. Yodelin' Kid from Pine Ridge (Republic; 1937). *Cast:* Gene Autry, Smiley Burnette, Betty Bronson, LeRoy Mason, Charles Middleton, Russell Simpson, Jack Dougherty, Guy Wilkerson, Frankie Marvin, Henry Hall, Fred "Snowflake" Toones, Jack Kirk, Bob Burns, Al Taylor, George Morrell, Lew Meehan, Jim Corey, Jack Ingram, Art Dillard, Art Mix, Bud Osborne, Oscar Gahan, Tennessee Ramblers, Champion (Autry's horse). *D:* Joseph Kane; *P:* Armand Schaefer; *St:* Jack Natteford; *Sc:* Natteford, Dorrell & Stuart McGowan. (G.B. title: *The Hero of Pine Ridge*) (0:54)

Gene Autry western with songs.

You and I *see* **The Bargain**

5377. You and Me (Paramount; 1938). *Cast:* Sylvia Sidney, George Raft, Harry Carey, Barton MacLane, Warren Hymer, Roscoe Karns, George E. Stone, Adrian Morris, Robert Cummings, Vera Gordon, Willard Robertson, Joyce Compton, Jack Mulhall, Bruce Cabot, Guinn Williams, Bernadene Hayes, Kit Guard, Arthur Hoyt, Egon Brecher, Carol Paige, Terry Ray (Ellen Drew), Meg Randall. *D:* Fritz Lang; *P:* Lang; *St:* Norman Krasna; *Sc:* Virginia Van Upp. (1:30)

A romantic comedy-drama of the marriage between two social outcasts. A box office flop.

5378. You Belong to Me (Paramount; 1934). *Cast:* Helen Morgan, Lee Tracy, Helen Mack, Lynne Overman, Dean Jagger, Clara Lou (Ann) Sheridan, Irene Ware, Arthur Pierson, David Holt, Edwin Stanley, Max Mack, Rev. Neal Dodd, Lou Cass, Mary Owen. *D:* Alfred Werker; *P:* Louis D. Lighton; *St:* Elizabeth Alexander; *Songs:* Sam Coslow, Arthur Johnston.

B musical-comedy-drama about the personal lives of some entertainers.

5379. You Can't Beat Love (RKO; 1937). *Cast:* Preston Foster, Joan Fontaine, Herbert Mundin, William Brisbane, Alan Bruce, Paul Hurst, Bradley Page, Frank M. Thomas, Berton Churchill, Harold Huber, Paul Guilfoyle, Barbara Pepper, Milburn Stone. *D:* Christy Cabanne; *P:* Robert Sisk; *St:* Olga Moore; *Sc:* Maxwell Shane, David Silverstein. (1:02)

On a dare, a playboy lawyer runs against an incumbant for mayor in this B comedy.

5380. You Can't Buy Everything (MGM; 1934). *Cast:* May Robson, Jean Parker, William Bakewell, Tad Alexander, Lewis Stone, Reginald Mason, Walter Walker, Claude Gillingwater, Mary Forbes, T. Roy Barnes, George Humbert. *D:* Charles Riesner; *P:* Lucien Hubbard; *St:* Lamar Trotti, Dudley Nichols; *Sc:* Eve Greene, Zelda Sears.

Hit comedy, based on fact of elderly female Wall Street wizard, Hetty Green.

5381. You Can't Buy Luck (RKO; 1937). *Cast:* Onslow Stevens, Helen Mack, Vinton Haworth (aka: Jack Arnold in smaller parts), Maxine Jennings, Paul Guilfoyle, Frank M. Thomas, Richard Lane, Murray Alper, Hedda Hopper, Dudley Clements, George Irving, Barbara Pepper, Willie Best, Edgar Norton, Margaret Fielding, John Kelly, Eddie Gribbon. *D:* Lew Landers; *St:* Martin Mooney; *Sc:* Mooney, Arthur T. Horman. (1:01)

B comedy-drama of a superstitious race track owner who is convicted of murder and escapes to prove himself innocent of the crime.

5382. You Can't Cheat an Honest Man (Universal; 1939). *Cast:* W.C. Fields (in his first film for Universal as Larson E. Whipsnade), Edgar Bergen (with Charlie McCarthy & Mortimer Snerd), Constance Moore, Mary Forbes, James Bush, Thurston Hall, Eddie "Rochester" Anderson, Charles Coleman, Edward Brophy, Frank Jenks, Ivan Lebedeff, Grady Sutton, John Arledge, Ferris Taylor. *D:* George Marshall, Edward Cline (unc.); *P:* Lester Cowan; *St:* Charles Bogle (Fields); *Sc:* George Marion, Jr., Richard Mack, Everett Freeman. (1:16) (video)

Classic comedy of circus owner Larson E. Whipsnade who is trying to get his daughter married off into a wealthy society family. Notable is a ping pong game at a society party and the legendary confrontations between W.C. Fields and Charlie McCarthy.

5383. You Can't Get Away with Murder (WB; 1939). *Cast:* Humphrey Bogart, Billy Halop, Gale Page, John Litel, Henry Travers, Harvey Stephens, Harold Huber, Joe Sawyer, John Ridgely, George E. Stone, Joseph Crehan, Herbert Rawlinson, Emory Parnell. *D:* Lewis Seiler; *As.P.:* Sam Bischoff; *Sc:* Robert Buckner, Don Ryan, Kenneth Gamet. (1:18)

Crime melodrama of a juvenile delinquent who takes a prison rap for a hoodlum. Based on the play "Chalked Out" by Lewis E. Lawes and Jonathan Finn.

5384. You Can't Have Everything (20th Century–Fox; 1937). *Cast:* Alice Faye (Judith Poe Wells), Ritz Brothers (themselves), Don Ameche (George McCrea), Charles Winninger (Sam Gordon), Louise Hovick (Gypsy Rose Lee in her film debut as Lulu Riley), David Rubinoff (himself), Tony

Martin (Bobby Walker), Arthur Treacher (Bevins), Phyllis Brooks (Evelyn Moore), George Humbert (Romano), Wally Vernon (Jerry), Jed Prouty (Mr. Whiteman), Robert Murphy (Barney Callahan), Inez Palange (Mrs. Romano), Howard Cantonwine (Tony), Margaret Fielding (Miss Barkow), Lynne Berkeley (Joan), Louis Prima (orchestra leader), Tip, Tap & Toe (Samuel Green, Ted Fraser, Ray Winfield), Frank Yaconelli (accordian player), Nick Moro (guitar player), Paul Hurst (truck driver), Gordon (Bill) Elliott (Lulu's friend), Sam Ash (publicity agent), William Mathieson (bagpiper), Hank Mann (cabby), Frank Puglia, George Davis, Dorothy Christy, Claudia Coleman, Clara Blandick, Robert Lowery, June Gale, Joan Davis, Tyler Brooke, Mary Gordon, Frances Drake. *D:* Norman Taurog; *P:* Lawrence Schwab; *St:* Gregory Ratoff; *Sc:* Harry Tugend, Jack Yellen, Karl Tunberg. (1:39) (video)

Musical-comedy which was one of the 38 top grossing films of 1936–37.

5385. You Can't Take It with You (Columbia; 1938). *Cast:* Jean Arthur (Alice Sycamore), Lionel Barrymore (Martin Vanderhof), James Stewart (Tony Kirby), Edward Arnold (Anthony P. Kirby), Mischa Auer (Kolenkhov), Ann Miller (Essie Carmichael), Spring Byington (A.A.N. for B.S.A. as Penny Sycamore), Samuel S. Hinds (Paul Sycamore), Donald Meek (Poppins), H.B. Warner (Ramsey), Halliwell Hobbes (DePinna), Dub Taylor (film debut as Ed Carmichael), Mary Forbes (Mrs. Anthony Kirby), Lillian Yarbo (Rheba), Eddie "Rochester" Anderson (Donald), Clarence Wilson (John Blakely), Josef Swickard (Professor), Ann Doran (Maggie O'Neill), Christian Rub (Schmidt), Bodil Rosing (Mrs. Schmidt), Charles Lane (Henderson), Irving Bacon (Henry), Chester Clute (Hammond), Harry Davenport (judge), Pierre Watkin, Edwin Maxwell, Russell Hicks, Byron Foulger, Ian

Wolfe, James Flavin, Pert Kelton, Kit Guard, Dick Curtis, James Burke, Ward Bond, Edward Keane, Edward Hearn, Robert Greig, John Hamilton, James Millican, Jordan Whitfield. *D:* (A.A.) Frank Capra; *P:* (A.A. for Best Picture) Capra; *Sc:* (A.A.N.) Robert Riskin; *Cinematographer:* (A.A.N.) Joseph Walker; *Editor:* (A.A.N.) Gene Havlick; *Sound Recording:* (A.A.N.) John Livadary. (2:07) (video)

Classic screwball comedy of an eccentric family which is based on the hit Broadway play by George S. Kaufman and Moss Hart with some story changes from the original. One of the 16 top grossing films of 1938–39 it placed #2 on the "10 Best" list of *Film Daily.*

You Can't Take Money (G.B. title) *see* **Internes Can't Take Money**

5386. You May Be Next (Columbia; 1935–36). *Cast:* Ann Sothern, Lloyd Nolan, John Arledge, Douglass Dumbrille, Berton Churchill, Robert Middlemass, Clyde Dilson, Nana Bryant, Gene Morgan, George McKay. *D:* Albert S. Rogell; *St:* Henry Wales, Ferdinand Reyher; *Sc:* Reyher, Fred Niblo, Jr. (G.B. title: *Panic on the Air*)

B comedy-melodrama.

5387. You Only Live Once (United Artists/Walter Wanger; 1937). *Cast:* Sylvia Sidney, Henry Fonda, Barton MacLane, Jean Dixon, William Gargan, Jerome Cowan, Charles "Chic" Sale, Margaret Hamilton, Warren Hymer, Ward Bond, Guinn Williams, Jack Carson (film debut), Wade Boteler, John Wray, Ben Hall, Jean Stoddard, Henry Taylor. *D:* Fritz Lang (his 2nd Hollywood film); *P:* Walter Wanger (his first to be released by U.A.); *St:* Gene Towne; *Sc:* Towne, Graham Baker; *Song Lyrics:* Paul Francis Webster. (1:25) (video)

Melodrama of a man framed for murder who escapes from prison and takes it on the lam with his wife. Partly based on the real life characters of Bonnie Parker and Clyde Barrow.

5388. You Said a Mouthful (WB/ F.N.; 1932). *Cast:* Joe E. Brown, Ginger Rogers, Sheila Terry, Guinn Williams, Preston Foster, Oscar Apfel, Selmer Jackson, Nat Pendleton, Harry Gribbon, Walter Walker, Edwin Maxwell, Frank Hagney, James Eagles, Anthony Lord, Mia Marvin, A.S. Byron, Harry Seymour, Bert Moorhouse, William Burress. *D:* Lloyd Bacon; *St:* William B. Dover; *Sc:* Robert Lord, Bolton Mallory. (1:15)

Joe E. Brown comedy of an inventor who comes up with an idea for an unsinkable bathing suit.

5389. You're a Sweetheart (Universal; 1937). *Cast:* Alice Faye (her only film for this studio), George Murphy, Ken Murray, Andy Devine, Frances Hunt, William Gargan, Frank Jenks, Charles Winninger, Donald Meek, Robert (Bobby) Watson, Samuel S. Hinds, Four Playboys, Noville Brothers, Malda & Ray, David Oliver, A.A. Trimble, Renie Riano, Ben Lewis, Edna Sedgwick, Casper Reardon, Bob Murphy. *D:* David Butler; *P:* B.G. (Buddy) DeSylva; *St:* Warren Wilson, William Thomas, Maxwell Shane; *Sc:* Monte Brice, Charles Grayson; *Art-Set Decoration:* (A.A.N.) Jack Otterson; *Songs:* title song, "Broadway Jamboree" & "Oh, Oh, Oklahoma" by Harold Adamson, Jimmy McHugh; "So It's Love" by Mickey Bloom, Arthur Quenzer & Lou Bring; & "Scraping the Toast" by Murray Mencher & Charles Tobias. (1:38)

A musical-comedy with the proverbial "puttin'-on-a-show" plot. Remade as *Cowboy from Manhattan* (Universal; 1943).

5390. You're Only Young Once (MGM; 1938). *Cast:* Mickey Rooney (Andy Hardy), Lewis Stone, Fay Holden, Cecilia Parker (Marian Hardy), Sara Haden (Aunt Milly), Ann Rutherford (Polly Benedict), Frank Craven, Eleanor Lynn, Ted Pearson, Charles Judels, Selmer Jackson. *D:* George B. Seitz; *Supervisor:* J.J. Cohn; *Sc:* Kay Van Riper. (1:18)

The second entry in the "Andy Hardy-Hardy Family" series and the first to introduce Lewis Stone as "Judge Hardy" and Fay Holden as "Mrs. Hardy."

5391. You're Telling Me (Paramount; 1934). *Cast:* W.C. Fields (who also starred in the earlier version), Joan Marsh, Larry "Buster" Crabbe, Adrienne Ames, Louise Carter, Kathleen Howard, Nora Cecil, Frederick Sullivan, Del Henderson, James B. Kenton, Tammany Young, Alfred Delcambre, Robert McKenzie. *D:* Erle C. Kenton; *St & Sc:* Walter de Leon, Paul M. Jones. (1:06)

Comedy of a small town down-and-out who is given a new lease on life by a visiting princess. A remake of *So's Your Old Man* (Paramount; 1926–27).

5392. Young America (Fox; 1931). *Cast:* Spencer Tracy, Doris Kenyon, Tommy Conlon, Ralph Bellamy, Beryl Mercer, Sarah Padden, Dawn O'Day (Anne Shirley), Louise Beavers, Robert Homans, Spec O'Donnell. *D:* Frank Borzage; *Sc:* William Conselman. (G.B. title: *We Humans*) (1:14)

Low-budget domestic drama of a youth, in trouble with the law. Based on the play by John Frederick Ballard.

5393. Young and Beautiful (Mascot; 1934). *Cast:* William Haines, Judith Allen, John Miljan, Joseph Cawthorn, Shaw & Lee, James Bush, Vince Barnett, Warren Hymer, Franklin Pangborn, James Burtis, Syd Saylor, Greta Meyer, Fred Kelsey, Andre Beranger, Ray Mayer, Lester's Hollywood Singers, Edward Hearn. *D:* Joseph Santley; *St & Adaptation:* Santley, Milton Krims; *Sc:* Dore Schary; *Additional Dialogue:* Al Martin, Colbert Clark. (1:03)

B budget Hollywood based romantic comedy.

5394. Young as You Feel (Fox; 1931). *Cast:* Will Rogers, Fifi D'Orsay,

Lucien Littlefield, C. Henry Gordon, Cecilia Parker, Brandon Hurst, Terrance Ray, Lucile Brown, John T. Murray, Rosalie Roy, Marcia Harris, Donald Dillaway. *D:* Frank Borzage; *St:* George Ade.

The first of two early attempts to film "The Jones Family." See also: *Business and Pleasure* (q.v.).

5395. Young Blood (Monogram; 1932–33). *Cast:* Bob Steele, Helen Foster, Naomi Judge, Henry Rocquemore, Charles King, Art Mix, Hank Bell, Harry Semels, Lafe McKee, Perry Murdock, Roy Bucko. *D:* Phil Rosen; *P:* Trem Carr; *St & Sc:* Wellyn Totman. (0:59)

Bob Steele western of a Robin Hood type who comes to the aid of an actress.

5396. Young Bride (RKO-Pathé; 1932). *Cast:* Helen Twelvetrees, Eric Linden, Arline Judge, Roscoe Ates, Cliff Edwards, Blanche Frederici, Polly Walters, Edmund Breese, Walter Percival, Allen Fox. *D:* William A. Seiter; *As.P.:* Harry Joe Brown; *Sc:* Garrett Fort; *Additional Dialogue:* Jane Murfin, Ralph Murphy. (Re-release title: *Love Starved*) (aka: *Veneer*) (1:16)

In this marital drama, a young woman eventually finds that her husband is a phony. Based on the play by Hugh Stanislaus Stange.

5397. Young Desire (Universal; 1930). *Cast:* Mary Nolan, William Janney, Alice Lake, Mae Busch. *D:* Lewis D. Collins. (1:09)

Low-budget drama of a carnival dancer and her tragic romance.

5398. Young Dr. Kildare (MGM; 1938). *Cast:* Lew Ayres (Dr. James Kildare), Lionel Barrymore (Dr. Leonard Gillespie), Lynne Carver (Alice Raymond), Nat Pendleton (Wayman), Jo Ann Sayers (Barbara Chanlor), Samuel S. Hinds (Dr. Steve Kildare), Emma Dunn (Martha Kildare), Walter Kingsford (Dr. Walter Carew), Truman Bradley (John Hamilton), Monty Woolley (Dr. Lane-Porteus), Pierre Watkin (Mr. Chanlor), Nella Walker (Mrs. Chanlor), Marie Blake. *D:* Harold S. Bucquet (feature directorial debut); *Sc:* Willis Goldbeck, Harry Ruskin. (1:21)

Premiere entry in a series of fifteen popular low-budget films of a young intern of Blair General Hospital who learns under the guidance of the cranky old Dr. Gillespie. Based on a book by Max Brand, the Kildare character was originally introduced in *Internes Can't Take Money* (q.v.). Also a TV series in the early 1960s.

5399. Young Donovan's Kid (RKO; 1931). *Cast:* Jackie Cooper, Richard Dix, Marion Shilling, Frank Sheridan, Boris Karloff, Fred Kelsey, Wilfred Lucas, Florence Roberts, Stanley Fields, Dick Alexander, Dick Rush, Harry Tenbrook, Philip Sleeman. *D:* Fred Niblo; *As.P.:* Louis Sarecky; *Sc:* J. Walter Ruben. (G.B. title: *Donovan's Kid*)

A notorious gunman is reformed by his girl and a six-year-old orphan in this drama based on a novel by Rex Beach. A remake of *Big Brother* (Paramount; 1923) with Tom Moore.

5400. Young Dynamite (Ambassador; 1937). *Cast:* Frankie Darro, Kane Richmond, Carleton Young. *D:* Leslie Goodwins; *P:* Maurice Conn.

Low-budget indie actioner.

5401. Young Eagles (Paramount; 1930). *Cast:* Charles "Buddy" Rogers (who also starred in *Wings*), Jean Arthur, Paul Lukas, Stuart Erwin, Virginia Bruce, James Finlayson, Jack Luden, Frank Ross, Stanley Blystone, Freeman Wood, Gordon DeMain. *D:* William Wellman (who also directed *Wings*); *St:* Elliott White Springs; *Sc:* William Slavens McNutt, Grover Jones. (1:11)

World War I actioner of American

fighter pilots and one who falls for a female spy. The film is actually a follow-up to *Wings* (Paramount; 1927), the first film to win an Academy Award for "Best Picture."

5402. Young Fugitives (Universal; 1938). *Cast:* Harry Davenport, Robert Wilcox, Dorothea Kent, Clem Bevans, Larry Blake, Mira McKinney, Henry Rocquemore, Tom Ricketts, Mary Treen, William (Billy) Benedict. *D:* John Rawlins; *P:* Barney A. Sarecky; *Sc:* Ben Grauman Kohn, Charles Grayson. (1:05)

B drama of an elderly man who promises a dying friend that he will find the man's son and give him the $25,000 he acquired over the years. Based on the story "Afraid to Talk" by Edward James.

5403. The Young in Heart (United Artists/Selznick International; 1938). *Cast:* Janet Gaynor (George-Ann Carleton), Douglas Fairbanks, Jr. (Richard Carleton), Roland Young (Colonel Anthony Carleton), Billie Burke (Marmy Carleton), Paulette Goddard, Minnie Dupree (Miss Fortune), Richard Carlson (film debut), Henry Stephenson, Lucile Watson, Eily Malyon, Irvin S. Cobb, Margaret Early, Tom Ricketts, Lionel Pape, Lawrence Grant. *D:* Richard Wallace; *Sc:* Paul Osborn, Charles Bennett; *Cinematographer:* (A.A.N.) Leon Shamroy; *Original Music Score:* (A.A.N.) Franz Waxman. (1:30)

Comedy of the Carleton family, a bunch of screwball con artists. Based on the novel "The Gay Banditti" by I.A.R. (Ida) Wylie.

5404. Young Man of Manhattan (Paramount; 1930). *Cast:* Claudette Colbert, Norman Foster, Charles Ruggles, Ginger Rogers (feature film debut), Leslie Austin. *D:* Monta Bell; *Sc:* Robert Presnell.

The romance of a movie gossip columnist and a sportswriter. Based on the novel by Katherine Brush, it was filmed at Astoria Studios in Long Island, N.Y. Notable as the feature film debut of Ginger Rogers in which she sings the ditty "I've Got It, But It Don't Do Me No Good," as well as coining the phrase "Cigarette me, big boy" which became a popular catch phrase of its day.

5405. Young Mr. Lincoln (20th Century–Fox; 1939). *Cast:* Henry Fonda (received an Acting Award from the National Board of Review for his portrayal of Lincoln), Alice Brady (Abigail in her final film — d. 1939), Marjorie Weaver (Mary Todd), Arleen Whelan (Hannah), Eddie Collins (Eph), Richard Cromwell (Matt), Donald Meek (Felder), Pauline Moore (Ann Rutledge), Judith Dickens (Carrie Sue), Eddie Quillan (Adam), Milburn Stone (Stephen A. Douglas), Spencer Charters (Judge Bell), Ward Bond (Palmer Cass), Cliff Clark (sheriff), Charles Tannen (Mr. Edwards), Francis Ford (Frank), Fred Kohler, Jr. (Scrub White), Kay Linaker (Mrs. Edwards), Russell Simpson (Woodridge), Edwin Maxwell (John Stuart), Charles Halton (Hawthorne), Robert E. Homans (Mr. Clay), Jack Pennick (Buck), Steven Randall, Jack Kelly, Dickie Jones, Harry Tyler, Louis Mason, Paul Burns, Frank Orth, George Chandler, Dave Morris, Dorothy Vaughan, Virginia Brissac, Robert Lowery. *D:* John Ford; *As.P.:* Kenneth MacGowan; *St:* (A.A.N.) Lamar Trotti; *Sc:* Trotti. (1:40) (video)

A classic biographical retelling of the early days of Abraham Lincoln when he was an aspiring lawyer. It was voted #5 on the "10 Best" list of the National Board of Review.

5406. Young Nowheres (WB/F.N.; 1929). *Cast:* Richard Barthelmess, Marion Nixon, Anders Randolf, Raymond Turner, Jocelyn Lee, Bert Roach. *D:* Frank Lloyd; *St:* I.A.R. (Ida) Wylie; *Sc:* Bradley King.

Low-budget drama set in a hotel of two employees accused of robbing a guest when caught in his room.

5407. Young Sinners (Fox; 1931). *Cast:* Dorothy Jordan, Hardie Albright (film debut), Thomas Meighan, Nora Lane, Edward Nugent, James Kirkwood, June (Lang) Vlasek (film debut), Cecilia Loftus, Edmund Breese, Gaylord (Steve) Pendleton, Lucien Prival, David Rollins, Billy Butts, Arnold Lucy, Yvonne Pelletier, Joan Castle. *D:* John G. Blystone.

Romantic drama.

5408. The Younger Generation (Columbia; 1929). *Cast:* Jean Hersholt, Lina Basquette, Ricardo Cortez, Rosa Rosanova, Rex Lease, Julanne Johnston. *D:* Frank Capra; *Sc:* Sonya Levien. (1:22)

Based on a story by Fannie Hurst, a young Jewish boy forsakes his ethnic roots to break into New York society, causing upset in his family.

5409. Your Uncle Dudley (Fox; 1935). *Cast:* Edward Everett Horton, Lois Wilson, William (Billy) Benedict, Marjorie Gateson, Rosina Lawrence, Florence Roberts, Jane Barnes, John McGuire. *D:* Eugene Forde; *St:* Howard Lindsay, Bertrand Robinson; *Sc:* Joseph Hoffman, Allen Rivkin, Dore Schary.

Comedy.

5410. Yours for the Asking (Paramount; 1936). *Cast:* George Raft, Ida Lupino, Dolores Costello, Lynne Overman, Skeets Gallagher, Edgar Kennedy, James Gleason, Betty Blythe, Olive Tell, Walter Walker, Keith Daniels, Robert Gleckler, Louis Natheaux, Ralph Remley, Terry Ray (Ellen Drew), Bud Flanagan (Dennis O'Keefe), Charles Requa. *D:* Alexander Hall; *P:* Lewis Gensler; *St:* William H. Wright, William R. Lipman; *Sc:* Eve Greene, Philip MacDonald, Harlan Ware.

B romance of a road house owner and a society girl.

5411. Youth on Parole (Republic; 1937). *Cast:* Gordon Oliver, Marian Marsh, Miles Mander, Milburn Stone, Peggy Shannon, Margaret Dumont, Wade Boteler. *D:* Phil Rosen.

B delinquency melodrama.

5412. Youth Takes a Fling (Universal; 1938). *Cast:* Andrea Leeds, Joel McCrea, Frank Jenks, Dorothea Kent, Isabel Jeans, Virginia Grey, Grant Mitchell, Henry Mollison, Brandon Tynan, Willie Best, Granville Bates, Oscar O'Shea, Marion Martin, Catherine Proctor. *D:* Archie Mayo; *P:* Joe Pasternak; *Sc:* Myles Connolly. (1:19)

Romantic hi-jinks involving love at first sight.

5413. Yukon Flight (Monogram; 1939–40). *Cast:* James Newill (Renfrew), Dave O'Brien, Louise Stanley, Warren Hull, William Pawley, Roy Barcroft, Karl Hackett, Jack Clifford, Bob Terry, Earl Douglas. *D:* Ralph Staub; *P:* Philip N. Krasne (Criterion production); *Sc:* Edward Halperin. (0:57) (video)

"Renfrew" Mountie melodrama involving a bogus trading post dealing in stolen gold. Based on the novel "Renfrew Goes North" by Laurie York Erskine.

5414. Zaza (Paramount; 1939). *Cast:* Claudette Colbert (doing her own singing as Zaza), Herbert Marshall, Bert Lahr, Helen Westley, Constance Collier, Genevieve Tobin, Walter Catlett, Rex O'Malley, Ernest Cossart, Duncan Renaldo, Dorothy Tree, Ann (E.) Todd, Monty Woolley, Janet Waldo, Robert C. Fischer, Clarence Harvey. *D:* George Cukor; *P:* Albert Lewin; *Sc:* Zoe Akins. (1:22)

Lavishly produced romantic drama of a French music hall performer who falls for a married man. Based on the play by Pierre Berton and Charles Simon and adapted by David Belasco to the American stage where it became a major hit for Mrs. Leslie Carter. Previous versions: (Famous Players; 1915) with Pauline Frederick and (Paramount; 1923) with Gloria Swanson. A red ink entry for the studios books.

5415. Zenobia (United Artists/ Hal Roach; 1939). *Cast:* Oliver Hardy (his only starring feature without Stan Laurel, as Dr. Tibbitt), Harry Langdon (Professor McCrackle), Billie Burke, Alice Brady, James Ellison, Jean Parker, June Lang, Stepin Fetchit (Zero), Hattie McDaniel (Dehlia), Wilfred Lucas, J. Farrell MacDonald, Clem Bevans, Hobart Cavanaugh, Chester Conklin, Tommy Mack, Philip Hurlic. *D:* Gordon Douglas (his only film as director); *P:* A. Edward Sutherland; *Sc:* Corey Ford, Arnold Belgard, Walter de Leon; *St:* Arnold Belgard, Walter de Leon. (G.B. title: *Elephants Never Forget*) (1:10)

Comedy of a doctor who heals an ailing elephant, only to have the grateful pachyderm follow him everywhere. Based on the story "Zenobia's Infidelity" by H.C. Brunner.

5416. The Zero Hour (Republic; 1939). *Cast:* Otto Kruger, Adrienne Ames (final film — ret.), Frieda Inescort, Willard Parker, Jane Darwell, Leonard Carey, J.M. Kerrigan, Donald Douglas, Ferris Taylor. *D:* Sidney Salkow; *Sc:* Garrett Fort.

B melodrama.

5417. Zoo in Budapest (Fox; 1933). *Cast:* Gene Raymond, Loretta Young, O.P. Heggie, Paul Fix, Wally Albright, Roy Stewart, Ruth Warren, Russell Powell, Frances Rich, Dorothy Libaire, Lucille Ward, Niles Welch. *D:* Rowland V. Lee; *P:* Jesse L. Lasky; *St:* Jack Kirkland, Melville Baker; *Sc:* Dan Totheroh, Louise Long, Lee. (1:25)

An offbeat love story which takes place in a zoo in Budapest, Hungary. Voted one of the year's "10 Best" films by the National Board of Review.

5418. Zorro Rides Again (Republic; 1937). *Cast:* John Carroll, Helen Christian, Reed Howes, Duncan Renaldo, Noah Beery, Richard Alexander, Bob Kortman, Nigel de Brulier, Jason Robards, Tom London. *D:* John English, William Witney; *Supervisor:* Nat Levine. (1:08) (video — serial only)

Feature version of the 12-chapter serial of the same name concerning the exploits of Zorro's great grandson.

Award-Winning Films

Following is a list of films which received recognition and critical acclaim from various institutions, namely: The Academy of Motion Picture Arts and Sciences, Academy Awards (A.A.), Academy Award Nominations (A.A.N.), *Film Daily's* "10 Best" list (F), the National Board of Review's "10 Best" list as well as Acting Awards (NBR), the New York Film Critics (NYFC), the *New York Times* newspaper's "10 Best" list (NYT), *Photoplay* magazine (P) and the Venice Film Festival (V).

Abraham Lincoln (1930) F, NYT
The Adventures of Robin Hood (1938) AA, AAN, F, NYT
The Adventures of Tom Sawyer (1938) AAN, V
The Affairs of Cellini (1934) AAN
After the Thin Man (1936) AAN
Alexander's Ragtime Band (1938) AA, AAN, F
Algiers (1938) AAN
Ali Baba Goes to Town (1937) AAN
Alibi (1929) AAN
Alice Adams (1935) AAN, NBR
All Quiet on the Western Front (1930) AA, AAN, F, NBR, NYT, P
All the King's Horses (1935) AAN
Angels with Dirty Faces (1938) AAN, NBR, NYFC
Anna Christie (1929–30) AAN, F, NYT
Anna Karenina (1935) AAN, F, NBR, V, NYFC
Anthony Adverse (1936) AA, AAN, F
Army Girl (1938) AAN
Arrowsmith (1931) AAN, F, NYT
Artists and Models (1937) AAN
As You Desire Me (1932) NBR
The Awful Truth (1937) AA, AAN, F
Babes in Arms (1939) AAN
Bachelor Mother (1939) AAN
Back Street (1932) F
Bad Girl (1931) AA, AAN, F, NBR, NYT
Balalaika (1939) AAN
Banjo on My Knee (1936) AAN
Barbary Coast (1935) AAN

The Barker (1928) AAN
The Barretts of Wimpole Street (1934) AAN, F, P
Beau Geste (1939) AAN
Becky Sharp (1935) V
Berkeley Square (1933) AAN, F, NBR, NYT
The Big Broadcast of 1936 (1935) AAN
The Big Broadcast of 1938 (1938) AA
The Big House (1930) AA, AAN, F
The Big Pond (1930) AAN
A Bill of Divorcement (1932) F, NBR, NYT
Black Legion (1936) AAN, NBR
Blockade (1938) AAN, NYFC
Born to Dance (1936) AAN
Boys Town (1938) AA, AAN, F
Breaking the Ice (1938) AAN
The Bride of Frankenstein (1935) AAN
The Bridge of San Luis Rey (1929) AA
Broadway Hostess (1935) AAN
The Broadway Melody (1928–29) AA, AAN, F
The Broadway Melody of 1936 (1935) AA, AAN, F
The Buccaneer (1938) AAN
Bulldog Drummond (1929) AAN, F, NYT
Cain and Mabel (1936) AAN
Camille (1936) AAN, NBR, NYT, NYFC
Captain Blood (1935) AAN
Captain Fury (1939) AAN
Captains Courageous (1937) AA, AAN, F, NBR, NYT, NYFC, P
Carefree (1938) AAN

The Case of Sergeant Grischa (1930)
AAN
Cavalcade (1933) AA, AAN, F, NBR,
NYT
Ceiling Zero (1935) NBR
The Champ (1931) AA, AAN, F
The Charge of the Light Brigade (1936) AA,
AAN
Cimarron (1930–31) AA, AAN, F, NBR,
P
City Streets (1931) NBR
Cleopatra (1934) AA, AAN
The Cock-Eyed World (1929) F
Come and Get It (1936) AA, AAN
Condemned (1929) AAN
Confessions of a Nazi Spy (1939) NBR
A Connecticut Yankee (1931) NYT
Conquest (1937) AAN, NBR
Coquette (1929) AA
The Count of Monte Cristo (1934) F, NBR
The Cowboy and the Lady (1938) AA, AAN
Crime Without Passion (1934) NBR
The Criminal Code (1930–31) AAN
The Crusades (1935) AAN
A Damsel in Distress (1937) AA, AAN
The Dancing Pirate (1936) AAN
Dangerous (1935) AA
The Dark Angel (1935) AA, AAN
Dark Victory (1939) AAN, F, NBR, NYT
David Copperfield (1934–35) AAN, F,
NBR, NYT, V
The Dawn Patrol (1930) AA
A Day at the Races (1937) AAN
Dead End (1937) AAN, F
The Devil Is a Sissy (1936) NBR
The Devil to Pay (1930) NYT
The Devil's Holiday (1929–30) AAN
Dinner at Eight (1933) F, NYT
Dishonored (1931) NBR
Disraeli (1929) AA, AAN, F, NYT, P
The Divorcee (1930) AA, AAN, F
Dr. Jekyll and Mr. Hyde (1931–32) AA,
AAN, F, NYT, V
Dodsworth (1936) AA, AAN, F, NYFC,
NYT
Doorway to Hell (1930) AAN
Drag (1929) AAN
Drums Along the Mohawk (1939) AAN
Dynamite (1929) AAN
East Lynne (1931) AAN
Emma (1932) AAN, F
Eskimo (1933) AA, NBR

Eternally Yours (1939) AAN
Every Day's a Holiday (1937) AAN
A Farewell to Arms (1932) AA, AAN, F,
NBR
First Love (1939) AAN
The First World War (1934) NBR
Five Star Final (1931) AAN, F
Flirtation Walk (1934) AAN
Flying Down to Rio (1933) AAN
Folies-Bergere (1935) AA
Forty-Second Street (1933) AAN, F
Four Daughters (1938) AAN, NBR, NYT
Four Devils (1928) AAN, NYT
Four Sons (1928) F, P
Frankenstein (1931) NYT, V
A Free Soul (1931) AA, AAN, F
The Front Page (1931) AAN, NBR, F
Fury (1936) AAN, NBR, NYFC, NYT
The Garden of Allah (1936) AA, AAN
The Gay Deception (1935) AAN
The Gay Desperado (1936) NYFC
The Gay Divorcee (1934) AA, AAN
The General Died at Dawn (1936) AAN
General Spanky (1936) AAN
The Gilded Lily (1935) NBR
The Girl Said No (1937) AAN
Girls School (1938) AAN
Glorious Betsy (1928) AAN
Go Into Your Dance (1935) AAN
Going Places (1938) AAN
Gold Diggers of Broadway (1929) F
Gold Diggers of 1933 (1933) AAN
Gold Diggers of 1935 (1935) AA, AAN
Gold Diggers of 1937 (1936) AAN
Golden Boy (1939) AAN
The Goldwyn Follies (1938) AAN
Gone with the Wind (1939) AA, AAN, F,
NBR, NYFC, NYT, P
The Good Earth (1937) AA, AAN, F,
NBR, NYFC, NYT
The Gorgeous Hussy (1936) AAN
Grand Hotel (1932) AA, F, NYT, V
The Great Victor Herbert (1939) AAN
The Great Waltz (1938) AA, AAN
The Great Ziegfeld (1936) AA, AAN, F,
NYFC, NYT, V
The Green Goddess (1930) AAN
The Green Pastures (1936) F, NBR, NYT
The Guardsman (1931) AAN, F, NBR,
NYT
Hallelujah! (1929) AAN, F, NYT
Hell's Angels (1930) AAN, F

Here Comes the Navy (1934) AAN
Hide-Out (1934) AAN
Hitting a New High (1937) AAN
Holiday (1930) AAN, F, NBR, NYT
Holiday (1938) AAN, NBR
The Hollywood Revue of 1929 (1929) AAN
The House of Rothschild (1934) AAN, F, NYT
The Hunchback of Notre Dame (1939) AAN
The Hurricane (1937) AA, AAN, F
I Am a Fugitive from a Chain Gang (1932) AAN, F, NBR
I Dream Too Much (1935) AAN
I Met Him in Paris (1937) NYT
If I Were King (1938) AAN
Imitation of Life (1934) AAN
In Old Arizona (1928) AA, AAN, F
In Old Chicago (1937) AA, AAN, F, NYFC
The Informer (1935) AA, AAN, F, NYFC
Intermezzo, A Love Story (1939) AAN
The Invisible Man (1933) NYT
The Iron Mask (1928-29) AAN
It Happened One Night (1934) AA, F, NBR, NYT, V
The Jazz Singer (1927) AA, AAN
Jezebel (1938) AA, AAN, NBR, V
Journey's End (1930) F, NYT
Juarez (1939) AAN, F, NYT
Just Imagine (1930) AAN
Kentucky (1938) AA
Kid Galahad (1937) V
King of Burlesque (1935) AAN
The King of Jazz (1930) AA
Lady and Gent (1932) AAN
Lady for a Day (1933) AAN, F
The Lady Objects (1938) AAN
The Last of Mrs. Cheyney (1929) F
The Last of the Mohicans (1936) AAN
Laughter (1929) AAN, NBR
Les Miserables (1935) AAN, F, NBR, NYT
The Letter (1929) AAN
Libeled Lady (1936) AAN
The Life of Emile Zola (1937) AA, AAN, F, NBR, NYFC, NYT
Lightnin' (1930) NYT
Little Women (1933) AA, AAN, F, NBR, NYT, P, V
Lives of a Bengal Lancer (1935) AAN, F, NBR, NYT
Lloyd's of London (1936) AAN

Lost Horizon (1937) AA, AAN, F, NYT
The Lost Patrol (1934) AAN, NBR, NYT
Love Affair (1939) AAN
Love Finds Andy Hardy (1938) F
Love Me Forever (1935) NYT
The Love Parade (1929) AAN, NYT
Mad About Music (1938) AAN
Madame Racketeer (1932) NBR
Madame X (1929) AAN, F
Made for Each Other (1939) NYT
The Magnificent Brute (1936) AAN
Make a Wish (1937) AAN
Make Way for Tomorrow (1937) NBR, NYT
Mama Loves Papa (1933) NBR
The Man from Blankley's (1930) NBR
The Man in the Iron Mask (1939) AAN
Man of Conquest (1939) AAN
Manhattan Melodrama (1934) AA
Manhattan Merry-Go-Round (1937) AAN
Marie Antoinette (1938) AAN, F, NBR, V
Marked Woman (1937) V
Maytime (1937) AAN
Men Without Women (1930) NBR
Merrily We Live (1938) AAN
The Merry Widow (1934) AA
A Midsummer Night's Dream (1935) AA, AAN, F
Min and Bill (1930) AA, F
Mr. Deeds Goes to Town (1936) AA, AAN, F, NBR, NYFC, NYT, V
Mr. Dodd Takes the Air (1937) AAN
Mr. Smith Goes to Washington (1939) AA, AAN, F, NBR, NYFC, NYT
Modern Times (1936) NBR
Morning Glory (1933) AA
Morocco (1930) AAN, NBR
Mother Carey's Chickens (1938) V
The Mouthpiece (1932) NYT
Mutiny on the Bounty (1935) AA, AAN, F, NBR, NYFC
My Man Godfrey (1936) AAN
Naughty Marietta (1935) AA, AAN, F, P
Night Must Fall (1937) AAN, NBR
Ninotchka (1939) AAN, F, NBR, NYT
No Greater Glory (1934) NBR
Northwest Passage (1939-40) F
Nurse Edith Cavell (1939) AAN
Of Human Hearts (1938) AAN, NBR
Of Mice and Men (1939) AAN, NBR
Old English (1930) F
The Old Maid (1939) F

One Hour with You (1932) AAN, NYT
One Hundred Men and a Girl (1937) AA, AAN
One in a Million (1936) AAN
One Night of Love (1934) AA, AAN, F, NYT, & Society of Arts and Science of N.Y.
$100 a Minute (1935) AAN
One-Way Passage (1932) AA
Only Angels Have Wings (1939) AAN
Operator 13 (1933) AAN
Our Daily Bread (1934) NYT
Outward Bound (1930) NBR, NYT
Pacific Liner (1938–39) AAN
The Patriot (1928) AA, AAN, F, NYT
Payment Deferred (1932) NBR
Pennies from Heaven (1936) AAN
Peter Ibbetson (1935) AAN
Pigskin Parade (1936) AAN
Portia on Trial (1937) AAN
The Prisoner of Shark Island (1936) NBR
The Prisoner of Zenda (1937) AAN
Private Lives (1931) NYT
The Private Lives of Elizabeth and Essex (1939) AAN
Private Worlds (1935) AAN
The Prizefighter and the Lady (1933) AAN
The Public Enemy (1931) AAN
Quality Street (1937) AAN
Queen Christina (1933) V
Quick Millions (1931) NBR
Raffles (1930) AAN
The Rains Came (1939) AA, AAN
Rango (1931) NBR
Rasputin and the Empress (1932) AAN, F
Ready, Willing and Able (1937) AAN
Reunion in Vienna (1933) AAN, NYT
The Right to Love (1930) AAN
Rio Rita (1929) F
The Roaring Twenties (1939) NBR
Roberta (1935) AAN, F
The Rogue Song (1929–30) AAN
Romance (1930) AAN, NBR
Romeo and Juliet (1936) AAN, F, NBR, NYT
The Royal Family of Broadway (1930) AAN
Ruggles of Red Gap (1935) AAN, F, NBR, NYFC, NYT
Sally (1929) AAN, NYT
San Francisco (1936) AA, AAN, F, P
Sarah and Son (1930) AAN
Scarface (1930–32) F, NBR

The Scoundrel (1935) AA, AAN, NYT
Second Fiddle (1939) AAN
Sequoia (1934) NYT
Shall We Dance (1937) AAN, V
Shanghai Express (1932) AA, AAN
She Done Him Wrong (1933) AAN, F, NBR
She Loves Me Not (1934) AAN
She Married a Cop (1939) AAN
The Sin of Madelon Claudet (1931) AA, F, V
Sing, You Sinners (1938) NBR, NYFC
Skippy (1931) AA, AAN, F, NYT
The Sky Hawk (1929) NYT
A Slight Case of Murder (1938) NYT
Smart Money (1931) AAN
Smilin' Through (1932) AAN, F, P
The Smiling Lieutenant (1931) AAN, NYT
Snow White and the Seven Dwarfs (1937) AA, AAN, F, NBR, NYFC, NYT, V
Something to Sing About (1937) AAN
Song of the Flame (1930) AAN
Souls at Sea (1937) AAN
Spawn of the North (1938) AA
Stage Door (1937) AAN, F, NBR, NYFC, NYT
Stagecoach (1939) AA, AAN, NBR, NYFC, NYT
Stanley and Livingstone (1939) F
A Star Is Born (1937) AA, AAN, F, NBR, NYT
The Star Witness (1931) AAN
State Fair (1933) AAN, F, NBR, NYT
Stella Dallas (1937) AAN
The Story of Louis Pasteur (1936) AA, AAN, F, NBR, NYT, V
Strange Interlude (1932) V
Street Angel (1928) AA, AAN, F, NYT
Street of Chance (1930) AAN, NBR
Street Scene (1931) F
Suez (1938) AAN
Surrender (1931) NBR
Suzy (1936) AAN
Svengali (1931) AAN
Swanee River (1939) AAN
Sweethearts (1938) AA, AAN, P
Swing Time (1936) AA, AAN
A Tale of Two Cities (1935) AAN, F
The Taming of the Shrew (1929) NYT
Tarzan, the Ape Man (1932) NBR
Test Pilot (1938) AAN, V
The Texas Rangers (1936) AAN
That Certain Age (1938) AAN

That Girl from Paris (1936) AAN
Their Own Desire (1929–30) AAN
Theodora Goes Wild (1936) AAN, V
There Goes My Heart (1938) AAN
These Three (1936) AAN, NYFC, NYT
They Had to See Paris (1929) NYT
They Won't Forget (1937) NBR, NYT
Thin Ice (1937) AAN
The Thin Man (1934) AAN, F, NBR, NYT
Three Comrades (1938) AAN, NBR, NYFC, NYT
Three-Cornered Moon (1933) NBR
Three Smart Girls (1936) AAN
Thunderbolt (1929) AAN
Tol'able David (1930) NBR
Tom Sawyer (1930) NYT
Top Hat (1935) AAN, F
Topaze (1933) NBR
Topper (1937) AAN
Trader Horn (1930–31) AAN
The Trail of the Lonesome Pine (1936) AAN
Transatlantic (1931) AA
The Trespasser (1929) AAN
Tropic Holiday (1938) AAN
Trouble in Paradise (1932) NBR, NYT
Two Seconds (1932) NBR
Under Western Stars (1938) AAN
Union Pacific (1939) AAN
The Vagabond King (1930) AAN
The Valiant (1929) AAN
Valiant Is the Word for Carrie (1936) AAN
Varsity Show (1937) AAN

The Virginian (1929) NYT
Viva Villa! (1934) AA, AAN, F, NBR, V
Vivacious Lady (1938) AAN
Vogues of 1938 (1937) AAN
Waikiki Wedding (1937) AAN
Way Out West (1936–37) AAN
Weary River (1929) AAN
Wee Willie Winkie (1936–37) AAN
Wells Fargo (1937) AAN
What Price Hollywood? (1932) AAN
When Ladies Meet (1933) AAN
When Tomorrow Comes (1939) AA
White Banners (1938) AAN
The White Parade (1934) AAN
White Shadows in the South Seas (1928) AA, NYT
Whoopee! (1930) AAN
Wings Over Honolulu (1937) AAN.
Winterset (1936) AAN, F, NBR, NYFC, NYT, V
With Byrd at the South Pole (1930) AA, F, NYT
The Wizard of Oz (1939) AA, AAN, F
The Women (1939) F, NYT
Wuthering Heights (1939) AA, AAN, F, NBR, NYFC, NYT
You Can't Take It with You (1938) AA, AAN, F
You're a Sweetheart (1937) AAN
The Young in Heart (1938) AAN
Young Mr. Lincoln (1939) AAN, NBR
Zoo in Budapest (1933) NBR

Bibliography

Autry, Gene, and Mickey Herskowitz. *Back in the Saddle Again.* Garden City, N.Y.: Doubleday, 1978.

Barbour, Alan G. *The Wonderful World of B-Films.* Kew Gardens, N.Y.: Screen Facts Press, c. 1968.

Bergen, Ronald. *The United Artists Story.* New York, N.Y.: Crown, c. 1986. Also by Octopus Books Ltd.

Blum, Daniel. *A Pictorial History of the Talkies.* New York, N.Y.: G.P. Putnam's Sons, 1958.

_____. *A Pictorial History of the Silent Screen.* New York, N.Y.: Grosset & Dunlap, c. 1953.

Corliss, Richard, ed. *The Hollywood Screen-writers.* New York, N.Y.: Avon Books, c. 1970, 1971, 1972 by Film Comment Publishing Corp.

Eames, John Douglas. *The M-G-M Story.* New York, N.Y.: Crown, c. 1985.

_____. *The Paramount Story.* New York, N.Y.: Crown, c. 1985.

Fenin, George N., and William K. Everson. *The Western.* New York, N.Y.: Grossman, c. 1973.

Fredrik, Nathalie. *Hollywood and the Academy Awards.* Beverly Hills, Ca.: Hollywood Awards Publications, c. 1969.

Geduld, Harry M. *The Birth of the Talkies.* Indiana University Press, c. 1975.

Green, Stanley. *Encyclopedia of the Musical Film.* Oxford, N.Y.: Oxford University Press, c. 1981.

Halliwell, Leslie. *Halliwell's Film Guide.* New York, N.Y.: Charles Scribner's Sons, c. 1983 (4th edition).

_____. *Halliwell's Filmgoer's Companion.* New York, N.Y.: Charles Scribner's Sons, c. 1985 (8th Edition).

Hirschhorn, Clive. *The Universal Story.* New York, N.Y.: Crown, c. 1983 (1987 edition).

_____. *The Warner Brothers Story.* New York, N.Y.: Crown, c. 1979.

Jewell, Richard B. & Vernon Harbin. *The RKO Story.* Octopus Books, Ltd., c. 1982. Published in the U.S. by Crown, N.Y.

Katz, Ephraim. *The Film Encyclopedia.* New York, N.Y.: Putnam, c. 1979.

McCarthy, Todd, and Charles Flynn. *Kings of the B's.* New York, N.Y.: E.P. Dutton, c. 1975.

McClure, Arthur F., and Ken D. Jones. *Heroes, Heavies and Sagebrush.* Cranbury, N.J.: A.S. Barnes, c. 1972.

Maltin, Leonard, ed.; Luke Sader, assoc. ed.; Mike Clark, Rob Edelman, Alvin H. Marill, Bill Warren, contributing eds.; Casey St. Charnez, video ed.; Ben Herndon, managing ed. *Leonard Maltin's TV Movies and Video Guide.* New York, N.Y.: Penguin Books, 1990 (1991 edition).

_____, ed. *TV Movies and Video Guide.* New York, N.Y.: New American Library, c. 1986 (1987 edition).

Martin, Mick, Marsha Porter, and Ed Remitz. *Video Movie Guide 1989.* New York, N.Y.: Random House, c. 1988.

781

Michael, Paul. *The American Movies Reference Book — The Sound Era.* Englewood Cliffs, N.J.: Prentice-Hall, c. 1969.

————, ed. *The Great American Movie Book.* Englewood Cliffs, N.J.: Prentice-Hall, 1980.

Miller, Don. *B Movies.* New York, N.Y.: Curtis Books, c. 1973.

————. *Hollywood Corral.* New York, N.Y.: Popular Library, c. 1976.

National Board of Review of Motion Pictures, Inc. *500 Best American Films to Buy, Rent or Videotape.* New York, N.Y.: Pocket Books, c. 1985.

The New York Times Directory of the Film. Arno Press, 1974.

Nicholls, Peter, ed. *The Science Fiction Encyclopedia.* Garden City, N.Y.: Roxby, Dolphin Books, Doubleday, c. 1979.

Nye, Douglas E. *Those Six-Gun Heroes.* Spartanburg, S.C.: ETV Endowment of South Carolina, c. 1982.

Okuda, Ted. *Grand National, Producers Releasing Corporation, and Screen Guild/Lippert.* Jefferson, N.C., and London: McFarland, 1989.

————. *The Monogram Checklist: 1931-1952.* Jefferson, N.C.: McFarland, c. 1987.

Parish, James Robert, and Michael R. Pitts. *Film Directors.* Metuchen, N.J.: Scarecrow, 1974.

Pitts, Michael R. *Western Movies.* Jefferson, N.C.: McFarland, 1986.

Publications International Ltd. *Rating the Movies for Homevideo, TV, and Cable.* Beeman House, c. 1985.

Quinlan, David. *The Illustrated Encyclopedia of Movie Character Actors.* New York, N.Y.: Harmony Books, c. 1985.

Scheuer, Steven. *TV Key Movie Guide.* New York, N.Y.: Bantam, c. 1966.

Shale, Richard. *Academy Awards.* Frederick Unger, c. 1978.

Shipman, David. *The Great Movie Stars — The Golden Years.* New York, N.Y.: Bonanza Books, c. 1970.

Thomas, Bob. *King Cohn.* London, England: Barrie & Rockliffe, c. 1967.

Trent, Paul. *Those Fabulous Movie Years: The 30's.* Barre, Mass.: Vineyard, c. 1975.

Tuska, Jon. *The Filming of the West.* Garden City, N.Y.: Doubleday, 1976.

————. *The Vanishing Legion.* Jefferson, N.C.: McFarland, 1982.

Weaver, John T. *Forty Years of Screen Credits.* Metuchen, N.J.: Scarecrow, c. 1970 (2 volumes).

Weldon, Michael, with Charles Beesley, Bob Martin and Akira Fitton. *The Psychotronic Encyclopedia of Film.* New York, N.Y.: Ballantine, c. 1983.

Zinman, David. *50 Classic Motion Pictures, the Stuff That Dreams Are Made Of.* New York, N.Y.: Crown, c. 1970.

Index

Buccola, Guy 4497

Buchanan, Edgar 3121

Buchanan, Elsa 555, 668, 1946, 2212, 2615, 3540

Buchanan, Jack 3034, 3475

Buchanan, Thompson 1206

Buchman, Harold 620, 795, 842/843, 1064, 1126/1127, 1478, 2238, 4097, 4893

Buchman, Sidney 16, 78, 182, 276, 493, 994, 1527, 1990, 2144, 2157, 2364, 2644, 2686, 3014, 3098, 3250, 4124, 4171, 5232

Buck & Bubbles 5050

Buck, Donald 2591

Buck, Frank 486, 1304

Buck, Pearl 1725

Buck the dog 563, 564, 849, 2897

Buckingham, Tom (Thomas) 207, 759, 1050, 1864, 1929, 3295, 3447, 4044, 4382, 4412, 4820

Buckland, Veda 1110, 3138, 4219

Buckler, Hugh 876, 2297, 2450, 2644

Buckler, John 362, 997, 1211, 5005

Buckley, Harold 355, 549, 1806, 2156, 3200, 3655, 4218

Bucknall, Nathalie 1413, 1494

Buckner, Robert Henry 107, 802, 1114, 1245, 1706, 2276, 2670, 3307, 5383

Bucko, Buck 1339, 1791, 1804, 4282, 4959

Bucko, Roy 287, 1339, 1791, 1804, 4282, 4959, 5395

Bucquet, Harold S. 568, 3323, 4047, 5398

Bud Flanagan (Dennis O'Keefe) 5410

Budd, Norman 529

Buell, Jed 1841, 2374, 2896, 3041, 3724,

3849, 3925, 4205, 4338, 4960

Buffalo Bill, Jr. (Jay Wilsey) 179, 296, 394, 1014, 1356, 1954, 2497, 2563, 3176, 3606, 3661, 3707, 3721, 3722, 3733, 5166

Buffington, Adele 249, 691, 1478, 1516, 1618, 1852, 1900, 1956, 2224, 2312, 2823, 3042, 3606, 3629, 4133, 5146

Bufford, Daisy 2275

Bulgakov, Leo 35, 3144

Bull, Frank 1558

Bull, Peter 2839

"Bulldog Drummond" (series) 159, 516, 517, 518, 519, 520, 521, 522, 523, 524, 591

Bullet the dog 3431

Bullock, Boris 1356, 1474, 2565, 3722, 3733

Bullock, Walter 1454, 1829, 2602, 3186, 3812

Bulwer-Lytton, Sir Edward 600, 2438

Bunce, Alan 4130

Bunn, Alfred 398

Bunn, Earl D. 2455

Bunny, George 2766, 5256

Bunny, John 5047

Bunston, Henry 2125, 2521

Bunston, Herbert 34, 90, 673, 1112, 1152, 1385, 2413, 2445, 2593, 2634, 3028, 3042, 3339, 3817, 4153

Bunuel, Luis 5365

Bupp, June 424

Bupp, Sonny 3252, 3785

Bupp, Tommy 140, 373, 595, 699, 818, 1079, 1408, 1650, 1977, 2004, 2055, 2248, 2591, 2682, 2752, 2773, 3145, 3430, 3427, 3561, 3776, 4495

Burani, Michelette 1236, 1255, 1456, 1623, 1673

Burbridge, Betty 287, 442, 791, 796, 891, 1707, 1902, 1953, 2040, 2180, 2308, 2487,

2777, 2897, 3065, 3188, 3228, 3418, 3458, 3609, 3663, 3766, 3771, 3829, 3942, 3993, 4212, 4357, 4397, 4866, 4993, 5259, 5366

Burch, John E. 1305, 1956

Burden, Douglas 4174

Burden, Shirley 255

Burfield, Joan (Joan Fontaine) 3246

Burger, Paul 660, 2596

Burgess, Betty 24, 2118

Burgess, Dorothy 29, 298, 361, 732, 1203, 1311, 1520, 1526, 1567, 1848, 1872, 2016, 2129, 2168, 2177, 2256, 2350, 2387, 2394, 2434, 2756, 2826, 2987, 3021, 3390, 3577, 3581, 3744, 3777, 3955, 4326, 4447, 4507, 5062, 5178

Burgess, Gelett 4965

Burgess, Harry 3077

Burgess, Helen 1116, 2350, 3222, 3574

Burgoyne, Ollie 2472

Burke, Billie 34, 251, 341, 470, 477, 588, 725, 874, 1092, 1141, 1246, 1255, 1326, 1391, 1481, 1679, 1769, 2924, 3107, 3167, 3381, 3384/ 3385, 3483, 3561, 3779, 4109, 4386, 4848, 4849, 5123, 5198, 5299, 5403, 5415

Burke, Brian 2407

Burke, Edwin 208, 482, 554, 938, 1309, 1631, 1826, 2608/2609, 2811, 3277, 3364, 3440, 5327

Burke, Frankie 108, 1912, 3424, 5342

Burke, James 28, 30, 172, 245, 563, 620, 737, 740, 782, 837, 944, 1000, 1009, 1091, 1119, 1428, 1475, 1757, 1977, 2245, 2248, 2287, 2372, 2399, 2510, 2595, 2601, 2323, 2748, 2802, 2915,

2759, 2795, 2829, 3228, 3418, 3434, 3458, 3715, 3766, 3823, 3829, 3839, 3993, 4910, 5259

Terhune, William 2315

Terrell, Kenneth 2612

Terrett, Courtenay 625, 984, 1302, 2105, 2678, 2734, 3748, 4941

Terris, Norma 572, 2854

Terry, Albert 2777

Terry, Alice 224, 1582, 1750, 5314

Terry, Bob 512, 765, 1147, 1422, 3330, 3415, 3788, 4232, 4235, 4284, 4329, 4339, 4430, 4486, 5199, 5413

Terry, Dick 868

Terry, Don 423, 960, 1349, 3444, 4401, 5018/5019, 5035, 5189, 5211, 5230

Terry, Ethelind 140, 2640

Terry, Frank 473

Terry, Linda 2723, 3474

Terry, Peggy 49

Terry, Phillip 217, 456, 531, 568, 1494, 2013, 2834, 3167, 3323, 5372

Terry, Richard (Jack Perrin) 2266

Terry, Robert 3989

Terry, Ruth 55, 2011, 2209, 2660, 4259

Terry, Sheila 234, 903, 1556, 1684, 1852, 2088, 2108, 2497, 2505, 2727, 3088, 3176, 3464, 3792, 3904, 4014, 4178, 4301, 4316, 4367, 4378, 4941, 5131/5132, 5193, 5388

Terwilliger, George 3587

Tetley, Walter 453, 2641, 3609, 4382, 4864

Tettener, John 2644

Tevis, Carol 3342, 4199

Thackery, William Makepeace 251, 5047

Thackrey, Eugene 164, 252

Thalasso, Arthur 268, 5069

Thalberg, Irving 113,

231, 321, 1719, 1725, 2445, 2875, 2927, 3204, 3246, 3387, 3926, 4274, 5174

Thalberg, Sylvia 724, 3032, 3276, 4508, 5018/5019, 5185

Than, Joseph 2730

Thatcher, Heather 245, 536, 1456, 1668, 2159, 2760, 4863

Thayer, Julia (Jean Carmen) 1808

Thayer, Tiffany 554, 1067, 2157, 2350, 4492

Theby, Rosemary 2752, 2942

Theilade, Nini 2957

Theodore, Pete 4097

Theodore, Ralph 937, 2444

Thesiger, Ernest 471, 3311

Thew, Harvey 137, 253, 1021, 1103, 1180, 1276, 1302, 1670, 2076, 2164, 2720, 2871, 3084, 3387, 3960, 4108, 4110, 4162, 4185, 4217, 4337, 4488, 4495, 4874, 4968, 5313

Thiele, Lawrence 1850

Thiele, Wilhelm (William) 211, 258, 470, 1128, 2297, 2618, 2654, 4408

Thoeren, Robert 2074

Thomas, A. E. 326, 397, 1259, 1639, 1730, 2037, 3246

Thomas, Augustus 138, 2898, 5286

Thomas, Billie "Buckwheat" 1594

Thomas, Brandon 657

Thomas, Elton (Douglas Fairbanks) 3012

Thomas, Evan 514, 2203, 2602

Thomas, Faith 828, 2020, 3762

Thomas, Frank M. 159, 194, 268, 318, 330, 373, 465, 714, 878, 892, 897, 956, 1020, 1129, 1130, 1257, 1269, 1484, 1683, 1743, 2491,

2744, 2806, 2815, 2887, 3004, 3019, 3070, 3229, 3409, 3684, 3927, 3967, 4053, 4690/4691, 4814, 5091, 5116, 5121, 5293, 5379, 5381

Thomas, Frankie 107, 456, 772, 1122, 2453, 2605, 3156, 3157, 3158, 3159, 3324, 5129

Thomas, Gretchen 926, 2849

Thomas, Jameson 260, 402, 481, 666, 832, 837, 918, 1068, 1237, 1283, 1645, 2087, 2245, 2265, 2406, 2410, 2454, 2508, 2596, 2611, 2648, 2701, 2812, 3002, 3005, 3042, 3216, 3247, 3276, 3353, 3556, 3949, 4015, 4069, 4202, 4453, 4903, 5334, 5356

Thomas, John 1842

Thomas, Lowell 380, 439, 2340, 3102, 4810

Thomas, Richard 80

Thomas, Robert 3823

Thomas, Virginia 5263

Thomas, William 575/576, 2163, 2347, 3374, 4311, 5389

Thompson, Charlotte 3739

Thompson, Clarence 2699

Thompson, Cliff 4935

Thompson, Duane 1541, 5074

Thompson, Fred 4341

Thompson, George 5234

Thompson, Hal 109

Thompson, Harlan 306, 649, 781, 1101, 1192, 1665, 1944, 2149, 2367, 2739, 2891, 3477, 3502/3503, 3556, 3918, 5297

Thompson, Nick 5087

Thompson, Irene 4935

Thompson, James "Slim" 3812

Thompson, Julian 5095

Thompson, June 4212

Thompson, Kay (and Her Radio Choir) 2829